P9-DMF-490

Personal Finance

Principles and Case Problems

Personal Finance
Principles and Case Problems

JEROME B. COHEN, Ph.D.
Professor of Finance and Dean (Emeritus)
Bernard M. Baruch College
City University of New York

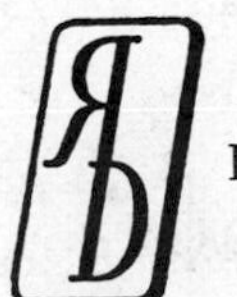

Fifth Edition 1975

RICHARD D. IRWIN, INC. Homewood, Illinois 60430

Irwin-Dorsey Limited Georgetown, Ontario L7G 4B3

Fifth Edition

First Printing, June 1975
Second Printing, December 1975
Third Printing, July 1976
Fourth Printing, December 1976

ISBN 0-256-01634-8
Library of Congress Catalog Card No. 74–27546
Printed in the United States of America

To Mina

Preface

THE TEMPO OF economic and financial change has accelerated so much in the last few years that any book dealing with personal finance quickly becomes outdated, necessitating a new edition. Devaluation of the dollar, floating exchange rates, soaring gold prices, stagflation, recession, large tax cuts, huge balance of payments deficits, bank failures, stock market declines, real estate retrenchment, a slump in new housing starts, double digit inflation followed by increased unemployment, and a subsequent multibillion-dollar peace time federal budget deficit, all have their combined impact on our personal incomes, expenditures, and borrowing, saving and investment patterns. Under such conditions better ways of getting and managing money become more important than ever.

In the past 35 years Americans have seen the value of their dollar cut by almost 75 percent. Since 1950 it has lost about half its value. If we can ever get back down to a 6 percent inflation, today's 27 cent dollar will be halved in another 12 years. The 12 percent rate we experienced recently would do the job in a mere 6 years. The story of the Vanishing American Dollar is as follows:

1975 = 27.1 cents	1950 = 57.7 cents
1970 = 35.8 cents	1945 = 77.2 cents
1960 = 46.9 cents	1939 = 100.0 cents

Headlines bemoan the end of affluence and the disastrous impact of financial disorder:

"Inflation Pinches Everyone"

"Economy Seen Changing Many Life Styles Sharply"

"The High Cost of Living It Up"

"Inflation Is Cruel to the Already Poor"

"Middle Income: The Fun's Gone"—"Low Income: Getting By Becomes Still More Difficult"

"The Squeeze on the Middle Class"

"Even The Well-To-Do Begin To Feel Inflation's Bite"

Taxes and dollar depreciation have taken their toll. It now takes an income of $21,080 to give you as much purchasing power as a $10,000 income provided in 1949. Even more striking, you have to earn $54,300 today to maintain the same standard of living as a $25,000 income provided 25 years ago.

If we say that middle class families are those with annual incomes of from $10,000 to $25,000, just over half of all U.S. families, 28.4 million, or 52 percent are included. About 39 percent had incomes of less than $10,000, while 9 percent had incomes of more than $25,000. The rising cost of middle class living was up from $13,000 for an urban family of four in 1967 to over $20,000 today, an increase in seven years of 53 percent!

A new, leaner life style is emerging in the United States. Higher costs are restricting gains in living standards. The rich feel this but little, social programs are helping the poor, but it is the middle class that is most troubled. It is losing the gains of the last 20 years. The blows suffered last year by the family with a middle range 1974 income of $14,466 included: a 14.3 percent rise in transportation costs; a 13.5 percent increase in housing costs; an 11.9 percent rise in food costs; a 26.5 percent increase in personal tax payments and a 21.6 percent rise in social security payments, plus boosts in real estate and sales taxes.

After nearly a generation of free spending and casual work habits, people are now trying to reduce debts and attempting to hold onto their jobs. More people are living alone. There has been a weakening of family ties. Social security, pensions, and medicare enable the elderly to live—precariously—apart from their grown children. Young people now move away from family restraints as soon as they find jobs. The number of nonfamily households has doubled in a little over two decades. The divorce rate has also doubled. The U.S. birth rate plunged from 26.6 per 1,000 in 1947 to 14.9 per 1,000 in 1974. The U.S. population is aging, though the greatest increase in population will come in the 18–39 age group. As we approach zero population growth, geriatrics will become more important than pediatrics, and nursing homes more numerous than day care centers.

How to manage personal finances in the face of such economic and financial uncertainties poses major challenges. You will face a host of perplexing financial choices over the next 40 or 50 years. Whether you handle them poorly or competently will go far toward determining the quality of your life style. If the following pages have any value, the measure of their worth will be the degree to which they will help you to reason wisely, to understand, and to come to sensible decisions on the host of financial dilemmas which will confront you over the next half century.

Since most of us have no funds to administer before we start earning an income, this book begins with income and occupation, the source of whatever financial resources the typical individual or family can acquire. Next, attention is shifted to basic expenditures which usually consume the major share of total income. Then comes the tax bite which each year seems to grow larger and larger. The remainder of the volume is devoted to that residual segment of resources, small though it may be, which can provide comforts, satisfactions, and security beyond the basic needs. At first this segment may be a mere emergency fund of dollars to fall back on in case of need. A combination of some of these surplus dollars and borrowing may bring the benefit of extra goods and services. As the savings grow, you normally think of the advantages of insurance, homes of your own, and the need for retirement income when earnings cease. Social security provides a base for life insurance programming, as well as for annuity and pension planning. Health care has become terribly important and costly. Automobile insurance, if you can get it, is more and more expensive. If you are fortunate in accumulating modest or even immodest surpluses, you have an investment problem on your hands and ultimately, since you can take nothing with you when you depart this life, the matter of the fair disposition of your accumulation must also be faced. This, in brief, is the order followed in the development of the subject.

A substantial upheaval has shaken the consumer's world over recent years. New and interesting developments have come so fast that a whole new body of laws and protective measures have been originated ranging from the new federal Consumer Product Safety Commission, the Truth in Lending and the Fair Credit Reporting laws to the Automobile Consumer Action Panels (Auto CAPs), Federal Warranty Standards Act, Security Investors Protection Act, The Real Estate Settlement Procedure Act, and no fault automobile insurance. There is a new awareness of the rights of and responsibilities to consumers. No longer does the caveat emptor (buyer beware) philosophy prevail. Consumer agencies have received recognition and achieved maturity. We have endeavored to capture and portray both the facts as well as the atmosphere of these developments. This new edition therefore reflects important developments in many fields ranging from consumer credit protection to health care to tax matters to investment innovations. A whole host of new procedures, programs, facts, and figures, too numerous to detail here, will be found in the pages which follow.

This text is designed for college use, essentially for one course, be it quarter, trimester, or semester. It may, however, easily be adapted to the double course by the simple expedient of spending one session discussing the principles of a given topic and the following session on the extensive case-problem material on that topic given at the end of each chapter and discussed in the Teacher's Manual. The case problems represent, as closely as possible, real-life situations and may, therefore, play a vital part in any course utilizing this text. Objective tests for each chapter will be found in the Teacher's Manual.

May 1975 JEROME B. COHEN

Acknowledgments

THE RANGE of topics covered in this volume is so diverse, detailed, and practical that it was essential to consult numerous experts. While any errors that remain are the author's responsibility, the assistance rendered by the writings and the cooperation shown by those versed in the various specialized topics is gratefully acknowledged. Hundreds of requests have gone forth for permission to use the fruits of their labor. Practically without exception it has been granted enthusiastically. So many experts in their own specialties have given advice or constructive criticism that it is impossible to mention them all in the brief space available here, much as one should like to do it. Some of them, however, have provided such substantial help that specific acknowledgment must be made.

I am especially indebted to Dr. Earl Nicks and Mr. Jeffrey A. Palca of the Insurance Information Institute; Mr. Milton Amsel and Ms. Joyce Morrissey of the Institute of Life Insurance; Dr. S. Lees Booth, Senior Vice President of the National Consumer Finance Association; Mr. V. G. Phelps, Assistant Vice President, Government Employees Insurance Corporation; Mr. Fred C. Cohn, Executive Vice President, Hugh Johnson & Co. Inc.; Mr. Robert W. Sterling and Mr. Jerome Sterling of M. C. Horsey & Co.; Ms. Denise Shulmister of the Health Insurance Association of America; Mr. John W. Hazard, Executive Editor of *Changing Times*, the Kiplinger Magazine, and Mrs. Gwen Fitzpatrick, Director of Promotion; Mr. Herman Spar, Vice President and Treasurer, Saks Fifth Avenue; Mr. Norman Guess of the Dartnell Corporation of Chicago; Ms. Margaret C. Dean, R.D., Food and Nutrition Consultant, American Red Cross; Mr. A. W. Cohen, Editor, Chartcraft Inc.; Mr. Allan Gruson, Actuarial Division, Metropolitan Life Insurance Co.; Ms. Ann V. Galvin, Vice President, Anchor Corp.; Mr. Herman Nickerson, Jr., Administrator, National Credit Union Administration; Mr. Arthur Vare and Mr. James Hunt of Kalb, Voorhis & Co., Mr. Graham M. Bright, Director of Information, Louis Harris & Associates Inc.; Mr. William Ruder of Ruder and Finn Inc.; Mr. Frank S. Endicott, Emeritus Director of Placement, Northwestern University; Mr. Paul Rivers of the Federal Reserve Bank of New York; Mr. Torrey Dodson, Second Vice President, TIAA-College Retirement Equities Fund; Mr. Fabian Linden, Director of Consumer Research of the Conference Board; Mr. Joseph Naar, Director of Information of the Conference Board; Prof. Lewis Mandell, Director, Social Science Research Institute, University of Maine; Mr. Meyer Zitter, Chief, Population Division, Bureau of the Census; Mr. N. Russell Wayne, Executive Editor of Value Line; Ms. Joyce E. Bryant, Director, Money Management Institute, Household Finance Corp.; Ms. Frances M. Moran, J.D., Assistant Vice President, the Keystone Company of Boston; Mr. Allen Silver, Editor/Publisher, FundScope, Inc.; Ms. Phoebe McConaughy, Managing Editor, Research, Life Insurance Agency Management Association; Dr. John Wilson, Senior Vice President and Chief Economist, Ms. Lora S. Collins, Vice President and Economist, and Mr. Arnold Pearlman, Associate Economist of The Chase Manhattan Bank NA; Mr. Norman Gottesman, Vice President, Indicator Digest; Mr. Richard Rush, Editor, *Art Investment Report*; Mr. Kenneth D. Campbell of Audit Investment Research; Prof. Paul M. Horvitz, Director of Research, Federal Deposit Insurance Corporation; Ms. Betty B. Peterkin, Food Economist, Research Division, U.S. Department of Agriculture; Mr. Earl Stephens, Assistant Vice President and Mr. Patrick J. McDonald, Managing Editor of Moody's Investors Service, Inc.; Mr. Joseph L. Oppenheimer, Vice President, and Mr. Joseph M. Gallagher, Vice President, Standard & Poor's Corp.; Mr. Robert Anderson, Editor, *The Outlook*, Standard & Poor's Corp.; Mr. Thomas Halley of Standard & Poor's InterCapital; Mr. Ben Rudolph of All Coverage Insurance Agency; Mr. Martin Karlin and Ms. Solidelle Wasser, Bureau of Labor Statistics (New York), U.S. Department of Labor; Dr. Allan O. Felix, Director of Education of the New York Stock Exchange; Mr. James Dines of James Dines & Co.; Mr. John D. Meyer of T. J. Holt & Co.; Mr. Dana H. Danforth, President of Danforth Associates; Dr. V. Grant, National Center for Educational Statistics, Office of Education, U.S. Department of Health, Education and Welfare.

To Ms. Mina S. Cohen a separate paragraph of appreciation and gratitude is required. While her contributions are not reflected in gross national product data, without her talents as an extraordinary researcher, and without her indomitable drive and perseverance, the complete revision and updating of this book would not have occurred.

J. B. C.

Contents

1

Income and Occupation

Experience keeps a dear school, but Fools will learn in no other.
Poor Richard's Almanack

YOU HAVE already made the first wise decision in managing your personal finances. You are in college, and experts estimate that the college graduate will receive an average of $231,696 more income during a lifetime than will the average high school graduate. There is a very high positive correlation between years of education and average lifetime earnings, as the following figures show:

Years of Education	*Average Lifetime Earnings*
Graduate study of 1 or more years	$823,759
College graduate (4 years or more)	710,569
High school graduate	478,873
Elementary school only	343,730

From the standpoint of maximizing income, it clearly pays to go to college; it also pays even more to graduate.

Recent figures[1] emphasize this relationship, as can be seen in the following listing of the mean annual income of men 25–34 years of age:

Elementary school	Less than 8 years	$ 5,699
	8 years	6,749
High school	1–3 years	7,856
	4 years	9,451
College	1–3 years	9,848
	4 years	17,480
	4 years or more	18,545
	5 years or more	19,672

[1] "Annual Mean Income, Lifetime Income and Educational Attainment of Men in the U.S. for Selected Years," U.S. Dept. of Commerce, Bureau of the Census, *Current Population Reports, Consumer Series* P–60 no. 92, March 1974.

Occupation and education have a good deal to do with determination of level of income. Generally speaking, it appears that heads of low-income families have had little formal education or training and are mainly unskilled workers, whereas heads of upper income families have had much more formal education, and this seems to have led them into either business or the professions. "Average family income tends to rise as the educational attainment of the head increases," according to the U.S. Census Bureau.

"We should all be concerned with the future," Charles F. Kettering once advised, "because we will have to spend the rest of our lives there." Your preparation for the future couldn't start off to better advantage. Personal finance is meaningful only if there is an adequate income to manage. If you pursue your present course, you are probably well on your way to a higher income bracket.

There is a school of thought, of course, that discounts the value of a college education and emphasizes experience. "Schooling and education are not synonymous: the educational content of time spent at school ranges from superb to miserable," Mincer states, and adds, "moreover, school is neither the only, nor necessarily the most important, training ground for shaping market productivities."[2] College does, however, guide millions toward satisfying goals.

While a college education has many rewards other than monetary benefits, these should not be overlooked. A higher percentage of young people are going to college these days, and of those who graduate many are going on to advanced degrees. Getting your college degree is step one in sound personal finance. Step two is tied in very closely—deciding what career or profession to pursue as your lifework. That's almost as hard as paying for college these days.

Intelligent Choice of a Career

In many instances a person finds himself in some occupation more or less by chance and not as the result of some well thought out plan. A hunch, a word from some friend, an inviting advertisement in a newspaper, parental advice, a "Help Wanted" sign on a building, or some other small impetus may land a person in a job in which a lifetime is spent. Often it works out pretty well; in other cases the person must wonder whether another calling might not have produced more satisfactory results.

---

[2] Jacob Mincer, *Schooling, Experience and Earnings,* New York: Columbia University Press, 1974, Introduction.

Progress has been made in devising aptitude and interest tests which can tell you the sorts of things you ought to be able to do satisfactorily and in which you may take a real interest. When we consider that a person sometimes spends nearly half of the waking hours on the job, it certainly seems sensible to strive to find work that will be congenial. We usually like interesting work that we have the ability to perform well. Aptitude tests are available in educational institutions and also in commercial testing centers in the larger cities throughout the United States. Let us assume you are about to choose a field for a career.

What input is needed to make the right choice in college? Employment probabilities, the expected monetary return, and your anticipated satisfaction return are all basic to your decision.

Teacher in Britain Decides to Switch to Bricklaying

PETERBOROUGH, England (UPI)—Kim Joyce, a teacher is quitting to become a bricklayer.

"Teaching just doesn't pay," said the 26-year-old teacher, who earns $67.50 a week as an elementary school instructor.

In Britain, many bricklayers are earning more than $250 a week.

New York Times June 27, 1973.

The occupational outlook to 1985 sees a projected growth of managers and administrators up from 8 million in 1972 to reach 10.5 million in 1985. The growth in professional and technical employment will continue faster than all others, from 11.5 million in 1972 to an expected 17 million in 1985.[3] An exception is the slow down in teaching. Engineering jobs are expected to grow rapidly, but at a slower rate than during the 1960s. While total employment will probably increase about 24 percent between 1972 and 1985, an increase of 37 percent is expected for white collar jobs.

What kind of jobs? Rapid growth is anticipated in industrial research and development, in health care, in computer programming and systems analysis, in personnel, and in other service functions. "Requirements for salaried managers are likely to continue to increase rapidly because of the increasing dependence of business organizations and government agencies on management specialists, according to "The U.S. Economy in 1985."

The majority of the 60 million job openings expected to become available between 1972 and 1985 will be open to persons who have not completed a full four years of college. While educational requirements will

[3] "The U.S. Economy in 1985," *Monthly Labor Review*, December 1973.

continue to rise for most jobs, college level training obtained through junior and community colleges will become increasingly important.

Manpower needs and the changing nature of the economy are interdependent. The job market shifts as an invention creates a new industry or automation wipes out an old one. Occupational choices may be narrowed because of the falling birth rate or increased competition from minorities.

'Orphans Preferred'

"Wanted," said the ad for Pony Express riders in 1860. "Young, skinny wiry fellows not over 18. Must be expert riders, willing to risk death daily. Orphans preferred. Wages $25.00 per week."

New York Times, August 13, 1970.

Demand in some careers like teaching, law, engineering, and business, follow a cyclical pattern.[4] Studies have found that they run through a four or five year cycle. A shortage in one field raises the salaries offered, which in turn attracts students, thereby increasing the supply. A surplus of talent, in turn, limits salaries and makes that career for a time unattractive to new entrants. For example, B.A.'s in education, which in 1970–71 were at their high of 177 thousand, dropped to 142 thousand in 1974, as the enrollment in elementary schools dropped and the demand for teachers lessened. As the accompanying Gallup poll indicates, however, financial realism is tempered by an equal insistence on career happiness. Despite the awareness of tight employment possibilities in education, teaching still held the highest appeal for college sophomores, juniors, and seniors. It was tied with medical care for top choice among freshmen.

Average annual openings expected between 1972 and 1985 are shown in Table 1–1 for selected occupations.

The job hunting graduate whose studies are more relevant to the times finds less difficulty. For example, one university urges all students, especially liberal arts majors, to take two tool courses—one in statistics and the other in computer programming—to make them more marketable when seeking work.[5]

Every undecided student may benefit from consulting the *Occupational Outlook Handbook* (842 pages) issued periodically by the U.S. Bureau of Labor Statistics. It not only deals with the employment outlook in over 850 occupations and 30 major industries—ranging from artists and ac-

---

[4] Jeffrey G. Madrick, "Careers with a Future," *Money*, April 1973, p. 24.

[5] "College Students' Big Goal Today: Earn a Living," *U.S. News and World Report*, December 30, 1974, p. 54. See also *Occupational Manpower and Training Needs*, Revised 1974 (Bulletin 1824) Bureau of Labor Statistics, 1975.

Gallup Poll

The question asked was, "What field or occupation do you plan to enter when you complete your education?"

The national results, by male and female students, follow:

	National 0/0	Men 0/0	Women 0/0
Teaching (college, high school, grade school)	23	17	32
Medical care (doctors, nurses, dentists, medical technicians, etc.)	14	10	20
Business	12	13	11
Law	10	13	5
Research and science	8	9	7
The arts (theater, music, painting, writing, crafts)	7	5	9
Social work (recreation, guidance counseling)	6	4	9
Engineering	4	7	†
Accounting/auditing	3	4	2
Government work (not including military)	3	4	2
Clergy (incl. religious and missionary work)	2	3	1
Military	2	2	1
Farming	1	2	†
Journalism/newspaper work	1	1	1
Sales	1	2	†
Service (airline hostess, cook, domestic help)	1	2	†
Urban planning	1	1	†
Miscellaneous	4	4	2
Don't know/no answer	6	7	6
(Totals)	109‡	110‡	108‡

† Less than 1 percent.

‡ Total exceeds 100 percent due to multiple responses.

New York Times, April 25, 1974.

Despite Nonsexist Name, It Still Sounds Like Work

By a *Wall Street Journal* Staff Reporter

WASHINGTON — "Brewmasters" are headed for extinction, the Labor Department decided.

In revising its massive Dictionary of Occupational Titles to eliminate age and sex connotations, the department has decided the job properly should be called "brewing director."

Among the 3,500 job titles that have been revised, "governess" has become "child mentor" and "headmaster" has been changed to "private school principal." A "maid" henceforth is a "houseworker," while a "valet" is a "gentleman's attendant."

The title "song and dance man" has become "song and dance person."

But the department's Manpower Administration, which makes the job-title decisions, says it hasn't decided how to change its own name.

Wall Street Journal, March 14, 1975.

countants to engineers, teachers, lawyers, and physicians—but also, where data are available, presents information on earnings, past, present, and prospective. Under each occupation listed are sections entitled "Nature of Work," "Where Employed," "Employment Outlook," "Training and Other Qualifications," "Earnings and Working Conditions," and "Where to Go for More Information."

TABLE 1–1
Expected Annual Occupational Openings, 1972–1985

Occupation	*1972 Employment*	*Expected Annual Openings*
Accountants	714,000	41,900
Architects	37,000	3,300
Chemists	134,000	6,800
Computer operating personnel	480,000	27,000
Counselors, school	43,000	2,900
Dentists	105,000	5,300
Draftsmen	327,000	17,900
Economists	36,000	1,500
Engineering and science technicians	707,000	39,600
Engineers	1,100,000	53,000
Geologists	23,000	1,100
Historians	24,000	1,500
Lawyers	303,000	16,500
Mathemeticians	76,000	4,200
Nurses	748,000	75,000
Physicians	330,000	19,000
Scientists	180,000	9,200
Social workers	185,000	17,500
Systems analysts	103,000	8,300
Teachers—College	525,000	24,000
Teachers—Kindergarten and elementary	1,274,000	105,000
Teachers—Secondary school	1,023,000	40,000

Source: *Occupational Outlook Handbook*, Bureau of Labor Statistics. Copies of the 1974–75 edition may be obtained from the Superintendent of Documents, U.S. Government Printing Office, Washington, D.C. 20402, at the cost of $6.85 each. If your college library is a government depository, it has a copy

Several abridged examples may give some indication of the usefulness of this volume:

> *Accountants.* Accountants numbered about 700,000, of whom about 20 percent were certified public accountants. About 3 percent of the CPAs, and 22 percent of all accountants are women.
>
> Employment of accountants is expected to increase rapidly through the 1980s as businesses and government agencies continue to expand in size and complexity. . . . Starting salaries of beginning accountants in private industry were $9,100. . . . Earnings of experienced accountants ranged between $11,900 and $17,400 depending on their level of responsibility and the complexity of the accounting system. . . . Beginning auditors averaged $9,600 a year, while experienced auditors' earnings ranged between $12,900 and $15,900. . . . Salaries are generally higher for accountants holding a graduate degree or a CPA certificate. More than 60 percent of all accountants do management accounting work. An additional 20 percent are engaged in public accounting as proprietors, partners, or employees of independent accounting firms. Other accountants work for federal, state, and local government agencies and a small number teach in colleges and universities.

Information about CPAs and aptitude tests given in many high schools, colleges, and public accounting firms, may be obtained from:

American Institute of Certified Public Accountants
666 Fifth Avenue
New York, New York 10019

Home Economists. About 120,000 persons were employed in home economics occupations. This figure includes an estimated 33,000 dietitians and approximately 5,300 cooperative extension workers who are discussed in separate statements elsewhere in the *Handbook*. Seventy thousand home economists are teachers: approximately 50,000 teach in secondary schools; more than 15,000 are adult education instructors; 5,000 teach in colleges and universities. . . . Home economists, especially those wishing to teach in high schools, may face some competition for jobs through the mid 1980s. Other areas . . . also may experience competitive job market conditions. . . . For those willing to continue their education toward an advanced degree, employment prospects in college and university teaching are expected to be good. . . . Cooperative extension workers on the county level averaged $10,300 while those on the state level averaged $14,200. . . . In general, home economists earn about one and one half times as much as nonsupervisory workers in private industry, except farming. . . . Home economics teachers generally receive the same salary as other teachers. The federal government paid home economists with bachelor degrees starting salaries of $7,700 and $9,500 depending on their scholastic record. Those with additional education and experience generally earned from $11,600 to $19,700 depending on level of responsibility.

A list of schools granting degrees . . . types of home economics majors offered in each school . . . and graduate scholarships are available from:

American Home Economics Association
1600 20th St. N.W.
Washington, D.C. 20036

Programmers. The programmer's job is to prepare step by step instructions for the computer to follow. . . . About 186,000 persons—about three-fourths of them men—worked as programmers. . . . The employment of programmers will grow rapidly over the next decade as the number of computer installations increases. Beginning salaries averaged $8,500 according to a Bureau of Labor Statistics survey in urban areas. Those in the North and West earned slightly more than the average, while workers in the South earned a little less. Programmers who worked for manufacturers and public utilities had higher earnings than those employed by banks and insurance companies. . . . Experienced business programmers averaged $11,000 a year. . . . Lead programmers averaged $14,400 and managers of programming $16,700 a year. . . . Additional information about the occupation of programmer may be obtained from:

Data Processing Management Association
505 Busse Highway
Park Ridge, Ill. 60068

A list of reading materials on career opportunities in programming may be obtained from:

Association for Computing Machinery
1133 Avenue of the Americas
New York, N.Y. 10036

Psychologists. Psychologists study the normal and abnormal behavior of individuals and groups in order to understand and explain their actions. . . . Psychologists often combine several areas of psychology in their specialty. Clinical psychologists are the largest group of specialists. . . . About 57,000 people, one fourth of them women, worked as psychologists. . . . More than 40 percent of the total worked in colleges and universities. . . . A Ph.D. degree—the mark of the full professional—is needed for many entrance positions. . . . Employment opportunities . . . are expected to be good through the mid 1980s . . . starting salaries for psychologists holding a master degree averaged about $11,000 a year. . . . Beginning salaries for those holding a doctorate averaged $13,000. . . . The average salary for Ph.D. psychologists in the Veterans Administration was about $21,000 a year. Psychologists who want to enter independent practice must meet certification or licensing requirements in an increasing number of states. . . .

For general information on career opportunities, certification or licensing requirements, and educational facilities and financial assistance for graduate students in psychology, contact:

American Psychological Association
1200 17th Street N.W.
Washington, D.C. 20036

Income, Occupation, and Education

In Table 1–2, as you can see, more than half of the households where the head holds a college degree are among the 29.9 percent of the total number with annual incomes over $15,000. The median income for the college graduate group was $17,011; for the high school graduate, $11,474; and for those who had completed eight years of elementary school it was $6,890, compared to the overall median income of $10,512.

There may be temporary periods when the job market for college graduates is occasionally depressed, but over the longer run, the college graduate tends to obtain the better paying position.

TABLE 1–2

Age, Education, Residence, Sex, and Race of Head—Households by Total Money Income in 1973 (households as of March 1974)

Subject	All Households (thousands)	Total Household Income: Total	Under $4,000	$4,000 to $4,999	$5,000 to $5,999	$6,000 to $6,999	$7,000 to $7,999	$8,000 to $8,999	$9,000 to $9,999	$10,000 to $11,999	$12,000 to $14,999	$15,000 to $24,999	$25,000 to $49,999	$50,000 and Over	Median Income (dollars)	Mean Income (dollars)
Age of Head																
Total	69,859	100.0	17.5	5.4	5.0	5.0	4.9	5.0	4.7	9.7	12.9	22.1	6.9	0.9	10,512	12,157
14 to 24 years	5,857	100.0	21.1	7.1	8.5	9.1	8.3	7.9	7.0	10.4	11.2	8.5	0.8	0.1	7,496	8,235
25 to 34 years	14,332	100.0	8.5	3.7	3.6	4.4	5.5	6.0	6.0	13.6	18.7	25.4	4.4	0.4	11,834	12,522
35 to 44 years	11,703	100.0	7.0	2.7	3.0	3.6	3.9	4.6	4.3	10.4	16.1	33.2	10.0	1.2	13,963	15,261
45 to 54 years	12,939	100.0	8.9	3.2	3.4	3.3	3.6	4.2	4.3	9.7	13.4	31.2	13.2	1.5	14,081	15,824
55 to 64 years	11,149	100.0	16.2	5.1	4.7	4.9	5.1	4.8	4.7	9.9	12.4	22.3	8.7	1.0	10,877	12,833
65 years and over	13,879	100.0	43.7	11.0	8.5	6.5	4.6	4.1	3.0	4.7	5.0	6.4	2.1	0.6	4,583	6,857
Educational Attainment of Head																
Total	69,859	100.0	17.5	5.4	5.0	5.0	4.9	5.0	4.7	9.7	12.9	22.1	6.9	0.9	10,512	12,157
Elementary: less than 8 yrs.	8,678	100.0	39.8	9.9	7.4	6.5	5.7	4.4	3.8	6.2	6.5	8.1	1.5	0.1	5,030	6,885
8 years	7,676	100.0	28.8	8.2	7.2	6.5	5.1	5.6	4.7	8.4	9.4	13.3	2.6	0.2	6,890	8,764
High School: 1 to 3 years	10,972	100.0	21.8	6.7	6.4	5.6	5.5	5.0	5.1	11.0	12.2	17.2	3.3	0.3	8,816	10,062
4 years	22,849	100.0	11.5	4.3	4.4	5.0	5.3	5.7	5.3	11.8	15.9	24.8	5.7	0.5	11,474	12,511
College: 1 to 3 years	9,142	100.0	11.1	3.7	4.2	4.6	4.3	5.3	4.8	9.8	15.1	27.9	8.3	0.9	12,449	13,701
4 or more	10,542	100.0	5.5	2.3	2.3	2.1	2.9	3.6	3.4	7.6	13.4	34.1	19.4	3.4	17,011	19,042
Total, Head 25 Years Old and Over	64,002	100.0	17.4	5.2	4.7	4.6	4.6	4.8	4.5	9.6	13.1	23.3	7.5	0.9	10,924	12,516
Elementary: less than 8 yrs.	8,566	100.0	39.9	9.8	7.2	6.5	5.7	4.5	3.8	6.2	6.5	8.2	1.6	0.1	5,034	6,902
8 years	7,538	100.0	28.6	8.2	7.2	6.5	5.1	5.5	4.7	8.4	9.5	13.5	2.7	0.2	6,928	8,816
High school: 1 to 3 years	10,037	100.0	20.6	6.6	6.2	5.1	5.4	4.9	5.1	11.2	12.7	18.5	3.6	0.3	9,254	10,396
4 years	20,245	100.0	10.8	3.9	3.9	4.3	4.8	5.3	5.1	11.8	16.3	26.9	6.4	0.6	12,034	13,032
College: 1 to 3 years	7,774	100.0	9.2	3.2	3.3	4.0	3.7	5.0	4.3	9.8	15.6	31.0	9.5	1.0	13,379	14,565
4 or more	9,843	100.0	4.8	1.9	1.8	1.8	2.5	3.2	3.1	7.5	13.4	35.6	20.7	3.6	17,776	19,717
Residence																
Total	69,859	100.0	17.5	5.4	5.0	5.0	4.9	5.0	4.7	9.7	12.9	22.1	6.9	0.9	10,512	12,157
Nonfarm	66,970	100.0	17.4	5.3	5.0	4.9	4.9	5.0	4.7	9.7	13.0	22.3	6.9	0.9	10,572	12,188
Farm	2,889	100.0	19.9	6.8	6.4	6.1	5.1	5.5	4.5	9.4	10.8	17.5	7.0	1.0	9,032	11,442
Sex of Head																
Total	69,859	100.0	17.5	5.4	5.0	5.0	4.9	5.0	4.7	9.7	12.9	22.1	6.9	0.9	10,512	12,157
Male	53,862	100.0	9.3	4.3	4.4	4.4	4.7	5.1	4.9	10.9	15.3	27.1	8.7	1.1	12,416	13,967
Female	15,997	100.0	45.7	9.2	7.3	6.8	5.6	4.7	3.8	5.7	5.0	5.3	0.9	0.1	4,478	6,064
Race of Head																
Total	69,859	100.0	17.5	5.4	5.0	5.0	4.9	5.0	4.7	9.7	12.9	22.1	6.9	0.9	10,512	12,157
White	61,965	100.0	15.9	5.1	4.8	4.8	4.7	5.0	4.7	9.9	13.4	23.3	7.4	1.0	11,017	12,627
Black and other races	7,894	100.0	30.4	7.8	6.9	6.2	6.0	5.5	4.6	8.4	9.0	12.3	2.8	0.2	6,730	8,471
Black	7,040	100.0	32.0	7.9	7.2	6.1	6.3	5.6	4.4	8.3	8.9	11.1	2.1	0.1	6,436	8,053

Source: U.S. Department of Commerce, Bureau of the Census, *Consumer Income* (Washington, D.C.: U.S. Government Printing Office, July 1974), Series P–60, No. 93.

Average Income in the United States

Perhaps it would help if you knew what the income of the average family and person in the United States is. Then you can judge your own position and outlook. The U.S. Bureau of the Census reports on incomes of families, of unrelated individuals, and of households. It answers such questions as: How many families are there in each income bracket? What is average annual family income? How does family income vary according to urban and rural residence, major source of earnings, color, size of family, type of family, age of head of family, and number of children?

FIGURE 1–1
Distribution of Money Income of U.S. Families—1973

1973 Income (dollars)	Families	Percent
Over 25,000	5,112,000 Families	9%
25,000		
	14,400,000 Families	26.0%
15,000		
	14,039,000 Families	25.5%
10,000		
	5,515,000 Families	10.0%
8,000		
	2,709,000 Families	4.91%
7,000		
	2,640,000 Families	4.79%
6,000		
	2,555,000 Families	4.69%
5,000		
	2,491,000 Families	4.5%
4,000		
	2,244,000 Families	4.1%
3,000		
	1,755,000 Families	3.1%
2,000		
	965,000 Families	1.7%
1,000		
	628,000 Families	1.1%
0		

Figures may not add up to 100 percent because of rounding.
Source: U.S. Department of Commerce, Bureau of the Census, *Consumer Income* (Washington, D.C.: U.S. Government Printing Office, July 1974), Series P-60, No. 93.

Of the nation's 55.1 million families, 14.5 percent of the total number, had incomes in 1973 of less than $5,000 (see Figure 1–1). On the other hand, 60.5 percent had incomes of $10,000 or more. At the top of the ladder, over 5 million families (or 9 percent of the total) received incomes of $25,000 per year or more. Figure 1–2 shows upward movement of family income and the increased number of families moving into the top level.

Although the median income for all families was $12,051, there was considerable variation, due to a number of factors.[6] For example, the

[6] "Median income" may be defined as that income below which (and above which) half of all the units fall. The median is not affected, as is the arithmetic mean (sometimes simply called the "average"), by a few high- (or low-) income units.

average income of nonfarm families ($12,151) was higher than that of farm families ($10,045). Marked differences characterized the income levels of white and nonwhite families. For the country as a whole, the median income of white families ($12,595), was almost twice that received by nonwhite families ($7,269). The median income of the nonwhite family was about 60 percent of the white family in 1973, an 8 percent increase over the median figure a decade earlier.

Family income varies according to the age of the chief breadwinner and according to who heads the family. The median income rose from $8,014 for families in which the head was under 25 years to $15,223 for

FIGURE 1–2
Families by Income

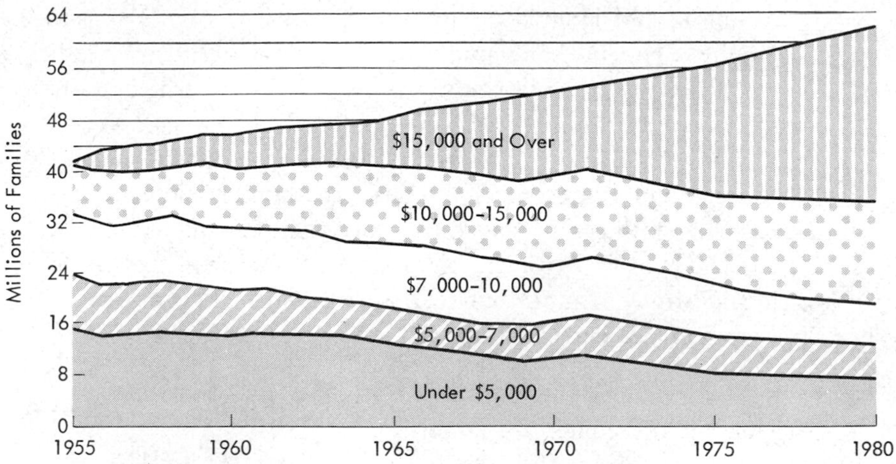

Source: U.S. Department of Commerce, The Conference Board, 1974/1975.

families in which the breadwinner was from 45 to 54 years of age. The median then declined to $6,426 for families in which the head was 65 years or older. Thus, middle age, the decade from 45 to 54 years, is the period of peak earnings. Families headed by males received considerably larger incomes ($12,965) than those headed by females ($5,797). This may be partly because families headed by females more often represent broken families, where the woman had not expected to assume the responsibility of providing for the family and may not have been well prepared for it. Also they may have had to put convenience of location and flexibility of hours above jobs with overtime or responsibility and so made less money.

Other factors also tend to move families up in the income scale. Important among these is the working wife. The proportion of husband–wife families with the wife in the paid labor force increased to 42 percent in 1973. The median income of the husband–wife families in which the wife was a paid worker was $15,237, while the median income for families in which the wife was not in the paid labor force was $11,418. Median family income where the wife worked at some time during the year rose by 37 percent on the average between 1962 and 1972; compared to a 28 percent rise for families where the wife had not worked at all.[7] Families in the income group of $15,000 and over gained the most as the proportion of working wives from that group rose from 33 percent in 1952 to about 50 percent in 1972.[8]

The upgrading in the occupational skills of the labor force reflected in an increase in the proportion of family heads employed in professional, technical, and kindred occupations has also raised the income of many families. The median family income where heads of families were so employed was $18,348 compared to the $13,730 which was the median income of all families with an employed head.

An increase in the proportion of families which have income from both earnings and other sources also raises the family income median. Families receiving both earnings and other sources of income had a median income of $12,720 in 1972, which was 14 percent more than that for families with income from earnings only. Those with incomes from multiple sources were 56.5 percent of all families.

Household Income

Income statistics are also collected in terms of households by the Census Bureau. The number of households in 1975 totaled 69.9 million. What makes a household different from a family? Household income is different from family income because it includes not only income of all related persons in the household, but also of any unrelated persons in the household. It also covers the income of one person households which tend to be relatively low. Between 1967 and 1975, there has been a shift toward smaller households and the relative number of households headed by women has increased. The average size of households is declining due to both the falling birthrate and the increasing proportion of both young and older adults who are living alone. In 1975 it had shrunk to 2.97 persons per U.S. household, the first time it has ever been below 3.

[7] *Finance Facts,* June 1974.

[8] *Current Population Reports,* Series P–60, no. 90, Bureau of the Census, U.S. Government Printing Office, Washington, D.C. 1973.

The median income of households was $10,512 according to the Census Bureau. Of total households 7.8 percent had incomes exceeding $25,000, 22 percent earned between $15,000 and $25,000, 23 percent between $10,000 and $15,000, 25 percent between $5,000 and $10,000 and 23 percent below $5,000. Household income rises until the head of the household reaches middle age and then declines. When the age of the head of the household is under 24 the median income is about $1,000 more than at the other end of the life span—at age 65 and over. It is highest between 35–54 years.

Education is a basic factor in determining amount of income. Those who had four or more years of college represented only 14.3 percent of all the households, but their mean income was 63 percent *above* the mean. At the other extreme, representing almost the same percent of households, (12.97) where the head had completed less than eight years of school, the mean was 58 percent *below* the mean for all households.

Differences in the characteristics of households are most pronounced at the high and low parts of the income distribution. Households with incomes of less than $3,000 tend to have few members, to live in small towns and the open country, and to be headed by persons 65 or more years of age. Retired persons, unskilled workers, widows, and students are most frequently found at this income level. Households with high incomes ($15,000 or more) are relatively larger in size, live in metropolitan areas, and are most frequently headed by persons between 35 and 64 years of age who are self-employed, in managerial positions, or in a profession.

A study on population change notes that "the new mores are making it more difficult to interpret the census data on households. . . ." Some communal arrangements are attempts to hold down expenses. "In other communes, whether the participants are single or married, the purposes are to explore new ways of living and of sharing experiences in accordance with the precepts of economic, social, religious, philosophical, or sexual theories—sometimes of several theories at once."[9] *The New York Times* listed 2,000 rural and urban communes.

Upper and Lower Income Groups—a Contrast

Although all groups in the nation have made real income gains, and there are fewer families in the lower fifth percentile than in 1967, the

[9] Lawrence A. Mayer, "New Questions about the U.S. Population," *Fortune*, February, 1971; Part II of series, "The U.S. Economy in an Age of Uncertainty." See also, *U.S. News and World Report*, Feb. 25, 1974, pp. 38–41.

top fifth still has the bulk of the national aggregate wealth—41.4 percent as compared to 42.7 percent in 1967. The income gap remains even though individuals move from one bracket to another. Figure 1–3 would indicate more families move upward each year. The *1974 Economic Report of the President* confirms that there has been very little change in the last 25 years in the relative shares of the national income. In 1947 the lowest fifth of families had 5.1 percent share of national income. Twenty-five years later it was 5.4 percent. The highest fifth in 1947 received 43.3 percent of national income, in 1972 its share was 41.4 percent. The top 5 percent share in 1947 was 17.5 and in 1972 was 15.9 percent.

Opposing forces working within this economic sector are changing its former general conformity. There is no longer unquestioned acceptance of hard work, deferred pleasures, and material goals. Although the new thinking has filtered into all age levels, the search for identity and new social values and concerns is especially strong among the young, affecting both their consumption demands and their productivity. Census Bureau data indicate that by 1980, 60 percent of the population will be under 35. One out of three adults under 35 will have had some college training. By reason of both numbers and purchasing power, this group, which is most susceptible to changing values, will have great influence.

Families headed by professional workers or by managers and administrators have higher median incomes ($19,120 and $19,215 respectively) than those headed by other types of workers. Self-employed professionals have

FIGURE 1–3
The Changing Pyramid of Income Distribution
(total families each year = 100%)

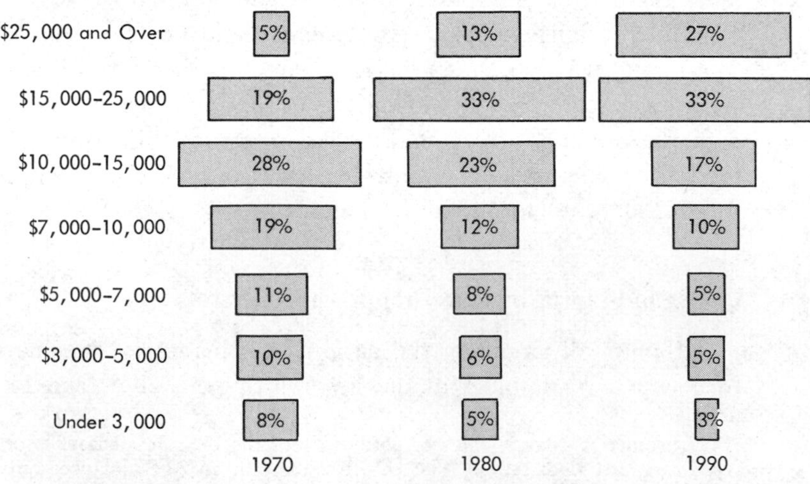

Source: The Conference Board and *Finance Facts Yearbook, 1974*.

the highest median income of all—$24,878. These are the families in the upper income levels.

In an article in *Fortune* 39 men are listed as new self-made multimillionaires ($50 million or more) to be added to a previous listing of 153 super-rich reported in a 1968 study.[10] Furthermore, of the estimated 210,000 millionaires in the United States today, roughly 5 percent are under 35 years of age.[11]

The Lower Income Group

About 23 million persons, or 11 percent of the population, were below the low income level in 1973. The federal government set the low income level (poverty level) at $4,550. The Census Bureau establishes a definition of poverty that is adjusted to reflect changes in the cost of living as measured by the Consumer Price Index. Households are classified as "poor" if total money income falls below specified levels.

The farm family poverty level is set lower than the urban family level. A single person with income of less than $2,300, a woman over 65 with income less than $2,123, a family of four with income less than $4,512, or a family of seven with income less than $7,359 are classified as "poor."

Poverty is most widespread among the aged, blacks, households headed by women, and those with little schooling. According to a labor department survey[12] of persons who live in poverty areas, the unemployment rate in a nonmetropolitan area is half that of those who live in a metropolitan area.

The number of white persons below the poverty level decreased from 28 million in 1959 to 15.1 million in 1973 (66 percent of the total poor). The number of nonwhites below the poverty level declined from 11 million in 1959 to 7.4 million in 1973, but its proportion rose from 28 percent in 1959 to 31 percent today. Numerically, two thirds of all the nation's poor are white.

One out of three families headed by women is in the low income category. When there are children in such families, almost half are below the poverty level. For black families headed by a woman, 64 percent are below

---

[10] Arthur M. Lewis, "The New Rich of the Seventies," *Fortune Magazine*, September 1973.

[11] *U.S. News and World Report*, February 25, 1974, p. 47.

[12] Poverty area is defined as one in which at least one fifth of the residents have incomes at or below poverty level. This is from a new series published quarterly, resuming the series discontinued in 1972, *Employment in Poverty Areas 1973*, U.S. Department of Labor, Bureau of Labor Statistics News, August 28, 1974.

the low income level, compared to 37 percent for white families with a female head.[13] Among females under 35 who head families, the incidence of poverty runs as high as 50 percent.[14]

Children of the poor are more likely to remain poor since they live mainly in households headed by women, who are less likely to work because of the children and therefore less likely to break the poverty barrier. Homes in which the male head has died, been divorced, disappeared, or become incapacitated are frequently in the poverty range.

Lack of schooling and low income are closely related. Men who had less than eight years of elementary school were 21.6 percent of all heads of family in the below low income level compared to the 5.4 percent who graduated high school. Female heads of family who had less than eight years of elementary school were 39.5 percent of the total in the poverty level, but even one year or more of college did not keep 15 percent of families with a female head from poverty. About half of all poor female heads who worked were in service occupations. Less than half of the poor families with a female head resided in the South. More than half lived in the North and West, and more than 60 percent in metropolitan areas.

Median income figures reflect the economic division between blacks and whites. While the median income figure for white families was $12,595, for black families it was $7,270 in 1973. From 1965 through 1970 the median income of blacks had been on the rise; but after 1970 the gain slowed. Before 1970 there had been a steady decline in the number of blacks earning under $3,000 and a sharp increase in those making above $10,000. A census report noted that between 1969 and 1973 the proportion of black husband–wife families with a working wife dropped as did the proportion of black families with two or more earners, reversing a trend begun in the 1960s. The South was an exception and the income gap there has narrowed between young black and white families where husbands and wives were both working. The earnings of black and white wives were about the same, but a higher proportion of black wives there contributed to the family income.[15] Approximately 7.4 million blacks and 15.1 million whites were below the low income level in the mid-70s.

---

[13] "Characteristics of the Low Income Population," *Consumer Income: Current Population Reports*, Series P–60, no. 94, July 1974.

[14] Fabian Linden, "The New Profile of Poverty," The Conference Board *Record*, August 1974.

[15] "The Social and Economic Status of the Black Population in the U.S.—1973," U.S. Bureau of the Census, *Current Population Reports*, Special Studies Series, P–23, no. 48, July 1974.

According to a study on poverty, it is not the verbal classifications, but living in an entirely separate economy that results as a family "ceases merely to have a low income but becomes poor."[16] For example, the poor may have to have a car in areas remote from jobs poorly serviced by mass transportation, because there is no other way to get to work, and this need seemingly conflicts with the necessity of buying food economically or getting medical help. When they patronize local food establishments—which they do out of loyalty, proximity, and the need for credit, or because of the inability to leave the neighborhood—they pay more. Poorly educated, they rarely read a paper and don't see where sales are advertised and thus pay a high price, further reducing their living standard.[17] Thus, "poor families are forced to adopt technologies appropriate to the nonpoor. And as a consequence, they are made even poorer." A "discretionary" luxury like a telephone is not such a luxury in a society where daily living needs require it and where to be without it, makes one not merely poor but isolated. The study's conclusion is that "it is better to be poor in a poor society than in a rich one." To be without education and therefore poor is to be alienated from society, because technology has made commonplace progress, information, skills, and techniques not shared.

In 1973 the population aged 65 and over was 20,602,000 or about 10 percent of the total, with a median income of $4,106 if male, and $2,119 if female. Consisting mainly of retired workers and widows, these make up roughly one fifth of poor households. Of all families in the 65 and over age group, 16.3 percent are below the poverty level. About 14.4 percent of white families and 35.5 percent of black families in this age range are included. Increases in pension and social security help somewhat and account for the continued decrease in the proportion of the aged poor. For families with a male head, social security accounted for the largest proportion of the income other than earnings, while for families headed by a female, public assistance income made up the majority of their total unearned income. To sum up, people defined as "poor" are more poor compared to the rest of the population today than in the past. In 1959 they had about one half as much income as the typical family, but in 1973 they had only a little more than a third as much.

---

[16] A. Dale Tussing, "Poverty, Education and the Dual Economy," *Journal of Consumer Affairs*, vol. 4, no. 2, Winter 1970. For a review of the various studies identifying the causes of poverty, see Robert F. Mogull, "Definition, Identification and Causes of Poverty," *Modern Society*, vol. 13, nos. 3–4, May–August 1970.

[17] Louis E. Boone and John A. Bonno, "The Plight of the Poor," *Business Studies*, North Texas State University, vol. 8, no. 1, Spring 1969—a study to determine whether the poor were paying more than average shoppers.

College Graduates and the Professions

Clearly, college graduates predominate among upper income families and spending units, and the heads of the upper income groups tend to be either professional men or businessmen. College graduates fill the ranks of the professions. The professions as a group have been expanding rapidly and will probably continue to grow. A major reason for the increase in the total number of workers in professional and related occupations has been the development of new professional fields. In 1870 the leading professions were the traditional ones—medicine, the ministry, law, and teaching. Nearly 75 out of every 100 professional workers were in these occupations. The "big four" professions of 1870 have all grown considerably since that time. The number of people in scientific, engineering, and closely related professions, however, is many hundred times greater today than in 1870. Other major professions, not recognized as separate occupational fields until the turn of the century, have also developed rapidly—for example, social work, accounting, and personnel management.

The growth of the professions has, of course, been accompanied by a

FIGURE 1–4
Earned Degrees, by Level—United States, 1962–63 to 1982–1983

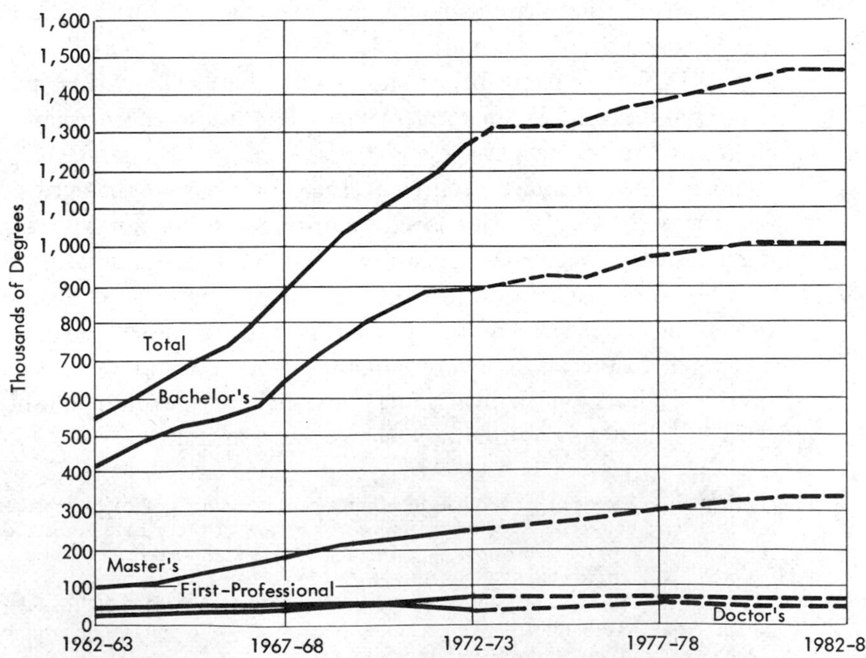

Source: *Projections of Educational Statistics to 1982–83*, Department of Health, Education and Welfare, 1973 edition.

considerable increase in the number of college students. The number of college students was 26 percent of the college age group in 1973, compared to 24 percent in 1967. Attendance at colleges and professional schools in 1982 is projected at 9.7 million. "If present trends continue, about 23 percent of persons in their late teens today can be expected to earn a bachelor's degree, 7 percent a master's degree and more than 1 percent a doctorate," as seen in Figure 1–4 and Table 1–3.

In recent years, business has been attracting gradually larger percentages of college trained men. Most of the high level administrative and specialized jobs that now exist in business are of fairly recent development. It was only about 75 years ago that really large scale industrial and commercial establishments such as we have today began to appear. Since 1920

TABLE 1–3
Earned and Projected Degrees, by Level

Level of Degree	*Granted 1962–63*	*Granted 1972–73*	*Projected 1982–83*
Bachelor's	416,400	896,000	999,000
First professional	27,100	50,000	64,500
Master's	95,500	252,400	337,700
Doctorate	12,800	33,000	52,200

Source: Projections of Educational Statistics to 1982–83, Department of Health, Education and Welfare, 1973 edition.

the number of students (male and female) graduating from business administration courses (colleges) have been increasing rapidly—from 1,500 in 1920 to 19,000 in 1940 and to 95,000 in 1970. Graduates with majors in the various specialties of business administration outnumber those in such large fields as engineering, law, and medicine.

College provides the essential training necessary to enter the more specialized professions, such as medicine, law, dentistry, and the technical phases of business, such as accounting, finance, and engineering. By and large, the nongraduate is barred from these fields. And because of preempting the highly specialized and technical occupations, the college graduate not only tends to earn more even at the outset of a career than the noncollege person, but the cash value of a degree increases with age, through the 45–54 year age category.

Women in the Professions

Approximately 38 percent of the women of working age in the United States are employed, compared to less than a fifth in 1890. Between 1930 and 1973, the number of women in the nation's working force rose from 10.4 million to almost 35 million. The number of women who received college degrees rose from 55,000 to 450,000 a year, and of women pursuing professional careers from 1.5 to 3.3 million. Four out of five of today's professional women are concentrated in seven professions: teaching, nursing, social work, library work, music, accounting and auditing, and work as technicians (medical and dental).[18] Women college graduates engage predominantly in teaching. Largely because of this, the college woman doesn't, on the average, do as well financially as her male counterpart. Over 60 percent of women college graduates go into teaching, which unfortunately is not one of the higher paying professions. A large number are underutilized in relation to their educational achievement. For example, one fifth of employed women with four years of college were working as service, sales, or clerical workers.[19]

Educated women are working in greater numbers than ever before. The higher a wife has climbed the educational ladder, the more likely she is to work—half the wives with a college degree are in the labor force against one fifth with less than five years of schooling. And the tendency for wives with higher educational attainments to work has increased while the proportion with less schooling who work has remained relatively constant. Moral—the man who marries an educated woman is more likely to be supported in the style to which he would like to become accustomed.

In 1940 there were just 4.2 million working wives. By 1950 the number was up to 8.6 million and by 1973, had jumped to 19.3 million or 42 percent of all wives in the population. Some of this increase can be explained by the population increase. But more significant has been the change in social attitudes concerning the employment of married women. Husbands no longer consider it a reflection on their earning ability if their wives have a paying job, and the earnings of these married women have contributed to higher standards of living, including the rise in home ownership and the increase in the number of college-educated youth.

The median income of the full time year round working women is $6,488 and has been increasing. If a college graduate, her median income was $9,771; working as a professional or technical worker, $9,093; or a manager or administrator, $7,667. A committee on the status of women in the economics profession reported that, "while women constitute 12 percent of the persons earning doctorate degrees in economics, they con-

---

[18] John B. Parrish, "College Women and Jobs—Another Look at the 1970s," *Journal of College Placement*, April–May 1971.

[19] *Underutilization of Women Workers* (Washington, D.C.: U.S. Department of Labor, Women's Bureau, 1971).

stitute only 7 percent of the economic faculties at major universities." But they are achieving more in the business world. About 15 percent of the membership of the National Association of Business Economists are women. The number of women enrolled in medical schools has more than doubled and is 15.4 percent of total enrollment. Medicine is the top earning profession for men and is the seventh highest for women, with a substantial number of women in the field (25,000 or 9 percent). Median earnings for the top ranking occupation for women were about half the earnings for the top ranking occupation for men.[20]

Among professional jobs, women account for 40 percent and earn 65 percent of what the men do. In the manager–administrator classification they are 18.4 percent of the total and their income is 53 percent of the male's income.[21] Changing jobs and geography had always been a handicap, but today, if relocation is part of advancement, it is regarded as discrimination for management to assume that a woman will not accept a transfer. Women have become more willing to be mobile and management is increasingly going out of its way to accommodate two careers in a family, even to the extent of job hunting for the other spouse—if they desire the talents of one of them.

New federal legislation has strengthened the enforcement of provisions which prohibits sex discrimination. Firms holding federal contracts are required to develop written affirmative action plans for recruiting, hiring, training and promoting women, and this is having an impact on the hiring policies of companies which are beginning to expand executive opportunities for women.[22]

What Professions Pay

Not all professions pay equally well. Medicine and law provide the highest average income. The teachers and the clergy get the least. Business and engineering lie in between. Of course, some corporation executives get handsome incomes running into six figures, but these are the fortunate few—the exceptions, not the average. A survey of administrative salaries in eastern corporations by the Dartnell Corporation of Chicago placed the average executive compensation at levels shown in Table 1–4.

The disparity between a beginner's salary and a seasoned executive's

---

[20] Dixie Sommers, "Occupational Rankings for Men and Women by Earnings," *Monthly Labor Review*, August 1974, p. 47.

[21] *U.S. News and World Report*, May 27, 1974.

[22] *Careers for Women in the 70s*, Women's Bureau Employment Standards Administration, U.S. Department of Labor, 1973.

TABLE 1–4
Executive Compensation in U.S. Corporations

Position	Total Compensation		
	Large Companies*	*Intermediate* Companies*	*Small* Companies*
President	$79,400	$51,600	$36,200
Chairman of the board	67,500	47,800	35,700
Executive vice-president	60,300	41,300	32,800
General sales manager	31,300	27,000	19,400
Top manufacturing executive	38,400	30,000	18,500
Treasurer	31,800	25,300	19,200
Controller	24,000	20,500	16,600
Secretary	28,200	21,000	16,200
Advertising manager	21,600	17,600	14,600
Top industrial relations executive	22,500	16,600	13,500
Purchasing manager	21,800	16,100	12,900
Office services manager	14,100	12,100	10,000
Credit manager	13,500	12,000	10,000

* Large companies are those with gross sales of $25–$100 million; intermediate companies have gross sales between $5 million and $25 million; small companies have gross sales under $5 million. Dartnell Corporation also has data for companies with over $100 million gross sales.
Source: The Dartnell Corporation, Chicago.

salary in business is much greater than comparable ranges in the professions. For example, a college graduate may start as an apprentice in business at $820 a month and ultimately hope to work his way up to the corporation's top executive ranks with a salary of $30,000 to $75,000 per year.

A study of the compensation of "junior executives" indicates that the average starting salaries rose as shown in Table 1–5. For a comparison of the average starting salaries of other professions see Table 1–6.

On the average, as Table 1–7 indicates, medicine appears to be the most lucrative of the professions, though it must be remembered that this is, in part, just compensation for much greater preparation than

TABLE 1–5
Average Annual Starting Salaries of Inexperienced Bachelor's Degree Graduates (recruited by business and industry from college campuses, 1950–1975)

Field	*1950*	*1960*	*1970*	*1975*
Engineering	$3,120	$6,120	$10,620	$12,744
Accounting	2,856	5,352	10,140	11,880
Sales	2,880	5,280	8,904	10,344
General Business	2,808	5,132	8,340	9,768

Source: Frank S. Endicott, *Trends in Employment of College and University Graduates in Business and Industry*, Annual Reports, Northwestern University, Evanston, Ill.

TABLE 1–6
The Graduating Class, 1975

College Women		*College Men*	
Field	*Average Monthly Starting Salary 1975*	*Field*	*Average Monthly Starting Salary 1975*
Accounting	$ 986	Accounting	$ 990
Engineering	1075	Engineering	1062
General business	840	Business admin.	814
Marketing-retailing	814	Sales marketing	862
Liberal arts	784	Liberal arts	776
Data processing	885	Production management†	928
Science	950	Chemistry	992
Math–statistics	918	Math–statistics	915
Other	825	Economics finance	851
		Other	872

Source: Frank S. Endicott, *Trends in Employment of College and University Graduates in Business and Industry* (29th Annual Report, Evanston, Illinois: Northwestern University, 1975).

most of the other professions require. As a physician, you would probably not begin practice until you were 27 or 28 years of age because of four years in medical school and one year as an intern and probably two years as a resident. Therefore, the much higher average compensation of physicians is partial payment for the lost years of earnings at the beginning of the career.

Specialization in medicine, as in all the professions, pays a handsome bonus over general practice. In the latest *Medical Economics* survey, general practitioners earned $42,336. Specialists in medicine, such as internists earned $47,229, general surgery netted $58,774 while obstetrics and gynecology paid $57,119 and pediatrics averaged $40,337.

Compensation for engineers favors the new entrant and is generous to the young practitioner but then levels off or declines and is not particularly rewarding to the experienced engineer. For example, beginning engineers averaged $11,904 per annum as a starting salary in 1974. The Engineering Manpower Commission Survey showed that, in 1970, those who entered the profession in 1960 were averaging $15,200 a year, those who entered in 1955 were averaging $16,800, those who started in 1945 were receiving $18,600, those who began in 1940 were averaging $18,800, while those who started in 1935 averaged 17,950. Thus the larger than average earlier rewards, fail to expand proportionally as the young engineer gains experience. Of course, we are speaking of averages. Some engineers, especially those who go into management, do very well indeed, much better than the average.

TABLE 1–7
Average Income in Five Major Professions, 1929–1972

Year	*Lawyers*	*Doctors*	*Dentists*	*Engineers*	*Teachers*	
					Public School	*College*
1929	$ 5,534	$ 5,224	$ 4,267	$ 3,616	$1,400	$ 3,050
1939	4,391	4,229	3,096	3,155	1,420	n.a.
1949	8,083	11,744	7,146	6,276	2,900	4,217
1951	8,730	13,150	7,743	7,120	3,123	4,692
1962	12,700	22,100	14,087	10,375	5,587	7,680
1970	27,960	40,550	29,500	17,000	8,844	13,284
1972	38,400	41,277	35,698	17,750	9,837	16,831

n.a. = not available.

Sources: *Lawyers:* "Income of Lawyers, 1929–48," *Survey of Current Business*, August, 1949, and Supplement, July, 1950; also "Incomes of Physicians, Dentists and Lawyers, 1949–1951," *Survey of Current Business*, July, 1952; also "Income of Lawyers in the Postwar Period," *Survey of Current Business*, December, 1956; *Lawyers in the United States: Distribution and Income, Part Two: Income* (Chicago: American Bar Foundation, 1958); also Reginald Heber Smith and E. Blythe Stason, "Income of Lawyers, 1959–1960," *American Bar Association Journal*, Vol. 49 (1963), pp. 732–34. *National Survey of Professional, Administrative, Technical and Clerical Pay* (Bulletin 1693 [Washington, D.C.: Bureau of Labor Statistics, U.S. Department of Labor, 1971]), *New York Times*, September13, 1971. American Bar Association Survey 1972, *Wall Street Journal*, August 3, 1973.

Doctors: "Income of Physicians, 1929–1949," *Survey of Current Business*, July, 1950, and July, 1952; also *Medical Economics*, December 21, 1970; *New York Times*, September 13, 1971. Medical Economics 1973.

Dentists: "Income of Dentists, 1929–1948," *Survey of Current Business*, January, 1950, and Supplement, July, 1950, and July, 1952; also *Survey of Dental Practice* (Chicago: Bureau of Economic Research and Statistics, American Dental Association, 1968—updated by Bureau, 1971). American Dental Association Survey 1973.

Engineers: Bureau of Labor Statistics, "Employment Outlook for Engineers," *Occupational Outlook Series* (Bulletin No. 968 [Washington, D.C.: Department of Labor]); also Engineering Manpower Commission, *Professional Income of Engineers* (New York: Engineers Joint Council, June 13, 1974).

Public school teachers (including principals and supervisors): Economic Status of Teachers (Washington, D.C.: Research Division, National Education Association, 1974), R4.

College teachers: George J. Stigler, *Employment and Compensation in Education* (Occasional Paper No. 33 ([New York: National Bureau of Economic Research, Inc., 1950]), p. 60. For all faculty ranks combined, average faculty salary in four-year undergraduate public and private institutions. See *Higher Education Salaries, 1961–62* (Washington, D.C.: Office of Education, U.S. Department of Health, Education, and Welfare, 1962). See also, the annual survey, *Economic Status of the Profession*, American Association of University Professors, and *Faculty Salary Schedules in Colleges and Universities*, annual, Research Division, National Education Association, *New York Times*, April 27, 1974 (73 figure $17,810).

The U.S. Department of Labor publishes an annual survey of earnings.[23] Chemists and engineers each are surveyed in eight levels. The first is the professional trainee level, typically requiring a B.S. degree. The highest level surveyed involves full responsibility over a very broad and highly complex and diversified engineering or chemical program. In 1974 average annual salaries ranged from $10,656 for chemist I to $34,476 for chemist VIII and from $11,904 for engineer I to $31,464 for engineer VIII.

Lawyers are classified in seven categories in the labor department earnings survey. Attorneys classified at level I are trainees with LL.B. degrees

[23] *National Survey of Professional, Administrative, Technical, and Clerical Pay*, March 1973 (Bulletin no. 1804, and U.S. Dept. of Labor, Office of Information, *News*, August 8, 1974).

and bar membership, who hold positions in companies other than law firms. Level VI is defined to include attorneys in charge of legal staffs. In 1974 average annual earnings ranged from $14,220 for attorney I to $38,184 for attorney VI. Again age and experience are factors.

The median earnings reported by statisticians ($18,000); computer scientists ($16,500), economists ($27,000), business ($22,000), systems analysts ($15,700), psychologists ($17,000), geologists ($14,000), oceanographers ($14,000), biochemists ($13,500), life scientists ($14,000), and soil scientists ($13,900) illustrate some of the possibilities available today.

Teaching, library work, and nursing are the poorest paying professions, possibly because of the larger percentage of women who enter these fields, work for a while, and then leave for marriage and a career as a housewife. As can be seen in Table 1-8, teaching and civil service provide lower earnings because of supposed advantages of tenure and security.

TABLE 1–8
Average Annual Salaries of Teachers Compared with Average Annual Earnings in Other Occupationl Groups, 1929–73

		Average Annual Earnings for Full-Time Employees Working for Wages or Salaries		
Calendar Year	*Average Annual Earnings of Public School Teachers*	*All Persons Working for Wages or Salaries*	*Employees in Manufacturing*	*Civilian Employees of Federal Government*
1929	$1,400	$1,405	$1,543	$ 1,933
1930	1,425	1,368	1,488	1,768
1939	1,420	1,264	1,363	1,843
1940	1,450	1,300	1,432	1,894
1949	2,900	2,851	3,092	3,361
1950	2,823	3,008	3,300	3,503
1959	4,863	4,558	5,215	5,682
1960	5,088	4,707	5,342	5,946
1969	8,180	7,098	7,775	9,424
1970	8,846	7,571	8,155	10,519
1971	9,414	8,061	8,638	11,503
1973	10,114	9,106	9,758	12,194

Source: *Economic Status of Teachers in 1972–73* (Washington, D.C.: Research Division, National Education Association, 1973.Table 41, p. 49, and Research Report, 1973 R3); U.S. Department of Commerce, *Survey of Current Business*, July 1974.

In a competitive world, no matter which career is selected, the best trained is usually more successful—and someone multitrained has even more marketable skills. The job hunting graduate whose career choice and preparation can fill the needs of the economy at the time is in demand.

Conclusion

The facts presented in this chapter and the additional data available in the sources here utilized should make it possible for you to estimate how much you can expect to earn in a given occupation. For example, if you plan to enter college teaching and obtain a position at a state university, to remain there for life, retiring at age 65, you can expect to earn approximately $10,662 the first three years as an instructor, about $13,300 the next five years as an assistant professor, approximately $16,400 for the next eight years as an associate professor, and an average of $21,500 thereafter as a full professor until retirement. Assuming you start teaching after you receive your master's degree at the age of 24 and teach until you are 65, you will earn approximately $767,186.

If you intend to be a physician, you will probably not begin practice until you are 27 or 28 years of age (because of four years in medical school and one year as an intern). From 30 through 34 years of age as an independent general practitioner, you can expect about $39,314 per annum; from ages 35 through 40, approximately $48,378; from ages 41 through 45, about $50,846; from ages 46 through 50, about $46,757; from ages 51 through 60, about $42,564—over 60, $30,524. Thus, lifetime income from 35 years of practice would total approximately $1,522,589.[24] Obviously, if you are equally capable of being either a college professor or a doctor and you choose the former, you are sacrificing about $755,403 of income over your lifetime.

While the particular profession or career you choose may have definite advantages in your eyes, you should be aware of the basic financial limitation or advantage and weigh clearly in your own mind all the relative advantages and disadvantages, not neglecting the financial factor. You should, of course, not be unmindful of aptitudes and of nonmaterial and spiritual values in making your choice. As you will see in the subsequent pages of this book, there are a great many major expenses you will encounter over a lifetime; and as you strive to surmount each financial hurdle, you may some day come to regret that you selected a field of endeavor which yields only two thirds, or a half, of the reward of another and perhaps, on reflection, equally attractive lifetime career.

A pioneering study on the average American "in pursuit of happiness" concluded that happiness depends on the "positive satisfactions" in life. Not unexpectedly, higher income was found to be a "positive satisfaction" and thus closely correlated with happiness.

---

[24] Does not include salary as intern and resident.

To those who are so fortunate as to still have the choice of their life's work before them, calculations of the type described in this chapter should be useful in helping to eliminate some of the haphazard guesswork and error involved in the difficult and basic decision of choosing an occupation for the rest of their lives. If the perplexities of the choice tend to get you down, do not be discouraged. Remember, "No matter how the statistics are grouped and regrouped, they always lead to just one conclusion: the financial success of the college man is a truly impressive thing."[25]

In addition, as the Carnegie Commission on Higher Education noted, "Going to college—any college—does give to the individual a chance for a more satisfying life and to society the likelihood of a more effective community."[26]

SUGGESTED READINGS

1. Bureau of Labor Statistics: (*a*) *Occupational Outlook Handbook,* Washington, D.C.: U.S. Department of Labor, 1974–75 ed.; (*b*) *Occupational Manpower and Training Needs,* Bulletin No. 1824, revised 1974.
2. *The Occupational Outlook* issued quarterly by the Bureau of Labor Statistics, U.S. Department of Labor.
3. F. T. Juster, ed., *Education, Income and Human Behavior,* National Bureau of Economic Research. New York: McGraw-Hill, 1975.
4. *Monthly Labor Review,* December, 1973. (*a*) R. E. Kutscher, "U.S. Economy in 1985—Projections." (*b*) Neal H. Rosenthal, "Projected Changes in Occupations."
5. U.S. Department of Commerce, Bureau of the Census, "*Income of Families and Persons in the United States*" in *Current Population Reports, Consumer Income.* Washington, D.C., latest year. Series P–60, No. 93.
6. (*a*) "Characteristics of the Low Income Population," *Current Population Reports, Consumer Income,* Series P–60, No. 98, annual. (*b*) "Annual Mean Income, Lifetime Income, and Educational Attainment of Men in the U.S. for Selected Years 1956–72," P–60, No. 92, March 1974. *Current Population Reports,* Bureau of Census, U.S. Dept. of Commerce. (*c*) "Household and Money Income and Selected Social and Economic Characteristics of Households," annual, Series P–60, No. 89 (*d*) "Social and Economic Status of the Black Population in the U.S.," annual, Series P 23, No. 48.

---

[25] Ernest Havemann and Patricia Salter West, *They Went to College: The College Graduate in America Today* (New York: Harcourt, Brace & Co., Inc.), p. 32.

[26] Quoted in *The New York Times,* October 6, 1971.

7. *Money*, a magazine published monthly by Time, Inc., Chicago. "Careers with a Future," Jeffrey G. Madrick, April 1973; "The Mysterious Case of Lawyer's Fees," Barbara Quint, March 1974.
8. Herman P. Miller, *Rich Man, Poor Man*. New York: Thomas Y. Crowell Co., 1971.
9. *National Survey of Professional, Administrative, Technical, and Clerical Pay*. Bulletin No. 1804. Washington, D.C.: U.S.: Department of Labor, Bureau of Labor Statistics, 1973.
10. C. Jencks et al. *Inequality*. New York: Basic Books, 1972.
11. Jacob Mincer, *Schooling, Experience and Earnings*. New York: National Bureau of Economic Research, 1974.
12. Jacob Mincer and Solomon Polachek, "Family Investments in Human Capital: Earnings of Women," *Journal of Political Economy*, March 1974.
13. Fabian Linden, "The New Profile of Poverty," *Conference Board Record*, August 1974.
14. Z. Griliches and W. Mason, "Education, Income and Ability," *Journal of Political Economy*, May 1972.
15. S. Weintraub, ed., "Symposium on Income Inequality" *Annals of American Academy of Political Science*, September 1973, pp. 1–173.
16. "The Earnings Picture for Women," *Federal Reserve Bank of Philadelphia Business Review*, July/August 1974.
17. Nancy Rudd, "Employment and Earnings of Women" *Consumer & Food Economics Institute*, ARS 62–5, U.S. Department of Agriculture, Fall 1973.
18. Dixie Sommers, "Occupational Rankings for Men and Women by Earnings," *Monthly Labor Review*, August 1974, pp. 34–51.

CASE PROBLEMS

1. Donald has a real aptitude for science. His father is a successful engineer and builder. Donald is having difficulty in deciding whether to become (*a*) a chemist, (*b*) a physicist, (*c*) a chemical engineer, or (*d*) an electrical engineer. Help him develop all the relevant facts on the four alternative fields in order to make a decision. (The Engineers Joint Council is located at 345 East 47th Street, New York, N.Y. 10017; as is The American Institute of Chemical Engineers and The American Institute of Electrical Engineers; The American Chemical Society is at 1155 16th Street, N.W., Washington, D.C.; and The American Institute of Physics at 335 East 45th Street, New York, N.Y. 10017)

2. Phil is majoring in political science and thinks he wants to go on to law school. He wonders whether it makes any difference which law school he enters, how much it will cost, and what he can expect to earn as a young

attorney. He also wonders whether he should take a first job as a junior in a large law office or apply to the legal department of a large corporation. Help him develop the relevant facts. (The American Bar Association is located at 1155 East 60th Street, Chicago, Illinois 60637)

3. Rita argues that an amazing social revolution has occurred in the United States in the last 25 years, that the income gap is narrowing, and that there is now a much more equitable distribution of income. Dick, whose family runs a retail business in a coal mining town argues that there is still unequal sharing of income and wealth and that the rich are getting richer. With whom do you side in this debate? Develop the relevant facts to support your side of the argument.

4. John is 32 years old, married, and has four children (ages 1, 3, 5, and 8). He teaches junior high subjects in a small New England town. He is presently receiving $7,500 per year. The maximum is $9,000 for his present position. For the last two years he had been working the night shift and summers in a local factory. For this he receives $140 per week (40 hours @ $3.50). In the summer he works a 45 hour week with time and a half for overtime. The school board tells him that he must give up his second job if he wants to keep his teaching position, as they feel that it is lowering the quality of his teaching. John knows that he can get a 45 hour per week job at the factory if he wishes. What are some of the things John should think about when making his decision?

5. Shirley was developing an inferiority complex at college because she thought her family was less well off than most others because her parents insisted she work part time and summers to help pay for tuition, room, and board. Her father owns a bookstore and earns from $10,000 to $12,500 a year. Her mother is a high school teacher and earns $9,500 annually. What facts and figures can you develop for Shirley to reassure her?

6. Marcia is a junior, majoring in English. She isn't quite certain what she wants to do when she graduates. She seeks your help in analyzing the vocational outlets for an English major. Help her develop the alternatives with respect to field, type of job, remuneration, opportunities for advancement, and where to go for additional information.

7. Joe is antiestablishment. His chief interests are (*a*) the protest movement, (*b*) girls, and (*c*) ecology. He is finishing his sophomore year and must pick a field in which to specialize in his junior and senior years. He does not come from a wealthy family and will have to earn his way after graduation, if he graduates. After talking with his advisor he is sent to the Dean of Guidance for specialization and vocational advice. Assume you are the Dean of Guidance, what would you suggest to Joe?

8. Betty and Marie are discussing the respective merits of library work and social work as career fields for women. Betty is introspective and shy. Marie is

energetic, outgoing, and vigorous. Help them marshal the facts, including suitability of the field, job opportunities, income to be expected in the first job and after five years, training required, and where to go for more information.

9. In high school, Raymond Durkin took the commercial course. He has had five years' experience as a bookkeeper in San Francisco; his present salary is $175 a week. Raymond knows that he does his present work well. He believes that with proper training he could become a successful certified public accountant. Since he has a wife (age 21) and one child (age 2), he has been able to save only $1,100. Should Raymond consider becoming a certified public accountant? How much different would his work then be? How could he get the training? How long would it take? Could he finance the training? Would it pay him to take it? Where should he go for more information about this field?

10. Carla wants to be a designer of women's or children's clothes. She feels she has had an aptitude for this from childhood. Her mother urges that she go to a four year liberal arts college and obtain her degree first before trying for a career in designing. Her father feels that she should go to a specialized school to develop her skill. What would you advise? Why?

11. Ben Weintraub's father owned a chain of retail shoe stores. He wanted Ben, who was about to begin his freshman year at the state university, to specialize in business in college and upon graduation to enter the family enterprise and train to take over. Ben, on the other hand, wanted very much to become a doctor, and he wanted his father to finance his four years at medical school after college. If you were Ben, what argument would you use to persuade your father?

2

Expenditures, Budgeting, and Consumerism

"What does Grandpa know about hardships? He only did without things . . . He never had to pay for them!"
Royal Bank of Canada

THE OLD TRUISM "You can't take it with you" has a modern counterpart, "You can't keep all you make." Taxes and dollar depreciation take their toll. Because of them it now takes an income of $21,080 to give you as much purchasing power as a $10,000 income in 1949. As you can see from Figure 2–1, there was a $1,112 tax bite out of the 1949 $10,000, leaving $8,888. You had to earn $21,080 in 1974 to have $8,888 of purchasing power left because taxes took away $3,666 and depreciation of the dollar cost $8,526 in lost purchasing power. Even more shocking, the $25,000 a year man of 1949 had to earn $54,300 in 1974 to maintain the same standard of living, as shown in Figure 2–1.

Unfortunately for most Americans, rising prices and rising taxes have become a way of life. We live in an era of inflation. You have to be over 40 to remember a year in which the price level declined. Prices in 1974 were 55 percent above their 1967 level. The steady erosion of the value of money shows no sign of ending. A leading investment firm (Hugh Johnson & Co.) estimates that over a ten year period this is what inflation may do to the value of your dollar.

Annual Rate of Inflation	*Value of the Dollar*
4%	−32.4%
6	−44.2
7	−49.2
8	−53.7
10	−61.5
12	−67.8

FIGURE 2–1
The Two Way "Squeeze," 1974

Income in 1974 Necessary to Equal 1949 Purchasing Power

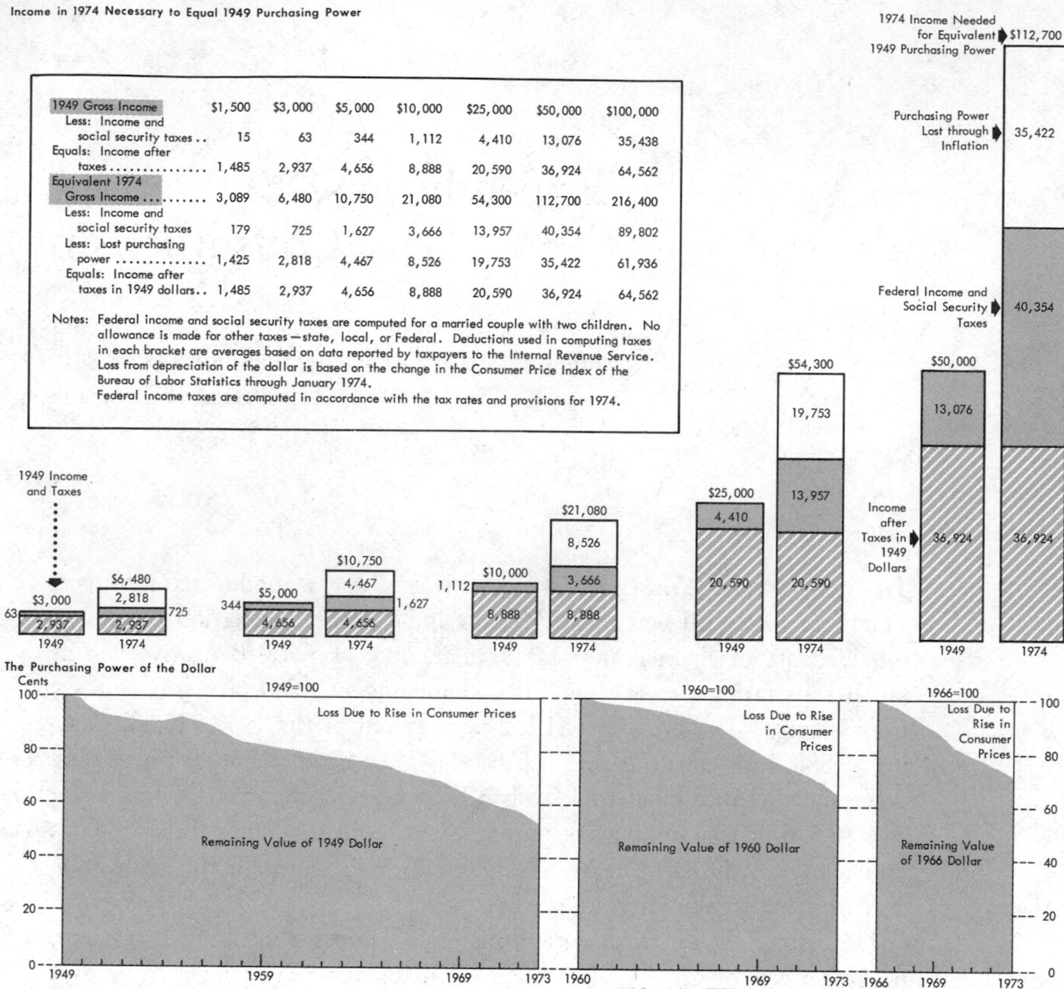

1949 Gross Income	$1,500	$3,000	$5,000	$10,000	$25,000	$50,000	$100,000
Less: Income and social security taxes . .	15	63	344	1,112	4,410	13,076	35,438
Equals: Income after taxes	1,485	2,937	4,656	8,888	20,590	36,924	64,562
Equivalent 1974 Gross Income	3,089	6,480	10,750	21,080	54,300	112,700	216,400
Less: Income and social security taxes	179	725	1,627	3,666	13,957	40,354	89,802
Less: Lost purchasing power	1,425	2,818	4,467	8,526	19,753	35,422	61,936
Equals: Income after taxes in 1949 dollars . .	1,485	2,937	4,656	8,888	20,590	36,924	64,562

Notes: Federal income and social security taxes are computed for a married couple with two children. No allowance is made for other taxes—state, local, or Federal. Deductions used in computing taxes in each bracket are averages based on data reported by taxpayers to the Internal Revenue Service. Loss from depreciation of the dollar is based on the change in the Consumer Price Index of the Bureau of Labor Statistics through January 1974.
Federal income taxes are computed in accordance with the tax rates and provisions for 1974.

Source: "Road Maps of Industry," No. 1735, April 1, 1974, from data from the Treasury Department, Bureau of Labor Statistics, and The Conference Board.

Inflation is personal. If you remember paying 25¢ for a hot dog then you can feel inflation when you pay 50¢ for a smaller hot dog. The *New York Times* cost 3 cents in 1948; 15 cents in 1974. A pair of blue jeans increased in price from $3.45 in 1948 to $11.25 in 1974. A ticket to a Broadway musical was $6 in 1948; $15 in 1974. A movie admission rose from 95 cents in 1960 to $3.50 in 1974. A loaf of bread soared from 20 cents in 1960 to 59 cents in 1974! Bad news for the traditionally minded bride who might want a five piece set of Royal Danish sterling flatware. The price has risen from $52.25 in 1964 to $186.00 in 1974. Overall inflation is measured formally by the Consumer Price Index.

Consumer Price Index

Using 1967 = 100 as a base (since January 1971), the CPI becomes a measure of today's prices in terms of a base year as seen in Figure 2–2. Prices are gathered from a variety of city and rural areas to achieve a geographical balance and are reported for a long list of basic items, such as food, housing, fuel and utilities, household furnishings, apparel and upkeep, transportation, and health and recreation. The CPI is published monthly by the Bureau of Labor Statistics covering the previous month. There are possible distortions in the CPI in that it is very slow to include new items or exclude those no longer in general use, and it does not reflect improvement or deterioration in products.

The CPI is a fixed weight index. Rising food prices, for example, get a weight of 22 percent in the index, but do not truly represent either the low income consumer who spends a larger proportion on food, or the upper income consumer who spends a smaller proportion on food. In addition while consumers vary their patterns of purchases as well as the

FIGURE 2–2
Consumer Price Index
(averages 1964–1968, by months 1969–1974)*

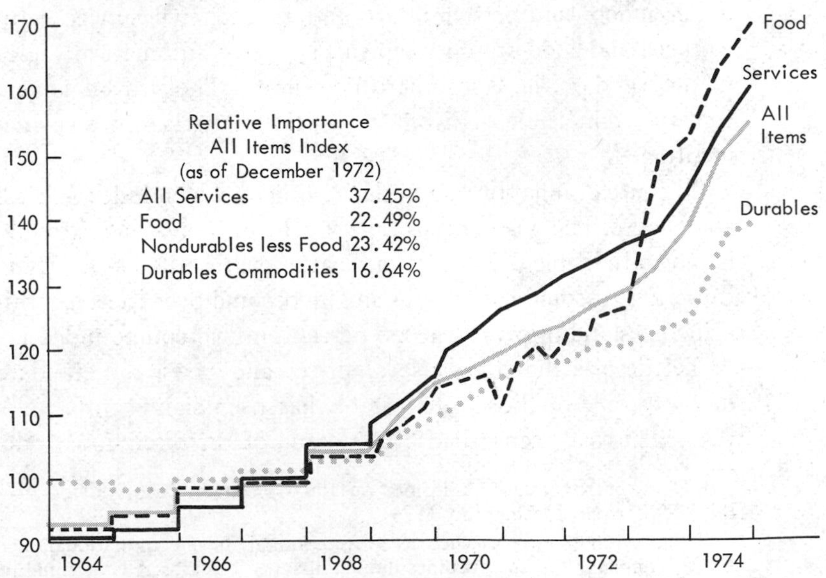

* Index: 1967 = 100
Source: Bureau of Labor Statistics and National Consumer Finance Association, *Finance Facts*, November 1974.

amounts purchased, the CPI assumes that consumer patterns of expenditure do not change. When real income increased in the period between 1963–1973, spending patterns naturally changed as demand grew for more luxury items and different necessity items. But the fixed weight index does not reflect this change.

To meet objections to the CPI the Bureau of Labor Statistics had planned to change the method of computing by broadening the base; by enlarging the current 400 items of the "market basket of goods and services" bought by urban wage earners and clerical workers and by shifting the weights given. The plan intended to reflect the expenditure of 80 percent of the population but was opposed by unions and by retired persons on the ground that the new index would give more weight to the spending patterns of the well to do and less to that part of the population which spends the larger proportion of their income on food, rent, fuel, and medical care. Objection was also made that the planned revision of the index would present an understated picture of inflation because it is these items whose prices are rising fastest that are most important to the budgets of lower income families.

Conflicting criticisms have resulted in a Bureau of Labor Statistics plan to retain the current Consumer Price Index for urban wage earners and clerical workers and also issue a second broader based Consumer Price Index for all urban households beginning in 1977. Almost 50 million people (29 million social security beneficiaries, 5 million wage earners under union contracts, military and federal civil service retirees, postal workers, and food stamp recipients) receive automatically escalated payments based on the Consumer Price Index.[1] The year's change of 12.2 percent shown in Table 2–1 would affect the automatically escalated payments mentioned.

The rate of inflation varies, depending on which index and which period you choose. The one verity is that it will continue. One extreme prediction is shown in Table 2–2, which indicates what a $10,000 family income and the prices of some basic items might become over the next three decades if incomes and prices rise at a 6 percent annual compounded rate.

Yet despite the sharp rise of prices and taxes, the standard of living of the people of the United States has risen significantly in the last ten years. This has been called "the decade of the discretionary dollar."[2] Fig-

[1] Denis S. Karnosky, "A Primer on the Consumer Price Index," *Federal Reserve Bank of St. Louis Review*, July 1974.

[2] The income concepts such as gross national income or national income are not exactly comparable with consumer money income. The closest is personal income which is defined as current income received by persons from all sources minus contributions for social insurance. Disposable personal income is the income remaining to persons

TABLE 2–1
Consumer Price Index (1967 = 100)

United States	Index for Dec. 1974	Percentage Change from Nov. 1974	Percentage Change from Dec. 1973	Point Change from Nov. 1974
All items	155.4	+0.7	+12.2	+1.1
Food	170.4	+0.7	+12.2	+1.2
Housing	159.4	+0.9	+13.7	+1.4
Transportation	143.4	0	+13.3	0
Health and recreation	147.5	+0.8	+10.9	+1.2

Sources: *New York Times*, January 22, 1975; Bureau of Labor Statistics.

TABLE 2–2
Income and Price Increases at a 6 Percent Annual Compounded Rate

Year	Income	Groceries	Color TV	Automobile	House
1970	$10,000	$ 20.00	$ 500.00	$ 3,000	$ 25,600
1975	13,382	26.76	669.11	4,014	34,258
1980	17,908	35.82	895.42	5,372	45,846
1985	23,965	47.93	1,198.27	7,189	61,351
1990	32,071	64.14	1,603.56	9,621	82,102
1995	42,918	85.84	2,145.92	12,875	109,871
2000	57,435	114.87	2,871.72	17,230	147,032

Source: *The Forbes Investor*, Forbes Investor Advisory Institute, New York, June 22, 1970.

ure 2–3 shows the projected tremendous growth of families with supernumerary income and indicates that by 1980 supernumerary income may be 22 percent of all income. As more families rise into middle and upper income brackets, they find themselves with larger shares of their income left over for discretionary spending after essential expenditures. This is due to the total expansion of the economy which for more than 100 years has been doubling itself every 16 years, unaffected by the cyclical setbacks experienced. An individual 24 years old now may see the economy increase eightfold over a lifetime, while a person 42 years old today may see the economy quadruple and a 62 year old may live to witness a doubling of the economy, if the same rate is maintained, and if double-digit inflation is contained.

after deducting personal tax and nontax payments to general government. It is the income of persons available for spending or saving. If you subtract necessary expenditures for essential needs and contractual payments, the remainder is discretionary income. The term "supernumerary income" according to the Conference Board refers specifically to all income in excess of $15,000 a year available to each family unit and represents a measure of consumer wealth for optional spending at that level and above.

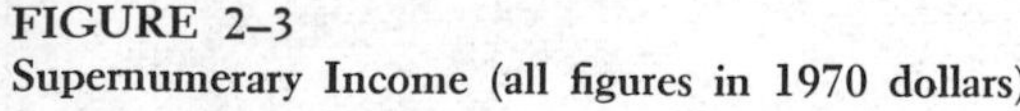

FIGURE 2–3
Supernumerary Income (all figures in 1970 dollars)

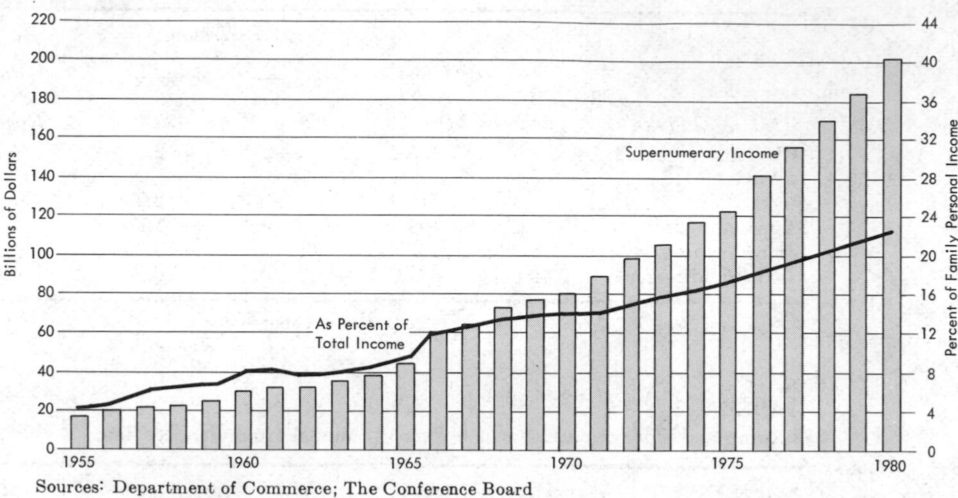

Sources: Department of Commerce; The Conference Board

The higher standard of living is reflected in new homes featuring garbage disposal units, dishwashing machines, electric refrigerators, electric washing and drying machines, and color television sets, which in the 1950s were available only to the wealthy. (See Figure 2–4.)

Lower income families found it increasingly difficult to have money left over after "expenses" (see Figure 2–5). Naturally the higher the income, the greater the discretionary income, but after discounting for inflation, real value declined and both groups depend more and more on credit.

As education levels rise, more wives work. Different age groups dominate the economy, causing cultural and social values to shift, and purchasing patterns to change. Today's emphasis in sales promotion on youth culture and home appliances is explained by the 42 percent of working wives and the 52 percent increase of 18 to 24 year olds in the population contrasted with a 14 percent increase for the entire population.

The Census Bureau projections for 1980 indicate a slowdown of total population growth to 11 percent while the 25 to 34 year age group grows by 45 percent. This will emphasize new consumption areas, especially as discretionary income is expected to rise somewhat. Nearly one out of three of these adults are singles who spend more of their income for luxury goods and services that most married, especially those raising a family, can only dream about. The unmarried woman between 18 and 35, for example, spends $100 to $150 more per year for clothing than do those with husbands. Half of the purchasers of sports cars and subcompacts are

FIGURE 2–4
The Mounting Possessions of American Families

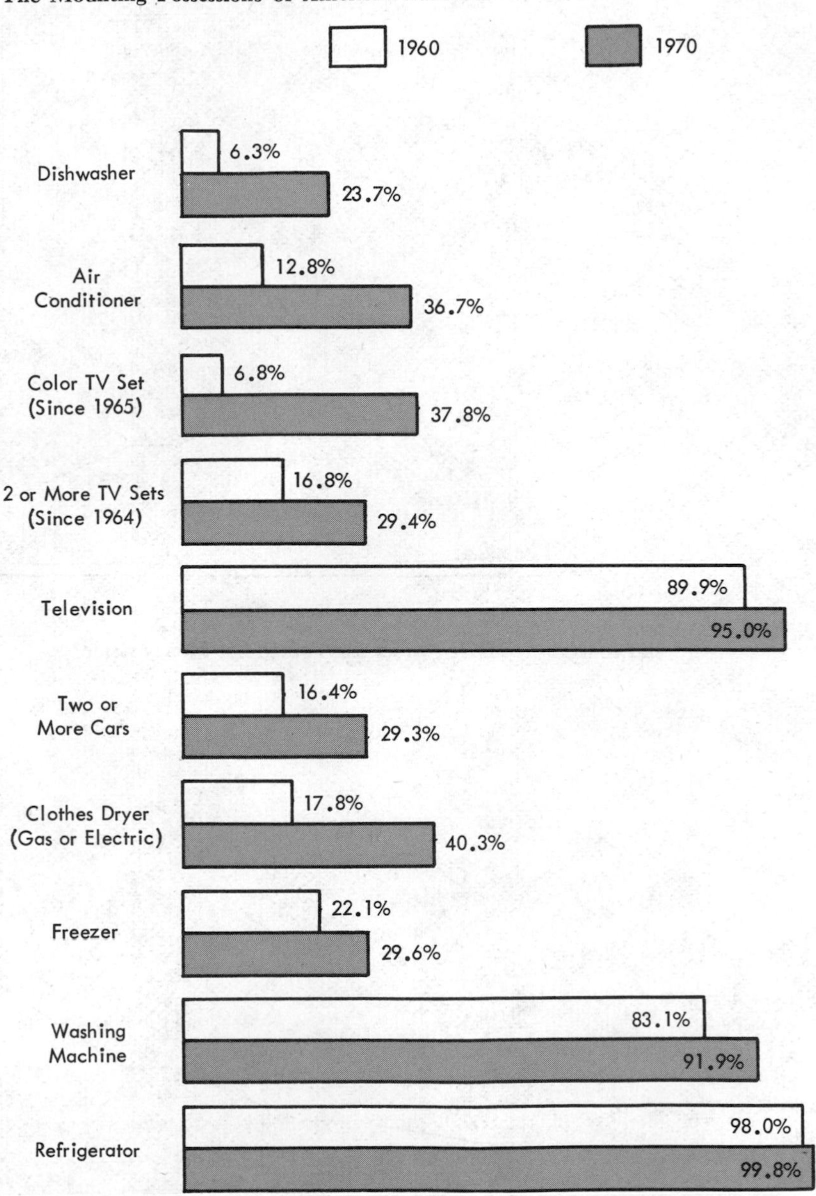

Sources: *New York Times,* December 9, 1970; Census Bureau; *Merchandising Week.*

FIGURE 2–5
Do You Have Money Left Over after "Expenses"?

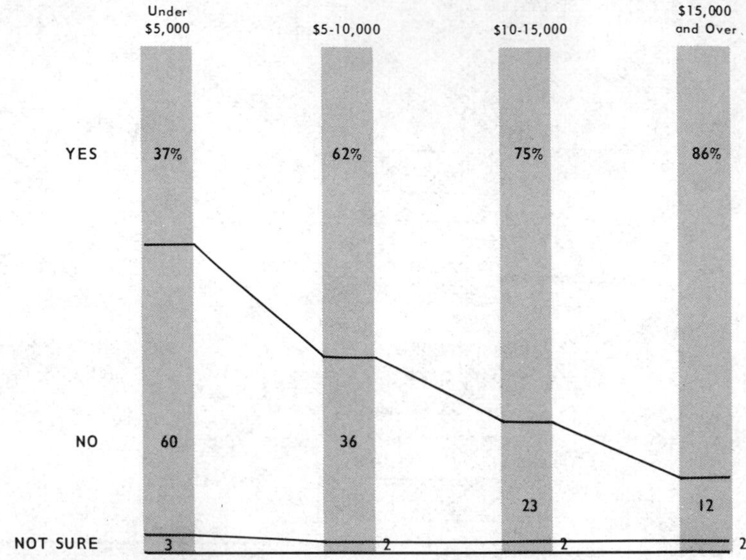

Has Inflation Made It Harder for You to Set Money Aside?

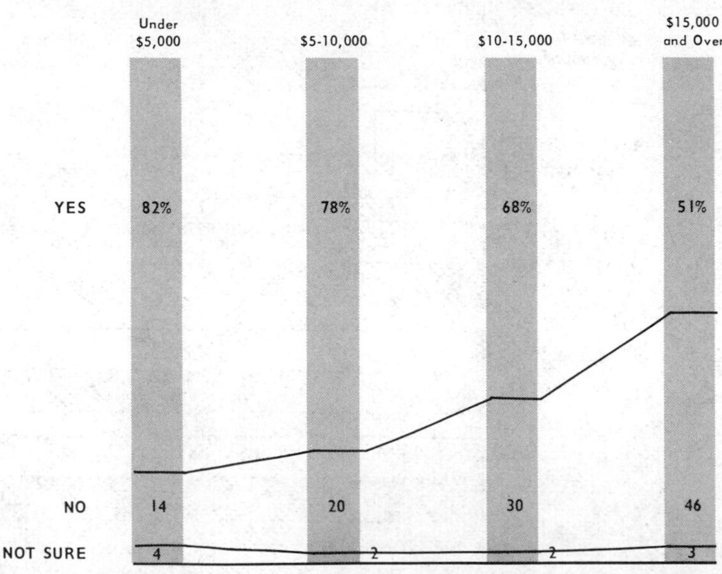

Source: "Public Attitudes Toward Money and Its Management," An Attitude and Awareness Study by Louis Harris & Associates for *Newsweek*.

singles. Insurance firms concentrate on the college market because two thirds of their business is with males 18 to 35 years old. More than 10 percent of that age group is single. Real estate experts estimate that almost one third of the new condominiums are being sold to singles. Bicycles, movies, and even Gerbers Products (once exclusively baby food, now marketing "Singles for Adults") are concentrating on the singles market.

At the same time more families are feeling the impact of the inflationary spiral and the need to plan the best use of their "real" income to get the most out of it. Budgeting sets priorities. If, as we have seen, inflation has become all too familiar then we need, as Federal Reserve Board Chairman Arthur F. Burns said, "the rediscovery of the art of careful budgeting of family expenditures."

Purpose of a Budget

A budget is a financial plan. Too often the purpose of a budget is misunderstood. Budgeting is not a dreary bookkeeping procedure of recording the details of every penny expended. Many people have assumed it to be just this and have quickly grown tired of keeping mountainous records of petty details.

The Royal Bank of Canada, Montreal, devoted a number of its monthly letters to the subject of family budgets. It stressed the fact that a budget is essentially a matter of planning, not of bookkeeping. Budgeting is a guide to spending and should not be looked upon as an inflexible pattern into which every penny of expenditure has to be fitted. The bank advised the family not to:

> . . . get into the habit of staying home at night, trying to find a missing 23 cents. No one can hope to budget 100 percent accurately, and only foolish persons try. With all his wizardry at mathematics, Einstein could never make his bankbook balance. Let us agree quite cheerfully that there must be some money that disappears as completely as if the mice had eaten it. One husband, going over his wife's records, came, every little while, on an entry: "HOK $1.50" or "HOK $3." He asked what it meant and was told "Heaven Only Knows."

Mindful that most people abandon budgeting when it becomes a matter of penny hunting record keeping, the bank suggests an extra category called "OIL" in the budget, amounting to about 2½ percent of the total. It states: "That's for oil for the troubled waters. It will cover mistakes and saves personal headaches. It will cover the $10 you lend to a friend and never get back; the $5 you spend on impulse when the budget makes no allowance for it."

The Continental Bank of Chicago offers similar advice. They say that you can go too far with money management. The reckless spender who keeps no financial records winds up with no money—but the man who knows his balance sheet by heart and keeps records on every transaction usually has no fun. They suggest an annual spending plan with a priority

"But in the past three years you've doubled your income, so actually we're no worse off than we were before."

Changing Times, The Kiplinger Magazine

system for both essentials and the most "meaningful" extras to be organized on a monthly spending basis subject to a review every few months.

Even Thoreau in the pastoral peace of Walden discovered that he needed a financial plan. In his book, *Walden,* he itemized his expenses during one eight month period and found they totaled $61.99, while his income from farming and odd jobs was only $36.78, and sadly concluded that his net loss came to $25.21. He was still part of a money economy.

No family ever has enough money. A budget is simply an application of willpower to the management of personal finances. It is a plan for spending, not simply a record of expenditures. It is designed to keep you out of financial trouble, to help you live within what—in terms of your wants and desires—is always an inadequate income. It enables you to set priorities in spending and to plan to get the most out of your money. If you were given $400,000 tomorrow, you would think very carefully about how best to use it—whether to spend or invest—and, if the choice were the former, on what. You would do some planning about the disposal of the $400,000. Well, if you average $10,000 a year in earnings between the ages of 25 and 65, you will control the spending of $400,000. Even though you obtain the money over a period of time, it would be well to ponder and plan its disposal, just as you would if you received it all at once.

It is not essential to budget, of course. If you live within your income easily, satisfy all your needs and wants, and manage to save in the bargain, then budgeting may be a waste of time for you. Some bright, competent people do their financial planning in their heads and do not stop to put it down on paper to see how it shapes up. But many people (and all responsible governments and successful business firms) estimate their income in advance and carefully plan its disposal—on paper. Because it brings one face to face with reality, the process may not be a pleasant one; but it is better to face facts ahead of time and trim your wants to your income. Some people find this process too onerous. They are the ones who went to debtors' prisons hundreds of years ago and who today have their cars repossessed, their furniture taken back. They pay extra and heavy charges to loan companies, have their salaries garnisheed and their property, if any, attached, and generally slip in and out of side doors to elude creditors' subpoenas and judgments.

Budget planning makes one think about alternatives in spending. The process of choosing makes you a wiser purchaser, although it may make you a sadder one, too. For example, is it more fun to entertain frequently or to be well dressed? Is laborsaving household equipment more important than the convenience of an automobile? Are temporary luxuries more to be desired than the security of a growing savings account? If drawing up a budget shows you that you may have to make such choices (and this irritates and aggravates you), do not blame it on the budget. Blame it on your income, because that is the real cause of your annoyance and frustration. It is not large enough to meet all your needs. The budget lets you see this fact ahead of time. If you wait to find it out through the spending process, you will be more annoyed later.

A Gallup Poll found that four out of every ten American families keep budgets; and of those that do, one out of three said they failed to stay within it. Gallup interviewers found that nearly half of all persons who have had a college education keep a budget, as compared with less than one third among persons whose education did not extend beyond grade school. This tends to indicate that people with larger incomes and higher standards of living use budgets more frequently than those who live in more modest circumstances. The two principal reasons given for not keeping a budget were "Not enough money, all spent anyhow" and "Don't need one, can live within means." Those who gave the first reason clearly misunderstod the purpose of budgeting and obviously would benefit from financial planning.

Components of a Budget

The components of a budget are determined wholly by the needs of the individual or family for which it is devised. For example, a college student's budget categories will differ considerably from those of a head of a family. A budget for a college student might have the following breakdown:

A. Income
   1. From parents
   2. From odd jobs during spring and fall semesters
   3. From summer work

B. Expenditures
   1. Tuition
   2. Fees
   3. Books
   4. Room and board
   5. Clothing, including laundry and cleaning
   6. Transportation or automobile upkeep
   7. Medical and dental care
   8. Donations
   9. Dues (fraternity, clubs, class)
   10. Newspapers, magazines, postage, and cigarettes
   11. Recreation and dates

A budget for a head of a family might be divided into the following categories:

A. Income
   1. From regular employment—salary or wages
   2. From additional employment or commissions
   3. From dividends, interest, or rent
   4. From bonuses, gifts, government, or other allowances

B. Expenditures
   1. Taxes
   2. Repayment of debts or installment payments
   3. Food
   4. Rent or mortgage payments
   5. Household operation—utilities, supplies
   6. Clothing, including laundry and cleaning
   7. Insurance

8. Home furnishings and household equipment
9. Medical and dental care
10. Contributions, gifts, subscriptions
11. Transportation or automobile expenses
12. Advancement
13. Personal allowances
14. Entertainment
15. Savings
16. Miscellaneous (OIL or HOK)

How to Budget

Clearly the point of departure in budgeting or financial planning is to estimate your annual income from all sources and then see how well or poorly it covers your estimated annual expenses. If it is apparent that your income will not cover them, then you can seek to increase your income, find ways and means of cutting expenses, or preferably do both.

You may possibly wish to keep records temporarily for two reasons. You may not be able to estimate one or another of the categories of proposed expenditures precisely enough in drawing up your original budget plan and may therefore wish to keep a record for a week or a month to see what that category of expenditure actually totals as a means of making a more exact annual or pay period estimate. Or, having drawn up your financial plan (budget), you may wish to check your ability to apply it by keeping an actual record of expenditures as a means of seeing how well you were able to conform to your financial plan.

How can you engage in budgeting without bookkeeping? Very simply. Once you have drawn up your annual financial plan, break it down on a per payday basis, and then set up a plan for spending for each pay period. When the pay check is cashed, put the cash in different envelopes, one for rent, one for food, and so on, with the amounts determined by the plan. Then, as you spend over the pay period, there is no need to keep a record of expenditures. If one envelope is consistently exhausted before the end of the period (say the food envelope, for example), you can either draw from the savings envelope to cover the deficit, thus saving less than you had planned, or you might try to reduce your expenditures for food by buying cheaper cuts of meat, for example, or by eating hamburger rather than steak.

Another useful arrangement is to have your monthly paycheck sent to your bank and to use checks to pay for all important expenditures. When the checks are returned by the bank with your statement, you can sort them out, total each category, and thus see whether you kept to or exceeded your plan. If you like to operate on a cash basis, you can use the envelope method; if you prefer to use a bank, then you can use your checking account to test your budget and eliminate the deadly record keeping which scares so many people away from budgeting.

Budget Forms

A considerable number of budget forms have been devised to meet varying situations. One of the best comprehensive series of budget forms, designed to emphasize the planning function, is published by the Money Management Institute of Household Finance Corporation, a large consumer finance company. These forms are found in a booklet entitled *Reaching Your Financial Goals.*[3]

The emphasis in this booklet is your planning—after you know your goals. It is very personal. The form "Your Savings for Goals" shown on page 46 in Figure 2–6 asks you to list the items you want, and then, to make you consider the matter practically, has you decide which you want now and which later, and in both cases to estimate costs. To satisfy these goals, you must know your income—which you list according to source. From income you subtract your fixed expenses, such as rent or mortgage payments, insurance, taxes, and installment payments. Ask yourself what regular bills must be paid on specific dates over the next year. Usually, it is impossible to pay these fixed expenses out of one paycheck. One of the best ways of planning to meet large bills is to chart the dates on which they fall due (see page 47). You can divide the total due into periodic payments and start a reserve fund. For example, if you are starting your budget in October and have a $120 insurance payment premium due in December, divide the total by three, setting aside $40 in each of the months of October, November, and December. From then on, you need set aside only one twelfth ($10) of the total.

The next step is to estimate, list, and substract "future, flexible expenses," such as clothing, household equipment, and home furnishings. These expenditures are all certain to appear, but they are sufficiently flexible in amount and time of occurrence to offer opportunity to adjust the budget (see page 48). If you do not know your day to day living costs, including such items as food, utilities, laundry, car upkeep, and

---

[3] This company also publishes a *Money Management Booklet Library* which includes 12 booklets, among which are: *Your Food Dollar, Your Clothes Dollar, Your Housing Dollar, Your Home Furnishings Dollar, Your Health and Recreation Dollar, Your Shopping Dollar, Children's Spending, Your Automobile Dollar, Your Equipment Dollar, Your Savings and Investment Dollar,* and *It's Your Credit—Manage It Wisely.* Information concerning these may be obtained by writing to Money Management Institute, Household Finance Corp., Prudential Plaza, Chicago, Ill., 60601.

entertainment, make rough estimates and then check them against performance over several pay or budget periods. A summary of the forcgoing can be listed on a form like "Make Your Spending Plan Balance" shown on page 49, which will enable you to get the whole picture in focus. If your spending plan is out of line with income, you now can analyze those elements that are causing the difficulties and see if they can be adjusted. It is at this point that most people have to stop and refigure. If nothing is left for savings, review your estimates. There may be places you can reduce expenditures—even temporarily. The form "Your Master Record of Spending and Saving" on page 49 will help you draw up a master plan of spending and saving on which you can list both what you plan to spend and what you actually spend in each period. If you find you are not living within your plan, you either adjust the plan—or yourself—to find what is best for you and your income. The *Reaching Financial Goals* booklet offers you that opportunity to consider again your goals, as you list them in a form entitled "Savings for Goals." Here, as you note the amount needed, you can also note the amount saved in each period, and when you can circle the total needed and saved, your satisfaction will make the next period easier. As you examine "Your Net Worth Statement" on page 46 periodically and realistically, you can judge if you are really headed toward your financial goal.

There are many other sources of budget forms for every need and purpose. The New York Life Insurance Company publishes an excellent *Family Finance Record Book*[4] as does the Royal Bank of Canada. The National Consumer Finance Association has a Family Budget Plan called "Budgeting Without Bookkeeping." The Institute of Life Insurance publishes what it calls "The Family Money Manager."[5] The budget of the

---

[4] Free copies may be obtained upon request in each case. The New York Life Insurance Company address is 51 Madison Ave., New York, N.Y. 10010; the Royal Bank of Canada's head office is in Montreal, Canada; National Consumer Finance Association is located at 1000 Sixteenth St. N.W., Washington, D.C. 20036. The First National City Bank of New York describes its "cash flow" approach to budgeting in its monthly consumer brochure *Consumer Views*.

[5] Copies may be obtained by writing to Institute of Life Insurance, 277 Park Avenue, New York, N.Y. 10017. See also its *A Discussion of Family Money—How Budgets Work and What They Do* (Woman's Division, Institute of Life Insurance, and *A Date with Your Future—Money Management for the Young Adult* (Educational Division, Institute of Life Insurance, Health Insurance Institute. *A Guide to Budgeting for the Family* (Home and Garden Bulletin No. 108 [Washington, D.C.: U.S. Department of Agriculture, 1973]); "A Guide to Budgeting for the Retired Couple," *Home & Garden Bulletin* No. 194 U.S. Department of Agriculture, 1973. *Helping Families Manage Their Finances* (Home Economics Research Report No. 21 [Washington, D.C.: Agricultural Research Service, U.S. Department of Agriculture]) *Paycheck Planning for You*—An Extension Publication of the New York State College of Human Ecology, Cornell University, Ithaca, N.Y. (prepared by Elizabeth Wiegand, 1974) are other sources for budgeting help.

FIGURE 2–6

YOUR SAVINGS FOR GOALS

Saving is setting aside money from your present income for use sometime in the future. The greatest incentive to save is provided when savings have a special purpose such as saving for college, a new car, a vacation, an emergency fund, or a down payment on a home.

Look at your goals listed on page 7. Are they still the things you want? When looked at objectively, goals often change—some becoming very important, others less necessary. Which of your goals are most important to you now? Write them down in the *Savings for Goals* chart below. Indicate the date needed and the estimated amount required to achieve each one. List regular planning periods at the top of each double column. As you put money aside each planning period, divide it among the listed items. In the first half of each double column, note the amount saved each planning period; in the second half, the amount saved to date. Circle the total saved when you have reached your goal.

The amount you can set aside for goals may not be as much as you would like. But when regular savings become a definite part of your money management plan you will be surprised at how quickly some of your goals can be reached.

Things We're Saving For	Date Wanted	Planning Periods																										
		Estimated Cost	Amount saved	Total saved	Amount saved	Total saved	Amount saved	Total saved	Amount saved	Total saved	Amount saved	Total saved	Amount saved	Total saved	Amount saved	Total saved	Amount saved	Total saved	Amount saved	Total saved	Amount saved	Total saved	Amount saved	Total saved	Amount saved	Total saved	Amount saved	Total saved

YOUR NET WORTH STATEMENT

WHAT DO YOU OWN		
Cash in checking accounts		
Cash in savings accounts		
Current value of government savings bonds		
Cash surrender value of insurance policies		
Equity in pensions		
Current value of annuities		
Current value of durable assets (car, house, furnishings and equipment)		
Cash value of ownership in a business		
Value of investment real estate owned		
Market value of securities		
Bonds		
Stocks		
Mutual funds		
Investment trusts		
Other assets		
TOTAL ASSETS		

WHAT DO YOU OWE		
Current bills outstanding		
Amount owed on instalment purchases		
Amount owed on personal loans . .		
Amount due on real estate mortgages		
Amount due on taxes		
Other liabilities		
TOTAL LIABILITIES		
YOUR NET WORTH (excess of assets over liabilities)		

YOUR FIXED EXPENSES

Which of the items below are your fixed expenses? List them on the forms on the following pages. Omit items deducted from your paycheck. Add additional items not listed. Consider carefully the total amount of your fixed expenses in relationship to your total income. This will give you an estimate of how much is left for flexible expenses. Also, if you are considering additional fixed expenses, it will help you to decide whether fixing more of your income will leave enough for other daily needs without lowering your level of living.

Housing
- Rent
- Mortgage payments

Taxes
- Federal income tax*
- State income tax*
- Local taxes
- Property taxes

Utilities and Home Services
- Telephone
- Gas
- Electricity
- Water
- Fuel
- Garbage pickup
- Cable TV

Instalment Payments
- Automobile
- Furniture or appliances
- Charge accounts
- Credit card accounts
- Personal loans
- Christmas Club plan

Insurance
- Life
- Automobile
- Health and accident
- Hospitalization
- Fire and theft
- Personal property
- Social security
- Other

Fees for Education
- Tuition
- Room and board
- Books
- Other

Transportation
- Automobile license plates
- Vehicle sticker
- Commuting fare
- Parking

Personal Allowances
- Husband
- Wife
- Children

Personal Improvement
- Music lessons
- Dancing lessons
- Other

Membership Dues
- Union
- Professional associations
- Clubs

Contributions
- Religious
- Charity

Emergency Fund
- Loss of job
- Illness
- Accident
- Major repairs

Subscriptions
- Newspapers
- Magazines

Others
- __________
- __________
- __________
- __________
- __________

* Estimate any additional payment beyond amount witheld from regular wages.

FIXED EXPENSES EACH PLANNING PERIOD

On the adjoining form list the *fixed expenses—rent or mortgage payments, utilities, instalment payments—which you will have each planning period.* Figure the annual amount needed for each expense. Divide the total by the number of planning periods during the year to determine the amount to set aside each planning period to meet these expenses. Projecting fixed expenses on an annual basis helps you to anticipate changes in your financial situation during the year and to review each expense in relationship to your total income.

Fixed Expenses Each Planning Period	Yearly Total	List Regular Planning Periods During the Year												
TOTAL														
AMOUNT TO SET ASIDE EACH PLANNING PERIOD														

FIXED EXPENSES WHICH OCCUR PERIODICALLY

List the *fixed expenses which will occur periodically during the year—taxes, insurance premiums, tuitions, etc.* Figure the annual amount needed for each expense. Divide the total by the number of planning periods during the year to determine the amount you must set aside regularly to meet these expenses as they occur. (If you are just beginning to build up a reserve fund for periodic expenses, you may wish to divide the annual amount needed for *each* expense by the number of planning periods until payment is due. For example, if you are planning on a monthly basis beginning in January and you have a $72 payment due in April, divide by 4, setting aside $18 in January, February, March and April. In May, however, you need set aside only 1/12, $6.00. When the $72 is due the following year, you will have the money on hand to meet that expense. While this system involves more figuring in the beginning, it enables you to meet large expenses during the current year and to build up reserves so you will have the money needed to meet these expenses the following year. After the first year, you should be able to average all expenses as described previously.)

Periodic Fixed Expenses	Yearly Total	List Regular Planning Periods During The Year												
TOTAL														
AMOUNT TO SET ASIDE EACH PLANNING PERIOD														

FIGURE 2–6 (concluded)

YOUR FLEXIBLE EXPENSES

Which of the items below are your ***flexible expenses?*** List them on the forms on the following pages. Add any items not listed. Some flexible expenses change seasonally, such as back to school clothing for children and prescription drugs and medications. Projecting these expenses on an annual basis allows you to anticipate and prepare for those changes.

Food
- Meals at home
- Meals eaten out

Clothing
- New clothes and accessories
- Laundry
- Dry cleaning
- Repairs and alterations

Household Equipment
- New appliances
- Remodeling or new furniture
- Repairs

Home Improvement
- Maintenance
- Remodeling
- Expansion

Household Supplies
- Cleaning supplies
- Small items for the home
- First aid supplies

Household Help
- Baby sitter
- Yard care
- Window washing
- Housecleaning

Gifts
- Birthdays
- Weddings and anniversaries
- Religious celebrations
- Showers
- Illness
- Graduation

Transportation
- Gasoline
- Repairs and upkeep
- Taxi
- Bus or train commuting

Contributions
- Religious
- Charities
- Service groups
- Professional groups
- Fraternal groups
- Social clubs
- Schools and colleges

Health
(not covered by insurance)
- Medical
- Dental
- Prescription drugs
- Medications

Personal Care
- Grooming aids
- Barber shop
- Beauty parlor

Entertainment
- Extra food
- Theater tickets
- Sports events

Recreation
- Hobbies
- Vacation
- Sports equipment

Miscellaneous
- Papers
- Magazines
- Stationery, postage
- Tobacco
- Others

Others
- ____________
- ____________
- ____________
- ____________
- ____________

FLEXIBLE EXPENSES WHICH OCCUR PERIODICALLY

On the adjoining form list the ***flexible expenses which will occur periodically—clothing, medical and drug expenses, home improvement, etc.*** Total the amount needed for each item. Divide by the number of planning periods during the year to determine the amount to set aside regularly to meet these expenses as they occur.

Periodic Flexible Expenses	Yearly Total	List Regular Planning Periods During the Year												
TOTAL AMOUNT TO SET ASIDE EACH PLANNING PERIOD														

FLEXIBLE EXPENSES EACH PLANNING PERIOD

List the ***flexible expenses which you will have each planning period—food, transportation, household supplies, etc.*** Total the amount needed for each item. Divide by the number of planning periods during the year to determine how much to set aside regularly to meet these expenses.

Flexible Expenses Each Planning Period	Yearly Total	List Regular Planning Periods During The Year												
TOTAL AMOUNT TO SET ASIDE EACH PLANNING PERIOD														

MAKE YOUR SPENDING PLAN BALANCE

Now that you are through with your estimating, it is time to make a trial plan to see if your expenses and income balance. Follow the five steps below to see how you are getting along.

	For One Planning period		For One Year	
1. ***What is your income?*** Enter income from pages 10 and 11				
2. ***What is the total of your fixed expenses?*** Enter the total of the fixed expenses which you will have each planning period and the allowance for fixed periodic expenses from pages 14 and 15				
3. ***What is the total of your flexible expenses?*** Enter the total of the flexible expenses which you will have each planning period and the allowance for flexible periodic expenses from pages 18 and 19				
4. ***Total items 2 and 3.***				
5. Deduct item 4 from 1. This is your ***Savings for Goals.***				

YOUR MASTER RECORD OF SPENDING AND SAVING

A money management plan helps you choose the ways you want to spend your money. However, a plan is meaningless unless it also is used to guide spending. When you are satisfied with your estimated figures for spending and saving, use the form below to compare what you actually spend with what you plan to spend each planning period.

You owe it to yourself to know where your money goes, but don't try to account for ***every*** penny spent. You and your family will weary of the tediousness of this.* If you have a checking account, you may find your checkbook is your way of keeping track of spending. If checks are made for cash, keep a list of items that were bought. Canceled checks, receipts and other records of payment can help you when figuring actual expenses. You may wish to keep small amounts of money for day-to-day living expenses in clearly marked envelopes or a purse for use as needed.

If expenses come within the set amounts, your plan is a success. If total expenses exceed income one month, look for ways to adjust spending so the two will balance the next planning period.

Remember, money management must be learned and practiced. Experience shows that it may take four to six planning periods to develop a workable spending and saving plan. However, your skill will increase with each planning period. Once you find the plan that is best for you, it will be easy to live with, and living within it will become second nature.

Using the form below, enter dates for each planning period during the year at the top of each double column. At the end of each planning period, record both planned and actual expenses in the spaces provided in the chart. You may wish to use pencil for ***planned*** figures and pen for ***actual*** figures.

Planning Periods																										
Fixed Expenses Each Planning Period (pages 14 and 15)	Planned	Actual	Planned	Actual	Planned	Actual	Planned	Actual	Planned	Actual	Planned	Actual	Planned	Actual	Planned	Actual	Planned	Actual	Planned	Actual	Planned	Actual	Planned	Actual	Planned	Actual
Allowance, Fixed Expenses Occurring Periodically (pages 14 and 15)																										
Allowance, Flexible Expenses Occurring Periodically (pages 18 and 19)																										
Flexible Expenses Occurring Each Planning Period (pages 18 and 19)																										
Balance Left Over or Savings for Goals (page 20)																										
TOTAL																										
INCOME (pages 10 and 11)																										

Source: *Reaching Your Financial Goals* (Chicago: Money Management Institute of Household Finance Corporation).

TABLE 2–3
A 'Sample' Budget for a Family of Four (In this hypothetical budget, a husband, wife and their two children under age 16, have a total after-tax income of $1,000 a month, or $12,000 a year.)

	Weekly	*Monthly*	*Annually*	*Percentages*
Income (take-home pay)	$231	$1,000	$12,000	100%
Housing	61	270	3,240	27
Food	51	220	2,640	22
Transportation	23	100	1,200	10
Clothing	21	90	1,080	9
Savings	18	80	960	8
Medical	12	50	600	5
Education/Recreation	12	50	600	5
Gifts/Contributions	7	30	360	3
Personal care	7	30	360	3
Job expenses	2	10	120	1
Life insurance	5	20	240	2
Miscellaneous or discretionary funds	12	50	600	5

Source: "You and Your Money" Newsletter published by the Savings Bank Association of New York State, June, 1973 issue.

Savings Bank Association of New York breaks the income and outgo into weekly, monthly and annual figures. Sometimes it is clearer that way. (Table 2–3).

Suggested Expenditure Patterns

Model spending patterns suggested for families at various income levels may be useful in enabling you to make sound decisions concerning your own proposed expenditures. For example, assume you have just graduated from college, married, and after passing the Federal Service Entrance examination, have been offered a position in Washington, D.C. at a salary of $8,055 per annum. You and your spouse proceed to Washington and are faced with the problem of renting an apartment. How much can you afford to pay in rent per month? An annual salary of $8,055 approximates $671 per month. But there are monthly income tax deductions (about $77) and also monthly pension retirement deductions (about $38), leaving a take-home sum each month of about $556. How much of this can you afford to spend for rent?

The American Bankers Association has prepared a table showing suggested distribution of income after income taxes (see Table 2–4). Looking down the first column, you find your monthly take-home pay figure falls closest to $525 per month. Then, looking across this line, in the two-in-a-family subdivision, it may be noted that the suggested proper expenditure

TABLE 2–4
Distribution of Monthly Income

(a) *Monthly Income*	*Number in Family*	*Savings*	*Food*	(b) *Housing*	*Clothing*	(c) *Transportation*	(d) *Other*
$ 315	2	$ 6	$ 79	$ 95	$16	$ 31	$ 88
	4	6	95	94	22	32	66
375	2	11	94	113	19	37	101
	4	8	112	109	26	37	83
425	2	13	102	123	26	43	118
	4	9	123	119	34	47	93
475	2	14	114	138	29	47	133
	4	10	133	133	38	52	109
525	2	21	121	147	37	52	147
	4	16	147	142	47	58	115
600	2	30	138	162	42	66	162
	4	24	168	156	54	72	126
650	2	39	143	169	52	72	175
	4	32	176	162	58	78	144
750	2	52	165	195	60	83	195
	4	45	195	188	67	90	165
850	2	68	179	212	68	93	230
	4	59	221	204	77	102	187
950	2	85	190	228	76	114	257
	4	76	237	228	86	123	200
1,050	2	94	210	252	84	126	284
	4	84	263	252	94	136	221

(*a*) After taxes and payroll deductions.
(*b*) Includes shelter, fuel, furnishings, appliances and equipment.
(*c*) Includes automobile purchase and operation, and public transportation.
(*d*) Includes religious and charitable gifts, recreation, education and miscellaneous.
Source: American Bankers Association, *Personal Money Management*.

for shelter is about $147 per month. If you spend more than this amount for rent, you will have to spend less in one of the other categories, such as food, clothing, other (which includes such items as personal expenses, and recreation), or savings. In all probability you will not be able to find suitable quarters for $147 per month in a high cost city like Washington, but will have to pay more. If you do, then you can expect to take the difference out of what otherwise would have been savings. If your spouse works earning $120 a week ($418 a month after taxes and retirement deductions), giving you a combined income of $974 per month, the table indicates that you can afford to pay about $228 per month for rent. Should you wish to pay $25 or $50 more, you will be able to save proportionately less.

Various sources have suggested different annual spending patterns. For example, the Pacific First Federal Savings and Loan Association publishes a slide rule "Family Budget Guide.[6] You set the scale to the column showing your gross monthly income and the number in your family. Then you read across to find suggested spending patterns. For example, if your family consists of a husband, wife, and one child, the patterns suggested at different levels of income may be seen in Table 2–5. Suggestions cover families of from two to five members.

These yardsticks serve only as models. Individual variations are not only necessary but desirable, since few families are exactly like the average at a given income level. Costs of living in different communities vary and must be taken into account. Any financial plan, therefore, must be personal and individual. What may be satisfactory for one may prove disturbing to another. The important thing is to have a plan—one that is flexible and that fits into your scheme of living.

Average Consumer Spending

You may also find it helpful in your own financial planning to know what average families in the United States actually spend and how these expenditures are divided among the various major categories, such as food, clothing, and shelter. An overall breakdown is shown in Figure 2–7. How does the average family spend its annual income? Budget studies of the Bureau of Labor Statistics, undertaken mainly to provide a continuing accurate basis for its Consumer Price Index, and personal consumption expenditure studies of the U.S. Department of Commerce, shed a great deal of light on current expenditure patterns of American families at various income levels.

How much income does it take for a four-person family to maintain an adequate but modest standard of living in the United States? The latest tool to help provide an answer to this question is the "Urban Family Budget," a study developed by the Bureau of Labor Statistics of the U.S. Department of Labor. Results of the latest study show the average annual budget cost for a family of four—husband, wife, son age 13, and a daughter age 8—to be $9,198 a year at a lower level, $14,333 at an intermediate level, and $20,777 at a higher level (see Table 2–6). Living in a metropolitan area cost a lower budget family 9 percent more than living in a nonmetropolitan area, an intermediate budget family 14 percent more and a higher budget family 19 percent more.

Family living expenses, including food, housing, clothing, transportation, medical care, and so forth, came to 80 percent of the total budget, at

[6] You can obtain a free copy by writing to the Pacific First Federal Savings and Loan Association, Eleventh and Pacific, Tacoma, Wash. 98401.

TABLE 2–5
The Family Budget Guide (three in family)

	Gross Monthly Income											
	$500	*$600*	*$700*	*$800*	*$900*	*$1000*	*$1100*	*$1200*	*$1300*	*$1400*	*$1500*	*$1600*
Federal withholding tax	41.80	59.40	72.20	91.40	104.20	127.70	144.30	173.10	192.30	221.10	240.30	270.30
Social security and medicare	29.25	35.10	40.95	46.80	52.65	58.50	64.35	64.35	64.35	64.35	64.35	64.35
Net monthly income	428.95	505.50	586.85	661.80	743.15	813.80	891.35	962.55	1043.35	1114.55	1195.35	1265.35
Food	144.50	160.25	170.25	185.25	193.25	203.25	214.75	230.00	245.75	267.75	285.50	306.50
Shelter	115.00	134.00	158.25	178.25	205.75	225.75	241.00	246.50	248.50	252.25	279.75	298.00
House operation	49.25	57.25	68.00	76.75	86.50	95.25	110.00	123.75	136.75	146.25	157.25	167.25
Clothing	52.25	61.50	73.50	83.00	92.25	103.25	115.00	116.75	117.50	120.00	127.75	136.25
Transportation	42.25	50.00	58.25	65.25	75.00	83.00	89.00	96.50	104.25	108.25	117.00	123.75
Personal	14.70	25.50	39.60	50.30	63.40	75.30	90.60	112.05	139.60	151.05	152.10	153.60
Savings	11.00	17.00	19.00	23.00	27.00	28.00	31.00	37.00	51.00	69.00	76.00	80.00

Source: Pacific First Federal Savings and Loan Association, 1974.

FIGURE 2–7
The Personal Income and Consumer Expenditure Dollar in 1973

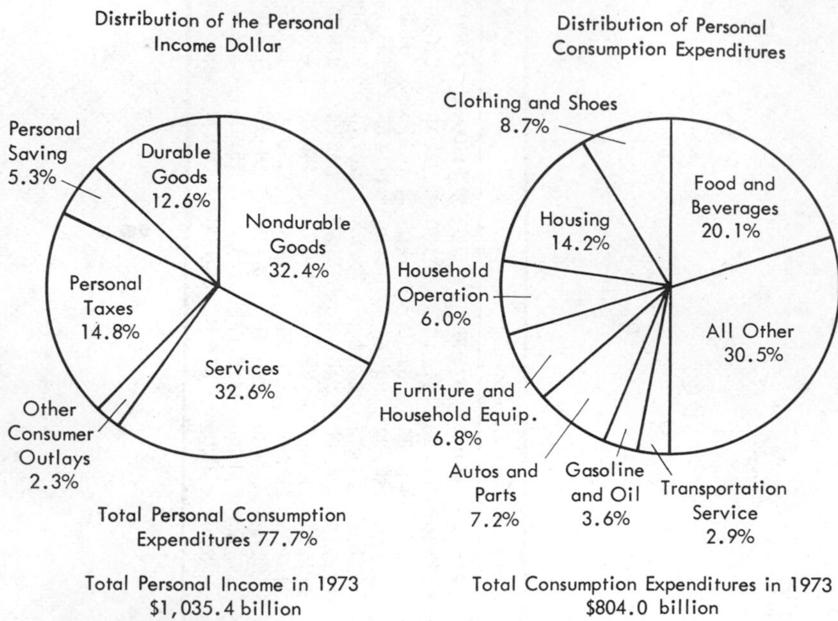

Source: Department of Commerce. *Finance Facts Yearbook*, 1974.

the lower level. The remaining 20 percent covered gifts and contributions, occupational expenses, life insurance, and social security and personal income taxes. In the intermediate budget, consumption costs represented 76 percent of the total budget. For the higher budget, these costs were 72 percent of the total budget.

The cost of all food (at home and away from home) was 37 percent of consumption costs in the lower budget, 33 percent at the intermediate, and 30 percent at the higher level. Similarly, medical care took 10 percent of the lower consumption costs, but only 7 percent and 4 percent at the intermediate and higher levels, respectively. Total housing (including not only shelter costs but also the cost of house furnishings and household operation) reversed this pattern. At the lower level, where shelter was provided by a rented dwelling unit, housing was 24 percent of all consumption costs. It was 30 percent in the intermediate and 33 percent in the higher budget. Roughly the same proportion (about 10 percent) was spent on clothing and personal care at all three levels, and for transportation the proportionate differences between the levels were small.

Using the budget developed for the four person city worker's family as a point of departure, the Bureau of Labor Statistics evolved a matrix of

TABLE 2–6
Summary of Annual Budgets for a Four Person Family at Three Levels of Living, Urban United States, Spring 1974

	Lower Budget	*Intermediate Budget*	*Higher Budget*
Total budget	$9,198	$14,333	$20,777
Total family consumption	7,318	10,880	14,976
Food	2,763	3,548	4,453
Housing	1,758	3,236	4,900
Transportation	643	1,171	1,521
Clothing	759	1,085	1,589
Personal care	231	310	439
Medical care	738	742	774
Other family consumption	423	786	1,297
Other items	415	662	1,113
Taxes	1,463	2,790	4,686
Social security and disability	553	780	787
Personal income taxes	910	2,010	3,899

Source: U.S. Department of Labor, Bureau of Labor Statistics.

equivalent scale requirements for families of different sizes and composition. For example, a three person household consisting of husband, wife, and a child under six would require only about 70 percent of the sum estimated for the budget-type family to maintain an adequate level of consumption. On the other hand, a five person household which includes three children would have to spend about 25 percent more than this standard budget-type family to maintain the equivalent consumption standards.

Table 2–7 contrasts the increase in consumer income with the price rise over the years 1965–1973.

Table 2–7
The Rise in Prices and Income 1965–1973

	Consumer Spending Power		*The Price Climb Record*	
Year	*Medium Family Income*	*Per Capita Disposable Personal Income*	*Wholesale Prices*	*Consumer Prices*
1965	$ 6,957	$2,436	96.6	94.5
1966	7,500	2,604	99.8	97.2
1967	7,933	2,749	100.0	100.0
1968	8,632	2,945	102.5	104.2
1969	9,433	3,130	106.5	109.8
1970	9,867	3,376	110.4	116.3
1971	10,285	3,605	113.9	121.3
1972	11,116	3,843	119.1	125.3
1973	12,051	4,295	134.7	133.1
	Up 73 Percent	Up 76 Percent	Up 39 Percent	Up 40 Percent

Source: *Wall Street Journal*, Sept. 23, 1974.

Raising children is pretty expensive these days. It costs the typical American family between $80,000 and $150,000 to raise two children and put them through college, according to a federal research study. This study, one of a series of reports for the Commission on Population Growth and the American Future, is thought to be the first to make complete long term estimates of the dollar cost of being a parent. The $80,000 figure is the estimated total of the direct cost of two children. The report also calculated the wages a woman could have earned if she had worked part time instead of staying home and caring for her children until the youngest reached age 14. Adding these wages raises the total to $150,000.

Consumption Costs for Different Family Types

How family consumption costs for an equivalent level of living vary for urban families whose size and composition differ from the budget family is shown in the Table 2–8.

TABLE 2–8
Annual Consumption Budgets for Selected Family Types, Urban United States, Autumn 1973*

Family Size Type and Age	*Lower Level*	*Intermediate Level*	*Higher Level*
Single person, under 35 years	$2,300	$ 3,420	$ 4,710
Husband and wife under 35 years:			
No children	3,220	4,780	6,590
One child under 6	4,080	6,050	8,340
Two children, both under 6	4,740	7,030	9,680
Husband and wife, 35–54 years:			
One child, 6–15 years	5,400	8,000	11,030
Two children, older 6–15 years†	6,580	9,761	13,450
Three children, oldest 6–15 years	7,630	11,320	15,600
Husband and wife, 65 years and over‡	3,360	4,980	6,860
Single person, 65 years and over§	1,840	2,730	3,770

* For details on estimating procedures, see "Revised Equivalence Scale," BLS Bulletin 1570–2.

† Costs for the BLS budgets for a four person family from which estimates for other family types are derived.

‡ Estimated from equivalence scale value of 51 percent of the base (four person) family. Costs based on detailed BLS budgets for a retired couple may differ slightly from estimates obtained by the scale value.

§ Estimated from equivalence scale value of 28 percent of the base (four person) family. May differ slightly from estimates obtained by applying a ratio of 55 percent to the BLS budget for a retired couple.

Source: U.S. Bureau of Labor Statistics.

Differences in Living Costs among Urban Areas

Area cost indexes not only represent different price levels but also include regional variations in consumption patterns, climate, modes of transportation, facilities, and taxes, as can be seen in Table 2–9.

TABLE 2–9
Cities Ranked by Annual Costs of Family Budgets

	High (*urban U.S. $18,201*)		*Intermediate* (*urban U.S. $12,626*)		*Low* (*urban U.S. $8,181*)
1	Anchorage	1	Anchorage	1	Anchorage
2	New York–Northeastern N.J.	2	Honolulu	2	Honolulu
3	Boston, Mass.	3	Boston	3	Boston
4	Honolulu	4	New York	4	San Francisco
5	San Francisco–Oakland	5	Hartford	5	Hartford
6	Milwaukee, Wis.	6	San Francisco	6	New York
7	Hartford, Conn.	7	Buffalo	7	Chicago
8	Minneapolis–St. Paul	8	Chicago	8	Champaign–Urbana
9	Buffalo, N.Y.	9	Milwaukee	9	Washington, D.C.
10	Chicago, Ill.	10	Washington, D.C.	10	Los Angeles
11	Washington, D.C.–Md. Va.	11	Philadelphia	11	Baltimore
12	Philadelphia, Pa.	12	Minneapolis–St. Paul	12	Philadelphia
13	Champaign–Urbana, Ill.	13	Champaign–Urbana	13	Seattle–Everett
14	Green Bay, Wis.	14	Detroit	14	Portland
15	Detroit, Michigan	15	Cleveland	15	Minneapolis–St. Paul
16	Los Angeles–Long Beach, Calif.	16	Indianapolis, Ind.	16	Detroit
17	Baltimore, Md.	17	Portland, Maine	17	San Diego
18	Cedar Rapids, Iowa	18	Seattle–Everett, Wash.	18	Milwaukee
19	Cleveland, Ohio	19	Cedar Rapids, Iowa	19	Buffalo
20	Kansas City, Mo.–Kansas			20	Indianapolis

Note: The three tabulations of cities ranked separately in each category starting with the most expensive in each, reveal no uniformity as to most costly. The cities listed are all above or equal to the urban U.S. figure for each type of budget. For the most part, southern states fall in the low cost category. It costs more to live in metropolitan areas than in nonmetropolitan.
Source: Bureau of Labor Statistics.

Public in Poll Sets $152 as Needed Pay for Family of Four

The American public estimates that an average minimum of $152 a week is needed by a nonfarm family of four to meet basic necessities, the Gallup Poll reported yesterday.

This is more than five times the $30 figure given in 1937 and 50 percent more than the $101 average offered in 1967.

In this national survey, 1,444 persons were interviewed during two periods in mid-February on the following question:

"What is the smallest amount of money a family of four (husband, wife, and two children) needs each week to get along in this community?"

The trend since 1937 and the averages are as follows:

1937	$ 30
1947	43
1957	72
1967	101
1969	120
1971	127
1973	149
LATEST	152

New York Times, April 10, 1974.

SPENDING PATTERNS

Food

Food expenditure declines proportionately with higher income. As earnings rise, consumers spend relatively less for basic necessities and are able to purchase proportionately more of comforts, luxuries, and nonessentials. But the explosive rise in food prices in 1973–74 hit low and middle income families, distorting budgets and causing hardship. The incredible rise in food prices and consequently in expenditures for food, may be seen in Figure 2–8. Useful sources for planning economic and nutritious meals on limited budgets are offered by the Department of Agriculture.

FIGURE 2–8
Food Prices and Food Expenditures

Figure 1

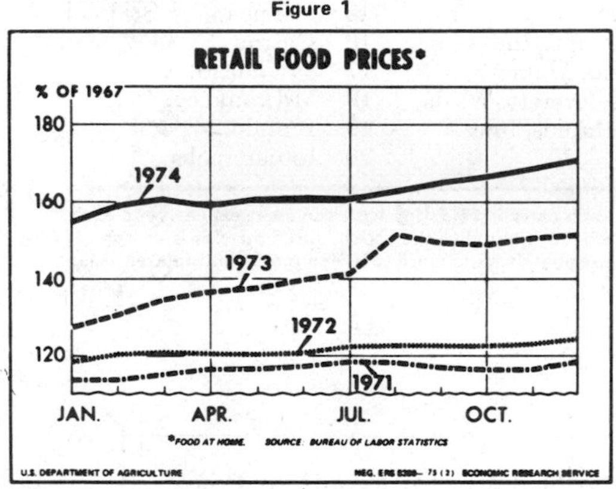

Figure 2

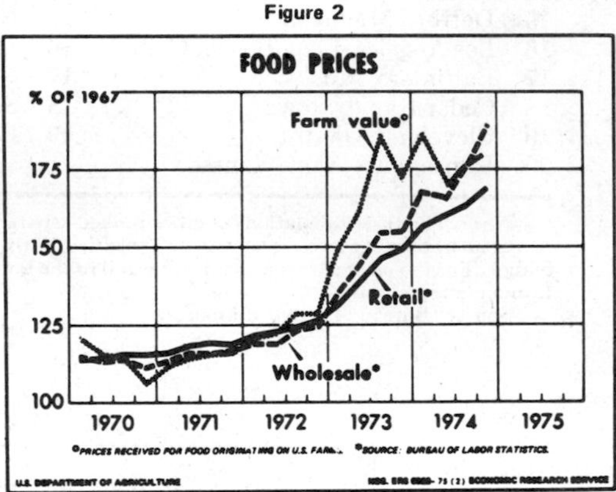

Figure 3

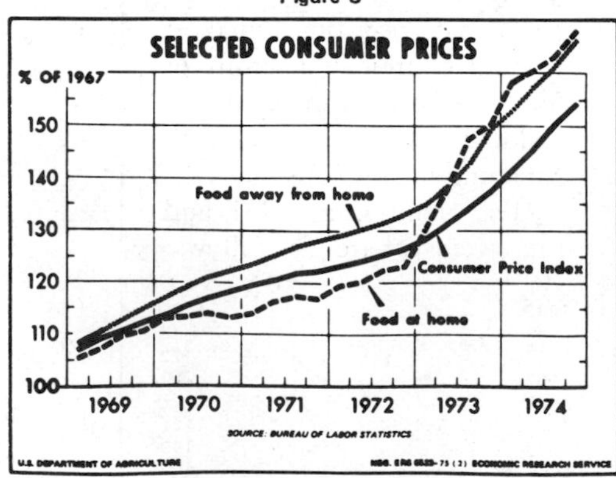

Figure 4

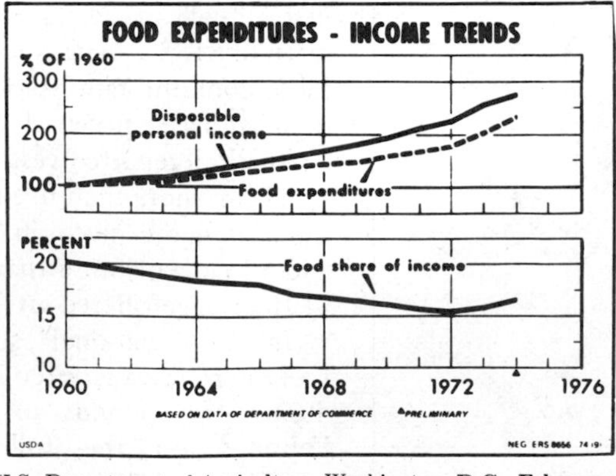

Source: *National Food Situation*, Economic Research Service, U.S. Department of Agriculture, Washington, D.C., February 1975.

Home economists claim that food costs can be cut and the diet still provide adequate nutrition. The Cooperative Extension of New York State, a three-way group combining representatives from Cornell University, the State University of New York, and the Department of Agriculture stated, "Since many Americans eat more protein than they need, perhaps careful shoppers should consider two ways to improve diet and save money. One way is to limit the amount of money spent on protein-rich foods, which include meats, poultry, fish, and eggs, to 38 percent of the total food budget. A second way is to select foods that are economic sources of protein." As illustrated in Table 2–10, items at the head of the list give more food for your money.[7]

The cost of one week's food at home is regularly estimated by the U.S. Department of Agriculture at three cost levels. The estimate is available for four regional areas (Northeast, North Central, South, and West). The composite U.S. average estimate of cost is shown in Table 2–11.

The American Red Cross, as a guide to its chapter workers in estimating family and individual living costs, suggests the food-cost scale shown in Table 2–12. Because of the many purposes for which chapter workers use the guide, food costs are computed on a standard cost basis with instructions for a supplementation in special situations.

Discount food stores seem to represent a growing trend among the big food chains. A&P Mart Discount Foods, an A&P subsidiary, trumpets its lower prices. A&P also has a small group of supermarkets called WEO (warehouse economy outlet). A–Mart prices are usually lower than A&P

---

[7] See also: *Family Food Buying—A Guide for Calculating Amounts to Buy—Comparing Costs*, Home Economics Research Report No. 37, Agricultural Research Service, U.S. Department of Agriculture, available from the Superintendent of Documents. For further information see:

Family Fare, Home and Garden Bulletin No. 1, Consumer and Food Economics Research, U.S. Department of Agriculture, U.S. Government Printing Office, Washington, D.C. 20402. A pamphlet giving basic nutrition facts, menus, market orders, and recipes.

Food for the Family with Young Children, Home and Garden Bulletin No. 5, U.S. Department of Agriculture, U.S. Government Printing Office, Washington, D.C. 20402.

Food for the Families with School Children, Home and Garden Bulletin No. 13, U.S. Department of Agriculture, U.S. Government Printing Office, Washington, D.C. 20402.

Food for the Young Couple, Home and Garden Bulletin No. 85, U.S. Department of Agriculture, U.S. Government Printing Office, Washington, D.C. 20402.

Food Guide for Older Folks, Home and Garden Bulletin No. 17, U.S. Department of Agriculture.

Consumer Leaflet 18 "Cut Food Costs When You Shop." Free from Mailing Room, Building 7, Research Park, Cornell University, Ithaca, N.Y. 14850.

Family Economics Review, A Quarterly Report on Current Developments in Family and Food Economics, Consumer and Food Economics Research Division, U.S. Department of Agriculture, Federal Center Building, Hyattsville, Md. 20782.

TABLE 2–10
Cost of Protein Sources (compared)

Food	Store Price (per lb.)	Cost of ⅓ R.D.A.	Usual Cooked Serving	Grams of Protein	Serving Cost Jan. '73	Serving Cost May '74
Dried lima beans	62c	16c	1 cup	14	4c	11c
Peanut butter	81c (18 oz.)	15	4 tbsps.	16	9	12
Pork & beans	31c	23	1 cup	16	10	18
Beef liver	97c	22	3 oz.	22	20	24
Chicken	47c	13	3 oz.	20	14	13
Eggs	71c (doz.)	20	2 large	12	13	12
Cottage cheese	68c	21	½ cup	16	11	17
American cheese	1.07	20	2 oz.	14	12	14
Tuna fish	54c (6½ oz.)	23	3 oz.	24	25	28
Hamburger	1.07	25	3 oz.	21	22	26
Milk	45c (qt.)	27	8 oz.	9	9	12
Ocean perch fillet (frozen)	1.18	34	3 oz.	16	16	27
Fish sticks	59c (10 oz.)	24	3 oz.	15	17	18
Chili con carne	60c (15 oz.)	33	1 cup	19	23	31
Whole ham	97c	33	1 slice (¼ lb. raw)	15	20	25
Frankfurters (all meat)	1.08 (8 in pkg.)	39	2	14	22	27
Beef chuck steak	88c	41	3 oz.	22	40	45
Round steak	2.03	51	1 slice (½ lb. raw)	40	85	1.02
Pizza	1.09 (15 oz.)	56	2 sections	14	28	39
Bologna	69c (8 oz.)	57	2 oz.	6	14	17
Bacon	1.07	50	4 slices	10	21	25
Rib roast	1.72	73	1 slice (½ lb. raw)	24	70	87
Sirloin steak	1.79	56	1 slice (½ lb. raw)	32	80	90

The costs of high-protein foods in New York City are figured on 60 grams of protein. The Federal Government's recommended dietary allowance (R.D.A.) per day is 65 grams for a man, 59 for a woman and 70 for a teen-ager.
Source: *First National City Bank* and *The New York Times*, June 6, 1974.

prices and WEO prices are less than A&P Discount prices, it is reported. Other chains have followed. For example, Food Fair has its Pantry Pride Discount food stores and also a Wholesale City. Acme Stores runs Super-Savers. While many supermarket executives balk at calling the new competitiveness a price war, a spokesman for Food Fair wasn't as reticent. "If it [discounting] gives the customer better value, and that's called a price war, then I'm for a price war." For the consumer, food discounting is good news indeed.

Buying in bulk by organizing local food co-ops, has become increasingly popular as a partially helpful solution toward cutting costs. Home gardens and home canning also provide considerable savings for those who can. Unit pricing, open dating on perishables and ingredient labeling help intelligent shoppers get better value for their food dollar. Reportedly, the federal food stamp program has been used extensively by college students to supplement inflation strained budgets, as well as by low in-

TABLE 2–11
Cost of Food at Home (estimated for food plans at three cost levels, April 1974, U.S. average)

	Cost for One Week			*Cost for One Month*		
*Sex–Age Groups**	*Low Cost Plan*	*Moderate Cost Plan*	*Liberal Plan*	*Low Cost Plan*	*Moderate Cost Plan*	*Liberal Plan*
Families						
Family of 2, 20–35 years†	$25.70	$32.20	$39.00	$111.30	$139.50	$168.90
Family of 2, 55–75 years†	20.90	26.60	31.70	90.30	115.60	137.30
Family of 4, preschool children‡	37.20	46.60	56.00	160.70	201.70	242.40
Family of 4, school children§	43.40	54.50	66.10	187.70	236.20	286.00
Individuals‖						
Children, under 1 year	4.90	6.10	6.80	21.10	26.40	29.30
1–3 years	6.30	7.80	9.30	27.10	33.80	40.20
3–6 years	7.50	9.50	11.20	32.40	41.10	48.70
6–9 years	9.20	11.60	14.30	39.90	50.30	62.00
Girls, 9–12 years	10.50	13.30	15.40	45.30	57.70	66.70
12–15 years	11.50	14.80	17.60	49.90	64.00	76.30
15–20 years	11.70	14.60	17.10	50.80	63.30	74.20
Boys, 9–12 years	10.80	13.60	16.30	46.60	59.10	70.50
12–15 years	12.60	16.40	19.30	54.80	70.90	83.40
15–20 years	14.60	18.30	21.80	63.30	79.40	94.50
Women, 20–35 years	10.80	13.50	16.10	46.60	58.50	69.60
35–55 years	10.30	13.00	15.40	44.70	56.30	66.80
55–75 years	8.70	11.10	13.10	37.60	48.20	56.80
75 years and over	7.90	9.90	11.90	34.20	42.80	51.70
Pregnant	12.70	15.70	18.40	54.90	68.10	79.60
Nursing	14.90	18.20	21.10	64.40	79.00	91.60
Men, 20–35 years	12.60	15.80	19.40	54.60	68.30	83.90
35–55 years	11.70	14.60	17.60	50.60	63.40	76.40
55–75 years	10.30	13.10	15.70	44.50	56.90	68.00
75 years and over	9.60	12.60	15.10	41.60	54.70	65.30

Note: These estimates were computed from quantities in food plans published in *Family Economics Review*, October 1964. The costs of the food plans were first estimated by using the average price per pound of each food group paid by urban survey families at three selected income levels in 1965. These prices were adjusted to current levels by use of *Retail Food Prices by Cities* released periodically by the Bureau of Labor Statistics.

* Age groups include the persons of the first age listed up to but not including those of the second age listed.
† Ten percent added for family size adjustment.
‡ Man and woman, 20–35 years; children, 1–3 and 3–6 years.
§ Man and woman, 20–35; child, 6–9 and boy 9–12 years.
‖ The costs given are for individuals in 4-person families. For individuals in other size families, the following adjustments are suggested: 1-person—add 20 percent; 2-person—add 10 percent; 3-person—add 5 percent; 5-person—subtract 5 percent; 6-or-more-person—subtract 10 percent.

Source: U.S. Department of Agriculture, Agricultural Research Service, Consumer and Food Economics Institute, Hyattsville, Maryland 20782.

come families with many children. How many stamps a student gets each month depends on the student's income and housing and tuition expenses. The student's living quarters must include cooking facilities. And he or she can have no more than $500 in savings. If you come from a middle or upper income household, however, you are not eligible for food stamps and if your parents claim you as an income tax dependent you are barred from the program.

TABLE 2–12
Family Food Budget Guide, May 1974 (cost per person for adequate food on standard budget)

Individuals—by Sex and Age	*Standard Cost*	
	Per Week	*Per Month*
Children, under 1 year	$ 6.40	$27.80
1 to 3 years	8.90	38.40
3 to 6 years	10.70	46.50
6 to 9 years	13.60	58.70
Girls, 9 to 12 years	14.60	63.30
12 to 15 years	16.80	72.60
15 to 20 years	16.30	70.80
Boys, 9 to 12 years	15.40	66.60
12 to 15 years	18.10	78.30
15 to 20 years	20.40	88.50
Women, 20 to 35 years	15.30	66.50
35 to 55 years	14.80	64.20
55 to 75 years	12.60	54.80
75 years and over	11.50	49.90
Pregnant woman	17.60	76.30
Nursing mother	19.90	86.30
Men, 20 to 35 years	18.30	79.30
35 to 55 years	16.70	72.30
55 to 75 years	14.90	64.70
75 years and over	14.40	62.40

Prepared by the food and nutrition consultant, national headquarters, for use by chapter workers in estimating family and individual food costs.

Note: In small families or in special situations the figures above should be supplemented to adjust family food costs.

The Standard Cost Budget Guide represents an adequate allowance for food for each individual in each age and sex group.

The basic figures used for calculating the standard cost budget were provided by the U.S. Department of Agriculture and the Bureau of Labor Statistics, February 1974. They are based on computations of average retail food prices in cities in the United States and the actual cost of food used by families at home to provide a nourishing diet.

Age groups include persons of the first age listed, up to but not including those of the second age listed.

All costs are rounded to the nearest $0.05.

Monthly costs are estimated on the basis of 4⅓ weeks in a month.

Source: The American National Red Cross.

Sample Food Price Changes

The same brands, in the same market, were used for basis of comparison.

	1969	*1972*	*1974*
Chicken of the Sea tuna, white meat, 7 oz.	$.36	$.51	$ .63
Maxwell House coffee 1 lb. can	$.74	$.90	$1.13
Del Monte fruit cocktail 17 oz.	$.28	$.32	$ .35
Wesson salad oil, 24 oz.	$.53	$.64	$ .87
Carolina rice, 3 lb.	$.52	$.59	$1.35
Welch's grape jelly, 10 oz.	$.26	$.32	$ .35
Bumble Bee salmon 7¾ oz.	$.73	$.85	$1.59
Golden Blossom honey 16 oz.	$.37	$.74	$1.05
Sun Maid raisins 15 oz.	$.34	$.47	$ .75

Source: local market survey, *New York Times*.

Housing and Household Operation

"Keeping up with the Joneses" is nowhere more manifest than in the purchase of homes, the upkeep of which is too expensive in terms of one's income, or in paying too high a rent because of the desire to live in a fashionable neighborhood. Some well-tested rules of thumb are available, but they are not easy to stay with and are more often ignored than observed. Detailed study of housing costs will be found in Chapter 12.

A family should not spend more than one week's net, take-home pay for the monthly rent. Many families probably exceed this limit, but the extra rental cost then comes at the expense of some other category of outlay, such as savings or recreation.

In purchasing a house, you should pay no more than three times your annual income. Thus, if you make $12,000 a year, you can afford a $36,000 house—no higher, though many families do go higher and then have to cut down elsewhere, on food, clothing, or savings, or go into debt more heavily than they should. Then there is the "1 percent rule." The total monthly cost of carrying a house, including all expenses—interest, taxes, repairs, painting,—is about 1 percent of the total cost of the house. Thus, a $20,000 house will involve monthly outlays and expenses of at least $200. To be safe, monthly mortgage payments should not exceed one quarter of the family's take-home pay.

In the BLS city worker's family budget, housing costs were slightly less than food costs, as a percent of the total budget, for families in lower and intermediate budget categories, but slightly more for families in the higher budget category. Housing costs, on the average took a higher percentage of the budget in urban areas than in nonmetropolitan areas. Budget costs were, in absolute terms, about $800 higher for homeowner than for renter families. However, this figure included an average of about $450 in payments on mortgage principal, an element of savings not included in the budget for renter families.

About 63 percent of all households now own homes compared to 55 percent in 1950. This doesn't tell the full story however. About 42 percent of households with the head under 35 years of age own their own home. Of households headed by those 35–54 years old, three of every four owned homes. The majority of renters are in the age brackets under 25 and over 44. More single persons, unrelated individuals, widows, and widowers have larger incomes today than previously and maintain their own quarters—usually apartments. Over 70 percent of those 65 and over hold title to their own homes, although they may live elsewhere for all or part of the year. With the trek to the suburbs and the sharp rise in homeownership, family expenditures for housing have increased. The rate of home ownership

TABLE 2–13
Home Ownership by Regions, 1970

Region	*Occupied Units*	*Owner Occupied Units*	*Renter Occupied Units*	*Percentage Owned*	*Percentage Rented*
Northeast	15,483,000	8,917,000	6,566,000	57.6	42.4
North Central	17,535,000	11,922,000	5,613,000	68.0	32.0
South	19,257,000	12,456,000	6,801,000	64.7	35.3
West	11,170,000	6,591,000	4,579,000	59.0	41.0
Entire United States	63,445,000	39,886,000	23,559,000	62.9	37.1

Source: Bureau of the Census. *Savings and Loan Fact Book 1974.*

varies from 50 percent for households with incomes under $3,000 to nearly 85 percent for those with incomes of $15,000 and over.[8] A regional comparison of renter and home owner may be seen in Table 2–13.

The portion of American households living in "substandard" dwellings declined from 48.6 percent in 1940 to 7.4 percent in 1970.[9] Rising property taxes, high interest rates on mortgages, lack of availability of mortgage funds and soaring costs of automobiles and gasoline make prospective homeowners hesitate. Many have been priced out of the market. Major household improvement projects once left to professionals are now attempted by the homeowners, after they hear the estimates. To lower the fuel bill, risen by 50 percent, the thermostat was lowered and the layered look became fashionable and practical. In general, housing costs have been rising dramatically as Figure 2–9(a) shows. You can see that maintenance and repair, homeownership, and shelter costs rose more sharply than all consumer prices. The average sales price for all new single-family houses in 1973 was $35,500, an 84 percent increase from 1963! See Figure 2–9(b).

As spending habits have shifted to cope with inflation, by emphasizing improvement of existing homes rather than new home purchases, some appliance buying has strengthened. To help economize on food costs by buying in bulk, shipments of home freezers, for example, rose sharply. And now, if an appliance doesn't work properly and you can't get satisfaction from the dealer or manufacturer, there is help available. Since 1970 the Major Appliance Consumer Action Panel (MACAP) set up by the appliance industry, attempts to correct the difficulty first by contacting the company. If the customer is still unhappy and the matter is not resolved then the MACAP tries.[10]

---

[8] *Finance Facts Yearbook, 1974.*

[9] *Social Indicators,* 1973, U.S. Office of Management and Budget, Statistical Policy Division. Compiled by Daniel B. Tunstall.

[10] See "Something Is Being Done about Appliance Gripes," *Changing Times, The Kiplinger Magazine,* May 1974, p. 12. The address of MACAP is 20 N. Wacker Drive, Chicago, Ill. 60606.

FIGURE 2–9(a)
Trends in Housing Costs (1967 = 100)

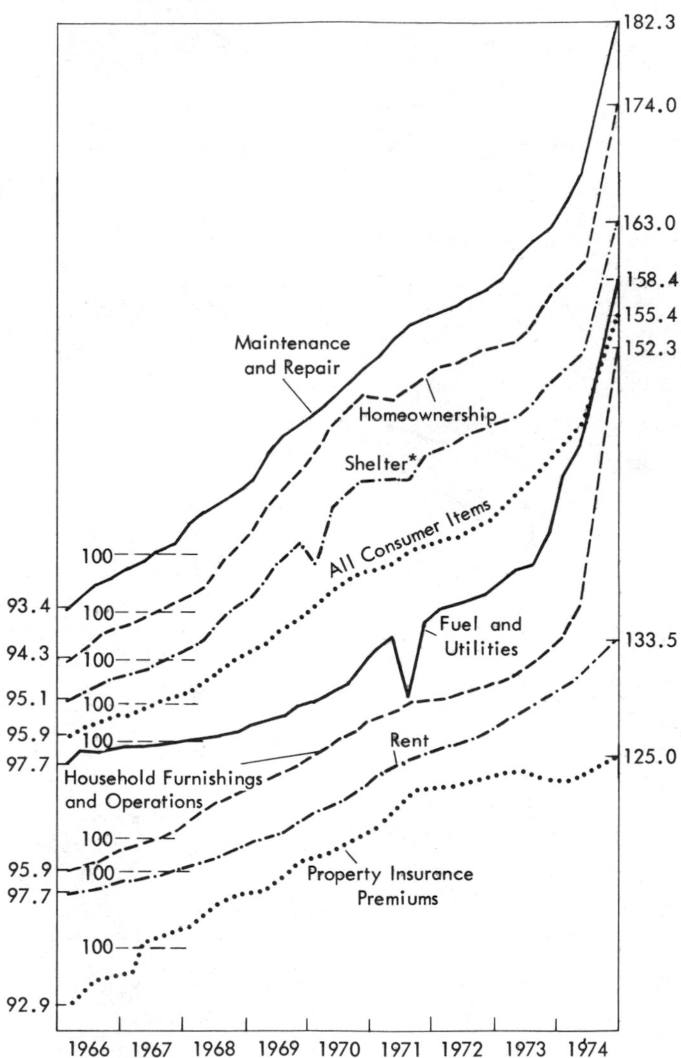

* Includes rent and home ownership items—purchase and finance costs, taxes' insurance, maintenance and repair; also includes hotel and motel rates (rent shown separately).

Source: *Road Maps of Industry,* No. 1746, the Conference Board, September 15, 1974.

The Discount Houses

A type of retailer who provides substantial savings for cash customers has developed over the past decade in the large cities and their suburbs. These retailers are known as "discount houses."

You will find discount stores in virtually all parts of the country. Some

FIGURE 2–9(b)
Average Sale Price of New One Family Homes

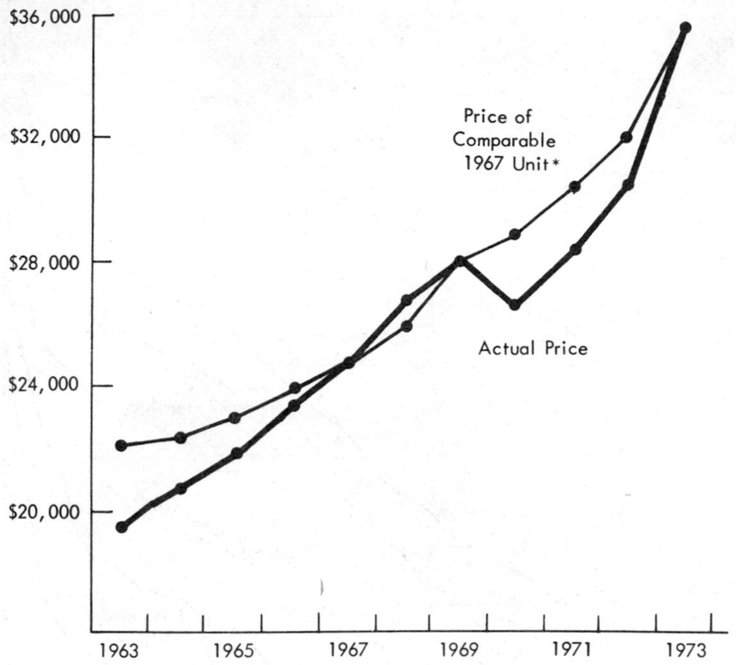

* Average sale price of units comparable to those sold in 1967.
Source: *Road Maps of Industry,* No. 1746, the Conference Board, September 15, 1974.

of the large ones are Zayre's; Two Guys, owned by Vornado, Inc.; Interstate Department Stores' White Front Stores; Kresge's K-Marts; Woolworth's Woolco; Arlan's; and E. J. Korvette. These discount houses sell nationally advertised, first quality, standard products, especially consumer durables and home appliances. They offer such merchandise as radios, television sets, pressure cookers, photographic equipment, baby carriages and baby furniture, toasters, electric mixers, electric shavers, watches, typewriters, records, sporting equipment, washing machines, air conditioners, refrigerators, and auto equipment and tires at discounts ranging from 15 to 30 percent.

Initially you might have found the discount store in a shabby part of town in cheap quarters in a second story loft. Today many have become huge, luxurious affairs in prime locations and suburban shopping centers. With the elimination of weaker stores, chains such as Kresge's K-Mart, Woolworth's Woolco, Korvette, and Zayre's have come to dominate the discount scene. How do these houses manage to sell at from 15 to 30 percent less than regular retailers? They trim costs; they sell at lower margins;

they ignore fair-trade laws, which usually provide very ample margins; they do a greater volume in fewer items than many department stores and thereby have lower unit costs; they have a large following because of their attractive discounts; they carry smaller inventories, reordering as needed more frequently. Basically they operate on a combination of higher volume and lower markups. Some of the larger houses now provide almost all the services of a full scale department store. The more reputable discount houses usually provide a manufacturers' guarantee on brand items.

It is useful to check prices. Those quoted as below list price may not be, or the reduction may be inadequate to offset the advantages of delivery, installation, servicing, or refund and exchange arrangements.

Catalogue showrooms have become to the discount industry, what the discount industry was to the conventional retailer a decade ago. On the principle that "if you can't fight them, join them" discounters' chains are incorporating catalogue showrooms. The catalogue discounter uses a catalogue of national brand items as his primary advertising and sales tool, and has a one of kind display in the showroom. The customer orders by mail or sees the display and receives the goods from the warehouse. The economy operation nets the cataloguer about 4 percent after taxes, compared to the discounter's 1.2 percent average net profit.

Clothing

Clothing expenditures absorb about 10 percent of the household budget. In contrast to food expenditures, which absorb a decreasing percent of the budget as income levels rise, clothing expenditures tend to rise percentagewise as income increases (Table 2–14). They also vary according to region. Most items sold west of the Mississippi are 10 percent higher. According to the BLS, clothing's costs are highest in San Francisco and Chicago.

As the family grows more affluent not only do outlays for clothing tend

TABLE 2–14
Clothing Expenditure at Varying Income Levels

After-Tax Income	*Clothing Costs*	*Clothing as a Percent of Living Cost*
\$ 5,000–\$ 6,000	\$ 602	9.6
6,000– 7,500	784	10.7
7,500– 10,000	1,009	11.3
10,000– 15,000	1,380	12.0
15,000 and over	2,176	12.6

Source: *Changing Times, The Kiplinger Magazine.*

to rise percentagewise but spending for the woman's wardrobe advances faster than for the man's. For example, at the $7,500 to $10,000 level, the women of the family spend about 57 percent of the family's clothing budget, but at the $15,000-and-above level, 67 percent.

Because of continued inflation the number of people sewing their own clothes has increased. Simplicity Pattern Company estimates that more than 45 million home sewers made some part of their own clothes—a number equal to half of all females over 12. Expenditures for fabrics, patterns, and notions amount to about 7 percent of consumer expenditures for clothing and accessories.

More casual living and the revolution in clothing styles emphasizing comfort and informality should have kept clothing costs down but inflation raised them. Wholesale clothing prices have risen sharply foreshadowing even higher store price tags. Inflation has made consumers somewhat reluctant to buy new outfits and the current strong trend in handbags and jewelry, neckwear, and sport shirts would seem to indicate that consumers are trying to dress up what they already have. When a simple cotton and polyester summer dress, that has only three yards of inexpensive material at $1.60 a yard, and a belt, costs the manufacturer $55.75 to make and which after $2 for taxes and $2 in profit he sells for 59.75 to the retailer; who in turn adds his overhead costs and salaries, advertising and merchandising expenses, $2 for taxes and $2 in profit to reach a price tag of $110, then its obvious why consumers are reluctant to buy and bankruptcies increase.[11]

Consumers who have been unable to do much about bread and milk prices or rent and gas costs are making their price resistance felt in apparel purchases. Clothing sales are down. As prices of children's clothing especially began to hurt, many families have increasingly turned to mail order catalogues which at least offer protection against overnight price hikes. Catalogue sales have jumped an average 25 percent.

Your Automobile

Perhaps one of the most striking observations that emerged from the Bureau of Labor Statistics budget studies is that the average family, and especially the lower income family, tends to spend almost twice as much on automobile operation and upkeep as on medical care and more than on clothing. Increased home ownership and the growth of suburban living have greatly extended the use of automobiles.

Table 2–15 indicates that a smaller percentage of upper income families

[11] *New York Times*, April 23, 1974.

TABLE 2–15
Household Ownership of Cars, 1972

Household Characteristic	*Total House-holds (millions)*	*Percent of Households Owning:* One Car	Two Cars	Three or More Cars	*Total Cars Owned by House-holds* (millions)*	*Percent House-holds Owning Current Model Car†*
Total	66.5	49.3	24.6	5.6	76.7	18.7
Income‡						
Under $3,000	10.9	35.3	4.9	.4	5.0	3.6
$ 3,000– 5,000	9.9	55.4	10.8	1.8	8.2	9.3
5,000– 7,500	11.7	61.0	20.1	3.1	12.9	14.5
7,500–10,000	10.0	59.1	27.7	4.5	12.8	20.9
10,000–15,000	13.9	49.3	38.0	7.6	20.6	26.6
15,000 and over	10.1	35.4	44.5	16.2	17.4	36.8
Age of head						
Under 25	5.3	59.1	20.2	2.1	5.6	21.0
25–34	13.0	57.5	27.4	1.9	15.4	20.8
35–44	11.9	46.2	34.2	7.1	16.2	19.4
45–54	12.7	40.9	31.6	13.6	18.4	25.3
55–64	11.0	49.9	23.5	5.8	12.6	18.6
65 and over	12.7	48.1	8.5	1.2	8.7	8.5
Race of head						
White	59.1	50.8	25.7	6.1	71.2	20.0
Black	6.9	38.4	14.9	1.3	5.0	7.5
Regions						
Northeast	16.6	46.6	21.7	4.4	17.1	19.0
New England	3.2	53.4	22.5	4.8	3.6	22.3
Middle Atlantic	13.4	45.0	21.4	4.4	13.5	18.2
North Central	18.6	50.7	26.4	6.3	22.8	18.9
E. North Central	13.7	49.4	27.3	6.1	16.8	20.3
W. North Central	4.8	54.4	23.6	7.0	5.9	15.1
South	20.2	49.3	25.1	5.3	23.3	18.8
South Atlantic	10.4	47.1	25.5	5.7	12.0	19.4
E. South Central	3.9	47.6	26.1	5.0	4.5	18.1
W. South Central	5.8	54.6	23.5	4.9	6.7	18.2
West	11.2	51.2	25.1	6.6	13.6	17.7
Mountain	2.4	56.1	24.9	6.3	3.0	19.3
Pacific	8.8	49.9	25.2	6.7	10.6	17.3
Residence						
Metropolitan	43.6	47.1	24.7	5.7	49.5	19.1
Central cities	20.5	45.4	17.5	3.5	18.6	14.5
Outside central cities	23.1	48.6	31.0	7.7	30.9	23.1
Nonmetropolitan	22.9	53.7	24.5	5.3	27.2	18.0

* Estimated (no adjustment for households owning more than three cars, or for household members not related to head who owned cars)
† 1971–1972 model year
‡ Households not reporting income level are distributed
Source: Department of Commerce & The Conference Board, 1974–75.

have cars, but those that do, have more than one car, to a greater percent than families in other income levels.

A vice president of car planning and research for Ford's development group admits, "More and more people view the automobile as an unfortunate necessity. As you are viewed more as a necessity, people are less tolerant of your shortcomings." The president of Chrysler predicted, "What type of car the customer buys, he is going to be more and more concerned about how well it works and whether he can get it serviced and repaired." In these days of high gasoline prices and shortages an important consideration is how many miles to the gallon the particular car can provide.

The status conscious pitch, the emphasis on styling and newness are, according to consumer surveys, not as important as they were. Instead, pollution, safety, quality of construction, insurance, repairs, and costs have become serious considerations. Legislation and regulation are developing in response.

Almost all makes of cars now meet the federal safety standard for bumpers which requires that models undergo five mile an hour front and rear barrier crashes without "safety related damages." There is however a wide variation in repair bills for damages among different models and makes, ranging from $43 to $119. At 10 or 15 miles an hour the damage and cost increased radically—in the case of one model to over $200.

There is no doubt that meeting these new standards will add to the price of the car. Manufacturers' percentage profit margins on luxury models can be five or six times that on the lowest priced model. The margins on extra-cost options are greater even than the profit margin on the most expensive basic machine. Maintaining profit margins plus the increased costs for the new safety devices, and the resultant price boosts further reinforces the trend toward smaller cars.

Higher prices stimulated the birth of car buying services that offer hefty discounts off the sticker price. Not all car models are available and the services are not interested in trade-ins. The dealers are scattered in different areas and transportation costs will add to the lowered price. To get the best price you should know how to figure the dealers' costs as distinguished from the sticker price.[13]

Consumer complaints about the high cost of auto repairs were investigated in a study of car repair shops in Dallas. What should have been a $1 charge for replacing a faulty distributor rotor of a 1969 Mustang ranged

[13] See *The Time-Life Book of the Family Car,* 1973, for details on how to figure the dealer's price.

from $54 for an unneeded valve job to a dozen other variations up to $130. Only one mechanic properly replaced the faulty distributor rotor and charged its true cost of $1. When questioned on why he didn't even charge for his labor, he replied, "It didn't hardly take any time."[14]

The Consumer Price Index indicates that auto repair costs have gone up 63 percent since 1967 and auto insurance 38 percent. Mechanics may be unable to pinpoint a problem because the complicated technology and modifications in each new model series have left them behind. There is also a reluctance to perform warranty work. Frequently the dealer receives less in reimbursement from the manufacturer than he would charge cash customers for the same work. There is delay, possibly due to difficulty in getting parts, possibly because the warranty is about to run out. This conflict between dealer and manufacturer is not to the advantage of the car owner.

The U.S. Office of Consumer Affairs reports that in state after state the number of complaints had increased more than seven fold in the last five years. Shoddy, unperformed work headed the list. A frequent complaint is that mechanics charge book prices based on work time, when the job probably has taken much less time. In shops where mechanics are paid by the amount of work turned out, no one wants to do a difficult job.

Legislation has been suggested that would require repair shops to provide customers with invoices detailing all work performed and all parts supplied. Certification of mechanics would raise the level of the quality of work done.

An experimental program establishing seven centers to handle consumer complaints has been jointly agreed upon by the National Automobile Dealers Association and Virginia H. Knauer, Special Assistant to the President for Consumer Affairs. These centers will have action panels to solve consumer complaints through nonbinding arbitration. The centers are to be in Denver, Cleveland, Salt Lake City, Portland, Chevy Chase, Md., Harrisburg, Pa., and Winter Park, Fla.

Misleading advertising and misquoted prices also exploit the unwary consumer. If a repairman says the price for a rebuilt motor is $119.50, he may not be telling the whole story, unless you ask. If he is unscrupulous, and waits until the motor is out of the car, before he lists the other items he says are needed for its proper, safe performance, there is little you can do at that point. An example given by the Better Business Bureau[15] is shown below:

---

[14] *Wall Street Journal*, April 21, 1971.

[15] No. 17 in Series, "Your Money's Worth," Better Business Bureau.

Rebuilt motor	$119.50	Clutch assembly	29.90
Labor to install	40.00	Throwout bearing	7.60
P.C.I. (explained as federal tax, but actually Production Cost Increase)	9.56	Pilot bearing	4.20
		Spark plugs	4.80
		Front pulley	11.60
		Oil pumps	14.00
Gaskets	6.10	Radiator repairs	14.00
Oil	3.60	Cracked block	40.00
Total	$304.86		

Table 2–16 shows the rise in selected repair costs in recent years.

The average person does not realize, when he first buys a car, how much more it takes to operate and maintain an automobile than he anticipates. The U.S. Department of Transportation recently made a survey of the cost of car upkeep, and its figures are shown in Table 2–17. Bear in mind that highway vehicles in the U.S. are presently consuming motor fuel at the rate of about 864 gallons each per year. You will notice that in Table 2–18 all cars operated at less miles per gallon at 60 miles per hour than at

TABLE 2–16
Comparison of Auto Repair Costs

	1969 Four Door Standard Chevrolet		*1974 Four Door Standard Chevrolet*	
Part	*Part Price*	*Labor**	*Part Price*	*Labor†*
Bumper	$123.45	$52.50	$221.28	$ 26.60
Grille	41.35	4.20	60.35	20.90
Hood	94.20	18.20	130.30	24.70
Front Fender	77.10	21.70	96.50	51.30
Total cost	$432.70		Total cost	$631.93

* Labor at $7 per hour.
† Labor at $9.50 per hour.
Source: Institute of Insurance Information.

TABLE 2–17
Cost of Operating a 1974 Car for Its 10 Year Life, 100,000 Miles

	Standard	*Compact*	*Subcompact*
Costs per mile (in cents)			
Depreciation	4.2¢	2.9¢	2.3¢
Maintenance, accessories, parts, and tires	3.4	2.7	2.5
Gas and oil (excluding taxes)	3.2	2.6	2.0
Garage, parking, tolls	2.0	2.0	2.0
Insurance	1.6	1.5	1.5
State and federal taxes	1.5*	1.2†	0.9‡
Total cost	15.9	12.9	11.2
Cost over ten years	$15,892.36	$12,879.53	$11,153.10

* 9.5 percent of cost.
† 9 percent of cost.
‡ 8.3 percent of cost.
Source: *Cost of Operating an Automobile*, U.S. Department of Transportation—Federal Highway Administration, April, 1974—study based on Baltimore, Maryland, area. The American Automobile Association also publishes a yearly study called "Your Driving Costs."

TABLE 2–18
Effect of Speed on Fuel Consumption Rates
(without use of air conditioning)

Test Car Number and Net Weight		Miles per Gallon at Selected Speeds					Percent Increase in Gasoline Consumption Caused by Increase in Speed*				
	(lbs.)	30	40	50	60	70	30 to 40	40 to 50	50 to 60	60 to 70	50 to 70
1	(4,880)	17.12	17.20	16.11	14.92	13.13	−0.05	6.76	7.97	13.63	22.70
2	(3,500)	19.30	18.89	17.29	15.67	13.32	2.17	9.25	10.34	17.64	29.80
2A	(3,500)	21.33	21.33	18.94	17.40	15.36	−0.01	12.64	8.85	13.28	23.31
3	(3,540)	23.67	24.59	20.46	14.83	13.42	−3.74	22.67	37.96	8.96	52.46
4	(3,975)	18.25	20.00	16.32	15.77	13.61	−8.75	22.55	3.49	15.87	19.91
5	(2,450)	31.45	35.19	33.05	30.78	22.82	−10.63	6.47	7.37	34.88	44.83
6	(3,820)	22.88	19.41	20.28	17.78	14.88	17.88	−4.29	14.06	19.49	36.29
7	(3,990)	15.61	14.89	16.98	13.67	11.08	4.84	−12.31	24.21	23.38	53.25
8†	(2,050)	(24.79)	(27.22)	(26.80)	(24.11)	n.a.	−8.93	1.57	11.16	n.a.	n.a.
9	(2,290)	21.55	20.07	19.11	17.83	16.72	7.37	5.02	7.18	6.64	14.29
10	(2,400)	22.72	21.94	22.22	21.08	17.21	3.56	−0.13	5.41	22.49	29.11
11	(5,250)	18.33	19.28	15.62	14.22	12.74	−4.93	23.43	9.85	11.62	22.61
12	(4,530)	20.33	20.00	17.50	16.17	14.86	1.65	14.29	8.23	8.82	17.77
Average (unweighted)		21.05	21.07	19.49	17.51	14.93	0.00	8.11	11.31	17.28	30.53

* Changes in this section marked with a minus (−) sign were decreases.

† Since vehicle #8 could not be operated satisfactorily at 70 miles per hour, its miles per gallon performances were omitted from the averages. They are, however, given in parentheses.

Source—U.S. Dept. of Transportation, Federal Highway Admin. *The Effect of Speed on Automobile Gasoline Consumption Rates*, October 1973.

50 and still less at 70 miles per hour. The average increase in fuel consumption when speed rose from 50 to 70 was 30.53 percent, and the 10 mile per hour increase in speed from 60 miles per hour to 70 showed a proportionately greater increase of 17 percent in fuel consumption.

About 64 percent of car sales are financed. Finance companies account for 19.7 percent, credit unions 15 percent and banks 65.3 percent. Loans are now being made available for longer than the usual 36 months. The extended loan is being offered to cushion the increased price of cars. But you must realize that the longer the loan runs, the higher your finance cost becomes, as the following example indicates:

Length of Loan	*Annual Percentage Rate*	*Amount of Loan*	*Amount of Interest Paid*
2 year loan (24 months)	11	$3000	$355.68
3 year loan (36 months)	11	$3000	$535.74
4 year loan (48 months)	11	$3000	$721.68

A new car depreciates fastest in the early months. If you trade your car before it is fully paid and there are many months to go—your equity will be less. The less equity, the more financing you'll need for the new car.

From another and different angle, as inflation decreases the value of your money and the longer the loan, the dollars you will use to repay the loan will buy progressively less—if inflation continues at a high rate. Thus the loan may be easier to repay, since it is a fixed dollar commitment over time. If you have accumulated savings, it is less expensive to finance a car purchase using the savings rather than a loan (see Table 2–19).

TABLE 2–19
Comparative Financing Choices

	36 Month Loan on ¾ Purchase Price—10% Annual Interest	*Savings Withdrawal Repayment in 36 Equal Installments, Interest Lost at 5.5%*
Standard	$517 or 1.3¢ per mile	$286 or 0.7¢ per mile
Compact	$356 or 0.9¢ per mile	$197 or 0.5¢ per mile
Subcompact	$291 or 0.7¢ per mile	$161 or 0.4¢ per mile

Source: *Cost of Operating an Automobile*, U.S. Department of Transportation—Federal Highway Administration, April 1974.

Medical and Personal Care

Consumer expenditure for medical and personal care rose to almost 10 percent of the average household budget over the last decade. Outlays in these areas have been rising faster than expenditures for all consumer goods. Increasing longevity, expanding medical and hospitalization programs, availability of new drugs, and the very sharp rise in the cost of professional services have been partly responsible. Health insurance plans have spread to the point where they cover three fourths of the population.

The Consumer Price Index of all medical services has increased 55 percent between 1967 and 1974. The index of physicians' fees rose 56 percent over the same period.

Americans spent over $104 billion on their health care in 1974. The average health bill for each American is $485, ten times as much as was spent at the end of World War II. In 1950 health care expenditures amounted to $12.1 billion and represented 4.6 percent of the gross national product. Now they are over $104 billion and represent 7.7 percent of the GNP. As in the past, payments for hospital care made up the largest share of the total national bill for health goods and services. On a per capita basis average hospital costs were $625.

The substantial rise in national health expenditures is the result of many factors—the growth in population, the rising prices per unit of services, the increase in the average per capita utilization of health services and supplies, and the rising level and scope of services through new techniques, drugs and treatment procedures. Of the increased billions spent since 1965 in personal health care expenditures 52 percent can be attributed to the rise in prices, another 10 percent was the result of population growth, and the remaining 38 percent was due to greater utilization of services and the introduction of new medical techniques.

These averages are not your medical costs—but they are detailed here as both guide and warning that with costs so high and steadily rising, even health insurance will not completely cover all medical expense. Provision for health care is an important budget item. Health care will be covered in detail in Chapter 10.

Education

Former low outlays on education shown in average consumer expenditure figures reflect the fact that Americans pay for elementary and secondary school education—and, to a limited extent, higher education—through taxes rather than private outlays. Putting a son or daughter through college these days, however, is likely to involve considerable expense and strain on the budget, as shown in Figure 2–10.

The cost of going to college has risen 32 percent for state residents

FIGURE 2–10
The Soaring Cost of Higher Education

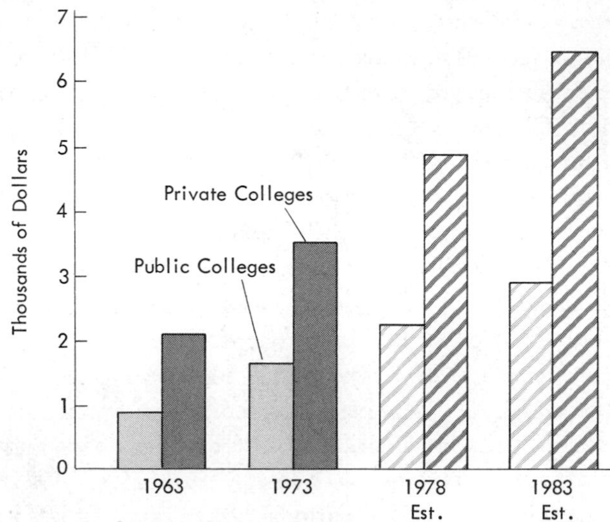

Note: Estimated future costs are based on a 5 percent annual inflation rate.

Source: Data, U.S. Office of Education. Reprinted from the February 2, 1974, issue of *Business Week* by special permission. © 1974 by McGraw Hill, Inc.

going to public colleges and 35 percent for out of state residents over the last five years. During the same period, costs for private coed colleges climbed 30 percent.[16] The following are examples found in each category. In 1964 Harvard's tuition was $1,760 and room and board was $1,130, making a total of $2,890, but for 1974–75, a year at Harvard costs $5,350 (not counting personal expenditures). Total cost for a Smith education in 1964 was $2,700, and for 1974–75, it is $4,560. For residents of Colorado, the university charged $1,070 a year in 1964, and in 1974–75, it is $1,893 (plus $1,366 for new residents). In 1964 the cost at the University of Florida was $926 and in 1974–75, it is $1,885 (plus $1,050 for new residents). Large private colleges in the Northeast are the most expensive; smaller public colleges in the South are the least expensive. The average cost of attending a publicly supported institution is $2,679 a year and exceeds $4,391 a year for a private institution of higher education. Additional living expenses above the fixed fee for room and board average around $1,500 and are higher in colleges located in or near big cities.

Even the state universities, however, require a substantial amount of

[16] Survey made by the Life Insurance Marketing Research Association, 1974–75. Annual editions of *College Costs* are available free through your local insurance agent.

money for attendance over four years. Tuition,[17] fees, and room and board costs for legal residents at the University of California (Berkeley) amount to $7,752;[18] at the University of Iowa, to $7,352; at the University of Minnesota, to $8,460; and at Ohio State, to $8,376. Supplementary charges for nonresidents range from $125 to $1,800 per annum. To become an engineer by attending California Institute of Technology now requires $18,124, or Carnegie Mellon, approximately $20,000.

Graduate work for professional degrees adds from one to four years of additional cost, depending on the field chosen. Fees for postgraduate work vary considerably as to both the course and the university. Tuition at law school for three years is about $3,000 a year. If we assume that room and board cost about $1,800 per year, a law degree would involve an expenditure of about $14,400. Since it takes four years, to earn a medical degree, the money cost of becoming a doctor (tuition, room, and board) would be about $20,200. A master's degree at a two-year graduate school of business will cost about $5,940 in tuition and $1,800 for room and board annually, or a two-year total of $9,540.

All these are substantial sums, and unless a family is well-to-do or begins to make provision long beforehand for college costs, it may have to deny this increasingly necessary and valuable privilege to its young.

> A graduate student applying for a scholarship was asked to state his principal reason for needing assistance. "My wife and I are now separated," he wrote, "and this has left me as my sole means of support."

As college costs have risen sharply, a variety of financial arrangements has been developed; including loans, insurance, savings plans, and so on. There is now a bewildering variety of solutions to the "Case of the Costly Tassel." Families can finance the spiraling costs of college education (*a*) out of current income, (*b*) out of savings, (*c*) by insurance, (*d*) by loans or scholarships, or (*e*) some combination of these four.

A student could once "work his way through college," but today this is difficult, and part-time employment can at best yield only a part of annual college costs. Meeting college costs out of current income has also become more difficult, since an average family's budget will require considerable rearranging to provide the average $2,500 per year for four years now required for college.

[17] For residents of the state. Tuition is usually higher for out of state residents.

[18] Tuition is free for residents of the state.

Savings and insurance are the two most prudent and foresighted ways to make sure that the money will be available, but they are used by only a minority of families. The earlier a family begins to save for college, the easier the task. If your child is three years old, you can accumulate $5,000 by the time he or she is 18 by saving about $16 a month at 6 percent. If you wait until the child is 13, the monthly amount will have to be almost four times as much to reach the same goal.

Insurance is another source of saving funds for college. A straight life policy over 18 years builds up a cash value through premium payments that can be used to pay college bills. The policy itself is a protection. If the insured parent dies the policy can pay for the college education.

Loans and Grants. In recent years loans have come into vogue to pay for part or all of the cost of a college education. Over $10 billion has been provided through federal grants and scholarships, G.I. bill and social security payments, state scholarships, institutional grants, and foundation and corporate awards. This does not include the large sums obtained through private loans which are state guaranteed.

There are a variety of federal financial aid programs for students, including the *Guaranteed Student Loan Program* which enables you to borrow directly from a financial institution such as a bank, credit union, or savings and loan association. The rules are complex but essentially permit undergraduates to borrow a maximum of $2,500 a year to a total of $7,500 at no more than 7 percent interest. For graduate study $10,000 may be borrowed. Depending on need, the federal government will pay the interest until after the student has left college. The loan must be repaid; repayment to begin between 9–12 months after graduation and must be completed within ten years. Colleges are required to determine the amount of money the family could contribute and recommend the amount of the loan. For students whose family income (above $15,000) places them outside the guaranteed loan category, getting a loan is not easy in a high interest money market. The paper work involved for such a student loan also makes a bank less interested. Defaults have been running high and students have been turning to bankruptcy proceedings to wipe out their repayment obligations after they graduate. Losses paid by the government on student loans rose from $27.5 million in 1972 to $112 million in 1974.

The National Direct Student Loan (NDSL) is for students who need a loan to meet educational expenses. They may borrow a total of $2,500 if enrolled in a vocational program or have completed less than two years toward a bachelor's degree; or a total of $5,000 if two years of study toward a bachelor's degree are completed; or $10,000 for graduate study. Repayment begins nine months after leaving school and the loan must be repaid within ten years, during which time there is a 3 percent interest payment charge on the unpaid balance. Application is made through the college financial aid officer. This loan is financed almost entirely by the Federal government. There are cancellation provisions for borrowers for only this type of loan to those who go into certain fields of teaching or military duty.

The College Work Study (CWS) *Program* provides a job opportunity to supplement other income. The college financial adviser determines the students to be employed, and the suitable jobs which may be as much as 40 hours weekly while classes are in session.

Basic Opportunity Grants (Basic Grants) provide a maximum of $1,400 a year, but anything the parents can contribute is deducted from the maximum. If parents can contribute more than $1200, the student is not eligible for this grant. Grants are government funds and need not be repaid.

Supplemental Educational Opportunity Grants (SEOG program) offer up to $1,500 a year for the student whose family's income is less than $9,000. Although eligible, a student may have difficulty in obtaining these funds which depend on the amount available at the particular college.

Special grants are available to veterans and their children, to those interested in nursing, to graduate students in city planning and in higher education careers, and to those in the fields of vocational rehabilitation, water pollution control research, and many others. Graduate foreign language fellowships, and National Science Foundation Fellowships, are also available.

United Student Aid. This program provides loan funds through a private nonprofit organization at rates no higher than 7 percent simple interest, with charges running from date of loan until repayment is completed. For a student who qualifies under federal law, the federal government will pay the 7 percent interest. All students will be required to pay an annual fee of 0.5 percent based on the amount of the loan.

A new government chartered agency called Sallie Mae (the Student Loan Marketing Association) provides a secondary market for government insured student loans. Sallie Mae lends money back to the holders of student loans so they can make more student loans. It is also buying loans outright with no strings attached. Proceeds from loans that Sallie Mae makes must go back into the student loan program within a year.[19]

State Aid. Each of the states has its own plan for providing guaranteed

---

[19] See "Tuition-Aid Trauma: Funds Shortage, Administrative Snarls Beset the Federal Student-Loan Program", *Wall Street Journal*, December 5, 1974, p. 34. Also "Five Federal Financial Aid Programs," HEW Fact Sheet, HEW Publication No. (OE) 74–17907, Department of Health, Education & Welfare, Washington, D.C. 1974.

student loans, made available through private lenders and for fixed amounts for study at acceptable institutions. The interest and principal are to be repaid beginning several months after studies are completed. The maximum repayment period is usually not more than 10 years, and maximum period for a loan is normally not more than 15 years. Special consideration is given those whose adjusted family income is under $15,000.

Private Bank Loans. Education loans are easier to arrange when interest rates are coming down, signifying that more money is available. Table 2–20 is an example of the charges and amounts on a purely personal loan basis from a savings bank. Commercial bank rates may be somewhat higher. Some colleges have established their own line of credit at the bank by agreeing to keep a minimum cash balance. This increases the number of loans that can be made.

Deferred Tuition. A number of colleges are offering variations of deferred tuition plans. Under one plan, students agree to pay .4 percent of

TABLE 2–20
Education Loans—Examples of Amounts Financed and Payments (annual percentage rate 11.40%)

1 Year Tuition Plan							
Amount of loan	*Annual Advances*	*12 Payments*	*Total Note*	*24 Payments*	*Total Note*	*36 Payments*	*Total Note*
$ 1,000	$1,000	$ 88.56	$ 1,062.72	$ 46.78	$ 1,122.72	$ 32.92	$ 1,185.12
2,000	2,000	177.10	2,125.20	93.50	2,244.40	65.90	2,372.40
3,000	3,000	265.70	3,188.40	140.30	3,367.20	98.80	3,556.80
2 Year Tuition Plan							
Amount of loan	*Annual Advances*	*36 Payments*	*Total Note*	*48 Payments*	*Total Note*	*60 Payments*	*Total Note*
$ 2,000	$1,000	$ 62.40	$ 2,246.40	$ 49.30	$ 2,366.40	$ 41.60	$ 2,496.00
4,000	2,000	124.60	4,485.60	98.60	4,732.80	83.10	4,986.00
5,000	2,500	155.80	5,608.80	123.30	5,918.40	103.80	6,288.00
6,000	3,000	187.00	6,732.00	147.90	7,099.20	124.60	7,476.00
3 Year Tuition Plan							
Amount of loan	*Annual Advances*	*48 Payments*	*Total Note*	*60 Payments*	*Total Note*	*72 Payments*	*Total Note*
$ 6,000	$2,000	$140.10	$ 6,724.80	$118.00	$ 7,080.00	$103.50	$ 7,452.00
9,000	3,000	210.10	10,084.48	177.20	10,632.00	155.10	11,167.20
10,500	3,500	245.09	11,764.32	206.64	12,398.40	181.12	13,040.64
12,000	4,000	280.30	13,454.40	236.20	14,172.00	206.90	14,896.80
4 Year Tuition Plan							
Amount of loan	*Annual Advances*	*60 Payments*	*Total Note*	*72 Payments*	*Total Note*	*84 Payments*	*Total Note*
$ 8,000	$2,000	$149.30	$ 8,958.00	$130.90	$ 9,424.80	$117.90	$ 9,903.60
12,000	3,000	224.00	13,440.00	196.30	14,133.60	176.90	14,859.60
14,000	3,500	261.40	15,684.00	229.00	16,488.00	206.40	17,337.60
16,000	4,000	298.60	17,916.00	261.70	18,842.40	235.90	19,815 60

their annual postgraduate income or a minimum of $29 for each $1,000 in tuition payment deferred. Repayment can stretch up to 35 years.

Tuition Plan Inc., a nongovernment loan program, offers parents loans repayable over a maximum six year period at an interest rate of 18 percent a year or 1.5 percent a month.

There appears to be a bewildering variety of student aid programs which seemed at first to favor the low income student, subsequently the middle income group, but which varies from college to college depending on admission pressures or the lack of them.

How Much Is Your Family Worth?

In addition to the budget and expenditure plan, it is sometimes advisable to draw up a family balance sheet from time to time, just as a business does. This is a statement of assets (things of value belonging to the family), liabilities (debts owed by the family), and the family's resulting net worth, all as of a particular time. A family's statement of condition, or balance sheet, might appear as shown in Table 2–21.

Such statements, if compared from year to year, will give some idea of the progress that the family is making (see Figure 2–11). More elaborate forms are obtainable at local banks, where they are customarily used to give the banker knowledge of the financial strength of those who seek credit from the bank.

One aspect of budgeting frequently ignored is preparation for financial security in retirement. This requires financial insight—long range planning and saving—so that accumulated resources yield the income which is needed, when it is needed. Where possible, a budget should allocate appropriate saving—not only for a house or an appliance but also for something as distant as retirement, taking into account the decline in the purchasing power of the dollar due to continued inflation.

TABLE 2–21
Balance Sheet of the Jones Family

Assets		*Liabilities*	
Cash	$ 261	Owed on home mortgage	$ 9,321
Savings bank books	576	Borrowed against life insurance	700
Cash surrender value of life insurance	2,072	Total Liabilities	$10,021
Furnishings at cost	936	Family's net worth	$11,324
Cost of home	$17,500		
Total Assets	$21,345	Total Liabilities and Net Worth	$21,345

FIGURE 2–11
Personal Balance Sheet

ASSETS	Five Years Ago	TODAY	Five Years From Now
Cash in bank			
Life insurance (paid-in value)			
Annuities (cash value)			
Real estate			
Furniture			
Automobile (trade-in value)			
Money due from others			
Other assets (cash value)			
Security investments:			
Government bonds			
Corporate bonds			
Stocks			
TOTAL ASSETS			
LIABILITIES			
Bills payable			
Loans payable			
Unpaid mortgage			
Other debts			
TOTAL LIABILITIES			
TOTAL ASSETS			
Less Total Liabilities			
NET WORTH			

Source: Merrill Lynch, Pierce, Fenner, and Smith, *How to Invest.*

Consumerism

Today's consumer has gone beyond the fundamental theory of *caveat emptor* (let the buyer beware), and instead is demanding that the buyer be informed. This demand has resulted in Truth in Lending, Truth in Packaging (Fair Packaging and Labeling Act), unit pricing in stores, and truth in credit rating. More than 35 federal agencies currently deal with the consumer affairs though it has been proposed that they be superseded by a single consumer agency. Since its reorganization in 1970, the Federal Trade Commission has become a veritable St. George against false advertising, announcing its intention to order all major industries to substantiate their advertising claims. FTC has also supported consumer demands for legislation to establish federal standards for fairness and clarity in warranties to protect the consumer, rather than the legal jargon that seems to protect the manufacturers against the consumer. A Congressional study of warranties found only one of 51 companies offered a guarantee free of loopholes. Corrective legislation (1975) requires that a company guaranteeing its products offer either a "full" warranty or a "limited" one clearly stated. If "full," the manufacturer must repair the product promptly and without charge after notification by the customer that something is wrong with it. If a number of attempts at repair (a reasonable number to be decided by the F.T.C.) failed to fix the item, the customer would be entitled to a replacement or money back. If the company wants to limit the duration of its guarantee it has to insert that limitation in the heading—e.g.—90 day warranty. If there are other limitations, the warranty would have to be clearly labeled as "limited."

Increasingly of late, states have passed protective consumer legislation. There has also been a strong movement in both state and federal areas for class action consumer suits in the courts, a formerly unacceptable concept. Many states have set up an Office of Consumer Affairs, or a Department of Consumer Protection and several have even developed "hot lines," which are statewide lines so that consumers can phone their complaints directly to the Office of the Consumer Counsel or Division of Consumer Protection.

Some of the nation's largest corporations have provided customer service departments to hear consumer complaints. Phone numbers (frequently toll free) and addresses have been made available so that customers can have some hope of action. Critics of these actions call them paper consumerism.

Under the guidance of the federal Office of Consumer Affairs, now under H.E.W., various industries have organized consumer panels for resolution of complaints. There exists FICAP (Furniture Industry Consumer Action Panel) and MACAP (major appliances), CRICAP (carpeting) and AutoCAP (automobiles).

Consumer product safety is the responsibility of the new independent federal agency—The Consumer Product Safety Commission. It has the power to develop and enforce uniform safety standards and ban hazardous products. It has set safety standards for more than 11,000 consumer products. The commission operates a toll free line that consumers may call for information.[20] The commission daily collects, via computer, injury reports coming from over 100 hospital emergency rooms around the country and, using this as a basis, plans product hazard lists that it issues to protect the consumer. It is alerted by an increase of injuries related to a specific product. An example of its strength was the agreement of a well-known manufacturer of baby cribs to recall thousands of its cribs and refund the purchase price and reasonable shipping charges because they failed to meet minimum federal safety standards.

---

[20] 800–638–2666.

The number of products being recalled is growing rapidly. As many as 25 percent of the country's 500 largest consumer goods companies were involved in recall campaigns in 1974. It is estimated that recalls will total at least 25 million product units a year throughout the rest of this decade. Product recalls are being spurred by a trend toward "defensive" recalls (companies increasingly are pulling back products before actual injuries or consumer complaints are reported), by a growing number of product liability actions in the courts, and by the increased activism of government agencies and consumer organizations.[21]

The knowledgeable consumer plans his purchasing at traditional sale time—the January and July clearance sales, the February furniture and bedding sales, the August "white" sales (sheets, linens, and so on), and the October coat sales. The informed buyer watches scales for full weight and reads labels for information on the product and on its care and takes advantage of all the consumer aids that exist, then becomes aware of the need for more.

The consumer has benefited from both the success of Ralph Nader's campaigns (especially, in the auto industry), and the headlines that highlighted the issues. The consumer has come a long way, when even the New York Telephone Company is required by the Public Service Commission, which invited customer suggestions on dealing with inadequate service, to rebate $1.50 per month to users with the worst service.

The consumer movement has become more powerful. It is drawing response from congressmen and commissions in asking for a more meaningful relationship between price and quality in the marketplace.

SUGGESTED READINGS

1. *Family Economics Review,* Consumer and Food Economics Research Division, U.S. Department of Agriculture. A free sample copy may be obtained by writing to Agricultural Research Service, U.S. Department of Agriculture, Hyattsville, Md. 20782. The *Review* is published quarterly.
2. *Sources of Consumer Information.* Obtainable from the New York State Department of Commerce, 112 State Street, Albany, N.Y.
3. *New York Life Family Finance Record Book;* also, Suzanne Hart Streit, *Marriage and Money.* Free copies may be obtained upon request by writing to the New York Life Insurance Company at Box 10, Madison Square Station, New York, N.Y. 10010.

---

[21] E. Patrick McGuire, "Product Recall and the Facts of Business Life," The Conference Board, *Record,* New York, February 1975.

4. *Your Driving Costs.* Latest annual edition obtainable from American Automobile Association, 8111 Gatehouse Road, Falls Church, Virginia 22042.
5. Sidney Margolius, *Paying for a College Education,* Public Affairs Pamphlet No. 404. New York: Public Affairs Committee, latest edition.
6. Sidney Margolius, *The Great American Food Hoax.* New York: Walker & Co., 1971.
7. *The Journal of Consumer Affairs,* official publication of the American Council on Consumer Interests; published semiannually by the University of Wisconsin Press.
8. In *Changing Times:*
"Guidelines for Updating the Family Budget," November 1974.
"Nutrition Labels: They Help You Buy Wisely, Eat Better," December 1974.
9. *The 1974 Buying Guide-Consumer Reports,* 256 Washington Street, Mount Vernon, New York 10550. A sample copy of the monthly *Consumer Report* will be sent on request by Consumers Union at the above address.
10. A *Guide to Budgeting for the Family,* Home and Garden Bulletin No. 108. U.S. Department of Agriculture. May be secured from the Superintendant of Documents, U.S. Government Printing Office, Washington, D.C. 20402.
11. *College Costs Today.* A free copy of the latest edition may be obtained by writing to the New York Life Insurance Company at 51 Madison Ave., New York, N.Y. 10010.
12. *Helping Families Manage Their Finances,* Home Economics Research Report No. 21 U.S. Department of Agriculture. Obtainable from the Superintendant of Documents, U.S. Government Printing Office, Washington, D.C. 20402.
13. Denis S. Karnasky, "A Primer on the Consumer Price Index," Federal Reserve Bank of St. Louis, July 1974.
14. Nicholas S. Perna, "Contractual Cost of Living Escalator," Federal Reserve Bank of New York, July 1974.
15. S. J. Prais and H. S. Houthakker, *The Analysis of Family Budgets,* Department of Applied Economics, Monograph Series #4. New York: Cambridge University Press, 1973.
16. Eleanor B. Sheldon, *Family Economic Behavior.* New York: Lippincott, 1973.
17. Robert Reichard, *The Figure Finaglers.* New York: McGraw-Hill, 1974.
18. Helen M. Thal, *Your Family and Its Money.* New York: Houghton Mifflin, 1973.

19. Arthur Watkins, *Dollars and Sense—A Guide to Mastering Your Money*. New York: Quadrangle Books, 1973.
20. In *Money:*
William B. Mead, "The Superinflation Squeeze," August 1974.
Avery Comarow, "A Budget Is Not Enough," July 1974.
Jeremy Main, "Bringing Your Budget Back to Earth," May 1974.
Merle E. David, "Managing Money in the First Year of Marriage," September 1973.
Paul Jankowski, "Keeping Calm about the Costs of College," February 1973.
21. William Robbins, *The American Food Scandal*. New York: Morrow, 1974.
22. Philip G. Schrag, *Counsel for the Deceived*. New York: Pantheon, 1972.
23. *Handbook for the Home*, U.S. Department of Agriculture, Washington, D.C.: Superintendent of Documents, 1973.
24. Donald A. Randall and Arthur P. Glichman, *The Great American Auto Repair Robbery*. New York: Charterhouse, 1972.
25. "Dictating Product Safety," *Business Week*, May 18, 1974, pp. 56–62.
26. *Family Food Buying: A Guide for Calculating Amounts to Buy and Comparing Costs*, U.S. Department of Agriculture, 1973.
27. *Your Money's Worth in Foods*, Home & Garden Bulletin No. 183, U.S. Department of Agriculture, January 1974.

CASE PROBLEMS

1. Clara and Edward Fedang had been married six years. They have two children, ages three and five. Ed, an engineer in a large New York City architectural construction firm, earns, $16,040 after taxes. Clara's father, who died some 15 years ago, left her an estate with a yearly income of $2,000 after taxes.

Clara and Ed had lived within their yearly income without budgeting, but they have not increased their savings in the last two years. This past winter they enrolled in an adult education course in personal finance. An assignment for one class was to develop a family budget plan. What should their budget include, both on an annual and on a monthly basis?

2. John Davis and Mary Doe (ages 25 and 22) are engaged to be married. Upon graduating from college, John went to work for a large company. He is now assistant manager of one of their branches at $200 a week. After high school, Mary went to secretarial school. She is now employed as secretary to a lawyer for $150 a week. John has saved $6,000, whereas Mary has saved $500 and has only two more monthly payments of $55 each to make before she will own free and clear a Ford Mustang which she bought new two years ago. Mary plans to work for a year or two after they are married in order that they

may furnish their home with things they probably could not otherwise afford. Both are anxious to plan carefully for the future. Their wedding is set for next June.

How much would you recommend that a couple in their position should budget for food? Clothing? Shelter? Other necessities? Savings?

What form or forms should they keep in order to compare actual expenditures with budgeted amounts?

They plan to live near to both of their places of employment. Since they are in a moderately large city, what should they plan to do with Mary's automobile?

3. Richard Roberts travels for a company which allows him 14 cents a mile for the use of his car. He drives about 2,000 miles a month on company business. Since he represents a financial organization which wants to make a good impression on its customers, he is expected to drive a relatively new car; but he uses the automobile so much that he figures he must "turn in his old car for a new one about every three years, anyway." In 1971 he turned in his 1968 five passenger Chevrolet coupe, which cost him $2,700 new, for the same model in the 1972 line, costing $3,100. He was allowed $950 for the old car, which he had run 81,000 miles.

Roberts thinks that his company is not paying him enough for transportation. He wants your assistance in working out a form or forms on which to keep track of all the expenses he incurs in connection with his automobile. What would you suggest? Enter reasonable figures for the various expenses you might expect him to have for the next year and compare the total with the amount he would collect from the company for 24,000 miles. Does it seem that 14 cents a mile is fair reimbursement? Would his expense per mile be different if he traveled only 5,000 miles a year on company business and continued to use his automobile for trips of his own approximating 3,000 miles a year? Would 14 cents a mile be fair reimbursement under these condition?

4. Ronald Graham, a junior, was elected treasurer of his college fraternity to serve for the year beginning July 1 and ending June 30. When he took office, the fraternity owned (*a*) its building, a brick structure, donated by a wealthy alumnus (it had cost $92,000), (*b*) furnishings which had been bought for $7,800, (*c*) supplies (chiefly canned goods) amounting to $710 at cost (*d*) a bank account with a balance of $3,700, and (*e*) an endowment fund of stocks and bonds which had been purchased for $16,823. At this time the fraternity owed various accounts payable amounting to $2,613 and a balance of $3,122 on its furniture. Prepare a balance sheet of the fraternity as of that date. Would you say that the fraternity is in a healthy financial condition? Why? Why not?

5. Bob and Janet Atkins have been married for four months. Bob has been employed for a year as an engineering salesman, and Janet has just started to teach, following her graduation from college. Their combined income after

taxes is $18,000; the savings account contains $800. Because of the city's excellent transportation system, Bob did not need a car previously, but he now needs one for periodic sales trips.

How should the Atkins plan the purchasing and financing of their car, keeping the family budget in mind?

6. Jane, age 24, was trying to decide whether to accept a certain job. The job was just what she had been looking for. The salary was $7,900 a year. The one problem preventing immediate acceptance of the position was transportation. The office was situated just outside the suburbs of the city, and there was no public transportation there. Jane investigated all possibilities, and she finally decided that she would either have to take a bus as far as she could and then be dependent on a car pool from that point to the factory or she would have to buy a car of her own. Jane was planning to share an apartment in the city with two other school friends. The rent of the apartment would be $220 a month. She had also incurred an educational debt of $320. How would a budget help Jane? What decisions should she make?

7. Sue Miller, age 22, has just graduated from a midwestern college. She has accepted a teaching position, to begin in September, in a small town about 50 miles from her home. After taxes and other deductions her pay is to be $8,020 a year.

Sue is planning to share an apartment with another teacher; her share of the rent would be $80 a month. Since both girls are good cooks, they believe that they can eat well for $75 each per month. During her senior year, it was necessary for Sue to borrow $350 (at 6 percent interest) from her college. According to the terms of the loan, the money should be paid back a year after her graduation date. Because her mother recently underwent an operation, Sue must remain at home during the summer and cannot take a summer job.

Sue is looking forward to buying a car as soon as possible, so that she can make weekend trips home. Being an avid golf enthusiast, she would like to join the local golf club.

How should Sue budget her income to accomplish what she wants to do?

8. Doris Gray and Betty James (ages 27 and 25) both teach kindergarten in a city of 25,000, not far from your home town. They each have $550 take-home pay every month. At present they room and board with Mr. and Mrs. Hassler, for $175 each per month. They would like a place of their own, so they are considering renting an apartment together.

Prepare a reasonable budget plan for each of them as you think it might be under present conditions. Enter representative figures for a period of a year on a form you consider appropriate. Compare the expenditures for the year with yearly income, nor forgetting that both have a summer vacation of approximately three months.

Set up a combined budget for the new conditions. Enter figures and compare with present yearly expenditures, making such assumptions as you think necessary.

Would it probably be financially beneficial to make the change? What other advantages and disadvantages do you see in the contemplated move?

9. Nancy and Robert Zander have an income of $250 a week. They used to live in an apartment for $135 a month. After saving some money and being left some by Nancy's mother, they bought a home for $27,000 in your community and thought they would be relatively free of dwelling expense for life. However, they are beginning to learn that this is far from true.

They ask you to help them devise a form or forms which will enable them to compare how much more or less expensive it is to own their home than to rent one. What is your suggestion? Enter reasonable figures for a year and compare the total with a year's rent at $135 a month. Are there any benefits other than financial from owning one's own home?

10. George and Nancy Green have budgeted $125 a month to run their new Chevrolet. George uses it to commute to work each day (48 miles each way), and the two of them use it evenings and for weekend travel to their camp (180 miles away), which is good for winter sports as well as summer activities. Insurance costs average $25 a month. Have they budgeted correctly? Explain.

3

The Tax Bite

Computation of Income Tax: Pauper Work
Ralph Noel

I'm proud to pay taxes in the United States. Only thing is—I could be just as proud for half the money.
Arthur Godfrey

MARK TWAIN, once asked what the difference was between a taxidermist and a tax collector, answered, "The taxidermist takes only your skin." We don't know who it was who said that the taxpayer is the only varmint expected to yield a pelt every year, but we do know you'd like to meet the mild little man who walked into the income tax collector's office, sat down, and beamed at everyone. "What can we do for you?" asked the receptionist. "Nothing, thank you," replied the little man. "I just wanted to meet the people I'm working for." If you stop to reflect, you do work for the government three or four months out of every year.

Today, the chief source of federal revenue is the income tax. It was originally introduced as a means of helping to finance the Civil War, but in its modern form it dates only from 1913.

Figure 3–1 shows the first Form 1040—on 1913 earnings. As you can see rates soared to 6 percent in the top bracket, on income of over $500,000. Exemptions—$3,000 for single persons, $5,000 for a married couple. Deductions were very liberal—For example, all dividends were deductible. Instructions took up all of one whole page.

At first, rates were very moderate; but two world wars and the state of the world today have caused the rates to rise to very high levels. The growth in the burden of the personal income tax may be seen from the fact that in 1915 a single person, with no dependents, earning $10,000 a

FIGURE 3–1
Form 1040 for 1913

TO BE FILLED IN BY COLLECTOR.

List No. ....

.... District of ....

Date received ....

Form 1040.

INCOME TAX.

THE PENALTY
FOR FAILURE TO HAVE THIS RETURN IN THE HANDS OF THE COLLECTOR OF INTERNAL REVENUE ON OR BEFORE MARCH 1 IS $20 TO $1,000.
(SEE INSTRUCTIONS ON PAGE 4.)

TO BE FILLED IN BY INTERNAL REVENUE BUREAU.

File No. ....

Assessment List ....

Page .... Line ....

UNITED STATES INTERNAL REVENUE.

RETURN OF ANNUAL NET INCOME OF INDIVIDUALS.

(As provided by Act of Congress, approved October 3, 1913.)

RETURN OF NET INCOME RECEIVED OR ACCRUED DURING THE YEAR ENDED DECEMBER 31, 191....

(FOR THE YEAR 1913, FROM MARCH 1, TO DECEMBER 31.)

Filed by (or for) .... of ....
(Full name of individual.) (Street and No.)

in the City, Town, or Post Office of .... State of ....

(Fill in pages 2 and 3 before making entries below.)

1. Gross Income (see page 2, line 12)	$			
2. General Deductions (see page 3, line 7)	$			
3. Net Income	$			

Deductions and exemptions allowed in computing income subject to the normal tax of 1 per cent.

4. Dividends and net earnings received or accrued, of corporations, etc., subject to like tax. (See page 2, line 11)	$							
5. Amount of income on which the normal tax has been deducted and withheld at the source. (See page 2, line 9, column A)								
6. Specific exemption of $3,000 or $4,000, as the case may be. (See Instructions 3 and 19)								
Total deductions and exemptions. (Items 4, 5, and 6)					$			
7. Taxable Income on which the normal tax of 1 per cent is to be calculated. (See Instruction 3)					$			

8. When the net income shown above on line 3 exceeds $20,000, the additional tax thereon must be calculated as per schedule below:

	INCOME.				TAX.			
1 per cent on amount over $20,000 and not exceeding $50,000	$				$			
2 " " 50,000 " " 75,000								
3 " " 75,000 " " 100,000								
4 " " 100,000 " " 250,000								
5 " " 250,000 " " 500,000								
6 " " 500,000								
Total additional or super tax					$			
Total normal tax (1 per cent of amount entered on line 7)					$			
Total tax liability					$			

Source: *Changing Times*, April 1973.

year paid a federal income tax of only $70. In 1929 the tax was $90. Today the tax is approximately $2,090. A married couple, with no dependents, earning $10,000 a year, paid $60 in 1915, $52 in 1929, and pays about $1,820 today. For the married couple with two dependents, comparable payments on a $10,000 income were $60 in 1915, $40 in 1929, and are $1,490 today.[1]

Or, to put it another way, the married couple, if the husband earned $100,000 a year, had $97,500 left over after taxes in 1915; they had $85,000 after taxes in 1929, and about $54,000 today. The single person earning

"We're not questioning your tips and donations - it wasn't necessary to bring proof!"

Courtesy: Jeff Keate and Chicago Tribune—New York News Syndicate, Inc.

$25,000 was able to retain $24,730 after taxes in 1915, $24,100 in 1929, and $17,810 today.[2]

As a result of high taxes and high prices, the married man (with two children) who made a $5,000 income would have to earn over $10,750 today to have the same purchasing power and to be as well off as he was

---

[1] Tax rates assume standard deductions taken.

[2] Assumes that the $100,000 and $25,000 figures are after taking deductions from adjusted gross income.

TABLE 3–1
Inflation and the Taxpayer

Inflation "robs" the taxpayer in a number of ways: As it pushes up a person's income, it often shoves him into higher tax brackets. Wages subject to the social security tax rise automatically with inflation. And inflation, of course, cuts the purchasing power of the taxpayer's dollars.

The tables below show inflation's impact in different income brackets on a married taxpayer, with two children, whose salary keeps pace with inflation—rising 11 percent in 1974 and assuming an 8 percent annual inflation rate until 1980.

In 1973			*In 1974*				*In 1980*			
Income	*Federal Taxes*	*Income after Taxes*	*Income Apace with Inflation*	*Federal Taxes*	*Inflation's Bite*	*Income after Taxes in 1973 Dollars*	*Income Apace with Inflation*	*Federal Taxes*	*Inflation's Bite*	*Income after Taxes in 1973 Dollars*
$ 5,000	$ 395	$ 4,605	$ 5,550	$ 506	$ 500	$ 4,544	$ 8,808	$ 1,248	$ 3,268	$ 4,292
7,500	927	6,573	8,325	1,112	715	6,498	13,212	2,230	4,748	6,234
10,000	1,490	8,510	11,100	1,732	928	8,440	17,616	3,320	6,180	8,116
15,000	2,397	12,603	16,650	2,845	1,368	12,437	26,424	5,481	9,054	11,889
20,000	3,392	16,608	22,200	4,000	1,804	16,396	35,231	7,973	11,784	15,474
30,000	5,812	24,188	33,300	6,902	2,616	23,782	52,847	14,314	16,658	21,875
40,000	8,902	31,098	44,400	10,583	3,351	30,466	70,463	21,759	21,055	27,649
50,000	12,547	37,453	55,500	14,920	4,021	36,559	88,079	29,246	25,434	33,399
75,000	23,067	51,933	83,250	26,713	5,603	50,934	132,118	47,962	36,381	47,775

Thus: In any income bracket a taxpayer whose wages or salary simply keep pace with inflation will suffer a decline in purchasing power as the higher income pushes him into higher tax brackets.

Source: Reprinted from *U.S. News & World Report*, copyright 1974, U.S. News & World Report, Inc.

in 1949. The $10,000 man must, to maintain his status, earn about $21,080 today, while the $25,000 a year man has to think in terms of an income of $54,300; the $50,000 a year man would have to earn $112,700. His federal income and social security taxes would have risen from $13,076 on an income of $50,000 in 1949 to taxes of $40,354 on an income of $112,700.

Inflation adds to the real burden of the income tax. If wages are increased to compensate for loss of purchasing power due to inflation, the taxpayer over time gets pushed into a higher tax bracket under a graduated

FIGURE 3–2

Where the Revenue Comes From (net income, in percent, fiscal 1974)

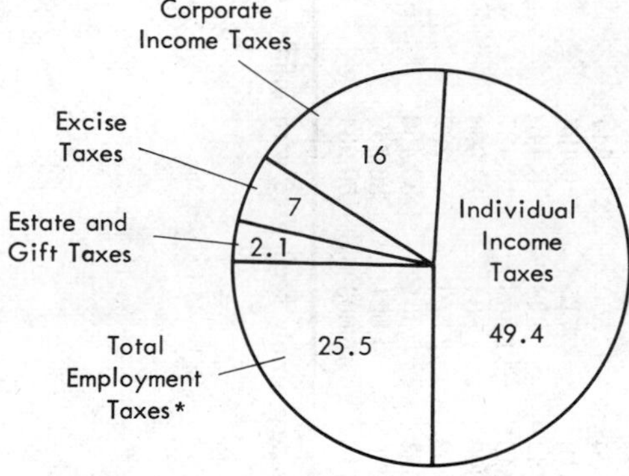

* Social security, railroad retirement, federal unemployment insurance taxes.

Source: Internal Revenue Service.

Who Pays What in Individual Taxes (how much is paid by various income levels; 1972 returns, filed in 1973)

*Income Level**	*Percent*
Under $5,000	2.3
5,000–9,999	14.3
10,000–14,999	21.4
15,000–19,999	17.8
20,000–24,999	10.5
25,000–29,999	5.9
30,000–49,999	10.1
50,000–99,999	9.1
100,000–199,999	4.4
200,000–499,999	2.4
500,000–999,999	.9
1,000,000 or more	1.1

* Adjusted gross income.

rate income tax structure. For example, using the excellent illustration from *U.S. News & World Report,* for a family of four with the breadwinner earning $20,000, income taxes and the social security payroll tax took $3,392, or 17 percent. Assume that the following year income rose equally to the rise in consumer prices of 11 percent. Earnings would thus total $22,200, an increase of $2,200. Taxes would rise taking 18 percent of income. And each dollar that remains will have less value in terms of real purchasing power. The family's spendable income of $16,608 in 1973 has shrunk to $16,396 in 1974, a loss of $212. See Table 3–1.

Assume that over subsequent years to 1980 inflation rises at an 8 percent annual rate. The $20,000 of 1973 becomes an income of $35,231 in 1980, but federal taxes now amount to $7,973 compared to the $3,392 of 1973. After higher taxes and inflation ($11,784), the family's income dwindles from $16,608 in 1973 to a buying-power equivalent of $15,474 in 1980, a loss of $1,134.[3] Table 3–1 illustrates the impact at various income levels.

There is really no "average" American taxpayer. Over 14 million Americans who filed income tax returns earned so little that they paid no tax. Of those who paid federal income taxes, the percentage distribution by income (adjusted gross income) level may be seen in Figure 3–2. Almost half (49.7) of the returns fell in the $10,000–$24,999 income range. Those reporting incomes of $50,000 and over accounted for 17.9 percent of total returns.

THE FEDERAL INCOME TAX LAW

Since practically everyone who works or has any income is subject to the federal income tax law, it is of the utmost importance that everybody have knowledge of at least its main provisions. Unfortunately, it has grown so complex that only those persons who devote most of their time and attention to it (tax experts) can really be fully conversant with it; and even they constantly run into troublesome situations where final decisions must be left to the courts.

Just how complex it has become can be seen from the fact that in a recent year one out of every five of the more than 75 million federal income tax returns filed was in error. Some 14 million returns were incorrect; 9 out of 10 paid too little, 1 out of 10 paid too much. Approximately $136 million was overpaid; $1.4 billion was underpaid. The Bureau of Internal Revenue has time and staff to examine only a limited number of all returns filed, and it does this largely on a sampling basis—except for the larger returns, all of which are examined. The larger your return, the more likely it is that you will face an audit. If you itemize your deductions rather than take the standard deduction, this increases the chance of an audit, especially if you take any large or unusual deductions. If you are self-employed, your chances of being investigated increase, and if you earn more than $20,000 in self-employment, there is more than a 50 percent chance of an examination. Usually about six out of every ten returns examined are found to be wrong.

Martinsburg Monsters

Electronic data processing (EDP) has now been extended nationwide. Performing arithmetic checks at speeds up to 250,000 numbers a second,

[3] "The Inflation 'Sleeper' in Your Income Taxes," *U.S. News & World Report*, December 30, 1974, p. 65. See also Avery Comarow, "Your Tax Bracket's Hidden Heights," *Money*, November 1974, p. 90.

this electronic computer system detects errors, discloses proper refunds and credits, and maintains a continuing account of your individual tax records. IRS keeps track of you by your tax identification number (social security number). Also, information returns are taking on an expanded role. Banks, brokers, and other businesses paying you $10 or more a year in dividends must report them to the Internal Revenue Service. Each information return contains your taxpayer's identification number.

"Martinsburg Monsters" are what Internal Revenue Service employees call the four huge computers at the National Computer Center at Martinsburg, West Virginia. On these machines are run the magnetic tapes of all the returns received at the Internal Revenue Service's seven regional processing centers. The tax return filed by the taxpayer first goes to one of the seven regional centers where the most vital information is placed on magnetic tape and then sent to Martinsburg, where for the next three years, before it is stored elsewhere, the taxpayer's return will be sent through the suspicious computers almost 200 times. The computers are programmed to look for errors, odd items, unusual changes, unlikely comparisons, and so on. Any taxpayer whose return is different from those in his class is immediately singled out for special attention. For example, a return listing $6,500 income and $2,000 in payment to charitable organizations is immediately spotted by the computer. If a taxpayer does not earn interest from savings accounts this year after collecting considerable interest for several years before, he too might be singled out. Doctors' incomes are lined up against others in the profession to compare income, deductions, and expenses. The same is done for other professions. Anything unusual or out of line singles out the return for an audit.[4]

The regional center gets shocks occasionally. In Austin, Texas, it was a quiet afternoon when a shriek pierced the air. A woman employee opened a return and found it soaked in blood (chicken's blood, the supervisor concluded) and the return was processed. Each year the seven regional centers are flooded with phony or humorous returns (see Figure 3–3), with shirts off taxpayers' backs, with teabags (symbolic of the Boston Tea Party) and with Band Aids because it hurts. One Form 1040 was reproduced on a shirt, another blown up on a 6-foot-long piece of butcher paper. One woman sent a lock of hair, saying she felt scalped after filling out the return. And a man included a handful of buttons, because, he said, "You got the shirt last year." One person sent in a comb, explaining that

[4] Mark B. Leeds, "How the IRS Looks at Your Tax Return," *Money*, March 1973; "If Your Tax Return is Audited," *Changing Times*, June 1973; "What IRS Auditors Will Overlook," *Money*, April 1974.

FIGURE 3–3

UNOFFICIAL FORM

1040XX COMBINED WITH FORM 1040(a.*.?! **INDIVIDUAL DEFICIT RETURN** INFERNAL REVENUE SERVICE **1974**

For the year January 1-December 31, 1974, or any dates within Chinese Year or other calendar preference.

Do Not Write in This Space

For Net Refunds of not more than $500,000.99

Notes: Before preparing this return, read "Ten Years in Stir," by Al Capone. Attach micro-encapsulation of blood sample, and note hospital preference. Note type of cell-block desired ☐ color TV ☐ private ☐ ward. Late return due to holding pattern delays not acceptable.

Write All You Want to Here

Print REAL Name, Please, and Address Below

Name____ Horoscope Sign____
Address____ Carte Blanche No.____
City____ State____ Zip____ Diners Club No.____
Name of your Bookie____ Phone No.____ Swiss Bank No.____

Your Filing Status Is this a joint return?____ Which joint?____ Living with wife?____ Why?____ Did you file a return last year?____ Did you tell the truth?____ (It's not too late to square yourself.) How much did you file?____ (If "Same", send copy of last year's return. We don't want to go through all of this again!)

INCOME

1. PAY DAY TOTALS (in dollars, bushels, or services received) .... $____
2. INTEREST (or have you lost it), PHONEY SALES, EXPENSE VOUCHERS .... ____
3. IOU'S YOU'RE SURE TO COLLECT, KICKBACKS, BRIBES, POKER, Etc. .... ____
4. TOTAL INCOME .... $____

DEDUCTIONS (This is the good part. Use your imagination.)

5. CONTRIBUTIONS PAID:
   - Fixing Traffic Tickets, less No. Unfixables .... $____
   - Business Expenses* (Entertainment, Name of Entertainment, or Friend. Limited to three 50-foot Yachts. All fuel disbursements involved, soda pop, bait, etc.) .... ____
   - Las Vegas Trips (Nobody wins. Put down the gross) .... ____
   - Paid to bowling, golf, pool and poker hustlers .... ____
   - Donations to Chicago 7; Red, White & Blue Panthers .... ____
   - Abortion Clinic support .... ____
   - Doormen, Hat-Check, Maitre D, Room-raiding officers, Plane ticket bribes, Amusement ticket under-plus-over-the-table assessments .... ____
   - Office raffles; welcome party, farewell party, get-well party, baby-coming, baby-not-coming, bachelor dinner, divorce party, reconciliation party, any-other-excuse-party donations... ____
6. OTHER DEDUCTIONS:
   - Mother-in-Law, Uncle Jake, Aunt Minnie, Dogs, Cats, Mynah Birds .... $____
   - Gasoline inflation, ABM inflationary effects, Wrong phone numbers, Postage stamp inflation, Bus fare increase**, Wrong change at supermarket .... ____
   - Lunches, Gifts to Purchasing Agents & Assistants .... ____
7. TOTAL DEDUCTIONS (Must exceed income. If not, start over and use more imagination) .... $____
8. NET INCOME (Transferred from Form 1040XYZ, line 3 to Form 1040ZYX, line 8, divided by one-half (whichever is smaller) of line 2 .... $____
9. NOT INCOME .... $____
10. LESS personal exemption in degrees Fahrenheit, divided by net weight at ringside, less two no trump, corrected to E.S. Time less elapsed time. (Note: No more than 24-column worksheets to be attached) .... ____
11. BALANCE OF NET DEFICIT TO BE REFUNDED (Stipulate preference: ☐ Confederate ☐ Scrip ☐ ADC credit vouchers) .... $____

GENERAL INSTRUCTIONS

Buy yourself an Excedrin (non-deductible) and hurry to the nearest tax expert you can find. If he refuses to help, turn him in as an Un-American.

*—See line 17a, section f, paragraph 3.

**—Stops once at every single house, twice at every double house.

AFFIDAVIT

I/we swear we're as confused as anybody by the simplified, simple Form 1040XX.
Subscribed and sworn at before me on this____day of____19____.

X____
Signature

XX____
Witness (bartender or Sick-iatrist suggested)

↓ Staple here all W-2's, Bus Transfers, Race Track Tickets, Laundry Receipts, 24-column (or less) work sheets ↑

Please note: We at PSI are not tax experts. We're as baffled by tax forms and reforms as you are. Our redesigned version of Form 1040 ought to convince you we both need help. Free copies (any quantity if you really want them) are yours.

Source: Printing Service, Inc., 1451 E. Lincoln, Madison Heights, Mich. 48071.

he didn't need it anymore because he had pulled out all his hair while figuring his taxes. One fellow sent along a sandwich bag full of mud, declaring: "This form is as clear to me as this mud."[5]

The Pay as You Go Plan—Withholding

Much of the income tax is collected through the withholding system. Under this system, the employer deducts part of your pay as tax and turns it over to the District Director of Internal Revenue or to a depository bank. The tax owed by you is determined after the close of your taxable year when you file your income tax return. You are then given full credit for the amounts withheld from your pay as shown by your withholding statement (Form W–2).

Wages subject to withholding include salaries, fees, bonuses, commissions, vacation allowances, dismissal and severance pay. Certain kinds of income such as payments for odd jobs, retirement and pension payments, etc., are not subject to withholding. Amounts received as scholarship and fellowship grants are not subject to withholding.

Two things determine how much tax your employer withholds from you. These are the amount of your salary and the number of withholding exemptions you claimed in a statement you are required to file with your employer on a Withholding Exemption Certificate (Form W–4). You are entitled to receive from your employer on or before January 31, *two* copies of a "withholding statement" Form W–2. This statement shows the total wages paid and the income tax and the social security tax withheld, if any, during the previous calendar year. One copy of the W–2 Form should accompany your tax return. The remaining copy is for your personal records.

Declarations of Estimated Tax

Because the withholding tax on wages is not sufficient to keep many taxpayers—particularly business owners, professional people, investors, and landlords—paid up on their income tax, they are required to file a declaration of estimated tax and to make quarterly payments in advance of the annual income tax return. This declaration is required of you if your estimated tax is $100 or more and

a. You can reasonably expect to receive more than $500 from income *not* subject to withholding, or

[5] "Some People Send in More Than Money with Their Tax Forms," *Wall Street Journal,* April 9, 1970.

b. You can reasonably expect gross income exceeding—

1. $20,000 and you are single;
2. $20,000 and you are a head of household, or a widower (or widow);
3. $5,000 for a married person not entitled to file a joint declaration;
4. $20,000 for a married person whose spouse does not receive wages but $10,000 for a married individual where both spouses receive wages.[6]

Normally, you file your declaration (Form 1040 ES) on or before April 15, along with your annual tax return. The return covers the previous year's income. The declaration estimates the current year's anticipated income. It must be accompanied by your first quarterly installment payment of the estimated tax. Payments are due April 15, June 15, September 15, and January 15.

"Do we get employee's discount?"

If you do not expect any considerable change in income from last year to this one, the whole estimating process can be simplified by using last

[6] If this isn't clear, what follows won't be either. You have three possible choices (*a*) go find an accountant, (*b*) call or write your nearest U.S. Internal Revenue office, or (*c*) drop the course.

year's income and last year's tax as your current year's estimate. If you do this, you will not be subject to any penalty even though your income and tax finally turns out to be much greater than the amount used in your declaration. Estimates do not have to be absolutely accurate. You are allowed a 20 percent margin of error before a penalty is imposed, and you are given an opportunity to change your estimate from quarter to quarter. You are liable for an additional charge of 9 percent a year for each underpayment. The addition is computed on the difference between 80 percent (66⅔ percent in the case of farmers) of the amount which you should have paid and the amount actually paid. For example, suppose you should have paid $1,000 but you only paid $600. Eighty percent of $1,000 is $800. Take 9 percent of the difference between $600 (what you paid) and $800 (80 percent of what you should have paid) and the penalty comes to $18. If your situation calls for a difficult estimate (for example, if last year's income was abnormally high), secure a Form 2210 from your District Director. It should be of considerable help in making your calculations.

Who Must File a Federal Income Tax Return[7]

You must file a return if you are a United States citizen or resident and your gross income is at least equal to the amounts shown below under your particular category:

1. Single—$2,050 ($2,800 if you are 65 or older. Under tax law you are considered to be 65 on the day before your 65th birthday!).
2. Married—$2,800 combined income ($3,550 if one spouse is 65 or older, $4,300 if both are 65 or older) and are eligible to file a joint return and are living together at the close of the tax year. However, the filing requirement for each spouse is $750 if:
   a. They file separate returns; or
   b. They do not live in the same household at the end of the year;
   c. Another taxpayer is entitled to an exemption for either spouse.
3. You had uncollected social security tax on tips.
4. You are self-employed and had net earnings from self-employment of $400 or more.

Note that you should file a federal income tax return if you had income tax withheld from your pay but did not have enough income to be required to file a return. By filing a return and claiming your personal

[7] For further information, see IRS Publication No. 528, *Information on Filing Your Tax Return,* Internal Reveune Service, Washington, D.C. A free copy may be obtained from any local IRS office.

exemption, you can get a refund, even though you are claimed as a dependent by another taxpayer.

Tax Forms

The two most commonly used forms for individual federal income tax returns are the Short Form 1040A (Figure 3–4) and the regular Form 1040 (Figure 3–5). Most taxpayers have a choice as to which form they use. You may use the Short Form 1040A if all your income was from wages, salaries, tips, dividends, and interest. You may not itemize deductions, however, if you use Short Form 1040A. To itemize deductions you must use Form 1040.[8]

If you have income from sources other than wages, salaries, tips, dividends and interest, such as, for example, alimony, rents and royalties, pensions and annuities, you must use Form 1040. You should also consider whether you qualify for any adjustments to income for sick pay, moving expenses, employee business expenses, or for any tax credits such as retirement income credit, investment credit, and foreign tax credit. If you are eligible for any of these provisions you should use Form 1040 rather than Short Form 1040A.

If you file Short Form 1040A no additional schedules are necessary. If you file Form 1040 you will probably also need one or more of the following schedules:

If you *itemize deductions* use Schedule A (Form 1040).
Sources of dividends and interest must be itemized in Schedule B.
Profit (or loss) from your business or profession is reported on Schedule C (Form 1040).
Gains and losses on sales or exchanges of property are reported on Schedule D (Form 1040) and Form 4797.
Supplemental Schedule of Income, Schedule E (Form 1040) is used to report income from pensions, annuities, rents, royalties, partnerships, estates, trusts, and small business corporations.
Farm income and expenses are shown on Schedule F of Form 1040.
Income averaging is computed on Schedule G (Form 1040).

---

[8] See *Your Federal Income Tax*, Publication No. 17, U.S. Department of the Treasury, Internal Revenue Service, Washington, D.C. latest edition. The pages which follow contain only highlight information current at the time of writing. Necessarily not all facets, aspects, rules and regulations are covered. For tax facts, advice, or information consult the Internal Revenue Service (toll free phones are listed in *Your Federal Income Tax*, p. 184) or an attorney, or a certified public accountant. The tax regulations are very complex and they are constantly changing. Consultations with competent sources are essential for up-to-date, accurate information.

If you claim retirement income credit, use Schedule R (Form 1040).
Use Schedule SE (Form 1040) to compute self employment tax.

If you use Short Form 1040A you may have the IRS compute your tax regardless of the amount of your income. If you use Form 1040 IRS will figure your tax if your income on line 15 (adjusted gross income) is $20,000 or less, and was only from wages, salaries, tips, dividends, interest, pensions and annuities, and you are willing to take the standard deduction. Thus if you wish to itemize deductions you cannot have the IRS figure your tax for you.

Form W–2 is not a tax return. It is a receipt which shows how much tax has been withheld from your salary. It must accompany your return as evidence of taxes withheld. If you work for more than one employer during the year you will have more than one Form W–2. Copy B of *each* Form W–2 must accompany your return.

> An income tax form is like a laundry list—either way you lose your shirt.
> —*Fred Allen*

Married Persons—Joint or Separate Return

Marital status is determined as of the last day of the taxable year. For tax purposes, a person is considered to be married for the entire calendar year if he or she is married on December 31, regardless of the date of the wedding. If you are divorced or legally separated on or before December 31, you are single for the entire calendar year for income tax purposes.

If either the wife or the husband dies before the close of the survivor's taxable year, the survivor is considered, for tax purposes, as having been married for the entire year. Thus, if the survivor did not remarry before the close of the taxable year, a joint return may be filed—except under certain limited circumstances—for both taxpayers by the surviving spouse.

In some states, which are known as "community property states" (Arizona, California, Idaho, Louisiana, Nevada, New Mexico, Texas, and Washington), the earnings of a married couple belong one half to the husband and one half to the wife, irrespective of who earned it. If, therefore, a husband and wife in a community property state file separate returns, it is mandatory that each shall report one half of the combined

FIGURE 3–4
Short Form 1040A

Short Form 1040A U.S. Individual Income Tax Return Department of the Treasury Internal Revenue Service **1974**

Please print or type

Name (If joint return, give first names and initials of both) | Last name | COUNTY OF RESIDENCE | Your social security number

Present home address (Number and street, including apartment number, or rural route) | Spouse's social security no.

City, town or post office, State and ZIP code | Occupation: Yours ▶ Spouse's ▶

Filing Status (check only one)

1 ☐ Single
2 ☐ Married filing joint return (even if only one had income)
3 ☐ Married filing separately. If spouse is also filing, give spouse's social security number in designated space above and enter full name here ▶
4 ☐ Unmarried Head of Household (See instructions on page 5) ▶
5 ☐ Widow(er) with dependent child (Year spouse died ▶ 19)

Exemptions Regular / 65 or over / Blind

6a Yourself . . ☐ ☐ ☐
b Spouse . . ☐ ☐ ☐ Enter number of boxes checked ▶
c First names of your dependent children who lived with you ______ Enter number ▶
d Number of other dependents (from line 26) . . ▶
7 Total exemptions claimed . . . . ▶

8 Presidential Election Campaign Fund . . . ▶ Do you wish to designate $1 of your taxes for this fund? . . Yes | No
If joint return, does your spouse wish to designate $1? . . Yes | No
Note: If you check the "Yes" box(es) it will not increase your tax or reduce your refund.

Attach Copy B of Forms W-2 and Check or Money Order here

9 Wages, salaries, tips, and other employee compensation. (Attach Forms W-2. If unavailable, see Instructions on page 3.) . . . 9
10a Dividends (if over $400, use Form 1040—see instructions) $........ 10b Less Exclusion $........ **Balance** ▶ 10c
11 Interest income (if over $400, use Form 1040) 11
12 Total (add lines 9, 10c, and 11) **(Adjusted Gross Income)** 12

- **If you want IRS to figure your tax, skip the rest of this page and see instructions on page 3.**
- **If line 12 is under $10,000, find tax in Tables 1–12 and enter on line 17, on back. Skip lines 13, 14, 15, and 16.**

13 **If line 12 is $10,000 or more,** enter 15% of line 12 but not more than $2,000 ($1,000 if line 3 checked) . 13
14 Subtract line 13 from line 12 14
15 Multiply total number of exemptions claimed on line 7 by $750 15
16 Taxable income (subtract line 15 from line 14) (Figure tax on amount on line 16 using Tax Rate Schedule X, Y, or Z, and enter on line 17, on back.) 16

Form 1040A (1974) Page 2

17 Tax, check if from: ☐ Tax Tables 1–12 **OR** ☐ Tax Rate Schedule X, Y, or Z . . 17
18 Credit for contributions to candidates for public office (see instructions on page 4) 18
19 Income tax (subtract line 18 from line 17). If less than zero, enter zero . . . 19
20a Total Federal income tax withheld (attach Forms W–2 to front) . . 20a
b Excess FICA tax withheld (two or more employers—see instructions on page 4) b
c 1974 estimated tax payments (include amount allowed as credit from 1973 return) c
21 Total (add lines 20a, b, and c) 21
22 If line 19 is larger than line 21, enter **BALANCE DUE IRS** Pay in full with return. Write social security number on check or money order and make payable to Internal Revenue Service ▶ 22
23 If line 21 is larger than line 19, enter amount **OVERPAID** . . . . . ▶ 23
24 Amount of line 23 to be **REFUNDED TO YOU** . . . . . . ▶ 24
25 Amount of line 23 to be credited on 1975 estimated tax . ▶ 25 | If all of overpayment (line 23) is to be refunded (line 24), make no entry on line 25.

Other Dependents

(a) NAME	(b) Relationship	(c) Months lived in your home. If born or died during year, write B or D.	(d) Did dependent have income of $750 or more?	(e) Amount YOU furnished for dependent's support. If 100% write ALL.	(f) Amount furnished by OTHERS including dependent.
				$	$

26 Total number of dependents listed in column (a). Enter here and on line 6d . . . ▶

Under penalties of perjury, I declare that I have examined this return, including accompanying schedules and statements, and to the best of my knowledge and belief it is true, correct and complete. Declaration of preparer (other than taxpayer) is based on all information of which he has any knowledge.

Sign here ▶ Your signature | Date ▶ Preparer's signature (other than taxpayer) | Date
▶ Spouse's signature (if filing jointly, BOTH must sign even if only one had income) | Address (and ZIP Code) | Preparer's Emp. Ident. or Soc. Sec. No.

☆ U.S. GOVERNMENT PRINTING OFFICE : 1974—O-548-290 52-07-38-972

FIGURE 3–5

Form **1040** US Department of the Treasury—Internal Revenue Service **Individual Income Tax Return** **1974**

For the year January 1–December 31, 1974, or other taxable year beginning ________, 1974, ending ________, 19__

Name (If joint return, give first names and initials of both) | Last name | COUNTY OF RESIDENCE | Your social security number

Present home address (Number and street, including apartment number, or rural route) | Spouse's social security no.

City, town or post office, State and ZIP code | Place label within block | Occupation: Yours ► Spouse's ►

Filing Status (check only one)
1 ☐ Single
2 ☐ Married filing joint return (even if only one had income)
3 ☐ Married filing separately. If spouse is also filing give spouse's social security number in designated space above and enter full name here ►
4 ☐ Unmarried Head of Household (See instructions on page 5) ►
5 ☐ Widow(er) with dependent child (Year spouse died ►19)

Exemptions Regular / 65 or over / Blind
6a Yourself . . . . . ☐ ☐ ☐ Enter number of boxes checked ►
b Spouse . . . . . ☐ ☐ ☐
c First names of your dependent children who lived with you ________ Enter number ►
d Number of other dependents (from line 27) . . . . ►
7 Total exemptions claimed . . . . ►

8 **Presidential Election Campaign Fund** . . . ► Do you wish to designate $1 of your taxes for this fund? . . . Yes / No. If joint return, does your spouse wish to designate $1? . . . Yes / No. **Note:** If you check the "Yes" box(es) it will not increase your tax or reduce your refund.

Please attach Copy B of Forms W-2 here

Income

9 Wages, salaries, tips, and other employee compensation (Attach Forms W-2. If unavailable, see instructions on page 3.) 9
10a Dividends (See instructions on pages 6 and 13) $______, 10b Less exclusion $____, Balance ► 10c
(If gross dividends and other distributions are over $400, list in Part I of Schedule B.)
11 Interest income. [If $400 or less, enter total without listing in Schedule B; If over $400, enter total and list in Part II of Schedule B] . 11
12 Income other than wages, dividends, and interest (from line 38) 12
13 Total (add lines 9, 10c, 11, and 12) 13
14 Adjustments to income (such as "sick pay," moving expenses, etc. from line 43) . 14
15 Subtract line 14 from line 13 (adjusted gross income) 15

● **If you do not itemize deductions and line 15 is under $10,000, find tax in Tables and enter on line 16.**
● **If you itemize deductions or line 15 is $10,000 or more, go to line 44 to figure tax.**
● CAUTION. If you have unearned income and can be claimed as a dependent on your parent's return, check here ► ☐ and see instructions on page 7.

Tax, Payments and Credits

16 Tax, check if from: ☐ Tax Tables 1–12 ☐ Tax Rate Schedule X, Y, or Z ☐ Schedule D ☐ Schedule G OR ☐ Form 4726 . . . 16
17 Total credits (from line 54) 17
18 Income tax (subtract line 17 from line 16) 18
19 Other taxes (from line 61) 19
20 Total (add lines 18 and 19) 20
21a Total Federal income tax withheld (attach Forms W-2 or W-2P to front) 21a
b 1974 estimated tax payments (include amount allowed as credit from 1973 return) . . . . b
c Amount paid with Form 4868, Application for Automatic Extension of Time to File U.S. Individual Income Tax Return . . . c
d Other payments (from line 65) . . . . d
22 Total (add lines 21a, b, c, and d) 22

Pay amount on line 23 in full with this return. Write social security number on check or money order and make payable to Internal Revenue Service.

Please attach Check or Money Order here

Balance Due or Refund

23 If line 20 is larger than line 22, enter **BALANCE DUE IRS** . . . . ► 23
(Check here ► ☐, if Form 2210, Form 2210F, or statement is attached. See instructions on page 7.)
24 If line 22 is larger than line 20, enter amount **OVERPAID** . . . . ► 24
25 Amount of line 24 to be **REFUNDED TO YOU** . . . . ► 25
26 Amount of line 24 to be credited on 1975 estimated tax. ► 26

If all of overpayment (line 24) is to be refunded (line 25), make no entry on line 26.

Sign here

Under penalties of perjury, I declare that I have examined this return, including accompanying schedules and statements, and to the best of my knowledge and belief it is true, correct, and complete. Declaration of preparer (other than taxpayer) is based on all information of which he has any knowledge.

► Your signature ________ Date ________ ► Preparer's signature (other than taxpayer) ________ Date ________

► Spouse's signature (if filing jointly, BOTH must sign even if only one had income) ________ Address (and ZIP Code) ________ Preparer's Emp. Ident. or Soc. Sec. No. ________

FIGURE 3–5 (continued)

Form 1040 (1974) Page 2

Other Dependents

(a) NAME	(b) Relationship	(c) Months lived in your home. If born or died during year, write B or D.	(d) Did dependent have income of $750 or more?	(e) Amount YOU furnished for dependent's support. If 100% write ALL.	(f) Amount furnished by OTHERS including dependent.
				$	$

27 Total number of dependents listed in column (a). Enter here and on line 6d . . . . . ►

Part I Income other than Wages, Dividends, and Interest

28 Business income or (loss) (attach Schedule C)	28	
29 Net gain or (loss) from sale or exchange of capital assets (attach Schedule D)	29	
30 Net gain or (loss) from Supplemental Schedule of Gains and Losses (attach Form 4797)	30	
31 Pensions, annuities, rents, royalties, partnerships, estates or trusts, etc. (attach Schedule E)	31	
32 Farm income or (loss) (attach Schedule F)	32	
33 Fully taxable pensions and annuities (not reported on Schedule E—see instructions on page 8)	33	
34 50% of capital gain distributions (not reported on Schedule D—see instructions on page 8)	34	
35 State income tax refunds (does not apply if refund is for year in which you took the standard deduction—others see instructions on page 8)	35	
36 Alimony received	36	
37 Other (state nature and source—see instructions on page 8) ►	37	
38 **Total** (add lines 28, 29, 30, 31, 32, 33, 34, 35, 36, and 37). **Enter here and on line 12** ►	38	

Part II Adjustments to Income

39 "Sick pay." (From Forms W-2 and W-2P. If not shown on Forms W-2 or W-2P, attach Form 2440 or statement.)	39	
40 Moving expense (attach Form 3903)	40	
41 Employee business expense (attach Form 2106 or statement)	41	
42 Payments as a self-employed person to a retirement plan, etc.—see instructions on page 9	42	
43 Total adjustments (add lines 39, 40, 41, and 42). Enter here and on line 14 ►	43	

Part III Tax Computation (Do not use this part if you use Tax Tables 1–12 to find your tax.)

44 Adjusted gross income (from line 15)	44	
45 (a) If you itemize deductions, check here ► ☐ and enter total from Schedule A, line 41 and attach Schedule A (b) If you do not itemize deductions, check here ► ☐ and enter 15% of line 44, but do NOT enter more than $2,000. ($1,000 if line 3 checked)	45	
46 Subtract line 45 from line 44	46	
47 Multiply total number of exemptions claimed on line 7, by $750	47	
48 **Taxable income.** Subtract line 47 from line 46	48	

(Figure your tax on the amount on line 48 by using Tax Rate Schedule X, Y, or Z, or if applicable, the alternative tax from Schedule D, income averaging from Schedule G, or maximum tax from Form 4726.) Enter tax on line 16.

Part IV Credits

49 Retirement income credit (attach Schedule R)	49	
50 Investment credit (attach Form 3468)	50	
51 Foreign tax credit (attach Form 1116)	51	
52 Credit for contributions to candidates for public office—see instructions on page 9	52	
53 Work Incentive (WIN) credit (attach Form 4874)	53	
54 **Total credits** (add lines 49, 50, 51, 52, and 53). **Enter here and on line 17** ►	54	

Part V Other Taxes

55 Self-employment tax (attach Schedule SE)	55	
56 Tax from recomputing prior-year investment credit (attach Form 4255)	56	
57 Tax from recomputing prior-year Work Incentive (WIN) credit (attach schedule)	57	
58 Minimum tax. Check here ► ☐, if Form 4625 is attached	58	
59 Social security tax on tip income not reported to employer (attach Form 4137)	59	
60 Uncollected employee social security tax on tips (from Forms W-2)	60	
61 **Total** (add lines 55, 56, 57, 58, 59, and 60). **Enter here and on line 19** ►	61	

Part VI Other Payments

62 Excess FICA tax withheld (two or more employers—see instructions on page 9)	62	
63 Credit for Federal tax on special fuels, nonhighway gasoline and lubricating oil (attach Form 4136)	63	
64 Credit from a Regulated Investment Company (attach Form 2439)	64	
65 **Total** (add lines 62, 63, and 64). **Enter here and on line 21d** ►	65	

Foreign Accounts Did you, at any time during the taxable year, have any interest in or signature or other authority over a bank, securities, or other financial account in a foreign country (except in a U.S. military banking facility operated by a U.S. financial institution)? ► ☐ Yes ☐ No
If "Yes," attach Form 4683. (For definitions, see Form 4683.)

community income. Taxpayers domiciled in these states have always divided their income for federal income tax purposes.[9]

Although married couples in noncommunity-property states cannot divide their income under state law, they can "split" their income for purposes of federal income taxation in joint returns. This equalizes federal income taxes on married couples in all states.

Married taxpayers may make a joint return and include all the exemptions, income, and deductions of both husband and wife. Even though one spouse has no income, husband and wife may still file a joint return. Ordinarily it will be advantageous, if married, to file a joint return using the "split income" method of computing the tax. It usually results in a lower tax than would result from the use of separate returns. This is because the tax is computed at the lower surtax rate which applies to each half of the income rather than at the higher surtax rate which would apply to the combined or total income. The surtax on one half of the taxable income when multiplied by two results in a total tax considerably less than if it had been computed on the total income as one sum.

Usually, but not always, the tax on a joint return is lower than the total tax of separate returns. Before making your decision as to which to use, you would do well to compute the total tax liability both ways and select the method resulting in the lower total tax.

Minors

An unmarried minor with a gross income of $2,050 or more during the tax year must file an income tax return. A minor is subject to tax on such earnings, even if under local law the parents have the right to them and may actually have received the money. A minor's income is not to be included in the parents' return. A minor should file an income tax return to get a refund if less than $2,050 is earned and income tax was withheld.

If your child is under 19 or is a student and qualifies as your dependent, you may also claim an exemption even though $750 or more is earned. If a minor with taxable income is unable to file an income tax return, the parent, guardian, or other person legally responsible must file it. If a minor's tax is not paid, that part of the tax attributable to compensation paid the minor is due and payable by the parent or guardian.[10]

[9] See IRS Publication No. 555, *Community Property and the Federal Income Tax*, Internal Revenue Service, Washington, D.C. A free copy may be obtained from any local IRS office.

[10] See IRS Publication No. 532, *Tax Information for Students and Parents*. A free copy may be obtained at your local IRS office.

Unmarried Persons as Head of Household

Any unmarried person required to maintain a household for the benefit of others is given a special tax concession of about one half the benefit that a married couple filing a joint return enjoys by reason of the split-income computation. If you are not married (or are legally separated) at the end of the taxable year, you qualify as a "head of household," provided you furnish over half of the cost of maintaining a home which, during the entire taxable year, except for temporary absences, was occupied as a principal residence both by yourself and by (*a*) any related person for whom you are entitled to an exemption or (*b*) your unmarried child, grandchild, or stepchild, even though such child is not a dependent. If your mother or your father, or both, qualify as your dependent and you maintain a home for one or the other or both, it is *not* necessary that you live in the same household to qualify as head of household. You may live in separate homes and still meet this test. A rest home or home for the aged qualifies as a household for this purpose.

When to File a Return

For most individuals, April 15 is the date when federal income tax returns must be filed. Returns, in most cases, can be filed at any time after the close of the taxable year up until midnight April 15. The April 15 deadline results from the fact that the Internal Revenue Code provides that income tax returns must be made on or before the fifteenth day of the fourth month following the close of the taxable year. For most persons filing individual income tax returns, the taxable year is the calendar year ending December 31. Therefore, the fifteenth day of the fourth month thereafter is April 15.

You may receive an automatic two month extension of time to file your tax return by filling out, in duplicate, Form 4868, "Application for Automatic Extension of Time to File U.S. Individual Income Tax Return." In filling out Form 4868, you must make a tentative tax estimate for the year. The original of the application must be filed, by the due date of the return, with the Internal Revenue Service Center for your area. You must also make full payment of any tax due with the application for the automatic extension. If you request an extension you cannot use Short Form 1040A when you file your return. If you need an additional extension beyond the 60 days you must file another form 2688, "Application for Extension of Time to File U.S. Individual Income Tax Return." This will not be granted as a matter of course and you must have substantial reasons.

How to Claim Your Exemptions[11]

You, as the taxpayer, are always entitled to at least one exemption for yourself. If, at the end of your taxable year, you were blind or were age 65 or older, you get two exemptions for yourself. If you were both blind and age 65 or over, you get three exemptions. You get exemptions for your wife (or husband) if you and she are filing a joint return. If you file a separate return, you may claim her exemptions only if she had no income and was not claimed as a dependent on another taxpayer's return for the taxable year. Otherwise your wife's (or husband's) exemptions are like your own—one, if she was neither blind nor age 65; two, if she was either blind or age 65; three, if she was both blind and age 65 or over.

If you were divorced or legally separated at the end of the year, you may not claim your former wife's exemption, even if you contributed all of her support.

The allowance for the personal exemption and exemptions for each dependent is currently $750. You can claim your personal exemption of $750 even if you are the dependent of another taxpayer.

> Some men never appreciate their children so much as when making out their income tax. —*Morton Gowdy*

Information Returns

In case you are ever tempted not to report part or all of your income, remember that the Internal Revenue Service has, by statutory authority, many sources which can be checked for information about your income. The "information at source" provision of the Internal Revenue Code requires every individual, partnership, or corporation to report certain payments to the Director of Internal Revenue.

In addition to Form W–2, which is filed for wages from which taxes have been withheld, there is another information return—Form 1099—which must be filed under certain circumstances. It is required when total compensation from sources of income such as rents, royalties, interest, dividends, alimony, annuities, wages not covered by withholding, and others, is equal to or exceeds certain limits.

---

[11] For further information see IRS Publication No. 501, "Your Exemptions and Exemptions for Dependents." A free copy may be obtained from your local IRS office.

What Income Is Taxable

If you win the Nobel or Pulitzer prize, you won't have to pay tax on the income from it! The law says that all kinds of income are subject to tax, with specific exceptions. This means that all income which is not specifically exempt must be included in your return, even though it may be offset by expenses and other deductions. Exempt income should be omitted entirely from your return.

The following are examples of income which *must* be reported:

Wages, salaries, bonuses, and commissions.
Tips and gratuities for services rendered.
Dividends and other earnings from investments.
Interest from bank deposits, bonds, and notes.
Pensions, annuities, and endowments.
Rents and royalties from property, patents, copyrights.
Profits from business or profession.
Profit from sale or exchange of real estate, securities, or other property.
Your share of partnership profits.
Your share of estate or trust income.
Contest prizes.
Gambling winnings.
Proceeds from lotteries, raffles, etc.
Alimony.
Jury duty fees.
Embezzled or other illegal income.

These are merely examples. The list is not all-inclusive, since all income, unless specifically exempt, must be reported.

The following are examples of income which should *not* be reported.[12]

Scholarship and fellowship grants.
All government payments and benefits to veterans and their families, with a few minor exceptions.
Dividends on veterans' government insurance.
Federal social security benefits.
Unemployment compensation.
Railroad Retirement Act benefits.
Gifts, inheritances, bequests.

---

[12] For further information, see IRS Publication No. 525, *Taxable Income and Non-Taxable Income,* Internal Revenue Service, Washington, D.C. A free copy may be obtained from any IRS office.

Workmen's compensation, insurance, damages, etc., for bodily injury or sickness.
Military allowances.
Payments to dependents of military personnel.
Relocation payments.
Interest on state and municipal bonds.
Accident and health insurance proceeds.
Casualty insurance proceeds.
Disability and death payments.
Life insurance proceeds upon death of the insured.

Even though tax has been withheld by your employer, the law requires you to report all your wages, salaries, fees, commissions, bonuses, and all other payments for your personal services. When your employer deducts taxes, insurance, union dues, savings bond subscriptions, social security, pension fund contributions, etc., from your pay, these amounts are still part of your wages, and you are required to report the total amount of your wages as if your employer had not made any deductions. You must also include in your wages all tips, gratuities, bonuses, and similar payments, whether you get them from a customer or from your employer. Legally these are not "gifts," even though people sometimes mistakenly call them by that name. If your employer pays part or all of your wages in merchandise, services, stock, or other things of value, you must determine the fair market value of such items and include it in your wages. Taxpayers who receive meals and lodging as part of their salaries must include in income the fair market value of the meals and lodging.

Adjusted Gross Income

Adjusted gross income is the balance remaining after deducting from *gross income* the following:

1. Expenses of a trade or business.
2. Expenses of a property yielding rents or royalties.
3. Expenses of travel, meals, and lodging while away from home at least overnight in the service of one's employer. You may also deduct transportation expenses incurred in connection with the performance of service as an employee even though you are not away from home.
4. Reimbursed expenses (other than those for travel, meals, and lodging while away from home overnight) incurred in the service of one's employer. Also moving expenses.

5. Allowable losses from a sale or exchange of property.
6. Sick pay, if it is included in your gross income.
7. Fifty percent of the excess of net long-term capital gains over net short-term capital losses.
8. Payments by self-employed persons to retirement plans.

Adjusted gross income is the amount you enter on line 15, page 1, of Form 1040. Some deductions are subtracted from *gross income* to determine the amount of *adjusted gross income.* Other deductions are subtracted only from *adjusted gross income* in arriving at the amount of *taxable income.*

The importance of *adjusted gross income* as a factor in determining your tax liability cannot be overemphasized. It governs the amount of the standard deduction you may claim if you do not itemize your deductions. It is used to determine the limitation on deductions for contributions and medical expenses if you do itemize your deductions. It is the basic figure used in determining your tax by the use of the tax table. If you are an employee working for a straight salary or wage and have no other income, your gross income and your adjusted gross income will usually be the same.

Dividends

Dividends representing distributions of earnings and profits by corporations and associations are taxable income. Those which are merely a return to the taxpayer of part of his investment are nontaxable.

Among taxable dividends, the following are included:

1. Dividends in cash.
2. Dividends in property (to be valued at market).
3. Stock chosen by the taxpayer in lieu of a cash dividend or vice versa.
4. Dividends which the taxpayer has consented to report as income.
5. Any payments supposed to be expenses but which are really dividends.

The following are exempt from tax as dividends:

1. Returns of capital (principal).
2. So called "dividends" (partial return of premiums) of mutual life or accident insurance companies or on government insurance.[13]

[13] So-called dividends from mutual savings banks, building and loan associations, savings and loan associations, credit unions, etc., are considered *interest* for federal income tax purposes and should be reported as *interest*.

3. Payments out of depletion reserves of oil, mining, or lumber companies, etc.
4. Stock dividends or stock rights which do not increase the stockholder's proportionate interest in the corporation.[14]

In some cases, a corporation distributes both a dividend and a repayment of capital at the same time. When the mixed distributions are made, the check or notice will usually show the dividends and the capital repayment separately. In any case, you must report the dividend portion as income. If you are the owner of stock held in the name of your broker, the dividend must be reported on your return.

You may exclude from your income $100 of dividends received from domestic corporations during your taxable year. If a joint return is filed and securities are held jointly, $200 of dividends may be excluded. If securities are held individually, each one may exclude $100 of dividends received from qualifying corporations, but one may not use any portion of the $100 exclusion not used by the other. For example, if the husband had $200 in dividends, and the wife had $20, only a total of $120 may be excluded on a joint return.

Interest

Interest income is usually taxable. You must include in your return any interest you receive or which is credited to your account (whether entered in your passbook or not) and can be withdrawn by you. All interest on bonds, debentures, notes, savings accounts, or loans is taxable, except for certain governmental issues. For example, the interest which is fully exempt from tax is interest from state and municipal bonds and securities (including political instrumentalities or subdivisions thereof, such as Port of New York Authority, the Indiana Toll Road Commission, State Industrial Development Boards, Oklahoma County Utility Services Authority, etc.

If you own U.S. savings discount bonds and are on a cash basis, you have a choice as to when you may report the interest: (*a*) You may elect to report the interest each year. If you do, the amount of interest to be included in income each year is shown on the table on the bond as the increase in redemption value, or (*b*) you may defer reporting the interest until the bonds are matured or cashed, in which case the interest must be included as income for that year. In most cases this is the more convenient

[14] See IRS Publication No. 550, *Tax Information on Investment Income and Expenses*. A free copy may be obtained from your local IRS office.

way. It is especially useful if your income fluctuates from year to year because then you can plan to cash your bonds and report the appreciation proceeds as income in a year in which your income is lower than usual, thereby minimizing taxes.

If you elect, however, to report the interest each year, you must continue to do so as to *all* U.S. savings discount bonds owned and those subsequently acquired. You may not change to another method unless you first receive permission to do so. If you are deferring the reporting of interest and wish to change to reporting the interest each year, you may do so without obtaining permission. However, in the year of change, you must report *all* interest on *all* such bonds which you own which was not previously reported.

Where interest on savings bonds is paid by check at stated intervals, the interest income thus received must be reported in the year in which it is received under the cash method.

Business or Profession

Profits from an unincorporated business or profession are taxable to the individual as income and therefore must be included in your personal income tax return.[15] A separate Schedule C, entitled "Profit (or Loss) from Business or Profession," is provided to enable you to subtract your costs from your receipts to arrive at net profit.

Generally, the costs you can deduct are the ordinary and necessary expenses of doing business—cost of merchandise, salaries, interest, taxes, rent, repairs, and incidental supplies. In the case of capital investments and improvements in depreciable property, such as buildings, machines, fixtures, and similar items having a useful life of more than one year, the law provides an annual depreciation allowance as the method of recovering the original capital cost tax-free. If some of your expenses are part business and part personal, you can deduct the business portion but not the personal portion. For instance, a doctor who uses his car half for business can deduct only half the operating expenses of the car and take depreciation on half the original cost of the car.

A partnership or similar business firm (not a corporation) does not pay income tax in the firm's name. Therefore, each partner must report in his personal tax return his share of his partnership's income and pay

[15] See *Tax Guide for Small Business,* Internal Revenue Service Publication No. 334. It may be obtained from the Internal Revenue Service free of charge. See also IRS Publication No. 463, *Travel, Entertainment, and Gift Expenses.* A free copy may be obtained from your local IRS office.

tax on it. As a partner you must include in income on your Form 1040 (Schedule E) your distributive share of partnership earnings which may be more or less than withdrawals. The partnership is required to file a Form 1065, which is an information return showing the results of its operations for the taxable year and the items of income, gain, loss, deduction, or credit affecting its partners' individual income tax returns. The partnership pays no income tax unless it has elected to be taxed as a corporation. Your distributive share of the partnership's income is your part of the partnership's business results whether distributed to you or not.

If, in the current taxable year, your business or profession lost money instead of making a profit or you had a casualty loss, you can apply these losses against your other income. If these losses exceed your other income, the excess, or "net operating loss," may be carried backward to offset your income for the three previous taxable years, and any remaining excess may be carried over to any or all of the five taxable years following the current one. If a carry-back entitles you to refund on either of the three previous years' taxes, you file Form 1045.

The social security tax for those who are self-employed is reported and paid as part of Schedule C of the personal income tax. The computation of your self-employment tax is made on the separate Schedule C, which, with attached Schedule SE, should be filed with your income tax return on Form 1040. The self-employment social security tax applies to every self-employed individual if he has at least $400 of net earnings from self-employment in a taxable year.

Sale and Exchange of Property

If you sell your house, car, furniture, stocks or bonds, real estate, or any other kind of property, the law requires you to report any profit in your tax return. Because of the many special rules for taxing the profit and deducting the loss from such transactions, a special form, Schedule D, is provided. Capital gains and losses will be considered in more detail later.

Annuities and Pensions

The government has granted a series of extra benefits in the tax law to older persons (65 and over). Yet the Internal Revenue Service seems determined to minimize these benefits by driving the recipients to an early grave through two of the most complex parts of the tax form. If an elderly person feels that senility has come upon him when he tries to understand and comprehend either the "Pension and Annuities" section of the tax law or the "Retirement Income Credit" schedule,[16] let him be reassured. It's just about as difficult at 25 or 45 as it is at 65.

The monthly payments you receive from social security when you retire are *not* taxable income, nor are veterans' pensions. If you receive any other kind of pension or annuity, however, it must be reported in Schedule E.

If your pension did not cost you anything and it was fully paid for by your employer, you must pay tax on the full amount you receive each year. If you and your employer each contributed a part of the cost of your annuity or pension and you will recover your contributions completely within three years from the date of your first pension payment, the amounts you receive are *not* taxed as income *until* you have recovered your contribution in full. All amounts received after you have fully recovered your cost are included in taxable income.

If you will not recover your cost within three years after your pension starts, your pension or annuity will be treated under the general rule for annuities. To understand this, take two aspirins, and then try to read the "simple" explanation of the "General Rule for Annuities" in the instructions accompanying Form 1040. We'll give odds that you won't follow it, but at the end there is a cute clause: "For other types of annuities which are not covered by these rules and for more detailed information, call or visit your Internal Revenue Service office." The whole thing makes you shudder at the prospect of living to 65.[17]

The Retirement Income Credit

This is the second, even less excusable horror, which the tax law inflicts on elderly retired persons. Cheer up, however, for you have until retirement to understand what follows, and if you read and study it once a year for the next 40 years, you may begin to understand the retirement income credit.[18]

If you are retired, or if you are 65 or over, and receive taxable pension or annuity payments, or have income from rents, interest, or dividends, you may be entitled to a credit against your tax for a certain percentage of

---

[16] Schedule R. If a retiree is eligible to and elects to have the IRS compute his or her tax it will also figure the retirement credit if the information for certain lines on Schedule R is provided.

[17] IRS Publication No. 575, *Tax Information on Pensions and Annuities,* Internal Revenue Service, Washington, D.C. Free copies are available from local IRS offices.

[18] For a complex but brief explanation, see IRS Publication No. 524, *Retirement Income and Retirement Income Credit,* Internal Revenue Service, Washington, D.C. Free copies are available from local IRS offices.

your retirement income. The retirement income credit is 15 percent of the retirement income limitation, or the total retirement income, whichever is less. To claim it you must fill out Schedule R of Form 1040. To do that you should have at least a Ph.D. in actuarial math, accountancy, tax law, and higher logic!

To qualify for the retirement income credit you must meet the age requirement, the prior earned income test, and have retirement income.

(*a*) The prior earned income test—you must have had at least $600 of earned income in each year for any 10 calendar years before the current year. It doesn't matter which years they were, and they need not have been consecutive years.

(*b*) Retirement income—if you met the prior earned income test, your next step is to determine whether you had any retirement income during the year which entitles you to the credit. Different rules apply for people under 65 and people over 65 years old.

If you are under 65, retirement income includes only a pension received from a public retirement system. Only the taxable portion of the pension is considered retirement income in computing the credit. If you are over 65 before the end of your taxable year, your retirement income includes all your taxable income from pensions, annuities, interest, dividends, and rents.

After you determine that you have received eligible retirement income, your next step is to determine how much, if any, is to be used in computing the credit. It is often possible under the rules to have retirement income and not be entitled to the credit. The credit is 15 percent of the lesser of (*a*) the retirement income you received during the year; or (*b*) $2,286 minus the total of certain pensions and annuities and current earned income.[19]

Rents and Royalties

The term *rents* includes income from real estate and the income from any other property. Royalties are received by authors and composers and for the use of inventions. People owning rented property must incur costs in connection with it. Ordinary expenses and repairs are deductible expenses. Capital expenditures or improvements must be added to the cost of the rented property and depreciated over its remaining life.

[19] The amount of $2,286 may be used where a joint return is filed by husband and wife and *both* are 65 years of age or over. In all other instances the amount will be $1,524. For further details on the computation, which will undoubtedly be changed a dozen times at least before you become eligible, see Chapter 14, of *Your Federal Income Tax*, 1975 edition, Internal Revenue Service, Washington, D.C.

If a taxpayer occupies a portion of a dwelling and rents out the balance of it, only those expenses chargeable against the rented portion are deductible. Rents and royalties are reported on Part II of Schedule E of Form 1040. However, if you hold an operating oil, gas, or mineral interest, you report gross income and expenses on Schedule C of Form 1040.

Miscellaneous Income

If you cannot find any specific place on your tax return to list some type of income, you should put it in Part I, line 37 of page 2, of Form 1040. This is the proper place to report amounts received as rewards or prizes; recoveries of bad debts, losses, etc., which reduced your tax in a prior year; and health and accident insurance benefit payments received by you as reimbursements for medical expenses which reduced your tax in a prior year.

DEDUCTIONS

There are two ways of taking deductions: (1) you may itemize these on Schedule A of Form 1040, or (2) you may claim the standard deduction. You should use the standard deduction only if it amounts to more than the total of your itemized deductions.

A husband and wife filing separate returns should use the method of claiming deductions most beneficial to them as a unit, even though it may be less advantageous to one of them. They both must use the same method of claiming deductions. If one itemizes deductions, the other must itemize. If one takes the standard deduction, the other must, too.

Charitable contributions, interest, and taxes of a nonbusiness nature (state income taxes or sales taxes, for example), medical and dental expenses, and certain losses and other expenses may be itemized in Schedule A of Form 1040.

It will usually be to your advantage to itemize your deductions if you are a homeowner paying interest and taxes; if you paid unusually large medical and dental bills during the year; made substantial contributions to qualified charities; paid significant state income taxes; or suffered a major uninsured casualty loss.

The standard deduction is an allowance used to reduce your adjusted gross income when you do not itemize your deductions. If your adjusted gross income is less than $10,000, the standard deduction is automatically considered in the tax table you use to determine your tax. If your adjusted gross income is $10,000 or more, your standard deduction, is limited to 16 percent of adjusted gross income, not to exceed $2,300 for a single person, and $2,600 for married couples. This is the amount you enter on line 45 of Form 1040 (or line 13, Short Form 1040A) when you compute your tax liability from the tax schedules, unless you elect to itemize your deductions.

The low income allowance has been designed to provide a tax-free allowance for low income taxpayers, thereby removing them from the tax rolls. In the case of certain taxpayers, this allowance may be $1,300. The allowance is automatically taken into consideration when one uses the Tax Tables rather than the Tax Schedules. The largest deduction is automatically considered in the Tax Tables. With the exception of married taxpayers who file separate returns, the standard deduction used in determining the tax reflected in the Tax Tables is the larger of the percentage standard deduction or the low-income allowance.

You may use the Tax Tables regardless of the source of your income if your adjusted gross income is less than $10,000, or on a joint return if the combined income of you and your spouse is less than $10,000 provided you do not itemize deductions.

How to Figure Depreciation as a Deduction

A professor owns a house or rents an apartment. Because his office space at the university is crowded and congested, he finds he can get little or no work done at his college desk, so he sets one or two rooms aside in his house as an office where he really accomplishes his research and writing. Many of the expenses connected with the maintenance and operation of this office are tax deductible under recent Internal Revenue Service rulings and court decisions. For example, he can write off (depreciate) his office furniture and equipment and the books he purchased for his research and writing.[20]

In the case of capital investments and improvements in depreciable property having a useful life of more than a year and owned for the purpose of making a profit from rents, royalties, business, or a profession, the tax law provides an annual depreciation allowance as the method of recovering the original capital cost tax-free. This means that you can spread the cost over as many years as the property is expected to be useful. These rules apply to a profession as well as to a business. For

---

[20] For an extended discussion of the various expenses which may be deducted, see *Educator's Tax Desk Manual*, latest edition, Executive Reports Corporation, Englewood Cliffs, N.J. See also Publication No. 508, *Tax Information on Educational Expenses*, obtainable free of charge from any IRS office.

instance, a lawyer can deduct the cost of his law books and a doctor can deduct the cost of his instruments *only* through the depreciation allowance.

The first step in figuring depreciation is to determine the useful life of each asset to be depreciated. The useful life of an asset depends on how long you expect to use it, its age when acquired, your policy as to repairs, upkeep and replacement, and other conditions. There is no average useful life which is applicable in all situations. Useful lives prescribed by the Internal Revenue Service, for depreciation purposes, are applicable to all assets used in a particular industry or business rather than to individual assets.[21]

Once you have made a reasonable estimate of the useful life of your property, you may divide its cost, less salvage value, if any, by the number of years of such useful life, and that is the amount you can deduct during each of these years. For example, suppose you own a house which has an estimated useful life of 40 years. If you rent the house to someone else, you can deduct from your rental income 2.5 percent of its cost (excluding the land cost) each year for 40 years. If you use the house as your own residence, you may *not* deduct depreciation. Depreciation may not be taken on property used for personal purposes exclusively, such as a taxpayer's automobile or home.

In addition to the "straight line" depreciation method described above, there are two others that may be used for property acquired from January 1, 1954, on: (*a*) the *double declining balance* method, and (*b*) the *sum of the years' digits* method.

Under the double declining balance method, a uniform rate of *twice* the straight line depreciation rate is applied each year to the *remaining* cost of the property (without adjustment for salvage value). The amount of depreciation taken each year is subtracted from the basis of the property before figuring the next year's depreciation, so that the same depreciation rate is applied to a smaller or declining balance each year.

In the sum of the years' digits method, you apply a different fraction each year to the basis of the property less its estimated salvage value. The denominator or bottom of the fraction is the total of the numbers representing the years of useful life of the property. Thus, if the useful life is five years, the denominator is 15 $(1 + 2 + 3 + 4 + 5 = 15)$. The numerator, or top of the fraction, is the number of years of life remaining at the beginning of the year for which the computation is made.

---

[21] For more detailed information see IRS Publication No. 534, *Depreciation, Amortization, and Depletion* obtainable free of charge from the Internal Revenue Service, Washington, D.C. This will also explain "additional first-year depreciation."

Model Tax Ruling Holds Beauty Is Never Obsolete

WASHINGTON, Nov. 13—The Internal Revenue Bureau told a group of models today that wrinkles were not tax deductible.

The girls had asked the bureau if they could make allowances on their income tax returns for bodily depreciation. They said that they were subject to "age, exhaustion and obsolescence." The bureau replied:

"Charm, beauty and talent, while undoubtedly of great value in your profession, are not generally recognized as depreciable for tax purposes. American beauty never becomes obsolete."

Thus, if the useful life is five years, the fraction to be applied to the cost minus salvage to figure depreciation for the first year is $\frac{5}{15}$. The fraction for the second year is $\frac{4}{15}$ and so on.

Take an example: Suppose a doctor buys a second car to use exclusively to make calls and not for personal use. He pays $3,500. The car has an estimated useful life of five years at the end of which its salvage (or trade-in) value is estimated to be $500.

Under the straight line method the annual depreciation is $600, computed as follows: Deduct $500 (salvage value) from $3,500 (cost of automobile), leaving $3,000. Then divide $3,000 by five (the number of years of useful life) to arrive at the annual depreciation of $600.

Under the double declining balance method, the rate of depreciation may not exceed 40 percent, that is twice the straight line rate of 20 percent above. The depreciation the first year is $1,400 (40 percent of the $3,500 cost). The depreciation for the second year is $840 (40 percent of $2,100, the unrecovered cost; that is $3,500 minus the first year's $1,400 depreciation).

Under the sum of the years' digits method, the depreciation would be $1,000 the first year. This is $\frac{5}{15}$ of $3,000 (cost of $3,500 less salvage value of $500). The depreciation the second year would be $\frac{4}{15}$ of $3,000, or $800, the third year, $\frac{3}{15}$ of $3,000, or $600, and so on.

A detailed comparison of the three methods may be seen in Table 3–2.[22]

How to Deduct Bad Debts

Bad debts not originally created or acquired in a trade or business (nonbusiness bad debts) must be treated as short-term capital losses.

[22] For further information see IRS Publication No. 534, "Tax Information on Depreciation." A free copy may be obtained from your local IRS office.

TABLE 3–2
Three Depreciation Methods

Year	Annual Depreciation: Straight Line (20 percent)	Double Declining Balance (40 percent)	Sum of the Years Digits
1	$ 600	$1,400.00	$1,000
2	600	840.00	800
3	600	504.00	600
4	600	302.40*	400
5	600	181.44*	200
Total	$3,000	$3,227.84	$3,000
Salvage value or unrecovered cost	$ 500	$ 227.84	$ 500

* Under the double declining balance method, depreciation must stop when the unrecovered cost is reduced to salvage value. Therefore, the fourth year only $211.68 of the $302.40 could be taken in depreciation and no depreciation could be taken the fifth year.

They are subject to the limitation on deductions for capital losses and should be reported in Schedule D of Form 1040.

Bad debts, with certain exceptions, are deductible if they become worthless during the year. But they must meet specific requirements in order to be deductible, and they must always be satisfactorily explained by the taxpayer. The explanation, if required, must show:

1. The nature of the debt.
2. The name of the debtor, and the debtor's relationship to the taxpayer, if any.
3. When the debt was created.
4. When the debt became due.
5. The effort made by the taxpayer to collect the debt.
6. How the debt was determined to be worthless.

For a debt to be worthless, it must not only be uncollectible but must also appear to be uncollectible at any time in the future. The taxpayer must take reasonable steps to collect the debt. He does not have to go to court, however, if it can be shown that a judgment, once obtained, would also be worthless. If a debtor, as lawyers say, is "judgment proof," then the judgment would be of no value. Bad debts must be shown to have existed in fact and in law. A taxpayer cannot, for example, claim a bad debt deduction for a debt which cannot be enforced in the courts. A gambling debt is a good example of an unenforceable debt.

Advances to relatives to tide them over financial difficulties may not be legally collectible debts, since they may be made without any fixed understanding as to repayment and may therefore be legally considered a gift rather than a loan.

Loans to children are presumed to be gifts. For example, loans or advances you make to a son or daughter to pay tuition expenses for necessary education generally are not a valid basis for a bad debt deduction.

Debts owed by political parties are not deductible. No deduction will be allowed any taxpayer, other than a bank, for any debt, regardless of how it arose, that has become worthless if owed by a political party or an organization that accepts contributions or makes expenditures in an effort to influence political elections.[23]

How to Deduct for Contributions

If you itemize deductions, you can deduct gifts to religious, charitable, educational, scientific, or literary organizations, and organizations for the prevention of cruelty to children and animals, *unless* the organization is operated for personal profit, or conducts propaganda, or otherwise attempts to influence legislation. You can deduct gifts to fraternal organizations if they are to be used for charitable, religious, etc., purposes. You can also deduct gifts to veterans' organizations, or to a governmental agency which will use the gifts for public purposes. The law does *not* allow for gifts to individuals, or to other types of organizations, however worthy.

The contribution deduction is now more complicated than it used to be. In general, contributions to most charities may be deducted up to 50 percent of your adjusted gross income (line 15 of form 1040). However, contributions to certain private nonoperating foundations, veterans organizations, fraternal societies, and cemetery organizations are limited to 20 percent of adjusted gross income.[24]

A contribution may be made in money or property (but not services). If in property, it is measured by the fair market value of the property at the time of contribution. For example, if you give $50 in old clothes to your church, it's as much a deductible contribution as if you had given cash. While you can deduct for gifts to organizations mentioned previously, you cannot deduct for dues or other payments to them for which

---

[23] For further information, see IRS Publication No. 548, *Tax Information on Deductions for Bad Debts*, Internal Revenue Service, Washington, D.C. A free copy may be obtained from your local IRS office.

[24] For further detail, see IRS Publication No. 526, *Income Tax Deductions for Contributions*, Internal Revenue Service, Washington, D.C. Certain limited political contributions may now be deducted under restricted circumstances. See also IRS Publication No. 561, "Valuation of Donated Property."

you receive personal benefits. For example, you can deduct gifts to a YWCA but not dues.

You *can* deduct gifts to:

Churches and temples.
Salvation Army.
Red Cross, Community Chests, and United Funds.
Nonprofit schools and hospitals.
Veterans organizations.
Boys Scouts, Girl Scouts, and other similar organizations.
Nonprofit organizations primarily engaged in conducting research or education for the alleviation and care of diseases such as tuberculosis, cancer, multiple sclerosis, muscular dystrophy, cerebral palsy, polio, diseases of the heart, etc.

You *cannot* deduct gifts to:

Relatives, friends, other individuals.
Social clubs.
Labor unions.
Chambers of commerce.
Propaganda organizations.

Interest as a Deduction

In general, interest on indebtedness is deductible if you itemize your deductions. Interest on mortgages, judgments, delinquent taxes, personal loans, and installment payments is deductible. Discount (interest paid in advance by being deducted from principal of the loan) is deductible on a cash basis only when the loan is fully paid, but taxpayers on the accrual basis may take the deductions as they accrue.

Probably the most common type of interest deducted is the interest paid on home mortgages. Monthly mortgage payments usually consist of repayment of principal and of interest. The former is not deductible, the latter is. If your records do not clearly show these two components, ask the lender to give you the exact breakdown. If you prepay your mortgage, any fee charged by the bank for this privilege is deductible as interest. If you purchase a cooperative apartment, you are entitled to deduct your portion of the interest payments on the indebtedness of the cooperative. Condominium apartment owners may deduct the interest they paid on the mortgage indebtedness of the project allowable to their share of the property.

If you receive income from renting part of your home, and have borrowed money for the purchase, repair, or alteration of the home, the "interest" expense must be allocated. The amount attributable to the rented portion is deducted on Schedule E of Form 1040, and the balance is deducted as a personal expense on Schedule A of Form 1040, if you itemize your deductions.[25]

Taxes as Deductions

Nonfederal taxes are generally deductible. They include state and local income taxes, personal property taxes, and real estate taxes (except those assessed for pavements, sewers, or other local improvements which tend to increase the value of your property). You can deduct state or local retail sales taxes if under the laws of your state they are imposed directly on the consumer, or if they are imposed on the retailer (or wholesaler, in the case of gasoline taxes) and the amount of the tax is separately stated by the retailer to the consumer.

Taxes chargeable to rents and royalties and taxes on property used in business may be deducted as business expenses in computing adjusted gross income. State income taxes are not deductible in computing adjusted gross income but may be taken as nonbusiness deductions. Social security taxes paid by an *employer* are deducted as business expenses, but the social security tax which you pay as an *employee* you are not permitted to deduct. Social security taxes paid by an employer on wages of domestic employees are not deductible, since in this case they are not business expenses but are considered federal excise taxes, whose deduction as a tax is prohibited by law.

In general, you cannot deduct any federal excise taxes on your personal expenditures, such as taxes on automobiles, tires, cosmetics, air and railroad tickets, telephone, and so on.

Taxes imposed on a previous owner of a property and paid by the taxpayer as part of the contracted purchase price should be included in the cost of purchased property. Municipal water bills, parking-meter charges, service fees, etc., are nondeductible as personal expenses but may be deducted as expenses of those in business. Real property and personal property taxes, and state and local gasoline taxes are deductible.

---

[25] If all this isn't clear, see Chapter 24, *Interest Deductions*, in IRS Publication No. 17, *Your Federal Income Tax for Individuals*, Internal Revenue Service, Washington, D.C. Also IRS Publication No. 545, *Income Tax Deduction for Interest Expense*, is available free at your local IRS office.

Federal income taxes, customs duties, gift taxes, estate taxes, and excise taxes are not deductible, nor are taxes paid by you for another person.[26]

Casualty or Theft Losses

A personal casualty or theft loss may be deductible to the extent that it exceeds $100. This deduction is allowed only to the person who owns the property. Special rules may apply if your property was in a disaster area.

Different rules apply for computing a casualty loss deduction on property used for personal purposes and property used for business purposes.

A casualty or theft loss on property used solely for personal purposes is deductible only to the extent that the loss exceeds $100 for each casualty or theft. A casualty or theft loss of business property or property held for the production of income is deductible in full, without regard to the $100 limitation.

To have a deductible loss you must have actually sustained one. For example, if a painting that cost you $5,000, but which was worth $10,000, was stolen, your deduction would be $4,900, your actual loss less the $100 limitation.

Casualty losses include:

1. Damage from a hurricane, tornado, flood, storm, shipwreck, fire, or accident.
2. Damage from an auto accident to the taxpayer's automobile caused by the faulty driving of either driver, if it was not caused by the willful act or willful negligence of the taxpayer.
3. Mine cave-in damage to your property.
4. Sonic boom damage from jet aircraft.
5. A loss from vandalism caused by agencies outside of your control, if the damage or destruction is sudden and unexpected.
6. Damage to trees and shrubs of an ornamental nature on residential property injured or destroyed by a casualty. To be deductible it must be established that there has been a decrease in the *total value* of the real estate.

Losses *not* deductible as casualties include:

1. Losses from the breakage of china or glassware through handling or by a family pet.

[26] For further information see IRS Publication No. 546, "Income Tax Deduction for Taxes." A free copy may be obtained from your local IRS office.

2. Disease. The loss of trees, shrubs, etc., on property used for residential purposes, as a result of disease, or fungus spread by beetles, insects, worms, etc.
3. Expenses incident to casualty, such as the personal injuries and the cost of temporary lights, fuel, moving, or rental of temporary quarters.
4. Termite or moth damage.
5. Progressive deterioration through a steadily operating cause and damage from a normal process. Thus, the steady weakening of a building caused by normal or usual wind or weather conditions is not a casualty loss.
6. Losses from nearby disaster. The reduction in value of property because it is in or near a disaster area that might again have a similar disaster is not a casualty. A loss is allowed only for the actual physical damage to your property resulting from the casualty.

A theft is the unlawful taking and removing of your money or property. It includes but is not limited to larceny, robbery, and embezzlement. The mere disappearance (mislaid or lost) of money or property from your person or your home is not a theft.

Nor is misrepresentation theft. For example, a seller assured a buyer of a property that a well produced an adequate supply of water. The well went dry after the buyer took possession. The buyer did not have a deductible theft loss due to the seller's misrepresentation.

You must be able to prove your loss and show that the amount of the loss is deductible. Sentimental values are excluded from consideration when determining the amount of loss. The amount of the loss to be deducted is measured by the fair market value of the property just before the casualty less its fair market value immediately after the casualty (but not more than the cost or other adjusted basis of the property), reduced by any insurance or compensation received.[27]

Dental, Hospital, and Medical Expenses

If you itemize deductions, you can take limited deductions for the amounts you paid during the year (not compensated by hospital, health, or accident insurance) for medical or dental expense for yourself, your wife, or any dependent who received over half his support from you. Ordinarily, the limit of deductions for dental and medical expenses is the amount by which they exceed 3 percent of your adjusted gross income;

---

[27] For further information see IRS Publication No. 547, "Tax Information on Disasters, Casualty Losses, and Thefts." A free copy may be obtained from your local IRS office.

you may deduct, disregarding the 3 percent limitation, one half of the amount you paid for medical insurance. This deduction, however, may not exceed $150. The balance is added to your other medical expenses and is subject to the 3 percent limitation. Your expenditures for medicines and drugs may be included in medical and dental expenses only to the extent they exceed 1 percent of your adjusted gross income. Taxpayers and dependents aged 65 or older as well as younger persons are subject to the 1 percent and 3 percent limitations. There is no maximum limitation on your medical expense deduction. Any reimbursement (insurance or otherwise) reduces the allowable deduction.

You can deduct payments to doctors, dentists, nurses, hospitals, and so on. Allowable deductions are limited to those expenses which are sustained "primarily for the prevention or alleviation of a physical or mental defect or illness." They include hospital, nursing, medical, laboratory, surgical, and dental services, eyeglasses, hearing aids, seeing-eye dog and its maintenance, supplies (including false teeth and artificial eyes and limbs), ambulance hire, and necessary travel for medical care. The amount paid for medicine and drugs may be taken into account only to the extent it exceeds 1 percent of your adjusted gross income. A prescription is *not* required as long as the medicine and drugs are legally obtained. You may not include the cost of toothpaste, toiletries, cosmetics, etc., in medicines and drugs. Medical expenses include sums paid for hospitalization, membership in certain associations which furnish medical service, and clinical care. Premiums for accident and health insurance which indemnifies for medical care of a specific injury are classed as medical expenses.

Burial and funeral expenses are not medical expenses, nor can you deduct for an illegal operation or for drugs or travel ordered or suggested by your doctor merely for rest or for change.[28]

If medical expenses are deducted in one year and reimbursement is received in a later year, the reimbursement must be reported as income in the year when received, but only to the extent that the reimbursement equals the deduction. Reimbursement to a taxpayer who took a standard deduction and did not take a specific medical deduction is not considered to be income. Insurance premiums paid to provide indemnification for loss of earnings are not a deductible medical expense, and any amount received under such a policy for loss of earnings is not taxable income.

---

[28] There are some very elaborate and subtle distinctions between what you may deduct and what may not be deducted. For further detail, see IRS Publication No. 502, *Deduction for Medical and Dental Expenses*. A free copy may be obtained from any IRS office, or by writing to the Internal Revenue Service, Washington, D.C.

An example will serve to make clear the medical deduction. Assume your adjusted gross income is $12,000. Your medical expenses for the year total $950. Three percent of $12,000 is $360. The first $360 of your $950 medical expense is *not* deductible. The remaining $590 *is* deductible.

Adjustments to Income for Sick Pay

If you are absent from work because of sickness or injury, the relationship of your weekly rate of sick pay to your regular weekly pay rate is a key factor in determining the amount of sick pay you may be able to exclude from your gross income.

You may exclude a limited amount of sick pay from your gross income if you meet the following three conditions:

1. You must have been absent from work because of sickness or injury. Neither needs to have been incurred in connection with your work.
2. You must have been absent longer than the required waiting period. To qualify for the sick pay exclusion your period of absence from work because of illness or injury must extend beyond the waiting period that applies in your particular case. Your waiting period depends primarily on whether your weekly rate of sick pay for the first 30 calendar days (or shorter period) of absence is more than, or is equal to, or is less than, 75 percent of your regular weekly rate of pay.
3. You must have been paid for the time you were absent under a sick pay plan financed by your employer.

The total wages you received, including amounts received for periods of absence because of illness or injury must be reported on line 9 of Form 1040. Then the amount of your exclusion is entered on line 39 of Form 1040.[29]

Care of Children and Other Dependents

A taxpayer who maintains a household may claim a deduction (not to exceed $400 per month) for employment related expenses incurred in obtaining care for any of the following members of his or her household: (*a*) A dependent of the taxpayer who is under the age of 15, (*b*) A dependent of the taxpayer who is physically or mentally disabled, or (*c*) A disabled spouse of the taxpayer.

[29] Details of how to compute the exclusion are given in IRS Publication No. 522, *Adjustments to Income for Sick Pay,* Internal Revenue Service, Washington, D.C. A free copy may be obtained either from your local IRS office or by writing to Internal Revenue Service, Washington, D.C.

The maximum deduction is $400 a month. The deduction limit is the same for a single person as for a married couple filing jointly. In the case of a married couple, the deduction is available only if a joint return is filed.

Employment related expenses are those incurred for the care of a child or a disabled dependent to enable the taxpayer to be gainfully employed.

Generally, the employment related expenses are deductible only if incurred for services in the taxpayer's household. A major exception to this rule, however, is in the case of child care, as distinguished from care of a disabled dependent. In the child care case the cost of services outside the taxpayer's home, day care center expenses, for example, may be claimed. The maximum deduction for expenses outside the household is $200 for one child per month, $300 for two children, and $400 for three or more children. The total deduction for all expenses, inside or outside the home, may not exceed $400 per month.

There is an income limitation, however. It is $35,000 for the year. If the adjusted gross income of the taxpayer exceeds $35,000 for the taxable year during which the expenses are incurred, the amount of the deduction must be reduced by 50 cents for each dollar of income above $35,000. If the taxpayer is married, the combined adjusted gross income of the married couple is considered.

There are a complicated set of other limitations for disabled dependents and an even more difficult set of requirements if a taxpayer has both a child and a disabled dependent. One thing the taxpayer can't do is employ a relative (son, daughter, etc.) to take care of a child or a disabled dependent and take a deduction for the wages paid. There are innumerable categories of relatives who can't be employed if the deduction is to be allowed.[30]

Expenses of Earning Nonbusiness Income

Taxpayers who itemize nonbusiness deductions may deduct nonbusiness expenses incurred in earning nonbusiness income, such as the income from securities and real estate. Such expenses must be necessary to the collection of income from, or to the conservation, maintenance, or management of, the property held to produce the income. For example, if you subscribe to an investment advisory service such as Standard and Poor's or Moody's, or if you pay a fee to an investment counselor, you

[30] For more information see IRS Publication No. 503, *Child Care and Disabled Dependent Care.* A free copy may be obtained at your local IRS office.

may deduct the expense. You can deduct the rental cost of a safe deposit box in which you keep securities but not the cost of a box used merely for jewelry and other valuables.[31]

Expenses for Education

Expenses for education may be deducted if primarily for the purpose of: (*a*) maintaining or improving skills required in your employment or other trade or business, or (*b*) meeting the express requirements of your employer, or the requirements of applicable law or regulations, imposed as a condition to the retention of your salary, status, or employment.

Expenses incurred for obtaining a new position, for meeting minimum requirements, a substantial advancement in position, or for personal purposes, are not deductible.[32]

If you receive a scholarship or fellowship grant (graduate or undergraduate), you may exclude the amount from your gross income, subject to certain limitations depending on whether or not you are a candidate for a degree.

To qualify for this exclusion the payment must be made primarily to further the recipient's education and training. The payment does not qualify, however, if it is made either (1) to compensate you for past, present, or future services, or (2) to allow you to pursue studies or research primarily for the grantor's benefit.

If you are a degree candidate, there is no limitation on the amount of fellowship grant or scholarship that may be excluded from your income and no restriction on the type of institution making the grant. There are limitations on nondegree students.

Payments that represent compensation for past, present, or future services performed by you are *not* excludable. Amounts received by students for services performed on a research project, which a university contracted to perform for a consideration, *are* compensation regardless of how such consideration is designated.

Normally, if the services are required of all candidates for a particular degree (whether or not recipients of scholarship or fellowship grants)

---

[31] For further information, see IRS Publication No. 550, *Tax Information on Investment Income and Expenses*, Internal Revenue Service, Washington, D.C. A free copy may be obtained from your local IRS office or from Washington.

[32] For more detail, see Chapter 19, "Employees' Educational Expenses," in *Your Federal Income Tax*, latest annual edition, U.S. Government Printing Office, Washington, D.C., 20402.

The IRS Spells Out the Tax Consequences of the New Tuition Deferral Plans

A growing number of colleges allow students to delay paying some of their tuition until they graduate and start earning a living. Under one plan, alumni have to pay the school a percentage of their income annually for up to 35 years. Thus, graduates with high earnings may wind up paying more than low wage earners. The maximum obligation is 150% of the deferred amount plus interest and premiums on life insurance the school carries equal to the graduate's unpaid balance. Low-paying students must at least repay the basic tuition without interest or premiums.

The IRS says it considers the deferred tuition a loan to the student, rather than taxable income. Interest on the delayed amount is deductible; principal payments aren't. The difference between the more affluent graduates' high payments and the poor alumni's relatively low outlays won't be considered taxable income to those paying less. The IRS adds that the "150-percenters" —those whose higher earnings force them to pay more than the sum of interest and the deferred amount—may deduct that excess as additional interest.

Wall Street Journal, Feb. 2, 1972.

as a condition to receiving the degree, the compensation for the service may be excluded.

If you are required, as a condition for receiving a scholarship, to agree to work for the grantor after completing your training, the scholarship is considered compensation for future services and thus must be included in gross income.[33]

Alimony Payments

Alimony or separate maintenance payments are expenses deductible by the husband when his wife or ex-wife must include them in income. If you are divorced or legally separated and are making periodic payments of alimony or separate maintenance under a court decree, you can

[33] For further detail and information, see IRS Publication No. 507, *Tax Information on Scholarships and Fellowships*, Internal Revenue Service, Washington, D.C. Free copies are available. See also IRS Publication No. 508, *Tax Information on Educational Expenses*, Internal Revenue Service, Washington, D.C. A free copy may be obtained at your local IRS office.

deduct these amounts. Such payments must be included in the wife's taxable income.

However, you may not deduct lump sum settlements, specific maintenance payments for support of children, or any voluntary payments not under a court order or a written separation agreement. Any alimony payment for which the ex-husband is allowed a deduction must be reported by the ex-wife as income.

If the decree, or some incidental legal instrument, specifies the total sum of an individual's alimony obligation and makes the total payable within ten years, no deduction is allowed. If the pay period is over ten years, each installment is a periodic payment and may be deducted, but not more than ten percent of the total sum may be deducted in any one year. Where no total sum is specified but the court orders periodic payments for life or until the ex-wife remarries, the payments are deductible. Obviously, from a tax viewpoint, how alimony payments are to be made is an important consideration.[34]

Automobile Expenses

The expense of running an automobile may be a business expense, a personal expense, or a combination of both. It depends on how the automobile is used. The costs of gasoline, oil, repairs, garage rent, insurance, and any other necessary operation and upkeep expenses are deductible for an automobile used in trade, business, or profession but not for one used personally. Deductions are also allowable for damages paid as a result of accidents which result from business use, provided, of course, that the taxpayer is not reimbursed by insurance, or otherwise, for the damages for which he is liable. Such deductions are not allowable if the car is used for personal purposes. Depreciation on the cost of an automobile used in trade, business, or a profession is also deductible, but it is not deductible if the automobile is used for personal pleasure. Taxpayers who use their automobiles to look after income-producing properties, yielding either rents or royalties, can deduct their automobile expenses from such income.

If you use your car for both business and for personal travel, you must apportion your expenses appropriately. To illustrate, suppose you are a consulting engineer and drove your car 20,000 miles during this year. Upon checking your records you find that 12,000 miles was for

[34] For further information, see IRS Publication No. 504, *Income Tax Deductions for Alimony Payments.* A free copy may be secured from your local IRS office or by writing to the Internal Revenue Service, Washington, D.C.

business travel and 8,000 for personal use. In this case 12,000/20,000, or 60 percent, of the total cost of operating your car may be claimed as a business or employment expense.

A simple alternate method is available for claiming automobile expenses. For business use of a family car you may take 15 cents a mile for the first 15,000 business miles and 10 cents a mile for any in excess of 15,000. Where you use a car for charitable work or for medical expenses such as trips to a hospital for treatments, you can claim expenses of 7 cents a mile.

Keep in mind that automobile business expenses are deductible from gross income to arrive at adjusted gross income rather than being a deduction from adjusted gross income to arrive at net income. This means that automobile business expenses may be used to reduce your gross income whether or not you itemize deductions.[35]

As far as personal expenses are concerned, taxpayers who itemize nonbusiness deductions may claim the following nonbusiness automobile deductions:

1. State and municipal property taxes on automobiles.
2. Interest on money borrowed on the security of an automobile.
3. Losses from fire, accident, storm, or theft not compensated for by insurance or otherwise.
4. Annual registration fees.
5. Damages to an automobile not compensated by insurance and not from a willful act of negligence of the taxpayer.
6. State and municipal sales taxes on the purchase of a car, accessories, or replacement parts.
7. State gasoline taxes.

Moving Expenses

If you moved to a new residence because you went to work for a new employer or transferred to a new place of work, you may be able to deduct the cost of the move.

You may deduct your allowable moving expenses even if you do not itemize your deductions.

To deduct moving expenses you must: (*a*) meet the 50 mile minimum distance requirement; and (*b*) meet the full time work requirement.

---

[35] For more detail, see *Automobile Income Tax Deductions,* latest annual revision American Automobile Association. A free copy may be obtained by writing to the Association at 8111 Gatehouse Road, Falls Church, Virginia 22042.

Fifty Mile Distance Requirement. To deduct the cost of moving to a new residence, your new place of work must be at least 50 miles farther from your former home than was your former place of work. For example, if your former place of work was 7 miles from your old residence, your new place of work must be at least 57 miles from your old residence.

Note that the minimum distance requirement does not apply to the location of your new residence.

The Full Time Work Requirement. In addition to the 50 mile minimum distance requirement, you must also meet one of the following time requirements.

1. Employees must work full time at least 39 weeks during the 12 month period immediately after their arrival in the general location of their new principal place of work. It is not necessary that you work for one employer for the 39 weeks, nor that the weeks be consecutive. It is necessary only that you be employed on a full time basis within the same general commuting area.

2. Self-employed persons will be allowed a deduction for moving expenses if during the 24 month period immediately following their arrival at the new principal place of work, they perform services on a full time basis during at least 78 weeks, of which not fewer than 39 weeks occur during the 12 month period immediately following the arrival at the new place of work.

Deductible Moving Expenses. These include the following items:

1. *Travel expenses* (including meals and lodging) for yourself and your family while en route from your old residence to your new residence. Your family includes any member of your household who had your residence as his principal place of abode before the move and who moved to your new residence with you. A servant, governess, chauffeur, nurse, valet, or personal attendant is not a member of your family.
2. *The cost of moving household goods* and personal effects of both you and members of your family. This includes the actual transportation or hauling from your old residence to your new one, the cost of packing and crating, in-transit storage, and insurance. The cost of shipping your automobile to your new residence is deductible.
3. *The cost of premove house hunting trips* (travel, meals, and lodging) after obtaining work.
4. *The cost of temporary quarters* (both meals and lodging) at the new location of work for up to 30 consecutive days.
5. *The costs of selling your residence* or settling your lease at the old location and purchasing a residence or acquiring a lease at the new

location. This includes broker's commissions, attorney's fees, "points" (to the extent not representing interest), and other similar expenses incident to the sale or purchase of a home. A loss on the sale of a residence is not deductible.

Limitations. The deduction for the expense of house hunting trips, temporary quarters, and selling your residence—items (3), (4), and (5) above—is limited to $2,500 overall, of which no more than $1,000 may be for house hunting trips and temporary quarters. For married persons filing separate returns, the limitations are $1,250 overall and $500 for house hunting and temporary quarters.

A self-employed person is not entitled to expense for house hunting or temporary quarters unless he has already made substantial arrangements to begin work at the new location.[36]

Miscellaneous Deductions

Many people pass up tax savings because they overlook obscure deductions, do not know about them, and do not take them. You are going to be paying income taxes for the rest of your life—a good many years—and it will pay you to familiarize yourself with present day complications of tax forms and tax rulings as early as possible in your career. Sooner or later, if you procrastinate, you will learn the hard way. It is really much more simple to spend a few hours now and straighten yourself out on a matter which will affect you all your life.[37]

For example, Tom Dobbins came back from two years' service in the Army. He weighed 158 pounds, whereas he had weighed 179 when he was drafted. He gave away all his old clothes to the Salvation Army because they did not fit. He could have deducted the fair market value of these, but he did not know about it. Then he got a job which required that he furnish small tools and a uniform at his own expense. He could have deducted for this, too, but he did not know that if you work for wages or a salary, you can deduct the ordinary and necessary expenses which you incur for your employer's benefit. He joined a union, because he had to as a condition of keeping his job; and he had to pay union dues, which he could have deducted. He had paid a fee to an employment agency for getting him a job, but he did not deduct that either, though he could have. His boss sent him to a neighboring town to do some repair

---

[36] Moving expenses are discussed in detail in IRS Publication No. 521, *Tax Information on Moving Expenses*, available free by sending a postcard to your local IRS office.

[37] For further information see IRS Publication No. 529, *Other Miscellaneous Deductions*. A free copy may be obtained at your local IRS office.

work. He used the company car to get there and back, but he had to stay over two nights. He could have deducted for meals and room, since he was not reimbursed for these outlays; but no one told him, and he had never read anything about taxes.

Generally speaking, if you operate a business or engage in a trade or profession, you can take a lot more deductions than if you are a wage earner. If you are an executive, the cost of a chauffeur to drive your car, used in business, is deductible; but a working wife may not deduct wages paid to a part time cleaning woman. If you are in business and entertain customers at dinner, you can deduct the cost of the dinners—yours and your customers—but an allowance paid by a husband to his wife for cooking dinner for him is not deductible, nor is the cost of the dinner. Traveling expenses, such as railroad fares, meals, lodging, tips, and so forth, incurred while away from home in the pursuit of your regular trade or business are deductible (in computing your adjusted gross income). But no deduction is allowable for traveling expenses that are personal in nature; this includes commuter's fares and similar costs of traveling between home and place of employment or business.

If you own your own home and use it solely for your personal residence, its depreciation, the cost of its restoration by repainting, the cost of insurance, or any loss on its sale represent personal expenses which are not deductible. If you own the house and rent it for income, all these expenses are deductible. Even maintenance costs of idle property, when you are attempting to rent or sell the property, are deductible. If you rent part of your house, you may deduct a proportionate part of the expense of running the house against rental income. If you are in business and your firm pays the expense of a membership in Kiwanis or Rotary, this is deductible; but if you pay your personal dues, it is not deductible. The legal expenses of a business are deductible, but you may not deduct legal fees paid for the preparation of a will or for securing a divorce.

The law specifically provides that no deduction shall be allowed for "personal living or family expenses, except extraordinary medical expenses." They are not part of the cost of operating a business or of producing income from investment property. The basic principle covering deductions applies to all taxpayers: if you seek a deduction you must point to some specific provision of law or regulations authorizing that deduction, and you must be able to prove that you are entitled to such a deduction. It is very important to keep records and receipts in case you are called upon for such proof.[38]

[38] See IRS Publication No. 552, *Recordkeeping Requirements*. A free copy may be obtained from your local IRS office.

CAPITAL GAINS OR LOSSES

In general, capital gains are profits from selling or exchanging any kind of property, except certain kinds when they are used or held in your trade or business. The capital assets you hold may be of two types: income producing and nonincome producing. Stocks and bonds purchased as investments are normally income producing; the house in which you live and your pleasure car are nonincome producing assets. The law requires that you report and pay a tax on any gains from the sale or exchange of either of these two types of capital assets and allows you to claim a loss and deduct in the case of the sale or exchange of income producing property, such as stocks or bonds, but not in the case of nonincome producing capital assets (such as the home in which you live or the pleasure car you drive). In the latter case, you pay a tax on the capital gain, if any, but can take no deduction for the capital loss, if any.

Capital and Noncapital Assets

Although most property is classified by the law as capital assets, there are certain kinds which are not so considered, including:

1. Stock in trade.
2. Real or other property of a kind includable in inventory.
3. Property held for sale to customers.
4. Depreciable property used in trade or business.
5. Real property used in trade or business.
6. A copyright; a literary, musical, or artistic composition; or similar property held by a taxpayer who personally created such property or acquired it from such creator by gift or transfer in trust.
7. Accounts or notes receivable acquired in the ordinary course of business.
8. Certain short term federal, state, and municipal obligations.

Accordingly, stocks and bonds are capital assets when held by individual taxpayers but are not when held for sale by a securities dealer. One's personal residence is a capital asset, but houses held for sale by a real estate dealer are not. A pleasure automobile is a capital asset, but one used in business is not, since it comes under category four, above.

If a capital asset is held six months or less, the gain or loss resulting from sale or exchange is short term. In general, any such profit is fully taxable and any loss is deductible in full. If a capital asset is held longer than six months, gain or loss resulting from its salc is long term. Short term capital gains and losses will be merged to obtain the net short term capital gain or loss. Long term capital gains and losses (taken into account at 100 percent) will be merged to obtain the net long term capital gain or loss. If the net short term capital gain exceeds the net long term capital loss, 100 percent of such excess shall be included in income. If the net long term capital gain exceeds the net short term capital loss, 50 percent of such excess shall be included in income.

The Tax Reform Act of 1969 sliced in half certain tax savings you were previously permitted to obtain through net long term capital losses. Prior to January 1, 1970, you were permitted to use up to $1,000 of the net long term capital losses to offset ordinary income, and if the net long term capital loss exceeded $1,000, it could be carried over and deducted from ordinary income in succeeding years until the loss was absorbed. Beginning in 1970 this was changed. Only 50 percent of your net long term capital loss can be used to reduce your income. Therefore $2,000 of net long term capital losses are needed to produce a $1,000 deduction, $1,000 to produce a $500 deduction, and so on. For example, in 1974 you had earnings of $10,000 and you claimed the standard deduction. You also had a net long term capital loss of $1,600. The capital loss you could use to offset income was $800 (one half of $1,600).

There was no change in the law concerning your net short term losses. As before you can use them, dollar for dollar, to offset ordinary income, up to a maximum of $1,000 in any one tax year and carry them over, dollar for dollar, until absorbed. There was also no change in the law concerning the use of your long term capital losses to offset capital gains, long term and then short term. As before, if you have long term capital losses of any amount, you can use them to offset an equal amount of gains, long term or short term. You must use long term losses first to offset any long term capital gains, and then use the remainder to offset any short term capital gains.

The tax on net long term capital gains will not normally exceed 25 percent because of the alternatives available to the taxpayer, providing his net long term capital gain does not exceed $50,000. He may either take half of his net long term capital gain and add it to his ordinary income and pay the customary income tax on the total, or he may pay a tax of 25 percent of the full net long term capital gain. He is permitted to choose whichever method gives him the lower tax.

If your net long term capital gains exceed $50,000, you are no longer permitted to apply a maximum tax rate of 25 percent to the whole of your net long term capital gain. You will pay a maximum of 25 percent on the first $50,000, but then you must pay 35 percent on the remainder of the net long term capital gain. And you may also be liable to the 10 percent tax on preference income.[39] If it applies to you, it will also apply to half of your net long term capital gains.

In the case of net short term capital gains, there is no alternative; nor is there any halving of the gain. The full gain is added to ordinary income, and the total is taxed at regular income tax rates.

It should be remembered that sales or exchanges of any property which is not used for business or held for the purpose of producing income may result in taxable profit, but losses cannot be deducted. This is the rule which requires one to pay a tax if you sell your home or television set for a profit, but does not allow you to deduct a loss thereon. The gain, however, is a capital gain; and if the property has been held for more than six months, it is a long term gain, and therefore only half of it need be added to ordinary income.[40]

Securities and Capital Gains

Obviously, it pays to hold your securities long enough to establish long term rather than short term capital gains, since the tax advantage is considerable. The holding period of six months, necessary to establish the long term gain, includes the day of sale but not the day of purchase. Every other day in the period—Sundays, holidays, business days,—is counted. Remember that *only one half* of your net long term capital gain need be added to ordinary income for tax purposes. The wealthier person, who may be taxed at 50 percent on the income tax scale, will prefer, in investments, to aim at capital gains rather than recurrent income, because the income will be taxed at 50 percent, but the long term capital gains will be taxed at a maximum of 25 percent if the net long term gain is $50,000 or less or at a 35 percent rate on that part of the gain that exceeds $50,000.

Frequently, investors sell some securities from their portfolio toward the end of the year to establish capital losses to offset earlier capital gains. They then buy back (after 30 days have elapsed) the securities at not very different prices, having by this means minimized their tax and yet not having changed their investment position materially. The tax law does not recognize losses, however, if the same stock is acquired either within 30 days before or 30 days after the tax loss sale.

---

[39] See section on "Preference Income," pp. 149–50.

[40] For further information see Chapter 32, "Reporting Capital Gains and Losses on Schedule D," in *Your Federal Income Tax*, latest edition, Internal Revenue Service, Washington, D.C.

When You Sell Your Home

The tax law has a special provision for homeowners who sell one house and buy another. If a taxpayer sells his principal residence at a gain and, within 18 months, buys another dwelling which is used as a principal residence, the gain is not taxable if the cost of the new dwelling equals or exceeds the sale price of the old one, but such gain is subtracted from the basis of the new home. You are allowed additional time in case of (*a*) construction of the new residence or (*b*) military service. If you begin construction of a residence, either before the sale of your old residence or within one year after the sale, and occupy it not later than 24 months after the sale, you will be considered to have purchased a new residence, and the nonrecognition of gain rule applies.

The rule provides that no tax is payable if a new residence is purchased and occupied within 18 months before or after the sale of the former residence at a profit, provided the cost of the new home equals or exceeds the selling price of the former home. The law takes the position that the new residence is in substance a continuation of the former investment in a home. To the extent that the former residence, however, sells for more than the cost of the new property, the gain is, therefore, taxable. A loss from the sale of one's residence is not deductible. The rule as to gains applies also, under certain conditions, to exchanges of one residence for another, to construction of a new residence, and to the acquisition of a new residence on which work must be done to make it fit for occupancy.

If an old residence costing $16,000 is sold for $30,000 (at a profit of $14,000), and a new residence is acquired for $34,000, the new residence takes as its basis (on which to compute later gain) the $34,000 cost diminished by the $14,000 profit on the former residence, or an adjusted basis of $20,000. This amounts to the cost of the old home increased by the additional investment ($4,000) in the new home. The apparent gain of $14,000 on the sale of the old home is not taxed but instead is used to reduce the cost of acquisition (basis) of the new house from $34,000 to $20,000. If, a few years later, you sell the new house for $40,000 and do not buy another, you will have a $20,000 capital gain, not a $6,000 gain.

If, to take another example, the taxpayer sells the original old home for $30,000 (at a profit of $14,000) and buys a new home for $24,000, does not invest $6,000 of the $14,000 profit made on the sale of the old home when the new home is bought, the part ($6,000) of the gain on the sale of the old property is taxable. In this case, the basis taken by the new home is $24,000 (cost) less $8,000 of nontaxable profit, or $16,000.

That is, if the sale price of your old residence exceeds the cost of your new residence, the gain on the sale is taxable to the extent of such excess.

Should you sell your new residence, to determine the gain on its sale, reduce its cost by the gain from the sale of your old residence which was not taxable. For example, if you sell your new residence—which cost, say, $28,000—for $32,000, and the nontaxable gain on your old residence was $8,000, your gain on the sale of the new residence is $12,000.

A *loss* on the sale or exchange of your residence is *not* deductible and has no effect on the basis of your new residence. If you have more than one residence, only the sale of your principal residence qualifies for the rule allowing postponement of the tax. For example, you own and live in a house in town and also own a beach house which you use in the summer. The town property is your principal residence; the beach house is *not*. Furniture, appliances, and similar items are *not* part of your principal residence. A houseboat, mobile home, or trailer may be your principal residence.

If you are a tenant-shareholder in a cooperative housing development and use as your principal residence the apartment you are entitled to occupy by reason of your stockholdings, that apartment qualifies as your principal residence. Ordinarily your basis will be the cost of your stock in the corporation which may include your allocable share of a mortgage (on the apartment building) that you are required to pay as a condition of retaining your stock interest. A condominium apartment is similar to a cooperative apartment. As in the case of the "co-op," your basis is your cost, which may also include your allocable share of the mortgage on the entire property if there is one.

A special benefit is provided for older persons. If a person 65 or over sells a residence for a gain, it is tax free if the adjusted sales price is $20,000 or less. The adjusted sales price is the amount realized less "fixing up" expenses, that is, those incurred within 90 days prior to sale. This tax relief applies only if the taxpayer used the property as a principal residence for at least five of the eight years before sale.

If the sales price is more than $20,000, the gain is tax free in the ratio that $20,000 is to the selling price. Assume the adjusted selling price is $30,000, for example, and the gain is $9,000. Only $6,000 of the gain is tax-free [$9,000 × ($20,000/$30,000)].[41]

---

[41] See IRS Publication No. 523, *Tax Information on Selling Your House*. A free copy may be obtained from your local IRS office or by sending a postcard to Internal Revenue Service, U.S. Treasury Department, Washington, D.C. See also IRS Publication No. 530, *Tax Information on Deductions for Homeowners*. A free copy may be obtained from your local IRS office.

OTHER PROVISIONS

Income Averaging

If your income increases substantially in any given year, it may be to your advantage to compute your tax under the income averaging method. The income averaging method permits a part of the unusually large amount of taxable income to be taxed in lower brackets, thus resulting in a reduction of the overall amount of tax due.

For "computation years" beginning after December 31, 1969, and for the "base period years" applicable to these computation years, the previous income averaging rules have been changed considerably. Under the new rules more types of income are averageable. Also, more individuals should be eligible to use this method and their averageable incomes should be larger.

You may choose this method of computing your tax if your averageable income for this computation year is over $3,000 more than 30 percent of the total of your adjusted taxable incomes for your four previous base years.

Here's how it works. Briefly, the income averaging method operates to tax a part (the averageable income) of the unusually large amount of income in the peak year at the same lower effective tax rate that applies to the first one fifth of this averageable income.

To provide a simplified example, take Mr. White, who is an eligible individual as defined later, a calendar year taxpayer, a bachelor, whose only source of income is, and has been, his salary. In 1974 he has taxable income of $20,000.

His taxable income for his base period years 1970 through 1973 was as follows: $7,000 in 1970, $8,000 in 1971, $4,000 in 1972, and $5,000 in 1973. The sum of these amounts is $24,000, 30 percent of which is $7,200.

Mr. White's averageable income for 1974 is $12,800, determined by subtracting $7,200 (30 percent of his total base period income) from $20,000. Since this is over $3,000, he may use the income averaging method.

Mr. White then computes his tax as follows:

1.	30% of total base period income (0.30 × $24,000)	$7,200.00
2.	⅕ of averageable income (⅕ × $12,800)	2,560.00
3.	Sum of items (1) and (2)	$9,760.00
4.	Tax on sum of items (1) and (2) (tax on $9,760)	$2,030.00
5.	Tax on 30% of total base period income (tax on $7,200)	1,398.00
6.	Tax on ⅕ of averageable income (item (4) minus item (5))	$ 632.00
7.	Tax on ⅘ of averageable income (item (6) multiplied by (4))	$2,528.00
8.	Tax for 1974 (sum of items (4) and (7))	$4,558.00

Under the regular method, his tax on $20,000 taxable income would be $5,230. Thus, he saves $672 by using the income averaging method.

Types of Income Eligible for Averaging. Almost all types of income are eligible for averaging. The only exceptions are premature or excessive distributions from self-employed retirement plans, trust accumulation distributions that you included in income under a special limitation on tax, and other items of income subject to a limitation on tax (excluding net long term capital gains).

Certain Benefits Not Allowable. If you choose the benefits of income averaging, you cannot take advantage of the following tax benefits in the same computation year:

1. Optional tax tables.
2. Alternative tax on capital gains.
3. Limitation on tax in the case of certain total distributions.
4. Exclusion of income from sources outside the United States or within U.S. possessions.
5. Maximum tax on earned income.

If you are eligible for any of these benefits, you should compute your tax under both methods to determine the one producing the lowest tax liability. You choose the income averaging method by attaching to your Form 1040 a filled in Schedule G, copies of which may be obtained from your Internal Revenue office.[42]

Cash or Accrual Accounting

Your return must be on a cash basis unless you keep accounts on the accrual basis. "Cash basis" means that all items of taxable income actually or constructively received during the year (whether in cash or property or services) and only those amounts actually paid during the year for deductible expenses are shown. Income is "constructively" received when the amount is credited to your account, or set aside for you, and may be drawn upon by you at any time. Thus, such income includes uncashed salary or dividend checks, bank interest credited to your account, matured bond coupons, and similar items which you can immediately turn into cash. The "accrual basis" means that you report income when earned even though not received, and deduct expenses when incurred, even though not paid within the taxable period. Most people find it more convenient to use the cash basis.[43]

---

[42] A complete discussion of income averaging, including a comprehensive example, may be found in IRS Publication No. 506, *Computing Your Tax under the Income Averaging Method*, available free by sending a postcard to your local IRS office.

[43] For further information see IRS Publication No. 538, *Tax Information on Accounting Periods and Methods*.

How to Figure Your Tax

To save arithmetic for the average taxpayer, the law provides tax tables which show the correct tax for any income up to $10,000. If your adjusted gross income is less than $10,000 and you do not itemize your deductions, you may use the appropriate Tax Table contained in the instructions accompanying Short Form 1040A, or Form 1040 to determine your tax. The standard deduction is an allowance used to reduce your adjusted gross income when you do not itemize your deductions. If your adjusted gross income is less than $10,000, the standard deduction is automatically considered in the Tax Table you use to determine your tax. The low income allowance has been designed to provide a tax free allowance for low income taxpayers, thereby removing them from the tax rolls. The allowance is automatically taken into consideration when you use the Tax Tables. With the exception of married taxpayers who file separate returns, the standard deduction used in determining the tax reflected in the Tax Table is the larger of the percentage standard deduction or the low income allowance. If you use the Tax Tables contained in the instructions you receive with your Short Form 1040A, or Form 1040, the number of your exemptions will determine the table to use in computing your tax.

If you itemize your deductions or if your adjusted gross income is $10,000 or more, you must use the Tax Rate Schedules, not the Tax Tables. However, if your income on line 15, Form 1040 is $20,000 or less, and consists only of wages or salaries and tips, dividends, interest, pensions, and annuities and you choose the standard deduction instead of itemizing your deductions, you may have the Internal Revenue Service

Women's Lib Is Leaving Its Mark on the Joint Tax Return

The IRS has long contended that if a couple files a joint return and has a refund coming, the IRS may apply the entire overpayment against any outstanding liability of either spouse. Recently, however, the IRS revoked that ruling. Under the new IRS stance, if a wife files jointly with her husband but pays the entire tax bill herself, none of the refund may be applied to the husband's separate tax liability for an earlier year.

The IRS says it's bowing to repeated court rulings that husband and wife have separate, rather than joint, interests in a refund. For instance, if one spouse dies or goes bankrupt, only that spouse's share of the refund goes into the estate or to the bankruptcy trustee.

Wall Street Journal, January 15, 1975.

compute your tax for you. If you are eligible to use Short Form 1040A you may ask the IRS to compute your tax no matter what your level of income.

You may pay your tax by cash, check, or money order. Check or money order are more advisable, since you have a receipt if you use the mail to file your return. Never send cash through the mail unregistered.

You have not filed a legal return unless you sign it. If its a joint return, both must sign. You do not need to have your return notarized, since your signature has the same legal effect as swearing to the truthfulness of your return.

Examination of Returns

In filing your return, you determine the amount of tax you owe the government according to your own calculation. The return must, however, be examined by the government before the amount of tax liability is officially determined. If the government finds that more tax is due, you have the right to appeal. More than 95 percent of such disputes are settled by agreements between taxpayers and field offices of the Internal Revenue Service. If they cannot agree, the taxpayer may appeal to the tax court or to the federal district court, circuit court, court of claims, or, finally, to the U.S. Supreme Court.

The government is allowed (by the applicable statute of limitations) three years from the filing of the return in which to examine it. This general rule is subject to three exceptions:

1. If a fraudulent return is filed, there is no limit to the time which the government may take to examine the return.
2. When no return is filed, the government may levy the amount it determines to be due at any time.
3. If more than 25 percent of total gross income reported is omitted from a return, the government has five years in which to assess a tax or to start court proceedings to collect.

Audits and Records

You must keep records to determine your correct tax liability. The law does not require any particular kind of record. Regardless of your bookkeeping system, your records must be permanent, accurate, and complete, and must clearly establish income, deductions, credits, and so on. Receipts, canceled checks, and other types of records are essential for explaining financial transactions.[44]

---

[44] See IRS Publication No. 552, *Record-keeping Requirements and a Guide to Tax Publications*. Free copies are available from the Internal Revenue Service.

If your return is selected for audit, you'll need your records to substantiate your return. There are three levels within the Internal Revenue Service at which agreement to the results of an examination may be reached. The first level is an *audit* by an examining officer, the second is a conference with a member of the District Conference Staff, and the third is a hearing with the Service's Appellate Division. If you wish you may have someone accompany you or represent you at any of the levels or at all of them. If you are not satisfied with the outcome, you may file a court suit, but this is costly. However, if you disagree with an increase in your income tax liability, as indicated in the notice of deficiency, you may ask for consideration of the deficiency by the U.S. Tax Court.[45] There is now a Small Case Division of the U.S. Tax Court. If neither the disputed amount of the deficiency, nor any claimed overpayment with respect to it, exceeds $1,500 for any one tax year, you may request that your case be handled in that court under the special procedures provided for small cases. It is simplified, expeditious, and informal. However, the decision cannot be appealed.[46]

Penalties

There are a whole series of penalties provided for in the tax law. There is a penalty for failing to file a declaration on time. A penalty is imposed if returns are not filed when originally due or within a period of extension, deferment, or postponement. A penalty in the form of interest at the rate of 9 percent must be paid on taxes not paid by their due date. There is a new penalty for failure to pay the tax on time—.5 percent per month of the amount unpaid with a maximum of 25 percent. In addition there is—as in the past—a 9 percent interest penalty. A similar penalty is charged if a declaration is filed but installments are not paid on time. When the taxpayer is able to satisfy the Internal Revenue Service that the delay was not caused by willful neglect but was the result of a reasonable cause, neither of these two penalties are levied.

If the tax is underestimated by more than 20 percent (33⅓ percent for farmers), a penalty may be levied. This penalty is not applicable if

---

[45] To obtain a copy of the rules for filing a petition with the court, write to the Clerk, United States Tax Court, Box 70, Washington, D.C. 20044.

[46] See IRS Publication No. 556, *Audit of Returns, Appeal Rights and Claims for Refund.* A free copy may be obtained by writing to the Internal Revenue Service, Washington, D.C. or from your local IRS office. See also "If Your Tax Return is Audited," *Changing Times,* June 1973; and "How People Are Taking on the Tax Man—and Winning," *U.S. News & World Report,* March 11, 1974; and "If Your Tax Return Is Challenged," *U.S. News & World Report,* March 10, 1975.

the taxpayer applied the current rates and exemptions to an amount not less than the previous year's income. There is, of course, no penalty if the sole reason for underestimation is an increase in tax rates. Severe fines and jail sentences may be imposed by the courts in cases involving large frauds.

Minimizing Taxes

The higher their clients' income, the more numerous are the ingenious techniques clever tax lawyers devise to enable wealthy clients to minimize taxes. The methods are fascinating to read about, but they can seldom be used by people of moderate income and are usually of little use to those who depend primarily on wages or salaries for income.

Just for future reference when you climb up into the $25,000 and over annual income bracket, let's look at a few of them. First, you can arrange to divide your income among members of your family. How? By gifts, by family trusts, and by family corporations. A married man earning $30,000 pays about $10,000 in taxes. Assume his father dies and leaves him $50,000 (after estate taxes). If he invests it at 6 percent, he can keep less than half of the $3,000 income he would receive. He doesn't need the income, and he feels it would be wasteful to receive it and then have to pay most of it in taxes. He has four children. They are young now, ages 1, 2, 3, and 4. Putting all four through college some day, he figures, will cost him about $20,000 each. He decides to create irrevocable trusts of $12,500 for each. Each will receive $750 a year income (at 6 percent) from his $12,500 trust until age 18 when the proceeds of the trusts will be paid to each over a four year period to finance the costs of a college education. Thus the father, by turning over his $50,000 inheritance to his children in irrevocable trusts, saves the taxes on the annual $3,000 income. Since $750 annually goes to each of the children, they pay no tax on it because each has a $750 exemption. They will remain $750 exemptions for the father, since he will continue to provide more than half their support.

A device, which is now being used by moderate income families, is the bunching of deductions in alternate years. In one year you take the standard 15 percent deduction. Deductions are then maximized by bunching into the second year the contributions, doctor's bills, property taxes, which you would normally pay each year. Assume, for example, you normally give $100 to the Community Chest in December. You postpone this contribution until the next month, that is January of the following year, and then at the end of the year in December you give again as you normally do. Thus in the first year when you took the 15 percent standard deduction you make no contributions. In the following year you make your donations both at the beginning and end of the year. By doing this with as many deductions as you can, you maximize your legitimate deductions.

When you are in the upper brackets, capital gains look much more attractive than income. That's why many a corporate executive prefers a stock option plan to a boost in salary. If the executive is in the 60 percent bracket, a $10,000 increase in salary leaves only $4,000, whereas an ability to buy shares of the company's stock and then sell them in the open market realizing a $10,000 gain will net $7,500.

As an actual example, consider the option granted in 1956 to Thomas J. Watson, Jr., the late president of the International Business Machines Corporation, giving him the right, *for 10 years,* to buy a total of 11,464 shares of the company's stock at $91.80 per share. Subsequently the stock soared to $600 per share. Assume Mr. Watson exercised his rights and bought the 11,464 shares. They would have cost about $1 million. Had he sold them at $600 a share, he would have had a total profit of $5.8 million on which he would have been taxed at the favorable capital gains rate. Had he exercised his rights but not sold the shares and held them until his death he would not have paid any income or capital gains tax on this considerable profit.[47]

It is to increase the opportunity for capital gains that many corporations in which insiders have large holdings deliberately keep dividend payments low. Plowing back earnings enhances the value of the company's stock and may ultimately mean a handsome capital gain.

Fortune reported that Mrs. Horace Dodge invested the entire estate her husband left her—$56 million—in tax exempt state and municipal bonds and, assuming a return at that time of 3.5 percent, had an annual tax free income of $1,960,000.

Recently, wealthy individuals seeking tax havens have been going in for oil and gas drilling programs and cattle breeding participations. Drilling for oil and gas is obviously risky and incredibly complex. The rich have usually provided the funds. The tax shelter arises from the high percentage write-off (80 percent to 100 percent) of intangible development and exploration costs allowed to be expensed. That, combined with the 22 percent depletion allowance, enabled highbracketed individuals to utilize income dollars that would otherwise have gone in taxes. Cattle breeding participations are somewhat similar to oil deals. They provide tax

---

[47] See Philip M. Stern, *The Rape of the Taxpayer* (New York: Random House, Inc., 1973); see also *The April Game*, by "Diogenes," Playboy Press, Chicago, 1973.

shelter in that you buy a participation, the expenses of raising the herd give you an annual tax loss deduction, while the sale of the herd at maturity provides a long term capital gain.[48] It isn't as easy as it sounds, and there are dangers of substantial losses in both types of operations.

The corporate expense account has often in the past been a favorite device for shifting personal expenses which would otherwise be nondeductible to corporate deductible business expenses. Under the guise of "business," for example, corporate officials have gone to Florida in the winter and Europe in the summer, have had their liquor, theater, restaurant, medical, dental, hospital, insurance, pension and annuity, and country club bills paid by their companies. Taxwise it has paid to be an "organization man." The Internal Revenue Service has been clamping down on these corporate "fringe" benefits.

There are a good many other devices and techniques but by the time you get to the $25,000 bracket, some of the old loopholes will have been plugged and new ones opened.

Minimum Tax on Tax Preferences

The Tax Reform Act of 1969 attempted to crack down, gently, on the tax shelters enjoyed by the wealthy. For example, it was reported to Congress that in 1969, 301 individuals who reported incomes of at least $200,000 paid no income tax at all. Their number included 56 with incomes of $1 million or more. The legislative response was the tax preference provision of the new act, which imposed a 10 percent penalty tax on certain types of tax sheltered income.[49]

A minimum tax now applies to a number of items that are considered to be of a tax preference nature. The tax is computed by first totaling all the items of tax preference, then reducing this amount by a specific exemption of $30,000 ($15,000 in the case of married persons filing separate returns). The excess is further reduced by the regular tax, and then the minimum tax is computed by applying a flat 10 percent rate against the balance.

Some of the items of tax preference are:

---

[48] Irving Schreiber, (ed.), *How to Use Tax Shelters Today*, Greenvale, N.Y.: Panel Publishers, 1973. See also *Tax Shelters For High Income Clients*, Practising Law Institute, New York, 1973.

[49] See "Outfoxing the Internal Revenue Service: That Tax Reform Act Left Shelters Intact, Many Taxpayers Find," *Wall Street Journal*, April 14, 1971. See also "Rep. Reuss Says Tax Loopholes Still Let Wealthy Avoid Paying," *New York Times*, January 3, 1972; and "Looking For Tax Shelters? There's Trouble Brewing," *U.S. News & World Report*, July 22, 1974.

1. *Capital gains.* This is one half of the amount by which your net long term capital gains exceed your net short-term capital losses for the year.
2. *Accelerated depreciation on real property.* This is the amount of the depreciation deduction during the year on real property that is in excess of the depreciation deduction that would have been allowable had the straight line method of depreciation been used.
3. *Stock options.* Upon the exercise of a qualified or restricted stock option, the amount by which the fair market value of the stock exceeds the option price at the time of exercise is an item of tax preference.
4. *Depletion.* This is the excess of your depletion deduction over the adjusted basis of the property at the end of the year (determined without regard to the depletion deduction for the year).[50]

However, one of the most widely used tax shelters was left untouched: income from state and municipal bonds is still tax free. To further redress the balance, the Tax Reform Act of 1969 provided for a reduction in the maximum tax rate on so-called "earned income." *Earned income* is a new tax term that covers salaries, bonuses, and other compensation paid currently, but excludes dividends, capital gains, and such deferred income as pensions and profit sharing income. Under this provision the maximum tax rate on earned income as defined was reduced from 70 percent to 50 percent in 1972 and thereafter.

Conclusion

As you have undoubtedly gathered by now, taxes are a very complicated subject; and, aside from studying the instructions and forms carefully, you should get expert advice if you are in doubt. The District Director's office will be glad to give you help at any time on a specific problem involving your own situation. Either visit the office, phone, or write. A hypothetical or theoretical question will not be answered, however. If you have a complicated tax situation, you would do well to consult a lawyer or an accountant with experience in handling tax matters. Their advice and suggestions may save you time, trouble, and money. Do not ever hesitate, however, to take the deductions and exemptions to which you feel you are really entitled. It is not fraud to become involved in a legitimate disagreement with the Internal Revenue Service. As Justice Learned Hand once held: "Nobody owes any public duty to pay more than the law demands."

---

[50] For further information see IRS Publication No. 525, *Taxable Income and Nontaxable Income*.

SUGGESTED READINGS

1. Treasury Department, Bureau of Internal Revenue, *Your Federal Income Tax—for Individuals,* Publication No. 17. Washington, D.C., latest edition. A copy may be obtained by writing to the Superintendent of Documents, U.S. Government Printing Office, Washington, D.C. 20402.
2. Treasury Department, Bureau of Internal Revenue, *U.S. Income Tax Form 1040 and Instructions for* [*Year*]. Washington, D.C., latest year. Free.
3. Other Internal Revenue Service Publications.

   The publications listed below may be obtained free by sending a postcard to any Internal Revenue office. IRS employees in these offices will also be happy to furnish you with any necessary forms you may need and to assist you if you need any help in the filing of returns.

Publication Number	
538	Accounting Periods and Methods, Tax Information on
519	Aliens, United States Tax Guide for
504	Alimony Payments, Income Tax Deduction for
520	American Scholars in the United States and Abroad, Tax Information for
556	Audit of Returns, Appeal Rights and Claims for Refund
548	Bad Debts, Tax Information on Deduction for
535	Business Expenses, Tax Information on
503	Child Care and Disabled Dependent Care
567	Civil Service (U.S.) Retirement and Disability Retirement, Tax Advice on
517	Clergymen and Religious Workers, Social Security for
555	Community Property and the Federal Income Tax
549	Condemnations of Private Property for Public Use
526	Contributions, Income Tax Deduction for
542	Corporations and the Federal Income Tax
551	Cost or Other Basis of Assets, Tax Information on
512	Credit Sales by Dealers in Personal Property
534	Depreciation, Tax Information on
547	Disasters, Casualty Losses, and Thefts, Tax Information on
561	Donated Property, Valuation of
508	Educational Expenses, Tax Information on
510	Excise Taxes for 1975, Information on
501	Exemptions and Exemptions for Dependents, Your
557	Exemptions for an Organization, How to Apply for
225	Farmer's Tax Guide
378	Federal Fuel Tax Credit or Refund for Nonhighway and Transit Users
349	Federal Highway Use Tax

Publication Number	
518	Foreign Scholars and Educational and Cultural Exchange Visitors
514	Foreign Tax Credit for U.S. Citizens and Resident Aliens
553	Highlights of 1973 Changes in the Tax Law
530	Homeowners, Tax Information on Deductions for
506	Income Averaging Method, Computing Your Tax under The
537	Installment and Deferred-Payment Sales
545	Interest Expense, Income Tax Deduction for
572	Investment Credit, Tax Information on
550	Investment Income and Expenses, Tax Information on
536	Losses From Operating a Business
502	Medical and Dental Expenses, Deduction for
529	Miscellaneous Deductions, Other
521	Moving Expenses—Tax Information on
564	Mutual Fund Distributions, Tax Information on
541	Partnership Income and Losses, Tax Information on
528	Preparing Your Tax Return, Information on
527	Rental Income and Royalty Income
540	Repairs, Replacements, and Improvements, Tax Information on
524	Retirement Income and Retirement Income Credit
560	Retirement Plans for Self-Employed Individuals
543	Sale of a Business, Tax Information on the
544	Sales and Other Dispositions of Assets
533	Self-Employment Tax, Information on
522	Sick Pay, Adjustments to Income for
558	Sponsors of Contests and Sporting Events, Tax Information for
532	Students and Parents, Tax Information for
559	Survivors, Executors, and Administrators, Federal Tax Guide for
554	Tax Benefits for Older Americans
509	Tax Calendar and Check List for 1975
571	Tax-sheltered Annuity Plans for Employees of Public Schools and Certain Tax-Exempt Organizations
505	Tax Withholding and Declaration of Estimated Tax
525	Taxable Income and Nontaxable Income
546	Taxes, Income Tax Deductions for
531	Tips for Federal Tax Purposes, Reporting Your
463	Travel, Entertainment and Gift Expenses
54	U.S. Citizens Abroad, Tax Guide for
570	U.S. Citizens Employed in U.S. Possessions, Tax Guide for
516	U.S. Government Civilian Employees Stationed Abroad, Tax Information for
513	Visitors to the United States, Tax Information for
539	Withholding Taxes From Your Employee's Wages

4. See *Changing Times:*
"Your Income Tax: 14 Mistakes That Could Cause Trouble," April 1973.
"If Your Tax Return is Audited," June 1973.
"You Can Save Now on Next Year's Taxes," July 1973.
"Do These Tax Rulings Affect You?" September 1973.
"Taxes: The Rules on Dependent-Care Costs," October 1973.
"New Tax Rulings That Could Affect You," January 1974.
5. *Federal Tax Course.* Englewood Cliffs, N.J.: Prentice-Hall, Inc., latest year.
6. *Automobile Income Tax Deductions,* latest annual edition, American Automobile Association. A free copy may be obtained by writing to the Association at 8111 Gatehouse Road, Falls Church, Virginia 22042.
7. *Educator's Tax Desk Manual,* Executive Reports Corporation, Englewood Cliffs, N.J., latest edition.
8. In *Money:*
"How the IRS Looks at Your Tax Return," March 1973.
"Eight Tax-Saving Ways to Happier Returns," March 1974.
"What the IRS Auditors Will Overlook," April 1974.
"Your Tax Bracket's Hidden Heights," November 1974.
9. Philip M. Stern, *The Rape of the Taxpayer,* New York: Random House, 1973.
10. *How to Prepare Your Personal Income Tax Return.* Englewood Cliffs, N.J.: Prentice-Hall, Inc., issued annually.
11. *Investor's Tax Guide,* issued annually by Merrill Lynch, Pierce, Fenner & Smith. A free copy may be obtained by writing to this firm at One Liberty Plaza, 165 Broadway, New York, N.Y. 10006.
12. *How to Prepare Your [Year] Tax Returns.* New York: Research Institute of America, latest year.
13. *Tax Guide for Small Business,* Internal Revenue Service Publication No. 334. Washington, D.C.: U.S. Government Printing Office, latest edition.

CASE PROBLEMS

1. John Daly sells magazines on commission in the city of Chicago and its suburbs. He finds it necessary to use his automobile a good deal in order to reach favorable areas in which to sell. Only infrequently is it possible for him to eat his luncheons at home during the week; occasionally he is forced to have dinner at a restaurant or hotel when he stays on his job until it becomes dark. To what extent may he deduct these expenses on his income tax return?

2. Roswell traded his Chevrolet sedan for a new Ford Galaxie. The dealer allowed $1,175 for the old car toward the purchase of the new automobile, which cost $3,960. Roswell had driven the Chevrolet 21,962 miles during the

three years he owned it, traveling between home and work and for general family use. What are the income tax implications?

3. Stanlaw earns $18,000 a year. He owns a camp on an island in a lake. Heavy rains cause the water in the lake to rise so high that damage of $2,500 is done to his boathouse and dock. Insurance which he has been carrying reimburses him the next year to the extent of $500. Which of these items enters into his income tax calculations? Why?

4. When Maddox and his wife were 64 years of age and had an adjusted gross income of $8,500, their medical expenses were $5,200 and those of their daughter, a junior in college, were $256. The following year, with an adjusted gross income of $8,100, their medical expenses amounted to $3,200 and those of their daughter were $186. How much could they deduct for medical expenses in each year?

5. Mary Jane Hancock is a widow with two children (ages 3 and 5). To help support her family, she works as a secretary at $155 a week. She finds it necessary to employ a housekeeper at $75 a week. In her estimation, the housekeeper costs her at least $10 more a week because of the food she eats. To what extent does the federal income tax law make provision for the housekeeper?

6. Biddle bought a 6 acre tract of land for $10,000. He divided the tract into 24 house lots. Improvements (roads, sewers, sidewalks, etc.) cost him $12,400. By November of the first year, he was ready to begin selling lots, but he had to wait for the selling season in the following spring. From June to August, he sold 16 lots—all he sold during the year. These lots were sold for $3,500 each. Biddle paid salesmen commissions of 15 percent for effecting the sales. What was the taxable profit? What can you tell about the tax?

7. Kerensky bought a two family frame house for $32,000 as of January 2. He estimated that the lot was worth $5,000. During the year he paid interest of $650, real estate taxes of $380, and fire insurance of $58. Miscellaneous painting cost him $134, and carpentry work for repairing the front steps amounted to $137. A new roof, guaranteed for 15 years, was installed for $1,500. The upper part of the house was rented throughout the year to Mrs. Kerensky's brother and his family at $155 a month. How should these facts appear on the joint tax return of the Kerenskys?

8. Kirkland earns $12,000 a year and lives with his wife and two children (ages 13 and 17). In computing his estimated tax for the year, Kirkland took an exemption of $750 for each of the children. By December 31, it is learned that the younger child earned $18 for baby sitting (for which no tax was withheld) and that the 17-year-old boy earned $728 (from which $15.60 was withheld) for his work as a caddy. Now what must be done?

9. In January, Emily Dirksen estimates that she will earn $9,300 in the current year. During the prior three years she was desperately ill and used up all her savings, but she is now fully recovered and back on the job. She calculates that the total tax on her earnings will be $1,430, but at the rate at which her employer is withholding for taxes from her salary, the total amount withheld for the year will be $1,280. The balance of $150 which she will have to pay as tax is brought about largely through her earnings from outside work on which no tax is withheld. Ms. Dirksen, because of her illness, feels out of touch with the federal income tax law, and asks you to refresh her memory as to her obligations under that law.

10. Putman is a teacher earning $9,200 a year. He lives in a southern community with his wife and two children (ages 2 and 4). His summer vacation period was spent at a school 1,000 miles from home, where he earned $1,200. Expenses of $682 were incurred by him for travel, meals, and lodging in connection with this employment. How should the above facts be entered on the return?

11. In March 1970, Smith bought a house as a residence for himself and his family at a cost of $15,000. During the next two years, he spent $1,000 for improvements to the house. In March 1974, he sold the house for $22,000. Six months later, in September 1974, he bought another home for $27,000. What are the income tax implications?

4

Charge Accounts, Credit Cards, and the Installment Plan

So far as my coin would stretch; and where it would not
I have used my credit.
Shakespeare

A CUSTOMER shopping for a record player in a large appliance store, finally located one to his liking. "What terms do you wish, sir?" inquired the salesgirl.

"Terms? I'll pay cash," replied the customer.

"Cash!" the astonished clerk exclaimed.

"I'll have to get the manager to see how to handle this."

This was meant to be funny but now an old fashioned idea has returned—cut rate prices for cash payments. As a result of an out-of-court settlement recently, American Express advised the retailers who honor its credit cards that it is permissible to allow discounts, "if such discount is clearly and conspicuously offered to all cash customers." Consumers Union had charged that American Express was illegally forbidding cut rate prices to cash customers at its client stores. Note that the discount must be clearly and conspicuously offered to all cash customers. A similar agreement has been made with Carte Blanche. The retailer who has to pay the credit company a service charge ranging from 2 to 8 percent on each transaction, but keeps all the profit from a cash sale may be understandably reluctant to publicize the opportunity for a discount. Similar court action has begun by various consumer groups against other credit card companies. Asking discounts for cash works—sometimes. Some merchants even volunteer the cash amount. There is even a cash credit card (UNIC) which advertises itself as an un-credit card. Its members, mostly on the West Coast, obtain discounts for cash.

The great rise in consumer indebtedness in recent years has been the subject of much debate. "The people who are most responsible for the dangerous increase in mortgage and short term consumer debt," says William H. Whyte, Jr., writing in *Fortune*, "are [the eminently respectable young] suburbanites; most of them are salaried members of large organizations; they are homeowners; they go to church; from one third to one half have gone to college; more will send their children to college; and about 65 percent of them vote Republican. And they are the true prodigals."

Fortune summed up: "The young people who some day will run our capitalist economy—how do they run their own? Atrociously. They are so bemused by the rhythm of equal monthly payments, they hardly think about the cost of money at all."

Consumer debt is now approaching $600 billion. Of this, over $375 billion is mortgage debt on family homes, while over $180 billion is in consumer credit of various forms. In 1941 total consumer credit was about $9 billion. The brief comparison shown in Table 4–1 highlights the changes in type of credit and shows it growth.

Under these circumstances, where no longer the privileged or the profligate were the main users of credit, the governments (federal, state and city throughout the nation) became conscious of their responsibilities toward the general public which were now involved. Thus, in the late 1960s and early 1970s, there is a new area of protective consumer legislation which shall be discussed.

It is the young marrieds who are responsible for most of the consumer debt. The *Survey of Consumer Finances* of the Survey Research Center,

TABLE 4–1
Growth of Consumer Credit, 1941–73 (in millions of dollars)

	End of Period				
	1941	*1950*	*1960*	*1970*	*1973*
Grand total	9,172	21,471	56,141	127,163	180,486
Automobile paper	2,458	6,074	17,658	35,184	51,130
Other consumer goods paper	1,929	4,799	11,545	31,465	47,530
Repair modernization loans	376	1,016	3,148	5,070	7,352
Personal loans	1,322	2,814	10,617	30,345	41,425
Total installment loans	6,085	14,703	42,968	102,064	147,437
Total noninstallment loans	3,087	6,768	13,173	25,099	33,049
Single payment loans	845	1,821	4,507	9,675	13,241
Charge accounts	1,645	3,367	5,329	7,968	9,829
Service credit	597	1,580	3,337	7,456	9,979

Source: *Federal Reserve Bulletin.*

University of Michigan, found that 59 to 67 percent of all families headed by those under 35 years of age, had incurred installment debt. "Young people are apparently willing to incur debt regardless of their income level. Furthermore, at each income level the incidence of installment debt declines with increasing age." "A large proportion of credit users in the younger age brackets apparently remain in debt most of the time," the Federal Reserve noted.

Credit Cards Are In, Paper Money Out, For Cornell Dining

Just as Marco Polo told incredulous Europeans that paper was being used as money in Cathay, so now travelers from Ithaca report that paper money will no longer buy sustenance at the academic caravanserai there.

Over the protest of a handful of humanists, plastic credit cards have been issued to members of the Cornell University faculty club. Cash is no longer accepted for meals.

Until a fortnight ago, one holdout insisted on paying in legal tender, even in the face of a 10 per cent penalty for cash.

It transpired that the School of Hotel Administration, which operates the faculty club, had installed the new computer credit system last January, partly to train students for their careers in what it calls the hospitality industry. It explained that the system had cost $25,000, and the faculty would simply have to contribute its share.

On this argument, the issue was put to a vote at a club meeting on May 8. On a motion to amend the house rules retroactively, the vote was 35-to-4 for plastic credit cards, instead of legal tender.

New York Times, May 23, 1974.

Families with incomes of $7,500 to $15,000 seem most likely to be credit users. After age 54, the older the family head the smaller the percentage of disposable personal income which is used for making installment payments. For example, some 59 percent of the families in the 18 to 24 and 68 percent in the 25 to 34 year-old groups had 10 percent or more of their disposable income committed to repayment of installment credit. By contrast, only 14 percent of those 65 and over had 10 percent or more of their disposable income committed to repayment of installment credit.

The most favorable attitudes toward installment buying were, as expected, found among the younger age groups. The most frequent argument advanced in favor of borrowing was that it was the only way that many families could buy certain things they needed. On the other hand, a sizable percentage held that credit encourages overspending and is expensive. The extensive use of credit coupled with the increasing rate of inflation has caused 3 in every 100 families to over extend themselves, with the expectation of the numbers rising to as many as 10 of every 100 families.[1]

The Nature of Consumer Debt

The use of consumer credit predominates in the purchase of durable goods. Of the total of $180 billion of consumer credit, some $147 billion is in installment debt, of which automobile paper accounts for about 34 percent of the total, as may be seen in Figure 4–1.

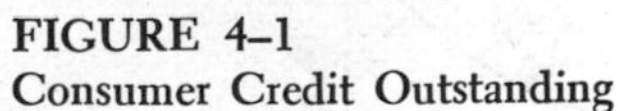

FIGURE 4–1
Consumer Credit Outstanding

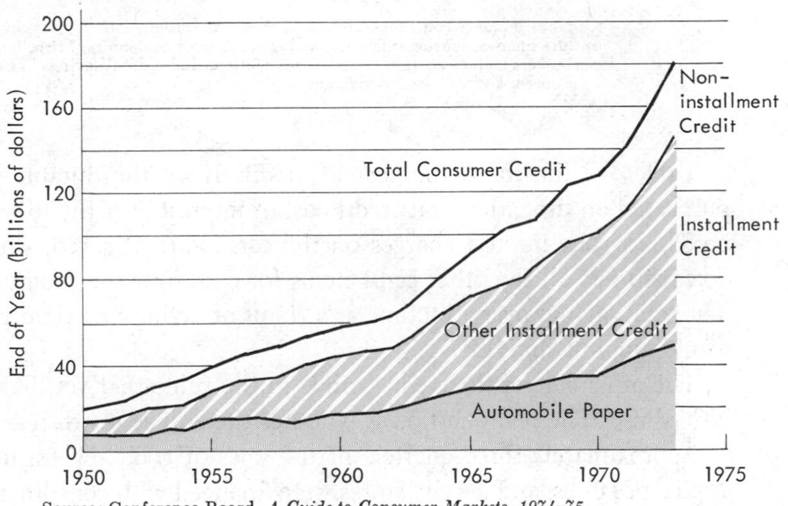

Source: Conference Board, *A Guide to Consumer Markets, 1974–75.*

Credit is used in the purchase of 66 percent of new cars and 49 percent of used cars. Almost half of purchasing families with incomes under $10,000 used credit to buy consumer durables such as appliances and furniture, while only one third of the purchasers with incomes exceeding $10,000 made use of installment credit. The sources of installment credit may be seen in Figure 4–2.

---

[1] Statement by Robert Gibson, President of the National Foundation for Consumer Credit which provides free counseling for families in financial trouble.

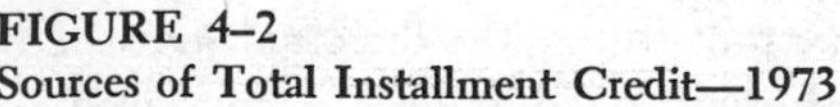

FIGURE 4–2
Sources of Total Installment Credit—1973

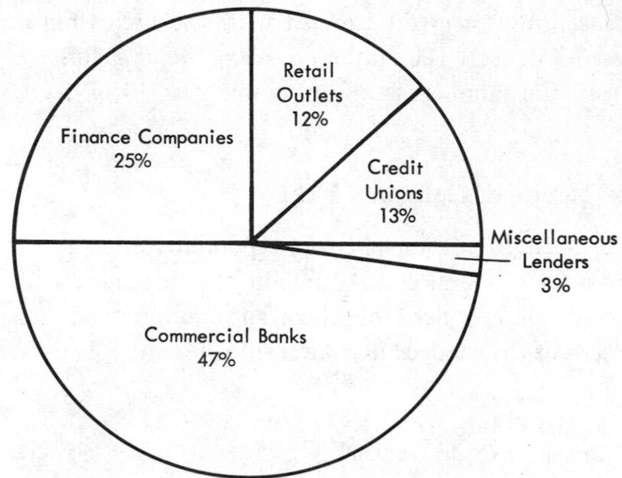

Note: Finance companies consist of those institutions formerly classified as sales finance, consumer finance, and other finance companies. Miscellaneous lenders include savings and loan associations and mutual savings banks.
Source: Federal Reserve System.

Table 4–2 illustrates the cost of credit. If all the durable items were purchased on time, the total credit cost of interest over the life span would be $8,128. The interest charges on the cars alone, if saved, would be sufficient to buy all the other eight items for cash over the family's life span. The total savings over a lifetime as a result of saving first then buying later would amount to $41,057.

The other side of the credit coin is in the value that you have from the NOW use. The real question is whether the cost is worth it to you.

Approximately three quarters of the sales of goods by furniture stores, appliance stores, and jewelry stores were financed with consumer credit and more than half the sales made by men's clothing stores, women's apparel stores, department stores, and mail-order houses were likewise financed.

Credit granting has changed completely within one generation. In the past, neighborhood food stores and company stores "locked in" customers by carrying accounts until payday, while nonfood retail chains insisted on cash purchases. Today the supermarket is almost completely cash while stores like Sears (almost 60 percent of its total sales are now on credit), Montgomery Ward (almost 50 percent), and J. C. Penney have revised this former cash only policy.[2]

[2] *Credit World*, vol. 58, no. 6 (March, 1970), p. 10.

TABLE 4–2
Cash Difference in "Buy Now–Pay Later" versus "Save Now–Buy Later"

	I	II	III	IV	V	VI	VII	VIII
	Cash Price per Item	*Number Bought over Family Life-Span*	*Total Cash Price over Family Life-Span*	*Total Cost over Family Life-Span If Bought on Credit 18%/yr. (12%/yr. for auto)*	*Total Credit Costs over Life-Span @ 18%/yr. (12%/yr. for auto)*	*Total Amount Saved If Monthly Credit Payment Saved Instead @ 4%/yr. Compounded Quarterly*	*Amount Interest Earned on Savings over and above Cash Price*	*Total Saved If Bought for Cash from Prior Savings*
Refrigerators	$ 300	3	$ 900	$ 1,068.75	$ 168.75	$ 1,232.24	$ 332.24	$ 500.99
Ranges	280	3	840	997.50	157.50	1,148.89	308.89	466.39
Washing machines	230	5	1,150	1,365.63	215.63	1,710.87	560.87	776.50
Automatic toasters	18	3	54	55.22	1.22	56.37	2.37	3.59
Electric sewing machines	135	2	270	320.62	50.62	554.12	284.12	334.74
Television sets	275	4	1,100	1,306.25	206.25	1,569.32	469.32	675.57
Vacuum sweepers	67	3	201	219.09	18.09	237.53	36.53	54.62
Living room rugs	150	3	450	534.38	84.38	615.50	165.50	249.88
Automobiles	3,255	13*	26,040†	33,266.08	7,226.08	56,808.94	30,768.94	37,995.02
Totals	$4,710		$31,005	$39,133.52	$18,128.52	$63,933.78	$32,928.78	$41,057.30‡

I. Average (mean) price of items rated by *Consumers Report* rounded off to even dollars.

II. Number bought over life-span based on service life expectancy of these items in USDA Report by Gail Pennock, divided into family life-span of 45 years (45 years calculated from average life expectancy of men and women today 69.9 years, and average marriage age—twenty years woman, 24 years man).

III. Column I times Column II. Cost per item times number of items bought over life-span.

IV. Column IV derived from use of constant ratio formula: $I = rp(n + 1)/2m$, where r = rate (18% or 12% for automobiles), p = principal, n = total number of installment payments, m = total number of installment payments in one year (12 months), and I = dollar amount of interest. I times Column II plus Column III = Column IV. (Assume installment payment period of two years.)

V. Column IV minus Column III = Interest only on those transactions.

VI. Savings based on monthly credit payment (derived from Column IV divided by Column II divided by 24 months each) equals monthly credit payment which is instead placed in savings account each month, earning 4% per year compounded quarterly. Method of compounding used equals 4% per year = 4.06% per year = (.0406). (The amount of interest earned on that installment payment if saved) plus Column IV = total amount saved.

VII. Column VI minus Column III. The amount left over after savings (over the equivalent installment period) has been used to pay cash for the item. The balance over and above the cash price is considered as "savings."

VIII. Column V plus Column VII. Interest saved by not making installment payment plus interest, on monthly savings over and above cash price equals total amount saved compounded over 45 years, total difference between these two methods of payment over life span of 45 years.

* Estimate. Usually the average American one-car family buys eight cars over its life-span.

† Although the average price per car was $3,255, the average additional dollar expenditure in purchasing another car was something like $2,003. Waddell therefore included the trade-in value and used the additional amount of dollar expenditure as the appropriate figure.

‡ Difference between "buying now–paying later" and "saving now–buying later" on these nine items (assuming installment payment period of two years per item).

Source: Frederick E. Waddell, "A-Borrowing, A-Sorrowing," *Journal of Consumer Affairs*, vol. 4, no. 1 (Summer, 1970), pp. 42–43.

"I stand for more credit, gentlemen! . . . we must give to the people who haven't money, the opportunity to spend it! . . ."

Courtesy: George Lichty, Publishers Newspaper Syndicate.

To sum up, of total consumer credit, installment credit is four times the volume of noninstallment credit. The financing of consumer durables has been the major factor in changes in consumer installment credit extensions and, in recent years, has amounted to between 60 and 70 percent of all installment credit extended during each year. Although noninstallment charge accounts are still a major form of consumer credit, they grew at a slower rate than installment sales.

Consumer credit in recent years has become easier and easier to obtain. Indeed, the consumer's problem is more how to resist it than how to get it. Merchants have found that it increases their volume. Customers buy more; and if they are tied to a store by a charge account or an installment contract, they tend to come back to that particular store because their credit is now known—has been established—and the initial red tape involved in opening an account need not be repeated.

THE CHARGE ACCOUNT

Charge accounts not so many years ago wore a sign of prestige. Only a limited number enjoyed the privilege of saying, "Charge it, please." Today charge accounts are a vital part of retail merchandising, and over half of all retail sales are done on a charge basis. Charge or "open account" purchases differ in a number of ways from installment purchases. Charge accounts do not call for a down payment; most installment transactions do. To installment prices are added carrying charges, which may or may not be disguised. Charge purchasers do not pay this extra cost for the use of credit; it is merged in the price of the article itself, which is paid by cash customers too. For very slow payment of end of month bills, a few stores used to add on a small carrying charge. On the other hand, many stores allowed charges to run up to 90 days without penalty. The average "30 day" account, a retail credit survey revealed, averaged 60–74 days, varying with the line of business. Now all charges are governed by the Consumer Credit Protection Act, known as the Truth in Lending law. For the customer who buys on a charge account, there is usually no contract to be signed and hence no right of repossession by the dealer should the customer fail to pay. That is, when you purchase on a charge account, you get title to the goods purchased. In most installment sales, title does not pass until the final installment is paid.

Revolving Credit

In recent years the charge account has become a flexible or revolving charge account. When merchants perceived that many customers were slow in paying at the end of 30 days, they decided to capitalize on this situation by imposing a finance charge and urging customers to add to their balances due by making additional purchases and permitting repayments in installments over 10 months. As the balance was reduced, additional purchases could build up the balance due and stretch out the required time to pay. This was, in a way, the adaptation of the "line of credit" concept which commercial bankers applied to business customers. It is also called open end credit.

Cost of Charge Accounts

The Consumer Credit Protection Act of 1968 requires that you be told how the finance charge is determined. This includes a statement of what is defined as an unpaid balance and what percentage is used to compute the finance charge.

Let's use the example of 1.5 percent per month. This seems to be an 18 percent (1.5 × 12) annual percentage rate, but it and your dollar charge will vary depending on the interpretation of unpaid balance. If a store does not credit partial repayments made during a billing period, but calculates the charge on the total, the result will be drastically different from what it would cost you if the partial payment had been taken into account. In a number of states there are suits pending in state courts challenging the 18 percent annual percentage interest rate on revolving open end credit accounts as violating the state usury laws. Some rates thus have been revealed to be higher than allowed under the usury laws of some states. On the other hand, you may appear to pay a lower rate because you may be billed several days after your purchase.

The store's bills must show the following information: the previous balance owed, date of transactions, the closing or billing date, payments made, new balance, finance charge with explanation, the required minimum payment, and its time deadline to avoid additional finance charges.

Figure 4–3 illustrates the old and new ways a department store handles the billing and unpaid balance. Table 4–3 shows how your unpaid balance faces varying finance charges in different states.

Methods of Computing Finance Charges—Open End Credit

1. *The previous balance method* is the most common and most expensive method to the consumer. If there is any balance left outstanding

FIGURE 4–3(a)
Illustrates the Old Monthly Statement

BILLING DATE	BALANCE FROM LAST BILL	CHARGES	CREDITS	PAYMENTS	BALANCE DUE
SEP 4 10	92.02	1.59		92.02	1.59

PAYMENTS, CREDITS, OR PURCHASES WHICH ARE NOT SHOWN ON THIS BILL WILL APPEAR ON YOUR NEXT MONTH'S STATEMENT.

INQUIRY REGARDING ANY ITEM SHOULD BE ACCOMPANIED BY THE SALES CHECK OR CREDIT SLIP.

BILLS ARE PAYABLE WHEN RENDERED.

SAKS FIFTH AVENUE, NEW YORK WHITE PLAINS • SPRINGFIELD • GARDEN CITY • BALA-CYNWYD • CHEVY CHASE • ATLANTA • CHICAGO • SKOKIE DETROIT • TROY • PHOENIX • BEVERLY HILLS • PALM SPRINGS • LA JOLLA • SAN FRANCISCO • PALO ALTO • ASPEN • PITTSBURGH • ST. LOUIS MIAMI BEACH • SURFSIDE • PALM BEACH • FORT LAUDERDALE • PRINCETON • NEW HAVEN • CAMBRIDGE • ANN ARBOR • SOUTHAMPTON • PETOSKEY

FIGURE 4–3(b)
Illustrates Method Required under Truth in Lending

Saks Fifth Avenue
611 FIFTH AVENUE, NEW YORK, N.Y. 10022

ACCOUNT NUMBER

11

OPTION ACCOUNT
CYCLE
MINIMUM PAYMENT DUE
$136.00

PLEASE SHOW ANY ADDRESS CHANGE

NUMBER AND STREET

CITY STATE ZIP CODE

$ AMOUNT ENCLOSED

PLEASE RETURN THIS PORTION WITH YOUR PAYMENT

REGULAR ACCOUNT TERMS: FULL PAYMENT OF NEW BALANCE IS DUE UPON RECEIPT OF STATEMENT.

OPTION ACCOUNT TERMS: YOU MAY PAY THE ENTIRE NEW BALANCE WITHIN 25 DAYS OF THE CLOSING DATE PRINTED ON THIS STATEMENT TO AVOID ADDITIONAL **FINANCE CHARGES.**

OR

IF YOU CHOOSE TO MAKE A PARTIAL PAYMENT (NOT LESS THAN THE MINIMUM PAYMENT DUE AS SHOWN ABOVE), A **FINANCE CHARGE** WILL BE ADDED, COMPUTED ON THE PREVIOUS BALANCE AFTER DEDUCTING PAYMENTS AND CREDITS AS PER THE SCHEDULE BELOW. IF A **FINANCE CHARGE** IS SHOWN IT WAS COMPUTED IN THIS SAME MANNER.

PAST DUE $38.00

REFERENCE MO DAY NO.	STORE	CHARGES	CREDITS	PAYMENTS
0530232	30	8.00		
0530232	30	10.30		
0530235	30	57.50		
0530233	30	22.00		
0530234	30	122.00		
0530232	30	10.80		
0530235	30	88.00		
0605029	30	38.00		
0605030	30	5.50		
0605003	30		36.00	
0611612	88	30.90		

BALANCE PAST DUE. PLEASE REMIT MINIMUM PAYMENT.
IF ALREADY PAID, THANK YOU.

CLOSING DATE MONTH DAY YEAR	PREVIOUS BALANCE	PAYMENTS & CREDITS	BALANCE SUBJECT TO FINANCE CHARGE	OPTION ACCOUNT FINANCE CHARGE	CHARGES	▼ NEW BALANCE ▼
061274	23258	3600	19658	294	39300	59252

ITEMS NOT SHOWN SHOULD APPEAR ON THE NEXT STATEMENT.
INQUIRIES SHOULD BE ACCOMPANIED BY SALES CHECK OR CREDIT SLIP

NEW YORK TELEPHONES: TO ORDER MERCHANDISE (212) PL3-4000
FOR SERVICE INQUIRIES (212) 691-1700

SAKS FIFTH AVENUE, NEW YORK SEE REVERSE SIDE FOR ALL STORE LOCATIONS

OPTION ACCOUNT - SCHEDULE OF **FINANCE CHARGES**

BALANCE SUBJECT TO FINANCE CHARGE	MONTHLY PERIODIC RATE	ANNUAL PERCENTAGE RATE
TO $ 500	1.50 %	18.00 %
OVER $ 500	1.00 %	12.00 %

at the end of the current period, the interest charged is figured on the amount outstanding at the beginning of the period. For example, you owe $200 at the beginning of February, and the finance charge is 1.5 percent per month or 18 percent per year. During February you paid $100. However, when the new balance is figured at the end of February, the 1.5 percent finance charge is figured on the $200 beginning balance (not the $100 ending balance) for a charge of $3.

2. *The average daily balance method* is less expensive for the consumer than the previous balance method. The finance charge is based on the average amount per day which you owe during the previous month. For example, suppose that you owe $200 on February 1 and that on February 14 you pay off $100. For the first 14 days of the month your balance was

TABLE 4–3
State Variations in Finance Charge Regulations

If You Reside in the State of	*Amount Subject to Finance Charge*	*Monthly Rate (%)*	*Annual Rate (%)*
Arizona California	$1,000 or less Over $1,000	1.5 1	18 12
Connecticut	Entire	1	12
Florida Georgia Illinois Maryland Massachusetts Michigan New Jersey New York Texas	$500 or less Over $500	1.5 1	18 12
Missouri	$500 or less Over $500	1.5 .75	18 9
Pennsylvania	Entire	1.25	15

therefore $200, and for the last 14 days your balance was $100. Thus the average daily balance for February was $150. The 1.5 percent finance charge is then taken on the $150 average daily balance for a charge of $2.25.

3. *The adjusted balance method* is clearly the least expensive of the three major methods, since the finance charge is based upon the remaining balance at the end of the month. Thus, the 1.5 percent finance charge would be figured on the $100 balance at the end of the month of February for a charge of $1.50. Retailers obviously are not too eager to use the adjusted balance method because it keeps the finance charges relatively low.

Many stores are switching to the average daily balance method because of mounting criticism of the previous balance method which had formerly been favored. If you have not understood your billing statement, and don't actually know what you are paying, as you can see it can be costly. The adjusted balance method is obviously better for the customer.

TABLE 4–4
Comparison of Computing Charges

Method	*Opening Balance Owed*	*Payments*	*Monthly Rate of Finance Charge*	*Actual Charge*	*Annual Rate of Finance Charge*
Previous balance	$200	$100	1.5%	0.015 × $200 = 3.00	36%
Average daily balance	200	100	1.5	0.015 × 150 = 2.25	27
Adjusted balance	200	100	1.5	0.015 × 100 = 1.50	18

Whichever the method, if the bill arrives within a day or so of the payment date, it is almost inevitable that a late payment results and angry, confused consumers complain of unfair service charges. The new Fair Credit Billing Act of 1974 now requires that bills be mailed at least 14 days before payments are due. If you check your bill to note how long it takes the company to post your payment from the day you sent it, it will help avoid late payments and you can also squeeze out a little extra "free" time.

Billing error caused by human or computer, is also receiving attention under another section. Within 30 days from the time a creditor mails his statement, a consumer who thinks there is an error must send a written, detailed notice of his complaint by registered or certified mail. The creditor can take no legal action nor communicate unfavorable credit information within the next 60 day period—subject to penalties, but must by that time either make the appropriate correction or show in writing why the original bill is correct.

The customer should also be careful lest any credits for overpayment or returns which may be unused for a while, do not disappear from the monthly statement and then from the account if it lies dormant for a while and the statement ceases to be sent.

Opening a Charge Account

To open a charge account is a simple matter. Application is made at the credit office, where a form is filled out giving such information as the name, address, age, spouse's name, employer's name and address, position held and length of service, names of other places where a charge account is maintained, and about three references, of which one is commonly the applicant's bank. If the applicant is a minor (usually under 21 years of age), a parent's or guardian's account will have to be used or have the account guaranteed by a parent or guardian.

A study of credit applications made in three metropolitan areas—Chicago, Milwaukee, and Minneapolis—of firms doing the major distribution of general merchandise there, the majority of whom operate on a nationwide scale, pointed out: "The 20 sample applications included 65 separate items varying in frequency of use from 100 percent to 5 percent—with a mean of 48 percent. There appears to be little consensus among credit managers as to what constitutes important information and consequently it may be concluded that a definitive rationale is lacking for requesting credit information."[3]

---

[3] Part I of a two-part study by Eugene F. Drzycimski of Marquette University, James E. Bell of Northern Illinois University, and William L. Kimball of Arthur Young & Co., March, 1970, p. 12.

Giving Credit to Women

Credit has not been a simple matter for women. As an example, a civil rights complaint was needed to prevent the Franklin State Bank of New Jersey from refusing an auto loan to a married woman (a financially independent attorney) without her husband's co-signature.[4]

Interest in the availability of credit for women sharpened after the National Commission on Consumer Finance held two days of hearings exclusively on this subject in 1972.

The First Women's Bank and Trust Company is about to open in New York. The president, Madeline McWhinney, formerly an economist for a federal reserve bank, promises "not to discriminate against men, either as employees or customers."[5]

In 1973 a group of Detroit women received a federal charter to start the Feminist Federal Credit Union.

To tell the story of these "exceptions" highlights the needs of the majority of women. In hearings on the subject of women and credit before the National Commission on Consumer Finance, Martha W. Griffiths, Congresswoman from Michigan, testified: "Men and women don't have equal access to credit. Banks, savings and loan associations, credit card companies, finance companies, insurance companies, retail stores, and even the federal government discriminate against women in extending credit. And they discriminate against women in all stages of life—whether single, married, divorced, or widowed; with or without children, rich or poor, young or old."[6] Retailers are slowly changing this policy under pressure, but it is not yet considered a right. J. C. Penney & Co. launched a campaign to give women credit cards in their own name—but the main office faced resistance in some branch credit offices. Montgomery Ward announced a screening program "to take all the subjectivity out of credit applications." But Sears, Roebuck appears to be discouraging separate credit cards for women—"very expensive for Sears to keep two accounts for one family."[7]

The credit head at one major retailing concern said, "This was sort of a shocker to us. Our business is primarily oriented to women. I'm afraid we didn't really know we had a problem."

The Retail Credit Co.—the nation's largest private investigator of individuals who apply for credit—agreed to honor requests by women to set up separate credit files in their own name so they can be evaluated independently.[8]

---

[4] Karolin Blackson, "Ms, Mrs. or Miss," *Consumer Credit Leader*, April 1974, p. 5.

[5] *Business Week*, January 12, 1974.

[6] *Wall Street Journal*, July 18, 1972.

[7] *Business Week*, January 12, 1974, p. 77.

[8] *Wall Street Journal*, April 25, 1974.

Lobbying, political pressure and media publicity by feminist groups achieved signal success through legislation in 1974. In one law equality was attained in the area of mortgage loans for residential housing where discrimination on the basis of sex is now forbidden. The other law which modified the Consumer Protection Act of 1968 becomes effective in October 1975. It bars discrimination in all types of consumer credit. The Federal Reserve Board must develop regulations within the year for various federal agencies to enforce. The Federal Trade Commission will supervise retail store credit, the Federal Deposit Insurance Corporation covers bank credit, and the Securities and Exchange Commission deals with stock transactions. The law provides for unlimited actual damages, but limits punitive damages to $10,000 per person. Provision for class action suits exist. On the state level 33 states prohibit credit discrimination against women.

Complications in legal property rights as well as tradition slow the elimination of discrimination. But finally, even when laws exist and guidelines have been changed, there is still a gap between policy and practice, between high level announcements and field operations.

The Credit Office and Investigation

The credit office contacts the references, usually by telephone or by sending forms to be completed and returned. In most of the larger cities the credit bureau can furnish all needed information about local applicants. The local credit bureau is a clearinghouse for the exchange of information among the merchants on the credit experience which each has had with the purchaser. Each firm supplies the bureau with all the details about its dealings with the credit applicant. The bureau is usually maintained by the joint contributions of all its members. A person with a good credit record may find that while waiting in the store's credit office, a phone call to the credit bureau may be sufficient to establish identity and past good record and permit the credit manager to approve the application without further delay.

If the credit applicant is unknown to the credit bureau, it will, at the store's request, make a detailed investigation of the applicant. Just what it looks for may be seen in Figure 4–4(a). If you have just moved from one city to another, the credit bureau in the city in which you are now applying for credit will get in touch with the credit bureau in the city in which you formerly resided via the national organization of credit bureaus, the Associated Credit Bureaus, Inc. In this way a person with a bad credit record may find it difficult to obtain credit anywhere in the country. Sometimes persons who fail to pay in one city and then move to another and establish themselves are located by the credit bureau network. The usual

FIGURE 4–4(a)

NAME AND ADDRESS OF CREDIT BUREAU MAKING REPORT

Credit Bureau of Anytown
1234 Main Street
Anytown, Anystate 95541

☐ IN FILE REPORT ☐ SINGLE REFERENCE ☐ TRADE REPORT
☐ EMPLOY & TRADE REPORT ☒ FULL REPORT ☐ PREVIOUS RESIDENCE REPORT

CONFIDENTIAL *Factbilt*® REPORT

FOR Bank of Anytown
P. O. Drawer Q
Anytown, Anystate 95542

Date Received 6/10/75
Date Mailed 6/12/75
In File Since 8/64

This information is furnished in response to an inquiry for the purpose of evaluating credit risks. It has been obtained from sources deemed reliable, the accuracy of which this organization does not guarantee. The inquirer has agreed to indemnify the reporting bureau for any damage arising from misuse of this information, and this report is furnished in reliance upon that indemnity. It must be held in strict confidence, and must not be revealed to the subject reported on, except by reporting agency in accordance with the Fair Credit Reporting Act.

REPORT ON (SURNAME):	MR., MRS., MISS, MS.	GIVEN NAME:	SOCIAL SECURITY NUMBER:	SPOUSE'S NAME:
ROGERS	Mr.	Andrew M.	562-24-2716	Laura

ADDRESS:	CITY:	STATE:	ZIP CODE:	SINCE:
10313 Spring St.	Anytown,	Anystate	95544	10/67

COMPLETE TO HERE FOR TRADE REPORT AND SKIP TO CREDIT HISTORY

PRESENT EMPLOYER	POSITION HELD:	SINCE:	DATE EMPLOY VERIFIED	EST. MONTHLY INCOME
Smith Hardware	Asst Mgr	5/70	6/11/75	$ 975

COMPLETE TO HERE FOR EMPLOYMENT AND TRADE REPORT AND SKIP TO CREDIT HISTORY

DATE OF BIRTH	NUMBER OF DEPENDENTS INCLUDING SELF:			
1/16/43	3	☒ OWNS OR BUYING HOME	☐ RENTS HOME	☐ OTHER: (EXPLAIN)

FORMER ADDRESS:	CITY:	STATE:	FROM:	TO:
Route 1 Box 85	That town	Anystate	12/65	10/67

FORMER EMPLOYER:	POSITION HELD:	FROM:	TO:	EST. MONTHLY INCOME
Crown Box Co	Foreman	8/64	5/70	$ 640

SPOUSE'S EMPLOYER	POSITION HELD:	SINCE:	DATE EMPLOY VERIFIED	EST. MONTHLY INCOME
Berg's Dept Store	Salesperson	4/72	6/11/75	$ 500

CREDIT HISTORY *(Complete this section for all reports)*

KIND OF BUSINESS	DATE REPORTED	DATE ACCOUNT OPENED	DATE OF LAST SALE	HIGHEST CREDIT	AMOUNT OWING	AMOUNT PAST DUE	TERMS OF SALE AND USUAL MANNER OF PAYMENT
B-451	6/11/75	1965	10/74	4,500	3,750	-	I-$90-1
D-888	"	1967	3/72	1,200	-	-	0-1
C-642	"	9/70	1/74	470	370	-	R-$20-1
H-509	4/10/75	4/68	2/71	1876	780	-	I-$50-1

Public Record - Financing statement 3/12/70 filed by City Loan Corp $1,000.

Source: Associated Credit Bureaus, Inc.

credit investigation is made by phoning the applicant's landlord, employer, bank, and trade references.

Credit bureaus are now using computers and to facilitate exchange of information a "Common Language" has been adopted. The common language is a code which uses a set of numerals combined with letters to tell everything the credit grantor wants to know about an individual's paying habits [see Figure 4–4(b)].[9]

[9] See "How To Use Form 100" and "How To Use The Common Language," Associated Credit Bureaus, Houston, Texas.

FIGURE 4–4(b)
Common Language for Consumer Credit

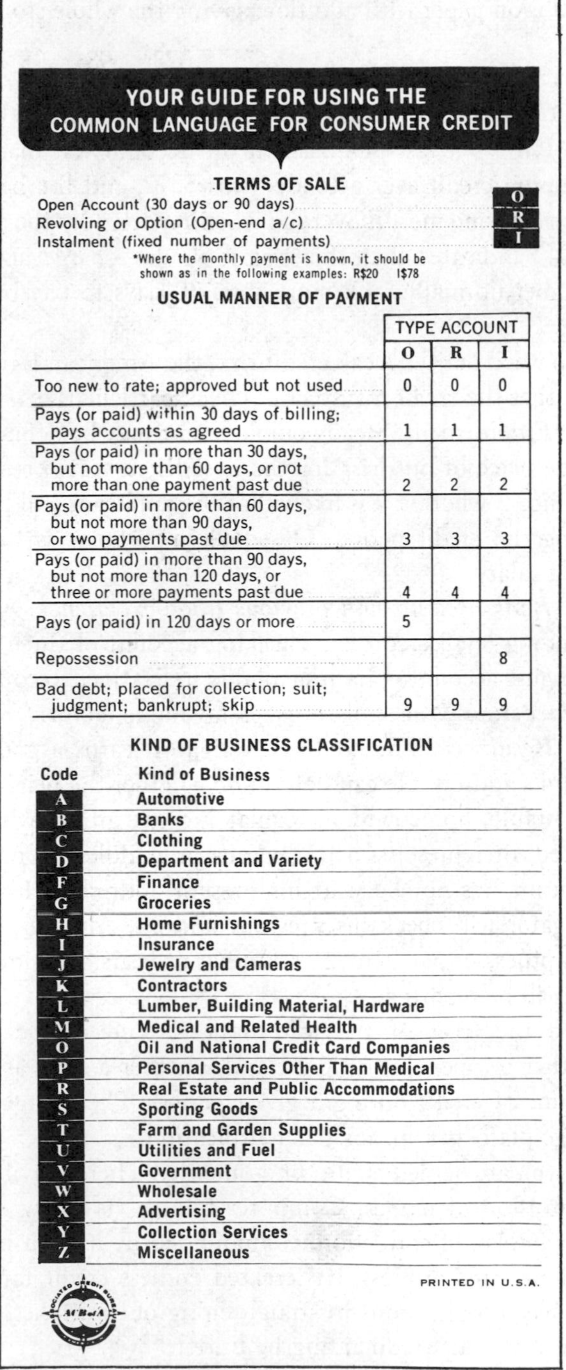

YOUR GUIDE FOR USING THE COMMON LANGUAGE FOR CONSUMER CREDIT

TERMS OF SALE

Open Account (30 days or 90 days)	O
Revolving or Option (Open-end a/c)	R
Instalment (fixed number of payments)	I

*Where the monthly payment is known, it should be shown as in the following examples: R$20 I$78

USUAL MANNER OF PAYMENT

	TYPE ACCOUNT		
	O	R	I
Too new to rate; approved but not used	0	0	0
Pays (or paid) within 30 days of billing; pays accounts as agreed	1	1	1
Pays (or paid) in more than 30 days, but not more than 60 days, or not more than one payment past due	2	2	2
Pays (or paid) in more than 60 days, but not more than 90 days, or two payments past due	3	3	3
Pays (or paid) in more than 90 days, but not more than 120 days, or three or more payments past due	4	4	4
Pays (or paid) in 120 days or more	5		
Repossession			8
Bad debt; placed for collection; suit; judgment; bankrupt; skip	9	9	9

KIND OF BUSINESS CLASSIFICATION

Code	Kind of Business
A	Automotive
B	Banks
C	Clothing
D	Department and Variety
F	Finance
G	Groceries
H	Home Furnishings
I	Insurance
J	Jewelry and Cameras
K	Contractors
L	Lumber, Building Material, Hardware
M	Medical and Related Health
O	Oil and National Credit Card Companies
P	Personal Services Other Than Medical
R	Real Estate and Public Accommodations
S	Sporting Goods
T	Farm and Garden Supplies
U	Utilities and Fuel
V	Government
W	Wholesale
X	Advertising
Y	Collection Services
Z	Miscellaneous

PRINTED IN U.S.A.

Source: Associated Credit, Bureaus, Inc.

How does the common language of credit reporting work?

A credit record reported as, "dee, oh–two," in a verbal report would look like this on paper with additions giving the whole story:

D 5/67 5/74 372 98 98 0–2

"D" is a department store where the consumer has been a customer since May 1967. The last purchase on the account was made in May 1974. The maximum credit ever extended was $372, and the balance owed was $98, which was one month overdue when reported by the store.

"0–2 indicates that this was a 30 day charge account. However, the customer normally took more than 30 days to pay but not more than 60 days.

To weed out the weak credit risk, the American Bankers Association suggests that the credit investigator check particularly:

a. Employment. Steady employment may be defined as being employed at one place of business for the past three years or more. Of primary importance is whether it is likely that the applicant will be gainfully employed during the credit period. Of equal importance is the verification of the stated salary.

b. Bank account and previous trade experience. A favorable feature in extending retail credit is a checking account of three figures or more. The two figure account is an unfavorable indication. Record of prompt payment at other stores is also, of course, a favorable factor.

c. Residence. The credit investigator learns a good deal from the applicant's address. He can determine whether the neighborhood is inhabited by a stable, homeowning, regular income group; whether the area is depressed, or represents a prosperous or middle income community. If the applicant has not been at his present address at least two years, the investigator will check his previous address. Also, the amount of rent and promptness of payment, the number of years of residence, and type of section will be reported.

On the basis of the information received, the credit office decides whether to open the account and whether a limit is to be placed on the amount of credit during a given period. The charge customer is given a charge plate as a means of identification.

If you are denied credit, find out why. There may have been an error, or a confusion of names. Computer billing, its many errors and slow, frustrating delay in correction, compounded by human mistakes in input and machine stubbornness, has created endless credit tangles. Despite the incredible complications in straightening out mistakes, it is essential to persevere lest your credit rating be hurt.

Fair Credit Reporting Act

Until recently a credit report was a secret document that might contain fact, error, fiction, hearsay, or invalid information unavailable to you but not necessarily to others whom you might not want to see it. Since April 25, 1971, the federal Fair Credit Reporting Act closed your file to snoopers and opened it to you. Unless you permit it or a court order compels it, your records are restricted to those—including government agencies—who must evaluate you for credit, insurance, or employment. Information may not be reported after it has become obsolete, i.e., 14 years after bankruptcies, or 7 for unfavorable matters, such as suits, judgments, liens, records of arrest, indictment, or conviction of a crime, except when the transaction involves credit on life insurance of $50,000 or more, or a job paying at least $20,000 annually.

If the consumer thinks a bank or credit file may contain unfair remarks, the information and the source may be requested in writing or by providing proper identification in person or by telephone. The law provides stiff penalties against persons who obtain a consumer credit report under false pretenses. If the consumer questions the information, the agency must reinvestigate and then, at no cost to the consumer, must inform those who have received employment reports within the preceding two years or credit reports within the last six months, concerning the results of the new investigation.

The consumer must be given written notice if personal interviews (of friends and others) are to be used in a credit investigation, and the consumer has the right to request disclosure of the nature and scope of the interview.

When making a consumer report, a consumer reporting agency must reverify all information which is not a matter of public information, if it has been more than three months since the adverse information was received.

Any person who, based on a consumer's credit report, increases the charge for, or denies a consumer credit or insurance, must inform the consumer of this action and provide the name and address of the reporting agency that furnished the report. The user of the report must also inform the consumer that if a written request is made within 60 days, the user will disclose the nature of the information.

A consumer can bring a civil damage suit against the agency or information user for willfully or negligently violating the act.

The Fair Credit Reporting Act is enforced by the Bureau of Consumer Protection in the Federal Trade Commission. Violations are subject to "cease and desist orders." Each violation of such an order is punishable by a $5,000 fine. The law also authorizes consumers to sue violators for damages. Punitive damages, as well as actual damages, may be imposed without specified limits, for willful violations.

The Fair Credit Reporting Act provides that you cannot be charged for an interview with a credit bureau, if within 30 days you have either been denied credit because of a credit report from a credit bureau or have received a notice from a collection department affiliated with the credit bureau. Under the same conditions, you cannot be charged for notification to previous recipients that information is being deleted from your file or for the addition of an explanatory statement.

Under certain circumstances, a credit bureau may make a reasonable charge for a consumer interview, but it must advise the applicant in advance of any charges. Complaints have come to the Federal Trade Commission that fees as high as $25 have been charged a consumer by credit reporting agencies for showing a consumer what is in the credit file—this under the guise of a "reasonable fee."[10] There have even been charges when the consumer has merely inquired of the existence of a file. Furthermore, it is alleged that credit bureau personnel do not fully disclose the information, but instead consumers must be able to interrogate, to ask the right questions in order to get the information they have a right to know.

You had to take the interviewer's word that all information had been disclosed. Files are not always updated. Name mix-ups are a problem. Following charges before FTC, hearings, and newspaper headlines on inaccurate reporting by investigators, one of the nation's largest credit investigation reporting companies agreed to allow individuals to read its reports on them to see for themselves what the files said.[11] Credit investigators told a Senate hearing of fees based on the number of reports completed each day—of consequent "zinging" or making-up information and reports. Witnesses gave examples of derogatory information based on rumor, gossip, and guess work.

Federal Trade Commission Chairman Lewis A. Engman objects to anonymity of sources ". . . if the investigative reporting industry cannot utilize sources that can be revealed—when it is these same sources whose personal opinions or observations contribute to denial of credit, insurance, or employment—then these sources are better not used at all."[12]

---

[10] Reported by Basil J. Mezines, Executive Director, Federal Trade Commission, in an address on the Fair Credit Reporting Act, June 15, 1971, New Orleans, La. For a free copy of *Consumers, Credit Bureaus, and the Fair Credit Reporting Act*, write Associated Credit Bureaus, Inc., 6767 Southwest Freeway, Houston, Texas 77036.

[11] *Wall Street Journal*, April 4, 1974.

[12] *U.S. News & World Report*, March 18, 1974; *Money*, February 1974; *Business Week*, April 6, 1974.

CREDIT CARDS

You may aspire to the fascinating world of credit cards and expense accounts. *The New York Times* reported on a man who did in a large and fraudulent way: "A 29 year old Alabamian landed at Kennedy Airport and was taken into custody after a $27,278 tour of Europe that he was accused of financing with a Diners' Club card, which he had obtained with a check that bounced." He had spent eight months in Europe running up bills at some of the finest hotels in Rome, Paris, Vienna, and Zurich, where he was arrested, while trying to rent a car and buy a watch.

Go now and pay later. Eat and charge it. It's the new way of life, and if you become a professional or an organization man, you will probably join the ranks of the millions who currently carry general purpose credit cards. The big three in this field are Diners' Club, American Express, and Carte Blanche. Half of all American families use at least one credit card. The average family has three, with the ones most widely held good only at a particular store or chain of stores. Use is above average among families with higher income, more education, young families with children, and families living in the suburbs.[13] The use of credit cards is directly related to the level of family income. Figure 4–5, for example, shows that 81 percent of families making at least $25,000 a year use a credit card. Despite this, a survey found that 75 percent of all persons interviewed said credit cards make it too easy to buy things they may not really want, or can afford. Half of all credit card holders use the debt feature of their credit cards the survey found. Lower and middle income families tend to value the credit feature of the cards more than the service benefits.

You can rent a car, stay at a hotel or motel, dine at expense account restaurants, hire an African safari, put your horse up at a Las Vegas horse motel where oats are free, buy anything from a mink coat to a salami, arrange bail, take a plane trip, make a long distance phone call to Tokyo or Teheran or Tallahassee, buy gasoline, or obtain an advance of cash, or pay your income tax up to $500 or medical, dental or hospital bills, all on credit cards. You can even play luncheon Russian roulette. A group of businessmen started it. Credit cards are laid face down on the table and the waiter picks one to pay the bill. Even culture comes via the credit card, thanks to an arrangement between the American Ballet Theatre and Diners' Club, and your credit card enables you to phone a reservation for the Metropolitan Opera!

In addition to the general purpose credit cards, there are gasoline cards issued by the oil companies, retail credit cards, telephone credit cards from

---

[13] Lewis Mandell, *Credit Card Use in the U.S.*, Institute for Social Research, Univ. of Michigan, Ann Arbor, Michigan, 1972.

FIGURE 4–5
Credit Card Use by Annual Family Income

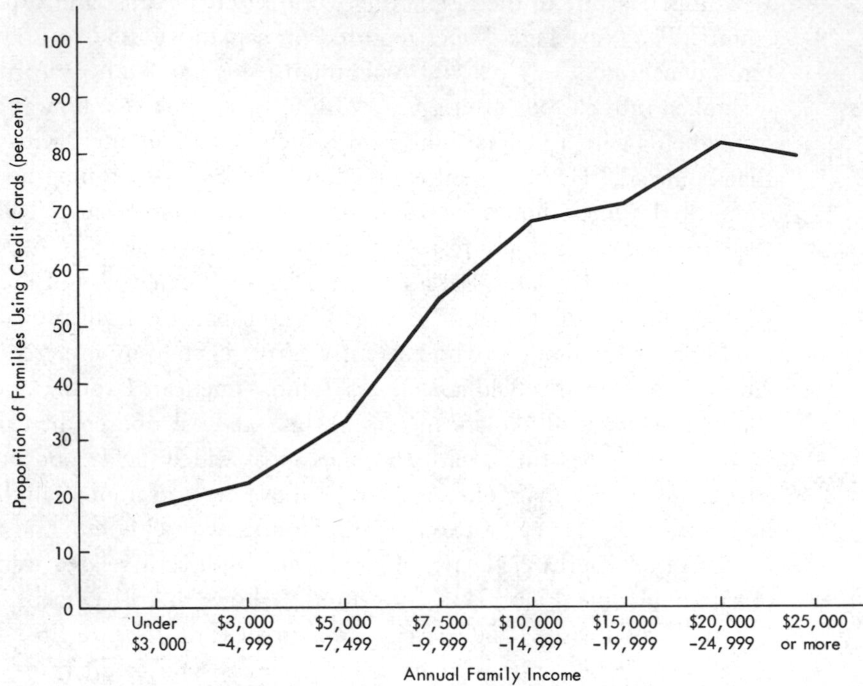

Source: Lewis Mandell, *Credit Card Use in the United States*, Institute of Social Research, University of Michigan, Ann Arbor, Michigan.

A.T.&T.; air travel cards of the Universal Air Travel Plan; car rental credit cards; and railroad travel cards good on almost all U.S. railroads; a total of 500 million credit cards. Paying cash has almost become passé. Sometimes a merchant will examine a bill more carefully to see if it is counterfeit than he will the signature on a credit card to see if it is genuine. "Plastic credit" can provide four months interest free use of money if you use the cards just after the billing date. Cards can be a source of quick cash loans. Multiple use of credit cards is shown in Table 4–5.

As has been said, "Debt is sinful, but charging is chic."

"Only the bank cards and travel and entertainment cards are intended to return a profit to their issuers. The oil companies and department stores use cards principally as marketing tools designed to solidify customer loyalty and increase sales."[14]

Credit investigations are quite costly to the general purpose credit card

[14] Irwin Ross, "The Credit Card's Painful Coming-of-Age," *Fortune* magazine, October 1971.

TABLE 4-5
Use of Combinations of Credit Cards (percentage distribution of families)

Type of Card Used	*Proportion of Families Who Use* Gasoline Cards	Bank Cards	Travel and Entertainment Cards	Store Cards
Gasoline cards	100	34	20	64
Bank cards	71	100	27	68
Travel and entertainment cards	72	47	100	63
Store cards	63	31	16	100

Note: The table reads: Of families who make use of bank credit cards, 71 percent also use gasoline credit cards.
Source: Lewis Mandell; *Credit Card Use in the United States.* Institute of Social Research—University of Michigan—Ann Arbor.

organizations, and they are now requiring a certain income level and upping their rejection rates, partly because of campaigns in various states to lower the finance charge by mandatory legislation. But at the same time, American Express now issues to the established card member a supplementary card, for an added small fee, for wife or child. It also issues an executive credit card (gold) if there is a participating bank in your area—which then enables you to draw on a line of credit amounting to $2,000 or more, permits deferred payment on all charges over $100 at your request, and is an open sesame to emergency funds in travelers checks, up to $500 in the United States and up to $1,000 in areas where a passport is needed.

The credit card companies cover costs and earn profits by charging members an annual fee, and by making deductions on the restaurant and other bills the companies pay on behalf of cardholders. Approximately three fourths of all general purpose credit charges are made in restaurants,

Connecticut Man Collects Credit Cards as a 'Hobby'

WINDSOR, CONN. (AP)—John Black has accumulated 437 credit cards, which he estimates have a potential credit value of $80,000.

He says he has credit cards from firms in 40 states and at least 12 cards from one oil company.

Despite his hobby, he keeps only one credit card in his wallet and uses that only in emergencies. He keeps his collection in a bank vault.

"With a potential value of $80,000, you've got to be a little apprehensive," he said.

Source: *New York Times,* May 13, 1974.

and this costs the restaurants from five to seven percent of the amounts billed. The credit card organizations deduct this when making payment. The restaurant which honors credit cards, therefore, probably takes this charge into account in setting its prices. It is likely to be what one might term an "expense account" restaurant, more costly than less pretentious restaurants which do not honor credit cards.

Credit Card Loss

Until recently, if you lost a credit card it could be costly. The courts previously held that a person losing a credit card was responsible for any bills run up by the finder unless the company was notified in writing of the loss. Since January 1971, an amendment to the Truth in Lending Act has made it harder for someone to use a stolen credit card. All cards newly issued are required to bear some type of identification, usually a picture or signature. It has been estimated that more than 150 million new cards are issued yearly.

The new rules also set new maximum penalties of a $10,000 fine or five years in prison, or both, for making unauthorized purchases totaling more than $5,000 on a credit card. No credit cardholder can be held responsible for more than $50 of unauthorized purchases by someone using a lost or stolen card.[15]

Even that liability does not exist if the company issuing the credit card has not notified the cardholder of his possible liability and provided him with a self-addressed, prestamped notice to be returned when the card is lost or stolen.

Certain elementary precautions should be taken. A list of credit cards should be kept in a place separate from the wallet in which they may be carried. Credit billings should be carefully checked against receipts, as charges could be doctored to boost the amount. A dishonest clerk could use the charge card to imprint blank slips, to be used later for unauthorized purchases, and you would receive the bill much later—too late.

American Express has been gradually re-issuing its 4 million cards with a magnetic stripe that has two tracks, one for the numeric code approved by the American Bankers Association and one sponsored by the International Air Transport Association (IATA) which has standard data and includes the card holder's name and number. With the combination of coded data and computer terminals, the credit card companies count on instant validation and telltale patterns of use to discourage fraud.

---

[15] Recent court decisions make this applicable to corporate users (employees and officials) as well as individual consumers. Cases cited in *Business Week*, June 8, 1974 are *American Airlines* v. *Remis Industries*—Court of Appeals, Second Circuit and *Credit Card Service Corp.* v. *FTC*, Court of Appeals, District of Columbia.

The illegal use of credit cards has been called a $20 million racket by the Better Business Bureau, which estimates that about one fifth of the 1.5 million cards annually reported lost are actually stolen. Hot credit cards sell for as much as $250 in some big cities, the bureau says, "where travelers' credit cards are accepted as readily as cash and no questions asked."

Bank Credit Cards

Bank credit cards have multiplied significantly in the last few years. Two dominant networks have emerged. *BankAmericard,* operated by Bank of America, the largest U.S. bank, extended its network outside of California by the franchise system,[16] and over four thousand banks throughout the country now handle this card.

Interbank Card Association, a nonprofit cooperative, serves as a clearinghouse in most states to interchange cards of its members, which range from individual banks to its biggest customer, *Master Charge*—which has almost 6,000 banks. The Interbank National Authorization System (INAS) is headquartered in St. Louis, Missouri, with a 24 hour, 7 day a week network system. It polls all nationwide on-line computers and terminals twice a second, picks up each authorization inquiry and authorization response and matches the messages.[17] This instant communication capability is also useful for broadcasting "hot card" information to Interbank Centers in a constant fight against fraud and theft.

A magnetic stripe with numeric coded data on bank credit cards readable by computer terminals and providing instant credit checks has been approved after long testing by the A.B.A.

Fear that the new bank credit cards with the magnetic stripe were easy to duplicate or alter led to a contest sponsored by the chairman of a subsidiary of Citibank who offered prize money to 22 teams of students at the California Institute of Technology—to prove it wasn't so! Instead the Cal Tech students found 22 ways to beat the system.[18] Some banks are still experimenting with other technologies—e.g., optical scanning, pin hole coding by laser or combinations of the several methods to provide more security.

Bank credit card losses are costing more than $350 million now—up from $200 million in 1970. For the first time, Master Charge and BankAmericard are participating in a joint credit card monitoring system in

[16] *U.S. News and World Report,* July 8, 1974 p. 50 reports an agreement with Intourist—Soviet Travel Commissariat by which BankAmericard will be accepted in 33 Russian cities.

[17] *Data Processor,* an IBM publication, February 1974, pp. 16–17.

[18] *Business Week,* August 11, 1973, pp. 120–122; *Wall Street Journal,* April 13, 1973.

New York City. A new network of banks, restaurants, and stores will be able to drop either credit card into an automatic reader, dial the bank's computer via a telephone line terminal and have an instant authorization.[19] As more terminals are installed and while equipment makers test for new technology to reduce losses by fraud, banks are of course, still distributing the credit cards.

Bank credit cards formerly were, for the most part, of regional nature, primarily because of the legal restrictions on branch banking and the consequent limited market for consumer lending. As interchange systems developed, cardholders of any bank in the system could use their cards to make purchases from any of the merchants signed up by other banks participating in the system. The bank credit card has extended the boundaries of banking geographically. Participating merchants find advantages in immediate credit received for all deposited slips, reduction in credit losses, fewer accounting and bookkeeping costs, and a decrease in their own credit needs.

The furor raised by the indiscriminate and unsolicited distribution of bank credit cards in the early expansion days resulted in enactment of an amendment to the Truth in Lending Act in October 1970, which forbade unsolicited mailing of credit cards. By that time the banks, however, had suffered loss through fraud, thieving, and poor risk accounts, and had therefore mostly discontinued the practice.

Bank credit cards are used primarily at retail stores in place of charge accounts or installment plans, although both BankAmericard and Master Charge have also been expanding into the travel and entertainment (T&E) field. The general purpose (T&E) card plans, such as American Express, Diners', and Carte Blanche, expect bills to be paid promptly. The banks, on the contrary, want cardholders to take their time about paying, because the outstanding balances are, in effect, installment loans at a maximum 18 percent annual rate of interest.

Interest rates and methods of computation vary from bank to bank. They also vary among the states depending upon the usury laws of the state. In some states where the maximum rate is low, banks are considering an annual fee for new members similar to that levied by the T&E cards. Paying finance charges on a credit card will cost you more than paying cash or borrowing the same amount from the bank or even getting a cash advance on your bank credit card as the following example indicates:

> The Chase Manhattan Bank's BankAmericard, for example, costs 1 percent a month—a maximum of 12 percent for 12 months—for a cash advance, while charges for purchases is 1.5 percent a month with a maxi-

---

[19] *Business Week*, June 22, 1974.

> mum of 18 percent a year. That means paying back $500 in one year as a cash advance will cost you $32.48, but paying off purchase charges of $500 in equal installments for 12 months will cost you $48.71. There is also the personal loan from a bank. If Chase Manhattan approves you as a risk, you can get $500 at a cost of $27.72 or 10.07 percent, over 12 months.

Banks like credit cards too—they provide additional income from interest on accounts and a percentage from the stores where the purchases are made. A number of banks also offer a credit card checking plan under which the customer writes a check which is charged to a credit card account. This is useful, where credit cards are unacceptable to the store and personal checks risky, because these checks against credit cards are viewed as bank guaranteed.

Banks have been prone to settle delinquent credit card accounts by using the funds in a depositor's account even without authorization. Congressional action against this procedure, known as "the set off," is expected.

As you will note in Figure 4–6 most of the increase in credit card activity is bank credit card use which was bank stimulated. In order to eliminate some of the paper work, bank credit card companies have joined the

FIGURE 4–6
The Credit Card Binge—Personal Credit Outstanding on Credit Cards

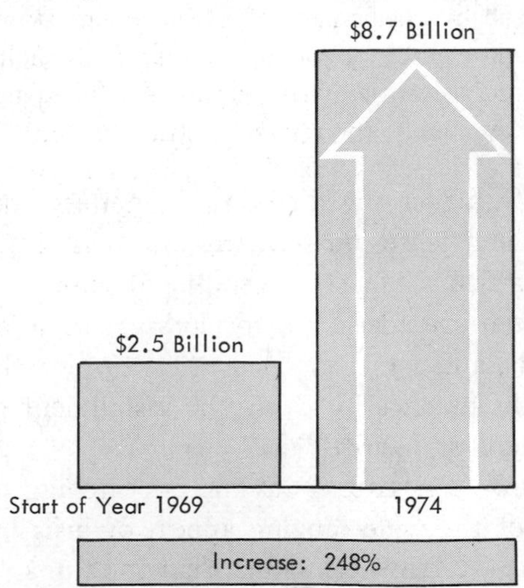

Most of the increase has come on bank credit cards—from $1.3 billion at start of 1969 to $6.6 billion in 1974. Credit on oil and other nonbank cards rose from $1.2 billion to just over $2 billion in the same period.

Source: Federal Reserve Board
Reprinted from *U.S. News & World Report*, Copyright 1974, U.S. News & World Report, Inc.

trend toward descriptive billing where the description of each item billed is printed on the statement itself (instead of the system where a copy of the sales ticket is returned to the customer with the statement). This is the next necessary step toward automated payments.[20]

If the next decade brings the expected "checkless cashless paperless" society, the banks moving toward the electronic cash and credit system will be ready to take consumer credit for retail charge sales out of the hands of retail merchants.

THE INSTALLMENT PLAN

Commonly about one fourth of all retail sales are made on the installment plan. About one out of every two households has some installment debt. Young households are more likely to have installment debt. Over 67 percent of the households with heads between 25 and 34 years of age have installment debt. The major holders of consumer installment credit are shown in Figure 4–7; and how that credit is used is shown in Figure 4–8.

In recent years it has become possible to buy anything from a baby carriage to a tombstone on the installment plan. As one sprightly author declared:

> The ordinary life cycle in the United States starts with a lay-away plan in the baby department of a convenient store, wends its way past the diamond counter of a credit jeweler, finds shelter beneath an FHA mortgage and is eventually laid to rest in a time-payment cemetery plot. After that presumably, the terms are strictly cash.[21]

Generally, higher priced consumer durables, such as automobiles, furniture, radio and television sets, washing machines, and refrigerators, have been the particular object of installment sales promotion, but the practice has now been extended even to clothing. In some stores all sales are on installments, and sometimes sellers try to hide the fact that they are engaging in the practice by giving the installment plan some such name as "Budget Plan" or "Thrift Plan."

"Sail Now—Pay Later" was the eye-catching headline in a newspaper, indicative of the wide ranging appeal of installment selling. "Own this boat today . . . ten years sooner than you think."

---

[20] "The Role of the Charge Card and the Evolving Payments System," *Review of Business*, St. Johns' University, Jamaica, N.Y., May/June 1974.

[21] Penn Kimball, "Cradle to Grave on Easy Terms," *New York Times Sunday Magazine*, June 1, 1952, p. 15.

FIGURE 4–7
Major Holders of Consumer Installment Credit

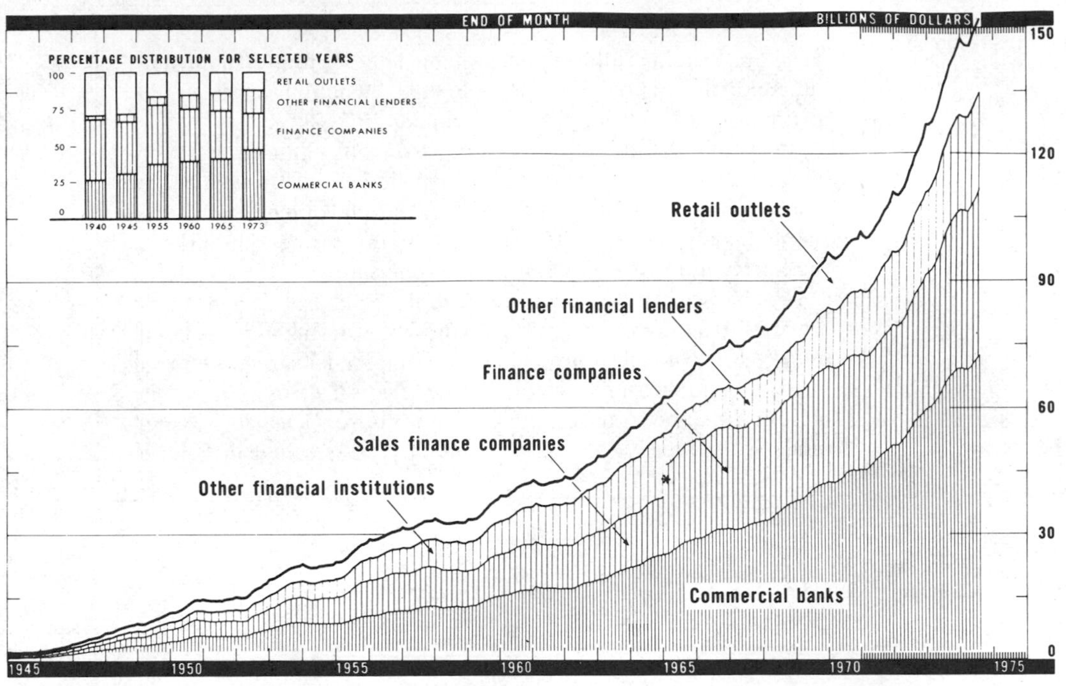

Source: *Historical Chart Book*, Board of Governors Federal Reserve System, 1974.

FIGURE 4–8
Uses of Consumer Installment Credit

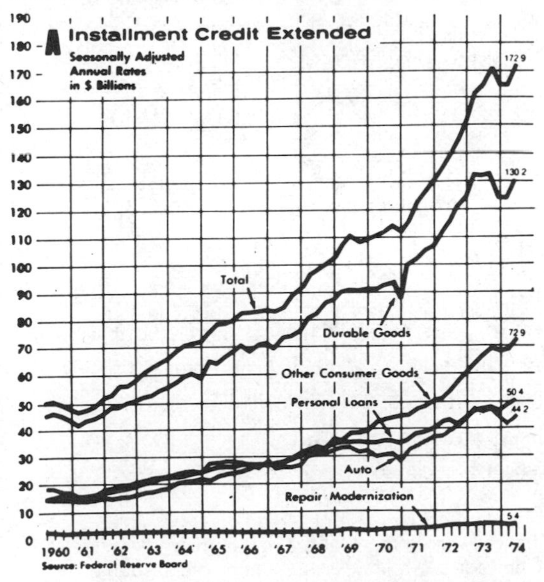

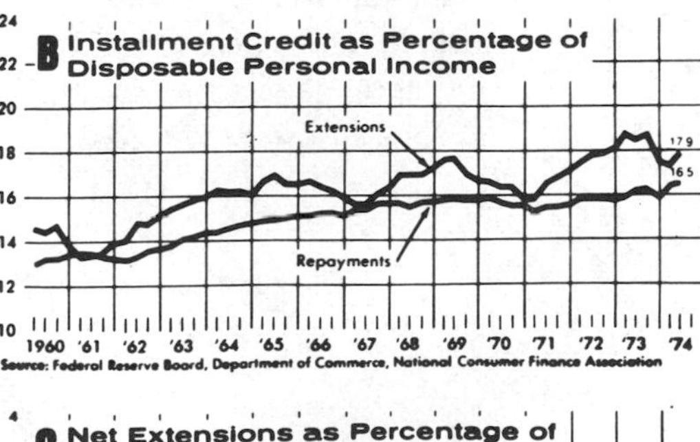

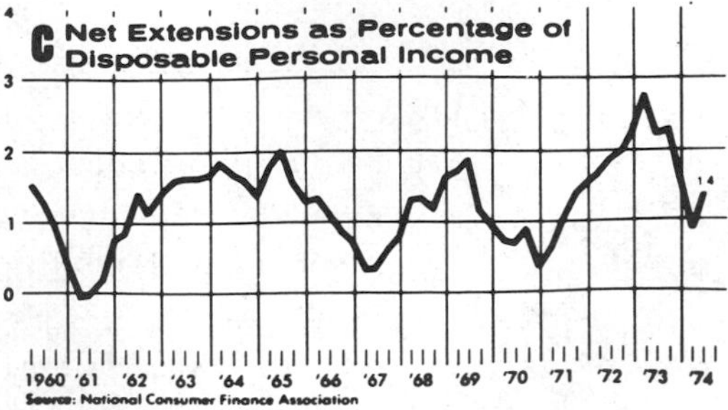

Source: *Consumer Credit Leader*, September 1974

The Hunt Goes Modern: Ride Now, Pay Later

LONDON, Oct. 19 (AP)—One of Britain's oldest fox hunts put the aristocratic sport of riding to hounds on the installment plan today.

"We feel it's in accord with modern trends," said Col. Sir Ralph Clarke, joint master of the Surrey and Burstow Hunt.

"We're very much against hunting being a rich man's sport," the colonel continued in an interview. "In fact, many of our members have very moderate means."

"Ten years ago," he acknowledged, dues in installments "would have been unthinkable."

Now one can join with very little down and the rest of the £40 annual membership fee spread out over the months.

The hunt also has started a family plan. For £65 husband and wife can belong. And children under 17 can come in for as little as £7 50s—all on the "never-never," as the installment plan is called in Britain.

Financial Vulnerability

A simple checklist has been devised by Professor Bymers to test the financial vulnerability of installment debtors.[22] There are three questions to answer:

1. How much cash do you have available to meet emergencies? Add what you have in savings accounts, in government savings bonds, and in your checking account. (You should consider the usual balance just before rather than just after payday.) This sum represents your liquid assets. Place a check in the A or F box.

	A		F
More than $500	☐	$500 or less	☐

2. How long are you committed to your present installment debt? To figure this, add your outstanding installment debts, and divide the total by the sum of installment debt payments you make each month. Even if some debts can be repaid in a few months and others run for a longer period, you divide by your current monthly payment because you are trying to estimate

[22] See Gwen J. Bymers, *A Financial Checkup on the Use of Credit*, rev. ed. (Ithaca, N.Y.: Cooperative Extension Service, New York State College of Human Ecology, Cornell University, December, 1968). Copies are available at 10 cents each from the Mailing Room, Building 7, Research Park, Ithaca, N.Y. 14850.

how long it will take you to complete repayment at your current rate. The result will be the number of months it will take to clear up your outstanding debt. Example:

Balance due on car	=	$1,230
Balance due on washing machine	=	110
Total Debt	=	$1,340
Car payments per month	=	$78
Washing machine payments per month	=	12
Total per Month	=	$90

$1,340 ÷ $90 = 14.8 + months

If the result is 12 months or less, you can be out of debt in less than one year. Check the A box. If the result is more than 12, as in the above example, it will take more than one year to liquidate your present installment debts. Check the F box.

	A		F
12 months or less	☐	More than 12 months	☐

3. How much of your monthly income is committed to installment debt payments? To obtain this figure, divide your monthly income after taxes by the total monthly installment debt payment estimated in (2). Example:

Monthly income (after taxes)	=	$575
Estimated monthly installment payments	=	$90
$90 ÷ $575	=	15.6%

If installment debt payments take less than 20 percent, check the A box; if they take 20 percent or more, check the F box.

	A		F
Less than 20 percent	☐	20 percent or more	☐

Three F checks mean "very vulnerable." Two F checks indicate vulnerability; either liquid assets are too small, or too large a portion of income is committed to debt repayment, or debt is likely to run too long. One F check may not be serious, while three A checks may indicate that the household can manage its installment debt without difficulty.

Protection for the Seller

Merchandise sold on the installment plan is usually paid for, with interest, in monthly installments which may range over a period of a year or more. Commonly the seller protects himself until he has received the total payment due. If the buyer has paid any substantial sum on the price at the time of his default, he is entitled to get that sum back, less the depreciation on the goods caused by wear and tear. The amount of depreciation will ordinarily be estimated by selling the goods a second time, frequently at auction, and seeing what they bring. Depreciation is the difference between what the installment seller sold the goods for originally and what the second, auction, sale brings in. For example, Smith bought a suite of furniture from a dealer on the installment plan for $600. He paid $100 down, got possession of the furniture, and agreed to pay the balance in 20 installments of $25 each. Title to the furniture was to remain with the seller until Smith paid the entire purchase price. After paying $200, Smith took sick, lost his position, and failed to make a payment which was due. The dealer took the furniture back. If the dealer sold it again at auction for $400, he would have to pay Smith $100, since the $300 he had received from Smith plus the $400 at the auction sale added up to $700, or $100 in excess of the original selling price of $600. Smith would lose $200 of his $300 paid because the furniture, as evidenced by the second sale, had depreciated $200.

An uninformed buyer, however, in the hands of a sharp seller, may not be able to discover what the furniture brings at the second sale; or the second sale may be rigged to establish a low price so that there need be no repayment. Only rarely does the defaulter recover what has already been paid.

When the goods or property which have been sold under the installment plan have been repossessed and resold, the proceeds of resale applied to payment of the debt may not be sufficient to cover the total amount. To satisfy this deficiency, a judgment may be secured against the debtor through court action. Thus the installment buyer may lose not only the cash paid and the article purchased but additional amounts as well.

From his thorough study of events leading up to default, Professor Caplowitz makes this observation:

> One might suppose that the better educated debtors in default would be more likely than the poorly educated to understand the conditions embodied in their contracts and would know that their obligations do not automatically end with the repossession. But oddly enough, this is not at all the case. In fact, the better educated seem to be more confused than

> the poorly educated in this matter. Thus, 49% of those who never graduated from high school understand that the repossession did not end their obligation, compared with 45% of those who did graduate from high school. (Among the relatively small number who attended college, only 45% understood the meaning of repossession.) Not only did formal education fail to differentiate those who did and did not understand their obligations following repossession, but education based on experience also makes no difference. Thus we expected that those debtors who had experienced debt problems in the past, especially those who had experienced prior repossessions, would be more likely than those in debt trouble for the first time to know that their obligations did not end with repossession. But this turns out not to be the case. There is no relationship whatsoever between the index of prior debt trouble and understanding of repossession. In fact, not even those who had experienced repossessions before had greater awareness of their obligations in the present instance.[23]

The seller, wishing protection against the buyer's creditors and against innocent purchasers from the buyer, is obliged to file a contract in a public office, such as the county clerk's, in certain states. For example, Simpson, a radio dealer, sold Thompson a television set but did not have the notice of his security interest recorded in a public office, as required by statute. Thompson used the television set for a month and then sold it to Hillman. Hillman received good title to the set because Simpson, through his failure to record the security interest, lost his rights in the television set when it came into the hands of an innocent third party.

If the goods are damaged, lost, or destroyed while the buyer is holding them and making payments, the loss falls upon the buyer, under most security agreements, and he must complete the payments. Since under these circumstances the buyer may have no financial means of meeting this obligation, the seller customarily is protected through insurance, which is paid for by the buyer. Since a down payment is frequently received, which further protects the seller, sellers commonly allow very liberal terms on installment sales, but these are usually more costly than the buyer realizes.

The Uniform Commercial Code

Since 1968 the Uniform Commercial Code, which was in effect in every state except Louisiana, deliberately changed all the terminology of past personal property security devices that had been used to protect the

---

[23] David Caplowitz with the assistance of Eric Single, *Debtors in Default*, Vol. I, Chap. 10 (New York: Bureau of Applied Social Research, Columbia University, 1970), p. 34.

interest of the creditor as security for the payment of a debt. Article 9 of the Code abolished all formal distinctions between chattel mortgages, conditional sales, trust receipts, and all other instruments based on passage of title but did not abolish their use. The new language instead refers to a *security interest*, which is synonymous with the older terms, and includes all the protective requirements needed to safeguard the secured party (the seller or creditor) until the buyer has completed payment for property which remains in his possession.

In the past, technicalities frequently voided the intent of statutes governing filing and recording requirements. The Code, in correcting this problem, simplified the requirements that must be met to give adequate public notice. The secured party perfects (validates) his security interest by

a. Possession of the negotiable instrument or other collateral. In the pre-Code era, perfection was often achieved by giving public notice of the lien claimed.

b. Filing of a simple notice known as a financing statement that the secured party has a security interest in the collateral described. In pre-Code days, the filing requirements not only had to conform to all the varied formalities of time, place, and detailed procedure but also required a precise and accurate description of the debtors' collateral and often a copy of the contract.

When there is a purchase money security interest (a loan to purchase goods), there is no need for filing a financing statement. However, the small loan company, which has no such purchase money security interest, to protect itself under the Code should file a financing statement.

Most merchants with a high volume of retail installment sales prefer to take the risk of not filing rather than deal with the cost and paper work involved. Frequently, as a substitute protection, a cosigner is required to the loan agreement, a situation—if you are asked—you should approach warily. It can change a personal relationship with a friend or relative into a business relationship with a company that you had not quite planned. If you are a cosigner on a loan, you are as responsible as the borrower—in case of default. You are just as liable to have a salary garnisheed or a judgment entered against you, and perhaps as a result, your credit rating may even be affected.

The Installment Contract

Unfortunately the average buyer fails to gain protection by reading carefully and understanding thoroughly all the papers signed in many transactions, including installment sales. For no good reason at all, a person feels embarrassed to take the necessary time to read a lengthy document in which a lot of important stipulations may appear in very fine print. For his own protection, he should most certainly read and understand before he affixes his signature to anything. It must always be remembered that sellers engage in many transactions of the installment type and obtain the services of able lawyers to see that they are protected to the utmost. The buyer engages in relatively few of these transactions and naturally does not know a great deal about them.

Some aspects of installment contracts to watch out for are:

The Add-On Clause. Add-on, or open end, contracts should be avoided by the consumer. This type of clause or contract is drawn to cover a succession of installment purchases and provides that the seller retains title or mortgage on each article until the very last one is paid for. A thousand dollars' worth of house furnishings, bought over several years, might be seized because the customer failed to meet a $20 payment on a recently purchased $100 item.

The Acceleration Clause. This provides that a default in one payment makes all other payments immediately due and payable. If the buyer is dishonest, this drastic safeguard is necessary. But an honest buyer may miss a payment date because of an emergency, perhaps sickness in the family or a temporary layoff from the job. Unscrupulous dealers take advantage of the acceleration clause to swoop down and immediately repossess the car, or refrigerator, or television set, and cart it off for resale without notice.

The Wage Assignment. The most drastic form of security in the installment contract may be the wage assignment. An obscure clause may give the dealer power of attorney to collect all or part of the buyer's paycheck or envelope if the buyer misses a payment. Most wage assignments are probably signed because the buyer does not know what he is signing. Long contracts in legal verbiage and fine type make it difficult for the buyer to read or understand the contract. The oversight may be encouraged if the document is headed simply "Contract" and fails to call the buyer's attention to the fact that he is signing away future wages. Wage-assignment abuses, like other shady practices, are restricted to a minority of installment dealers. That such abuses threaten the legitimate dealer as well as the unwary customer is indicated by the suggestion of the National Association of Sales Finance Companies that state laws prohibit any wage assignment made before actual default on the installment contract.

Originally the installment contract was used to sell only products for which there was a definite resale market. If an individual lagged behind in payments on a piano or a car, the dealer could repossess and probably make up the unpaid balance by reselling the item. The merchandise itself was adequate security, until the installment dealers, trying to conquer new markets, made their items so "easy" that often the unpaid balance exceeded the resale value of the article. At the same time, they went into new fields, selling "soft goods," such as clothing, for which resale value was either low or nil. Resale of a repossessed pair of pants brings little. As added security for deals such as these, the wage assignment came into prominence.

The legal process of attaching the debtor's wage is known as "garnishment" or "garnisheeing wages." By court order, the employer of the debtor is obliged to pay all or a certain percentage of the wages of the debtor (buyer) to the creditor (installment seller) until the debt is paid in full. Some states limit by law the percentage of a wage earner's salary which may thus be taken by a creditor at any given pay period or prohibit assignment entirely under certain conditions. Some employers dislike being bothered with legal forms and with the added bookkeeping routine involved in turning over wages to a creditor. They therefore fire employees whose wages are garnisheed.

One of the most cruel causes of default judgments, ruined credit and garnisheed salaries is the "sewer service" or the practice of filling out false affidavits that the process had been served. Thousands of such judgments are issued yearly when the purchaser stops payment on faulty merchandise and a store or loan company sues for nonpayment on an installment contract. Its lawyer issues a summons on the person being sued, who has usually 10 days to appear in court to answer the suit. If he does not appear, and the process server swears in an affidavit that he delivered it in person or tried to, then the court can declare the defendant in default. The next step is the marshall's attempt to collect—and the purchaser might have been completely unaware of the entire proceedings.

Garnishment. The 1968 federal Consumer Credit Protection Act has a section on garnishment that became effective July 1, 1970. It provides that the amount of an individual's disposable earnings for any workweek which may be subjected to garnishment may not exceed the lesser of the following:

1. Twenty-five percent of his disposable earnings for that week, or
2. The amount by which his disposable earnings for the week exceed 30 times the federal minimum hourly wage prescribed under the Wage and Hour Act at the time such earnings are payable.

There is also a prohibition against discharging an employee for garnishment of earnings for any one indebtedness. The act also provides that where a state law is more restrictive than federal laws the provisions of the state law shall govern. For example, in New York the amount which can be reached by garnishment did not rise to 25 percent but remained at the 10 percent in effect under the state law.

A Supreme Court decision declared unconstitutional Wisconsin's wage garnishment law and by implication, the laws of other states that permit debt collection practices that freeze a portion of a worker's wages without first granting him a hearing in court. The legal defense had claimed that "workers who are pressed for cash sometimes are forced to pay up even though they might be able to prove fraud or some other misdeed by the finance company if the case ever went to court." These other states are Alaska, Arkansas, Arizona, California, Idaho, Iowa, Minnesota, Montana, New Hampshire, Oklahoma, Utah, Vermont, Washington and Wyoming.

The "Balloon Contract." A contract which has as its final installment a payment substantially in excess of the preceding installments is known as a "balloon contract." For example, the contract may call for 11 monthly installments of $25 each and one (the 12th payment) of $300. This is a highly undesirable type of payment arrangement because total charges paid by the purchaser are higher because of the necessity of refinancing at least once and sometimes two or three times. To illustrate, an example cited by *Business Week* may be used. It should be noted that the balloon contract is usually found in the financing of automobiles. *Business Week* stated:

> Here's how a typical "$100 down and $40 a month" deal worked in Cleveland:
>
> | | |
> |---|---:|
> | Advertised price of the car | $1,795.00 |
> | But a heater is necessary | 60.00 |
> | So that the cost now stands at | 1,855.00 |
> | Add state tax on $1,855 | 56.65 |
> | Add cost of title transfer, etc. | 6.36 |
> | So the total cost is | 1,918.00 |
> | The buyer is talked into paying | 118.00 |
> | Leaving a balance to be financed of | 1,800.00 |
> | Two years insurance | 194.00 |
> | Which brings the price back to | 1,994.00 |
> | Add interest at 6% and carrying charges for two years | 269.00 |
> | And, as the owner drives away he owes | 2,263.00 |
>
> Notes are $40 a month (as advertised) for 23 months, with a "balloon note" for the balance falling due in the 24th month. So:
>
> | | |
> |---|---:|
> | The buyer makes 23 monthly payments at $40 each | $ 920.00 |
> | And the balloon note amounts to | 1,343.00 |
>
> Meanwhile, the car has depreciated to perhaps $1,450 at the end of the first year, and perhaps in the same proportion during the second. At any

rate, the owner can't afford to pay out $1,343 in a lump sum. So he refinances the 24th note for another two years. It works this way:

Amount of the balloon note	$1,343.00
Add another two years' insurance	181.00
Add interest and carrying charges for another two years	200.00
And the buyer starts paying again on	1,724.00

(Remember this is on a two-year-old car that was advertised at $1,795.)

And so he makes 23 more payments at $40 each	$ 920.00
And he runs smack up against another balloon note this time for (the car is now four years old)	804.00
So he adds another two years insurance	120.30
And another two years interest and carrying charges	146.90
And he starts the fifth year paying on	1,071.60
So he makes 23 more payments of $40 each	920.00

And at the end of six years he finds (if he bothers to add it up) that he has paid out $2,878 in cash, that he still owes $151.60, and that his car is now worth perhaps $150.

Obviously, a balloon contract is to be avoided. Now, under Truth in Lending, the payment must be clearly labeled "*balloon.*" This is intended to act as a warning signal to the consumer.

Cost of Installment Financing

In one way or another a seller must be paid for financing the buyer who acquires goods on credit. The various expenses of investigation, collecting, bookkeeping, repossession, reconditioning, reselling, bad debts, and insurance must be covered, either by an inflated price for the article sold, by separate fees and charges, or by inclusion in the charge of interest. In the past, though a nominal rate of 5 or 6 percent may have been quoted, analysis of the charges usually revealed that the real rate was often far in excess—and it had to be in order to cover the cost of the service rendered.

Suppose an article selling for $75 is sold with a 20 percent down payment, the balance to be paid in installments over a period of nine months. If a charge of 6 percent of $75 is made for the service rendered, it amounts to $4.50.

But the 1st	month the buyer has the use of	$60.00
the 2nd	month the buyer has the use of	53.33
the 3rd	month the buyer has the use of	46.67
the 4th	month the buyer has the use of	40.00
the 5th	month the buyer has the use of	33.33
the 6th	month the buyer has the use of	26.67
the 7th	month the buyer has the use of	20.00
the 8th	month the buyer has the use of	13.33
and the 9th	month the buyer has the use of	6.67

One way to look at these figures intelligently is that if the buyer had the use of \$60 the first month and only \$6.666 during the ninth, he had the use of

$$\frac{\$60 + \$6.66}{2} = \frac{\$66.66}{2} = \$33.33$$

on the average for the nine month period. Since \$4.50 was paid for this accommodation (for nine months), it amounts to paying \$6.00 for a year's use of an average amount of \$33.33.

Now,

$$\frac{\$6}{\$33.33} \times 100 = \frac{\$600.00}{\$33.33} = 18 \text{ percent.}$$

The Time Honored 6 Percent

Interest rates were often not given at all in installment contracts. When they were given, they were seldom what they seemed. Usually they were disguised as forms of the time honored 6 percent. In the course of the years, 6 percent had come for many people to be synonymous with "fair return." As one merchandiser put it, "Six percent has sex appeal for the customer."

When installment sellers, who were to be repaid in equal installments, stated their charge (say 6 percent) as a percentage of the total unpaid balance at the start, since this balance was reduced by installment payments, the average balance outstanding during the term of the installment contract was only about half the original unpaid balance. Therefore, the true rate, in the absence of other manipulations and distortions, when payments were spread over a year, was roughly twice the stated rate.

"One percent a month" appears to be a reasonable charge; but depending on the way it's calculated, it is much more than it seems. It is 12 percent a year if levied on the new reduced unpaid balance each month; but if levied as a percentage of the total unpaid balance at the beginning of the contract, it is about 24 percent, since, over a year, the average balance outstanding is only half the original unpaid balance.

The Role of the Sales Finance Company

You may sign an installment agreement to purchase an automobile from a dealer only to find that you must make your payments to a finance company. Often you are immediately told of the arrangement; sometimes you are not. The reason the dealer utilizes a finance company is that in many cases he does not have sufficient capital of his own to finance the volume of business he can do if he sells on time. Therefore, he uses a finance company, which pays him at the time the car is sold, thus replenishing his capital while, at the same time, financing the extension of credit to the purchaser. The finance company extends the credit and relieves the dealer of this obligation, thus freeing his capital for more rapid turnover.

There are nearly 4,000 sales finance companies and offices operating throughout the country, holding about one fourth of all consumer installment paper outstanding. They account for about 30 percent of the total automobile paper but commercial banks have 55 percent. The giants in the field are General Motors Acceptance Corporation, which finances General Motors cars; CIT Financial, which finances Ford cars, grants home modernization loans, and finances other consumer durable sales; Commercial Credit Corporation, which finances Chrysler cars; and Associates Investment Company, which finances miscellaneous auto paper. Sears, Roebuck has established the Sears, Roebuck Acceptance Corporation.

Sales finance companies have increased the absolute amount of their loans on automobiles over the last decade, but the relative importance of this type of lending—traditionally their specialty—has declined as the companies stepped up activity in other areas such as financing other retail consumer goods. About two thirds of all new car purchases are financed on the installment plan, and notes on such car purchases are averaging about $3,000 each.

In shopping for auto credit, several surveys found that banks charged the lowest rates, national sales finance companies were a close second, and local finance companies charged the highest rates.

Finance companies are anxious to have an absolute promise to pay from the purchaser, which cannot be impaired by any disputes or claims between the dealer and the purchaser. Frequently, however, the purchaser will not find servicing or repairs satisfactory, or will claim an inferior or damaged product was received and will, therefore, refuse to pay. To guard against this, the finance companies have employed a variety of devices. One attempt to deal with the problem has been to provide in the contract that the purchaser will settle all claims with the dealer directly and will not set up any such claim in an action brought by the finance company. The courts, however, have been loath to enforce such a clause and have held against the finance companies where the purchasers had legitimate grievances.

Holder in Due Course

The "holder in due course" doctrine is the legal reason for the consumer credit tangle that results when the car or appliance bought from the dealer on credit is found unsatisfactory. You complain to the dealer, but the credit contract has been sold to a bank or finance company or loan company who is the "holder in due course." If the company refuses responsibility for the defective item, you can sue the original dealer. If you stop payment to bring pressure on the dealer, the company that holds your financial agreement can take action against you. You must continue to pay for the worthless item. Frequently the signed financing contract includes a "waiver of defense" clause, in which the purchaser agrees not to raise any claims against a subsequent holder of the paper.

Thirty five states have statutorily affected the holder in due course doctrine to some degree.[24] Seven states including New York and Massachusetts have limited holders in due course on most installment contracts. Twenty others have restrictions on certain types of credit transactions, such as auto sales. Arizona gives a consumer 90 days to raise any claim against holders in due course. The California Supreme Court ruled that consumers can sue both the company that defrauded them and the finance company to whom the contracts were assigned even if the finance company may not have been part of the fraud.

Consumer groups are lobbying to establish the principle that responsibility for the retailer's performance follows the note. If the retailer defaults on the warranty or fails to give the services contracted for, the consumer should be able to force the retailer to right the wrong—even by stopping payment. This shifts the responsibility to the holder of the note, who would therefore want to be sure of the reliability of the retailer before buying the note. The proposal would require the face of the note drawn up by a retailer to have printed on it the fact that any third party buying the note is subject to legitimate claims the consumer might make as a result of the business transactions. It would also forbid any agreement causing the consumer to waive any legal rights to make such claims. This proposal would eliminate the traditional holder in due course practice as it has applied to consumer sales, and another device known as "confession of judgment." In "confessing judgment," a debtor signs away the right to contest the validity of a debt.

The purchaser is almost as helpless when a credit card is used for the purchase of an article. The credit card contract holds the card holder

---

[24] National Consumer Law Center Inc., Boston, Mass., June 1974.

responsible for all indebtedness and relieves the issuer of the card of any liability for problems concerning the merchandise.

Credit Life Insurance

A purchaser on the installment plan is often required to buy (*a*) credit life insurance and (*b*) credit disability insurance. The purpose is to protect the seller or the finance company in case the buyer dies or becomes disabled and cannot continue to pay off installments due.

If the dealer wants to sell you credit life insurance, you must be told the cost and asked to sign a statement saying you want the insurance. If the dealer won't sell the car without the insurance and you agree, the full amount for the insurance must be included in the finance charge and in the annual percentage rate. A recent study asserts that most purchasers regard the insurance protection favorably.[25]

PROTECTION FOR THE BUYER

The Regulation of Installment Selling

Regulation of installment selling falls into two categories: (*a*) federal regulation of unfair practices, and (*b*) state regulation.

Federal regulation of unfair trade practices is largely the responsibility of the Federal Trade Commission. For example, the Commission drafted "trade practice rules covering the automobile 'pack' and related practices." It declared: "The primary purpose of the trade practice rules is to provide for the elimination and prevention of concealed 'packing' and other related practices in the financing of motor vehicles." The rules provide that the seller must furnish the purchaser with the following detailed itemization of his cost in the installment purchase of a motor vehicle:

a. The cash delivered price, including specified extras.
b. The amount allowed in trade-in or down payment or both.
c. The amount unpaid on the cash selling price, which includes item (*a*) less item (*b*).
d. The cost of insurance, the coverage provided, and the party or parties to whom the insurance is payable.
e. The amount of official fees charged.
f. The amount of unpaid balance to be financed (sums of items [*c*], [*d*], [*e*]).

[25] *Consumer Credit Life and Disability Insurance*, edited by Charles L. Hubbard, College of Business Administration of Ohio University, Athens, Ohio, 1973.

g. The finance charge.

h. The time balance owed by the buyer to the seller (sum of item [*f*] and item [*g*]), the amount and number of installments to be paid, and the time covered.

Under the Commission's rules, it is an unfair trade practice to conceal or to fail or refuse to disclose in a written agreement any of the items enumerated above. Since Truth in Lending emphasizes the disclosure of all formerly hidden charges, the Federal Trade Commission now uses this added power of enforcement.

The Federal Consumer Credit Protection Act

After some years of debate, Congress passed and the President signed the Consumer Credit Protection Act in 1968, already discussed in part in connection with the cost of charge accounts (pages 163–66). The act does not limit any charge for credit that may be made, but it does require disclosure of credit terms, including clear disclosure of the finance charge.

Under Title I of the Truth in Lending Act (from which the Consumer Protection Act gets this substitute name), which became effective July 1, 1969, the main purpose was to require creditors to make clear to consumers the exact amount of the finance charge to be paid for the extension of credit (See Figure 4–9). The rules and regulations for truth in lending were spelled out by the Federal Reserve in Regulation Z. Disclosure of credit terms is expected to help consumers by allowing them to decide if the charges are reasonable and to help them compare the cost of credit by making comparisons and shopping for the best credit terms.

The *finance charge* and *annual percentage rate* are the two most important concepts embodied in Regulation Z. They are designed to tell you at a glance how much you are paying for credit and the relative cost of that credit in percentage terms. In general, *the finance charge,* which must be stated in dollars and cents, is the total of all costs imposed by the creditor and paid either directly or indirectly by the consumer or another party in connection with the extension of credit. It includes such costs as interest and time price differential, that is, any difference between the price of an item sold for cash and an item sold on credit. It also includes amounts paid as a discount; service, transaction, activity, or carrying charges; loan fees, "points"—extra sums figured as a percentage of the loan amount and charged in a lump sum—; finder's fees or similar charges; fees for an appraisal; investigation or credit report (except in real property transactions); and premiums for credit life insurance that are required by the creditor as a condition for obtaining credit.

FIGURE 4–9
Truth in Lending—Consumer Credit Cost Disclosure

Seller's Name: ______________________ Contract #______
____

RETAIL INSTALLMENT CONTRACT AND SECURITY AGREEMENT

The undersigned (herein called Purchaser, whether one or more) purchases from ______________(seller) and grants to ______________ a security interest in, subject to the terms and conditions hereof, the following described property.

QUANTITY	DESCRIPTION	AMOUNT	
Description of Trade-in:			
	Sales Tax		
	Total		

Insurance Agreement

The purchase of insurance coverage is voluntary and not required for credit. (Type of Ins.) insurance coverage is available at a cost of $__________ for the term of credit.

I desire insurance coverage

Signed______________ Date________

I do not desire insurance coverage

Signed______________ Date________

PURCHASER'S NAME______________
PURCHASER'S ADDRESS______________
CITY__________ STATE______ ZIP______

1. CASH PRICE $______
2. LESS: CASH DOWN PAYMENT $______
3. TRADE-IN ______
4. TOTAL DOWN PAYMENT ______ $______
5. UNPAID BALANCE OF CASH PRICE $______
6. OTHER CHARGES:
______________ $______
______________ ______
7. AMOUNT FINANCED $______
8. FINANCE CHARGE $______
9. TOTAL OF PAYMENTS $______
10. DEFERRED PAYMENT PRICE (1+6+8) $______
11. ANNUAL PERCENTAGE RATE ______%

Purchaser hereby agrees to pay to______________ ______________ at their offices shown above the "TOTAL OF PAYMENTS" shown above in ______ monthly installments of $__________(final payment to be $__________) the first installment being payable __________ 19______, and all subsequent installments on the same day of each consecutive month until paid in full. The finance charge applies from (Date)

Signed______________________

Notice to Buyer: You are entitled to a copy of the contract you sign. You have the right to pay in advance the unpaid balance of this contract and obtain a partial refund of the finance charge based on the "Actuarial Method." [Any other method of computation may be so identified, for example, "Rule of 78's," "Sum of the Digits," etc.]

This form, when properly completed, will show how a creditor may comply with the disclosure requirements of the provisions of paragraphs (b) and (c) of §226.8 of Regulation Z for the type of credit extended in this example. This form is intended solely for purposes of demonstration and it is not the only format which will permit a creditor to comply with disclosure requirements of Regulation Z.

Source: Board of Governors, Federal Reserve System, Exhibit C—"Consumer Credit Cost Disclosure."

The *annual percentage rate* represents the relationship of the total finance charge to the total amount financed. It must be computed to the nearest one quarter of 1 percent. The method of computation depends on whether the credit is open end or of the installment type. For credit other than open end, the annual percentage rate must be computed by the "actuarial method," or the "U.S. rule." In fact, companies are likely to use government prepared tables or similar commercially produced schedules from which the relevant figures can be taken.[26] See Table 4–6 for an example of a page from a manual for computing the annual percentage rate.

In the case of installment sales and loans, the information given to you must include the total amount being financed; an itemized account of charges being made; the total finance charge in dollars; the finance charge as an annual percentage rate; the number, amount, and due dates of payments to be made; any charges that will be added for late payment of installments; a description of any security the creditor will hold; penalties, if any, for prepayment; and whether the installments include any "balloon" payments—a payment more than twice the amount of a regular installment.

Keep in mind that the act requires that facts about the credit charge be stated. It does *not,* however, fix or specify in any way maximum or minimum charges for credit. Nor does it cover credit transactions within states that request and obtain exemption because their laws have the same requirements as the federal law and adequate provision for enforcement.

The advertising of credit is also regulated. The act provides that (1) no credit grantor shall advertise that any specific periodic credit amount or installment can be arranged unless the creditor usually or customarily arranges credits for such amounts or with installments for that particular period, and (2) that no credit grantor shall advertise any credit terms less conspicuously or with less emphasis than any other credit terms.

Furthermore, in the advertising of credit transactions for installment purchasing, the law requires that if any lender advertises the rate of the finance charge, it must be expressed as an "annual percentage rate." Also, if the amount of any down payment or that no down payment is required is advertised, or the amount of any installment payment, or the dollar amount of any finance charge, or the number of installments, or the period of repayment, all the following items must be stated.

1. The amount of the installment credit or loan.
2. The amount of the down payment, if any.

[26] The actuarial method or the United States rule, *Story* v. *Livingston* (1839) 38 U.S. 359, is a method for computing the simple annual rate on the declining balance. The actuarial method assumes that a uniform periodic rate is applied to a schedule of installment payments such that the principal is reduced to zero upon completion of the payments. The actuarial rate is such periodic rate multiplied by the number of periods in a year. See *Truth in Lending: Law and Explanation* (Chicago: Commerce Clearing House, Inc., 1968), p. 18.

TABLE 4–6

Sample Page from Table for Computing Annual Percentage Rate for Level Monthly Payment Plans

EXAMPLE

Finance charge = \$35.00; Total amount financed = \$200; Number of monthly payments = 24.

SOLUTION

Step 1–Divide the finance charge by the total amount financed and multiply by \$100. This gives the finance charge per \$100 of amount financed. That is, \$35.00 ÷ \$200 = .1750 x \$100 = \$17.50.

Step 2–Follow down the left hand column of the table to the line for 24 months. Follow across this line until you find the nearest number to \$17.50. In this example \$17.51 is closest to \$17.50. Reading up the column of figures shows an annual percentage rate of 16%.

NUMBER OF PAYMENTS	ANNUAL PERCENTAGE RATE															
	14.00%	14.25%	14.50%	14.75%	15.00%	15.25%	15.50%	15.75%	16.00%	16.25%	16.50%	16.75%	17.00%	17.25%	17.50%	17.75%
	(FINANCE CHARGE PER \$100 OF AMOUNT FINANCED)															
1	1.17	1.19	1.21	1.23	1.25	1.27	1.29	1.31	1.33	1.35	1.37	1.40	1.42	1.44	1.46	1.48
2	1.75	1.78	1.82	1.85	1.88	1.91	1.94	1.97	2.00	2.04	2.07	2.10	2.13	2.16	2.19	2.22
3	2.34	2.38	2.43	2.47	2.51	2.55	2.59	2.64	2.68	2.72	2.76	2.80	2.85	2.89	2.93	2.97
4	2.93	2.99	3.04	3.09	3.14	3.20	3.25	3.30	3.36	3.41	3.46	3.51	3.57	3.62	3.67	3.73
5	3.53	3.59	3.65	3.72	3.78	3.84	3.91	3.97	4.04	4.10	4.16	4.23	4.29	4.35	4.42	4.48
6	4.12	4.20	4.27	4.35	4.42	4.49	4.57	4.64	4.72	4.79	4.87	4.94	5.02	5.09	5.17	5.24
7	4.72	4.81	4.89	4.98	5.06	5.15	5.23	5.32	5.40	5.49	5.58	5.66	5.75	5.83	5.92	6.00
8	5.32	5.42	5.51	5.61	5.71	5.80	5.90	6.00	6.09	6.19	6.29	6.38	6.48	6.58	6.67	6.77
9	5.92	6.03	6.14	6.25	6.35	6.46	6.57	6.68	6.78	6.89	7.00	7.11	7.22	7.32	7.43	7.54
10	6.53	6.65	6.77	6.88	7.00	7.12	7.24	7.36	7.48	7.60	7.72	7.84	7.96	8.08	8.19	8.31
11	7.14	7.27	7.40	7.53	7.66	7.79	7.92	8.05	8.18	8.31	8.44	8.57	8.70	8.83	8.96	9.09
12	7.74	7.89	8.03	8.17	8.31	8.45	8.59	8.74	8.88	9.02	9.16	9.30	9.45	9.59	9.73	9.87
13	8.36	8.51	8.66	8.81	8.97	9.12	9.27	9.43	9.58	9.73	9.89	10.04	10.20	10.35	10.50	10.66
14	8.97	9.13	9.30	9.46	9.63	9.79	9.96	10.12	10.29	10.45	10.62	10.78	10.95	11.11	11.28	11.45
15	9.59	9.76	9.94	10.11	10.29	10.47	10.64	10.82	11.00	11.17	11.35	11.53	11.71	11.88	12.06	12.24
16	10.20	10.39	10.58	10.77	10.95	11.14	11.33	11.52	11.71	11.90	12.09	12.28	12.46	12.65	12.84	13.03
17	10.82	11.02	11.22	11.42	11.62	11.82	12.02	12.22	12.42	12.62	12.83	13.03	13.23	13.43	13.63	13.83
18	11.45	11.66	11.87	12.08	12.29	12.50	12.72	12.93	13.14	13.35	13.57	13.78	13.99	14.21	14.42	14.64
19	12.07	12.30	12.52	12.74	12.97	13.19	13.41	13.64	13.86	14.09	14.31	14.54	14.76	14.99	15.22	15.44
20	12.70	12.93	13.17	13.41	13.64	13.88	14.11	14.35	14.59	14.82	15.06	15.30	15.54	15.77	16.01	16.25
21	13.33	13.58	13.82	14.07	14.32	14.57	14.82	15.06	15.31	15.56	15.81	16.06	16.31	16.56	16.81	17.07
22	13.96	14.22	14.48	14.74	15.00	15.26	15.52	15.78	16.04	16.30	16.57	16.83	17.09	17.36	17.62	17.88
23	14.59	14.87	15.14	15.41	15.68	15.96	16.23	16.50	[illegible]	17.05	17.32	17.60	17.88	18.15	18.43	18.70
➡ 24	15.23	15.51	15.80	16.08	16.37	16.65	16.94	17.22	(17.51)	17.80	18.09	18.37	18.66	18.95	19.24	19.53
25	15.87	16.17	16.46	16.76	17.06	17.35	17.65	17.95	[illegible]	18.55	18.85	19.15	19.45	19.75	20.05	20.36
26	16.51	16.82	17.13	17.44	17.75	18.06	18.37	18.68	18.99	19.30	19.62	19.93	20.24	20.56	20.87	21.19
27	17.15	17.47	17.80	18.12	18.44	18.76	19.09	19.41	19.74	20.06	20.39	20.71	21.04	21.37	21.69	22.02
28	17.80	18.13	18.47	18.80	19.14	19.47	19.81	20.15	20.48	20.82	21.16	21.50	21.84	22.18	22.52	22.86
29	18.45	18.79	19.14	19.49	19.83	20.18	20.53	20.88	21.23	21.58	21.94	22.29	22.64	22.99	23.35	23.70
30	19.10	19.45	19.81	20.17	20.54	20.90	21.26	21.62	21.99	22.35	22.72	23.08	23.45	23.81	24.18	24.55
31	19.75	20.12	20.49	20.87	21.24	21.61	21.99	22.37	22.74	23.12	23.50	23.88	24.26	24.64	25.02	25.40
32	20.40	20.79	21.17	21.56	21.95	22.33	22.72	23.11	23.50	23.89	24.28	24.68	25.07	25.46	25.86	26.25
33	21.06	21.46	21.85	22.25	22.65	23.06	23.46	23.86	24.26	24.67	25.07	25.48	25.88	26.29	26.70	27.11
34	21.72	22.13	22.54	22.95	23.37	23.78	24.19	24.61	25.03	25.44	25.86	26.28	26.70	27.12	27.54	27.97
35	22.38	22.80	23.23	23.65	24.08	24.51	24.94	25.36	25.79	26.23	26.66	27.09	27.52	27.96	28.39	28.83
36	23.04	23.48	23.92	24.35	24.80	25.24	25.68	26.12	26.57	27.01	27.46	27.90	28.35	28.80	29.25	29.70
37	23.70	24.16	24.61	25.06	25.51	25.97	26.42	26.88	27.34	27.80	28.26	28.72	29.18	29.64	30.10	30.57
38	24.37	24.84	25.30	25.77	26.24	26.70	27.17	27.64	28.11	28.59	29.06	29.53	30.01	30.49	30.96	31.44
39	25.04	25.52	26.00	26.48	26.96	27.44	27.92	28.41	28.89	29.38	29.87	30.36	30.85	31.34	31.83	32.32
40	25.71	26.20	26.70	27.19	27.69	28.18	28.68	29.18	29.68	30.18	30.68	31.18	31.68	32.19	32.69	33.20
41	26.39	26.89	27.40	27.91	28.41	28.92	29.44	29.95	30.46	30.97	31.49	32.01	32.52	33.04	33.56	34.08
42	27.06	27.58	28.10	28.62	29.15	29.67	30.19	30.72	31.25	31.78	32.31	32.84	33.37	33.90	34.44	34.97
43	27.74	28.27	28.81	29.34	29.88	30.42	30.96	31.50	32.04	32.58	33.13	33.67	34.22	34.76	35.31	35.86
44	28.42	28.97	29.52	30.07	30.62	31.17	31.72	32.28	32.83	33.39	33.95	34.51	35.07	35.63	36.19	36.76
45	29.11	29.67	30.23	30.79	31.36	31.92	32.49	33.06	33.63	34.20	34.77	35.35	35.92	36.50	37.08	37.66
46	29.79	30.36	30.94	31.52	32.10	32.68	33.26	33.84	34.43	35.01	35.60	36.19	36.78	37.37	37.96	38.56
47	30.48	31.07	31.66	32.25	32.84	33.44	34.03	34.63	35.23	35.83	36.43	37.04	37.64	38.25	38.86	39.46
48	31.17	31.77	32.37	32.98	33.59	34.20	34.81	35.42	36.03	36.65	37.27	37.88	38.50	39.13	39.75	40.37
49	31.86	32.48	33.09	33.71	34.34	34.96	35.59	36.21	36.84	37.47	38.10	38.74	39.37	40.01	40.65	41.29
50	32.55	33.18	33.82	34.45	35.09	35.73	36.37	37.01	37.65	38.30	38.94	39.59	40.24	40.89	41.55	42.20
51	33.25	33.89	34.54	35.19	35.84	36.49	37.15	37.81	38.46	39.12	39.79	40.45	41.11	41.78	42.45	43.12
52	33.95	34.61	35.27	35.93	36.60	37.27	37.94	38.61	39.28	39.96	40.63	41.31	41.99	42.67	43.36	44.04
53	34.65	35.32	36.00	36.68	37.36	38.04	38.72	39.41	40.10	40.79	41.48	42.17	42.87	43.57	44.27	44.97
54	35.35	36.04	36.73	37.42	38.12	38.82	39.52	40.22	40.92	41.63	42.33	43.04	43.75	44.47	45.18	45.90
55	36.05	36.76	37.46	38.17	38.88	39.60	40.31	41.03	41.74	42.47	43.19	43.91	44.64	45.37	46.10	46.83
56	36.76	37.48	38.20	38.92	39.65	40.38	41.11	41.84	42.57	43.31	44.05	44.79	45.53	46.27	47.02	47.77
57	37.47	38.20	38.94	39.68	40.42	41.16	41.91	42.65	43.40	44.15	44.91	45.66	46.42	47.18	47.94	48.71
58	38.18	38.93	39.68	40.43	41.19	41.95	42.71	43.47	44.23	45.00	45.77	46.54	47.32	48.09	48.87	49.65
59	38.89	39.66	40.42	41.19	41.96	42.74	43.51	44.29	45.07	45.85	46.64	47.42	48.21	49.01	49.80	50.60
60	39.61	40.39	41.17	41.95	42.74	43.53	44.32	45.11	45.91	46.71	47.51	48.31	49.12	49.92	50.73	51.55

Source: Board of Governors of the Federal Reserve System, Exhibit G—"Truth in Lending—Consumer Credit Cost Disclosure."

3. The number, amount and due dates or period of installments scheduled.
4. The finance charge expressed as an annual percentage rate.

The Supreme Court upheld a Federal Reserve Board rule which specifically imposes the Truth in Lending Act's disclosure requirements on sales where payment is to be made in more than four installments and where the cost of credit is included in the sale price and is not separately stated. The case involved a Florida widow who signed with Family Publications Service, Inc. to purchase a five year subscription for four magazines. The contract required her to make a down payment of $3.95 and thirty monthly payments of $3.95. There was no mention of the total purchase price of $122.45.[27]

Repossession

Sales of repossessed merchandise, especially automobiles, offer an avenue of abuse. Frequently there is no requirement for public sale. Repossession when only one or two payments remain may wipe out the entire equity the purchaser has established. Ethical dealers find ways of avoiding such repossessions, but some firms, particularly in the used car field, appear to specialize in repossession. They draw up contracts, such as those with "balloon clauses," which encourage delinquency and then, when a payment cannot be met, seize the car without notice and either sell it at a rigged sale or collect excessive fees for its return to the customer. In larger cities, in a number of states, dozens of cars are reported to the police as stolen, though in fact they have been repossessed without notice to the installment purchaser.

In many jurisdictions, collateral can be retaken without notice to the purchaser if it does not involve breach of the peace. Breaching the peace, in this connection, is generally interpreted as breaking into a garage, removing a car from a private driveway, or taking a car from a resisting installment buyer. When a purchaser in default will not surrender a car peacefully, a writ of replevin is served on him by the sheriff. In some states, if the collateral is retaken without notice to the purchaser, he may redeem the collateral within 10 days after the retaking by tendering the amount due under the contract, together with any expenses incurred by the seller; but he frequently does not know about this legal right or may not have or be able to obtain the funds to take advantage of it.

---

[27] *Wall Street Journal*, April 25, 1973. For another detailed illustration see *Changing Times*, February 1974, Table p. 22. This demonstrates the minimum payment trap.

In New York State in 1970 a federal court ruled that it was unconstitutional to take property by force without a court order, thus overturning a 700 year old English precedent that had been accepted procedure for creditors. In the historic Fuentes case (1972) the Supreme Court in a 4 to 3 decision seemed to have made invalid laws that did not allow notice and where repossession took place before any hearing was held. The court did not question the power of a state to seize goods "before a final judgment to protect creditors as long as these creditors have tested their claim through the process of a prior hearing." They also exempted situations where seizures were required by public interest such as to collect taxes, protect the public from misbranded drugs or contaminated food. But two years later in May 1974 the Court upheld a Louisiana statute (*Mitchell* v. *W. T. Grant*) that permitted an installment seller to obtain a writ to seize property when payments were overdue without notice to the purchaser—or a hearing. Perhaps these conflicting opinions will be reconciled by the Supreme Court's agreement to hear an appeal from a Chicago man protesting the Illinois' law that allowed his car to be reclaimed by a bank without notice or hearing, for default of payment and transfer title back to the dealer for resale. This case is expected to be heard in 1975.

The Role of the Federal Trade Commission

In December, 1970, the FTC reported on a five city (Boston, Chicago, Los Angeles, Philadelphia, and San Francisco) study of six major categories of complaints accounting for 48 percent of the total 8,800 complaints reported. In order of ranking:

1,272 (14.38%)	Failure to deliver merchandise that has been paid for.
780 (8.81%)	Truth in Lending violations.
657 (7.42%)	Defective work or services.
617 (6.99%)	Inferior merchandise.
508 (5.74%)	False advertising.
413 (4.62%)	Refusal to grant refunds.

The FTC is participating with other federal, state, and local agencies in the formation of consumer protection coordinating committees. It furnishes computer services to these committees for compilation and analysis of complaints, and for correlation of enforcement activities. The cease and desist order used by the FTC to correct law violations under its jurisdiction has an extra power in application to the Truth in Lending Act, since disregard of that order is as if it were a violation of the Federal Trade Commission Act itself.

Annual Percentage Rate
(Consumer Credit Policy Statement #5)

It has come to the attention of the FTC that many retailers and lenders are using terms such as "5% Add-on" or "$6.00 per hundred" to describe the rates which they charge on consumer credit transactions. The Commission believes that the use of such terminology is confusing to consumers and is violative of the Truth in Lending Act and Federal Reserve Regulation Z.

No use should be made in advertising or in other communications with consumers of the add-on or discount rates, whether in percentages or dollars per hundred. Under the Truth in Lending Act and Regulation Z, only the annual percentage rate may be used in advertising the cost of consumer credit, and Truth in Lending contemplates that the annual percentage rate should be used in all oral or written communications to consumers rather than the previously popular add-on or discount rates. Continued use of such confusing terminology may be violative of both Truth in Lending and Section 5 of the Federal Trade Commission Act.

FTC News Summary, December 1971

As part of its education policy, the FTC had been issuing detailed releases of a series of Consumer Credit Policy Statements. In the second such statement, it alerted the public to practices that some credit granters have used to deceive consumers into thinking that the Truth in Lending Act and Regulation Z required them to (*a*) impose finance charges where none had been before, or (*b*) discontinue a discount for prompt payment, or (*c*) discontinue certain kinds of no finance charge deferred payment plans, such as 30–60–90 day accounts and other similar actions—none of which was true.

According to a nationwide survey of credit compliance with Truth in Lending, the FTC found that 86 percent of the major creditors using retail installment contracts are in substantial compliance with the law. Sampling was done at random in 115 of the largest cities in the country. New car dealers were found to be in best compliance in contrast to used car dealers and jewelry stores, which were in the lowest category. Home improvement concerns, television and appliance dealers, and furniture stores were in between. Those who used consumer credit in less than 50 percent of their sales complied more than those who used credit on a larger scale. Sixty-nine percent of the total sample were in complete compliance with Truth in Lending.

There are nine federal agencies involved in Federal Reserve Regulation Z enforcing, as well as Truth in Lending and Consumer Credit Cost Disclosure. Figure 4–10 shows which agency handles what.

State Regulation of Installment Selling

Starting with Indiana in 1935, some 45 states have passed legislation concerned with regulating installment selling in the interest of consumers. The Indiana statute applies to all lines of installment selling. Under it, Indiana's State Department of Financial Institutions is empowered to set maximum finance charges for various lines of installment merchandise. Maximum penalties which may be assessed for late payments are prescribed. Minimum rates of rebate for prepayment of installments are required, not only on the finance charge but also on the insurance charge. The "add-on" clause is outlawed.

A Wisconsin statute is restricted to the automobile business. Dealers, salesmen, finance companies, and manufacturers' representatives are licensed by the state, and a license is subject to revocation if the dealer willfully defrauds any retail buyer or if he fails to furnish him with required information. The seller must give the buyer a complete copy of the installment contract, listing the cash sale price, down payment, trade-in allowance, amount of each installment payment, an exact statement of the insurance coverage in force, and the difference between the cash and the time price. Buyers have the right to complain to the State Banking Department if they think their contracts are unfair. In New York State both the Motor Vehicle Law and the Retail Installment Sales Act, which covers all goods other than motor vehicles, set ceilings on credit charges which installment sellers may ask. A number of states now set maximum credit charges which can be imposed in installment sales.

A national consumer protection organization has been formed by state, county, and city consumer agency officials to exchange information on consumer problems and solutions. It plans to remain separate from the government administration as an organization and to press for consumer legislation. The report of the National Commission on Consumer Finance entitled *Consumer Credit in the U.S.* was released in 1973 and contained 85 recommendations in its 216 pages of 12 chapters, each devoted to a phase of consumer credit. The Commission created by the Federal Consumer Credit Protection Act for this purpose no longer exists, but its report is expected to shape new and workable consumer credit regulation. Continuous change is characteristic of this field.

FIGURE 4–10

TO FIND OUT MORE

If you have any questions about Truth in Lending, you can get information from the federal agency which enforces the law for a particular business. The nine agencies involved, and the businesses they cover, are listed at the end of this leaflet. The law provides criminal penalties for willful violators.

You as an individual may sue if a businessman fails to make the required disclosures. You may sue for twice the amount of the finance charge—for a minimum of $100, up to a maximum of $1,000—plus court costs and reasonable attorney's fees.

FEDERAL AGENCIES

From the list that follows, you will be able to tell which Federal agency covers a particular business. Any questions you have should be directed to that agency.

Retail, Department Stores, Consumer Finance Companies, and all other creditors not listed below

1. Division of Consumer Credit
Federal Trade Commission
Washington, D.C. 20580

National Banks

2. Comptroller of the Currency
United States Treasury Department
Washington, D.C. 20220

State Chartered Banks that are members of the Federal Reserve System

3. Federal Reserve Bank serving the area in which the State member bank is located.

State Chartered Nonmember Banks that are insured by the Federal Deposit Insurance Corporation

4. Federal Deposit Insurance Corporation Regional Director for the Region in which the nonmember insured bank is located.

Savings Institutions insured by the Federal Savings and Loan Insurance Corporation and members of the Federal Home Loan Bank System (except for savings banks insured by Federal Deposit Insurance Corporation)

5. The FHLB's Supervising Agent in the Federal Home Loan Bank District in which the institution is located.

Federal Credit Unions

6. Regional Office of the Bureau of Federal Credit Unions, serving the area in which the Federal Credit Union is located.

Airlines and other creditors subject to Civil Aeronautics Board

7. Director, Bureau of Enforcement
Civil Aeronautics Board
1825 Connecticut Avenue, N.W.
Washington, D.C. 20428

Meat Packers, Poultry Processors and other creditors subject to Packers and Stockyards Act

8. Nearest Packers and Stockyards Administration area supervisor.

Creditors subject to Interstate Commerce Commission

9. Office of Proceedings
Interstate Commerce Commission
Washington, D.C. 20523

Source: Board of Governors of the Federal Reserve System, Washington, D.C., 20551.

SUGGESTED READINGS

1. Gwen J. Bymers, *A Financial Checklist on the Use of Credit*. Ithaca, N.Y.: New York State College of Human Ecology, Cornell University, latest edition.
2. *Finance Facts Yearbook,* Educational Services Division, National Consumer Finance Association, published annually. A free copy may be obtained by writing to the Association at 1000 Sixteenth Street, N.W., Washington, D.C. 20036.
3. Martin J. Meyer, *Credit Cardsmanship*. Lynnbrook, N.Y.: Farnsworth Publishing Co., 1971.
4. ——— *How to Turn Plastic into Gold,* Lynnbrook, N.Y.: Farnsworth Publishing Co., 1974.
5. *Buying on Time,* State of New York. Latest edition. A free copy may be obtained by writing to the New York State Banking Department, Two World Trade Center, New York, N.Y. 10047.
6. David Caplowitz, with assistance of Eric Single, Research Study, *Debtors in Default,* vol. I. New York: Bureau of Applied Social Research, Columbia University, January, 1970.
7. *What Truth in Lending Means To You,* free pamphlet, Board of Governors of the Federal Reserve System, Washington, D.C. 20551.
8. *What You Ought to Know About Federal Reserve Regulation Z—Truth in Lending—Consumer Credit Cost Disclosure*. Booklet available from Board of Governors, Federal Reserve System, Washington, D.C. 20551.
9. *Changing Times, The Kiplinger Magazine*
"New Rules That Protect Your Credit Rating," April 1971.
"Are You Using All Your Truth in Lending Rights?" November 1973
"The Big Name Credit Cards & How They Compare," Sept 1973
"A Time for Cash, a Time for Credit," August 1973
"Don't Just Pay That Charge Account Bill. Read It—," February 1973
"If You're Dunned to Pay a Bill," March 1974
10. Sidney Margolius, *Buyer, Be Wary,* Public Affairs Pamphlet, No. 382, 1971.
11. ———, *A Guide to Consumer Credit,* Public Affairs Pamphlet, No. 348A, 1971.
12. Michael Kawaja, "The Regulation of the Consumer Finance Industry, a Case Study of Rate Ceilings and Loan Limits in New York State," Studies in Consumer Credit, No. 3. New York: Columbia University, Graduate School of Business, 1971.
13. Summary of Hearings on Debt Collection Practices, National Commission on Consumer Finance, in *The Banking Law Journal,* April, 1971.

14. Dale L. Reistad, "Beyond the Credit Card," *Bankers Magazine*, Spring, 1971.
15. Thomas Russell, *Economics of Bank Credit Cards*, New York: Praeger, 1975.
16. Robert A. Hendrickson, *The Cashless Society*, New York: Dodd Mead & Co, 1972.
17. Robert H. Cole, *Consumer and Commercial Credit Management*. 4th ed. Homewood, Ill.: Richard D. Irwin, Inc., 1972.
18. *Report of the National Commission on Consumer Finance and Consumer Credit*, 1973. Superintendent of Documents, U.S. Government Printing Office, Washington, D.C. 20402.
19. Lewis Mandell, *Credit Card Use in the U.S.* Institute for Social Research, University of Michigan, Ann Arbor 1972.
20. *Consumer Credit Life & Disability Insurance*. ed. by Charles L. Hubbard, College of Business Administration of Ohio University, Athens, Ohio 1973.
21. *The Dun & Bradstreet Handbook of Credits and Collections*. Harold T. Redding & Guyon H. Knight III, Thomas Y. Crowell, New York, 1974.
22. Prudence Brown, "Debt Takes a Holiday," *New York Magazine*, November 13, 1972.
23. "When Credit Investigations Dig Into Your Affairs" *U.S. News & World Report*, March 18, 1974.
24. "Credit-Card and Check-Credit Plans at Commercial Banks," *Federal Reserve Bulletin*, September 1973.

CASE PROBLEMS

1. Visit the largest local department store that has a revolving credit plan. Compare the price of a household appliance (*a*) if bought for cash, (*b*) if bought under the revolving credit plan, (*c*) if payment is delayed for a month beyond the billing date.

2. Visit your local Chevrolet or Ford dealer. Select any standard four door sedan model and find out what the finance charge and the annual percentage rate would be if you made the minimum down payment permitted and paid the balance in equal monthly installments over a three year period. Then visit your local bank and find out what the finance charge and the annual percentage rate would be if you borrowed an amount equal to the balance you would owe on the car to be repaid over the same period of time. Compare the rates and give your conclusion as to which would be preferable for you.

3. Select either (*a*) a given standard model television set, or (*b*) a standard model electric refrigerator, or (*c*) a window air conditioner, and visit five stores

or dealers, both cash and credit. Ask the basic price, and charge for purchasing under an installment plan, and installation costs for (*a*) or (*b*) or (*c*). Finally, compare the annual percentage rate for the installment offers with the cash offers. What conclusions do you draw from this study?

4. Visit the manager of your local credit bureau. Ascertain from him how the operation of the Fair Credit Reporting Law has affected the work of his bureau. Ask if you can see your credit record—if not, why not. If a charge is requested ask how much and why. Ask under what circumstances you can get a report of your record without charge. Inquire if there is any adverse information in your file and if so what it is. Write a report detailing the results of your visit.

5. The Household Fair Department Store advertised a standard-make refrigerator for $325 cash. This article may also be purchased on an installment plan, the terms of which are:

a. Down payment—25 percent of cash price.
b. Charges—0.5 percent per month on the original balance financed, payable with and in addition to the down payment.
c. Contract terms—balance financed payable in 12 equal monthly payments.

What is the total amount of the credit service charge? What is the annual percentage rate? Would you be willing to purchase on such terms? For help in solving the problem visit a local department store.

6. Visit any three large local stores that have charge accounts and extend revolving credit. Inquire which method of computing charges they use, whether the *previous balance* method, the *average daily balance* method, or the *adjusted balance* method. Find out from each of the stores what the annual percentage rate charge would be if you made a $90 purchase and paid over three months. Write a brief report describing the answers and indicate your conclusion as to which store you would choose for your purchase and why.

7. Jim and Mary, newlyweds, are about to buy furniture for their apartment. They can make a substantial down payment, but in addition they need credit amounting to $300. They figure they can pay this balance in 10 months. The store where they plan to make their main purchases figures that the monthly payments will have to be $33. They consider the possibility of borrowing the money and paying cash. A small loan company in the neighborhood offers rates of 2 percent a month. A bank offers such loans at a 6 percent discount with an added $2 fee for investigation. Assuming that they can get the credit at either place, what is your advice to Jim and Mary? Support your conclusions with annual percentage rate and dollar cost figures. For help in solving this problem visit a local furniture store, a local bank, and a small loan company.

8. Make a check list of *your* state and local laws and regulations covering: annual finance charge, consumer credit costs, credit cards, revolving credit,

charge accounts, repossession, usury limits, credit insurance charges, wage assignments or garnishment, holder in due course, balloon contracts, and add-on clauses.

9. Robinson bought a television set for $400. He paid $100 down. The balance was to be paid in 20 monthly installments, each of which amounted to $19. After he made 10 monthly payments he lost his job. The seller repossessed the set, spent $55 to recondition it, and sold it for $300. Robinson thinks the seller owes him some money. Discuss. If the seller sold the repossessed set for $200, how much do you think he should seek to recover from Robinson as a deficiency? If the seller sold the repossessed set through an agent who charged 25 percent commission, would your answer be different?

10. *The Poor Pay More* is the title of a provocative book. To ascertain if this is so in your area, visit a TV and radio appliance store, located in a "poverty" or "ghetto" section. Select a store that advertises and sells primarily for credit. Select any standard RCA or Zenith color TV set and find out what it would cost if you paid for it on installments over 18 months. Ascertain the total cost including the finance charge. Then ask what it would cost if you paid cash. Next visit a department store in a central shopping area, and, using the same model color TV set, ascertain the prices for the same two methods of purchase. Finally, visit a discount appliance store in a central shopping area and find out the cash price. If the discount store also sells on the installment plan, find out the total cost if you paid for the set over 18 months. What conclusions do you reach? From this experience do the "poor pay more"?

5

Obtaining a Loan

If you want the time to pass quickly, just give your note for 90 days.
Farmer's Almanac

He who goes a borrowing, goes a sorrowing.
Poor Richard's Almanack

BENJAMIN FRANKLIN'S view of borrowing may have been logical in an age when people went to jail if they could not pay debts, but today we have moved more to the view that a wise and judicious use of credit can materially aid our careers and ease our way. Over half of all the nation's families are in debt, to some extent. Many have borrowed to buy houses and some to buy cars or TV sets; others have made loans to meet emergencies such as sudden illness or funeral expenses, or to pay moving expenses to another city to obtain a better income. A number have gone into debt to help put their children through college, and many have borrowed to pay off other debts.

Personal debt today is over $600 billion, two thirds of it representing mortgage loans which people have obtained to purchase homes. A third consists of "consumer credit," to enable consumers to buy cars, meet doctors' bills, and so on. The funds came from a variety of institutions and individuals—from banks, consumer finance companies, sales finance companies, retailers, insurance companies, savings and loan associations, credit unions, fraternal organizations, loan sharks, pawnbrokers, relatives, and other sources. Indeed, a complete list of sources of small loans is astonishingly diverse.

Your credit is probably better than you think. You probably are not aware of the number of lenders who would be glad to help you if you gave them a chance. In fact, millions are spent in advertising each year to persuade you to do just that. And yet the chances are that when you need and want a loan, you will be embarrassed at the prospect of seeking one, become emotionally upset, and lose some of the good judgment you would normally exercise in any other business transaction. The emergency that induces us to borrow may leave us disturbed and troubled and so distracted by the intense need to obtain the money that straight thinking goes by the board.

It would be well, therefore, to become acquainted with the various sources of loans, the services offered, the requirements, the different rates charged, and the different methods of computation before the emergency or crisis occurs which induces the borrowing. Few want to get into debt; but sooner or later many of us do, and for some it proves to be a very painful lesson which could have been partially avoided if the emergency had been faced coolly because the borrower had previously determined which lenders are reliable, how much could be borrowed, on what terms, and so on. The borrower with such knowledge may then calmly apply for the loan as a business transaction, without fear or apology or emotion. Since a wide variety of financial institutions want to make loans, there is no need to approach the lending institution as if seeking a favor. Thus, if you need a loan, you should go out and shop for it. If your credit standing warrants it, most of them will want to lend to you. Ironically, your credit standing improves if you have once borrowed and repaid. If you have never borrowed you have no credit rating. If reliable lenders refuse—unreliable ones (loan sharks) only spell trouble.

Shopping for a Loan

When you shop for a loan, there are a variety of things to look for; but the two most important are the reliability of the lender and the real total cost of the loan. The former is easier to ascertain than the latter. Any national or state commercial bank with a personal loan department, any insurance company or mutual savings bank, may be considered a reliable lender. An easy test to use for any other type of lender is whether or not it is licensed by the state in which it operates. If there is no state license then beware! The large personal loan companies which operate on a national scale are reputable and sound business enterprises, but some of the very small, local companies, even though licensed by the state, may charge concealed and exorbitant rates. The lender who has no office—who just lends at the corner drugstore or barber shop, or who comes around to your home or office or factory gate—is almost invariably a loan shark and someone from whom you should stay away.

How Much Debt Can You Afford?

It's been so easy to get into debt over the past decade that many people have overdone it. If you are in debt, or contemplating the plunge, there are a number of yardsticks you can use to judge your position. First, your total debts should not exceed 20 percent of your annual (take home) salary. Under this rule, if your annual take home pay is $6,000, you can incur about $1,200 of debt as a maximum. Second, your total debt should not exceed the amount that you can pay off with 10 percent of your income over 12 to 24 months. Assume your take home pay is $500 a month. If you used 10 percent, or $50, to pay off what you owe, you could incur a debt of from $600 to $1,200, depending on whether you had one or two years to pay it. Thirdly, what you owe should not exceed a third of your "discretionary" spending (or saving) for the year. By discretionary spending we mean what you have left to spend from your income after you have made essential expenditures such as those for food, shelter, and clothing. For example, assume your take home pay is $500 a month ($6,000 a year) but that expenditures for rent, food, clothing, essential personal allowances, and so forth, come to $3,600. This leaves $2,400 for discretionary spending or saving. Taking one third of this would suggest a maximum debt of about $800. Naturally these are flexible rules, but applying them in your own case will give you a range within which to operate.

Table 5–1 would indicate that the middle range of income has a higher ratio of debt income. Studies reveal that it is within this range that the mismanagement of borrowing availability, overdraft checking account privileges and multiplicity of credit card debt occurs.

TABLE 5–1
Families in Debt: What They Owe

Average Income	*Average Debt*	*Ratio of Debt to Income*
Less than $3,000	$ 99	4.3%
$3,000–$4,999	328	8.1
$5,000–$5,999	659	12.0
$6,000–$7,499	796	11.6
$7,500–$8,499	963	11.9
$8,500–$9,999	1,140	12.3
$10,000–$12,499	1,229	10.9
$12,500–$14,999	1,247	9.2
$15,000–$19,999	1,137	6.8
$20,000 or more	917	3.2

Source: *Changing Times, The Kiplinger Magazine*, June 1974.

Changes in family needs are reflected in the changing ratio of debt to income—declining from 81 percent in the young family (head under 35 years), to 78 percent for the growing family (head 35–54 years), to 41 percent for the contracting family (head 55–64 years), to 38 percent for the retired family (head 65 years and over), see Figure 5–1. "The typical customer is a skilled or semi-skilled worker with an income of $6,000 to $12,000 a year, who frequently owns his own home. Almost 80 percent of personal loans are obtained to consolidate previously accumulated debt and to get an extension of time to pay it off. In fact, the average borrower

FIGURE 5–1
Average Financial Ratios of Families, by Age Groups

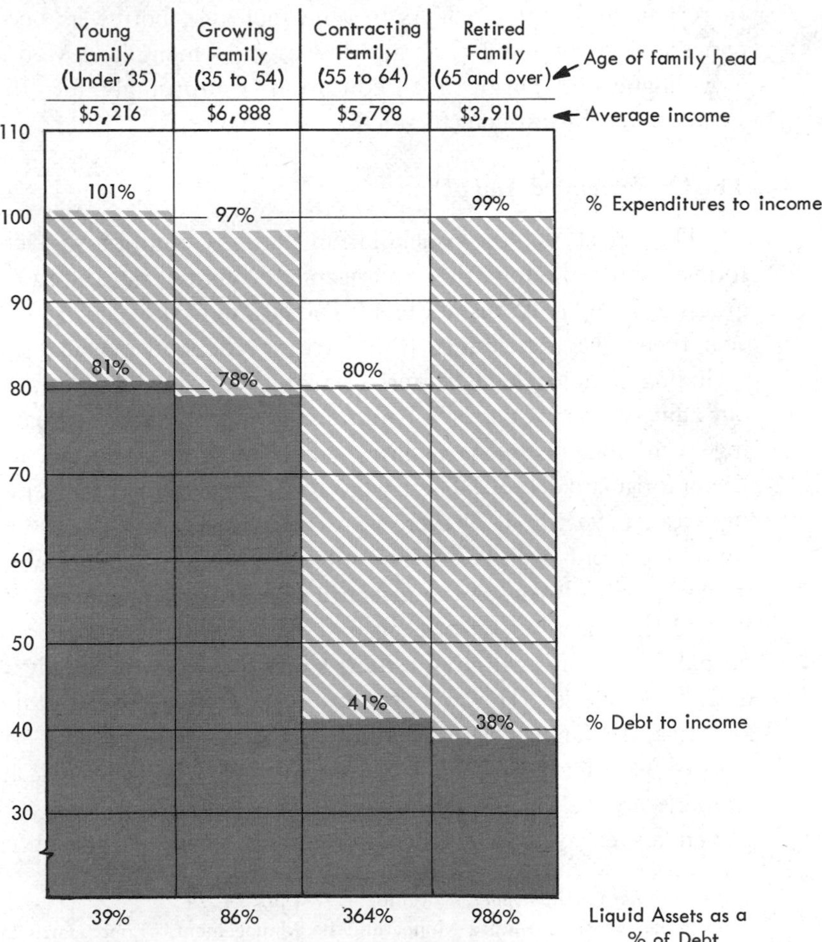

Source: Department of Agriculture from *Finance Facts Yearbook*, 1974

takes out a new loan three times before managing to liquidate his existing balance: he stays in debt to the finance company for 39 months."[1]

Consumer Attitudes toward Borrowing

More people would rather save than borrow for something they "need," according to a survey by Louis Harris & Associates for *Newsweek*. Yet, with the exception of the lower income group sampled, there is no longer any stigma attached to borrowing.[2] The affluent exhibit the least fear of being in debt. Fewer than one in three feel that borrowing is a reflection on their ability to live within their income. When asked what are the main disadvantages of borrowing, the answers "too costly" and "burden of repayment" were cited. As income increases, borrowers become more concerned over interest costs and less over payment size. Many indicated a willingness to borrow for "education," surprisingly few for "travel/vacation" or "investment in stocks" (see Figure 5–2).

The Overextended American

"The Society for the Amelioration of the Condition of Debtors" was formed shortly before the American Revolution by a forward looking group of New York businessmen. Today almost 180,000 Americans each year themselves seek refuge from excessive debt in personal bankruptcy, including some under Chapter XIII of the Federal Bankruptcy Act. In our affluent society, personal bankruptcies have been rising sharply, resulting in millions of dollars of losses to creditors and personal hardship to the unfortunate debtors. There were 163,000 personal (nonbusiness) bankruptcies in 1965; in 1970 there were 178,000. The 1974 figure of 168,000 was 8.4 percent over 1973.[3] The all time high of 208,329 was recorded in 1967 and had marked the fifteenth straight year of increase. California topped the state by state listing and with six other states combined reported 49 percent of all nonbusiness bankruptcies but had only 29 percent of U.S. population. However, the same states (California, Ohio, Illinois, Alabama, Indiana, Tennessee, and Georgia), have receded from their high of 54 percent in 1967. Arkansas, Maine, Massachusetts, and North Carolina are well below the national averages.

Lenders engaged in extending credit have formed credit counseling

---

[1] *Consumer Credit Leader*, November 1973, pp. 14, 24.

[2] "Public Attitudes toward Money and Its Management," Louis Harris & Associates for *Newsweek*, New York, p. 28–38.

[3] Statistics from Bankruptcy Division of the Administrative Office of the United States Courts, *Annual Report of the Director*, 1974.

FIGURE 5–2
Why People Borrow

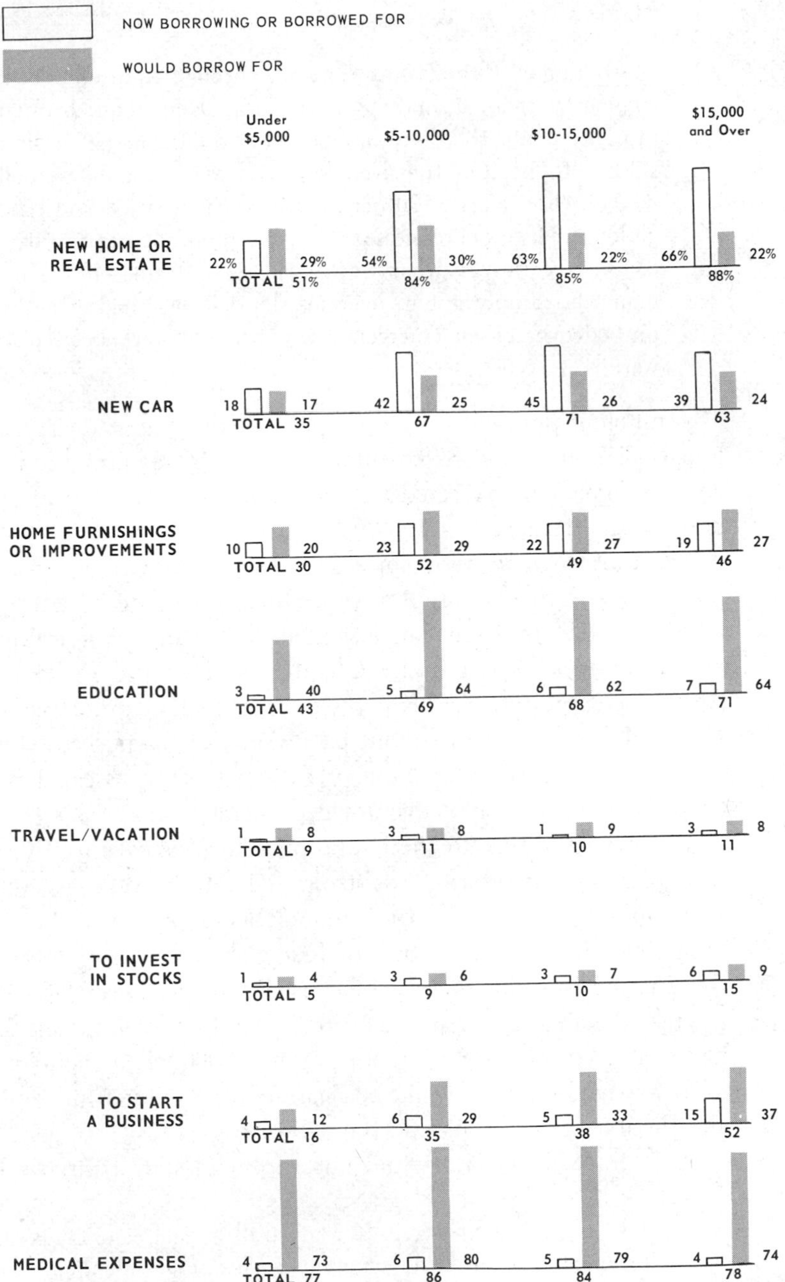

Source: "Public Attitudes Toward Money and Its Management," study conducted by Louis Harris & Associates for *Newsweek* magazine.

services and centers throughout the country to advise hard pressed debtors. Recently the president of the National Foundation for Consumer Credit said:

> In working with thousands of people through counseling centers, we have come up with an accurate portrait of the Overextended American. For one thing he is not the disadvantaged ghetto citizen that he is so often considered to be. On the average, he is a reasonably well-off, blue-collar worker who makes $500 per month. He is married and has two or more children. His indebtedness is in the neighborhood of $3,000. He may be a compulsive buyer—what we call a credit drunk—but generally he is a man who simply got in over his depth unwittingly, bit by bit, or was pushed over by an emergency which could have been planned for but wasn't.

A different personal bankrupt (perhaps the largest on record—$59 million of liabilities and $25.6 million of assets) Lammot du Pont Copeland Jr. agreed to pay creditors between 10 cents and 20 cents on the dollar over the next ten years.[4]

For those who cannot cope with their personal debts and seek the protection of the bankruptcy procedure, there are usually two courses to follow: the insolvent can either file a "straight" or ordinary petition or he can seek shelter under Chapter XIII of the Federal Bankruptcy Act.[5] Once a person has his debts discharged he cannot file again for six years but need not worry about paying any of his unsecured debts. However, property such as a house or car may be repossessed if pledged as collateral and payments have not been made.

Until the addition to the bankruptcy law, passed in 1970, a consumer who had been freed from debts in federal proceedings could be sued again in state courts for the same debts. Now such state actions are brought under the jurisdiction of federal bankruptcy referees, who make the final decision on these debts—usually on the issue of whether there has been "material misrepresentation." If a debtor who earns $5,000 a year had concealed other debts amounting to $2,000 when the loan application form was made out, it would be regarded as "material misrepresentation" and the referee would require the debtor to pay.

A debtor who previously did not appear in state court to defend him-

---

[4] *Wall Street Journal*, May 8, 1974, May 20, 1974, and Nov. 15, 1974.

[5] In the unlikely event that you want further information on this subject, see Thomas M. Ryan, "Economic Relief for the Honest Debtor," *Consumer Credit Leader*, May 1974; also Robert J. Cole, "Personal Finance," *New York Times*, November 8, 1973; Jerome L. Meyers, "How to Go Bankrupt and Start Over," *New York Magazine*, Sept. 10, 1973.

self in a suit (either because he did not know he was being sued or because he thought the federal bankruptcy proceedings under Chapter XIII had ended the matter), was faced with a state court judgment. The 1970 law offers some relief in that the creditors must see that the debtor's lawyer is advised of any new action—presumably while he still has a lawyer during the bankruptcy proceedings.

A poorly publicized alternative, if a debtor has some regular income, is the "wage earner plan" under Chapter XIII of the Bankruptcy Act. Under it, a person files a petition in U.S. District Court for approval of a budget that sets aside basic monthly living expenses plus a specified amount to be paid to creditors. These plans are administered by court appointed trustees and usually last about three years. Expenses are paid by the debtor and amount to about 7.5 percent of the money the court pays to the creditor. The advantages are protection from dunning or garnishment of wages. A two year study of the bankruptcy system completed by a nine member commission created by congressional resolution made some drastic recommendations. A major proposal was to abolish the device of "reaffirmation"—a method by which a debtor waives the right to the discharge of the debt—after the Bankruptcy Court has cleared the debt. This can happen when a debtor has not fully disclosed all debts in the original application for a loan (often to insure that the loan would be granted). The creditor might then be able to persuade the debtor to "reaffirm" the debt or face suit over the false loan papers. This proposal would eliminate, as a basis for denial of bankruptcy, the use of a false financial statement.

Most of those legally released from debt through bankruptcy proceedings use credit again. According to David R. Earl, chairman of the state board that supervises collection agencies in Oregon and author of the book *The Bankruptians*, about 80 percent of those who do use credit again are in debt trouble within five years "to the point of repossession and collection procedures. Within 7 years, 10 percent of bankrupts file for bankruptcy again and within 10 years, the figure reaches 20 percent."[6]

A different viewpoint is expressed by Herbert S. Denenberg—author of a newly published "Consumer's Guide to Bankruptcy," currently Special Advisor for Consumer Affairs to the Governor of Pennsylvania and formerly Pennsylvania Insurance Commissioner. He is quoted as saying, "by going bankrupt you may improve your credit rating. Creditors know that (by law) you can't go bankrupt again for six years. Plus the system shoves

[6] Richard A. Shaffer, "Debtors' Dilemma," *Wall Street Journal*, November 5, 1970. For a different point as expressed by Herbert S. Denenberg, see *New York Times*, January 8, 1975.

credit down your throat. An astounding number of bankrupts are doing it for a second time, so obviously they have been able to reestablish credit." His guide is intended to inform consumers that bankruptcy is a citizen's right under the U.S. Constitution.

Excessive garnishment of wages or salary to pay off debt is one of the main forces that lead to personal bankruptcy. Garnishment means any legal procedure through which the earnings of any individual are required to be withheld for payment of any debt. The 1968 Consumer Credit Protection Act provides a federal limitation on garnishment. The maximum part of the aggregate disposable earnings of any individual for any workweek which is subjected to garnishment may not exceed (*a*) 25 percent of his disposable earnings for that week, or (*b*) an amount by which disposable earnings for that week exceed 30 times the federal minimum hourly wage, whichever is less. It is expected that this federal limitation on garnishment will have some moderating impact on personal bankruptcies.

How Much Will the Loan Cost?

If, in shopping for a loan of $100, repayable in equal monthly installments over a 12 month period, one lender required you to repay $10.07 per month; another $9.75; a third $8.87; and a fourth $8.67, and all other factors were equal, you would probably be inclined to borrow from the lender who quoted the lowest rate, namely $8.67. Over the year you would save $16.80 by borrowing from the last rather than the first lender. These were actual rates. The first lender was a small personal loan company, the second was a large national consumer finance company, the third was a credit union, and the last was the personal loan department of a very large commercial bank.

Before Truth in Lending, rates were often not quoted on this simple, comparable basis, and it was frequently difficult to know exactly what comparable costs were. There were different ways of measuring costs. Lenders used varying methods of charging for loans, and in some cases there might be several scattered charges instead of a single one. Interest can be discounted, added on, or figured on the declining balance. The latter is the less expensive of all methods, as you only are paying for what you are still using.

Tables 5–2 and 5–3 illustrate clearly the difference in showing the cost of a small loan before and after Truth in Lending. You will notice in Table 5–2 that if you borrow $100 for six months your payment would be $18.15 per month and under this old method you had no way of

TABLE 5–2
Illustration of Incomplete Borrowing Information before Truth in Lending

Amount of Loan	*Number and Amount of Monthly Payments* 6 Payments	12 Payments	15 Payments	20 Payments
$ 50	$ 9.08			
75	13.62	$ 7.31	$ 6.06	
100	18.15	9.75	8.08	$ 6.41
200	36.13	19.33	15.98	12.65
300	54.02	28.82	23.80	18.80
400	71.53	38.00	31.31	24.64
500	88.83	46.94	38.57	30.22

The company's charge is 2.5 percent per month on balances of $100 or less, 2 percent per month on that part of the balance in excess of $100 and not in excess of $300, and 0.5 percent per month on that part of the balance in excess of $300, up to a maximum of $500.

knowing how much of it was payment of principal and how much was finance charge. You therefore did not know the interest rate you were paying and could not compare it with other loan sources to see if you were getting the best buy. For example, in Table 5–2, the borrower will repay $9.75 per month for 12 months if his loan is $100 and he elects to pay it back over a year; 12 × $9.75 = 117 – $100 = $17, the true dollar cost of the loan.

This "true dollar cost" is one of two basic methods of measuring and comparing costs. You add up all the money that you pay the lender from the time you apply for the loan until it is repaid, including all fees, and then subtract the amount of cash you get from the lender. The difference is the true dollar cost. It is the real figure you are looking for, but it affords

TABLE 5–3
New York Small Loans—Finance Charges and Annual Percentage Rate under the Actuarial Method

	6 Months		*12 Months*		*24 Months*		*36 Months*		*48 Months*	
Amount	*Charge*	*APR*	*Charge*	*APR*	*Charge*	*APR*	*Charge*	*APR*	*Charge*	*APR*
50	4.42	30.00	8.44	30.00	16.96	30.00				
100	8.90	30.00	16.88	30.00	34.16	30.00				
200	16.72	28.21	31.84	28.25	63.76	28.18				
400	30.56	25.78	58.28	25.89	116.24	25.82	177.44	25.69		
600	42.48	23.89	80.64	23.95	160.08	23.85	243.84	23.70		
800	53.62	22.63	101.68	22.70	201.76	22.61	306.64	22.47		
1000	64.28	21.72	122.00	21.82	242.00	21.75	367.64	21.62		
1500	88.74	20.02	168.48	20.12	333.12	20.05	504.84	19.94	683.52	19.82
2000	112.00	18.96	212.20	19.04	419.20	18.99	634.84	18.88	858.88	18.77
2500	134.72	18.25	255.08	18.33	503.36	18.28	761.96	18.19	1030.40	18.09

Note: 2.5%—$100; 2%—$300; 1.5%—$900; 1.25%—$2,500.
Source: Adapted from *Cost of Personal Borrowing in the United States*, Financial Publishing Company, Boston.

an accurate comparison only when two loans have the same length and method of repayment. When they do not, then it is better to use the second basic method, the annual percentage rate, which is the method required in Truth in Lending. This will enable you to compare costs when loans differ in length and payment plans.

In the dollar cost illustration given in Table 5–2, you might imagine at first glance that the true annual rate was 17 percent. You paid $17 for a loan of $100 over a period of a year. Offhand, that looks like 17 percent, but it is not. Why? Because you did not have the use of the whole $100 for a complete year. During the second month you would have the use of only $^{11}/_{12}$ of the loan, during the third month only $^{10}/_{12}$ of the loan, and so on, and during the final month only $^{1}/_{12}$, so that, for the whole year, you would have had, on the average, the use of only about $50. To approximate the annual percentage rate, you need only apply the following constant ratio formula:

$$r = \frac{2mI}{p(n+1)},$$

where

r = the annual rate percentage charged,
m = the number of payment periods in one year (12 if you are repaying monthly, regardless of the number of months you take, and 52 if you are repaying weekly, regardless of the number of weeks you actually take),
I = true dollar cost of the loan,
p = the net amount of the loan,
n = the number of repayments you actually will make.

Applying this formula to the illustration above, of the $100 loan, repayable over a year, which cost $17, we find

$$r = \frac{2 \times 12 \times 17}{100(12+1)} = 31 + \text{percent.}$$

Thus, it is apparent that the annual rate of interest is about 31 percent under the constant ratio method. As illustrated by Table 5–3, it is 30 percent under the actuarial method.

In the past one had to apply this formula to each case as one shopped for a loan before comparative costs became clear and evident. Now all you need do is compare the annual percentage rates disclosed as required under the Consumer Credit Protection Act. These rates are computed under the actuarial method and usually are therefore slightly lower than the rates that would result from use of the constant ratio formula.

You might be surprised at how many people—even now with the advent

TABLE 5–4
Awareness of Interest Costs

Type of Loan	Percentage of "Don't Knows" 1969	1970
First mortgages	27	13
Home improvement	35	27
New automobiles	27	21
Used automobiles	40	34
Appliances and furniture	58	42
Personal loans	43	28
Retail charge accounts	48	32

Source: "Ignorance Shown on Interest Rates," *New York Times*, February 7, 1971, p. 24.

of the Truth in Lending Act, which forces lenders to disclose the annual percentage rate—still do not know what actual interest rates they are paying. The percentage of "don't knows" was disclosed in a recent survey by the Federal Reserve Board. The results are shown in Table 5–4. Note, however, that since 1969, when the act went into effect, there has been an increase in consumer awareness of credit costs. Figure 5–3 illustrates the increase in this awareness with higher income levels.

FIGURE 5–3
What Is Your Main Consideration When Deciding to Take Out a Loan?

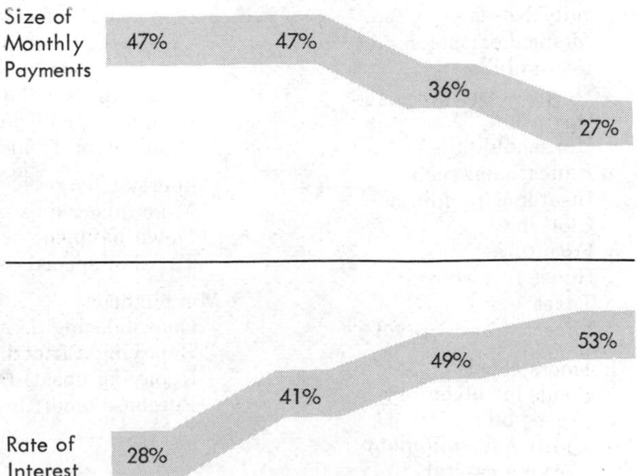

Source: "Public Attitudes toward Money and its Management" study conducted by Louis Harris & Associates for *Newsweek* magazine.

Differences among Lenders

Prospective borrowers will find that lenders differ not only in their charges but in the security or collateral required, in the extent of the credit risks taken, in size of loans, and in length of time allowed for repayment. Some lenders require comakers, or cosigners; others require a specific pledge of collateral, such as the signing of a chattel mortgage on household furniture or an automobile. Others will grant loans merely on the borrower's signature if the credit investigation indicates that there is a reasonable probability that the loan will be repaid. Some will not extend credit to unemployed persons or to those whose income is below a certain level. Most lenders will want to know why you need the money or for what you propose to use it. Some banks will not grant loans where the proceeds are to be used to repay old debts, while, on the other hand, a leading personal finance company reports that 30 percent of its loans are to pay family debts already contracted. Figure 5–4 lists some of the main purposes for which personal loans are granted.

The length of time for which loans are made varies from a few months to as much as three years. Some lenders will not bother with very short term loans of a month or two. Others will not lend for as long a period as three years even when repayment is on a monthly basis. Personal loans run in size anywhere from $10 to $32,500. Some lenders are limited by law to a maximum amount of $500; others will not wish to bother with a loan of $50 or less. To obtain the kind of loan you want, on the most

FIGURE 5–4
Some of the Useful Purposes for Which Personal Loans Are Made

Family Needs
- Medical expenses
- Dental bills
- Hospital charges
- Operation
- Household bills
- Educational costs
- Insurance premium
- Clothing
- Furniture
- House furnishings
- Taxes
- Vacation and Travel

Business Needs
- Goods for inventory
- Urgent bills
- Additional equipment
- Working capital

Motor Car Purposes
- Purchasing cars and trucks —new or used
- Using car as collateral
- Fire, theft, collision insurance
- Public liability insurance

Property Charges
- Modernization or improvements
- Down payment on home
- Taxes or special assessments

Miscellaneous
- Consolidating debts
- Repaying a friend for a loan
- Repaying unsatisfactory loan
- Purchase securities for investment

favorable terms available, it is useful to shop around before you make your commitment. You cannot expect to do as well by waiting until the emergency is upon you and then rushing to the first lender within range. Perhaps a survey of different types of lenders and their policies will show you why this is so.

Borrowing on Life Insurance Policies

One of the least expensive ways of obtaining a personal loan is to borrow on your life insurance policy. After the first two or three years, most life policies, except term insurance, accumulate a "cash" or "loan" value, which increases each additional year the policy is in force. This "cash" or "loan" value for each year of the policy's life is shown in a table in your contract. This also tells you at what rate the company will lend you the cash you need against the "loan" value of the policy. You will pay from 5 to 6 percent, depending on the company and your contract, which is better than you can do elsewhere. On veteran's U.S. government insurance the rate is 5 percent. These are true annual rates, so that the real dollar cost for a loan of $100, borrowed for a whole year and repaid, not in monthly installments, but all at the end of the year, is only $5 or $6.

The insurance company cannot turn you down when you ask for a loan within the limit of the "cash" value of your policy. Cash value builds up gradually, so that in 12 to 13 years it roughly equals the total of premiums paid in. Your right to obtain the loan is part of the contract, and your credit standing, good or bad, has nothing to do with your right to the loan, providing premiums have been paid and the policy is in force. In some states the law permits the company to postpone the loan for a period of from 90 days to 6 months, but this privilege is rarely invoked. The purpose of this provision is to protect the company against a "run" on its reserves. At a time of crisis or emergency or depression, such a large number of policyholders might, in one short period, ask for funds that the company's liquid assets might become depleted. Apart from this provision, however, you can get your loan at any time merely by requesting it. There is no credit investigation and no extra fee, and the company does not ask, nor has it any control over, what you do with the proceeds of the loan.[7]

---

[7] In 1970 and in 1973–74 interest rates on corporate and government bonds soared to record highs. This prompted many individuals to borrow against the cash values of their life insurance policies at rates established in the policy years earlier, namely, about 5 percent to 6 percent. The individual could then purchase U.S. Treasury bills at yields of up to 9 percent, thereby making a 2 percent to 3 percent differential on their borrowed funds.

Each year insurance companies make new policy loans totaling hundreds of millions of dollars and have total loans outstanding of several billion dollars. There is little relationship between new loans made in any year and the total of loans outstanding because there is no set period of time for repayment of a policy loan. You can take as long or as short a period as you want to repay, and indeed you do not need to repay at all if you so choose.

The companies encourage but do not demand that such loans be repaid. If the interest charge is not paid, it is usually added to the loan. Whenever the policy becomes payable, whether due to death or maturity, any outstanding loan is deducted from the amount of the claim the insurance company pays. This unique feature of a policy loan has both advantages and disadvantages. The loan reduces your insurance protection, and there is a constant temptation to postpone repayment because there is an absence of pressure. On the other hand, if you just cannot repay the loan, your salary is not garnisheed, nor your car or household furniture taken from you.

Savings Bank Passbook Loans

You can obtain a personal loan at relatively low rates using your savings account as collateral. As Table 5–5 shows, the largest savings bank in the country charges 7.50 percent—annual percentage rate—for a loan repayable over 12 months, or 24 months or 36 months.

TABLE 5–5
Examples of Amounts Financed and Payments (annual percentage rate 7.50 percent)

Cash to Borrower	*Finance Charge*	*Total of Payments*	*Monthly Payments*
12 month loan			
$ 576.32	$ 23.68	$ 600	$ 50
1,037.38	42.62	1,080	90
2,881.60	118.40	3,000	250
24 month loan			
$ 555.56	$ 44.44	$ 600	$ 25
1,000.01	79.99	1,080	45
2,777.81	222.19	3,000	125
36 month loan			
$ 803.70	$ 96.30	$ 900	$ 25
1,446.66	173.34	1,620	45
4,018.50	481.50	4,500	125

Source: Bowery Savings Bank.

The reason savings bank passbook loans carry a relatively low rate is that the loan is fully protected by your savings account. The bank takes no risk. Why would you in effect want to borrow your own money? Why not draw out the savings and use the funds instead of borrowing?

There are several answers. Many people after making numerous small deposits slowly over a considerable time do not want to withdraw their savings suddenly. If they borrow, they continue to earn interest. Thus the loan costs little. If they earn 5.25 percent and pay 7.25 percent, the net cost is 2 percent, and when they repay the loan they still have the savings account paying 5.25 percent. In addition, psychologically there is more pressure on the average person to repay a loan than to rebuild a savings account. Furthermore, when interest is credited quarterly if left until the end of the quarter, you may lose interest for two thirds of a quarter if you withdraw your savings during the last month of that quarter. The loss is even greater when interest is credited semiannually if funds are on deposit for the half year and you withdraw in the fifth or sixth month.

Personal Loan Departments of Commercial Banks

At one time commercial banks looked down upon consumer loans and would have little to do with them. Today, commercial banks are the largest source of such funds, sharing the field with the small loan or consumer finance companies. Of total consumer loans outstanding, amounting to over $147.4 billion, commercial banks account for 47.2 percent, consumer finance companies for 25.2 percent, credit unions for 13.3 percent, retail outlets for 12.3 percent, and other financial institutions for 2 percent.

There are two main reasons why the commercial banks have led in the granting of small loans. They are able to make them at rates considerably below those charged by consumer finance companies. Yet they have found the business quite profitable and have, therefore, through advertising, gone after it vigorously.

In recent years, commercial banks have developed several new plans to give them a greater share of the consumer loan market. The two most popular have been charge account banking and revolving personal loans. The basic tool of the charge account system is the credit card, issued to those who meet the bank's credit requirements. With this card the consumer can charge purchases at any store belonging to the bank's plan. When a purchase is made, the customer signs a sales slip which, in effect, is a note to the bank. At the end of the month the customer gets a single bill from the bank covering all purchases. He then has the choice of either paying in a lump sum or of spreading payments over a number of months and paying a fee—1 percent or 1.5 percent a month—on the unpaid balance. The credit is revolving. As the account is paid down, new purchases may be made.

Revolving personal loans, on the other hand, sometimes called Check-Credit, or Readi-Credit, do not involve a credit card. The customer simply applies for a "line of credit" based on ability to make monthly repayments. If the bank allows 24 months for repayment and the borrower can afford to repay $50 per month, then he can apply for a $1,200 "line of credit." Upon approval, after a credit investigation, the borrower gets a special book of checks to use in drawing in the $1,200 account that the bank sets up for him. Popularly known as a "guaranteed checking account" because the borrower will receive an identification card issued by the bank, which provides check cashing privileges where the customer is unknown, and where a regular personal check might be refused. The borrower is charged only for the amount actually used. The usual charge is 1 percent a month on the outstanding balance. As in all revolving plans, the credit is rebuilt, up to the designated ceiling, as the account is repaid. The main advantage of the revolving personal loan plan is that you can buy what you want where you want.

A variation is the Checking Plus account. It's an overdraft system which permits you to write checks in excess of the balance in your account. You fill out an application for such an account, and the bank sets up a credit reserve for you from $400 to $5,000, depending on your needs and your ability to repay.

Once the reserve is set up, you don't need to use it unless you want to do so. It doesn't cost anything if it isn't used. But you can write a check for more than you have in your checking account. Money sufficient to cover it is transferred automatically into your checking account from your credit reserve. The reserve is available when you need it. You can draw on it up to the limit of your approved credit. And, as you repay, you rebuild your credit reserve so that you can use it again.

Each month you receive a credit reserve statement showing the amount, if any, which has been transferred to your checking account and the amount you have to repay. Once your credit reserve is established, no advance notice to the bank is necessary to use it. You just write your usual check. No one knows that you are using credit. And your canceled checks are returned to you, unlike in other revolving check plans.

Banks found that they could handle personal loans at the traditional discount rates charged on commercial loans, since the installment method of repayment for the personal loan made the annual percentage rate of return on the loan roughly double the stated discount rate. For commercial banks, stated discount rates on the full amount of the loan ranged from 4.75 to 13 percent. Since loans are repaid in equal monthly installments and only about half of the full amount of the loan is outstanding for the entire repayment period, the annual percentage rates range from 9 to 27 percent, with 12 or 13 percent as a common average. The way in which commercial banks have adapted their discount rates to the new requirements of the Truth in Lending Act may be seen in Table 5–6. What was formerly stated as a 5.75 percent discount rate on loans repayable in 12 months now is stated as an 11.08 annual percentage rate. If repayable in 24 months, the 5.75 discount rate becomes a 12.02 annual percentage rate, while for loans repayable over 36 months the 5.75 percent discount rate becomes 12.74.

Banks predominate in financing automobile loans, holding $31.3 billion of outstanding paper in contrast to the $11.9 billion held by finance companies, the $7.6 billion that credit unions have, and the $0.3 billion in the hands of auto dealers. Rates vary from 9 to 24 percent annually and are secured. The trend toward longer car loans is not necessarily advantageous.

A two year loan of $3,000 at 11 percent annual percentage rate (APR) brings a total interest charge of $355.68. A three year loan at the same rate would cost $535.74 and for four years would cost $721.68. By this time your car will have depreciated considerably. If you trade your car before it is fully paid for, you lose equity in reverse ratio to the number

TABLE 5–6
Thirty-Six Payment Chart with 12.74 Annual Percentage Rate (formerly 5.75 percent discount rate)

Amount Financed	*Finance Charge*	*Total of Payment*	*Monthly Payment*
$ 29.79	$ 6.21	$ 36	$ 1
59.58	12.42	72	2
89.37	18.63	108	3
119.16	24.84	144	4
148.95	31.05	180	5
1,370.34	285.66	1,656	46
1,400.13	291.87	1,692	47
1,429.92	298.08	1,728	48
1,459.71	304.29	1,764	49
1,489.50	310.50	1,800	50
2,561.94	534.06	3,096	86
2,591.73	540.27	3,132	87
2,621.52	546.48	3,168	88
2,651.31	552.69	3,204	89
2,681.10	558.90	3,240	90

of payments left. The less equity, the more financing your new car will cost.

Increasingly, banks throughout the country are changing from discount rates to calculating them on a simple interest basis. As a result of full disclosure of interest rates, borrowers had found that a discounted loan is not to their advantage, since they pay the interest in advance and have to borrow more to get the amount they need. Especially if some installments are paid ahead of time—or if the remaining balance is paid in lump sum ahead of schedule it costs more than if calculated under the simple interest method even though both methods are figured at the same rate. This is because the simple interest method charges on a declining balance; you pay only on what you still owe. Truth in Lending disclosure has also raised questions about an old banking practice of figuring interest on a year of 360 days. Exact simple interest requires using the exact number of days in a calender year—365. Otherwise, the bank is increasing the real rate of interest.

Why are many commercial banks able to make personal loans at lower costs to borrowers than most other lenders? They obtain their loan funds from bank depositors at very low cost, whereas the consumer finance companies frequently borrow their funds from the banks. Most of the overhead of the bank's operation is paid for out of earnings on commercial loans, and very little needs to be charged to the personal loan department. Rent is a good example. In the small loan company, the borrowers carry the entire burden; in the commercial bank, they bear only a very small share.

Losses on personal loans of commercial banks are very small, perhaps because they select their credit risks more carefully; perhaps because they prefer secured loans, although they do make single signature loans; and perhaps because they encourage automobile and home improvement loans, which run to larger amounts, and tend to shy away from very small loans for short terms. What probably happens is that the better credit risks seek, and are accepted by the banks, while the poorer risks, knowing their own status, stay away from the banks and go initially to consumer finance companies. The result is that the range of applicants for credit from loan companies is poorer in the first instance than in the case of banks. This suggests, of course, the advisability of trying a commercial bank first, if you want to borrow. If you are accepted, fine; if not, you can always try elsewhere.

Are You a Good Risk?

The American Bankers Association *Bank Manual on Personal Loans* sheds interesting light on what banks look for in granting or refusing personal loans. The first question the bank asks itself is, "Does the applicant have adequate borrowing capacity?" People frequently want to borrow to "consolidate other debts," and in this case the bank wants to know about *all* the other debts; then it will seek to determine whether the borrower's income is sufficient to meet living expenses as well as cover the monthly payments on the consolidated debt. The *Bank Manual* declares: "Income must balance living expenses and the liquidation of all debts. There can be no other deferment of debts while the borrower is liquidating one set of obligations. Only in the rarest instance should the borrower be left with any monthly payments except those to the bank."

If you want a home improvement loan, the bank will want to be sure that your income is sufficient to meet living expenses, to pay interest and principal on your mortgage, to pay taxes, and to meet the monthly installments on your improvement loan as well. If you are applying for a car loan, the bank will want to be sure that you can make repayments on the debt even when your pocketbook is under the added strain of paying for gasoline, tires, repairs, and the other expenses which a car involves. In short, the bank will in every case ask itself, "Does the applicant have adequate income?" The most common reason for rejecting a loan is lack of income from which repayment can be made. Personal loans are, in a great majority of cases, loans against future income; and if, after careful, down-to-earth calculation, it becomes apparent that future income will not be adequate, the loan application is likely to be rejected. As a rule of thumb, banks tend to limit advances to an amount which will require monthly payments that are no greater than 10 percent of the borrower's income.

The banker is concerned with three important factors: the character of the borrower; ability to repay, not out of present capital but from future income; and, finally, the borrower's capacity for using the money beneficially. In a credit investigation the banker asks himself three more questions about the borrower in addition to the income estimation: "Does he work where he says he works?" "Does he live where he says he lives?" and "Does he pay his bills?" The banker uses various means to check each. The prospective borrower will be asked to fill out an application, and this form is then checked by phone or spot investigation. One side of such an application form is shown in Figure 5–5. This investigation is conducted quickly, and if everything is found to be as stated the applicant will be notified quickly of the approval of the loan request. When he returns to the bank to obtain the funds, he will be asked to supply additional information. The ABA *Manual* declares:

> With the check in his hand, made payable to the borrower, the banker should ask for information regarding close relatives not living with the borrower, the names of two or three friends, and the names and ages

FIGURE 5–5

FORM DESIGNED AND APPROVED BY CONSUMER CREDIT DEPT. AND BANK MANAGEMENT COMMISSION AMERICAN BANKERS ASSOCIATION

APPLICATION FOR PERSONAL LOAN
(INCLUDING DIRECT INSTALMENT SALES FINANCING)

NAME ______________________ (DATE) ________

TO ______________________ (BANK)

(FILL ALL BLANKS, WRITING "NO" OR "NONE" WHERE NECESSARY TO COMPLETE INFORMATION)

AMOUNT OF LOAN APPLIED FOR ______________________ DOLLARS $______

PURPOSE: PROCEEDS OF THIS LOAN, IF GRANTED, ARE TO BE USED AS FOLLOWS: ______________________

THE ________ DAY OF EACH MONTH IS MOST CONVENIENT FOR MAKING PAYMENTS.

FOR THE PURPOSE OF OBTAINING THE AFOREMENTIONED LOAN, THE UNDERSIGNED MAKES THE FOLLOWING STATEMENT OF ______ FINANCIAL CONDITION AS OF THE ______ DAY OF ____________, 19___, AND CERTIFIES TO THE ABOVE-NAMED BANK THAT THE INFORMATION HEREINAFTER SET FORTH IS IN ALL RESPECTS TRUE, ACCURATE AND COMPLETE AND CORRECTLY REFLECTS THE FINANCIAL CONDITION OF THE UNDERSIGNED ON THE DATE AFOREMENTIONED.

PERSONAL

HOME ADDRESS ________ CITY ________ STATE ________ PHONE ________

NUMBER OF YEARS AT THIS ADDRESS ________ NUMBER OF YEARS IN THIS COMMUNITY ________ PREVIOUS ADDRESS (IF AT PRESENT ADDRESS LESS THAN TWO YEARS) ________

AGE ______ MARRIED—YES ☐ NO ☐ IF YES, NAME OF SPOUSE ________ NUMBER OF DEPENDENTS INCLUDING WIFE ________

NAME OF NEAREST LOCAL RELATIVE ________ ADDRESS ________

EMPLOYMENT

FIRM ________

ADDRESS ________ PHONE ________

KIND OF BUSINESS ________

YOUR POSITION ________

NAME AND TITLE OF SUPERIOR ________ HOW LONG WITH THIS EMPLOYER ________

PREVIOUS EMPLOYER ________ HOW LONG ________

IF SPOUSE IS EMPLOYED, WHERE? ________

IF IN BUSINESS FOR SELF, PLEASE STATE

FIRM OR TRADE NAME ________

ADDRESS ________ PHONE ________

KIND OF BUSINESS ________

YOUR INTEREST IN THE BUSINESS ________ HOW LONG ________

TRADE REFERENCES ________

PREVIOUS EMPLOYER ________ HOW LONG ________

MONTHLY INCOME

SALARY, WAGES AND COMMISSIONS ________ $______

SALARY OF SPOUSE (IF EMPLOYED) ________ $______

OTHER INCOME (STATE SOURCE) ________ $______

TOTAL MONTHLY INCOME ________ $______

MONTHLY EXPENSE

RENTAL OR MORTGAGE PAYMENTS ______ $______

ESTIMATED LIVING EXPENSE (FOOD, UTILITIES, INSURANCE, ETC.) ______ $______

PRESENT CONTRACT OBLIGATIONS ______ $______

TOTAL FIXED EXPENSES ______ $______

BALANCE, INCOME OVER EXPENSE $______

BANKING

CHECKING ACCOUNT $________ BANK ________ SAVINGS ACCOUNT $________ BANK ________

HAVE YOU HAD A PREVIOUS LOAN WITH US? YES ☐ NO ☐ TYPE OF LOAN ________ YEAR? ________

LIFE INSURANCE

AMOUNT $________ CASH VALUE $________ AMOUNT BORROWED ON INSURANCE $________

COMPANY ________ BENEFICIARY ________

SECURITIES

FACE VALUE (BONDS) NUMPER OF SHARES (STOCKS)	DESCRIPTION OF SECURITY	MARKET VALUE	INCOME RECEIVED LAST YEAR
		$	$

> of any of the borrower's children and whether they are in school. . . . The purpose in getting this additional information which is sometimes difficult to obtain at the time the application is being taken (and difficult just because the applicant does not want any one checking with his relatives or his friends), is that such information is necessary in the event of a "skip." Experience will show that a skip can usually be traced if the collector has information regarding two or three friends, two or three relatives, or a child or two in school.[8]

Credit Scoring Systems

A number of financial institutions have experimented with credit scoring systems as a means of more readily discriminating between good and poor credit risks. Weighted values, points, are assigned to various credit characteristics. For example, a homeowner may receive 25 points; a renter who has lived in the same place for five years or more, 15 points; a new renter, 0 points; and a boarder, −10. A person may receive 25 points for having held a position as a supervisor for the past five years; a clerk on the job one year, 5 points; a construction worker on a temporary job, 0 points; and an unemployed person, −20. Elaborate studies have been made to develop point scores for identifiable credit characteristics of good borrowers and to detect signs indicative of possible or probable default.

In one scoring system a probability table such as is shown in Table 5–7 was developed. A lender using a scoring system associated with this table might decide to reject all prospective borrowers with scores of 400 or less, thereby sharply increasing the probability that loans granted (to those with scores of 401 or better) would be repaid.

An effective scoring system enables risk to be determined more from a lending organization's accumulated experience than from the "human element" based on the judgment of an individual credit man, which may influence the lender to refuse credit unfairly.[9]

"Numerical point scoring to determine the quality of a borrowers' credit risk ignores the color of a man's skin, the neighborhood in which he lives, and/or his political leanings. It asks only if he has the capacity to pay his obligations, if there is some likelihood that this ability will continue

---

[8] *A Bank Manual on Personal Loans* (New York: Consumer Credit Department, American Bankers Association), pp. 12–13. See also *Analyzing the Cost Factors of Installment Lending* (New York: American Bankers Association).

[9] Herbert J. H. Roy and Edward M. Lewis, "Overcoming Obstacles in Using Credit Scoring Systems," *Consumer Finance News*, vol. 55, no. 4 (October 1970). See also H. J. H. Roy and E. M. Lewis, "Credit Scoring as a Management Tool," *Consumer Credit Leader*, vol. I, no. 4 (September 1971).

TABLE 5-7
Credit Risk Probability Table

Credit Score (points)	*Number Bad*	*Number Good*	*Total*	*Probability of Going Bad*
200–300	5	1	6	83% (5 ÷ 6)
301–400	10	10	20	50 (10 ÷ 20)
401–500	13	25	38	34 (13 ÷ 38)
501–600	24	115	139	17 (24 ÷ 139)
601–700	19	140	159	12 (19 ÷ 159)
701–800	19	260	279	7 (19 ÷ 279)
801–900	6	200	206	3 (6 ÷ 206)
Over 900	4	240	244	2 (4 ÷ 244)

throughout the term of the loan—and if he has shown a certain degree of responsibility in prior credit dealings."[10] Such a point score can be shown to an applicant and be an objective explanation for a refusal of a loan. The opposite was also true, the low risk applicant was recognized, and could be given the opportunity of a larger loan.[11]

Credit Unions

A credit union is a cooperative association, whose members accumulate and pool savings and make loans at reasonable rates to each other from the accumulated funds. The National Credit Union Administration insures credit union accounts to $40,000. The insurance is mandatory for federal credit unions and available to state chartered credit unions on an optional basis, assuming they meet the necessary financial conditions. To borrow from a credit union, a person must be a member or become a member.

Out of the funds accumulated from savings, loans may be made to members. Credit unions will make very small loans, at times for as little as $5 or $10—loans of a size which other lending institutions tend to avoid. The federal law permits unsecured loans up to $2,500 and adequately secured loans in larger amounts, depending on the size of the credit union. The board of directors of each federal credit union has authority to fix lower maximum limits for loans and to revise them as the credit union grows. Repayments may be made weekly, semimonthly, monthly, or according to any other agreed upon schedule, extending up to but not over five years for unsecured loans and ten years for secured loans. Applications for loans

[10] William D. Coakley, "Small Loan Credit Scoring," *Industrial Banker*, February 1971, p. 12.

[11] Richard J. Zaegel, "After Ten Years of Credit Scoring," *The Credit World*, July 1971, pp. 14–16.

are passed upon by a credit committee elected by the members. Secured loans, as in the case, of other lenders, may be backed by comakers, assignment of credit union shares, or by chattel mortgages on property, household equipment, or an automobile.

The charge on credit union loans may not exceed a maximum of 1 percent per month on unpaid balances, inclusive of all charges and fees. This is a maximum true annual rate of 12 percent a year, or roughly equivalent to 6 percent discounted. Thus the dollar cost is a maximum of $6.50 for $100 for a year, or $12.50 for 24 months. Each credit union fixes its own rate within this limit. Occasionally charges are as low as 0.5 percent per month. Rates can be low because, as cooperatives, credit unions usually have little or no expense for rent, salaries, investigations, collections, or federal income taxes. Because the members are usually known to the credit committee, credit investigation is reduced to a minimum.

Even if the prospective borrower is not known to the committee, the credit union (since it is formed by people who work together or have a common church or union or fraternal society or live in the same housing project) seldom has difficulty in securing reliable information quickly, with little or no expense.

Frequently, the employer will regularly deduct the payment due to the credit union from the employee's paycheck or salary envelope, thus reducing collection costs for the union to zero. If an employee leaves the firm, his final paycheck may be held back until he permits the deduction to pay the credit union advance in full. In this way, the firm becomes a collector for the credit union. In some cases the service is free of charge, in others, the credit unions pay a fee for payroll deductions. The treasurer of a credit union is the only official who may receive a salary, but other officers contribute their services without charge. Little expenditure for advertising is necessary, since knowledge of the credit union travels by word of mouth among those eligible to join. At times, pamphlets are issued and circulated, but their cost is small. For reasons such as these, credit union costs are relatively low, and it can afford to lend at rates which only large commercial banks can match, or better. Furthermore, losses on loans are quite low. Actual statistics of federal credit unions show that losses charged off amount to about .29 percent of total loans. In 1973 credit unions had almost $22 billion in total loans outstanding compared to $4.4 billion in 1960.

Consumer Finance Companies

One out of every five American families is going to borrow some money from a finance company this year. By the year's end, these families will owe the consumer finance companies and personal loan divisions of sales finance companies over $37.2 billion of which 45 percent or $16.6 billion are in personal loans. Small loans are big business. Next to commercial banks, consumer finance companies are second in volume of small loans extended to personal borrowers. They range in size from the nationally known Beneficial Loan Corporation and Household Finance Corporation to the small local company which does a strictly neighborhood business. There are some 2,961 finance companies in operation of which 58 had short and intermediate credit outstanding of $100 million or over.[12] Most states regulate this type of lending under provisions of small loan laws.

State regulation will be of little help if you succumb to the lure of an attractive mail solicitation offering you a loan of $600—no collateral, no cosigners, no security required. According to a story related in *The New York Times,* a finance company from Kentucky could charge you a total of $866.75 for the use of that $600 over a 27 month period, while the parent company of that same company would only be able to collect $161.60 for a similar loan if you made it in New York.[13] All this could be done with full compliance with Truth in Lending, which only requires disclosure. Disclosure would show that you paid at a rate of 34.75 percent if the mail advertisement of "only $31.57 a month" caught you.

Forty nine state statutes legally provide for special companies to make small loans. In about half of the states with small loan laws, consumer finance companies make larger installment loans under the provisions of other laws commonly known as industrial loan laws or consumer discount acts, and in a few states under general interest laws.

Maximum Rate. Alaska allows 3 percent on the first $400 of the loan, 2 percent thereafter to $800, and 1 percent thereafter from $800 to $1,500. In most other states the maximum rate is 3 or 2.5 percent per month, and a higher rate is charged on the first $100, $200, or $300 of a loan balance and a lower rate on the rest. For example, in New York the rate is 2.5 percent per month on the first $100, 2 percent on the next $200, and 1.5 percent on the amount from $300 to $900 and 1.25 percent from $900 to $2,500. In recent years, there has been a trend for small loan laws to permit the use of add-on rates, i.e., dollar amounts computed on and added to the original amount lent. Ohio's small loan law is of this type and provides the following maximum charges: $16 per year per $100 on the original amount of the loan to $500; $9 per year per $100 on the original amount between $500 and $1,000; and $7 per year per $100 on the original amount between

---

[12] *Finance Facts Yearbook* (Washington, D.C.: National Consumer Finance Association, 1974), p. 58.

[13] *New York Times,* September 2, 1970.

TABLE 5–8
Summary of Maximum Loan Size

Amount	Number of States	State
Unlimited	4	Delaware, Mississippi, Missouri, Tennessee
$32,500	1	Utah
30,000	1	Idaho
27,500	1	Indiana
25,000	5	Colorado, Oklahoma, Wyoming, Kansas, Louisiana
10,000	2	California, Nevada
7,500	1	South Carolina
5,000	3	New Hampshire, North Carolina, Oregon
3,000	3	Massachusetts, Nebraska, Wisconsin
2,500	9	Rhode Island, South Dakota, Texas, Arizona, Florida, Georgia, Montana, New Mexico, New York
2,000	2	Maine, Ohio
1,800	1	Connecticut
1,500	3	Alaska, Michigan, Vermont
1,200	3	Kentucky, Minnesota, West Virginia
1,000	5	Iowa, New Jersey, North Dakota, Virginia, Washington
800	1	Illinois
600	1	Pennsylvania
500	1	Maryland
300	2	Alabama, Hawaii

Note: Arkansas constitution forbids a rate above 10 percent simple interest. No special laws for consumer credit transactions.
Source: National Consumer Finance Association.

$1,000 and $2,000. Under "stepped" rates (a usual procedure) your repayments will first be applied to the lowest interest part of the loan, leaving the highest interest rate part to last the longest.

Maximum Loan Size. Formerly $500 was the maximum size of the small loan law—now more than 30 states permit over $2,000. The permissable size of the loan is steadily rising. Kansas law was $2,100. It is now $25,000. Louisiana had a limit of $300 which rose to $25,000 also. Florida went from $600 to $2,500, New York from $1,400 to $2,500. Seventeen states place the maximum below $2,000, 12 are above $10,000, and only 4 have no ceiling—leaving 20 whose maximum ranges from $2,000 to $10,000 (see Table 5–8). Some states which have low loan ceilings have other laws which permit loans to a much higher ceiling.[14] Usury laws, limiting the rates to be charged for loans, are intended for the protection of the poor. According to some experts[15] they hurt those they are meant to protect since

[14] See *Consumer Finance Rate and Regulation Chart* (Washington, D.C.: National Consumer Finance Association, 1974).

[15] Norman N. Bowsher, "Usury Laws Harmful When Effective," *Monthly Review Federal Reserve Bank of St. Louis*, pp. 16–23, August 1974.

by decreasing possible available credit (at high rates), a greater share goes to lower risk applicants who would have been able easily to get credit anywhere. The poor risk whose need is great is caught between the high cost of repayment or no loan.

The charges of consumer finance companies and credit unions are customarily stated as a monthly percentage of the balance of the unpaid principal. Consequently, the effective annual cost to the borrower is 12 times the monthly rate. Two principal methods of setting rates are the "flat" rate and the "graduated" rate. The former approach uses the same monthly rate regardless of the size of the loan extended, but only a minority of states use this method. Most states require lower rates as the size of the loan increases. For example, Illinois has a fairly typical three step rate: 3 percent per month on the first \$150, 2 percent on the amount between \$150 and \$300, and 1 percent on the amount between \$300 and \$800. The lower rates do not apply to the entire loan but only to the part above a certain amount. Taking into account the lower rates on larger amounts of loan balances, true annual rates range from 13 to 36 percent. Dollar costs on a \$100 loan, repayable over 12 months, are generally \$13 to \$20 and average about \$18 or \$19. The larger the loan, the lower will be the cost per \$100, since a sliding scale of rates is often used. The interest cost can vary for an identical loan in different states because of the differing legal loan rate provisions. It should be noted that, under most small loan laws, the stated rate *must* be calculated on the decreasing periodic balance, not on the entire original credit. Banks are not subject to this regulation, and neither are installment sellers. Small loan companies and credit unions are, however. While the consumer finance companies lend to all income and occupation groups, their borrowers include a higher proportion of low income wage earners and salaried people than does the average bank.

The small loan company is specially designed for people without established credit, and its charges are set to cover the costs of extensive investigations and more elaborate collection procedures even on the very small loans. The average size of consumer finance loans has been rising. Most loans are made to families in the \$5,000 to \$12,000 income brackets. Household Finance Corporation recently surveyed its borrowers and found they were industrial or office workers with an average monthly income of \$882 (see Table 5–9). The average size of its more than 1.5 million loans was \$1,258. It also found that people borrow principally to consolidate other debts (see Table 5–10). The loans are to pay off creditors who will not or cannot wait. The new loan brings order and a respite, in the form of one loan and one monthly installment, to the theretofore harried debtor.

A study comparing personal loans of consumer finance companies with those made by a group of banks found that about half of the bank borrow-

TABLE 5–9
Distribution of Loans by Occupation of Borrower (type of job)

Occupation	*Number of Loans Made to Borrowers in Each Occupation as Percent of Total Loans*
Proprietors, managers, and officials (excluding farm)	7.94
Craftsmen, foremen and kindred workers	14.19
Operatives and kindred workers	24.91
Laborers, except farm and mine	10.47
Clerical and kindred workers	12.39
Sales persons	3.81
School teachers	1.29
Professional and semiprofessional workers (except teachers)	2.39
Unemployed, pensions or independent income	2.10
Occupations not reported	.00
Farmers and farm managers	.20
Farm laborers and foremen	.36
Domestic service workers	.32
Protective service workers	2.25
Other service workers	7.05
Members of Armed Forces	10.33
Total	100%

Average size: $1,258.10
Total number loans: 1,573,000

Source: Household Finance Corporation, 1973.

ers were white collar workers and half blue collar, whereas only about one quarter of the consumer finance company borrowers were white collar and three quarters were manual workers. Consumer finance company borrowers, in the main, came from somewhat lower income brackets than did bank borrowers. Fewer bank borrowers were under 30 years of age, and more over 40 years than were consumer finance company borrowers.

A little more than half of the loans made are on the borrower's signature alone. Most of the remainder are protected by a security interest on the borrower's household possessions. This may be more a psychological than a material security for the loan company, since it does not often take possession of such property; and indeed the legal costs of doing so, in relation to the small secondhand resale value of the furniture, make foreclosure of a security interest uneconomic. But the average borrower, not knowing this, will try to avoid the ignominy and neighborhood disgrace which the removal of his furniture would entail. A small percentage of loans are secured by pledges of automobiles or insurance or by the added security of a cosigner. A prospective borrower will be asked to fill out a financial statement, and at the first interview the loan company official will ask questions

TABLE 5–10
Distribution of Loans by Principal Use of Borrowed Money

Use of Loan	*Number of Loans Made for Each Use as Percent of Total Loans*
*To consolidate existing debts	32.87
Automobile purchase or repairs	19.28
Travel and vacation expenses	9.53
Miscellaneous	7.28
Home furnishings and appliances	5.48
Assist relatives	4.29
Household repairs	4.08
Miscellaneous equipment	3.63
Medical, dental and hospital	3.01
Clothing	2.64
Taxes	2.12
Insurance	1.31
Moving expenses	1.28
Education	.95
Business for self	.70
Payment on real estate loansfl	.69
Funeral expenses	.52
Fuel	.23
Food bills	.10
Not reported	.01
Total	100%

* All loans are classified under the heading describing the use to which the larger part of the loan applied. Where several bills are paid and no major purpose appears, the loan is classified under the heading "To Consolidate Debts."
Source: Household Finance Corporation, 1973.

for the investigation record. When this is checked and completed by the company investigator and it is decided to grant the loan, the applicant will be called in and asked to sign a note and may also be asked to sign a security interest (chattel mortgage). He will then be given the proceeds of the loan, and a "loan statement and receipt book."

Considering the variety and complexity of the small loan laws in the United States, it would seem desirable to have some uniformity. The attempts to secure uniformity by the National Conference of Commissioners on Uniform State Laws have been met by attack from business groups who want to limit the right of entry into the field and from consumer groups who want to set a ceiling on rates. The Uniform Consumer Credit Code is based on the principle of free entry and competitive credit charges. After four years' work by a special drafting committee, the code was completed in 1969, and as of now, five states had adopted it. Its purpose is to replace the hundreds of overlapping and conflicting state laws governing consumer credit transactions, including usury statutes and small loan laws.

Consumer organizations, while agreeing that the Uniform Consumer Credit Code is an improvement over many state laws, are afraid that it will weaken consumer protection in states that have strong consumer legislation and would enable states to be exempt from the federal Truth in Lending Act.[16]

Loan Sharks

Loan sharks are lenders of money who operate outside the pale of the law. In the field of credit, they are the bootleggers. While occasionally unethical *licensed* lenders will take advantage of an unwary borrower and overcharge, the term *loan shark* is reserved for those who operate without license or supervision and who violate the letter of the law as well as its social purpose. Loan sharks flourish in states which do not have effective small loan laws.

If someone offers to lend you $5 today if you promise to repay $6 a week later, on payday, beware! He is a loan shark. The "five for six" racket is an old and lucrative one and still mulcts many an unsuspecting borrower. If you pay one dollar for the use of five for one week, you are being charged interest at the rate of 20 percent a week, or an incredible, 1,040 percent per year. No wonder many an industrial worker will find a friendly fellow at the factory gate ready to accommodate him. Borrow $10 from him until payday two weeks later and you will usually pay back $12. A $2 charge on $10 for two weeks is 520 percent a year.

Even worse than the exorbitant interest charge is the loan shark's practice of making it difficult, often impossible, for the borrower to repay the principal. The loan shark is glad to have the borrower fall behind in payments of principal, as long as interest is paid; and, indeed, in order to mire the borrower still more deeply, the loan shark may grant another loan to enable the borrower to keep up the interest payments on the first loan.

Loan Shark Schemes

The schemes and devices whereby the loan sharks sidestep the law and ensnare victims are myriad. A common device is salary buying. The victim does not borrow; he "sells" the loan shark part or all of his salary. In the middle of the month, for example, the borrower sells $20 of his salary, due at the end of the month, for $18 cash. The loan shark appoints the bor-

[16] For further information on the Uniform Consumer Credit Code, see "A Summary of the Uniform Consumer Credit Code," prepared by Nathaniel E. Butler, Educational Director, National Conference of Commissioners on Uniform State Laws.

rower his agent to collect the salary at the end of the month and deliver it. The borrower is threatened with prosecution for embezzlement if delivery is not made. Frequently, no attempt is made to collect the full amount which was "sold," but only the charges are collected and the loan is renewed for another two weeks. This goes on and on. Many states now have statutes which prohibit salary buying, but a number do not, and it is still widespread.

Another illegal procedure used is to have the borrower sign a note for an amount in excess of the sum actually loaned and then charge interest on the fictitious amount of the signed note. A borrower will frequently submit to this because of desperation for a loan. Another technique is endorsement selling. The loan will not be made unless it is endorsed. Luckily, "someone" just happens to be available who, for a fee, will endorse the note. Or two offices, usually run by the same people, claim to be broker and lender. Application for the loan has to be made through the "broker," who then submits it to the "lender." The broker's "commission" is in reality, of course, illegal interest.

Sometimes only one loan shark may be involved in the so called brokerage plan. For example, assume you want to borrow $50 in a state which does not have a small loan law. By means of a card handed to you as you leave work, you are told that a Mr. Smithson arranges loans. When you go to see him, he explains that he does not lend money himself but that he will serve as a broker, for a fee, and arrange a loan for you. For the $50 loan his brokerage fee will be $18.50 and the interest $1.42. If you agree, he gives you the $50 and asks you to sign a note for $69.92 payable in eight biweekly installments of $8.74. If you do not stop to calculate, and the average borrower does not, you will have agreed to a loan at a yearly interest rate of more than 260 percent.

A sale of goods—valueless goods—may be tied in to a loan. In this case, the borrower, as a condition of the loan, must buy some valueless ornament or costume jewelry for, say, $25. He will then be granted a $50 loan with the lender taking a note for $75. An even more vicious variation occurs where the lender gives the borrower who needs cash badly an order on a grocery store for $15 worth of groceries. The store, which is in league with the lender, cashes the order for only $10, but the borrower must repay $15 on the next payday. In some cases, loan sharks will refuse to lend unless the borrower buys costly life, health, and accident insurance, which must be purchased through an agent in league with them and where part of the commission must be kicked back to the loan shark. Legislative and court records indicate that in some cases over 80 percent of the premiums paid by the borrowers are returned by the agents to the lenders.

The borrower usually does not want anyone to know about this debt, and the illegal lender is well pleased to have the loan kept secret. Everything is done quietly—at first. There is no red tape. No one knows—only borrower and lender. No credit investigation, no cosigners, no calls to employer or landlord to verify job and residence claims. But this initial secrecy boomerangs, for should the borrower fail to pay an installment, the loan shark threatens to tell the borrower's family, his employer, or the neighbors. He may even appear at the borrower's office and loudly denounce him as a "crook and deadbeat." In more extreme cases, borrowers who are late in payments or who try to pay off the principal entirely are beaten up.

Under the Consumer Credit Protection Act it is now a federal offense to engage in "an extortionate extension of credit." This is defined as the use, or threat of use, of violence to obtain repayment of a loan. Thus the FBI is now involved in investigating loan shark activities. If certain factors are present in connection with an extension of credit, there is prima facie evidence that the extension of credit is extortionate. One of these is a rate of interest in excess of 45 percent per annum.

Congress claimed authority to make loan sharking a federal crime because of its jurisdiction over bankruptcies and matters affecting interstate commerce. In granting a hearing on November 16, 1970 to Alcides Perez, convicted in federal court of using threats of violence to extort high interest payments from a butcher named Alexis Miranda, the Supreme Court undertook to decide if money paid to Perez could be assumed to flow into organized crime syndicates and affect interstate commerce—and therefore if Congress acted constitutionally in enacting the Consumer Credit Protection Act. Mr. Miranda had testified that he had been forced to repay $6,520 on a loan of $5,000 and that he still owed $6,700 when he went bankrupt. On April 26, 1971, the Supreme Court in an eight-to-one decision upheld the conviction of Perez in "unlawfully using extortionate means in collecting and attempting to collect an extension of credit in violation of Title II of the Consumer Credit Protection Act." The Court found that "Title II is within Congress' power under the commerce clause to control activities affecting interstate commerce and Congress' findings are adequate to support its conclusion that loan sharks who use extortionate means to collect payments on loans are in a class largely controlled by organized crime with a substantially adverse affect on interstate commerce."[17]

Loan sharks flourish mainly in those states which do not have effective small loan laws or in those where the stringency of the small loan laws,

---

[17] Supreme Court of the United States, April 26, 1971; 426F 2nd 1073 Affirmed.

limiting rates to say 10 percent a year, has driven the legitimate small loan company out of the state because it cannot profitably do business at such a rate. There were several cases where, in battles in state legislatures over whether or not to pass a small loan law, the agents of the illegal lenders, when it became apparent that their lobbying efforts to prevent the passage of the small loan law had failed, turned around and lobbied for very stringent regulation, with a low maximum annual rate of 10 percent or less. They knew that the latter would be as effective in insuring their continued operation as the former. Texas, for example, once relied entirely on its 10 percent a year usury law and as a result was, for a time, the leading loan shark state. While exact statistics are, of course, not available, the best estimates are that illegal lenders do in excess of $200 million of business annually in the United States.

Pawnbrokers

You will probably never need to resort to a pawnbroker, but for thousands of families he is still a possible factor in emergency credit. The role of the pawnbroker has diminished greatly since the advent of the small loan company, but there is still no other lender who will let you have $5 for a few days at legal rates of interest or who will lend $100 on five minutes' notice, without any investigation of your credit standing or lack of it.

A pawnbroker lends money on the security of personal effects, household or sporting goods, jewelry, furs, and so on, left by the borrower. The contract by which loans of this description are effected is called a "pawn" or "pledge," and the same terms are also applied to articles deposited. The pawn or pledge must have resale value, and the pawnbroker, who through long experience has become an expert judge of values, appraises it in terms of the price he can get for it on resale. He will probably lend 60 to 90 percent of the estimated resale value; that is, he allows a margin of safety in case he is forced to sell the pledged article to recover his loan.

If his offer is accepted, he gives the borrower the money and a ticket which identifies the merchandise and gives the borrower the right to redeem it at any time within a given period by repaying the amount loaned plus interest. The article is left at the pawnshop as security for the loan. If the loan is not repaid within the specified time, or, if no time is specified, then within a reasonable time as defined by state law, the pawnbroker may sell the pledged article and retain the proceeds if this sum does not exceed the amount of the loan plus accumulated interest. If there is, by chance, a surplus, it is supposed to be turned over to the borrower.

A pawnbroker's loan is unlike most others previously described. You never have to pay back a pawnbroker's loan if you do not want to or cannot. You do not even have to pay interest. The pawnbroker cannot force you to do either, nor will he ever try to find you to take you to court or garnishee your salary, for you sign nothing. His security is the article you pledged; and if you fail to repay the loan, he simply sells the article. Even if you repay the loan, you do it in a lump sum, not in installments; and you can pay it back at any time within the overall period. Interest charges range from 2 percent a month all the way to 10 percent a month, depending upon the state. A common rate is 3 percent per month. Thus you would pay from 20 cents to $1 a month (30 cents in the case of a 3 percent rate) on each $10 borrowed.

Who borrows from pawnbrokers? Obviously, only persons in desperate need, those with no cash reserve to fall back on in an emergency and with no certain future income. They want cash quickly and are in no condition to hold out or bargain; if the cash offered for the pledge seems very low, they usually take it, nevertheless. They have very little choice. It is partly for this reason that unscrupulous pawnbrokers were able to take advantage of borrowers at one time, and this subsequently led to regulation. Laws were passed in many states which provided for licensing, set maximum rates, provided for state supervision, and required that a record be kept of all loans, the name of the borrower, the date, the payment, and so on. The Federal Trade Commission insists that pawnshops, since they are lenders, comply with the provisions of Truth in Lending. They must tell their customers how much they charge at an annual rate and how much the loan costs in dollars and cents.

As an idea of how complicated this can get, in New York, loans of more than $100 are levied at an annual rate of 24 percent a year for the first six months and at a rate of 12 percent a year for the second six months, or at a rate of 18 percent a year for one year. For loans under $100, the rate is 36 percent a year for the first six months and 24 percent a year for the second six months, or 30 percent a year if kept for a year. In St. Louis, the rate is 24 percent a year; in Chicago, it is 36 percent, and in Los Angeles it works out to 30 percent a year. The redemption period also varies.[18]

Remedial Loan Societies

Out of the need to help a poverty stricken borrower using his last possessions to get cash before resorting to charity or public relief, and out of

---

[18] *Changing Times*, February 1972, p. 34.

the desire of philanthropic citizens to prevent persons in such desperate straits from being subjected to excess charges, grew the remedial loan society. These are semiphilanthropic pawnshops, the most famous of which is the Provident Loan Society of New York. Formed in 1894, over its first half-century the Society made 20,005,350 loans aggregating $1,055,227,046. It has made loans for as little as 25 cents and for as much as several thousand dollars; currently the Society makes 100,000 loans a year.

Its interest rates are the lowest known for pledge loans. It no longer regards itself as a remedial loan society. Its rates are 1.5 percent per month (18 percent per annum) computed for exact number of days on any loan not exceeding the sum of $100, and 1.5 percent per month for the first six months, and after that 1 percent for each succeeding month (15 percent per annum) computed for exact number of days on the part of any loan in excess of $100.

Provident loans involve no investigation of credit, income, or employment. This assures absolute privacy. Ordinarily a Provident loan requires only a few minutes; loans on elaborate jewelry may require slightly longer. Once the appraisal is made the borrower receives the full amount of the loan and is not required to repay either the principal or the interest for a full year. Loans can be made by mail, the same day that collateral, such as jewelry, silverware, U.S. stamps or coins are received, providing that with such a shipment there is included a signed statement that the articles are owned free and clear.

The loan may be outstanding for a year before the pledge is sold. Interest is not deducted in advance, and loans may be repaid fully or partially at any time during the year at the convenience of the borrower. At any time during the life of the loan, the payment of interest due plus a small reduction of principal will extend the loan for another year. The Society advises the borrower never to destroy an expired loan ticket without first inquiring if a surplus is due. Any surplus realized above the loan amount when the pledge is sold at public auction is paid to the borrower on presentation of the loan ticket. If the sale results in a loss, it is borne by the Society.

Co-sign?

If you're asked to co-sign a note—don't! If you do anyway, here is a list of what you might try to do to protect yourself:

1. Try to persuade the lender to promise in writing that he will try to collect from the borrower before tackling you.
2. Maybe you can co-sign or guarantee only part of the note.

3. Ask the lender to notify you if the buyer is ever late with his payments. Maybe you can influence the borrower.
4. Get all the information on the loan that you can under Truth in Lending.
5. Hope you won't be needed. If so, compensate by thinking of it as a possible tax deduction.

Delinquency

Delinquent loans are up 19 percent—even for banks—due to the inflation and the economy. According to the American Bankers' Association survey . . . it is the highest rate in the decade since it began making the surveys. The delinquency rate for autos rose 29 percent; for mobile home loans, 3 percent; recreational vehicle loans, 59 percent; and home improvement loans, 45 percent.

"While loan delinquency rates are on the rise, they're still low when expressed as a percentage of total loans outstanding, and frankly, it is amazing that they are low when there is so much continuous encouragement to get people to spend more," according to Fabian Linden, Director of Consumer Economic Research for the Conference Board. The families with fairly high level of income, accustomed to ample credit, are in debt as inflation has cut into their discretionary income creating hopefully temporary problems. Blue collar workers, the purchasing power of whose weekly spendable income has declined, according to government statistics, have been squeezed by installment payments, and face more long term difficulty.

The Consumer Credit Counseling Service, a nationwide nonprofit organization that tries to help debtors manage their finances and repay creditors on a pro rata basis, is supported by banks, businesses and community groups. The Service has professional counselors who give free personalized money management plans that are realistic. The client sums up debts in detail, surrenders charge plates, gives up credit, arranges to budget a certain sum each month. The Counseling Service arranges a repayment program with the creditors in exchange for no dunning, no garnishment, no repossession.

Conclusion

Shopping for a loan is a complicated business, but it obviously pays to shop, since it may mean the difference between paying 5, 40, or 520 percent for your money. Generally speaking, an insurance company, commercial bank, or credit union will be your least expensive source of personal credit;

TABLE 5–11
Sources of Personal Loans Compared

Lender	*Charge for $100 Repayable in One Year*		*Range of Loans*
	True Dollar Cost	*Annual Percentage Rate*	
Insurance company or Veterans Administration	$5–$6*	Range, 5–6%* Common, 6%	Loan value of policy v. a. 94% of cash value of policy
Savings banks or savings and loan associations	$7.25–$9*	Range, 7¼–9% Common, 7½%	Up to full value of savings account, or 90% of value of savings and loan assn. shares
Commercial banks, personal-loan department	$5.25–$7.00	Range, 10–14% Common, 11.50%	$100–$10,000
Credit union	$6.50 maximum for federal credit—generally also for state credit unions	Range, 6–12% (Max., 1% per mo.) Common, 12%	$5—maximum of 10% of the credit unions assets to any one member
Consumer finance companies	$10–$24	Range, 16–42% Common, 30%	$10–$32,500, varying with the state a few states unlimited
Loan sharks	$50–$1,040	Range, 50–1040% Common, 260%	$5–$1,000
Pawnbroker	$24–$120*	Range, 24–120%* Common, 36%	$1–$500
Remedial loan society	$15–18*	Range, 15–18%* Common, 15½%	$1–$2000

* On the assumption that repayment does not occur in installments but rather in one lump sum at the end of the year and that interest is paid at the time of repayment, not deducted in advance.

Collateral Needed	*Other Characteristics*
Insurance policy with cash value	No due date. If interest and principal are not paid, no legal action will be taken, but deductions will be made when policy becomes payable. No questions asked about purpose of loan. No credit investigation. Repayment on installment basis; \$10 or more on life insurance and \$5 or more on V.A.
Savings account or savings and loan assn. shares	No credit investigation necessary, but must have savings account or savings and loan shares.
Varies—single signature; cosigner; chattel mortgages on cars or household goods, etc.	Credit investigation necessary. Loans both installment and single payment. Purpose of loan must be approved. Rate must be quoted in terms of annual percentage rate (simple annual interest) and repayment usually on monthly installment basis.
Anything acceptable to credit committee	Maximum rate is 1% per month *on unpaid balances* for federal credit unions. Repayable in installments. Must be a member of credit union to borrow. Purpose must be approved.
Generally, chattel mortgage or signature	Rates quoted on monthly basis, up to a maximum of 3½% *on unpaid balance.* In most states, monthly rate is graduated according to size of loan; thus, in New York State, 2½% on first \$100; 2% from \$100 to \$300; 1½% from \$300 to \$900; 1¼% from \$900 to \$2500. Purpose of loan must be approved. Repayment on monthly installment basis.
Varies greatly	No credit investigation; purpose of loan of no importance; due date on principal will be ignored if interest paid regularly; frequently strong-arm methods used to collect.
Pawn or pledge	Rates usually quoted on monthly basis: 2–10% per month. Usually 60–90% of estimated resale value of pledged property is loaned. No credit investigation. Purpose of loan no concern to lender. Single-payment loans usual. Repayment unnecessary.
Pledged property, signature, chattel mortgage, comaker	Rates usually 1% per month on unpaid balances. Loans need not be repaid. Single-payment or installment loans. No credit investigation necessary on pledge loans. Usually one year allowed to repay loan before pledge is sold. Loans not discounted.

personal loan and consumer finance companies are somewhat more costly; while illegal and unlicensed lenders are simply extortionate. If you shop around for your loan ,where you borrow is likely to depend on your credit standing, because if it is good—if your prospective future income is adequate and regular—you will need to go no further than the commercial bank or credit union. If these institutions are reluctant to help you, a consumer finance or personal loan company may. If you cannot get a loan, however, it means that men skilled at analyzing people's finances have decided you should not borrow, since you have little or no prospect of paying back. If they could with reasonable safety lend to you, they would. If they will not, there are always the pawnshops; and of these, the best are the remedial loan societies. As between resorting to a loan shark and going to a pawnbroker, it seems quite clear that the latter is preferable. Table 5–11, showing sources of personal loans, may serve to provide a useful comparison and summary.

SUGGESTED READINGS

1. *Finance Facts Yearbook,* published annually. A free copy may be obtained by writing to the National Consumer Finance Association, 1000 Sixteenth Street, N.W., Washington, D.C. 20036.
2. S. Lees Booth, *Report on Nonbusiness Bankruptcies by States.* Washington, D.C.: National Consumer Finance Association, annual.
3. *Consumer Finance Rate and Regulation Chart,* published annually by the National Consumer Finance Association. A free copy may be obtained by writing to the Association at 1000 16th St., N.W., Washington, D.C. 20036.
4. "Summary of Hearings on Debt Collection Practices, National Commission on Consumer Finance," *Banking Law Journal,* Vol. 85, No. 4 (April 1971).
5. Credit Union National Association (CUNA), *Credit Union Yearbook.* Madison, Wis., latest edition (issued annually). A free copy may be obtained on request.
6. In *Changing Times*—
   "Do You Owe Too Much?," June 1974
   "Here's a Break for Borrowers," April 1974
   "If You're Dunned to Pay A Bill," March 1974
   "A Time for Cash, A Time for Credit," August 1973
   "Is It Smart to Borrow on Your Life Insurance?," December 1972
   "Should You Borrow from a Small Loan Company?" November 1972
   "If You're Asked to Co-Sign a Note," March 1972
   "Ever Use a Pawn Shop?" February 1972

7. *Consumer Credit in the United States*—Report of the National Commission on Consumer Finance, Superintendent of Documents, U.S. Government Printing Office, Washington, D.C. 1973
8. Sidney Rutberg, *Ten Cents on the Dollar or the Bankruptcy Game*. New York: Simon & Shuster, 1973.
9. David Caplowitz, *Consumers in Trouble—A Study of Debtors in Default* —N.Y.: Appleton, 1973.
10. Gary Hendricks and Kenwood C. Youmans with Janet Keller, *Consumer Durables and Installment Debt*—Institute for Social Research—University of Michigan, Ann Arbor, 1973.
11. Jerome I. Meyers, *Wipe Out Your Debts and Make a Fresh Start*. New York: Chancellor Press, 1973.
12. "How to Borrow Money Cleverly," *New York Magazine*, January 24, 1972.
13. Walter F. Emmons, "Collection Practices Today," *Credit*, National Consumer Finance Association, Washington, D.C., February 1975.
14. *Cost of Personal Borrowing in the United States*, Charles H. Gushee, (ed.) Boston: Financial Publishing Co., annual.
15. Stanley Morganstern, *Legal Regulation of Consumer Credit*, Dobbs Ferry, N.Y.: Oceana Press, 1972.
16. David T. Stanley and Marjorie Girth, *Bankruptcy: Problem, Process, Reform*, Washington, D.C.: Brookings Institution, 1971.
17. Edgar R. Fiedler and Maude R. Pech, *Measure of Credit Risk and Experience*—National Bureau of Economic Research, N.Y. 1971
18. *Truth in Lending—What it Means for Consumer Credit*—Public Information Department, Federal Reserve Bank of Philadelphia, 1970.
19. Caroline Donnelly, "Struggling Back from Debt," *Money*, January 1975.
20. George M. Treister, "The New Bankruptcy Rules," *California State Banking Journal*, 1973, pp. 522–27.
21. Herbert S. Denenberg, "A Consumer's Guide to Bankruptcy," Pennsylvania Insurance Department, Harrisburg, Pa., 1975.

CASE PROBLEMS

1. If there is a credit union in your locality, interview the chairman of the loan committee and discuss:

a. The general economic status of those who borrow from the credit union.
b. The credit tests the union uses for loan applicants.
c. The costs of granting loans.
d. The loss experience of the union.
e. The collection procedure followed in case a borrower is late in paying installments.

In your opinion, why might this be a good place to obtain a loan?

2. If there is a small loan company in your town, arrange an interview with the manager and discuss:

a. The general economic status of the loan company's borrowers. Does the manager think they differ as a group from those who go to a commercial bank for small loans?
b. The credit tests the company applies to loan applicants.
c. The cost of granting small loans, both absolute and annual percentage rate.
d. The loss experience of the company.
e. The collection procedure the company follows if installments are not paid when due.

State whether you would do business with this institution and explain your reasons.

3. If there is a commercial bank with a small loan department in the town in which your school is located, arrange an interview with the manager and collect information on:

a. How an applicant's credit status is investigated and checked.
b. What the loss experience of the bank has been on small loans.
c. What fees, if any, the bank charges on a small loan in addition to the stated interest.
d. What security or collateral the bank requires.
e. What collection procedure the bank follows if the borrower is late in his payments.

What are the advantages or disadvantages of having a small loan from this bank?

4. The Home Bank agrees to lend you $100 at a discount rate of 6 percent, plus an investigation fee of $3. If the loan were payable in 12 monthly installments, what is the annual percentage rate? Explain whether this rate is too high.

5. If Ms. Roble borrows $300 at a discount rate of 6 percent and agrees to repay the loan in one payment at the end of a year, what is the annual percentage rate she is paying? If, on the other hand, she borrows $300 at a discount rate of 6 percent and agrees to pay back the loan in 12 monthly installments of $25 each, what is the annual percentage rate?

6. Jason wants to borrow $250 from a personal loan company. He has no collateral. He is told that he can have the money only if he can find a satisfactory comaker for his note. He approaches Yarrow, a fellow worker in an automobile factory. How would you react if you were Yarrow?

7. Barrows has a $10,000 life policy with the John Hancock Mutual Life Insurance Company in Boston. The policy now has a loan value of $3,000. Upon writing to the company, he is told that 6 percent per annum is charged on loans. He also is told that he may surrender the policy for $3,000. He wonders

why he should pay any interest at all for the use of his own money. Discuss what he should do.

8. Joan Firestone works for the Connelly Company. The company established a credit union for its employees several years ago, but Joan knows little about it. She needs to borrow $150 right away. She is about to seek a loan from a local personal finance company when a friend advises that she contact the credit union. Why?

9. Clark meets Gonsalves. They start talking about personal finance companies. Clark says it is always better to deal with one of the giants in the business or better yet with a commercial bank. What are his reasons?

10. Homer, a bachelor, has just been released from the hospital after a serious operation. The doctors have told him that he must spend at least three months recuperating. Homer currently owes $600 to various creditors and his savings have been depleted by his illness. His company pays all employees on sick leave half their regulary salary—or $80 a week in Homer's case. He also has a $10,000 life insurance policy which has a cash surrender value of $3,000. What should he do?

11. Lytell and Makepeace meet after having made their payments at a personal finance company. Lytell says next time he will borrow from the local remedial loan association. Makepeace does not agree. He says that he has had dealings there and that he likes dealing at the personal finance company better. What are their respective arguments?

6

Using Your Bank

A bankbook makes good reading—better than most novels.
Sir Harry Lauder

THE MODERN bank is a department store of finance. It performs a wide variety of services for you, but the one you will probably find most useful and convenient, perhaps the first service everyone uses at a bank, is the checking account. According to a Louis Harris poll, more than 68 percent of adult Americans now use a regular checking account. Roughly 450 million checks are written weekly and the number continues to grow by 10 percent a year. In recent years there has been talk about electronic money —a checkless, cashless society—computer governed punch button credit card finance—but the flood of checks continues.

Why are checking accounts so universally used? Well, it's a most convenient way to pay. There is a vast saving in time and effort. You can pay by mail, sit at your desk and write out your checks and not have to run from store to store or office to office and possibly stand in line to pay bills. A check allows you to pay the exact amount due. It represents safety because you don't have to carry large sums of cash around. Furthermore it provides an automatic receipt. Your canceled check, which is returned to you after it has been cashed, is a receipt. You can keep your accounts straight through checkbook stubs, the bank's monthly statement to you, and the returned canceled checks. A check is simply an order to your bank to pay someone you name an amount of money you have on deposit. Sooner or later you will need to write a check, and once you open an account and try it, you'll never be without a checking account. It's a tremendous convenience. You may frequently be asked to name your bank in connection with transactions involving credit, such as opening a charge account, or renting a house or an apartment. And as an extra touch, banks are offering checkbooks in all varieties of style—Pucci print and flower decorated in color with your name and address imprinted on the checks and the checkbook personalized, all for a nominal fee.[1] At the same time as checking account advantages are increasingly recognized, it has become increasingly difficult to cash a check, especially where you are unknown. This has become true even with a handful of identification cards—all of which might have been stolen. For this reason, the "line of credit" or "reserve checking" accounts have gained an added value. Stores regard them as "guaranteed accounts" because the I.D. given by the bank with those accounts indicates the credit is good and the stores accept such checks willingly. It may even be difficult to cash your own check in your own bank. Some big city banks issue personal check cashing cards to all account holders that can be read by a computer terminal to see if there is sufficient funds. Others provide "convenience" cards for cashing limited amounts if you have a bank credit card. There are probably some banks that trust their customers!

Check Processing

Suppose you sent your parents who live in Los Angeles a check to buy themselves a gift. You are working in New York. Let's assume that they cannot immediately decide what they want to buy, and so they deposit the check in their local bank in Los Angeles, which, in turn, deposits it to its credit at the Federal Reserve Bank in San Francisco, since it is part of Federal Reserve District 12 of which San Francisco is headquarters. The Federal Reserve Bank of San Francisco sends the check to the Federal Reserve Bank of New York for collection. The Federal Reserve Bank of New York sends the check to your bank, which deducts the amount of the check from your account. Then your bank authorizes the Federal Reserve Bank of New York to deduct that amount from its reserve on deposit with the Federal Reserve Bank. Then the Federal Reserve Bank of New York pays the Federal Reserve Bank of San Francisco from its share in the Interdistrict Settlement Fund. Finally, the Federal Reserve Bank of San Francisco credits the Los Angeles bank where your parents deposited your check with the amount of the check, and the Los Angeles bank credits your parents' account. This transaction is multiplied on the order of 450 million times each week. Since it is in the heart of the nation's financial district, the New York Federal Reserve Bank is one of the busiest. Figure 6–1 will show you how it copes with its problems.

[1] For an interesting analysis of why some people do not want checking accounts see Robert F. Schlax & Sidney Levy, "A Qualitative Analysis of Why People Do Not Have Checking Accounts," a Bank Marketing Association Research Publication, 1971.

FIGURE 6–1

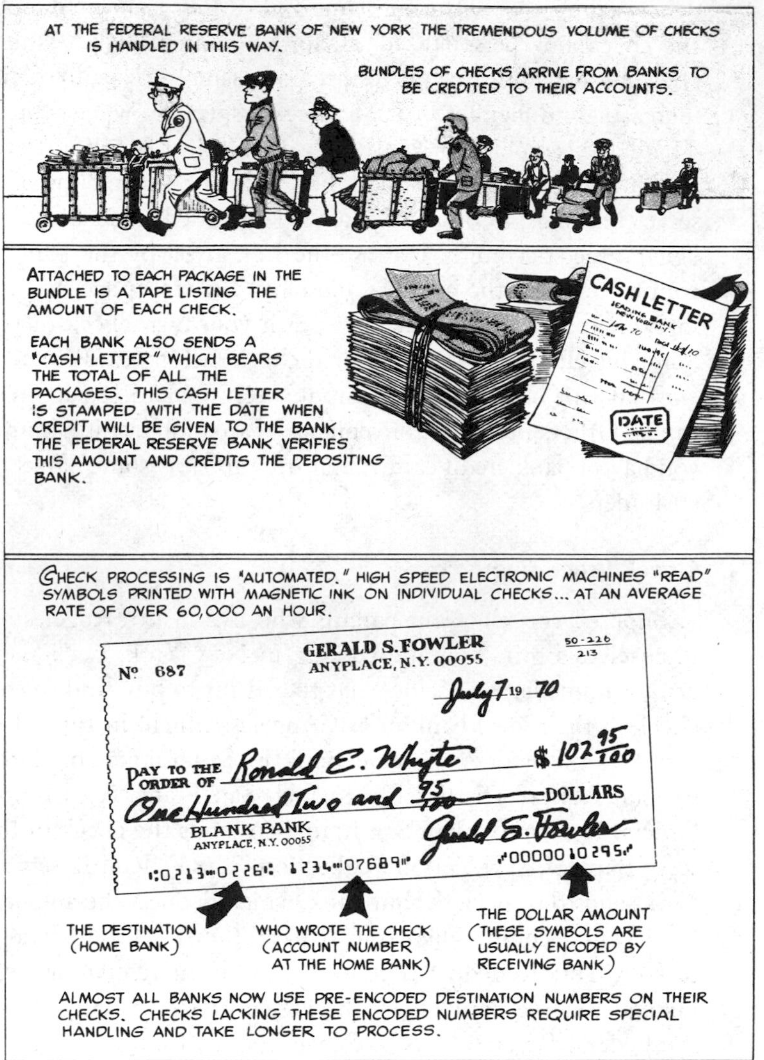

Kinds of Accounts, Balances, and Service Charges

There are regular personal checking accounts and special checking accounts. The regular account requires that a minimum balance be maintained, generally from $100 to as much as $800. These are usually referred to as "free" checking accounts, since there are no charges imposed if the depositor maintains the required balance. The majority of banks are turning to this type of program. Charges vary from flat charges to scaled charges

FIGURE 6–1 (continued)

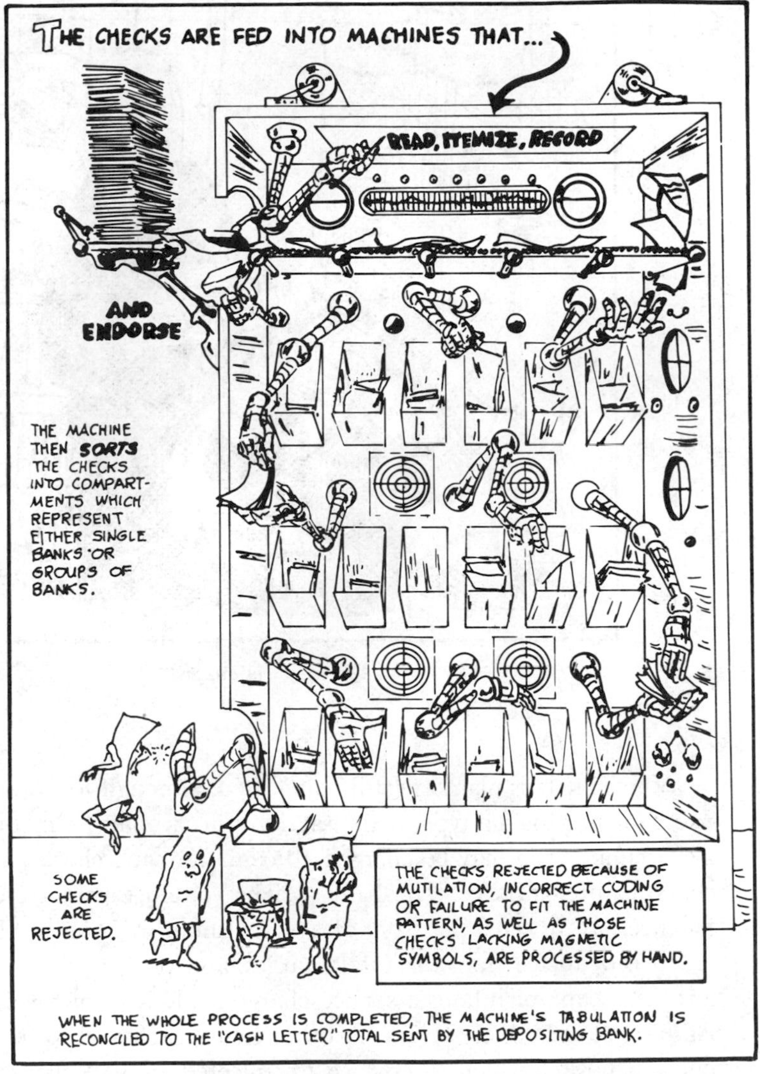

Source: *The Story of Checks*, Federal Reserve Bank of New York.

if the depositor's balance falls below his required minimum. (These charges run from $1 to $4.) Some banks still analyze accounts, computing the cost of the "activity" or items processed (i.e., checks drawn, deposits made, etc.) and allow a credit based on the average balance maintained. If the cost is greater than the credit or "expense" allowed, the amount is charged. A small amount is charged, too, if the average balance falls below the minimum required.

"All I ever get is checks!"

Wall Street Journal

Where analysis plans are still being used, although less usual, you pay a fixed amount for the type of transaction plus a monthly maintenance fee. For example, you may be charged 10 cents for each check paid, and a 75 cents maintenance fee. The bank assigns you an earnings credit on your balance, say 10 cents per $100 of average monthly balance. The earnings credit is deducted from the total charges, and you pay the net amount, if any. The bank maintains a service charge analysis form for each account. Additional charges are levied for other items, such as a $1.00 charge for a check deposited which is returned uncollected, or a $4 charge for a check you write which is returned because of insufficient funds.

You may, of course, open a checking account in which no minimum balance is required with $1. Special checking accounts have been devised over the last two decades to encourage the use of commercial banks by those who find it difficult to maintain a consistent minimum balance. These special accounts are known by various names, such as "Pay-As-You-Go Checkway," "Check-Master," "Chex," "Thrifti-Checks," and so on, but there are a number of features common to all. The depositor needs only enough money on deposit to cover any check written. A special

TABLE 6–1
Your Choice of Check Plans

The check system offers you two ways of paying for your account. Both are clear and easy to understand. You choose the plan that suits you best. The one that's least expensive for you. All the benefits and extra services available are the same with both plans. Only the fee structure is different.

The Special Check Plan. With this plan, there is no minimum balance requirement. You pay a monthly fee of 75¢, plus 10¢ for each check drawn.

The Regular Check Plan. If you use this plan, there is no charge per check. No matter how many checks you write. The monthly fee is based on the lowest balance in your account during the month. And, if you keep a balance of $500 or more, your account is free. Here's the complete story:

Lowest balance during month	*Monthly fee*
$500 and over	Free
$400 to $499	$1.00
$300 to $399	$2.00
$200 to $299	$3.00
$ 0 to $199	$4.00

Which Plan is Best for You? That's easy to decide. Just estimate the number of checks you write each month and the lowest balance in your checking account. The table below will show you whether you should have a regular (R) or special (S) plan.

Checks Written	*Lowest Balance*				
	Below $200	*$200s*	*$300s*	*$400s*	*$500+*
0	S	S	S	S	R
5	S	S	S	R	R
15	S	S	R	R	R
25	S	R	R	R	R
35	R	R	R	R	R

checkbook, containing 20 checks, is issued and a fee of 10 cents is charged against your account when the check is paid. Normally there is a monthly 75 cent service or handling charge imposed as well.

Since the service charge usually does not come to very much each month, the convenience of having and using a checking account more than compensates for the cost. You should choose the type of account—either special checking account or regular checking account with minimum balance and no fee—best suited to your finances (see Table 6–1). If you can afford to keep a minimum balance large enough to avoid service charges, it is a good idea to do so. But if you cannot do this, it should not prevent you from enjoying the convenience of a checking account. Over most of the country, the charges on special checking accounts appear to be small and reasonable. If there are a number of banks in your community, shop to see which has the most reasonable service charge consistent with your financial position and requirements.[2]

[2] See Jeremy Main, "Putting Your Bank's New Look to Work," *Money*, April 1974.

No matter what the type of account—regular, special, or business—there are service charges which vary from bank to bank for a varied number of special services which you may require. See Table 6–2 for such charges.

Opening an Account

To open an account is a simple matter and takes only a few minutes. The six steps involved may be listed as follows:

1. The necessary information about the new customer—place of birth, address, telephone number, occupation and employer, names of parents and places of birth—is obtained by the bank.
2. The bank's service charges are explained so that there may be no misunderstanding.
3. Signature cards are made out by the new customer, in the same form that they are to appear on the checks, so that tellers may later verify the signature on all checks until they get to know the customer well.
4. A receipt for the initial deposit, in the form of an official receipt slip, which is a duplicate copy of the deposit slip, is issued. Most banks have now abandoned the passbook in favor of the multiple copy deposit slip. Some fully automated banks provide multiple copy deposit slips that have the customer's name imprinted and also have the bank's ABA routing number and the customer's account number in MICR (Magnetic Ink Character Recognition) characters.
5. The customer is supplied with a checkbook, which in the case of fully automated banks has the customer's name and sometimes the address printed on each check, as well as the bank's ABA routing number and the customer's account number in MICR characters. The customer can reorder supplies of imprinted checks from time to time on a form supplied by the bank and a small charge may be made for the checks. The checkbook may also contain deposit tickets imprinted like the checks with the customer's name (and address) and MICR account number.

Usually an account is opened in the name of one depositor alone. A husband and wife, however, often open a joint account, with right of survivorship. Then each of them can draw checks on the same account. In case of the death of a person who has an account in one name alone, no other person, except the legally appointed executor or administrator of the estate, can draw on the account. Sometimes this may tie the account up for months before the court takes action.

Usually the survivor or survivors of a joint account can arrange with little difficulty to continue drawing checks on the account; they must merely give the tax authorities assurance that all taxes due will be paid. When two

TABLE 6–2
A Service Charge Rate Schedule

Special Fee Plan (special checking)	
*Additional statements	0.75
Checks deposited returned unpaid	0.50
Checks on us certified	0.50
*Checks on us returned (insufficient funds, uncollected funds or postdated)	4.00
*Checks paid (per check)	0.10
Immediate credit	1.00
*Monthly maintenance charge	0.75
Overdraft (accounts overdrawn in excess of $5)	4.00
*Stop payments	3.00
Note: Charges for other applicable services are the same as those for regular checking accounts	
Miscellaneous Charges	
Passbook, lost, stolen, or destroyed	1.00
Photostats—paid checks (per check) (10 or more checks—0.75 each)	1.00
Photostats—ledger sheets (per sheet)	1.00
Stop payments—personal money orders	3.00
Dormant Christmas Club accounts—per year (charged annually during the month of March)	4.00
Dormant savings accounts—per year (charged annually during the month of March)	4.00
Unclaimed balances—per year (charged annually on May 31st at rate of 1.00 per month on each account except those which represent official or certified checks and or personal money orders)	12.00
**Regular Fee Plan—Personal Accounts*	
Deposit and check activity have no effect on Regular Fee Plan. Charges for other applicable services are the same as those for business accounts.	
Lowest balance	
$500 and over	Free
$400 to $499	1.00
$300 to $399	2.00
$200 to $299	3.00
$ 0 to $199	4.00
Securities Transactions Charges	
Securities accepted for exchange	15.00
Securities received or delivered vs. payment or receipt	6.00
Securities received for redemption	6.00
Securities transfers (per issue)	6.00
Securities transfers—legal—per issue (transfers to or from the name of a fiduciary—i.e. trustee, executor, etc.). Consult Securities Department for fee when a large number of issues are involved.	12.00
Signature guarantees (per certificate)	0.50
Substitution of collateral (each issue)	2.00
Temporary safekeeping (items held in) per month each receipt	1.00

* Processed automatically by computer. All other charges or units must originate at branch office.

or more persons use the same account, care must be exercised to avoid confusion and not to draw checks for more money than is in the account. Each should keep a full and clear record of every check drawn, and frequently the complete record should be brought together so that both will know just what has been deposited and withdrawn.

In some states, the law does not automatically assume that the balance in a joint account goes to the survivor. It has been held that the survivor's right may be lost by proof that the decedent did not intend to make any gift, before his death, of his contribution to the account. This may apply to checking or commercial accounts as well as to savings accounts.

Monthly Statements

Customarily, banks prepare monthly statements of each account and submit them, with canceled checks, to the depositors, in person or by mail. They do not necessarily prepare them as of the end of the month; to spread the work, one third may be ready as of the 10th, one third as of the 20th, and the remaining third as of the end of the month. Those that operate on a monthly basis may, in order to get the statements out promptly, record transactions up to the 25th of the month only, with later transactions appearing on the next month's statements. If all transactions for the month are recorded on the statements, depositors will probably not be able to obtain them till a few days after the beginning of the next month, since preparing statements for distribution takes some time. Most of the larger banks now use computers to speed up the preparation of the monthly statement.

Making Deposits

Deposits are made to regular checking accounts by filling out a deposit ticket. The depositor inserts name and the date, then fills in the various amounts which are to be deposited. To the right of "bills" or "currency" he inserts the amount of paper money being deposited. The total of coins and silver is entered to the right of these terms, unless the slip calls for "rolled coins" on one line and "loose coin" on another. The amount of each deposited check is listed separately, below. It is good practice to identify the bank on which each check is drawn. Each bank has a number, which appears on its printed checks near its name. This number is good identification of the bank; it is much quicker and easier to write than is the bank's full name. After all items have been listed, the total deposit should be added and entered in the proper space at the bottom of the ticket. The multiple copy deposit slip is presented to the receiving teller, along with the items being deposited. The teller will stamp and receipt the multiple copy deposit ticket and return one copy for the depositor's record. Of course, the deposit should be entered on the proper stub in the checkbook. This will be useful in balancing your checking account when you receive your monthly statement.

Some banks have eliminated duplicate deposit tickets and provide instead a machine receipt. Copies of deposit slips or receipts should, of course, be saved because in the absence of a passbook they constitute your record of deposits. If you lose your copy of the deposit slip or receipt, it isn't too serious because it only records a deposit and the bank, of course, has a duplicate record. Another person cannot get your money simply by finding your lost deposit slip or receipt. Your signature on a check is the only way money can be withdrawn from your account.

It is a good plan, and often saves difficulty, to deposit promptly all checks received. There is a possible danger that the person who drew the check may die, and the bank will then refuse to pay the check. Or there may no longer be sufficient funds in the account when the check is finally presented for payment.

In addition to cash and checks, other items that may be deposited with the bank for collection include promissory notes, postal money orders, and bond interest coupons. When depositing the latter, it is necessary to fill out an ownership certificate, which is sent to the Federal Reserve Bank in the district in order that the government may see that it receives the income tax on the amount involved.

You can bank by mail. After your initial deposit you can handle all transactions—deposits and withdrawals both—by mail. Most banks will provide self-addressed (printed) and franked envelopes, without charge, for this purpose. Frequently, banks have special provisions for receiving deposits outside of regular banking hours. They may provide a small door (to be opened by a key furnished to the depositor, through which the deposit may be dropped into a chute connecting with a vault) or other device. The after-hours deposit box may not require a key. It may be self-closing like a mailbox. Also some banks have drive-in windows which are open longer than regular banking hours.

Certified Checks

There are occasions when a certified check is required in payment. When, for example, in a real estate transaction, the parties meet at the registry of deeds to "pass papers," the seller should deliver a deed to real estate only in exchange for cash or for a check which is certified by a bank. The prospective buyer can make out a check payable to himself, present it at the bank for certification, and then endorse the check to the real estate seller when it is found that everything is in order and the deal is to be consummated. If the deal falls through, it is a simple matter for the disappointed buyer to deposit this check, payable to himself, to his own account again. If the check is made payable to the real estate seller in the first place and is then not used, it is sometimes a bit more troublesome to have it canceled and to have the amount of the certified check credited back to the buyer's account.

When the check is first presented to the bank for certification, the bank ascertains immediately whether there is enough money in the account to cover the check. The check is then stamped "certified" across its face, the stamp also bearing the name of the bank and a space for a proper officer

Check 'Carries' Long Way

BENNET, NEB. (AP)—Checks that bounce are not uncommon, but LeRoy Ringland, a farmer living near here, found one that had "flown." When a tornado destroyed the home of Ed McClure, a farmer living near Blue Springs, Neb., a blank check with Mr. McClure's imprinted name on it was blown some 40 miles before coming to earth near Bennet.

New York Times, May 10, 1974.

to append his signature. By its certification the bank guarantees that sufficient funds have been set aside to pay the check when presented. In other words, the bank guarantees payment on the check. The amount of the check is immediately subtracted from the depositor's balance, and an offsetting credit is made to the bank's "Certified Checks" account, which thereby records the liability of the bank. A small charge is sometimes made for certification, but usually banks will certify without charge for regular customers. When the certified check is cashed, the bank retains it for its records; and it includes a slip, stating the amount of its charge for cerification, when it returns the other canceled checks to the depositor. The recipient of an ordinary check can also present it to the bank for certification if, for one reason or another, it is not to be cashed immediately; the effect is that the bank is responsible for payment later rather than relying on what may or may not be in the depositor's account when the check is cashed.

Why the Bank May Not Honor a Check

As Figure 6–2 indicates, there are some 19 reasons why a bank may not honor a check drawn upon it. Of these, the following seven are the most important:

1. There may not be sufficient funds in the depositor's account to cover the check. Normally, depositors are immediately notified when such checks are presented at the paying teller's window, and the checks are turned back to persons who present them. The person writing a bad check is usually given, by law, a certain number of days to make the check good. If it is not made good, the act becomes an offense under the bad-check law, and the maker becomes subject to prosecution.

2. The check may have been altered. If you make a mistake in writing a check, you cannot erase or cross out. The check will not be honored. It is best to tear up the check on which you made a mistake and write another if you are using a regular checking account. If you have a special checking account and you spoil a check for which you have already paid, the bank will exchange it for a new check without extra charge.

3. The signature may not be genuine. Every bank keeps a file of signatures of all depositors. The signature card you signed when you opened your account is consulted in case of doubt. The bank must know its depositor's signatures because if a forged check is cashed, it cannot be charged against the depositor's account. If the bank pays out money on a forged check, it is paying out its own money and not that of the depositor. Banks protect themselves from such losses by carrying forgery insurance.

4. The check may have been postdated, or the words and figures on the check may not agree. A postdated check cannot be paid until the date specified, although at times a busy bank teller may by accident pay a check

FIGURE 6–2

Returned to..

By

CAMBRIDGE TRUST COMPANY

CAMBRIDGE, MASS.

ADVISED RETURN ITEM C. O'K RNC

ACCOUNT CLOSED	INFORMAL
ACCOUNT TRUSTEED	NO ACCOUNT
BANK ENDORSEMENT MISSING	NO FUNDS
CHECK ALTERED	NOT SATISFIED WITH SIGNATURE
DATED AHEAD	NOT SUFFICIENT FUNDS
DRAWN AGAINST UNCOLLECTED FUNDS	PAYMENT STOPPED
ENDORSEMENT MISSING	RECEIPT OF PAYEE
ENDORSEMENT UNSATISFACTORY	SENT US IN ERROR
GUARANTEE OF AMOUNT	SIGNATURE INCOMPLETE

SIGNATURE MISSING

which is dated ahead. If the words and figures on a check do not agree, many banks will refuse to cash it and will return it unpaid. Some, however, will pay the written amount, because by law the written amount has precedence over the figure. Upon proper authorization, bank employees sometimes make corrections on such checks.

5. There may be a stop order on the check. This will be discussed later.

6. A check may not be cashed by a bank after it has received notice of the death of the person who wrote it.

7. The party who requests payment must be entitled to receive it, upon presentation of proper identification. Banks will not cash checks for unidentified strangers even when the checks are drawn on the bank and the signature of the person who wrote the check has been verified. Identification satisfactory to the bank is required to cash a check. Many large banks now issue identification cards to depositors so that checks can be cashed at any branch.

> If a man's after money, he's money-mad; if he keeps it, he's a capitalist; if he spends it, he's a playboy; if he doesn't get it, he's a ne'er-do-well; if he doesn't try to get it, he lacks ambition. If he gets it without working for it, he's a parasite; and if he accumulates it after a lifetime of hard work, people call him a fool who never got anything out of life.—*Victor Oliver*

Avoiding Overdrafts

In England it has been an accepted practice to borrow from the bank by overdrawing one's account, being charged interest on the overdraft. Although this practice has not been generally followed in the United States, overdrafts are common. When a check for which there are insufficient funds on deposit is presented for payment in this country, the bank may refuse payment and return the check to the person tendering it, along with a slip stating that payment is refused because of insufficient funds. An alternative is for the bank to notify the depositor and allow an opportunity to cover the check before payment is refused. When banks are lenient and honor the check, they are making a forced loan. This is done not from choice but because of the fear of injuring the depositor's standing. Many overdrafts result because the customer does not keep an accurate record of her deposits and her withdrawals; she gets confused as to her correct balance. These overdrafts are innocently created. However, others are deliberately created because of shortage of funds, and checks are issued against the hope of obtaining funds by the time the check is presented for payment. The practice is so prevalent and so troublesome that it is becoming rather common for banks to penalize offenders by making a charge, such as $3–$5 for each overdraft. Another procedure is for the banks to regard the overdraft as a loan and charge a low interest rate. You can prevent overdrafts by keeping accurate records. Every time you make a deposit, add it to the previous balance in your own checkbook. Before you write a check, enter the date, number, payee, and deduct the amount from your balance as shown on your check stub.

Stopping Payment

If you write a check and later for some reason do not want the bank to pay it, you may ask the bank to stop payment. Commonly, you will be asked to fill out a form, giving the number and amount of the check, its date, and the name of the person to whose order it is payable (see Figure 6–3). This is good procedure when a check is lost. It is also useful if after giving a check you cannot obtain what you were supposed to receive for it, or if what is received is not of the agreed quality or quantity.

After the bank receives a stop notice from the depositor, it puts a tab or colored flag on the record of the depositor's account and notifies all tellers who might possibly cash the check. If the check should be presented, it will be refused, ordinarily. Most banks insert a clause in the stop payment form, which must be signed by the drawer of the check to stop it, relieving the bank of any liability if by oversight or error one of its employees pays a check after it has been stopped.[3] With a computerized operation, however, it is practically certain that the check will be stopped.

An oral stop payment order is binding on the bank for 14 days and a written order is good for six months—subject to renewal. Neither a certified check nor a cashier's check can be stopped by such an order. Sometimes the stop payment order can create a problem for the bank, as was reported in a *New York Times* article when a wife ordered a stop payment on a check drawn by her husband on their joint account. The bank honored the check, and a court upheld the bank's position.[4]

How to Write a Check

Checks should be written clearly, completely, and in ink. Make it a practice to fill out your check stub before you write the check itself. There

---

[3] See *Stop Payment Procedure*, Bank Management Commission, American Bankers Association, latest edition.

[4] *New York Times*. May 16, 1968.

FIGURE 6-3

STOP PAYMENT ORDER

OFFICE NO.________________ DATE________________

CHEMICAL BANK NEW YORK TRUST COMPANY

☐ REGULAR
☐ SPECIAL
☐ OTHER
____

DEAR SIRS:

PLEASE STOP PAYMENT OF ACCEPTANCE / CHECK / NOTE DRAWN BY THE UNDERSIGNED ON OR PAYABLE AT YOUR OFFICE.

NO. DATED OR DUE ________________

FOR $ PAYABLE TO THE ORDER OF ________________

____

IT IS EXPRESSLY UNDERSTOOD AND AGREED THAT SHOULD THIS ITEM BE CERTIFIED AND/OR PAID THROUGH INADVERTENCY OR OVERSIGHT, YOU WILL IN NO WAY BE HELD RESPONSIBLE.

A DUPLICATE WILL / WILL NOT BE ISSUED UPON RECEIPT OF YOUR ADVICE.

YOURS VERY TRULY,

TELEPHONE ORDER

	TIME	BY
RECEIVED		
TO AUDIT DEPT.		

____
ACCOUNT NUMBER

____
(PRINT NAME OF ACCOUNT)

____
ADDRESS

____
AUTHORIZED SIGNATURE

Do not write below line — for Bank use only

Noted by:
P & R TELLERS

DATE RECEIVED________________

TIME RECEIVED________________ ________________

____

VOUCHERS AND CURRENT WORK CHECKED________________ ________________

CERTIFICATION CLERK________________

ADJUSTER________________ BOOKKEEPER________________

are six different items to be written in ink on the face of the check itself.

1. *The date* should be written first, and it should be the date on which the check is drawn. A check dated as of a Sunday is as good as any other. Since some people may refuse to accept it, however, you might just as well date it the previous day. Ordinarily, checks should not be postdated (dated ahead). Such a check cannot be paid by the bank before the day whose date it bears, unless it is done through oversight. Postdated checks are sometimes issued to creditors when the debtors' accounts do not as yet have enough on deposit to cover them. The creditors are asked not to cash them before the date that they bear, by which time the debtors hope to have enough on deposit to cover them.

2. *The check number* should be filled in next. For your own convenience and use in record keeping, every check you write should be numbered and the same number should be entered on the corresponding stub. If you order supplies of name imprinted checks from your bank, they may bear printed consecutive numbers if you so request. It speeds balancing your checkbook.

3. *The payee's name* should be written after the printed words "PAY TO THE ORDER OF." (The payee is the person or company or organization to whom the money is to be paid.) Spell the name correctly. Instead of making the checks payable to "Bearer" or "Cash," it is usually better to name a specific person or company as payee. Then the check will bear the endorsement of the payee when it is cashed and will serve as a better receipt for the amount paid. Furthermore, a check drawn to "Cash" can be cashed by anyone, and thus the loss of a check made out to "Cash" is the same as losing currency.

4. *The amount in figures* (after the payee's name) should be written close to the dollar sign to prevent other figures from being inserted between. Although you are not responsible beyond the original sum, it is best to prevent the possibility of this happening. The correct way to express dollars and cents is: $\$17^{50}/_{100}$.

5. *The amount in words* should be written on the following line. It should be started as far to the left as possible so that no one may insert a word before it and thereby raise the amount. Of course, the two expressions of the amount should be in agreement. The Uniform Negotiable Instruments Law gives preference to the amount written out in words in case they do not agree. The word "dollars" is usually printed on the checks. To prevent anything being inserted between the amount and the word "dollars," it is considered good practice to insert a wavy line, as in Figure 6–4. When the amount is less than $1.00—89 cents for instance—it can be written out as "None $^{89}/_{100}$," or "Eighty-nine cents only." In figures, "$^{89}/_{100}$," "none $^{89}/_{100}$," or "89 cents" can be used.

FIGURE 6–4
Writing a Check

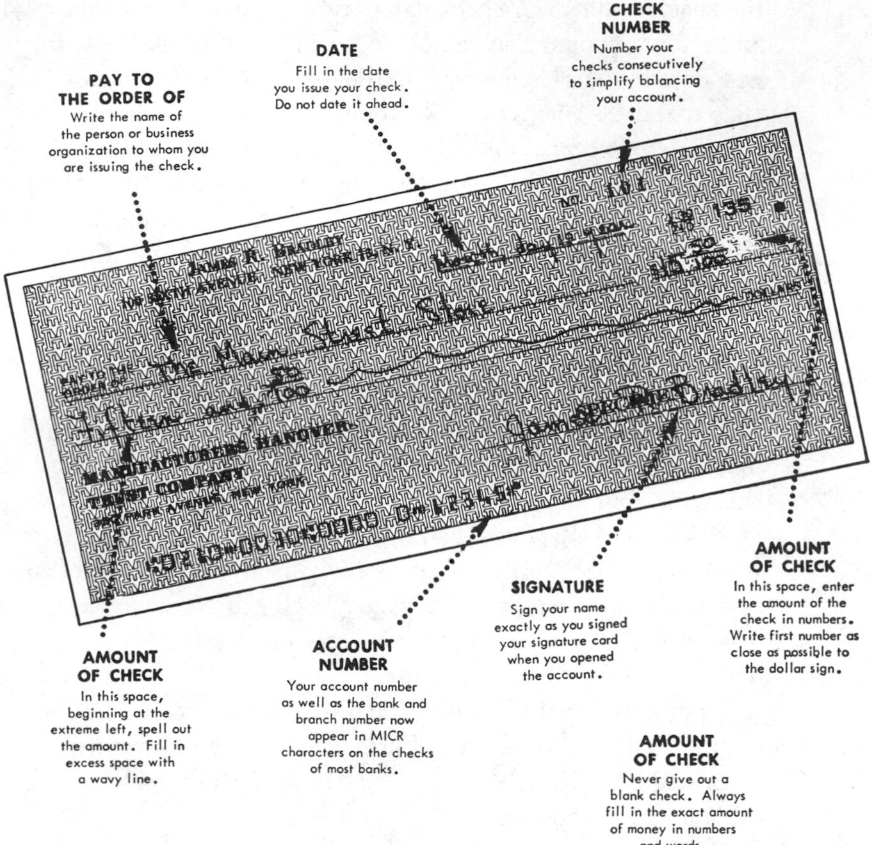

6. *Your signature* should be written in exactly the same way as you signed it on the signature card which you filled out for the bank. If the signature is reasonably legible, it helps. Never sign a blank check. Write your signature only after all other blanks have been filled in. Do not cross out, erase, or change any part of a check. The bank will probably not accept it because such alterations give too much opportunity to forgers. Mark the stub void and tear up the check.

Sometimes you may draw a check and find you don't have enough funds to cover it. Perhaps your arithmetic was a little shaky and you made a mistake and you have overdrawn. Perhaps you forgot a check that is still "outstanding" and the reconciliation of your bank statement was too optimistic. You are now worrying about having written a check for money that isn't there. Relax.

Rancher Inks Check on Cowhide—Bank Honors It

Temperatures throughout the Southwest have been high much of the summer. This probably has nothing to do with the fact that Joe M. King, a rancher, spent some time recently inking a $500 check to himself on a six-by-three-foot cowhide.

Equally improbable was Mr. King's explanation: "I didn't have a blank check handy."

Whatever the reason for writing this unusual check, Mr. King presented it last week to be cashed at the downtown Tuscon office of the Valley National Bank of Phoenix, Ariz. Jeanne Rudolph, a teller, was a bit taken back. But such checks were nothing new to Gil Bradley, a vice president and manager of the office.

"It is perfectly negotiable, although perhaps unwieldy," he reportedly said.

Mr. Bradley has made a study of unorthodox checks, the bank noted in reporting the event. It disclosed these results of his research:

¶A check written on a paper bag was presented for payment recently at the office of a competitor bank in Tucson.

¶An employer in the Northwest paid off his men with checks written on shingles.

¶A Canadian lumberjack wrote his checks on birchbark peeled from a tree.

Mr. Bradley also found that checks had been written on hard-boiled eggs, watermelons and even boiler plate. In the last instance, the bank cancelled the check with a rented blowtorch.

If a check is worded correctly, has a valid signature and there are sufficient funds in the account upon which it is drawn, Mr. Bradley asserts, it will be honored.

Honored, but perhaps not welcomed. Because of the advent of automatic check sorting and electronic bookkeeping, the American Bankers Association has issued stern injunctions to its members to discourage such oversize and unmanageable checks.

Neither Mr. Bradley nor anyone else at the Valley National explained why they had not made another suggestion to Mr. King—that he use a counter check available in most bank offices.

New York Times

There is a service called "No Bounce Checking" which several large metropolitan banks offer. It provides a line of credit to an agreed amount at no advance cost—and a low bank rate when used. Simply stated this means that the bank will cover your check up to a limited maximum at a small cost. This is also known as "writing your own loan."

Your Check Stub

Every deposit you make and every check you write, including blank check forms mentioned above, should be entered on your stub record. This is your only means of keeping an accurate record of your bank account and of reconciling your figures with the bank statement you receive at the end of the month. In fact, your stub is so important that it is advisable to fill out the stub *before* you write the check so that you won't forget it. Enter the check number, the date, the amount of the check, the name of the person or company to whose order the check is payable, and what you are paying for, all in the space on the stub. Then, if a month later you are asked if you paid that particular bill, you can look back over your stubs and see exactly when you did. For one example of the proper way to fill out a check stub see Figure 6–5.

FIGURE 6–5

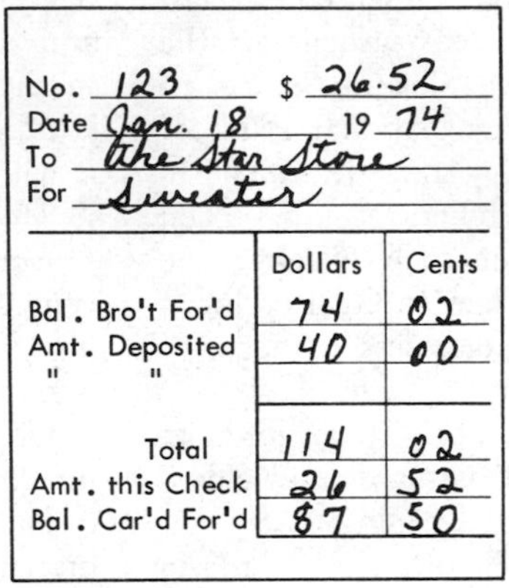

No. 123 $ 26.52
Date Jan. 18 19 74
To The Star Store
For Sweater

	Dollars	Cents
Bal. Bro't For'd	74	02
Amt. Deposited	40	00
" "		
Total	114	02
Amt. this Check	26	52
Bal. Car'd For'd	87	50

How to Endorse Checks

Before you can cash or deposit a check made out to you, you must sign it on the back, preferably custom dictates, at the extreme left end. This is known as endorsement. If you want to take a check which has been made out to you and give it to another person in payment for something, you must first endorse it and then the other party must also endorse it before it can be cashed or deposited. If your name is misspelled or incomplete, write your first endorsement in the same way—and then write your correct signature.

You should never endorse a check until you get to a bank. If you endorse a check beforehand and then lose it, the finder may possibly cash it. By endorsement the person to whom the check is made out passes title to the check to someone else. If you lose a check made out to you, you may be able to arrange to have payment on it stopped *providing you haven't endorsed it.*

There are several methods of endorsing (see Figure 6–6). The most common is for you merely to write your name on the back of the instrument across the left hand end. This is a *blank* endorsement, and since it makes the check payable to bearer, it may be dangerous. With a blank endorsement a check can be transferred from person to person and is payable to anyone holding it. The only time when a blank endorsement is safe is when the check is being cashed in a bank. The blank endorsement should be placed on the check after the endorser arrives at the bank. If a check is made payable to your order and you endorse it and then lose it, whoever picks it up or finds it may be able to cash it. To prevent such a loss, you may resort to the protection of a *restrictive* endorsement or a *special* endorsement. The *restrictive endorsement,*

For deposit only
Rita Andrews

allows the check to be used only for deposit in your account, assuming for the moment that you are Andrews. Restrictive endorsement means that you endorse the check for a special purpose only. This type of endorsement is always recommended when checks are mailed and then it is best to write "For deposit only" before signing your name.

Pay to the order of Steven Andrews
Rita Andrews,

negotiates the check to Steven Andrews, who must, in turn, endorse it in order to pass title to it. The chief advantage of this endorsement is

FIGURE 6–6

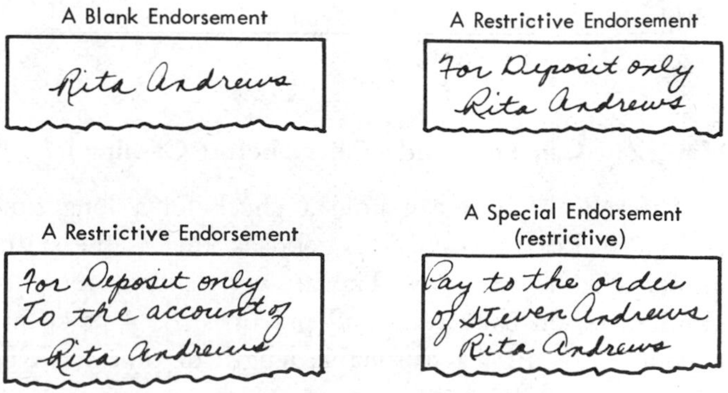

A Blank Endorsement

Rita Andrews

A Restrictive Endorsement

For Deposit only
Rita Andrews

A Restrictive Endorsement

For Deposit only
To the account of
Rita Andrews

A Special Endorsement (restrictive)

Pay to the order
of Steven Andrews
Rita Andrews

that the check can be cashed only by the specified party. It is possible to convert a blank endorsement into a special endorsement by inserting the words "Pay to the order of" and a person's name above the blank endorsement.

A check, of course, is a negotiable instrument. When you receive a check and endorse it, giving it to someone in payment, you are responsible if it turns out to be bad, even though you passed it along in good faith. You, in turn, can try to get your money back from the person who gave it to you in the first place. If your checkbook should be lost or stolen and your name is forged for fantastic sums, you are not responsible; but notify the bank immediately.

2 Experts Tell Bankers How to Spot Forgeries

PITTSFIELD, MASS., May 12 (AP)—Two experts are making the rounds at Massachusetts banks, teaching tellers how to spot a bad check. And the experts, Ronald D. Strelnick and Edward F. Welch, know what they're talking about—they're both convicted check forgers.

"We've perpetrated these frauds," said Mr. Welch, who is 51 years old and is still serving time at the Berkshire House of Correction for interstate transportation of bad checks. "It gives us the credibility the bank officer lacks."

Mr. Strelnick, 31, was released from the Pittsfield prison April 3 after completing an 18-month sentence for check forgery.

The two men conduct "prevention workshops," including a 30-minute videotape of a con artist in action, and explanations of various methods used to pass bad checks.

Mr. Welch has been released from the prison, accompanied by a deputy, to conduct the sessions in western Massachusetts. He is eligible for parole in July but says he does not know if his work will influence the parole board to release him.

New York Times, May 13, 1974.

How Long Can You Hold a Check before Cashing It?

Theoretically, you can hold a check for a long time, but it isn't a good idea. Legally, a check is good as long as the statute of limitations allows—usually six years. The answer depends more on facts and circumstances, on bank rules and practices. As a practical matter, a check becomes stale after a reasonable length of time has elapsed. In general, banks usually refuse to honor checks more than six months old. "Reasonable time" is as long as the bank feels it can collect the funds. Staleness of a check does not make it bad or void. It merely puts the bank on notice that irregularities may exist—that something may be wrong and therefore it shouldn't be paid. Under such circumstances, the bank will not pay the check without obtaining the maker's consent.

Unless a check is presented to the bank for payment within a reasonable time after it is issued, the maker of the check will be relieved of liability on it if the payee suffers a loss by reason of the delay. What constitutes a reasonable time depends on the circumstances in each case. Ordinarily, a reasonable time is determined by the length of time it would take an ordinarily prudent person to present the check for payment under similar circumstances. Williams gives Stone a check for $100 drawn on the Bankers Bank. Although the bank is only a few blocks away, Stone, being busy, does not deposit the check. He remembers it and presents it for payment five weeks later. Meanwhile, Williams died. At worst the check may not be honored at all; at best payment will be delayed until Williams' estate is settled.

How to Reconcile Your Balance

Usually the depositor receives a bank statement and canceled checks once a month. The statement shows the balance at the beginning of the month or on the previous closing date, all individual charges for checks and notes paid and service charges, and the balance at the end of the month or on the new closing date. For several reasons, the ending balance on the bank's statement probably will not be in agreement with the depositor's checkbook stub balance as of the same date. Therefore, it is necessary to reconcile the two balances. All checks drawn, if the depositor has been keeping his record correctly, have been deducted by the depositor from the balance at the bank. Some of these checks have, however, probably not yet been presented to the depositor's bank for payment; they are therefore said to be "outstanding." Since these checks, nevertheless, were given by the depositor in payment for something, the proper procedure is to deduct them from the bank's balance on the reconciliation statement, for which the depositor can use any spare piece of paper or a form frequently provided for the purpose on the reverse side of the bank statement. The bank has already deducted service charges, and in that respect is nearer to the true cash balance than is the balance shown on the checkbook stubs. The checkbook, moreover, may show credits for deposits which are still "in transit," i.e., have not yet been credited by the bank. Therefore, if deposits in transit are added to the bank's final balance and outstanding checks are deducted from it, we should usually be able to ascertain the true cash balance.

The depositor has two objectives: (1) to prove that the story told by the checkbook stubs is in agreement (reconciles) with the same story as told by the bank statement and (2) to ensure that the checkbook stubs reveal the true cash balance for the ensuing period. It is important to you to keep your checkbook in agreement with the balance in your account at the bank. Be sure to enter each check on the check stub and subtract that amount from the balance in your checkbook. In this way you can avoid overdrawing your account and having your checks returned unpaid.

As soon as you receive a statement of your account and your canceled checks from the bank, look them over carefully. If no errors are reported, the account will be considered correct by the bank. The following procedure is recommended to balance your record with the bank's statement of your account:

1.	Sort checks numerically or by date issued.	
2.	Reduce your checkbook balance by the amount of any service charges not previously recorded.	
3.	Enter statement balance here..........................	$..........
4.	Check back each paid check to your checkbook stubs and make a list of all checks issued but not yet paid by the bank. Enter and subtract the total of these unpaid checks here...	$..........
		$..........
5.	Enter and add any deposit in transit by mail or made later in transit than the date of this statement..................	$..........
6.	This balance should be the same as your checkbook balance..	$..........

Perhaps a simple illustration will clarify the procedure. Let us suppose that your bank statement reveals a final balance of $1,732.49, whereas your checkbook stubs show that you ended the month with $1,536.29. When you compare the canceled checks returned by the bank with the record of checks drawn according to the stubs, you find that check No. 62 for $88.29 and check No. 67 for $109.45 are still outstanding. Inspection of the bank statement shows service charges of $1.54 not yet recorded on the checkbook stubs. You can arrive at the true cash balance by two independent methods.

One method is to start with the bank's balance of $1,732.49 and reconcile it with the checkbook stub balance of $1,536.29:

Balance on bank statement..............................		$1,732.49
Less: Outstanding checks: No. 62.................	$ 88.29	
No. 67.................	109.45	197.74
Total..		$1,534.75
Plus: Service charges..................................		1.54
Balance shown on checkbook stubs.......................		$1,536.29

Or you can begin with the checkbook stub balance of $1,536.29 and reconcile it with the balance of $1,732.49 on the bank statement:

Balance on checkbook stubs		$1,536.29
Add: Outstanding checks:		
No. 62	$ 88.29	
No. 67	109.45	197.74
		$1,734.03
Less: Service charges		1.54
Balance as shown by bank statement		$1,732.49

Now that you have reconciled the one story with the other, you must remember to deduct the service charge of $1.54 from your checkbook stub balance in order that you may begin the next month with your true cash balance of $1,534.75. Canceled checks, bank statements, and checkbook stubs should be retained for a reasonable number of years. The ordinary statute of limitations provides that creditors must bring action for recovery of debts within six years or lose the right to sue for them. In case of dispute as to whether a bill has been paid, a canceled check may prove to be an effective receipt.

Automation, Computers and MICR

To clear, collect, and process the billions of checks we write each year, banks have had to resort to automation. Computers and MICR have come into vogue as the answer. The odd looking numbers at the bottom of checks serve a very useful purpose. They allow checks to be read and sorted automatically by new electronic machines and enable computers to post accounts and print statements.

The four initials MICR (which stand for Magnetic Ink Character Recognition) denote these new developments in banking. Those funny numbers at the bottom of checks are readable both by humans and by magnetic sensing devices. They are printed on checks using an ink containing iron oxide, like the coating of magnetic recording tapes. A permanent magnet on the machine magnetizes the iron oxide in the ink on the checks, making the numbers ready to be read by the machine. Each numeral gives off a different electrical impulse. These signals given off by the magnetized characters can be used to operate such equipment as sorting machines, which work at the rate of more than 1,000 a minute.

Checks carry two sets of figures at the bottom: the first, at the left, is the American Bankers Association routing symbol, the number of the bank on which the check is drawn and the city and Federal Reserve district in which it is located. This is equivalent to the printed number in the upper right hand corner of the check. Thus, for example,

$$\frac{1\text{–}12}{210}$$

where the 1 stands for New York, N.Y., 12 for the Chemical Bank, and 210 for the New York Federal Reserve Bank (2 for 2nd district), (1 for head office, not branch), (and 0 for immediate availability), becomes in MICR:

⑆0210⑉0012⑆

This is then followed by the number of your account at the bank. Thus the check can be automatically sorted and sent back to the right bank and to the right account. In addition, when the check is presented for collection, additional figures may be added by the use of an inscriber, a machine by which MICR characters may be inscribed on deposit slips or on checks. For example, it is customary now to inscribe the amount of the check in MICR. This permits processing by a computer which can then adjust accounts and issue daily statements. In large banks there are delivered each morning, before the bank opens for business, computer compiled sheets showing the closing balance in each account at a given branch as of the close of the most recent clearing the night before. Thus the teller knows how much is in every account and does not need to call the head office to find out. Also the monthly statement is put together by the computer.

In this age of intercontinental ballistic missiles, the larger urban banks now each have a depository in more remote locations, where duplicate sets of account records, statements, deposit slips, and so forth, are available in case of atomic attack. Daily computer tabulations are sent to these depositories to keep accounts up to date, and officials of one bank estimate that the bank could open for banking transactions at the remote location with a complete, up-to-date set of records within 48 hours after an atomic attack. Whether anyone would or could show up to make a deposit or withdrawal is another question.

Instant Cash—Money Machines

Diebold, Inc., has recently introduced a new automated system, and some banks have adopted it to enable customers to make withdrawals during hours when banks are normally closed. The system, called the "MD 400 Automatic Teller System" involves four steps. First, the bank customer is issued an "Insert Card" which looks like an ordinary credit card. The card is embossed with the customer's name, account number, expiration date, and other standard information. When the customer wishes to make a cash withdrawal, the card is inserted into the automatic teller, a piece of equipment which may be installed outside the bank for customer convenience. The customer pushes buttons on a panel to inform the "teller" the amount of cash requested, and indicates on the buttons the six-digit "secret number" which identifies the account. If the number is incorrect, the equipment will light up a panel saying, "TRY AGAIN." If the card has expired or been stolen and reported "hot," the equipment will not return the card (nor distribute cash). Instead, it will light up, "CARD RETAINED." Finally, if everything is in order, the machine will return the card and then distribute the requested cash. Simultaneously, the equipment will record the transaction for the bank's records.

Checkless Banking

Consumer resistance, as much as technical limitation, is slowing electronic banking. Banks benefit through reduction of paper work and its cost. A check goes through ten hands before returning to its writer. The customer however wants a canceled check as a record. Today's world demands legal records of everything even though electronic services show transactions on statements. The Federal Reserve Bank of Atlanta commissioned a study that showed people in its area did not react favorably toward pre-authorized bill payments or checkless payment systems. A worker's comment typified others' feelings, "I like looking at the weekly pay check even though the money goes quickly." It was also found that checkless payroll plans are regarded unkindly by workers who keep the exact sum of their pay a secret from their spouse. But it has begun. California has SCOPE (Special Committee on Paperless Entries) and Georgia has COPE (Committee on Paperless Entries) as functioning electronic fund transfer systems, cooperating with the regional Federal Reserve Bank. A company delivers its payroll to its bank on computer tape. The bank then electronically transfers an employee's pay, through the Federal Reserve Bank, to the individual's bank where it is credited to each employee's account before the bank opens on pay day.

To function effectively electronic point of purchase terminals should be placed in all retail outlets where customers can use cards that would automatically debit their bank accounts and credit the store's. But these terminals each cost around $500, and it is at this point that banks hesitate. One sweetener is the Federal Reserve's offer of the use of their 44 automated computer centers being set up around the country to speed clearing of checks—from several days to one. Finally, both banks and their customers are united in enjoying the use of the "float"—extra use of money represented by checks in transit. Electronic banking will eliminate this.

Capabilities of the IBM cash issuing terminal have been expanded. Previously, the terminal enabled bank customers to withdraw cash and inquire about the current balance in their accounts. Now, new optional features will also let them deposit checks or cash, make loan payments, obtain printed records of transactions, and transfer funds from one account to another, at any hour. The terminal can dispense cash, in denominations of either $5, $10 or $20, as specified by the bank.

To make deposits or loan payments, the customer, after identifying himself to the terminal, simply presses the appropriate keys and inserts an envelope containing the deposit into a covered deposit slot. Customers can also make payments by keying instructions to deduct funds from checking, savings or credit card accounts. A new receipt printer can record each transaction and issue a receipt to the customer.

EFTS (electronic funds transfer systems) is not yet cashless, checkless society but its current operations are eliminating floods of paper. Automated finances, cash cards, electronic money are making more feasible banking where you shop and/or shopping where you bank.[5]

Other Uses of Your Checking Account

There are many other valuable and convenient uses of your checking account. For example, you can arrange, as a permanent matter, to have your salary check sent directly to your bank and deposited automatically to your credit. Thus you can avoid the semimonthly or monthly chore of getting your paycheck and taking it to the bank to deposit.

There is now a "dividend deposit plan." Under it your dividend checks on any stock you own will be mailed directly by the disbursing agent to your bank for deposit in your account. This helps avoid the problem of checks going astray or piling up in a mailbox while a family is away on vacation.

On the disbursing side, you can arrange with your bank to have it automatically pay your utility bills or your insurance premiums, or buy a U.S. government bond for you each month, deducting the cost from your account. In the case of utility and insurance bills, the companies are notified to send their bills or notices to your bank, and you authorize your bank to pay them as received, deducting the amount from your account, and notifying you, of course, of the payments.

Some banks go even further; there is a monthly payment insurance

---

[5] For detail see *U.S. News and World Report*, August 5, 1974 and September 16, 1974.

premium plan. If you have a large annual insurance bill coming due, the bank will pay it for you in one lump sum, and you can then repay the bank in equal monthly installments. You can either pay in the cash each month or they will deduct the amount from your account. No assignment of the policy is necessary. A small charge is levied for this service, which is, of course, a loan.

A number of commercial banks have adopted revolving check-loan account plans in the past few years. They are offering under a number of different names, such as Cash Reserve Checking or Checking Plus, the opportunity to write checks for more than you have in your account —up to a point. This special service is offered as a line of credit depending on your needs and ability to repay.

Under these plans a credit limit is set for each borrower, usually 12 times the agreed monthly payment, and a book of checks is given which can be used at any time so long as the unpaid balance does not exceed the credit limit. Monthly payments are one twelfth of the line of credit, regardless of the amount of the unpaid balance, as long as some balance is outstanding. These plans involve a service charge, usually 15 cents a check, plus interest on the unpaid balance.

Other Ways to Transfer Funds

If you want to transfer funds to someone at a distance who does not know you very well and who will therefore not accept your personal check, there are several alternative possibilities.

1. A *certified check*. Most banks make no charge for certifying a personal check of one of their depositors. You can send a certified check, but the limitation is that you will not have a receipt. The bank assumes liability on the check because of its certification, and it may, therefore, retain the canceled check.

2. A *cashier's check*. This is a check which the bank draws on itself. It can be used by nondepositors. If you do not have a checking account at a bank, you can nevertheless ask for a cashier's check made out payable to the order of the distant party that you want to pay. You give the bank the appropriate amount. They give you a check drawn by the bank on itself payable to the order of the party you name. The charge for this is usually 50 cents per check—usually no charge if you have an account. The limitation is the same as in the use of the certified check. You have no personal receipt in the form of a canceled check, since the bank keeps it. In contrast to the certified check, the cashier's check is used mainly by those who do not have checking accounts.

3. *Bank money order or register check.* These have grown rapidly in use in recent years for domestic transfers of sums up to $500. These cost between 40 and 50 cents, depending on the bank. They contain a space for the sender's name and have a detachable stub or record copy which serves as a receipt and bears (for identification) the same serial number as the main part of the money order itself.

4. *U.S. postal and American Express money orders.* Both the U.S. Postal Service and the American Express Company sell money orders. Postal money orders, of course, are for sale at any U.S. post office. The rates for postal money orders are as follows for orders from: $0.01 to $10—25 cents; $10.01 to $50—35 cents; or $50.01 to $300—40 cents. American Express retail outlets are being phased out. Money orders can be purchased at banks or American Express offices and cost somewhat more than postal money orders.

5. *Telegraphic transfers of funds.* If you want to transfer money in a hurry, you can do so by telegram. Money orders, of course, are sent by mail and this takes time. If the need to transfer funds is urgent, then you can go to the nearest Western Union office, pay the clerk the amount to be transferred, the fee involved, and the cost of the telegram. The clerk will then send a telegram to the company's office nearest to where the person you want to pay lives, instructing that office to pay the amount. The check drawn is either delivered to the payee by a company messenger or the payee is reached by telephone and asked to come to the telegraph office to receive payment. The cost of a telegraphic money order, which is naturally much more than either a bank or a postal money order, depends on (*a*) the amount of money sent, (*b*) the distance over which the telegram must be sent, and (*c*) the amount of traffic between the sending and paying locations. In addition there is a federal tax on the transaction.

6. *Sending money abroad.* You can use either international postal money orders or American Express or bank drafts. For small amounts the postal money order is less expensive. The rates are for orders from: $0.01 to $10—45 cents; $10.01 to $50—65 cents; $50.01 to $300—75 cents. In transmitting larger sums than $100 the bank draft is much more convenient. While rates will vary somewhat from bank to bank, the following is typical of current charges for amounts: up to $100—$1; $100 to $300—$2; $300 to $2,000—$2.75; For sums over $2,000—.125 percent with a maximum of $25. A remittance abroad can be sent by cable, airmail, or regular mail, depending on the speed with which it is desired to effect the transfer. You, of course, pay the cable or air mail costs. The American Express charge is more than the bank charge.

Traveler's Checks

If you are going on a trip, you will find many opportunities to make use of traveler's checks. It is, of course, hazardous to carry large amounts of money with you. Your personal checks are not generally acceptable. Traveler's checks usually cost 1 per $100 and are issued in denominations of $10, $20, $50, $100, and $500 and even $1,000.

The banks are glad to issue these checks, not so much because of the charge of $1 per $100, which they give in part or in full to their agents who sell the checks for them, but rather because of "the large float": the use of the money which they have for the period that elapses between the time the checks are sold and the date they are cashed. When the checks are purchased, the buyer signs each check with his usual signature at the upper left. Later, for identification, he signs the same signature at the lower left in the presence of the person cashing the check for him.

The checks are generally sold to the buyer in a folder, which contains a form on which to record the serial numbers and the places and dates where each was cashed. Uncashed checks can be replaced if lost or stolen, providing records of purchase and serial numbers have been kept. Perhaps needless to say, the record should not be kept in the same place as the checks. American Express Company, Bank of America, Cook's, First National City Bank of Chicago, First National City Bank of New York, and Republic National Bank of Dallas, among others, all issue traveler's checks. You will find that hotels, motels, restaurants, gas stations, and large stores are universally acquainted with traveler's checks and accept them readily. They are a real convenience in traveling. You may keep your traveler's checks as long as you like. They are good until used, and there is no time limit on them.

Countersigning must be done in the presence of the person accepting the check. On occasion the double signature requirement has presented difficulties. In one instance the countersignature of an American abroad was questioned. He agreed that the original signature was much more shaky, but observed that he had purchased the checks after imbibing rather freely of cognac. To obtain a comparable signature, he suggested, in all seriousness, that the prospective acceptor of his checks take him to a nearby bistro for a few cognacs.

To have available large sums in traveling, you would use a *traveler's letter of credit*. These are issued by a bank to a customer preparing for an extended trip. The customer pays for the letter of credit, and the bank issues it for a specified period of time in the amount purchased. The bank furnishes a list of its foreign offices and its correspondent banks, where drafts drawn against the letter of credit will be honored. The bank also identifies the customer by exhibiting a specimen signature of the purchaser on the folder enclosing the list of correspondent banks. The purchaser may go to any bank listed, draw a draft against the letter of credit, and receive payment. The letter of credit then operates like a mobile checking account, letting you cash checks or drafts as you travel. Each bank that honors a draft endorses on the letter of credit: the date a payment was made, its name, and the amount it paid out against the letter of credit.

Promissory Notes and Drafts

When buying a house, borrowing from a bank or other institution, or buying on credit, one often signs a promissory note (see Figure 6–7 for compliance with Truth in Lending). Although checks and drafts are orders to pay, notes are promises to pay. To a note there are two parties: the maker and the payee, in addition to any endorsers who appear thereon. In the case of drafts, however, there are usually three parties: A orders B (the bank, when a check is involved) to pay C. Notes may be due on demand or at a fixed and determinable future time. In order to hold the maker, the note must be presented for payment before it is barred by the statute of limitations, time of which differs among the various states. The safest course is to present it promptly when due. In order to hold endorsers, a time note must be presented to the maker for payment on the due date, whereas a demand note must be presented within a reasonable time. Endorsers of notes are liable in the same order as was mentioned in the case of checks. Likewise, they may endorse in the same ways (blank, special, or restrictive), and their liabilities are similar.

Drafts and notes are governed by the Uniform Negotiable Instruments Law. As we have seen in the case of the check, a draft is an order drawn by one party (drawer) on another party (the drawee), ordering payment to a payee, who may be the drawer or another party. Drafts drawn and payable in the United States are domestic drafts, whereas drafts drawn in this country and payable in a foreign country (or vice versa) are foreign drafts. Foreign drafts are sometimes called "bills of exchange." When a bank draws a draft (check) on another bank, the instrument is called a "bank draft." A draft drawn by a seller to obtain payment for merchandise is known as a "trade acceptance"—the buyer obtains the merchandise when he "accepts" the draft. He accepts the draft by writing his acceptance and signature on the face of the instrument, very much as a bank certifies a check and thereby promises to pay it. A "sight draft" is payable at sight or presentation, whereas a "time draft" is payable in a given number of days after date of acceptance.

Drafts are used by sellers to expedite payment. The initiative comes from the seller. Frequently, a seller will not part with the goods until the buyer accepts the draft drawn on him. Sometimes a draft, with an order

FIGURE 6–7

Example of disclosures on a promissory note for non-sale credit for which a finance charge is added to the amount financed and the obligation is repayable in installments.

PROMISSORY NOTE

____________________, ____________________
(City) (State)

____________19____

For value received, undersigned maker(s), jointly and severally, promise to pay to the order of _________________________ at the above place _________________________ dollars ($______) in ______ consecutive monthly payments of $________, each beginning one month from the date hereof and thereafter on the same date of each subsequent month until paid in full. Any unpaid balance may be paid, at any time, without penalty and any unearned finance charge will be refunded based on the "Rule of 78's". In the event that maker(s) default(s) on any payment, a charge of ________ may be assessed.

1. Proceeds $__________
2. ________________ (Other charges, itemized) __________
3. Amount financed (1+2) $__________
4. FINANCE CHARGE __________
5. Total of payments $__________

ANNUAL PERCENTAGE RATE __________ %

Signed ______________________________

____

____

This form, when properly completed, will show how a creditor may comply with the disclosure requirements of the provisions of paragraphs (b) and (d) of §226.8 of Regulation Z for the type of credit extended in this example. This form is intended solely for purposes of demonstration and it is not the only format which will permit a creditor to comply with disclosure requirements of Regulation Z.

Source: Federal Reserve Board, Exhibit D, "Consumer Credit Cost Disclosure."

bill of lading attached, is given to the seller's bank with instructions to have the bill of lading handed to the buyer (through a correspondent bank) only after he has accepted the draft drawn on him. It is even more satisfactory for the seller if the arrangement is for the buyer's bank to accept (and promise to pay) the draft. A draft drawn on a bank and accepted by it is known as a "banker's acceptance." Accepted drafts, being the equivalent of promissory notes, can be discounted (sold) to banks and are, therefore, a source of ready money even before the due dates. The discount is the amount of money deducted from the face value of the note or draft by the bank.

Sometimes a borrower can obtain money only if he secures a co-maker to sign his note with him. In other cases, the lender will require that the maker secure the endorsement of some financially able person. Persons who lend their signatures as accommodation co-makers or endorsers often live to regret the act; a co-maker will have to pay the amount of the note if the maker fails to do so, just as an accommodation endorser can be called upon to pay the amount upon due presentment and due notice of dishonor.

Bank Services—Loans

The wide variety of bank loan services are covered in more detail in Chapter 5, Obtaining a Loan; Chapter 2, Expenditure and Budgeting and in Chapter 12, on Housing. But some listing is needed here so that you will be aware that they exist. There are personal loans to meet emergencies, or for a vacation and travel, and loans to consolidate debts and thereby reduce interest costs. There are many educational loans available—varying from bank to bank and state to state—which finance education at all levels and may even include a life insurance coverage equal to the outstanding balance of the loan at no extra cost.

You can borrow not only to meet large scale medical or dental expenses but also to buy a boat, or a low cost property improvement loan, financed in advance (before you select your contractor or the boat)—and "on the spot" as some banks say—for which all you need do to qualify is to show that you have a steady job or income and are of legal age. Most of these loans do not even require a checking account in the bank where you are applying for the loan. Auto loans are available on the same basis, and while some banks offer to take your application by mail, a large New York bank is willing to do it on a Dial-A-Loan service 24 hours a day, 7 days a week.

Other Bank Services

Many banks are providing income tax service for a small charge, processed by computer. The bank tax service will minimize your tax payment by automatically selecting the method that results in the lowest tax payment based on the information you provide. If your taxes are higher than you anticipated the bank will help with a tax loan.

Savings accounts have become increasingly popular with commercial banks, useful to the bank in providing additional sources of money and useful to the depositor in the convenience of one stop banking (see Figure 6–8). There are accounts that provide quarterly or even monthly statements (unlike the regular passbook account) showing all deposits and withdrawals together with interest earned during the period. There are special accounts with minimum deposit and fixed guaranteed rate of interest through a definite period and subject to withdrawals at fixed times under definite restrictions. Called Nest Egg Deposits or Golden Passbook accounts, they resemble the certificates of deposit which also offer guaranteed interest, flexibility in selecting maturity dates, automatic renewal if desired, and a choice in manner and frequency of interest payments.

Although commercial banks have expanded their savings accounts, they are resisting fiercely the savings banks' attempt to enter a commercial bank domain—checking accounts. These savings bank accounts called NOW (Negotiable Order of Withdrawal accounts) are noninterest bearing by federal law except in Massachusetts and New Hampshire. While they look and act like checks, but are called payment orders or pay orders, they differ technically in not being "demand" accounts but subject to a 60 days advance notice of withdrawal—a provision rarely invoked.

Commercial bank savings accounts are protected against loss through insurance up to $40,000 for each account which is in a bank insured by the Federal Deposit Insurance Corporation. Further details on types of accounts covered will be discussed in Chapter 7, on Savings.

Six of every ten commercial banks in the United States provided credit card services to their customers at the end of 1974, and one in ten operate a check credit plan. It is expensive credit because of the flexibility of repayment, but while the maximum amount is set, it remains open end and eliminates the need for a borrower, as long as his credit is good, to process a separate loan as formerly had been the custom. In fact, the larger banks are encouraging this use of line credit instead of installment loans as an easier method of consumer loans. Because the bank credit cards have the standard waiver of defense clause which places the user at the mercy of a retailer who sells defective merchandise, the banks are

FIGURE 6–8

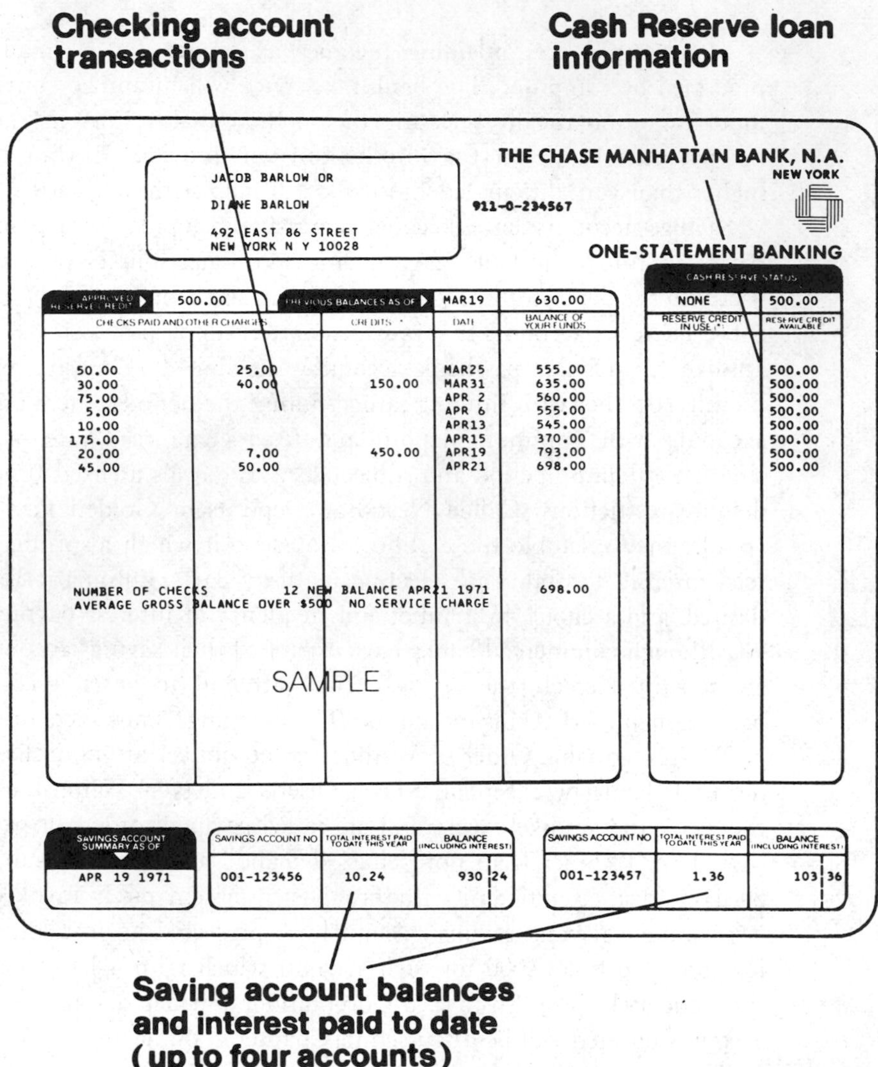

caught in the midst of legislative attempts to limit the holder in due course doctrine. The seller collects immediately from the bank and the bank from the buyer. The bank is then either in the position of "being responsible for the performance of merchants all over the world" or of suffering large losses in a protection of buyers' rights.

All of the listed innovations (see box) have become fairly usual throughout the country since that time. The banks are becoming innovative in reaching the public. In Oregon, U.S. National Bank set up four

CITICORP UNVEILS UNITS THAT OFFER NEW WAYS TO PAY

Bank's Consumer-Loan Offices Provide Payment Orders That Work Like Checks

NEW YORK—Citicorp, a diversified bank-holding company, has unveiled a hybrid consumer-finance operation in four states that offers such services as advance mortgage commitments and credit lines with facilities for writing check-type payment orders.

The new operation, called Citicorp Person-to-Person Financial Centers, is a division of the company's Nationwide Financial Services Corp. unit. A total of 15 offices have been opened in Denver, New Orleans, Phoenix and Salt Lake City.

Among the major departures from usual small loan companies, the Person-to-Person centers offer a checking-type service connected to a line of credit. Under the plan, a customer is given a line of credit and a book of payment orders, almost identical to checks.

The customer can use the payment order in the same way he uses checks. The order is then cleared through the nation's banking network in the same way as is a check, finally clearing through First National City Bank, Citicorp's flagship. Once cleared it shows up as a borrowing on the customer's account, and interest charges are imposed.

Wall Street Journal, October 8, 1974.

electronic teller machines in off premises shopping centers. "We want to take our services to the customer's doorstep" explains the bank's chairman and chief executive officer. Rudolph C. Pesci of U.S. National believes "that product innovation is as important to banking as to softgoods." If we approach it the way Procter & Gamble does, we should get the same results, he insists.[6]

The Everything Account of Citibank in New York includes cashing personal checks at any branch, purchase of money orders, cashier checks without usual service charges, systematic savings transferred from checking account to savings account, credit card privileges, unlimited purchase of travelers checks, reduced costs on personal and auto loans, personalized checks, unscrambled bank statement, a minimum cost safe deposit box and a checking account with line of credit, unlimited checks and no required balance all for $4 a month.

In California, Wells Fargo advertises its Gold Account covering rela-

[6] *Business Week*, June 22, 1974.

Something New at the Bank

Commercial banks gear most of their activity toward one goal—making profits by attracting deposits. It's a competitive game, and to keep ahead of the competition, some provide more varied services and more conveniences than others. Some examples:

Superchecks. Want to pay as many as 40 bills at one time with one check? Such a service is available to customers of the First National Bank & Trust Co. of Macon, Ga. Beside the names of merchants printed on the form you simply write in the amount you wish each to receive. The bank takes care of the disbursements. With variations, the plan is being used by such banks as the United Bank of Denver, Wachovia Bank & Trust Co. of Winston-Salem, N.C., and the First National Banks of Nevada; Phoenix, Ariz.; Memphis, Tenn.; Lake Forest, Ill.

Money machines. To get cash in a hurry, you don't even have to enter the Seattle First National Bank or the Marine Midland Bank-Western of Buffalo. These are among the banks that have installed instant money machines on their outer walls for round the clock access. You feed a coded card in the slot, set the dial at $25 or $50 and out comes the money!

Push-button banking. Some banks—a branch of the Surety National in Los Angeles is one—are out of touch with their customers, deliberately. In these robbery-free facilities, customers have only TV contact with the tellers, who are located on another floor and carry out their business via pneumatic tubes and electronic cash drawers.

One-statement banking. More and more institutions, such as the Beverly Bank in Chicago, are sending out one comprehensive monthly statement showing such things as checking and savings balances, the line of credit available, plus installment credit and mortgage figures.

Better teller lines. Innovations in this troublesome area range all the way from express lines and fully manned windows on Mondays, Fridays, and paydays to a single master line that feeds people to the next open teller station. In Baltimore, customers at Equitable Trust receive a numbered card and sit drinking free coffee and reading magazines until their turn is indicated on a large electronic callboard.

Lobby displays. Some bank lobbies provide playpens and toys to soothe infants, color TV's, adding machines for customers' use, beauty contests, art exhibits and flower shows. In San Diego, Southern California First National often has pettable animals borrowed from a local zoo.

Tax returns. The Columbus, Ohio, City National Bank & Trust Co. and an estimated 500 other banks prepare income tax returns for a nominal fee of $5 to $15 or so. Generally, these are computer-run.

Life insurance. A small number of banks—including the Jefferson State Bank in Chicago—provide their savers with life insurance protection through insurers, the premiums either being deducted from the interest earnings or paid indirectly through a low rate of interest. With Jefferson State's plan, savings of up to $2,500 are matched by an equal amount of life insurance until you reach 60, the coverage falling with the balance. Interest is 2½%.

Changing Times: The Kiplinger Magazine, December 1971, p. 8.

tively the same items for $3. It competes on TV with United California Bank which makes a similar offer (United Account) for $2 as does the Bank of America with its All-in-One Checking plan and Security Pacific (Combined Account).[7] If you are not rich or famous, but feel you need professional help in financial management and you have some assets, Cleveland's Union Commerce Bank will help for a fee. It's a comprehensive package—"will provide financial planning tools, budget controls, a bill paying service, record keeping, and a reserve credit line." All this, on a personal basis for a $50 initial charge, $15 a month fee for 15 transactions plus 38 cents for each additional item.

To avoid teller lines—for check deposits only—Chemical of New York has a quick deposit envelope that includes a deposit slip, is sealed, dropped in the quick deposit box, and a receipt is mailed to you the same day.

City National Bank & Trust Co. of Columbus, Ohio tested an electronic banking system in 30 stores in a suburb. A customer's bank card was inserted in a computer terminal at a store. After confirmation that the customer had money in the bank, the computer simultaneously credited the store's account and debited the customers.[8] It has also been tried by other banks in different sections of the country.

The Comptroller of the Currency ruled that federally chartered banks may install electronic terminals anywhere—which would not be considered as bank branches. These terminals linked to the bank's computers would enable a customer to withdraw cash from his account, transfer funds between checking and savings accounts and make purchases by credit. For example, if the customer chooses to pay on credit, the terminal would inform the bank that a credit purchase had been made and the bank would bill the customer as in a normal credit card purchase. Automatic tellers in retail outlets would dispense cash to a customer and credit the withdrawal to his account.

National banks were urged to delay opening such terminals in any state that prohibited state chartered banks from doing likewise. The Comptroller said "he expects the terminals . . . will change the face of the banking industry."[9]

Bank Secrecy Act

Based on the Supreme Court decision of 1974, banks must keep a record of all depositors' identities, copies of all checks over $100 and all

---

[7] *Business Week,* March 23, 1974.

[8] *Money,* April 1974, p. 30.

[9] *Wall Street Journal,* December 13, 1974.

loans over $500 except mortgages. The bank must report any transaction in which $5,000 (including traveler's checks) passes in or out of the country and in which $10,000 is withdrawn or deposited within the country. Since 1973, when the law went into effect, the banks have been photocopying checks at the rate of 30 billion a year—none of which is supposed to be divulged to anyone—except under proper legal authority. An amendment has been proposed that would make it illegal for the banks to furnish any information without notifying the customer first.[10]

Safe Deposit Boxes

The safe deposit box is a metal container kept under lock and key in a section of a bank's vault for customers' use. The boxes are kept in small compartments, each with a separate lock. They are rented with the compartment to depositors and other customers for an annual rental, varying wih the size of the box but ranging from $8 per annum for the smallest box to $600 for the largest. A typical small box is 2 × 5 × 22, that is 2 inches deep, 5 inches wide, and 22 inches long. A very large one is 45 × 47 × 22. Each customer has an individual key to the safe deposit box that is rented. The bank also has a separate key to each box. The box cannot be opened unless both keys are used, the customer's key opening one set of tumblers, and the bank's key opening another set to release the lock.

A safe deposit box is an excellent place in which to keep a variety of valuable papers, such as insurance policies, savings bank passbooks, stock certificates, bonds, real estate deeds, car titles, valuable receipts, and even unused jewelry. If the renter of the box dies and the key is not found, the box is opened, either by drilling or by a factory man, in the presence of authorized legal officers and the executors. If the box is in the joint names of husband and wife, the survivor will not have access to the box after the death of the other, until certain formalities are over. The box is immediately and temporarily sealed when the bank receives notice of death and may not be reopened until a tax officer is present to take an inventory of the contents of the box for estate and inheritance tax purposes.

Something expensive or difficult to replace(for example, discharge papers from the Army) belongs in a safe deposit box. If a stock certificate is lost or stolen, you can replace it only by furnishing an unlimited liability indemnity bond. This costs 3 percent of the market value of the stock.

---

[10] For further information see Congressman Fortney Stark, "There's No Financial Privacy in Banks," *Bankers Magazine*, Winter 1975.

Every precaution is taken by a bank to safeguard the contents of a box. Carefully constructed steel vaults are guarded by alarms and police protection. Every entrant to a safe deposit department is carefully identified. In addition, insurance policies are carried to protect boxholders against possible loss because of fire, flood, and other hazards. Bank employees cannot get into your box when the box is rented because the bank loses possession of one of the two keys necessary to open the box, and the bank has no master key which will open every box. If you lose your key, it is usually necessary to destroy the lock by drilling into it. Sometimes, however, it is possible to bring a factory representative to the bank to open the box.

It is wise to have an accurate current list of the contents of safe deposit boxes to estimate values in case of loss. Banks do not insure the contents, although they do insure themselves for negligence. Even in cases where a bank employee has stolen the contents of a safe deposit box—a highly unlikely example because of the security surrounding the area—a bank is not liable. There is no way for a bank to know what a customer has placed in a box unless he tells them and then there is no way for a bank to know whether they should believe him. Several insurance companies are marketing a group rate insurance to allow banks to cover the contents of the safe deposit boxes automatically. If not covered by insurance, a customer would have to sue the bank and prove negligence. Thus you deposit in a safe deposit box at your own risk!

After four days of complex argument in Federal Court in Newark, John Jacob Astor 3d accepted a $350,000 out-of-court settlement from the First Jersey National Bank, which, he charged, had misplaced or lost $465,000 worth of diamonds he had left 20 years ago in a safe deposit box. The 62-year-old Miami Beach social figure and financier said he had put the diamonds, including a 25.84-karat oval that once belonged to Eugenie, wife of Emperor Napoleon III of France—in the box in 1954 while involved in divorce proceedings with his second wife, Gertrude. During remodeling of the bank in 1963, he was asked in writing to move his treasures to another box. But he ignored the letter and the bank transferred the diamonds. Mr. Astor contended they were missing when he tried to claim them two years ago. The bank in court admitted that, after the box switch, as many as 41 persons might have had access to the contents of the box.

New York Times, April 5, 1974.

Providing Trust Services

Most banks have a division specializing in managing estates and trusts. While this service, for a proper fee, is usually limited to those with a sizable estate, banks willingly share nuggets of practical advice on these matters in monthly bulletins available to the public.[11]

Investment Management Service

This division of the bank devotes itself to complete management of portfolios, usually with a minimum of $25,000, providing investment advice and supervision of the portfolio plus record keeping and custody of securities on an annual fee basis. The bank usually prefers to handle these matters on a "discretionary account" basis, meaning they can act without the client's consent. They can offer a client a stock investment service which allows the purchase of any of selected common stocks through an automatic monthly charge of between $20 and $500 to the checking account. The bank collects a service charge on each transaction plus a brokerage fee. Given your consent, your dividend can automatically be reinvested in your stock.

The two services of trusts and investment are intertwined when the bank has been named as trustee under a will or as trustee of a trust established during a person's lifetime. See Chapter 17 for more information.

Looking Ahead

The concept of multiple bank service packaging has been developing from the many services offered but now made easier through the uses of electronic data processing. The nearer certainty of the electronic future has been the catalyst precipitating the struggle now upsetting the previous delicate balance between commercial and savings institutions. Each had had its special advantage.

The commercial banks had their checking accounts but had to pay lower interest on their savings accounts than thrift banks. Savings institutions had the market for mortgage money and could attract deposits by higher interest rates. As the credit crunch made depositors withdraw funds seeking still higher interest, savings banks opened NOW accounts to attract deposit money. Commercial banks with their package plans

---

[11] For excellent coverage, write for *How to Do More for Your Family*, Personal Trust Division, Irving Trust Company, One Wall St., New York, N.Y. 10015.

Billie Jean King Rallies to Bank

Billie Jean King will head a new equal lending program at the Lincoln Bank designed to end sex discrimination, the institution announced yesterday in Philadelphia.

Norman Denny, chairman of the bank, also announced the appointment of the tennis star to the bank's 16-member board of directors.

He said that 53 percent of the population was female, and "they're second-class citizens as far as banks are concerned." He promised equal treatment for both sexes in loan applications and in promotions to executive positions.

New York Times, May 1, 1974.

moved into thrift areas. Competition sharpened. To the savings bankers, the NOW accounts are an admission to the electronic fund transfer system of the future and consequently survival.

The Presidential Hunt Commission Report tends toward an elimination of the differences between the two systems. Proposals for the future would eliminate interest ceilings on savings accounts, give thrift banks the right to issue credit cards and checking accounts, and make consumer loans. Commercial banks would have more leverage to invest in mortgages as ceilings on VA and FHA mortgages would be eliminated. All these proposals expand choices for consumers, and by sharpening competition would improve the quality and convenience of all services. The combination of expanding financial desires and the availability of expanding financial services, stimulated by the attractive advertising of their availability and the convenience of banking branches, would make the neighborhood bank as familiar as the neighborhood candy store used to be.

SUGGESTED READINGS

1. Martin Mayer, *The Bankers,* Weybright & Talley, New York, 1975.
2. *Banking in the Age of Consumerism,* proceedings of the ABA, 1973 National Marketing Conference, American Bankers Association, 1974.
3. Christopher Elias, *The Dollar Barons.* New York: Macmillan Publishing Co., 1973.
4. *The Bank Book* by Morgan Irving, as audited by Charles Sopher. Boston: Little, Brown & Co., 1973.
5. "Putting Your Bank's New Look to Work," *Money,* April 1974.

6. *The Bankers Magazine:*
   Congressman Fortney ("Pete") Stark, Jr., "There's No Financial Privacy in Banks," Winter 1975.
   Christopher Elias, "Let the Bank Customer Beware," Winter 1974, pp. 49–54.
   Robert W. Haas, "Bank Marketing in the Age of Consumerism," Winter 1972, pp. 39–44.
7. "Helpful banker—new things he offers," *U.S. News and World Report,* February 5, 1973.
8. *Personal Money Management,* American Bankers Association, latest edition. A free copy may be obtained from your local bank.
9. *The Story of Checks,* Federal Reserve Bank of New York, latest edition. A free copy may be obtained by writing to the bank at 33 Liberty Street, New York, New York 10045.
10. New York State Banking Department, (a) *A New York Consumer's Guide to Banking and Borrowing,* and (b) *What Every Consumer Asks About Bank Deposit Accounts,* 2 World Trade Center, New York, N.Y. 10047, 1974.
11. *Changing Times, The Kiplinger Magazine:*
    "It's Getting Harder to Cash a Check," October 1973.
    "Coming—A Shakeup in Banking," February 1974.
12. Arthur Halley, *The Moneychangers,* Doubleday, New York, 1975.

CASE PROBLEMS

1. John and Sally Yates are a young married couple who believe they should have a checking account. Should the account be opened in the name of John, or Sally, or in the names of both jointly? Why? What are the various advantages and disadvantages?

2. Elizabeth and Benjamin Lake have a joint checking account. The checkbook is kept by Elizabeth at home. She is always careful to record all deposits she makes and all checks that she draws. The checkbook shows a balance of $200 and she is about to draw a check for $180. Unknown to her, Benjamin, while on a business trip away from home, mailed in deposits to the bank in the amounts of $150, $175, and $200. He also, using checks he had taken along from the checkbook, drew checks of $125, $105, $100, and $280 on the joint account. What is the correct balance of this account at present before Elizabeth draws her check?

3. John Jamison has acquired enough money so that he feels he should have some sort of checking account. He wants to pay about five bills a month by check. What are the relative merits of a regular checking account as against a special checking account for him?

4. Helen Ford opened a checking account at the Broadway Bank. At the end of a month, her checkbook showed a balance of $222.16. She compared this with the balance ($283.17) on her bank statement, which she had just received at the bank. Before leaving the bank, she asked a teller what the probable reasons were for the discrepancy. What do you suppose he told her? Before noting the balance of $222.16 in her checkbook, Helen had just added a deposit of $50 and had cashed a check for $22. When she arrived home, she looked over the canceled checks returned by the bank and found that three of the checks she had drawn during the month (for $20, $27, and $43.44) were missing. From the bank statement she learned that the bank had made a service charge for the month of $1.43. Reconcile the balances. How much money has she in the bank at the present moment?

5. When Peter Green completed graduate school, he accepted a position with the Bisco Corporation, which was located about 300 miles from his home town, where he had had a checking account for over five years in a large commercial bank. The Bisco Corporation is located 10 miles from a town whose population is 5,000 and which has two old but small commercial banks. Green wants your advice as to whether to retain the checking account he now has or to close it out and open a new one in one of the banks in the town. What advice would you give him if he were running a grocery store doing both a charge and a cash business? Is the large bank safer than the small ones? Why?

6. Grace Smith, a student in college in New York City, maintains a checking account in the Chase Manhattan Bank. Being short of funds for a planned trip to Europe, she writes to her father in San Francisco for financial assistance. About a week later, she receives from him a check for $400, which she immediately deposits. Grace and the receiving teller at the bank both overlook the fact that Grace has failed to endorse the check, which is payable to her order. Since Grace is to leave in less than a week, she makes several purchases in the next few days, giving checks which she believes will be charged almost entirely against the $400 received from her father. What will happen?

7. James Donnelly received a check for $450 from Peter Lyons, drawn on a local bank. James took the check to the bank on which it was drawn and had it certified so that he could use it to pay for some land he was going to purchase in a couple of months. In the interim, the bank, which was not insured by the Federal Deposit Insurance Corporation, failed. How do the parties stand?

8. When Janet Sheridan graduated from college and left home, she made it a practice to send her mother $100 on the first of every month. Janet mailed her mother a check for $100 on May 1, 1975. On May 20 the mother wrote that she had not yet received the check and was worried because she had not yet paid her rent, which was due on the first of the month. Janet lived 200 miles from her mother. What could Janet do to remedy the situation?

9. Edward Downing runs a small business which he owns. At the beginning of the month, both his checkbook and his bank statement showed a balance of

$1,522.63. During the month he made deposits totaling $1,732.63, and he also left at the bank for collection three promissory notes (for $392.63, $282.71, and $26.28) which he did not enter in his checkbook (preferring to wait until he received a notice from the bank that they had been collected). Checks drawn during the month totaled $2,264.13. The bank statement at the end of the month showed a balance of $1,995.46 after a service charge of $3.52 had been deducted. Four of the checks he drew (for $90, $67.14, $82.51, and $92.86) were not among the canceled checks returned by the bank. At that time, the checkbook showed a balance of $991.13. Reconcile the balances. How much does Downing have available to spend? Did the bank collect the notes?

10. Alice Gordon went into her bank and bought 10 traveler's checks, each of $10 denomination, for which she paid the bank $101. She noticed that the clerk spent quite a little time explaining the checks to her, making out forms, and so on. She wondered how her bank and the bank that issued the traveler's checks could afford to give all the required service for only $1. It was eight months later before she cashed half of the checks. Discuss why the bank is interested in this kind of transaction.

7

Savings and Savings Instruments

Money makes money
And the money
That money makes
Makes more money.
Poor Richard's Almanack

BENJAMIN FRANKLIN provided one of the most dramatic examples of the ability of money to multiply itself under the impetus of compound interest. In 1791 Franklin bequeathed the sum of $5,000 to the inhabitants of Boston with the proviso that the sum be allowed to accumulate for 200 years. By 1891 the fund had grown to $322,000. From it the Franklin Union Building, a technical school in Boston, was paid for and the remainder was set aside for a second hundred years of accumulation. By 1970 this second century fund had reached $2,307,694.

Over the years, Americans have rather consistently adhered to the habits of thrift suggested and advanced by their ancestors, and the consequent enormous capital accumulation channeled into productive facilities has made the United States the most advanced industrial country in the world. If there is any one single factor which distinguishes advanced from underdeveloped countries, it is the ability of the former to accumulate savings and funnel them into productive economic activity. Most individuals find, likewise, that unless and until they can accumulate a fund to fall back upon in emergencies or use to take advantage of opportunities for personal advancement, business success, or investment profit, progress in economic status comes but slowly. What would your answer be to the question in Figure 7–1?

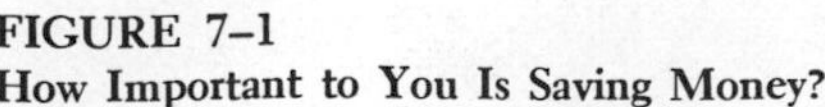

FIGURE 7–1
How Important to You Is Saving Money?

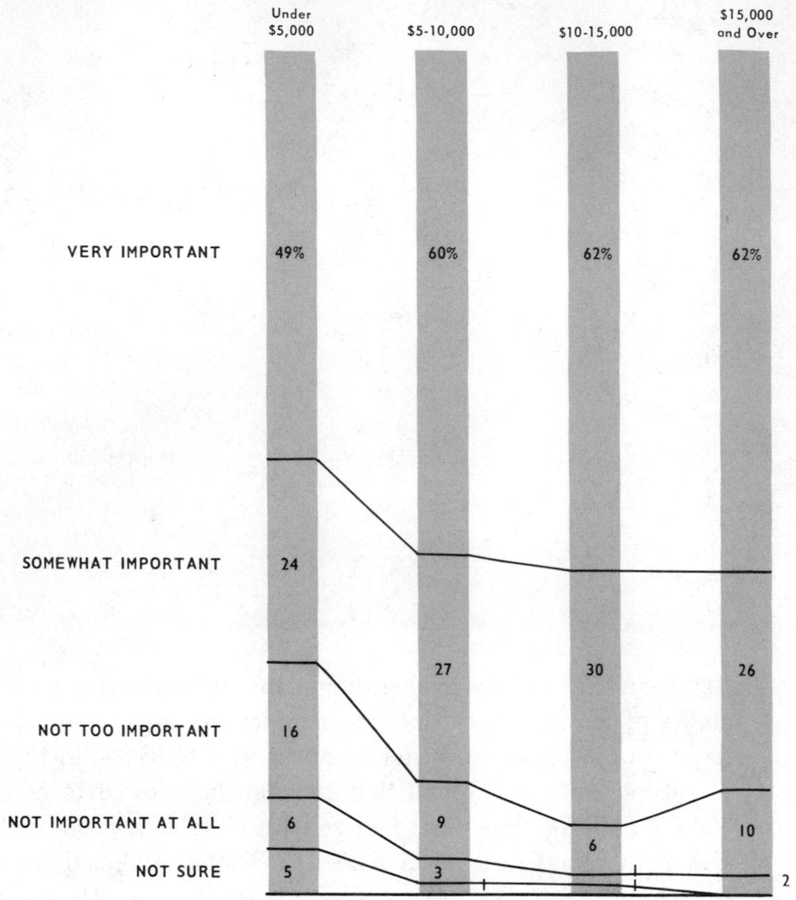

Source: *Public Attitudes toward Money and Its Management*, study conducted by Louis Harris & Associates for *Newsweek* magazine.

Forms of Savings

Savings can take many forms, can be held and used in many different ways. From simple to complex, the range includes keeping cash under the mattress; accumulating cash balances in bank demand deposits; holding savings deposits, accounts in credit unions, or shares in savings and loan associations; building equities in pension funds, annuities, or life insurance; buying savings bonds or other government securities; buying capital assets such as homes, personal small business enterprises, or corporate stocks or bonds. While this chapter deals primarily with "liquid" forms of savings (deposits, savings accounts, savings bonds), it is worth noting that an individual who pays for a home in monthly installments on a mortgage is saving just as effectively as one who puts comparable sums in a savings bank. Most life insurance policies involve not only the purchase of protection but a large element of savings as well.

A Savings Plan

One can save haphazardly, putting aside any surplus that seems to be left over after essential expenditures of the moment have been made, or one can draw up and try to stay with a savings plan (long term, short term, or both). The latter usually results in more systematic, consistent, and therefore larger savings, just as spending is made more efficient by the use of a plan. But there is no perfect savings plan, and there is no plan that will fit every family. A good savings plan will involve at least five elements. In order of priority these are:

1. A decision, and it should be a realistic one, as to how much of annual, monthly, or weekly income may really be considered surplus and thus available for savings. It should be remembered that the average family is probably engaged in a considerable amount of contractual saving—paying premiums on life insurance, contributing to a pension fund each month via payroll deduction, and this may leave less room for voluntary saving.

2. How large a cash reserve can you and should you maintain? No matter how well ordered one's life may be, there are always emergencies that strain one's finances; and when they come, it is better to be able to fall back on a cash reserve in the bank—or in other forms of savings that can be readily liquidated—than to have to borrow at once. By consensus, it is felt that an adequate emergency fund should be the equivalent of three months' salary. This would work out as follows:

Annual salary	*Emergency fund*
$ 5,000	$1,250
7,500	1,875
10,000	2,500
15,000	3,750
20,000	5,000

The Louis Harris & Associates survey concludes that the higher the income the more people have savings plans and the more they are confident they will achieve their goals as seen in Table 7–1.

3. How much life insurance (not just a policy, but an insurance plan) will provide reasonable security for your dependents? Can you afford this? Will you have any surplus left over after providing for this? It may be

TABLE 7–1

	Under $5,000	$5,000–$10,000	$10,000–$15,000	$15,000 and Over
Do you have a plan worked out to set money aside for special purposes?				
Yes	27%	61%	71%	79%
No	73	39	29	21
Will you reach your goal?				
Yes	32	49	65	77
No	51	39	26	16
Not sure	17	12	9	7

that (2) and (3), or (2) alone, will be your only form of savings. About 83 percent of American families have some life insurance, averaging $28,800 per insured family.[1]

4. Is your surplus large enough to permit you to meet (2) and (3) and, in addition, buy a home—assuming, of course, you want to own your own home? If you live in a very large city or have no children, you may prefer to rent. This will be discussed in a later chapter.

5. After meeting (2), (3), and (4), do you have any money left over for other forms of savings, such as investments? If so, what are your objectives?

One can look in vain for a place to put savings that will be safe, liquid, inflation resistant, and yield a large return. There is no such place. One or more of these elements must be sacrificed in whole or in part to achieve the others; and in the formulation of a savings plan, considered judgments must be made.

Various Savings Instruments Meet Different Objectives

There are various savings instruments to meet different objectives. If you want a high return on your savings, you cannot expect safety of principal. If you want safety of principal, you cannot expect the same instrument to provide a good hedge against inflation. Under most conditions, if you want liquidity, you cannot hope for long term growth. If you want certainty of continued income, you cannot expect a high yield. There is presented in Figure 7–2 a comparison of the various outlets for savings, showing how different income levels favor different forms of saving.

Quite clearly, no one instrument or institution combines all savings objectives successfully. Those instruments which combine safety and

[1] *Life Insurance Fact Book, 1974* (New York: Institute of Life Insurance).

FIGURE 7–2
If You Found a Way to Save an Extra $5,000, What Would You Do with It?

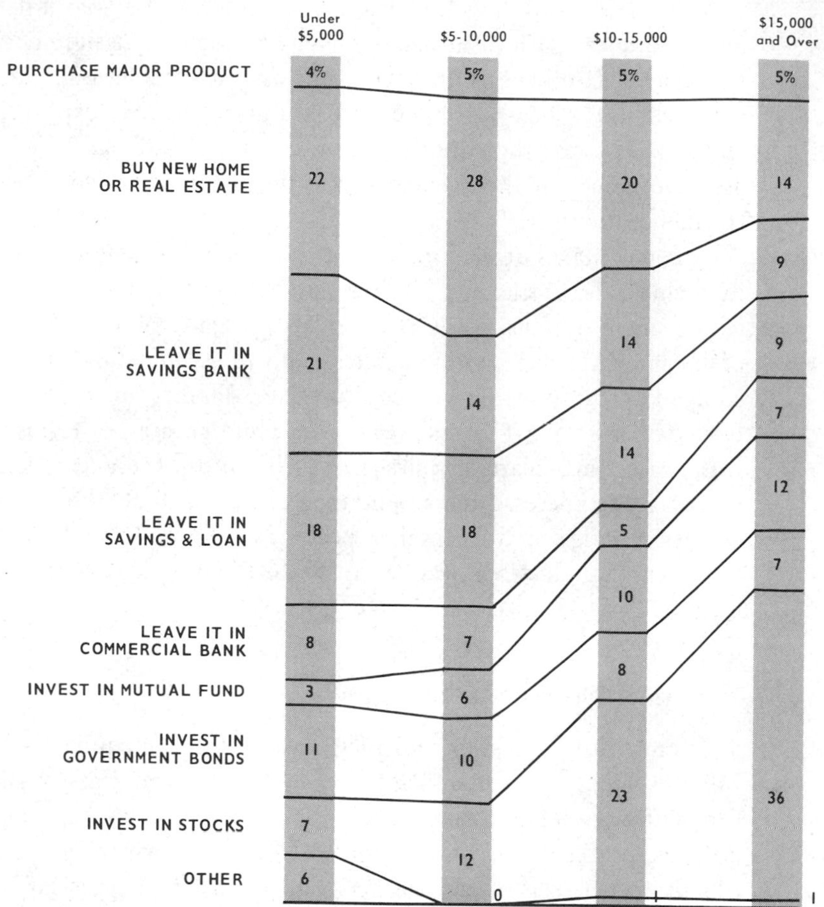

Source: *Public Attitudes toward Money and Its Management*, study conducted by Louis Harris & Associates for *Newsweek* magazine.

liquidity sacrifice return and possibility of growth, while for a number of instruments the reverse is true. Your income level and your savings objectives should determine your choice. If you need a reserve against financial trouble or loss of a job, you will want a very different type of savings instrument than if you are trying to protect yourself against long run (secular) inflation and loss of purchasing power. If you can spare the money for a period of years, you will want a different medium than if you expect to use the fund as a down payment on a house a year or two from now. Many families have several objectives and therefore spread their funds, choosing several rather than one form of savings.

Savings Patterns

Who saves and how much depends on how savings are measured and who does the measuring. If savings are defined as liquid assets,[2] the younger the family head the smaller the asset accumulation, and as is to be expected, the older the higher. In education, similar expectations were realized. The less the education of the family head the lower the liquid assets holdings on the average, while the more advanced the education, the higher they were.

Different stages of the life cycle of the family bring significant variations in savings and dissavings. Savings, or accumulation of liquid assets by young single persons, while frequent, is generally limited by insufficiency of income. Marriage and the setting up of a household are usually accompanied by numerous expenditures for durable goods and thus some degree of dissavings. Several years after children are born, positive saving rises again, particularly as purchases of life insurance and houses tend, at this stage, to increase the importance of contractual, though not liquid, savings. Savings tend to reach a peak after the children have left home, but then that develops less incentive to save and, with retirement, less income.

How Much Do We Save?

It's not easy to answer this question in a firm, unequivocal way. Why? Well, because different federal agencies define and classify "savings" in different ways. The one most useful to our purpose is the personal savings estimate of the U.S. Department of Commerce which is derived as the difference between disposable personal income and personal outlays, obtained in the national income estimates. As Table 7–2 shows personal saving, while rising in volume in recent years, has been relatively stable when considered as a percentage of disposable income, varying from a low of 4.9 percent to a high of 8.2 percent over the past two decades. Figure 7–3 shows where this income went, while Figure 7–4 illustrates the relative stability of the saving. As shown in Figure 7–5 individuals' financial investments rose from $38.1 billion in 1960 to $130.8 billion in 1973. Eighty percent of these assets were in banks and savings institutions, life insurance and pension fund reserves.[3] Traditional outlets of saving were jolted by frantic efforts at least to keep pace with the rising inflation, and the soaring short term interest rates appeared to many to provide the solution. What

[2] Liquid assets include savings accounts, certificates of deposit, checking accounts, and U.S. government savings bonds.

[3] *Business in Brief*, No. 115, April 1974, Chase Manhattan Bank N.A.

TABLE 7–2
Personal Savings in the United States, 1951–73 (dollar figures in billions)

Year	*Disposable Personal Income*	*Personal Outlays*	*Personal Saving*	*Saving as Percent of Disposable Income*
1951	$226.6	$209.3	$17.3	7.6
1953	252.6	234.3	18.3	7.2
1955	275.3	259.5	15.8	5.7
1957	308.5	287.8	20.7	6.7
1959	337.3	318.3	19.1	5.7
1961	364.4	343.3	21.2	5.8
1962	385.3	363.7	21.6	5.6
1963	404.6	384.7	19.9	4.9
1964*	438.1	411.9	26.2	6.0
1965	473.2	444.8	28.4	6.0
1966	511.9	479.3	32.5	6.4
1967	546.3	506.0	40.4	7.4
1968	591.0	551.2	39.8	6.8
1969	634.4	596.2	38.2	6.0
1970	691.7	635.5	56.2	8.1
1971	746.4	685.9	60.4	8.0
1972	802.5	749.9	52.5	6.5
1973	903.7	829.3	74.3	8.2

* Series revised in 1964.
Source: U.S. Department of Commerce, National Income Division, *Survey of Current Business.*

developed was the process known as "disintermediation" by which individuals withdrew funds from savings accounts and shifted them into high interest money market instruments. People shopped for higher returns. Savings depositors moved their money from lower paying accounts to higher interest bearing four to six year certificates, frequently in the same bank.

Savings Institutons

The American people have accumulated a great volume of savings and they have chosen a variety of forms and institutions in which to place these savings. Most people still prefer safety to maximum return, but the inflationary pressures of recent years increased the popularity for a time of savings forms, such as stocks and real estate, in which the risk of fluctuating principal is present. But with the collapse of the stock market in 1973–74 and the inflation induced high short term interest rates, savers shifted to money market investments such as U.S. Treasury bills, bank certificates of deposits, federal agency notes, and so forth. On the other hand, some individuals are still so cautious and distrustful of financial institutions that

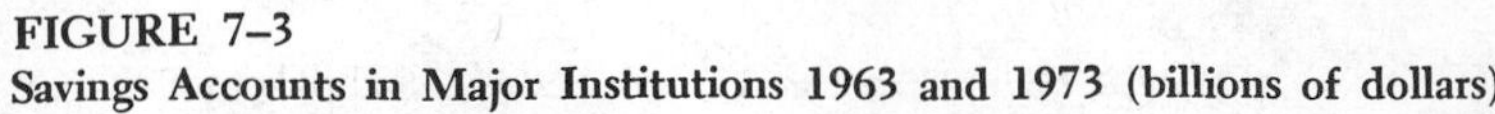

FIGURE 7–3
Savings Accounts in Major Institutions 1963 and 1973 (billions of dollars)

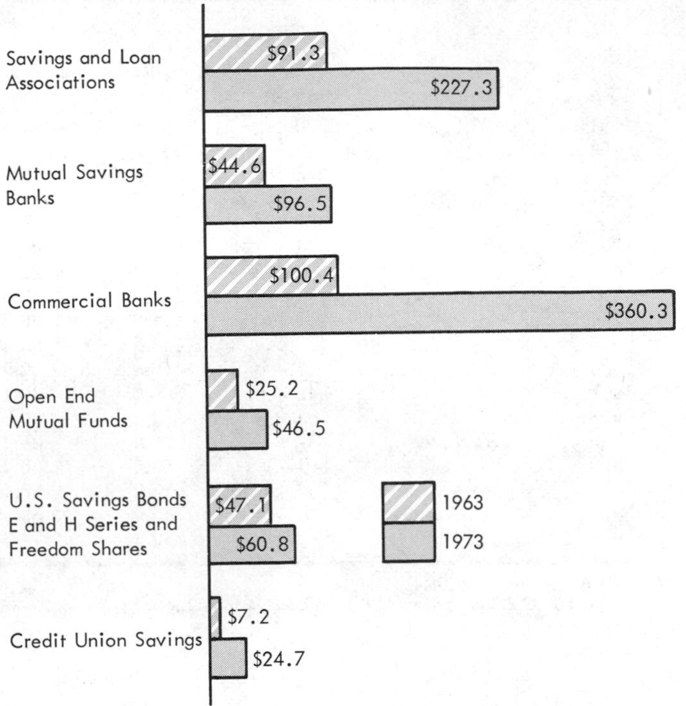

Source: Credit Union National Association, Inc. *Yearbook* 1974. A copy of the latest edition may be obtained by writing to CUNA International, Inc., 1617 Sherman Ave., Madison, Wisconsin 53701.

they prefer to keep their savings in the form of cash, which they hoard on their persons or hide in their houses. This is certainly the most liquid form of savings, but it is hardly the safest.

From time to time, stories appear in the newspapers telling of eccentric persons, old recluses, the uneducated, and the slightly insane, who upon death are found to have on their persons or premises anywhere from $1,000 to $250,000 in cash. Now and then one reads of old immigrant couples whose life savings were lost or stolen because they kept the cash wrapped in newspaper in their rooms. For every case that reaches the press, there are doubtless dozens that do not. There is, of course, no way of knowing how much of the $65 billion of currency "in circulation" is being hoarded by savers, how much distrustful people have hidden beneath mattresses, or how much gamblers and racketeers keep in safe deposit boxes (because they do not wish cash to become a matter of record through a deposit) but the total must be considerable.

The disadvantages of cash as a form of savings are quite apparent. The money is lost or stolen much too easily, and it earns no income. One

FIGURE 7–4
Personal Savings as a Percentage of Disposable Personal Income

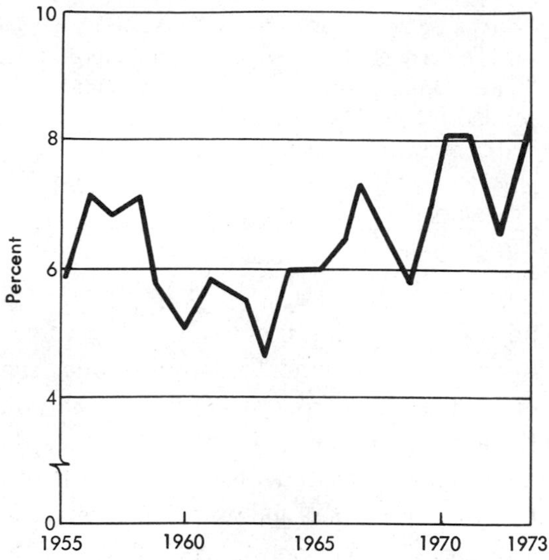

Source: Data, Department of Commerce; chart, *Savings and Loan Fact Book*, 1974.

FIGURE 7–5
Average Annual Financial Investment by Individuals (in billions of dollars)

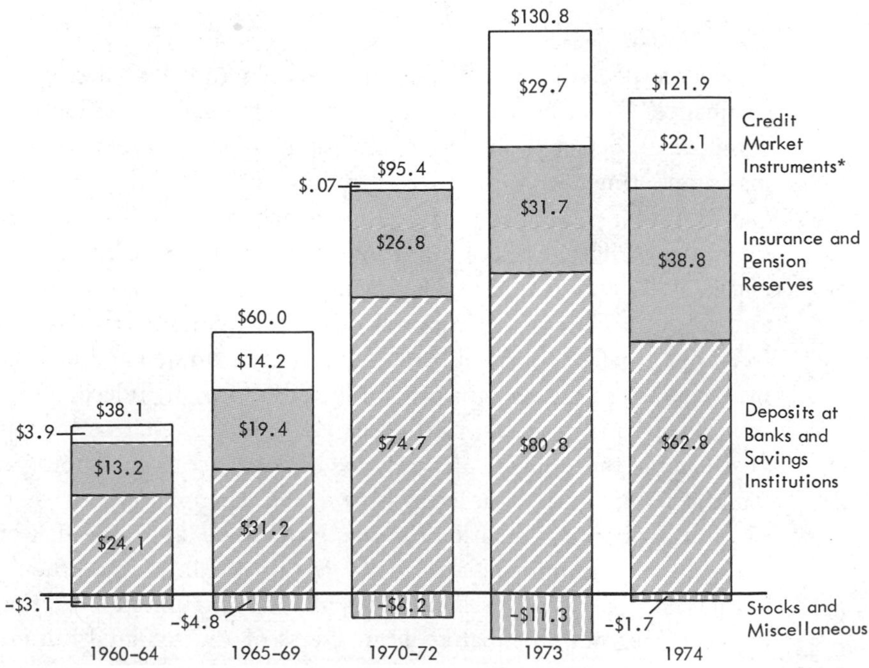

* Credit market instruments: U.S. government securities, state and local government securities, corporate bonds, commercial paper and mortgages.

Source: Data, Federal Reserve System; chart, *Business in Brief*, Chase Manhattan Bank N.A.

Hid Life Savings, Thief Takes All

DALLAS, TEX., April 16—A. C. Mallory, 44, last night reported his life savings of $7,800 taken from its hiding place under his house. Mallory said the money was in two pint fruit jars suspended in a pillow case under a hallway trap door. He said he had been saving the money since he was 12 and never kept it in a bank.

Associated Press

is reminded of the eccentric old lady who confided to her neighbor that she kept her money at home, hidden in a coffee can. "But," reminded the neighbor, "you're losing interest." "Oh, no, I'm not," the old lady insisted serenely; "I'm putting away a little extra, just for that." With deposit insurance covering commercial banks, savings banks, and savings and loan associations, credit unions, and government savings bonds available, there is no longer need to "put away a little extra" to achieve safety. A survey of these institutions as savings media, will indicate this. Life insurance, real estate, and securities will be discussed in later chapters.

Save at a Commercial Bank?

The commercial bank has frequently been called a "department store of finance" because it performs so many financial functions. It grants commercial, personal, mortgage, and other types of loans. It receives demand and time deposits (that is, it has both checking and savings accounts); it rents safe deposit boxes, performs investment services and gives investment advice, handles collections, issues letters of credit and traveler's checks, sells and redeems U.S. savings bonds, performs trust functions, and provides Christmas Club and other systematic savings schemes.

At one time, commercial banks paid interest on demand deposits. They no longer do so because the law no longer allows it. Indeed, with the rise in costs of bank operations in recent years, service charges have been imposed upon the demand deposit or checking account. These vary from bank to bank. Since no interest is paid, most people do not use checking accounts or demand deposits for saving purposes; and indeed, where they maintain a minimum balance, they try to see to it that their account neither falls below nor rises too much above the required level. Funds kept in a checking account materially in excess of the required minimum balance earn no income for the owner, nor, of course, does the minimum balance. The bank keeps the income from the minimum balance to cover the cost of the checking service rendered and to yield a reasonable profit.

Over 14,000 commercial banks located throughout the United States, however, also maintain "savings," "thrift," "special interest," or "compound interest" accounts, as they are variously called. These are time deposits, and to them more than 90 million depositors have entrusted more than $273.5 billion. In some communities the commercial bank is the only available institution where an individual may deposit savings and receive interest. On these time deposits, commercial banks pay interest rates which have been about 0.5 percent lower than those paid by savings and loan associations. Rates vary with changes in economic activity, but in the past few years or so, commercial banks have paid savers 5 percent annually. The so called Golden Passbook account, in which the saver leaves his money in the bank for at least a three month period (usually with a $500 minimum deposit), returns about 5.5 percent to savers.

Checks may not be drawn on time deposits. A time deposit differs from a demand deposit in that the bank, in the case of the former, may require the depositor to wait a period of time to receive his money, usually 30 to 60 days from the day he asks to withdraw it. Virtually all banks refrain from exercising this privilege in normal times; they invoke it only when necessary, in times of panic or crisis, when a run on the bank is threatened. In the case of a demand deposit, on the other hand, the bank does not have this privilege and must pay out funds as depositors ask for them; otherwise the bank is regarded as insolvent and is closed. Savings depositors in a commercial bank are creditors of the bank, in contrast, as we shall see, to depositors in a mutual savings bank or in a savings and loan association, who, in effect, are also owners of the institution.

Do You Know How Interest Is Computed on Your Savings Deposit?

Not only do banks vary according to the basic rate of interest they pay but they differ as to the method and timing used in computing interest on savings accounts. You will be amazed to know that the American Bankers Association found that at least 54 different methods were used. The Association has noted the following:

> Surveys made years ago emphasized the fantastic variations in interest paid on identical accounts by the use of different methods. If a sum of money is on deposit throughout an interest period, the amount of interest at any given rate would not vary regardless of method. The variation in the amount of interest payable depends on the method of de-

termining the balance on which interest should be paid. The activity in savings accounts is the basis for the varying methods of computing interest.

There are four principal methods of calculating interest based on activity in the account.

Method 1: Fifo. Under Fifo (first in, first out) withdrawals are deducted first from the starting balance of the interest period and then, if the balance isn't large enough, from subsequent deposits. In effect, that means you lose interest on withdrawals from the start of the interest period or the earliest deposit dates rather than from the date you actually took the money out. Some banks charge withdrawals against the beginning balance of the interest period; others against the first deposits of the interest period. The latter method provides more interest for the saver although both calculations are relatively unfavorable as we shall see.

Method 2: Low Balance. Under this method, interest is computed on the *minimum* balance on deposit in a savings account for the entire interest period, which may be a half year or a quarter. No interest is paid on deposits made in the midst of the interest period.

Method 3: Lifo. The last in, first out method of computing interest is one in which funds withdrawn are deducted from those funds most recently deposited within the stated interest period, such as a quarter or a half year, whatever the crediting period may be. Accrued interest lost as a result of a withdrawal against deposits under this method is less than under Fifo since the withdrawal dollars here had less time to earn interest.

Method 4: Day of Deposit to Day of Withdrawal (DD–DW). Under the daily interest method, all funds earn interest for the actual number of days they remain on deposit. The highest cost to the bank and highest yield to the saver are present in the day of deposit to day of withdrawal method. The use of this method has spread rapidly in recent years, principally in large banks in metropolitan areas around the country.

The method of treating withdrawals is extremely important. You, as a saver, are favored by a method which charges withdrawals against the most recent deposit, and you are hurt by one which charges them against the beginning balance of the period or first deposits. Let's assume that your bank charges withdrawals against the first deposit, and you make your first deposit on January 20. You deposit another $100 on August 10, a third $100 on October 1, and then you withdraw $100 on December 1. Assuming the bank is paying interest from the first of the semiannual period and they charge the $100 withdrawal against the January 20 deposit, as in Fifo you lose all interest on that deposit even though it has been in the bank for over 10 months. If, on the other hand, it's charged against the last deposit, as in Lifo the one made on October 1, you lose nothing, since interest on that would not start until the following January 1.

Date	Withdrawals	Deposits	Balance
Jan 20		$100	100
Aug 10		$100	200
Oct 1		$100	300
Dec 1	$100		200

Now what does all of this mean? It may seem confusing at first, but it's important to you as a saver to understand it clearly. You ought to avoid banks that use Methods 1, 2, and 3, and favor those that use Method 4. One aspect ought to be quite clear. Method 1 tends to discourage withdrawals, and also customers, since the yield is less. In Method 4, the bank starts paying interest on the day of deposit. Suppose you deposited $100 on January 20 of any given year. Under Method 4, your deposit on January 20 would start earning interest beginning January 20. Thus under Method 4, you would earn interest for the exact number of days of deposit.

A comparison of the interest computation in Table 7–3 for the two methods—Method 1 (Fifo), which benefits the saver least, and Method 4 (DD–DW), which benefits him most, will illustrate how this works. The calculation is done using a nominal 1 percent to illustrate—which can be multiplied by the current interest rate to arrive at the actual interest.[4]

Obviously, therefore, several different banks could state that they pay interest at the rate of 5 percent per annum, but, depending on how they compute your minimum balance or the amount to be used for crediting interest, the variations in what you actually got might be as extreme as $3.78 to $7.59 for a half-year as shown in Table 7–4. It would pay, therefore, to deposit savings funds in a bank which uses Method 4. You would do well to study the various methods banks use and then choose the bank using the method most favorable to you.

An examination of the methods now in use reveals that most of them penalize the overactive or in-and-out saver. Indirectly, this benefits the true saver, as the benefits between semiannual and quarterly compounding, even over a fairly long period of time, do not make as much appreciable difference as does the activity of the account and the method of bookkeeping. Table 7–5 illustrates this.

The rate of interest and method of calculation are most important in determining the return, but other factors such as the length of the interest period and the grace period affect the return too. The longer the grace

---

[4] *Savings and Time Deposit Banking* (New York: American Institute of Banking, American Bankers Association, 1968).

TABLE 7-3
Comparison of Interest Computation of Fifo and DD-DW Methods

Date	Withdrawal	Deposit	Interest	Balance	Interest Memo
Fifo method:					
January 1				$1,000.00*	$4.96†
April 1		$1,000.00		2,000.00	7.45‡
May 15		1,000.00		3,000.00	8.74§
May 20	$1,000.00‖			2,000.00	3.78#
July 1			$3.78	2,003.78	
DD-DW method:					
January 1				1,000.00*	4.96†
April 1		1,000.00		2,000.00	7.45‡
May 15		1,000.00		3,000.00	8.74§
May 20	1,000.00**			2,000.00	7.59††
July 1			7.59	2,007.59	

* Operating balance.

† Calculation of anticipated interest as if no additional deposits or withdrawals are to be made:

$$\$1,000 \times 1\% \times \frac{181 \text{ days}}{365 \text{ days}} = \$4.96.$$

‡ Calculation to cover additional deposit:

$$\$1,000 \times 1\% \times \frac{91 \text{ days}}{365 \text{ days}} = \$2.49$$

$$\$4.95 + 2.49 = \$7.45.$$

§ Calculation including $1,000 additional deposit:

$$\$1,000 \times 1\% \times \frac{47 \text{ days}}{365 \text{ days}} = \$1.29$$

$$\$7.45 + 1.29 = \$8.74.$$

‖ $1,000 withdrawal on May 20 calculated against balance of $1,000 on Jan. 1.

Anticipated interest of:

$$\$8.74 - \$1,000 \times 1\% \times \frac{181 \text{ days}}{365 \text{ days}} = \$4.96$$

$$\$8.74 - 4.96 = \$3.78 \text{ (interest for the 6 months).}$$

** Deposit of $1,000 on May 15 earned interest for five days—equal sum withdrawn on May 20.

†† Anticipated interest of $8.74—interest loss calculated:

$$\$1000 \times 1\% \times \frac{42 \text{ days}}{365 \text{ days}} = \$1.15$$

$$8.74 - 1.15 = \$7.59.$$

TABLE 7-4
Summary of Interest Earned Using the Four Methods (same activity patterns as in Table 7-3)

Method	*Amount of Interest for Period*
Low balance	$4.96
Fifo	3.78
Lifo	7.45
DD/DW	7.59

TABLE 7–5

Years $1,000 Is on Deposit	*Interest Accumulated when Compounding Is—*			
	Annual	*Semiannual*	*Quarterly*	*Monthly*
1	$ 50.00	$ 50.62	$ 50.94	$ 51.16
2	102.50	103.81	104.49	104.94
3	157.62	159.69	160.75	161.47
4	215.51	218.40	219.89	220.89
5	276.28	280.08	282.04	283.36
10	628.89	638.62	643.62	647.01

Source: Time-Life Book, *Family Finance*, p. 314 (New York, 1970).

period (usually at the beginning of the interest period) and the shorter the interest period, the greater the saver's freedom to make withdrawals and deposits without losing interest.[5]

Is Your Deposit Insured?

Of the 14,123 commercial banks operating in the United States, over 98 percent are members of the Federal Deposit Insurance Corporation. Each depositor is protected to an upper limit of $40,000 if the bank should fail. For this insurance, each bank contributes semiannually to the Deposit Insurance Fund based on its total deposits. When a failing insured bank is closed, the Insurance Fund either pays the depositor in cash or opens another account in his or her name for the same amount in a solvent, going bank. The money in this new account may be withdrawn at once.

The $40,000 protection limit applies to a single depositor in a given bank, regardless of the number of accounts he may have. A person who has a $2,000 balance in a checking account in a given bank, and a savings account with a $39,000 balance in the same bank, would be insured for $40,000 (not $41,000); if he had only the savings account, he would be fully insured for the $39,000. If his savings account balance were $42,000, he would be insured for only $40,000. The insurance coverage is based upon deposits maintained by a person at a single insured bank, not upon his total deposits throughout the banking system.

The law limits insurance basically to $40,000 for any one depositor in any one bank but does not prohibit you from splitting your funds among a number of banks. Moreover, if you are married, your own deposit, your spouse's separate deposit account, as well as your joint deposit, *with right of survivorship*, are each separately insured to the maximum of $40,000,

[5] *Selecting A Savings Account* by Nancy Rudd, Summer 1973, Agricultural Research Service ARS 62–5 U.S. Dept. of Agriculture, pp. 17–19.

even though they are all in the same bank. If you have accounts in the main office and a branch or in several branches of one insured bank, the accounts will be added together in determining your insurance, since the FDIC considers the main office and all branches as one bank.[6]

Deposits of a partnership are insured separately from the individual deposits of each of the partners if the individual and the partnership are engaged in an independent activity. If you act as a trustee, guardian, administrator, executor, agent, or in some other fiduciary capacity, deposit accounts which you open and maintain in any or all of these capacities are insured separately from the deposits in your individual account. In fact, you can maintain deposits in an insured bank in each of the following rights and capacities and be separately insured to the maximum of $40,000 on each of the accounts shown below:

John Doe	40,000
Mary Doe	40,000
John Doe and Mary Doe, joint account with right of survivorship	40,000
John Doe, Mary Doe, and Richard Doe, joint account with right of survivorship	40,000
John Doe, executor of estate of (name) deceased	40,000
John Doe, trustee of (name) irrevocable estate	40,000

All trust interests created by the same person in the same bank for the same beneficiary must be counted toward the one insurance of $40,000. If the account is a revocable trust and there is another account at the same bank in the name of the grantor of the trust, then it is counted as one account under the insurance. If an estate of a deceased is divided into separate accounts at the same bank as held by an executor and by an administrator, these accounts are regarded as one account.

Except to the extent that the annual assessment which the insured bank pays to the Insurance Fund adds to the cost of banking operations and thereby reduces the income available for payment to savings depositors and stockholders, there is no direct charge to the individual depositor for deposit insurance. If you should, therefore, ever have a choice between placing funds in an insured bank or depositing in one that is not insured, your decision should not be difficult. The 200 odd small, state chartered, noninsured banks (all national banks must be members of the FDIC) are, however, able to survive in their noninsured status largely because they are, in almost all cases, the only bank in the small town in which they are located, and inhabitants of the town thus have little choice.

---

[6] A copy of *Your Insured Deposit*, issued by the Federal Deposit Insurance Corporation, giving all essential facts about insurance coverage, may be obtained by writing to the Information Office Federal Deposit Insurance Corporation, 550 17th St. N.W., Washington, D.C. 20429.

Savings Banks

From the organization of the first saving bank more than 150 years ago, these institutions have successfully weathered panics, wars, and depressions and have grown in size and importance in the American economy until today they hold deposits of more than $96.4 billion in some 27 million accounts. Of the 486 mutual savings banks located in 18 states and Puerto Rico, about half are at least 100 years old and the 100 largest each have deposits in excess of $214 million dollars. Twenty mutual savings banks have deposits greater than $1 billion. Bowery Savings Bank, New York, heads the list with deposits of over $3.3 billion.

In contrast to commercial banks, mutual savings banks have no stockholders. All earnings, after operating expenses are met, go to benefit depositors either directly, in the form of dividends, or indirectly, as additions to reserves which increase depositors' protection. The U.S. Supreme Court has defined a mutual savings bank as "an institution in the hands of disinterested persons, the profits of which, after deducting the necessary expenses of conducting the business, inure wholly to the benefit of the depositors, in dividends or in reserve surplus for their greater security."[7]

Your deposit in a savings bank is usually evidenced by a passbook, in which the bank enters all deposits and withdrawals. This you keep in your possession, and it is a duplicate of the bank's own record of your account. More and more savings banks offer "statement" accounts with an identification card taking the place of the passbook. Under such plans, periodic statements are sent to the depositor showing deposits, withdrawals, interest credits, and the savings balance.

Additional protection of depositors' funds is provided by careful supervision of savings banks' investments by state banking authorities and by the provision requiring banks to set aside a part of earnings as a reserve or surplus. In most states, the reserve or surplus must be built up to a specified percentage of deposit liabilities, which varies from state to state. Furthermore, about two thirds of the mutual savings banks are insured by the Federal Deposit Insurance Corporation in exactly the same way as are both demand and time deposits of commercial banks. In the event of default, savings bank time deposits in the insured banks would be paid off in just the same way as both demand and time deposits in commercial banks. The insured deposit, up to a maximum of $40,000 would be paid in cash within 10 days after the date of final closing of the failed bank, or the insured depositor would have his account transferred to a solvent, insured banking institution.

---

[7] *Huntington* v. *National Savings Bank*, 96 U.S. 388, 395.

WOMAN HAS TROUBLE 'BANKING' ON LAMPS

MEDFORD, MASS., (UPI)— A Massachusetts woman may not be so sure now that lampshades are safer than banks.

The woman, who did not want to be identified, said that she had been stitching her savings into the linings of lampshades since the 1930s.

"I'm not crazy or anything, it just seems to me lampshades are safer than banks," she said.

Recently, she said, she forgot which lampshades had the money and threw out two of them containing a total of $2,500.

Sanitation workers had picked up the rubbish and were leaving the woman's street when she ran up to them and explained the situation.

The workers went to the dump, emptied the contents of their truck and spent half an hour sifting through the junk. They found the lampshades and the money.

"I'm thankful there are good, clean honest men working for the city of Medford," the woman said.

"I guess that's all the thanks we needed," said Victor Ferri, sanitation yard foreman.

New York Times, May 10, 1972.

The average interest rate rose from 1.90 percent in 1950 to 3.47 percent in 1960, to 5.25 percent in 1973. About 97 percent of the 486 mutual savings banks are now paying 5.25 percent interest. The average regular account in a mutual savings bank amounts to $3,876.

Opening a savings account is a very simple procedure. The prospective depositor walks into the bank; steps up to the reception desk where accounts are opened; fills out a signature card, which also contains space for address and other information which will help in identification, such as the names of mother and father; makes an initial deposit, which often need not be more than $1; and receives a passbook in which deposits, withdrawals, and interest credits are entered by the bank or a record folder to enter these transactions. The passbook must be presented along with a deposit slip or withdrawal slip, duly filled out, every time that a deposit or withdrawal is made. Forms are available which may be sent to the bank with the passbook if the depositor wishes to do business by mail in free postage paid envelopes supplied by the bank. Care should be taken not to lose the passbook.

Some of the accounts that may be opened at a savings bank are:

Individual Accounts. Owned only by one person, adult or minor. You are the sole owner, and the money is payable only to your order. It can be opened with a small amount, usually as little as $1, and can be increased to the limit prescribed by the law in your state.

Joint Accounts. May be opened by two persons, most frequently by a husband and wife. Either may deposit or withdraw. In case of the death of one of them, the balance is payable to the survivor. Such an account is opened "Richard Doe or Jane Doe—payable to either or the survivor."

Voluntary Trust Accounts. Can be opened by you in trust for a child or other person. The account is controlled by you during your life; after your death, it is payable to the person named as beneficiary. The trust is revocable in the sense that you have the right to change the beneficiary at any time. Such an account is opened "Richard Doe in trust for Mary Doe."

Custodial Accounts. If you open such an account for a minor, in New York State, for example, it is under the New York Uniform Gifts to Minors regulations. The account is irrevocable and becomes the property of the minor when the legal age is reached. It can be expended in whole or in part *for the minor's benefit* up to this age, however.

Lease Security Account or Landlord Trust Account. An interest bearing account for benefit of tenants whose lease security deposits must be placed in such an account.

Fiduciary Accounts. If you are appointed as executor or administrator of an estate or as guardian for a minor or for an "incompetent" person, you may open an account, called *fiduciary,* for the funds entrusted to you.

Organization Accounts. These are accounts in the names of nonprofit organizations, such as religious groups, lodges, clubs, fraternal organizations, and so on.

School Savings Accounts. Over 2 million savings bank accounts are owned by students, who deposit and withdraw in schools cooperating with the savings banks. Thus habits of thrift are learned directly at an early age.

Payroll Deduction Accounts. May be opened by any business firm for the convenience of its employees. The employee authorizes his company to deduct from his wage each payday a stated amount and to deposit it directly in his savings bank account.

Special Accounts. If you wish to accumulate funds for a special purpose —such as insurance, taxes, travel, U.S. savings bonds—the bankbook can be marked accordingly. These are regular accounts on which dividends are paid. Funds may be withdrawn at any time, but the banks ask that a small balance be left if you intend to save for the same purpose the next year. This avoids the expense and inconvenience of having to open a new account each year.

Christmas, Chanukah, and Vacation Club Accounts. You accumulate extra money by depositing a fixed amount—$2 to $20 a week—and in 50 weeks you receive a check by mail for the total you have deposited plus dividends at the rate of 5 percent a year compounded daily from dates of deposit.

Other Savings Plans. The Tax Saving Retirement Plan for self-employed individuals—known as the Keogh Act—can be fulfilled with deposits in a savings bank subject to approval by the Internal Revenue Service. The deposits increase by dividends compounded quarterly until at least retirement at age 59½ but not later than age 70½, at which time they are then subject to income tax.

The Bill-Me-Monthly Club uses the softest sell of all in its effort to encourage regular monthly savings. The bank sends you a postage paid envelope with a deposit slip monthly at the time you say you usually pay your bills.

Time Deposit Savings Certificates are offered to provide a range of guaranteed rates of interest higher than on regular accounts but require a minimum deposit of $1,000 and usually a two to seven year maturity. See Table 7–6. Before you buy a higher rate certificate it is essential to balance the pleasure of the higher interest rate with the disadvantage of losing the use of your money for a fairly long period, and in addition the possibility of a penalty if you withdraw your money before the allotted time. On $10,000 deposited at 7.5 percent the interest for one year is $750. If the deposit is withdrawn during the year, the interest drops to the passbook rate of

5.25 percent or	$525.00
plus a penalty loss of one quarter.	(−131.25)
Total interest =	$393.75 = 3.94% Annual interest

Retirement Savings Account or Automatic Payout Plans. Under this arrangement, the bank will mail you checks in the amount you specify—monthly, quarterly, semiannually, or annually, as you instruct. A minimum balance and minimum payment are usually required. As an example: a deposit of $1,000 will with interest (not guaranteed in advance) provide payments of $25 a month for three years and eight months.

Abandoned Accounts. Although it is hard to believe people sometimes forget a savings account. If a passbook has not been presented for a specified number of years, an account is legally deemed abandoned. If the depositor is not then located by advertising, banking law usually requires that the balance be turned over to the comptroller of the state. Even then, the balance may be reclaimed by the depositor from the comptroller. To guard against this, it is best to have dividends entered at least once a year and to keep the bank informed of all changes of address. Change of address cards can be secured free of charge at your local post office.

TABLE 7–6
The New Pattern of Savings Accounts

	Start With	*1 Year*	*2 Years*	*2½ Years*	*3 Years*	*4 Years*	*5 Years*	*6 Years*	*7 Years*
8.17% effective annual yield on 7.75% a year. 6 or 7 year Term Savings Accounts*	$ 1,000							$ 1,602.24	$ 1,733.21
	10,000							16,022.47	17,332.10
7.90% effective annual yield on 7.50% a year. 4 to 6 year Term Savings Accounts*	1,000					$ 1,355.45	$ 1,462.53	1,578.06	
	10,000					13,554.52	14,625.31	15,780.69	
7.08% effective annual yield on 6.75% a year. 2½ to 4 year Term Savings Accounts†	1,000			$ 1,186.50	$ 1,227.88	1,314.85			
	10,000			11,865.03	12,278.85	13,148.52			
6.81% effective annual yield on 6.50% a year. 1 to 2½ year Term Savings Accounts†	1,000	$ 1,068.11	$ 1,140.87	1,178.97					
	10,000	10,681.16	11,408.72	11,789.79					
6.00% effective annual yield on 5.75% a year. 90 days to 1 year Term Savings Accounts†	1,000	1,060.02							
	10,000	10,600.26							
5.47% effective annual yield on 5.25% a year.‡ Regular and Day-of-Deposit to Day-of-Withdrawal Accounts.	1,000	1,054.66	1,112.32	1,142.23	1,173.13	1,237.26	1,304.90	1,376.23	1,451.47
	10,000	10,546.67	11,123.22	11,422.35	11,731.30	12,372.62	13,049.00	13,762.35	14,514.70

* Minimum $1,000 deposit, interest guaranteed when held to maturity.

† Minimum $500 deposit, interest guaranteed when held to maturity.

‡ Dividends compounded daily, credited quarterly when $25 remains on deposit to end of quarter. (Dividends on 5.25% accounts not guaranteed.) Dividends must remain on deposit a full year to earn the 5.47% yield.

Courtesy The Manhattan Savings Bank, New York, N.Y.

Other Services. In addition to these services, savings banks perform a variety of others, such as making mortgage loans, student loans, passbook or personal savings loans, home improvement loans, co-op apartment loans; and providing safe deposit facilities, money orders, traveler's checks, low cost savings bank life insurance, and financial counseling. Just as the commercial bank is offering a comprehensive package of financial services so, too, the mutual savings banks are becoming family financial centers to satisfy all aspects of consumer financial needs.

NOW Accounts. The shadow of EFTS (electronic fund transfer system discussed in Chapter 6, *Using Your Bank*) becoming stronger has been partly responsible for the surfacing of the long smoldering intention of savings banks to compete in the check issuing field. If their savers were going to be frozen out of the multitude of services functioning through EFTS they would lose them. As we have seen the Federal Reserve gave its blessing and support to EFTS to facilitate the check clearing process. For future survival the savings banks want to take part in that flow.

In 1973 savings institutions in Massachusetts and New Hampshire were allowed to continue paying interest on accounts that had checking privileges. These are called NOW (negotiable order of withdrawal) accounts. The customer is charged a small sum per check.

Federal law presently bars commercial banks from paying interest on checking accounts and savings and loan institutions from offering them. Since mutual savings banks were not mentioned, they are trying a non-interest paying, thinly disguised version of checks called NOW (negotiable order of withdrawal), or WOW (written order of withdrawal), EZ Pay, or payment account, or a checking account by any other name. Savings banks in New Jersey and Maryland have for several years been offering checking accounts, but the size of the New York savings bank market made it more of a threat to commercial banks and these accounts are now the subject of litigation. The NOW accounts pay bills if you have money in your account—just as in the commercial account. They do not provide, however, for overdrafts or certified checks.

Savings and Loan Associations

In recent years, savings and loan associations have grown more rapidly than mutual savings banks. In 1925 deposits in mutual savings banks were about twice the size of those in savings and loans. By 1954 the two competitors had roughly equal amounts of deposits, but by 1973, savings and loan associations had close to $227 billion in deposits, more than twice the $96 billion of mutual savings banks. Perhaps the major reason for their more rapid growth is that savings and loan associations are found in all 50 states and in Puerto Rico, Guam, and Washington, D.C., while mutual savings banks are located in only 18 states plus Puerto Rico. Yields on deposits in savings and loan associations are currently about similar to those paid by mutual savings banks and commercial banks.

A savings and loan association is a locally owned and privately managed thrift and home financing institution. It gathers together the savings of individuals and uses these savings to make long term amortized loans (that is, loans whose principal is reduced regularly) to purchasers of homes. These loans are made for purposes of construction, repair, purchase, or refinancing of houses, and their repayment is secured by first mortgages. They total 85 percent of the assets of the associations. There are now about 5,244 savings and loan associations in the United States, of which some 3,204 are state chartered and 2,040 federally chartered.[8] A decline in the total number of associations has been paralleled by the growing concentration of assets in fewer associations, although the majority remain moderate sized. However, 554 associations with assets of more than $100 million each held 59.3 percent of all savings association assets. Of total savings and loan associations, 87 percent are mutually owned. All federal associations are mutually owned. The remaining 13 percent operate as stock companies and have almost 21 percent of all deposits.

The first association was established in 1831 in a suburb of Philadelphia with 37 members. Each member agreed to save a certain amount each month. As funds accumulated, they were loaned to one of the members to build a home. Since the funds were limited, some members of the group had to postpone their home ownership plans while waiting for adequate funds to accumulate. It soon became apparent that to provide a regular flow of funds for steady home financing it was essential to invite other savers to join the association. This was done, and the number of savers came to outnumber the borrowers. Today some 55 million savers have contributed more than $272 billion, which in turn has been loaned, for the most part, to almost 12.2 million mortgage borrowers. The average account is $3,785; the average loan is $16,875.

Most savings and loan associations are mutual corporations which distribute their earnings to those who save or invest in them. All savers in these mutual institutions are legally part owners. From their own number they elect boards of directors to guide the associations. All federally chartered associations must be members of the Federal Home Loan Bank System and the Federal Savings and Loan Insurance Corporation. Federal

---

[8] Known also as "savings associations," "building and loan associations," "cooperative banks" (New England), and "homestead associations" (Louisiana). See *Savings and Loan Fact Book, 1974* (Chicago: United States Savings and Loan League, latest edition). A copy may be obtained by writing to the League at 111 East Wacker Drive, Chicago, Ill. 60601.

charters are granted by the Federal Home Loan Bank Board, an agency of the federal government. Application to establish a state chartered association is usually made to the state banking department. In many of the states, membership in the Federal Home Loan Bank System and in the Federal Savings and Loan Insurance Corporation is required by authorities issuing new state charters. State chartered savings and loan associations, which constitute the majority, may or may not be members of the Home Loan Bank System; but federally chartered associations must join. Advantages of membership in this reserve banking system have proved so great that the institutions now affiliated with the Home Loan Bank System represent 98 percent of all the assets of operating savings and loan associations. The liquidity of the associations is furthered, since they may borrow from the Home Loan Bank on the security of mortgages which they pledge.

The Federal Savings and Loan Insurance Corporation, a federal agency, which insures savings accounts in covered associations up to a maximum of $40,000, was established in 1934. It provides the same kind of protection to savers in covered savings and loan associations as the FDIC does for depositors in banks.

The insured association pays an annual premium to the FSLIC of 1/12 of 1 percent per annum on its savings accounts to meet the cost of this insurance. There is no direct cost to the individual saver, however. Just as in the case of the FDIC coverage, one person may have insured accounts in more than one insured association and may receive $40,000 of insurance protection on each account.

At one time a savings account in a savings and loan association could not be called a deposit, and as a result, a variety of different names and types of accounts developed, with "share accounts" being the generally accepted technical definition. The law was amended in 1968 to permit savings associations to use the term "deposit" with payments on them to be called interest. By 1970 changes in regulations and practices made it possible for an association to issue more than 10 different types of accounts. The accounts differ in the maximum interest rate that can be paid, the time over which the account must be held, and the minimum balance required. After 1966 the FHLB was given the power to set rates, formerly at the discretion of individual managers.

Types of Savings Accounts

Although losing popularity because of a lower rate of interest, passbook accounts are still one of the two major types of savings accounts at savings and loan associations. The interest rate is 5.25 percent. Any amount may be added or withdrawn at anytime. Accounts that require 90 day notice of withdrawal require no minimum balance but carry a higher interest rate, 5.75 percent.

The certificate accounts, the second major type of savings instrument, are issued in fixed amounts with fixed maturities at higher interest rates, ranging from 5.75 to 7.5 percent. They represent more than half of the total savings held by the associations.

Normally the associations will pay out savings and repurchase shares on demand. Furthermore, the safety of the savings and loan association is ultimately assured by (*a*) its ability to borrow from the Home Loan Bank in time of need, (*b*) its reserves, (*c*) its holdings of cash and government bonds, (*d*) the amortized nature of its mortgages, which usually insures an adequate margin of safety should it have to foreclose property and sell it, (*e*) the regular monthly repayments of principal which flow in on amortized mortgages, (*f*) the VA and FHA guarantees on a considerable share of its mortgage holdings, and (*g*) the insurance of accounts up to a maximum of $40,000 each.

Credit Unions

A credit union is a cooperative association organized to promote thrift among its members and to accumulate savings out of which loans are made, at reasonable rates of interest, to members only for useful purposes. Credit unions are not new. The credit union movement in the United States is usually dated from 1909, when Massachusetts passed the first state credit union law. Since then, most of the states have passed similar laws. The Federal Credit Union Act, providing for the chartering and supervision of federal credit unions, was passed in 1934. Today there are both state and federally chartered credit unions numbering about 23,500 and having more than 29.4 million members. The nearly 13,000 federal credit unions have approximately half of the $31.8 billion in assets for all credit unions combined.

The federal credit unions are supervised by the National Credit Union Administration, an independent agency created in 1970. The state credit unions are regulated by the state banking departments. There are over 10,000 state chartered credit unions with a membership of 13.5 million, assets of $15.1 billion, with average savings per member of $966.

Membership in a federal credit union is limited to persons having a common bond of occupation or association and to groups within a well defined neighborhood, community, or rural district.[9] For this reason, most credit unions remain small. There is a movement now to stretch the

[9] Mark J. Flannery, "Credit Unions as Consumer Lenders in the U.S.," *New England Economic Review*, Federal Reserve Bank of Boston, July/August 1974.

meaning of common bond. For example, to join the Wisconsin State Central Credit Union, you only need live in the state. The first credit union organized to meet the financial needs of women—gender being the common bond—was chartered in Detroit and now has over 900 members.

Two thirds of all credit unions in the United States have assets under $500,000. Savings by members are made in the form of share purchases, each share being valued at $5. Savings may be made in amounts as small as 25 cents per month and may be withdrawn at will, although the credit union's board of directors may require two months' notice for withdrawal of funds, as in a savings bank. This provision is seldom invoked. Regular saving of small sums by members is encouraged; the cultivation of the habit of systematic thrift is a basic purpose of credit unions. Average shareholdings (savings) per member of federal credit unions amount to about $910.

Joining a credit union is easy. Not much money is needed. In fact, credit unions are primarily intended for people who do not have much. The membership entrance fee generally is only 25 cents. A minimum investment of at least one share is required. A credit union is run by its members, and each member is entitled to only one vote regardless of the number of shares held. Once you are a member, two kinds of service are available: (1) savings facilities and (2) loan service. Money is deposited in a credit union very much as in a savings bank. Savings may be used to buy shares on which dividends are paid. These usually range from 3 to 7 percent a year, with federal credit unions limited to paying the latter as a maximum. As in savings and loan associations, savers are owners, not creditors. Sums due members comprise over 85 percent of the liabilities of federal credit unions. Earnings come largely from loans to members. Many people join a credit union to obtain a loan. In addition to interest to savers, credit unions are the only financial institutions that pay interest refunds to their borrowers. Usually this has been 10 percent of the interest paid by the borrower.

Since October 1970, savers in all federal credit unions and all state credit unions that apply and meet the standards of the administration, are insured up to $40,000 by the National Credit Union Administration through annual premiums of 1/12 of 1 percent of the total amount of the member accounts. The National Credit Union Share Insurance Fund consists of these assessments and income from the investment of the funds balances.

In keeping with the drive toward a national electronic funds transfer system, credit unions are developing a "share draft" plan, similar to the savings banks' NOW payments, so that they too will be participating along with bank checks when the system becomes a functioning reality. The only bank in the United States owned by credit unions—the Kansas Credit Union League—was bought in 1974 in Lancaster, Kansas (pop. 279) to gain access to the Federal Reserve System and through it to the future E.F.T. The Lancaster bank provides its credit union depositors with an "expand a check" program enabling a depositor to write a check when he wants a loan which when processed through the bank's data system is credited to the depositor's loan account with the credit union.

U.S. Government Savings Bonds

This form of savings is now used by about 24.5 million families, or about one half of all the families in the United States. Recently, the total amount of savings bonds outstanding was $64.1 billion, a sum that, over the years, has been steadily rising. In 1973 interest rates on U.S. savings bonds were increased to 6 percent in order to make them more competitive with other forms of savings.

Series E. These are appreciation rather than current income bonds. That is, they are purchased at 75 percent of the maturity (par) value and increase in value by the accretion of interest periodically, so that, over a period of time, the inherent value gradually rises to the full par value at final maturity. In contrast, the current income bond (Series H, for example) requires full payment initially of the par value; interest is paid directly to the holder by check every six months; and at maturity the bondholder receives back the same amount that he paid originally.

Series E bonds purchased after June 1, 1969, mature in 5 years after the issue date, and pay 6 percent interest, compounded semiannually. Originally, the old Series E bonds ran for 10 years and paid 2.9 percent if held to maturity. Over the years, the period to maturity has been shortened in order to raise effective yields, so that Series E rates would be more competitive. All Series E bonds now carry an automatic 10 year extension privilege, while those bonds issued prior to June 1, 1949, have had two 10 year extensions. In other words, holders of E bonds may continue to receive returns equivalent to the current 6 percent rate for at least 10 years after their bonds reach maturity. The holder need not act to receive the extension, since as long as they hold the bonds the extension is automatically granted.

The rate of interest paid on E bonds has always been staggered, with lower rates paid in the earlier years and higher rates in the latter years, to provide a financial incentive for individuals to retain their bonds to maturity rather than cash them in at an earlier date. If held six months, new E bonds yield 3.73 percent; if held one year, 4.50 percent; if held two years, 4.7 percent; and five years, 6 percent.

Present Series E bonds are issued in denominations of $25, $50, $75, $100, $200, $500, $1,000, and $10,000 (maturity value). For these you pay $18.75, $37.50, $56.25, $75, $150, $375, $750, and $7,500, respectively. To buy a bond which will pay $100 in 5 years, you pay $75; to buy one which will pay $500, you pay $375. Purchases are limited to $10,000 maturity value, or $7,500 issue price, for each calendar year.

A notable feature of U.S. savings bonds, apart from their unquestioned safety, is the redemption provision. In contrast to all other government and corporate securities, which will be paid off by issuers in cash only at maturity, U.S. savings bonds may be redeemed at any time, after two months from issue date, without advance notice, at any financial institution which is an authorized paying agent, at any Federal Reserve Bank or branch, or at the office of the Treasurer of the United States. Not only is there no penalty attached (the full amount originally paid is given back) but accumulated interest is also paid to the date of redemption from the date of issuance if held for at least six months. Furthermore, U.S. savings bonds are not callable by the Treasury prior to maturity. Redemption values at different stages are shown in Table 7–7. It should be noted that no interest as such is paid on appreciation bonds. The return comes to the saver in the form of the difference between what was paid for the bond originally ($18.75, for example) and what is received if redeemed before maturity ($21.39 if held three years), or the sum received when cashed at maturity ($25.00).

Series H. This is a current income, not an appreciation, bond, bearing an investment yield approximately equal to that of the E bond. It is issued in denominations of $500, $1,000, and $5,000 and these are the amounts the saver pays when he buys the bond. The original purchase price and the amount payable at maturity are the same. The return (interest) is paid by the government by check semiannually beginning six months after issue date. The yield is 5 percent the first year, 5.80 percent for the next four years and 6.50 percent for the second five years. The yield over the entire life of the bond, however, averages out to 6 percent (see Table 7–8). Series H bonds are redeemable *at par* any time after six months from issue date. This is a most unusual feature in a current income bond. Usually, corporate bonds of this type will not be redeemed by the issuer until call or maturity, and if in the interim the investor wants his money, he must sell the bond in the market, finding someone who will buy it at a price which may be less than par. Thus, the Series H bond provides a safe investment with no risk of market fluctuations. It offers an ideal savings plan for the indi-

TABLE 7–7
Revised Series E Bond, Effective December 1, 1973, Schedule of Redemption Values and Investment Yields

Period (years and months after issue)	(1) Redemption Values during Each Half Year Period (values increase on first day of period)								Approximate Investment Yield (annual percentage rate)		
	$18.75† *(25.00)*‡	*$37.50* *(50.00)*	*$56.25* *(75.00)*	*$75* *(100)*	*$150* *(200)*	*$375* *(500)*	*$750* *(1,000)*	*$7,500* *(10,000)*	*(2) From Issue Date to Beginning of Each Half Year Period*	*(3) From Beginning of Each Half Year Period to Beginning of Next Half Year Period*	*(4) From Beginning of Each Half Year Period to Maturity*
0–0 to 0–6	$18.75	$37.50	$56.25	$ 75.00	$150.00	$375.00	$ 750.00	$ 7,500		3.73%	6.00%
0–6 to 1–0	19.10	38.20	57.30	76.40	152.80	382.00	764.00	7,640	3.73%	5.34	6.25
1–0 to 1–6	19.61	39.22	58.83	78.44	156.88	392.20	784.40	7,844	4.54	5.00	6.37
1–6 to 2–0	20.10	40.20	60.30	80.40	160.80	402.00	804.00	8,040	4.69	4.98	6.57
2–0 to 2–6	20.60	41.20	61.80	82.40	164.80	412.00	824.00	8,240	4.76	5.24	6.83
2–6 to 3–0	21.14	42.28	63.42	84.56	169.12	422.80	845.60	8,456	4.86	5.39	7.15
3–0 to 3–6	21.71	43.42	65.13	86.84	173.68	434.20	868.40	8,684	4.95	5.53	7.59
3–6 to 4–0	22.31	44.62	66.93	89.24	178.48	446.20	892.40	8,924	5.03	5.92	8.29
4–0 to 4–6	22.97	45.94	68.91	91.88	183.76	459.40	918.80	9,188	5.14	6.09	9.48
4–6 to 5–0	23.67	47.34	71.01	94.68	189.36	473.40	946.80	9,468	5.25	12.93	12.93
5–0*	25.20	50.40	75.60	100.80	201.60	504.00	1008.00	10,080	6.00		

* Maturity value reached at 5 years and 0 months after issue.
† Issue price.
‡ Denomination (redemption value).

TABLE 7–8

Revised Series H Bond, Effective December 1, 1973, Schedule of Semi-Annual Interest Checks and Investment Yields

Period of Time Bond Is Held after Issue Date	Amounts of Interest Checks for Each Denomination				Approximate Investment Yield (annual percentage rate)		
	*$500**	*$1,000**	*$5,000**	*$10,000**	*From Issue to Each Interest Payment Date (percent)*	*For Half-year Period Preceding Interest Payment Date (percent)*	*From Each Interest Payment Date to Maturity (percent)*
.5 years	$10.50	$21.00	$105.00	$210.00	4.20	4.20	6.12
1.0 years	14.50	29.00	145.00	290.00	4.99	5.80	6.15
1.5 years	14.50	29.00	145.00	290.00	5.25	5.80	6.17
2.0 years	14.50	29.00	145.00	290.00	5.38	5.80	6.20
2.5 years	14.50	29.00	145.00	290.00	5.46	5.80	6.24
3.0 years	14.50	29.00	145.00	290.00	5.51	5.80	6.28
3.5 years	14.50	29.00	145.00	290.00	5.55	5.80	6.32
4.0 years	14.50	29.00	145.00	290.00	5.58	5.80	6.37
4.5 years	14.50	29.00	145.00	290.00	5.60	5.80	6.44
5.0 years	14.50	29.00	145.00	290.00	5.62	5.80	6.51
5.5 years	16.28	32.56	162.80	325.60	5.69	6.51	6.51
6.0 years	16.28	32.56	162.80	325.60	5.75	6.51	6.51
6.5 years	16.28	32.56	162.80	325.60	5.80	6.51	6.51
7.0 years	16.28	32.56	162.80	325.60	5.84	6.51	6.51
7.5 years	16.28	32.56	162.80	325.60	5.87	6.51	6.51
8.0 years	16.28	32.56	162.80	325.60	5.91	6.51	6.51
8.5 years	16.28	32.56	162.80	325.60	5.93	6.51	6.51
9.0 years	16.28	32.56	162.80	325.60	5.96	6.51	6.51
9.5 years	16.28	32.56	162.80	325.60	5.98	6.51	6.51
10.0 years†	16.28	32.56	162.80	325.60	6.00	6.51	—

* Issue price, redemption, and maturity value at all times, except that bond is not redeemable during first 6 months.
† Maturity reached at 10 years and 0 months after issue date.

vidual who wants a bond that pays interest by check every six months. Compare the H bond with the E bond in this respect. The annual limit on the purchase of H bonds by any single individual is $10,000.

How Savings Bonds Are Registered

E and H bonds may be purchased by individuals and registered in one of three ways: (*a*) in the name of one person, e.g., "Richard Roe, 418 Main Street, Sunrise, Iowa"; (*b*) in the name of two persons as co-owners, e.g., "Richard Roe *or* Mrs. Mary L. Roe, 418 Main Street, Sunrise, Iowa"; or (*c*) in the name of one person, with one beneficiary, e.g., "Richard Roe, 418 Main Street, Sunrise, Iowa; payable on death to Carla Lee Roe." In the case of co-ownership, (*b*), either co-owner, whichever has possession of the bond, can cash it by endorsement without the consent or endorsement of the other. At times this may be an advantage, at times a disadvantage, depending on circumstances. In case of the death of one of the co-owners, it is an advantage, since the other is then the sole owner of the bond without establishing proof of death or having it transferred to his name. In (*c*) only one beneficiary may be named, and to eliminate or change the beneficiary, through reissue, the permission of the original beneficiary must be obtained. The beneficiary, upon death of the registered owner, may keep the bond until maturity or have it reissued in his name alone or with a designated beneficiary, after providing proof of death of the original owner. All savings bond buyers must now provide their social security number at time of purchase.

Savings Bonds—Advantages and Disadvantages

The savings bond offers investors and savers some very valuable features. There is an advantageous combination of safety and yield. The 6 percent paid compares favorably with the yield from other savings media, and the safety is unequaled elsewhere. The option to redeem before maturity is a unique privilege in a savings bond. You get compound interest, and the income from your bond is exempt from state and local income and personal property taxes.

In addition, the Series E bonds offer the holder the alternative of deferring federal income taxes on the increase in redemption value—which is itself considered as interest—until the holder actually redeems the bonds, presumably at an advantageous time.[10]

[10] Series E are now more than 30 years old and the oldest—still not retired—are now worth double their original face value.

A tax free savings plan for education is possible through purchase of E bonds. If they are bought in the child's name with the parent as beneficiary, *not* co-owner, they can be reported on the child's income tax return, listing the increase in value for the first year. Unless income exceeds $2,050, no tax will be due. Thus, when the bonds are cashed to meet college costs, all the accrued interest is free from federal income tax.

There is probably no security available to savers or investors that is as safe as a U.S. savings bond. It is actually safer than cash. Your dollars can be lost or stolen, but if savings bonds are lost, stolen, or destroyed, owners may obtain substitute bonds, under provisions of the law and regulations, upon filing proper proof of loss or theft or destruction. For such a contingency, it is a good idea to keep a record of the bonds you own, by serial number, amount, and issue date. Keep the list separate from the bonds, so that you will have one if the other is lost. Then, if your bonds disappear, write to the Bureau of the Public Debt, Division of Loans and Currency, 536 South Clark Street, Chicago, Illinois 60605, stating the serial number (with prefix and suffix letters), the issue dates (month and year), and your name and address. The Division will then send you a special form to fill out in order to obtain the issuance of substitute bonds. The Division keeps records of savings bonds by both names of owners and serial numbers and now social security numbers; so even if you do not have the serial numbers or issue date, they still can probably help you. Since this takes much longer and there is greater difficulty involved, it is much wiser to keep a record separate from the bonds themselves.

Unlike the other stocks and bonds, United States savings bonds are purchasable without payment of any commission. Banks sell or redeem them free of charge, and you can buy or redeem them at any time. There is no problem of marketability, no pricing problem, no unfortunate experience of buying high and selling low. You can always get your money back at any time you want it—not only the amount you put in but interest on your money to the date of redemption as well. Series E bondholders may exchange their bonds at current redemption values for current income H Bonds, if of $500 or more—also with tax deferred rights.[11]

Systematic Savings Plans

Different financial institutions have developed a variety of systematic savings plans. The country's largest savings bank has come up with an

[11] Freedom Shares, no longer being sold, had a 5 percent annual yield. Series A, B, C, D, F, G, J, or K, also not sold, have reached maturity and are no longer earning interest. Series A–D can be redeemed by being cashed at a bank; others can be forwarded by a bank to the Federal Reserve.

ingenious "Packaged Savings" plan. Under it one deposit a week brings you a three-way package: (*a*) a constantly increasing bank balance, (*b*) a steadily growing number of U.S. savings bonds, and (*c*) savings bank life insurance. You can arrange to pay in $3, or $5, or $10 a week for 5 years, or 10 years, or 20 years. The bank publishes tables to show what each amount will accumulate over a stated period in each of the three resource categories. Table 7–9 shows one page from the bank's descriptive booklet which contains a whole range of other tables for varying amounts over varying periods.

If you intend to put a child through college, you should begin to save right now toward accumulating the estimated $15,000 cost as shown in Table 7–10.

Your own retirement plan to supplement social security or other pension begins small if you start at age 25. Fifty dollars a month saved until you reach 65 will add up to $24,000, see Table 7–11(a). Based on an average interest rate of 5.25 percent being earned and compounded quarterly, the power of money at work will increase your own savings to a cumulative principal amount of $82,113. In each of the 15 years after your retirement you will be able to withdraw from the bank $660 a month of combined

TABLE 7–9
The Packaged Savings Plan (plans available for ages 1 month to 70 years)

Starting Age	*Cash* in the Bank*	*Savings Bank Life Insurance†*	*U.S. Savings Bonds (face value)*
$5 a week for 10 years brings you all three			
20	$1,650	$5,000	$500
25	1,560	5,000	500
30	1,440	5,000	500
35	1,290	5,000	500
40	1,090	5,000	500
45	1,330	3,000	500
50	1,130	3,000	500
55	860	3,000	500
$10 a week for 10 years brings you all three			
20	$3,730	$10,000	$500
25	3,550	10,000	500
30	3,310	10,000	500
35	3,010	10,000	500
40	2,620	10.000	500
45	2,100	10,000	500
50	3,100	5,000	500
55	2,650	5,000	500

* The cash in bank figure does not include cash dividends which will be paid to you.

† In addition, you will receive yearly cash dividends, as earned, on your policy. Your straight life insurance policy, of course, may be kept in force after 10 years with no increase in premium. Or you may convert your insurance into its cash value, or accept a reduced amount of paid-up insurance.

Source: The Bowery Savings Bank.

Table 7–10
Annual Savings That Will Make $15,000 Available to Pay for a 4 Year College Education from Age 18 through 22 (dividend rate of 5.25 percent compounded daily)

Present Age of Child	*Number of Years to First College Year*	*Annual Savings Necessary to Build College Fund of $15,000*
1	17	$ 528
2	16	579
3	15	636
4	14	703
5	13	779
6	12	870
7	11	977
8	10	1,106
9	9	1,265
10	8	1,467
11	7	1,722
12	6	2,066
13	5	2,550
14	4	3,277

Note: This schedule is based on the premise that a college fund should wisely be in hand by the time college starts. Interest earned on "extra money" available for the second, third, and fourth years is a good inflation hedge.
Source: New York Bank for Savings.

principal and interest, as shown in Table 7–11(b). If you don't touch the principal, dividends alone will give you $359 a month for the rest of your life. Combined, over a 15 year period, you will have received a total of $118,800, or a $94,800 gain over what you paid in, due to interest accumulated over the 40 years.

The power of compound interest alone will double your capital at 4 percent in 17½ years, at 5 percent in 14½ years, and at 6 percent in just 12 years. The "rule of 72" is an easy way to estimate how long it will take to double your money. Just divide the percent of interest into 72. If, for example, your money is earning 6 percent it will double in 12 years. If it is earning 9 percent it will double in 8 years. And the power of interest compounded daily instead of quarterly as some banks are offering, affects the nominal rate as shown in Table 7–12.

If you are one of those who find it difficult to save, there are a number of ways which will help make it easier. Your firm, if you so request, will probably deduct a specified sum from your paycheck and send it directly to your bank. Social security and corporate dividend checks can be deposited directly. You can have your firm deduct for savings bonds, too, or have your bank buy one a month for you from your account. You can open a Vacation Club or Christmas Club account at a savings bank, or

Table 7–11 (a)
How Much Would You Have at Age 65?

Your Present Age	*At Age 65, Your Account (including dividends) Will Be Worth*	*Amount You Will Have Actually Deposited by Age 65*	*If You Leave the Principal Intact, Dividends Alone Will Give You This Amount Monthly for the Rest of Your Life*
If You Save $50 a Month...			
25	$ 82,113	$24,000	$ 359
30	60,524	21,000	265
35	43,919	18,000	192
40	31,148	15,000	136
45	21,325	12,000	93
50	13,769	9,000	60
55	7,957	6,000	34
If You Save $100 a Month:			
25	$164,226	$48,000	$ 719
30	121,049	42,000	530
35	87,839	36,000	385
40	62,296	30,000	273
45	42,650	24,000	186
50	27,538	18,000	120
55	15,915	12,000	69
If You Save $200 a Month:			
25	$328,452	$96,000	$1,439
30	242,099	84,000	1,061
35	175,679	72,000	770
40	124,593	60,000	546
45	85,300	48,000	373
50	55,077	36,000	241
55	31,831	24,000	139

Source: Dime Savings Bank of New York, August 1974.

Table 7–11 (b)
Typical Monthly Withdrawal Amounts

When you reach retirement age, you may prefer to use part of your principal each month as part of your income. Whatever you leave in the bank, of course, continues to earn interest. If you use both interest and principal, here are typical examples of the approximate amount you could withdraw each month over a period of 10 to 15 years.

*Amount of Principal at Age 65**	*Monthly Withdrawal (interest plus principal) for 10 Years*	*Total Principal and Interest Received*	*Monthly Withdrawal (interest plus principal) for 15 Years*	*Total Principal and Interest Received*
$124,593	$1,337	$160,440	$1,002	$180,360
82,113	881	105,720	660	118,800
42,650	457	54,840	343	61,740
27,538	295	35,400	221	39,780

All figures are calculated at the dividend rate of 5.25 percent a year compounded daily from day of deposit which will yield 5.47 percent when deposits remain in your account for a year. The rate of dividends depends on earnings, and therefore no specific rate can be guaranteed. Also, these figures are gross and make no allowance for income taxes to which savings dividends, like all other taxable sources of income, are subject. The tables assume therefore that any taxes due will be paid from other income sources.

* Selected examples derived from column 2 of Table 7–11(a).

Source: Dime Savings Bank of New York, August 1974.

TABLE 7–12
Compounded Rates of Return

	Compounded	
Nominal Rate	*Quarterly*	*Daily 365 days* $\left(\frac{365}{360}\right)$
4.0%	4.06%	4.14%
4.5	4.58	4.67
5.0	5.09	5.19
5.5	5.61	5.73
6.0	6.13	6.27
6.5	6.66	6.81
7.0	7.18	7.35
7.5	7.61	7.90
8.0	8.24	8.45

start the bonus savings plan at a savings and loan association. Or you can resort to the very familiar device of saving one kind of coin—a dime, a quarter, or a half dollar. Every time you get one in change, you put it apart from the rest of your change in a separate pocket and then, when you get home, drop it in a coffee tin set aside for savings.

It helps to save if you have some definite purpose or goal in mind, one preferably which is realizable (see Figure 7–6).

Disintermediation, Savings and Double Digit Inflation

For someone in the 25 percent federal income tax bracket, a 5.25 percent return on a savings account yields only 4.1 percent after taxes. See Table 7–13 for comparable illustrations. Such a return in a period of double digit inflation caused an outflow (disintermediation) of money from thrift institutions into higher yielding short term investments such as Treasury bills or notes of federal agencies (Figure 7–7 illustrates why). Three month Treasury bills which are exempt from state and local income taxes rose to yield as much as 8–9 percent. The minimum investment in Treasury bills now is $10,000, but there was a time in the recent past when they could be bought in denominations of $1,000. Obligations of the Federal Intermediate Credit Banks come in $5,000 denominations and have a higher return over a shorter period than thrift institutions offer. The minimum purchase of securities of the Federal Land Banks is $1,000.

Citicorp (the holding company of First National Citibank of New York), offered a novel type of note with a floating rate of one percentage point higher than the average rate on three month Treasury bills. Initially sold in blocks of $5,000, the notes later could be traded in $1,000 denomi-

FIGURE 7–6
Saving for What?

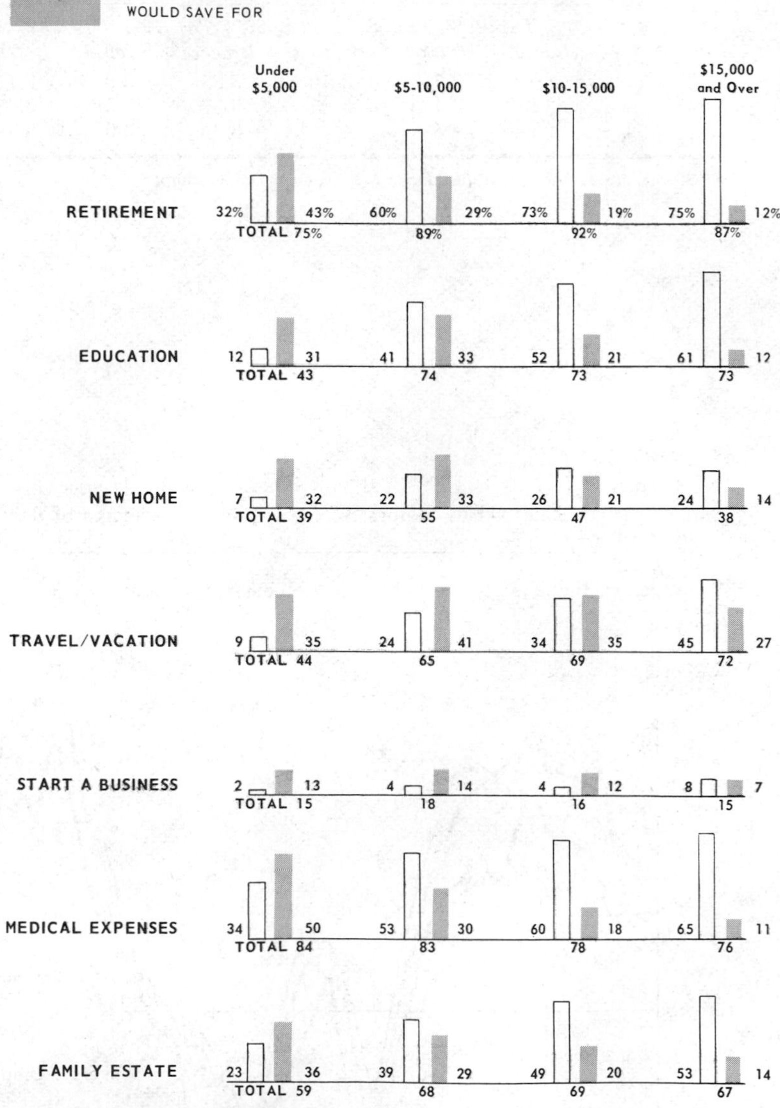

Source: *Public Attitudes toward Money and Its Management*, study conducted by Louis Harris & Associates for *Newsweek* magazine.

TABLE 7–13
Net Interest Returns after Taxes

	Your Net after Taxes						
Interest	*20% Tax Bracket*	*25% Tax Bracket*	*30% Tax Bracket*	*35% Tax Bracket*	*40% Tax Bracket*	*45% Tax Bracket*	*50% Tax Bracket*
5.0%..........	4.0	3.75	3.5	3.25	3.0	2.75	2.5
5.5.............	4.4	4.125	3.85	3.575	3.3	3.03	2.75
6.0.............	4.8	4.5	4.2	3.9	3.6	3.3	3.0

Source: *Money Maxims*, Oppenheimer Management Corporation.

FIGURE 7–7
No Contest
Money Market Rates versus Savings Accounts (monthly averages of daily figures)

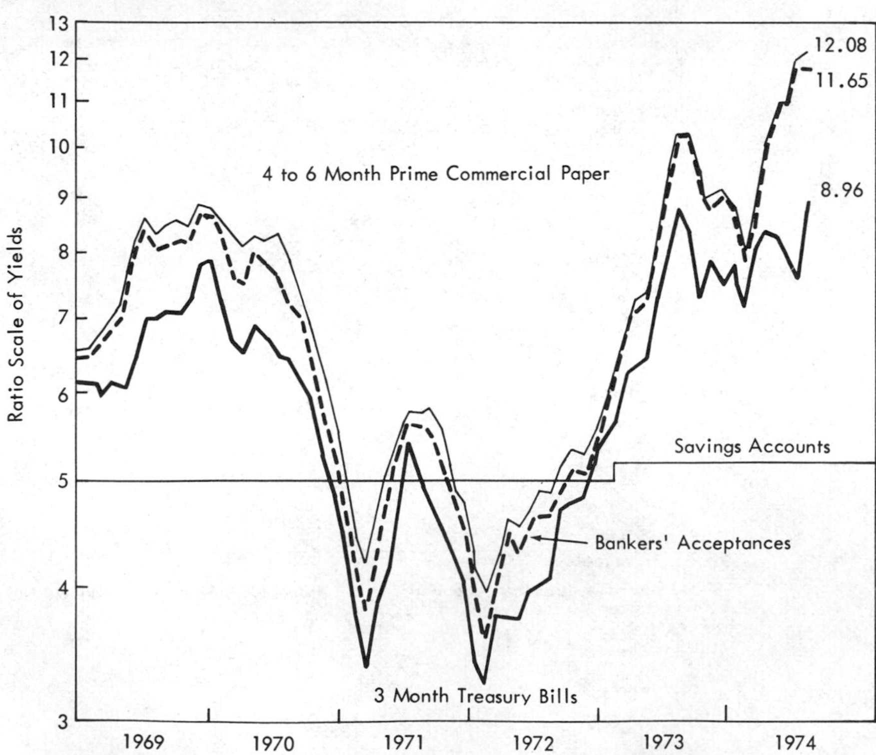

In the 1974 money market the knowledgeable investor pulled funds out of savings accounts to take advantage of record-breaking interest rates available in short term instruments in the money market.
Latest data plotted, August, prepared by Federal Reserve Bank of St. Louis.

nation. These notes are not insured by the FDIC. The storm that rose from savings banks and savings and loan associations that feared further loss in funds because of the attractiveness of this offer, brought subtle pressure from the SEC and Citicorp altered its original plan and agreed to delay possible redemption of the notes for a year, instead of six months. After the initial year, notes could be redeemed every six months at the option of the holder. It further agreed to an interest rate of 9.7 percent for the first year instead of the original floating rate.

Chase Manhattan and TransAmerica Financial followed with similar floating rate note offerings. Although sold for a 25 year period, investors could redeem them with interest twice a year. Twice a year they receive a new interest rate.

TABLE 7–14
Loss in Value of Personal Savings as a Result of Depreciation of the Dollar (1940 dollar = 100)

Year Ended	*Total Personal Savings (billions of dollars)*	*Buying Power of $100*	*Loss of Purchasing Power if Each Year's Savings Are Maintained until 1973*
1940	$ 3.8	$100.0	68.6%
1945	29.6	78.2	59.7
1950	13.1	59.1	46.7
1955	15.8	52.1	39.5
1960	17.0	47.4	33.5
1965	28.4	44.8	29.7
1970	56.2	38.1	17.3
1971	60.2	35.7	11.8
1972	49.7	33.4	6.0
1973	54.8	31.4	—

Excerpted from *Financial Planning Workbook*, published by Kalb, Voorhis & Co. Washington, D.C.

Investors who had thronged savings banks years ago when the 6 percent certificate of deposits were first issued, turned out in equally large numbers at all the Federal Reserve Banks throughout the country to buy the 9 percent Treasury notes, 33 month maturity, offered in $1,000 denominations, in 1974.

Formerly content with savings accounts, inflation has made American savers more sophisticated. They were attracted to short term funds investing solely in short term money market instruments. These funds accepted investors with a minimum of $1,000, and allowed sales or redemptions on a daily basis. The funds charged an annual management fee of 1 percent of their average daily net assets. An example is Dreyfus Liquid Assets, Inc.[12]

[12] See Chapter 16.

There were also money brokers who sold participation interests in $100,000 certificates of deposit (CDs). They pooled the money of small investors until there were enough funds for a $100,000 CD which had no interest rate limitation and which would otherwise, because of the minimum amount required (usually $100,000), not be available to the small investor. These are but a few of the ways in which the small investor has tried to cope with double digit inflation. Table 7–14 emphasizes the main reason for this massive disintermediation.

Conclusion

Sooner or later, at one time or another, every family or individual sets out to save. It may be the result of a New Year's resolution and may last but two days, or, because of the nature of one's personality, it may take hold and last a lifetime. Some people can save and some people can't. It takes will power, self-denial, patience, and perseverance, and these qualities are not present in everyone. Level of income is not of overriding importance. There are some who can set aside something out of $5,000 a year income, while others find it difficult to make ends meet on $50,000 a year. If you can save, it makes life smoother. If you lose your job, you have a cushion to fall back on and can take longer to look around and perhaps get a better job than if you have to take the first thing that comes along. If there is sudden illness or surgery, financial tragedy does not accompany the physical distress. Vacations, automobiles, better furnishings, a home—all are more easily within your reach. You may be able to accumulate a modest financial beginning for a small business which in time may develop into a bigger one. You may be able to provide security and self-support for your old age instead of having to depend on the charity of others. It is surprising how small sums set aside regularly cumulate rapidly into substantial and usable surpluses.

SUGGESTED READINGS

1. *Your Insured Deposit*, Federal Deposit Insurance Corporation. A free copy may be obtained by writing the Corporation at 550 17th Street, N.W., Washington, D.C. 20429.
2. National Credit Union Administration, *Credit Union Statistics, NCUA Quarterly*, and *Annual Report*. A free copy may be obtained from the Administration at 2025 M Street, N.W., Washington, D.C. 20456.
3. *The Credit Union Yearbook*, issued annually, Credit Union National Association. A free copy may be obtained by writing to the Association at Filene House, 1617 Sherman Ave., Madison, Wis. 53701.

4. *Savings and Loan Fact Book*. Chicago: U.S. Savings and Loan League, issued annually. A free copy may be obtained by writing to the League at 221 North LaSalle Street, Chicago, Ill. 60601.
5. *Personal Money Management*. American Bankers Association, 1120 Connecticut Ave., N.W., Washington, D.C., 20036.
6. S. Rose, *Savings and Loans Break Out of Their Shell*," *Fortune*, September 1972.
7. *Changing Times, The Kiplinger Magazine:*
   "Take Another Look at U.S. Savings Bonds," March 1975.
   "Managing Your Savings for the Highest Return," December 1973.
   "Maybe We Need 'Truth in Savings,' Too," February 1971.
8. *National Fact Book of Mutual Savings Banking,* issued annually. A free copy may be obtained by writing to the National Association of Mutual Savings Banks, Suite 200, 1709 New York Avenue, N.W. Washington, D.C. 20006.

CASE PROBLEMS

1. Letitia Church, a recent college graduate, earns a net of $450 a month. She is anxious to save money for a trip to Europe two years hence, but she never seems to have any money left over to save. When she cashes her check on payday, she has an irresistible urge to buy new clothes, and she barely manages to pay for rent and food. She works for a company which has a credit union, a savings bond a month plan, Christmas Club, and an arrangement with a local bank for depositing employees' checks directly in the bank. What savings plan would you suggest for Letitia?

2. Carroll Robinson and his wife Doris (both age 30) have bought and furnished a home. They have two children (ages 8 and 2). After providing for all regular expenses, they have about $50 left over each month for emergencies and capital expenditures. How would you advise them to invest the money? Why?

3. Mabel and James (both age 25) were married a year ago. They live in a four room apartment which they rent for $250 a month. Both are working, their total income being $1,150 a month, of which they are just beginning to save $100 through careful budgeting. They want to accumulate their savings toward a down payment on their own home. Where would you advise them to put their savings? How expensive a house do you think they should plan to buy? If everything goes along smoothly, how long will it take to accumulate the down payment? While they are saving for the down payment, should they put any funds elsewhere for emergencies? Why?

4. John Sullivan is a construction engineer who lives in a community which has a long, cold winter, during which he is often without work for a couple of months. He is age 48, and Kathleen, his wife, is age 45. Their three children

are ages 8, 13, and 19. When he works, John finds he has about $350 a week after taxes, of which they manage to save about $50. Where can they put it to best advantage? Is it enough for their needs, considering that they own their home?

5. John and Lydia have accounts in a regular savings Day of Deposit Day of Withdrawal Account and a two year certificate account. Lydia has just gone to the hospital because of a serious illness; she may be there for a while. John thinks he should have $2,000 at hand immediately and is about to make a withdrawal from the certificate account although it has a year to maturity to yield that amount. What other alternatives does he have?

6. Alice and Lawrence Toddhunter have been investing about $25 a month for years in Series E bonds and have been taking advantage of the extended maturities. They now believe that future savings should be invested in something which will provide a cash income every year. They own their own home, believe that they have adequate insurance, and have no children. They do not believe that they have the knowledge and experience to invest in other than government issues. What investment would you advise?

7. The Dandis family came to this country only a few years ago. They have saved $2,000, which they keep at home. What are disadvantages of this method of handling their savings? What alternative suggestions do you have for them?

8. For the last 15 years, Belle and Raymond Lynch and their three children (ages 14, 8, and 6) have been able to save nothing despite the fact that both work. On the death of Raymond's mother, they were left $10,000. How should they invest this money?

9. John Smith is a printer who works for Art Crafts, Inc., which makes and sells calendars on a large scale. His company is sponsoring a new credit union, to which it offers free quarters and $500 a year toward expenses. John is popular among the employees and is elected to be the operating head of the credit union at a salary of $1,500 a year. The company will pay him for his duties at the credit union and will free him from his regular work to the extent necessary. So far, 150 employees have joined the credit union out of a total of 700. What advantages will they have? How much time per week would you expect John to have to spend on the new job? What sort of records would he have to keep? Where would you advise him to keep credit union cash? Of what advantage will the credit union be to the sponsoring company?

10. The only place for savings in your fairly small community is the time deposit department of the People's Bank, which pays 5 percent per annum and which has always given the impression that it is not anxious for business. You are asked to join a group of persons who are interested in establishing a federal savings and loan association in your community. You are a graduate of a collegiate school of business administration and work as chief accountant for a

local factory, where you earn $14,000 a year and feel that the future is anything but bright for you. The community is thriving and growing. What advantages or disadvantages for the community do you see in establishing the federal savings and loan association? Are there personal reasons why it might be advantageous for you to join? Others in the community argue that what is needed is a good credit union. Why? Is there room for both? Why?

8

Life Insurance

A man's dying is more the survivors' affair than his own.
Thomas Mann

In 1850 conditions were such that the expectation of life at birth in the United States was only about 40 years. As a result of a century of scientific, social, and economic progress, which probably has no counterpart in all human history, the baby born today can be expected, on the average, to live to age 70, if it's a boy, to 77, if it's a girl. Thus, within four generations, the expectation of life has risen by about 30 years, or by two-thirds (see Table 8–1). If you are 20 years old now, male, having survived the extra

TABLE 8–1
The Lengthening Life Span–Comparison of Life Expectancy at Various Ages in the United States, 1850–1975

	You Are Male and				*You Are Female and*			
		Age				*Age*		
If in—	*Just Born*	*20*	*40*	*60*	*Just Born*	*20*	*40*	*60*
1850	40.4	40.1	27.1	15.3	43.0	41.7	29.9	16.7
1900	46.6	42.0	27.6	14.3	48.7	43.6	29.1	15.2
1960	67.4	50.1	31.6	15.9	74.1	56.2	37.1	19.7
1975	70.9	52.9	34.3	17.8	77.0	58.5	39.3	21.5

Source: U.S. Department of Health, Education and Welfare.

hazards and perils of the teen ages, you can expect to live another 52.9 years. If you are a girl, you are obviously anything but the "weaker sex." On the average, you can expect to live to 77, or seven years longer than the average male. A girl of 20, today, can look forward to another 58.5 years.

The Money Value of a Man

In a very interesting book entitled *The Money Value of a Man,* the late Dr. Louis I. Dublin, then a vice president and chief statistician of the Metropolitan Life Insurance Company, attempted to estimate the amount of the present worth of a man's future earnings, in excess of expenditures on his own person, assuming the man is subject to existing mortality conditions. While his grim purpose was to find the amounts which the family of a deceased person would have to have at its disposal to replace its share of his earnings if he had not died, his interesting calculations may be presented in a somewhat cheerier frame. If a young woman of age 20 (the average age at which females in the United States marry) marries a young man of 22 (the average age at which males in the United States marry) and he is earning $9,000 a year, she is acquiring $387,000 of future income. As Dr. Dublin noted: "Little do we ordinarily realize how great these amounts are even in the case of relatively small income."[1]

Actually the calculation of the money value of human life is a bit complex. Let's take a simplified version as it might be worked out in court in an automobile accident case. Assume that a young architect, Fuller Plans, aged 26, is killed in an automobile accident by a drunken driver. Mr. Plans is a college graduate, leaves behind a widow and two small children aged four and two. According to the laws of the state in which the accident took place, Mrs. Plans can sue for the present value of her deceased husband's expected lifetime earnings less his cost of maintenance.

The first step in preparing such an estimate would be to calculate the amount Mr. Plans might have earned between the ages of 26 and 64 without making any allowances for growth in his income or discounting his income to present value. Reference to Census Bureau tables shows that assuming no growth and no rate of discount, a young professional, aged 26, a college graduate, might expect to earn $392,000 between the ages of 26 and 64.[2]

But Mr. Plans' earnings would have grown over his working lifetime. The second step in the calculation requires the assumption of a growth rate. Assuming a 4 percent annual increase in his earnings, Fuller Plans could expect to earn $948,000 over his working lifetime.

But there is a third step which requires that Plans' lifetime earnings be

[1] Louis I. Dublin and Alfred J. Lotka, *The Money Value of a Man*, rev. ed. (New York: Ronald Press Co., 1946), p. 147. For a more recent version, see "The Economic Value of Human Life" by Dorothy P. Rice and Barbara S. Cooper, in *American Journal of Public Health*, vol. 57, no. 11 (November, 1967).

[2] See Herman P. Miller and Richard A. Hornseth, *Present Value of Estimated Lifetime Earnings* (Technical Paper No. 16 [Washington, D.C.: Bureau of the Census, U.S. Department of Commerce, 1967]).

discounted to present values. This is to allow for the fact that a dollar one expects to receive 35 years from now is not worth a dollar today. A given sum is normally worth more today than an equal sum at some future date, because the funds can be profitably invested in the interval. Interest is the premium paid to reflect the fact that any given sum can be put to profitable use over a period of time. It follows that the value of money which is not currently available but will become available some years hence must be discounted for the interest which could be earned in the interim. This is why the present value of a dollar to be received in the future is always less than 100 cents.

How much less depends on the discount rate assumed. Alternative assumptions are possible. Will Mrs. Plans put her money award in common stock and average a 9 percent return over the years or will she put it in a savings account and receive 5 percent? The higher the discount rate, the lower the present value of future earnings. The lower the discount rate, the higher the present value of future income.

Assume a 5 percent discount rate, which means investment of the award in a savings account with a minimum risk of financial loss. Then, with an annual increase in productivity of 4 percent per annum and a discount rate of 5 percent per year, it can be ascertained from the Census Bureau's tables that the present value of Mr. Plans' expected earnings between the ages of 26 and 64 is $316,000.

There remains a final step in this calculation: estimating Mr. Plans' probable maintenance costs during his working lifetime. If we assume $1,000 a year as his personal maintenance costs apart from his family's, then, referring again to Census Bureau tables, $29,000 would have to be subtracted from the present value of his expected lifetime earnings in order to allow for the cost of his maintenance.

If the court accepted the calculations and assumptions in this example, it would then award Mrs. Fuller Plans $287,000 as the present value of her husband's expected lifetime earnings, excluding the cost of his own maintenance.

Since the purpose of *The Money Value of a Man* was to estimate how much insurance a man would have to carry to enable his family to continue its level of living unchanged in the event of his death, it assumed various levels of income per annum, and a very simplified version of this concept may be seen in Figure 8–1. Of course, not many of us can afford enough life insurance fully to replace our lifetime earnings should we be taken away prematurely, but life insurance is now recognized as the quickest way for a young person to build an estate to provide adequate protection for a family.

FIGURE 8–1

ONE HUNDRED AVERAGE MEN AT AGE 25	FORTY YEARS LATER AT AGE 65
Looking forward with enthusiasm to 40 years of living, earning and— Ultimate Financial Independence	Gone .... 36 Still working.............. 5 Dependent—unable to work... 54 Financially Independent.... 5 100

THE MONEY VALUE OF LIFE

AGE	YEARS OF EARNINGS TO 65	AVERAGE MONTHLY EARNINGS							
		$400	$500	$600	$700	$800	$1,000	$1,200	$1,500
25	40	$192,000	$240,000	$288,000	$336,000	$384,000	$480,000	$570,000	$714,000
30	35	186,000	210,000	252,000	294,000	336,000	420,000	504,000	630,000
35	30	144,000	180,000	216,000	252,000	228,000	360,000	430,000	538,000
40	25	120,000	150,000	180,000	210,000	240,000	300,000	360,000	450,000
45	20	96,000	120,000	144,000	168,000	192,000	240,000	264,000	336,000
50	15	72,000	90,000	108,000	126,000	144,000	180,000	216,000	270,000
55	10	48,000	60,000	72,000	84,000	96,000	120,000	144,000	180,000
60	5	24,000	30,000	36,000	42,000	48,000	60,000	72,000	90,000
65	0	0	0	0	0	0	0	0	0

How much of this money will you have at 65?

Who Owns Life Insurance?

Almost everyone sooner or later. The number of people in the United States who own some form of life insurance now totals over 145 million. A study by the Institute of Life Insurance found that 86 percent of all families owned some form of life insurance. In families headed by college graduates, 81 percent held life insurance. Where family income was $10,000 to $20,000, some form of life insurance was owned by 95 percent. There are over 369 million life policies in force in the United States, amounting to $1.8 trillion. The size of the average new ordinary life policy is $13,310, and the average amount of life insurance owned per insured family is $28,800.[3]

Sharing Risks by Insurance

Insurance is a plan by which large numbers of people, each in some danger of possible loss, the time of which cannot be foreseen or prevented,

[3] For greater detail, see *Life Insurance Fact Book* (New York: Institute of Life Insurance, latest ed.). Free copies may be obtained by writing to the Institute at 277 Park Avenue, New York, N.Y. 10017.

are brought together for mutual protection so that when one of the group suffers a loss, it will be made good, partly or wholly, from the contributions of the entire group. In other words, all members of the group contribute small sums regularly and beforehand in order to make good particular losses to the individuals who suffer them.

Perhaps the best way to understand this is to look at fire insurance first. Only a few houses in each community are damaged or destroyed by fire each year. This rate of destruction can be determined from past experience, so that it is possible to estimate approximately the cost that all must pay in order that those who suffer losses can be compensated. The only other question is: "Will past experience be a reliable guide to future losses?" The same principles apply to life insurance. But while a house may never catch fire, everyone must someday die.

Insurance is possible because of the law of probability, large numbers, or the law of averages. If you toss a penny just once, you have no way of knowing whether you will get heads or tails; but if you tossed it a million times, you could be pretty sure of getting very close to 500,000 of each. Insurance companies have skilled mathematicians, known as "actuaries," who study the proportion of people who die at various ages. These actuaries calculate rates of mortality based on hundreds of thousands of cases, and the results are compiled in mortality tables, which insurance companies use as the basis for calculating the rate to charge for insuring any particular person.

Mortality Tables and Premium Rates

A very basic mortality table, the Commissioners Standard Ordinary Table of Mortality, compiled by the National Association of Insurance Commissioners, shown in Figure 8–2, is based on the experience of life insurance companies. It starts with 10 million cases at birth. It follows them through to age 99. For each year it shows how many of the original 10 million will still be living and how many will die; it calculates the death rate per 1,000 at that age (see Figure 8–3).

For example, at age 20, of the original group 9,664,994 are still alive. That year, 17,300 may be expected to die, which means that the death rate is 1.79 per thousand.[4] That is, out of 10,000 people at age 20, 1.79 per 1,000, or approximately 18, will die before reaching age 21. Thus, 10,000 college students, all age 20, could easily figure out how to insure themselves and what to pay, *for one year*. They can be reasonably certain that 18 of them will die within the year, but, of course, they do not know which 18.

[4] The rate is figured not on the original 10 million but on the 9,664,994 still alive.

FIGURE 8–2
1958 CSO Mortality Table, Commissioners Standard Ordinary

Age	Number Living	Number Dying	Death Rate per 1,000	Expectancy, Years	Age	Number Living	Number Dying	Death Rate per 1,000	Expectancy, Years
0	10,000,000	70,800	7.08	68.30	50	8,762,306	72,902	8.32	23.63
1	9,929,200	17,475	1.76	67.78	51	8,689,404	79,160	9.11	22.82
2	9,911,725	15,066	1.52	66.90	52	8,610,244	85,758	9.96	22.03
3	9,896,659	14,449	1.46	66.00	53	8,524,486	92,832	10.89	21.25
4	9,882,210	13,835	1.40	65.10	54	8,431,654	100,337	11.90	20.47
5	9,868,375	13,322	1.35	64.19	55	8,331,317	108,307	13.00	19.71
6	9,855,053	12,812	1.30	63.27	56	8,223,010	116,849	14.21	18.97
7	9,842,241	12,401	1.26	62.35	57	8,106,161	125,970	15.54	18.23
8	9,829,840	12,091	1.23	61.43	58	7,980,191	135,663	17.00	17.51
9	9,817,749	11,879	1.21	60.51	59	7,844,528	145,830	18.59	16.81
10	9,805,870	11,865	1.21	59.58	60	7,698,698	156,592	20.34	16.12
11	9,794,005	12,047	1.23	58.65	61	7,542,106	167,736	22.24	15.44
12	9,781,958	12,325	1.26	57.72	62	7,374,370	179,271	24.31	14.78
13	9,769,633	12,896	1.32	56.80	63	7,195,099	191,174	26.57	14.14
14	9,756,737	13,562	1.39	55.87	64	7,003,925	203,394	29.04	13.51
15	9,743,175	14,225	1.46	54.95	65	6,800,531	215,917	31.75	12.90
16	9,728,950	14,983	1.54	54.03	66	6,584,614	228,749	34.74	12.31
17	9,713,967	15,737	1.62	53.11	67	6,355,865	241,777	38.04	11.73
18	9,698,230	16,390	1.69	52.19	68	6,114,088	254,835	41.68	11.17
19	9,681,840	16,846	1.74	51.28	69	5,859,253	267,241	45.61	10.64
20	9,664,994	17,300	1.79	50.37	70	5,592,012	278,426	49.79	10.12
21	9,647,694	17,655	1.83	49.46	71	5,313,586	287,731	54.15	9.63
22	9,630,039	17,912	1.86	48.55	72	5,025,855	294,766	58.65	9.15
23	9,612,127	18,167	1.89	47.64	73	4,731,089	299,289	63.26	8.69
24	9,593,960	18,324	1.91	46.73	74	4,431,800	301,894	68.12	8.24
25	9,575,636	18,481	1.93	45.82	75	4,129,906	303,011	73.73	7.81
26	9,557,155	18,732	1.96	44.90	76	3,826,895	303,014	79.18	7.39
27	9,538,423	18,981	1.99	43.99	77	3,523,881	301,997	85.70	6.98
28	9,519,442	19,324	2.03	43.08	78	3,221,884	299,829	93.06	6.59
29	9,500,118	19,760	2.08	42.16	79	2,922,055	295,683	101.19	6.21
30	9,480,358	20,193	2.13	41.25	80	2,626,372	288,848	109.98	5.85
31	9,460,165	20,718	2.19	40.34	81	2,337,524	278,983	119.35	5.51
32	9,439,447	21,239	2.25	39.43	82	2,058,541	265,902	129.17	5.19
33	9,418,208	21,850	2.32	38.51	83	1,792,639	249,858	139.38	4.89
34	9,396,358	22,551	2.40	37.60	84	1,542,781	231,433	150.01	4.60
35	9,373,807	23,528	2.51	36.69	85	1,311,348	211,311	161.14	4.32
36	9,350,279	24,685	2.64	35.78	86	1,100,037	190,108	172.82	4.06
37	9,325,594	26,112	2.80	34.88	87	909,929	168,455	185.13	3.80
38	9,299,482	27,991	3.01	33.97	88	741,474	146,997	198.25	3.55
39	9,271,491	30,132	3.25	33.07	89	594,477	126,303	212.46	3.31
40	9,241,359	32,622	3.53	32.18	90	468,174	106,809	228.14	3.06
41	9,208,737	35,362	3.84	31.29	91	361,365	88,813	245.77	2.82
42	9,173,375	38,253	4.17	30.41	92	272,552	72,480	265.93	2.58
43	9,135,122	41,382	4.53	29.54	93	200,072	57,881	289.30	2.33
44	9,093,740	44,741	4.92	28.67	94	142,191	45,026	316.66	2.07
45	9,048,999	48,412	5.35	27.81	95	97,165	34,128	351.24	1.80
46	9,000,587	52,473	5.83	26.95	96	63,037	25,250	400.56	1.51
47	8,948,114	56,910	6.36	26.11	97	37,787	18,456	488.42	1.18
48	8,891,204	61,794	6.95	25.27	98	19,331	12,916	688.15	.83
49	8,829,410	67,104	7.60	24.45	99	6,415	6,415	1,000.00	.50

Source: National Association of (State) Insurance Commissioners.

FIGURE 8–3

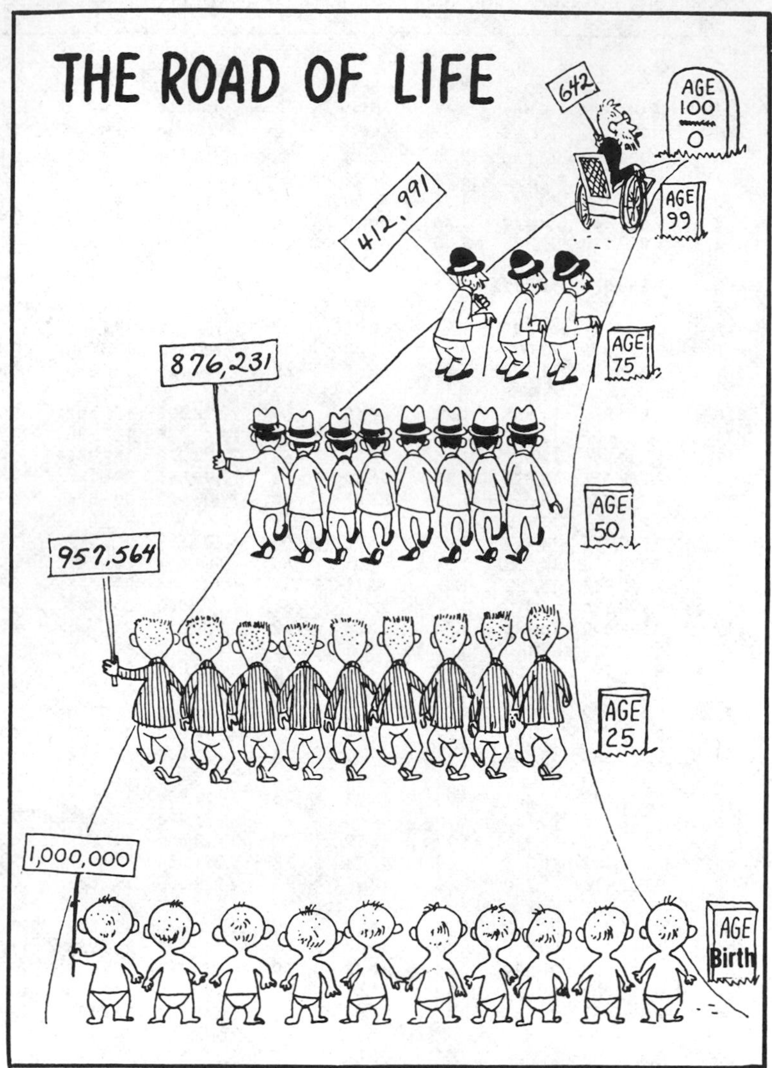

The story of the Road of Life is depicted in the CSO Table of Mortality shown in Figure 8–2. Visualize a million people at birth, starting down this road. By age 25, there are 957,564 living. By age 50, 876,231 remain. Only 412,991 are alive at age 75, and there are only 642 left at age 99.

Courtesy: Life Insurance Marketing and Research Association, Hartford, Conn.

If they wanted to be certain that the families of each of the 18 who died would receive a payment of $1,000, they could each (10,000) contribute $1.80, thus establishing a fund of $18,000, out of which $1,000 could be paid to the families of each of the unfortunate 18 who were to die. Each student would be paying for pure protection, and there would be nothing left over from the insurance fund at the end of the year. If the same group, now 9,982, wanted to insure in the same way, the next year, from age 21 to age 22, each would have to contribute a little more than the $1.80 of the year before, first, because there are fewer contributors and, second, because 18 more of them will die the second year. More and more will die in succeeding years. The group left to contribute each year will become progressively smaller. The payments to be made each year will grow larger. Thus the cost of insurance will rise steadily. By age 60, of the original 10,000, 20 year old college students, 2,034 will have died, leaving 7,966 living. In the 61st year, 162 more will die. To pay the beneficiaries or the estates of each the sum of $1,000 would require $162,000. Thus, each of the 7,966 survivors at age 60 would have to contribute $20.34. And each year thereafter, fewer survivors would have to pay steeply increasing amounts. This approximates the simplest form of insurance—term insurance—which will be described later. Rates are low when the average age of the insured is low, but they climb steadily, until old surviving members can hardly pay the premiums (see Figure 8–4).

Level Premium Policies and Reserves

But the insurance company faces a somewhat different problem. It will be asked, say, to insure the 10,000 for life, and they will want to pay the same amount each year. Sooner or later all will die, and each estate will receive $1,000. How much must the company charge? There will be a total of 10,000 payments by policyholders of the group to the company the first year, plus 9,982 the second year, and so on. According to the mortality table, these add up to a total number of annual payments made by this group, over all the years, of 508,703.

A total of $10 million must be paid by the insurance company; and since the company will collect 508,703 equal installments from policyholders, simple division indicates that the annual payment (premium) will be $19.66. Under this plan, the group will pay the insurance company more than is necessary to meet the claims in the early years, and the extra amount will be available for investment. The money which is accumulated to help pay future claims is known as the "reserve." It is only partly made up of the premiums paid. The rest comes from interest earned on the com-

FIGURE 8–4

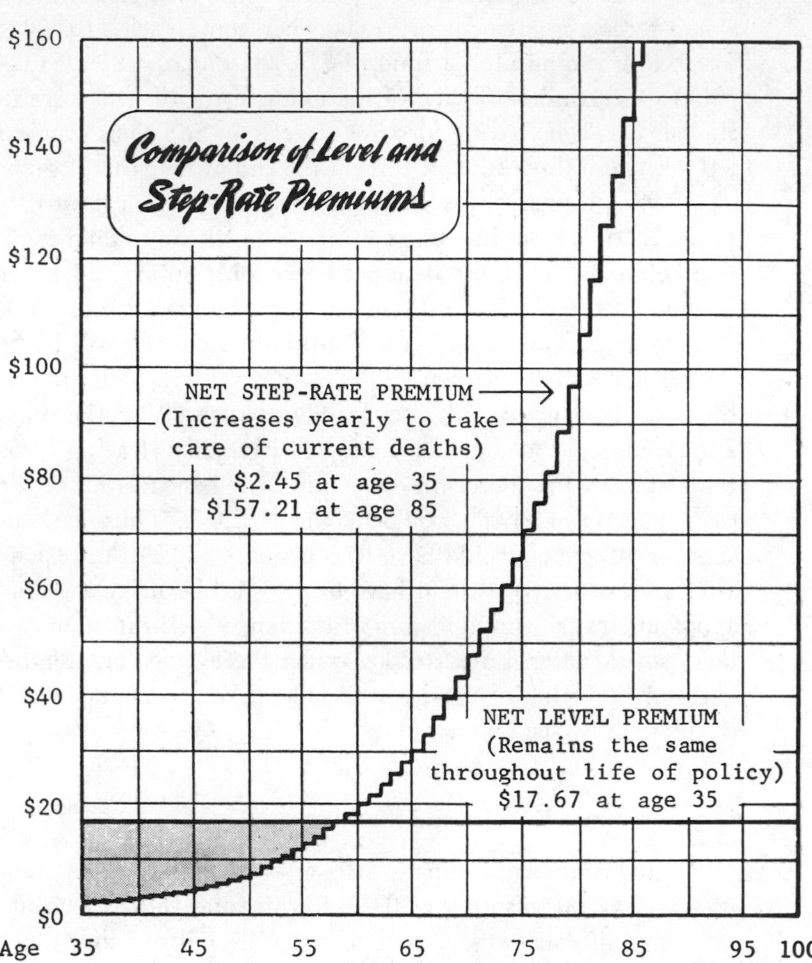

By paying the difference indicated by shaded portion below the level premium line, the company accumulates funds which offset the yearly increases occurring in later years.

Source: Life Insurance Marketing and Research Association.

pany's investment of this reserve. These earnings can be used to help pay claims. This reduces what the policyholder would otherwise have to pay. Therefore, the company, before it can determine the premium rate, must estimate the interest rate it can expect to earn on its reserve funds. Generally this has been calculated at 3 percent, even though in recent years the figure of 5.88 percent has been the actual rate of return. This benefits the participating policyholder for the particular year. The insurance companies maintain the 3 percent because they must estimate and the 3 percent is a safe, conservative rate.

For example, if 3 percent interest is earned, each member of the group need pay a premium of only $9.56 a year instead of $19.66. In other words, the total payments over the years for everybody need be only $4,863,201 instead of $10 million, in that an average of $10.10 a year for each member is paid toward the cost of insurance by interest earnings, or a total for everybody of $5,136,799.[5]

Legal Reserves and Premium Rates

In the level premium policies, one pays more than the current cost of insurance in the early years but less in the later years. Consequently, a reserve fund accumulates to one's credit. This, together with future premium payments and interest earnings, makes it possible to pay death benefits in later years when level premiums alone would be insufficient because of increasing death rates. The difference between the level premium and the old step rate premium may be seen in Figure 8–4. The policyholder can borrow against his pro rata share of the reserve fund; or if he wishes, he can surrender the policy and collect it as cash value. Thus, level premium insurance provides a savings or investment feature along with pure protection or insurance. Collecting more funds than are needed in the earlier years of life creates definite obligations on the part of the company to its policyholders. These obligations are called "policyholders' reserves" or "legal reserves" and are carefully supervised by the state, for on the ownership of assets equal to these reserves (which are really liabilities) depends the company's solvency. The reserve is separate from surplus and is not available for distribution as dividends.

When basic premium rates are set, something must be added to cover the cost of running the insurance company. This charge is known as the "loading." Efficient companies hold expenses low. Thus the premium charged you for life insurance depends on three factors: (*a*) the real cost of insurance based on mortality experience, (*b*) the return earned on the reserve accumulated under level premium policies, and (*c*) the costs of running the insurance company.

How Much Insurance Should I Buy?

A student once asked his professor, "Skipping all the details, how much insurance should I carry and what's the best policy for me?" The professor thought for a moment and then said, "Skipping all the details,

[5] For a more detailed explanation, see R. Wilfred Kelsey and Arthur C. Daniels, *Handbook of Life Insurance* (New York: Institute of Life Insurance, latest ed.). A free copy may be obtained by writing to the Institute at 277 Park Avenue, New York, N.Y. 10017.

just tell me when you are going to die and whether you'll have any dependents or not at the time. Then I'll answer your question."

How much life insurance is enough? This has been a puzzle for a long time. You can answer it, however, if you examine your needs.[6] In fact, you can list them and come to a pretty definite answer. Naturally, a college student at 18 or 20 isn't thinking about death and, consequently, your first and most immediate need may not even occur to you. It's—

1. ***Cleanup Expenses.*** The high cost of your dying will hit your family. There will be medical bills, hospital bills, funeral costs. There may also be bills and loans to pay as well as your final tax remittance. Based on the experience of others, these costs will range from $1,000 to a half-year's income.

2. ***Family Period Income.*** The second essential need you face is to provide a minimum monthly income for your dependents, if you have any. If there are two or three young children, it will be difficult, if not impossible, for the wife to go off to work to support them. To stay home and take care of them, she needs a minimum monthly income. It's been estimated that the surviving family can live three quarters as well as before on half the income. You won't be able to duplicate your present income, but you won't need to because part of your present budget involves your own expenses. If you are covered under social security, then your wife and children will receive monthly survivors benefit payments until the youngest child is 18, or 22 if still in school. Payments to the wife will cease when the youngest child reaches 18, but will continue to the student directly if in school until the end of the term in which the 22d birthday is reached. Social security payments to the widow will resume when she reaches 60. In estimating the need for minimum monthly income until the little ones grow up, figure from one third to one half of your present monthly income.

3. ***Pay Off the Mortgage.*** If you live in a house which you "own," but on which the bank has made a substantial mortgage loan, this is your next need to be taken care of by insurance. There is no need for estimating here. You know the exact monthly cost of interest and principal repayment on your mortgage. And there's a special insurance policy designed just to handle this situation. If your wife wants to keep the house and continue to live in it, you can buy a policy—reducing term insurance—which will pay off the mortgage. On the other hand, if she is likely to want to sell the house and move back with her parents, then all you need is enough in-

[6] For a detailed study see: The Life Insurance Deficit of American Families: A Pilot Study, E. Scott Maynes and Loren V. Geistfeld *Journal of Consumer Affairs,* Summer 1974.

surance to enable her to meet the mortgage payments for six months or a year so that she doesn't have to sell the house under pressure.

4. ***An Emergency Fund.*** Savings may provide this, but if not, you'll have to use insurance to set it up, provided of course, you can afford the cost. Every family needs an emergency fund in case of major illness, an accident, sudden hospitalization, and other misfortunes. It's a sort of "reserve for contingencies," and for young families something between $500 and $1,000 is about right.

5. ***Income for the Wife's Middle Age.*** Remember social security payments to your family cease when the youngest child reaches 18 or 22. They don't resume again until your widow reaches 60. This gap is known as the "blackout period" in the insurance man's jargon. Perhaps you can provide a monthly income for your wife during this blackout period until social security payments resume at 60.

6. ***Income for the Wife's Old Age.*** When your wife's social security payments resume, they will range from approximately $83.20 to $335.40 per month for the rest of her life, depending on what your average earnings were.[7] You may be able to supplement this by monthly insurance payments, but as the head of a young family, it isn't likely that you'll be able to afford the cost of reaching this far into the future.

7. ***A College Fund for the Children.*** This is your next goal, and we use the term "goal" advisedly. Paying for your child's college education is a goal; buying groceries for the family when the youngster is in first grade is a need. If your income permits the extra insurance cost involved, by all means buy the special kinds of policies devised to cover the cost of four years at college.

8. ***Retirement Income.*** Almost all the insurance you buy to cover the previous expenses can be converted, as you will see, to provide retirement income if you are lucky enough to live long enough to retire. But you may find you want a higher monthly retirement income even after you take into account social security benefits. If so, insurance, using endowment policies perhaps, or annuities, can provide it. As your income rises and your children grow older, you'll want to look into this possibility, but right now it's probably the most expendable goal on the list.

As seen in Figure 8–5, every income level finds life insurance about equally important for financial security but for differing reasons. Those under $10,000 are more concerned about funeral expenses and leaving a debt free estate. Those over $10,000 place greater emphasis on savings, education for children, and retirement.

---

[7] Subject to cost of living escalation.

FIGURE 8–5
Is Life Insurance an Important Part of Your Financial Security?

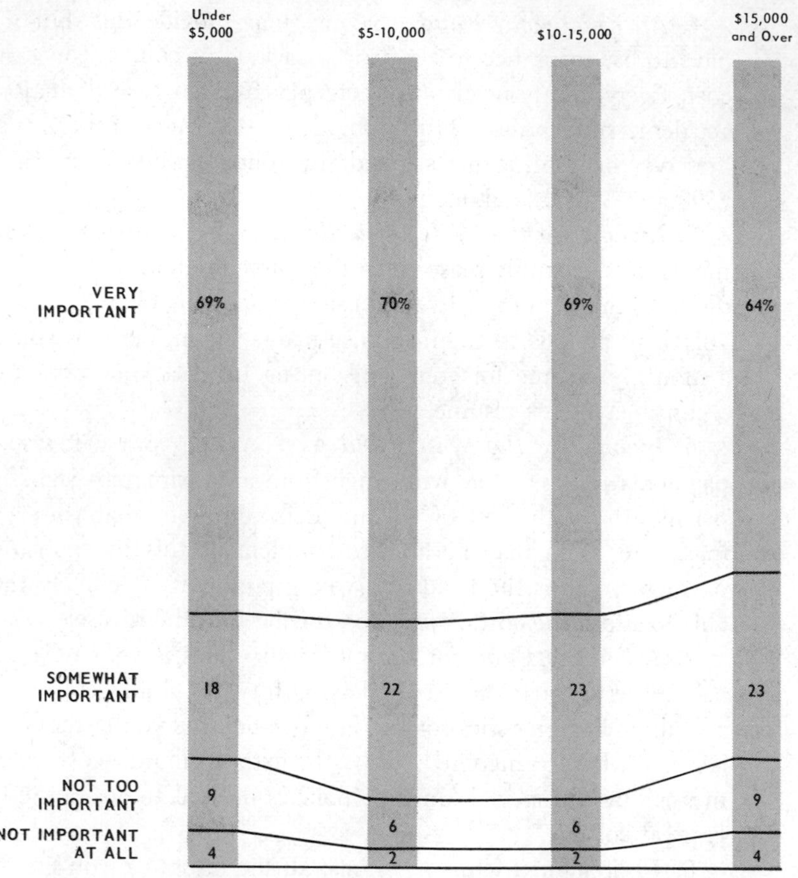

Source: *Public Attitudes toward Money and Its Management*, study conducted by Louis Harris & Associates for *Newsweek* magazine.

Changing Times, The Kiplinger Magazine, has devised a table (shown in Figure 8–6) to enable you to pin down your insurance needs in money terms and to offset against each need the cash resources you may already have accumulated to meet it.[8] You'll probably need an insurance agent to assist you with this form, but it's the way a skilled agent would go about helping you figure out how much insurance you need.

Can you afford what you need? Perhaps not. Then, having listed the needs in order of priority and essentiality, you do the best you can within your financial capacity. Remember the average family spends about 3 per-

[8] "How Much Life Insurance Do You Need?" *Changing Times, The Kiplinger Magazine*, January 1972.

FIGURE 8–6

cleanup expenses / **cash available**

cleanup expenses			cash available		needed from life insurance
medical care	$		*savings*	$	
funeral			*social security death benefit*		
debts & bills			*group insurance*		
taxes			*other*		
insurance loans			*other*		
estate settlement					
extra family expense					
total needed	$	*less*	*total available*	$	= $

mortgage			cash available		needed from life insurance
			savings	$	
			other		
balance outstanding, or payments pending sale	$	*less*	*total available*	$	= $

family's monthly expenses			monthly income available		needed monthly from life insurance
housing	$		*social security*	$	
utilities & household operation			*investments*		
food			*earnings*		
clothing			*other*		
medical care			*other*		
incidentals (car, personal, recreation)					
total needed	$	*less*	*total available*	$	= $

emergency fund			cash available		needed from life insurance
			savings	$	
			investments		
			group insurance		
			other		
estimated need	$	*less*	*total available*	$	= $

wife's monthly expenses to age 62			monthly income available		needed monthly from life insurance
			investments	$	
			earnings		
			other		
estimated budget (follow family-period headings)	$	*less*	*total available*	$	= $

wife's monthly expenses after age 62			monthly income available		needed monthly from life insurance
			investments	$	
			social security		
			other		
estimated budget (follow family-period headings)	$	*less*	*total available*	$	= $

special funds			cash available		wanted from life insurance
for	$		*investments*	$	
for			*other*		
total wanted	$	*less*	*total available*	$	= $

Source: Adapted from *Changing Times, The Kiplinger Magazine.*

cent of its disposable personal income on life insurance. This is about what you can afford. It's a good bench mark to stay close to in paring your list of needs to your financial ability.

What Kind of Policy Shall I Buy?

If you have only a certain limited amount of money to spend on life insurance and you find that for one type of policy you have to pay $4.30 per $1,000 of insurance protection. For another you have to pay $41.60 per $1,000. Or, for a given expenditure of $100, one policy you can buy provides $19,000 worth of protection while another provides only $2,100 of insurance. You will begin to think about the kinds of policies available and the differences among them (see Table 8–6, page 371). Naturally you may wonder at these large differences and the reasons for them. Various kinds of policies offer differing advantages and limitations. To be able to buy insurance intelligently, you'll need to examine and understand the basic differences.[9]

Kinds of Life Insurance

Life insurance may conveniently be grouped as follows:

1. Ordinary
   a. Term
   b. Straight or whole life
   c. Limited payment (20 or 30 years) life
   d. Endowment
   e. Combination plans
2. Group
3. Industrial
4. Credit life insurance

When you buy life insurance, you receive a *policy* which is the contract between you and the company. The money you send to the company at regular intervals to pay for your life insurance is known as the *premium*. The person you name to receive the money from the policy if you should die is the *beneficiary*. A *contingent beneficiary* may also be named to receive the money if the beneficiary dies before you do. The *face value* of the policy is the amount stated on the first page of the contract that will be paid in case of death, or in the case of an endowment policy, at ma-

[9] A panel discussion among experts on the differing values of the various types of life insurance may be found in *Money*, June 1973, pp. 24–28.

turity. As you pay premiums on your policy, a certain amount of reserve accumulates to its credit. This is called its *cash value*. The *loan value* is the amount you may borrow on your policy while it is still in force. Usually, this is close to the cash value.

Ordinary Life Insurance

Ordinary insurance is sold on an individual basis for larger amounts than industrial insurance, and premiums are usually paid by check or at the insurance company office on a quarterly, semiannual, or annual basis. Nearly half of the total number of policies issued are ordinary policies but account for more than half of the total value of life insurance in force in the United States today. Generally, the smallest amount for which an ordinary policy is written is $1,000; the average size of such policies in force today is $7,230. When we remember that many of these policies are written for $5,000, $10,000, $25,000, and $50,000, it is not difficult to see why they all add up to a very substantial amount of insurance. They are usually written with level premiums (annual premiums fixed in amount and continuing at the fixed amount throughout the life of the policy), and in most cases provide both living and death benefits.

By "living benefits" we mean the values which exist in most life insurance policies which enable you to benefit while you are still alive. These living benefits include the ability to convert an ordinary policy to retirement income at 65, the ability to surrender the policy for cash, the ability to borrow against it, matured endowments, disability benefits, dividends, and the "nonforfeiture" provisions, which will be explained subsequently. Life insurance companies pay more money to living policyholders than to families of policyholders who have died. Last year 58 percent of insurance company payments were "living benefits" (see Figure 8–7). Death benefits, of course, are the sums paid to beneficiaries upon the death of the insured. The various ways in which the death benefits can be paid are known as "settlement options." They too will be explained later.

Term Insurance

When you buy term insurance, you buy pure insurance protection and nothing else. Everyone seems to know that if a policy is bought from a fire insurance company and is not canceled, nothing will be collected from the company unless there is a fire; the policy will be worthless when the time for which it has been written has expired. Exactly the same sort of situation exists for a person who buys term insurance from a life insurance com-

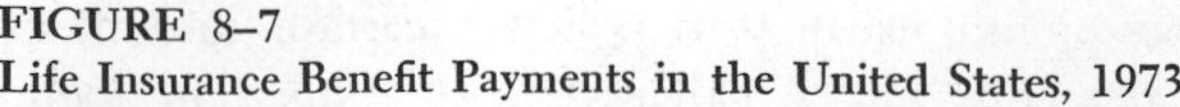

FIGURE 8–7
Life Insurance Benefit Payments in the United States, 1973

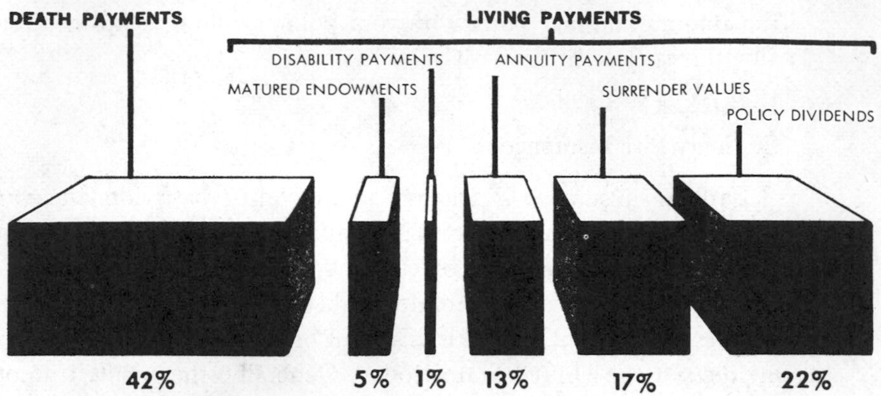

Source: Institute of Life Insurance

pany. If death comes within the term of the policy, the company will pay the beneficiary the face value of the policy; but if the insured is still living at the expiration of the time for which the policy was written, then the policy is of no value. Term policies are usually issued at level premiums for terms of 1, 5, 10, or 15 years; sometimes they are written to expire at age 65. Some companies write one year term policies which are renewable one year at a time for a given number of years—perhaps 5 or 10—without further medical examination. The insured pays the lowest premium the first year, and a higher premium each succeeding renewal. Such a policy has the lowest possible premium in the first year, because it is not averaged for the later years, when the age of the insured and the risk of dying will be greater. A five year policy with a level premium would tend to have a premium equivalent to what would be paid in the third year of renewal of a one year term policy. It is usually advisable to purchase a term policy which is renewable, without another medical examination, for a fairly large number of years, if it can be obtained, since you may later want the protection longer than you had originally planned. Many term policies are convertible into permanent types of life insurance policies, but on the policies into which you convert, you must pay premiums based on your age at time of conversion, which premiums will naturally be higher than they would have been if these policies had been taken earlier. The chief advantage of the conversion feature is that you know that you can have the policy if you want it; you need take no medical examination at time of conversion.

If you buy straight life or endowment insurance, you not only buy protection but in addition pay enough so that for all practical purposes you have a savings account with the insurance company. This is the reason your policy has a cash surrender value or loan value. Since term policies have no savings or investment feature, they are accordingly the least expensive form of insurance to buy in the short run and at young ages. Another way to express it is that a given amount of money will buy a larger face amount of term insurance than of straight life or endowment. For example, as Figure 8–8 shows, if you can spend (at age 20) only $100

FIGURE 8–8
What Insurance $100 a Year Will Buy (policies bought at age 20)

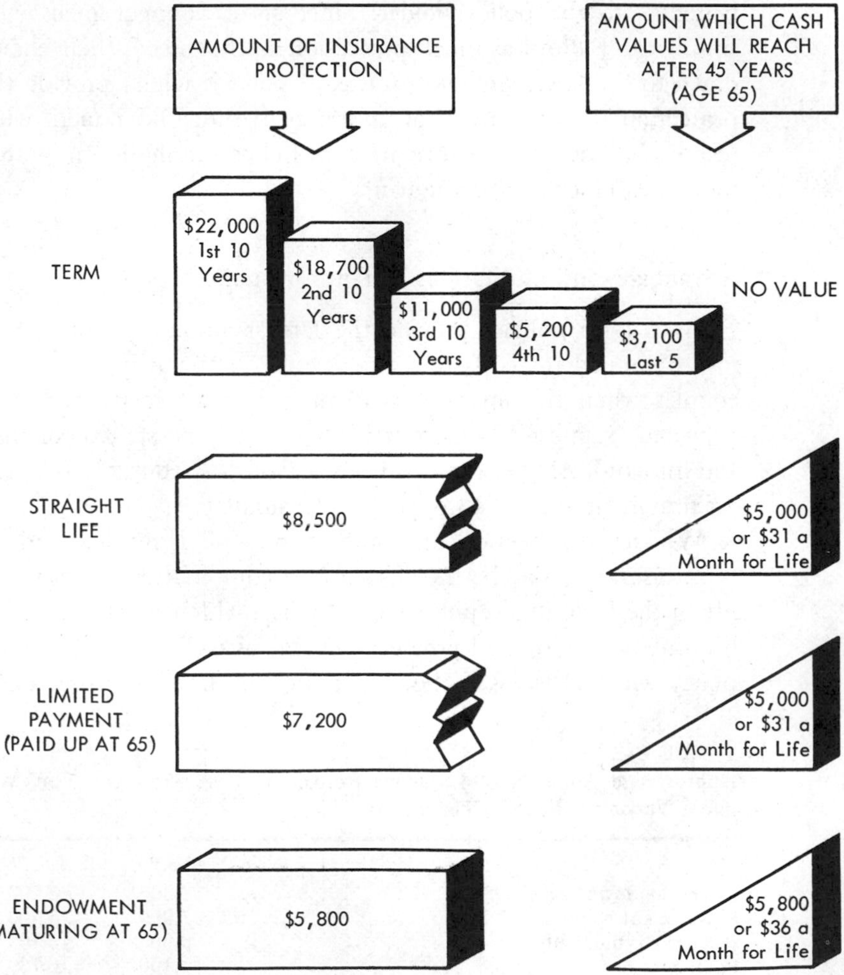

These are the four basic kinds of life insurance policies. Straight life insurance and limited payment policies can give lifetime protection. Term insurance cannot be purchased after age 65; the term insurance rates shown here are for a term policy which will call for a new physical examination every 10 years. Figures are approximate.

Source: Institute of Life Insurance.

annually for insurance, this amount will provide $22,000 of term insurance protection as against only $8,500 of straight life, or $7,200 of limited payment life, $5,800 of endowment (at age 65) insurance.

It should be clear, therefore, that term insurance may be, temporarily, the most convenient insurance for a young family to buy when it needs a maximum amount of protection but cannot afford to pay the larger annual premiums which other forms of insurance require. To generalize: at the younger ages, term insurance costs only about a third of the cost of straight life insurance and about one tenth of what 20 year endowment insurance costs. But remember that term insurance provides no "living benefits" to the policy holder. Since most younger men with families simply can't afford as much protection as they need, their choice narrows down to the lower premium forms of policies which provide the greatest protection for what they can afford to spend. Older men, whose family responsibilities may be less, may wish less emphasis on protection and more on an income at retirement.

Advantages and Limitations of Term Insurance

Since term policies provide the largest amount of protection for the lowest immediate cost, they are useful, temporarily, for young married couples when the husband is earning a small salary and offspring are expected. Suppose $150 a year is all that can be spared for insurance on the husband. As you can see from Table 8–2, your $150 a year achieves maximum protection through term insurance.

Whenever protection, and protection alone, is needed, and at low cost, term insurance may be the answer or a combination of term and straight life in the form of a family income policy, which combines temporary and lifetime protection and provides "living" as well as "death" benefits. This policy will be discussed shortly. If the sole need is protection while the

TABLE 8–2
Approximate Amounts of Insurance Protection That $150 per Year Will Purchase under Varying Policies at Three Ages

Type of policy	*Age 25*	*Age 35*	*Age 45*
20-year endowment	3,300	3,200	3,000
Endowment at 65	7,900	5,200	3,000
20-year payment life	6,600	5,100	3,900
Payments to 65	10,100	6,700	3,900
Straight life	10,900	7,900	5,200
5 year convertible and renewable term	32,000	27,700	15,500
10 year convertible and nonrenewable term	33,000	22,900	11,900

Source: Institute of Life Insurance.

children are growing up, term insurance will provide it at lower cost than other ordinary policies. Another typical use of term insurance is to protect your family against mortgage foreclosure in the event of your death. You can buy a decreasing term policy where the amount and premium on the insurance will decline at exactly the same rate as the amount of the mortgage which you are paying off month after month. If you should die at any time during the mortgage term, the amount of insurance payable under the policy will cover the remaining amount of the mortgage. Frequently, the family income or family maintenance policy is used not only to protect the wife and children from loss of the home but to provide additional protection as well.

It should be remembered, however, in the case of term insurance, that if the insured lives beyond the term of the policy, the policyholder will have nothing—no income in old age, no paid up insurance, no cash surrender or loan value. Other types of ordinary policies provide all these features. Term insurance only provides death benefits provided you die within the stated term or an extension thereof. Term policies have no "living benefits." The term policy accumulates no reserve funds from which you can get cash or a loan. Furthermore, renewal rates get very high as you grow older. For short periods, term insurance costs less than other insurance; for a longer period—as for life—it costs more. Term insurance does not help in an investment or savings program, nor is it the best kind of insurance to carry as one grows older, because the premiums become so large as to be prohibitive for most people. The cost at age 40 doubles at age 50 and triples at age 55. Since the premium for a term policy pays only the cost of protection during the term of the policy, the policy seldom has any *nonforfeiture* values, which permanent policies have. Thus, if unemployment or sickness make it impossible to keep up the premiums, since there is no reserve available, the policy will terminate at the end of the grace period, usually 30 days from premium due date.

Some term policies have *renewal* privileges, which give the right to renew the policy for another term, at a higher rate, without proving one's insurability at the end of the original policy term. Some term policies, also, can be converted into a permanent form of insurance within a definite period of years specified in the contract, generally without a medical examination. You should never buy a term policy which does not have these two features: renewability and convertibility, both without requiring a medical examination. This is important, because there may come a time when you may not be able to pass an insurance examination or when rates on your renewable term policy become quite high. You may then want to convert to a permanent plan, and you should be sure that your term policy permits you to do so even if you are not in good health. Several life insurance companies offer whole life or term policies whose face value increases automatically in line with the consumer price index, until they are doubled. Naturally an indexed policy has a much higher premium cost than a regular policy.[10]

The variation in rates among the various types of term insurance may be seen in Table 8–3.

TABLE 8–3
Rates for Various Types of Term, Modified, and Straight Life per $1,000 of Insurance for Policies of $10,000

Kind of Policy	*Age When Bought* 25	35
One year term, convertible and renewable	$ 5.47	$ 6.20
Five year term, convertible	4.74	5.05
Ten year term, convertible	5.19	7.09
Five year term, convertible and renewable	5.33	6.04
Ten year term, convertible and renewable	5.35	6.24
Term to age 65	7.87	10.81
Modified life, first five years	5.71	7.21
Modified life, after first five years	14.15	20.05
Straight life	13.35	18.61

Source: Institute of Life Insurance.

Straight or Whole Life Insurance

A straight or ordinary life policy is a plan of insurance for the whole of life with premiums payable until death. It has the lowest premium rate of any permanent policy on the level premium plan. It is the most widely used, and it is a good all-purpose policy, which meets many different needs and family situations. A level premium is paid throughout life (with premiums stopping sometimes at a ripe old age), and the face of the policy is payable to the beneficiary upon the death of the insured. Because the level premiums in the early years of the policy are in excess of mortality and other costs, they are reserved and in effect act as savings combined with protection. In the later years these reserves or savings make it possible to keep the premium level even though mortality and other costs are greater than the premium.

This type of policy combines protection with saving; but since the premium, and therefore the saving, is moderate, the cash surrender or loan value also grows at a moderate rate. It fits the needs of those who wish to secure protection for beneficiaries and do some saving in addition.

---

[10] *Money* August 1974, p. 30.

It provides both "living" and "death" benefits. If the death of the insured occurs, the beneficiary is paid the face of the insurance policy. On the other hand, if the insured lives, the straight life policy can be borrow against or cashed in. The loan value is the amount which may be borrowed with the policy as sole collateral. But you cannot eat your cake and have it too: if you surrender the policy for its cash value, the protection will be gone; if you borrow on the policy your beneficiary will receive on your death the face value of the policy reduced by the amount of the loan and any unpaid interest thereon.

If, some day, the holder of a straight life policy wishes, say upon retirement, to discontinue premium payments, any one or, if the policy is large enough, a combination of the following alternatives can be selected:

1. Continue the protection at a reduced amount for the balance of his lifetime.
2. Continue the full amount of protection for a definite period of time.
3. Cancel the policy entirely in return for a cash settlement of guaranteed amount, plus dividends, if any.
4. Discontinue life insurance protection and elect to receive an income from the policy for a certain limited period of time or for life.

In the next chapter it will be shown that social security provides something for the old age of many people but that in many cases it must be supplemented to provide reasonable retirement comforts. Savings built up through life insurance can help in supplementing social security benefits, and indeed, modern insurance programming builds from the social security base to meet family needs more adequately.

Whole or straight life combines protection, savings, and retirement income at a minimum yearly cost. It has the lowest premium rate of any permanent policy on the level premium, legal reserve plan. The premium rate, however, is higher than the rate on a term policy because, if the policy is continued, it must some day be paid as a claim, whereas a term policy is paid only if the insured dies within the term. In the straight life policy, the increasing risk of death is averaged over the years at a level premium. For example, as Figure 8–9 indicates, if you buy $10,000 worth of whole life insurance at age 20, you will pay $115.50 per annum over the ensuing years until death. A renewable five year term policy for the same amount would cost you $52.80. But if you kept renewing the term policy every five years, at age 50 you would pay $144 per annum, more than the whole life policyholder; and when you renewed at age 60 (the last time you would be permitted to renew), you would pay $330.30 a year for the next five years. At age 65, your term policy would expire and could not be re-

FIGURE 8–9
Approximate Cash Values of the Four Kinds of Life Insurance ($10,000)

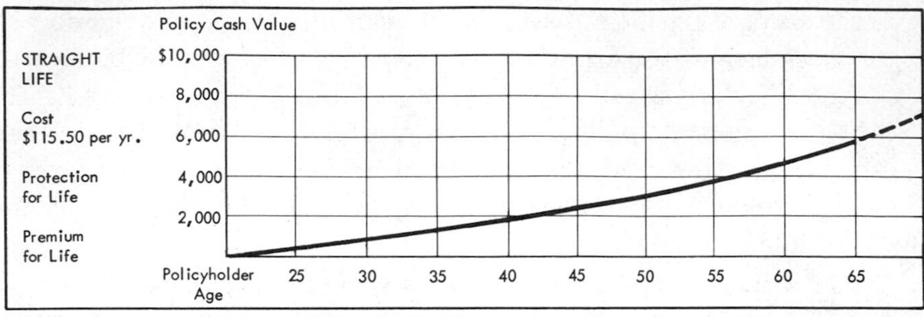

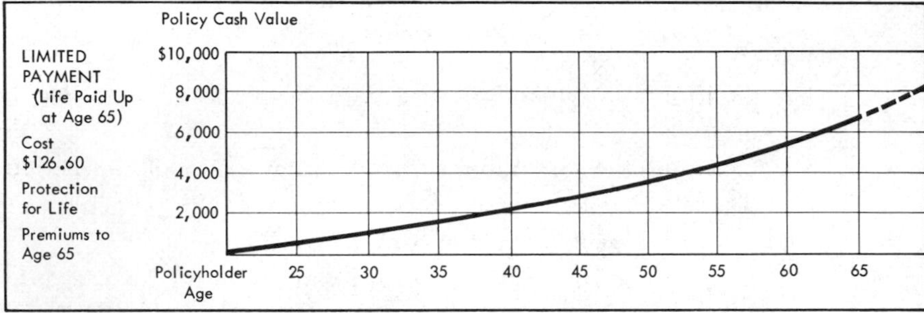

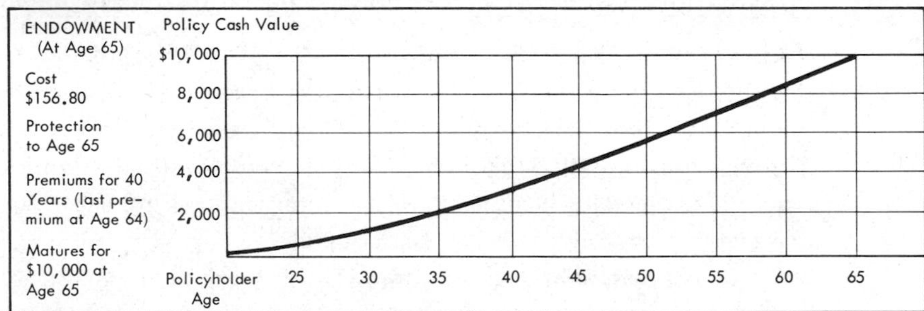

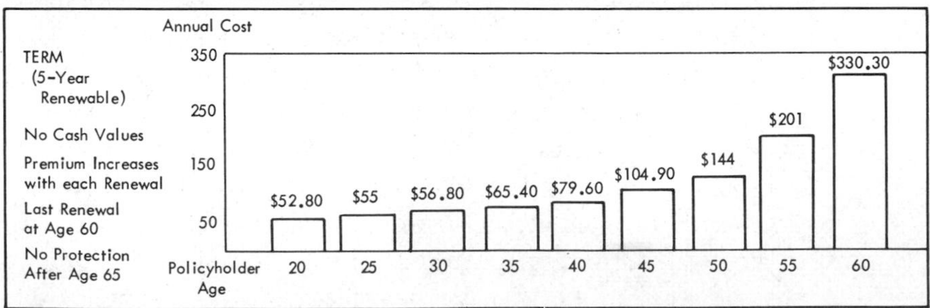

Here are four $10,000 life insurance policies bought by people who are 20 years old. Approximate cash values and costs are shown in this chart. The limited payment policy becomes "paid up" at age 65, and the endowment "matures" at age 65.

Source: Institute of Life Insurance.

newed again. You would have no accumulation to show for your 45 years of payments, although, of course, you had protection over this period. The holder of the straight life policy, however, wished to stop paying premiums at age 65—and any whole life policyholder can exercise this privilege—could give up the policy and receive $5,910 (the cash surrender value) in cash or as income over a period.

Loan opportunities are most desirable in a period of tight money and high interest rates, since you can borrow freely against your own policy and at a fixed rate—usually lower than the going rate. (See Figure 8–10.) If the loan is repaid, the borrower has had the use of his money at lower cost than the current market rate, the interest on the loan is tax deductible and

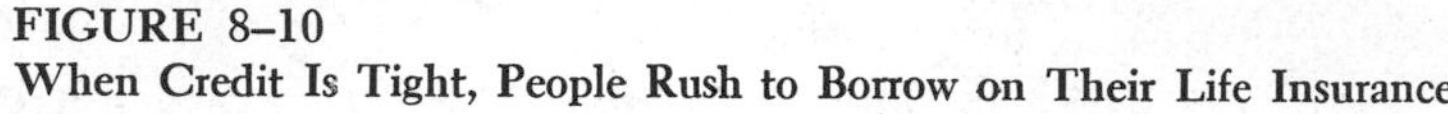

FIGURE 8–10
When Credit Is Tight, People Rush to Borrow on Their Life Insurance

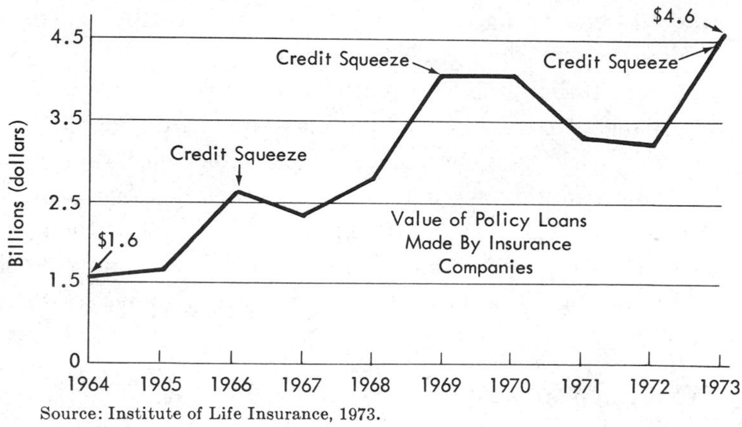

Source: Institute of Life Insurance, 1973.

the face value of the policy is unimpaired. If the loan is not repaid, the only penalty is the decreased value of the policy which may seem justified if the purpose of the loan was, for example, to provide a college education for the future beneficiary. Between 1945–65 the percent of policy loans outstanding as a percentage of life insurers assets was 5 percent. The record high was 18.3 percent, set in 1932. In 1974 the figure was 8.3 percent.

Payment of Premiums

It is preferable, if possible, to pay premiums on an annual basis. However, arrangements can usually be made to pay semiannually, quarterly, or even monthly. In the latter cases, the company does not have the use of the total premium as soon, and it must, therefore, be paid interest for the delay. In addition, several payments in each year rather than one single premium payment increase the costs of sending out notices and keeping the records, so that it may cost you 8 to 10 percent extra to avail yourself of the privilege of making partial payments. Of course, the average person is paid weekly or monthly; and it is somewhat of a hardship to pay a large insurance premium at one time, just as it is to pay a large real estate or income tax bill. One way out of the difficulty is to take out several smaller policies, instead of one larger one, having each payable in a different month, providing, of course, that you stay with ordinary insurance and do not resort to industrial. Each of the smaller policies can be paid on an annual basis, with staggered due dates, thus achieving the economies of annual payment for the policyholder.

The extra cost in not paying annually may or may not be considered interest—depending on whose viewpoint. Insurance agents and the Internal Revenue Service say it is not interest (therefore not tax deductible), but some professional experts think it should be so considered. By whatever name, it costs you 8–10 percent extra. Only one in five pay annually—reaping savings many others could achieve by doing some financial planning. Another method is a plan whereby your bank automatically places in a special account during the year preceding the annual premium date an appropriate amount from your regular account and then pays the premium when due. The bank makes no extra charge for this service.

What Happens if You Can't Pay Your Premium?

In a permanent policy, where a cash value has been built up, you don't usually lose the policy. The nonforfeiture provisions come into play. If you are temporarily unable to meet your premium payments, you can borrow against the cash value of your policy and thus continue payments through the loan. If it looks as if you will be unable to resume payments again, or if you become 65 and you don't want to continue to pay premiums, you can choose one of the various nonforfeiture options.

Every permanent policy, of which the whole or straight life policy is the most popular, has the built-in "nonforfeiture values." There are three kinds of nonforfeiture or guaranteed values:

1. Cash Value. This is the money you will get if you give up your permanent life insurance policy. A policyholder who has purchased life insurance on the level premium plan has paid premiums which were more than needed to pay claims in the earlier years, thus building up a fund of assets with which to meet claims in later years. It follows that if he withdraws, there is an accumulation of assets out of the premiums paid by him to which he is entitled.

The cash value is his share of this accumulation. It will be paid to him as guaranteed in his insurance contract and as required by law. It may be taken in a lump sum or in a series of regularly recurring payments over a period of years providing it amounts to $1,000 or more. The longer you have your policy, the more your cash value will be (see Table 8–4). Today, many people reaching retirement arrange to take their cash value in the form of income that will be paid for life over the retirement period. Some requests for cash reflect an upset in family finances as a result of unexpected illnesses or loss of a job. Though life insurance is not designed as a way of preparing to meet such financial difficulties, it may help more in this way, in some cases, than it would if kept in force as regular life insurance coverage.

You can borrow against your cash values at any time; if you die before the loan is repaid, the payments to your beneficiaries will be reduced by the amount of the loan and any interest owed. In an emergency, then, the loan provision of your life insurance policy can be used to secure money or to pay premiums due. Some policies have a special provision for the latter, called the "automatic premium loan." If this provision is in your policy, your company will automatically pay any premium that is not paid when due. The company will charge such premiums as loans against your policy to the extent of the available loan values. The policy continues in force until such time as the total loan against the policy equals the cash value. At that time the policy terminates without further value.

2. ***Reduced Paid-Up Life Insurance.*** This is a nonforfeiture or guaranteed value you can use if you want to keep some protection but are not in a position to or do not wish to pay any more premiums. The amount of your insurance will be reduced, as may be seen in Table 8–4. For example, if you bought a $1,000 policy at age 20 and at age 65, because of illness, were unable to continue paying premiums, you could arrange to have $857 of paid-up insurance as long as you lived without any further payments of premiums. That is, if you have a permanent life policy, the paid-up insurance feature will protect you for life without further premium payments, but the insurance is reduced in amount to what your net cash value will buy as a single payment at your attained age.

3. ***Extended Term Insurance.*** Suppose you can no longer pay premiums on your policy but want to continue the maximum amount of protection as long as possible. Extended term insurance gives you continued protection for the full face value of your policy (less any loan outstanding) for a limited length of time. As Table 8–4 indicates, if, at age

TABLE 8–4
Table of Approximate Cash, Loan, and Nonforfeiture Values for Straight Life Policy Issued at Age 20*

Premiums Paid to Age—	*Paid-Up Insurance*	*Cash Value (loan values, subject to the "loans" clause)*	*Extended Term Insurance*	
			Years	*Days*
25	$ 81	$ 21	6	219
30	252	76	20	106
35	406	142	24	349
40	537	218	25	347
60	815	515	18	87
65	857	591	15	348

* For each $1,000 of the face amount of the policy free from indebtedness and without dividend accumulations or paid-up additions. Paid-up insurance will be adjusted to the nearest dollar. Above figures are nonparticipating.
Source: Institute of Life Insurance.

65, you were unable to continue to pay premiums on the $1,000 policy you bought at age 20, you could continue to enjoy the protection of the full face value of your policy, without paying any more premiums, for an additional 15 years and 348 days. The time is determined by what your net cash value will purchase when used as a single payment to buy the extended term protection at your attained age.

Combination Policies

The straight life policy has many variants—in fact, the insurance companies are constantly trying to devise new contracts which meet the needs of certain people better than the older forms. Thus we hear of *family income* and *family maintenance* policies, of *family* policies and of *modified life*. These are combinations of whole life and term policies. A 20 year *family income* policy provides that if the policyholder dies within 20 years after taking out a policy, the beneficiary will be paid $10 a month for each $1,000 of the policy for the balance of the 20 years *after the policy was taken out*. At death or at the end of the 20th year, depending upon the contract, the beneficiary receives, in addition, the face value of the policy or its equivalent in the form of income. Such a policy is a combination of decreasing term insurance and a straight life insurance policy. If the insured lives on beyond the 20 year term, the whole life portion of the policy can be continued at the rate for straight life in effect when the policy was bought. The premiums on these combination policies run only a little higher than those for ordinary life policies, and for families with young children they are often excellent.

For example, if a man who has a wife and a one year old baby takes out a 20 year, $10,000 family income policy and dies three years later, the policy will assure the widow and child of $100 a month income until the child is age 21. Then the face of the policy will become due and payable to the widow, either as a lump sum or as income. If the man had lived, he could have continued paying on the policy as an ordinary whole life policy after the 20 year period was up.

The way in which the family income policy combines permanent life insurance and term insurance is shown in Table 8–5, where $10,000 straight life is combined with enough decreasing term insurance to provide $100, $150, or $200 per month for a period of 20 years from the date of purchase. The policy provides that if the head of the family dies during the family protection period, then the monthly income will be paid until the end of the term or family period. At that time, the $10,000 of permanent protection will be paid in a lump sum or may be taken in the form of an income. If the insured outlives the family protection period, there is

TABLE 8–5
Illustration of Family Income Policy, Insured Age 30 (basic policy, $10,000 straight life)

	Family Income per Month		
	$100	*$150*	*$200*
Approximate annual premiums:			
For $10,000 straight life	$150	$150	$150
For family income rider	$ 43	64	85
Total for family income policy	$193	$214	$235
Term insurance provided in addition to $10,000 straight life:			
1	$ 14,360	$ 21,540	$ 28,720
2	13,810	20,715	27,620
3	13,250	19,875	26,500
4	12,670	19,005	25,340
5	12,070	18,105	24,140
6	11,460	17,190	22,920
7	10,830	16,245	21,660
8	10,190	15,285	20,380
9	9,530	14,950	19,060
10	8,850	13,275	17,700
11	8,150	12,225	16,300
12	7,430	11,145	14,860
13	6,690	10,035	13,380
14	5,930	8,895	11,860
15	5,150	7,725	10,300
16	4,350	6,525	8,700
17	3,530	5,295	7,060
18	2,680	4,020	5,360
19	1,810	2,715	3,620
20	920	1,380	1,840

Source: Institute of Life Insurance.

simply a straight life policy for $10,000—the term portion having run out. At or near the end of this 20 year period, the policy generally provides for a reduction in premium to that of the $10,000 straight life policy.

Family maintenance policies are similar, except that a 20 year policy of this kind would pay its monthly income for 20 years *after the death of the insured,* should death occur within 20 years after purchase of the policy. To illustrate the difference: suppose that two women buy policies of the two types in 1975 and that both die in 1985; the beneficiaries under the family income policy will receive a monthly income until 1995 and will then receive the face of the policy, while the beneficiaries under the family maintenance policy will receive a monthly income until 2005 and will then receive the face of the policy. Naturally, therefore, family maintenance policies cost more, since the company faces the possibility of having to extend the monthly income payment over a longer period. Both kinds of insurance are available in 10 year and 15 year as well as 20 year policies.

Modified life is a type of policy which starts as term insurance and then after a stated period, usually five years, automatically changes to whole life at a higher premium. During the first five years the low term premium rate prevails. The basic purpose of modified life, of course, is to provide permanent insurance for young people who aren't yet in a position to pay for it. It is therefore a very useful policy for newlyweds or for the young family.

The *family* (not to be confused with family income) policy is one of the insurance industry's combinations of term and straight life. It provides a "package" of insurance coverage for the whole family—husband, wife, and children. The policy is issued in $5,000 units with each unit providing $5,000 of whole life insurance for the husband, $1,250 of term insurance for the wife, if she is the same age as her husband, and $1,000 of term insurance for each covered child. The wife's insurance coverage is more if she is younger than the husband and less if she is older. The premium is not affected by the number of children covered. Children born after the plan is issued are automatically eligible for children's coverage when they are 15 days old, at no extra premium.

Extra protection policies also combine term and ordinary life. There are "double," "triple," and even "quadruple" protection policies. The double protection policy, for example, may be $1,000 of straight life with $1,000 of term tacked on. Triple protection adds $2,000 of term to the $1,000 of whole life, and so on. The term portion usually runs until age 60 or 65 and then expires leaving the straight life protection only. These policies give less "extra" protection in the early years than a comparable premium expenditure on a family income policy, but the "extra" protection lasts longer—to 60 or 65.

Preferred risk policies are regular policies issued at specially reduced rates to those who are in very good health, in safe occupations, and who will buy a large minimum amount of insurance, usually $25,000 or $50,000. The rate is significantly less than for regular type policies. If you are going into the professions and enjoy excellent health, inquire about the preferred risk policy. For those who qualify, it means buying regular insurance at very favorable rates.

High risk cases have more chance to get insurance at normal rates today because improved statistics and changed attitudes in the thinking of insurers make it possible. Asthma, diaphragmatic hernia, even some forms of skin cancer are acceptable, but not diabetes. The deaf, the blind, those with mental or nervous conditions, airline pilots, people who go into bankruptcy may soon find coverage less expensive.

Limited Payment Life Policies

Limited payment life policies are straight life policies with the one difference that premium payments are not made for life but for a limited term, such as 20 or 30 years. They have been called "hurried-up" ordinary life policies. Since the insured contracts to make fewer premium payments, naturally those that he does make will have to be larger; for the insurance company is obligated to insure him for his lifetime. Since the insured makes larger payments and makes them during the first 20 or 30 years the policy is in force, the cash (and loan) value accumulates faster than it does in the straight life policy.

The limited payment life policy is attractive to those who for one reason or another want to cut short the burden of paying premiums. Often the insured wishes to complete premium payments before earnings start to decline. He may have a "life-begins-at-forty" philosophy and aim to have many of his obligations squared away by middle age so that he will have less to encumber a free and easy existence from his forties or fifties to the end of his days. Of course, this puts a larger burden on his most active working years than if he spread the load over a longer span. Sometimes, fear that work will not be available later leads to the decision to strike while the iron is hot and pay while earnings are at their peak. This is particularly true of professional athletes, movie stars, etc.

For a young person, especially with family responsibilities, limited payment life is not the best plan. You get less protection for your premium dollar than you would if you bought ordinary life. A 22 year old with $200 a year to spend on insurance would get about $16,900 of straight life protection; and only $9,600 for 20 payment life. Of course, if you can afford it and if you outlive the premium paying period, there is a big advantage. Your insurance is paid up. You are insured for life, but you need make no more premium payments. A life paid-up at 65 policy makes a good deal more sense than a 20 pay life if you are under 30 and insist on a limited payment plan. It's less costly for one thing. At age 22, life paid up at 65 will cost only $12.46 per $1,000 compared to $19.69 for 20 pay life and $11.22 for straight life. Since your highest earning period may be from 40 to 65, there is no need to try and pay off your insurance by 40, although there is a good deal more sense in trying to get it paid up by 65.

Endowment and Retirement Income Policies

Both of these policies place the emphasis on savings rather than on protection. Both cost more than any other type of policy. An endowment policy is one that is written for a given period of time and for a stated face value. Endowment at 65 and 20 year endowments are the most common types. If you die before the stated period is up, your beneficiary receives the full face value. If you live until the maturity of the policy, you receive the full face value. Once you have received the full face value on maturity, however, you are no longer insured. The company has paid off under the contract, and the policy terminates.

Naturally, since the cash value must build up to the face value by the time the contract period is up, an endowment premium is much more costly than any other type of policy. As you can see from Table 8–6, a 20 year endowment would cost $41.60 per $1,000 face value for a 22 year-old as compared with $11.22 for straight life and $19.69 for 20 payment life.

There is a great difference, of course, between a limited payment life and an endowment policy. When you are finished paying on a limited payment life policy, you are insured for life but you collect nothing, although your cash value has built up to about three fifths of the face value. On the other hand, in the case of the endowment, once you have finished paying (*a*) you are no longer insured, (*b*) you collect the face amount of the policy, and (*c*) the policy terminates.

For young people, endowments are not very sensible. As insurance protection, it's very expensive and as savings it's costly. You can see from the figures above that $1,000 of protection at age 22 costs $30.38 more if you buy it as an endowment than if you buy it as straight life. Ah, yes, you say, but I'm saving the difference. Perhaps you are, perhaps you're not.

TABLE 8–6
What a $100 a year Premium Will Buy in Life Insurance (male age 22)

	Type of Policy	*Annual Rate per $1,000 Insurance*	*Amount of Insurance $100 a Year Will Buy*	*Cash Value at Age 65 per $100 Annual Premium*	*Monthly Life Income at Age 65, Men (10 years certain)*
1.	Term (5 year renewable and convertible)	$ 4.30	$19,000	None	None
2.	Term (10 year convertible, nonrenewable)	4.04	22,000	None	None
3.	Straight life	11.22	8,000	$4,660	$30.75
4.	Life—paid-up at 65	12.46	7,200	4,968	31.10
5.	Modified life (5 years)*	13.92	6,800	4,683	28.00
6.	Family income (20 years) $10 monthly	14.65	7,700	4,504	28.19
7.	Endowment at 65	15.73	5,700	5,700	35.68
8.	Twenty payment life	19.69	4,400	3,036	19.00
9.	Retirement income at 65	22.60	4,000	6,250	38.50
10.	Twenty year endowment	41.60	2,100	Matured (age 42)	

* Cost of the first five-year term insurance is $5.60. Then the cost rises to $13.92 at age 27 for whole life.
Source: Institute of Life Insurance.

Suppose you have a 20 year endowment and you die in the 19th year. What your beneficiary receives is 95 percent of your savings and almost no insurance. Had you bought straight life, or a family income policy, and saved the difference in premiums, your beneficiary would have gotten both the full face amount of the insurance and your savings as well. Every young family needs life insurance, but they don't need the most expensive kind. If you must buy an endowment, the endowment at age 65 is much less costly $15.73 per $1,000 when purchased at age 22, (see Table 8–6) than a 20 year endowment, and makes more sense for a younger man.

The retirement income policy differs from the endowment in that it pays a monthly income from the date of its maturity rather than a lump-sum cash amount. It is, of course, an insurance policy and therefore has a stated face value and pays a death benefit of this amount to your beneficiary if you should die before the maturity date. However, to build cash value to pay the retirement income, the reserve behind the policy builds up very rapidly and in time exceeds the face value. If you die after that has happened, your beneficiary will receive more than the face value of the policy. He or she will receive the full cash value, which is now greater than the face value. It's no sudden windfall, though. It's your accumulated savings. A retirement income policy is expensive—less expensive than a 20 year endowment, more expensive than an endowment at age 65.

Sometimes parents take out endowment policies, maturing at ages 17 or 18, on children, to provide funds for a college education. Generally speaking, in families of moderate income, practically all life insurance should be placed on the wage earners, without whose income the family finances would be sadly crippled.

Money for a college education can be accumulated, if the parent lives, by saving the money in a savings bank or savings and loan association. If it is desired to combine protection with saving for a college education through life insurance, the policy should be taken out on the life of the parent, the child being thus assured of cash for an education if the parent dies; whereas, if the insurance were on the life of the child, the parent's death might result in the policy's lapsing before a sufficient sum had accumulated for the desired education. (For a small extra premium, however, a clause can usually be added to a child's policy waiving further premiums should the head of the family die or become disabled before the child reaches a certain age.) If the parent lives, the cash surrender or loan value of the policy can be used, if necessary, to meet part of the child's college costs. Thus, in insuring to cover the costs of a college education, as well as in other general life insurance situations, the best principle to follow is to have the insurance placed on the life of the breadwinner rather than on that of a dependent.

Some Comparisons

The many different kinds of policies described thus far may be a bit puzzling. Stop then and try to put all this together, to compare and contrast. Study Table 8–6. The range of policies is from those with maximum protection and minimum (or no) savings to those with less protection (per premium dollar) and more savings. The term policy provides maximum protection and no savings for your premium money. The 20 year endowment provides the least protection and the maximum savings for your premium dollar. Generally speaking, the more costly the insurance, the faster it is building a cash value and, therefore, the more it is emphasizing savings. This may be all right for the established person of 40–45 with married children, but for the young person of 20–25, the emphasis should be placed on protection.

Insure Your Insurability

A rider is available to add to a regular insurance policy. Designed primarily for young people who can purchase only a limited amount of insurance at first, it gives you the right to purchase additional insurance later at standard premiums, within certain limits, even if your health should become impaired making you uninsurable under ordinary circumstances.

The rider, which can generally be purchased up to age 37, gives you the right to buy more insurance as specified intervals, without a medical examination, in amounts equal to the face value of the basic policy. The number of option dates depends on your age when you buy the basic policy. For example, on a policy purchased at age 22, you can buy up to $10,000 more (if the face value of your basic policy is $10,000 or more) at ages 25, 28, 31, 34, 37 and 40. Thus you could buy an additional $60,000 of insurance, until age 40, regardless of the condition of your health or the type of job you hold. At age 23, for example, the rider would cost approximately $1.52 a year for each $1,000 of insurance you add at any option date. The rider doesn't buy the insurance for you. It simply gives you the right to buy the insurance regardless of health. You pay the standard premium for your age each time you buy an extra policy. The rider is an option to buy insurance tomorrow. It doesn't add to your insurance today.

Group Insurance

Would $5,000 of life insurance offered to you for an annual premium of $25 interest you? It should. It's quite a bargain, and it may well be your introduction to life insurance. It's group insurance, of course, the kind a firm might make available to you when you start your first career job. Increasingly, responsible firms are providing employees with group life insurance, where the employer pays at least half, sometimes all, of the premium cost. Usually, the amount of group insurance you can buy is equal to at least one year's salary.

Group insurance is usually term insurance written under a blanket (master) policy issued to an employer or sponsoring association on all or some of the members of the group. Group insurance usually costs less per $1,000 of protection than ordinary insurance. Since the groups are frequently large—often running into the thousands—with all being covered by one sale, the selling cost is low per thousand dollars face value of insurance, even though considerable effort may be expended in arranging the details so that the needs of the group will be satisfied. Another factor making for lower costs is that the employer does much of the bookkeeping, since he makes collection through payroll deductions from employees of their share of the premium and pays the insurance company one sum covering the premium for the whole group. In many ways it resembles a wholesale operation rather than a retailing of insurance. Costs of group insurance are so low that eligible employees who can use the added insurance protection should think twice before passing up the opportunity to obtain it. Group insurance generally is written for one year, renewable.

One of the chief advantages of group insurance is that no medical examination is required of the members of the group. Risk is spread sufficiently because of the very size of the group itself—varying perhaps from a low of about five persons to a high of thousands in some of the larger organizations. By means of group insurance, some persons obtain life insurance protection who, because of the status of their health, might otherwise be unable to obtain it. One disadvantage is that you cannot borrow against the policy.

The employer pays some part of the premium cost and often all of it. His contribution may be reduced, if because of favorable experience, a dividend on the master policy is returned to him. Each member of the group is given an individual certificate indicating his rights in the group contract. Generally, regardless of age, each employee pays the same amount per $1,000 of protection.

In some cases, group insurance is now being written as a combination of term and straight life. Therefore, it may carry no cash surrender or loan provisions. It customarily terminates when the employee leaves the job with the employer, whether before or at retirement age. It is, however, a common provision to allow employees covered by group insurance to convert it into the standard forms of straight life or endowment within 30 days after severing their employment. Since group insurance usually does not cover retired employees—or at least to a smaller extent than when they were actively employed—this very fact cuts down claims against the insurance company and is a further reason for the low cost of this type of insurance.

An increasing number of employers are making group life insurance available to their retiring employees, in lesser value after 65, and at minimum or no cost to them. Other employees face a gap in financial planning requiring a decision on conversion at high premiums to straight life or adjusting either to less insurance as the group policy ends—or to none at all. This affects all levels of incomes, with those at the lower level relying almost completely on social security. Even those who can afford conversion, finding that a straight life no-dividend policy of $10,000 that at age 30 would cost $150 annually, now at age 65 will cost $670 a year, might hesitate.

If your first job offers group insurance, don't turn it down. It protects a new family, the cost is very low, the employer pays all or part of the premium, you won't need to take a medical examination, and you can convert to ordinary insurance, in most cases, if and when you leave the company. There are over 88 million individual certificates under 338,000 master group life insurance policies outstanding in the United States. The average amount per employee is $7,900.

Industrial Insurance

Industrial insurance, which is sold in small sums of less than $1,000, involves weekly premiums (usually of small amounts of 10 cents, 25 cents, or 50 cents) collected at the home by the insurance agent. Since the agents must visit the home, write receipts for very small sums, enter amounts in their record books, possibly chat briefly with the family, and often find people are not at home and have to come back again, it can readily be seen that this type of insurance must be relatively expensive.

One large company pays the policyholders 10 percent of the premiums for each full year that they make payments at the company's offices instead of depending on the agent to call at the residence to collect. Of course, the contact at the homes frequently leads to sales of insurance that might otherwise not be made. The name of this insurance is derived from the fact that it is usually sold to industrial workers who are paid weekly and, therefore, find it convenient to pay for insurance weekly.

Industrial policies are rarely written for more than $500 of protection. Because of their small weekly cash premiums, more policies of this type were written than any other sort. The little protection they afford, however, makes all of them together amount to but a small fraction of total life insurance protection in force. These policies were particularly useful to pay funeral expenses, and it was not unusual to find a half-dozen of them in force in a single family (covering both parents and children).

About 75 million industrial policies are in force today, amounting to $40.6 billion; this compares with total life insurance outstanding of $1.8 trillion (369 million policies). Death benefits payable annually on industrial policies now run to $476.7 million a year. Because of the small amount of protection under each policy, medical examinations are sometimes (particularly on children) not required.

Usually, industrial policies are issued on the basis of the soliciting agent's recommendation and the applicant's own statements as to medical history and present condition of health. If the insured warrants that she is in "sound health," receives a policy, and then dies within a year or two, the company may investigate, find that the state of health had been misrepresented, and reject the insurance claim. If an examination is required, it may be less thorough than in ordinary policies, in order to keep the cost in line with the small premium. There is 20 percent higher mortality experience for industrial policyholders than for others—another factor making for high cost of industrial insurance.

Policy lapses are large, sometimes amounting to as much as new policies written, in spite of the fact that the agent is penalized for allowing these policies (technically, "in his debit") to lapse. Thus the life of these policies is short. Moreover, the cost of writing the policies and agent's commissions must be absorbed so soon that we have another of the causes of high cost.

A number of the largest insurance firms no longer sell industrial insurance and have where possible upgraded the amount of the policies in force to make monthly rather than weekly payments possible. The relative decline in new purchases of industrial policies is due both to the inflationary character of our economy and to the wider prevalence of group policies, making it possible for workers to be more easily covered at their place of employment.

Savings Bank Life Insurance

Savings bank life insurance has many advantages. Among them are the lower cost—because you must buy it directly from the bank in person or by mail, there is no commission—and the variety of plans available, all of which pay dividends beginning the first year, which may then be used to reduce premium payments or to buy additional amounts. The major disadvantage is that this type of insurance is available in only three states—New York, Connecticut, and Massachusetts—and you must either live or work in the state where you purchase it. Table 8–7 indicates the low rates on savings bank life insurance at ages 21 and 23.

Credit Life Insurance

There has been a phenomenal growth in credit life insurance over the last decade paralleling the growth of consumer credit. Credit life insurance is written through lenders on the lives of borrowers and installment purchasers. It assures full payment of loans in the event of death, thus leaving survivors in the debtor's family free of his indebtedness. More than 77.5 million policies are outstanding for a total of $101.2 billion. The average amount covered per policy or certificate under credit life insurance is $1,304.

TABLE 8–7

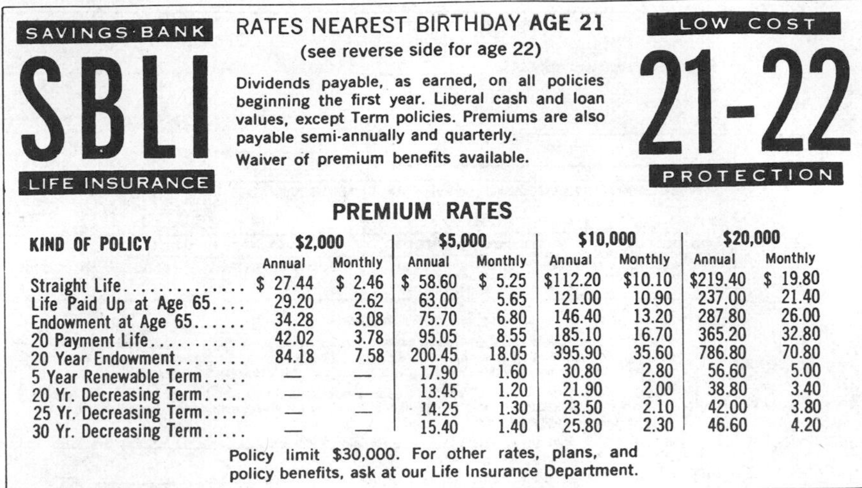

SAVINGS BANK **SBLI** LIFE INSURANCE

RATES NEAREST BIRTHDAY **AGE 21**
(see reverse side for age 22)

Dividends payable, as earned, on all policies beginning the first year. Liberal cash and loan values, except Term policies. Premiums are also payable semi-annually and quarterly.
Waiver of premium benefits available.

LOW COST **21-22** PROTECTION

PREMIUM RATES

KIND OF POLICY	$2,000 Annual	$2,000 Monthly	$5,000 Annual	$5,000 Monthly	$10,000 Annual	$10,000 Monthly	$20,000 Annual	$20,000 Monthly
Straight Life	$ 27.44	$ 2.46	$ 58.60	$ 5.25	$112.20	$10.10	$219.40	$ 19.80
Life Paid Up at Age 65	29.20	2.62	63.00	5.65	121.00	10.90	237.00	21.40
Endowment at Age 65	34.28	3.08	75.70	6.80	146.40	13.20	287.80	26.00
20 Payment Life	42.02	3.78	95.05	8.55	185.10	16.70	365.20	32.80
20 Year Endowment	84.18	7.58	200.45	18.05	395.90	35.60	786.80	70.80
5 Year Renewable Term	—	—	17.90	1.60	30.80	2.80	56.60	5.00
20 Yr. Decreasing Term	—	—	13.45	1.20	21.90	2.00	38.80	3.40
25 Yr. Decreasing Term	—	—	14.25	1.30	23.50	2.10	42.00	3.80
30 Yr. Decreasing Term	—	—	15.40	1.40	25.80	2.30	46.60	4.20

Policy limit $30,000. For other rates, plans, and policy benefits, ask at our Life Insurance Department.

SAVINGS BANK **SBLI** LIFE INSURANCE

RATES NEAREST BIRTHDAY **AGE 23**
(see reverse side for age 24)

Dividends payable, as earned, on all policies beginning the first year. Liberal cash and loan values, except Term policies. Premiums are also payable semi-annually and quarterly.
Waiver of premium benefits available.

LOW COST **23-24** PROTECTION

PREMIUM RATES

KIND OF POLICY	$2,000 Annual	$2,000 Monthly	$5,000 Annual	$5,000 Monthly	$10,000 Annual	$10,000 Monthly	$20,000 Annual	$20,000 Monthly
Straight Life	$ 28.88	$ 2.60	$ 62.20	$ 5.60	$119.40	$10.70	$233.80	$ 21.00
Life Paid Up at Age 65	30.92	2.78	67.30	6.05	129.60	11.70	254.20	22.80
Endowment at Age 65	36.48	3.28	81.20	7.30	157.40	14.20	309.80	27.80
20 Payment Life	43.84	3.94	99.60	8.95	194.20	17.50	383.40	34.60
20 Year Endowment	84.32	7.58	200.80	18.05	396.60	35.70	788.20	71.00
5 Year Renewable Term	—	—	18.20	1.65	31.40	2.80	57.80	5.20
20 Yr. Decreasing Term	—	—	13.90	1.25	22.80	2.10	40.60	3.60
25 Yr. Decreasing Term	—	—	14.95	1.35	24.90	2.20	44.80	4.00
30 Yr. Decreasing Term	—	—	16.35	1.45	27.70	2.50	50.40	4.60

Policy limit $30,000. For other rates, plans, and policy benefits, ask at our Life Insurance Department.

Most credit life insurance is written on a group basis and is, therefore, relatively inexpensive. However, there have been repeated instances of abuse all over the country with some lenders or installment dealers adding on from 50 to 100 percent of the actual cost of the premium as a "pack," thus overcharging the unsuspecting borrower. See Figure 8–11 which illustrates how Truth in Lending attempts to show you your real costs.

To sum up the comparison of the different types of insurance, over the years the average size of policy for each is shown in Table 8–8.

FIGURE 8–11

DISCLOSURE STATEMENT OF LOAN

BORROWERS (NAMES AND ADDRESSES): LENDER: LOAN NO.__________ Date__________

(STREET ADDRESS)

(CITY) (STATE) (ZIP)

TOTAL OF PAYMENTS	FINANCE CHARGE	AMOUNT FINANCED	ANNUAL PERCENTAGE RATE:	CREDIT LIFE INSURANCE CHARGE	DISABILITY INSURANCE CHARGE	PROPERTY INSURANCE CHARGE
$	$	$	%	$	$	$

PAYABLE IN: CONSECUTIVE MONTHLY INSTALLMENTS	DUE DATE OF PAYMENTS			AMOUNT OF PAYMENTS			
	FIRST:	OTHERS: SAME DAY OF EACH MONTH	FINAL:	FIRST: $	OTHERS: $	FINAL: $	RECORDING FEE $

INSURANCE

PROPERTY INSURANCE, if written in connection with this loan, may be obtained by borrower through any person of his choice. If borrower desires property insurance to be obtained through the creditor, the cost will be $__________ for the term of the credit.

CREDIT LIFE AND DISABILITY INSURANCE is not required to obtain this loan. No charge is made for credit insurance and no credit insurance is provided unless the borrower signs the appropriate statement below:

(a) The cost for Credit Life Insurance alone will be $__________ for the term of the credit.

(b) The cost for Credit Life and Disability Insurance will be $__________ for the term of the credit.

I desire Credit Life and Disability Insurance.	I desire Credit Life Insurance only.	I DO NOT want Credit Life or Disability Insurance.
(Date) (Signature)	(Date) (Signature)	(Date) (Signature)

REBATE FOR PREPAYMENT IN FULL. If the loan contract is prepaid in full by cash, a new loan, refinancing or otherwise before the final installment date, the borrower shall receive a rebate of precomputed interest computed under the Rule of 78's.

DEFAULT CHARGE. [The creditor should set forth the amount, or method of computing the amount, of any default, delinquency, or similar charges payable in the event of late payments.]

SECURITY

DESCRIPTION

A. ☐ This Loan Is Secured By a Security Agreement of Even Date covering..................

The Security Agreement will secure future or other indebtedness and will cover after-acquired property.

☐ Motor Vehicle(s): Make- .... Serial No: ....

☐ Household Goods & Appliances of the following description:..........

☐ Other: (Describe) ....

B. ☐ This Loan Is Unsecured.

I ACKNOWLEDGE RECEIPT OF A COPY OF THIS STATEMENT.

Borrower: ....

Witness: ....

This form, when properly completed, will show how a creditor may comply with the disclosure requirements of the provisions of paragraphs (b) and (d) of § 226.8 of Regulation Z for the type of credit extended in this example. This form is intended solely for purposes of demonstration and it is not the only format which will permit a creditor to comply with disclosure requirements of Regulation Z.

Source: Federal Reserve System.

How Life Insurance Policies Pay Off

If you married a dancer with maximum figure and minimum brain, better study the "settlement options" in your life insurance contract carefully. It just wouldn't make sense to leave $25,000 or $50,000 in a lump sum. If, on the other hand, your mate has the family's Phi Beta Kappa key, makes out the budget, pays the bills, fills out the income tax forms, and so forth, you may not have to read the following section so carefully.

TABLE 8–8
Average Size Life Insurance Policy in Force in the United States

Year	*Ordinary*	*Group*	*Industrial*	*Credit*
1920	$1,990	$ 960	$150	$ 200
1930	2,460	1,700	210	200
1940	2,130	1,700	240	150
1950	2,320	2,480	310	360
1960	3,600	4,030	390	680
1965	4,660	5,060	450	850
1966	4,940	5,360	450	840
1967	5,150	5,730	470	870
1968	5,450	6,070	480	910
1969	5,770	6,470	490	950
1970	6,110	6,910	500	1,000
1971	6,440	7,170	520	1,080
1972	6,790	7,530	530	1,190
1973	7,230	8,010	540	1,300

Note: Data are revised, "Credit" is now limited to life insurance on loans of ten years' or less duration. "Ordinary" and "Group" include credit life insurance on loans of more than ten years' duration.
Sources: *Spectator Year Book* and Institute of Life Insurance.

Should a lump-sum cash settlement ever be considered? Is it always wiser to favor a set monthly payment for life? Is the choice a matter of personality—adventure versus security—or is there any economic reasoning involved? The advantages of the lump sum choice would be most felt in an era of high interest rates and capital gains when investment opportunities are more plentiful. Additional considerations are age, other income, and the background of knowledge needed for investment decisions.

Apart from a lump sum cash settlement, there are four settlement options, as Table 8–9 shows. All four are explained in your life insurance policy. If the *interest* option is chosen, the company holds and invests the money until the beneficiary needs it; in the meantime, it sends out regular checks for the interest which this money has earned. If an *amount* option is chosen, a regular income of as much money as you want per month will be paid until the money and interest are gone; for example, if you have a $10,000 policy and want $100 a month, the company will be able to pay you this amount for nine years and five months. If you chose a *time* option, the company will pay, for the period you specify, a monthly amount fixed to last for the period selected; for example, if you wish some income for at least 20 years, the company will pay $54 a month for the 20 years. If the *lifetime income* option is chosen, a regular income is paid as long as the person named to receive it lives; the monthly amount will be less for a younger person, more for an older person.

If the insurance company has contracted to pay monthly installments for a certain number of years and the beneficiary dies before payments are

TABLE 8–9
The Four Optional Settlements for $10,000 (as income rather than a single cash payment)

The interest option:	
Money left at interest until the family asks for it	$275 a year at 2¾% interest, until the money is withdrawn*
The amount option:	
A regular income of as much money as you want, paid until money and interest are gone	$100 a month for 9 years and 5 months, or $200 a month for 4 years and 4 months
The time option:	
A monthly income to last as many years as you want, paid until money and interest are gone	10 years income of $95 a month, or 20 years income of $54 a month
The lifetime income option:	
A regular income guaranteed for the person's lifetime	$57.60 a month for life (for a woman 65 years old) $67.25 a month for life (for a man 65 years old)

* This is the legally guaranteed rate in a typical contract. Companies actually pay about 5 percent and higher now.
Source: Institute of Life Insurance.

completed, remaining payments will be made to the estate of the insured in the absence of a second, named beneficiary. You, as the insured, may either choose the plan by which settlement is to be made or leave the choice of settlement options to your beneficiary. Some people have their insurance payable to a bank as trustee and indicate in a trust agreement how the money is to be used. The method you select should take into consideration the financial capacity of your beneficiary and his or her needs.

The interest payment option is the most widely used, providing safety for the principal and flexibility in interest payments. Both the amount option and the time option are forms of installment payments, most advantageously used in advanced age, or over a period when children are growing up.

The lifetime income option is used mainly to provide for a widow, children, or dependent parents. There are several options within this choice:

1. You can provide the largest life income for the beneficiary under a life only annuity which then forfeits the remainder of the principal if the beneficiary has an early death.

2. Another possibility provides a refund to a second beneficiary, either in lump sum or installment payments of the difference between the principal and the amount paid to the first beneficiary.

3. A variation helpful to a widow with small children provides set payments for a fixed period after the original beneficiary dies.

Lately some insurance companies have been offering a 6 percent and higher interest return to those who will leave their matured endowment policy money or life insurance benefits on deposit for five more years. It could doubly benefit a widow. It gives her a good return during a period in which she can make plans and also provides a lump sum five years later, at which time, she, as an older women, can purchase higher annuity income with the insurance proceeds.

Beneficiaries

When you take out a policy, you have the right to name a beneficiary to whom the policy is payable in case of your death. You may also retain the right to change the beneficiary later, if you deem it wise to do so.

If a beneficiary is not named, the proceeds will be paid to the insured's estate, where they will be subject to creditors' claims and to inheritance taxes. In some states, the proceeds are subject to inheritance taxes, even when there is a named beneficiary; but sometimes amounts of less than about $10,000 escape this tax if left to immediate relatives. A federal estate tax applies to estates where there is a net value over $60,000. It also applies when the proceeds go to a named beneficiary if the insured retained such incidents of ownership in the policy as the right to change beneficiaries, to borrow with the policy as sole security, or to surrender the policy for cash.

At times it is sensible to name a contingent beneficiary to receive the proceeds if the primary beneficiary should predecease the insured. Frequently, children are named *contingent* beneficiaries. If the children are young, money for them may perhaps be better left to a trustee, to be administered for their benefit. Possible future children should be included in the wording. In the event that one child dies, his share may be left to his children or be divided among his brothers and sisters. Since this is all very technical, the average person will have to depend for guidance on a life insurance agent, who, after a few years of experience, is well versed in these complexities and usually can render good advice or can obtain it from others in the company. If you get to the point where your estate is substantial, then it will be advisable to secure the services of a competent attorney who knows a good deal about estate planning.

What's in Your Life Insurance Policy?

"The big print gives it to you, the fine print takes it away," a lawyer once remarked in reading a contract. In the case of your insurance policy, however, the fine print confers many more benefits than it takes away.[11]

Have you ever taken the time to read your life insurance policy? Do you know the benefits it offers to you and to those for whom you bought the protection?

Most likely your policy came to you carefully folded. On its back you will notice your name, your policy number, its amount, and the date it was issued. The amount of your premiums and the type of policy are also written here.

Open your policy. On the first page you will find the main part of the contract. Your policy states that the XYZ Life Insurance Company insures your life. You are called the *insured.* The company agrees to pay $________, the *face amount,* to the person you have named, called the *beneficiary.* In return, you promise to make a periodic payment, called a *premium,* to the company. If you fail to make the premium payment within the *grace period* (usually 31 days after a premium is due), your policy *lapses,* which means that the policy comes to an end, unless it can be kept in force on a different basis by *nonforfeiture provisions,* such as *cash value, reduced paid-up* insurance, or *extended term* insurance, all previously described. Sometimes, after your policy has lapsed, you may put it into full effect again (*reinstate it*), provided (*a*) you have not turned it in for cash, (*b*) that you again qualify as a good risk (*are insurable*), and (*c*) that, of course, you pay the overdue premiums plus interest. Your policy will be *incontestable* after either one or two years, usually two. During this initial period the company has the opportunity to check the information you gave in your application. After the period of contestability, the company cannot withdraw from the contract or contest it.

Your policy will probably have a number of special clauses. Life insurance policies will not pay off for death by suicide if it occurs during a stated period, usually the first year or two of the contract. The *suicide clause* states that the company will return the premiums paid in case of suicide during this period. There are occasionally other *limitations of coverage,* which at times exclude payment when death results from abnormal risks, such as travel in dangerous places or by dangerous means of conveyance, or death due to war, if there is a *war clause.*

In some states, the law permits you to include in the settlement arrangements a so-called *spendthrift clause,* which protects your beneficiaries from the claims of their own creditors. In most states, your life insurance,

[11] The Institute of Life Insurance, will send you, gratis, a specimen "Institute Life Company" contract to enable you to see what a representative policy is like. It will also send you a copy of its booklet *What's in Your Life Insurance Policy?* Both of these publications, especially when read together, are very useful.

if payable to named beneficiaries rather than to your estate, is already protected from the claims of your own creditors, unless it can be shown that funds were purposely diverted in order to bypass the creditors.

Your policy may contain *waiver of premium* and *double indemnity* riders. Under the former, any premiums which fall due after the beginning of total and permanent disability will be waived. In effect, the company will pay them. Disability must occur before you reach a certain age, usually 60, and before the policy matures, if it is an endowment. The disability must last for at least six months before premiums will be waived.

The accidental death benefit, or *double indemnity*, provides that an additional sum, equal to the face of the policy, will be paid if death occurs by accidental means. Accidental death must occur within a certain time after the injury, usually 90 days, and before a certain age, usually 60 or 65. The double indemnity rider usually says that certain causes of death are not covered.

Both riders require small additions to the premium to cover the extra cost to the company, but both enjoy wide favor, especially the waiver of premium, without which many incapacitated insured persons would be forced to drop their policies. Life insurance thus protects against "economic death," whether casket or disability. The latter, however, must be total and permanent. Partial or temporary disability comes under *health insurance*.

Commissions, Dividends, and Reserves

A number of questions always come up in class discussion on these three points. The first one invariably is: "How much of my premium goes to the insurance agent as his commission?" The answer depends on the type of policy and on whether you mean first year commission or that on your premium payments in subsequent years. Naturally, since a greater effort is involved in initially selling the policy, the first year commission is higher than those of subsequent years. On an ordinary whole life policy, the average agent in many states receives about 50 percent or more of your first year's premium. Thus, if you buy $10,000 of whole life at say age 23 and pay a $200 annual premium, the agent will get about half of this the first year. On term insurance policies, it will be a smaller percentage on, of course, a smaller premium. On 1 year renewable term, he will get about 20 percent; on 5 or 10 year renewable term about 30 percent. For the next nine years, after the first, the agent receives 5 percent on most policies, according to state regulations.

"Why do some companies pay 'dividends' on policies, while others do not?" First of all, the term *dividends* as used in insurance parlance does not mean the same thing as it does in finance and investments. In insurance, a dividend is a partial return of your own money; it is a *refund* of part of the premium you paid. To make this clear, a number of other things need to be explained first.

Insurance companies are of two kinds: stock and mutual. Policies are of two kinds: participating and nonparticipating. A stock company is similar in its corporate organization to any other corporation. The stockholders own the capital and surplus. They take the risk of loss and are entitled to any profits. The stock company sells life insurance at guaranteed rates, guaranteed neither to increase nor decrease. Because of competition, the premium rates are kept as low as possible. If they are too low, the stockholders take a loss; if they are more than is exactly sufficient, there is a profit. Most stock companies issue only nonparticipating policies.

A mutual company, on the other hand, is "a cooperative association of persons established for the purpose of insuring their own lives." There are no stockholders to receive any profits nor to absorb losses. Nearly all mutual companies issue only participating policies. Hence, the gross premium rates in mutual companies are higher than stock company rates to cover all contingencies. Mutual company rates are usually set high enough so that there is usually a refund, which the insurance company calls a dividend, to the policyowner, after the policy has been in force for a certain time.

Policies sold with a higher gross premium and a subsequent refund (dividend) are called participating policies. Those sold on a lower guaranteed rate without refund are called nonparticipating. The Institute of Life Insurance declares:

> Life insurance dividends are a return to policyholders of the unused portion of premiums paid. They are refunds given after actual costs have been determined. Premiums on participating policies are purposely set at a higher rate than would normally be necessary in order to provide funds which might be needed for unforeseen emergencies. At the end of each year, the company totals the amount actually paid for death claims and operating expenses, and determines the amount of money earned on investments. After the amount required by law has been added to the policy reserve fund, another portion may be added to supplementary reserves for the policyholders benefit. The excess is then returned as policy dividends. Since nonparticipating policies do not pay dividends, the premiums you pay represent the actual cost of your policy.[12]

[12] *Your Life Insurance and How It Works.* Institute of Life Insurance, New York. A free copy may be obtained by writing to the Institute at 277 Park Ave., New York, N.Y. 10017.

Premiums do vary from company to company. If you do "shop" for insurance, then, be sure that when comparing rates of a stock and a mutual company, you compare net premium rates, not gross. That is, ask for the rate after the refund dividend, not before. A 1973 Congressional hearing on life insurance before the Senate Antitrust and Monopoly Committee supports a full disclosure of costs and the use of the "interest adjusted" method as a technique of comparing costs of similar policies. This thinking found expression in two model rules approved in a recent meeting of the 50 state insurance chiefs. Wisconsin and Arkansas have just adopted implementing regulations.

Basically this method takes into account the possible investments a policyholder might make with the excess funds used to pay the excess premiums of the earlier years of a life insurance policy. Based on actuarial risk premiums are higher than need be in the early years to keep the costs down in the later higher risk years. Furthermore if dividends are paid by one company regularly and by another in a lump sum after many years, although the total amounts may be the same, the policyholder of the second company has suffered by not having the use of the money during that time.

The model rules of the insurance commissioners propose a formula to calculate these costs at the tenth and twentieth anniversaries of the policies. This procedure is designed to reveal the cost differences in companies' policies.[13] Beware of swapping policies—you not only lose the cash loan values you have built up, but you will have to pay a higher premium because you are older. It pays to research before you buy your policy or switch in the early years, rather than later.

Just as the term "dividend" when used in the insurance sense is misunderstood, generally so is the word "reserves." There is a misconception that the term "reserves" maintained by insurance companies represents surplus or accumulated profits. It does not. U.S. insurance companies are "legal reserve" companies, that is, they are required by law to set aside part of the premium you pay in a reserve fund to meet their future liability to your beneficiary. Thus the reserve does not represent either earned surplus or profit but is the amount of money which together with future premiums and interest earnings will insure the ability of the company to

---

[13] See: "Life Insurance: Now you Can Spot the Low Cost Policies," *Changing Times, The Kiplinger Magazine*, March 1971, pp. 6–10. The study is titled *Cost Facts on Life Insurance*, the National Underwriters Company, 420 E. Fourth Street, Cincinnati, Ohio 45202. A copy of the study costs $25. Also *Changing Times, The Kiplinger Magazine* June 1973 and June 1974; *A Shopper's Guide to Term Life Insurance*, Pennsylvania Insurance Dept., Harrisburg, December 1972; *A Shoppers Guide to Straight Life Insurance*—Pennsylvania Insurance Dept., Harrisburg, June 1973; latest *Consumers Union Guide to Life Insurance;* and "Life Insurance Firms are Pressed to Tell Differences in Costs of Competing Policies," *Wall Street Journal*, March 8, 1974.

carry out policy obligations whenever they mature. This is the primary reason why reserves are required by law. The way in which the reserve behind your policy builds up as you continue to pay premiums may be seen in Table 8–10 and in Figure 8–12. The "net amount which the company has at risk" decreases as the reserve behind the policy builds up. Another way of looking at this is that increasingly your savings (cash

TABLE 8–10
Approximate Cash Values of Whole Life and 20 Year Endowment Policies (per $1,000)

	At End of Year							*At Age*	
Age	*2*	*3*	*4*	*5*	*10*	*15*	*20*	*60*	*65*
Whole life* ($1,000) CSO 3.5–3 percent									
20		1	11	21	76	142	218	515	591
25		5	16	28	94	170	256	494	573
30		10	23	38	115	201	298	467	551
35		16	32	48	137	235	342	433	522
40	3	21	40	59	161	271	388	388	484
45	6	27	49	72	187	309	435	309	435
50	8	34	59	84	214	347	480	214	347
55	12	40	69	98	243	383	520	98	243
60	20	52	84	117	272	416	559		117
65	28	64	99	133	296	449	591		
20 year endowment† ($1.000) CSO 3 percent									
20	43	84	127	172	416	689	1,000		
25	42	89	127	172	416	689	1,000		
30	42	84	127	172	417	689	1,000		
35	42	84	128	173	417	688	1,000		
40	42	83	127	172	415	685	1,000	1,000	
45	40	83	127	172	414	681	1,000	681	1,000
50	40	83	126	171	411	676	1,000	411	676
55	39	82	126	171	408	667	1,000	171	408
60	41	84	128	173	402	651	1,000		173
65	43	86	130	173	393	634			

* Nonparticipating.
† Participating.
Source: Best's Flitcraft Compend (A. M. Best Co., Morristown, N.J.) Courtesy Institute of Life Insurance.

value) are accumulating to enable the company to pay its liability to your beneficiary. The longer your policy runs (assuming it is permanent insurance and not term), the more the accumulation of your savings reduces the company's "risk."

Pointers for Policyholders

As a policyholder, be sure to do these five things, which will help you and your beneficiaries:

1. Read Your Life Insurance Policy. Be sure you understand its basic provisions and benefits, as well as its limitations and restrictions. If you have any questions, do not hesitate to ask your agent; or write to the company or to your state insurance department.

2. ***Keep Your Policy in a Safe Place.*** Actually your policy has no value to a stranger who might find or take it. Moreover, your company will issue a duplicate policy if yours should be lost or destroyed by fire. A safe deposit box is a good place to keep the policy, but it has the disadvantage that, after the death of the insured, the box may not be opened except by court order. Let your beneficiaries or attorney know where your policies are, for, in order to obtain payment, your beneficiary must turn the policy over to the company or give reasonable proof of loss.

3. ***Keep Your Company Informed of Your Address.*** Each year a number of policyholders move without either leaving a forwarding address or notifying their insurance companies. There may be dividend checks to be mailed to you; or if you let your policy lapse, the company will want to

FIGURE 8–12
How Cash Values Build Up for $10,000 of Insurance for Each of Four Types of Life Insurance Policies Taken Out at Age 22*

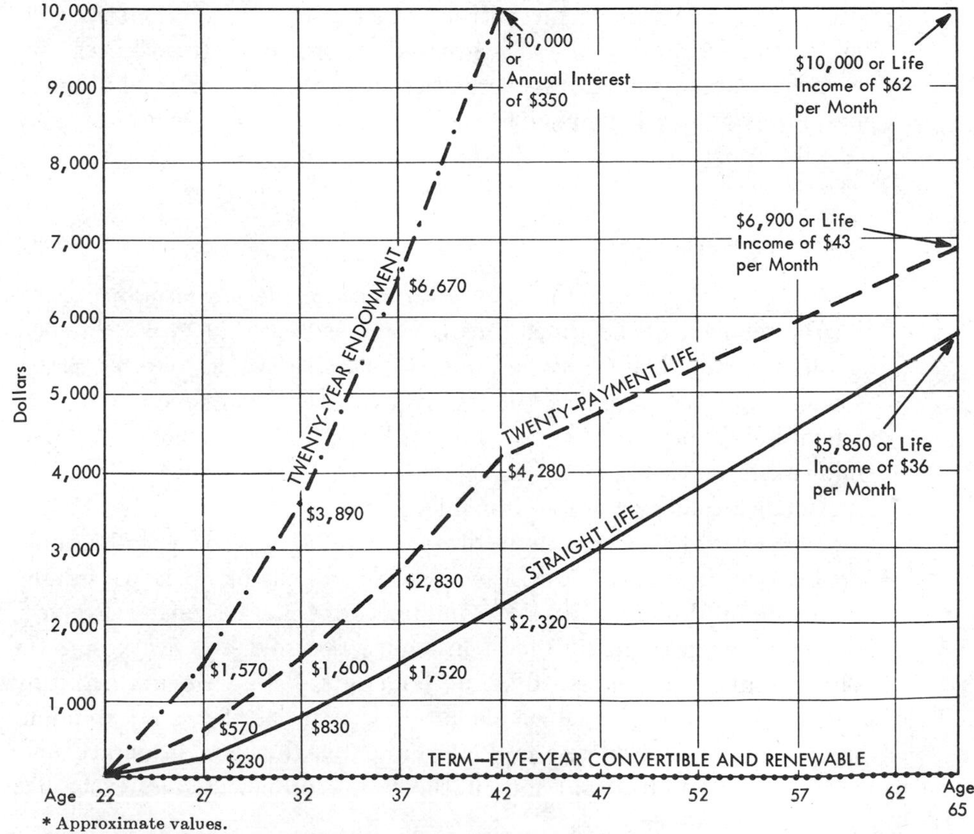

* Approximate values.
Source: Institute of Life Insurance.

mail you a form on which to indicate your choice of nonforfeiture options.

4. Discuss Your Insurance Program with Your Family or Other Beneficiaries. It is usually advisable to have them share in the planning from the outset and to discuss with them each addition to or change in the program. It is a good idea also to leave a letter outlining your insurance policies and indicating any choices the beneficiary may have in the settlement of the policies. It may be well to point out (*a*) that no outside assistance is needed in order to collect the insurance money and (*b*) that your life insurance agent will help your beneficiary fill out the "proof of claim" papers and assist in selecting a settlement option if the choice is left to the beneficiary.

5. Review Your Insurance Program Periodically. We live in a changing world. A program for insurance which is sensible for any of us when we are 20 years old may no longer fit our needs when we are age 40 and may be ridiculous when we are 60 years of age. Inflation is diminishing the value of your coverage, which should be increased an equal amount to offset the loss. Consequently, the wise person will review his insurance periodically, perhaps every 5 or 10 years, and consider its adequacy, not only alone but in connection with his other assets and the persons who look to him for protection. Able insurance agents, bank trust officers, investment counsel, and attorneys are often helpful in assisting the ordinary person to rearrange a complete financial program so that it will reasonably meet the apparent needs.

Government Insurance

During World War I, the U.S. government made life insurance available for members of the armed forces. Veterans of World War I, in good health, may still obtain it (total limit $10,000). Known as "United States Government Life Insurance," it was issued as five year renewable term, straight life, 20 payment life, 30 payment life, 20 year endowment, 30 year endowment, and endowment at age 62.

Insurance sold by the government to soldiers in World War II and those who served thereafter up until April 25, 1951, is known as "National Service Life Insurance." NSLI was issued to eligible persons in any amount from $1,000 to $10,000 in multiples of $500. Originally, five year level premium participating term insurance was sold. All five year term policies applied for and issued before January 1, 1946, were automatically extended for an additional period of three years at the same premium rates by an act of Congress in 1945. Presently, the term insurance may be renewed prior to expiration of the term, for new terms, every five years, without a physical examination, at the premium rate for the then attained age. It may also be converted into any one of six permanent plans: ordinary life, 30 payment life, 20 payment life, 20 year endowment, endowment at age 60, or endowment at age 65.

NSLI insurance was one of the best insurance buys ever offered, and those who have it should retain it. The cost was and is very low, for a variety of reasons. There was no loading charge, that is, the government paid the costs of the insurance operation out of budgetary funds, with no charge by way of premiums. Veterans who died in service, or later, as a result of service connected disabilities, had death benefits paid from government appropriations rather than from insurance reserves. Dividends have been very generous. It has been reported that 67 cents has been paid out in dividends for every dollar collected in National Service Life Insurance premiums. The dividend windfall resulted primarily because fewer World War II veterans died than experience had indicated. There are many favorable clauses and features, as, for example, settlement option No. 4, refund life income, which, for the NSLI low rate, no commercial insurance company can match. The advantage of refund life income is that not only may the beneficiary choose to receive the proceeds of the policy in monthly installments as long as he or she lives but if, upon his or her death, the amount paid out in these monthly installments has not equaled the face amount of the policy, the remainder is paid to the contingent beneficiary.

Veterans of the Korean conflict, that is, all those called to active duty for 31 days or more on and after June 27, 1950, as well as those who served after the war, until January 1, 1957, were treated differently under the Servicemen's Indemnity and Insurance Acts of 1951, which became effective April 25, 1951. They were automatically covered by a free indemnity against death in active service for $10,000, less any NSLI or USGLI in force at time of death. This free indemnity protection, at no charge to the servicemen, continued for 120 days after separation from service. The insurance was payable only to surviving spouse, child or children, parent, brother, or sister; and the insured could name one or more beneficiaries within this permitted class. The $10,000 indemnity was payable in 120 equal installments of $92.90 per month.

Within 120 days after they were released from active service, but before January 1, 1957, veterans who were *not disabled* could apply for a five year level premium term policy that could be renewed every five years at the premium rate for the then attained age. This insurance was at first not convertible to any other form of government life insurance, nor did it pay dividends. No physical examination was needed to obtain it, only payment of the first premium. A veteran was allowed to take out from $1,000 to $10,000 of this term insurance, less any other government life insurance in force at the time of application. In 1958 the law was changed to permit conversion to any of a variety of permanent plans.

Servicemen's Group Life Insurance (SGLI), first offered in 1965, is group life insurance originally intended to cover servicemen going into a combat zone who would otherwise be limited to commercial policies with war exclusion clauses. It is term insurance with no cash surrender values.

The SGLI program is supervised by the Veterans Administration, but it is operated under an arrangement with nearly 600 commercial insurance companies. Unless refusal to join is submitted in writing, all members of the uniformed services are automatically insured for $20,000, for which $3.40 a month is deducted from their pay. While still on active duty, one had the right to convert to an individual commercial policy up to within 120 days after separation without regard to physical condition.[14] The advantage of conversion is especially desirable for the service disabled veteran who might otherwise have difficulty in getting commercial insurance at standard rates.

A veteran separated after August 1, 1974 is automatically covered by SGLI but he must make application and pay the first premium before 120 days have passed. SGLI is the "insurance company" for the next five years, after which, the group policy can be converted into an individual policy with any company then participating in the SGLI program.[15]

Insurance and Inflation

Life insurance is particularly vulnerable to inflation due both to its fixed dollar and lengthy contracts. This has tended to more than double the purchase of term policies and motivate the idea of variable insurance policies.

Variable life insurance offers a death benefit based on a guaranteed minimum that would rise and fall depending on the result of the investment of its premiums in the stock market. Naturally it would cost more. If a 35 year old man is now paying $200 a year for $10,000 of conventional life, the variable policy would cost $220, which could have bought $11,000 of conventional coverage. In deciding upon the variable policy he would be gambling on the state of the market at the time of his death.

[14] For further information, write Office of Servicemen's Group Life Insurance, 212 Washington Street, Newark, N.J. 07102. See also *Federal Benefits for Veterans and Dependents*, Veterans Administration Information Service, latest edition, Washington, D.C.

[15] Veteran Insurance Act of 1974.

Additional costs would result from the considerable expense of the administrative detail for annuity accounts requiring daily evaluation and computation of the unit value. Sample variable policies have been approved by almost half of the state regulatory agencies, and almost all have accepted it either by statute, regulation, or clearance of contract.

The SEC requires registration of variable insurance contracts prior to sale. Since they bear an investment risk they must fulfill the disclosure requirements of financial information as is the case with common stock and mutual funds. The pertinent disclosure would cover "the nature of the risk borne by the contract holder and a clear discussion of such costs as sales charges, administrative and mortality charges, risk charges and management fees." Agents selling variable contracts must register as securities representatives. But sales commissions on life insurance are regulated by the states and are quite large in contrast to the limitation placed on a mutual fund salesman.

Another of the ways in which insurance companies have sought to protect themselves against inflationary hazards was either to acquire a mutual fund, affiliate with one, or start one. Over 150 life insurance companies sell mutual funds or variable annuities. To meet the Securities and Exchange Commission's approval, insurance companies have set up separate accounts for their variable annuity pension plans. Both large and small companies are now involved in variable annuity plans which may provide differing income payments varying with the current value of the investments on which the annuity is based or may be a combination of both fixed and variable types under one contract.[16] Group annuities issued under insured pension plans remain the largest and fastest growing area.

Conclusion

Although you now understand the basic differences in kinds of policies, you have found not only that there are variations within variations in different companies but that there are many methods of evaluating costs.

In addition to cost comparisons, other factors to consider are: premiums vis à vis your budget, estimated dividends in participating policies, and options that suit your individual needs.

Life insurance, with its triple purpose of replacing income, meeting emergencies, or supplementing income on retirement serves best when a particular plan fits your particular needs and goals and offers some protection for an uncertain future.

---

[16] See Chapter 9 for a discussion of fixed and variable annuities.

SUGGESTED READINGS

1. R. Wilfred Kelsey and Arthur C. Daniels, *Handbook of Life Insurance*. New York: Institute of Life Insurance, latest edition. A free copy may be obtained by writing to the Institute at 277 Park Ave., New York, N.Y. 10017.
2. *Life Insurance Fact Book*. New York: Institute of Life Insurance, latest annual number. A free copy may be obtained by writing to the Institute at 277 Park Ave., New York, N.Y. 10017.
3. *Decade of Decision*, a life and health insurance primer for college students. New York: Institute of Life Insurance. A free copy may be obtained by writing to the Institute.
4. *Facts You Should Know about Life Insurance*. Write Educational Division, National Better Business Bureau, 1107 Seventeenth St., N.W., Washington, D.C. 20036, for latest edition.
5. *What's in Your Life Insurance Policy?* New York: Institute of Life Insurance, latest edition. A free copy may be obtained by writing to the Institute.
6. *How Much and What Kind of Life Insurance Should I Own?* Connecticut Mutual Life Insurance Co. Hartford, Conn. 06115. A free copy may be obtained by writing to the company. Also A *Buyer's Guide to Individual Life Insurance*.
7. William J. Sheppard, *A Shopper's Guide to Resolving Insurance Complaints*, Pennsylvania Insurance Department, Harrisburg, Pennsylvania 17120 (free, mail a self-addressed large envelope with 20 cents postage affixed).
8. *Federal Benefits for Veterans and Dependents*, Veterans Administration Information Service, free booklet, 66 pages, latest edition. Write any regional office of the Veterans Administration.
9. *A Shopper's Guide to Term Life Insurance* and *A Shopper's Guide to Straight Life Insurance*, Pennsylvania Insurance Department, Harrisburg, Pennsylvania 17120 (free, postage required).
10. *In Changing Times, The Kiplinger Magazine*

    "New Kind of Life Insurance Policy," January 1975.

    "Sizing up the Agent Who Sells You Life Insurance," October 1974.

    "They're Selling College Kids Bad Buys in Insurance," March 1974.

    "A Young Family's Best Bet in Life Insurance," November 1973.

    "What Kind of Life Insurance Should You Buy?" September, 1971.

    "Life Insurance—Now You Can Spot the Low Cost Policies," March, 1971.

    "How Much Life Insurance Do You Need?," January 1972.

    "How Should Your Life Insurance Pay Off? May, 1970.

    "When is Term Insurance the Best Buy?" March, 1970.

"Six Fine Points to Check in Your Life Insurance Policy," July 1973.
"Buy Life Insurance That Pays Dividends," May 1972.

11. *A Date with Your Future-Money Management for the Young Adult.* New York: Institute of Life Insurance, Educational Division, 1971.
12. Virginia B. Puder, "The Revolution in Life Insurance," *Financial Analysts Journal,* July–August 1970.
13. Joseph M. Belth, "*Life Insurance—A Consumer's Handbook.*" Indiana University Press, 1973.
14. Jeffrey O'Connell, "Living with Life Insurance," *New York Times Sunday Magazine,* June 2, 1974.
15. In *Money*
    Jeremy Main, "How Much Life Insurance Is Enough?" January 1974.
    "Who Needs Straight Life Insurance," June 1973.
16. E. Scott Maynes and Loren V. Geistfeld, "The Life Insurance Deficit of American Families:" A Pilot Study *The Journal of Consumer Affairs,* Summer 1974, pp. 37–60.

CASE PROBLEMS

1. Sally and Charles Donaldson, 30 and 32 years old respectively, are working for the same concern. Together, they earn about $19,000 per year after taxes, but Charles has chronic heart trouble and is frequently ill. They have one child. They have a five year term policy with no conversion clause which expires next year. They also have Blue Cross and Blue Shield coverage. Their employer is now offering group life insurance, and they are wondering if they should take it. What is your advice?

2. Jack Jamison, age 35, is earning $10,000 annually. He and his wife, Mary, have no children. Jack's company provides for early retirement at age 60 on a pension amounting to about one half of average salary for the prior 10 years, and he plans to take advantage of this opportunity. With this in mind Jack decides to purchase a $20,000, 20 payment life insurance policy? Is he wise?

3. Martin Skoler is 25 years old. He lives with his widowed mother and is just about to set up a law practice. Martin's mother is self-supporting and her home is paid for. Now he is thinking of buying some life insurance and is trying to decide which kind would be best for him. What would you suggest?

4. Mildred Becker is a 40 year old accountant with an income of $25,000 a year. She is married and has four children ranging from 3 to 10 years old. She already carries a $10,000 straight life insurance policy and would now like to take out enough insurance to protect her family until the youngest child reaches 21. What insurance program would you suggest for her?

5. While the family was growing up, James Colson and his wife paid premiums on $20,000 of endowment insurance, which has matured, and on

$30,000 of straight life insurance, with annual premiums of $600. The children are now grown up and prosperous. James's wife has just died. He is 67 years old, is worth $80,000, and wonders what to do about the straight life insurance. What would you advise?

6. Grace Robinson (age 26) is a kindergarten teacher. She is single; her father, mother, and two older brothers are living. An agent tries to sell her $5,000 of 5-year term insurance. Should she buy it? Explain.

7. John Sullivan (wife and two children, ages 6 and 9) has a $20,000 term policy which is expiring. It is convertible into straight life (cost, $18 per $1,000) or endowment (cost, $40 per $1,000). The family has been able to save little. They have had difficulty paying the premium on the term policy. What should John do?

8. Peter Quirk's job pays well ($200 a week), but it is not steady. Sometimes he is out of work for three months at a time. He has a wife and three small children (ages 2, 4, and 5). As long as he has work, the family feels that it can spend about $250 a year for insurance. The agent tells him he ought to buy a $10,000 straight life policy. Do you agree?

9. Joseph, Patrick, and Michael are three brothers. Joseph took out a $10,000 term policy. Patrick bought a $10,000 straight life policy. Michael bought a $10,000 10 year endowment policy. Three years later they were all killed in one automobile accident. Each left a wife and two small children; their other assets were negligible. What did each policy do for the family involved?

10. Jack Gunnison is 22 years old. He and his wife have decided to take out a $10,000 straight life policy on him. The cost is $11.22 annually per $1,000 of insurance. After necessary expenses of running the home, they have $400 left over each year for other things. They are expecting a baby. Gunnison is strong and healthy and drives a truck for a living. The agent advises them to take a 20 payment life policy which will cost $10 extra per $1,000 per annum. What are the arguments pro and con? Do you think the limited payment life policy is preferable in their case?

11. Lawrence and Martha Washington have three children (ages 4, 6, and 7). They own their home and have sufficient insurance for current protection and old age. Their principal worry is concerned with their children's education. An agent tries to sell them a $10,000, 10 year endowment policy on each of the children. Would that be a good policy to buy?

12. Ronald Smithers (two children, ages 19 and 23) works for the Jonas Corporation. He and his wife think that, with $20,000 of straight life insurance, they have enough insurance. What they have costs $224 a year, which seems to be large in relation to what he earns ($110 a week). The Jonas Company offers Smithers a group participation of $4,000 of insurance for 60 cents per

month per $1,000. Smithers is 50 years old, and his health is beginning to fail. Should he take the group insurance?

13. Frank Jackson (age 57) has paid his premiums faithfully on his straight life policy for 30 years. Now he is in ill health and has retired. His company has pensioned him, and the pension is just enough to support him and his wife. They live in a rented apartment. He can no longer afford to pay the insurance premiums. What should he do?

9

Social Security, Annuities, and Pensions

The essence of social insurance is bringing the magic of averages to the rescue of the millions.

Winston Churchill

SOCIAL SECURITY

YOUR LITTLE white and blue social security card represents a combination of retirement pension, life insurance, and disability protection which may be worth more than $100,000 to you and your dependents.

Johnnie Wilson, 25, of Okmulgee, Oklahoma, was an operator of heavy equipment with a highway construction crew. Recently, the young father of two children was paralyzed when he injured his back in an automobile accident.

While Johnnie is undergoing a program of therapy at the Okmulgee Rehabilitation Center—a treatment that will last at least two years—he and his family will receive over $400 a month in social security payments as part of the social security disability insurance benefits program. Most people believe that social security is something that only "old" people need think about, but that is not true for 25 year old Johnnie Wilson, who said, "Without social security, I don't know what I would have done."[1]

Richard A. Harder of Bay Port, Michigan, has the rare distinction at 17 to receive a monthly check for $64 as a disability payment based on

---

[1] Social Security Administration, Office of Public Affairs, Press Office, Baltimore, Md., April, 1971. (Although social security records are confidential, persons mentioned gave permission to be quoted.)

his own work credit. He had worked on construction in 1967, 1968, and 1969 and had earned the six quarters of coverage required, while at school, so that when his routine high school TB checkup disclosed that he needed medical care, he was hospitalized, continued his schooling in the hospital, and graduated with his class, all the while receiving his monthly check until he recovered.

Thanks to social security, Mrs. Betty Stiltner, a bride of one year, and a daughter born two months after the tragic death of the 21 year old father in a car accident, will be assured a monthly income, because the young husband had worked for several years under social security. Checks will come until the child becomes 22 years old and if it is at school full time.[2]

Captain Riley Leroy Pitts, the first black American officer to receive the Medal of Honor, left a young widow with two small children. Social security could not bring back the husband and father lost in Vietnam, but it could make living easier for the survivors. The $425 a month that will come until the youngest child finishes college will amount to over $80,000.[3]

Student Benefits

You are mistaken if you think of Social Security only as retirement insurance for the far distant future. Today 95 out of 100 children under 18 and their mothers can count on monthly cash benefits if the working father dies. The families of the disabled worker are also covered—and such unmarried children up to age 22 can collect benefits based on a parent's (in some cases grandparent's) earnings. Medicare now goes to people who have been getting social security disability benefits for two years, regardless of age. Wives, husbands, or children of an insured person of whatever age as well as the insured person, are eligible for dialysis treatment or kidney transplant.

If you are between 18 and 22, you are eligible for social security payments if one of your parents gets social security disability or retirement benefits and you are unmarried and a full time student at an educational institution. You are also eligible if you are disabled. If you were over 18 when a parent died and you fulfill the previously stated requirements, you can receive benefits as a student until you are 22.

If you attend college but have not completed the requirements for a bachelor's degree, your checks can continue until the end of the semester

[2] The *Gallipolis Tribune*, Gallipolis, Ohio, February 7, 1971.

[3] Social Security Administration Reports.

or quarter in which you become 22. If you attend a trade or vocational school, your checks can continue until you complete your course or for two months after the month you reach 22, whichever comes first.

Your checks will stop earlier if you marry, stop attending school, or reduce your attendance below full time.

Who Is a Full Time Student? Under the social security law, you're a full time student if you attend a university, college, or junior college in the United States and the college considers you to be in full time attendance according to its standards for day students.

If you attend high school or trade or vocational school, you're a full time student if: (*a*) you're considered in full time attendance by the school; (*b*) you're enrolled in a course of study lasting at least 13 weeks; and (*c*) you're enrolled for at least 20 hours a week.

You're not eligible for student benefits if you are paid by an employer to attend school because he asked or required you to do so.

Benefits are payable to either the student, parent, or a legal representative if the student agrees. Benefit payments are made during a vacation period of not more than four months providing you are a full time student at the end of that time. If you are working as well as studying, your annual earnings must not exceed $2,520. If they do, you lose $1 for every $2 you earn. If your benefit payments depend on your parent, his or her earnings above $2,520 will affect you.

If you are a student who became eligible after you were 18, you must apply. Benefits do not come automatically. Even if you apply late, you can receive payments retroactively for as many as 12 months.[4]

About 600,000 young Americans are receiving in excess of $500 million annually from social security—more than from all the scholarship funds made available by colleges and universities.

If you were told that you had inherited $116,815—free from income and estate taxes—you would be interested, wouldn't you? You would want to know more about it. Well, social security can yield this amount and more. How?

If the father of two children, one 14 and the other 11, dies after having paid social security taxes on an average of $6,100 in salary annually in covered employment:

a. His widow will receive a lump sum death payment of $255.
b. His two children and their mother will receive payments of $554.60 a month until the 14 year old reaches 18. Over a four year period, this will amount to $26,620.80.

---

[4] *Social Security Checks for Students 18–22*, Social Security Administration, Publication No. SSA–10048.

c. His younger child and the mother will then receive benefit payments of $454.60 a month until the second child reaches 18. This will amount to $38,186.40.

The young mother's benefit stops when there is no longer a child eligible for payments. However, she will begin receiving widow's benefits when she reaches age 60. She will then draw $216.70 a month for the rest of her life. Assuming that she lives to age 80, she will receive $52,008, making a grand total of $116,815.20.

As the amounts deducted from paychecks for social security increase over the years, so also will the benefits.

The Social Security Act

Congress first passed the Social Security Act in 1935, but it has been amended a number of times, adding categories of people covered and increasing the amount of individual benefits and the amounts paid in taxes. One out of seven Americans is now receiving social security checks, while nine out of ten workers in the United States are covered.

Only about 22,000 people were entitled to benefit payments for the month of January 1940, when monthly benefits started; about 400 of them, now 95 years or older, have received more than 380 benefit checks each. The first social security check ever issued went to Mrs. Ida M. Fuller, of Brattleboro, Vermont who passed away in 1974 at the age of 98. Her total contribution was less than $22 and, counting the check received in January 1974, her payments totaled $19,685.[5] Today 92 percent of the people over 65 are receiving social security benefits, or could receive them if they were not still working.

Although the Social Security Act covers a wide variety of social insurance, unemployment insurance, public assistance, and health and welfare services, the federal government administers only the old age and survivors insurance and disability insurance programs and our discussion will be confined to this. Under it, those who work in employment or self-employment covered by the law make social security tax contributons during their working years to provide, as a matter of right and not as a matter of need, an income for themselves and their families when earnings cease in old age, and for their families in case of their death. Some 116 million living persons in the United States are fully insured and over 30 million are already receiving monthly benefits. Of those receiving benefits, 19 million are retired workers and their dependents, 7.2 million are survivors of insured workers, nearly 4 million are disabled workers.

---

[5] American Association of Retired Persons *Bulletin,* January 1974.

In 1940 the total personal income of the nation amounted to $78 billion and included income from social security of $35 million or 0.04 percent of total personal income. In 1973 the total personal income was $1.036 trillion and the comparable social security figure was $63.3 billion or 6 percent of the total. Approximately 14 percent of the population is receiving all or part of their income from the Social Security Administration. As you can see from Figure 9–1, the aged in the population have steadily increased in number.

FIGURE 9–1
U.S. Population

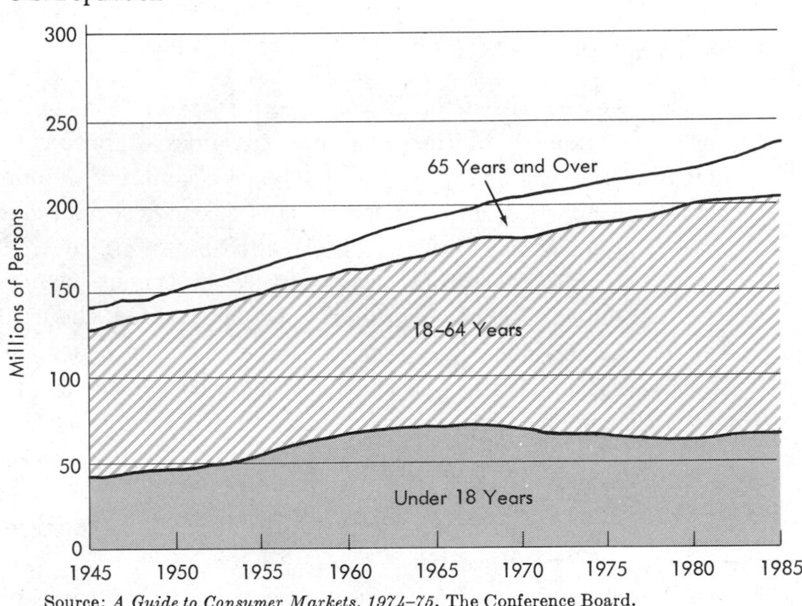

Source: *A Guide to Consumer Markets, 1974–75.* The Conference Board.

Changes in the Law

Many of the amendments to the basic law have been two part: (*a*) an escalation of benefits to match inflation and (*b*) an escalation of the wage base to match rising wage levels. Beginning in January 1975, if the Consumer Price Index (CPI) increases 3 percent or more in the specified base period it will trigger an automatic increase in social security benefits equal to the rise in the cost of living. At that point, the tax base is also raised. A CPI which measures price increases for urban workers would not seem to be the best instrument for measuring a retiree's costs. The needs differ. A retiree spends proportionately more income on food, housing, and medical care including drugs, while an urban worker will spend more on transportation, clothing, education, than the retiree does.

The "across the board" increases in benefits were made to ease the financial problem of today's aged. In 1950 a retired couple found that the average social security benefit met half their budget, but today it meets less than one third. Cost of living increases in rent and food, for the aged, tend to offset the social security increase in the fight to make ends meet.

On the other hand, Figure 9–2 draws the opposite conclusion that bene-

FIGURE 9–2
Average Retirement Benefits (selected years 1950–1973)

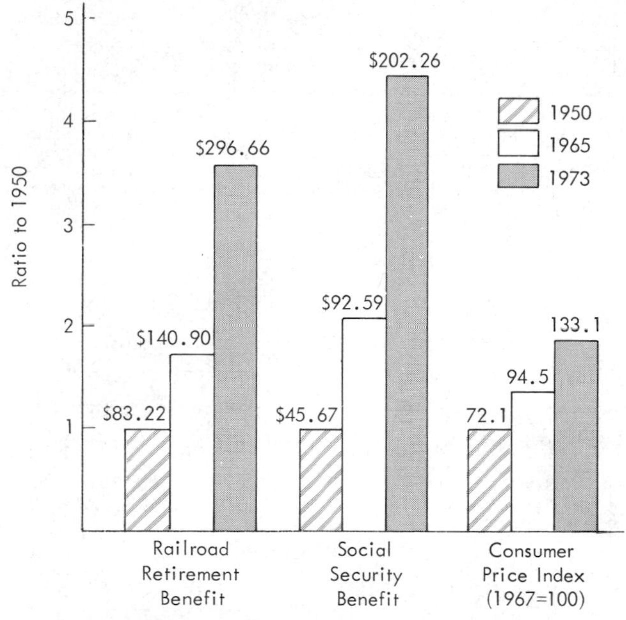

Note: Benefit amounts shown are generally for the third month following the effective date of the amendments. Data for 1973 include the 11 percent increase signed into law on January 3, 1974 of which 7 percent will be effective in March and 4 percent in July.

Source: Data, U.S. Railroad Retirement Board; chart, *Finance Facts*, April 1974, National Consumer Finance Association.

fits have not only kept pace with the cost of living but have increased purchasing power over 1950: by 80 percent for a railroad retirement annuity; by 125 percent for social security.[6] The contradiction can best be explained by your position on the ladder. If you were above average you may have been able to make ends meet; below average you would have difficulty. The across the board increase benefit in social security was partly lost for those who could ill afford the 6.4 percent increase in optional Medicare insurance premiums for doctor's bills.

[6] *Finance Facts,* April 1974.

TABLE 9–1
Benefits for a Worker Retiring at Age 65

Maximum Monthly Benefit		*In Years to Come**	
1940	$ 41.20	1975	$ 330.30
1951	$ 68.50	1980	$ 493.70
1953	$ 85.00	1985	$ 636.30
1955	$ 98.50	1990	$ 810.50
1959	$116.00	1995	$1,037.40
1962	$121.00	2000	$1,376.50
1966	$132.70	2010	$2,366.90
1968	$156.00	2025	$5,114.10
1970	$189.80		
1972	$216.10		
1973	$266.10		
1974	$304.90		

* Benefits will automatically rise with average consumer prices in the U.S., even if Congress votes no further boost in payments. Based on assumptions that inflation will gradually slow to 3 percent by 1978, then hold level at that figure, the maximum benefits that might be paid in future are listed.

Note: Inflation will erode much of the buying power of the increase in benefits.

Source: U.S. Dept. of Health, Education and Welfare as printed in *U.S. News & World Report*, July 15, 1974. Copyright 1974 U.S. News & World Report, Inc.

The new amendments will have the effect of providing in the future more generous maximum benefits to the middle income worker who is now only in the early stages of a working career. For those already a long time in the labor force, the maximum benefits will rarely apply, since their earlier contributions have been at a lower tax rate and on a lower base. This will affect the average earnings on which the computation of benefits is based.

Thus it will be years before a worker can retire at age 65 with average annual earnings of $14,100 (new maximum taxable base earnings effective 1975) to receive a monthly benefit of about $475, because of all the previous years of much lower covered yearly earnings from $3,000–$6,600 (which were effective from 1937 to 1967). The average now is at the most $6,132, with a maximum monthly retirement benefit of $304.90. As an illustration of past reality and future hopes, Table 9–1 lists the changes.

The median annual income for elderly couples last figured in 1972 by the Bureau of Labor Statistics was $5,513. Table 9–2 is a comparative picture of living costs for a retired couple in selected cities and areas in the United States. It shows where living is comparatively easier.

Kinds of Benefits

Broadly speaking, there are now three different kinds of benefits, namely, "retirement" benefits (or what we previously called "living" bene-

TABLE 9–2
Cost of Living for Retired Couple in Selected Cities

	A "Minimum Budget"	*A Moderate Budget*	*A Comfortable Budget*
Northeast			
Boston	$4,208	$6,415	$10,013
Buffalo	$4,089	$5,916	$ 8,708
Hartford	$4,290	$6,170	$ 9,002
Lancaster	$3,680	$5,313	$ 7,693
New York area	$4,220	$6,353	$ 9,557
Philadelphia	$3,701	$5,668	$ 8,433
Pittsburgh	$3,742	$5,446	$ 8,070
Portland	$3,886	$5,625	$ 8,055
North Central			
Cedar Rapids	$3,731	$5,360	$ 8,028
Champaign-Urbana	$3,835	$5,620	$ 8,268
Chicago	$3,743	$5,538	$ 8,288
Cincinnati	$3,563	$5,111	$ 7,463
Cleveland	$3,871	$5,577	$ 8,166
Dayton	$3,671	$5,158	$ 7,709
Detroit	$3,789	$5,484	$ 8,458
Green Bay	$3,620	$5,273	$ 8,054
Indianapolis	$3,845	$5,554	$ 8,178
Kansas City	$3,801	$5,416	$ 8,209
Milwaukee	$3,784	$5,487	$ 8,130
Minneapolis–St. Paul	$3,825	$5,444	$ 7,992
St. Louis	$3,737	$5,375	$ 7,854
Wichita	$3,638	$5,200	$ 7,697
South			
Atlanta	$3,428	$5,005	$ 7,465
Austin	$3,385	$4,914	$ 7,411
Baltimore	$3,662	$5,287	$ 7,841
Baton Rouge	$3,326	$4,788	$ 7,156
Dallas	$3,462	$5,025	$ 7,735
Durham	$3,622	$5,140	$ 7,437
Houston	$3,479	$5,039	$ 7,725
Nashville	$3,605	$5,199	$ 7,688
Orlando	$3,676	$5,055	$ 7,323
Washington, D.C.	$3,937	$5,618	$ 8,289
West			
Anchorage	$5,175	$6,900	$ 9,778
Bakersfield	$3,580	$5,161	$ 7,652
Denver	$3,696	$5,260	$ 7,860
Honolulu	$4,221	$6,038	$ 8,844
Los Angeles area	$3,851	$5,496	$ 8,473
San Diego	$3,733	$5,304	$ 7,994
San Francisco–Oakland	$4,151	$5,919	$ 8,732
Seattle-Everett	$4,072	$5,724	$ 8,325

Source: U.S. Department of Labor, Autumn 1973 prices.

fits), "survivors" (or "death") benefits, and "disability payments." When you become age 62 and retire, you and certain members of your family can become eligible for monthly insurance payments if you are fully insured. After you reach age 72, the payments may be made even if you have not

TABLE 9–3
Types of Payments and How You Must Be Insured for Each

Monthly Payment to	*If You Are*
Retirement:	
You as a retired worker and your wife and child	Fully insured
Your dependent husband 62 or over	Fully insured
Your divorced wife 62 or over and unmarried	Fully insured
You as a retired worker over 72 with fewer than 6 quarters of coverage	Transitionally insured
Your survivors at your death:	
Widow 60 or over	Fully insured
Widow or widower (regardless of age) if caring for your child who is entitled to benefits	Either fully or currently insured
Dependent child	Either fully or currently insured
Dependent widower 62 or over	*Both* fully and currently insured
Dependent parent 62 or over	Fully insured
Dependent divorced wife (regardless of age) if caring for your child who is entitled to benefits	Either fully or currently insured
Lump sum death payment	Either fully or currently insured
Disability:	
You and your dependents if you are totally disabled for work	Fully insured and meet specified work requirements

retired. In the event of your death at any age, certain members of your family may receive insurance payments if you were either fully or currently insured at time of death.

If you become totally disabled and are unable to work, you may become eligible for monthly payments if you have social security credit for at least five years in the 10 year period ending when you become disabled. The different kinds of payments under the three major categories and the ways in which you must be insured for each are shown in Table 9–3. You will notice that you are eligible for retirement benefits only if you are fully insured, whereas most survivors benefits are payable to your family if you are only currently insured.

What is the difference between being fully and currently insured, and how do you become insured?

Becoming Insured

To become eligible for monthly payments for yourself and your family, or for your survivors to get payments in case of your death, you must first have credit for a certain amount of work under social security. Social security credits are called "quarters of coverage." You can get social security credit for up to four quarters in a year. You may have earned social security credit (quarters of coverage) by working in employment covered by the law at any time after 1936 and in self-employment covered by the law after 1950.

Most people who work for someone else get one quarter of coverage fore each calendar quarter in which they are paid total wages of $50 or more, including the cash value of wages in kind.[7] If you receive wages of $14,100 or more during the year, you get credit for all four quarters of that year even if you receive no wages in some of the quarters. If you are self-employed, you get social security credit for four calendar quarters for each taxable year in which you have net profit of $400 or more from self-employment covered by the law. If your net profit is less than $400 for any year, it does not count for social security.

There is no age limit. You get social security credit for work covered by the social security law no matter how young or how old you are. Most jobs, businesses, and professions are now covered by social security. Active duty in military service is also under social security. Your base pay is credited to your social security record. If you should stop working under social security before you have earned sufficient credit to become insured, no benefits will be payable to you. If you should later return to work covered by social security, regardless of your age, both your past earnings and any additional earnings will be combined in determining whether you qualify for benefits.

Fully Insured. For monthly benefits to be payable to you and your wife or husband in your old age, or to your aged widow or widower, or aged dependent parents in case of your death, you must have worked under social security long enough to become "fully insured."

Just how much credit you must have to be fully insured depends upon the year you reach 62, or upon the date of your death or disability if you die or become disabled before reaching that age.

The amount of work a person needs to be covered varies from 1½ years to 10 years, depending on his or her age. Any worker who dies before his 28th birthday is insured with as little as 1½ years of work under social security and death benefits and benefits to qualified survivors will be paid.

A worker is fully insured if he or she has any one of the following:

a. Forty quarters of coverage (10 years) acquired any time after 1936.
b. One quarter of coverage for every four calendar quarters that have elapsed between December 31, 1950, and December 31 of the year

[7] Wages in kind (such as meals or a room) do not count, however, if they are paid for work in private households, on farms, or in the Armed Forces.

prior to the year of death or retirement. Coverage may have been acquired any time after 1936. Minimum required coverage is six quarters.

c. In the case of a worker who attains the age of 21 after 1950, one quarter of coverage for every four calendar quarters that have elapsed between December 31 of the year in which he or she became 21 and December 31 of the year prior to the year of death or attainment of retirement age, with a minimum coverage of six quarters.

The liberalization of coverage in paragraphs (*b*) and (*c*) allowed older people who had not earlier been covered, since they could not otherwise have been able to attain 40 quarters of coverage, to achieve fully insured status.

Currently Insured. You will be currently insured if you have social security credit for at least 1½ years work or six quarters of coverage within the three years before you die or become entitled to retirement benefits.[8]

How to Estimate Your Benefits

The exact amount of old age and survivors or disability insurance benefits payable on your social security account can't be figured until a claim for benefits is made by you upon your retirement, or by your family in case of your death. This is because the benefits must be figured from the record of your earnings right up until the year that you retire or die.

But it's not hard to estimate how much would be payable to you and your dependents if you were now 65 and retired, and also how much would be payable to your family in the event of your death at this time.[9]

Benefits are based on *average* yearly earnings. If your earnings in the future are higher than they have been up to now, your actual benefits may turn out to be higher than this estimate. If your earnings go down or if you are out of work for any long period of time, your actual benefits may be lower.

Old Age Retirement Payments.[10] If you are fully insured, you and certain members of your family can be paid monthly benefits when you are 65 or over (benefits are payable as early as age 62 if the worker is fully

---

[8] See *Your Social Security*, SSA–10035, Social Security Administration, U.S. Department of Health, Education, and Welfare, Washington, D.C.

[9] You may choose to retire between age 62 and 65 and take reduced benefits (see Table 9–4).

[10] *Social Security Benefits—How You Earn Them—How Much Credit You Need*, SSA–10047, Social Security Administration, U.S. Department of Health, Education, and Welfare, Washington, D.C.

insured, but in a reduced amount to take account of the longer period over which benefits will be paid). It is not necessary to stop work completely to get benefits.[11]

The amount of your payments is figured from your average earnings under social security. The more regularly you work under social security and the higher your earnings, the higher your benefits will be.

Most people may figure their average yearly earnings by the following method:

1. Count the number of years to be used in figuring your average earnings as follows:
   If you were born before 1930, start with 1956.
   If you were born after 1929, start with the year you reached 27.
   Count your starting year and each year up until (but not including) the year you reach 62. (If you became disabled or died, the year this occurred would be listed for disability or death benefits.) At least five years of earnings must be used to figure retirement benefits and at least one and a half years to figure disability or survivor benefits.
2. List the amount of your earnings for all years beginning with 1951. (In case of death or disability, earnings in the year of death or the year disability began would be included.) Do not count *more than* \$3,600 for each year 1951 through 1954; \$4,200 for each year 1955 through 1958; \$4,800 for each year 1959 through 1965; \$6,600 for 1966 and 1967; and \$7,800 for 1968 through 1971; \$9,000 for 1972; \$10,800 for 1973, \$13,200 for 1974, and \$14,100 for 1975.
3. Cross off your list the years of lowest earnings until the number remaining is the same as your answer to step 1. (It may be necessary to leave years in which you had no earnings on your list.)
4. Add up the earnings for the years left on your list, and divide by the number of years you used (your answer to step 1).

The result is your average yearly earnings covered by social security over this period. Look at Table 9–4 and estimate your benefit from the examples given there.

Within two years, it is expected that all benefits will be paid into bank accounts electronically, without a check written or a long bank line to wait on for cashing. Instead of mailing checks (with the danger

---

[11] *You Can Work and Still Get Social Security Benefits*, SSA–10092, Social Security Administration, U.S. Department of Health, Education, and Welfare, Washington, D.C. There is strong pressure to remove the earnings limitation on those drawing benefits at ages under 72, as it has been for those over 72.

TABLE 9–4
Examples of Monthly Social Security Payments

	Average Yearly Earnings Since 1950*									
Benefits Can Be Paid to	*$923 or Less*	*$3,000*	*$3,500*	*$4,000*	*$5,000*	*$6,000*	*$7,000*	*$8,000*	*$9,000*	*$10,000*
The worker										
Retired at 65 / Under 65 and disabled	93.80	194.10	210.40	228.50	264.90	299.40	335.50	372.20	393.50	412.40
Retired at 62	75.10	155.30	168.40	182.80	212.00	239.60	268.40	297.80	314.80	330.00
Wife of worker										
At 65	46.90	97.10	105.20	114.30	132.50	149.70	167.80	186.10	196.80	206.20
At 62, with no child	35.20	72.90	78.90	85.80	99.40	112.30	125.90	139.60	147.60	154.70
Under 65 and one child in her care	47.00	102.70	130.90	162.00	224.00	249.90	262.40	279.20	295.20	309.40
Widow of worker										
At 65 (if worker never received reduced retirement benefits)	93.80	194.10	210.40	228.50	264.90	299.40	335.50	372.20	393.50	412.40
At 60 (if sole survivor)	74.90	138.80	150.50	163.40	189.50	214.10	239.90	266.20	281.40	294.90
At 50 and disabled (if sole survivor)	56.80	97.10	105.30	114.30	132.60	149.80	167.80	186.20	196.80	206.30
Widowed parent and one child	140.80	291.20	315.60	342.80	397.40	449.20	503.40	558.40	590.40	618.60
Maximum family payment	140.80	296.80	341.30	390.50	488.90	549.30	597.90	651.40	688.70	721.80

* Generally, average earnings are figured over the period from 1951 until the worker reaches retirement age, becomes disabled, or dies. Up to 5 years of low earnings or no earnings can be excluded. The maximum earnings creditable for social security are $3,600 for 1951–1954; $4,200 for 1955–1958; $4,800 for 1959–1965; and $6,600 for 1966–1967. The maximum creditable in 1968–1971 is $7,800 and, beginning in 1972, $9,000, 1973, $10,800; 1974, $13,200, and 1975, $14,100, but average earnings usually cannot reach this amount until later. Because of this, the benefits shown in the last column on the right generally will not be payable until later. When a person is entitled to more than one benefit, the amount actually payable is limited to the larger of the benefits.

Source: Social Security Administration.

of being lost or stolen) deposits will be recorded on magnetic tape, which will be forwarded to commerical banks or regional collection centers to be processed into accounts without any checks written. Even before that day comes, the Social Security Administration will send your check directly to your bank for deposit if you tell them to do so.

Payments at Varying Ages

Special payments can be made under the social security program to certain people 72 and over who do not qualify for full social security benefits. These payments are intended to assure some regular income for older people who had little or no opportunity to earn social security protection during their working years.

If you decide to start receiving benefits before you are 65, the amount of your monthly benefit will be reduced according to the number of months you are under 65. For example, if you retire at 60 you will receive $247 a month, but if you wait until 65, it becomes $316 a month. A widow of an insured worker may start receiving benefits as early as age 60 if she decides to accept a reduced monthly amount. The closer you are to 65 when you start receiving payments, the smaller the reduction will be. If you elect to retire at age 62 you will receive roughly 80 percent of what you would get if you had waited until age 65 to retire. Are you better off financially retiring at 62 or at 65? It depends, among other things, on how long you expect to live! If you die before 75, you'd come out ahead if you had begun at 62. If you die after 75, you'd probably have been better off waiting until 65 to retire.

Figure 9–3 would indicate that the benefits of retirement programs are adequate to attract increasing numbers. Other reports from business and unions indicate that many would like to retire, but fear of inflation keeps them working another year to add to the pension. Perhaps one could conclude that individual circumstances such as private pensions and extra discretionary income help form the decision.

Family Payments

Monthly payments can be made to certain of your dependents (*a*) when you are receiving old age or disability insurance benefits, or (*b*) when you die.

These dependents are:

a. Unmarried children under 18 years of age or between 18 through 22 if they are full time students.

FIGURE 9–3
More and More Workers Are Retiring Early on Social Security

At start of 1964, 2,600,832 workers had retired on Social Security before age 65—or 25.3 per cent of all retired workers collecting benefits.

At start of 1969, 4,967,975 workers had retired before age 65—or 40 per cent of all retired workers collecting benefits.

At start of 1974, 8,077,366 workers had retired before age 65—more than half, or 52.6 per cent, of all retired workers collecting benefits.

Thus: In the past decade, the number of workers on early retirement under social security has tripled—while the proportion of all retired workers who retired early has doubled.

Data from U.S. Social Security Administration.
Source: *U.S. News & World Report*. Copyright 1974 U.S. News & World Report, Inc.

b. Unmarried children 18 or over who were severely disabled before they reached 18 and have remained so since.

c. A wife, or widower, regardless of age, if caring for a child who is getting payments based on the worker's social security account.[12]

d. A wife 62 or widow 60 or older even if there are no children entitled to payments.

e. A widow 50 or older (or dependent widower) who becomes disabled not later than seven years after the death of the worker or, in the case of a widow, not later than seven years after the end of her entitlement to benefits as a widow with a child in her care.

f. A dependent husband or widower 62 or over.
  1. Dependent widower 60 or over.
  2. Disabled widower 50 or older.

After the death of an insured worker, benefits may *also* be paid to:

g. Dependent parents at 62.

h. A divorced wife, if she is not working and over 62 and had been

[12] The U.S. Supreme Court held that a widow or widower is entitled to "survivor's benefits." March 20, 1975.

married to him for 20 years, or if she has in her care his child who is also entitled to payments.

i. A widower with dependent children.

Before February, 1968, benefits could be paid to children of a deceased mother only if she had worked under social security coverage for at least one and a half years out of the last three years. In 1967 the mother of four—William, age 19; Robert, 15; Jack, 11; and Barbara, 5—died. The father, about to retire from the Air Force on June 30, 1968, checked on social security benefits for his children and found they could collect nothing because his wife had not worked since 1947, when William, her oldest was born, even though she had worked for five years prior to 1947. The law has since been amended to provide the same rules of coverage for all workers, regardless of sex.

If a person becomes entitled to monthly benefits based on the social security account of more than one worker, only one benefit can be received and it will be the larger of the two. For example, a woman who is eligible for benefits based on her own earnings and also for wife's benefits based on the earnings of her husband will receive an amount equal to the larger of the two benefits. She will not receive both.

Working Wives. If a working wife elects benefits on her own earnings record at age 62, before her husband retires, she has reduced her pension for life. She may later qualify as a wife, on her husband's earnings—if she desires. If she has never worked, she qualifies on her husband's earnings. The working wife who has contributed to social security during her working life has gained no advantage for that contribution over the non-working wife who will receive exactly the same benefit from a husband's earnings. A working husband and working wife each paying social security taxes pay more than a man making the same income would pay.

The disability pensions work against the working wife since payments are made only if the worker has coverage for five out of ten years before the disability. Since the working wife may have quit for a while to care for a family, she is handicapped in meeting that requirement.

Housewives are now seeking recognition in dollar terms for services as housekeeper, cook, babysitter, nurse, both for social security retirement and disability insurance. The costs of replacing these varied functions in case of disability, can be ill afforded in most households. The homemaker's real economic contribution is not now part of the GNP unless someone is hired as a replacement while she works at something else. Although housework is difficult to measure, various studies have done so. A Chase Manhattan survey found housewives working 99.6 hours a week at tasks that would cost $235.40 to purchase.[13] *Changing Times* concluded that in a typical family a housewife not employed outside the home does work equal to $5,600 a year, which dips to $3,600 if she works outside the house.[14] If a housewife is considered a home economist, her value in terms of a professional, would increase. If she joins the work force at a later age, after her children are older, still another disadvantage for her will be the low salary base which will prevent her from qualifying for a significant social security benefit.

Lump Sum Death Payment

After your death, in addition to regular monthly survivor payments to your spouse and children under age 18, a lump sum of three times the amount of your monthly benefit may be paid to your widow or widower if you were living together. If there is no widow or widower, the person who paid the burial expenses can be repaid up to the amount of the lump sum. The payment may be three times the primary monthly insurance benefit, but not more than $255.

How Social Security Taxes Are Paid

Federal old age and survivors insurance is paid for by a contribution (or tax) on the employee's wages and on the self-employed person's earnings from trade or business. If you are employed, you and your employer will share equally in the tax. If you are self-employed, you pay two thirds as much as the total payment of employee and employer would on the same amount of earnings.

If you are employed, your contribution is deducted from your wages each payday. The employer sends your contribution and a matching contribution to the Internal Revenue Service. Employers of household workers may use a special envelope report. If you are self-employed, you must report your earnings and pay your contribution each year when you file your individual income tax return. As long as you have earnings that are covered by the law, you continue to pay the social security tax regardless of your age. Table 9–5 shows the tax rates and the scheduled increases. For those who pay the maximum, the tax has risen faster than pensions have—from $30 in 1940 to $824.85 in 1975.[15] See Table 9–6.

[13] *Wall Street Journal*, August 7 1973.

[14] *Changing Times*, June 1973, p. 24 and "What a Housewife Is Worth," April 1973.

[15] *Money*, October 1974, p. 35, "The Squeeze Ahead for Social Security," William B. Mead.

TABLE 9–5
Contribution Rate Schedule Payable by Employers and Employees

Year or Period	Percent of Covered Earnings: For Retirement, Survivors, and Disability Insurance	For Hospital Insurance	Total
1973	4.85	1.0	5.85
1974–77	4.95	0.9	5.85
1978–80	4.95	1.1	6.05
1981–85	4.95	1.35	6.30
1986–2010	4.95	1.5	6.45

Source: Social Security Administration.

TABLE 9–6
Social Security Taxes and How They Grow

	Taxes: Maximum Paid by Workers (matched by employers)	Maximum Paid by Self-Employed Persons*
1937–49	$ 30	—
1950	45	—
1951–53	54	$ 81
1954	72	108
1955–56	84	126
1957–58	94.50	141.75
1959	120	180
1960–61	144	216
1962	150	225.60
1963–65	174	259.20
1966	277.20	405.90
1967	290.40	422.40
1968	343.20	499.20
1969–70	374.40	538.20
1971	405.60	585
1972	468	675
1973	631.80	864
1974	772.20	1,042.80
1975	824.85	1,113.90
1980	1,179.75	1,579.50
1990	2,070.45	2,728.50
2000	3,386.25	4,462.50
2011	6,705.00	7,650.00

* Self-employed people were not covered until 1951.

Note: The wage base on which social security taxes are levied, now $13,200 ($14,100 in 1975), will automatically rise with inflation and average wages in U.S., under current law. Payroll tax rate, now 5.85 percent for workers and employees, is set to rise gradually over the years, reaching 7.45 percent by the year 2,011, and to 8.5 percent for self-employed by 1986. Based on assumptions of moderating wage hikes the maximum taxes that might be levied in selected years beginning with 1975 are listed.

Source: Reprinted from *U.S. News and World Report*, Copyright 1974 U.S. News and World Report Inc.

Beginning January 1, 1975, earnings from employment or self-employment up to a total of $14,100 a year are subject to the social security tax.

From the social security tax report, your wages and self-employment income are posted to your individual record by the Social Security Administration. This record of your earnings will be used to determine your eligibility for benefits and the amount you will receive.

Self-Employed

You pay the social security self-employment contribution for each year in which you have self-employment income of $400 up to the amount of income subject to the same limitation which the law sets for earnings (see Table 9–7).[16] In 1951 the maximum self-employment social security tax was $81. By 1975 it had risen to $1,113.90!

TABLE 9–7
Contribution Rate Schedule for Self-Employed People

	Percent of Covered Earnings		
Period	*For Retirement, Survivors, and Disability Insurance*	*For Hospital Insurance*	*Total*
1973	7.0	1.0	8.0
1974–77	7.0	0.9	7.9
1978–80	7.0	1.1	8.1
1981–85	7.0	1.35	8.35
1986–	7.0	1.5	8.5

Source: Social Security Administration.

Special Refunds

Your social security taxes apply only to the first $14,100 of your earnings in any calendar year. If you have more than one employer, each different employer must deduct the tax from the first $14,100 of the wages he pays you in a year. You should keep a record of your employers' names and addresses and of the wages paid by each. If the total tax withheld is more than that required for wages of $14,100 you may claim the excess tax as credit on your income tax return for that year.

---

[16] *Special Information for Self-Employed People*, SSA–10022, Social Security Administration, U.S. Department of Health, Education, and Welfare, Washington, D.C.

Claiming Benefits

Benefit payments, whether retirement, disability, or survivors, monthly or lump sum, are not made automatically. *An application for benefits must be filed before monthly payments or the lump sum can be paid.* The application should be filed promptly. Only 12 months of back payments can be made when an application is filed late; years of payments may be lost. The lump sum may be paid only if an application is filed within two years after the death of an insured person. Benefits payable to a child or to an incompetent adult are usually paid for his use to a parent or near relative. The place to file a claim is the nearest Social Security Administration field office. There you and your family will receive, free of charge, any help you need to make out the claim papers. If, because of sickness or distance, you cannot go to the social security office, you may write or telephone. The local post office or a phone book will furnish the address of the nearest social security office.

Five Times for Action

There are five times when it is especially important to consult the social security office:

If a Worker in Your Family Dies. Some member of the family should inquire promptly at the social security office to learn if survivors insurance benefits are payable.

If You Become Disabled. If you become disabled after you have been in work covered by social security, you should get in touch with your social security office. You and your dependents may be eligible for monthly payments.

When You Are Near Retirement Age. When you approach 65 (62 if not working or working for low earnings), get in touch with your social security district office. Application for benefits may be filed three months in advance of retirement age, but even if you do not plan immediate retirement, you should get information about your social security rights. You need not be completely retired to get social security benefits.

When You Are 72. At age 72 benefits are paid no matter how much is earned. If you work after you start receiving benefits your wages are subject to social security and medicare taxes regardless of your age. A worker who delays retirement until 72 receives a 7 percent increase in benefits (1 percent for each year) but only he—and not his dependents or survivors benefit.

Every Three or Four Years. Check with the Social Security Administration periodically for a record of your earnings. If you wait too long, you lose the chance to correct any error, since there is a 3 year, 3 month, 15 day time limit for any such change. The statement does not show the amount of contributions you or your employer paid except indirectly.

Checking Your Account

Each employer is required by law to give you receipts for the social security taxes deducted from your pay. This must be done at the end of each year and also when you stop working. These receipts will help you check on your social security account because they show not only the amount deducted from your pay but also the wages paid you.

FIGURE 9–4

REQUEST FOR STATEMENT OF EARNINGS

ACCOUNT NUMBER →

DATE OF BIRTH → MONTH | DAY | YEAR

Please send me a statement of the amount of earnings recorded in my social security account.

NAME { MISS / MRS. / MR. ______

STREET & NUMBER ______

CITY & STATE ______ ZIP CODE ______

} Print Name and Address In Ink Or Use Typewriter

SIGN YOUR NAME AS YOU USUALLY WRITE IT ______

Sign your own name only. Under the law, information in your social security record is confidential and anyone who signs someone else's name can be prosecuted.
If your name has been changed from that shown on your social security account number card, please copy your name below exactly as it appears on that card.

Source: Social Security Administration.

You may check your own record as often as once a year by writing to the Social Security Administration, P.O. Box 57, Baltimore, Maryland 21203, and asking for a statement of your account. You can get an addressed postcard form at any field office for use in requesting wage information (see Figure 9–4). It costs 10 cents a page for a copy of your record. Minimum fee is $1, so if your record is less than ten pages it will be free.

If an error has been made in your account, the field office will help you get it corrected. Even though the statement of earnings does not show your contributions or your employers', it will show if your earnings have been reported. If reported, contributions would have to have been made. Your receipts will check both and reveal any error. It's the earnings on which benefits are paid, not on the contributions.[17]

When Payments Stop

When you become entitled to monthly old age or survivors insurance payments, you will receive a check each month unless certain events occur. The law lists some events that will stop the payment of monthly checks for only one or two months or for some longer period, and some that end your right to receive payments. These events are listed below. You must report promptly to the Social Security Administration if any of them happen in your case.

If You Work after Payments Start.[18] If you are under 72 years of age and are receiving monthly payments as a retired worker and you earn more than $2,520 in a year, benefits will be reduced by one half the amount over $2,520. You work throughout a year and earn $3,300 which is $780 above the minimum. Your benefit is normally $150, but deductions of $390 will only be taken against the benefit in those months during which you earned more than $210. Regardless of your total earnings for a year, benefits will be payable for any month in which you neither earn wages of more than $210 nor perform substantial services in self-employment.

The decision as to whether you are performing substantial services in self-employment depends on the amount of time you devote to your business, the kind of services you perform, how your services compare with the services performed in past years, and other circumstances of your particular case.

Earnings from work of any kind, whether or not it is covered by the social security law, must be counted in figuring the amount of benefits due for a year. Total wages (not just take home pay) and all net earnings from self-employment must be added together in figuring up your earnings for the year. However, income from savings, investments, pensions, and insurance does not affect your old age or survivors insurance.

In the year in which you first become entitled to benefits, you must count your total earnings for the entire year in determining the amount of benefits that can be paid to you.

After you reach 72, you can earn any amount and still get payments for the months in which you are 72 or over.

---

[17] See *Your Social Security Earnings Record,* SSA–10044, Social Security Administration, U.S. Department of Health, Education, and Welfare, Washington, D.C.

[18] See *You Can Work and Still Get Social Security Benefits,* SSA–10092.

Investment Income Does Not Affect Benefit Payments. People who don't get benefit checks because their earnings from work are too high sometimes wonder why others, with good incomes from stocks, bonds, or real estate, are nevertheless paid benefits. The reason is that the purpose of the program is to insure against loss of earnings from *work* because of age.

Social security is not intended as a substitute for private savings, pension plans, and insurance protection. It is, rather, intended as a foundation upon which these other forms of protection can be built.

WEDDING CUTS DOWN BENEFITS

PORTLAND, ORE. (AP)—Spencer Armstrong and his bride lost $90 a month in social security benefits when they were married. But, said the 84-year-old Armstrong, the couple won't have it any other way.

"I don't care what anybody does to us, we're not going to live in sin" he declared.

Armstrong and his wife, Beulah, 82, found out this week their combined benefits from social security would be less than when they were single. And now, they said, they won't be able to afford the monthly rent at McKenzie Manor.

Before they were married last April, the two got $412 a month in benefits. Now they get $322 a month, and the rent at the rest home is $408.

What the elderly couple will do next isn't certain, with the single exception: "I never spoke nothing but the truth in my life nor did nothing wrong, not even run a red light," Armstrong said. "And I won't start now."

Source: *Sarasota Herald Tribune*, July 13, 1974.

Events That End Payments. If any person receiving monthly benefit payments as a dependent or as a survivor gets married, the right to payments generally stops if the new spouse is working. An exception is made in the case of the widow who remarries after the age of 60. If she could have qualified for benefits on her deceased husband's record, she may still get benefits. She would receive one-half of her deceased husband's retirement benefit, or (at 62) the amount of the wife's benefit on her husband's record—whichever is larger. The same provision applies to widowers who remarry after 62.

Payments to a wife or dependent husband are ended if a divorce is granted.

A widow under 60, or the wife or divorced wife, under 62, of an insured person may receive payments only while she has in her care a child who is also entitled to monthly payments.

Payments to a child stop when the child marries, unless child is disabled and marries another social security beneficiary.

When a child entitled to benefits reaches age 18, or 22, if a full time student, payments are stopped unless he is disabled. When the child of a deceased insured person is adopted, his payments end unless the adopting person is the child's stepparent, grandparent, aunt, or uncle.

When any person receiving monthly benefits dies, payments are ended. The last payment in such cases is for the month immediately before the month of death.

If a person receiving disability benefits recovers or returns to work, payments (and any payments to dependents) will stop, but not right away—he will be given a chance to test his ability to work and to adjust. If he goes to work despite a severe handicap, benefits will continue to be paid for as long as 12 months. If a beneficiary recovers from a disability, benefits will continue to be paid for three months.

Supplemental Security Income System

This new program for the elderly poor began in January 1974 and helps those whose income does not exceed $227 a month if single; or $315 for a married couple. They must have less than $1,500 (single) $2,250 (couple) in assets and be 65 or older, or blind, or disabled. The program provides $140 a month to meet basic living expenses of a single person and $210 for a couple. These payments replace the joint state–federal programs of public assistance for the aged, blind, or disabled. Owning a home (if the value is not over $25,000) does not disqualify, or a car (valued at not over $1,200) or an insurance policy (depending on value) but other assets will. One can earn a total of $85 a month and still receive payments. These payments come from the general funds of the U.S. Treasury, unlike social security payments. A person may receive both social security and supplemental security income, if eligible. The Social Security Administration will run the program and, in agreements with 36 states, will also determine eligibility for *Medicaid* on behalf of the state.

Military Service

After 1957. Members of the Armed Forces have been covered by social security in the same way as people in civilian employment since January 1, 1957, under the Servicemen's and Veterans' Survivor Benefits Act of 1956. They receive social security credit for their base pay for active duty, and their share of the social security tax is deducted from their base pay, just as the social security tax of civilian workers is deducted from their wages. In addition, for each quarter they receive additional earnings credits of $300. The credits do not appear on their earnings statement but are counted automatically when a claim for benefits is made. Military service since January 1, 1957, appears on the social security earnings record and can be counted toward both military retirement pay and social security benefits.

Before 1957. Since 1950 the Congress has enacted laws giving *free* social security wage credits of $160 for each month of active military service from September 16, 1940, to December 31, 1956. These credits count the same as actual earnings of $160 a month in determining whether a veteran has enough credits for a social security benefit and in figuring the amounts a veteran and family can receive in social security benefits.[19]

If You Become Disabled[20]

If you become disabled before age 65, you may qualify for monthly disability benefits, as if you had reached 65 and your spouse and children are also paid monthly benefits. The time element is very important in applying for disability benefits—too long a delay in making an application may result in your losing benefits. However, benefits are payable retroactively up to 12 months.

How Disabled Must You Be? To be found disabled under the social security law, you must have a condition so severe that, in the words of the law, it makes you unable to "engage in any substantial gainful activity."

Your disability must be expected to last for at least 12 months or be expected to continue for a long and indefinite time. Payments start with the month following the five month waiting period.

How Much Work Is Required? In general, if you have social security credit for at least 5 years in the 10 year period ending when you become disabled, you have enough work to quality for disability insurance benefits —if the disability began at age 31 or later.

If you become disabled before you are 31, you need credit for one and one half years of work in the years before you become disabled, subject to a six quarter minimum. Unmarried disabled persons under the age of

---

[19] See *Social Security for Servicemen and Veterans* SSA–10031, Social Security Administration, U.S. Department of Health, Education, and Welfare, Washington, D.C.

[20] See *If You Become Disabled,* SSA–10029, Social Security Administration, U.S. Department of Health, Education, and Welfare, Washington, D.C. Also, *Disabled? Find out about Social Security Disability Benefits,* SSA–10068.

22 can get payments based on the earnings of a parent or in some cases—a grandparent.

A person whose eyesight is so poor that the law considers him blind no longer needs to have substantial work in recent years to get benefits. It is enough to be "fully insured."

Proof of Your Disability. When you apply for disability insurance benefits, your social security office will give you a medical report form to have filled in by your doctor or by a hospital or clinic where you have had treatment. If your earnings from work are in excess of $200 per month it will ordinarily be deemed to demonstrate your ability to perform substantial gainful activity, and therefore indicates you are not disabled.

The Amount of Your Disability Benefit. The amount of your monthly disability insurance payment is the same as the amount of the old age insurance benefit you would get if you were retired. Figure your average earnings as if you reached 62 at the time you became disabled.

Unfortunately many disabled are further handicapped if they have the private disability insurance which frequently has an offset clause. A disabled worker is granted a fixed monthly benefit from this policy which is in addition to his social security, but every dollar increase in social security benefits causes his private insurance benefits to decrease by a dollar. Offset provisions are currently prohibited in three states—Illinois, Massachusetts, and New York.

Account Number Cards

If you are employed or self-employed in any kind of work covered by the Social Security Act, you must have a social security card. Your card shows your account number, which is used to keep a record of your earnings. You should use the same account number all your life, for the number on your social security card distinguishes your account from the social security accounts of other people who have names similar to or exactly like yours. Both your name and account number are needed to make sure you get full credit for your earnings. Show your card to each employer so that when reporting your wages he may use your name and account number exactly as they appear on the card.

Your nearest social security office used to issue a social security card or a duplicate card to replace one that had been lost. Now all cards and numbers will be issued from the Baltimore headquarters because of the increasing importance of the number. Applicants are prescreened against central files for error or the issuance of more than one number to the same individual. If you have no number, and are going to look for your first job, apply early as there may be delay. If your name has been changed, ask your social security office for a new card showing the same account number and your new name.

Your card is a symbol of your social security account. The benefits payable to you or to your family are figured from the earnings recorded in your social security account.

There is an ever increasing use of the social security number as identification for other purposes, such as income tax, civil service records, as a veterans hospital admission number, and as a military service number. The Social Security Administration repeatedly assures the public this use will not affect the confidential nature of social security records. Programs exist to provide a social security number to children entering school, or to those now at the ninth grade level.

The need for careful identification has intensified because more than 900 employers and the Armed Forces now make social security reports on reels of magnetic tapes prepared by electronic computers. The Social Security Administration's computers then read and record the information directly at tremendous savings without human intervention and the possibility of human transcribing errors. Of course, the original input by the human could have errors—not eliminating the need for checking. There is no escape if you feel overwhelmed by being just a number; the Social Security Administration reports that even the 2,141 Micronesian islands along the equator in the Pacific have started a social security system.

Proof of age is needed to receive the first payment of medicare and social security. The identification number is not sufficient. If you have neither birth nor baptismal certificate, one of the following could be a substitute:

School record.
Federal census record (from the U.S. Census Bureau).
Marriage record.
Employment or union record.
Hospital record.
Birth certificate of a child showing age of a parent.

You must send the actual document, which will be returned. No photocopy is acceptable unless it is certified by the custodian of the record.

For those born abroad, usable documents are a foreign passport, immigration record, or naturalization certificate (all of which are illegal to photocopy).

However, even a dated baptism cup has been accepted as proof.

Social Security and Insurance Programming for Death or Retirement

One insurance broker tries to get families to think about retirement and death by showing a chart entitled "A Financial Forecast for Age 65." "Take 100 men starting out at age 25," he declares; "40 years later, nine out of ten are either dead—or dead broke!" While the figures are not accurate, the chart does get people to stop and think.

Today it is possible to have a skilled insurance agent sit down with you and show you, by simple charts and tables, how to build a considered program, within your resources and capabilities, for family financial security in the event of your untimely death or for your own benefit when retirement is at hand.

Modern insurance programming builds on a social security base and adds to meet felt needs—within the limit of financial capacity, of course. Even those insurance agents who were originally opposed to social security now recognize that it was one of the best things that could have happened to their industry. Why? Simply because without social security the average middle income family could not afford sufficient insurance to provide for essential needs in case of either premature death or retirement. Now, with part of the burden met by social security, it is easier to show the average family that the amount of insurance it requires for meeting minimum needs is, coupled with social security benefits, financially attainable. As a result, insurance is sold more easily—and more intelligently; and, what is most important, the average family is somewhat closer to financial security than it was previously.

In the following pages are presented case studies of four relatively young families with continuing responsibilities for raising children. The insurance programs worked out for them are shown, and the tie-up with social security. Three are from the files of the Institute of Life Insurance, one from TIAA. Were the families a little older or a little better off, annuity programs could be linked with insurance and social security, looking toward comfortable retirement. It should be remembered, however, that it is usually possible to take the cash value of ordinary life insurance at retirement and use it for monthly payments. Also pensions are now coming to play an increasing role in the retirement picture.

Each situation is different, and a program prepared for one family will hardly fit the needs or resources of any other. You can have a plan tailored to your situation, developed by the agent of any good insurance company, who will figure out your social security payments due in the event of death, will show you how to make the best use of your government life insurance, if you have retained it, and then will point out the gaps and indicate how much it would cost to fill them, in whole or in part. You can build a program gradually, as your resources and earning power grow; but if you have a program, you will be able to see where you are going and plan wisely instead of either ignoring your responsibilities or trying to meet them in a hit or miss, illogical way.

FOUR LIFE INSURANCE PROGRAMS WITH A SOCIAL SECURITY BASE

The following are case studies of typical owners of life insurance, and you will be interested to see what these life insurance programs are like. The programs were tailor made by these families with the help of their life insurance agents. They will not fit just anybody. But they will help you to see how families are using life insurance, along with social security,[21] to provide for their financial needs.

The George Kents

George Kent, 31; his wife, Mary, 25; and their three children—Roger, four, Billy, two, and Virginia, one—live in Minneapolis, where George is employed by a public bus line. George earns a weekly salary of $200. This is the total income for the family.

They own $40,000 of life insurance, including two ordinary straight life, and one family plan and group insurance on George available through his employer. Their premiums total about $412.42 a year. Their policies, each on Mr. Kent's life, are as shown in Table 9–8.

Figure 9–5 shows the combined social security and insurance income for the Kent family in the event (*a*) that George Kent dies now (this is shown

TABLE 9–8
George Kent's Life Insurance Policies

Policy Number	*Age at Purchase*	*Amount and Kind*	*Premiums*
1	20	$10,000 whole life	$115.50
2	22*	5,000 whole life family plan	92.40
3	24	10,000 whole life	129.50
4	26	15,000 group life	75.00

* Bought by George's parents and paid for by them until he was 21.

[21] It should be noted that social security payments are now tied by escalation to price level changes and therefore the social security payments shown in the following case example may not reflect anything more than the situation as of mid-1974. Payments at retirement especially are likely to be very different.

FIGURE 9–5
Income Distribution—the Kents' Life Insurance Program

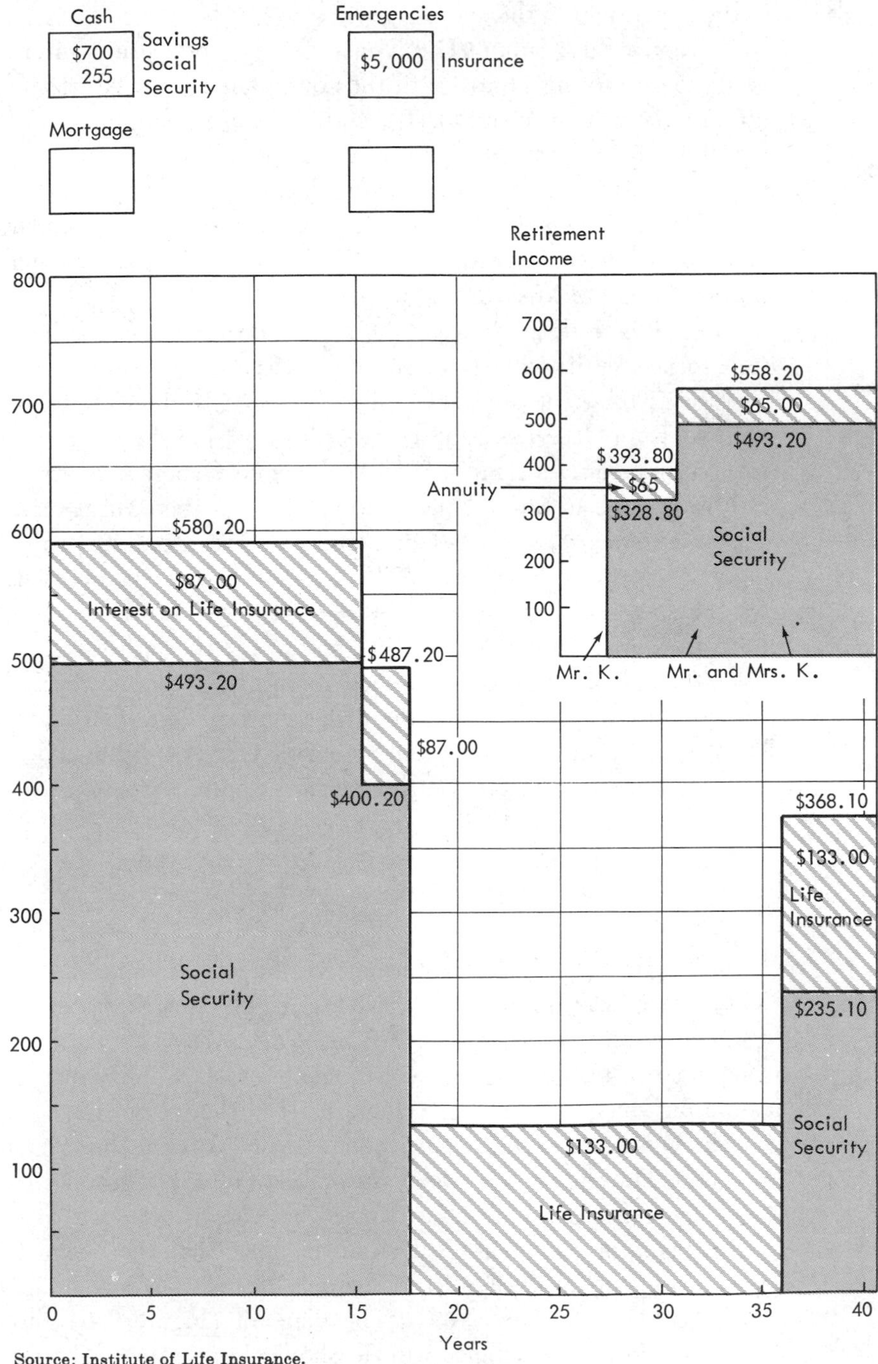

Source: Institute of Life Insurance.

in the lower portion of the diagram) or (*b*) that George Kent lives through a normal retirement period (shown in the retirement income box in the upper right of the diagram).

If George Kent Should Die Now. George's program is intended, first of all, to care for his family until the youngsters are grown. If George dies now, his life insurance and social security will furnish an income of $580.20 monthly until Billy is age 18. Then Mrs. Kent will receive $487.20 monthly until Virginia is 18, when the income drops to $133.00 per month, which is the income from the $35,000 life insurance policies settlement option selected for life by Mrs. Kent. The $133 a month insurance payment will run for the rest of Mrs. Kent's life.

Policy 2 is to be used to pay the bills at the time George dies. In addition, social security will pay a lump sum of $255 at that time.

When Mrs. Kent is 60, she will receive $235.10 monthly for as long as she lives from George's social security plus the $133 she has been receiving from insurance for a total of $368.10. She and George know there will be at least enough to care for the children through the critical years.

At Retirement Time. When George is 65 years old, he can stop working. His social security will pay $328.80 a month; and when his wife reaches 65, this social security income will increase to $493.20 for as long as they both are living. To supplement this, he can use the cash values of his two $10,000 whole life policies to purchase an immediate joint life and survivorship annuity to provide $65 a month as long as either one of them lives. His group life policy expires when he retires. Figure 9–5 thus shows how his life insurance and social security benefits combine to take care of the minimum needs of his family.

The Dawsons

The Dawsons live in California, where Mr. Dawson is a mechanic. They have two children—Jack, who is eight, and Margaret, four. Mr. Dawson is now 32 years old, and his wife is 28. Their annual income amounts to $14,500, but this will probably increase. They own their own home, on which there is a $15,000 mortgage at the present time.

Mr. Dawson has taken particular care in planning his life insurance program. The company he works for does not offer any group life or retirement insurance plan, but he is covered by federal social security.

An inventory of their life insurance shows that they own a total of $47,000 of insurance, all on Mr. Dawson's life, as shown in Table 9–9.

If Mr. Dawson Dies Now. The diagram (Figure 9–6) shows what Mr. Dawson's life insurance will do should he die now. There will be a monthly income of $80 from the life insurance policies left at interest until Margaret is age 18. Added to that will be an income from Mr. Dawson's social security ($602.10 until Jack is age 18 and then dropping to $508.40 until Margaret is 18).[22]

Because the social security income stops when Margaret is 18, Mr. Dawson has arranged for the bulk of his life insurance to provide $84 a month income for Mrs. Dawson for the rest of her life. When Mrs. Dawson is age 60, the social security income will start again and pay her $242.40 a month as long as she lives. Added to that will be $84 a month from his insurance, thus increasing her monthly income to $326.40.

TABLE 9–9
John Dawson's Life Insurance Policies

Policy Number	*Taken at Age*	*Amount and Kind*	*Annual Premium*
1	20	$ 2,000 straight life	$ 31.10
2	22	15,000 straight life	168.30
3	26	5,000 straight life	70.80
4	28	10,000 term to 65	85.90
5	29	15,000 reducing term	52.10

Policy 5 is a $15,000 reducing term policy purchased to pay off the mortgage. As Mr. Dawson's income increases, he can convert the $10,000 term to 65 to an ordinary policy adding to his permanent life insurance program. This will give him a total of $32,000 in permanent life insurance. Policy 1 plus a $255 lump sum from social security will be used to pay Mr. Dawson's final expenses.

At Retirement Time. Chances are that Mr. Dawson will live to see his children grown and with families of their own. Then this program will provide a retirement income for him and his wife. At age 65 his policies will have a total cash value of about $16,840. Mr. Dawson will continue about $2,000 of his insurance. The cash values of the balance will be used to purchase an immediate joint and survivor annuity for retirement. This will be sufficient to pay them a monthly income of $90 for as long as they both are living. From Mr. Dawson's social security there will be an income of $338.90. When they both are 65, the income from social security will be $508.40 a month. Thus, for the first three years of his retirement, he will have a combined (insurance plus social security) monthly income of $428.90, and thereafter it will rise to $598.40.

---

[22] If Margaret is a full time student to 22, her own benefit will be $254.20 per month.

FIGURE 9–6
Income Distribution—the Dawsons' Life Insurance Program

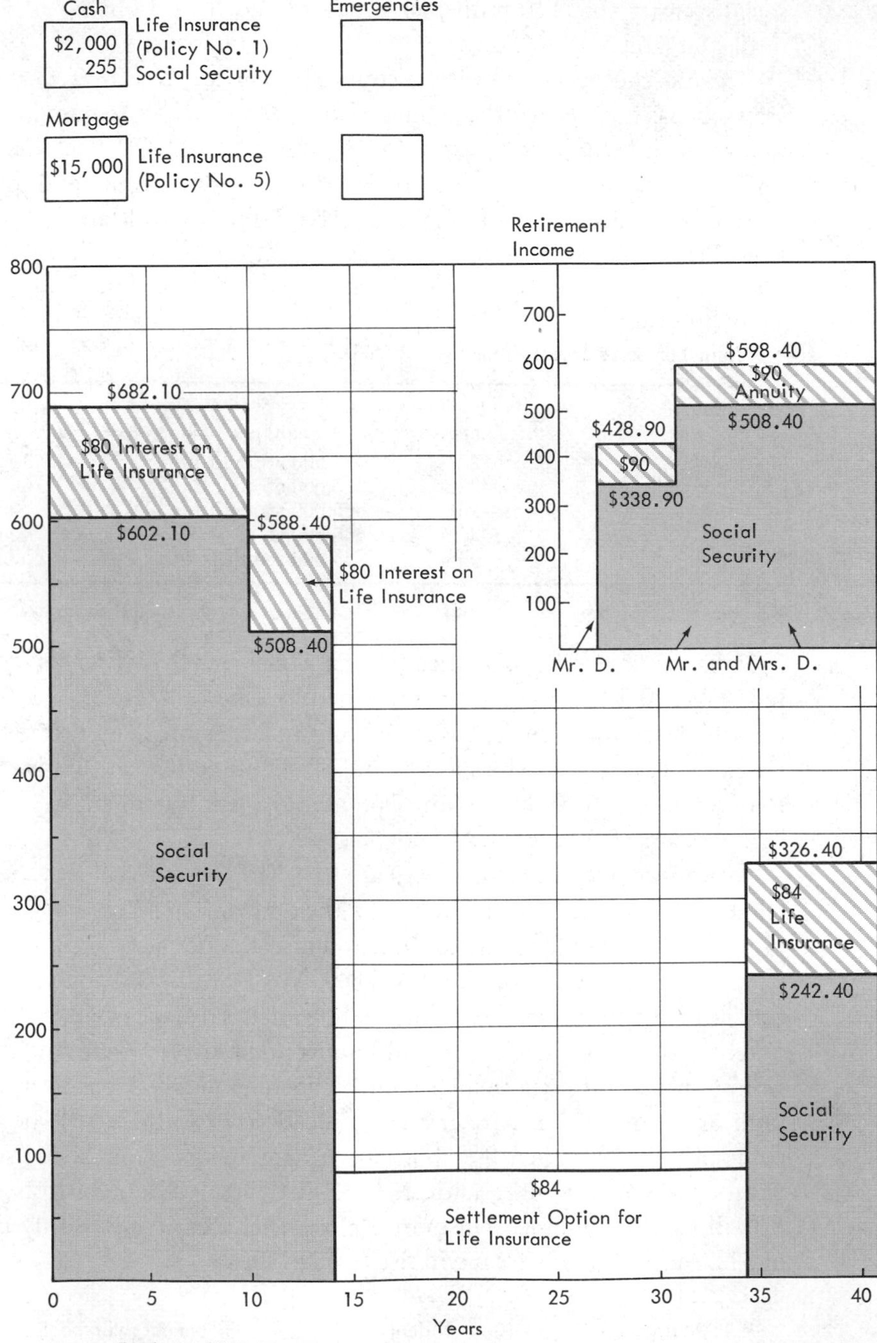

Source: Institute of Life Insurance.

The Crawfords

Bill Crawford is age 32. He and his wife Jean, age 28, have a little boy, four years old. Bill works as a pharmacist and earns $14,800 a year. He is covered by social security, and he owns his own home, which has only a small mortgage.

The Crawfords' resources are the home which cost $35,000 and is worth more now; five life insurance policies totaling $54,000, and $825 in savings in the bank and $650 in government bonds. Their life insurance policies are shown in Table 9–10.

TABLE 9–10
Bill Crawford's Life Insurance Policies

Policy Number	*Taken at Age*	*Amount and Kind*	*Annual Premiums*	*Retirement Values at age 65*
1.	20	$ 2,000 straight life	$ 31.10	$1,182 or $7.40 a month for life
2.	24	$20,000 5 year renewable and convertible term*	68.30	$10,680 or $70.70 a month for life
3.	25	$10,000 30 payment life	170.30	$6,900 or $43 a month for life
4.	26	$10,000 straight life family income ($100)	178.95	$5,690 or $35 a month for life
5.	30	$12,000 straight life	185.80	$6,612 or $41 a month for life

* Converted at age 33 to straight life.

Use of Resources if Bill Should Die. Figure 9–7 shows what would happen. There would be $2,255 cash, consisting of $2,000 from life insurance and $255 from social security. This would take care of the funeral and other last expenses. The $1,475 in savings and bonds would remain for subsequent emergencies. As may be seen in the diagram, Mrs. Crawford would receive $740.66 a month until Bill, Jr., is 18, ($549 from social security and $91.66 from interest on life insurance plus $100 from family income). Although her social security benefit stops at this time, she will continue to receive $100 from the family income benefit until Bill, Jr., is 20. One $10,000 policy will be used to pay Bill, Jr.'s, college expenses. The proceeds of the other policies will be used to purchase a monthly income of $171 for Mrs. Crawford for life. This will supplement her salary if she goes to work and her social security benefit when she decides to retire. Her combined income on retirement will be $432.70 ($261.70 from social security and $171 from life insurance).

FIGURE 9–7
Income Distribution—the Crawfords' Life Insurance Program

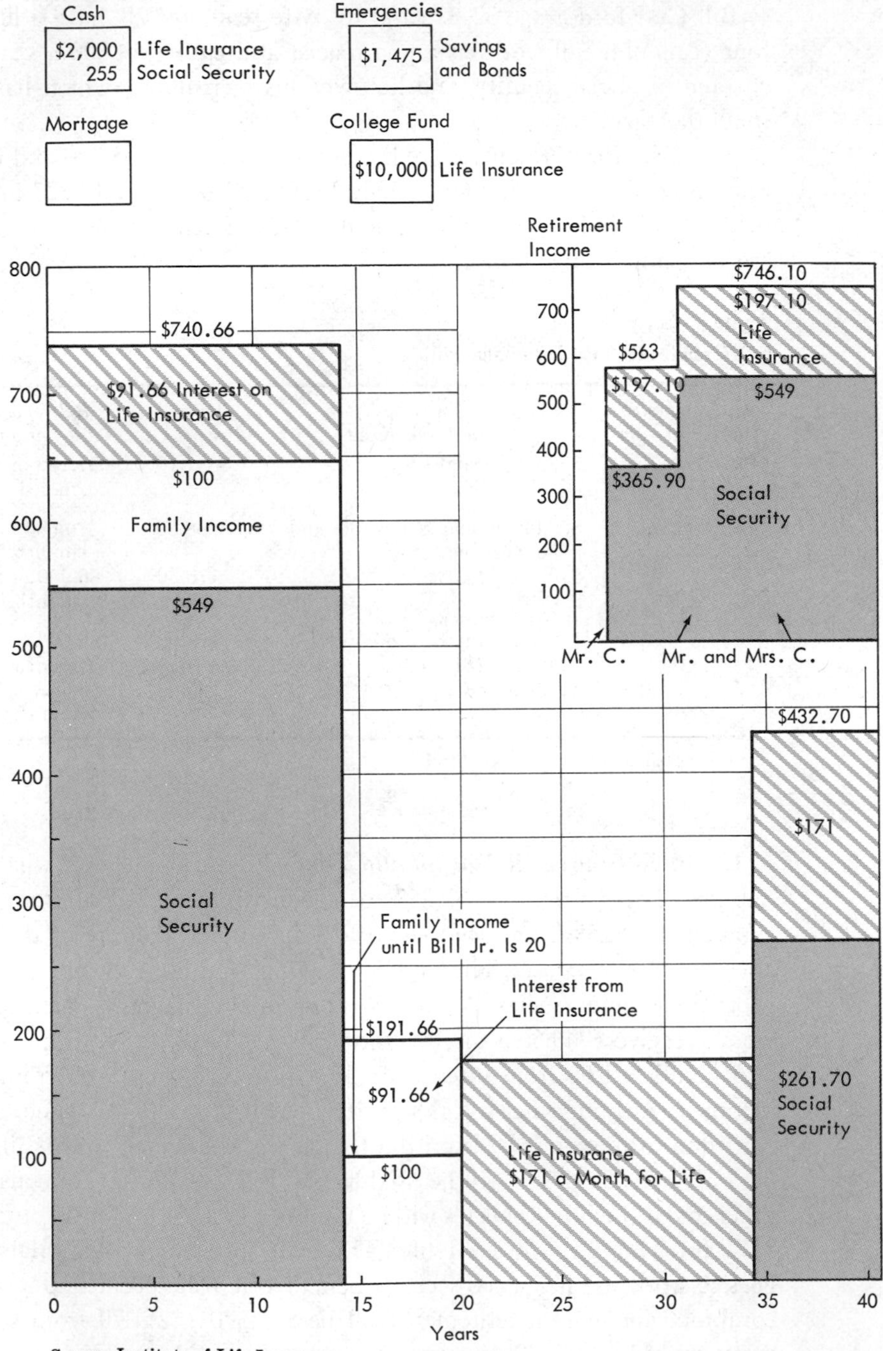

Source: Institute of Life Insurance.

Use of Resources if Bill Lives. If Bill lives to retire, the combined insurance policies (monthly income from cash values) will provide $197.10 a month for life. Social security will provide $365.90 for Bill alone; then, when Mrs. Crawford becomes age 65, the combined social security payment will rise to $549.00 and total monthly income to $746.10. Thus they will be fairly well protected in their old age, apart from any other savings or investments which they may accumulate.

The Walkers

Ralph Walker, aged 33, has just been promoted to associate professor at the college where he teaches. His wife Jean is also aged 33, and their children Robert and Jane are 5 and 1, respectively. In addition to his salary of $20,000 a year, Ralph's employing institution contributes an amount equal to 10 percent of salary to a fully vested pension plan for which he has just become eligible. The pension plan is funded by individual annuity contracts issued by Teachers Insurance and Annuity Association (TIAA) and the accumulated contributions are available as a death benefit if Ralph should die before retirement. The college also has a group life insurance plan that gives each employee coverage equal to one year's salary. Ralph's life insurance payable to Jean if he dies, is shown in Table 9–11.

TABLE 9–11
Walker's Life Insurance Policies

Policy Number	*Age*	*Amount and Kind*	*Yearly Premium*
1.	25	$ 5,000 whole life	$ 70
2.	—	20,000 group life	144
3.	33	75,000 decreasing term	276 (before dividends)

If Ralph Should Die Now. In considering plans for family security recently, Ralph concluded that if he died he would want Jean to have $5,000 for final bills, for which policy #1 is earmarked, income equal to at least three-fourths of his present salary while the children are growing up, college funds for the children, and as much provision for lifetime security as possible for Jean. To help meet these objectives he has just purchased the new $75,000 TIAA life insurance policy (#3). He selected decreasing term insurance to keep the outlay as low as possible and to recognize future increasing death benefits building up in the pension plan. He pays approximately $170 a year for this policy, net after dividends, in addition to the cost of the other coverage.

FIGURE 9–8
Income Distribution—the Walkers

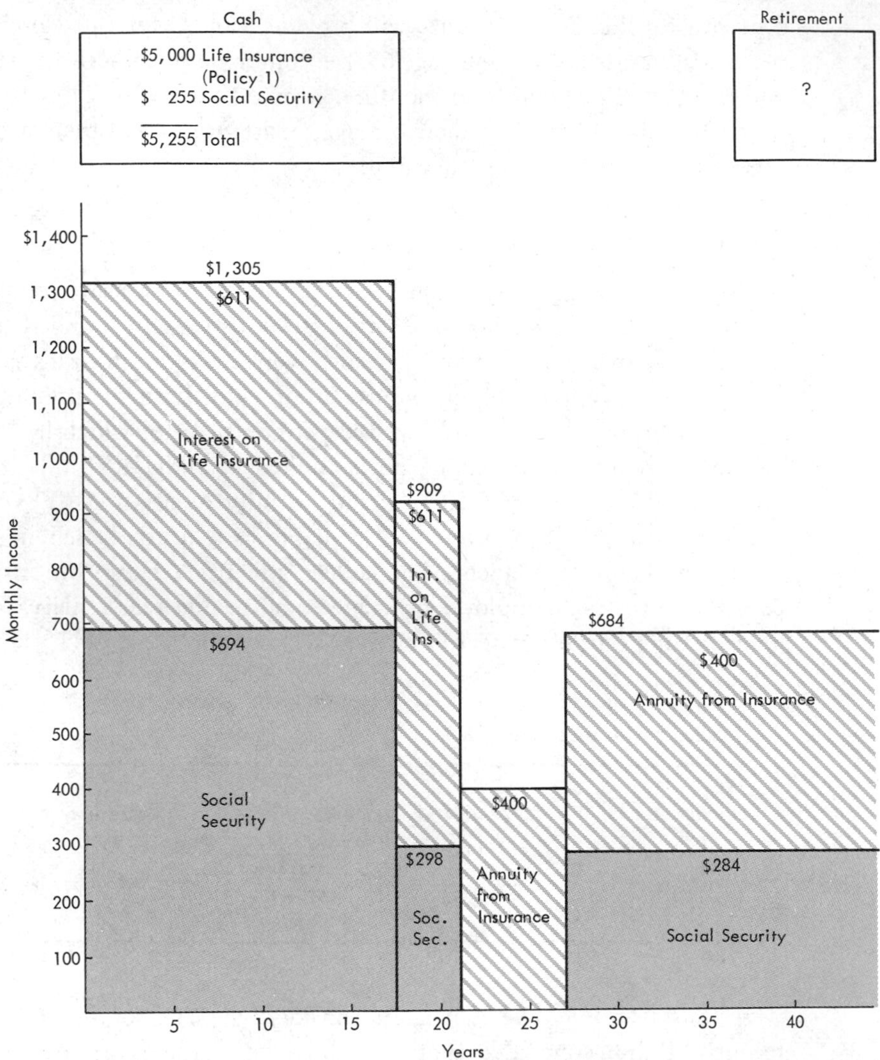

Source: Teachers Insurance & Annuity Association (TIAA)

Should Ralph die now, social security would produce about half the desired family income until the children are aged 18; followed by a reduced benefit while the younger child is under age 22 and attending college; Jean could begin receiving a widow's benefit commencing at her age 60. As shown in Figure 9–8, with social security benefits, Ralph's objective for family income while the children are growing up can be met by leaving the $95,000 of insurance money with TIAA to pay interest, holding the principal intact for future use; assuming college expenses for the children require Jean gradually to use up $40,000 of the principal (reducing her interest income as the principal is withdrawn). She will then have the remaining $55,000 to provide a life annuity starting after the youngest child is aged 22. As shown in Figure 9–8, this annuity income would be supplemented by the social security widow's benefit which starts when Jean is 60.

At Retirement Time. It is anticipated when Ralph retires at age 65 the pension program would provide retirement income equal to approximately 40 percent of his salary at the time of retirement, assuming his present salary increases at the rate of 5 percent a year. Social security benefits will bring the anticipated retirement income for Ralph and Jean to approximately 50 percent of that final salary.

There is no retirement box in Figure 9–8 because it would have to forecast a professor's salary 32 years hence, just prior to Ralph Walker's retirement. We can safely assume that over 32 years Walker will be promoted from associate to full professor. But what will full professors be earning in the year 2007—$50,000 a year? $100,000 a year? $150,000 a year?

ANNUITIES (FIXED AND VARIABLE)

You may look at some of these cases of retirement income in old age and say to yourself "the total combined income from social security and insurance may be enough for some but it's not enough for me." Those of you who don't feel that way can skip the rest of this chapter. But all prospective entrants into the upper income brackets read on. You'll learn a bit about "annuities," a subject of interest to upper middle income (and on up) groups. At 20 you may not find the subject all absorbing; at 40 you'll be much more interested, especially if your income exceeds $25,000 a year, as it probably will—either due to your own competence or to inflation.

The word *annuity* comes from the Latin word *annus,* meaning "year." Thus, in origin, an annuity is annual payment. Today, however, any fixed, periodic payment (weekly, monthly, quarterly, or yearly) for a given period of time or for life is an annuity.

An annuity is a contract that provides an income for a specified period of time, such as a number of years or life. A life annuity is a way of taking a certain sum of money, or building up a fund, and then using it up month by month, year by year, principal as well as interest thereon, and yet being absolutely sure that you will not run out of money as long as you live. That is the reason why anyone who is planning to retire some day, whether soon or in the distant future, ought to know something about annuities.

Insurance provides protection against dying too soon. An annuity, strange as it sounds, provides protection against living too long. Annuities may be bought by payment of a lump sum or by installment payments. The same companies that sell life insurance also sell annuities; the same care in choosing a company from which to buy insurance should be used in choosing a company from which to buy an annuity.

The Annuity Principle

Annuities are based on the principle of a group of people getting together and sharing risks. Individually, these people could not spend their savings without fear of outliving their principal. Some would die before their principal was exhausted, but others would live long after their money had disappeared. As members of a group of annuitants, however, each of these people can turn all or part of his savings over to a life insurance company and secure in exchange a promise that the company will pay him a regular income for life. While a life insurance company does not know how long any individual member of the group will live, it does know approximately how many in a group will be alive at the end of each successive year. A company can thus calculate the amount of annuity payments for each member of the group. The annuitant receives a certain income each year. Moreover, if he is over 50 years of age, he would have a greater assured income for life than he could safely obtain by investing the same amount otherwise. For example, a man of age 65 can obtain an income equal to 8 percent of his investment in a straight life annuity. In general, no medical examination is required for any annuity unless it includes insurance features.

Payments for Annuities

Suppose a person of age 40 has $50,000. It would be possible to give the $50,000 to an insurance company in return for the promise of the company to make a small monthly payment for life, to begin immediately. Or, if he needed no immediate income from his money, he would get a much larger monthly payment if he allowed the $50,000 to grow at interest with the company and began to receive the monthly payments for life when he became 60, 65, or 70 years of age. The later the payments begin, the greater each one will be. If he had no such lump sum to give the company, he could build an equivalent accumulation through regular installments over a period of years and in return obtain monthly payments later on.

Who Is Protected

The ordinary life insurance policy gives protection primarily to beneficiaries in the event the insured dies and secondarily builds up cash surrender (and loan) values for the insured; the annuity policy is primarily for the benefit of the insured (the annuitant) and only secondarily of benefit to others. Since life insurance gives protection to others in the event the insured dies and annuity policies are primarily for the benefit of the insured (the annuitant), their purposes and use are therefore very different. To put it briefly, life insurance is primarily to protect others; annuities are to protect oneself. It should be remembered, however, that the proceeds of life insurance policies are often paid out to beneficiaries in the form of annuities. Or the insured may take the cash value of a policy—or, in the case of an endowment, the maturity value—and elect to receive the money in the form of an annuity.

Effects of Rates of Interest upon Income

As you get older, you will begin to think of the time when you will no longer be able to earn an income. If you are fortunate, you may perhaps have saved some money, which may be earning interest in banks, be coming to you from insurance companies, or be invested in securities or in real estate. It is only natural to ask yourself whether you will be able to live in retirement on the income which your accumulated assets will provide. These days it takes $100,000 (a rather large sum of money for most of us) to provide an annual income of $5,000 to $8,000. Suppose you manage to accumulate $100,000 but you feel that you must have $11,000 a year; you will perhaps conclude that you will have to sell some of your assets, as time passes, to supplement your income. Such a procedure will naturally leave less assets to produce income, and you will probably envisage yourself selling more and more assets as the years go by, and then you will begin to worry that you will be destitute before you die.

Annuities Assure a Maximum Income

It is in such a situation that an annuity comes to the rescue. If you turn your money over to an insurance company in return for an annuity policy that guarantees you a given monthly income for life, you can be sure that you cannot possibly outlive your money, unless perchance you make a poor choice of an insurance company which fails. Of course, you may also worry lest you give the insurance company $100,000 today and die after receiving only a few monthly payments. In that case the insurance company would retain the balance of what you paid (plus earnings thereon) so that it could pay other annuitants who lived beyond expectation. We shall see later that there are ways, at a price, to avoid such a worry. In fact, annuities remove so much worry that this is often said to be the reason that annuitants live longer than others.

Kinds of Annuities

Annuities are sold both to individuals and on a group basis. Group annuities are for pension plans and are outside the scope of this book.[23] Group or individual, the same kinds of contracts are available, and an employer has about the same array to choose from when setting up a pension plan that you have when you shop for an annuity.

Every annuity has three variables: how you pay for it, when you collect, and how you collect. In the same fashion, every annuity contract has a three part name. One part specifies when you collect; one, how you pay; and one, how you collect. For example, a single premium, deferred, straight life annuity is one (*a*) for which you pay a lump sum in a single premium; (*b*) on which the company starts paying you a periodic income at a future date, e.g., when you become age 65; (*c*) with an income for as long as you live, but all payments stop at your death. Figure 9–9 sets out these three classification points for quick reference and shows you the various types of annuities available.

Immediate Annuities

When a person pays the insurance company a lump sum and wants annuity payments to begin without delay, we have an immediate annuity. We also have smaller periodic payments than if payments were to begin later. To obtain such an annuity of $100 a month at age 40, you would have to spend over $30,000. By the time you were 65 you could probably buy it for a little over half that amount. Ordinarily, people buy immediate annuities just about the time they want to have payments to them begin, i.e., when they are older and approaching retirement. They want this income to begin almost at once and to continue as long as they live.

---

[23] For a discussion of group annuities see *Handbook of Life Insurance* (New York: Institute of Life Insurance), pp. 55–56.

FIGURE 9–9

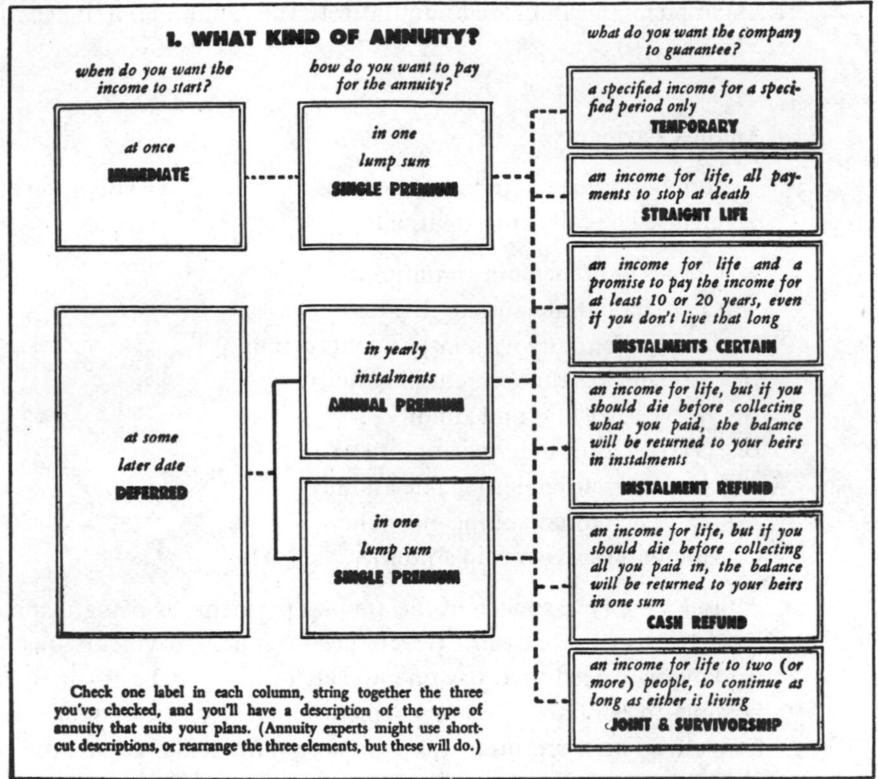

Source: *Changing Times, The Kiplinger Magazine.*

Deferred Annuities

Payments on deferred annuities begin at some time in the future, whether they are paid for in a lump sum or by a series of installments. If paid for in a lump sum, the person who buys such an annuity must ordinarily have saved and invested the money in some other way. He must, therefore, have assumed the risks involved in accumulating the money. When paid for in installments, the company assumes the burden of investing the money as received and paying the annuitant beginning with the arrival of the contracted date for payments to start. Naturally, more people can undertake to buy annuities on the installment plan than can produce a lump sum with which to buy them. In many company pension plans, employer and employee cooperate to pay the installments, which eventually produce an accumulation that provides a retirement income for the employee. The younger person is likely to prefer the annual (or installment) payment deferred annuity, while the older one is more likely to prefer the single premium, immediate annuity. If you think about it, you'll realize why this is so.

Annuity Payments

Annuitants have various options as to how they will receive annuity payments. The following are usual:

A. Types of immediate annuities.
   1. Straight life annuity.
   2. Life annuity with installments certain.
   3. The installment refund annuity.
   4. The cash refund annuity.

B. Variations of deferred annuities.
   1. The retirement income annuity.
   2. The retirement income policy.

C. Joint and survivorship annuities.

Although we have spoken of the annuity payments as being made monthly—on the theory that most people need frequent payments, just as while working they need their pay on a weekly or monthly basis—it is, of course, possible to contract to have payments made quarterly, semiannually, or annually. The more often the company must make payments, the more costly it is because of mailing, bookkeeping, and clerical expense and, furthermore, because of loss of interest involved in making payments sooner. Another factor making the cost of monthly annuity payments more than that of quarterly, semiannual, or annual payments is that some people live long enough in the year they die to collect some monthly payments, whereas their death would eliminate payments to be made at the end of a following quarter, half, or full year.

The Straight Life Annuity

The straight life annuity is the original and basic type of annuity. It is purchased for a lump sum premium, and annuity payments are immediate. It does not have a cash value. Payments cease, and there is no value left in the policy, upon the annuitant's death, no matter how soon he dies. This type of annuity (returning to the annuitant both principal and interest) provides the annuitant with the largest possible payments, but there is no value left in his policy should he die even a month or two after buying the policy. Notice that this type of annuity protects the annuitant only and provides nothing for his dependents beyond what they obtain out of the payments made to the annuitant. It is something like a pension for life: when the pensioner dies, the pension ceases, regardless of how many dependents the pensioner leaves. An indication of the cost of a straight life annuity at different ages may be seen in Table 9–12.

TABLE 9–12
Single Premium Payment, Immediate Annuities—Nonparticipating (January 1, 1973 rates)*

	Single Premium Purchase Price for Annuity of:			
Age Last Birthday	*$100 Annually*	*$50 Semiannually*	*$25 Quarterly*	*$10 Monthly*
Life—Male				
30	$1,626.45	$1,653.54	$1,667.08	$2,011.33
35	1,557.93	1,585.02	1,598.56	1,929.10
40	1,476.33	1,503.42	1,516.96	1,831.18
45	1,380.66	1,407.75	1,421.29	1,716.39
50	1,277.37	1,304.46	1,318.00	1,592.43
55	1,171.71	1,198.80	1,212.34	1,465.64
60	1,060.65	1,087.74	1,101.28	1,332.37
65	943.43	970.52	984.06	1,191.71
70	820.51	847.60	861.14	1,044.20
75	697.56	724.65	738.19	896.66
80	584.20	611.29	624.83	760.63
85	477.53	504.62	518.16	632.62
Life—Female				
30	$1,686.91	$1,714.00	$1,727.54	$2,083.89
35	1,631.37	1,658.46	1,672.00	2,011.23
40	1,565.23	1,592.32	1,605.86	1,937.87
45	1,487.23	1,514.32	1,527.86	1,844.26
50	1,397.76	1,424.85	1,438.39	1,736.91
55	1,296.64	1,323.73	1,337.27	1,615.56
60	1,183.69	1,210.78	1,224.32	1,480.01
65	1,058.71	1,085.80	1,099.34	1,330.04
70	924.89	951.98	965.52	1,169.46
75	790.17	817.26	830.80	1,007.79
80	651.85	678.94	692.48	841.81
85	531.72	558.81	572.35	697.66

* Note: For purchase payments in excess of $15,000, yields income more favorable as amount of purchase payment increases.
Source: Metropolitan Life Insurance Company.

Life Annuity with Installments Certain

The straight life annuity is not favored by some people, who dislike the idea of a contract that might pay them an income for only a few months and then stop if they died at that time. These people feel that they would like some close relative to get something out of their purchase money besides the few payments they received. Actually, of course, the company does not get the apparently unused part of the purchase money. This money, according to the risk sharing principle, goes to other annuitants who live a long time and receive much more than their purchase money.

To meet the objection to the straight life annuity, however, a life annuity with installments certain was developed. This not only pays an income to the annuitant for life but if death occurs within the guaranty period, the income payments for the balance of the guaranty period are paid to a beneficiary selected by the annuitant. This period is usually from 10–20 years and is often expressed as 120 or 240 months. The company is obligated to pay income benefits, in any case, for 10 or 20 years. There is no risk sharing or life annuity principle involved until after the end of that time.

Since, on this type of annuity, the company cannot benefit from the very early death of the annuitant, payments to the annuitant must be less than those on a straight life annuity. If the annuitant lives and receives payments for 4 years and payments have been guaranteed for 10 years, the beneficiary receives the payments for 6 more years, making, together, 4 and 6—the 10 years certain. The beneficiary may elect to receive the six years' payments in one lump sum, which will, however, be smaller than the total amount he would have collected had he waited to receive it in installments over the six years. Should the annuitant live and collect for a longer period than 10 years, the policy would terminate on his death, and no value would remain for the beneficiary.

The Installment Refund Annuity

The installment refund annuity also pays an income to the annuitant for life. But if the annuitant dies before he has received as much money as he paid for the annuity, income payments are continued, in installments, to his beneficiary until total payments equal the amount paid.

The Cash Refund Annuity

A cash refund annuity is also a life annuity, but the company guarantees to pay out (all told) a sum equivalent to the cost of the annuity policy, either to the annuitant if he lives or to the annuitant and his beneficiaries in the event that he does not live long enough to collect it all. If $10,000 is paid for such a policy and the annuitant dies after receiving $2,000 in payments, $8,000 would still be due the beneficiaries, making a total of $10,000 to be paid out by the company. A policy of this type assures the annuitant that no part of his principal (but not interest) will be lost. For this guaranty the annuitant must pay by accepting smaller annuity payments (sometimes as much as 20 percent smaller) than could be received without it. In contrast to the installment certain annuity, where the beneficiary is paid for the remainder of the guaranteed installment periods, under the cash refund annuity the beneficiary is paid the remainder of the total amount of the annuity in one lump sum.

A straight life annuity is advisable for the person who wishes to receive the largest possible income for his money. A life annuity with installments certain or a cash refund annuity is advisable for the person who not only wants a lifetime income but who also wishes to provide some payment to his beneficiary in the event of his early death. The income to the annuitant is less, it should be remembered, under the installment refund and cash refund than under the straight life annuity, since additional benefits are provided.

Variations of the Deferred Annuity

All deferred annuities have initial payments which begin at a stipulated time in the future, i.e., payment is deferred. A deferred life annuity begins paying at some date after that of original purchase; and when it starts, it pays for life. This annuity may be purchased by a single premium. More often, it is paid for over a period of years. Deferred annuities are usually bought by people who do not need or who already have adequate life insurance protection.

Any annuity under which the income payments are deferred is commonly called a "deferred annuity." A *true deferred annuity has no cash value and no death benefit*. For example, assume you start buying a deferred annuity, on the installment plan, at age 35 and that you pay in $500 a year. Payment to you on this annuity is to start at age 65 under the terms of your contract. If you should become unemployed at age 60 and should wish to draw out the funds accumulated under the annuity, you cannot do so. It has no cash surrender value. If you should die at age 60, after having made payments of $500 a year for 25 years (for a total of $12,500), your estate would receive nothing from this annuity, since there is no death benefit. Offsetting this, it has the advantage of providing maximum income per dollar of premium to those surviving beyond the deferred period. Because so many people misunderstand the "all or nothing" nature of the benefits and because it fits the needs of so few people, only occasionally do life insurance companies sell this annuity contract.

Most individual retirement plans that are popularly known as deferred annuities are actually savings plans. These generally include some insurance but no annuity element during the deferred period. These contracts build up a fund which is used at the end of the deferred period to buy an immediate annuity. The two most popular plans of this type are (*a*) the retirement income annuity and (*b*) the retirement income policy.

The Retirement Income Annuity. The companies give various names to this plan, which is issued to meet the needs of people who want to save regularly for a life income but who need no insurance protection. This contract is really an accumulation at interest of premiums paid, less expenses. The amount accumulated by the end of the deferred period is used to buy a life annuity of the straight life, or more often of the refund, type. The usual unit for this contract is $10 of monthly retirement income at the selected age, which is generally 65.

Added to each unit of retirement income is a very small amount of life insurance protection—just enough, in fact, to provide a death benefit during the early years of the policy equal to all premiums paid. After that time, the savings accumulation exceeds the total of premiums paid and becomes the death benefit, the insurance element ceasing. As the savings accumulation builds up, the death benefit likewise increases.

Prior to the maturity date, the policy has a cash surrender value and also a loan privilege equal to the savings accumulations. During the early years of the policy, due to sales expenses and insurance costs, the cash and loan values will be less than the total of premiums paid.

A retirement income annuity enables you to set aside funds regularly for retirement. Your beneficiary will receive at least the amount of the premiums you paid if you die before the retirement age. You can borrow on the accumulated fund in case of need. You can cash the policy in if your situation changes, and, except for the early years, you will get back at least what you paid in.

The Retirement Income Policy. This is a variation of the retirement income annuity. It includes a substantial insurance element coupled with each unit of $10 of monthly income at the retirement age selected. The insurance element ranges from $1,000 to $1,500. In all other respects this contract is identical in principal to the retirement income annuity.

The retirement income policy fits the needs of many types of people. Single persons often find that the insurance furnishes them all the protection they need, while the policy directs their premium dollars principally toward filling retirement needs. People with dependents who have purchased nearly all the insurance protection that they want and now wish to strengthen their retirement program find this policy helpful. It adds to their insurance protection, which is an advantage, while it lays principal stress on building a retirement income.

The Joint and Survivorship Annuity

Joint and survivorship annuities are especially useful where it is desired to have a retirement income for both husband and wife. They receive the annuity jointly during the life of both of them, and then payments of like (or lesser—often two thirds) amounts are made to the survivor as long as he or she lives. This type of annuity may meet the needs of an elderly couple with no dependents.

A larger monthly payment can usually be obtained by stipulating that the survivor (usually wife) is to receive two thirds of what was received while both were living, rather than the full amount.

There are deferred joint and survivorship annuities, similar to immediate joint and survivorship annuities, except that annuity payments do not begin immediately. While the immediate joint and survivorship annuity must be purchased on a single premium basis, the deferred joint and survivorship annuity is often purchased on an annual premium (installment) basis. As in the case of the true deferred annuity, the deferred joint and survivorship annuity is rarely sold, because death of either before the "maturity" date would terminate the contract and provide no benefit to the survivor.

One of the principal advantages of an immediate joint life and survivorship annuity is that much of the need for life insurance is eliminated. For example, if a man and a wife have such an annuity, providing sufficient income for their needs, the husband would have to carry insurance sufficient only to cover cash for final expenses and one year's readjustment income, because the wife will be supported by the annuity income even after his death.

Life insurance policies can be and are paid off in joint and survivorship annuities. The way to look at a life insurance policy, in this connection, is not in terms of the face amount but rather in terms of the amount of income it will produce. More people use life insurance policies with their annuity income options to provide joint and survivorship income than use the joint and survivorship annuity contract to accomplish the same result. The cost of a single payment, immediate, joint and survivorship annuity of $10 monthly is shown in Table 9–13.

The Cost of Annuities

The price of an annuity is based on the amount of income it will pay. You can look at price in two ways: you can take the amount you can pay and see what income it will buy, or you can take the income you want and see what it will cost. The amount you will pay for a given income—say,

TABLE 9–13
Joint and Survivor Annuity—Nonparticipating Single Payment for $10 Monthly* (January 1, 1973 rates)

	Female Age			
Male Age	*10 Years Younger*	*5 Years Younger*	*Same Age*	*5 Years Older*
45	$2,066.62†	$2,013.51†	$1,959.92†	$1,908.98†
46	2,053.03†	1,998.26†	1,943.04†	1,890.54†
47	2,038.87†	1,982.19†	1,925.13†	1,870.94†
48	2,024.12†	1,965.30†	1,906.17†	1,850.18†
49	2,008.80†	1,947.60†	1,886.18†	1,828.26†
50	1,992.90†	1,929.07†	1,865.15†	1,805.18†
51	1,976.71†	1,911.06†	1,845.49†	1,783.89†
52	1,959.84†	1,892.12†	1,824.67†	1,761.31†
53	1,942.32†	1,872.25†	1,802.69†	1,737.45†
54	1,924.13†	1,851.44†	1,779.56†	1,712.30†
55	1,905.27†	1,829.71†	1,755.27†	1,685.87†
56	1,886.22†	1,808.83†	1,732.66†	1,661.93†
57	1,866.40†	1,786.91†	1,708.76†	1,636.59†
58	1,845.82†	1,763.95†	1,683.55†	1,609.87†
59	1,824.48†	1,739.94†	1,657.05†	1,581.75†
60	1,802.38†	1,714.89†	1,629.24†	1,552.21
61	1,780.43	1,691.06†	1,604.12†	1,525.52
62	1,757.55	1,666.07†	1,577.57	1,497.31
63	1,733.80	1,639.90	1,549.27	1,467.56
64	1,709.20	1,612.51	1,519.53	1,436.29
65	1,683.74	1,583.95	1,488.35	1,403.50
66	1,658.67	1,557.14	1,460.29	1,374.70
67	1,632.65	1,529.03	1,430.67	1,344.29
68	1,605.66	1,499.61	1,399.47	1,312.27
69	1,577.70	1,468.88	1,366.71	1,278.64

* For purchase payments in excess of $15,000, yields income more favorable as amount of purchase payment increases.

† These are the values for a 10 year certain contract because they are more advantageous to the purchaser than the life rates in these age combinations.

Source: Metropolitan Life Insurance Company.

$100 a month—depends on what income plan you select, how old you are when payments begin, and whether you are a man or a woman.

Things to remember about costs are:

1. The older you are when the income is to start, the less you will pay. In the case of an immediate annuity, the older you are when you buy, the less your cost will be.

2. With a deferred annuity, the younger you are when you sign up, the less your annual premium cost will be. The lower premiums result from spreading payments over a longer period and from the interest your payments can earn.

3. The total of annual premiums paid for an annuity of so much a

month will be less than the single premium you will pay for an immediate annuity of the same amount beginning at the same age. All of the latter comes out of your pocket, whereas the annual premiums are built up with the aid of compound interest.

4. At the same age, a woman pays more than a man for the same income, because women, on the average, live longer and collect more.

5. For each dollar of income, you pay least if you take a straight life plan, most if you take a cash refund joint and survivorship plan.

Life insurance premiums are based on an "integral" age, which is usually on the basis of the insured's age as of his last birthday. Annuity premiums, however, change with each month. Life insurance premiums increase as one gets older; premiums for immediate annuities decrease the older one is and the shorter the time for which the company contracts to make payments. It is sensible for one to buy life insurance just before his age changes and to buy a life annuity just after attaining a higher age. Annuity rates for women are higher than for men of equal age because women have a longer expectation of life. For life annuities it is customary to charge women the same rates that are charged men who are five years younger, since this measures approximately the difference in length of life.

Most immediate annuities are nonparticipating, whereas more and more deferred annuities are being written on a participating basis. Medical examinations are not required for annuities that combine with them no insurance protection: the poorer one's health, the less likelihood there is that the company will have to pay for a long time. Various combinations of annuities and insurance have been worked out by insurance companies to fit particular needs.

Fixed Annuities and Investments

The major limitation of fixed annuities is that they provide a fixed dollar income, which is not protected from shrinkage in purchasing power due to inflation. On the other hand, putting all one's retirement funds into investments might be too risky; or if safety is desired and a more conservative investment policy is therefore pursued, the resultant income might not be sufficient to meet needs.

People choose fixed annuities for all sorts of reasons, ranging from taxes to timidity. The tax advantage is that money put into annuities during your working years earns interest, but you do not need to pay income taxes on the interest until you actually collect it; and then your income and your tax bracket will presumably be much lower. Timidity enters because people mistrust their ability to invest wisely, especially their ability to handle the somewhat complicated operation of continuing to invest while using up capital gradually over the retirement period. They cannot live on earnings alone; their capital fund to start with is not large enough; and they must, therefore, gradually draw on principal, but there is the danger that they may use it up too rapidly, live longer than they anticipated, and thus face destitution. The annuity relieves them of such worries.

In the fixed annuity versus investment debate, you will find that annuities gain in popularity in recession or depression, when investments lose their luster, whereas, in boom and inflation, when the fixed dollar income from annuities purchases less and less and stock investments are rising in value and yielding capital gains, the annuity looks less attractive.

Variable Annuities

To combine the safety advantages of fixed annuities with the long run inflation hedging protection of common stock investment, the "variable" annuity has been developed. The variable annuity is an annuity providing a life income, not of a fixed number of dollars but of variable amounts keyed to an underlying common stock investment portfolio. Under a variable annuity your premiums are invested primarily in common stocks and provide a retirement income that increases as stock prices and dividends increase, and decreases as they decline. A fixed annuity, on the other hand, invests your premiums primarily in bonds and mortgages and provides a guaranteed fixed dollar annuity income that does not change in amount from year to year, except as extra dividends are added.

In the words of a former president of the Metropolitan Life Insurance Company:

> The so called variable annuity is similar to a true annuity in that premiums are paid to the issuing company by the annuitant, presumably during his working years. At retirement the company makes payments periodically to the annuitant—generally speaking over the remaining years of his life. The difference, however, and a vast difference it is, is that in the variable annuity type of contract the premium payments to the company are to be invested in equities, which to all intents and purposes, means common stock, and the issuing company makes *no* commitment as to any dollar amount that will be paid to the annuitant during the period of retirement. The issuing company merely undertakes to make payments based on the annuitant's pro rata share of the then market value of the common stock fund in which his payments have been invested.

How the Variable Annuity Developed

Inflation has reduced the purchasing power of the dollar by more than 50 percent over the past 25 years. It was fear of inflation and its debilitating impact on retirement income which gave rise to the variable annuity.

The modern variable annuity was first developed by the Teachers Insurance and Annuity Association of America. It established the College Retirement Equities Fund (CREF) in 1952 to enable college teachers who were contributing to the TIAA retirement system (buying an individual fixed dollar annuity) to have up to one half[24] of their contribution (including the college's contribution) go toward the purchase of a CREF variable annuity, with the balance going to TIAA to purchase the fixed dollar annuity.

Based on careful studies of investment and price trends over a previous 70 year period, the TIAA concluded:

1. It is unwise to commit *all* of one's retirement savings to fixed dollar obligations, since decreases in the purchasing power of the dollar can seriously reduce the value of a fixed income annuity. Increases in the purchasing power of the dollar, on the other hand, improve the status of the owner of a fixed income annuity.

2. It is equally unwise to commit *all* of one's retirement savings to equity investments, since variations in prices of common stocks are much too pronounced to permit full reliance on them for the stable income needed during retirement. Changes in the value of common stocks and other equities are by no means perfectly correlated with cost of living changes, but they have provided a considerably better protection against inflation than debt obligations.

3. Substantial problems exist whenever an individual has the option to invest a large single payment in *either* an equities fund or a fixed dollar fund. If $10,000 had been invested in common stocks in 1929, there would have been a drop in value to $2,600 in 1932. (Since the price level also fell, the purchasing power would have been $3,250.) Likewise, if $10,000 had been invested in government bonds, a savings account, or a life insurance fund in 1914, it would have declined *in purchasing power value* to $5,000 in 1920. (Both figures exclude interest and dividend additions.)

4. Therefore, the TIAA concluded, contributions to a retirement plan which are invested partly in fixed dollar obligations, such as bonds and mortgages, and partly in common stocks offer promise of providing retirement income which is at once reasonably free from violent fluctuations

---

[24] It may now be up to 75 percent of their contribution or as little as 25 percent.

in amount and from serious depreciation through price level changes.[25]

Some 375,000 college teachers are now contributing to the College Retirement Equities Fund,[26] and today most major insurance companies are offering variable or balanced annuities in addition to fixed annuities. In addition, a growing number of companies have provided in their pension plans for either the variable or the balanced annuity. What's the difference between the two? Well, first of all, an *annuity,* as we have seen, is a series of monthly payments. A *life annuity,* for example, provides monthly payments for your lifetime. A *fixed dollar annuity,* is a series of regular monthly payments which continue for your lifetime in a fixed dollar amount each month. A *variable annuity* is a series of monthly payments which will continue for your lifetime, but varying in dollar amount from month to month. Money used for this type of annuity is placed in a Variable Contract Account Investment Fund, which is invested primarily in common stocks. The dollar amount of monthly variable annuity payments will vary according to the investment results, including dividends and market value changes, of the investment fund. A *balanced annuity* is a combination of a variable annuity and the fixed dollar annuity.

Over the long term, common stock values have tended to move in the same general direction as the cost and standard of living. Over the short term, they have generally changed more rapidly and sometimes have moved in opposite directions. A retirement income could have unpleasant drops when the variable annuity payments go down as a result of falling common stock prices. That's why the balanced annuity concept was developed. The variable annuity balanced by the fixed was thought to provide offsetting protection. The fixed dollar annuity would provide a base income and protect against falling stock prices, while the variable annuity would provide the hedge against inflation, theoretically. The TIAA–CREF combination is a *balanced annuity.* TIAA is the *fixed dollar* component; CREF is the *variable* annuity segment.

How the Variable Annuity Works

Suppose you decide to set aside $50 a month over a period of years for a variable annuity.

1. The funds you pay in would be placed in the insurance company's

---

[25] Adapted from William C. Greenough, *A New Approach to Retirement Income,* Teachers Insurance and Annuity Association of America, 730 Third Ave., New York, N.Y., 10017, latest edition.

[26] A prospectus of this Fund may be obtained by writing to the TIAA.

variable contract account and invested separately, from the company's regular insurance or annuity funds, primarily in common stocks.

2. Each $50 monthly payment, after deduction of a specified allowance for expenses, would be applied to credit you with a number of Variable Contract Account Units, determined by the current dollar value of an accumulation unit. The dollar value of an accumulation unit would go up and down depending on changes in the value of the assets in the account. Each $50 that you paid might buy a different number of units. The dollar value of the units credited to you would change each month. The company makes no dollar guarantees. Its liabilities for the variable annuity are always in terms of the current value of its assets.

3. When you retire, all of your Variable Contract Account Units would be converted, on a basis set forth in your contract, into a fixed number of annuity units. As in a straight life annuity you are guaranteed a payment each month for as long as you live. But instead of providing for the payment each month of a fixed number of dollars, your variable annuity contract will provide for the payment each month of the current value of the fixed number of annuity units credited to you.

Thus the dollar amount of each payment would depend on the dollar value of an annuity unit when the payment is made. The dollar value of an annuity unit would change from month to month, according to the investment results of the account, in much the same way as the Variable Contract Account Units. For example, if you were entitled to a payment of 10 annuity units each month and the dollar value of the common stock assets behind each annuity unit fell from $10.00 to $9.50 and then rose to $11.00, with change in market trends, your retirement income over the three months would be $100, $95, and $110 for each month, respectively.

You may find of interest the trend in CREF annuity unit values since they were first made available in 1952. The performance is shown in Figure 9–10, and in Table 9–14.

The CREF experience has been a favorable one. Regular participation in CREF gained for the individual the benefits of dollar cost averaging, which results in a lower average cost for the shares purchased than the average of the prices paid, since more shares are obtained at lower than at higher prices.

CREF's annuity and accumulation units have different values because they perform different functions. During the years when a participant and the college are paying premiums to CREF, the accumulation unit value determines the number of accumulation units purchased with each premium payment and measures the market value of the participant's current share of the CREF portfolio (see Figure 9–10). When the participant re-

FIGURE 9–10
CREF Annuity Unit Values since 1952 (annuity year, May through April)

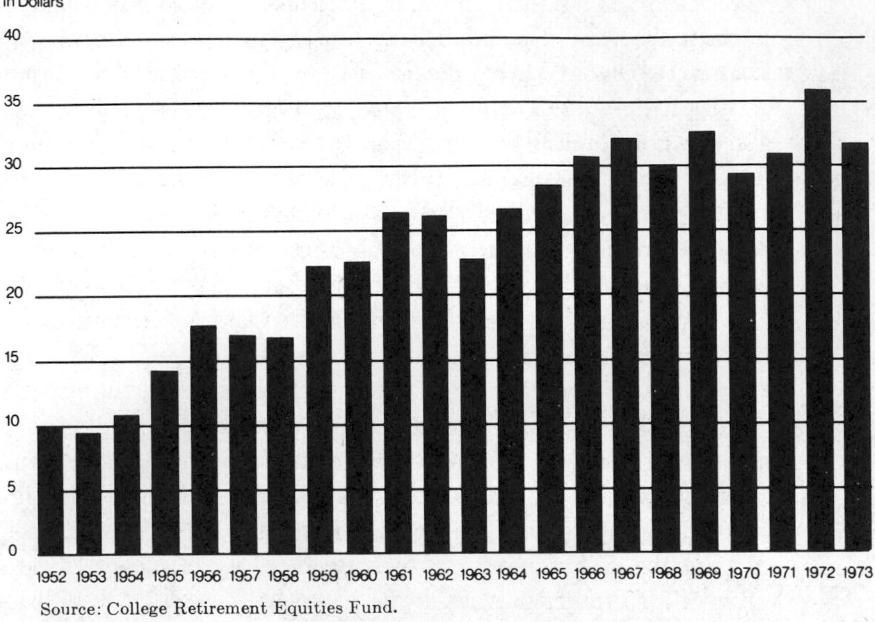

Source: College Retirement Equities Fund.

tires, the annuity unit is used as a basis for spreading payment of his CREF holdings over his retired lifetime. At retirement, the participant can choose among various options, including ones that provide continuing life income to the wife or husband after the annuity owner's death. The value of the annuity unit is therefore affected by actuarial factors as well as invest-

TABLE 9–14
CREF Annuity Unit Values since 1952

Annuity Year (May through April)	*Annuity Unit Value*	*Annuity Year (May through April)*	*Annuity Unit Value*
Initial value	$10.00		
1953–54	9.46	1964–65	26.48
1954–55	10.74	1965–66	28.21
1955–56	14.11	1966–67	30.43
1956–57	18.51	1967–68	31.92
1957–58	16.88	1968–69	29.90
1958–59	16.71	1969–70	32.50
1959–60	22.03	1970–71	28.91
1960–61	22.18	1971–72	30.64
1961–62	26.25	1972–73	35.74
1962–63	26.13	1973–74	31.58
1963–64	22.68		

ment experience. Table 9–14 shows CREF's annuity unit values from 1953–54 through 1973–74.

One Insurance Company's View

Of the large insurance companies, Prudential pioneered in sponsoring the development of the variable annuity, first under group contracts and then under individual contracts. It did so because of the purchasing power risk involved in the fixed annuity. It also did so because of three basic forces:

1. The lengthening years of retirement.
2. The increasing cost of living.
3. The rising standard of living.

The average retirement age used to be close to 70 years. Now there is a trend toward earlier retirement. Most people do not work beyond 65, and many retire in their late fifties or early sixties. Also the retiree may be expected to live longer. Earlier retirement and longer life combine to lengthen the years of retirement. The longer you live in retirement, the greater the impact of the increasing cost and standard of living on the adequacy of your retirement income.

Over the longer term, inflation has significantly reduced the purchasing power of the dollar. In inflation, a retired person living on a fixed income is forced to adjust to proportionately less goods and services. This becomes a particularly acute hardship in the face of the rising standard of living, as wages and salaries of the working population increase fast enough to keep up with price rises (see Figure 9–11).

Prudential's research led it to conclude, as did CREF's, that over the longer term, the price of a diversified group of common stocks would generally have tended to change with changes in average wages, changes in average wages reflecting the combined effect of changes in (1) the cost of living, and (2) the standard of living. This led to the conclusion that the variable annuity based on a diversified group of common stocks would tend to keep pace with changes in the economy and at the same time provide a retirement income you can't outlive! See Figure 9–11 (bottom).

A variable annuity is expressed in terms of "annuity units." An annuity unit has a dollar value, called the annuity unit value. It goes up or down each month, depending on whether the investment results of Prudential's investment fund are at a rate higher or lower than the "Assumed Investment Result."

In computing the first payment of the variable annuity, it is usually

FIGURE 9-11
Cost of Living

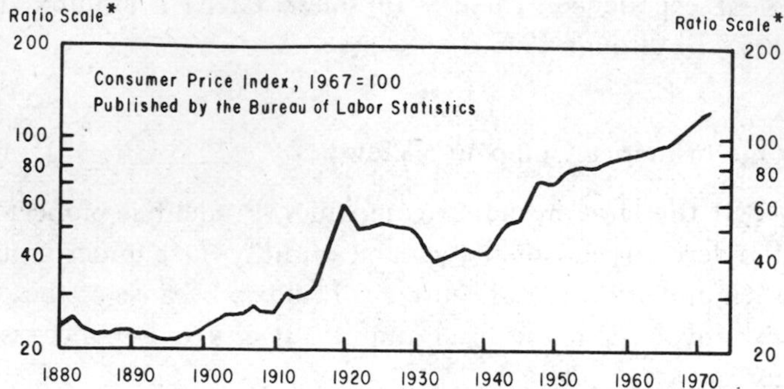

Standard of Living

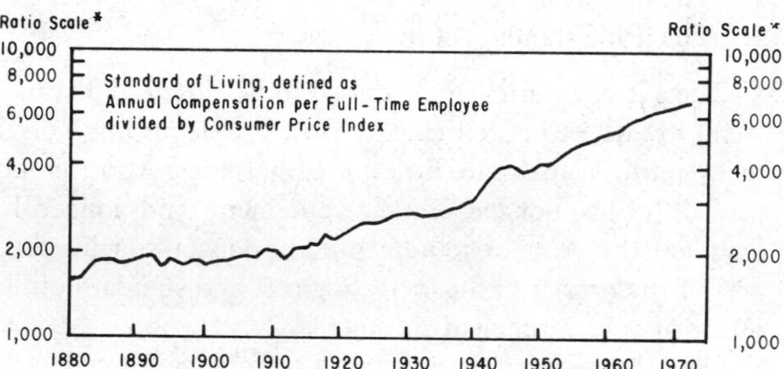

Common Stock Prices Compared with Wages

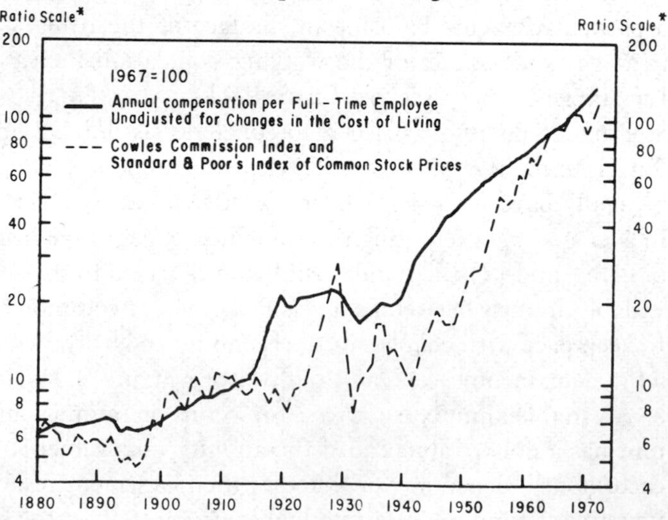

* These charts show relative rates of change, since equal distances on the scale correspond to equal percentage changes.

Source: Courtesy of the Prudential Insurance Company of America; wage data from *Historical Statistics of U.S.* and *Survey of Current Business.*

assumed that there will be a given percentage increase, say 4 percent or 4.5 percent, or 5 percent, or 5.5 percent in the value of the fund, from the combination of investment income and realized and unrealized gains. If it turns out that the value of the investment fund increases at exactly this assumed investment result, then the successive variable annuity payments will not vary at all but will be equal to the first payment. If the results of the investment fund for any month are greater than say 4 percent (an illustrative assumed investment result), then the next payment will be higher and correspondingly, if the results are less than 4 percent, then the next payment will be lower. See Table 9–15 for an actual example of how the actual investment results of Prudential's variable contract account investment fund varied from an assumed investment result of 4 percent yer year.[27]

TABLE 9–15
A History of Annuity Unit Values (December 1962 = $1.00)

For Annuity Payments in	*Variable Contract Account Investment Fund*											
	Jan.	*Feb.*	*Mar.*	*Apr.*	*May*	*June*	*July*	*Aug.*	*Sept.*	*Oct.*	*Nov.*	*Dec.*
1963........	$1.08	$1.10	$1.14	$1.11	$1.14	$1.19	$1.21	$1.17	$1.17	$1.23	$1.21	$1.23
1964........	1.22	1.25	1.29	1.31	1.32	1.31	1.31	1.32	1.34	1.31	1.34	1.33
1965........	1.34	1.34	1.39	1.43	1.40	1.46	1.44	1.36	1.38	1.43	1.48	1.52
1966........	1.52	1.54	1.55	1.53	1.51	1.55	1.46	1.44	1.43	1.29	1.27	1.32
1967........	1.36	1.36	1.46	1.48	1.55	1.63	1.55	1.57	1.64	1.62	1.65	1.59
1968........	1.59	1.63	1.55	1.51	1.50	1.63	1.64	1.63	1.60	1.61	1.67	1.70
1969........	1.79	1.72	1.71	1.63	1.69	1.72	1.71	1.61	1.51	1.57	1.52	1.60
1970........	1.54	1.52	1.40	1.47	1.47	1.33	1.22	1.19	1.28	1.34	1.38	1.36
1971........	1.41	1.50	1.55	1.57	1.62	1.68	1.62	1.62	1.54	1.59	1.58	1.51
1972........	1.49	1.61	1.62	1.67	1.67	1.68	1.71	1.68	1.67	1.72	1.70	1.70
1973........	1.73	1.80	1.75	1.68	1.67	1.61	1.60	1.58	1.64	1.60	1.66	1.66
1974........	1.47	1.45	1.44	1.43	1.41	1.36	1.31	1.29	1.18	1.08	0.95	1.08

Notes: The Annuity Unit Values shown in this table reflect the extent to which the actual investment results of Prudential's *Variable Contract Account Investment Fund* varied from an *Assumed Investment Result* of 4 percent per year.

The Annuity Units for your plan are based on this fund. It was established in 1962 and consists primarily of common stocks. The investments of this fund are selected by Prudential in accordance with the long-term view of a prudent investor, concerned with the potential for capital gains as well as dividends. Dividends are reinvested as received. The selection of stocks is well diversified over many industries and many geographical areas.

The Annuity Unit Values in this table are taken to the nearer cent and cover the period from December, 1962, to December, 1974. The values in this period should not be considered a prediction of future investment results.

Source: Courtesy of the Prudential Insurance Company of America.

Why Not Invest in Common Stock Directly?

Why not buy common stock directly and provide this variable income in retirement by a systematic liquidation of your investments over your

[27] For further information, see Prudential's publications: (*a*) *New Directions in Pension Planning,* and (*b*) *Focusing on Your Future.* For copies of the latest editions, write to The Prudential Insurance Company of America, Prudential Plaza, Newark, N.J. 07101.

retirement period? There is one big reason why you can't. You can set up an investment program, but you can't predict how long you will live. Therefore, after retirement, you can't know how much of your principal it is safe to spend each year. You might figure on drawing down your money over, say, 15 years—and then live only half as long. Or you might still be hale and hearty after 20 years—but with all your money gone.

Only an insurance company, spreading the mortality risk on a sound actuarial basis over a large group of people can guarantee you a distribution of your savings over your full retirement lifetime no matter how long you may live. The insurance company can do this because, dealing with a large number of annuitants, the "losses" on those who live longer than the "average" will be offset by "gains" on those who do not live as long as the average. By enabling you to use up your principal as well as the return on it, over the retirement period with income guaranteed for life no matter how long you may live, annuities generally provide a higher monthly return than comparable forms of direct investment.

Conclusion

The chief advantage of the variable annuity from the purchaser's point of view is that it helps to provide a hedge against retirement income being diminished in purchasing power due to continuing inflation. The chief disadvantage, on the other hand, is that it subjects retirement income to the vagaries of the stock market and may result in a diminution of retirement income in a period of stock market decline.[28]

YOUR COMPANY PENSION PLAN

When you graduate and are deciding which job to take, check the pension plan of each of the companies that have made you an offer. Today most medium and large corporations provide attractive retirement plans. A generous plan will enable you to use funds that you might otherwise husband for retirement.

Will you contribute to the plan or does the company pay all the cost? Practice varies. When you contribute, by payroll deduction, benefits may be larger. At any event all the income the money earns during your working years is tax free until your retirement. In some companies there is no payroll deduction on the first $5,000 or $10,000 of income but a significant contribution from higher compensation. Plans vary widely in this respect.

---

[28] "Shrinking Benefits: Retirees Who Picked 'Inflation Insurance' See Pensions Wither," *Wall Street Journal*, September 10, 1974.

How much will you get? Here, too, it is hard to generalize. Some plans are tied to profit sharing; others use formulas and pay benefits without any formal relationship to profit. Pensions may be based on length of service or on level of salary, or on both. The company, for example, may pay 1 percent for each year's service. The 1 percent may be on your average salary or it may be on your salary for the five years prior to retirement. The latter would probably be more advantageous, since your last five years' salary is likely to be higher than your average salary with the firm. Almost all corporate pensions are in addition to or on top of social security benefits.

Is the plan vested? What happens if you serve for a number of years but leave the company for another job, prior to the official retirement age? Vesting is your right to share in the money your employer has contributed to the pension fund in your behalf, even if you leave before retirement.

The company's pension fund may be invested by a bank or trust company, in which case when you retire, your pension benefits are paid directly from the trust fund. Or the pension fund may be handled by an insurance company, in which case pension funds are in effect used to purchase annuities payable to you upon your retirement.

What form will the pension take? Usually you receive a monthly check for as long as you live. Under some plans widows and survivors get nothing after the death of the pensioner. However, many plans offer other options. One is the "years certain" option. You can elect to receive a somewhat smaller monthly payment with the assurance that whether you live or not it will be paid to you or to your widow for 5, 10, or 15 years, that is, for a certain specified period. Or you can choose the "joint and survivor" option. If you die, the same or reduced payment is made regularly to your widow for as long as she may live.

Clearly there are many variations and ramifications of corporate pension funds—many more than have been explored here. And plans and provisions change over time. You will want to examine the pension and retirement provisions of a company job offer as one of the important features, just as you certainly will weigh salary, location, type of work, and opportunities for advancement.

The Pension Reform Act of 1974. This was enacted to correct abuses which had developed in private pension plans over the years. It's a very complicated statute, but several provisions may be of interest to you. Any employee who is at least age 25 and has one year on the company payroll must be taken into the pension plan—assuming the firm has one—and must be given credit for past service up to three years.

Companies are not required, under the new law, to set up retirement plans, or told precisely how benefits are to be computed; but where plans are operating—new or existing ones—employees must be permitted to accumulate pension credits in some fair and orderly way. For example, vesting is now required, with a choice of several options, but under any of the options an employee must become at least 50 percent vested after 10 years of service and 100 percent vested at 15 years, regardless of age.

In the past, even full vesting has not always guaranteed a worker the pension earned. Thousands of employees lost out when their companies failed, merged with others, or simply dropped pension plans. Now companies with pension plans must meet new standards of financing or funding. Formal pension funds will have to be managed and administered under trust arrangements or invested through an insurance company. Pension plan assets will have to be made independent of the future fortunes of the employer. Companies will now be required to "fund" currently the normal costs of pension rights as they accrue.

Extending the protection concept to pensions, a new Pension Benefit Guaranty Corporation now has been set up to insure all of a worker's vested benefits up to certain limits. The guarantee will be for a benefit amount up to 100 percent of a workers average pay in the five years of highest earnings, but no more than $750 of monthly pension at the start. That $750 ceiling is to rise with general wage levels.

The 40 million private industry employees who are not covered by any pension plan other than social security are now allowed to set up their own tax free retirement plans. Under the new law, these workers may create Individual Retirement Accounts, or IRAs, and an eligible employee may place as much as 15 percent of his or her pay in an IRA, up to a maximum of $1,500 a year, and take a tax deduction for the amount. This deduction is available even for those who claim the "standard" deduction, rather than itemize.

Funds put into IRAs must be invested in one of three ways: (*a*) they can be used to buy special annuities that will not begin to pay off until age 59½, or (*b*) they can be invested in a special type of Treasury bond that currently pays 6 percent, or (*c*) the money can be put into a trust to be administered by a bank or other approved institution.

The annual earnings from the invested funds, as well as the income put aside each year, is tax free. Withdrawals of funds from IRAs, at age 59½ or later, will be fully taxable income, though usually at lower rates than people pay in working years.[29]

---

[29] "How New Pension Law Will Affect You," *U.S. News & World Report*, August 26, 1974; "Worker, Bosses Alike Face Many Unknowns in New Pension Law," *Wall Street Journal*, August 28, 1974; "New 1974 Pension Reform Highlights," *Commerce Clearing House*, Chicago, 1974.

Pensions for the Self-Employed[30]

If, instead of going to work for a company, you set up your own small business or enter one of the professions, the provisions of the Self-Employed Individuals Tax Retirement Act of 1962, popularly known as the Keogh Act, as amended by the Pension Reform Act of 1974, will interest you. The act permits self-employed persons to establish tax favored retirement plans for themselves.

If you are self-employed as an accountant, architect, author, decorator, dentist, doctor, farmer, lawyer, or are an owner or partner in an unincorporated business and receive self-employment income from personal services rendered, you can set up a retirement plan and be eligible for tax benefits under the act.

The self-employed person can determine what the annual contribution to the retirement fund will be—up to the maximum set by law. For a sole proprietor, or a partner with more than a 15 percent capital or profit interest, the upper limit is 15 percent of earned income but not more than $7,500. For example, a dentist earning $20,000 a year can contribute 15 percent or $3,000 to a plan. A doctor, netting $40,000 a year, may contribute $6,000, tax free.

Under the old law, self-employed persons were allowed to put aside, tax free, up to 10 percent of their earnings, but no more than $2,500 a year. Starting in 1974, however, they were able to set aside up to 15 percent of earnings, with a top limit of $7,500. For beginning, low earning self-employed, $750 can be set aside tax free, no matter how small earnings are.

The tax advantage you receive is that you can deduct your annual contribution to your retirement plan from your taxable income. Furthermore, the income or capital gains from your invested fund are free from taxes until withdrawn. You will not be taxed until you actually receive distributions upon retirement. By that time your tax rate may be lower than in your active earning period.

There are some limitations, of course. You cannot withdraw funds until you reach age 59½ without incurring tax penalties. However, earlier distribution is permitted in case of permanent disability. Also your beneficiaries can receive benefits upon your death, even though that occurs before age 59½. If you set up a plan for yourself, you must also set up a plan for all your employees who have completed three years of continuous service at the date of the plan's adoption. Full tax deduction is permitted,

---

[30] See Internal Revenue Service Publication 560, *Retirement Plans for Self-Employed Individuals,* which may be obtained free of charge by sending a postcard to Internal Revenue Service. See also IRS Publication 566, *Questions and Answers on Retirement Plans for the Self-Employed.* This too may be obtained free of charge from your local IRS office.

however, for contributions made on behalf of "regular" employees. Also, you are restricted as to how you can invest the money. You have four main choices:

a. You may put the money into a trust.
b. You may purchase annuity contracts from an insurance company.
c. You may open a special "custodial" account with a bank, which account can be invested wholly in mutual fund shares, or wholly in annuity, endowment, or life insurance contracts issued by an insurance company.
d. You may purchase special U.S. government "retirement" bonds. Those bonds can't be cashed until you are 59½, unless you die or become disabled earlier.

The self employment retirement plan must be approved by the Internal Revenue Service, which also provides a plan number. Most large banks, brokerage houses, mutual funds, and insurance companies have master and model plans already approved. Also, many trade and professional associations have developed group plans involving, for example, group annuity contracts, or mutual fund plans.

Setting up a self-employed retirement plan isn't simple. The act is more complicated than has been indicated above. If and when you decide to take advantage of the act, consult a lawyer, or an accountant, or your insurance man, or your local banker. They will know about details and all changes which are likely to occur in this area between now and the time you may want to act.

THE ADEQUACY OF SOCIAL SECURITY AND RETIREMENT INCOME

The foregoing discussion of social security, annuities, and pensions does not pretend to be an exhaustive treatment of all ramifications of the subject. It should, however, give you a fairly good indication of your future stake in the programs. A family may receive benefits from social security which could otherwise be obtained only by having saved thousands of dollars or by having insurance policies upon which thousands of dollars of premiums had been paid.

In view of the fact that high living costs and high taxes are making it difficult for many families to save adequately in order to have reasonable income for survivors in case of the wage earner's death or for the wage earner in retirement, the forced saving of social security and pension plans

FIGURE 9–12
Retirement Planner—to Estimate Today How Much You Will Need Tomorrow

Use this planner to determine what you must put aside in order to have the monthly retirement income of your choice beginning at age 65 for life, according to the mortality table indicated below.

WE WILL NEED A MONTHLY INCOME OF .... $______
(approximately ⅔ of present expenses)

We shall have assured monthly income from:
Investments .... ______
Social Security .... ______
Pensions .... ______
Other .... ______

TOTAL MONTHLY INCOME ASSURED .... $______

ADDITIONAL INCOME NEEDED MONTHLY .... $______

USE CHART TO CALCULATE MONTHLY SAVINGS OR LUMP SUM REQUIRED AT YOUR PRESENT AGE TO PLAN RETIREMENT AT AGE 65

Match figure to closest dollar amount in this column.

Monthly amount required at retirement		YOUR PRESENT AGE 25	30	35	40	45	50	55	60
$200 ($22,696)*	lump sum	3,224	4,115	5,251	6,702	8,554	10,917	13,933	17,783
	or monthly	15	20	27	38	54	83	143	326
400 ($45,392)*	lump sum	6,448	8,229	10,503	13,404	17,108	21,834	27,867	35,566
	or monthly	30	40	54	75	109	167	286	652
600 ($68,088)*	lump sum	9,672	12,344	15,754	20,106	25,662	32,752	41,801	53,399
	or monthly	45	60	81	113	164	251	430	978
800 ($90,784)*	lump sum	12,896	16,458	21,006	26,809	34,216	43,669	55,734	71,132
	or monthly	60	80	108	151	218	334	573	1,304
1,000 ($113,480)*	lump sum	16,120	20,573	26,257	33,511	42,770	54,586	69,667	88,915
	or monthly	75	100	136	189	272	417	716	1,630

*Accumulation at age 65. All figures are based on 5% interest compounded annually. These figures are calculated on a fixed interest rate compounded annually and assuming no fluctuation in value of principal. The figures are not intended to be a projection of any investment results. Mutual fund shares of course may rise or fall in value and the dividends may vary in amount. No adjustment has been made for income taxes. Annuity figures use 1951 GA male table at 5%.

TO PLAN RETIREMENT AT AGE 60 USE AGE BRACKET 5 YEARS OLDER THAN YOUR OWN AND ADD 16% TO REQUIRED LUMP SUM OR MONTHLY INVESTMENT

For a combination of savings already accumulated and future monthly savings, simply use column for your age. Take lump sum required, then deduct amount already saved and find nearest balance in that column. This will show you what you must set aside each month.

EXAMPLE: At age 40, $20,106 is required for $600 a month at retirement. If you already have $7,000 set aside, you'll still need $13,106. The closest figure to this in the Age 40 column is $13,404 which is equal to $75 a month.

Source: The Oppenheimer Fund, Inc.

may indeed prove a blessing to many who, in its absence, would be forced into going on relief rolls.

If your prospective retirement benefits don't seem sufficient and you want higher income in retirement, the use of the "Retirement Planner" shown in Figure 9–12 may be helpful.

SUGGESTED READINGS

1. *Your Social Security*, SSA–10035, Social Security Administration, U.S. Department of Health, Education, and Welfare, Washington, D.C., latest edition.
2. *If You Become Disabled*, SSA–10029, Social Security Administration, U.S. Department of Health, Education, and Welfare, Washington, D.C., latest edition.
3. *You Can Work and Still Get Social Security Checks*, SSA–10092, Social Security Administration, U.S. Department of Health, Education, and Welfare, Washington, D.C., latest edition.
4. *Your Social Security Earnings Record*, SSA–10044, Social Security Administration, U.S. Department of Health, Education, and Welfare, Washington, D.C., latest edition.
5. *Social Security Benefits for Students 18–22*, SSA–10048, Social Security Administration, U. S. Department of Health, Education, and Welfare, Washington, D.C.
6. *Facts on Aging*, Office of Aging, U.S. Department of Health, Education, and Welfare, Washington, D.C.
7. *Social Security Information for Self-Employed Farmers*, SSA–10066, Social Security Administration, U.S. Department of Health, Education, and Welfare, Washington, D.C.
8. *Social Security Benefits—How to Estimate the Amount*, SSA–10047, Social Security Administration, U.S. Department of Health, Education, and Welfare, Washington, D.C.
9. *Social Security Benefits for People Disabled Since Childhood*, SSA–10012, Social Security Administration, U.S. Department of Health, Education, and Welfare, Washington, D.C.
10. *Special Information for Self-Employed People*, SSA–10022, Social Security Administration, U.S. Department of Health, Education, and Welfare, Washington, D.C.
11. *Social Security Information for Young Families*, SSA–10033, Social Security Administration, U.S. Department of Health, Education, and Welfare, Washington, D.C.

12. *Changing Times, The Kiplinger Magazine:*
"The New Pension Law Could Be Good News For You," December 1974.
"Do-It-Yourself Pensions," January 1975.
"What a Housewife Is Worth," April 1973.
"A Special Report on Social Security—New Tables You Can Use Now," October 1973.
"Your Social Security: How to Protect It," October 1971.
13. *Commerce Clearing House,* Chicago:
a. Pension Reform Act of 1974, Law and Explanation, (4892).
b. Explanation of Pension Reform Act of 1974, (4891).
c. New Tax Saving Plans for Self-Employed, (4890).
d. New 1974 Pension Reform Highlights, (4348).
e. 1974 Social Security and Medicare Explained, including Medicaid, (4935).
f. New 1974 Social Security Benefits, Including Medicare, (4936).
14. "How New Pension Law Will Affect You," *U.S. News & World Report,* August 26, 1974.
15. "Pension Reform's Expensive Ricochet," *Business Week,* March 24, 1975.
16. W. R. Sloane, "Life Insurers, Variable Annuities and Mutual Funds: A Critical Study," *Journal of Risk and Insurance,* March 1970.
17. D. A. West, and G. L. Wood, "Risk Attitudes of Annuity—Prone Investors," *Journal of Risk and Insurance,* March 1970.
18. "Planning a Retirement Program," *Teachers Insurance and Annuity Association College Retirement Equities Fund Bulletin,* latest edition.
19. "The Push for Pension Reform," *Business Week,* March 17, 1973.
20. *Money:*
Jeremy Main, "The Good Life Costs Less After 65," May 1973.
Jeffrey G. Madrick, "The Case for Spending It Now," October 1973.
William B. Mead, "The Squeeze Ahead for Social Security," October 1974.
21. Peter Langier, *You Can Collect From Social Security Regardless of Age and Income.* Saugatuck, Conn.: World Publications, 1973.
22. Carolyn Shaw Bell, "Social Security: Unfair to Those Who Pay It Unfair to Those Who Receive It," *Challenge,* July/August 1973, pp. 18–22.
23. "Social Security: The Real Cost of Those Rising Benefits," *Fortune,* December 1973, p. 80.
24. Edwin L. Dale, Jr., "The Security of Social Security—The Young Pay for the Old," *New York Times Magazine,* February 11, 1973, pp. 8, 40–45.

25. Robert C. Alberts, "Catch 65," *New York Times Magazine,* August 4, 1974.

26. Special Report on Social Security—"Promising Too Much to Too Many" *U.S. News & World Report,* July 15, 1974, pp. 26–30.

CASE PROBLEMS

1. Joe Bartlett first became covered by social security on January 1, 1956. He is now 62 and will retire July 1, 1978, at age 65. His average earnings are $8,000. When he retires, how much will his monthly benefits be? His wife is now age 56. His children are ages 17 and 24. How is each member of the family covered?

2. Malcolm Watson earns $5,350 from his free lance writing, apart from his $17,500 salary in an advertising firm. How does social security cover this?

3. When George McNair (annual earnings, $14,000) received his monthly salary, he found that $70 had been deducted as his social security payment. He figured that this was too much because at that rate he would be paying $840 a year. What mistake had been made?

4. Ralph Vinal now earns $120 a month working part time. Do his present earnings cancel his social security benefits? Mr. Vinal will be 73 years old next week. He is offered a part time job paying $200 monthly, but he is afraid to take it because he does not want to lose his social security. What does the law say about this?

5. Francis O'Connor was covered by social security from July 1, 1964. His average wages amounted to $7,500 a year. He died in November, 1974. What benefits should his wife (age 29) and his two children (ages 2 and 7) have received? How long do they receive benefits?

6. Pete Grant was injured in an accident in the steel plant where he works. Since then, for the last 10 months, he has been receiving company benefits. Should Mr. Grant, instead of just being content with the company compensation, have done something about applying for social security benefits? To what benefits, if any, is he entitled? Explain.

7. Rita Ramirez is 19 and she has been living alone with her father, a disabled World War II veteran since her mother died when she was six years old. She is a business major at college and is afraid she may have to drop out because her father can no longer afford the college expense and she does not want to get a loan. Someone told her that social security would help, since her mother had worked in a department store before she died. But Rita says that was too long ago. What are the facts in this situation?

8. Mrs. Stephens, a court stenographer, left four children all under 18 when she died in an auto accident last year. Her husband is working, and they had a modest savings account. For what social security benefits are they eligible?

9. Paul Vincent has been working for 10 years and just wrote the Social Security Administration for his first statement of past earnings. When it came, he checked his papers and found a mistake made by his second employer five years ago. What can he do?

10. Mrs. Karen Gorse cannot find her birth certificate and remembers only that her family left Iowa when she was a child of two. She plans to retire in a year. What can she do to present proof of age?

10

Health Care

With health—everything is a source of pleasure, without it nothing else, whatever it may be, is enjoyable.
Schopenhauer

A TWO AND ONE HALF YEAR OLD girl developed nephrosis from a bee sting, and other complications, such as diabetes, allergy, and cataracts, resulted from the medication used. This girl is not cured yet, and the bills are not all in, but so far that bee sting has cost the family $57,794.[1]

Fiction? Not at all. A real life story! Fortunately, as medical costs have risen, the insurance device has been adapted to meet them. It is now possible to obtain insurance to meet the two essential needs in any accident or illness: (*a*) to provide funds to help pay the medical and hospital bills involved and (*b*) to provide for the continuance of income while a breadwinner is ill or disabled.

HEALTH COSTS

Medical needs for the individual are unpredictable, almost impossible to budget. One severe illness, or a number of minor ones in a short period, can wreck the family budget and bring on indebtedness. A hospitalized illness "involves a severe physical shock, a high emotional crisis, and a large economic expenditure." In one year illness cost families of the United States $104.2 billion. The average hospitalized illness costs in the neighborhood of $625, apart from loss of income, and in some cases the cost rises to several thousand dollars. Last year one out of every seven persons in the United States was hospitalized. The average cost per hospital stay ranged from a low of $476.64 in Wyoming to a high of $1,287.74 in New York.

[1] *Wall Street Journal*, May 7, 1970, p. 1.

On a daily basis the range was from $68.62 in South Dakota to $148.80 in Alaska.

On a per person basis, health spending averaged $485. Direct out of pocket payments averaged $149.[2] The cost of medical care over the nation rose by 55 percent between 1967 and 1974; charges for hospital rooms went up more than 100 percent and national health expenditures for physicians' services rose by 56 percent over the same period.

Figure 10–1 compares the increase in all items in the Consumer Price Index with the greater increase for items of health care.

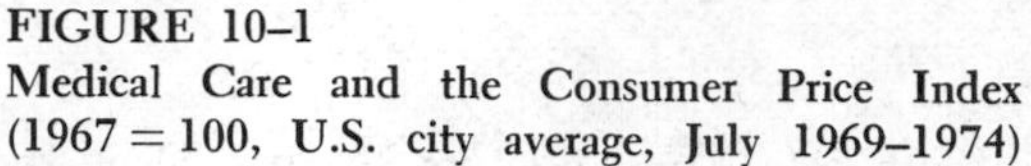

FIGURE 10–1
Medical Care and the Consumer Price Index (1967 = 100, U.S. city average, July 1969–1974)

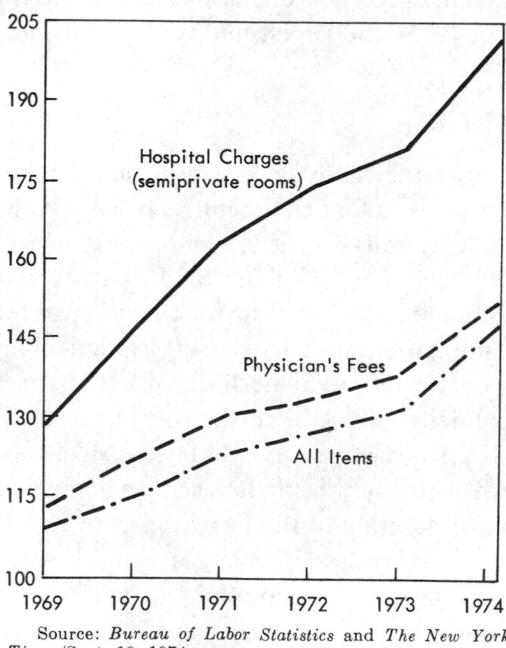

Source: *Bureau of Labor Statistics* and *The New York Times*/Sept. 19, 1974.

Table 10–1 would indicate a decrease in the ratio of population to physician. The map (Figure 10–2) showing the maldistribution of physicians may be one explanation for the many contradictory statements that there is both scarcity and plenty of available physicians.

A government publication notes that the need for physicians is expected to increase by as much as 50 percent between 1968 and 1980. This would

[2] Nancy L. Worthington, "National Health Expenditures, 1929–1974," *Social Security Bulletin*, February 1975.

TABLE 10–1
Physicians—Population Ratio

Year	*Physicians per 100,000 Population*
1950	141
1955	142
1960	141
1965	147
1970	158
1971	165
1972	167
1973	171

require about 20,000 new doctors a year. "More than 16,689 doctors were licensed in 1973—the largest one year gain in medical manpower ever."[3]

Filling a Need

The National Health Service Corp. has attempted to redistribute medical professionals so that communities that have fewer than one doctor for 4,000 residents will benefit. In return for two years of service, young doctors who join are paid about $12,000 a year in salary and are forgiven 60 percent of their personal loans. In exchange for three years of service 85 percent forgiveness is offered. New legislation being planned encourages a young doctor to give some form of national service in return for the federal subsidies given toward the cost of the training. A similar idea, begun by the University of New Mexico Medical School seniors to fill a health care gap, is now being funded by a grant from the Bureau of Health Manpower Education of the Department of Health, Education and Welfare. The students needed practical clinical experience and the isolated areas needed medical care. Another program offers "supernurses," of whom there are now 10,000, to fill the gap. Usually they practice in association with physicians jointly providing more effective health care. On occasion when the supernurses act independently, some insurers have, at times, balked at reimbursing patients for their bills. Some doctors are critical of what they term these "second class doctors."[4]

A special Harris opinion poll on doctors reported that large sections of the public feel doctors jam too many patients into office hours, have raised their fees to take advantage of medicare and medicaid, are reluctant to make house calls. People complain that general practitioners are mainly a

[3] *New York Times* July 23, 1974, quoting the American Medical Association.

[4] *Wall Street Journal*, July 3, 1974.

FIGURE 10–2
Poor Distribution of Physicians

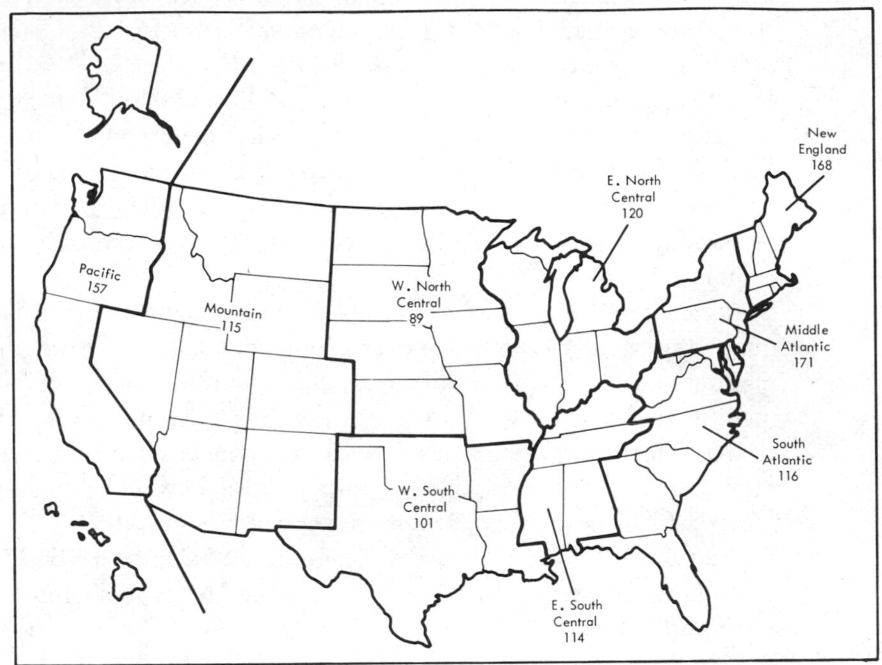

Note: Numbers are physicians per 100,000 population.
Source: *New York Times*, April 28, 1971.

referral source and say that doctors should concentrate more on preventive medicine.[5] In a recent year, more than four out of five physicians reported they were specialists. "Medicine in the United States is no longer experiencing a trend toward specializations. It is specialized."[6]

The medical profession is also unhappy about the public. The number of malpractice suits has increased to the extent that insurance companies are paying out millions more than they take in on premiums. Premium costs in most states have tripled in two and a half years. In California which leads the nation in malpractice actions, premiums rose more than 400 percent since 1968. Since malpractice suits have become more common, doctors engage in "defensive medicine"—more tests, X-rays, and consultants than usual—which raises costs to the patient.

As the following example illustrates, physician and hospital costs have skyrocketed. A simple appendectomy may cost, in all, about $1,200 ($400 for the surgeon, $150 for the anesthetist and operating room, $550 for

[5] *Washington Post*, November 9, 1970.

[6] *Socioeconomic Issues of Health*, American Medical Association, Chicago, 1973.

hospital room at the rate of $110 a day for five days in a semiprivate room, $50 for drugs in the hospital, and about $125 in fees for diagnosis and for visits to the general practitioner before and after the operation)—in addition to loss of income for a month. Further, if you need special nursing care, a registered nurse charges $45 for an eight hour shift, and sometimes necessity requires special duty private nurses in the hospital on a round the clock, 24 hour basis. If you can use a practical nurse at home after the operation, it will cost about $36 for a 12 hour day. When the family with an income of less than $15,000 is confronted with such costs, it is in trouble.

Accident and sickness can (1) cut off family income, (2) quickly wipe out savings slowly accumulated over a long period, or (3) leave a hopeless muddle of debt, or (4) be so costly that a family cannot afford all the medical services it needs. For these reasons, increasing millions have turned to prepayment insurance plans to ease the monetary pains of heavy hospital, surgical, and medical bills. And increasingly public funds bear a larger share of the medical care cost as shown in Figure 10–3.

A study by the Committee for Economic Development (CED) notes that there are large gaps of health coverage for certain groups in the population.

> The uninsured were concentrated among the poor. As many as 64 percent of people with family incomes of less than $3,000 and 43 percent in families with incomes of $3,000 to $5,000 were uninsured.
>
> As many as 44 percent of nonwhites were uninsured, compared with 19 percent of all whites.

FIGURE 10–3
Who Pays the Nation's Health Bill? (public funds now pay 40 percent)

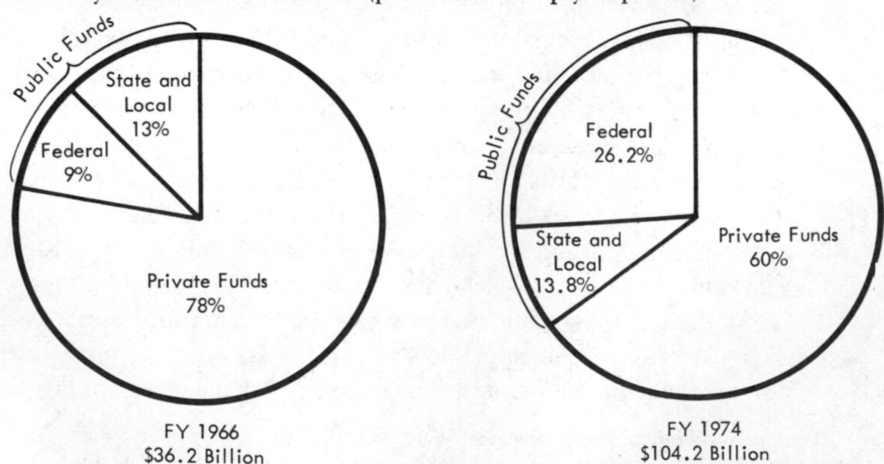

Source: Social Security Administration, U.S. Department of Health, Education and Welfare, 1975.

Among the categories of people less often insured were the unmarried (24 percent were not insured), the widowed (29 percent), the divorced (30 percent), and the separated (49 percent).

People with various kinds of disabilities were also often uninsured. Among those limited in some degree by disability in pursuit of their major activity, 30 percent of those under 65 were not insured. Among those unable to carry on their major activity, as many as 51 percent were uninsured.

The uninsured were also often to be found among the unemployed. In many instances, even brief periods of unemployment result in a loss of protection, despite many efforts to extend coverage during interruptions of work and sustained unemployment.

Occupations in which coverage is relatively limited include service workers (26 percent) and farm workers (52 percent).[7]

Surveys indicate that most Americans are not really sure of what their health insurance policies cover. When they discover the omissions it is too late. It has been said that "buying adequate health insurance may be the single most difficult purchase a consumer may ever make." The legalese and the hidden booby traps in the small print make evaluating a policy difficult. The following pages should help clarify some aspects.[8]

Prepaid Voluntary Medical Care Insurance

Accident and sickness (health) insurance has usually been used broadly to provide two very different kinds of protection: (*a*) "health" or "medical care" insurance plans, including the cost of hospitalization, surgical, limited medical, major medical catastrophes, and comprehensive medical care; and (*b*) "disability" insurance plans, compensating injured persons for the loss of a part or parts of the body, such as an arm or a leg or an eye, *or* for the loss of earnings through disability. For an early example of how it all began see Figure 10–4.

The former type now covers some 182 million persons in the United States, the latter some 76 million. There has been a striking increase in recent years in the number of people in the United States who have been covered by voluntary insurance, especially group insurance, against some part of the costs of medical care. The number of those who had some protection against the costs of hospital care, for example, was less than 6

---

[7] *Building a National Health-Care System,* Committee for Economic Development, Research & Policy Committee, April 1973, pp. 63–64.

[8] For a discussion of guideposts see *Diagnosing Your Health Insurance* by Warren Boroson in *Money,* September 1974, pp. 39–51.

FIGURE 10–4
A Pioneer in Prepaid Voluntary Medical Care Insurance (what the benefits were in 1904)

SOUVENIR OF THE
SUMMER-NIGHTS FESTIVAL
OF THE
Gas Companies Employees Mutual Aid Society of New York
To be held at the **Manhattan Casino**, 155th St. & 8th Ave.
New York City
FRIDAY EVENING, JULY 22, 1904

EMPLOYEES OF THE GAS COMPANIES OF NEW YORK CITY
should join the Society for the following reasons:
1. Your family or friends will receive - - - - -
$300.00 AT YOUR DEATH
if you pay into the Society one and two-third cents per day. - - - - - - - - - - - - - - -
2. If you are sick you will have the care of a good
DOCTOR, AND $6.00 A WEEK
for twelve (12) weeks. You pay only one (1) cent per day or thirty (30) cents a month extra into the Society for this benefit. - - - - - - - - - -
3. If you are sick more than the twelve (12) weeks during which time you received $6.00, the medical attendance of the Society's Doctor continues until you are fully recovered. - - - - - - - - -
4. During illness, in nearly all cases - - - - - -
MEDICINES ARE FURNISHED FREE
5. That the Society may do this, the Consolidated Gas Company of New York, contributes fifty (50) cents for every dollar that the member contributes. The company supplies the medical attendance without cost to the Society. - - - - - - - - - - -
Where can you make a better Investment?
If not now a member consult the Financial Secretary of your Branch, Station or Department in which you are employed at once for your own good, and he will start you in the right direction to become one of us.

Total benefits paid since organization to July 1, 1904,	$62.400.00
Total cash on hand July 1, 1904,	$24.706.24

O. H. LABARRE, 407 FOURTH AVE., N. Y.

Source: *Your Medical Care and Sickness Benefits*, courtesy of Consolidated Edison Employees' Mutual Aid Society, Inc.

million in 1939. Figure 10–5 shows the growth since then. Today more than 89 percent of our population are covered by some form of voluntary medical care insurance.

While disability insurance was the more popular type prior to World War II, medical care insurance has now superseded it in importance, as more and more people have come to realize that the chances of their losing an eye, or an arm, or a leg are minute compared to the prospect that they will, at some point, land in a hospital to have an appendix removed or some infectious disease cured. Health insurance, can be

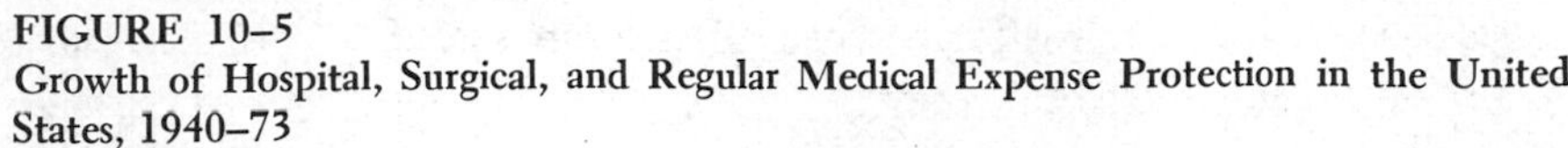

FIGURE 10–5
Growth of Hospital, Surgical, and Regular Medical Expense Protection in the United States, 1940–73

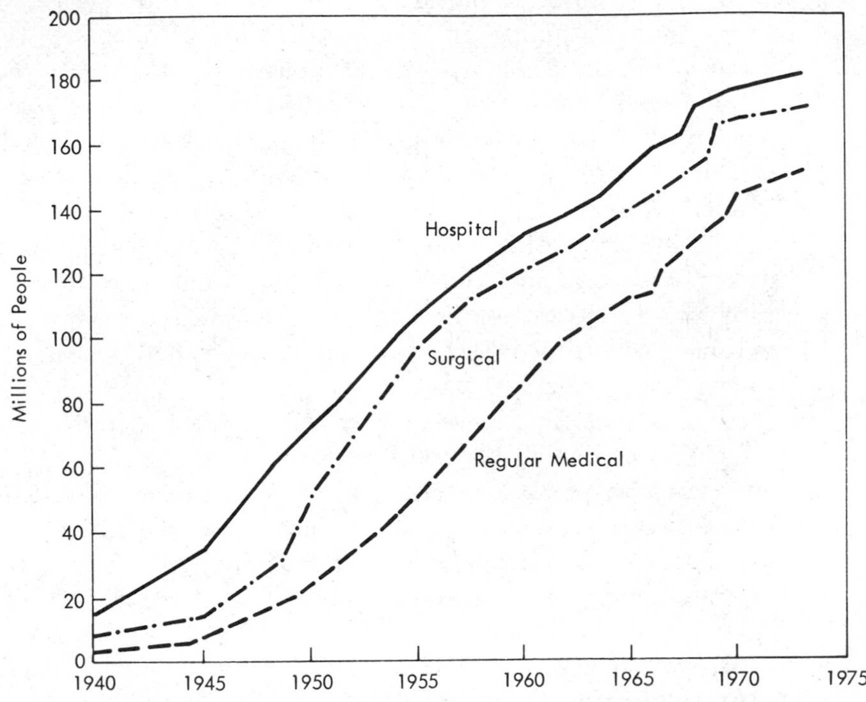

Source: Health Insurance Council.

considered in five categories: (a) disability insurance (b) hospital expense insurance, (c) surgical expense insurance, (d) regular medical care insurance, (e) major medical expense insurance. When a health insurance plan covers hospital, surgical, and nonsurgical medical insurance, it is often referred to as a "base" or "basic" plan. When the basic plan is combined with a major medical plan, it is called a comprehensive plan.

Loss of Income or Disability Insurance

Protection against loss of income resulting from sickness or accident is the oldest form of voluntary health insurance. This type of insurance pays benefits when you are unable to work because of sickness or accident. The problem which looms large in cases of illness or accident is the loss of wages or salary during the period needed to regain one's health. The economic cost of accidents add up to $30.4 billion—a dollar amount required to pay for property damage, legal, medical, surgical and hospital costs, the administrative costs of insurance and loss of income resulting from absence from work.[9]

Policies of this type provide as much as 50 to 65 percent of wage earners' normal earnings for a specified period of disability. Usually a company will not pay more than three quarters of the regular weekly or monthly income for a very good reason: if a person were able to buy a policy which paid as much or more than what was earned while working, there would be strong incentive toward feigned illnesses and delay in returning to work.

Disability can be interpreted many ways in your contract. If you can do any kind of gainful work—not necessarily your usual job—the company may say you are not disabled. It may not recognize partial disability as coming within the coverage—or it may be generous, which, of course, costs higher premiums.

The possibility that disability is caused by illness increases as you get older. The noncancellable policy that covers both accident and illness offers effective protection and value for your money. The longer the payments covered, the higher the premium cost. If you try to balance the long period by a small amount of disability payment so as to reduce expenses, you are working against yourself statistically. Most disabilities last for a relatively short period. Based on averages, you give yourself better protection by buying higher coverage for a shorter period.

Disability payments under social security have been liberalized recently and should be taken into consideration in planning your disability insurance. Previously, benefits were paid only to those whose disability was expected to continue indefinitely or result in death. Now short term disability is covered, with payments beginning 5 months after incapacitation and lasting 12 months or more.

The longer the waiting period, the more inexpensive the insurance. To avoid small claims, costly in paper work and overhead, the insurance companies will pass the benefit to the insured person in either larger monthly income or longer coverage. In determining the length of the waiting period, the insured should consider the amount of personal savings and other disability payments that can be used for living expenses during this period. For the long term, the best policy, then, is the one with a moderately long waiting period, noncancellable, and guaranteed renewable until the day the policyholder reaches a certain age.

The number of persons protected by group loss of income plans through private industry and government is greater than those covered by in-

[9] *Insurance Facts, 1974,* Insurance Information Institute, 110 William St., New York, N.Y. 10038.

dividual policies. This is true also of other forms of health insurance, since most of the people who have health insurance today obtain it as members of employed groups.

Consider two actual cases, one involving an individual policy, the other an example of a group policy. Mary O'Brien graduated from State College two years ago. She is 25, single, with no dependents now, teaching school in Illinois, earning $9,400 a year. As part of her health insurance protection, she has purchased a policy which, at an annual premium cost of $66.08, will pay her a monthly income of $200 for five years in case she is disabled by an accident or illness which prevents her from earning a living. Since Mary rooms with another teacher, her rent is low, and she feels she can save enough money from her salary to cover her possible expenses if she buys the policy with a 30 day waiting period rather than one with a 7 day waiting period. This will reduce her premium costs by 25 percent.

Our second case is that of a young bachelor attorney, Robert Farmer, Jr. He's 26, graduated from Yale Law School, earns $16,400 a year. At a premium cost of $106 a year, he recently purchased a policy through his bar association which, if he becomes disabled as a result of an accident, will pay him $150 a week for seven years starting from the first day of the accident, or $150 a week for seven years starting from the eighth day of sickness or first day of hospital confinement. Under this policy he has lifetime protection, wherever he goes, as long as he is a member of this bar association. For most new noncancellable policies, the benefits for sickness and accident are the same. Long term policies (over five years) all go to age 65 when on a group basis.

Under-20 Employees Most Accident Prone

Don't trust anyone under 20 years of age—when it comes to being accident-prone in an office environment—reports the Health Insurance Institute.

A five year life insurance company study of office accidents showed that falls are the single greatest cause of disabling accidents and that employees under 20 are the most accident-prone of any age group.

The accident rate dropped through ages 30 to 59, the study found, then, rose slightly between the ages of 60 to 64.

The study also indicated that while male office workers have about as many accidents as females, men sustain more disabling ones.

Source: *Health Insurance News*, May 4, 1970.

Women, who account for 38 percent of the American work force, have trouble getting disability insurance. Four out of ten working women are mothers and 36 percent of these have children under 6 years of age. A woman alone or supporting children or whose income is needed for the family would be in financial difficulties, if disabled and her earnings lost. Her disability insurance would cost twice the amount a man would pay. In contrast, a free lance male artist, working at home, if disabled would have no problem. A woman artist in the same situation would find her indemnity automatically reduced 50 percent.[10] Although insurance companies claim women have much more illness than men, social security disability claims in 1970 were 5.3 men per 1,000 and 3.9 per 1,000 for women. The insurance industry supports its unequal treatment of women needing disability insurance by insisting they are only part time workers, despite Department of Labor statistics that a married woman with children works 25 years and a single woman an average of 45 years.

Hospital Expense Protection

More than 9 out of 10 persons in the United States are now protected through voluntary programs against the costs of hospital care in the event of accident or illness. Over 182 million people have this biggest single form of coverage in the field of health protection. Insurance companies provide about 50 percent of the coverage. Hospital expense protection provides benefits toward the payment of hospital charges for room, board, and miscellaneous services. Benefits have been steadily liberalized and expanded since this form of coverage began its major growth some two decades ago. Present day coverage usually includes payment for use of an operating room and for laboratory and X-ray examination, medicines, and all other services incidental to medical care and treatment which are furnished by the hospital. You are allowed so much per day up to a maximum number of days, usually 120 to 365. Pioneered by Blue Cross, hospital expense insurance is now sold by all the major insurance companies as part of their total health insurance package.

Over a period of a year, the actuarial risk involved in a possible serious illness requiring hospitalization is about 7 percent for a 30 year old male, 12 percent for a female in the same age bracket, and 5 percent for a child.

Hospitalization costs have risen higher than any other health cost. The average cost of room and board in hospitals across the nation is about $110 a day, exclusive of any medical care. Blue Cross rates nationally

---

[10] *New York Times*, February 9, 1974.

have been steadily rising, to meet increased hospital costs, for which unnecessary usage is partly blamed. Studies have shown that more patients today occupy beds to gain insurance coverage for tests and minor operations that could be done at less cost outside but for which they have no insurance.

To minimize this, a plan known as PAT (preadmission testing) has been tried in various areas. New York Blue Cross repays in full all presurgical testing providing that it is completed seven days before a scheduled surgery and it is done in the same member hospital where the surgery takes place. The Harvard University Community Health Plan in New England, and some suburban Los Angeles communities as well as some larger private insurance companies, are using PAT. Increasingly additional areas are adopting this practice.

Surgery without hospitalization—sometimes known as verticare or ambulatory surgery is practiced now in one out of seven hospitals in the American Hospital Association. By eliminating overnight stays for minor surgery, it frees beds for the more seriously ill, cuts hospital medical expenses for room service charges, nursing care, laundry bills, allows the operating room to be more fully utilized and saves money and time for the patient. Variations of the plan provide for checking in for breakfast and getting home in time for dinner or allowing patients to come for surgery between 4 and 9 P.M. after having had presurgical tests early in the day and so are free to spend the time between at home or at work.[11] George Washington University Hospital in Washington, D.C., using this system since 1966, had to hospitalize only 1 percent of its 14,000 patients. A 20 minute cataract operation allowed the patient to leave the hospital shortly afterwards, check into a nearby hotel and visit his surgeon daily instead of spending days in the hospital.[12] Currently 63 of the 74 U.S. Blue Cross plans pay the full cost of outpatient care.[13]

Another pressure on hospital beds is caused by the lack of post hospital facilities—convalescent or nursing homes. A spot survey of 50 representative hospitals showed that 8.3 percent of their beds were occupied by holdovers who no longer needed hospital care, while on that day "hundreds of persons awaited admittance, a good many of whom were classified as emergency or urgent cases."[14] A number of Blue Cross plans have developed a workable method for cutting costs as follows:

---

[11] *U.S. News & World Report*, February 18, 1974.

[12] *New York Times*, February 2, 1974.

[13] *Wall Street Journal*, January 4, 1974.

[14] *New York Times*, March 19, 1971. Statement by Dr. Joseph R. Brennan, head of the Hospital Utilization Committee of Kings County Medical Society, New York.

1. The amount Blue Cross will pay per day for a bed patient is determined in advance. The hospital is then responsible for keeping within this limit or itself bearing the cost of the difference.
2. Most hospitals now have a utilization committee which reviews every admission and checks lengthy stays.
3. A home care posthospital program has been initiated which, with the doctor's approval, is covered by Blue Cross.
4. A recently completed detailed study of hospital costs and uses has been made through a new Blue Cross computer program.

Similar procedures are being tried in such states as Maryland and Connecticut where Health Services Cost Review Commissions are attempting surgery on operating costs. These efforts are being watched as possible models by other states.[15]

If through fear of rising hospital costs, you are considering a supplementary insurance policy offering extra cash when hospitalized, study carefully what the large advertised sums amount to when broken down by day payments and remember that the usual hospital stay for those under 65 is about a week. Will that extra premium cost give an adequate return? Equally important: look at the small print. Do you get immediate coverage for all possibilities as of the time you sign, as the big print seems to say—or is there a subtly worded exemption requiring a long wait before benefits will be paid on a physical condition you had before the policy went into effect?

Mail Order Health Insurance

Practitioners of the big promise and little return may be found among the mail order insurance companies. Small by comparison with the giants of the health insurance industry, is the mail order share, but its growth in new business is leaping. Promises of $1,000 a month cash free when you go to the hospital sound great, until you realize that most hospital stays average five days and benefits usually start after the sixth day. Also, while everyone is accepted without an examination, the insurance company doesn't pay claims if they result from ailments you had two years before the claim. It's the insurance company that decides if you had the ailment when the policy was issued—even if you didn't know of it. Some ads promise $50,000 hospital payments, giving hope of coverage in a catastrophic illness. Usually a long term illness patient is shifted to a

[15] *Wall Street Journal*, December 10, 1974.

nursing home, rarely stays long enough in the hospital to benefit from such a claim, and nursing homes are not covered.

While state regulatory agencies, the Senate Antitrust and Monopoly Subcommittee, and the Federal Trade Commision, are continuing to expose the deceptive language and statistics, the small print exclusions, and to control the misleading or deceptive advertising, it is really your own obligation to read the offers carefully to see if the supplementary coverage fits your needs and covers probable possibilities. The famous person endorsement does not prove you will be getting your money's worth.[16]

Surgical Expense Protection

The next largest form of protection in the field of voluntary accident and health coverage is surgical expense protection. The number of persons with this form of coverage now totals more than 169 million. A later development than coverage for hospital care, surgical expense protection has shown the more rapid growth over recent years. If the services of a surgeon are needed, the protection provides payments in accordance with a schedule of fees fixing maximum reimbursement for each type of operation.

The policy you buy prescribes the maximum the insurance company will pay according to the schedule. If an operation costs more than the sum the company will pay under the schedule, you pay the difference. The cost of the policy bears a direct relationship to the maximum the company contracts to pay. The higher the maximum, naturally the higher the cost; the lower the maximum, the lower the cost.

Regular Medical Expense Protection

In the development of voluntary accident and health coverage, regular medical expense protection came third, following the growth of hospital and surgical benefits. Its growth has been essentially a post-World War II phenomenon. In 1941 it was estimated that there were only about 3 million persons with regular medical expense protection. Today more than 152 million carry this type of coverage.

This type of coverage pays for visits to a doctor's office or for his visits to you at your home or in a hospital, as well as diagnostic, X-ray, and laboratory expenses. The maximum number of calls for each sickness or

[16] For a detailed discussion see *Consumer Reports*, May 1973, pp. 304–310.

$10,000 3-Day Medical Bill For Man Who Died Queried

YREKA, Calif., Nov. 30 (AP)—Emil A. Liloiva accrued a medical bill of more than $10,000 in the last 70 hours of his life, and the administrator of his estate wants doctors to justify every cent.

Mr. Liloiva was wheeled unconscious into Siskiyou General Hospital last Dec. 11 and died three days later after two unsuccessful heart operations.

"I don't think you should charge $11,000 or $12,000 for dying," Charles Hurley, the Siskiyou County Administrator, said Monday. "I want the claims proved." Earl Van Wagoner, administrator of the hospital, acknowledged that the bill was high, but said that the hospital would make only $250 after expenses.

A doctor has filed suit against Mr. Liloiva's estate to force payment of the bill. An insurance company paid $6,672 and the balance was passed on to Mr. Hurley for payment by the estate, whose estimated value is less than $4,000.

New York Times—December 1, 1974.

injury is usually specified in the policy. Some companies will not write this type of policy because they feel it is a cost that should be budgeted rather than insured. They will, however, provide for it in combination policies, either surgical–medical, or comprehensive. The Blue Shield organization sells different kinds of general medical policies depending upon your income. Figure 10–6 shows how the more traditional types of coverage have grown.

Major Medical Expense Coverage

Major medical expense coverage is designed to help meet the catastrophic costs resulting from very serious illnesses and from prolonged disability. Broadly speaking, the financial benefits under this form of coverage are paid toward virtually all kinds of health care prescribed by a physician. Major medical has had a very rapid growth.

For those who may be hospitalized for long periods, or those who require extensive treatment by medical specialists, it is a form of protection against large medical bills not covered by the usual type of hospital and surgical plans. As one authority put it: "Major medical takes up where the basic health plans stop." Major medical expense insurance ordinarily pays benefits whether hospitalization is involved or not. Major medical

FIGURE 10–6
Percent of Population with Private Health Insurance by Type of Coverage (selected years 1955–73)

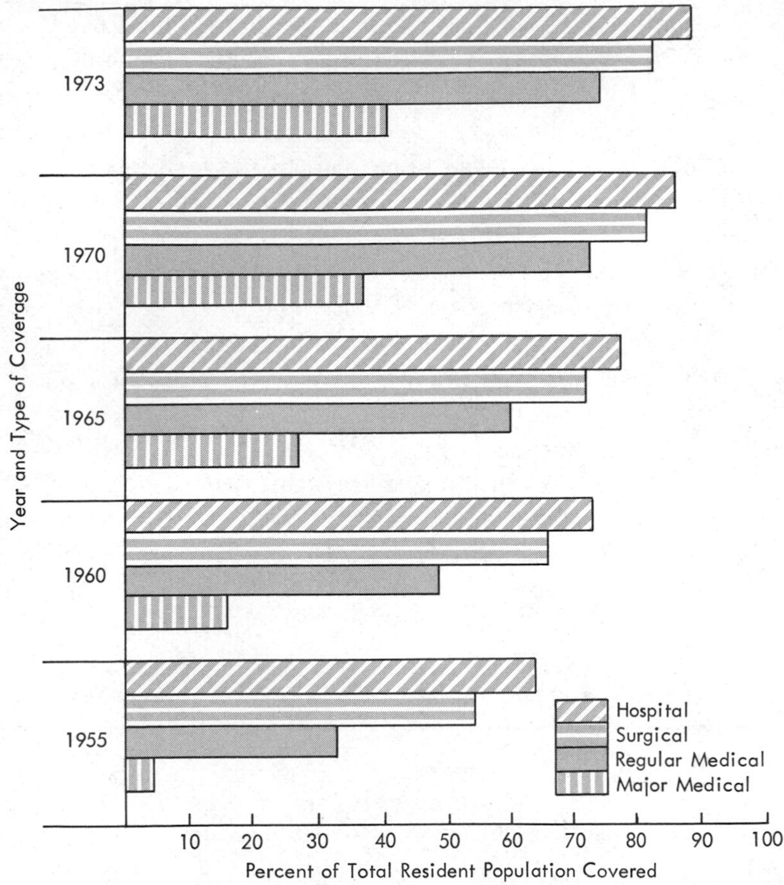

Source: Health Insurance Council, 1973; New York, Health Insurance Institute, *Source Book of Health Insurance Data*, 1970; *Socioeconomic Issues of Health* (rev. ed. Chicago: American Medical Association, 1973).

policies, furthermore, insure against expense arising from almost any conceivable medical cause, not just rarities like polio, spinal meningitis, or a selected list of diseases. A few policies exclude mental illness, but most in group insurance don't.

There are three distinguishing features of major medical insurance: (1) There are high maximum limits, ranging from $5,000 to $50,000 or more, as many as 44 percent have $50,000 coverage. The maximum may apply to any one illness, to a policy year, or to a lifetime. (2) A deductible provision, similar to that found in most automobile collision policies, is used in major medical. This is to eliminate what would otherwise be an undue burden of many small claims, excessive in number and costly to handle and process. The deductible is the beginning amount of medical expense which the policyholder himself must pay before insurance coverage takes effect. The deductible amounts commonly range from $100 to $1,000, with $250 or $500 most usual. The higher the deductible, the lower the premium. (3) The third feature is the "coinsurance" clause. This requires the policyholder to pay part of the total bill, over and above the deductible. The purpose is to prevent demands for excessive medical service.

What does major medical cost? Most major medical policies are sold under group plans. Don Thomas purchased a major medical policy through his dental association. It had a $15,000 maximum benefit, a $100 deductible clause, and a 20 percent coinsurance provision. It cost but $49.50 per annum.

Let's see how major medical works. Don Thomas developed a severe case of hepatitis which necessitated an extended period of hospitalization followed by a long convalescence at home. He is covered by a basic plan and by major medical insurance. His expenses are shown in Table 10–2.

As you can see, of a total bill of $8,460 Don paid only $1,112; major medical paid $4,048, about half the bill.

TABLE 10–2

	Total Charges	*Covered by Base Plan**	*Covered by Major Medical*
Hospital room and board:			
50 days @ $80 per day	$4,000	$2,200	$1,800
Other hospital charges:			
X-rays, blood tests, medicines, etc.	1,010	800	210
Registered nurses:			
$90 per day for 30 days	2,700	. . .	2,700
Physicians' fees	750	300	450
Totals	$8,460	$3,300	$5,160
Less: Deductible of $100			−100
Balance subject to coinsurance			5,060
Less: Coinsurance at 20%			−1,012
Amount paid by major medical			$4,048

Summary:	
Paid by base plan*	$3,300
Paid by major medical	4,048
Paid by patient	1,112
Total	$8,460

* Hospital room and board and general medical expense.
Source: Health Insurance Institute.

Comprehensive Medical Insurance

Now popular is the combination type of health insurance that ties together the basic plans of hospitalization, surgical expense, and regular medical expense protection with major medical insurance into one big package policy called "comprehensive." It began in 1954 with about 100 policies in force covering 50,000 employees and their families. It is currently estimated that over 24 million people have this type of policy.

The Federal Employees Health Program offered by a consortium of health insurance organizations is one of the largest group comprehensive major medical plans in force, covering in excess of 1.5 million persons. See Table 10–3, which illustrates what the different groups offer in comprehensive major medical plans in benefits, exceptions, and costs. The program consists of a high and low option, with about three fourths of the persons included selecting the high option. The high option described here has a $50,000 maximum a year for each enrollee and each member of his family, with exhausted benefits automatically restored in the amount of $2,000 per person a year until the top limit is again reached. If family expenses exceed $10,000 in any given year, they are paid in full.

A similar plan sponsored by the Teachers Insurance and Annuity Association is available to colleges, universities, independent schools and other nonprofit institutions engaged in education or research.[17] Premiums vary among institutions, but in each it is an averaged monthly rate, one amount for employee insurance and other for dependent coverage. Most institutions contribute a substantial portion of the premium. Prepaid medical plans and health maintenance organizations (HMOS) usually provide comprehensive medical care (see pages 491–93).

Dental Insurance

With emphasis on total health care today, one of the latest types of health care coverage is prepaid dental insurance. This is a fast growing area of coverage. Only 550,000 persons were covered in 1960, but it is currently estimated that 13 million persons have some type of dental care insurance. The need exists since it has been estimated that over one half of the adult population does not have any annual dental examinations or treatment. About 20 percent of adults and 50 percent of children have

---

[17] For a free copy of a booklet describing the plan, write to TIAA, 730 Third Avenue, New York, N.Y. 10017. Other booklets available include: *Planning a Retirement Program, Collective Life Insurance, Group Life Insurance,* and *Group Fatal Disability Benefits Insurance.*

TABLE 10–3
Federal Employees Health Benefits Program

Monthly individual and family premiums and examples of extra charges and limitations on selected benefits for federal enrollees of the nineteen comprehensive group practice plan carriers and the two government-wide plans; January 1, 1974.

Plan	*Monthly Premiums*[1] *Individual*	*Family*[2]
Columbia Medical Plan Columbia, Maryland	$22.73	$66.54
Compcare, Wisconsin	$27.52	$71.52
Community Health Care Center Plan New Haven, Connecticut	$22.51	$63.55
Family Health Program Long Beach, California	$25.96	$71.91
*Group Health Association, Inc. Washington, D.C.	$26.56	$67.75
Group Health Cooperative of Puget Sound, Seattle, Washington	$18.92	$50.07
Group Health Plan St. Paul, Minnesota	$20.95	$58.11
Harvard Community Health Plan Boston, Massachusetts	$26.41	$72.11
*Health Insurance Plan of Greater New York (HIP)-Blue Cross[3]	$17.88	$50.31
Kaiser Community Health Foundation Ohio Region	$23.92	$65.67
Kaiser Foundation Health Plan Northern California Region	$21.58	$55.97
Kaiser Foundation Health Plan Southern California Region	$27.24	$70.76
Kaiser Foundation Health Plan Colorado Region	$22.53	$60.13
Kaiser Foundation Health Plan Hawaii Region	$19.11	$56.49
Kaiser Foundation Health Plan Oregon Region	$18.70	$50.16
Metro Health Plan Detroit, Michigan	$32.91	$80.34
Rhode Island Group Health Assn. Providence, Rhode Island	$21.75	$59.97
Ross-Loos Medical Group Los Angeles, California	$22.40	$54.19
Western Clinic Tacoma, Washington	$21.47	$52.80
*Blue Cross–Blue Shield (Government-Wide Service)	$25.74	$62.77
*Aetna (Government-Wide Indemnity)	$22.79	$56.70

* "High Option" or "Premium" Benefits of these plans.

[1] Government pays $9.51 for individual coverage and $23.69 for family coverage except for three exceptions for individual coverage as Gov't contribution cannot exceed 50% of premium (HIP—$8.94; Group Health Cooperative of Puget Sound—$9.46; Kaiser Foundation Health Plan, Oregon Region—$9.35).

[2] Family is two or more.

[3] HIP secures hospitalization through Blue Cross; other plans provide or self-insure for hospitalization.

Source: Compiled by Group Health Association of America, Inc., 1717 Massachusetts Ave., N.W., Washington, D.C. 20036 (202)483-4012.

			Extra Charges	
			Physicians Care	
Hospitalization	*Maternity*	*Office or Clinic Visits*	*Home Calls*	*Prescription Drugs*[5]
No limit	$100	$2	$5 first call $2 second call	$2 each prescription
365 days	...	...	...	No coverage
485 days	...	...	...	30% of prescription cost
$15,000 per confinement	...	...	$6 each call	$1 each prescription
No limit	First $50 hospital	...	$5 first call each illness	20% after first $50
No limit	$250	...	...	Covered in full
365 days	...	...	$3 day; $5 night	Reduced cost
No limit	...	$1	$5	No coverage
365 days	Hospital charges over $150	...	$2 night	No charge from designated pharmacy; 20% in excess of $25 if obtained else- elsewhere
365 days	...	$1	$5 first 2 calls each illness	$1 not in excess of smallest therapeutic package or 34 day supply, whichever is greater
365 days	$60	$1	$3.50 day; $5 night	Wholesale price; $1 minimum
†150 days	$100	Reasonable charge for injections	$5	50% of wholesale price
365 days	...	$2	No coverage	$1 for each prescription not to exceed a 60 day supply
365 days	$60	$1	$5	$1 not in excess of smallest therapeutic package or 34 day supply, whichever is greater
‡180 days	...	$1	$3	$1 not in excess of smallest therapeutic package or 30 day supply, whichever is greater
No limit	...	...	$4 day; $6 night first call each illness	$1.07 (or retail price if less) for each prescription per 5 week supply
No limit	...	...	$5 first call each illness	Covered in full
365 days	...	...	$5	No coverage
30 days; 80% of next 60 days	$50	$1	$3; additional charge outside Tacoma limits	No coverage
365 days		First $100 of physician's bills beyond Basic Benefits + 20% thereafter[4]		Covered under Supplemental Benefits subject to deductible and coinsurance
Rm. & Bd.; first $1000 plus 80% there- after other expenses; 80% after first $50; $250,000 maxi- mum per person		First $50 of medical ($25 if hospital deductible used) + 20% thereafter		Covered under Other Hospital and Surgical and Medical Expenses, subject to deductible and coinsurance

† Reduced rates for next 215 days of hospitalization.

‡ Reduced rates for next 185 days of hospitalization.

4 Basic Benefits cover essentially all physician care in hospital, including intensive care and physician anesthetist, and specified nonhospital physician services without deductible or coinsurance.

5 If drugs are prescribed by a plan physician and obtained from the plan or plan affiliated pharmacy with the exception of prescription coverage under Group Health Association, Inc. Blue Cross–Blue Shield, and Aetna where drugs may be obtained where so desired.

never seen a dentist.[18] Dental insurance is making inroads into this market.

Dental coverage is provided primarily on a group basis, although there are a few policies issued on a nongroup basis. The principal suppliers are Blue Cross–Blue Shield Associations, state dental societies, insurance companies, and local group dental practice plans.[19]

A typical dental prepayment plan would pay 75 or 80 percent of the cost of treatment after a $25, $50, or $100 deductible. There is also a maximum amount payable of between $600 and $1,000. Covered expenses include diagnostic services, such as examinations, consultations, and X-rays; preventive procedures, including cleaning, polishing, and application of fluorides; oral surgery for extractions and surgery; restorative treatment with amalgam, porcelain, or plastic restorations, and gold restorations, crowns, and jackets; endodontics and periodontics procedures for treatment of diseases of the teeth and gums; and prosthodontics procedures which includes construction, placement, or repair of bridges and dentures. Orthodontic treatment when done purely for appearance sake, is often not covered. The dental plans can be designed in various ways to pay for the above services after the necessary deductibles and coinsurance provisions have been met. There are scheduled plans that place dollar limits on the covered dental procedures with the excess being paid by the patient. Part of a table of allowances would read as follows:

Cleaning	$ 7.00	Removable space maintainer	$ 50.00
X-ray	15.00	Peridontal scaling, per arch	15.00
Extraction	7.00	Crowns, porcelain	105.00
Silver filling, two surfaces	12.00	Root canal treatments, one canal	65.00

There are also plans that will pay for all reasonable and customary charges. The bill submitted by the dentist is paid subject to the deductible and coinsurance provisions. If the bill is more than the scheduled fee, the patient may be required to pay the difference.

Sometimes dental coverage is incorporated into comprehensive medical coverage or with other plans. When this is done, the dental bills may be either on a scheduled basis or on a reasonable and customary fee basis. If combined with major medical, the dental expenses are tied to the deductible in the major or comprehensive medical contract. Costs vary for dental coverage, but for a family the premium could range from $9 to $30 per month.

---

[18] "Coming: A New Way To Pay Dental Costs," *U.S. News and World Report*, September 21, 1970.

[19] Lou Joseph, "Dental Insurance: A Developing Success Story," *Today's Health*, March, 1970, p. 48.

Other Special Health Insurance Coverages

There are four other types of health coverages that are available in addition to the more traditional ones discussed previously. They are prescription drug coverage, eye care insurance, special nursing home care, and rehabilitation coverage. Many of these plans are tied to the other more common forms of health insurance where there are specific exclusions for these items. Prescriptions drug coverage may include all drugs ordered by a doctor on an outpatient basis. Eye coverage would include examinations, treatments, and the cost of eye glasses. Nursing home insurance benefits would be paid when an individual is not a patient in a regular hospital but receives nursing care in an extended care facility. Rehabilitation coverage is often made a part of disability income plans. Here payments are made to help restore the disabled worker to a productive life following a serious accident or illness. Primarily benefits are paid to help finance the retraining of the injured person.

Paying Your Part

That part of your bill which insurance does not pay can still be a worrisome expenditure for you. If you decide to pay your bill in installments the Truth in Lending Act is not involved. But if the hospital, doctor, or dentist makes a specific agreement with you to pay the costs in more than four installments, then, at that time, Regulation Z requires written disclosure of all applicable points of information even if no finance charge is involved (see Figure 10–7). This is to prevent misunderstanding on any one's part of the amount due.

Types of Organizations Which Provide Voluntary Medical Care Insurance Protection

Medical care insurance at present is provided by three large groups of organizations: (*a*) the nonprofit Blue Cross and Blue Shield plans; (*b*) the casualty, life, and other commercial insurance companies; (*c*) a number of organizations independent of the first two groups, including industrial and labor union plans, consumer cooperatives, private medical groups, some medical societies, community organizations, and others. Blue Cross is concerned primarily with hospital insurance; Blue Shield with surgical, limited, and general medical service insurance; the independent organizations provide either hospital, surgical, or comprehensive medical care. None of the Blue Shield plans provides for group practice of medicine, while many of the independent plans do. Figure 10–8 indicates each one's share of the market.

FIGURE 10–7
Medical Bills and Truth in Lending

This disclosure is in compliance with the Truth in Lending Act

Dr. John Doe
10 Main Street
Washington, D. C.

____
(Patient's Name)

____

____
(Patient's Address)

1.	Cash Price (Medical Fee)	$500
	Less: Cash Down Payment (Advance Payment)	100
2.	Unpaid Balance of Cash Price	400
3.	Amount Financed	400
*4.	FINANCE CHARGE	NONE
5.	Total of Payments (3+4)	400
6.	Deferred Payment Price (1+4)	500
*7.	ANNUAL PERCENTAGE RATE	NONE

The "Total of Payments" shown above is payable to Dr. John Doe at the address shown above in 10 monthly installments of $40.00, the first installment being payable ____________________, 19__, and all subsequent installments are due on the same day of each consecutive month until paid in full.

____________________ ____________________
(Date) (Patient's Signature)

* These items may be omitted if there are no charges for credit. In such case, the form may include affirmative disclosure of this fact.

Blue Cross

In 1929 a group of teachers in Dallas, Texas, realized that *individually* a serious illness requiring hospitalization would impose a cost upon any one of them beyond their resources. Millions of other Americans had found themselves in this plight but had done nothing about it; these Dallas teachers did. They figured that, as a *group*, they could easily pay

FIGURE 10–8
Private Health Insurance Benefit Payments by Type of Insurer, Selected Years, 1955–1973

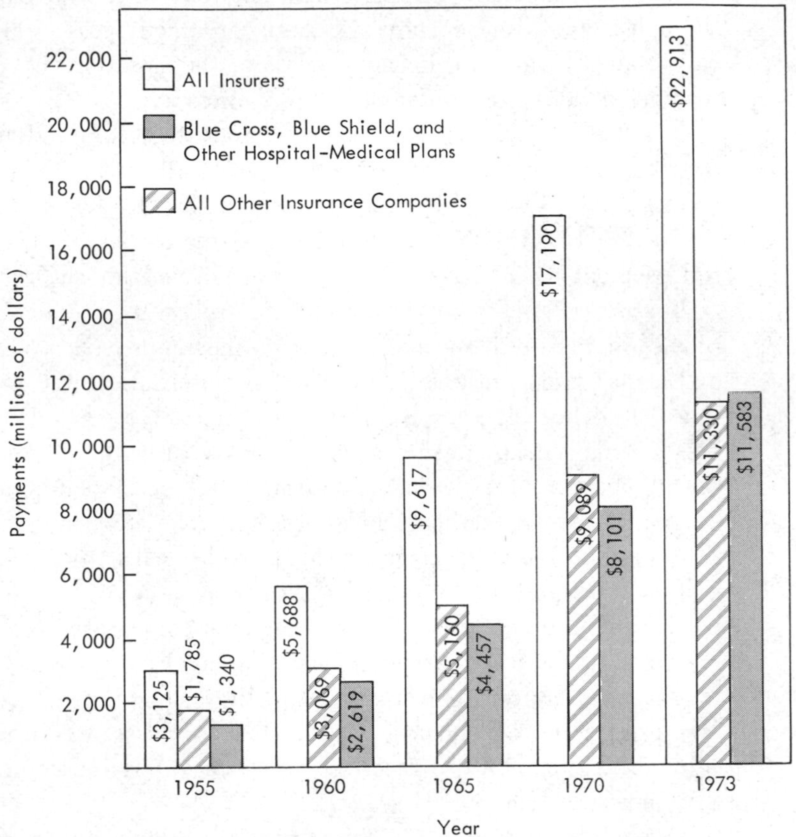

Source: Health Insurance Council, 1974; New York, Health Insurance Institute, *Source Book of Health, Insurance Data*, 1974; *Socioeconomic Issues of Health* (rev. ed. Chicago: American Medical Association, 1973).

all the hospital bills they were likely to incur. So they worked out an arrangement with Baylor University Hospital to provide, for $3 per teacher per school semester, 21 days of hospital care to any one of them who needed such care. This was the beginning of Blue Cross. By 1938 Blue Cross membership had reached half a million. Today it is over 80 million, with 74 Blue Cross plans in the United States and 1 in Puerto Rico.

Rates. More than 40 percent of those who hold some form of insurance against the costs of hospital care are insured through 75 nonprofit, tax free, autonomous Blue Cross plans. A majority of these plans contract with hospitals to provide most or all of their services in semiprivate accommodations with a minimum of additional charges. If you are a member of Blue Cross, the rate you pay depends on the type of plan you select and where you live and work. There are contracts for individuals or for a family (including all unmarried children under 19), enrolled either through a group or separately. Group enrollment costs you less. Rates vary from plan to plan, largely because of the variation in hospital costs in different areas and different benefits offered.

In general, hospital protection in semiprivate accommodations for 120 days will cost an individual from $120 to $254 a year in premiums and from $250 to almost $400 for a family. Table 10–4 shows rates under one of the 120 day Blue Cross plans and for the 21/180 day plan with full payment for 21 days and 50 percent covered for the next 180 days.

Benefits. Benefits differ somewhat but follow a general pattern. Some provide more care than others, and some allow more special services. Most of the standard contracts provide full hospitalization 120 or more days in a year, or for each admission. In most areas it is customary to provide bed, board, general nursing care, customary drugs, special diets, use of operating room, anesthesia, laboratory tests, special equipment such as oxygen, X-ray examinations, and so on, as part of the semiprivate service.

Room and board coverage provided by the plans varies from coverage in full in semiprivate accommodations to per diem allowances. All the participants are entitled to full coverage in semiprivate accommodations regardless of the cost. The plans provide an allowance, equal to the hospital's average semiprivate charge, toward the cost of a private room. With rare exceptions, dependents are entitled to the same benefits as the subscriber. Since 1969 Blue Cross plans began paying more outpatient than in-hospital claims.

Typical Limitations. Contracts usually exclude admissions for diagnostic care, rest cures, and blood, blood plasma, or blood donor services. Mental care in a general hospital is covered by 64 plans within limitations. Only 9 of the 75 plans exclude all dental care, with most allowing

TABLE 10–4
Rates for Blue Cross Plans

	Group Enrollment		*Nongroup Enrollment (direct payment)*	
Type of Contract	*Monthly*	*Annually*	*Quarterly*	*Annually*
Rates for 120 day plan:				
Individual	$12.99	$155.88	$63.36	$253.44
Family	29.76	357.12	99.96	399.84
Rates for 21/180 day plan:				
Individual	9.98	119.76	38.40	153.60
Family	24.93	299.16	82.35	329.40

benefits when such care is necessitated by accident. Maternity hospital costs are usually covered if conception took place while covered under a Blue Cross contract that provides maternity benefits. In states that have no fault automobile insurance contracts are being revised to avoid duplication of payment for injury, from both Blue Shield–Blue Cross and no fault automobile insurance.

Organization. The plans coordinate enrollment, public relations, and statistical research through the Blue Cross Association, but each Blue Cross plan exercises complete local independence over the benefits and rates included in its contracts. The plans arrange with local member hospitals to furnish care to subscribers, and they pay for the hospitalization according to the contract agreement. Almost all Blue Cross plans have a working agreement which allows for transfer of their subscribers from one plan to another when a subscriber moves to another community. A second agreement gives benefits to a subscriber hospitalized in any community serviced by Blue Cross, whether or not it is in the home area. Although most of the emphasis is on group enrollment, all the plans enroll individual subscribers. Approximately one out of every three persons in the United States now belongs to Blue Cross.

Blue Shield

While Blue Cross is entirely a hospitalization insurance plan, mostly on a service basis, its allied Blue Shield plan covers the costs of physicians' services, mostly on a cash indemnity basis.

Blue Shield was established in 1946 by a group of nine predecessor plans known as "Associated Medical Care Plans." It was sponsored by the American Medical Association and is known as the "Doctors' Plan." Stress is placed on the fact that under it the subscriber has free choice of physician.

Over 71 million subscribers received payments of about $3.3 billion against some of the costs of physicians' services (mostly surgery and nonsurgical treatment in the hospitals) under the 71 nonprofit Blue Shield plans last year.

The largest number of Blue Shield subscribers, some two thirds, are enrolled under service programs, in which participating doctors accept the Blue Shield allowances as full payment for subscribers whose incomes are within predetermined levels. The service programs are for families with limited incomes; the cash indemnity programs for those of higher incomes. In recent years, Blue Shield service plans have developed higher income ceilings to keep pace with rising income levels.

The Blue Shield plans contract with participating physicians to accept payment according to a standard fee schedule. Claims are paid according to two distinct methods. The newest of these "the usual customary and reasonable charge" program provides payment in full to physicians for covered services based on their usual and customary fee in the given locality in which they practice. The second payment method "indemnity" represents the allowance of a fixed dollar amount toward payment for medical care. If your income is above the ceiling set by the medical plan in your area, you may be charged the difference between the participating physicians' regular fee and the amount set in the Blue Shield fee schedule. If you select a nonparticipating physician, you are allowed cash indemnity up to the amount set in the Blue Shield fee schedule, and you make your own financial arrangements with the physician. Blue Shield plans are either sponsored directly by a medical society or are officially approved by it. Generally speaking, the majority of Blue Shield surgical–medical coverage is added to a Blue Cross hospitalization enrollment. In some states they have merged. Like the Blue Cross, Blue Shield plans provide for transfer from plan to plan without a waiting period. Each plan designs its own local program.

Blue Shield generally offers two kinds of coverage: (*a*) surgical–medical and (*b*) general medical. No new surgical only contracts are being written—although the old ones still exist. The surgical–medical coverage includes allowances toward doctor's fees for surgery performed in the hospital, or in the doctor's office, or in your home, and maternity allowances under family enrollment *plus* medical care in the hospital when no surgery is involved. The general medical care coverage provides all the benefits given in the surgical–medical plan *plus* home and office medical care and specialists' consultation. Supplemental major medical is also offered in a majority of the plans.

The Blue Shield plan that costs least and offers minimum benefits for lowest incomes is the Two Star Better Benefits Plan where participating doctors will accept most Blue Shield allowances as paid in full payment. The next higher level for eligible income and rates for surgical medical care under higher medical allowances is the Three Star Better Benefits Plan. The highest level of rates and allowances is under the Executive Indemnity Plan.

What You Pay. The cost of Blue Shield coverage varies with the scope of covered services, local medical economics, and local patterns of utilization. As an indication of the range involved, monthly rates for most widely held group service benefit medical–surgical programs ranged from $2.55 to $5.00 for individuals, and from $7.25 to $15.00 for family coverage. You will want to check your local organization to determine the current rates in your area.

Prepaid Medical Plans

There are over 859 nonaffiliated health insurance plans that provide health care benefits on a prepayment or insurance basis. These plans are independent of Blue Cross–Blue Shield and insurance companies. Although they cover only 5 percent of all persons in private health insurance organizations, they make a significant contribution to the health insurance field. These plans consist of community group or individual practice plans, employer–employee union plans, private medical group clinic plans, and private dental group or dental service plans, some contract with hospitals, some own their own. Each membership has been able to obtain that type of plan which meets its own particular needs, generally providing comprehensive medical care in home, doctor's office, group clinic, or hospital as required.

The community health plans are usually group practice plans, under which full health benefits are usually provided. In the United States, there are approximately 30 community group practice plans, with 90 to 95 percent of the total subscribers belonging to the nine largest plans. Of these the largest is the Kaiser Permanente Medical Care Program with its 2.5 million members. It operates in California, Oregon, Hawaii, Colorado, and Ohio and includes 2,100 doctors in nearly every specialty. Exact coverage varies by region and contract. As an example, $55.97 a month is the cost for a family of three in northern California covering surgery and hospital care, but each visit to a doctor costs $1; maternity benefits are an extra $60, and drugs are low cost. There are no personal doctors and whatever can be routinized is; dental care is excluded, as is psychiatric care or hospital treatment for alcoholism or drug abuse.

Nonetheless, the National Advisory Commission Report on Health Manpower found the quality of the plan's medical services was "equivalent, if not superior to that available in most communities." In addition, the average member's medical care cost was "20 to 30 percent less than it would be if he obtained it outside." The plan's cost control is "due almost entirely to the elimination of unnecessary health care, particularly hospitalization." While the general population averaged 137.9 hospital admissions a year per 1,000, Kaiser cut its admissions to only 80 per 1,000. Kaiser's patients stayed only 6.65 days compared to a national average of 7.8 days, according to the Commission.

Another reason for cost control is the year end bonus given partner doctors (after three years on a straight salary) dependent on how successfully the group has been in living under its budget for the year.

The automated screening program to detect and thereby prevent illness which was started by the Kaiser group has become the model for the Health Insurance Plan of New York's computerized testing center, which will check for more than 50 possible medical ills, take a medical history in both English and Spanish before the patient sees a doctor. It is intended to make preventive medicine available to large numbers at low cost and with a limited use of medical manpower.

There are 100 such multiphasic health centers now existing. It is expected that they will expand tenfold within the next five years. Comprehensive medical care and preventive medicine seem to have a natural affinity, further enhanced by the possibility of cutting costs and improving medical care.

The community individual practice plans provide benefits with a choice of physician from a local panel. Although most of these plans are small, one of the largest is the Health Insurance Plan with almost 800,000 subscribers serving the metropolitan area of New York. This particular plan offers benefits providing surgery, obstetrical care, and in-hospital physician visits as well as comprehensive physician services. Also available at an additional charge are dental care benefits.

The Health Maintenance Organizations (HMOs)

The one stop health care centers already in existence received extra encouragement and grants from the new law approved in December 1973 authorizing the Department of Health, Education, and Welfare to spend $325 million over a five year period to expand HMOs.

The law provides that an employer of more than 25 persons must offer this plan, where a qualified HMO is available, as one alternative health insurance plan. The law mandates such benefits as diagnostic mental health services and dental care for children. This raises problems for the more than 120 existing plans serving 8 million subscribers because to add these services would make the plans too expensive to market. Without these services they cannot be certified under the law.

The law permitted enrollees to pay medicare premiums, and deductibles directly to an HMO and receive medicare services from the doctors, and hospitals operated by the HMO. Thirteen states permit medicaid recipients to join.

The goal is preventive medicine—providing comprehensive care from checkups to surgery. Each plan operates from a fixed revenue pool obtained from monthly prepayments. Each doctor has an incentive to pare expenses because not only salaries but year end bonuses are paid from the surplus the organization earns. Hospital costs are the largest part of the nation's rising health bill. If the HMO shifts the emphasis of care to the doctor's office and reduces the use of hospitals, the patient benefits at less cost.

In addition to the Kaiser Permanente plan, the 27 year old Group Health Corporation of Puget Sound in Seattle, the 44 year old Ross-Loos Medical Group in Los Angeles, the 30 year old Health Insurance Plan of New York, the 40 year old Group Health Association, Inc. of Washington, D.C., and the 30 year old St. Louis Labor Health Institute are all successful versions of the prepaid comprehensive health plans.

The employer–employee union plans operating under jointly managed welfare funds, employers, and employee benefit associations or unions, are somewhat different from the community plans in that more of the participants are covered for physicians' office care, dental care, drugs, appliances, and nursing home care, while fewer are covered for hospital care, surgery, or in-hospital visits. The two largest plans are the United Mine Workers of America and the National Association of Letter Carriers. Both of the plans offer services to about 1.0 million enrollees.

Although there are about 30 private medical groups operating in the United States, mostly small, the largest is the Ross-Loos Medical Group in Los Angeles, California, with an enrollment of over 150,000. This is a prepayment plan with relatively comprehensive hospital and physicians services available to participants.

The majority of the independent groups are cooperative organizations controlled in their financial, economic, and general policy by the members. However, in the medical sphere and in the relationship between the doctor and the patient, the professional medical staff has complete control. Most of the member plans provide direct service to covered individuals, while others offer cash indemnity payments. Some plans provide hospitalization to their members through Blue Cross; others have made their own arrangements with hospitals.

Professional Standards Review Organizations (P.S.R.O.s)

The quality of medical care given to patients whose costs are paid in whole or in part by taxpayer money is soon to be reviewed by 182 local doctor groups under a national program. This program with its two prolonged goal for medical care of the highest quality and lowest cost is highly controversial. If it works, it is expected to be adapted for general use if and when national health insurance is enacted. Peer review is not new. Several large comprehensive medical prepayment plans have used it for a long time to monitor costs and complaints. Hospital bed utilization review had been a practice for some time. But this is the first national mandated program to function in hospitals and HMOs.

Commercial Insurance Company Plans

Over 108 million people now hold hospital expense policies issued by the insurance companies: 83 million under group policies. About 100 million persons now hold commercial insurance policies (approximately 84 million under group coverage) against costs of surgery. Some 86 million were covered by insurance companies for regular medical expense protection. And some 95 million persons obtained major medical expense protection through insurance companies. They accounted for much of the major medical, comprehensive, and loss of income (disability) policies. Of the $22.9 billion of health insurance benefits paid, the insurance companies provided $11.3 billion, or 48.7 percent (see Table 10–5).

TABLE 10–5
Health Insurance Benefits Paid (millions of dollars)

	Type of Insurance Organization		
Type of Benefit	*Insurance Companies*	*Blue Cross–Blue Shield and Others*	*Total*
Hospital*	$ 5,392	$ 7,699	$13,091
Surgical/Medical†	3,810	3,884	7,694
Disability	2,128	—	2,128
Total	11,330	11,583	22,913

* Includes major medical.
† Includes dental expense.
Source: Health Insurance Council, 1974.

Types of Commercial Policies

There are so many varieties, shapes, and sizes of policies that for the most part generalization is useless. Two $10,000 face value policies which purport to pay this amount if you or some member of your family contracts one of a number of dread diseases may be as different as day and night. The list of diseases may differ. One list may contain many diseases no longer widespread in the United States. One policy may have a specific exclusion for travel abroad and pay only if you contract the disease in the United States. One may cover members of the family from the ages of 21 through 65 only, while the other covers both children and older members as well. It is essential to read the policy you contemplate buying very carefully. Generally, the lower the cost the greater the limitations, exclusions, and exceptions and therefore the less potentially useful is the policy.

The cost of any commercial health insurance policy depends upon the extent of benefits provided. You may pay $20 a year for very limited benefits or larger sums for contracts that offer much more. Those which pay many claims on small illnesses are expensive. Others which pay large benefits on types of claims which do not occur often cost the company less. You can buy a program which covers only the extremes of loss of limb or accidental death; and since these are rare occurrences, the cost is little, and the odds are small that you will ever use the policy. At the other end of the scale you can, for a substantial premium, buy a comprehensive policy providing $50,000 or more in various medical benefits, guaranteed renewable for life.

Over the last decade, insurance companies have made a number of real advances in broadening their coverage in the health insurance field. They now write policies covering not only the customary loss of income, hospital expense, surgical expense, and general medical expense insurance, but they have expanded into major medical expense, guaranteed renewable for life policies, and special health insurance policies for the aged.

Some 700 of these life insurance companies belong to the nonprofit trade association known as the Medical Information Bureau, which has a computerized centralized file of health data on insurance applicants which it keeps in coded form for seven years and makes available with certain safeguards to other members. In tune with these consumer oriented times, all companies belonging to this cleaning house must now notify applicants for insurance, in writing, that significant medical history or conditions may be provided to the Medical Information Bureau. Several of the large private insurance companies have taken direct roles in forming plans and many others have been influential in support of new HMOs. Ten major insurance companies have joined with Massachusetts Blue Cross, Harvard Medical School and some of its teaching hospitals to provide comprehensive care such as the Harvard Community Health Plan—a university sponsored prepaid medical care for a metropolitan community.

This push away from the traditional fee for service of the usual medical practice and toward prepaid programs, would move more patient care away from expensive hospital use and toward preventive health care in the clinics. A public health service study of Washington area federal employees found that those who had conventional health insurance had twice the rate of hospital admission as those with HMO coverage.

"It says, 'If you can read this the contract will have to be renegotiated.' "

Major medical insurance is now provided by 305 companies—ranging from high benefit maximums of $5,000 to $50,000 or more of which 97.5 percent have a $10,000 maximum 80 percent have $20,000 and 44 percent have $50,000 or more. Of the group policies issued, 99 percent now provide some coverage for nervous or mental disorders. Guaranteed renewable health insurance policies are now offered to the public by more than 360 insurance companies. These cannot be terminated by the insurance company prior to the age limit stated in the policy, and premiums can only be modified on a policyholder class basis. Increasingly, hospital, surgical, and major medical policies guaranteed for lifetime are being made available.

Health Insurance for Older People

With the advent of medicare, health insurance for those 65 and over changed drastically. Many older persons had been without funds to provide adequate health services for themselves, and traditionally had found health insurance difficult to buy, and, if available, very costly. When policies already held lapsed, they were frequently not renewable. Prior to the passage of medicare, suppliers of health insurance provided some private health coverage for the aged. Blue Cross, Blue Shield, and commercial insurance companies extended coverage to provide nongroup policies for persons over 65 years of age including a limited right to conversion when an employee retired. Group type health plans were also offered through a mass enrollment program for a specified period on a state, regional, or nationwide basis. However, when the government sponsored medicare became effective, many private plans could not compete, and as a result private coverage has shown a substantial decline.

Medicare Benefits

Medicare, an important addition to the Social Security Act, became law on July 30, 1965, took effect one year later, and was subsequently amended. It provides two different kinds of health coverage for people 65 and older:[18]

Part A—*Hospital Insurance* (Basic Plan) will pay most of the cost of services in a hospital or extended care facility or as a home care patient receiving services from a participating home health agency. Included are the cost of rooms, meals, regular nursing services, and the inpatient cost of drugs, supplies and other necessary equipment.

Part B—*Medical Insurance* (Supplementary Plan) will help pay for part of the cost of doctors' services as well as certain medical costs and services not covered by the basic plan.

All social security and railroad retirement beneficiaries 65 or over are automatically entitled to hospital insurance and need not take any action. Other persons who are eligible must apply for it at a social security office. Disabled persons who have been receiving disability benefits for 24 consecutive months are eligible. People under 65 or their dependents who need kidney transplants or dialysis for kidney treatment are eligible for medicare if they worked as little as 1½ years. Those not eligible when reaching 65 will need a certain number of quarters of social security coverage to get hospital insurance.

There is no extra charge for hospital insurance for those now 65 or older. Eligibility for medicare is not affected by whether you are working or retired. If you receive social security payments you are entitled to

[18] U.S. Department of Health, Education, and Welfare. Social Security Administration, *Your Medicare Handbook*, SSA 10050, issued annually.

Part A, hospital insurance, but you must pay extra for Part B, medical insurance.

Hospital Insurance Program—Medicare Part A

The law requires an annual review of hospital costs under medicare and an adjustment of that portion of the bills for which the medicare beneficiary is responsible, according to a set formula. Therefore, all coverage is subject to yearly changes. Public funds paid for nearly two thirds of personal health care spending for the aged. Medicare met 40 percent of it.

A Health, Education, and Welfare Department statement quotes the social security commissioner as saying that the hospital deductible amount "is intended to make the medicare beneficiary responsible for expenses equivalent to the average cost of one day hospital care." In 1966, when medicare began, it was $40; it is now $92.

In similar fashion the dollar cost of a hospital stay of more than 60 days, a posthospital extended care stay of more than 20 days, or a hospital stay that draws on the lifetime reserve of 60 additional days in the same benefit period has been increased.

Currently, the hospital insurance program, Part A of medicare, will pay the cost of covered services for the following hospital and posthospital care:

1. Up to 90 days in any participating general care, tuberculosis, or psychiatric hospital in each benefit period with all covered costs paid for the first 60 days except for the first $92. For the next 30 days, all covered costs are met above $23 per day. A "benefit period" starts on the first day you enter as a patient. It ends after you have been out of a hospital or extended care facility for 60 consecutive days.

2. If more benefit days are needed, the lifetime limit of an additional 60 days can be used, but any additional days used reduces this lifetime limit. The program pays for all covered expenses for these additional days beyond $46 a day. It should be noted that treatment in a mental hospital has a lifetime limit of 190 days. Outpatient services for diagnosis such as X-ray, blood tests, and other tests within a 20 day period are paid 80 percent by hospital insurance after you pay the first $60.

3. Up to 20 days in an extended care facility (defined as a qualified facility furnishing skilled nursing care and related services) are completely covered. Also covered are an additional 80 days for each benefit period, if needed after a hospital stay of at least three days. For such additional days you pay $11.50 per day with medicare covering costs above this amount per day.

4. This coverage also applies to 100 home health visits and may be used for as long as one year after your most recent discharge from a hospital or from an extended care facility where you received covered services.

5. For services in a hospital or extended care facility, benefit payments will cover the cost of services in semiprivate accommodations plus the cost of drugs, supplies, and most services customarily furnished by the institution.

6. Some services are not covered. No payment will be made under hospital insurance for the services of a physician, but they are covered under Part B, medicare insurance. Payment will not be made for private nurses, cost of the first three pints of blood, or for items furnished for the patients' convenience such as telephone, television, or personal services.

Medical Insurance Coverage—Medicare Part B

Part B, medical insurance (supplementary plan) will help pay for part of the cost of doctors' services as well as certain medical costs and services not covered by the basic plan.

For medical insurance, however, there is a charge of $6.70, which is deducted from social security benefit checks each month. If not on social security, the premium must be paid to the Social Security Administration every three months in advance. Those who are eligible and refuse medical insurance, pay a premium that is 10 percent higher for each full year that enrollment was possible, if they later want it. The federal government pays half of the cost of medical insurance, and the medicare beneficiary pays the other half. As was the case for hospital insurance, the extra payment medical insurance premiums also face a required yearly review. Premiums have been steadily increasing to meet rising physician fees. Although prices generally have risen 4 percent a year, doctors' fees rose approximately 6 percent. Each year about one third of the nation's doctors increase their fees by 20 to 25 percent. Because of the age of the patients and the nature of their illnesses, it is understandable that the use of physicians' services for this group in the population is increasing by 2 to 3 percent per year.

The current premium is $6.70 a month, compared to the original $3.00 when the program began. Until now, the premiums were based more on political decisions than on actuarial estimates. Two conflicting truths complicate the financing of medicare. It is unfair to freeze physicians fees—the only professionals to be so treated—and equally unfair for the 23.7 million aged to bear the whole inflationary burden at a time in life when they are least able to do so. For physicians' services a person 65 or older paid three and one-half times more than one 18 or younger and his average hospital bill amounted to ten times more.[19]

The medical insurance program will help pay for the following services:

1. Physicians' and surgeons' services in a hospital, doctor's office, home, or elsewhere, including services of medical doctors, osteopaths, and certain services of dentists involving surgery or setting of fractures of the jaw and the services of podiatrists.

2. Up to 100 home health visits under an approved plan by a health home agency each year with no need for prior hospitalization. This is in addition to the 100 visits provided under the hospital insurance program. Even if you have not been in a hospital, if home health services by a physical therapist, a home health aide, or other health workers are ordered by a doctor and are furnished by a home health agency that take part in medicare, it can be provided. A visit is counted each time a health care service calls. If both a visiting nurse and physical therapist come at the same time, it is counted as two visits.

3. A number of other medical and health services include diagnostic services, X-ray or other radiation treatments, surgical dressings and splints, casts, and rental of medical equipment.

4. Rental or purchase of durable medical equipment such as wheelchairs, hospital beds, oxygen equipment, and crutches when the doctor prescribes it. If the equipment is rented, medicare pays monthly as long as the doctor deems the equipment needed. If the item is bought, to be paid for over a period of time and the medical need ends prior to that time, medicare payments stop when the medical need stops.

5. Medical supplies furnished by a doctor in his office, services of the office nurse, and the cost of administering drugs, if these are part of the services. Outpatient physical therapy services performed in a participating facility and certain ambulance services are all covered.

6. Physicians' charges for clinical laboratory, X-ray, and radiological services when you are in a hospital. All reasonable charges for these services are paid for under Part B, medical insurance.

Medical insurance does *not* pay for the full cost of these services. The insured patient pays the first $60 in each calendar year for these services and then pays 20 percent of the remaining costs. The medical insurance pays 80 percent of the reasonable charges for additional services, beyond the $60 deductible. For example, if covered medical bills were $500 in a given year, the medical insurance program would pay $352; the patient would pay $148, the first $60 plus 20 percent of the remaining $440. It

[19] *HEW News*, April 19, 1974.

is important to note that there is only *one* $60 deductible each year and not a separate deductible for each kind of service. Doctors treating medicare patients can also accept assignment and receive the prevailing fee directly from medicare.

The medical insurance program does not cover some services, such as the cost of routine physical checkups, drug prescriptions and patent medicines, eyeglasses and examinations, hearing aids, ordinary dental treatment, orthopedic shoes, personal comfort items, and the first three pints of blood.

Financing the Medicare Program

Part A, the basic hospital insurance, is paid for by payroll deductions from employees and their employers, and by self-employed persons. Both the employee and the employer pay the same rate.

The rate as of 1975 is 0.9 percent of the first $14,100 earnings in a year. The contribution for hospital insurance (medicare, Part A) is included in the 5.85 percent social security rate paid by both the employer and the employee. The total top tax is $824.85, which divided into its component parts means $126.90 for hospital insurance and $697.95 for social security benefits—.9 percent for hospital insurance (medicare) and 4.95 for social security totaling 5.85 percent. These rates are subject to change—usually upward as the social security law is amended.

For the self-employed based on the earnings base, the rate is 7.9 percent combined, of which 0.9 percent is medicare and 7 percent is the social security rate. This results in a total tax of $1,113.90 of which $126.90 is for medicare (hospital insurance, Part A) and $987 is for social security.

Part B of medicare, the medical part is paid monthly by automatic deductions from social security checks for each person. You can reject coverage. However, anyone who is 65 or over and who enrolls for medical insurance is not under any obligation to continue it beyond one calendar quarter after notifying the social security office. Thus, if the insured does not like the program or the increase in the premium rate, there is the opportunity to drop out of the program. Even if one does drop out, there is a chance to get back in, but only one chance. Those eligible are permitted to sign up again in one of the "general enrollment periods" between January 1 and March 31 within three years after they had canceled their medical insurance.

Supplementary Policies

There are a number of separate private policies offered to the aged that build on medicare and seek to fill in the gaps and add to coverage of the government plan for a relatively small premium.

Blue Shield and Blue Cross have developed Senior Care, which pays a large part of the first deductible under hospital insurance and a large part of the deductible in the charges from the 61st through the 90th day and provides full coverage for semiprivate room, board, and services from the 91st day through the 120th day in any Blue Cross hospital. It pays part of the per diem cost not carried by medicare in an extended care facility, and the 20 percent balance not covered by medicare for surgical–medical services. It pays slightly less but comparable sums in non-Blue Cross hospitals. Senior Care benefits are automatically paid after your medicare benefit, so that there is no need to submit a separate claim.

Two areas not covered under these plans are private nursing in and out of the hospital and out of hospital prescription drugs—both of which are high expense items.

Two private insurance policies that extend medicare coverage to 365 days are the Aetna Life Senior Major Medical Expense policy and Guardian Life, Guardian 65 Health Insurance policy. Since the average hospital stay for a medicare patient is 11½ days, which is usually more than covered by medicare's 60 day period, these policies are mainly useful for catastrophic illnesses.

In addition to covering copayments, as does Senior Care, these commercial policies also provide for the two important areas of nursing and drugs not covered by Senior Care. By excluding the first 30 days of an illness which medicare would normally cover from such extra days, the policy rates become lower.

Health care expenditures for a person over 65 has shown a marked increase rising from $445 in 1966 to $1,052 in 1973.[20] Two thirds of the cost was borne by third parties (government, private health insurance, philanthropy, and industrial programs). An aged individual's out of pocket expenses amounted to an average of $311 of that $1,052 bill. While his total costs had risen $600 over that period, his out of pocket expenses had increased $75. Most of this was for drugs and nursing home care.

Nursing Homes

Faced with the problem of a sick, elderly parent, you will not find a happy solution in a nursing home. Highly expensive, physically condemned by almost every investigation, relatively scarce, overcrowded, cheerless, with underpaid, inefficient staffs, a large number of the homes cannot be used for medicare patients, since they do not meet the standards set.

Today there are over 16,000 nursing homes in the United States; 73

[20] "Age Differences in Medical Care Spending," May 1974 *Social Security Bulletin*.

percent are operated for profit, 27 percent nonprofit. They provide care for over one million residents or about 5.2 percent of the U.S. population aged 65 or over. The homes can be divided into the following categories: those certified as extended care facilities by medicare, or those certified as skilled nursing homes or intermediate care facilities by medicaid. The latter comprise 73 percent of the nation's nursing homes and 26 percent of these have multiple certification. The certified homes provide care for 84 percent of all residents of nursing homes. Those homes not certified, care for only 16 percent of all patients although they comprise 27 percent of all homes. The national average cost per resident per day was $16.14 and only 14 percent of nursing homes had an average cost per resident above that.[21]

Medicaid

In addition to medicare, there was also enacted into law, in 1965, Title XIX, of the Social Security Act establishing a federal–state medical public assistance program called Medicaid. Each state, at its option, makes payments to providers of medical services for recipients receiving cash maintenance payments from the state (public aid) and for others who are medically indigent and need help in meeting medical expenses. The individual states control the expenditures under Medicaid, and the federal government will pay up to 50 percent of the cost in high income states and up to 83 percent of the cost in low income states. In order for the state to qualify for federal reimbursement, the state must provide hospital care, outpatient care, doctors' services, nursing home care, and laboratory and X-ray services.

Toward National Health Insurance?

There is such widespread dissatisfaction with many aspects of our present health system that groups as disparate as the American Medical Association, private insurance companies, the Health, Education, and Welfare Department, labor organizations, and various senators and congressmen are all offering naturally differing plans for some form of national health insurance.[22] Who is to pay for the 15 million surgical operations a year and the 1 billion drug prescriptions?

---

[21] "1973–74 Nursing Home Survey," *Monthly Vital Statistics Report*, Sept. 5, 1974, National Center for Health Statistics.

[22] "National Health Insurance Is on the Way," *Business Week*, January 26, 1974; "*Agreed: Here Comes National Health Insurance*," Alice M. Rivlin, *New York Times Magazine*, July 21, 1974; "Health Insurance for Everyone," *U.S. News & World Report*, February 11, 1974.

The private insurance companies are concerned because they fear that, despite rising rate charges, there will be a breakdown in the plan because of spiraling costs. Although the average major medical insurance plan may pay up to $20,000, a patient in a big city hospital with a serious illness can face a bill that exceeds even that. When doctor's fees jump by 8.5 percent and hospital charges by 10.7 percent in one year, private insurance companies affected by the inflationary spiral are ready for a change.

Fears of policy cancellation, difficulties in conversion from group to individual coverage on change of job or other status, doctor shortages, overcrowded hospitals, nonexistent or understaffed neighborhood clinics —these are some of the inadequacies of medical services.

It is generally agreed that savings would occur if (*a*) instead of every hospital within an area providing duplicate expensive equipment, each would specialize in a particular field; (*b*) less expensive outpatient facilities were made available as a substitution for longer stays in hospital beds; (*c*) more paraprofessionals were trained to relieve doctors in routine detail, making the doctor's expertise more readily available when needed and (*d*) some incentive were offered to reduce costs. These suggestions receive support from people of every shade of opinion. Endorsement of some form of national action is also widespread.

The Louis Harris Survey reports that 54 percent of the American people favor a comprehensive federal health insurance program which "would combine government, employer, and employee contributions into one federal health insurance system that would cover all medical and health expenses," while 28 percent are opposed.[23] In response to questions by the survey the average family reported health insurance payments of $133 per year and willingness to pay $186 per year for comprehensive health coverage.

None of the plans suggested over the last few years would provide full coverage at that low a figure at today's inflated prices. Until there are compromises on the issues of how workers and employers contribute to premiums, how much federal money should be contributed, whether federal, state, or private agencies should administer the system, there can be no agreement on how much coverage there should be.

In such a climate of readiness, proposals for national health insurance abound, varying greatly as to breadth of benefit and cost. There have been more than 20 such bills introduced in Congress lately, with more than 400 representatives and senators either introducing or cosponsoring them. Some favor only catastrophic coverage—others are "cradle to the grave advocates."

---

[23] The Louis Harris Survey, April 1974.

A study by the Committee for Economic Development concludes:

> We recommend that national health insurance coverage be provided through a three category system:
>
> 1. Employers should be required by statute to provide a minimum level of employment based insurance protection for all employed persons and their dependents for specified basic benefits under qualified plans.
> 2. Medicare would continue to cover aged persons under the social security system and those eligible for disability benefits under both the social security and railroad retirement acts, with certain modifications in benefit provisions.
> 3. Federally sponsored community trusteeships should be established to assure basic benefits for all persons ineligible under the above categories. These would include the poor and near poor, people between jobs as well as the long term unemployed, part time employees not qualified for employment based plans, and the self-employed. Also covered in this category would be aliens, the temporarily disabled, and people regarded as uninsurable by customary insurance standards to the extent practically and legally feasible. Agencies of state and local government should be able to perform the trustee role in which they are qualified."[24]

The face of national health insurance is not yet recognizable, but that it has a foreseeable future is certain.

Conclusions on Health Insurance

It is the general consensus that a large sector of the population is not receiving adequate health care and that change and action to expand the capacity of the health service to meet the demands is necessary. It is also felt that currently health care costs are excessive.

Increase in health manpower, more emphasis on prepaid health maintenance organizations, extensive development of preventive medicine, more availability and usage of extended care facilities, and neighborhood health centers are all agreed upon needs.

The method and amounts for funding these accepted goals are the controversial heart of the current debate on health care, its rising costs, its delivery and effectiveness.

SUGGESTED READINGS

1. *Medicare and Social Security Explained.* Chicago: Commerce Clearing House, latest edition.

[24] *Building a National Health-Care System,* Committee for Economic Development. A statement by the Research and Policy Committee, April, 1973.

2. Sylvia A. Law, *Blue Cross: What Went Wrong?* New Haven, Conn.: Yale University Press, 1974.
3. *Changing Times, The Kiplinger Magazine*: "How to Choose a Nursing Home" January 1974. "Health Insurance: A Drive to Make Policies Fit Promises," April 1973.
4. *Your Medicare Handbook,* SSA 10050, Social Security Administration, U.S. Department of Health, Education, and Welfare. Annual.
5. *A Brief Explanation of Medicare,* SSA 10043, Social Security Administration, U.S. Department of Health, Education, and Welfare.
6. *Health Insurance For the Disabled Under Social Security*. Washington, D.C.: U.S. Department of Health, Education, and Welfare, Social Security Administration, latest edition. SSA 10068
7. *Source Book of Health Insurance Data.* New York: Health Insurance Institute, latest edition.
8. Herbert S. Denenberg, *Citizens Bill of Hospital Rights*. Pennsylvania Insurance Department, Harrisburg, Pa., 1973.
9. ——— *A Shopper's Guide to Surgery*. Pennsylvania Insurance Department, Harrisburg, Pa., 1972.
10. ——— *A Shopper's Guide to Health Insurance*. Pennsylvania Insurance Department, Harrisburg, Pa., 1972.
11. ——— *A Shopper's Guide to Dentistry*. Pennsylvania Insurance Department, Harrisburg, Pa., 1973.
12. *Blue Cross and Blue Shield Fact Book*. Annual, free. Published by the Associations. Write to the Blue Cross Association, 840 North Lake Shore Drive, Chicago, Illinois 60611; also National Association of Blue Shield Plans, 211 East Chicago Avenue, Chicago, Illinois 60611.
13. Victor R. Fuchs, (Ed.), *Essays in the Economics of Health and Medical Care,* National Bureau of Economic Research, New York, 1972.
14. "Mail Order Health Insurance," *Consumer Reports,* May 1973.
15. In *Money:*—
    "Diagnosing your Health Insurance," September 1974.
    "An X-Ray Analysis of Doctor's Bills," August 1973.
16. *Building a National Health Care System,* Committee for Economic Development, New York, 1973.
17. Eveline M. Burns, *Health Sciences for Tomorrow: Trends & Issues,* University Press of Cambridge Series, Dunellen, 1973.
18. Edward M. Kennedy, *In Critical Condition: The Crisis in America's Health Care,* New York: Simon & Schuster. (paper) Pocket Books, Inc. 1973.
19. Davis W. Gregg & Vane B. Lucas, (Eds.) *Life & Health Insurance Handbook,* 3rd ed. Homewood, Ill. Dow Jones–Irwin, Inc., 1973.

20. "Prepaid Group Practice that Works," Kaiser Permanente Organization, *Forbes,* March 15, 1973.

21. M. B. Rothfeld, Sensible Surgery for Swelling Medical Costs—Health Maintenance Organizations," *Fortune,* April 1973.

22. G. Hodgson, "Politics of American Health Care," *Atlantic,* October 1973, pp. 45–61, December 1973 discussion, January 1974 discussion.

23. Charles G. Oakes, *The Walking Patient and the Health Crisis,* University of South Carolina Press, 1972.

24. John Krizay and A. Wilson, *The Patient As Consumer—Health Care Financing in the United States.* Lexington, Mass.: Lexington Book, D. C. Heath & Co., 1974.

25. Victor R. Fuchs, *Health, Economics, and Social Choice.* New York: Basic Books, 1975.

CASE PROBLEMS

1. Brooks Elliott is a young lawyer, aged 27. He is still a bachelor. He earns $18,000 a year. His small law firm does not provide any fringe benefits—no hospitalization or health insurance of any sort. He feels a vague need for some sort of medical insurance protection. What kind of coverage should he have?

2. Rogers had formerly worked for a company which provided Blue Cross and Blue Shield for its employees. When he left the company, he paid for his family certificate individually ($300 a year). On his new job he is offered the opportunity to take $10,000 of group life insurance in combination with hospital and surgical benefits similar to those provided by Blue Cross and Blue Shield, at a cost to him of $360 a year. Rogers is married, has two children (ages 8 and 10), and earns $18,000 a year. He wonders whether he should drop Blue Cross and Blue Shield. What advice would you give him?

3. Worthen has a wife and three children (ages 8, 14, and 19). He earns $13,000 annually. He carries family membership in Blue Cross and Blue Shield. His eldest son, John, has just become 19 years old and will no longer be covered by the family membership. Upon inquiry, he is told that it will cost him $38.40 per quarter for 21/180 Blue Cross and $12.32 quarterly for Blue Shield in a separate membership for John—a total of $50.72 a quarter, or $202.88 a year. Should he take the separate membership for John?

4. Fred North is earning $180 a week. He is 48 years old, has a wife (age 43) and two children (ages 16 and 18). The family has always been frugal, with the result that they own their home and automobile and have $6,782 in a savings bank. In addition, a $10,000 straight life insurance policy has been carried on North for the last 20 years. Fred's employer now makes Blue Cross and Blue Shield available to his employees. A family membership including both sorts of benefits will cost North $39 a month. He hesitates whether to avail himself of the opportunity. What do you advise?

5. Mrs. Catherine Howard received payment on her medicare claim. One of her doctor's bills was $22, but she only received $12—and the notation on the benefit sheet read "payment reflects the medicare allowable amounts." What is the basis under medicare for medical payments?

6. Leonard Reynard has been ill several times this year, and each time made a claim for medical repayment under his major medical insurance coverage. Each time he received much less than he had paid, always with an explanation about 20 percent coinsurance and $60 deductible—none of which seemed very clear. He continued to file claims and at the end of the year finally received some additional money. Why did he receive the money then? Explain what he did not understand about deductibles and coinsurance.

7. Your father has just become 65. He knows you are taking a course in personal finance and he writes to you for advice and information on medicare. He wants to know how he is covered. He asks what the hospitalization portion covers and what he must pay for it. He asks what the medical portion covers and whether he should purchase coverage. Finally he inquires about Senior Care, what it is, what it covers, and what it will cost. Write an appropriate answer to each of his questions.

8. At this writing a great national debate is underway about the future nature of the nation's health care system, its costs and benefits, and its financing, public or private. Write to your Congressman and ask for copies of the various bills which have been submitted in the House and in the Senate on health care. Also write to the Secretary of the U.S. Department of Health, Education, and Welfare in Washington, D.C. for information on the various alternative proposals. After you have read and studied the material received, outline the several different proposals and explain which one you personally would favor.

9. Tests show that Mariam Snorton, 33, needs a mastectomy operation. She works as a secretary at the University, has Blue Cross and Blue Shield coverage. She wonders if she is eligible for coverage for this operation and if not what alternative sources of financing there are. She also is uncertain of the cost of such an operation. Can you advise her?

11

Automobile, Fire, and Property Insurance

Your own property is concerned when your neighbors' house is on fire.
Horace

Every 13 seconds a fire breaks out somewhere in the United States. Annual losses due to fire now amount to more than $2.3 billion. Every homeowner knows that he needs fire insurance. Some time back it was customary to buy fire insurance as a separate policy, perhaps add extended coverage or additional extended coverage or buy a separate personal liability policy. Today the trend is to purchase a package policy covering a large number of risks and perils.

INSURANCE ON THE HOME

This is a complicated insurance area, and you need to understand certain terms to know what the insurance agent means. *Property* insurance provides financial protection against loss or damage to property caused by such perils as fire, windstorm, hail, explosion, riot, aircraft, motor vehicles, vandalism and malicious mischief, riot and civil commotion, smoke, and so on. *Liability* insurance affords financial protection for injury to persons or property of others for which you may be held liable. *Burglary and theft* insurance protects financially against loss of property due to burglary, robbery, or larceny. *Comprehensive personal liability* insurance reimburses the policyholder who becomes liable to pay money for damage or injury to others. *Fire* insurance covers losses caused by fire and lightning, as well as the resultant damage caused by smoke and water. *Extended coverage* insurance protects you against loss or damage to your property caused by windstorm, hail, smoke, explosion, riot, vehicles or falling aircraft. It is provided in conjunction with the fire insurance policy. A *homeowners* insurance policy is a package type which includes fire and extended coverage, theft, and personal liability coverage in a single policy. *Multiple peril insurance* policies combine many perils previously covered by individual policies of fire and casualty companies. The homeowners policy is one example. Others are the commercial property policy, the tenant's policy, the farm owner's policy, and so on.[1]

The Homeowners Policy

This package policy comes in several forms—basic, broad, or comprehensive. The nature of the perils covered in each case may be seen in Figure 11–1. The advantage to the homeowner is obvious. You have only one policy and one premium to worry about, and by packaging a number of perils in one policy, the insurance companies are able to offer the policy at 30 to 40 percent less than that of separately purchased coverages.

The homeowners policy provides both property insurance and liability coverage. Property coverage includes your house or dwelling and your garage. Your personal property is insured including household contents and other personal belongings used, owned, worn, or carried by you or your family. The protection applies both at home and away from home. If you wish, this coverage may apply to the personal belongings of your friends while they are on your premises. Certain limits are set on the amount of coverage on money, stamps, jewelry, and furs. If you want to recover full value for loss or damage to such items, you should have them covered under separate policies. You are also insured for additional living expense when damage to your home requires you to live elsewhere, in a hotel, for example, while a house damaged by fire is being repaired. Automobiles, although personal property, are not protected under a homeowners policy.

Against what perils is your property insured under the homeowners policy? It depends on the form (see Figure 11–1). The *Basic Form* insures against 11 named perils. The *Broad Form,* which is the most popular, covers 18 perils. The *Comprehensive Form* is a so called "all risks" contract. Actually, no policy gives you protection against every possible peril. Generally speaking, an "all risks" contract is one that covers you for everything

---

[1] See Insurance Information Institute's "*Insurance Facts,*" latest annual edition. A free copy may be obtained by writing to the Institute at 110 William Street, New York, N.Y., 10038.

FIGURE 11–1
Perils against Which Properties Are Insured—Homeowners Policy

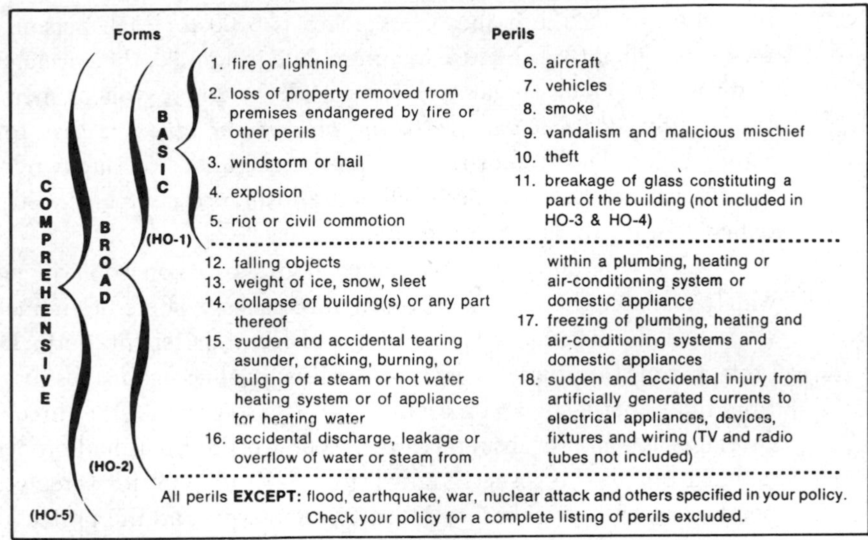

Source: Insurance Information Institute, "A Family Guide to Property and Liability Insurance."

except—and then it lists the exceptions. In the Comprehensive Form, perils excluded are earthquake, flood, war, nuclear attack. The major difference between the Comprehensive Form and the other forms of the homeowners policy is that the comprehensive form lists the perils you are *not* insured against while the other policies list the perils you *are* insured against. The former names the exclusions; the latter names the perils.

Liability coverage in all forms of the homeowners policy include comprehensive personal liability, medical payments and physical damage to the property of others. *Comprehensive personal liability* protects you against claims arising from bodily injury to others or damage to their property. For example, suppose your neighbor slips and falls on your icy steps, suffers a head injury which impairs vision, and then files suit for damages. Your insurance company will represent you in court, and if the court verdict goes against you, damages will be paid by your insurance company up to the limit of your policy. A note of caution: in states where workmen's compensation insurance is required by law, the personal liability coverages under the homeowners policy do not provide coverage if a cook, housekeeper, maid, or other servant, is injured.

Medical payments coverage protects you when persons are accidentally injured on or away from your premises if the injury is caused by you, members of your family, or your animals. The insurance company reimburses the injured party, regardless of who is at fault, for medical and surgical services incurred within one year of the accident. The basic amount of this protection under the homeowners policy is $500 for each person. Unlike medical payments in the case of automobile insurance, the coverage in the homeowners policy applies only to outsiders—not to you or members of your family. *Physical damage to the property of others* is easy to understand. A child kicks a football through the neighbor's picture window. Under the parent's homeowners policy the insurance company will pay the damages up to the limit of the policy.

If you live in an apartment, rented house, or co-op you will now find widely available the same sort of insurance package offered to homeowners. It's called the Residence Contents broad form, or tenants form H0–4. It protects your furniture and your personal belongings against loss or damage from the 18 perils shown on Figure 11–1. It also provides the three liability coverages as well. For insurance on $25,000 worth of personal property in a city apartment, the cost will range from $200 to $600 for three years, depending on city, neighborhood, construction type, and fire protection.

How Much Property and Liability Insurance Do you Need?

It is difficult to estimate needs because you cannot know ahead of time how large the claim or suit against you may be. Even against persons of average means, jury awards may be very high. Therefore, most people, especially those who have assets, salaries, or other income to protect, should carry at least $25,000 of liability insurance. As to property insurance, the amount you need depends on the replacement value of your house and personal property. If your home burned to the ground, how much would it cost, at today's prices, to replace it? Replacement cost is the basis for determining how much property insurance is enough.

Assume your house would cost $25,000 to rebuild and that your household contents are valued at $10,000. To receive full payment (replacement cost) for partial loss or damage to your house under the homeowners policy, you need insure it for only 80 percent of replacement value. Eighty percent of $25,000 is $20,000, and it is the basis for determining the amount of the other property coverages under a homeowners policy. In the case of a broad form homeowners policy, the property and liability protection would be as shown in Table 11–1.

What would such coverage cost? Based on a $25,000 frame house in a specific midwestern town, a comparison of costs for basic, broad, and comprehensive forms of the homeowners policy would be as shown in Table 11–2. Keep in mind that these figures are only an example of what

TABLE 11–1
Homeowners Policy—Broad Form

	Amount of Coverage	
	Insured to Value	*Insured at 80%*
Property coverages		
Dwelling	$25,000 (full value)	$20,000 (80% of full value)
Appurtenant private structures	2,500 (10% of dwelling)	2,000 (10% of dwelling)
Unscheduled personal property	12,500 (50% of dwelling)	10,000 (50% of dwelling)
Additional living expenses	5,000 (20% of dwelling)	4,000 (20% of dwelling)
Liability coverages		
Personal liability	$25,000 (each occurrence)*	$25,000 (each occurrence)*
Medical payments to others	500 (each person)*	500 (each person)*
Physical damage to property of others	250 (each occurrence)	250 (each occurrence)

* Larger amounts are available.
Source: Insurance Information Institute.

one person might pay for this coverage. For various reasons your coverage may cost more, or less. Costs vary according to territory, water supply available for fire fighting, efficiency of fire department, type of construction, and other factors.

TABLE 11–2
Comparison of Coverage Costs for a $25,000 Frame House

	Insured to Value		Insured at 80%	
Coverage	*Cost per Year*	*Cost per Month*	*Cost per Year*	*Cost per Month*
Basic Form—11 perils*	$ 76.00	$ 6.33	$ 61.00	$ 5.08
Broad Form—18 perils*	$ 82.00	$ 6.83	$ 66.00	$ 5.50
Comprehensive Form—"all risks"*	$181.00	$15.08	$157.00	$13.08

* $100 deductible.
Source: Insurance Information Institute.

Inflation and Insurance

In many states you can obtain homeowners inflation protection which provides for an automatic increase in the amount of insurance protection provided by your policy whenever the cost of living and building construction rises due to inflation. The automatic adjustment can work in several ways. Many policies provide for an increase in the protection every three months at the rate of 1 percent of the face of the policy. There is at least one policy available that increases the protection monthly, based on changes in the Composite Construction Cost Index computed by the Department of Commerce and changes in the Consumer Price Index computed by the Department of Labor. Under either plan there is no charge for the additional coverage during the policy period. However, when the policy is renewed, the premium is adjusted, based on the new amount of insurance. Insurance experts say that many homes are underinsured since construction costs have increased more than 50 percent since 1967. Therefore an automatic annual increase in coverage of 4 percent may not be adequate in light of the inflated replacement cost. Some insurance companies have developed tables that estimate what these costs might be. Factors including the number of room units, the type of construction, and the materials used provide the primary expense estimate which must then be multiplied by an area cost modifier to take into consideration the varying material and labor costs to figure fairly accurately the replacement cost.

Separate Policies

You may be the old fashioned type and prefer to buy your coverages in individual policies, as the need appears to develop even though it will cost you more. Or you may feel you do not need protection against as many perils as the homeowners policy covers. You may just want to get down to basics and buy fire insurance, for example, and nothing else. In that case read on. If you are mainly interested in cars, however, skip to page 524.

Fire Insurance Policies

Fire insurance reimburses for the replacement value (less depreciation) of property destroyed, not for its original cost. Fire insurance policies were typically written for one, three, and five years with the premium fixed for the length of the policy. Now it is customary to write them for periods of one and three years, with some companies writing what is referred to as a one year continuously renewable until canceled policy. The reason for dropping the five year policy and discouraging the use of the three year coverage is that fire losses and insurance rates have increased rapidly during the past decade. The arson rate is ten times as high as in 1950. A policy with a shorter life permits adjustment of rates more quickly to meet losses and economic change.

When you buy fire insurance, a "form" or "endorsement" is attached to the standard contract by the company. It contains all the personal details of the contract, the amount of insurance, for example, a description of the property covered, its location, the owner, and so on. The form, or endorsement, becomes part of the contract. In fact, without it the standard policy insures nothing. Basically all provisions fall into two categories:

1. The provisions that explain the risks covered and the risks excluded.
2. The provisions that should be considered before a loss occurs and those that should be considered after a fire.

Annual Fire Premiums

Annual premiums for fire insurance vary widely, depending on construction, use, location, nearness to a hydrant, adequacy of water supply, fire-fighting facilities, and other factors. Fire insurance rates are customarily expressed as the number of dollars or cents which would be charged for $100 of insurance for one year. Thus a rate of 20 cents means that you pay 20 cents for each $100 of fire insurance protection. An $8,000 policy would thus cost $16. Under the best conditions an annual rate approaching 10 cents per $100, or $1 per $1,000, of insurance may be expected, whereas the rate can be as much as $8 per $1,000 under extremely unfavorable conditions. A rate in the neighborhood of $3.20 per $1,000 has been fairly typical for an ordinary frame house, but, like everything else, there is a tendency for rates to go up. Some companies will reduce the rate if a smoke detection system is installed. The Hanover Insurance Company is offering a 5 percent discount to families of nonsmokers.

Extended Coverage on Fire Policies

Since fire insurance is designed only to reimburse the loss resulting from fire or lightning, it is sensible to consider whether additional insurance should be carried to protect against other hazards. *Extended coverage* offering protection against damage by cyclone, tornado, hurricanes, hailstorms, windstorm, and such unrelated things as damage caused by a motor vehicle or an airplane, or explosion, riot, or smoke damage is often added to fire policies. The fee for extended coverage is small, ranging from 4 to 20 cents per $100 of protection for one year. The fire insurance companies have also developed another "endorsement" or "clause" which may also be added to your fire policy. This is called *additional extended coverage* and protects against water damage from plumbing and heating systems; vandalism and malicious mischief; glass breakage; ice, snow, and freezing; fall of trees; and collapse. The rate for additional extended coverage is 6 cents for $100 of protection for one year. Most extended coverage policies and all additional extended coverage policies are sold only with $50 deductible clauses.

In the suburbs of a large city, where fire fighting facilities are adequate, the cost of $20,000 of fire insurance would be about $120 for three years; extended coverage would cost another $64, and additional extended coverage $32 more. Rates vary so greatly from area to area, from city to city, and for different types and construction of buildings that it is dangerous to generalize. Check your local rates with two or three companies. They should be the same per $100 of protection desired for your particular piece of property.

Many buyers of home owner's policies are not aware that price competition exists. A combination of state laws and industry sponsored proposals began in 1970 to phase out standard set rates and substitute "open rating." Insurers had historically been exempted from antitrust laws because they had used standard rates based on a broad sampling of losses not available to any one company. The Insurance Services Office, the industry owned rating service, is now supplying raw data to insurers on prospective losses and expenses to allow them to formulate their own rates. The "open rating" now used in many states allows companies to change rates before notifying the insurance regulatory authorities, a practice previously forbidden. Rates have been cut over widespread geographic areas, increasing competition. In New York State, for example, there is as much as 50 percent divergence for identical coverage in the prices offered by some 180 insurance companies doing business in the state.

Cancellation

There is a commonly misunderstood fact that deserves mention. If one buys a fire policy and wants to cancel it he will probably not receive a pro rata refund of his premium but will receive a refund based on a short rate table contained in or on the policy. The effect is to return to him considerably less than the pro rata amount which the company will refund if it decides to cancel the policy. If the company wishes to cancel, it must give you written notice five days (in some states ten days) before the insurance is to be terminated. The purpose is to give you a few days to seek protection from some other company.

Coinsurance

Many people underinsure their properties either because they expect a fire loss, if it occurs, to be only a small percentage of the total value of the property, or because, having bought the property and originally taken out the fire insurance some years back, they have not taken into consideration the subsequent appreciation in value of property due to inflation.

In those states having a "coinsurance" clause in the standard fire insurance contract, the underinsurer is often surprised and shocked to find that only part of the amount of fire loss can be recovered from the insurance company, even though the face amount of the policy actually exceeds the amount of the fire loss. This sounds surprising and complicated, but it is really easy to understand.

A coinsurance clause, which most people do not bother to read, or if they do read, do not understand, might appear as follows:

> It is a part of the consideration of this policy, and the basis upon which the rate of premium is fixed, that the insured shall at all times maintain insurance on each item of property insured by this policy of not less than 80 (the rate may vary from state to state) percent of the actual cash value thereof, and that failing to do so, the insured shall be an insurer to the extent of such deficit, and in that event shall bear his, her or their proportion of any loss.

What does this mean? It merely says that if you fail to carry insurance amounting to 80 percent of the value of the property, in the event of a loss you must share the loss with the insurance company and may collect only that proportion of the loss which the amount of insurance you actually have bears to the amount of insurance you should have under the coinsurance clause. For example, if you own a property valued at $20,000, you should, under a typical coinsurance provision, carry $16,000 worth of fire insurance. Suppose that you carry only $8,000 of fire insurance and that a fire occurs, causing an $8,000 loss. You will be surprised to find that you cannot collect the whole $8,000 from the insurance company. You are a coinsurer with the company for one half the loss, since you were carrying only one half ($8,000) of the insurance you should have been carrying ($16,000); and you will collect only $8,000/$16,000, or one half of the loss, namely, $4,000.

If you have a coinsurance clause in your fire policy, then the following simple formula will apply:

$$\frac{\text{Amount of insurance carried}}{\text{Amount of insurance required}} \times \text{Amount of loss} = \text{Amount collectible.}$$

Some people believe that in the event of any loss, either partial or total, the property owner is entitled to collect only that percentage of his loss which is stated in the coinsurance clause. For example, they think that if a man owns a building worth $20,000 and carries $16,000 of insurance with an 80 percent coinsurance clause, he will collect only 80 percent of any loss. Thus, if he has a $2,000 loss, they believe he would collect only $1600. This impression is incorrect. He would collect $2,000. He will collect in full any loss up to $16,000, since he has purchased the full protection required, namely, 80 percent of the value.

The true purpose of the coinsurance clause is to distribute the cost of fire insurance equitably among property owners, and it has been widely adopted by insurance companies. For example, North and West each own buildings valued at $10,000. North, gambling on the fact that most fires result in partial losses, purchases only $2,000 of fire insurance. West, the more sensible property owner, carries $8,000 of coverage. If both call on their insurance company to reimburse them in the event of $2,000 fire losses each, North, the property owner who gambled, would in effect be seeking the same indemnity as West, although North has paid only one quarter of the premium West paid. Because of coinsurance North would collect only $500, while West would be paid $2,000.

The fairness of coinsurance is demonstrated by the companies' willingness to grant a reduction in the rate or cost of insurance for the acceptance of this clause. It provides an incentive to the owner to insure the property fully and to increase his insurance when there is an appreciation in values. Fire insurance rates would be higher were it not for this clause. Coinsurance is generally considered the fairest method yet devised for equalizing the cost of insurance between those who carry complete coverage and those who attempt to get away with only enough to cover small losses.

Things to Watch in Fire Policies

Fire policies may be unknowingly voided for various reasons stated in the policy. You will not know about these unless you read your policy carefully. For example, if you leave your house unoccupied for more than 60 consecutive days, you may void your policy. If you add a room, you may need more insurance. Does your policy cover your household furnishings as well as the house itself? If so, do you have an inventory of the furnishings, so that you can prove your loss in the event of fire? Your insurance broker can give you a room by room form which makes inventory taking easier. Put the completed inventory in your safe deposit box. Some homeowners take their inventories with a camera, photographing each room and then putting the pictures in a safe deposit box. If household furnishings are covered, you may also have a 10 percent off-premises clause in the policy, protecting your personal property away from your home. You may not know about this, suffer a fire loss while traveling, and fail to collect. Policies cover losses due to damage by water used to extinguish the fire. They also cover the cost of removing debris.

The 10 percent provision is important in three instances.

1. Ten percent of the insurance on your dwelling can be applied to cover losses on other buildings on your premises. Suppose your house is insured for $12,000. Your garage burns down. The company will pay up to 10 percent of $12,000, or $1,200 on the loss of the garage. If the garage was worth $1,200, the 10 percent clause would pay for it in full. If it was worth $1,000, that is the amount the insurance company would pay. If the garage was worth $1,500, you could collect only $1,200.

2. Up to 10 percent of the household contents coverage can be applied to any additions, alterations, or improvements you may make should they be destroyed by fire. For example, you live in a rented apartment. Since the landlord won't paint it you do. If fire should break out and ruin the apartment, you can collect not only for your household contents but for the cost of your paint job as well.

3. Finally, the 10 percent protection on household contents covers your personal property even though away from home. You are traveling. Fire breaks out in the hotel where you are staying. You flee to the street. Your luggage is destroyed by fire. You can collect up to a maximum of 10 percent of your fire insurance coverage.

If you are forced to rent a hotel room or apartment temporarily because your dwelling was destroyed by fire, the insurance company will cover the cost of your actual expense for rental of temporary quarters up to a maximum of 20 percent of the insurance on the dwelling. You cannot, however, receive more than one twelfth of the 20 percent for rental expense for any one month. For example, you have insured your house for $24,000. A fire breaks out and you are forced to live in a hotel for three months while repairs are being made. The insurance company will not pay more than $400 a month toward your hotel bill (20 percent of $24,000 is $4800, 1/12 of $4800 is $400 maximum per month).

When You Have a Fire Loss. There are four things to do:

1. Report the loss to the company at once.
2. Safeguard the remaining property.
3. Prepare an inventory of lost or damaged property.
4. Submit "proof of loss" supported wherever possible by bills, vouchers, and canceled checks showing how much you paid for things lost.

It is an excellent idea to call your insurance agent right away and to sign nothing until you have discussed your loss with him. A loss is payable, as a rule, 60 days after the property owner's sworn statement, called the "proof of loss," is received by the company. Most companies pay claims in much less time, however. The company will probably send its adjuster to inspect your loss.

In large cities there are licensed "public adjusters," who persuade the harassed and excited homeowner who has just suffered a fire loss to sign a paper authorizing the "public adjuster" to represent the homeowner in dealing with the insurance company. The homeowner may initially be glad to have someone else handle the problem for him, until he finds that the public adjuster gets 10 percent or more of everything the insurance company pays. Either deal with the insurance company adjuster, who will be sent around to inspect your loss, yourself or have your agent do it for you. There is no need to hire a public adjuster.

If you and the company adjuster cannot agree on the value of what was lost, take the matter to your agent. If the agent agrees with you, he can ask the insurance company for a special investigation. You may get a better settlement. If, however, you still cannot agree, your policy provides that the dispute may be settled by two appraisers, one selected by you and the other by the company. These two then select a competent and disinterested umpire, and the dispute is then arbitrated. But you pay half the costs of appraisal and arbitration. While you may not want to go this far because of the expense, do not settle for an unsatisfactory sum simply because you are in a hurry to get your check. The adjuster, while normally fair, may perceive this or count on it, and you may get less than you would have received if you had been more determined.

Do not underinsure. Remember the coinsurance clause. On the other hand, don't overinsure. It doesn't help. For example, your property is worth $22,000. You insure it for $30,000. A fire causes a total loss. You can collect only $22,000, the value of the property destroyed, not $30,000. Read your policy carefully. Ask your broker to explain those things that you do not understand. Find out how coinsurance affects you. Know what your policy covers. Make an inventory, and keep it somewhere other than on the insured premises, preferably in a safe deposit box. Do not settle hastily. When you have done all this, you will have reasonable protection.

Other Separate Policies on the Home

A householder, transplanting a shrub, hadn't finished when darkness came. That night a neighbor started across the lawn, fell into the hole and broke a leg. He sued and was awarded $9,500 damages. As a homeowner, you may want separate policies for your protection. If someone visiting you slips on the porch steps and falls and breaks his back, you may find yourself facing a costly lawsuit for damages, even though you had nothing to do with the accident. It was on your property, and you may thus be liable.

1. A *comprehensive personal liability policy* covering your legal liability

for bodily injury, illness, death, or property damages suffered on your property by a nonmember of your family may be purchased for a small premium. A $25,000 policy (with $500 for medical payments) costs only $21. You can buy larger policies, of course, for slightly higher annual premiums. For only about $4 a year, you can quadruple your $25,000 coverage—a prudent precaution in the face of today's fairly common high awards. The *comprehensive personal liability policy* is well worth its small cost and is a must not only for the homeowner but for the apartment tenant as well. If you live 10 stories up and your air conditioner falls out of the window and kills someone, or if your bathtub or washing machine runs over due to your negligence and ruins the neighbor's paint job below, *comprehensive personal liability* is a very useful policy to have.

2. A *personal articles floater* is very useful. It insures specifically listed items such as furniture, clothing, sporting goods, cameras, linens, rugs, silverware, luggage, furs, and books, both in the home and away from it, against almost all risks of loss or damage with a few such minor exceptions such as moths, vermin, and dampness. A personal property articles policy is a good idea for valuables costing $500 or more—with each article appraised and listed separately. There's no geographical limitation—the property is covered no matter where you take it. Rates vary depending on where you live and the items insured. Fine arts insurance rates vary widely, but a typical premium is $3.50 per $1,000 of value or $35 a year for your $10,000 Dufy. Rate is on a sliding scale downward above $10,000. It's wise to keep all bills of sale in a safe place, such as your safe deposit box. Ironically—where it is most needed—it is difficult to buy floater coverage in a high crime risk area.

For each item covered there is a minimum premium of $25. Furs cost about $1 a year for each $100 of value in most places. In Chicago, however, where fur thefts have been heavy, they go up to $5 for mink. Jewelry coverage across the country varies from a high of $5 per $100 to a low of 90 cents per $100. In the Los Angeles area the rate went from $1.50 to $4 in the last ten years. Walter Hoving of Tiffany advises going without insurance—"If you're rich enough, you can stand a good robbery."[2] In case of a robbery, the loss can be taken as an income tax deduction. You can get a lower insurance rate for jewelry normally kept in a bank vault; however, this doesn't apply to furs kept in storage. Some states will not permit a company to cancel a jewelry coverage after a theft, until the policy lapses. After that, it is up to the company. Jewelry thefts of more than $100 are tax deductible, minus the insurance paid. For the wealthy, a tax

---

[2] *New York Times*, December 3, 1973.

loss might be cheaper than insurance. Since most homeowners policy forms now limit theft coverage on unscheduled jewelry and furs to $250 in the aggregate, for each loss, those who possess valuable jewelry or furs should consider the additional premium.

3. *Theft* insurance covers burglary, robbery, and larceny. You will want residential theft insurance covering both the stealing of property from your home and also damage to home and property by thieves. This will cost from $25 to $35 per $1,000 of protection for one year. You'll want your theft insurance to cover not only burglary, robbery, and larceny but also "mysterious disappearance" (its just gone but you don't know how!) and also "theft damage." The last is important. Often burglars will twist, shatter, and break far more than they steal. A "broad form" theft policy will cover all this whereas the "limited" form is more restricted.

It is no longer regarded as "mysterious disappearance," but as theft, when you leave a ring on a washstand in a restaurant and return shortly after to find it gone. But, if something disappears and you have no idea what happened, that can only be covered by a special policy. Such a policy will cover circumstances which in themselves do not necessarily suggest theft.

4. *Low cost flood insurance* has become recently available to home owners under a program subsidized by the federal government. Otherwise rates would be very high as the only persons who would want insurance would be those almost certain to have losses. Insurance is available through the Federal Insurance Administration of the U.S. Department of Housing and Urban Development and administered by the National Flood Insurance Association consisting of approximately 100 private insurance companies. Protection is provided against losses caused by the overflow of inland or tidal water or the unusual and rapid accumulation or run off of surface waters from any source. It can be purchased through local agents in about 3,000 communities in the United States at an annual premium cost of 25 cents for each $100 on the building up to $35,000 on a one family house and from $30,000 to $100,000 on two to four family structures. The coverage for contents of residential buildings may be up to $10,000 at an annual cost of 35 cents per each $100.

Why You Might Not Get Insurance

Getting and keeping insurance has become more difficult, as the risks mount, for home, property, and car insurance, as companies have become less eager to meet the demands for such insurance. Since the basis for writing insurance has always been the actuarial tables which, until recently, reflected the normal trend over the years, the companies have just not been prepared for the rise in auto thefts and home burglaries, or the inflation in medical and legal costs, and in car repairs on accident claims. The exclusion policy of selling only to arbitrarily selected good risks has been their way of staying solvent, but it leaves many unprotected. If you have made too many claims—even legitimate ones—you run the risk of a canceled policy or one not renewed. One answer has been to increase the deductible (since under the circumstances you hesitate anyway to make small claims), therefore lowering your own premium rate and, in that way, perhaps balancing the costs of higher premium charges.

Government Assisted Programs

The underlying principle of insurance—the spreading of risks among many—has been converted into only insuring those least likely to make claims. Those desperate for protection, and most in need of it, cannot get it. The Federal government and some states have moved into the void. There are laws providing for pools into which all the bad risk cases are placed. Some states have also mandated coverage on fire insurance. Fire insurance is based on full metropolitan areas—not on sections or individual buildings within the area. Deteriorating areas or those with high crime rates had difficulties in the past, but after the riots, large sections of many cities were completely ignored by the insurance companies. The President's Commission on Insurance in Riot Affected Areas recommended that states set up pools to take in all reasonable risk for fire insurance, including riot protection under the extended coverage endorsement with federal reinsurance provided by the Department of Housing and Urban Development. In 26 states, Puerto Rico and the District of Columbia, the pool is called FAIR (Fair Access to Insurance Requirements), and although providing limited maximum coverage, it is one of the largest property insurers.

Traditionally, insurance companies are state regulated by Commissioners of Insurance. At one time, when the Supreme Court declared insurance interstate and subject to antitrust laws, federal regulation seemed likely. But Congress acted to exclude insurance companies from such provisions and provided for federal action only where the states did not. There have since been some tentative steps in this direction of federal action.

Since August 1971, federal government crime insurance has been sold where private insurance is not available at reasonable rates, or where state governments have taken no action. The program is operated by the Department of Housing and Urban Development in Connecticut, Illinois, Maryland, Massachusetts, Florida, Kansas, New Jersey, Tennessee, Missouri, New York, Ohio, Pennsylvania, Rhode Island and Washington, D.C. Relatively few policies have been sold since the program began. HUD claims there has not been enough public education that the policies exist. The insurance companies claim that there has been little need; hence few sales. The program's future is in doubt.

Premium rates for both business and home insurance will be based on crime statistics furnished by the Federal Bureau of Investigation for each area and will be uniform throughout a Standard Metropolitan Statistical Area. This means that the rates will be the same for the inner city as in the suburbs in that area. Maximum coverage for homes is $10,000 and for business $15,000.

The Federal Crime Insurance program places the onus for taking all needed protective measures on the insured. If an individual presents a claim for loss due to burglary, he will have to show that he had not been negligent in taking proper precautions, such as installing appropriate locks and bolts. Policies may be bought from local insurance agents.

AUTOMOBILE INSURANCE

Next to the home and its contents, the automobile is typically the most expensive family possession. Aside from the original purchase price and upkeep (discussed in Chapter 2), the automobile is costly to its owner in other ways. Insurance is expensive, repair costs too high to go uninsured and the possibility of a disastrous jury award to an injured person too great not to be covered by liability protection. Those who underinsure risk mortgaging a large share of future earnings to pay increasingly high jury awards. Those who do not insure can be a menace to everyone else. Every state has some form of financial responsibility law which requires a person involved in an automobile accident to furnish proof of financial responsibility up to a certain minimum. Usually this requirement is met by the purchase of liability insurance in the minimum amount set by the state in which your car is garaged.

Some states such as New York, Massachusetts, and North Carolina have laws which require that liability insurance be carried as a prerequisite to obtaining license plates and registration for the car. Other states require that a motorist who is uninsured and involved in an accident would lose his license regardless of fault.

A poll conducted by Louis Harris and Associates, sponsored by the Sentry Insurance Company and termed "the most comprehensive and candid survey of public attitudes and perceptions of the insurance industry to date" found, among other things, that:

> 73 percent favored requiring insurance companies to provide five year policies that could not be canceled and for which premiums could not be raised.
>
> 66 percent felt drivers 29 years of age and younger were treated less fairly than others.
>
> 31 percent felt that nonwhites are treated less fairly than others.
>
> Nearly four in five policyholders felt most insurers would refuse to insure them if they were high risks, and half said they felt insurance companies were quick to cancel policies after one accident.
>
> Only two out of five home or automobile policyholders felt their companies would readily pay the full amount of a claim, while close to half felt there was delay.
>
> More than half felt that premium discounts should be offered for cars with more safety features than required.[3]

Kinds of Automobile Insurance

Last year, more than 56,000 people died in automobile accidents and 5 million more were injured. There have been three times as many deaths from automobile accidents since the 1900s in the United States than battle deaths in our Armed Forces covering a period from the Revolutionary War until the present. Over half of the automobile accidents occur on weekends. Death struck every ten minutes last year, and every seven seconds someone was injured in an automobile accident.

There are six basic automobile insurance coverages. They are:

1. Bodily injury liability.
2. Property damage liability.
3. Medical payments.
4. Comprehensive physical damage.
5. Collision.
6. Protection against uninsured motorists.

Coverage is decided on classification of age, sex, marital status, driver training, and how the car is used—its purpose, age, and mileage. The most favored are married people between the ages of 30 and 65 who drive for

---

[3] "The Sentry Insurance National Opinion Study: A Survey of Consumer Attitudes in the U.S. Towards Auto and Homeowners Insurance," conducted by Louis Harris & Associates Inc. and the Dept. of Insurance, The Wharton School, University of Pennsylvania, January 1974.

pleasure, or only a short distance to work. While insurance companies favor these refinements, the Federal Insurance Administrator disapproves on the principle that it is a means of isolating risks. Although the states regulate rates, it does not mean that all companies within a state charge the same coverage or services. Insurance companies compile statistics on claims relating to cars garaged within a rating territory and set their basic rates accordingly.

The six basic automobile insurance coverages are available in many combinations and for varying amounts. Table 11–3 shows what each protects. In some cases they can be purchased separately, but large numbers of owners of private passenger cars prefer a package policy, either in the form of the Family Automobile Policy or the Special Automobile Policy. Experienced drivers and insurance experts will tell you that the basic coverages of bodily injury and property damage are an absolute must. To be without these is to run the risk of financial disaster. Think of paying a damage award of $250,000 over your lifetime out of your earnings.

TABLE 11–3
A Summary Chart of Automobile Insurance Coverages

	Principal Applications			
Coverages	*Policyholder*	*Other Persons*	*Policyholder's Automobile*	*Property of Others*
Bodily injury				
Liability	No	Yes		
Medical payments	Yes	Yes		
Protection against uninsured motorists	Yes	Yes		
Property damage				
Liability			No	Yes
Comprehensive physical damage			Yes	No
Collision			Yes	No

Source: Insurance Information Institute.

Bodily Injury Liability Insurance

This pays for injury, sickness, disease, or death of others for which you may be legally liable, including claims for damages for care and loss of services, because of accidents involving your automobile, up to the limits of the policy.

Who is protected? You, all other members of your family, and all those who may on occasion drive your car with your permission. Members of your family are covered even when driving someone else's car, as long as the owner has given them permission. What is covered? Bodily injury liability insurance provides protection in the form of legal defense when claims or suits are brought against you by or on behalf of people injured or killed by your automobile.

Costs of Bodily Injury Liability Insurance

Amounts of bodily injury coverage are usually spoken of in such terms as: "ten, twenty," "twenty-five, fifty," or "one hundred, three hundred." They are usually written 10/20, 25/50, 100/300. In each case the first number refers to the maximum, in thousands of dollars, that the insurance company will pay for injury to any one person. The second number is the limit they will pay for all of the injuries resulting from any one accident. This means that the insurance company agrees to protect the insured up to $10,000 for bodily injuries to or death of any one person, and, subject to the same limit for each person, up to $20,000 for bodily injuries or death involving two or more persons in a single accident. Premium rates for such protection vary greatly from place to place. In rural areas, where the chance of hitting people is considerably less, 10/20 bodily injury liability protection may be obtained for less, whereas in the larger cities its cost may amount to five or six times as much. Often you will hear insurance agents refer to bodily injury and property damage limit, combined, as "ten, twenty, and five." The first two numbers refer to bodily injury liability and the last one to property damage insurance in thousands of dollars. Actual costs for varying limits for five large cities in the United States are shown in Table 11–4.

It's not uncommon for a jury to award an injured person $60,000—or more. If this happened to you and you had 10/20/5 coverage, your insurance company would pay only $10,000 and you would be personally liable for the remaining $50,000. It doesn't cost very much more in the way of an additional premium to increase your bodily injury coverage. If we assume that 10/20 costs $55, then the comparative cost relationships shown in Table 11–5 would prevail. Note that in the third assumption, bodily injury coverage is five times as great as in the first assumption, but the increase in cost is only $19 a year on each $100 of premium. In the last example, the bodily injury coverage is more than doubled, yet the increase in premium is only $8 more.

Thus the extra protection can be gained at relatively little extra cost. Juries, of course, take no notice of, and are in no way bound by, your insurance limits in any damage suit against you. You may carry 10/20 and a jury may award $50,000 damages, if you gravely injure or cripple someone.

TABLE 11–4
Comparative Automobile Insurance Rates in Five Cities

	New York (Manhattan)		*Washington, D.C.*		*Chicago (Evanston)*		*Dallas*		*San Francisco*	
Coverage Available	"*A*"	"*B*"	"*A*"	"*B*"	"*A*"	"*B*"	"*A*"	"*B*"	"*A*"	"*B*"
Bodily injury liability										
$10,000/$20,000	$ 46.20	$ 78.05	$ 60.10	$136.30	$ 87.30	$198.00	$27.00	$ 63.00	$ 94.70*	$214.80*
$20,000/$40,000	55.90	94.45	71.50	162.30	103.90	235.70	32.00	75.00	100.70	228.40
$25,000/$50,000	58.20	98.40	74.00	167.90	107.40	243.70	33.00	78.00	104.00	236.00
$50,000/$100,000	65.15	110.05	81.20	184.10	117.80	267.30	36.00	86.00	114.20	259.10
Property damage liability										
$5,000	$ 44.00	$ 78.20	$ 37.10	$ 84.10	$ 36.60	$ 82.90	$34.00	$ 80.00	$ 48.10	$109.20
$10,000	46.20	82.10	39.00	88.50	38.50	87.40	36.00	84.00	50.60	114.80
$25,000	47.50	84.45	40.10	90.90	39.60	89.70	37.00	87.00	52.00	118.00
$50,000	49.70	88.35	42.00	95.30	41.40	93.90	38.00	91.00	54.50	123.60
No fault coverage										
Full basic personal injury protection (PIP)	37.80	63.85			14.30	32.50				
$200 ded basic PIP	31.35	53.00								
Extended PIP rate per vehicle	3.00	3.00								
Additional PIP rate per vehicle	9.00	9.00								
Excess PIP dependents					39.00	39.00				
Excess PIP no dependents					28.90	28.90				
$2,500 PIP							15.00	17.00		
$5,000 PIP							23.00	25.00		
$10,000 PIP							33.00	35.00		

Coverage										
Automobile medical payments										
$1,000	$ NW	$ NW	$ 6.20	$ 13.90	$ 11.20	$ 25.40	$ 7.00	$ 9.00	$ 16.40	$ 37.20
$2,000	NW	NW	8.10	18.30	13.30	30.10	NW	NW	18.40	41.60
$3,000	NW	NW	9.10	20.70	14.30	32.50	NW	NW	19.30	43.70
$5,000	*extended* 1.00	1.00	11.10	25.10	16.30	36.90	11.00	14.00	21.40	48.40
$10,000	*extended* 2.00	2.00					15.00	18.00		
Uninsured motorists										
$10,000/$20,000	$ 2.00	$ 2.00	$ 3.10	$ 3.10	$ 5.00	$ 5.00	$ 5.00	$ 4.00	$ 16.20	$ 16.20
Fire, theft comprehensive										
Non deductible	$ 96.00	$ 96.00	$ 21.90	$ 49.60	$ 27.30	$ 62.00	$23.00	$ 20.00	$ 35.10	$ 79.70
$50 deductible	57.00	57.00	11.90	26.90	13.00	29.50	13.00	10.00	15.60	35.40
Collision or upset										
$25 deductible	$201.00	$385.05	$116.10	$263.40	$132.60	$300.90	NW	NW	$192.00	$447.00
$50 deductible	134.00	256.70	77.40	175.60	88.40	200.60	$66.00	$211.00	131.30	298.00
$100 deductible	91.00	174.25	61.00	138.40	65.00	147.50	55.00	177.00	94.90	215.00
Towing and labor costs										
$25,000	$ 2.00	$ 2.00	$ 1.40	$ 1.40	$ 2.30	$ 2.30	$ 2.00	$ 2.00	$ 3.00	$ 3.00

Note: "*A*"—For a car driven to and from work with no male drivers under 25; "*B*"—For a single 18 year old male driver with driver training credit having principal use of the car to and from work. All quotations are based on a 1971 Ford Galaxie 8 cylinder, 4 door sedan.

NW – Not Written.

* Minimum financial responsibility limit is $15,000/$30,000.

Source: Government Employees Insurance Company.

TABLE 11–5
Comparative Costs of Bodily Injury Liability Coverage

Assume That	*10/20 Costs You*	*$55*
Then.	25/50 would cost about	$68
Then.	50/100 would cost about	$74
Then.	100/300 would cost about	$82

The insurance company will pay $10,000 if there is only one person injured. You will have to pay the remaining $40,000 either out of savings or future income. It is thus well worth the small added cost to buy all the bodily injury liability coverage you can afford.

The Cost of Being Young or Irresponsible

Automobile insurance rates are based, principally, on the dollar amount of claims paid out over a period of time. The more insured accidents you and your friends have, the more claims insurance companies must pay. The more claims paid, the higher the cost of your automobile insurance. The highest rate is paid by the unmarried male under 30 years of age who owns or is the principal driver of the car. The base annual rate in a large city for bodily injury and property damage liability on passenger cars with no young driver is $124—but in the same city, the rate for a young man who has just reached the legal driving age and owns a car is $250 a year. However, if he is a graduate of a standard driver education course, he could save about $55 a year. Compare rates for A and B drivers in Table 11–4.

In general, the reason costs are higher for younger people is that they are involved in more accidents than those over age 30. Last year, those under age 30 were responsible for 48.9 percent of all accidents even though they accounted for only 32.4 percent of all drivers. Drivers aged 20 to 24 were involved in the highest rate of fatal accidents. Interestingly—marriage makes a difference, as Figure 11–2 shows. The young married male pays a lower rate.

The most widely used rating system reduces the cost of auto insurance to young drivers year by year, as Figure 11–2 indicates. The cost of insurance varies from group to group, dependent on driving records and accident rate. Rate discounts are allowed women drivers if they are the only operators resident in their households. In some states, drivers over 65 with good records are eligible for a discount, as are youthful drivers of a family car resident at a school more than 100 miles from home. Safe-driver plans in effect in most states offer a lower rate if everyone in the household who

FIGURE 11–2
Rates Go Down as Young Drivers Grow Older

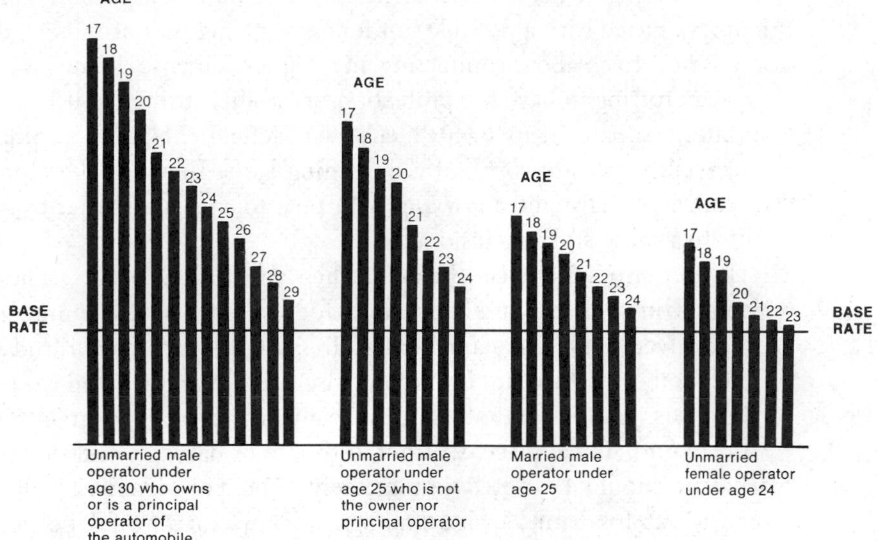

Note: Based on a driver classification plan used by a large segment of the business in many states. These comparisons of gradations are for private passenger cars used for pleasure where all operators have "clean" driving records. Adjustments in premiums are made for cars used to drive to work, used for business, or used on a farm. Adjustments are also made for youthful operators with driver training credit, drivers with "unclean" driving records, and owners of more than one car. In many states, premium discounts are available to students with outstanding scholastic records.

Source: Insurance Information Institute.

drives the family car has a "clean driving record," which means no serious traffic law violation for the preceding three years and no accident where you were at fault.

In most states, many companies offer a student who ranks in the upper 20 percent of the class or has a B average or better, a discount up to 25 percent on rates. Some companies offer a discount to drivers between 20 and 24 if they have successfully completed a driver education course.

Not only youth but motor power adds to cost. The higher performance, or "muscle" cars, carry a higher premium cost, regardless of the driver's age. With these cars, as a three year study by Nationwide Insurance found, age made no difference in the number of accidents. The lure of motor power defeated the caution that is said to come with age.

The Farmers Insurance Group (the nation's third largest auto insurer) offers nonsmoker auto insurance in most states west of the Mississippi with discounts of about 20 percent.[4]

---

[4] *New York Times*, November 1, 1973.

Insurance Companies and Lawsuits

The average person involved in an automobile accident is apt to feel helpless. Faced with a possible suit for a staggering sum of money, the problem is how to go about conducting an adequate defense. In such a situation it is comforting to have the protection of liability insurance because the insurance company at its own expense will defend the insured. Since insurance companies are constantly defending suits, they are therefore expert in knowing what to do and which attorneys to engage in order to bring the suits to a successful conclusion.

It is essential to collect the facts when an accident occurs. The obvious items of information are the name, address, and license number of the other driver, as well as name and address of the car's owner and registration number of the car. Important also are the names and addresses of passengers, injured or not, and especially witnesses who might later be hard to find. Time, place, weather, estimate of damage, and details of the accident should be noted immediately. The police officer will make a report, but his name, badge number, and precinct would be helpful information for corroborative support, if needed.

The defendants must hold themselves ready to appear in court, but every move they make is guided by experienced lawyers provided by the insurance companies; one often feels that this defense is worth the total cost of the insurance. As the insurance company states in Figure 11–3, bodily injury liability insurance is "your protection against loss of home, income and life savings should your car injure or kill others and you be held liable. This includes bail bond expenses, defense of all suits, court and other costs." The insurance company, thus, will pay all legal costs as well as bail bond premiums of up to $200 if you are involved in a bodily injury or property damage suit. A fairly new casualty insurance known as "umbrella" insurance which is a personal catastrophe liability policy issued on top of basic insurance coverage, became available as escalating jury awards made more people aware of such a need. The underlying insurance and the "umbrella" insurance need not be provided by the same company.

Property Damage Liability Insurance

Property damage liability insurance is your protection against financial loss should your car damage the property of others and you be held liable. This second important type of automobile insurance pays for damages caused to the property of others, for which you are legally liable, up to the limits of the policy. It includes damage to another automobile, damage to

FIGURE 11–3

GEICO® GOVERNMENT EMPLOYEES INSURANCE COMPANY
1705 L Street, N.W., Washington, D. C. 20036
A Capital Stock Company Not Affiliated with U. S. Government

TO ORDER YOUR POLICY

1. Insert all missing automobile and registration information.
2. Check below each coverage desired and compute the total premium separately for each car to be insured. Fill in the total policy premium.
3. Select payment terms.
4. Answer all questions on the reverse side.
5. Indicate mailing address corrections in space provided below.
6. Mail application with your payment in postage-paid return envelope.

Mailing Address Corrections:

Name And Mailing Address

Rated location, if not City and State shown in mailing address: Washington, D.C.

PLEASE FILL IN ALL MISSING INFORMATION (EXCEPT SHADED AREA BELOW)

OFFICE USE ONLY	Identification	D #	Line	Trans.	NIS.	No. Units	Occup.	Mail St.

Rated State	Source	Terr.	City Code	St. Cd.	Policy No.	T. Date
	109					

CAR 1	Year	Make (Trade Name)	No. Cyl.	Symbol	NAII	Class
	1971	Ford	8	4		NR

Model (Impala, F-85, etc.)	Body Style (4 Dr., Sta. Wgn., etc.)	State of Car Registration
Galaxie	4 Dr. Sedan	D. C.

Operator's License No. as recorded on your driver's license State	Serial or ID No. as shown on vehicle Registration Card

CAR 2	Year	Make (Trade Name)	No. Cyl.	Symbol	NAII	Class

Model (Impala, F-85, etc.)	Body Style (4 Dr., Sta. Wgn., etc.)	State of Car Registration

Additional rating information for compact and 1965 and later model automobile(s). Check appropriate boxes		Serial or ID No. as shown on vehicle Registration Card
	FOR COMPACT CAR(S) ONLY	1965 or LATER MODEL CAR(S)—Is HP over 300?
Car #1	☐ Check ONLY if hp. exceeds 130	☐ No ☐ Yes If "Yes," give exact hp. ....
Car #2	☐ Check ONLY if hp. exceeds 130	☐ No ☐ Yes If "Yes," give exact hp. ....

COVERAGES AVAILABLE

Coverage descriptions and insurance ordered are subject to policy terms and conditions.

A — BODILY INJURY LIABILITY

Not available without Coverage B.

Your protection against loss of home, income and life savings should your car injure or kill others and you be held liable — includes bail bond expenses, defense of all suits, court and other costs. Pays up to the first limit for any one person and up to the second limit for two or more persons injured or killed.

Other limits available if desired.

B — PROPERTY DAMAGE LIABILITY

Not available without Coverage A.

Your protection against financial loss should your car damage the property of others and you be held liable. Pays for damages caused by your car to the property of others up to the limit you select.

Other limits available if desired.

C — AUTOMOBILE MEDICAL PAYMENTS

Not available without Coverages A & B.

Pays expenses for Medical, Dental, Surgical, Hospital, Funeral, etc., to each person for injury or death caused by accident. Protects everyone in your automobile. Also protects you and household relatives in other automobiles or through being struck by an automobile.

J — UNINSURED MOTORISTS

Not available without Coverages A & B.

The "Family Protection" coverage which pays damages that you, household relatives and passengers in the insured automobiles are legally entitled to recover because of bodily injury or death caused by uninsured or hit-and-run automobiles. Pays up to the first limit for one person and up to the second limit for two or more persons injured or killed.

Only quoted limit is available. In Minn., other limits are available.

H — FIRE, THEFT — COMPREHENSIVE

Not available without either Coverage E or Coverages A & B.

Broad form protection for loss caused other than by Collision. Includes fire, theft, glass breakage, riot, windstorm, hail, etc. The deductible applies to all damage except by fire. Also available on mobile homes and campers.

Only quoted limit is available.

D — FIRE, THEFT — Combined Additional

Not available without either Coverage E or Coverages A & B.

Same as described in "H" above except glass breakage not covered and a $25 deductible amount applies to loss by malicious mischief or vandalism. Written on mobile homes, campers, and truck type vehicles used commercially.

Only quoted limit is available.

E — COLLISION OR UPSET

Protection for loss or damage to YOUR CAR caused by collision with another object or by upset of your automobile, for the amount of each loss in excess of the deductible amount. Also available on mobile homes and campers.

Only quoted limit is available.

I — TOWING & LABOR COSTS

Not available without other Coverages.

Pays up to the limit indicated per claim for disablement of your car. Includes labor cost at place of disablement and towing costs. Parts not covered.

Only quoted limit is available.

Coverage	LIMITS OF COVERAGE (Recommended Minimums are in Red)	CAR No. 1 ANNUAL PREMIUM	CAR No. 1 Premium of Coverage Selected	CAR No. 2 ANNUAL PREMIUM	CAR No. 2 Premium of Coverage Selected
A	$10,000 $ 20,000	$ 60.10 ☐		$ ☐	
A	$20,000 $ 40,000	$ 71.50 ☐		$ ☐	
A	$25,000 $ 50,000	$ 74.00 ☐	$	$ ☐	$
A	$50,000 $100,000	$ 81.20 ☐		$ ☐	
A	$ /$ M	$ ☐		$ ☐	
B	$ 5,000	$ 37.10 ☐		$ ☐	
B	$10,000	$ 39.00 ☐		$ ☐	
B	$25,000	$ 40.10 ☐	$	$ ☐	$
B	$ 50,000	$ 42.00 ☐		$ ☐	
C	$ 1,000	$ 6.20 ☐		$ ☐	
C	$ 2,000	$ 8.10 ☐		$ ☐	
C	$ 3,000	$ 9.10 ☐	$	$ ☐	$
C	$ 5,000	$ 11.10 ☐		$ ☐	
J	$ 5,000/$10,000	$ ☐		$ ☐	
J	$10,000/$20,000	$ 3.10 ☐	$	$ ☐	$
H	Full Coverage	$ 21.90 ☐		$ ☐	
H	$ 50 Deductible	$ 11.90 ☐	$	$ ☐	$
D	Car 1: Actual Cash Value or $ Car 2: Actual Cash Value or $ (Stated Amount applies only if inserted herein.)	$ ☐	$	$ ☐	$
E	$ 50 Deductible	$ 77.40 ☐		$ ☐	
E	$100 Deductible	$ 61.00 ☐	$	$ ☐	$
E	$150 Deductible	$ ☐		$ ☐	
I	$25.00	$ 1.40 ☐	$	$ ☐	$

TOTAL ANNUAL PREMIUM FOR EACH CAR Car No. 1 $ .... Car No. 2 $ ....

PAYMENT TERMS: (If no premium is quoted, a $40.00 minimum payment must be enclosed. Checks, drafts and money orders are accepted subject to collection only.)

PAYMENT TERMS (CHECK ONE)

☐ **Payment in Full (Due with application)**

☐ **4 - PAYMENT PLAN***
1st Payment - 25% of Annual Premium plus 50 cents service charge - Due with Application
2nd Payment - 15% of Annual Premium - Due 45 days from effective date
3rd & 4th Payment - 30% of Annual Premium - Due 3rd & 6th month of policy.

☐ **6 - PAYMENT PLAN* (Available only when Annual Premium is more than $150.00)**
1st Payment - 25% of Annual Premium plus 50 cents service charge - Due with Application
2nd Payment - 15% of Annual Premium - Due 45 days from effective date
3rd, 4th, 5th & 6th Payment - 15% of Annual Premium - Due 3rd, 5th, 7th, & 9th month of policy.

*A notice will be mailed to you when each installment is due. A service charge of 50 cents will be included in the bill for each installment.

TOTAL ANNUAL POLICY PREMIUM $

ENCLOSED IS $ ....
☐ Check ☐ Money Order
Please do not send Currency, Coin or Stamps.

U-15-DC (9-71)

PLEASE ANSWER ALL QUESTIONS ON REVERSE SIDE

or destruction of another's property of any description, and the loss of the use of the property damaged. It is customary to write property damage and bodily injury liability insurance together.

Bear in mind that damage to your own car is *not* covered under property damage liability. This insurance is available in amounts ranging from $5,000 to $100,000. Either $10,000 or $25,000 is generally purchased and rates vary according to age of drivers, location, and use of car.

Both property damage insurance and bodily injury insurance cover you if you are driving someone else's car. It also covers anyone driving your car with your permission. Your policies, of course, cover anyone you invite to ride with you.

It doesn't cost much more in the way of an additional premium to increase your property damage liability coverage. In an area where your property damage liability coverage of $5,000 costs $32 a year, then increasing it to $10,000 would cost $34 a year or increasing it to $25,000 would cost $35 a year.

Automobile Medical Payments

Under this coverage the insuring company agrees to pay, up to the limits of the policy, medical expenses resulting from accidental injury. It applies to you and your immediate family whether in your car, someone else's, or if struck while walking. Passengers and guests riding in your car are covered also. The insurance company agrees to pay all reasonable expenses incurred within one year from the date of the accident for necessary medical, surgical, X-ray, and dental services, ambulance, hospital, professional nursing and even funeral services, up to the limits declared in the policy. Payment is made regardless of who is at fault, or if no one is at fault. Amounts available range from $500 to $10,000. These limits apply to each individual injured.

One insurance company will double the amount of medical payment they will make if you are wearing a seat belt at the time of the accident. If you have $500 coverage and your medical expenses are $600, your total bill will be paid by the company.

Premiums vary according to the dollar amount of claims paid in each locality. The range of rates might run as shown in Table 11–6.

Collision Insurance

Collision insurance provides reimbursement for damage done to *your own automobile* through collision or upset regardless of who was responsible. It doesn't cover damage done to the other fellow's car. That's covered by the property damage insurance you carry, assuming the accident was your fault. Put it this way. If the accident was the other fellow's fault, his property damage insurance will pay your damages. His own collision insurance will pay his own damages. If he had no insurance, your collision insurance can cover your car, but your company has the legal right to proceed against him to recover the sums it paid to you. If the accident was your fault, your property damage insurance pays the other fellow, and your collision insurance pays you.

More people would doubtless have this protection if it did not cost so much. The cost varies with the protection provided, the type of automobile insured, and the locality. On a new automobile of average worth in one of our larger cities the premium is higher, whereas it would be less than half that much in a smaller place and still less for an older car. One common device used to reduce the cost of this insurance is for the insured to agree to pay for the first $100 or $250 of the damage, the insurance company being responsible only for the balance. This is known as "deductible collision." Insurance companies are able to write policies with such "deductible" clauses at lower premiums because such a clause saves them from having to pay for a host of accidents each of which involves little damage. Devices of this sort are rather common in insurance; the insured can buy protection more cheaply if he will bear a small initial part of the risk himself. Because of the cost of collision insurance, some automobile owners decide to bear the cost themselves if an accident occurs. Often, however, you are forced to take collision insurance when you must finance the purchase of a car by borrowing. The cost of $100 deductible collision insurance (the most usual type written) varies, depending upon type of car and locality. For example, in an area of the country where collision insurance is average, a person with a good driving record and no youthful drivers in the family, who uses a 1974 four door Chevrolet Impala for pleasure only, could purchase $100 deductible for $92 a year, or with $250 deductible for $55 a year.

TABLE 11–6
Comparative Costs of Medical Payments Coverage

Assume That	*$500 costs*	*$8*
Then	$ 1,000 would cost about	$10
Then	$ 2,000 would cost about	$12
Then	$ 5,000 would cost about	$15
Then	$10,000 would cost about	$23 a year

Comprehensive Physical Damage Insurance

Careful owners almost always insure their automobiles against fire and theft. The annual premium amounts to only a few dollars. In fact, a comprehensive policy affording protection against malicious damage, vandalism, glass breakage, windstorm, or anything except collision and upset, in addition to fire and theft, can be purchased for $20–$100 per annum, depending on location. Reimbursement is made on the basis of the actual cash value of the vehicle when the loss or damage is incurred. In some of the larger cities, losses to companies on this type of insurance have been so large due to petty thefts and vandalism that a number of the companies have either refused to write such policies for cars that are not garaged, or have introduced a $50 deductible clause. If the theft or vandal's damage amounts to less than $50, the car owner cannot collect from the insurance company. This relieves the companies of thousands of small claims which are costly to service and permits them to write the insurance less expensively. If the cost of repairing the damage is more than $50, the first $50 is paid by the insured.

If a theft of personal property occurs when your car keys are in the hands of an authorized parking attendant, you are protected through your Homeowners Insurance policy, since it is recognized that garages and parking lots require that you surrender the keys to your car, and under these circumstances, your property is not considered unattended. If you leave the car unlocked and unattended elsewhere, you are not protected against theft of personal property.

If your automobile is stolen, your comprehensive policy will compensate you for the cost of substitute transportation, whether rented car or taxi. Usually you cannot collect more than $10 a day for this, and there is an overall limit. Sometimes companies allow the local car rental rate. The theft of the car must have been reported to the police and, of course, to the insurance company. Your insurance does not cover things you leave in the car, only the car itself or parts thereof such as tires, battery, and so on.

A flourishing national industry with sources in the big cities and outlets both here and abroad is auto theft that thrives on professional specialists and efficient organization which is able both to neutralize the manufacturer's safeguards and to fatten on owner carelessness.[5] The following excerpt explains in part the rising costs of auto insurance.

> Even the thieves are able to justify their work. A veteran, very professional thief who lives in New Jersey reasons, "What I do is good for

[5] Peter Hellman, "Stealing Cars is a Growth Industry," *New York Times*, June 20, 1971.

> everybody. First of all, I create work. I hire men to deliver the cars, work on the numbers, paint them, give them paper, maybe drive them out of state, find customers. That's good for the economy. Then I'm helping working people to get what they could never afford otherwise. A fellow wants a Cadillac but he can't afford it; his wife wants it but she knows he can't afford it. So I get this fellow a nice car at a price he can afford; maybe I save him as much as $2,000. Now he's happy. But so is the guy who lost his car. He gets a nice new Cadillac from the insurance company —without the dents and scratches we had to take out. The Cadillac company—they're happy too because they sell another Cadillac.
>
> "The only people who don't do so good is the insurance company. But they're so big that nobody cares *personally*. They got a budget for this sort of thing anyway. So here I am, a guy without an education, sending both my kids to college, giving my family a good home, making other people happy. Come on now—who am I really hurting?"[6]

In more than 48 states if you buy a second hand car now you can be reasonably sure you have a clear title to the car, since a certificate of ownership is usually filed with the Motor Vehicle Bureau. If you are in a state that does not require title registration, not only are the premiums for theft loss on comprehensive insurance coverage higher, and the percent of stolen cars recovered much smaller, but you might have unknowingly bought a stolen car, added improvements, and then have absolutely no redress when it is claimed by its legal owner. Since the car theft rings operate interstate, such a disaster can also happen within a title registered state, as the car could have been stolen from a state that has no such law.

Protection against Uninsured Motorists

This coverage applies to bodily injuries for which an uninsured motorist, or a hit-and-run driver, is legally liable. It applies to the policyholder and family whether occupying their car, someone else's, or while walking. It also applies to guests occupying the policyholder's car. The insuring company agrees to pay damages to injured persons to the same extent that it would if it had carried insurance on the uninsured or unknown motorist.

The advantage of protection against uninsured motorists is immediate payment from your insurance company for hospital bills and medical costs. Assuming the uninsured motorist is at fault, it may take some time before an agreement can be reached on the amount you should receive for your injury. Furthermore, the uninsured motorist may have little or no property or money and may never be able to pay. The amount of protection you can

[6] *New York Times*, June 20, 1971.

purchase under this coverage is limited to the liability required under the financial responsibility laws of your state. Cost of this protection is so small that automobile owners who know about it are seldom without it.

Suggested Cautions

Automobile insurance policies vary in cost from company to company. Shop for yours. Ask four or five companies to send you their quotations. Open rating or competitive pricing is a reality in auto insurance as well as in home coverage.[7]

There are mutual companies and stock companies and in their competition, there may be benefits for you. The kind of agent you select will affect your choice. He may represent only one company on a commission basis, may be a salaried employee of a particular company, or can be independent —representing several companies. Naturally, the advice and usefulness to you will be determined both by his personality and his relationship to the company that insures you. If he fears jeopardizing his connection with the company by advancing too many claims, you should be aware of that possibility in making your insurance decisions.

If you eliminate collision insurance on the theory that it's cheaper to bear the loss, you may find it more difficult to collect from the other driver, since there is no insurance company interested in pressing your claim.

Read the policy—there may be advantages of which you are unaware. There may also be limitations. For example, if you delay in reporting an accident, you may lose your coverage, as your policy could have a clause with such a time limit. Read it even if it is difficult to read. Legislators as well as insurers agree that it is anything but simple to say something in simple language. Especially is this true in offering a comprehensive policy and describing it in nontechnical language acceptable to the legal experts.

Assigned Risks

The assigned risk is one whose driving record is so bad that it is difficult, if not impossible, to obtain the various automobile insurance coverages through regular channels. Sometimes, as in the case of males under 25, it is the high accident rate of the whole group which makes it difficult for the new applicant in this age category to obtain any insurance at all, even though there is no accident record as yet. Companies cannot be compelled to accept applicants, and where they anticipate they will lose more in pay-

---

[7] See for example A *Shoppers Guide to Pennsylvania Automobile Insurance*, Pennsylvania Insurance Department, Harrisburg, Pennsylvania, April 1972.

ments of claims than the premiums they receive, they will refuse to write insurance. Some companies withdraw from a high risk territory. In some states, an assigned risk pool has been set up by all auto insurance companies licensed to, and doing business in the state. Each company agrees to accept a proportionate share of the "poor risks."

Some states are eliminating the pool and have organized a joint underwriting association which pools expenses and losses, but whose members write policies directly, offering faster and better service and in many plans increasing the coverage above the former maximum of 10/20 and also providing medical payment and physical damage policies. One state, Maryland, has eliminated the insurance industry and has set up a state insurance fund to service assigned risks offering bodily injury, property damage and collision coverage.

A person who is so classified by reason of having been rejected by at least three companies within 60 days applies to the assigned risk pool, pays an application fee, and is usually assigned to one of the companies. He will probably have to pay the highest rate the company charges because of his assigned risk status. This may be as much as 50 percent more than in the normal market. This insurance is only for one year.

The introduction of no fault insurance which mandates insurance coverage for all, temporarily swells the numbers involved in assigned risk status. A company would be understandably leery in accepting a 30 year old who had never been insured before, although he had driven for years. Some states have devised procedures for dealing with the influx by offering credit against future assigned risks to companies which voluntarily will write a percentage of this insurance. The Assigned Risk Plan now known as the Automobile Insurance Plan covers about 4 percent of all automobile insurance written, and it is growing steadily.

There are wide variations, not only in companies but also in areas, which are included. According to testimony given in a recent Senate study on auto insurance problems, chaired by Senator Philip A. Hart, the inclusion can result from a personal decision of the insurance investigator, be based on the unchecked gossip in the community, or be linked to an official blacklist of occupations (including ministers, taxi drivers, beauticians) or families with a potential youthful driver. It is said that ministers are included in the list because they "drive as if God will provide."[8]

In states where the assigned risk driver pays more, the surcharge is based on the point system imposed by the state for traffic violations. A Depart-

---

[8] See Robert J. Cole, "Personal Finance: Insurance Analysts Tell of Problems of Motorists in Assigned-Risk Plan," *New York Times*, August 3, 1970; see also Robert J. Cole, *New York Times*, Dec. 31, 1973.

ment of Transportation study (the Reinmuth-Stone Report) found that in many states such a policyholder must pay the entire premium at once—or within 30 days. Because the cost is higher, this means an extra hardship. However there is a "take out" procedure, in which a driver who has had no accidents for three years becomes a "clean driver" and in some states is returned to the normal market.

Group Auto Insurance

Group policies on a payroll deduction plan are being used in some universities and corporations to provide the insurance otherwise difficult to purchase—and surprisingly, it can be purchased at a discount.

More than 3 million are now issued through 2,500–3,000 such plans. Savings average 15 percent. Unlike group life or group health insurance, mass merchandised auto insurance—as the insurance companies call it—is individual coverage sold to members of a group. Employers generally do not contribute beyond making the initial arrangements and providing a payroll deduction option. Labor unions view it as an attractive fringe benefit that does not add to costs. Large corporations such as Delta, Franklin Mint, Lockheed Aircraft Corp., Consolidated Edison Co. of New York have these plans. Insurance companies have mixed reactions. Sales and overhead costs decrease because of the group, but so do commissions. Employees can rejoice over the clout of the company behind them or be disturbed over the lack of personal advice and service in this arrangement.

Repair Insurance

Auto repair costs have risen 63 percent since 1967. A number of insurers thinking this is therefore the right moment are testing the acceptance of a low cost insurance policy covering "mechanical breakdowns." The Kemper Insurance Group will pay the cost of repairing—subject to a $50 deductible—or replacing parts under a policy whose premiums range from $63 to $234 depending on the car. The Motors Insurance Co. (owned by General Motors Acceptance Corp.) is testing in a few states a policy that offers coverage that is an extension of the warranty. The American Road Co. (owned by Ford Motor Credit Co.) is for vacationers and offers protection for $15 for either 30 days or two separate 15 day periods. The policy covers three quarters of repair bills up to $250 caused by mechanical failure and pays for three quarters of reasonable expenses including food, lodging, car rental, towing, and road service up to $225.

No Fault Insurance

Under our present liability or fault system, each case of property damage or personal injury must be decided on its own merits to determine whose is the legal responsibility for losses suffered. The two year, $2 million study made by the U.S. Department of Transportation indicates that only 48 percent of seriously injured victims, including fatalities, received some reparation under the fault insurance system.[9] One federal study indicates "that it costs $1.07 to deliver one dollar in benefits under the present system; another that consumers receive only 44 cents in recovery on the premium dollar spent. This cost benefit ratio is drastically lower than those of other major forms of insurance." "Fifty-five percent of those who were killed or sustained personal injury in auto accidents received no benefits to themselves or to their estates at all from the automobile tort liability system."[10]

"Out of every personal injury liability insurance dollar, approximately 60 cents goes for operating expenses. The expenses of insurance companies account for 28 cents. Lawyer fees, claim adjustment, and other litigation costs amount to 32 cents, leaving only 40 cents for victims."[11] The average delay between the date of accident and final settlement of fault insurance claims for all cases of serious injury and deaths, whether settled in or out of court, is 16 months. The delay problem is most serious in urban areas. Studies show that auto accident cases take 17 percent of the time of U.S. judges and contribute greatly to the backlog.

No fault is a term used to describe a system of automobile insurance in which the insuring company pays the policyholder for his own personal or bodily injury, instead of protection against claims made for losses he may cause to others. It does not cover property damage.

The "no fault" basis eliminates the need to prove the "other fellow" responsible for the accident so you can collect from him. Under the fault or tort system, if you are even partially to blame, under the "contributory negligence" principle you would be unable to collect anything. Under "no fault," each injured person would be compensated partly or completely by his own insurance company regardless of who was to blame. Under the "fault" system, the company insuring the person who is liable pays damages

---

[9] Department of Transportation, *Economic Consequences of Automobile Accident Injuries* (Washington, D.C.: U.S. Government Printing Office, April, 1970), vol. 1, p. 47.

[10] Speech by Mrs. Virginia H. Knauer, Special Assistant to the President for Consumer Affairs, May 25, 1971, before the 21st International Conference of the Planning Executives Institute.

[11] Dennis F. Reinmuth, "Automobile Insurance in the 1970's Decade of Change," *Michigan Business Review*, May, 1971, p. 24.

to the innocent party. The demand for change has led more than 21 states and the Commonwealth of Puerto Rico to adopt forms of no fault auto insurance. Massachusetts in 1970 was the first state to pass a no fault law.

The Massachusetts Act requires no fault coverage of up to $2,000 for hospital and medical expenses and 75 percent of income loss while retaining the right to sue for higher losses and property damage. Victims may still sue for pain and suffering if medical expenses exceed $500 or if death or specified permanent injury, such as dismemberment or loss of eyesight results from an accident. A 1973 study of the Massachusetts Court System by Professor Allan I. Widiss of the University of Iowa Law School found that since enactment automobile insurance claims filed in Massachusetts District Courts (small claims) decreased by 90 percent, while claims filed in the states' five Superior Courts were cut by anywhere from 40 to 60 percent. A study by the actuarial firm of Millman and Robertson done for the U.S. Department of Transportation estimated a 25 percent reduction in insurance premiums.

Puerto Rico has had "no fault" legislation longer than any other area. Its compulsory noncancellable plan provides 90 cents of every premium dollar for benefits. The owner of a car must pay a Puerto Rican government agency $35 a year for coverage or he cannot get a license plate. The plan pays all of an auto accident victims' medical and hospital expenses, as well as up to $5,000 for loss of a limb or sight, and up to $15,000 in survivor's benefits. The plan also pays 50 percent of lost income (up to $50 a week the first year, $25 the second year) and has been so successful that the actuarial rates indicate that the compensation can be raised without raising the rates. In its first year, $17.5 million was collected in premiums and $6 million paid or set aside in benefits for 28,000 accident victims and survivors.

One of the most controversial issues is over the right to sue for "pain and suffering." These claims over and above medical costs and economic losses form the basis for many auto accident suits and are usually responsible for the most expensive litigation. On one hand, a basic right is limited and so is a legitimate claim for those whose expenses and injuries are beyond that provided by no fault. On the other hand, litigation is the avenue through which minor injuries have become inflated claims, and which have been responsible for high insurance premiums. The American Trial Lawyers Association would preserve the rights of all "innocent parties" to sue. They also favor a low dollar limitation, if there is to be one, on lawsuits. Advocates of no fault support limiting liability suits for damages to a relatively few most serious cases. As Herbert Denenberg wrote, when he was Pennsylvania Insurance Commissioner:

> Under no fault you could only sue for the pain and suffering caused by very serious injuries. . . . There has to be some way to separate phony, exaggerated or minor claims for pain and suffering from the important ones. The way to do it is to create a *can sue* threshold. Once you have passed the threshold, your pain and suffering is considered serious and you can sue for these hard to measure losses. One type of threshold is a certain dollar value of medical expenses—for example, $1,000. Another type of threshold would limit suits to injuries causing severe disfigurement, lasting disability, or death. . . . The more "right to sue," the more lawsuits. The more lawsuits, the more money for people who now make their living in the fault system. If a $1,000 threshold had to be crossed before lawsuits could be started for pain and suffering losses there would be fewer lawsuits. And with a $2,500 threshold there'd be hardly any lawsuits. That's why people who make a living in the fault system want a low threshold like $250, or none at all.[12]

Most of the 20 states have adopted compulsory first party and liability insurance and restrictions on the right to sue. Several other recently enacted state laws have optional insurance and where the right to sue is unrestricted. Major variations in each state involve dollar limits on medical and hospital expenses (unlimited in some states), funeral or burial expenses, lost income from earnings, and the amount to be paid a person hired to perform essential services that an injured nonincome producer, such as a housewife, is unable to perform; also conditions governing the right to sue which usually include death, serious injury and a point at which medical expenses reach a certain amount. Most laws emphasize prompt payment of claims—usually within 30 days and with a penalty of interest if unpaid after that.

A uniform law proposed by the National Conference of Commissioners on Uniform State Laws calls for unlimited medical benefits and up to $200 a week for an unlimited period for lost earnings and other losses. Suits would be allowed only under most limiting conditions. The insurance industry has recently voiced support of state no fault laws partly because they have decreased costs and partly to prevent federal legislation. Most of them are automatically extending their liability insurance policies to provide policyholders traveling in other states and Canada at no additional cost with required "no fault" coverages, as more states adopt no fault insurance. About 26.3 percent of the nation's population is covered currently by compulsory plans that include restrictions on litigation. All of the states still retain the tort liability system under which payments for auto damages are based on proof of "fault" on the part of the person against whom a claim

[12] Herbert S. Denenberg, *A Motorists Guide Through No Fault*, Insurance Department, State of Pennsylvania, July 1973, p. 3.

is brought. Federal proposals have been debated for years. Supporters would set minimum guidelines that would go into effect if any state failed to pass its own legislation.

A Harris poll of attitudes toward auto and home insurers showed that consumers actually feel the services offered are improving, compared with a growing discontent with auto makers and home builders.

SUGGESTED READINGS

1. Insurance Information Institute, *Family Guide to Property and Liability Insurance*, New York, 1974. A free copy may be obtained by writing to the Institute at 110 Williams Street, New York, N.Y. 10038.
2. Jeffrey O'Connell and W. H. Wilson, *Car Insurance and Consumer Desires*. Urbana, Ill.: University of Illinois Press, 1970.
3. Jeffrey O'Connell, *The Injury Industry—and the Remedy of No-Fault Insurance*, Commerce Clearing House, Chicago, 1971.
4. "No-Fault Auto Insurance," *Forbes*, January 15, 1972.
5. Dennis F. Reinmuth, "Automobile Insurance in the 1970's Decade of Change," *Michigan Business Review*, May 1971.
6. U.S. Department of Transportation, *Economic Consequences of Automobile Accident Injuries*, vol. 1. Washington, D.C.: U.S. Government Printing Office, April, 1970.
7. U.S. Department of Transportation, *Causation Culpability and Deterrence in Highway Crashes*. Washington, D.C.: U.S. Government Printing Office, July, 1970.
8. Herbert J. Denenberg, "A Motorists Guide Through No Fault," Pennsylvania Insurance Dept., Harrisburg, Pennsylvania, 1973.
9. "Insurance—The Road to Reform," *Consumer Reports*, April 1971.
10. Peter Hellman, "Stealing Cars is a Growth Industry," *New York Times Magazine*, June 20, 1971.
11. Mel Mandell, "Can You Outsmart the New York Car Thief?" *New York Magazine*, April 19, 1971.
12. *Changing Times, The Kiplinger Magazine:*
    "Coming: Better Ways to Insure Problem Drivers," November 1974.
    "How To Collect on House or Auto Insurance," December 1970.
    "How To Buy Auto Insurance Today," July 1971.
13. "Shopping for Insurance," *Consumer Reports*, December 1972.
14. W. M. Apple, "Understanding Your Homeowners Policy," *Consumers Research* Magazine, September 1973.

15. "No-Fault Automobile Insurance—Progress Report," *Consumer Reports,* October 1973.

16. *Money:*
   Avery Comarow, "How to Emerge Undented from Car Crash Claims," January 1975.
   Jo Degener, "Stealing a Look at Your Theft Insurance," December 1974.
   William B. Mead, "A Precrash Course in No-Fault Car Insurance," June 1974.
   Caroline Donnelly, "Ordeal by Fire Insurance," July 1974.

CASE PROBLEMS

1. Peter Crosby bought a home for $30,000. Pete and his wife were very insurance conscious and wanted their house to be fully protected by fire insurance. They purchased an insurance policy in the amount of $30,000 with extended coverage and additional extended coverage. For reasons of health, he and his wife closed the house last winter and went to Florida. The necessary precautions to prevent freezing of pipes were taken. However, upon their return from Florida, they found that the pipes had burst and there was much water damage to the house. Floors were swollen and ceilings damaged. He notified the insurance company and an adjustor was sent to investigate the damage. Mr. Crosby was amazed to hear the adjustor say he was sorry, but he could not compensate them for the damage. Explain.

2. Ann and Frank were married a year ago. They have just bought a frame house for $24,000. He earns $12,000 a year. She keeps house. What essential insurance coverages should they have for their home? They ask you to write to three insurance companies for them, get rates and examples of policies and advise them what to purchase.

3. Joc Brown bought firc insurancc with an 80 pcrccnt coinsurancc clause some years ago, when the value of his property was $20,000. His insurance agent now suggests purchasing additional insurance. What should Mr. Brown do? Why?

4. Clara Rogers has just started teaching. She's 24, unmarried. Because she wasn't able to find housing near the school where she teaches, she bought a new Ford Galaxie and now drives back and forth to work (7 miles each way). Assuming she works in a town in your state, what basic insurance coverage should she have for her car? Prescribe an automobile insurance policy or policies for her, and determine how much it will cost her annually.

5. In Mandell's town, bus fares have just been increased to 55 cents a ride. He lives in a state with a financial responsibility provision in the law. Mandell has been married five years and has a child of three years. He works in a

grocery store 5 miles from his home, earning $130 a week. It is his opinion that if he bought an old car, it would cost less to commute to work in it than it now costs on the bus, that he would not need insurance, and that the automobile would be available for use evenings and weekends. He could park it in the yard behind his flat. Should he get the car? Could he drive uninsured in your state? If not what is the minimum insurance he would be required to have on the car? What would it cost?

6. Halley had just bought a home. It is worth $35,000 and the land is worth $10,000. The Halley family consists of Halley (age 38), his wife (age 33), and three children (ages 12, 8, and 5). Halley is a dentist and averages a net income of $26,000 a year. He carries $22,000 of straight life insurance, owns securities worth $14,386, and has $3,800 in savings accounts and $1,183 in his checking account. Since he has noticed that most fires in connection with residences cause damage amounting to from $1,000 to $4,000, he believes that if he carries $10,000 of fire insurance on the house he will be amply protected. What do you think of his plan? What would you suggest he do instead?

7. King, a salesman who travels by automobile, owns his home and has $1,800 in the bank. He buys a new car for $3,600, using $900 of his funds for a down payment. When the bank (from which he borrows the balance of the money necessary to acquire the automobile) gives him a statement of the total amount he owes to it, he notices that he is being charged $150 for a year's collision insurance. He argues that he does not want the collision insurance, but the bank insists that he must have it. What will be the outcome, and why?

8. You have just reached your 20th birthday. Your folks have given you a new Toyota for your birthday. What insurance will you have to take out as a new car owner and exactly what will it cost you for a year?

9. Does your state have a no fault automobile insurance law? If so what are its provisions and how does it differ from the previous system? If your state does not have a no fault law, have bills for one been introduced in your state legislature? If so what specifically do they propose? Would you favor or oppose passage of such a bill? Why?

12

Buying a Home

I never saw an oft-removed tree nor yet an oft-removed family that throve so well as those that settled be.
Poor Richard's Almanack

WHEN YOU look into a new field, it's useful to get your terms straight right at the beginning. Here are some expressions that you will encounter whenever you set out to buy a home:

GLOSSARY FOR HOME BUYERS

One of the preliminaries in buying a house is the reading of real-estate ads. This can be a confusing process. So to help the prospective home buyer, this magazine has compiled its own handy glossary of real-estate terms and phrases. It follows (even if all the definitions don't—quite):

OWNER LEAVING TOWN—He's hoping to retire to Florida on the proceeds.

SELDOM HAVE WE BEEN PRIVILEGED TO OFFER SUCH A BUY—A white elephant, the kind with eight bedrooms and a 1908 bath.

MAGNIFICENT VIEW—The nearest bus stop is at least five miles away.

IMMEDIATE OCCUPANCY—You'll get in sometime between the date set by the builder and next Christmas.

PRICED WELL BELOW THE MARKET—been trying to unload this one for some time.

TWENTY MINUTES FROM TOWN—Forty minutes from town unless you have a police escort.

SPACIOUS DINING ROOM—Will hold a table.

A SETTING OF NATURAL CHARM—You get rid of the poison ivy yourself.

NEEDS SOME REDECORATING—It will take the Army Engineers to fix this one up.

RAMBLER—Anything under three stories.

SEMIDETACHED—Semiattached.

ALL MODERN IMPROVEMENTS—Has inside plumbing.

LOT BEAUTIFULLY LANDSCAPED—Has a tree on it that looks like a buggy whip.

SUBSTANTIAL CASH REQUIRED—You couldn't afford it.

ONLY TWO LEFT—There were three originally.

Source: *Changing Times, The Kiplinger Magazine.*

To Buy or to Rent?

The old argument whether to rent or to buy is almost never resolved on the basis of a careful financial investigation. For one thing, the average home buyer couldn't make the detailed comparison. Even when the experts try, they have to use a contrived, artificial example which doesn't reflect real facts and which provides only a very hedged answer with a lot of "ifs" and "buts."

One such attempt began by assuming a landlord had an 8 percent return on his money and a homeowner an equal benefit.[1] The landlord passes his costs on to the tenant, such as: management costs, allowance for vacancy periods, higher maintenance costs (since tenants are not usually as careful as owners), and tax payments on his capital investment. Other costs such as utilities, local taxes, and insurance are the same for both. Under this formula the homeowner has a slight advantage since the hidden costs of home ownership go into the rent bill. The homeowner's advantage lies in the savings on deductability of mortgage interest and property taxes.

Increased equity from the forced saving of capital growth in mortgage payments plus the expectations that the value of the home will increase at the rate of 4 percent a year can make a homeowner feel that there are economic as well as emotional satisfactions.

Based on the purchase of a $40,000 house—$10,000 down payment and a 25 year mortgage at 8.5 percent interest, the costs of home ownership over that 25 year period will amount to more than $136,000, which includes the following:[2]

$43,000 in interest (8.5 percent interest—25 year mortgage)
$49,974 in property tax bills (3 percent of the value of house each year)
$8,327 in homeowner's insurance, (0.5 percent of the value of the house each year)
$33,317 in home maintenance (average 2 percent of value of the house annually)

Building equity in home ownership is, however, an effective hedge against inflation.

Inflation and Home Ownership Costs

Inflation seems to be putting the goal of owning your own home out of reach. Over the past ten years the cost of buying and running a home has

[1] Prof. John P. Shelton's complicated computation may be found in *Land Economics*, February 1968, pp. 59–72. "Cost of Renting vs. Owning a Home."

[2] "Owning a Home Is Costly But It Beats Renting," Sylvia Porter—*Sarasota Herald Tribune*, May 16, 1974. See also "Buy a House or Rent? A Fresh Look at the Options," *Changing Times*, April 1975.

soared by about 107 percent. Over the last five years the price of a typical new house rose from $27,900 to $38,600, an increase of almost 40 percent. With median family income at about $13,100 the average family can no longer afford to buy a new house.

Median family income has since 1969 lagged behind soaring housing costs. Over the last five years electric bills have risen 47 percent, repairing a furnace 48 percent, re-siding a house 54 percent, painting a room 65 percent, reshingling a roof 72 percent, and fuel oil bills have risen 109 percent.

Buying a house, once an ordinary expectation of young Americans, is now too expensive for 60 percent of all families, the vice president of the National Association of Home Builders told a congressional committee. "Its getting impossible for a person making $17,000 or $18,000 a year to buy a house."

On the average, monthly costs on today's $38,600 house after a down payment of $8,000, run to about $350, covering mortgage payments, taxes and insurance. This is 67 percent more than the $210 a month it cost to carry a typical 1969 house. Property taxes are up 35 percent, interest rates 20 percent, water and sewer bills 40 percent.

Rents have risen too, but not as much as the costs of home ownership, according to the consumer price index. On a 1967 = 100 base the rent index in December 1974 was 129.3, while the index for home ownership costs was 151.4. Young families with limited income facing larger cash down payments, difficulty of getting mortgage loans, high interest rates on mortgages, often now have no choice but to rent.[3] For families headed by women, where income is lower than for the average family, this is even more probable.

The last Census statistics show that the North Central region of the United States had the highest rate of owner occupancy while the Northeast had the lowest. Homeowners outnumbered renters in every state but Hawaii and New York and the District of Columbia. California had the highest number of owner occupied units; New York the largest number of rented units. Nationally 37 percent of all households lived in rental housing.

Home ownership is related directly to the age of the head of the household: from the age of 35–54 almost three out of four own their homes, over 70 percent of those over 65 are homeowners. Income obviously affects home ownership: of those with income under $7,500 a year, about half are homeowners. As the income rises so does the homeowner proportion, be-

---

[3] Lucie G. Krassa, "Rental Housing in the U.S." *Family Economics Review*, Winter 1974. Consumer and Food Economics Institute, U.S. Department of Agriculture.

coming over 85 percent beginning at the $15,000 income bracket. The percentage of homeowning blacks increased to 41.6 percent—or nearly 2.6 million persons. The Census also reported that 4.6 percent of all American households own second homes.

Transfer costs of homeowning must be included in evaluating renting versus owning. It is estimated that the average homeowner moves every eight years. The costs of buying and selling thus reduce his advantage. It is also estimated that the average house increases in value by about 5 percent a year, and in desirable suburbs as high as 10 percent. Your investment improves the longer you stay. There is little equity accumulated in the first 7–10 years of home ownership, as most of the payments go to paying interest charges and allowance must be made for depreciation. If we add points and the brokerage fee which are also paid at this time, the transfer of ownership can cost about 10 percent of the selling price.

While capital appreciation and building equity through mortgage payments increase the value of the real estate you own, the renter might have made the same financial gain using his available capital in other investments. One more caveat on the advantages of homeowning, lies in the realization that the profits of real estate ownership somewhat disappear when you sell and then must purchase another home—value has risen under similar conditions—even though you benefit from a tax advantage in the sale.

Decision Making

The choice of owning a home or renting is difficult, expensive, and more varied today. There are fewer one family homes available in proportion to the growing population. Because land is valuable, sewage facilities overtaxed, and heating only half the expense where walls are shared the townhouse has become more popular. Apartment buildings are more profitable to build. Condominiums and co-ops offer the mixed joys of ownership. Added choice can also be found in mobile homes and attached townhouse communities.

The difficult part of the decision is in coming to terms with high housing prices, high mortgage rates (if the credit is available) in an inflationary period.

The following example illustrates the choice: Buy now—or wait.

> The answer to this question, however, is that—assuming that on average the purchase price of a house increases by 10 percent a year, a reasonable assumption in this era—you will not save by waiting for lower mortgage rates to buy your house. To illustrate:

You Purchase Your House Now

Purchase price	$35,000
Down payment of 10 percent	$ 3,500
Amount of mortgage	$31,500
Term of mortgage	25 years
Monthly payment at:	
7 percent	$222.71
8 percent	$243.18
9 percent	$264.60
10 percent	$286.34

You Wait One Year to Buy

Purchase price of home (up 10 percent)	$38,500
Down payment of 10 percent	$ 3,850
Amount of mortgage	$34,650
Term of mortgage	25 years
Monthly payment at:	
7 percent	$244.98
8 percent	$267.50
9 percent	$291.06
10 percent	$341.97

To make the comparison clear: say you buy the $35,000 house now and commit yourself to a 9 percent mortgage over 25 years as against buying one year from now and getting the same mortgage for 8 percent over 25 years.

—Your down payment is $3,500 against $3,850, a saving of $350 in the down payment if you buy now.

—Your monthly payment at 9 percent is $264.60 as against $267.50 a year from now even at a full 1 percent lower rate.

—Your saving on the mortgage by buying now is $2.90 per month, $34.80 per year, and over the 25 year period, $870.

—Your total savings by buying now are $350 on the down payment and $870 on the mortgage over 25 years or $1,220.[4]

When there is a limited availability of housing credit, new home buyers have an easier time getting financing if the lending institutions have working arrangements with large developers. Large companies transferring employees may have financial clout in both the sale and purchase of new homes. If you can't fit into those categories, mortgage money can be scarce.[5]

The decision to buy or to rent is usually made on the basis of needs and wants. A young couple, recently married, may prefer to rent for a variety of reasons. They may both work and they want to be within easy transportation range of their jobs. In a city this may mean rental housing. His career isn't set yet. He may change jobs several times, or be transferred by the company. Her career possibilities are also a basic consideration.

---

[4] Sylvia Porter column, *Sarasota Herald Tribune,* July 10, 1974.

[5] "No Deal: Mortgage Squeeze Makes Buying a House a Very Tough Task," *Wall Street Journal,* October 11, 1974.

Other factors of importance enter into the rent-or-buy decision. The convenience in having the landlord make repairs, provide maintenance, service, and sometimes utilities, at his expense, are advantages in renting. Adding to the problems of homeowning are the costs of garbage and trash collection, heating fuel, and water costs, as well as the difficulty of finding skilled repairmen. On the other hand, renters may have problems about keeping pets, playing musical instruments, or turning the volume on their stereo too high. A more serious problem for renters is that at the time they sign the lease, they don't know what the rent will be when it's time to renew the lease several years later. The choice can be an emotional one—the freedom from responsibility compared to the joy of roots attract different personalities. Status goals play a part. In second or third generation immigrant families, or mobility conscious upward bound working class families, home ownership symbolizes having arrived successfully. The desire for privacy, or for socializing, independence and a concern and love for the land, or security and the need for proximity to transportation and convenient shopping all motivate the decision. It should be noted that while the number of owner occupied units increased by over 7 million, the percentage increased by a mere 1 percent over the last decade.

How Much Can You Afford for a House?

One bank loan officer uses two basic rules: first, the amount of a loan should not exceed two times the gross yearly income; second, monthly payments for borrowing, including mortgage payments, should not exceed a fourth of the gross monthly income. Since the mortgage affects how much house you can afford, these rules offer a useful basis for judgment.

One method for figuring out how much of your income you can devote either to renting or to buying a home is to list your expenses and income—either on a monthly or a yearly basis—as shown in Figure 12–1. Now subtract "Your total expenses" from "Your total take home pay." You get the

FIGURE 12–1

What is your total income? . . . . $____

What are your withholdings for income taxes, retirement, social security benefits, hospitalization insurance, and any other deductions from your wage or salary . . . . $____

Subtract the second figure from the first.

Your total "take home pay" is . . . . . $____

Monthly savings budget . . . . $____

Food and clothing . . . . $____

Medical care . . . . $____

Life insurance . . . . $____

Recreation . . . . $____

Utilities and fuel . . . . $____

Automobile expenses . . . . $____

All other expenses (membership dues, contributions, charge accounts, installment purchases, etc.) . . . . $____

Add these up.

Your total expenses are . . . . $____

TABLE 12–1
Income Available for Housing: How Much Mortgage Can You Afford?

For (years)	*$100 per Month Available ($1,200 per year) for Loan of:*	*$200 per Month Available ($2,400 per year) for Loan of:*	*$300 per Month Available ($3,600 per year) for Loan of:*	*$400 per Month Available ($4,800 per year) for Loan of:*	*$500 per Month Available ($6,000 per year) for Loan of:*
At 6%					
20 years	$13,940	$27,890	$41,840	$55,780	$69,730
25 years	15,500	31,000	46,510	62,010	77,510
30 years	16,660	33,330	50,000	66,660	83,330
At 7%					
20 years	12,880	25,770	38,650	51,540	64,430
25 years	14,140	28,280	42,430	56,570	70,720
30 years	15,010	30,030	45,040	60,060	75,070
At 8%					
20 years	11,940	23,890	35,840	47,780	59,730
25 years	12,950	25,900	38,860	51,810	64,760
30 years	13,620	27,240	40,870	54,490	68,110
At 9%					
20 years	11,110	22,220	33,330	44,440	55,550
25 years	11,904	23,800	35,710	47,610	59,520
30 years	12,420	24,840	37,260	49,680	62,110
At 10%					
20 years	10,350	20,700	31,050	41,400	51,750
25 years	11,000	22,000	33,000	44,000	55,000
30 years	11,380	22,770	34,160	45,550	56,940

Source: United States Savings and Loan League.

figure, $———, which is the amount of money you can afford to pay for a roof over your head. This figure is referred to as your *income for housing.*

Now that you have your income for housing, either on a yearly or monthly basis, consult Table 12–1. Find your housing income in the table to learn the amount of the loan you can afford. The figures in this table include not only principal and interest charges on a mortgage but also estimate an allowance for taxes, maintenance, and insurance as well. Suppose you have found that your income for housing is $100 a month. According to Table 12–1 this would, for example, permit you to afford a home loan of $11,940 at 8 percent for 20 years. This figure represents what you should be able to finance from your current income. It does not, of course, include your down payment. If you can afford a down payment of $2,000, then you will be able to buy a house selling for about $13,940. The higher the down payment, the lower your monthly cost.

A Limit to Cost

If a family is going to buy a home, it is most important to buy one which can be paid for comfortably. The usual rule is that the family should buy a house at a price not exceeding 2½ times the family's annual income. This means that a family with annual earnings of $13,000 should try to be content with a home costing about $32,500. Since in many parts of the country this ($13,000) is a fairly typical family income today, and since it is not easy to find suitable new housing costing $32,500 or less, it is obvious that many families will be tempted to pay more in order to become homeowners. Yet they cannot do so without making substantial sacrifices of other things they would like to have. To a greater or lesser degree, we can have one thing only by doing without something else that we would like to have. Our thoughts and feelings are changeable, however. We may decide to buy a house even when it is obvious that we can do so only by dispensing with other things we want. Later we may decide that the burden of home ownership is costing us too many other pleasures which we crave. It is, therefore, probably wise for most families to limit the price for a home to about 2½ times the family's annual income. There are unanticipated costs of home ownership that should also be kept in mind (see Table 12–2).

Another useful rule is that rent or housing costs per month should not exceed more than one week's take home pay. Since the monthly housing cost is usually roughly 1 percent of the total purchase price of the house, a $16,000 house is likely to cost $160 a month to carry (this will vary somewhat, depending on size of mortgage and cash down payment). Obviously, if your take home pay is $120 a week, this is too expensive a house for you. Another measure would be annual carrying costs of approximately 25 percent of annual income. There are probably as many yardsticks as there are experts, but you must notice that they all express some form of caution.

Women applying for mortgage credit with their husbands, in the past were discriminated against even though employed, if they were of child bearing age. A financial lender—bank or savings and loan association—would probably have weighted her salary at half or not at all.

Now a new federal law forbids discriminatory conditions or terms imposed on a woman, if not on a man in the same economic circumstances. Many states now have similar regulations about lending institutions under their jurisdiction.

One bank has developed a very simple form for quickly estimating whether or not to grant a proposed mortgage loan. This is shown in Figure 12–2. In the bottom half of this form, if the ratio of income to carrying charges is less than 20 percent, the loan will be granted. If it exceeds 25 percent, it will be rejected. If it falls between 20 and 25 percent, it will be studied carefully by the mortgage loan officer and becomes a matter for his critical judgment. In a period of tight money, it would probably be rejected. In a period of easier money, it might well be granted.

TABLE 12–2
The Cost of Taking the Plunge

The financial burden of home ownership keeps piling up long after you've made the down payment and budgeted for the monthly mortgage installments. There are improvements to be made, decorating schemes to be tried, necessities to be bought. And single people are as likely as families to start sinking their money into things they never thought they'd need. Here's what a single home buyer in Virginia spent in the first six months after making the move from a rented one bedroom apartment to a new three bedroom townhouse with a mortgage.

20 percent payment on house	$ 7,200
Settlement costs	1,324
Better locks for doors	69
Window shades	203
Tile for entrance area	54
Wall to wall carpet	767
Storm windows	389
Total cash expenditure, excluding mortgage payments	$10,006

Month to month expenses added more. Cash outlays for all of last year broke down like this:

Mortgage payments (principal, interest, taxes, insurance)	$3,252
Utilities	346
Water and sewer	93
Dues to community association	150
Repairs	45
Total outlay	$3,886

By comparison, it would have cost an estimated $175 per month, utilities included, to rent a one bedroom apartment in the same area, making a 12 month outlay of $2,100. For someone inexperienced or unprepared, the difference of $1,786 in out of pocket living expenses could have caused a serious crimp in the budget.

Income tax deductions that go with owning a home compensated for some of the increased expense, of course. Property taxes and interest on the mortgage amounted to $2,663—a hefty deduction on both the federal and state returns. Altogether, itemized deductions cut this single homeowner's state and federal income taxes by about 10 percent each.

Source: *Changing Times—Kiplinger Magazine*, January 1973.

A House Built to Specifications

Naturally, if a family has a home built to its specifications, it should expect to be able to get a house meeting those specifications; but it is common for persons not used to reading blueprints to get quite a surprise when they see the house which was built from them. Sometimes it is far different from what they imagined it would be. As they see the house going up, it is

FIGURE 12–2
Credit Analysis for a Mortgage Loan

CREDIT ANALYSIS

Servicer	FHA. VA.
Subdivision	Sales Price
Property	VA. Value
	FHA. Value
Borrower	FSB. Commitment
	Mortgage Amount
Commitment Date	VA. Guaranty
	Term
	Int. Rate

APPROVED

(A) MORTGAGORS MONTHLY INCOME		(B) MONTHLY CARRYING CHARGE		RATIO-INCOME TO CARRYING CHARGES	
1. Mortgagor	$	1. Princ. & Int.	$	B to A-1	%
2. Other Income		2. Taxes		B to A-1-2	%
		3. Insurance		B to A-1-2-3	%
		4. Water Rent		INCLUDING (4)	%
3. Co-Mortgagor		5. M.I.P.			
4. Co-Bondsman		TOTAL	$		
TOTAL	$				

not unusual for them to discover things that they want changed to make the house (in the family's opinion) what they had visualized. To make these changes, much more expense may be involved than can be comfortably financed. In a great many cases it is wise to secure the services of a competent architect, who may charge from 12 to 15 percent of the total construction cost, to draw plans that will suit the family's needs and wants and to see that the contractor is building according to specifications. Honest and able architects and builders can do much to smooth the path of the unwary person who for the first time is having a house built, for it can be very expensive.

Building your own home is usually a long, costly, and often bitter process; and if your funds are limited and your patience short, it is not a good idea. Figure 12–3 shows a few of the construction features of a house, and

FIGURE 12–3

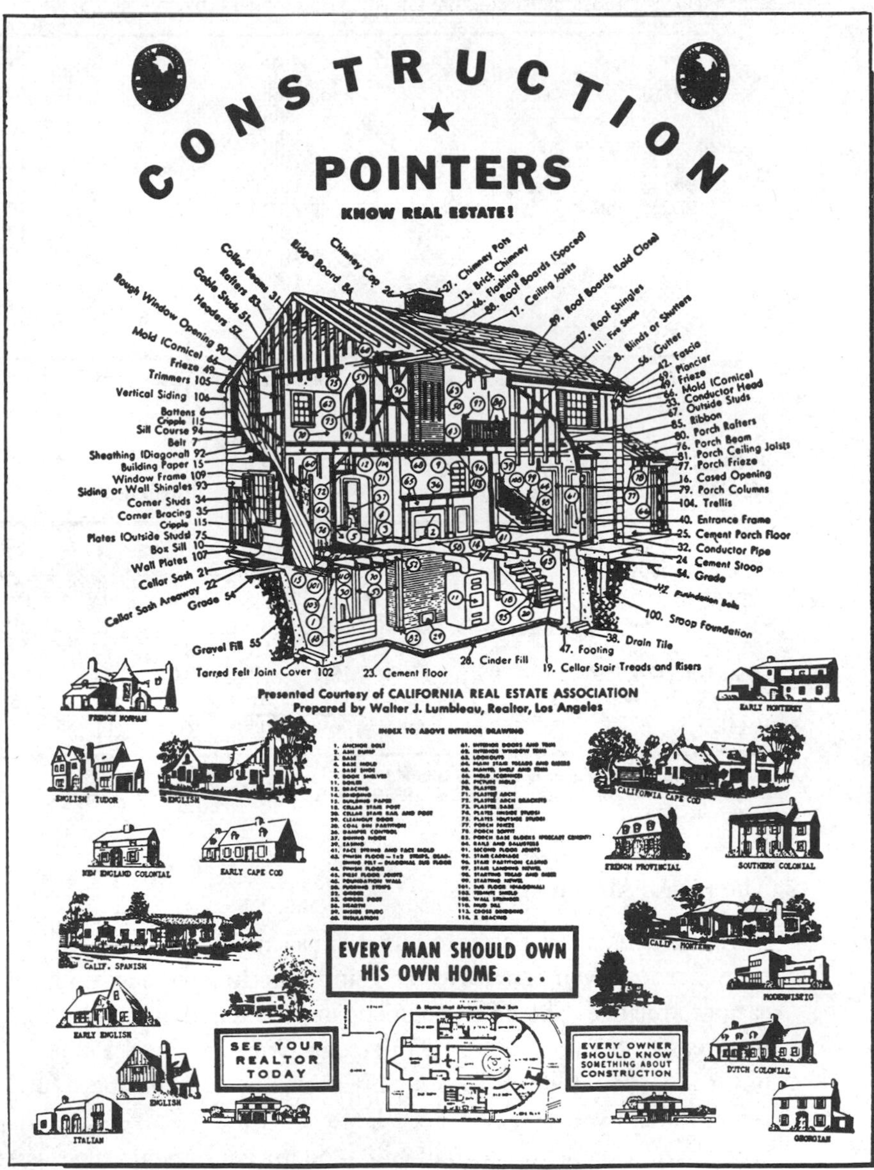

you can see how much study and time it will take to acquire enough information to talk intelligently with your architect and contractor. If you do decide to build, a construction loan can be obtained. Table 12–3 shows how costs have risen—while Table 12–4 tells how these costs are reflected in the selling price of new homes in varying price ranges.

TABLE 12–3
Boeckh Index of Residential Construction Cost (1967 = 100)

Year	*Index*	*Year*	*Index*
1954	70.4	1965	90.4
1955	72.5	1966	94.3
1956	75.7	1967	100.0
1957	77.2	1968	107.3
1958	77.9	1969	116.2
1959	80.5	1970	122.4
1960	81.8	1971	132.8
1961	82.0	1972	145.8
1962	83.4	1973	159.2
1963	85.2	1974	171.9
1964	87.6		

Source: E. H. Boeckh and Associates. *Savings of Loan Fact Book,* 1974.

TABLE 12–4
New One Family Homes Sold, by Sales Price (percentage distribution)

Sales Price	*1966*	*1967*	*1968*	*1969*	*1970*	*1971*	*1972*	*1973*
Under $15,000	15%	11%	8%	6%	4%	3%	2%	1%
$15,000 to $19,999	30	27	22	21	31	24	17	8
$20,000 to $24,999	21	21	22	21	23	22	21	14
$25,000 to $29,999	16	17	19	18	15	17	20	19
$30,000 to $34,999	9	11	13	13	10	11	13	17
$35,000 and Over	10	12	17	21	19	23	28	41
Total	100%	100%	100%	100%	100%	100%	100%	100%

Note: Components may not add to totals due to rounding.
Source: Bureau of the Census and Department of Housing and Urban Development. *Savings & Loan Fact Book,* 1974.

The House Already Built

In most cases it is better to buy a house already built—preferably a new house; at least you can see what you are getting. A new house is usually easier to finance. The down payment may be less than an old house which may require between 20 and 33 percent. You may need $7,000 in cash to buy a $20,000 old house—a probably good buy in more space for your dollars, although you may also need large sums for repairs and perhaps modernization. Where you merely add modern equipment, such as rewiring, plumbing, heating-cooling, or are doing inside alteration, such as installing a bathroom or kitchen, a contractor may be adequate. But if you want to create new space or alter the old, an architect is needed to save money and prevent mistakes. His fee ranges from 12 percent to 15 percent of construction costs.[6]

[6] For a useful checklist, see "Business Dealings with Architect and Contractor," Small Homes Council–Building Research Council, at the University of Illinois, One E. St. Mary's Road, Champaign, Ill. 61820.

If you are going to buy a used house which requires extensive remodeling to make it suit your needs, it may ultimately cost more than a new house. Things which have already cost money have to be removed and scrapped, and substitutes have to be installed at further expense. Then, again, there is always the danger that the remodeled home will be a hodgepodge, inferior to one built from scratch to a carefully drawn plan. Some houses built in former days, however, have materials and workmanship that can be duplicated today only with difficulty. They are apt to be large, with big rooms, and, in some climates, high heating expense. Of course, any house more than 5 or 10 years old requires more in the line of repairs than most of those which have just been built. Older houses, however, may be cheaper and perhaps better buys for those who are content to live in them as they are and not undertake extensive remodeling.

In buying an older house some questions you may want to think about—apart from the larger question of remodeling—are:

a. How recently has it been painted? If four or five years ago, you might be in for a $1,000 to $1,500 paint job right away, unless you can do it yourself.

b. How old is the roof? If a new one is needed, it costs $40 to $70 a square (100 sq. ft.) in asphalt shingle, $200 to $300 a square in slate and $125 in tile. If it sags there may be a weakened foundation—$15,000.

c. What is the shape of the heating plant? How about the wiring? Basement cracks ($200 to $1,000)?

d. Are the gutters and downspouts about to fall apart? Moisture retained in walls? Paint peeling?

e. Try all the faucets—test for water pressure. New piping will cost $1,500 to $3,000.[7]

Location and Transportation

Land cost is a variable factor which is closely related to both location and convenience. The same house that would cost $50,000 within a 15 mile radius of Times Square in New York City might sell for $20,000 if 100 miles away. It has been found that the cost of land declines to the extent that people must pay extra and higher transportation costs to get to and from it. The land cost for the average house doubled over the last decade. A house that is conveniently near to good bus or train service has a considerable advantage for most families. Railroad commuting fares were once small enough to occasion little comment, but they are now an important expense. The cost of transportation, which for a typical move from city to

[7] *Business Week*, "Personal Business Supplement—Home Remodeling," July 20, 1974, pp. 87–97.

suburb may add more than $100 to previous monthly transportation costs, should not be overlooked in computing future estimated total monthly housing costs.

Schools

If there are children in the family, it becomes necessary to consider whether a house is conveniently situated, not only to elementary schools but also to junior high schools and high schools as well. Investigate the present school tax and the prospects for the future. If a new school is badly needed and the community quite properly authorizes it, you may find your school tax suddenly doubled. If you are considering a new development, most likely populated by young families, this will be especially true.

Stores

As a result of high labor and transportation costs, grocery stores and meat markets no longer make a practice of delivering orders to the extent that they did in former years. The high cost of living and increased mobility have also caused more and more people to take advantage of the lower prices charged by chain stores and supermarkets. A home which is conveniently situated near a local or even a major shopping center, so that daily shopping can be accomplished with a minimum of time and effort will, because of this advantage, be found to merit serious attention.

Other Conveniences

Proximity to churches and synagogues, clubs, lodges, and other community activities are also things to be remembered when choosing a home site. The lay of the land (topography) in the immediate vicinity of the home is also important. The view from a home on a high hill can be an inspiring sight, but it takes effort to climb the hill. When one is young, the trip may not be difficult in a car on even on foot, but in later years, age may make the journey troublesome. In some of our climates, coping with slippery, icy streets may cause trouble for those still young and able. Therefore, consider well the location of the proposed home site; view it carefully by day and by night, in all seasons, and try to imagine how suitable it will prove to be for your family at present and in the future. It is a human failing to enthuse over the first view of a given spot; but sometimes familiarity with it may breed despair.

Environment

Whether the neighborhood is populated with families that probably would prove to be congenial is worth noting. There are young people's neighborhoods, where older persons feel out of place; and there are neighborhoods filled with older persons, where growing children find it hard to meet suitable playmates. Everything may be fine about some location except for the absence of a suitable place for the children to play. Remembering Alfred Marshall's remark that it is common for things to have a period of growth, a period of leveling off, and a period of decline, one should give thought to the present status of a proposed home site. Does it appear to be one that will increase in value and draw in more people who would be acceptable to the family, or has it reached its zenith, or is it already on the downgrade? Are there local building codes determining zoning, lot size, and sidewalks and curbs which would keep property values more stable? The house you buy should conform in price and size to the other houses around. A $25,000 house in a $15,000 neighborhood has less resale value. This matter of choosing a place in which to live is not one for quick, offhand decision. A chart showing the more important points you should check before buying is shown in Figure 12–4.

The Lot

For most purposes, a level, rectangular lot of reasonable size is preferred by most people. Blasting away cliffs, digging garages into hillside cellars, and getting automobiles out of sunken garages on icy pavements can be expensive and provoking. Corner lots may seem attractive from some points of view, but to some of us they mean extra sidewalks from which to remove snow. More land than the family can reasonably use and service involves a useless financial burden. A lot with 100 feet of frontage and a like depth—a little less than a quarter-acre—should prove ample for most families, unless they want a vegetable or flower garden. More than this can lead to quite a chore of lawn mowing and, in some localities, a considerable expense for water. Presence of sheltering trees may mean freedom from oppressive heat in summer or blistering winds in winter. The direction the lot faces has bearing on the placing of the house. Large windows facing north and south are cooler than those facing east and west. With windows facing south you receive more winter sunshine, keeping the house warmer and saving on heating bills.

FIGURE 12–4

POINTS TO CHECK BEFORE YOU BUY

Here are 20 points to consider about any neighborhood. To compare two different houses or neighborhoods, rate one in column a, the other in column b. Use check marks; then figure the scores as indicated below. Don't be discouraged if you don't have a lot of "good" checks. This is a tough test.

	a	b
"Good" checks × 3	___	___
"Fair" checks × 2	___	___
"Poor" checks × 1	___	___
Total scores	___	___

	GOOD	a	b
shopping	*Local shopping center within walking distance; major shopping area within 4 miles.*		
churches & amusements	*Available within 2 miles.*		
community pride	*Well-kept lawns and gardens. Houses in good repair, painted and neat.*		
neighbors	*Mostly people not much better off nor much worse off than you, most of whom are likely to share some of your tastes and interests.*		
police & fire protection	*Well-trained, adequately equipped, full-time paid forces in the locality.*		
schools	*Good schools within ½ mile, off important thoroughfares.*		
playgrounds	*Within 15-minute walk. Separate facilities for preschool and older groups.*		
trash & garbage disposal	*Several public or private collections weekly.*		
street layout	*Streets gradually curved to slow traffic, fitted to land contours, intersections at right angles or close to it.*		
transportation	*Convenient bus or car stop, frequent service, less than 30 minutes' ride to work.*		
growth trend	*In direct path of growth of city's most desirable residential areas.*		
lay of the land	*Moderately sloping, rolling land, readily drained.*		
trees	*Numerous scattered trees, well developed, likely to remain healthy because original land level has not been changed.*		
water	*Public water supply with mains in place.*		
sewerage	*Public sanitary sewer system.*		
protection against encroachment	*Area zoned against undesirable uses like railroad tracks, cemeteries, cheaper residential areas. Restrictions rigidly enforced.*		
traffic	*No thoroughfare through neighborhood, existing or potential. Lot on dead-end street.*		
hazards	*No hazards—such as airport, gas or oil storage tanks—for considerable distance.*		
privacy	*Spacious lots with houses arranged to give maximum seclusion to each.*		
nuisances	*Nothing in vicinity to produce noise, smoke, soot, dust or odors.*		
ADD CHECK MARKS			

FAIR	a	b	POOR	a	b
Local shopping within 1 mile; major shopping area within 4 miles.			*More than 1 mile to any store; major shopping area more than 4 miles away.*		
Available within 3½ miles.			*More than 3½ miles away.*		
Mostly a well-kept neighborhood but with a few exceptions.			*Well-kept property exceptional. Numerous overgrown, littered vacant lots.*		
Mostly people of somewhat higher, or lower, economic and social standing than yours, but a few in your bracket, too.			*Everybody a few steps above, or below, your rung on the ladder. You'd be a novelty in the neighborhood.*		
Part-time or volunteer forces maintained by community organization.			*Protections skimpily provided for or absent.*		
Good schools up to 3 miles away, with school bus or other transportation provided.			*More than 3 miles to nearest schools.*		
Available, but it takes more than 15 minutes to get there.			*None provided.*		
Public or private collection once a week.			*None provided.*		
Mostly curved, limited traffic streets—including yours—but some through streets.			*Rigid waffle squares unrelated to traffic flow or land contours.*		
Adequate service at rush hours, 30 to 45 minutes to work.			*Infrequent service, more than 45 minutes to work.*		
Not directly in path of growth of most desirable sections but far enough out to avoid encroachment by undesirable development.			*Not in path of desirable development, close to existing and undesirable development*		
Steep but accessible land or flat land that is well drained.			*Very flat, low-lying land that may have drainage or sewerage problems. Filled land.*		
Few mature trees or nothing but newly planted trees.			*Barren land, land overgrown with brush, or deep fill that will kill existing trees.*		
Community water system.			*Individual wells.*		
Community sewer system, installed by developer with provision for continued operation.			*Individual septic tanks or cesspools.*		
Shielded from undesirable uses by buffer areas like golf courses, parks, stream valleys.			*Adjacent undesirable areas, zoning inadequate or lacking.*		
Neighborhood split by street carrying through traffic, but it's not your street.			*Lot located directly on heavily traveled street.*		
One or more hazards in vicinity but at some distance.			*Nearby hazards.*		
Medium-sized lots but with houses located to give as much seclusion as possible to each.			*Small lots with houses lined up in rows, staring at each other.*		
Only possible sources of nuisances considerable distance away. Prevailing winds blow in opposite direction.			*Nuisance sources nearby and to windward.*		

Source: *Changing Times, The Kiplinger Magazine.*

Other Exterior Features

Is the design standard? Unusual styling may be very interesting and attractive, but it may also narrow your market for resale at a later date. A man built a strikingly modernistic home at a cost of $110,000 in a small, conservative Ohio city. It was a most unusual and very attractive house. A few years later he accepted an offer of a much better position in another city. After commuting (week ends) for two years between the two cities while trying to sell the house for what it cost him, he finally let it go for $54,000.

Has the lot been graded away from the house? This is to permit proper drainage of surface water. Have dry wells or splash blocks been provided at the drainpipes to carry roof rainwater away from the foundation walls assuring a warm, dry basement?

Another thing to check is the landscaping of the grounds around the house. Is there shrubbery circling along the perimeter of the property to provide privacy? How is the lawn? If it needs redoing, it's a costly business. Have concrete walks and curbing been installed? Also, is there a finished driveway, either concrete or asphalt? You'll need them to avoid dust and dirt, and if they are not there, it's another expense to add them.

Are you so far out in exurbia that sewerage, water, garbage disposal, and so on, create continuing headaches and expenses? In other words, does the property have a public sewer system, community water, and garbage and refuse collections? Are there adequate street lighting facilities? Have the streets been surfaced and deeded to the municipality so that they are a community responsibility? Absence of such utilities or community services is likely to involve future assessments, or higher taxes to provide for their installation and upkeep. Check on zoning, taxes, and extra assessments.

Appraising the Lot

Since the investment involves so much money for the average family, whether one has a house built to order or buys an existing one, you must be sure that you are getting reasonable value for your money. If you plan to build you must first select a lot which will suit your needs. How are you to know that the price being asked for it is fair? There are at least two things that you can do to assure yourself. First, you can use the comparison or market method, commonly used by real estate appraisers. This consists of comparing the price asked for the particular lot with the prices at which other comparable lots are being offered. Such a procedure takes time and effort; but if it is carried out intelligently, it prevents paying a price far out of line from what other people are paying for such properties.

Most families have to borrow from some financial institution a large part (sometimes 70 or 80 percent) of what they pay for a home. The bank will, through its investment or mortgage committee, usually composed of persons of long experience in the real estate field, assure itself of the value of the property which is to serve as security for the loan. The prospective homeowner can profit from the advice obtained from such an institution as to the value of the lot (and buildings, if any). Experienced bank mortgage loan officers know more about the value of a lot than the average person can learn in a reasonable time. Since financial institutions which make a business of lending on home mortgages often charge a modest fee for appraising property (so that they can state how much they feel able to lend with it as security), it is often advisable to pay for this service even though it is not certain that you will have to borrow in order to buy. Some careful persons submit applications to two or more institutions, and pay the required fees, simply to secure assurance that the price to be paid is not excessive.

The family, therefore, which independently does a reasonably competent job of deciding whether the price at which a lot is offered is fair, and then gets support for its decision by obtaining the opinion of impartial experts, should not pay an unduly high price. However, it must be remembered that sellers who ask a certain price for a given property are frequently ready to do business, if necessary, at a lower price; bargaining over real estate prices is rather common, especially at times when real estate is not selling readily.

Appraising the House

The fair price for having a house built can be obtained by having a few contractors bid independently for the privilege of building a house for which plans and specifications drawn by an architect are presented for the contractors' study. Care should be taken to secure the services of a competent and honest architect to prepare the plans and specifications and to allow only contractors of good general reputation to bid. The financial instability of many contractors, who are frequently mere carpenters who have decided to go into business for themselves, is so notorious that it is only common sense to make sufficient investigation to determine that the contractor can and will perform the work competently for the agreed price.

The National Established Repair, Service, and Improvement Contractors Association suggests you check bank references; contact at least two wholesale suppliers who sell materials to the contractor and talk with at least three homeowners whose houses have been finished within the last year. It is wise to be sure that the contractor has public liability insurance —a protection to you in case of property damage or injury to third persons.

A detailed written contract covering brands and quality grades of materials, room by room, is vital for your protection. The contract should also include a provision for sketches (subject to your approval) and a starting and finishing date.

If an old house is being considered, there are other things, besides using the comparison method, which a family can do to assure itself of the value of the property. Banks and dealers in builders' supplies can give information as to present building costs per cubic foot and per square foot of living space for houses of various sorts (frame, or brick, or stone). A typical family of four requires a house with 1,300–1,400 square feet of living area. Climate and area cause the price per square foot to vary considerably. Costs are less in the South—about 5 percent less in suburban Atlanta than in a northern city.

Detailed door and window hardware, better bathroom tiling, or finer lighting fixtures, and extras such as a large or beautiful parcel of land, extra large garage, or a fireplace add to value and cost. Sometimes it is cheaper in the long run to consider a more expensive house per unit cost than to plan to add the extras to an inexpensive one at what will be a higher cost later. For example, the cost of finishing a dormered attic ranges from $2,000 to as high as $5,000 depending on materials used and layout.

With such information it is possible to approximate how much a house would cost to build new. If we deduct from this cost an allowance for the fact that the building is partially worn out, we can get a figure (cost less depreciation) for the value of the building which may prove of some help in knowing whether the price being asked for it is reasonable.

Another useful method, although more usually applied to commercial or business property, is to find the valuation of the property by capitalizing the net income. A simple way to approximate this method is to decide how much a property should rent for, as compared with what other, similar properties are commanding. If we think that the property should rent for $100 a month, application of the 1 percent rule will tell us that the property in question should be worth something like $10,000. If we wish to make a more detailed and careful study, we can start with the $100 rent figure, which we think is about right, convert it to a $1,200 annual basis, and subtract the estimated yearly expenses (depreciation, taxes, repairs, insurance, interest, etc.), to try to find the net annual income. Suppose the expenses, as best we can judge them, will amount to $600. Then we expect the net income to be $600 ($1,200 – $600). If we think the net income ($600) should be 5 percent of the value of the property, we divide $600 by 5 and multiply this result ($120) by 100 to get 100 percent or $12,000, the value of the property by this method. The hardest thing about this method is to decide at what rate (we used 5 percent) to capitalize the net income. Using 8 percent would give $7,500 as the value of the property. A rate of 6 percent would lead to the $10,000 value indicated by the 1 percent rule.

Generally, it will be found helpful to try to obtain a value figure by two or three methods (comparison, cost less depreciation, and capitalization of income). If they lead to different results, you have something to think about. You can compromise here and there while you try to arrive at the one figure which in your judgment best expresses the real value of the property. Armed with such an estimate and fortified by what you can learn from others, you should have a much better understanding of the value of the property you are considering than has the average buyer.

Examining the House

You have never bought a house before, and when the real estate agent ushers you into the gleaming new house, aside from your wife's noting with approval the colorful ceramic tile and flocked wallpaper of the bathroom and the mechanical wonders of the modern kitchen, with its dishwasher, garbage disposal, refrigerator, trash compactor, washing machine, dryer, and so on, all of which will probably require periodic visits from a mechanic to service, how do you tell whether or not the house is soundly constructed? What do you look for, and how will you know what is right and what is not right?

A checklist for your guidance is presented in Figure 12–5. Merely glancing at it will indicate what a complicated job you face. Floors, doors, machines, walls, electrical outlets, windows, heating unit, insulation, fans or ventilators, basement, storage, plumbing, roofing, sewage disposal, and so on, all must be considered and examined. You cannot possibly know whether the strip flooring is good or bad; whether the doors will warp; whether good or bad "dry wall," "sheetrock" board, "fiber" board, or plastered wall has been used and finished properly; whether the windows will continue to open and close a month hence or after a heavy rain; whether the heating system is adequate or not; whether the basement-less house has adequate crawl space and foundation vent openings or, if there is a basement, whether it is going to drain properly if it leaks a little or a lot; whether insulation thickness in the attic is adequate or not; or whether the plumbing is designed to hold up for 12 months or 12 years. Since you know little or nothing about such things and it is very costly to learn the hard way by buying, moving in, and waiting to see, the best suggestion we can offer is to get expert advice.

The time and expense of getting expert advice is well worthwhile; you

FIGURE 12–5

Checklist for Use in Buying or Building a Home

This checklist is offered to aid you in selecting your home. The list does not cover everything but does include the principal items which you should consider.

CHARACTERISTICS OF PROPERTY (Proposed or existing construction)

Neighborhood

Consider each of the following to determine whether the location of the property will satisfy your personal needs and preferences:

		Remarks
Convenience of public transportation	☐	
Stores conveniently located	☐	
Elementary school conveniently located	☐	
Absence of excessive traffic noise	☐	
Absence of smoke and unpleasant odors	☐	
Play area available for children	☐	
Fire and police protection provided	☐	
Residential usage safeguarded by adequate zoning	☐	

Lot

Consider each of the following to determine whether the lot is sufficiently large and properly improved:

Size of front yard satisfactory	☐
Size of rear and side yards satisfactory	☐
Walks provide access to front and service entrances	☐
Drive provides easy access to garage	☐
Lot appears to drain satisfactorily	☐
Lawn and planting satisfactory	☐
Septic tank (if any) in good operating condition	☐

Exterior Detail

Observe the exterior detail of neighboring houses and determine whether the house being considered is as good or better in respect to each of the following features:

Porches	☐
Terraces	☐
Garage	☐
Gutters	☐
Storm sash	☐
Weather stripping	☐
Screens	☐

Interior Detail

Consider each of the following to determine whether the house will afford living accomodations which are sufficient to the needs and comfort of your family:

Rooms will accommodate desired furniture	☐
Dining space sufficiently large	☐
At least one closet in each bedroom	☐
At least one coat closet and one linen closet	☐

FIGURE 12–5 (continued)

Remarks

- Convenient access to bathroom ☐
- Sufficient and convenient storage space (screens, trunks, boxes, off-season clothes, luggage, baby carriage, bicycle, wheel toys, etc.) ☐
- Kitchen well arranged and equipped ☐
- Laundry space ample and well located ☐
- Windows provide sufficient light and air ☐
- Sufficient number of electrical outlets ☐

CONDITION OF EXISTING CONSTRUCTION

Exterior Construction

The following appear to be in acceptable condition:

- Wood porch floors and steps ☐
- Windows, doors, and screens ☐
- Gutters and wood cornice ☐
- Wood siding ☐
- Mortar joints ☐
- Roofing ☐
- Chimneys ☐
- Paint on exterior woodwork ☐

Interior Construction

- Plaster is free of excessive cracks ☐
- Plaster is free of stains caused by leaking roof or sidewalls ☐
- Door locks in operating condition ☐
- Windows move freely ☐
- Fireplace works properly ☐
- Basement is dry and will resist moisture penetration ☐
- Mechanical equipment and electrical wiring and switches adequate and in operating condition ☐
- Type of heating equipment suitable ☐
- Adequate insulation in walls, floor, ceiling or roof ☐

The following appear to be in acceptable condition:

- Wood floor finish ☐
- Linoleum floors ☐
- Sink top ☐
- Kitchen range ☐
- Bathroom fixtures ☐
- Painting and papering ☐
- Exposed joists and beams ☐

Are You Sure . . .

That the basement will stay dry after heavy rains?
That the foundations are sound?
That there has been no TERMITE damage?
You'd better get EXPERT ADVICE on the condition of existing construction, if you want to *be sure* the house is a good buy.

Source: Veterans Administration.

do not want to buy a house with termites, a leaky roof, a wet basement, a poor foundation, or defective floors, walls, or ceilings without knowing exactly what you are getting into. Extensive repairs to correct such defects may be very costly. Hire an expert to look the house over for you if you think you are interested in it; go out to the house with him when he examines it; have him explain his observations to you. And if he notes a number of things that need to be corrected and you do want to buy the house, insist that the builder or seller agree *in writing* to make the necessary changes or corrections. Do not be content with oral assent. Get it in writing. Then you can be half-sure that it will be done. Many a naïve and unsuspecting purchaser has taken a builder's word for it that a leaky basement would be fixed and has then waded around in hip boots for six months while waiting for the contractor to get around to the repair work. Before you take title, insist that the seller agree in writing to do the repairs, and specify that they be done before the date you plan to move in.

In some areas, local real estate brokers, as a sideline, act as appraisers. In other areas, professional engineers estimate the condition of a house. The Society of Real Estate Appraisers has members who are qualified to tell what the house is worth and what is wrong with it. These professionals charge $50 to $200, depending on the value of the house. Another source with branches in major big cities is the Nationwide Real Estate Inspectors Service, Inc.

A third is the National Home Inspection Service with offices in 30 metropolitan areas. This firm will examine the condition of the major structural, mechanical, and electrical elements of the house you want to buy and give a detailed report. If roof, walls, ceiling, basement, plumbing, heating, and so on are sound, the company will guarantee its inspection against unforeseen defects for one year. The fee for inspection and insurance is $110 for the first year, and $85 annually thereafter. A one year termite guarantee is $25.

These inspectors are not appraisers. Real estate salespeople actually represent the seller. A survey of 10,000 new home owners by the National Association of Home Builders, on problems they had shortly after moving in, revealed that 29 percent had to make minor repairs, 27 percent had difficulties with the plumbing, 20 percent complained about defective doors and windows.[8] If you are buying an older house or having a new one built under VA or FHA financing, the construction will have to meet certain standards. An FHA appraisal costs less (about $40) than the usual

[8] "Ins and Outs of Inspecting a House" or "40 Ways to Look at a House," *Money*, Avery Comarow, July 1973, pp. 20–27.

fee, and includes a report on needed repairs or changes, eliminating another expensive engineers' report.

Warranties

A warranty program for new houses has been started by the National Association of Home Builders. Known as HOW (Home Owners Warranty Program) it includes a ten year warranty against major construction defects, a two year warranty on installation of plumbing, heating, electrical, and cooling systems and a one year protection against faulty workmanship and defective materials. The plan is to be administered by local building groups who will pay the cost ($2 for each $1,000 of a home's sales price). The warranty becomes effective only when the buyer takes title.

Financing the Home

Once you have selected the house you think you want to buy, your next step is to arrange for financing. If you are in the position of most, you will be able to make only a modest down payment, 25 percent or less, and will need to get the rest of the purchase price by mortgage from a financial institution. When contemplating making a down payment, no family should thoughtlessly decide to part with all of its cash resources for this purpose. It should always strive to retain something in the bank for meeting emergencies.

According to a recent survey made by the Federal Reserve Board, 18 percent of home buyers reported they did not know the interest rate on their mortgages. This sad situation is an improvement over the last survey's results, which found 27 percent unaware of one of the most important financial facts in their lives.

The Truth in Lending Act and Regulation Z apply to home purchase credit costs with certain exceptions. In the purchase of real estate, unlike in the purchasing of a used car, the law does not require the costs for appraisal or credit rating reports to be included in the finance charge, but does say that these fees must be reasonable. Therefore, it is necessary not only to shop around for the best annual percentage rate but also for comparison of the other costs. This Consumer Credit Protection Act (its other name) does require that if "points" (see page 594) are charged, they must be shown as part of the finance charge, since they change the annual percentage rate which must be shown. On first-lien mortgages (when you are signing a mortgage to finance the purchase of a home), the lender does not have to spell out the amount of the finance charge in dollars and cents but the annual percentage rate must be given.

Another exception is that your right to cancel a credit transaction within three days does not apply when you are financing the purchase of your home, but only when you are making improvements. In repair or modernization loans and other instances you have the right to cancel a credit arrangement within three business days if your residence is used as collateral for credit.

If it can be arranged, the prepayment privilege—or the right to pay off your mortgage ahead of time—should be included in the agreement, instead of the usual prepayment penalty. The privilege gives you the opportunity to take advantage of favorable circumstances when they exist and so possibly lighten your debt burden. In inflationary times, the banks give discounts to homeowners who make partial or full prepayment on their mortgages. The banks can make more profit lending out these funds at a current higher interest rate.

When interest rates vary dramatically in a short time, it is possible to renegotiate the terms of your loan, but there are certain caveats to bear in mind. It is possible to refinance the mortgage at another bank or your own, but if the new expense equals the difference—or comes close—it may not be worthwhile. For example, if you can get a 7.5 percent mortgage on your 25 year $25,000 loan instead of its 8.5 percent current rate, the idea looks attractive. But if a prepayment penalty of 2 percent, or $500 on the old loan (since the rate was computed on 25 years and you are paying sooner), is added to a service fee of 1 percent, or $250, to the new lender, and there is a new title search and title insurance cost of $500 and other costs for paper work, adding up to a grand total of about $1,400, you want to be sure you are really saving and not just appearing to save. Unless you have at least eight years more of mortgage time left, you will not have saved much, since only then will you have reduced your monthly payment from $201 to $185, a saving of $192 a year, or in eight years, the amount of $1,536.

Variable Mortgages and Flexible Payment Plans

As we have seen the standard mortgage loan has fixed monthly payments for 20 or 30 years. The monthly payment, using the same percentage in down payments on a standard new house has increased 85 percent in the period from 1965 to 1973, while average wage and salary income during that same period rose 57 percent.

Believers in flexible payment plans point out that this makes it very difficult for the new buyer of a home in an inflationary period, to pay the early years of the fixed mortgage, whereas as time and inflation move on, both the home buyers' income and equity in the house grow, making it easier to pay the later payments. The idea of a graduated payment schedule would ease the problem for new buyers but the lender would object to low payments that would be mostly interest and no repayment of principal. Linking variable rate mortgages pegged to an index of money market rates sweetens the idea for lenders and makes more mortgage money available. While the lender does not like being locked into unrealistically low rates over a long period, the homeowner relishes it. Each favors a different kind of elasticity—the borrower in payment, the lender in rate.

The Federal Home Loan Bank Board has raised to $55,000 the maximum loan a savings and loan association can make and to $45,000 the amount it would insure. It will allow flexible mortgages in which for the first five years home buyers will pay only interest; repayment of principal can begin in the sixth year.

The variable interest rate mortgage has been getting increasing attention, with its built-in mobility to cope with the shifting interest rates. Under the variable interest rate mortgage loan monthly payments rise or fall depending on changes in interest rates. About 10 percent of savings and loan associations have been using variable interest rate mortgages. Government guaranteed mortgages such as VA and FHA cannot carry variable interest clauses, and their use is limited in some states by the usury laws.

Where to Go for a Mortgage Loan

Most home loans on mortgages today are made by savings and loan associations, savings banks, commercial banks, insurance companies, and individuals. Of these, only the savings and loan associations specialize exclusively in lending on mortgages. They (including cooperative banks in Massachusetts, homestead associations in Louisiana, and building and loan associations generally) make a business of obtaining savings from the public and putting this money to work earning interest by lending it out on mortgages, largely on residences. They have from 80 to 95 percent of their funds invested in mortgages. Savings banks have invested about 50 percent of their funds, on the average, in recent years in real estate mortgages; commercial banks, as their name implies, endeavor to put most of their money to work in commercial loans and place only relatively small percentages of assets in mortgages; insurance companies have large bond portfolios and have gone actively and extensively into the market for residential mortgages. Many persons like to do business with a local institution if it offers terms and advantages comparable with those that can be obtained elsewhere. It is not unnatural, therefore, someone seeking a mortgage loan often drops into the local savings and loan association, savings bank, or commercial bank to talk it over. If a person wishes to do business with an insurance company, then contact would be with a local real estate broker who usually acts as loan correspondent for one or more insurance companies. Real estate mortgage loans may also be obtained from individuals, but they usually cost more than if secured from a financial institution. Figure 12–6 illustrates the share each lender has in the mortgage loan market.

FIGURE 12–6
Mortgage Loans Outstanding on One to Four Family Nonfarm Homes, by Type of Lender (year-end 1950 and 1973)

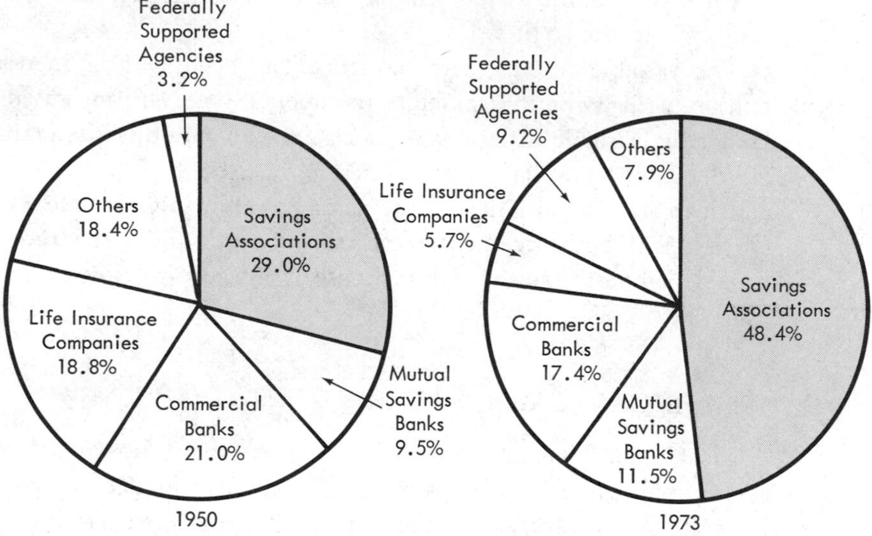

Source: Data, Federal Home Loan Bank Board; Federal Reserve Board; Chart, *Savings & Loan Fact Book*, 1974.

The Old Type Straight Mortgage

When a loan is made on the security of a mortgage, the mortgagee—the lender—makes the loan to the mortgagor—the homeowner or borrower—in return for a promissory note secured by the mortgage of the property and adequate insurance thereon. The promissory note can be payable in any number of years, depending on agreement. They were known as "straight mortgages" because there was no provision for partial payment of the principal of the loan during the period for which the note was written; customarily, only the interest was paid periodically—every quarter, every half year, or every year. At the end of the note's term, it really became a demand instrument, full payment of which could be demanded immediately. Many borrowers would forget about the principal until the full amount of the note was due and payable when the note matured, and then they would attempt to renew the loan for another term of years. Many promissory notes were permitted to run for years, in some cases for 15 or 25, with only interest payments made during the interim. If the note came due in a prosperity period, there might not be any difficulty in renewing it; but if it came due in a recession, the borrower could lose the property.

For several reasons the straight mortgage is now thought to be disadvantageous. The lender, on the one hand, continues to have just as much money at risk throughout the years in spite of the fact that the security for the loan (the house on the land) is depreciating year after year. The borrower, on the other hand, goes through the period of the note paying merely interest till maturity, at which time the full amount of the note must be paid and this is generally impossible.

In case the loan was called at the maturity of the note the borrower would have to get a second loan to pay off the first, or run the danger of having the mortgage foreclosed (property sold to secure whatever money it would provide, to apply on the note). In event of foreclosure, if the note was not satisfied fully by the sale of the property, there was a good chance that the borrower could be held for the deficiency, since he had not made good on his promise as evidenced in the note. Another difficulty with the straight mortgage, from the point of view of the borrower, was that he frequently could not borrow enough on one mortgage of this type (the risk to the lender being what it was) and was forced to borrow the balance on a second mortgage, which, because of the greater risk, commanded a higher rate of interest.

Under the straight mortgage, the borrower had to accumulate the funds to pay off his total obligation. If he went to a savings and loan association, the borrower obtained a favorable straight mortgage, in that the period for which the promissory note was written was long enough to permit him to build up share value (he was obliged, as a condition of the loan, to buy shares of the association on the installment plan; he received dividends on his share investment) sufficient to pay off his note at maturity. The way it worked amounted to borrowing in one place, saving in the same place, and finally using the savings to pay off the borrowings. Usually he paid a higher rate on his borrowings than he earned on his savings. And he owed the full amount of his borrowings till the day when he had saved enough to pay off the loan in full at one time; his payments (savings) meantime did nothing to reduce his borrowings.

It is easy to see how disadvantageous such a loan could be for a borrower. Suppose $10,000 were borrowed at 6 percent per anuum, the interest, therefore, being $600 a year. When the borrower had saved, say, $6,000, on which we shall assume that he was earning 5 percent per annum, i.e., $300, it was really costing him $300 net a year to have the use of $4,000 net, which is a cost of 7.5 percent. The larger his savings became, the higher would be the effective rate of interest which he was paying.

The Amortized or Direct Reduction Mortgage

The old straight type mortgage has gone out of favor because both government and private mortgage financing agencies insist on the amortized mortgage. They want the loans paid off in the foreseeable future—during the economic life of the building. The direct reduction or amortized mortgage is thus named because the borrower makes a fixed monthly payment which not only includes interest (and perhaps taxes and insurance) but also reduces the principal of the mortgage debt.

The earlier monthly installments include primarily interest and only small amounts of principal repayment. As the principal is gradually reduced, a larger and larger percentage of the monthly payment is applied to repayment of principal, until the loan is entirely repaid. Under this plan, interest at the stipulated rate is figured on the reducing unpaid balance of your loan. Thus, as the regular payments of the fixed monthly amount are made, the part of the payment needed to pay interest becomes less, and the part applied to reducing the loan becomes greater.

As compared with the old type straight mortgage, the amortized mortgage requires a higher monthly payment but results in a very large saving in interest costs. For example:

Under the old type straight mortgage:
You make a mortgage loan of $20,000.
You do not make payments to reduce the principal of the mortgage.
You make 240 monthly payments of $133.33.
You pay in interest, over 20 years at 8 percent per annum, $32,000.
You still owe the original mortgage of $20,000.

Under the amortized mortgage:
You make monthly payments of $167.29 to pay both interest and reduce the principal.
You pay in interest, in 20 years at 8 percent per annum, $20,149.60.
Thus you save $11,850.40 in interest costs and the principal is entirely paid off at the end of the 20th year.

Obviously, the amortized mortgage is a much better arrangement for the borrower. Table 12–5 illustrates monthly mortgage payments on an amortized basis.

In the past it was frequently found that borrowers had not kept up their tax and insurance payments; today, to prevent trouble from this source, it is a common practice for borrowers to add to their monthly payments for principal and interest one twelfth of estimated yearly tax and insurance payments. The lending institution keeps this in a special "escrow" account and uses it to pay the taxes and insurance when due. Taxes in arrears for one or more years would seriously shrink the security (property value pledged for the loan), since the government has a first lien for property taxes. The lender could not afford to take a chance on the borrower letting the insurance lapse.

TABLE 12–5
Monthly Payments, Including Amortization and Interest, Required to Liquidate a Loan of $20,000

Interest Rate (percent)	*Payment Period (years)*				
	10	*15*	*20*	*25*	*30*
6%	$222.05	$168.78	$143.29	$128.87	$119.92
7	232.22	179.77	155.06	141.36	133.07
8	242.66	191.14	167.29	154.37	146.76
9	253.36	202.86	179.95	167.84	160.93
10	264.31	214.93	193.01	181.75	175.52
11	275.51	227.32	206.44	196.03	190.47
12	286.95	240.04	220.22	210.65	205.73

Perhaps an illustration is in order. Let us suppose that Joe Jones owns a house valued at $20,000 and borrows $10,000, with the house mortgaged as security for his promissory note. The direct reduction loan has been reduced to $6,000, but then Jones loses his job and he can no longer keep up his payments. After giving due notice of the default in the newspapers, the lending institution proceeds to have the property auctioned off at a foreclosure sale (expense, $150) and bids the property in, itself, at the sale for $5,000. If it is then found that real estate taxes are in arrears in the amount of $1,000, the creditor will have to pay this sum to the local political subdivision (city or town) to clear the title. To the borrower's obligation for $6,000 the creditor can add the foreclosure expense of $150 and the tax payment of $1,000, making the total amount due from the borrower, $7,150. If the $5,000 received from the sale of the property is credited against the total due, there is a deficiency of $2,150 for which the borrower is still technically liable; but since Jones is out of a job, it will probably be difficult to collect anything from him, and the creditor will accordingly have to take a loss of $2,150. If Jones had kept his taxes paid to date, the creditor's loss would have been $1,000 less. That is why lending institutions insist that money for tax payments be accumulated monthly, when interest and principal payments are made.

Mathematics of Direct Reduction Loans

The mathematics of direct reduction mortgage loans of 15, 20, or 25 years, payable in monthly installments, are too complicated for the average borrower to comprehend; and indeed, lenders use mathematical tables to determine quickly the monthly payment required to amortize a given loan at a certain percentage for a fixed period. Your local bank or savings and

TABLE 12–6
Monthly Payment Necessary to Amortize a Loan

9½% MONTHLY PAYMENT NECESSARY TO AMORTIZE A LOAN

TERM / AMOUNT	20 YEARS	21 YEARS	22 YEARS	23 YEARS	24 YEARS	25 YEARS	26 YEARS
$ 100	.94	.92	.91	.90	.89	.88	.87
200	1.87	1.84	1.81	1.79	1.77	1.75	1.74
250	2.34	2.30	2.27	2.24	2.21	2.19	2.17
300	2.80	2.76	2.72	2.68	2.65	2.63	2.60
400	3.73	3.67	3.62	3.58	3.54	3.50	3.47
500	4.67	4.59	4.53	4.47	4.42	4.37	4.33
1000	9.33	9.18	9.05	8.93	8.83	8.74	8.66
1500	13.99	13.77	13.57	13.40	13.25	13.11	12.99
2000	18.65	18.35	18.09	17.86	17.66	17.48	17.32
2500	23.31	22.94	22.62	22.33	22.07	21.85	21.64
3000	27.97	27.53	27.14	26.79	26.49	26.22	25.97
3500	32.63	32.12	31.66	31.26	30.90	30.58	30.30
4000	37.29	36.70	36.18	35.72	35.32	34.95	34.63
4500	41.95	41.29	40.71	40.19	39.73	39.32	38.96
5000	46.61	45.88	45.23	44.65	44.14	43.69	43.28
5500	51.27	50.46	49.75	49.12	48.56	48.06	47.61
6000	55.93	55.05	54.27	53.58	52.97	52.43	51.94
6500	60.59	59.64	58.79	58.05	57.39	56.80	56.27
7000	65.25	64.23	63.32	62.51	61.80	61.16	60.60
7500	69.91	68.81	67.84	66.98	66.21	65.53	64.92
8000	74.58	73.40	72.36	71.44	70.63	69.90	69.25
8500	79.24	77.99	76.88	75.91	75.04	74.27	73.58
9000	83.90	82.57	81.41	80.37	79.45	78.64	77.91
9500	88.56	87.16	85.93	84.84	83.87	83.01	82.24
10000	93.22	91.75	90.45	89.30	88.28	87.37	86.56
10500	97.88	96.34	94.97	93.77	92.70	91.74	90.89
11000	102.54	100.92	99.50	98.23	97.11	96.11	95.22
11500	107.20	105.51	104.02	102.70	101.52	100.48	99.55
12000	111.86	110.10	108.54	107.16	105.94	104.85	103.88
12500	116.52	114.68	113.06	111.63	110.35	109.22	108.20
13000	121.18	119.27	117.58	116.09	114.77	113.59	112.53
13500	125.84	123.86	122.11	120.56	119.18	117.95	116.86
14000	130.50	128.45	126.63	125.02	123.59	122.32	121.19
14500	135.16	133.03	131.15	129.49	128.01	126.69	125.52
15000	139.82	137.62	135.67	133.95	132.42	131.06	129.84
15500	144.49	142.21	140.20	138.42	136.84	135.43	134.17
16000	149.15	146.79	144.72	142.88	141.25	139.80	138.50
16500	153.81	151.38	149.24	147.35	145.66	144.16	142.83
17000	158.47	155.97	153.76	151.81	150.08	148.53	147.16
17500	163.13	160.56	158.29	156.28	154.49	152.90	151.48
18000	167.79	165.14	162.81	160.74	158.90	157.27	155.81
18500	172.45	169.73	167.33	165.21	163.32	161.64	160.14
19000	177.11	174.32	171.85	169.67	167.73	166.01	164.47
19500	181.77	178.90	176.37	174.13	172.15	170.38	168.80
20000	186.43	183.49	180.90	178.60	176.56	174.74	173.12
20500	191.09	188.08	185.42	183.06	180.97	179.11	177.45
21000	195.75	192.67	189.94	187.53	185.39	183.48	181.78
21500	200.41	197.25	194.46	191.99	189.80	187.85	186.11
22000	205.07	201.84	198.99	196.46	194.22	192.22	190.44
22500	209.73	206.43	203.51	200.92	198.63	196.59	194.76
23000	214.40	211.01	208.03	205.39	203.04	200.96	199.09
23500	219.06	215.60	212.55	209.85	207.46	205.32	203.42
24000	223.72	220.19	217.08	214.32	211.87	209.69	207.75
24500	228.38	224.78	221.60	218.78	216.28	214.06	212.08
25000	233.04	229.36	226.12	223.25	220.70	218.43	216.40

154

MONTHLY PAYMENT NECESSARY TO AMORTIZE A LOAN 9½%

TERM / AMOUNT	20 YEARS	21 YEARS	22 YEARS	23 YEARS	24 YEARS	25 YEARS	26 YEARS
$25500	237.70	233.95	230.64	227.71	225.11	222.80	220.73
26000	242.36	238.54	235.16	232.18	229.53	227.17	225.06
26500	247.02	243.13	239.69	236.64	233.94	231.53	229.39
27000	251.68	247.71	244.21	241.11	238.35	235.90	233.72
27500	256.34	252.30	248.73	245.57	242.77	240.27	238.04
28000	261.00	256.89	253.25	250.04	247.18	244.64	242.37
28500	265.66	261.47	257.78	254.50	251.60	249.01	246.70
29000	270.32	266.06	262.30	258.97	256.01	253.38	251.03
29500	274.98	270.65	266.82	263.43	260.42	257.75	255.36
30000	279.64	275.24	271.34	267.90	264.84	262.11	259.68
30500	284.31	279.82	275.87	272.36	269.25	266.48	264.01
31000	288.97	284.41	280.39	276.83	273.67	270.85	268.34
31500	293.63	289.00	284.91	281.29	278.08	275.22	272.67
32000	298.29	293.58	289.43	285.76	282.49	279.59	277.00
32500	302.95	298.17	293.95	290.22	286.91	283.96	281.32
33000	307.61	302.76	298.48	294.69	291.32	288.32	285.65
33500	312.27	307.35	303.00	299.15	295.73	292.69	289.98
34000	316.93	311.93	307.52	303.62	300.15	297.06	294.31
34500	321.59	316.52	312.04	308.08	304.56	301.43	298.64
35000	326.25	321.11	316.57	312.55	308.98	305.80	302.96
35500	330.91	325.69	321.09	317.01	313.39	310.17	307.29
36000	335.57	330.28	325.61	321.48	317.80	314.54	311.62
36500	340.23	334.87	330.13	325.94	322.22	318.90	315.95
37000	344.89	339.46	334.66	330.41	326.63	323.27	320.28
37500	349.55	344.04	339.18	334.87	331.05	327.64	324.60
38000	354.21	348.63	343.70	339.34	335.46	332.01	328.93
38500	358.88	353.22	348.22	343.80	339.87	336.38	333.26
39000	363.54	357.80	352.74	348.26	344.29	340.75	337.59
39500	368.20	362.39	357.27	352.73	348.70	345.12	341.92
40000	372.86	366.98	361.79	357.19	353.11	349.48	346.24
40500	377.52	371.57	366.31	361.66	357.53	353.85	350.57
41000	382.18	376.15	370.83	366.12	361.94	358.22	354.90
41500	386.84	380.74	375.36	370.59	366.36	362.59	359.23
42000	391.50	385.33	379.88	375.05	370.77	366.96	363.56
42500	396.16	389.91	384.40	379.52	375.18	371.33	367.88
43000	400.82	394.50	388.92	383.98	379.60	375.69	372.21
43500	405.48	399.09	393.45	388.45	384.01	380.06	376.54
44000	410.14	403.68	397.97	392.91	388.43	384.43	380.87
44500	414.80	408.26	402.49	397.38	392.84	388.80	385.20
45000	419.46	412.85	407.01	401.84	397.25	393.17	389.52
45500	424.12	417.44	411.53	406.31	401.67	397.54	393.85
46000	428.79	422.02	416.06	410.77	406.08	401.91	398.18
46500	433.45	426.61	420.58	415.24	410.50	406.27	402.51
47000	438.11	431.20	425.10	419.70	414.91	410.64	406.84
47500	442.77	435.79	429.62	424.17	419.32	415.01	411.16
48000	447.43	440.37	434.15	428.63	423.74	419.38	415.49
48500	452.09	444.96	438.67	433.10	428.15	423.75	419.82
49000	456.75	449.55	443.19	437.56	432.56	428.12	424.15
49500	461.41	454.14	447.71	442.03	436.98	432.48	428.48
50000	466.07	458.72	452.24	446.49	441.39	436.85	432.80
55000	512.68	504.59	497.46	491.14	485.53	480.54	476.08
60000	559.28	550.47	542.68	535.79	529.67	524.22	519.36
65000	605.89	596.34	587.90	580.44	573.81	567.91	562.64
70000	652.50	642.21	633.13	625.09	617.95	611.59	605.92
75000	699.10	688.08	678.35	669.74	662.09	655.28	649.20

155

Source: Financial Publishing Company, Boston, Mass.

loan association will undoubtedly have a copy of *Expanded Payment Tables for Monthly Mortgage Loans*, published by the Financial Publishing Company of Boston. One page of this 224-page volume is shown in Table 12–6. From it you can see, if you look down the first column (on page 578), that to amortize a loan of $10,000 at 9.5 percent over a 20 year period, a monthly payment of $93.22 is required. To pay off the same loan over a 25 year period, look across the $10,000 line to the 25-year column, and you will see that a monthly payment of $87.37 is required. Table 12–7 may be more useful to you, since it shows the annual payment necessary to amortize a loan of $1,000 over any period from 2 to 40 years and at any rate from 6 to 12 percent. By dividing the annual payment by 12, you can get the approximate monthly payment required; and then, if your loan is a

TABLE 12–7
Annual Payment Necessary to Amortize a Loan of $1,000

ANNUAL PAYMENT
NECESSARY TO AMORTIZE A LOAN OF $1000

RATE / YEARS	6%	6⅛%	6¼%	6⅜%	6½%	6⅝%	6¾%
2	545.44	546.40	547.35	548.31	549.27	550.22	551.18
3	374.11	374.98	375.85	376.71	377.58	378.45	379.32
4	288.60	289.42	290.25	291.08	291.91	292.74	293.57
5	237.40	238.21	239.02	239.83	240.64	241.45	242.27
6	203.37	204.17	204.97	205.77	206.57	207.38	208.18
7	179.14	179.94	180.73	181.53	182.34	183.14	183.94
8	161.04	161.84	162.64	163.44	164.24	165.05	165.85
9	147.03	147.83	148.63	149.44	150.24	151.05	151.86
10	135.87	136.68	137.49	138.30	139.11	139.92	140.74
11	126.80	127.61	128.42	129.24	130.06	130.88	131.71
12	119.28	120.10	120.92	121.75	122.57	123.40	124.23
13	112.97	113.79	114.62	115.45	116.29	117.13	117.97
14	107.59	108.42	109.26	110.10	110.95	111.79	112.64
15	102.97	103.81	104.66	105.51	106.36	107.21	108.07
16	98.96	99.81	100.66	101.52	102.38	103.25	104.12
17	95.45	96.31	97.17	98.04	98.91	99.79	100.66
18	92.36	93.23	94.10	94.98	95.86	96.74	97.63
19	89.63	90.50	91.39	92.27	93.16	94.05	94.95
20	87.19	88.08	88.97	89.86	90.76	91.66	92.57
21	85.01	85.91	86.81	87.71	88.62	89.53	90.45
22	83.05	83.96	84.86	85.78	86.70	87.62	88.55
23	81.28	82.20	83.12	84.04	84.97	85.90	86.83
24	79.68	80.61	81.53	82.47	83.40	84.34	85.29
25	78.23	79.16	80.10	81.04	81.99	82.94	83.89
26	76.91	77.85	78.79	79.74	80.70	81.66	82.62
27	75.70	76.65	77.61	78.56	79.53	80.50	81.47
28	74.60	75.56	76.52	77.49	78.46	79.44	80.42
29	73.58	74.55	75.52	76.50	77.48	78.47	79.46
30	72.65	73.63	74.61	75.59	76.58	77.58	78.58
35	68.98	69.99	71.01	72.04	73.07	74.10	75.14
40	66.47	67.52	68.57	69.63	70.70	71.77	72.85

RATE / YEARS	6⅞%	7%	7⅛%	7¼%	7⅜%	7½%	7⅝%
2	552.14	553.10	554.06	555.01	555.97	556.93	557.89
3	380.19	381.06	381.93	382.80	383.67	384.54	385.42
4	294.40	295.23	296.07	296.90	297.74	298.57	299.41
5	243.08	243.90	244.71	245.53	246.35	247.17	247.99
6	208.99	209.80	210.61	211.42	212.24	213.05	213.87
7	184.75	185.56	186.37	187.18	187.99	188.81	189.62
8	166.66	167.47	168.28	169.10	169.91	170.73	171.55
9	152.68	153.49	154.31	155.13	155.95	156.77	157.60
10	141.56	142.38	143.21	144.03	144.86	145.69	146.52
11	132.53	133.36	134.19	135.03	135.86	136.70	137.54
12	125.07	125.91	126.75	127.59	128.43	129.28	130.13
13	118.81	119.66	120.50	121.36	122.21	123.07	123.93
14	113.49	114.35	115.21	116.07	116.93	117.80	118.67
15	108.93	109.80	110.67	111.54	112.41	113.29	114.17
16	104.99	105.86	106.74	107.62	108.51	109.40	110.29
17	101.55	102.43	103.32	104.21	105.11	106.01	106.91
18	98.52	99.42	100.32	101.22	102.12	103.03	103.95
19	95.85	96.76	97.67	98.58	99.50	100.42	101.34
20	93.48	94.40	95.32	96.24	97.17	98.10	99.03
21	91.37	92.29	93.22	94.16	95.09	96.03	96.98
22	89.48	90.41	91.35	92.29	93.24	94.19	95.15
23	87.77	88.72	89.67	90.62	91.58	92.54	93.51
24	86.24	87.19	88.15	89.12	90.08	91.06	92.03
25	84.85	85.82	86.78	87.76	88.73	89.72	90.70
26	83.59	84.57	85.54	86.53	87.51	88.50	89.50
27	82.45	83.43	84.42	85.41	86.41	87.41	88.41
28	81.41	82.40	83.39	84.39	85.40	86.41	87.42
29	80.45	81.45	82.46	83.47	84.48	85.50	86.53
30	79.58	80.59	81.61	82.62	83.65	84.68	85.71
35	76.19	77.24	78.29	79.35	80.42	81.49	82.56
40	73.93	75.01	76.11	77.20	78.30	79.41	80.51

ANNUAL PAYMENT
NECESSARY TO AMORTIZE A LOAN OF $1000

RATE / YEARS	7¾%	7⅞%	8%	8⅛%	8¼%	8½%	8¾%
2	558.85	559.81	560.77	561.74	562.70	564.62	566.55
3	386.29	387.16	388.04	388.91	389.79	391.54	393.30
4	300.25	301.09	301.93	302.77	303.61	305.29	306.98
5	248.81	249.64	250.46	251.29	252.11	253.77	255.43
6	214.68	215.50	216.32	217.14	217.96	219.61	221.27
7	190.44	191.26	192.08	192.90	193.72	195.37	197.03
8	172.37	173.20	174.02	174.85	175.67	177.34	179.00
9	158.42	159.25	160.08	160.92	161.75	163.43	165.11
10	147.36	148.20	149.03	149.88	150.72	152.41	154.11
11	138.39	139.23	140.08	140.93	141.78	143.50	145.22
12	130.99	131.84	132.70	133.56	134.42	136.16	137.90
13	124.79	125.66	126.53	127.40	128.27	130.03	131.79
14	119.55	120.42	121.30	122.18	123.07	124.85	126.64
15	115.06	115.94	116.83	117.73	118.62	120.43	122.24
16	111.18	112.08	112.98	113.89	114.79	116.62	118.46
17	107.81	108.72	109.63	110.55	111.47	113.32	115.18
18	104.86	105.78	106.71	107.63	108.56	110.44	112.32
19	102.27	103.20	104.13	105.07	106.01	107.91	109.81
20	99.97	100.91	101.86	102.81	103.76	105.68	107.61
21	97.93	98.88	99.84	100.80	101.76	103.70	105.65
22	96.11	97.07	98.04	99.01	99.98	101.94	103.92
23	94.48	95.45	96.43	97.41	98.39	100.38	102.37
24	93.01	93.99	94.98	95.98	96.97	98.97	100.99
25	91.69	92.69	93.68	94.69	95.69	97.72	99.76
26	90.50	91.50	92.51	93.52	94.54	96.59	98.65
27	89.42	90.44	91.45	92.48	93.50	95.57	97.64
28	88.44	89.47	90.49	91.53	92.56	94.64	96.74
29	87.55	88.59	89.62	90.66	91.71	93.81	95.93
30	86.75	87.79	88.83	89.88	90.94	93.06	95.19
35	83.64	84.72	85.81	86.90	87.99	90.19	92.41
40	81.63	82.74	83.87	84.99	86.12	88.39	90.67

RATE / YEARS	9%	9¼%	9½%	9¾%	10%	11%	12%
2	568.47	570.40	572.33	574.26	576.20	583.94	591.70
3	395.06	396.82	398.58	400.35	402.12	409.22	416.35
4	308.67	310.37	312.07	313.77	315.48	322.33	329.24
5	257.10	258.77	260.44	262.12	263.80	270.58	277.41
6	222.92	224.59	226.26	227.93	229.61	236.38	243.23
7	198.70	200.37	202.04	203.72	205.41	212.22	219.12
8	180.68	182.36	184.05	185.75	187.45	194.33	201.31
9	166.80	168.50	170.21	171.92	173.65	180.61	187.68
10	155.83	157.54	159.27	161.01	162.75	169.81	176.99
11	146.95	148.69	150.44	152.20	153.97	161.13	168.42
12	139.66	141.42	143.19	144.98	146.77	154.03	161.44
13	133.57	135.36	137.16	138.97	140.78	148.16	155.68
14	128.44	130.25	132.07	133.91	135.75	143.23	150.88
15	124.06	125.90	127.75	129.61	131.48	139.07	146.83
16	120.30	122.17	124.04	125.92	127.82	135.52	143.40
17	117.05	118.94	120.84	122.75	124.67	132.48	140.46
18	114.22	116.13	118.05	119.99	121.94	129.85	137.96
19	111.74	113.67	115.62	117.58	119.55	127.57	135.77
20	109.55	111.51	113.48	115.47	117.46	125.58	133.88
21	107.62	109.60	111.60	113.61	115.63	123.84	132.25
22	105.91	107.91	109.93	111.96	114.01	122.32	130.82
23	104.39	106.41	108.45	110.51	112.58	120.98	129.56
24	103.03	105.08	107.14	109.21	111.30	119.79	128.47
25	101.81	103.88	105.96	108.06	110.17	118.75	127.50
26	100.72	102.81	104.91	107.03	109.16	117.82	126.66
27	99.74	101.85	103.97	106.11	108.26	116.99	125.91
28	98.86	100.99	103.13	105.29	107.46	116.26	125.25
29	98.06	100.21	102.37	104.54	106.73	115.61	124.67
30	97.34	99.51	101.69	103.88	106.08	115.03	124.15
35	94.64	96.89	99.14	101.41	103.69	112.93	122.32
40	92.96	95.27	97.59	99.92	102.26	111.72	121.31

Source: Financial Publishing Company, Boston, Mass.

multiple of $1,000, you can multiply the monthly figure by the number of times $1,000 goes into your loan to get your approximate monthly payment. For example, a loan of $1,000 at 7 percent amortized over 20 years will require an annual payment of $94.40, or a monthly payment of $7.87. A $10,000 loan at 7 percent amortized over 20 years would mean an annual payment of $944, or a monthly payment of $78.66.

For each mortgage loan that is made, an individual amortization

TABLE 12–8
Amortization Schedule

Schedule of Direct Reduction Loan

RATE %	PAYMENT $	LOAN $
7.00	207.92	10,500.00

TERM: YEARS	MONTHS	PERIODS
5		60

Prepared by Financial Publishing Company, Boston

PAYMENT NUMBER	PAYMENT ON INTEREST	PAYMENT ON PRINCIPAL	BALANCE OF LOAN
1	61.25	146.67	10,353.33
2	60.39	147.53	10,205.80
3	59.53	148.39	10,057.41
4	58.67	149.25	9,908.16
5	57.80	150.12	9,758.04
6	56.92	151.00	9,607.04
7	56.04	151.88	9,455.16
8	55.16	152.76	9,302.40
9	54.26	153.66	9,148.74
10	53.37	154.55	8,994.19
11	52.47	155.45	8,838.74
12	51.56	156.36	8,682.38
13	50.65	157.27	8,525.11
14	49.73	158.19	8,366.92
15	48.81	159.11	8,207.81
16	47.88	160.04	8,047.77
17	46.95	160.97	7,886.80
18	46.01	161.91	7,724.89
19	45.06	162.86	7,562.03
20	44.11	163.81	7,398.22
21	43.16	164.76	7,233.46
22	42.20	165.72	7,067.74
23	41.23	166.69	6,901.05
24	40.26	167.66	6,733.39
25	39.28	168.64	6,564.75
26	38.29	169.63	6,395.12
27	37.30	170.62	6,224.50
28	36.31	171.61	6,052.89
29	35.31	172.61	5,880.28
30	34.30	173.62	5,706.66
31	33.29	174.63	5,532.03
32	32.27	175.65	5,356.38
33	31.25	176.67	5,179.71
34	30.21	177.71	5,002.00
35	29.18	178.74	4,823.26
36	28.14	179.78	4,643.48
37	27.09	180.83	4,462.65
38	26.03	181.89	4,280.76
39	24.97	182.95	4,097.81
40	23.90	184.02	3,913.79
41	22.83	185.09	3,728.70
42	21.75	186.17	3,542.53
43	20.66	187.26	3,355.27
44	19.57	188.35	3,166.92
45	18.47	189.45	2,977.47
46	17.37	190.55	2,786.92
47	16.26	191.66	2,595.26
48	15.14	192.78	2,402.48
49	14.01	193.91	2,208.57
50	12.88	195.04	2,013.53
51	11.75	196.17	1,817.36
52	10.60	197.32	1,620.04
53	9.45	198.47	1,421.57
54	8.29	199.63	1,221.94
55	7.13	200.79	1,021.15
56	5.96	201.96	819.19
57	4.78	203.14	616.05
58	3.59	204.33	411.72
59	2.40	205.52	206.20
60	1.20	206.20	207.40*

The final payment is usually somewhat different from the regular payment, and is shown starred on the last line.

224

Amortization Schedules

Starting with the payment as shown in this book an amortization schedule can be constructed showing the allocation of each payment into interest and principal, also the balance outstanding after each payment has been made. Proceed by (1) computing the interest on the previous balance; (2) deducting this from the payment; and (3) crediting the remainder as a repayment of principal. As a specimen in the column to the left we give the amortization schedule for a loan of $10,500 at 7% payable over 5 years by monthly payments of $207.92.

Note that the final payment is usually several cents smaller than the regular payment. This is because the tabulated payment is always a fraction of a cent too large. (If, however, the payment were 1¢ less, the final payment would be slightly larger).

Amortization schedules for loans of any amount, interest rate, and term or payment may be obtained from the publisher of this booklet.

Source: Financial Publishing Company, Boston, Mass.

schedule is prepared and given to the borrower. An example of such a schedule is shown in Table 12–8. As you can see, this covers a loan of $10,500 at 7 percent for five years. The required monthly payment is $207.92, and the schedule shows each of the 60 monthly payments that must be made, indicating how much goes to interest, how much to repay principal, and what the balance of the loan is.

The rate of interest you pay affects the total cost of your home. A variation of one half of 1 percent may amount to several thousand dollars over the period of the loan, as Table 12–9 shows.

TABLE 12–9
Effect of Interest Rate on Cost of a $20,000 Loan over 25 Years

Percent	*Monthly Payment (principal and interest)*	*Total Interest (over 25 years)*
6	$129	$18,600
6.5	135	20,440
7	141	22,390
7.5	148	24,330
8	154	26,280
8.5	161	28,200
9	168	30,220
9.5	175	32,370
10	182	34,460

Source: U.S. Department of Agriculture, *Selecting and Financing a Home* (Home and Garden Bulletin No. 182, [Washington, D.C.: U.S. Government Printing Office]).

The amount of interest you pay may exceed the original loan if you spread the payments over a very long period, as Table 12–10 illustrates.

From the creditor's view point, this seems reasonable. You have borrowed and had the use of the money for a longer term, and, naturally, you must pay more interest. If, for example, you borrowed $10,000 at 7 percent for five years, your payments would be $198.02. In the next five years, you would make 60 payments of this amount: $198.02 × 60 = $11,881.20.

TABLE 12–10
Effect of Repayment Period on Cost of a $20,000 Loan at 9 Percent

Payment Period (years)	*Monthly Payment (principal and interest)*	*Total Interest*
5	$415	$ 4,910
10	253	10,400
15	203	16,490
20	180	23,160
25	168	30,220
30	161	37,820

Source: U.S. Department of Agriculture, *Selecting and Financing a Home* (Home and Garden Bulletin No. 182 [Washington, D.C.: U.S. Government Printing Office]).

This $11,881.20 would pay off the $10,000 of principal and provide $1,881.20 for interest.

If $10,000 were borrowed at 7 percent for 20 years, monthly payments would be only $77.53 each, but there would be 240 (20 × 12) of them: $77.53 × 240 = $18,607.20. After paying off the $10,000 principal, there would be $8,607.20 remaining for interest. Compare the two interest totals: $1,881.20 in the case of the five year loan and $8,607.20 in the 20 year loan; the 20 year loan costs $6,726.00 more for interest than the corresponding loan written for only five years. Now consider the 30 year maturity. If $10,000 were borrowed at 7 percent for 30 years, monthly payments would be only $66.54 each, but there would be 360 (30 ×12) of them: $66.54 × 360 = $23,954.40. Not only would you be paying $23,954.50 for a $10,000 house, but the total interest of $13,954.40 would be $12,073.20 more than if you had been able to pay off the loan in five years. The chief justification for the longer period is that it makes the monthly payments small enough so that the borrower can meet his obligations. It might be difficult for the average person to make monthly payments of $198.02, whereas many persons could pay $66.54 monthly without spending more than a reasonable portion of income for payments on the house.

Thus you can see why, with the trend to the amortized mortgage and the sharp increase in the prices of houses, the tendency has been to write mortgages with longer maturities so as to bring the required monthly payment within financial reach of the average family. Formerly, the straight mortgage ran for 5 years on the average, and mortgages for more than 15 years were virtually unknown. Today, however, savings banks and savings and loan associations are making 25 and 35 year loans. With today's high real estate prices, few persons can afford the large monthly payments necessary to pay off a large mortgage in as short a period of time as 5 or 10 years.

Down Payment

The larger the down payment, the lower the interest cost will be, as Table 12–11 indicates. For example, in the purchase of a $20,000 house, if the down payment is only $3,000 and a $17,000 mortgage loan is obtained at 9 percent for a 30 year period, the total interest cost amounts to $32,244. If, however, you can raise an additional $4,000 for a down payment, bringing the total down payment to $7,000 and the mortgage loan is held to $13,000, then the interest cost for the same 30 year, 9 percent loan amounts to $24,659, and you save $7,585 in interest charges.

TABLE 12–11
Purchase of $20,000 Home and Interest Paid for Various Amounts Borrowed at 9 Percent

Down Payment	*Mortgage Amount Borrowed*	*Monthly Payment*		*Total Interest Paid*	
		For 20 Years	*For 30 Years*	*Over 20 Years*	*Over 30 Years*
$3,000	$17,000	$152.96	$136.79	$19,710	$32,244
$4,000	16,000	143.96	128.74	18,550	30,346
$5,000	15,000	134.96	120.70	17,390	28,452
$6,000	14,000	125.97	112.65	16,232	26,554
$7,000	13,000	116.97	104.61	15,072	24,659

But it is foolish to make such a large down payment in cash that there is little or nothing left in the bank with which to meet emergencies. Temporary unemployment, sickness, need to replace a leaking roof, sudden breakdown of the heating system, and other possibilities too numerous to mention make it very desirable to have an emergency fund of several hundred dollars in the bank. If your mortgage payments are not met on time, the loan is in default; after a few months of default (generally about three or four), the lending institution, under the terms of the mortgage contract, has the right to begin proceedings (foreclosure) to sell the property and apply the proceeds from the sale (cash received) to the debt. Unless you have the wherewithal to keep up your mortgage payments, you may lose your home. While worrying about your inability to meet mortgage payments, you will (in the absence of ready cash) also be worrying about where food and other necessities are to be obtained. If a reasonable down payment cannot be made without leaving the family stripped of adequate reserves for the unexpected, it is doubtless better to defer acquiring a home until more money has been saved.

A very different approach suggests that since inflation reduces the real cost of repayment, it would be wise to borrow as much as possible and make a minimum down payment. The bigger mortgage can be paid off with dollars that will have less purchasing power then than they do now. Then, too, having a mortgage that can be transferred to another buyer later at a lower rate than the prospective buyer can obtain new mortgage money may make selling easier.

Taking Over a Mortgage. A real bargain would be to find the perfect house with an old VA loan of 6.5 percent for which the present owner had made a very small down payment, and on which he wants repayment of his down payment and mortgage payments to date plus a fair profit. Since the VA will allow transfer of the loan to you as the new owner if your credit is good, you will have managed a big saving. You and the seller will also be able to avoid several closing costs, for example, placement fee of 1 percent, survey costs, document fees (for you); prepayment penalty and points (for him).

An owner who has an FHA insured mortgage on his home can sell the home or trade it without paying off the insured mortgage in either of two ways. The FHA and the lender who holds the mortgage can agree to substitute the new owner's name on the mortgage, thereby releasing the old owner from his personal liability. The original owner can sell without the consent of the FHA and the lender, but will still be liable for the mortgage. An FHA mortgaged house usually has a low down payment and so, if it has a lower mortgage rate, it too is a big buy—but like the similar VA example, harder to find than property covered by a conventional mortgage (neither FHA nor VA).

A conventional mortgage can be assumed without requiring the lender's consent, but it leaves the seller of the house still liable to the original lender if the buyer fails to meet the mortgage payments. Under these circumstances, the seller must take all careful precautions to be sure the buyer who assumes the mortgage is financially responsible.

The Purchase Contract

When you have selected the house, given some thought to the financing, and decided to buy, the builder or seller will usually require a cash deposit as evidence that you really intend to go through with the deal. Make certain when you hand over the deposit that you get a signed agreement from the seller providing for a refund of your deposit if you are unable to obtain financing or if the builder or seller fails to go through with his part of the agreement. You may also expect to be requested to agree that if you fail to comply with your pledges, you will forfeit your deposit. Such clauses are customary and usual in sales agreements. Try to be sure that the person to whom you are making the payment is reliable. Some prospective purchasers have lost their deposits to persons who were dishonest or who went bankrupt.

The seller will also expect you to sign a contract of purchase. This sales contract is a legal agreement containing legal terms with which the average person is unfamiliar. Each term has specialized meaning based on tradition, court decisions, precedents that vary from state to state and not translatable by common sense interpretation. It may be called a binder —a bid, a deposit receipt, earnest money agreement, a memo, an offer to buy—but it is a contract and therefore binding in all the details of the agreement you are signing.[9] You must therefore be sure that your interests are protected because the other party to thc transaction is under no obligation to advise you as to the meaning and effect of the clauses contained therein. Since you will need a lawyer at some point in the proceedings, this is the time to consult one to be sure you are not signing future problems for yourself. If the agreement is drawn by the other side to the deal, have it carefully studied by your own attorney before your signature is appended. Once you bind yourself to the agreement, you must abide by its consequences. Before you sign anything, be sure that you know to what you are agreeing and that you are able to comply with the financial arrangements. Neither party need do anything not specified in the contract, which is subject to negotiation.

The sales contract should cover the following points:

1. The sales price should be specified in the contract. For your protection, it is usually best if the contract states that the sales price is not subject to change. Some builders' contracts contain a so called "escalator" clause which permits them to increase the price because of future cost increases. Such clauses should be avoided, but some builders may insist upon them. If they do, and you agree, you should insist upon a maximum beyond which you will not go, just to protect your financial status.

2. The sales contract will state the amount of cash payment which will be required from you and the method of financing the balance. It must state the annual percentage rate, but under the Consumer Credit Protection Act, mortgage credit for the purchase of a home need not show the total amount of the finance charge in dollars and cents. Nor are charges for credit reports and appraisal fees included in the annual percentage rate for this type of mortgage loan. However if "points" are to be paid, this must be shown. If the loan were for home improvements, not purchase, then all charges must be shown in dollars and cents. If the contract requires that you must arrange to obtain a loan for the balance due, it should provide that any cash deposit you make will be refunded to you if you cannot obtain appropriate financing.

3. The contract should require the seller to deliver the property to you on or before an agreed date, often 30 days after closing, and should set forth your right to withdraw and get your deposit back if the property is not delivered on time.

4. If you are buying a new house, it is desirable to have indicated in the contract (or by separate written agreement) what responsibility the builder will assume after you move in. You will want him to agree in

---

[9] American Bar Association, *Your Home Buyer's Guide.*

writing to correct any defects due to poor material or workmanship within a limited period after you move it, without any cost to you. If the landscaping and seeding was not completed before you took possession, you may find that you will have to do it yourself unless there is an obligation in writing to complete the work.

5. In the case of new construction, the contract should provide that the builder will complete the home in accordance with definite plans and specifications, which you should either review or have reviewed for you by an expert for a small fee. Furthermore, you should be provided with a copy of the plans and specifications for your retention.

6. You should not sign any contract containing a so called "safety" or "escape" clause which would enable the builder or seller to back out of the contract any time he wants to unless you also have similar rights. If you do sign such a paper, be sure it specifies that the builder or seller must advise you in writing on or before a definite date that he will accept or that your offer will expire and you will be free to get your money back.

7. Be sure you have protection against mechanics' liens. Have a seller agree to indemnify you for any losses due to unpaid bills for labor or materials. Unlike other purchases, the buying of a home often carries with it a liability for unpaid claims on the part of those who supplied labor or materials for the house. If the bills for labor or materials are unpaid when one takes title, craftsmen or tradesmen holding the unsatisfied bills can under certain circumstances file liens (mechanics' liens) against the house and collect from the purchaser.

8. There should be a clause protecting you against a defective title and providing for the return of the down payment or for clearing the title in case the search should prove the title to be defective.

These are just a few of the items to check. Legal documents are complicated, and your best bet will be to retain a lawyer. The small fee may save you a large loss or an unhappy experience.

Deeds and Titles

Do you know the difference between an open end and a closed mortgage; between a quitclaim and a warranty deed; between dower and curtesy; between encroachment and encumbrance; between joint tenancy and tenancy in common? Probably not! But you ought to before you buy a house!

A *deed* is a written instrument which is used for the purpose of transferring the title to real estate from one party to another. The one who transfers the title to the real property by means of the deed is called the *grantor;* the one to whom the title is transferred is called the *grantee.* There are two principal kinds of deeds: (*a*) *quitclaim deeds* and (*b*) *warranty deeds.*[10] The quitclaim deed (sometimes called a "release deed") conveys to the grantee whatever title the grantor may have had in the property and throws upon the grantee the risk as to whether there is good or bad title to the property or no title at all. A warranty deed conveys title, and, in addition, the grantor warrants that his title to the property and his right to transfer it are unencumbered and not defective. If property is transferred by a warranty deed and it is later discovered that the title was defective—that the seller did not have good title to the property—the purchaser may proceed at law to recover from the seller for breach of the warranty. However, if the seller dies, or becomes bankrupt, or leaves the area and cannot be traced, the warranty deed may be no better than the quitclaim deed. The best protection is a thorough title search and title insurance.

Naturally, when you make as large a purchase as a house (and the land on which it stands), you will want to be as sure as you can that you really own it, that no one with a prior, unsettled claim will come along and dispute your title. This quest for certainty has, therefore, led people to want something more than the deed. By and large, it only conveys whatever title the seller had to the property. He believes and says he had an unimpaired title. But to try and make sure, prudent and cautious people have devised four techniques for checking the safety of their titles.

1. The first method used is the *abstract.* This involves having someone, usually a lawyer or a title guarantee company, trace and write up the history of the ownership of the property. The resulting legal document, the abstract, indicates if there are any liens or claims still outstanding, and if so, states just what they are. All legal transactions, deeds, mortgages, sales and so on, which involved the property in the past are recorded in the abstract, which may therefore be quite lengthy. It does *not* evidence or guarantee title, but if the search has been careful and thorough and no unsettled claims appear, it provides reassurance.

2. A *certificate of title* may be used in some areas in place of the ab-

---

[10] There are also *special warranty deeds and deeds of bargain and sale.* In the former case, the grantor simply warrants that he did not at any time in the past execute any deed or mortgage or place an encumbrance on the property, not mentioned in the present deed. The warranty and liability extends only to this, therefore, and if it later develops that some prior owner had granted some claim and had not transferred a clear title, the grantor of the special warranty deed cannot be held liable. In the bargain and sale deed the consideration for which the property is transferred is recited and one or more warranties may also be explicitly stated. If such is the case, the bargain and sale deed falls midway between the quitclaim and the warranty deeds. If not, the bargain and sale deed resembles a quitclaim deed. It is best to demand and get a regular warranty deed. If the seller does not want to grant it, then don't buy!

stract. It is merely a certification by an attorney that he has examined all records affecting the property and that in his opinion there appear to be no unsettled or prior liens or claims. Thus he is in effect certifying that in his opinion the purchaser is receiving a valid title. But he is not guaranteeing this and if his search has been made with due care, the attorney cannot be held liable if in fact some obscure claim does arise to impair title.

3. The *Torrens certificate*[11] is one issued by a governmental unit evidencing and registering title to real property. In the United States it is used mainly in large cities. It is a safer and faster method than either the abstract or certificate of title, since an official recorder or registrar issues a certificate stating ownership after all those who could possibly have a claim or lien are notified and invited to sue. If no suit develops, as is usually the case, then a court orders the registrar to record the title in the new owner's name and issue a certificate to this effect.

4. There is *title insurance*. A title guarantee company searches the records and having established to its own satisfaction that a clear title is being transferred, writes a policy in favor of the new owner, for a fee, insuring him against any loss from the possibility of defects in the title, other than those which may be stated in the policy. If a lawsuit should arise, the title company will defend for the owner and pay the expenses and costs involved. While title insurance is now found mainly in the larger cities, its use is growing.

As protection, therefore, from a defective title, the prospective purchaser should always have the title searched either by a competent lawyer or by a title guarantee company. If he is borrowing to finance the purchase, the lender may insist on this and will, in addition, take out title insurance up to the amount of the loan for protection. The purchaser, too, will find it a good idea to buy title insurance covering not the amount of the loan but the full cost of the house, in order to protect his equity in the property. Title insurance taken by the lender protects only the lender. It does not protect the equity of the borrower-owner.

It is customary to have deeds and mortgages recorded in the registry in some public office, such as a county courthouse. Failure to do so may result in a later recorded deed or mortgage taking precedence over an earlier unrecorded deed or mortgage. The theory is that the public is

---

[11] The so called "Torrens system" of registering titles to land is in force in some of our states. Under this system, one who wishes to have his title to land registered may have the title examined by an official examiner of titles. If this examiner finds that the title is valid he issues a certificate of title. All later transfers of the property are noted on this certificate and in later transactions affecting the property search, back of this registration, need not be undertaken.

entitled to rely on the status of titles as revealed by the public records. Thus the seller's title, and that of those who sold to him, can be examined and traced back to insure that the present purchaser is receiving a valid, nondefective title.

Title to real property may be held by one person alone or by two or more persons together. If it is held by one person, it is said to be an *estate in severalty*. Persons holding real property jointly may have taken title as *joint tenants* or as *tenants in common*. Under the common law, if two or more persons took title to real property together under the same instrument, it was interpreted to be joint tenancy, the principal feature of which was that if one of the joint tenants died the survivor took the whole property, and nothing passed to the heirs of the deceased joint tenant. Most states have now superseded the common law by statutes which provide for *joint tenancy with rights of survivorship* or *tenancy by the entirety* (limited to husbands and wives only; neither spouse can transfer any interest during their joint lives without consent of the other).[12] Both have the same essential feature as did the common law joint tenancy. If one of the joint tenants dies, the survivor takes the whole property, and no part of it passes to other legal heirs. If you are buying property jointly with your spouse and both wish to have it all fall to one on the death of the other, you may take title in this fashion. Depending on the laws of your state, it can be arranged by your lawyer at the closing, but since this may result in income, gift, or inheritance tax consequences it is important to consider the possible results in advance.

Tenancy in common is different. When two or more persons hold shares in property under separate instruments or under one instrument which shows that each has a separate or individual interest in it, there is *tenancy in common*. On the death of one of the tenants in common, his share goes to his heirs and not to the surviving tenants in common. If ownership of real property involves a corporation as one of several owners, then there must be a tenancy in common, since a corporation cannot be a joint tenant. The statutes now generally provide that all conveyances or devises to two or more persons shall be deemed to be tenancies in common unless specifically expressed to be joint tenancies, and that heirs shall receive the land as tenants in common. For wealthy persons the tax aspects of how title is taken and passed become quite important.

Even though a married man or woman owns real estate in his or her

---

[12] Neither, acting alone, can dispose of his or her interest to a third party. Tenancy by the entirety, which is a form of joint tenancy limited to husbands and wives only, is not recognized in community property states since it is not necessary. See Robert Kratovil, *Real Estate Law* (New York: Prentice-Hall, Inc., latest edition).

own right, in some states good title cannot be passed to another person without having wife or husband join in the deed to release *dower* or *curtesy*. By common law, dower is the wife's right to a life interest in one third of her husband's real property in the event of his death. Dower and curtesy (the husband's right in his deceased wife's property, providing the couple had a child, even though the child may have predeceased the mother) still exist unimpaired in some states. In most states, these rights have been much modified by statute; and if you are acquiring real property, it would be worthwhile to find out about the law in your state.

In many states a *homestead status* can be placed upon the house you buy. Under these state statutes, the property is declared to be the home of the parties and is then protected from seizure for liability for debts. The amount of property exempted under the right of homestead differs in the several states; and in the same states, more is allowed in the country than in a city. Some states fix this amount by area, some by value, and some by both. It is usually provided that a husband cannot transfer a homestead estate without his wife's consent. In many states, on the death of the husband, the widow or minor children succeed to the homestead right.

Final Settlement, or Closing the Loan

After the house is ready and financing has been arranged, the lender will set a date for "settlement" or "closing." Settlement day is the occasion when the property officially becomes yours. You will also remember it as the "paper signing" day. Among the papers you sign is the *note* or *bond* or other evidence of debt which is used in your area. This document is your promise to repay the loan with interest within a specified period of time, and it will show the repayment terms by means of an amortization schedule. Another paper you will sign is the *mortgage* or *deed of trust*, which is a conditional lien and serves as security for the note or other evidence of the debt. Most of this document is devoted to outlining the rights of the lender in enforcing payment on the debt, including the right to "foreclose the mortgage" (take over the property) should you fail to make prompt payment of interest, principal, taxes, and insurance, or neglect the property so that it is not in a good state of repair. The mortgage is recorded with the county clerk (or other proper official) in the county, town, or city in which your property is located. It remains on record there as a lien or claim against your property until the loan has been paid off.

A *title search* will have been made and you will probably have purchased a *title insurance policy* to protect you from any loss as a result of any defect in the title. You will receive a copy of this policy. A *survey* will also perhaps have been made showing the exact boundaries of your property, and you will receive a copy of this. You should also receive a copy of the bond, the mortgage, and the deed—the legal document conveying title to you. The original will probably have been sent to the proper local official for recording. Thus you should receive five documents: the *bond,* the *mortgage,* the *deed,* the *survey,* and the *title insurance policy,* as well as receipts for all payments you make. Ask for copies of all papers. Ordinarily they will be provided. Obviously, closing is a complicated business involving a number of legal documents which you have probably never seen before. Do not be afraid to ask questions about any or all of them; but even if you do ask many questions, you probably will not know or cover all the angles, and therefore it is a very good idea to have your lawyer along with you. The fee for this service will be well worth it in the reassurance and peace of mind that comes from knowing that everything is being arranged properly.

Closing costs will probably run higher than you anticipated. These are the fees which you will have to pay at the settlement for all the various documents that have been drawn and services rendered in connection with your buying the house, borrowing, and taking title. An example of average closing costs provided by a survey of banks for a $25,000 home purchase involving a $15,000 mortgage loan is as follows:

Expenses:		
Legal fees		$200.00
Recording fees		10.55
Survey		75.00
Appraisal		75.00
Mortgage and title policy fee		126.00
State mortgage tax		87.50
Total closing costs		$574.05
Funds collected for delivery to mortgagee (the bank):		
Taxes (3 months at $50.00), if due*	$150	
Interest*	30	
Hazard insurance premiums (2 months)	14	
Total other funds to be in hand at closing	$194	$194.00
Total		$768.05

* Pro rata if already paid by seller.

These closing costs are only an example. Exact costs will vary widely among the localities because of different procedures and requirements.

Approximate closing costs on purchases of houses ranging in price from $20,000 to $40,000 may run as follows:

Survey	$75–$200
Title fee	$100–$400
Mortgage tax	$110–$300
Recording fees	$10–$20
Title insurance	$125–$200
Bank's lawyer	$150–$200
Buyer's lawyer	$100–$500
Engineer	$35–$200
Advance real estate taxes Advance insurance	That amount required for the next due payment date

Closing costs as revealed in a national survey by the Department of Housing and Urban Development and the Veterans Administration average about $558.

In an attempt to limit unreasonably high settlement costs Congress passed the Real Estate Settlement Procedure Act in December 1974. This law requires advance disclosure of all settlement costs. The lender is required to provide the buyer and seller with an itemized list when the loan arrangements are made—but not later than 12 days before the closing. The measure also prohibits kickbacks from title insurance companies to lawyers or banks. While it does not mandate reduction in premiums, in theory this should result.

Escrow

Under the Real Estate Procedure Act limits were placed on escrow requirements. The buyer must have the money on hand for the equivalent of one month's real estate taxes plus water and sewerage taxes as well as a fire insurance policy covering the house. This money held in escrow by the lender is paid out when the insurance and tax bills come due. Mean-

TITLE INSURANCE

A young executive whose wife left him decided to teach her a lesson.

He put their house up for sale, persuaded a woman friend to pose as his wife and together they signed away the interest in "their" home.

Some time later, after the new owners had already moved in, the real wife showed up and demanded her rightful interest in the property. Was all lost? Were the new owners ruined?

They had bought title insurance. They turned the problem over to their insurance company, which paid the wife the money that was legally hers.

Source: Robert S. Cole, "Title Insurance Agents Gallop to Rescue Many in Distress," *New York Times*, March 14, 1971.

while most banks and lending agencies invest these funds in short term high interest bearing notes, while giving no interest to the owners of the money. Consumer groups have made the payment of interest by these financial institutions on these accounts one of their objectives.

Tax Savings for the Homeowner

The homeowner, in contrast to the renter, does have a definite tax advantage. The homeowner may deduct from adjusted gross income in computing net taxable income (*a*) interest paid on a mortgage loan, (*b*) real estate taxes, and (*c*) any casualty losses in excess of those compensated for by insurance.

Assume *A* rents an apartment and *B* owns a house, and both have the same adjusted incomes after all other deductions. In addition, however, *B* pays $370 in real estate taxes and $530 interest on a mortgage. Now assume that both *A* and *B* are in the same income tax bracket of 30 percent. *A* cannot take further deductions (and probably would elect to take the 10 percent deduction instead of itemizing), but *B* can claim another $900 in deductions ($370 + $530) which will save him $270 in income taxes (0.30 × $900).

Ordinarily, if you sell your house at a higher price than you paid for it, you will be taxed (at capital gains rates) on the profit. If you buy another house within 18 months of the sale of the old one, and the new house costs at least as much as or more than you received for the old one, you can avoid the capital gains tax on the profit from the old house. This was explained in more detail in Chapter 3. If you sell your old house and build a new one, the 18 month rule is extended. You have 24 months following the sale to build and move in. Furthermore, you can start construction 12 months before you sell. The 18 or 24 months rule where you buy or build applies only to your "principal residence." It doesn't apply to a summer house, for example. It also applies, however, when you sell and then buy a co-op apartment or a condominium apartment. If instead of realizing a profit on the sale of your old house you take a loss, you cannot deduct the loss either from other capital gains or from regular income.

If you sell your old house at a profit and don't buy another house, you can minimize your capital gains tax by adding to the original cost of the house all capital improvements put into it during your ownership. Also, you can add your initial buying costs such as attorney's fees, title search charges, and so on. Finally, you can subtract from the price received all sales costs such as attorney's fees, broker's commission, cost of advertising, "fix up" costs prior to sale, and so on.

An individual who is 65 or older is permitted to exclude from gross income any capital gain up to $20,000 of the sale price of his personal residence provided the property had been owned and used by him as his principal residence for at least five years during the eight year period preceding the sale. If the adjusted sales price is over $20,000, an election may be made to exclude part of the gain. Only one election to exclude gain may be made during the taxpayer's lifetime.

According to the Tax Foundation, Inc., every state has adopted some form of tax concession for homeowners who are 65 years or older and who have a minimum income. Federal legislation is pending. The relief takes different forms. In Connecticut where the income ceiling is $7,500, a rebate is given depending upon the income. In New York it takes the form of a 50 percent reduction in assessed valuation. In New Jersey it is a flat $160 reduction in the homeowner's property tax bill. The Bureau of the Census reports that those 65 years or older paid more than 8 percent of their incomes for real estate taxes while all other age groups paid about 4 percent. Homeowners generally paid an average of $21 in real estate taxes for every $1,000 of market value for their homes. Regional figures ranged from $29 in the Northeast to $14 in the South.

Points

Frequently, in periods of tight money, the lending institution may require you, the borrower, to pay "points." A point is 0.125 percent of interest or 1 percent of the face value of the mortgage loan. For example, if you have an 8 percent mortgage of $20,000 for 20 years, and are required to pay 4 points, the payment amounts to 4 percent × $20,000 or $800. The $800 is deducted immediately from the face value of the loan; therefore, you receive the use of only $19,200 in credit—not the full $20,000. Furthermore, your mortgage payments are actually something more than the 8 percent stated rate, since your interest costs are based on a loan of $20,000, or $800 greater than the amount you actually receive. The 4 points are equal to 0.5 percent. Each point is worth 0.125 percent of interest. The interest charged is 8.5 percent. The shorter the maturity of the mortgage, the greater is the true rate of interest in the case where points are present. The more cash you put up, the less likely you are to pay heavily in points, which can go as high as 10 or 12. The amount of points you may have to pay also depends not only on the liquidity of money in general, but also in your area, the lender involved, and the house you are buying. In some states they are forbidden on conventional loans, and although both the VA and FHA frown on points, they have been known to be merely added to the selling price by the builder or seller, and so passed on to the buyer. In fact, since VA and FHA mortgages are usually at lower rates than the conventional mortgage, they have been known to require more points. At times points are assessed against the seller, especially in the case of FHA and VA loans where it is illegal to charge the buyer points. The VA and FHA insure repayment, but they can't make a lending institution give you a loan, and as can be seen in Table 12–12, they raise rates to meet market conditions.

Difficulties exist when the usury laws in some states prohibit mortgage loans at greater than the stipulated rates. Suppose that in your state the law limits mortgage rates to 7 percent, but that free market rates are 7.5 percent. The lending institutions cannot therefore lend at equitable rates, thus, they may charge points to raise the true rate of interest that they receive. In states, such as Connecticut, for instance, where there is no

TABLE 12–12
FHA Maximum Interest Rates—Home Mortgages (Sec. 203) (historical series)

Rate (percent)	*Period*	*Rate (percent)*	*Period*
4.25	4/24/50–5/1/53	8	12/2/70–1/12/71
4.5	5/2/53–12/2/56	7.5	1/13/71–2/17/71
5	12/3/56–8/5/57	7	2/18/71–8/9/73
5.25	8/6/57–9/23/59	7.75	8/10/73–8/24/73
5.75	9/24/59–2/1/61	8.5	8/25/73–1/21/74
5.5	2/2/61–5/28/61	8.25	1/22/74–4/14/74
5.25	5/29/61–2/6/66	8.5	4/15/74–5/12/74
5.5	2/7/66–4/10/66	8.75	5/13/74–7/5/74
5.75	4/11/66–10/2/66	9	7/6/74–8/15/74
6	10/3/66–5/6/68	9.5	8/16/74–11/25/74
6.75	5/7/68–1/23/69	9	11/26/74–1/19/75
7.5	1/24/69–1/4/70	8.5	1/20/75–3/1/75
8.5	1/5/70–12/1/70	8	3/2/75 to date

maximum on mortgage rates, they can go to 9–9.5 percent, for example, and points make it even higher.

The state usury laws, varying from state to state, have ironically hurt the mortgage borrower, the very person the laws are supposed to protect. The idea behind these laws was to insure that the borrower would not have to pay very high interest rates, but when free market rates climbed sharply to 8 percent and a state law prohibited rates above 7 percent, the lending institutions might choose to stop granting mortgages, since the law restricted them from charging the current competitive rate. In this case, the prospective borrower could not obtain a mortgage, since none were available, even if he were willing to pay 8 percent, because the state would not allow him to pay it.[13] When tight money causes this situation to become general, state legislatures often raise their usury rates to make mortgage money available. Pennsylvania's new law permits the usury ceiling to be adjusted month by month.

It should be noted that points paid by a buyer can be deducted as an interest expense from income tax. The seller cannot deduct the points, but can include them in the costs when computing the profit or loss on the sale of the house. The Truth in Lending law requires that points be disclosed.

FHA Insurance

Your lender may ask you if you wish FHA insurance on your loan, or, for protection, may insist that you apply for it. Under an FHA insured mortgage, you borrow from your lending agency, and then the U.S. government, through the Federal Housing Administration, insures the lending agency against any loss of principal if you fail to meet the terms and conditions of your mortgage. Under the FHA plan, you pay an "insurance fee" of 0.5 percent, computed monthly, on the outstanding amount of the principal for the full term of your loan. This is in addition to the normal interest on your loan. You also pay an FHA "processing or application fee" when you apply for the loan. This FHA insurance fee, to which you and millions of other home buyers contribute, is used to build up a fund to take care of the losses when homeowners default on their mortgages and foreclosures become necessary. It protects the lender, not you; but you do derive some benefits from FHA insurance. The FHA will not insure loans of more than $45,000 on one family dwelling.

An advantage of an FHA insured loan is that the property is inspected carefully by an FHA appraiser; and if judged not to be worth what you expect to pay for it, you will learn this in time to avoid an unwise commitment. If you are building your own house, or if the builder from whom you expect to buy has an FHA construction loan, the FHA will supervise each step in the building of your house, and the builder or contractor will have to comply with the exacting standards of the FHA. The FHA staff will check the construction several times while it is under way to see that its specifications and conditions are met. It may thus be worth the extra 0.5 percent to be reassured that your house is being constructed properly and checked by an impartial outside agency. There is also a negative sort of benefit, in that if you did not apply for FHA insurance, your lender

[13] See David J. Brophy, "The Usury Law: A Barrier to Home Financing," *Michigan Business Review*, January, 1970, pp. 25–31.

might be forced to charge you a higher rate of interest, because of assuming the greater risk. You will note that FHA mortgage insurance plays a relatively small role in the home financing field as shown in Figure 12–7. Conventional markets offer quicker processing, lower down payments and more realistic interest rates today.

FIGURE 12–7
Number of New One Family Homes, by Type of Financing (thousands of units)

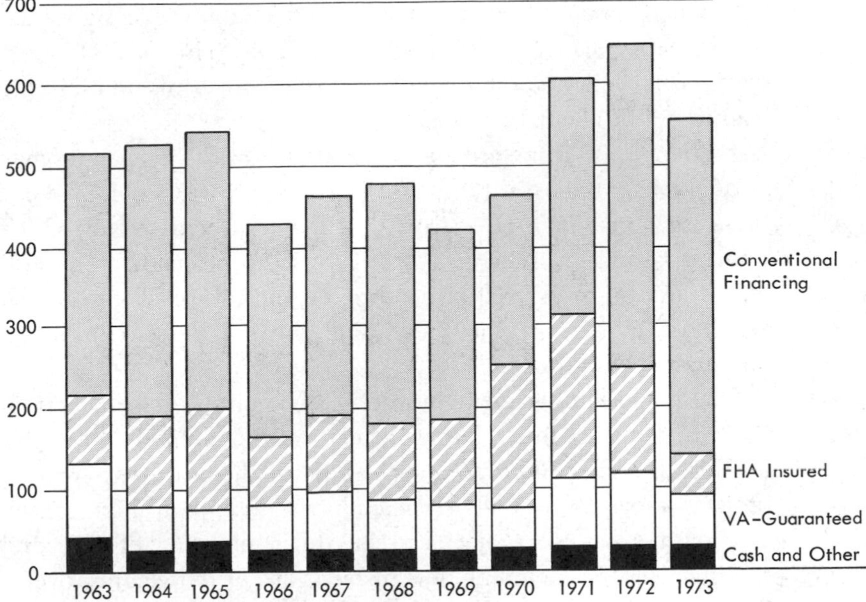

Note: Excludes homes sold with type of financing not reported.
Source: The Conference Board, "Road Maps of Industry" #1746 September 15, 1974.

FHA Insured Home Improvement Loans

Want to borrow to install air conditioning, wall to wall carpeting, or a swimming pool in the back yard? The FHA won't help you do this. But it will help if you want to add a room, or bath, or redo the porch, or roof, or put in a new heating system or septic tank. The FHA has a program for *insuring,* not making, loans for home improvements.

You can obtain FHA insured loans to enlarge your house, for new flooring, plumbing, wiring, painting, plastering, fences, driveways, sewerage, pumps, insulation, landscaping, lawn sprinkling systems, and so on. You cannot secure them for swimming pools, barbecue pits, TV antennas, tree surgery, furniture, fixtures, appliances, and the like. The purpose of the loan must be for a permanent, structural improvement.

The FHA insures your lender. For this the FHA collects a premium of 0.5 percent of the net proceeds of the loan. The insurance, by protecting the lender, helps you get the loan, because the lender is encouraged to make what is a virtually riskless loan. You can, of course, obtain a non-FHA insured home improvement loan from various commercial lenders, but it will cost you more, because the lender is taking the whole risk.

The FHA Title I loans are for a maximum of $10,000 with annual percentage rate varying from 8.83 percent to 10.57 percent depending on the amount and term of the loan. They require no cosigner and rarely more security than your signature on the note. The maximum maturity is seven years. The rate on a similar conventional bank home improvement loan would be about 12 percent.

Section 203K loans are for a maximum of 20 years and may be for normal rehabilitation if the house is at least 10 years old. If not that old, these loans may be used to correct a major structural fault or repair the result of a disaster, such as a fire. Loans can be made from $12,000 per family unit up to $17,400, depending on the cost levels in the area. Rates are those current in the area, plus the 0.5 percent FHA insurance premium.

The home improvement business is booming—20 percent more spent this year than last to modernize or expand the family home. A trade publication, *Building Supply News,* estimates there are two modernization projects every year for each of the country's 40 million single family homes. The most expensive project can be the remodeling of the kitchen, averaging $965 and including new installations of refrigerator, oven, lighting fixtures, and floor covering. Significant savings result when the do-it-yourselfer contributes what has become known as "sweat equity." A survey based on written response to a questionnaire conducted by National Family Opinion, Inc. of Toledo and the Bureau of Building Marketing Research found that more than 900,000 families add rooms to their homes each year. Converting basement space to rooms was about $500 cheaper per room than attic space, and so five times more were converted.

Why the boom? In a time of scarce costly mortgages and rising home prices and hesitancy as to what to do, home remodeling becomes a solution. Lenders are willing to make remodeling loans because they yield more (12–15 percent per 5–10 years) than a mortgage loan. You can borrow up to 90 percent of your equity. Experts suggest plans with an eye directed toward adding to the future sales value of your house. "Your remodeling dollar comes back 100 percent on resale if it is spent on adding new space to the house, 75 percent if you modernize existing rooms, and 50 percent if you add fancy luxuries such as patios and pools."

Some remodeling jobs "creating new living space in an attic can even bring a $2 for $1 return if the new rooms are big and well finished." Warning is given against "overbuilding" in a house that is surrounded by others less costly if resale is a primary goal.[14]

A decision on financing method depends on a number of factors, some of the most important being the kind and amount of indebtedness already existing on the property, the borrower's own financial condition, and the type and extent of improvements to be made. Sometimes, however, depending on circumstances, it might be more advantageous to refinance and include the cost of the improvements in a new mortgage.

When you use your home as security in financing a home improvement job, the lender must provide you with the proper forms and notice of your right to cancel without obligation within three business days. The contractor, if payment is allowed in more than four installments, must wait until three days have passed before beginning work unless you, by letter or wire (no telephone call) waive your right, due to an emergency. The purpose of this section of the Truth in Lending law is the protection of your home against high pressure or unscrupulous dealers who trick you into agreements that you would like to void after some thought.[15]

The FHA regional office has on file a list of companies and individuals who are thought to have done unsatisfactory work on jobs financed by FHA, and while the FHA will not spell out details, this list is available for inspection.

Death, Mortgages, and Insurance

Will you live to pay off the 20 year mortgage on your home? One out of four homeowners aged 40 will not. One out of ten aged 25 will not. One out of six aged 35 will not. But statistics do not really matter when *you* are the one. What will happen to your family if you die prematurely and there is an unpaid mortgage? In a way, a mortgage is a one sided contract. It protects the lender and the investment in every possible way. For this protection the lender has:

---

[14] Personal Business Supplement, *Business Week* "Instead of Buying, Home Remodeling," July 20, 1974 pp. 89–97.

[15] See *Home Improvements*, No. 5 in the Series "Your Money's Worth," published by the Better Business Bureau of Dallas. For a copy write them at 106 Elm Street, Dallas, Tex. 75201 for the latest edition.

1. A mortgage on your home.
2. A bond signed by you and your wife.
3. A fire insurance policy.
4. A title insurance policy.
5. Monthly payments from your income.

But unless you tie your insurance program to your mortgage, you have no protection against death or adversity, such as unemployment or financial reverses. The leading insurance companies have all developed plans which, by the use of decreasing term insurance (on top of ordinary life) over the life of the mortgage, matching the decreasing principal owed, guarantee your family the home free and clear of debt if you should die. In addition, they provide a reserve fund that you can draw upon if financial reverses hit during your lifetime and threaten your ownership of the house. Any good insurance agent will explain what one company calls its "assured home ownership plan." It is a sound idea and well worth investigating when you buy a home and obtain a mortgage loan. FHA insurance is designed primarily to protect the lending institution. Mortgage redemption insurance protects the widow.

POLICY LIFTS MORTGAGE

DENVER, Nov. 6 (AP)—A widow paid off a $9,000 mortgage on her home at a cost of $9.46.

Her husband, George Smart, 31, applied for life insurance to pay the mortgage last Saturday. He had passed the necessary physical examination the day before. He died Sunday.

Courtesy New York Post

Do You Want to Sell?

As the seller you pay the brokerage commission—usually 6 percent of the price. In return you get a number of services. There are several kinds of agreements to be made with brokers.

Sole Contract. Just one broker has the right to work on selling the house. But if the owner sells it, the broker gets no commission.

Exclusive Right to Sell. Same as above, except that the broker gets a commission even if you sell the house. Both types have very limited exposure to possible buyers.

Open Listing. You simply have as many brokers as you wish list your house. But who will bother—if he has no special advantage?

Multiple Listing. All local brokers included in the listing can handle the house. Brokers in other areas may forward customers. You can deal with one broker, but have the selling efforts of all.

The Co-op

The purchaser of a cooperative apartment buys an interest in a non-profit corporation which will own and run the buildings that form the cooperative. In this sense the owner of a co-op apartment is a landlord, but in his responsibility to the board of directors of the co-op, he is also a tenant.

A member of the cooperative does not directly own his apartment. He owns a membership certificate which carries the right to occupy his apartment and participate in its management as a member of the board or as a voter. Mortgage charges, real estate taxes, cost of maintenance, repairs, replacements and administration are budgeted annually and divided among the owners in proportion to the number of shares equal to the value of the apartment, and are payable by each owner. The sale of an apartment is done by the transfer of shares in the corporation. Anyone who is approved by the co-op board can buy shares. The sale of the unit—if at a profit—is subject to a capital gains tax. The cooperative has a blanket mortgage. When buying into a co-op it is important to see if it is held by a reputable institution, to check its rate of amortization or its time for refinancing. If the latter comes too soon, and in a period of rising interest rates, it would mean higher maintenance costs for you.

Co-op versus Leasing. Carrying charges for a co-op may be lower than the rental prices for a similar apartment. Also, the co-op owner has income tax benefits because of his share in real estate. He may deduct his share of the interest on the co-op's mortgage, his share of the real estate taxes the co-op pays.

The tenant has the advantage of using his capital in any investment venture, since it is not frozen into the cost of the apartment. He need not worry about the sale of his apartment in the future, nor whether he can recoup his investment. While he knows his rent may go up, he does not have to share increased maintenance costs with other co-op owners if there is a high vacancy rate, unexpected repair expense, or increased fixed maintenance charges.

The co-op buyer should check whether the maintenance budget includes adequate reserves for major repairs or replacements. He should compare the total cost and valuation of the prospective co-op building with those of similar buildings in the same or comparable neighborhoods.

Even after he carefully and deliberately buys in a co-op where the major part of his maintenance fee would include mortgage interest and amortization charges, he will soon find, if current trends continue, that his costs will grow faster proportionately as fixed expenses rise sharply through increased fuel costs, payroll pacts, inflation-affected repair costs—and even an increased assessed valuation of property for rising real estate taxes. Not only are there a limited number of moneyed buyers around but today's higher costs and interest rates necessitate financing increasingly when purchasing cooperatives. New banking laws in some states, for example, now permit both savings and commercial banks to offer housing type loans using co-op shares as security, instead of the personal loans at short term and high interest rates which were the only possibility before. Some states allow financing up to 75 percent of the purchase price for a maximum term of 20 years to be repaid in equal installments of principal and interest. Frequently prepayment without penalty is allowed. The regulations are better than no loan but mortgage loans on a house are far more favorable.

Co-op or Condominium?

The condominium is closer to true ownership. The purchaser actually gets a deed to his own apartment, plus an undivided share in the halls, elevators, heating equipment, and other common facilities. Condominium housing is not the same as cooperative housing. The chief differences between the two are:

1. In condominiums, individuals take title to their units; in cooperatives, an individual has a stock ownership in the cooperative and the right of occupancy to a specific unit.

2. In condominiums, individuals vote on a proportionate basis; in cooperatives, each individual has one vote regardless of the size of his unit.

3. In condominiums, individuals are taxed separately on their units; in cooperatives, individuals pay their share of taxes on the project in their monthly carrying charges.

4. In condominiums, individuals are responsible only for mortgage indebtedness and taxes involving their own property and their proportionate share of the expenses of operating the common property, and have no mortgage indebtedness, tax, or other liability for the other properties; in cooperatives, each individual is dependent upon the solvency of the entire project.

5. The condominium owner can sell his apartment to anyone else—

more freely than the co-op owner, who is bound by the need to have the purchaser approved by the board of directors. A prospective purchaser of a co-op must assume the seller's pro rata share of the unpaid indebtedness under the blanket mortgage. Therefore, a co-op seller must find a buyer with enough cash. The would-be purchaser of the condominium, on the other hand, can mortgage his unit to finance his purchase—like any other home buyer.

The FHA has been authorized to provide mortgage insurance—under the National Housing Act of 1961—for condominiums which provide ownership of apartments in multiple dwellings.

Some insurance companies provide insurance tailored especially for condominium owners. If fire or accident occurs on the common property of the condominium each unit owner is liable for damage and assessed accordingly. A common practice of renting out the condominium during the owner's absence requires a special type of coverage against loss or damage.

The condominium apartment is treated like a separate parcel of real estate—even separately assessed and taxed. In the cooperative apartment, if an owner does not pay his share of the maintenance charges, they must eventually be distributed among the other owners. But this is not the case in the condominium.

If a stockholder-tenant (cooperative) violates the terms of agreement (lease), he may be dispossessed in the same manner as a defaulting tenant (renter). The condominium owner cannot, in absence of special statutory authorization, be ousted from possession for infraction of the bylaws or regulations.

One experienced condominium owner notes that while it is true that the owner of a condominium unit is legally free to sell his apartment to whomever he chooses, actually he is apt to accept a stipulation in the Articles of Condominium that any new owner be acceptable to the board and that the condominium association will have the prior right to purchase at the market price. "Most owners," he says, "are willing to accept this because it means the characteristics which made the complex suitable for him in the first place, will not be drastically changed."

Condominiums as well as co-ops run the whole gamut from luxury to lower cost. Speculation and high profits create a special danger for each to the prospective homeowner. In the co-op area, profit hungry owners of rental property may push co-opting upon tenants and unload property at self serving sales prices and management contracts which prove to be expensive to the new co-op association. For the individual owner it may mean higher maintenance costs to pay the resultant high mortgage debt the association faces. It may also mean long delay in occupying an apartment paid for, if a reluctant tenant occupant won't move without court action. In many states new regulations increase the percentage of tenants' approval required before co-opting can take place. This is a protection for both current tenants and future owners.

The future condominium owner faces a different possible risk. Overexpansion in building as well as speculative buying and selling of units under construction, during a seemingly booming market, may not only increase prices but also lead to foreclosure. It is possible that the investor who puts down 10 percent on a condominium unit under construction will lose the deposit if the project folds.

Other special condominium risks to the prospective buyer result from large areas of nonexistent consumer protection provisions. The expectation is that half the population will live in condominiums within 20 years. Fifty-seven percent of new housing in Cleveland, Ohio, 83 percent in Bridgeport, Connecticut, and 45 percent in Milwaukee, Wisconsin, is condominium housing. This rush to condominium living has bared many problems—lack of state regulation and possible conflicting or minimal regulation among several federal agencies.[16] In 1974, however, the state of Florida, long a condo mecca, after two years of public hearings and commission study, passed a comprehensive condominium regulation law tightening the reins on developers in an effort to eliminate the various abuses which had been observed. For example, developer control of common areas and recreational facilities was made much more difficult to achieve. Also the developer's ability to dominate the condominium association was curbed. Buyers are given 15 days in which they may cancel a contract for the purchase of a condo unit.

A major source of trouble comes from builders retaining title to common parking and recreational facilities and charging exorbitant fees for their use. If the condominium owner fails to pay, the developer can foreclose on his unit. Sometimes title to the land is kept and leased back to the buyers for 99 years. Builders warranties, usually a year in length, often run out before the last owner moves in.

Condominium boards may discover that they have to cope with a costly long term management agreement built in by the developer. The ads promise "Carefree Condominium Living." But as some one said, "its true, the developer doesn't care, and nobody else cares either."

---

[16] In an effort to guide buyers, a booklet "Questions About a Condominium—What to Ask Before You Buy," has been published by HUD and may be obtained by writing the Office of Public Affairs; Department of Housing and Urban Development, Washington, D.C. 20410. See also "Condominium Crack Down," *Barron's*, April 14, 1975.

If you are a typical condo buyer you probably rented before buying and belong to one of two distinct age groups. The first group are between 45 and 64 years old, have grown families and are seeking a smaller home. The second age group—25 to 34 are most likely young professionals—either single or two person households.

When You Buy—A Baker's Dozen

1. Check on the reputation of the builder.
2. Make sure you know what you are buying and what you are responsible for.
3. Read all the legal documents—with the aid of a lawyer.
4. Find out if the developer is retaining the right to manage the project and whether residents can fire him.
5. Make sure the management fee includes everything, so you don't face unexpected assessments for use of common and recreational facilities.
6. If the developer promises "maintenance free living," is this exterior or interior?
7. What kind of warranty do you have on all equipment?
8. Don't allow your deposit to be co-mingled with the developer's funds. They should be held in escrow.
9. Read the operating budget. It should clearly spell out assessments and services.
10. Check the estimated real estate taxes.
11. What are the restrictions on the resale of your unit?—or leasing?
12. Has the developed provided reserve funds to correct construction flaws after the buyer moves in?
13. Who pays maintenance costs for unsold units? You don't want to.

Mobile Homes

The most common type mobile home is the single unit 12 feet wide by 65 feet long. There are "expandables" which telescope inside the home during highway movement and at the homeside can add 60 to 100 square feet to a room. There are double wide units with 28 foot living rooms. The current average price is $8.50 per square foot, including furnishings and appliances. The average new mobile home costs from $7,800 to $11,000 nationally, with an average resale value of $5,000. There are extremes, though, especially in California, Florida, and Arizona where you can find five star rated mobile parks and mobile homes whose facades, landscaping, and furnishings cost as much as $78,125. Four out of five mobiles have become "immobile mobiles" and are being treated like permanent housing. Park space can be rented or purchased. Rents in luxury Western parks run from $95 to $225 a month compared to Eastern rentals of $80 to $120 a month. When you examine the average price for a mobile home, the growth of the industry from 103,700 in 1960 to almost 600,000 today, is understandable (see Figure 12–8). The mobile homes cater to both ends of the housing market—95 percent are in the below $5,000 sector and the remainder is super luxury. Many mobile home manufacturers have gone into mobile park development to insure a place for their products.

Extras to Buy. Although furniture, drapes, carpeting are included in the purchase price, the extras to buy are frequently required by mobile home communities. These may include steps with handrails for the outside door, skirting to conceal the wheels, supports or piers to provide a foundation.

Standards and Improvements. More than 75 percent of the mobile homes produced today are built to established national standards. They were developed by the American National Standards Institute (ANSI) for mobile homes.[17] However there have been criticisms of high fire risk and lack of state and federal supervision.

Financing. The VA may guarantee or make direct loans to finance mobile home purchases up to a maximum of $10,000 for a mobile home and up to $17,000 where a lot is also purchased for the home. The GI can later use the loan benefits to purchase a conventional home once the mobile home loan is paid off. The purchase price for a mobile home is much lower than for a house, but an additional cost of renting ground in one of the 22,000 mobile parks must be considered. Financing was formerly more like car insurance—a shorter term, higher rate of interest, no amortization, and a fairly fast depreciation. The FHA also can insure mobile home loans up to $10,000 and for as long as 12 years. Comparative rates are shown in Table 12–13.

If the mobile home is made up of two or more modules, the loan limit rises to $15,000 and can last for 15 years. Minimum down payment is 5 percent of the first $6,000. The maximum annual percentage rate of the finance charge ranges from 7.97 percent to 10.57 percent, depending on the amount and term of the loan. Payments must be in equal monthly installments. An FHA Title I loan is applicable on a mobile home only if it is the borrowers' principal residence and not a summer home. It must be on a site that meets FHA requirements.

---

[17] *Buying and Financing a Mobile Home,* HUD Publication No. 243, U.S. Government Printing Office, September 1973.

FIGURE 12–8
Total Shipments of Mobile Homes, Selected Years (thousands of units)

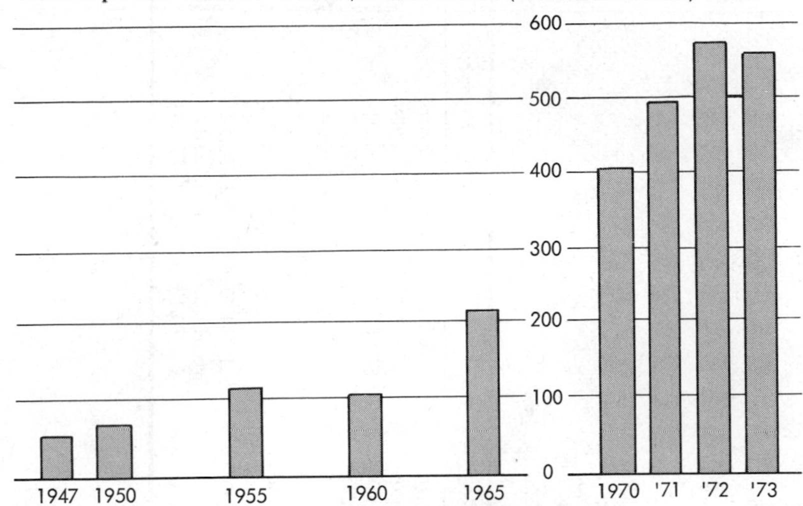

Source: The Conference Board, Road Maps of Industry #1745 September 1, 1974, "Housing Characteristics."

The mobile home buyer can expect lower charges for insurance, utilities, taxes, and maintenance, and he also has the opportunity to change his location. An experienced owner warns, however, that if you try to move a mobile home off the original site, you may have a difficult time finding another place to park it. People have often had to buy a new mobile home to gain entry into a desirable mobile home park. Also the resale values of mobile homes are low. Mobile home values usually go down like car values, say 20 percent depreciation the first year, 10 percent the second and third, and 5 percent for each of the next few years.

Town House

The very opposite in housing also has found a new appeal, the town house—called the brownstone in New York but available also in most of the older areas of other big cities—has had a revival through renovation for those who want space, prefer city living, and seek a bargain. In areas already successfully converted, there are few bargains left as prices escalate. Taxes are usually lower than in the suburbs. Most houses are so built that it is possible to create separate apartments and by renting to tenants pay off the mortgage, perhaps even live rent free. Renovation is possible by either of two extremes. An architect and a contractor supported by a goodly sum of thousands can do a beautiful job. Or as *Business Week*

TABLE 12–13
Mobile Home Loans

	Conventionally Financed		HUD-FHA Financed		
Term of Loan	*5 Years (60 months)*	*7 Years (84 months)*	*7 Years (84 months)*	*10 Years (120 months)*	*12 Years (144 months)*
Mobile home price	$5,500.00	$6,500.00	$5,000.00	$6,500.00	$ 7,500.00
Down payment	1,650.00	1,625.00	250.00	350.00	450.00
Balance to be financed	3,850.00	4,875.00	4,750.00	6,150.00	7,050.00
Interest rate	8% Add on	8% Add on	8.88%*	8.39%*	8.14%*
Equal to a simple interest rate of:	14.13%	13.69%			
Annual interest cost	308.00	390.00			
Total interest paid for entire term of loan	1,540.00	2,730.00	1,644.57	2,955.12	4,014.27
Total cost of mobile home (including down payment)	7,040.00	9,230.56	6,644.57	9,455.12	$11,514.27
Amount of monthly payments (including interest)	89.83	90.54	76.13	75.88	76.84

* Annual interest percentage rate.

suggests "More often brownstoners do as much work as they can themselves." Costs can be cut by a third, and you'll "live in the midst of the debris as you make repairs." If this is your decision, you'll probably need guidance.

Townhouses are no longer purely urban as the name would imply. The term now refers to attached houses with shared "party" walls wherever they may be. In a recent survey, for the Urban Land Institute, of residents in 49 townhouse projects on both the East and West coasts, two out of five of the owners replied they planned to stay five or more years. But 75 percent would not move to another townhouse.[18] The reasons offered were lack of privacy, noise, and monotonous development views.

Home ownership has become identified with other than the single family home. An increasing use of residential units in "cluster zoning" for better land use in suburbia has been another answer to meet the rising cost of the limited amount of land available within commuting distance from city jobs.[19] This trend toward multifamily, garden apartment house communities seems under way—especially when planned with the recreational and environmental "amenities" that compensate for the loss of privacy of individual lots. By clustering the residential units, land areas are available for tennis courts, swimming pools, and golf courses. Changing life styles has shifted emphasis to human ecology—new communities that are planned unit developments with elements of "togetherness" around the community swimming pool or neighborhood village shopping center.

Prefab Housing

Prefabricated houses used to be temporary summer homes or inexpensive, unsubstantial shelters hedged in by zoning laws and building codes. Today they are available in choice of design, range in price up to $40,000 (not including the lot), and in many areas have become acceptable. Restrictions on their use are being removed. Financing prefabs is easier today than in the past. There are still problems. To get the home erected, you frequently must employ the one local firm in the area that specializes in this type of housing, regardless of its reputation for the quality of its work and no matter which company sold you the prefab. It is also often necessary to adapt plumbing and electrical equipment to fit existing codes. But construction costs are cheaper and the time element halved, and so prefab housing has become an acceptable choice for a growing number.

---

18 Take a Fresh Look at Townhouses," *Changing Times*, August 1973 p. 35.

19 "Housing Comes Cheaper by the Fourplex," *Business Week*, October 28, 1972 p. 54.

Conclusion

The projections indicate a stable population growth for adults age 20–39 (the home making stage) in the next decade. Some prophets envision a life style geared to townhouses and recreational activity, others hope that the problems of little credit and high cost will vanish so that the dreams of

FIGURE 12–9
Growing Up in the 1970s—Net Population Change by Age Group

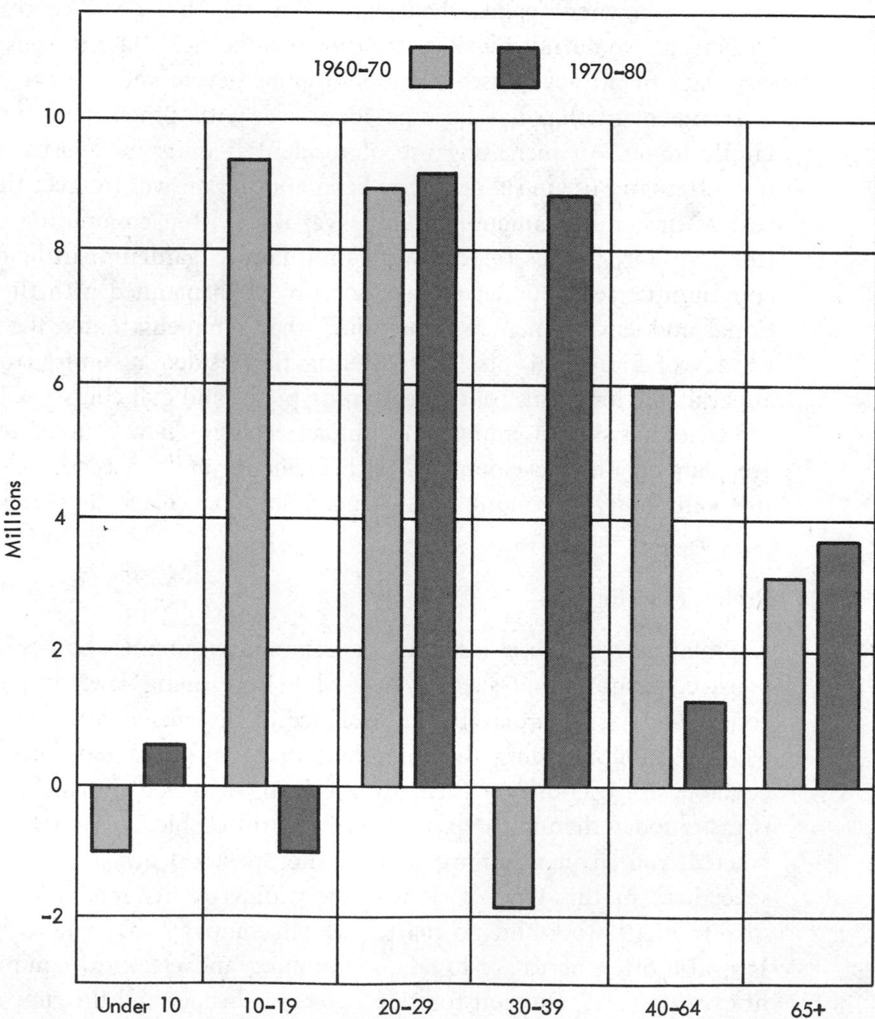

There will be fewer teen-agers by 1980, but about 9 million more Americans in their twenties and another 9 million in their thirties. Comparatively few people were in their thirties—the peak home buying ages—in the past decade.

Source: Lawrence A. Mayer, "New Questions About the U.S. Population," *Fortune*, February, 1971. Courtesy of *Fortune Magazine*.

one family housing can again be realized. There is talk of a revolution in housing happening imperceptibly in that the realism of costs have made the one family home obsolete. Whatever the manner, the increased numbers shown in Figure 12–9 will have to be housed.

SUGGESTED READINGS

1. *Real Estate Review:*
   George Cline Smith, "Housing in the Seventies—Realism vs. Euphoria," Spring 1971.
   John A. Stastny, "Homebuilding in the Seventies," Spring 1971.
   Richard L. Ragatz, "The Expanding Market for Vacation Homes," Summer 1973.
   Emmanuel B. Halper, "People and Property—Looking Out for the Homebuyer," Summer 1973.
   Harold A. Davidson, "The Future of the Mobile Home Market," Winter 1974.
   Arthur H. Hartwig, "Quiet Revolution in Mobile Home Financing," Winter 1974.
2. *Changing Times, The Kiplinger Magazine:*
   "Buy a House or Rent? A Fresh Look at the Options," April 1975.
   "How to Pick a Really Good Mobile Home," March 1975.
   "Do Home Improvements Pay Off?" December 1974.
   "Facts You Should Know about the New 'Flexible Mortgages,'" July 1974.
   "The Legal Side of Owning a House," July 1973.
   "What's Happening to the Cost of Building a House," June 1973.
   "How to Buy a House in Five Easy Steps," February 1973.
   "Should a Single Person Buy a House," January 1973.
   "A Mobile Home vs. a House—How the Costs Compare," January 1971.
3. *Money:*
   Avery Comarow, "Ins and Outs of Inspecting a House," July 1973.
   Carol Moore, "You Can Fix Up An Old House But Is It Worth It?" November 1974.
   William B. Mead, "Mortgages: The Unreal Crisis in Real Estate," December 1974.
4. "Why it costs so much to sell a house?" *Forbes*, October 15, 1972.
5. Federal Publications on Consumer Information Index available on order from Public Documents Distribution Center, Pueblo, Colorado 81009.
   "Closing Costs 1973" 4 pp. 146B—free.
   "Cooperatives vs Condominiums 1973"—4 pp. 148B—free.

6. R. W. Semenow, "Buying or Selling a House; Pitfalls to Watch For," *U.S. News and World Report*, May 7, 1973.
7. Daniel R. Fredland, *Residential Mobility and Home Purchase*, Lexington, Mass.: Lexington Books 1974, D. C. Heath.
8. James N. Karr, *The Condominium Buyer's Guide*. Frederick Fell Publishers, New York 1973.
9. "Home-Buyer's Checklist" published by the National Homebuyers and Homeowners Association—a non-profit public interest organization—Pamphlet $1—from the association, 1225 19th Street N.W.—Washington, D.C. 20036. 1974.
10. *A Place to Live—Housing Policy in the States*, Council of State Governments, Lexington, Kentucky, 1974.
11. "House Construction—How to reduce costs," U.S. Dept. of Agriculture, *Home & Garden Bulletin* no. 168, 1973.
12. "Financing the Nation's Housing Needs," Committee for Economic Development, April 1973.
13. "13 Million Families are Held Housing-Deprived," Joint Center for Urban Studies of MIT and Harvard, December 1973.
14. "Don Quixote Rides Again," *Forbes*, August 1, 1974. (on condominiums).
15. Melvin Mencher, "*The Fannie Mae Guide to Buying, Financing and Selling Your Home*. New York: Doubleday & Co. 1973.
16. Betsy & Hubbard Cobb, *Vacation Houses*. New York: Dial Press, 1973.
17. Peter Hellman, "A New Way to Buy a Co-op," *New York Magazine*, January 24, 1972.
18. "Condominium Crack Down," *Barron's*, April 14, 1975. See also Stephen L. Williams, "The Great Condominium Ripoff," Research Publications, Boston, 1975.
19. "Financing for Home Purchases and Home Improvements—A Guide to Financing Costs and Home Buying Ability," Federal Housing Administration, Washington, D.C., latest edition. A free copy may be obtained by writing to the Office of Public Information of the FHA.
20. Arthur M. Watkins, *How Much House Can You Afford?* New York. New York Life Insurance Company, latest edition. A free copy may be obtained by writing to the company at Box 10, Madison Square Station, New York, N.Y. 10010.
21. Center for Auto Safety, "Mobile Homes, The Low Cost Housing Hoax," New York: Grossman Publishers, 1975.

CASE PROBLEMS

1. Ellen and John are both graduating college in June. They are to be married the day after commencement. They have both been offered positions in

Chicago. He will be earning $165 a week. She will be earning $130 a week. They have surveyed housing possibilities and have narrowed down their choices to two alternatives. They can rent a three room apartment in the heart of town for $325 a month. They can buy a new five room house in a suburban development for $26,160 ($10,000 down, 8.5 percent, 30 year mortgage for balance). Which would you choose? Why?

2. Ring earns $12,000 a year. He has a wife and two children (ages 2 and 4). Since he and his wife are good savers, they already have $8,000 in the bank. They decide to buy a $25,000 home ($9,000 down). The bank informs them that they may borrow $16,000 for 10 years at 8 percent or for 20 years at 8.5 percent. Ring and his wife do not like having a debt hanging over their heads, and they naturally prefer the lower interest rate; so they are inclined to borrow for 10 years at 8 percent. Are they wise?

3. Martin earns $450 a month. He is paying $140 rent. He can buy a suitable home for $17,500, of which he can borrow $12,000 on a 20 year mortgage at 8 percent. This, he figures, is cheaper than renting. What do you think?

4. Rollins borrowed $7,500 on his $18,000 home from the local savings and loan association. A fire caused $2,000 damage to the property, which sum the insurance company paid to the association. Rollins wants to repair the property, but he has no money. Can anything be done?

5. Jane and William Carleton have been married three years. The birth of their daughter, Linda (now 7 months), made them decide to give up living in an apartment in town and instead buy a house in the suburbs. They have decided on a $25,000 house. In shopping for financing they have received the following offers:

a. $8,000 down, $17,000 mortgage at 8.5 percent for 30 years.
b. $8,000 down, $17,000 mortgage at 8.5 percent for 25 years.
c. $5,000 down, $20,000 mortgage at 8 plus 0.5 percent FHA insurance fee, for 25 years.
d. $8,000 down, $17,000 mortgage at 8.5 percent for 20 years.

Which should they choose? Why?

6. Martha and Sam Winkler decide to buy a $35,000 house. They are offered the following financing possibilities:

a. $5,000 down, $30,000 mortgage for 30 years at 9 percent.
b. $10,000 down, $25,000 mortgage for 30 years at 9 percent.
c. $15,000 down, $20,000 mortgage for 30 years at 9 percent.
d. $17,500 down, $17,500 mortgage for 20 years at 9 percent.

Assuming they have the savings to make up to a $20,000 down payment what should they do? Why?

7. In the town of X, the only lawyer, young and inexperienced, gave an

opinion that the title to the home Young is buying from Bright is good and is in Bright's name, but Young hates to trust the lawyer's opinion entirely in the matter of this $40,000 deal. What can Young do?

8. Ralph and Ethel Gould are 28 and 26 years of age. They live in Minnesota. A 10 room house, 30 years old, which they like, comes to their attention. It is common knowledge that houses cost $3,000 a room to build in their town, and ordinary rooms are nowhere near as large as the rooms in the house in question. They feel that they have an opportunity to make a very attractive purchase for $25,000. Since the price is reasonable why do they hesitate?

9. Raymond and Ruth Wilkes have three children (ages 2, 5, and 7). Raymond is a lawyer earning $18,000 net a year. They have been living in a house which was rented to them for $225 a month, but this house has been sold and they must move. In their town, properties for sale are hard to find. One that is available has four bedrooms, is 30 years old, and is being offered for $25,000. A new house large enough for the family would cost at least $34,000. No rental property is vacant. Outside of $20,000 of straight life insurance which Raymond has carried, the family has been able to do little saving. What should they do?

10. Jane and Frank Prince have been married three years. He earns $140 a week; she earns $100. They have saved enough money to buy furniture for five rooms, and they have $2,600 in the bank. Recently they have become interested in buying a home. They discovered a Cope Cod cottage which is three years old, in good condition, and whose price seems right ($20,000). It can be bought for $8,000 down on a 20 year mortgage at 8 percent. What would you advise them and why?

13

Introduction to Investments

A bull can make money in Wall Street; a bear can make money in Wall Street; but a hog never can.

—Not Confucius

"THRIFT IS a wonderful virtue, especially in an ancestor," someone said. If your father or grandfather had had the foresight to buy 300 shares of Minnesota Mining and Manufacturing in 1913 at $1 a share, then 300 shares would have become 115,200 shares as a result of successive stock splits. Near its 1974 high, each share was worth about $78,[1] bringing the value of the original modest investment of $300 up to $8.9 million. What's more, at that point, the investment would also yield $144,000 a year in dividends.

Or perhaps one of your ancestors bought 100 shares of International Business Machines (IBM) in 1913 at a cost of $4,450. Without further cash investment, as a result of stock splits and stock dividends, this would, at its peak in 1974, amount to 74,150 shares with a market value of $18.8 million,[2] compared with the original investment of $4,450.

Nor are investment opportunities of this type a matter of the early 1900s. They have been available in the more recent past as well. For example, to cite several cases: (*a*) A $1,000 investment in Food Machinery stock in 1932 was worth $100,000 by 1946. (*b*) The old Homestake Mining gold stock rose from 81 in 1931 to 544 in 1936. (*c*) The stock of the Cross Company soared from $1 a share in 1950 to $80 in 1955. (*d*)

---

[1] Written when MMM was near its 1974 high of 80½. Subsequently it fell to a low of 43¼.

[2] Written when IBM was at its 1974 high of 254. Subsequently IBM fell to a low of 150½.

Control Data rose from 37½ cents a share (adjusted for a stock split) in 1958 to a high of $165½ in 1967; (*e*) Burroughs Corporation rose from 22⅛ in 1965 to a high of 252¾ in 1973, while (*f*) Telex, Inc., increased from 50 cents (adjusted for a stock split) to 44½ in 1972; and finally (*g*) Fleetwood Enterprises, a builder of mobile homes, jumped from 87½ cents to 49½ in 1972.

What goes up often comes down, however, in the market. Burroughs fell to 61⅜ in 1974; Telex to 2½; and Fleetwood to 3½. LTV, a conglomerate, which traded as high as 169½ in August, 1967, fell to 7½ in 1974, a decline of 98 percent. Some of the so called "performance stocks" took a terrific beating. Four Seasons Nursing Centers dropped from $90 to $1 in a year. Minnie Pearl, subsequently renamed Performance Systems, went down from $23 to 50 cents, while National Student Marketing Corporation dropped from $36 late in 1969 to 87½ cents in 1970. Avon Products fell from 140 in 1973 to 18⅝ in 1974; Polaroid from 149½ to 14⅛. Now if you'd like to know more about the fascinating subject of investments, the next few chapters offer a brief introduction.

Single Proprietorships

In general, business is organized as (*a*) single proprietorships, (*b*) partnerships, and (*c*) corporations. A business operated by an individual as a single proprietorship does not issue stocks and bonds. Ordinarily, such a business has no piece of paper which evidences ownership in it (unless there is a bill of sale). It belongs to its owner just as his house, clothing, or dog, belongs to him. He merely uses his property, or part of it, in conducting a business. If there are debts of the business, they are also his debts, for which he is liable without limit. These debts are usually accounts payable (evidenced by no formal paper) or notes payable (secured or unsecured). There are approximately 9.5 million proprietorships in the United States.

Partnerships

A partnership is a business operated under an agreement by two or more individuals (partners). It does not issue stocks and bonds. The only formal evidence of ownership that is commonly found in such an organization is a written partnership agreement which sets forth the various interests and rights of the partners. Partnerships are governed by special laws applicable to partnerships, but in general the partners are personally liable without limit for the debts of the partnership. There are about 936,000 partnerships in the United States.

Corporations: Common and Preferred Stocks

It is only the corporation which issues stocks and bonds. When we are stockholders, we own part or all of a corporation; when we are bondholders, we are creditors of a corporation. A corporation in the eyes of the law is a legal entity apart from its owners. It is itself a legal person brought into existence under an act of the legislature. In legal language, a corporation is an artificial (not natural) entity (being) existing only in contemplation of law. This artificial person (the corporation) has only the rights and privileges which its creator (the legislature or lawmaking body) gives it. Ordinarily it has such rights as the power to own property in its own name, incur obligations to others (debts), sue, and be sued. This artificial person, which commonly is the possessor of valuable properties, is owned by its stockholders. As evidence of their ownership, they hold printed or engraved certificates of ownership known as "stock certificates." An individual certificate may show ownership of one or more shares or interests in the corporation. When all shares have the same rights in the corporation, they are known as "common shares" or "common stocks." If some of the shares have superior rights (as compared with other shares) to dividends or assets in event of liquidation (termination) of the corporation, they are "preferred shares." There are approximately 1.7 million corporations in the United States.

Federal and State Charters

Both the federal legislature (Congress) and our state legislatures can create corporations, but most, nowadays, are given their charters by the states. Formerly the legislatures voted in each case whether or not to charter an individual corporation. If they persisted in this practice today, when so many corporations are formed, they would have little time for anything else. At present, therefore, it is customary for a legislature to pass an enabling act, a general incorporation law, whereby those who follow the provisions in the act may apply to the designated authorities for a charter. This makes application for a charter a fairly straight forward procedure; but since some states are more generous toward corporations than others, there is always the question of determining in which state to apply. The corporate charter dictates the amount of stock, common and preferred, which is authorized. That part of the authorized stock which is issued and outstanding (usually in return for cash, property, or services) constitutes the ownership of the corporation.

Limited Liability

When we discussed single proprietors and partners, it was said that ordinarily they are liable for debts of their businesses without limit. In the case of the single proprietor, this means that if the business cannot pay its debts, the proprietor must pay them with other private funds if available. Whenever a partnership cannot pay its bills, the partners can be compelled to pay them out of any other of their personal resources. The stockholders of a corporation are in a happier position. Remember that the law regards the corporation itself as a person; if the corporation cannot pay its bills, nobody else has to pay its bills for it. Thus, the shareholders have limited liability; they can lose only what they have invested in the corporation. It is for this reason that after a corporate name in England and Canada we find the word "Limited," usually abbreviated to "Ltd." (for example, Imperial Chemical Industries, Ltd.).

COMMON STOCK

Occasionally one finds common stock divided into two classes—A and B, for example. Although common stock generally has voting power, it may be found that one class has voting control and the other is denied it. When the Dodge brothers sold their automobile company, a new company was formed to buy the business. The latter sold securities of several types to the public (including nonvoting common stock) to raise money for the purchase. Finally, a relatively small block of voting common stock was sold to the Chrysler Corporation, thus giving Chrysler the control of the Dodge operation, which permitted Chrysler to consider Dodge cars a product of Chrysler. This is not the only instance of nonvoting common stock in the automobile business. Henry Ford died in 1947, at which time he owned about 1.9 million shares in the Ford Motor Company. He left most of his holdings (1,805,000 shares) as a tax free gift to a charity, the Ford Foundation, but this stock had no voting power. The rest of his stock (95,000 shares) had all the voting power and was bequeathed to his heirs; it vested control of the company in them. The net result was that the Ford family was saved the difficulty of trying to raise a huge sum for taxes, although it retained control of the business, and the world got the benefit of a large part of the wealth which the free enterprise system allowed Henry Ford to accumulate.

Despite its occasional use, nonvoting common stock is frowned upon as a general proposition. It is felt that if common stock is residual with respect to income (gets only what is left), it should, at least, have the power to vote. Since 1926, nonvoting common stock has not been eligible for listing on the New York Stock Exchange, and it is not often encountered today in the United States, though it is quite usual in Canada.

Par and No-Par Stock

Prior to 1912, when New York State first permitted the issue of no-par stock, all stock issued had to have a face or par value. This was the value mentioned in the stock certificate. To creditors it was supposed to mean that that much money or its equivalent had been given by the stockholders to the corporation in return for the stock (as a fund for creditors' protection), or that the creditors could sue to have the deficiency paid to the corporation if it sold the stock for less than par (at a discount).

Although the par value may have meant something at or about the time the stock was issued originally, after a while it became practically meaningless; few stocks continued to sell at anything like their par value. In fact, some people were deceived into thinking that a stock selling for $45 must be worth more because a par value of the more or less customary amount of $100 was mentioned on the stock certificate.

Today, most states provide for the issue of no-par value shares. They can be sold for whatever they will bring in the market. There is at present a fairly widespread view that par value is only a legal fiction. Thus it is recognized that no-par stock represents a share of ownership which is valued from time to time at whatever investors estimate it is worth. In contrast, par value stock is tagged with an artificial fixed value, which seldom remains the market's valuation for long. For example, E. I. du Pont has a par value of 5 for its common, which has ranged, in recent years, in the market from a low of 92 to a high of 293¾. Coca-Cola common has no par value; the market price has ranged from 12 to 150. No-par stock may be sold initially at whatever the market will bring.

In many cases today, primarily for tax purposes, corporations assign a nominal stated value of $5 or $10 a share to their stock when initially issued, regardless of the price at which stock is first sold. The investor today is generally little concerned whether stock has par value or no-par value or stated value. Market value is the important consideration.

Book Value, Market Value, Earnings Value

What is a given share of common stock worth? This is a key question which has been discussed and written about extensively. It is clearly not related to par value. Is it book value? Book value may be defined as the total assets (using values carried on the company's books) of the company less its debts and preferred stock. It is the value at which the common shares are carried on the company's books together with the surplus and reserves. It is largely an accounting concept and usually not too useful.

Market value is the price set in the market as a result of the forces of supply and demand at work. It's what one person is willing to pay for a share and what another person is willing to sell it for—one person's bid, another's asking price. Market value or market price, however, doesn't tell you whether the stock is a good buy or a poor buy; whether it is overvalued or undervalued. The price of a certain company's share may be high because few shares are outstanding. Superior Oil Company's shares sold from $1,200 to $1,500 per share prior to a 10 for 1 split in 1965. Another company's shares may sell at low prices because there are a great many shares outstanding.

What is most important in determining the value of the shares of a company over the long run? The answer is earnings and dividends. To state it, at this point, as simply as possible, shares tend to sell over the longer run at a multiple of earnings. For example, if the company is likely to earn $3 a share next year and stocks tend to sell at 15 times earnings, then the shares should be worth and sell at $45 a share. For certain growth stocks whose earnings are expected to grow rapidly from year to year, a higher multiple may be regarded as appropriate—25 times prospective earnings, for example. In that case the stock should sell at $75 a share based on prospective earnings of $3 a share next year.[3]

Common Stocks as an Investment

Since common stocks are residual as to assets and earnings, the common stockholders may, in the event of reorganization or liquidation, receive only what is left after ordinary creditors, bonds, and preferred stocks have had their rights satisfied. Common stocks are subject to risk and fluctuations in value varying with the earnings and profits of the corpora-

---

[3] It's more complicated than this, but this gives you an idea of one method of valuing common stocks. For more detail see Chapter 5, "Valuation of Common Stocks," in Jerome B. Cohen, Edward D. Zinbarg and Arthur Zeikel, *Investment Analysis and Portfolio Management*, rev. ed. (Homewood, Ill.: Richard D. Irwin, Inc., 1973).

tion, with the business cycle, and with general trends in the stock market.

The three chief advantages of common stock, however, which have had a strong appeal to investors are (*a*) ability to participate financially in the economic growth of the country over the next few decades, (*b*) possible capital gains, and (*c*) a hedge against inflation, over the long run.

Common stock investment may be one of the more effective financial means of participating in the coming growth and change in the American economy over the next generation. It is estimated that our present popula- tion, with the business cycle, and with general trends in the stock market. 2000. GNP will have grown from $975 billion in 1970 to perhaps $1,800 billion in 1980 and to $3,500 billion in 2000. Consumers bought 9.5 million cars per year in the early 1970s. In 1980 they are likely to buy 14 million cars and by the year 2000 some 28 million a year. Financial sharing in the economic rewards of growth may be obtained by judicious investment in common stock.

Substantial capital gains may be realized in common stocks. Such gains are not possible, of course, in fixed dollar obligations, such as bonds or savings accounts. For example, you could have picked up shares of the common stock of Northern Pacific Railroad, before World War II, for a low of $3.75 and a dozen years later sold them for as much as $94.37. In the case of Du Pont, it could have been purchased in the late thirties for $22 (adjusted for stock split) and sold in recent years as high as $293¾ per share. Minnesota Mining and Manufacturing went from 50 cents (adjusted) per share to $119¾; Natomas from $4⅛ a share to over $130½; and Avon Products from 12 cents (adjusted) a share to $140. You have to exercise exceptional judgment to find and time these capital gains correctly. Some people bought A.T.&T. at $310 a share in 1929 and had to sell it at $70 a share in 1933. More recently, others may have bought Itek Corp. at $172 a share and later had to sell it at $4⅞ a share.

Common Stocks as a Hedge against Inflation

Common stocks have been usually regarded as a good *long run* hedge against inflation. From time to time in our history, the rise in the price level has reduced the purchasing power of the dollar, so that those who have to live on fixed, or relatively fixed, dollar incomes find themselves seriously pinched. It has become customary to speak of a 40 cent dollar. What is meant, of course, is that because of the rise in the price level and the decline in the value of the dollar, the dollar now buys only 40 percent as much goods as did a dollar in 1945. Thus you need more dollars if you want to buy the same amount of such items as food, clothing, shelter, entertainment, and the like, that is, maintain your standard of living.

One's purchasing power would, by *average* common stock investment, have been preserved; and that is why we speak of common stocks as being a hedge against inflation. The long term, secular, upward trend of common stock prices may be seen in Figures 13–1 and 13–2. But note the short term setbacks shown in Figures 13–3 and 13–4. Occasionally a long term common stock investment will do considerably more than protect against secular inflation. An investment in 100 shares of Eastman Kodak, bought for $10,000 in 1901, would have been worth, with dividends, about

FIGURE 13–1
Investment Risk (common stocks and value of the dollar since 1897)

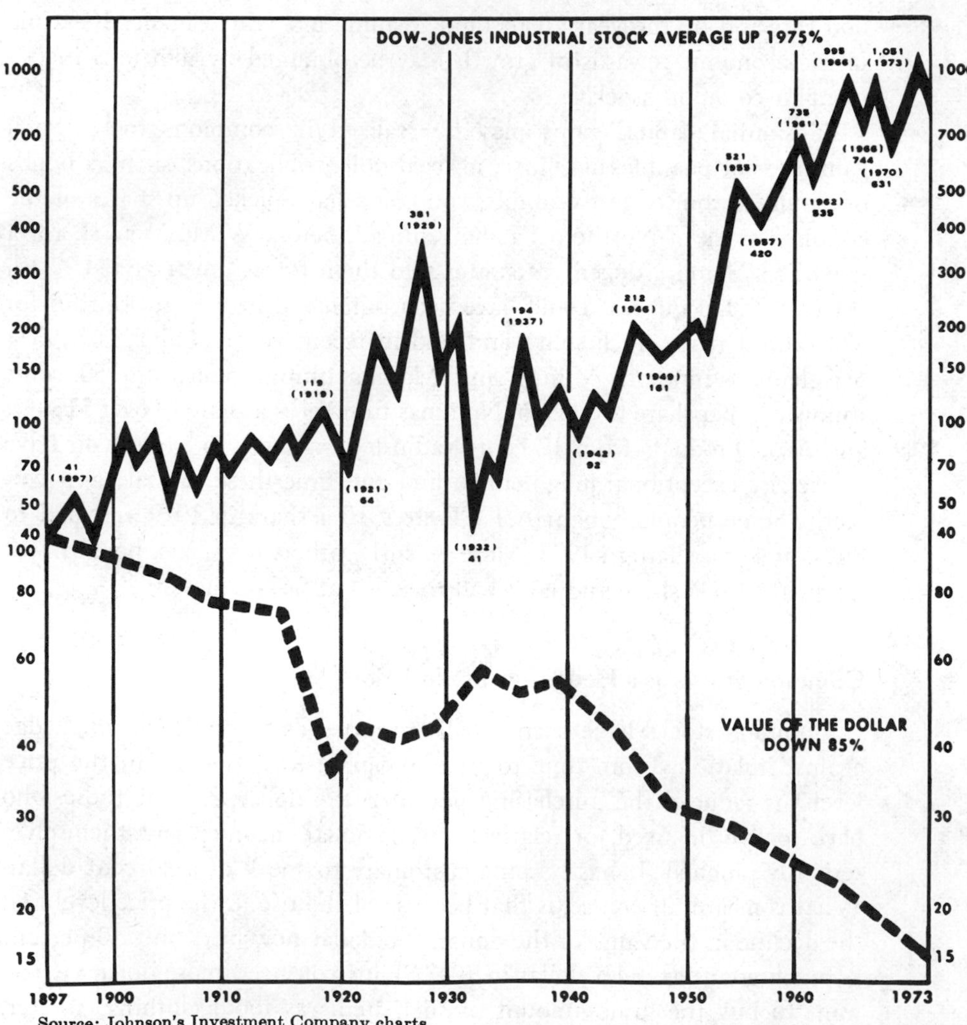

Source: Johnson's Investment Company charts.

FIGURE 13-2
Trend in Common Stock Dividends and Prices Compared with Consumer Prices

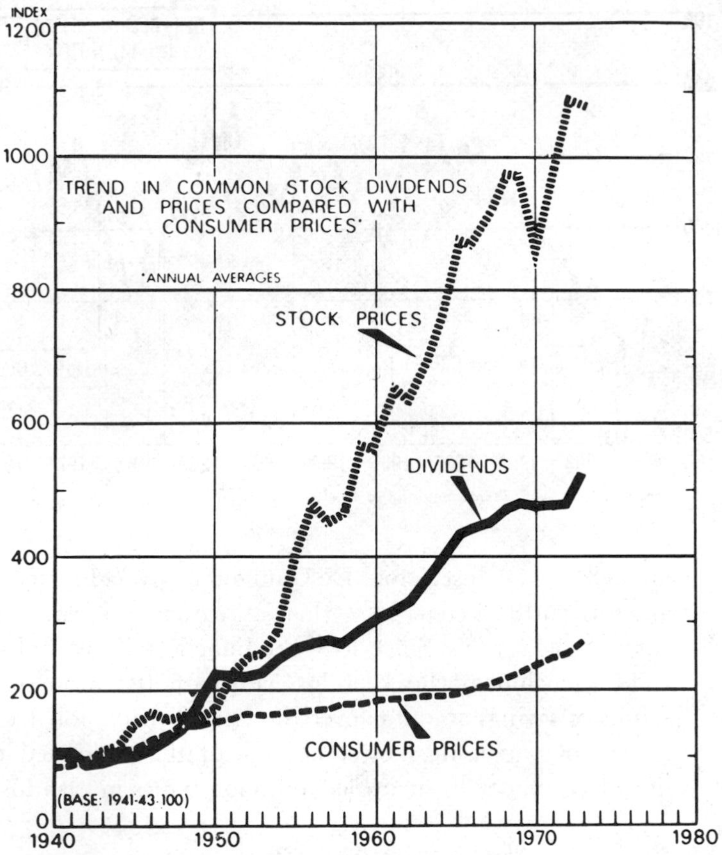

Note: All lines are plotted from annual averages, thus do not show fluctuations within each year. Consumer Prices based on Bureau of Labor Statistics' Index. Dividends and Stock Prices based on Standard & Poor's "500" stocks.
Source: New York Stock Exchange.

$2 million,[4] while 100 shares of Sears, Roebuck bought in 1906 at $5,700 would have been worth about $1.8 million.

Consider this in another light. In 1914 the French franc was worth 19½ cents; by 1920 its value had dropped to 7 cents; when France temporarily returned to the gold standard in 1928, the franc was worth less than 4 cents. All that time the price of stocks (and of gold) in France was rising proportionately. With the Nazi invasion of France in 1940 the franc went down to 2 cents; by 1946 it was down to less than a

[4] This assumes warrants and rights not exercised. If all warrants and rights had been exercised through investment of additional capital, present number of shares would total 37,113 amounting to a market value of $3.1 million.

FIGURE 13–3
Dow Jones Industrial Monthly Closing Averages

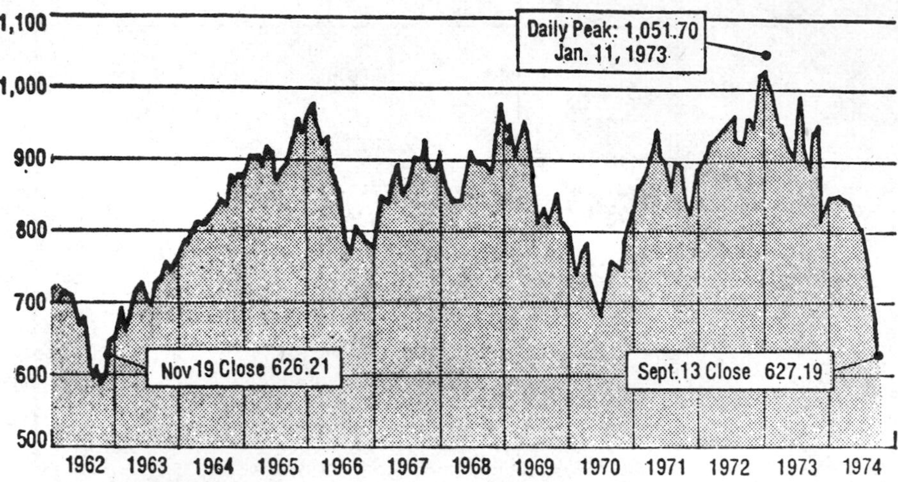

Source: *The New York Times*, September 14, 1974.

cent (0.84 cent). Just before De Gaulle took over the official value of the franc was but 0.23 cents—less than a quarter of a cent—and in the free market it sold for less. Since 1914 the franc lost 99 percent of its value.

The Frenchman who kept his wealth in the form of cash or bank deposits or savings accounts over the last 40 years probably had little left in terms of purchasing power because of the continued decline in the value of his money. If he owned a million francs in cash in 1914, it would

FIGURE 13–4
The Value Line Composite Average (more than 1,500 stocks)

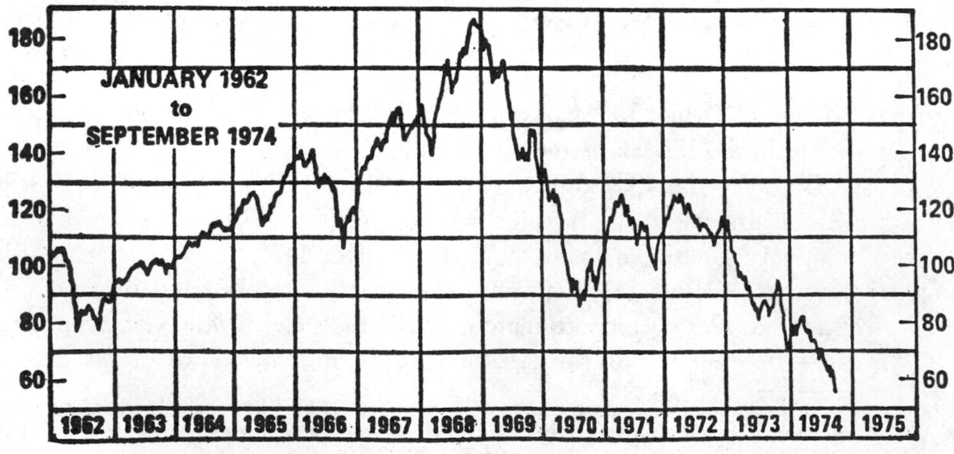

Source: *Value Line*, September 13, 1974.

have bought what approximately $200,000 U.S. dollars could purchase at that time. If he had kept his million francs in cash and spent them just before the revaluation of the franc, they would buy only what $2,380 U.S. dollars could purchase. But if he had put his million francs in select common stocks or in gold in 1914, he would have preserved his purchasing power over the years. Living costs, for example, rose 1,800 percent in France during and after World War II; common stock prices almost kept pace—they rose 1,600 percent.

In a study for the National Bureau of Economic Research, "Common Stock Values and Inflation," Professor Phillip Cagan concluded:

> The common stocks represented in the indexes examined here have more or less maintained their real value over long periods of currency depreciation except mainly for hyperinflations and war devastation. . . . In short, the data presented here indicate that a comprehensive group of stocks will protect against inflation, apart from hyperinflation or wartime devastation, but not concurrently. Compared with bonds or other fixed value assets, stocks if broadly selected pass the test as an inflation hedge only for long term holdings. In the United States, given these limitations, they have performed especially well.[5]

A study by the Anchor Corporation indicates that living costs rose in 61 percent of the 1 year periods since 1871 and in 64 percent of the 10 year periods. When longer periods were tabulated, it was found that living costs increased in 72 percent of the 15 year periods, 79 percent of the 20 year periods and in 94 percent of the 30 year spans. Whether they have invested for one year or longer, investors have had inflation in store for them more than half the time since 1871. Over 20 year spans they have experienced inflation three quarters of the time; over 30 year spans, nearly all the time.

Stock prices rose in 67 percent of the one year inflationary periods and in 9 out of 10 of the longer periods of rising prices. Since 1871 common stock prices have increased in value in 95 percent of the 20 year periods and in all 30 year periods of rising living costs. Increases in stock prices matched or bettered increases in the cost of living in 72 percent of all 10 year periods, 82 percent of the 15 year periods, 90 percent of all 20 year periods, and 91 percent of all 30 year periods of inflation and rising stock prices (see Figure 13–5).[6]

---

[5] Philip Cagan, "Common Stock Values and Inflation: The Historical Record of Many Countries," National Bureau Report Supplement 13, National Bureau of Economic Research, New York, March 1974.

[6] See *Common Stocks and the Cost of Living over the Last Century, 1871–1974* (Elizabeth, N.J.: Anchor Corporation).

FIGURE 13–5
Common Stocks and the Cost of Living over the Last Century 1871–1974 (1871 = 100)

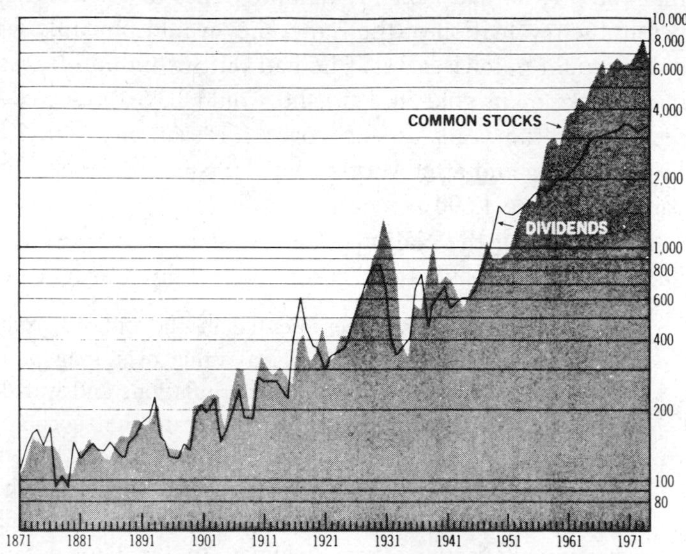

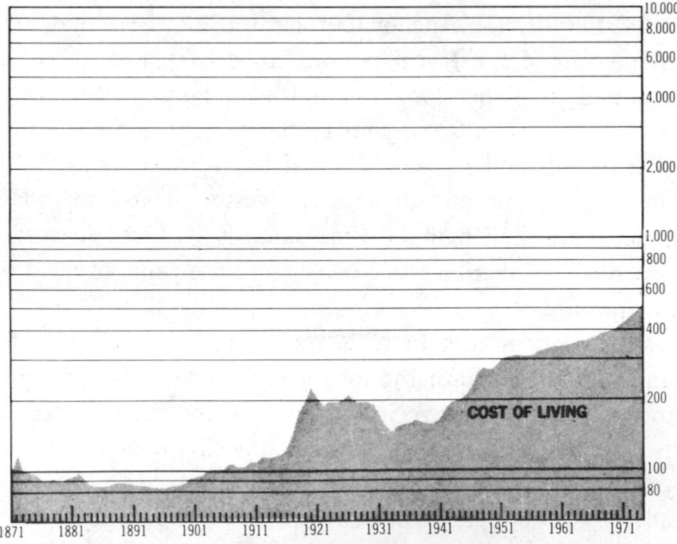

Stock prices (January 1) Standard & Poor's Index of Industrial Stock Prices.

Dividends (annual total) For the years 1925 to 1974, Standard & Poor's Index of Dividends of Industrial Stocks was employed. For prior years, the Cowles Commission Index of Dividends on Industrial Stocks was adjusted to the Standard & Poor's Index.

Cost of living (annual average) The U.S. Bureau of Labor Statistics Index of Living Costs (annual average) is used continuously throughout the study.

Source: © Anchor Corporation, May 1974.

Fixed dollars have clearly lost value. Between 1953 and 1973, the costs of a postcard rose from 1 cent to 8 cents, subway fare from 5 cents to 35 cents, a loaf of bread from 18 to 45 cents. Over the 1964–73 decade, while the cost of living rose 49.7 percent and the value of the dollar fell 33.2 percent, the investment changes shown in Table 13–1 occurred.

Let's suppose you were a General Motors shareholder using dividends to purchase the family car. In 1939 a small Chevy cost around $700. That year, also, GM paid a $3.50 dividend. So ownership of 200 shares would have allowed you to enjoy a car "on the company." Since then GM split its stock 2 for 1 in 1950, and 3 for 1 in 1955—your 200 shares would now have grown to 1,200. Total dividends of $4,080 paid on those shares will buy a new car today.

TABLE 13–1
Percent Change

	1960–70	*1964–73*
New York Stock Exchange Index	+62.3%	+29.8%
S & P 500 Stock Index	+58.6%	+30.0
Dow-Jones Industrial average	+36.2%	+11.5
Insurance stocks	+95.7%	+75.1
Bank stocks	+75.4%	+82.7
Utility stocks	+19.2%	−29.4
Rail stocks	+19.8%	+12.7
Cost of living	+33.3%	+49.7
Value of the dollar	−25.0%	−33.2
Cash	00.0%	00.0
Municipal bonds	−27.2%	−21.9
Long-Term government bonds	−25.1%	−20.0
Preferred stocks	−30.6%	−45.1
High-Grade corporate bonds	−31.7%	−34.1

Source: Johnson Investment Company.

If you had purchased 100 shares of General Electric in early January of 1950, you would have received $340 in dividends that year. And $269.95 of that income would have bought a good General Electric 12 inch black and white table model TV set. Since then those 100 shares have grown, through a 3 for 1 stock split in 1954, to 300 shares. Dividends totaling $780 were paid on those shares in 1970. Today a greatly improved General Electric 18 inch color television table model sells for $380, which is only 40 percent more than the smaller black and white TV set cost in 1950. However, income from the stock increased 105 percent.[7]

The contemplation of any investment action today must be based upon the protection of capital against inflation. The following projections

[7] From *Dividends Over the Years* (New York Stock Exchange, 1971).

of annual increases in the cost of living over the next 10 years and the resulting declines in the value of the dollar bring this problem into clear focus.

If the Annual Cost of Living Increases	*The Value of the Dollar Will be Down*
4% per year	32.4%
5	38.6
6	44.2
7	49.2
8	53.7
10	61.5
12	67.8

But Stocks Can Go Down Too

Several limitations should be noted. First, the results shown for the past are not necessarily indicative of results to be expected in the future. The next decade may not be as inflationary as the last. If there is deflation, of course, common stock values shrink. The investor who has bought common stock outright (not on margin) in sound companies and who can afford to hold (is not forced by need for funds to sell) may not be hurt at all by a short period deflation, but one who is forced to sell may be hurt severely. Table 13–2 shows what happened to the unlucky investor who went into the market in 1929, picked a dozen sound stocks, but was forced to sell in 1932 to obtain funds on which to live.[8] Obviously, as good

TABLE 13–2
A Dozen Good Common Stocks, 1929–32

Company	*1929*	*1932*
Anaconda Copper	174⅞	3
A.T.&T.	310¼	70¼
Chrysler Corporation	87	5
Du Pont	503	22
General Motors	224	7⅝
Montgomery Ward	156⅞	3½
New York Central	256½	8¾
Standard Oil of New Jersey	83	19⅞
Standard Oil of California	81⅞	15⅛
Sears, Roebuck	197½	9⅞
U.S. Steel	261¾	21¼
Western Union	272¼	12⅜

[8] For a fascinating account of the stock market boom of the late twenties, the 1929 crash, and the immediate aftermath see Frederick Lewis Allen, *Only Yesterday* (New York: Harper & Bros., 1931), and Edward Angly, *Oh, Yeah* (New York: Viking Press, 1931). See also John Kenneth Galbraith, *The Great Crash, 1929* (Boston: Houghton Mifflin Co., 1955).

as common stocks are as a hedge against long term secular inflation, the investor who may be forced to sell in a shorter term deflation hardly finds this an advantage.

Just how frequently market slumps occur may be seen in Figure 13–6. The severity of the decline varies but market setbacks on numerous occasions are customary and not exceptional.

Another limitation is that, even in an inflationary decade, some stocks

FIGURE 13–6
Market Slumps Since 1929—How the Latest Sell-Off Compares

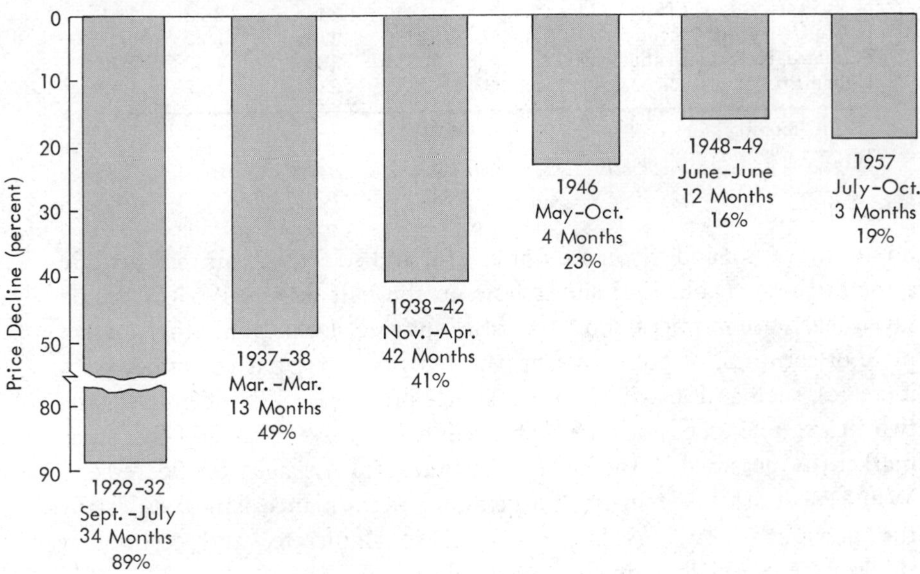

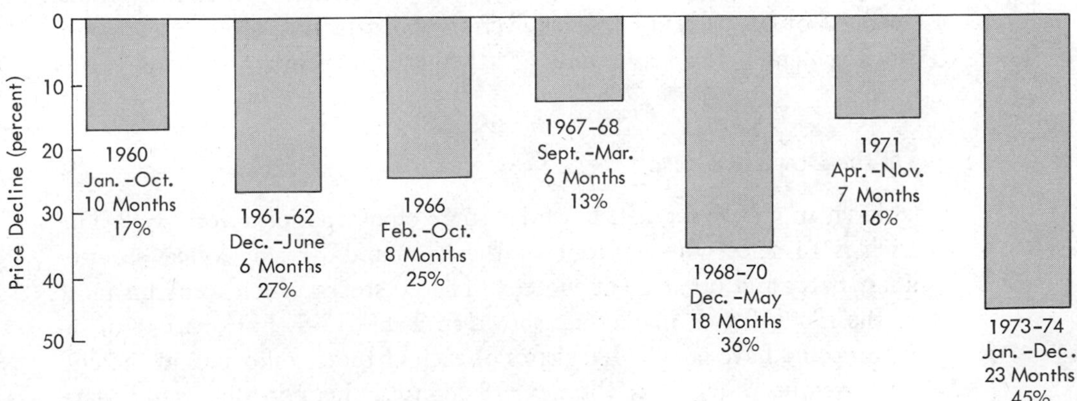

Duration of each major decline starting with the market crash of 1929–32, and the percentage drop in stock prices, as measured by the Dow Jones Industrial average.

Source: Chart adapted and reprinted from *U.S. News & World Report*, September 9, 1974. Copyright 1974, U.S. News & World Report, Inc.

TABLE 13–3
Market Laggards, 1965–70

Company	*Price**		*Earnings*	
	1965	*1970*	*1965*	*1970*
United States Steel	$55⅞	$39½	$4.62	$2.72
American Telephone & Telegraph	70½	53⅞	3.41	3.99
Allied Chemical	58¼	28	3.14	1.56
Northwest Airlines	35⅝	29	2.50	2.11
Continental Airlines	20	13⅞	1.26	0.32
Swank, Inc.	41⅛	20¾	2.03	1.51
Celanese Corporation	92	64½	5.10	3.51
N.Y. State Gas & Electric Corp.	48⅝	34⅜	2.79	2.81
Falstaff Brewing Corp.	40½	11⅜	1.22	0.27
Standard Kollsman Industries, Inc.	26⅛	13¾	1.52	*D* 0.42
Helme Products, Inc.	23⅝	21¾	1.47	1.17

* High for the year
D = deficit
Source: *Financial World, Stock Factograph Manual* (5th ed.; New York, 1971).

do not move up; and if you are not careful and selective, you may acquire some of these. Table 13–3 shows how, in the half decade 1965–70 which saw a sharp rise in prices, some securities suffered declines in either market price or earnings, or both. In fact, short periods of rapid consumer price increases, such as 1969–70 when consumer prices rose 12 percent over the two years, may see stock market declines. During 1969–70, the stock market (as measured by the Dow-Jones Industrial Average) fell 36 percent. While most stocks declined, the glamour, performance issues, especially the previously very popular computer, conglomerate, and technology stocks were especially hard hit (see Table 13–4).

Again in 1973–74 consumer prices rose very sharply while stock prices declined by 38 percent.[9] In fact over the half decade, 1969–74 common stock, generally, did very poorly as a hedge against inflation.

Up the Down Staircase

Even in a bear market, however, some stocks perform very well. The trick is to select the few out of the thousands. Even skilled security analysts try and often don't succeed. The 20 stocks which went up most in the 1969–70 bear market are shown in Table 13–5. For $82,700 an investor could have bought 100 shares of each of these companies at the end of November 1968. Over the next 18 months, this portfolio would have grown to $173,000, a gain of 109 percent, while the New York Stock

[9] Consumer prices rose 21.7 percent between January 1973 and December 1974.

TABLE 13–4
Collapse of "Performance" Stocks

Thirty growth stocks lost 81 percent of their value in the 1969–70 crash, just a shade under the drop in history's worst market break.

	Stock Price		
	*1967–68 High**	*1970 Low*	*Extent of Decline*
Computer stocks			
Control Data	163	28	83%
Sperry Rand	65	18	72
Mohawk Data	111	18	84
University Computing	186	13	93
I.B.M.	375	218	42
Data Processing Financial	92	6	94
Leasco Data	57	7	88
Levin-Townsend	67	3	96
National Cash Register	81	29	64
Electronic Data Systems†	162	24	85
Average decline of computer stocks			80
Technology stocks			
Polaroid	141	51	64%
Xerox	115	65	43
Optical Scanning†	146	16	89
Texas Instruments	140	61	57
Itek	172	17	90
Recognition Equipment†	102	12	88
Fairchild Camera	102	18	82
EG&G	72	9	88
General Instruments	63	11	83
Kalvar†	73	11	85
Average decline of technology stocks			77
Conglomerate stocks			
Litton Industries	104	15	86%
Gulf & Western	66	9	87
Ling-Temco-Vought	135	7	95
Bangor Punta	61	5	93
Kidde	87	15	82
A-T-O	74	6	92
Teledyne	72	13	82
Northwest Industries	60	8	87
Textron	57	15	74
United Brands	58	12	80
Average decline of conglomerate stocks			86
Average decline of all stocks			81

* Several stocks reached highs after 1968; in such cases, the post-1968 high is used.
† Over-the-counter stocks for which bid price is given.
Source: *New York Times*, January 1, 1971.

TABLE 13–5
Bulls in a Bear Market

	Stock Price (end of month)		Percent In-crease
	Nov. 1968	*Feb. 1970*	
1. Telex*	$28⅜	$134¼	373.1%
2. New Process	19†	65⅛	242.8
3. U.S. Natural Resources	11¾	31¼	166.0
4. Kleinert's	13⅝	35⅞	163.3
5. Milgo Electronic	24½	62⅜	154.6
6. Digital Equipment	54.67†	112¾	106.3
7. Automatic Data Processing	23.42†	46½	98.6
8. McIntyre Porcupine Mines*	78	153	96.2
9. Jeannette Glass	12.81†	25	95.1
10. Walt Disney Productions*	77.94†	147⅝	89.4
11. Coro	18⅛	32½	79.3
12. Savin Business Machines	34.69†	61⅞	78.4
13. Wackenhut	18⅝	32¼	73.2
14. BTU Engineering	9½	16⅜	72.4
15. Drug Fair-Community Drug	19¼	33	71.4
16. Peabody Galion	15.53†	26⅝	71.4
17. Christiana Oil	10¾	18¼	69.8
18. Copper Range*	45.48†	77⅛	69.6
19. Monroe Auto Equipment*	28*	47¼	68.8
20. Roosevelt Raceway	28	47	67.9

* Listed on New York Stock Exchange (others traded on Amex).
† After adjustment for stock splits or stock dividends.
Source: *Fortune*, April, 1970.

Exchange index fell by 18 percent. Again in the 1973–74 bear market some stocks rose against the tide.

Even in the 1973–74 bear market certain performance types did well: gold stocks, Dome Mines rose from 68 to 155, Homestake Mining from 23 to 70⅞, Campbell Red Lake from 35⅞ to 79; semi conductors, National Semi-Conductors from 23 to 108⅝ and Texas Instruments from 74⅜ to 138⅞; sugar stocks, Great Western United rose 200 percent, Holly Sugar 109 percent. The ability to pick next year's performance stocks, or those that will move up in a down market is a skill akin to alchemy or astrology but handsomely rewarded.

Who Owns Common Stock

Wall Street and its counterparts in other American cities—La Salle Street in Chicago, Montgomery Street in San Francisco, Marietta Street in Atlanta, and State Street in Boston—once teemed with individual investors.

There are now more than 30 million shareholders. Nearly 1 out of 4 adults is now a shareowner as compared with 1 out of 8 a decade ago.

Women shareholders about equalled male. The average shareholder had an annual household income of $13,500. Of the 30 million shareowners 58.4 percent had household incomes of under $15,000, while 41.6 percent had incomes of $15,000 or more. Only 14.5 percent had household incomes of $25,000 or more. The median age of the shareholder population was 48 in 1970 compared with 39 for those who became shareholders for the first time since 1962.

Nineteen million shareowners have portfolios worth less than $10,000. Most of these same people, who can be defined as "small investors" also had incomes of less than $15,000, in 1970.

Over 50 percent of the nation's adult shareholders have attended college. In the past five years, the greatest shareholder growth occurred among individuals having four or more years of college experience. Reflecting the trend toward more education for greater numbers of Americans, 10 million college graduates—36 percent of all shareholders—now own stock. While the educational level is rising nationwide, the proportion of shareowners in the better educated groups is growing at a somewhat faster rate than the total number of all persons in these groups. Together, college graduates and those who attended college account for 56 percent of the nation's shareowners in 1970.[10]

Housewives and retired persons constitute 37 percent of all shareowners —a higher percentage than any employed group. Professional and technical people form the largest category of employed shareowners, more than doubling since 1965 to a total of 6.3 million or 22 percent of all shareowners. Here again, the influence of rising educational levels in the general population appears to be the primary reason for the predominance of professional persons among employed shareholders.

Despite the seeming spread of stock ownership a recent study found that most stock is owned by the rich. Based on an extensive sample of tax returns, it was found that the top 0.2 percent of U.S. families who had incomes in excess of $100,000 owned 30.2 percent of all stock, while the top 1 percent with incomes in excess of $50,000 owned 51.1 percent of all stock.[11]

Investment Objectives and Common Stocks

You would not think of going into a drugstore and asking for a dollar's worth of medicine. You would want a certain kind of medicine to treat a

---

[10] See New York Stock Exchange, *Census of Shareowners* and New York Stock Exchange, *Fact Book*, 1974, p. 50.

[11] Marshall Blume, Jean Crockett, and Irwin Friend, "Stock Ownership in the United States: Characteristics and Trends," *Survey of Current Business*, November 1974.

particular condition or illness. In just the same fashion, you do not buy $1,000 worth of securities. You want a certain type of security to meet a particular aim or objective. Generally, three major objectives are discernible in investments: growth (or capital gains or appreciation), income (either high or moderate with stability), and safety (no dollar loss of capital invested). The largest brokerage house in the country, Merrill Lynch, Pierce, Fenner & Smith, classifies the three major kinds of securities in terms of these objectives as shown in the accompanying tabulation:[12]

Type of Security	*Growth*	*Income*	*Safety*
Common stock	Best	Variable	Least
Preferred stock	Variable	Steady	Good
Bonds	Generally none	Very steady	Best

Common stocks are, on the average, better for growth than are other types of securities, because they reflect the earning power and the prospects of a company. Common stocks are called "equities" because they receive what is left of earnings after the companies' fixed charges are paid. Since what is left over goes to common stockholders, when a company prospers and its earnings rise, almost all the increase goes to benefit the common stock.

Another qualification is that while, for the whole range of common stocks, income is characterized as variable, some common stocks have paid regular dividends for decades and have been a steadier source of income than many of the railroad bonds which went into default over the first half of the century. But some common stocks have not done well. Judgment and selection play an important role, and that is why we speak of common stock income as "variable."

Again, to say that common stocks are "least" safe, using a term of comparison, may perhaps give the impression that they are *not* safe. This is not what is meant. Many common stocks are not only good, sound investments; they have survived more business setbacks than many bonds, which, though originally considered safe, subsequently went into default. The common stock of the Bank of New York, which has paid dividends uninterruptedly for more than 190 years, is a much safer investment than were the bonds of the Missouri-Kansas-Texas Railroad. Generally speaking, though, common stocks vary more in price than either preferred stocks or bonds. If by "safety" is meant the assured return of the same

[12] From *How to Invest*, published by Merrill Lynch, Pierce, Fenner & Smith, New York (latest edition). A free copy may be obtained on request by writing to this company at One Liberty Plaza (165 Broadway), New York, N.Y., 10006.

number of dollars one put into an investment, then there is no certainty that a given common stock will, if sold next year, bring in the same number of dollars paid for it today. If you must sell in a recession then common stocks may not return the same number of dollars, but the fixed value security (bonds) faces an interest rate hazard in the upward phase of the cycle.

Common stock price appreciation may preserve purchasing power in the long run under inflation, whereas the fixed value security, even though it may return the same number of dollars, shrinks in real terms. Furthermore, the same disability attaches to the income of fixed value securities. Therefore, one must conclude that, in investments, safety is a relative term; that in seeking safety or protection against certain hazards, such as price decline, you necessarily expose yourself to hazards of other types, such as loss of purchasing power due to inflation. There is, then, in investments, never absolute safety.

Risk and Return

Total return is a concept which must be understood for common stock investing. Total return on common stock is what you earn by combining dividend return and price appreciation (capital gains). Current yield, or the purchase price divided into the annual dividend, is only part of the picture. Assume you paid $60 for a share of common stock and receive an annual dividend of $3.00. The current yield is 5 percent ($3.00 ÷ $60. = 5 percent). Compared to a high grade bond yield of 8 percent, the return on stock may not seem particularly attractive. But if the price of the stock was 7 percent higher at the end of the year, then the total return on the common stock would be 12 percent, a favorable return compared to 8 percent on the bond. A basic study by Lorie and Fisher, covering all common stocks listed on the New York Stock Exchange, found that over the entire period, 1926–1965, the average annual rate of return compounded annually, was 9.3 percent.[13]

A more recent analysis by Standard & Poor's concluded that "even after factoring in the sharp recent setback since early 1973, total return as expressed in terms of the S & P composite index of 500 common stocks averaged 6 percent annually for the ten years and five months through May 1974. Slightly more than half of this represented dividend yield

---

[13] Lawrence Fisher and James H. Lorie, "Rates of Return on Investment in Common Stock: The Year-by-Year Record, 1926–1965," *Journal of Business*, University of Chicago, vol. 41, no. 3, July 1968, pp. 291–316. The study assumed reinvestment of dividends and assumed the investor was tax exempt.

(compounded quarterly); a bit less than half, net appreciation. Such a return on your investments would have provided a good hedge against inflation; the average annual increase in the cost of living over this period was 4.1 percent."[14]

Most individual investors are risk averters. They seek a maximum return for the level of risk they are willing to assume. It has been generally assumed, though never proven, that the greater the risk undertaken the greater the return. It is more likely that the greater the risk undertaken the greater the loss. Risk can be expressed in either qualitative or quantitative terms. Major types of investment risks to which investors are vulnerable are:

1. Business risk (i.e., a decline in earning power), which reduces a company's ability to pay interest or dividends.
2. Market risk (i.e., a change in "market psychology"), which causes a security's price to decline apart from any fundamental change in a company's earning power.
3. Purchasing power risk (i.e., a rise in prices or decline in the value of the dollar), which reduces the buying power of income and principal.
4. Interest rate risk (i.e., a rise in interest rates), which depresses the price of fixed income type securities.
5. Political risk (i.e., price-wage controls, tax increases, changes in tariff and subsidy policies, etc.)

Common stocks are most vulnerable to (1), (2), and (5). Bonds are subject to (1), (3), (4), and (5). No securities are free of all risks. Even U.S. government bonds are subject to (3) and (4).

The effort to quantify risk has centered on the use of the *beta* coefficient. This is a method of measuring risk which relates the volatility of a stock or a portfolio to the volatility of the market as a whole.

Beta seeks to anticipate what will happen to a stock or to a portfolio of stocks given a change, up or down, in the total market. A high risk stock, a volatile stock, has a high beta; a low risk stock a low beta. If a stock moved exactly as the market moved it would have a beta of 1. General Motors has a beta of about 1. It tends to move with the market. If it was more volatile than the market, its beta would be above 1. For example, a stock with a beta of 2 should move up twice as fast as the market moves up. If less volatile than the market, its beta would be below 1. A.T.&T. is an example. But stocks seldom behave precisely as they are

---

[14] "Investing for Total Return," Standard & Poor's, *The Outlook*, Midyear Forecast Issue, June 24, 1974, p. 703.

supposed to, which is where another measure, *alpha*, comes in. It is used to account for change in a stock's price not attributable to its beta.

Suppose, for example, that the market advances by 5 percent over a year's time. If a stock has a beta of 1, it should go up by 5 percent. If, instead, it went up 15 percent, the 10 percent difference between the anticipated and the actual performance would be the stock's alpha. If a stock had a beta of 2—a more volatile or riskier stock—and it went up by 15 percent in the same year the market advances by 5 percent, it would have an alpha of 5 because, based on its beta, it should have gone up 10 percent, twice as much as the market.

According to beta theory, there are two possible ways of achieving superior portfolio performance. One is to forecast the market more accurately (an impossible task) and adjust the beta of your portfolio accordingly. If you foresee a substantial market rally, you might buy some high beta stocks and sell some low beta stocks to raise your portfolio to a beta level of say 2. If you are wrong and the market drops, your portfolio will, of course, decline twice as much.

The second way of obtaining above average performance is to achieve a positive alpha, or "excess return." When one stock has a higher or lower rate of return than another stock with the same beta; when it does better or worse against the market than its beta would have predicted; this is said to be due to its alpha factor, or the various residual nonmarket influences unique to each stock. If you can select enough stocks with positive alphas, your portfolio will perform better than its beta would have indicated for a given market movement.

But as you add more stocks to a portfolio, you tend to diversify away both the chance of obtaining a positive alpha, as well as the risk of getting a negative alpha. Your portfolio's volatility will also become very much like the market as a whole. A fully diversified portfolio, if there is such, would have a beta of 1 and an alpha of 1. Interesting?[15]

Objectives and Types of Common Stock

A young person, with good earning power, who has surplus funds to invest will seek a very different kind of investment from that sought by an

[15] For further information on this subject, see *Investment Analysis and Portfolio Management*, rev. ed. by Jerome B. Cohen, Edward D. Zinbarg, and Arthur Zeikel, (chapters 17 and 18), Homewood, Ill.: Richard D. Irwin, Inc., 1973; also William G. Shepard, "How Alpha-Beta Works," *Business Week*, April 22, 1972; Burton G. Malkiel, A *Random Walk Down Wall Street*, W. W. Norton, Inc., New York, 1974 and James H. Lorie, and Mary T. Hamilton, *The Stock Market: Theories and Evidence*, Homewood, Ill.: Richard D. Irwin, Inc., 1973.

elderly couple who must live on the income from a $100,000 lifetime accumulation which they have invested. The young person will either seek speculative gains, or, if wiser, will invest in growth stocks, which, over the years, may yield substantial capital gains, though current income may be low. The elderly couple will seek as high an income as they can attain consistent with stability and relative safety.

"Growth stocks" are those of companies usually, though not always, paying relatively low current returns because earnings are being plowed back. They are considered attractive because of future prospects. In earnings they have been doing better than the industry average or are expected to do so. The rate of growth must be greater than the rate of population increase. Furthermore, earnings tend to move forward from cycle to cycle and are only temporarily interrupted by business recessions. The growth company suffers less of a setback than the average company, recovers more quickly, and moves forward more rapidly. Today certain mobile home, leisure time, pollution control, business service, electronic, instrument, cosmetic, pharmaceutical, office equipment, and other companies are regarded as "growth" companies. An example of 140 rapid growth stocks screened by Standard & Poor's computer, based on growth rate criteria, may be seen in Table 13–6. Growth stocks may not only appreciate in value over time, if held, they yield substantial income as well (see Table 13–7). These are the results for one decade and may not necessarily be valid for some subsequent period.

The elderly couple seeking maximum return consistent with the greatest stability and least risk, and willing to forego growth possibilities, might invest in what one large brokerage house calls "*heirloom stocks*," i.e., those that have paid dividends uninterruptedly for from 35 to 180 years. Table 13–8 shows the "blue chips," as these high grade, relatively safe stocks are called, that were selected from the list to provide good return and stability. All of the companies shown had paid dividends uninterruptedly for over 60 years.

Or our elderly couple could have picked "defensive" stocks of equally high quality and almost as long an uninterrupted dividend record. By "defensive" stocks are meant shares of a company which is likely to do better than average, from an earnings and dividend point of view, in a period of deteriorating business. If a business recession is feared, a growing interest tends to develop in these recession resistant companies. While these stocks lack the glamour of certain market leaders, they are characterized by a relatively high degree of stability, an attribute much to be desired when the economy faces a period of uncertainty. Utility stocks are usually regarded as defensive issues since their slow (5 to 7 percent per

TABLE 13–6

RAPID GROWTH STOCKS

This list of 140 stocks is the end product of screening the many thousands of issues in the Standard & Poor's data base. Through this process we have eliminated stocks with highly erratic earnings, and those with recent adverse trends, despite good over-all performance. While the process is intended to point out those stocks with strong growth trends, the results are not to be regarded as a "buy" list.

Growth rates show the compounded annual rate of per share earnings for the past five years. To maximize the importance of the current trend of earnings, the "last 12 months" figure is substituted for the sixth or oldest year in instances where late interim earnings are available.

Principal criteria used: (1) if growth in share earnings over the past five years has been steady, it must have amounted to at least 7% per annum, compounded; (2) if growth has been interrupted in only one year and the decline has been less than 5%, annual growth must have been at least 10%; (3) if growth has been interrupted in more than one year, or in one year the decline has been more than 5%, annual growth rate must have been at least 12%.

Selections have been limited to issues with more than 750,000 shares outstanding and to those with earnings of at least $0.25 a share in the last full year.

Range 1974 (Fractions in 8ths) Hi	Lo	Recent Price	P-E Ratio	Listed	Growth Stocks	Yr. End	Earnings $ Per Sh. 1972	1973	Last 12 Mos.	Growth Rate % 5-Yr. Tr	Last 12 Mo
58	38^{2}	40	15	•	Air Prod. & Chem.	Sp	1.40	1.83	^{6}2.67	12	18
17^{6}	12	12	8	•	Albertson's, Inc.	Ja^{74}	1.19	1.45	^{4}1.54	15	17
32^{7}	15^{6}	19^{2}	22	•	Alcon Laboratories	Ap^{74}	△0.72	0.87	0.87	20	20
15	11^{3}	13^{4}	10	♦	Amer'n Business Prod.	Dc	0.90	1.07	^{6}1.34	13	17
34^{4}	16^{2}	16^{2}	13		Amer'n Greetings 'A'	Fb^{74}	1.07	1.20	^{5}1.24	19	16
44^{7}	31^{4}	31^{5}	24	•	Amer'n Home Prod.	Dc	△1.08	1.25	^{6}1.34	12	12
41^{3}	27^{5}	28^{4}	24	•	Amer. Hospital Supply	Dc	1.00	1.13	^{6}1.21	11	11
45^{2}	31^{4}	32^{4}	25	•	AMP, Inc.	Dc	0.90	1.23	^{6}1.32	19	17
101	69	75^{4}	14	•	ARA Services	Sp	4.63	5.12	^{6}5.38	11	11
25	18^{2}	18^{4}	17	♦	Augat, Inc.	Dc	0.77	0.96	^{6}1.08	35	28
44^{7}	33^{2}	36^{3}	23	•	Avery Products	Nv	0.93	1.39	^{5}1.58	13	19
43^{3}	22^{5}	23^{3}	16	•	Baker Oil Tools	Sp	1.08	1.17	^{6}1.50	14	16
36^{7}	22^{6}	27^{4}	24	•	Bandag, Inc.	Dc	0.68	0.96	^{6}1.14	51	43
48^{5}	29^{2}	30	28	•	Baxter Laboratories	Dc	0.77	0.95	^{6}1.09	13	18
40	27^{4}	27^{4}	32		Betz Laboratories	Dc	0.62	0.74	^{6}0.86	13	19
57^{5}	44^{4}	45^{4}	15	•	Big Three Industries	Dc	2.06	2.51	^{6}3.03	17	18
41^{4}	27	27^{3}	26	•	Black & Decker	Sp	0.71	0.87	^{6}1.06	13	16
113	80^{3}	81	24	•	Burroughs Corp.	Dc	2.35	3.00	^{6}3.31	16	15
66^{4}	51^{4}	51^{4}	13	♦	Carnation Co.	Dc	3.23	3.64	^{6}3.95	12	11
26^{4}	18	18^{4}	6		Chart House	Dc	1.87	2.50	^{6}2.94	34	40
28	13	13	9		Chemed Corp.	Dc	1.15	1.34	^{6}1.42	13	13
46^{2}	28	29^{4}	13	•	Citicorp	Dc	△1.78	□2.14	^{6}2.35	14	15
29^{4}	22^{6}	23^{4}	8		Clark (J.L.) Mfg.	Nv	□2.15	2.52	^{5}2.88	13	14
127^{6}	76^{4}	79^{2}	21	•	Coca-Cola	Dc	3.19	3.60	^{6}3.79	13	12
52	37^{6}	38^{6}	17	♦	Cross (A. T.) Cl A	Dc	1.62	2.13	^{6}2.28	27	23
23	17	17^{4}	9	•	Crown Cork & Seal	Dc	1.58	1.81	^{6}2.03	12	13
32^{4}	18	18	10		Daniel Int'l	Sp	1.36	1.57	^{6}1.79	38	23
54^{2}	22^{6}	36^{4}	7	♦	Data Documents	Sp	•1.93	•2.85	^{6}5.58	11	24
39	21^{2}	21^{4}	20	•	Data General	Sp	0.49	0.83	^{6}1.08	68	88
51^{2}	23^{4}	29	17		DEKALB Ag. Research	Au	1.13	1.41	^{5}1.72	24	24
122^{6}	84^{2}	84^{2}	22	•	Digital Equipment	Jn^{74}	2.16	3.80	3.80	25	25
34	27^{6}	30^{6}	13	•	Dillon Companies	Jn^{74}	2.05	2.46	2.46	23	23
22^{7}	11^{1}	11^{5}	21	•	Dr Pepper Co.	Dc	0.43	0.51	^{6}0.55	18	17
41^{2}	28^{1}	31^{3}	7	•	Dover Corp.	Dc	3.18	3.95	^{6}4.61	15	15
70	50^{1}	62^{4}	15	•	Dow Chemical	Dc	2.07	2.94	^{6}4.28	13	23
34	22^{3}	23^{3}	16	•	Echlin Mfg. Co.	Au	1.05	1.32	^{5}1.47	25	24
26^{7}	13^{4}	14^{1}	12	•	Eckerd (Jack)	Jl	0.77	1.02	^{4}1.14	27	21
39^{4}	29^{1}	29^{2}	28		Economics Lab.	Jn	0.79	0.94	^{3}1.04	13	13
59^{4}	45^{6}	45^{6}	30	•	Emery Air Freight	Dc	1.07	1.38	^{6}1.53	20	22
24^{6}	16	17^{2}	18		Extracorporel Med.	Jn	0.50	0.73	^{3}0.95	52	48
60	35	35	12	•	First Int'l Bancshares	Dc	△2.29	△2.64	^{6}2.90	16	14
21^{2}	14^{3}	14^{6}	13	•	Fort Howard Paper	Dc	0.98	1.08	^{6}1.17	14	14
64^{4}	20^{1}	20^{4}	7	•	Foster Wheeler	Dc	□2.25	2.85	^{6}3.12	13	14
20	12	13^{4}	10	•	Franklin Mint	Dc	0.83	1.12	^{6}1.33	57	42
16^{4}	9	12^{6}	14		Friendly Ice Cream	Ap^{74}	0.71	0.79	^{7}0.88	18	15
38^{2}	24^{2}	27^{4}	18	•	Gannett Co.	Dc	△1.14	1.41	^{6}1.52	18	17
47^{6}	26	40^{6}	14		Gen'l Crude Oil	Dc	1.46	1.75	^{6}2.84	24	31
59^{7}	39^{2}	39^{2}	12	•	General Mills	My^{74}	2.81	3.18	3.18	13	13
36^{2}	24	25^{3}	19	•	Genuine Parts	Dc	1.13	1.30	^{6}1.36	17	14
55^{6}	22	22	7		Gilbert Assoc. 'A'	Dc	1.44	2.21	^{6}3.12	29	32
37^{4}	28^{6}	30^{4}	20	♦	Grainger W. W. Inc	Dc	1.00	1.37	^{6}1.50	20	21
25^{7}	13^{1}	15^{4}	8	♦	G.R.I. Corp.	Nv	0.95	1.79	^{5}2.02	52	43
194	125	125^{1}	21	•	Halliburton Co.	Dc	3.75	5.04	^{6}6.06	12	16
25	18^{2}	18^{2}	17	♦	Harland (John H.) Co.	Dc	0.84	1.01	^{6}1.10	20	18
40^{2}	22^{2}	22^{6}	9	•	Heller (W. E.) Int'l	Dc	2.03	2.25	^{6}2.48	13	12
47	20^{1}	22^{1}	8	•	Helmerich & Payne	Sp	1.70	△2.08	^{6}2.94	23	23
52^{2}	27^{6}	27^{6}	11	•	Heublein Inc.	Je^{74}	□2.11	2.57	2.57	15	15
92^{2}	68	68^{2}	29	•	Hewlett-Packard	Oc	1.40	1.89	^{4}2.32	16	21
22^{4}	15^{2}	16^{5}	14	•	Hunt (Phil. A.) Chem.	Dc	0.62	△1.07	^{6}1.17	17	22
30	22^{4}	25^{4}	14	•	Illinois Tool Works	Dc	1.23	1.61	^{6}1.84	14	16
254	196^{2}	198^{4}	16	•	Int'l Bus Machines	Dc	8.83	10.79	^{6}12.23	11	14
43^{2}	28	28	33	•	Int'l Flavor & Frag.	Dc	0.60	0.76	^{6}0.85	17	18
119^{3}	85^{5}	87^{4}	31	•	Johnson & Johnson	Dc	2.15	2.59	^{6}2.84	19	18
25^{6}	19^{1}	21	18	♦	Johnson Products	Au	0.65	0.92	^{5}1.14	19	21
23^{6}	12^{6}	13^{2}	6	♦	Kaneb Services	Dc	1.34	△1.56	^{6}2.10	19	21
92^{4}	56	56^{5}	15	•	Kerr McGee	Dc	2.14	2.52	^{6}3.71	11	20
11	6^{2}	6^{7}	9		Koss Corp.	Jn	0.41	0.60	^{3}0.73	82	61
26	17^{4}	21	25		Lawson Products	Dc	0.53	0.72	^{6}0.85	36	31
24^{6}	13^{2}	13^{6}	18		Lawter Chemicals	Dc	0.52	0.66	^{6}0.75	16	17
82^{6}	59^{6}	60^{1}	24	•	Lilly (Eli)	Dc	1.85	2.26	^{6}2.46	15	16
40^{2}	20^{6}	20^{6}	26		Loctite Corp.	Jn^{74}	0.60	0.80	0.80	34	34
70	37^{6}	37^{6}	19	•	Longs Drug Stores	Ja^{74}	1.66	1.93	^{4}2.01	19	16
52^{2}	30^{2}	30^{2}	18		Lowe's Companies	Jl	1.08	1.50	^{4}1.64	28	28
42^{3}	33	38^{4}	18	•	Lubrizol Corp.	Dc	1.30	1.81	^{6}2.10	15	18
43^{6}	33^{2}	36	24		Mallinckrodt Inc.	Dc	0.98	1.31	^{6}1.53	17	19
26^{2}	17^{2}	18^{7}	13	•	Malone & Hyde	Jn	1.19	1.32	^{3}1.43	13	13
25^{7}	15	17^{2}	12	•	Mapco, Inc.	Dc	0.70	1.05	^{6}1.39	19	27
35	13	13^{3}	10	•	Marion Laboratories	Jn^{74}	1.15	1.39	1.39	22	22
26	17^{2}	19^{2}	23		Mary Kay Cosmetics	Dc	0.56	0.70	^{6}0.83	34	34
46	33^{6}	33^{6}	17	•	Masco Corp.	Dc	1.41	1.81	^{6}2.00	23	25
63^{2}	36^{2}	37^{1}	25	•	McDonald's Corp.	Dc	0.94	1.31	^{6}1.50	35	33
53	19	27	28		Medtronic, Inc.	Ap^{74}	0.81	0.96	0.96	32	32
86	60	60	23	•	Merck & Co.	Dc	1.99	2.40	^{6}2.56	13	13
32^{6}	22^{4}	23	13		Mervyn's	Ja^{74}	1.15	1.63	^{4}1.72	30	26
57^{2}	36	36	32		Millipore Corp.	Dc	0.81	△1.02	^{6}1.14	19	18
42^{2}	30^{4}	36^{4}	14		Moore (Samuel)	Ja^{74}	1.36	2.23	^{4}2.53	35	35
57	45^{6}	45^{6}	19		Moore Corp.	Dc	1.62	1.93	^{6}2.37	11	14
31^{6}	21	21^{2}	16	•	Nalco Chemical	Dc	1.01	1.25	^{6}1.32	13	15
44^{6}	32^{2}	34	12	•	Nashua Corp.	Dc	2.15	2.55	^{6}2.93	12	14
47^{4}	34^{6}	36^{2}	31	•	Nat'l Chemsearch	Ap^{74}	0.88	1.16	1.16	22	22
25^{1}	10^{7}	11^{5}	9	•	Nat'l Semiconductor	My^{74}	0.32	1.32	1.32	68	68
56^{4}	37^{3}	37^{3}	13	•	Nat'l Starch & Chem	Dc	2.23	2.68	^{6}2.89	15	19
26	12^{2}	15^{6}	12		Northrop, King	Sp	0.54	0.95	^{6}1.34	36	45
75^{4}	35^{4}	35^{4}	17		Ocean Drill & Exp.	Dc	△1.26	1.66	^{6}2.14	22	24
11	6^{4}	6^{4}	5	♦	Ohio Sealey Mattress	Nv	0.87	1.18	^{5}1.26	23	21
26^{6}	10^{1}	10^{3}	4	•	Overseas Shiph'ldg Gr	Dc	△1.60	2.08	^{6}2.54	21	24
50^{6}	35^{4}	46	9		Pacific Lumber	Dc	3.00	4.58	^{6}5.04	20	22
35^{2}	18^{4}	19^{3}	10	•	Pacific Petroleum	Dc	0.98	1.42	^{6}2.00	17	36
14^{6}	11^{1}	13^{7}	10		Pay'n Save Corp.	Ja^{74}	0.92	1.24	^{4}1.36	19	19
32	12	15^{5}	11	•	Peabody Galion	Sp	1.04	1.28	^{6}1.47	40	26
71^{6}	41^{3}	41^{6}	12	•	PepsiCo., Inc.	Dc	3.05	3.36	^{6}3.51	10	9
40	22^{2}	23^{4}	24	•	Perkin Elmer	Jl	0.77	0.91	^{4}1.00	13	12
45	25^{2}	26^{4}	14	•	Pfizer, Inc.	Dc	1.50	1.74	^{6}1.95	11	11
61^{3}	42^{6}	43^{2}	15	•	Philip Morris, Inc.	Dc	2.33	2.71	^{6}2.91	20	18
24^{2}	15^{2}	17^{7}	11	•	Pizza Hut	Mr^{74}	1.08	1.53	^{6}1.69	32	38
30	18^{7}	20^{5}	13	•	Quaker State Oil Ref	Dc	1.09	1.36	^{6}1.56	18	17
46^{7}	34	34^{1}	14	•	Ralston Purina	Sp	1.87	2.22	^{6}2.49	12	10
41^{6}	29^{2}	29^{2}	19		Roadway Express	Dc	1.20	1.34	^{6}1.56	34	34
25^{4}	10^{6}	11^{1}	11	•	Robins (A.H.)	Dc	0.89	0.97	^{6}1.02	13	13
47^{7}	24^{7}	29	11	•	Sabine Royalty	Dc	1.50	1.85	^{6}2.57	24	28
19	10	12^{7}	14	♦	Sambo's Restaurants	Dc	0.54	0.76	^{6}0.91	45	43
75^{7}	46^{6}	47^{3}	22	•	Schering-Plough	Dc	1.44	1.97	^{6}2.13	22	23
133^{6}	87^{6}	91^{1}	29	•	Schlumberger, Ltd.	Dc	1.94	2.53	^{6}3.16	16	20
28^{2}	13^{5}	15^{2}	12	•	Searle (G. D.)	Dc	1.02	1.24	^{6}1.32	14	15
66^{2}	30	30	13	•	SEDCO Inc.	Je	1.42	△1.76	^{3}2.27	13	15
22^{2}	14	14	13		Sigma Int'l, Ltd.	Mr^{74}	0.82	1.07	^{6}1.12	19	18
23^{2}	19^{6}	20	13		Southland Financial	Dc	△1.26	△1.35	^{6}1.57	26	21
45	26^{1}	26^{3}	14	•	Squibb Corp.	Dc	△1.60	1.80	^{6}1.89	11	11
43^{2}	26^{6}	28	20	•	Standard Brands Paint	Sp	1.02	1.17	^{6}1.37	21	19
16	10	11^{7}	8		Sullair Corp.	Dc	0.90	1.29	^{6}1.57	26	31
41^{4}	27	27	17		Tennant Co.	Dc	1.08	1.50	^{6}1.63	21	24
28^{7}	14^{5}	15^{5}	3	•	Tesoro Petroleum	Sp	1.32	1.90	^{6}5.36	37	50
50^{6}	24^{4}	24^{4}	10		TexasCommerceBk'shr	Dc	△1.89	□2.28	^{6}2.51	16	14
115^{6}	73	75	18	•	Texas Instruments	Dc	2.17	3.67	^{6}4.13	21	27
21^{1}	9	10^{2}	9	•	Texas Oil & Gas	Au	0.72	0.93	^{5}1.13	24	26
49^{5}	31^{6}	32^{4}	17	•	Thomas & Betts	Dc	1.42	1.80	^{6}1.96	12	16
47^{1}	30^{6}	32^{4}	10	•	Tidewater Marine Serv.	Mr^{74}	2.03	2.79	^{6}3.15	16	21
63	48^{4}	58^{6}	12	•	Union Camp	Dc	2.57	4.01	^{6}5.08	14	22
88^{2}	54^{2}	68^{7}	26	•	Upjohn Co.	Dc	1.58	2.33	^{6}2.64	12	17
52^{7}	33^{4}	40^{6}	18	•	Utah Int'l	Oc	1.39	1.81	^{4}2.25	16	18
27^{4}	17	17	9		Vaughan-Jacklin	Je^{74}	1.34	1.82	1.82	41	41
34^{2}	16	21^{2}	18	•	Vetco Offshore	Ap^{74}	0.67	1.19	1.19	42	42
24^{5}	13^{7}	19	10	•	Wallace Busin. Forms	Jl	1.24	1.48	^{4}1.93	9	11
20^{4}	13^{5}	15^{2}	15	•	Wal-Mart Stores	Ja^{74}	0.70	0.93	^{4}1.01	49	38
19	14	14^{6}	11		Wettreau Inc.	Mr^{74}	1.18	1.34	^{6}1.39	11	11
77	45^{3}	54^{2}	10	•	Williams Cos.	Dc	3.94	4.65	^{6}5.63	11	13
44^{3}	33	34^{1}	14	•	Winn Dixie Stores	Je	1.98	2.12	^{3}2.48	11	12
19^{6}	14^{6}	17^{7}	4		Worthington Ind	My^{74}	2.14	4.01	4.01	46	46
127^{1}	85^{3}	85^{3}	21	•	Xerox Corp.	Dc	3.16	3.80	^{6}4.06	17	15
55	36^{6}	36^{6}	12		Yellow Freight Sys	Dc	2.21	2.51	^{6}2.99	24	27

Superior numbers preceding Last 12 Mos. earnings indicate month where different from annual ([1]for Jan. [2]for Feb. etc.) Listed: •NYSE. ♦ASE.

◦ Source: Standard & Poor's *Stock Summary*, September 1, 1974.

TABLE 13–7

Dynamic Growth of Principal Value and Income Return

Often overlooked is the *income potential* of growth stocks—just as dramatic as that for capital appreciation.

If in 1960, for instance, you had been looking at the stocks shown below, you might not have selected any of them because current income yield was low—only 1.17% for Avon Products. Yet, if you had bought them at that time, look at the higher yields you would now enjoy on the "cost" prices of your 1960 investments.

Merck paid \$.53 a share in 1960, a yield of 2.13%. The yearly dividend payments have nearly quadrupled since. The investor who bought it then would now be receiving \$2.00—*an annual yield of 8.04%* on his original purchase price of 24⅞.

In selecting growth stocks, capital and income *potential* is far more important than "current yield."

	1960			1970			
Stock	*Market Price* 1/31*	*Dividend for Year*	*Income Yield*	*Market Price 1/31*	*Dividend for Past Year*	*Present Income Yield on 1960 Price*	*Gain in Principal Value since 1960*
Avon Products	\$25¾	\$.30	1.17%	\$158	\$1.80	6.99%	+514%
Eastman Kodak	22⅝	.49	2.17	77⅞	1.22	5.39	+244
IBM	72⅛	.52	0.72	335¼	3.60	4.99	+365
McDonnell-Douglas	3⅞	.15	3.87	20¾	.40	10.32	+435
Merck	24⅞	.53	2.13	101	2.00	8.04	+306
Am. Home Products	25⅝	.70	2.73	64⅝	1.40	5.46	+152
AMP. Inc.	7¾	.13	1.68	50½	.48	6.19	+552
CBS	15½	.56	3.61	43¾	1.40	9.03	+182
Kerr-McGee	23¾	.60	2.53	92¼	1.50	6.32	+288
Nalco Chemical	9½	.25	2.63	61	.62	6.53	+542

* Adjusted for stock splits and stock dividends.

Source: Merrill Lynch, Pierce, Fenner & Smith,

TABLE 13–8
Selected Blue-chip (Heirloom) Stocks

Company	*Dividends Paid Uninterruptedly for at Least—*	*Price Range 1960–74*
Chesebrough-Pond's	93 years	7¾–92
E. I. du Pont de Nemours	72	84½–293¾
General Electric	77	27⅛*–75⅞
First National Bank of Boston	192	19¾–50
New England Tel. & Tel. Co.	90	21½–57¾
Eastman Kodak	74	20¼*–151¾
Travelers Corp.	112	15⅝*–54¼
Norfolk & Western R. R.	75	49⅝–150⅝
A. T. & T.	95	39⅝*–75
Texaco	74	15*–45⅛

* Adjusted for stock split.

annum) but steady growth rate tends to hold up in recession years as well as in boom years. They are sensitive to interest rate changes, falling in price if interest rates rise sharply, and increasing in price if interest rates decline, as they usually do in recession periods. Over the 1965–1975 decade, however, they performed poorly.

In addition to utilities, the shares of gold mining companies theoretically are good defensive issues. In bear markets, gold shares usually rise and pay higher dividends. The so-called "habit forming product" companies also suffer relatively little even in a fairly severe business adjustment. This makes the shares of tobacco, snuff, soft drink, gum, candy bar, and similar companies "defensive." Also, with social security and unemployment insurance and welfare, the earnings of packaged foods and grocery chain companies tend to be maintained under less favorable business conditions.

At the opposite pole from "defensive" stocks are the "cyclical" stocks —those which often furnish impressive rewards when business conditions are improving rapidly but which suffer most when business conditions are falling off. The preeminently cyclical stocks are found in the automobile, steel, cement, paper, machinery, building materials, coal, railroad, and railroad equipment industries. U.S. Steel, Johns-Manville, General Motors, International Paper and Anaconda Copper are examples of stocks which would be classified as cyclical. Such stocks may pay excellent dividends and may go up in price sharply in the prosperity phase of the business cycle but will tend to decline in price and reduce or even pass dividends during the downward phase.

The two tiered market, which fell apart in 1973–74, separated the glamour growth (or performance) stocks from the cyclicals, by sharply different (p/e) price/earnings evaluations. For example, at a time when Ford was selling at 9 times earnings, Chrysler at 10 times earnings, Bethlehem Steel at 9.5 times earnings, U.S. Steel at 11 times earnings, Giant Portland Cement at 9.4 times earnings, Norfolk & Western Railway at 10 times earnings; Simplicity Pattern was selling at 51 times earnings, Winnebago Industries at 73 times earnings, Tropicana Products at 54 times earnings, Levitz Furniture at 86 times earnings, Walt Disney Productions at 78 times, and McDonald's at 70 times earnings, to contrast a few. Since these high price/earnings ratios were discounting the future well into the hereafter, they were washed out in the 1973–74 market decline.

Minnie Pearl, a fried chicken franchise firm, was renamed Performance Systems, Inc. and went public in 1968. At that time, the company reported revenues of $13 million and earnings of $3.5 million under an accounting system that counted the total cost of a franchise as income, although only a small percentage was put down in cash. The shares soared to a high of $67 in 1968. By 1972 they sold for six cents a share. This is what Wall Street would agree was a *speculative* stock.

Webster defines "speculation" as a "transaction or venture the profits of which are conjectural. . . ." In this sense all common stock investment is speculative. A purchaser of stock has no promise, no certainty, that the funds received ultimately when the shares are sold will be more, less, or the same as the dollars originally paid. Because they provide a variable, rather than a fixed dollar outcome, all common shares are speculative in Webster's sense. But in the flexible parlance of Wall Street, a speculative stock has a more limited meaning. High flying performance stocks are speculative; "hot" new issues are speculative; penny oil and mining shares are speculative. The speculative glamour issues can usually be identified by their very high price/earnings ratios. For example, when the Standard & Poor's 500 were selling at 17 times earnings, some of the leading performance issues, or "concept stocks," such as Memorex, Automatic Data Processing, Levitz Furniture, Bausch & Lomb, and others were selling at 60, 70, and even 80 times earnings.

At an advanced stage of a bull market, small, little known companies go public and offer their low priced shares to an enormous speculative demand. Prices of new issues soar, doubling or tripling within days or weeks. When a postmortem is undertaken months or years afterward, the "hot" new issues are either liquidated, or liquidating, or selling for pennies. Four Seasons Nursing Homes was a hot new issue when it went public at $11 a share in May 1968. It soared to more than $100 a share in the same year. After a two for one split, it shot up again to $90.75 a share in 1969. It went into receivership in 1970, and by 1972, was down to 25 cents a share.

A number of those associated with the issue were indicted for alleged fraud.

Possibly the lowest level of speculative issues are the penny mining and oil shares. One broker-dealer specializing in such shares circulated market reports and offers extensively by mail, and his combination packets read like a stamp dealer's. In one report he plugged Trans-Mountain Uranium at 2 cents a share. The packet offer was a combination of "1,000 Trans-Mountain, 1,000 Santa Fe, and 5,000 Globe Hill Mining for $63.75 with a bonus of 1,000 United Empire Gold thrown in" for good measure.

The only term appropriate for those who buy penny oil and mining shares is "gambler." The lure that, perhaps once in 2,000 cases, a small outlay will pay incredible dividends, draws people in; but most of these wildcat fly by nights have as much prospect as Cheyenne Oil Ventures (sold by the now defunct Tellier & Co. of New Jersey for 15 cents a share), of which, in its offering circular, it was stated: "The U.S. Geological Survey has prepared a map which indicates that the immediate area of this structure is not considered by it as favorable with respect to its relative likelihood of yielding commercial quantities of oil as those areas of the United States which have yielded oil in commercial quantities." Thus the prospective purchaser was, in effect, told—if he took the trouble to read the fine print in the offering circular—that no oil of commercial value was likely to be found; but this apparently did not deter those who wanted to get in on a "good thing" on the "ground floor."

Common Stocks: Individual versus Institutional Investors

Common stock investment, then, can range from buying shares in the First National Bank of Boston, which has paid dividends uninterruptedly for the past 191 years, to paying 15 cents a share for Cheyenne Oil Ventures, Inc. Obviously, with so wide a diversity in common stocks, generalizations are both difficult and hazardous. One thing is quite clear, however. In recent years, individual investors, have been turning away from direct investment in the market. The proportion of stock held by institutional investors has been increasing while the share held by individuals has been declining. The exodus of the smaller investors from the market accelerated in 1973–74 with the surge of inflation, the sharp rise in interest rates and the drop in stock prices. The lure of high short term interest rates led many investors into short term instruments such as Treasury bills, bond anticipation notes and revenue anticipation notes (Bans and Rans), government agency securities, floating rate notes, and tax anticipation notes (Tans).

TABLE 13–9

INSTITUTIONAL FAVORITES

TABLE C

ISSUE	Industry	Closing Price Feb. 15	Instit'l Holdings Cos.	Instit'l Holdings Shs. (000)	Ind. Div. Rate $	% Yld. on Ind. Div.	¶Sh. Earn. Last 12 Mos. $	P-E Ratio
Int'l Bus. Mach.	58	233½	1137	14222	5.12	2.2	[12]10.79	22
General Motors	7	50⅛	782	15952	4.90	9.8	[12]8.34	6
Exxon Corp.	61	82½	751	18551	4.55	5.5	[12]10.89	8
Amer. Tel. & Tel.	85	51¾	693	22453	3.08	6.0	[12]4.98	10
General Electric	24	55⅞	686	16789	1.60	2.9	[12]3.21	17
Eastman Kodak	5	100¼	663	11208	1.91	1.9	[9]4.04	25
Texaco Inc.	61	27⅞	602	26011	2.00	7.2	[12]4.75	6
Xerox Corp.	58	107	597	9796	1.00	0.9	[12]3.80	28
Sears Roebuck	76	83½	429	6072	1.85	2.2	[10]4.27	20
Ford Motor	7	44½	410	11539	3.20	7.2	[12]9.13	5
Mobil Oil	61	45½	398	10550	3.05	6.7	[12]8.28	5
Minn. Mng. & Mfg.	56	70	385	7655	1.25	1.8	[12]2.62	27
Gen'l. Tel. & El'trcs.	85	24¾	378	12750	1.72	6.9	[12]2.87	9
duPont (E.I.) Nem.	17	158½	374	16931	5.75	3.6	[12]12.04	13
First Nat'l City Corp.	11	37⅞	363	16853	0.72	1.9	[12]2.14	18
Atlantic Richfield	60	96½	356	7197	2.00	2.1	[12]4.76	20
Westinghouse Elec.	24	21¼	354	13265	0.972	4.5	[12]1.82	12
Gulf Oil	61	22⅛	352	11956	1.50	6.8	[12]4.06	5
Int'l Tel. & Tel.	26	26⅜	350	10247	1.40	5.3	[9]4.10	6
Stand. Oil of Indiana	60	90⅞	339	5221	3.20	3.5	[12]7.33	12
Merck & Co.	22	73½	335	7169	1.40	1.9	[12]2.40	31
Dow Chemical	17	54⅜	331	8525	1.00	1.8	[12]2.94	18
Goodyear T. & Rub.	77	16	326	11521	1.00	6.2	[12]2.53	6
Union Carbide Corp.	17	33¼	322	8923	2.10	6.3	[12]4.78	7
Burroughs Corp.	58	180	314	4305	1.00	0.6	[12]6.01	30
Texas Util.	92	20⅞	307	8417	1.08	5.2	[11]2.01	10
Phillips Petroleum	60	48¼	305	7409	1.40	2.9	[12]3.05	16
Stand. Oil (Calif.)	61	28	287	11786	1.70	6.1	[12]4.97	6
Pfizer Inc.	22	37¾	281	8707	0.73	1.9	[12]1.74	22
Caterpillar Tractor	42	58¼	280	5809	1.60	2.7	[12]4.32	13
Int'l Nickel of Can.	55	37¼	280	8087	1.35	3.6	[12]3.04	12
Amer. Home Prods.	22	36⅞	277	10976	0.708	1.9	[12]1.25	29
Warner Lambert	22	34	272	11451	0.76	2.2	[9]1.73	19
Southern Co.	92	16½	254	6688	1.38	8.4	[12]2.07	8
Int'l Paper	64	47⅝	245	7677	1.69	3.5	[12]3.60	13
Avon Products	21	47	244	5814	1.48	3.1	[12]2.34	20
Honeywell Inc.	26	72⅝	242	2752	1.40	1.9	[12]5.12	14
Penney (J.C.) Co.	76	70¾	240	3740	1.12	1.6	[10]3.10	23
Deere & Co.	41	44¾	238	6996	1.56	3.5	[10]5.75	8
Kresge (S.S.)	74	33¾	237	1292	0.20	0.6	[10]1.14	30
Continental Oil	60	42⅜	235	7438	1.60	3.8	[12]4.81	9
Monsanto Co.	17	54¾	235	4848	2.00	3.7	[12]6.90	8
So. Calif. Edison	92	18¾	233	6209	1.56	8.3	[12]2.70	7
Coca-Cola	82	110⅜	227	2999	1.90	1.7	[9]3.52	31
Polaroid Corp.	5	71	227	5385	1.40	0.5	[12]3.05	23
Chase Manhattan Cp.	11	50¼	226	3167	2.20	4.4	[12]5.15	10
Com'w'th Edison	92	29⅞	222	4261	2.30	7.7	[12]3.16	9
Florida Pwr. & Lt.	92	25¼	220	5029	1.22	4.8	[12]3.09	8
Sperry Rand	24	38⅝	219	8851	0.66	1.7	[9]3.14	12
Procter & Gamble	80	84¾	216	3294	1.80	2.1	[12]3.62	23
Bristol-Myers	22	46⅛	214	4391	1.32	2.9	[12]3.16	15
Fed. Dept. Stores	76	32¾	211	4475	1.08	3.3	[10]2.60	13
Virginia Elec. & Pwr.	92	15⅜	210	6387	1.18	7.7	[12]2.13	7
Amer. Elec. Pwr.	92	26	208	2825	1.90	7.3	[12]2.85	9
Weyerhaeuser	16	36	208	13024	0.80	2.2	[12]2.74	13
Gillette Co.	23	33¾	205	4533	1.50	4.4	[9]2.80	12
RCA Corp.	24	18½	203	8068	1.00	5.4	[9]2.27	8
Johnson & Johnson	49	102¼	199	2948	0.55	0.5	[9]2.49	41
Central & So. West	92	15⅞	193	8277	1.12	7.1	[12]1.72	9
Morgan (J.P.)	11	58	198	4689	1.60	2.8	[12]3.89	15
General Foods	33	27	189	3154	1.40	5.2	[12]2.35	11
Houston Lt. & Pwr.	92	27⅞	188	3537	1.48	5.3	[12]3.05	9
Schering-Plough	22	64⅛	185	5410	0.62	1.0	[9]1.91	34
Halliburton Co.	62	153½	181	2824	1.12	0.7	[12]5.04	30
Alcan Aluminium	50	35⅝	179	6469	1.00	2.8	[12]2.42	15
Aetna Life & Caslty	36	61¼	173	4344	2.16	3.5	[9]6.99	9
Philip Morris	89	104½	172	5733	1.40	1.3	[12]5.42	19
Amer. Cyanamid	17	20¾	1710	3206	1.40	6.7	[12]2.37	9
Kennecott Copper	51	39¾	171	4282	2.00	5.0	[12]4.81	8
Sterling Drug	22	27	169	5078	0.65	2.4	[12]1.29	21
Pacific Gas& Elec.	92	23⅝	165	5899	1.88	8.0	[12]3.23	7
Upjohn Co.	22	56⅛	165	5621	0.88	1.6	[9]2.21	25
Illinois Power	92	24	161	2462	2.20	1.7	[12]2.51	15
Texas Instruments	26	96	159	5091	0.68	0.7	[12]3.67	26

¶ Period ended indicated by superior numbers: [1]for Jan., [2]for Feb., etc.

Source: New York Stock Exchange, *Growth Leaders on the Big Board*, Spring 1974, p. 17.

It is estimated that total institutional holdings of NYSE listed stock amounted to about 45 percent of the NYSE list at the end of 1973 in contrast to less than 15 percent at the end of 1949. Institutional favorites are shown in Table 13–9. Companies having the largest number of shareholders may be seen in Table 13–10. They tend to attract the small investor.

College endowment funds, commercial banks, savings banks, insurance companies, pension funds, and, of course, mutual funds invest in common stocks. Their portfolio holdings and changes in investment choices—what they sell off and what they acquire, from year to year—can be studied, and the individual in his investment choices can thus obtain, without cost, the benefits of skilled investment managers' decisions. For example, some insights into how a big investment manager picks stocks for its customers' accounts is provided by the First National City Bank of New York. The bank distributes a 40 page booklet setting forth its general policies and specific criteria for selecting stocks in keeping with its fiduciary responsi-

TABLE 13–10
NYSE Companies with the Largest Number of Common Stockholders of Record, Early 1974

Company	*Stockholders*	*Company*	*Stockholders*
American Tel. & Tel.	2,934,000	Detroit Edison	175,000
General Motors	1,283,000	Commonwealth Edison	172,000
Exxon Corp.	725,000	Niagara Mohawk Power	169,000
Int'l Business Machines	557,000	Greyhound Corp.	165,000
General Electric	537,000	Litton Industries	165,000
General Tel. & Electronics	430,000	Transamerica Corp.	165,000
Ford Motor	341,000	Standard Oil (Indiana)	164,000
Gulf Oil	333,000	American Electric Power	164,000
Texaco Inc.	310,000	Westinghouse Electric	161,000
Consolidated Edison	308,000	Int'l Tel. & Tel.	157,000
U.S. Steel	302,000	Pacific Gas & Electric	156,000
RCA Corp.	295,000	General Public Utilities	154,000
Sears, Roebuck	267,000	Phillips Petroleum	153,000
Standard Oil of Calif.	253,000	Northeast Utilities	150,000
Tenneco Inc.	233,000	Pan Amer. World Airways	147,000
Eastman Kodak	233,000	Xerox Corp.	138,000
Bethlehem Steel	227,000	Atlantic Richfield	136,000
du Pont de Nemours	217,000	Int'l Harvester	136,000
Mobil Oil	216,000	Penn Central	135,000
Chrysler Corp.	209,000	Pennsylvania Power	135,000
Occidental Petroleum	196,000	American Motors	130,000
Public Service Elec. & Gas	192,000	American Brands	129,000
Union Carbide	188,000	Cities Service	124,000
Philadelphia Electric	184,000	El Paso Natural Gas	122,000
Columbia Gas	175,000	Reynolds Industries	120,000
		American Can	120,000

Source: New York Stock Exchange, *Fact Book*, 1974.

bilities.[16] It also provides a list of the largest holdings of all common stocks in its fiduciary accounts as well as an example of holdings in a typical common stock trust fund.

Rights

"Rights" are privileges granted to stockholders to buy new shares at a price generally below the prevailing market. By state law or corporate charter, stockholders (generally common stockholders only) are given a preemptive right to buy a proportionate part of any new stock issued, or other securities which can be converted into stock, in order that they may retain their proportionate ownership in the company. Suppose that Company A has 100 common shares outstanding, of which Jenny Jones owns 10. If the corporation is successful and it is felt that earnings would be even better if the company had more money with which to work, it may be decided to sell 50 additional shares. If Ms. Jones has the right to buy 5 of the new shares (generally expressed as 10 rights, i.e., one for each old share), she can, by exercising her right, acquire 5 shares to add to the old 10, allowing her to retain 10 percent ownership in the company. Although preemptive rights are not so important as they used to be, in the days when corporations were small, and although it is the trend to deny them to stockholders in corporate charters whenever state law does not make them mandatory, some of our biggest and best corporations find corporate rights the instrumentality by which additional corporate funds can often be obtained advantageously.

By way of illustration, the American Telephone and Telegraph Company has made use of rights for years. When it needs new money, it can offer its stockholders additional shares. If the stock is selling at $45 a share, stockholders feel they are getting a bargain when they are told that they can buy the additional stock at, say, $40 a share. The result is that the company sells practically all of the new issue to its shareholders.

Even though stockholders do not have preemptive rights, it is common financial practice to grant them privileged subscription rights. Since the stockholders have had experience with the company's stock, why should they not be among the best customers for an additional issue of the company's stock if the company has been successful? Furthermore, if the new

---

[16] *The Investment Management Group of First National City Bank 1974 Review*, New York, 1975: See also "Telling More at Citibank," *Business Week*, March 9, 1974, p. 140. For further information on the activities of institutional investment managers and their selections, see the magazines *Financial Analysts Journal* and *Institutional Investor*.

stock is offered at a price materially below the market price of the old stock, the equity of the old stockholders would be diluted if they were not given rights to acquire a proportionate amount of new stock.

What to Do with Rights

A right is a valuable instrument; it is the privilege of being able to buy for less the equivalent of what has been and is selling for more. There are three things that can be done with a right:

1. Do nothing.
2. Exercise it.
3. Sell it.

To do nothing is very foolish, since a right has value only so long as it is used (exercised). Rights are usually issued for only short periods—two weeks or a month. If you do nothing with your rights you will find that their value evaporates. In spite of repeated warnings, however, we constantly read of people who, through ignorance, do not take proper action to preserve their interests. Of course, it takes money to exercise rights (you have the right to buy for a certain price, but you must have the price). It is only by exercising rights, however, that a stockholder can end up with proportionately as large an interest in the company as was held before the new stock was issued. If you do not have the money to exercise your rights, you should sell them (any stockbrokerage firm can sell them for you) before they lose their value.

The Value of a Right

There is a formula for computing the theoretical value of a right. This formula rests on the assumption that the corporation can earn the same percentage on the money received for new stock as it was earning on the total market value of the old stock. If this is not a fact or if investors do not believe it is a fact, the price at which rights will sell in the market will differ from the theoretical value. The formula is

$$V = \frac{M - S}{N + 1},$$

in which:

V = Value of a right;
M = Market value of a share of old stock;
S = Subscription price of new stock;
N = Number of old shares necessary to have the privilege of buying a new share.

This formula is to be used to calculate the theoretical value of a right when the old shares are sold and the rights which attach thereto are sold along with them. In the financial market this condition is expressed by saying that the stock is sold "cum rights" or "rights-on." When the time comes when the stock alone (without the rights) is sold (called "ex-rights" or "rights-off"), we use the formula

$$\frac{M - S}{N}.$$

We may illustrate the use of the first formula by a simple illustration. Suppose a company has $1 million of stock outstanding (10,000 shares, each of $100 par) and has been earning $100,000 yearly, so that the stock is selling in the market at $200 a share. Now the company decides that it could earn 10 percent on $1.5 million of new money, so it decides to give its stockholders the right to buy a new share at $150 for each old share held:

$$V = \frac{M - S}{N + 1},$$

$$V = \frac{\$200 - \$150}{1 + 1},$$

$$V = \frac{\$50}{2},$$

$$V = \$25.$$

Now suppose that Jenny Jones had one share of the old stock. It was worth $200 in the market (including the $25 right inherent in it). If she sold the right, she would still have a share worth $175. The share and the $25 in her pocket would keep her $200 intact. If she used (exercised) the right and paid $150 along with it, she would have two shares, each worth $175, or $350 for the two, representing her former investment of $200 and her additional investment of $150 more. We now see that if she failed to do anything with the right, she would end up with merely $175 in the old share and would have suffered a shrinkage in her investment of $25. The $25 should preferably have been received in cash through sale of the right or invested in new stock, rather than have been lost through shrinkage of the investment.

After the old stock sold, ex-rights, it would presumably be worth $175 in the market, other things being equal. The right to buy for $150 the equivalent of what was selling for $175 would surely be worth $25:

$$V = \frac{M - S}{N}$$

or

$$\frac{\$175 - \$150}{1} = \frac{\$25}{1} = \$25$$

The essential thing to note is that when rights are issued, value leaves the old stock. This value should be turned into cash (by selling the right) or invested in new stock (by exercising the right). If nothing is done, the value is lost. Naturally, it would be better to sell rights than to exercise them if, for any reason, it were felt that it would not be good to make a further investment in the same stock.

Warrants

Warrants are options to buy securities, generally common stock, at a given price. They are at times issued in connection with reorganizations; at other times we find them offered in connection with the initial sale of securities which would not sell satisfactorily without the help of the warrants (to "sweeten" the offering). Nondetachable warrants may be sold only along with the securities to which they are attached; detachable warrants may be sold separately. Rights are relatively short lived, whereas warrants are good either for a period of years or indefinitely until exercised. Warrants fluctuate more than the stock to which they apply, and in this sense they are more speculative.

"$500 to $104,000 in 4 years" is the way an advertisement about warrants begins. It tells the amazing but true story of the R.K.O. warrant. In 1940 the Radio-Keith Orpheum Co. (R.K.O.) reorganized after some years of bad fortune. The old common stockholders seemed to fare badly. For each old share, they received only one sixth of a share of new common stock plus one warrant, good to buy one share of new common stock from the company at $15 per share. In 1942 R.K.O. common was selling at a low of 2½ and with general pessimism rife, the chance of R.K.O. common ever selling above $15, at which point the warrants would begin to have some actual value, seemed slim. R.K.O. warrants were, therefore, selling on the New York Curb Exchange at only 1/16, or 6¼ cents, per warrant. But the picture changed in four years. The R.K.O. common stock advanced to a high of 28⅛ on the New York Stock Exchange. The right to buy R.K.O. common at $15 per share from the company when it was selling on the open market at $28 per share was worth $13, and the warrants did sell at exactly $13 on the American Stock Exchange (then the New York Curb Exchange). That is the story of the R.K.O. warrant—$500 invested in these warrants in 1942 was worth $104,000 just four years later.

From this illustration you can see how much more the warrant lends itself to a capital gain in a rising market than does the common stock itself.

Between 1942 and 1946, R.K.O. common stock went from $2.50 a share to $28. Therefore, a $500 investment in the stock appreciated to $5,625. But between 1942 and 1946 R.K.O. warrants went from 6¼ cents to $13. Therefore, a $500 investment appreciated to $104,000.

Even more startling is the history of Tri-Continental Corporation perpetual warrants. They could have been purchased in 1942 at 1/32nd or slightly more than 3 cents per warrant. By 1969 this warrant rose to a high of 75¾, so that $500 invested in Tri-Continental *warrants* in 1942, if held to 1969, could have been sold for $1,212,000. If the same $500 had been invested in Tri-Continental *common* at the 1942 low, it would have been worth $48,451 in 1969. Compare the performance of the common and warrants.

But while the leverage of warrants allows them to rise faster than the common in advancing markets, they also fall more sharply than the common in bear markets. For example, in the 1969–70 bear market, Ling-Temco-Vought warrants fell from a high of $82 to a low of 2¼; Strategic Systems warrants fell from $42 to 50 cents; TWA warrants fell from $80 to $4⅝. Atlantic Richfield Oil warrants fell from 47¼ in 1969 to 1½ in 1972. Warrants pay no return, no dividends, and at times expire and lose all value. There are now about 300 actively traded warrants. They are listed on both the American and New York Stock Exchanges. Interesting warrants are now outstanding, but this is an area primarily for the sophisticated investor.[17]

PREFERRED STOCK

From an investment point of view, preferred stocks are more like bonds than common stocks. The return on the investment, if one gets it, is fixed and limited. Of course, preferred stock, unlike most bonds, has no maturity, and the preferred stockholder is a stockholder, i.e., an owner, not a creditor. Ordinarily a corporation gets into little difficulty by foregoing dividends on its stock, common or preferred. Preferred stocks are issued to attract investors who wish a safer and less changeable income than they could get from common stocks. For most of the last 30 years, preferred stocks of high grade have tended to yield more income than high grade bonds, but this extra payment is largely to compensate for extra risk.

The rights of the preferred stockholder are to be found in the corporation's charter. Dividends on preferred stock may be cumulative or non-

[17] For more detail, see Sidney Fried, *Speculating With Warrants,* latest ed., R. H. M. Associates, 220 Fifth Avenue, New York, N.Y. 10001.

cumulative. Cumulative dividends which are not paid when they should regularly be paid (ordinarily once a quarter) accumulate for the benefit of the preferred stockholder and must be paid, as a matter of law, when earnings of the corporation permit, before dividends can be paid on the common. If the preferred is noncumulative, the stockholder has no special claim for dividends which have been passed.

Ordinarily, the return on preferred stock is definite, and the owner of preferred stock does not share in earnings beyond his stated 5, 6, or more percent. In some cases, however, a special type of preferred stock is issued, known as "participating preferred." In the case of participating preferred, the stock is permitted to share in earnings, if they are large enough to so warrant, in excess of the stated rate of dividend. Such a stock is entitled to its regular dividend and then, after the common shares receive a similar rate of dividend, participates with the common stock in the balance of the earnings distributed as dividends.

Some preferred stock is callable, that is, the issuing company can retire the stock, usually at a premium of 5 percent or more. Only when market conditions make it impossible to issue callable preferred stock will preferred stock without a call provision be issued.

Although preferred stock represents ownership and cannot be secured like a debt, there have been instances where a fund has been provided to assure future dividend payments. There have also been sinking funds used to provide for retirement of preferred stock. Such devices may make the preferred stock easier to sell. Sometimes preferred stock is issued with a conversion feature which allows it to be exchanged for common stock at a given ratio. Convertible preferreds have been popular because they give the cautious investor a steady return but also provide a hedge against inflation, since conversion into common is possible. Such conversion proves advantageous when earnings increase and common stock rises in price. Ideally, the best preferred to buy would be cumulative, participating, convertible preferred, but there are few such animals.[18]

BONDS

A bond is a formal evidence of a debt in which the borrower promises to pay the lender a specified amount with interest at a fixed rate, payable on specified dates. It differs from a stock in that it constitutes a debt of

[18] For further information see *Preferred Stock Guide*, latest annual edition, Salomon Brothers, One New York Plaza, New York, N.Y. 10004; see also *Understanding Preferred Stocks and Bonds*, and *Understanding Convertible Securities*, New York Stock Exchange, 11 Wall Street, New York, N.Y. 10005. Free copies of these booklets may be obtained by request.

the issuing corporation rather than a share in the ownership of the business. Interest on bonds is a fixed charge which the borrowing corporation must pay, whether it has sufficient income or not. If it misses an interest payment, it is said to be "in default," and reorganization or bankruptcy will follow.

The volume of bonds, listed and unlisted, outstanding in the United States is greater than all stock issues, but most of the bonds are held by institutional investors, such as insurance companies, banks, and so on. Relatively few individuals—and then only the wealthier ones—own corporate bonds. Indeed, for the investor of average means, the amount of time and energy that would be necessary to obtain a good grasp of the complexities of bond investment, and the exposure to interest rate and purchasing power risks associated with bond investment, may make such investment difficult.

The Case for Bonds

The purchaser of a bond limits income return and largely foregoes the prospect of capital gain, appreciation, or speculative profit. If, despite these sacrifices, serious risk of loss is still possible, as is the case when a corporate bond is purchased, particularly if it is not of the highest grade, is it worth it?

Mr. George Wanders, former editor of the *Bond Buyer*, in stating the case for bonds, tells a fable:

> Once upon a time a stock hare and a bond tortoise set out on an investment race. The hare had all the best of it for a while, what with fat dividends, good business prospects, and a boom on the New York Stock Exchange. The tortoise merely plugged along, paying a stipulated rate of interest. Almost everyone cheered the hare and bet on it, but there were a few who favored the tortoise, partly because as trustees of savings banks they had no alternative under state law.
>
> This fable ends in the traditional way. The stock hare lagged after a time and took a dividend nap. The bond tortoise kept going and in the end paid the investors rather handsomely and also returned to them the entire original investment.

There is nothing farfetched in this approach to the investment problem. It reflects the theory that stocks have the better of it in prosperity, while bonds come into their own and are really appreciated in recession or depression. The rule is not invariable, for there are corporations in which a stock investment has proved, over the years, a better proposition than almost any bond investment. Some of our leading corporations have no bonded debt, and an equity, representing ownership, is the only possible way of investment in such cases. Campbell Soup, International Flavors and Fragrances, Simplicity Pattern and INA, for example, have no bonded indebtedness.

The wealthier investor, whose financial needs require that a portion of his capital be subjected to no more than minimum risk, may turn to high grade bonds. Common stocks, even those of investment grade, may represent a greater risk than do high grade bonds because they represent a share of ownership in a business, whose profits will necessarily vary with changes over time.

There are at least five reasons for favoring high grade bonds. (*a*) When the economic going gets rough and dividends on stock may be omitted, interest payments on high grade bonds may continue. (*b*) If it gets too rough, and a company ends in the bankruptcy court, the bondholder ends up with the assets and the stockholder gets little or nothing. (*c*) In a recession, the prices of high grade bonds tend to go up. This is because investor demand now concentrates upon those securities which continue to pay interest and which appear to be able to weather the storm. The increased demand concentrated on a limited supply sends the price up. The opposite is true, of course, in a prosperity period, when investor demand turns away from the fixed and limited returns on a high grade bond. There is also a lessening of investor demand because the purchasing power of the fixed and limited return is diminishing. The bond offers no hedge against inflation. The really high grade bond, however, is a hedge against deflation. (*d*) There are numerous individuals of substantial means whose requirements for fixed income securities cannot be met by U.S. savings bonds. (*e*) Wealthier investors find that the tax exempt features of state and municipal bonds are quite attractive.

If you or your parents are in this latter category there is a simple formula which will show you the percentage yield which a bond or other security with fully taxable income must give in order to provide an after-tax yield equivalent to a given tax exempt yield. Find your tax bracket and then apply this formula:

$$\text{Tax exempt yield} \div (100\% - \text{Tax bracket } \%) = \text{Taxable equivalent yield}$$

Assume you are in the 55 percent tax bracket. If you can buy a 6 percent tax exempt bond what would an alternate investment with fully taxable income have to yield to provide 6 percent after taxes?

$$6.00\% \div (100\% - 55\%) = ?$$

$$\frac{6.00\%}{45\%} = 13.33\%$$

Your fully taxable investment would have to yield 13.33 percent to give an after tax return of 6 percent for someone in the 55 percent tax bracket.

Bond Ratings

When you first become interested in a particular bond, an initial step in finding out something about it is to go to one of the financial services, such as Standard & Poor's or Moody's, and see what rating they have assigned to the bond. While these financial services are not infallible, their experts are accustomed to judging the relative merits of fixed income securities, and the rating will give you a clear idea of the approximate quality of the bond. It is a useful orientation for looking further into merits, or lack of them, of the proposed purchase. It may be that when you see the rating assigned, you will no longer be interested in the bond, since it may be classed as speculative; and you would have little interest in buying a speculative bond, which is really a contradiction in terms. The Standard & Poor's Bond Ratings are as shown in Figure 13–7. The other services have similar classifications; they differ only in the symbols assigned and vary little in the method of classification. While these services can be obtained in banks, brokerage houses, or large libraries, Standard & Poor's publishes a *Monthly Bond Guide*, which provides, among other information, the bond ratings.

A sample from this *Bond Guide* is shown in Figure 13–8. You will note that bonds are described by:

1. The name of the company.
2. The type of bond or security.
3. The interest paid.
4. The maturity date.

Thus, "General Tel. Co., Ohio, 1st 7⅝s 2001" means the first mortgage bond issue of the General Telephone Company of Ohio paying 7⅝ percent interest per annum and maturing in 2001.

Bond Prices, Coupons, and Yields

Usually, though not always, bonds are issued in denominations of $1,000. This is the par or face value stated on the bond, and it is the amount on which interest is computed. The bond rate, sometimes called the "coupon" rate in the case of coupon bonds, is the simple interest rate, stated in the bond, at which the interest payment is computed. If you

FIGURE 13–7
Standard & Poor's Bond Ratings

CORPORATE BONDS

BANK QUALITY BONDS—Under present commercial bank regulations bonds rated in the top four categories (AAA, AA, A, BBB or their equivalent) generally are regarded as eligible for bank investment.

AAA Bonds rated AAA are highest grade obligations. They possess the ultimate degree of protection as to principal and interest. Marketwise they move with interest rates, and hence provide the maximum safety on all counts.

AA Bonds rated AA also qualify as high grade obligations, and in the majority of instances differ from AAA issues only in small degree. Here, too, prices move with the long term money market.

A Bonds rated A are regarded as upper medium grade. They have considerable investment strength but are not entirely free from adverse effects of changes in economic and trade conditions. Interest and principal are regarded as safe. They predominantly reflect money rates in their market behavior, but to some extent, also economic conditions.

BBB The BBB, or medium grade category is borderline between definitely sound obligations and those where the speculative element begins to predominate. These bonds have adequate asset coverage and normally are protected by satisfactory earnings. Their susceptibility to changing conditions, particularly to depressions, necessitates constant watching. Marketwise, the bonds are more responsive to business and trade conditions than to interest rates. This group is the lowest which qualifies for commercial bank investment.

BB Bonds given a BB rating are regarded as lower medium grade. They have only minor investment characteristics. In the case of utilities, interest is earned consistently but by narrow margins. In the case of other types of obligors, charges are earned on average by a fair margin, but in poor periods deficit operations are possible.

B Bonds rated as low as B are speculative. Payment of interest cannot be assured under difficult economic conditions.

CCC-CCC Bonds rated CCC and CC are outright speculations. with the lower rating denoting the more speculative. Interest is paid, but continuation is questionable in periods of poor trade conditions. In the case of CC ratings the bonds may be on an income basis and the payment may be small.

C The rating of C is reserved for income bonds on which no interest is being paid.

DDD-D All bonds rated DDD, DD and D are in default, with the rating indicating the relative salvage value.

Canadian corporate bonds are rated on the same basis as American corporate issues. The ratings measure the intrinsic value of the bonds, but they do not take into account exchange and other uncertainties.

MUNICIPAL BONDS

Standard & Poor's Municipal Bond Ratings cover obligations of all states or sub-divisions. In addition to general obligations, ratings are assigned to bonds payable in whole or in part from special revenues.

AAA-Prime—These are obligations of the highest quality. They have the lowest probability of default. In a period of economic stress the issuers will suffer the smallest declines in income and will be least susceptible to autonomous decline. Debt burden is not inordinately high. Revenue structure appears adequate to meet future expenditure needs. Quality of management would not appear to endanger repayment of principal and interest.

AA-High Grade—The investment characteristics of bonds in this group are only slightly less marked than those of the prime quality issues. Bonds rated AA have the second lowest probability of default.

A-Upper Medium Grade—Principal and interest on bonds in this category are regarded as safe. This rating describes the third lowest probability of default. It differs from the two higher ratings because there is some weakness, either in the local economic base, in debt burden, in the balance between revenues and expenditures or in quality of management. Under certain adverse circumstances, **any one such weakness** might impair the ability of the issuer to meet debt obligaitons at some future date.

BBB-Medium Grade—This is the lowest investment grade security rating. Under certain adverse conditions, several of the above factors could contribute to a higher default probability. The difference between A and BBB ratings is that the latter shows **more than one** fundamental weakness, whereas the former shows only one deficiency among the factors considered.

BB-Lower Medium Grade—Bonds in this group have some investment characteristics, but they no longer predominate. For the most part this rating indicates a speculative, non-investment grade obligation.

B-Low Grade—Investment characteristics are virtually non-existent and default could be imminent.

D-Defaults—Interest and/or principal in arrears.

FIGURE 13–8
Standard & Poor's Bond Guide

42 Con-Dal

Title-Industry Code & Co. Finances (In Italics) / Individual Issue Statistics — Exchange	Ind / Interest Dates	*Chgs. 1970* / S&P Quality Rating	*Times Earn. 1971* / Eligible	Bond Form	*1972* / Legality (Ct Ma NH NJ NY)	*Yr. End*	*Cash &Eqv* / Redemption Provisions — Refund Earliest/Other	*Current Assets* / Call Price — For S.F.	*Liabs* (Million $)	*Date* / Call Price — Regular	*L. Term Debt (Mil $)* / Out-st'd'g (Mil $)	*Debt % Prop* / Underwriter Firm	Year	*Interim Times Earn. — Period* / Price Range 1960-71 High	1960-71 Low	*1972* / 1972 High	*1973* / 1972 Low	1973 High	1973 Low	Mo. End Price Sale(s) or Bid	Curr Yield	Yield to Mat.
Continental Tel Corp	*67c*	....	....		....	*Dc*	*36.5*	*220*	*205*	*9-73*	*942*	*66.1*										
•Notes 9⅝s '75	fA15	BBB	X	R	- - - - -		....	....		NC	65.0	H17	'70	110	100	108⅞	106	106⅞	100¾	s103¾	9.28	7.11
Control Data	*20*	....	....		....	*Dc*	*433*	*4082*	*2090*	*12-72*	*1712*	*476*										
SF Deb 5s '85	Mn	BBB	X	R	- - - - -		....	†100.42		†103.30	32.0	D1	'65	100⅝	64	77¾	68	77	71	74	6.76	8.64
•xs SF Deb 5½s '87	jD	BBB	X	R	- - - - -		....	100		†103.70	50.4	H16	'67	90	60	81	75	82⅜	73½	s77⅜	7.11	8.26
[1]***Corn Products***	*27c*	*3.48*	*2.99*		*3.55*	*Dc*	*78.6*	*539*	*300*	*12-72*	*175*	*38.1*										
•SF Deb 5¾s '92	fA15	AA	X	R	- ✓- - ✓		[2]102.89	100		†103.68	90.7	D4	'67	100	75	89	84	87⅛	78¼	83½	6.89	7.39
•Sub Deb 4⅝s '83	aO	A	X	CR	- - - - -		[3]100	....		[4]100¾	33.9	Exch	'58	106	64	82	77	82	70⅞	77⅛	6.00	8.05
Corning Glass Works	*29*	*5.01*	*4.19*		*5.82*	*Dc*	*49.5*	*371*	*184*	*6-73*	*★124*	*21.8*		*6 Mo Jun*		*6.34*	*5.41*					
SF Deb 7¾s '98	mN15	AA	X	R	- ✓✓- -		[5]103⅞	[6]100		†107¾	50.0	L3	'73	....	....	....	....	100¼	99	100¼	7.73	7.72
Cousins Mtg. & Eq. Inv.	*56*	△*10.74*	△*2.47*		△*1.67*	*Au*	*18.9*			*8-73*	*70.0*											
•xw Sub Deb 6½s '82	Ms	NR		R	- - - - -		....	....		[7]100	30.0	M5	'72	....	....	88½	80	89	74	80	8.13	10.16
Crane Co	*13g*	*1.36*	*1.44*		*1.61*	*Dc*	*32.1*	*288*	*124*	*12-72*	*245*	*93.5*										
•SF Deb 6½s '92	Jd	BBB	Y	R	- - - - -		[2]103½	100		†104.70	35.8	D5	'67	102⅞	72½	89½	83	85⅝	77½	79½	8.18	8.76
•Sub SF Deb 7s '93	Ao	B	Y	R	- - - - -		....	[8]100		†107	18.0	0	'68	100	69	89¼	82	87½	73	s73	9.59	10.23
•Sub SF Deb B 7s '94	jJ	B	Y	R	- - - - -		....	....		[8]107	.52.1	0	'69	82½	63	85	81	84½	70⅝	s74½	9.40	9.93
Credithrift Financial	*26a*	*1.24*	*1.31*		[9]*1.42*	*Dc*	*82.1*			*9-73*	*167*											
•Sr Notes 9¾s '75	Ao15	BBB	X	R	- - - - -		....	....		NC	20.0	M5	'70	108½	97⅞	108	104½	107½	99¾	100½	9.70	9.32
•Sr Deb 8s '92	Fa	BBB	X	R	- - - - -		z[10]102.70	[5]100		[11]103.30	25.0	M5	'72	....	....	102¾	98	103½	85	91⅝	8.73	8.94
[12]***Crocker Citizens Natl. Bk***	*10*	....	....		....	*Dc*					*245*											
Notes 4.60s '89	Ao	NR		R	✓- ✓- -		....	100		†102.53	60.1	L4	'64	102⅜	60¼	79⅜	75½	79⅞	69½	75⅛	6.12	7.33
Crown Cork & Seal	*16b*	*5.19*	*6.88*		*8.69*	*Dc*	*4.80*	*175*	*105*	*12-72*	*31.2*	*14.7*										
•SF Deb 4⅜s '88	Ms15	A	X	CR	- - - - -		....	†100.89		†103.29	17.0	d1	'63	101¼	60	74⅝	72½	75	70⅝	s73⅜	5.96	7.44
Crown Zellerbach	*50*	*3.37*	*2.80*		*3.36*	*Dc*	*70.6*	*390*	*124*	*12-72*	*★385*	*46.1*										
•SF Deb 8⅞s 2000	Ms15	A	X	R	- - - - -		[13]105.475	[4]100		†108.03	125	L4	'70	.111	97⅜	112¼	109¼	112½	103⅞	104¼	8.51	8.46
[14]***Crucible, Inc***	*66c*	*2.29*	*2.35*		*2.57*	*Dc*	*62.0*	*379*	*105*	*12-72*	*217*	*100*										
•SF E Bonds 6⅞s '92	jD15	BBB	X	R	- - - - -		[2]103.31	100		†104.64	29.0	G2	'68	103⅛	68½	88½	80	90	83	83½	8.23	8.66
Cummins Engine	*41c*	*5.66*	*4.75*		*2.06*	*Dc*	*8.43*	*231*	*123*	*12-72*	*101*	*59.0*										
•SF Deb 8⅞s '95	aO15	A	X	R	- - - - -		[13]103.823	[7]100		†106.499	30.0	F2	'70	107	98	111	107	109	99½	100	8.88	8.88
SF Deb 7.40s '97	Ao	A	X	R	- - - - -		[11]103.70	[5]100		†107.03	20.0	F2	'72	....	....	101½	99	100¾	91	97	7.63	7.67
Cutler-Hammer, Inc.	*24b*	*3.38*	*3.80*		*3.94*	*Dc*	*12.8*	*130*	*44.1*	*12-72*	*40.2*	*95.3*										
SF Deb 5¾s '92	Mn	A	X	R	- - ✓- -		[2]102½	†100.56		†103.80	15.2	M9	'67	100⅝	62½	81½	74	79½	73	76	7.57	8.32
[15]***Dallas Power & Light***	*72a*	*3.33*	*3.06*		*3.06*	*Dc*	*5.92*	*26.4*	*41.4*	*8-73*	*247*	*47.3*		*12 Mo Nov*		*3.12*	*2.71*					
1st 2⅞s '79	Ao	AAA	X	CR	✓✓✓✓✓		....	†100.38		†100.76	10.0	K2	'49	86	64½	79.878	77⅞	79⅝	77½	79	3.64	7.83
1st 2¾s '80	Jd	AAA	X	CR	✓✓✓✓✓		....	†100.42		†100.90	24.5	F2	'50	82¾	61⅛	76½	73	76	73¼	75	3.67	7.77
1st 3½s '83	Ms	AAA	X	CR	✓✓✓✓✓		....	†100.85		†101.52	9.00	S1	'53	90½	60	74¼	71¼	74¼	70½	72	4.86	7.84
1st 3⅛s '86	Fa	AAA	X	CR	✓✓✓✓✓		....	100.35		101.40	10.0	F2	'56	83½	53¾	65½	62⅝	65⅜	61¾	63¼	4.94	7.90
1st 4¼s '86	jD	AAA	X	CR	✓✓✓✓✓		....	†100½		†102.42	10.0	H2	'56	99⅞	63½	74¼	71¼	73½	69¼	70¾	6.01	7.90
1st 4¼s '93	Fa	AAA	X	CR	✓✓✓✓✓		....	100.79		103.28	25.0	K2	'63	101	58¼	69	66	67⅞	62⅝	64	6.64	7.94
1st 4⅞s '96	Jj	AAA	X	CR	✓✓✓✓✓		....	†100.65		†104.08	20.0	H2	'66	100¾	63⅜	74¾	71⅛	73⅛	67	68¼	7.14	7.95

Uniform Footnote Explanations—See Page 1. Other: [1]Now CPC Internat'l. [2]From 1977. [3]By Purchase Fund. [4]From 1978. [5]From 1983. [6]From 1984. [7]From 1981. [8]From 1974. [9]Fiscal Sep'72 & prior. [10]From 1977, z100. [11]From 1982. [12]Now Crocker Nat'l Corp. [13]From 1980. [14]Now Colt Industries. [15]Subsid of Texas Util.

Source: Standard & Poor's *Bond Guide*, January 1974.

buy a bond for a $1,000 par value and the stated rate of interest is 10 percent, you will be paid $100 a year interest, or $50 every six months if interest is paid semiannually. The price quoted for bonds is usually expressed as a percentage rate of the par value. That is, a year after you have purchased your $1,000 bond, you may find it quoted in the newspaper at 98. This does *not* mean it is worth only $98. It means that the bond may be purchased for 98 percent of par value: $980 for a $1,000 bond, or $98,000 for a $100,000 bond.

If you needed funds at the time and decided to sell your bond for $980, the person who bought it would receive $100 a year from the corporation whose obligation it was. When you receive $100 a year on an investment of $1,000, your return—10 percent—is the same as the stated interest rate on the bond; but the new purchaser, assuming he holds it just one year and then resells it to someone for $980, has received $100 for one year on an investment of $980. Clearly, he has received a return of more than 10 percent. His current yield, not the stated rate (coupon rate), on the bond was:

```
         .1020408
980)100.000000
     98 0
      2 000
      1 960
         4000
         3920
          8000
          7840
```

or 10.20 percent.

"Yield" is not to be confused with "stated" or "coupon" rate. The latter is fixed once and for all when the bond is originally issued and governs the fixed amount which the corporation pays each year to whoever happens to own the bond. The former (the yield) is determined by the price you pay for the bond. If you pay less than par for the bond, the yield will be more than the coupon rate. If you pay more than par, the yield will be less than the coupon rate. To state it in another way: yield varies inversely with price. The lower the price you pay for the bond, the higher the yield; the higher the price you pay, the lower the yield.

But the current yield does not tell the whole story with respect to returns on bonds. When you buy a bond below par (at a discount) and hold it to maturity, you receive not only the current yield, as described above, but also the difference between your purchase price ($980) and the par value ($1,000) at which the corporation will redeem the bond at maturity. This extra $20 must be added to your income from the bond over the period you hold it to determine the true yield to maturity. In the same fashion, if you pay more than par for the bond (assume $1,020) and hold it until maturity, you will get back only $1,000 from the company. Thus you will lose $20, which must be subtracted from your income from the bond over the period you hold it in order to arrive at the true yield.

If the bond is bought at a discount, the difference between the purchase price and the redemption value is a gain for the investor. If you divide this difference by the number of years in the remaining life of the bond, you may consider the result an average annual gain. If the bond were bought at a premium, this result would be an average annual loss. Now, if you add this average annual gain to, or subtract the average annual loss from, the total interest payment received in a year, you get the average annual income from the investment. The investment at the time of purchase is the price paid; but the investment at the time of redemption is the redemption value; so the average of these two could be considered as an average investment. The average annual income divided by the average investment gives the approximate true yield.

An illustration may clarify this. Take the previous case of the 10 percent bond purchased for $980 in the market and assume that it has 10 years to run to maturity and that you hold it for the 10 years. You saw that the current yield was 10.20 percent, but you realize that this is not the true yield because, over the 10 years, you will receive a $20 gain. Your average investment was $980 + $1,000 ÷ 2, or $990. If you divide the $20 gain over ten years, you received an extra $2.00 a year. Add this to the $100 you received in interest from the company each year, and you have an average annual income of $102.00 on an average investment of $990. Your approximate yield is then:

```
        .103030
990)102.000000
     99 0
      3 000
      2 970
         3000
         2970
```

or 10.30 percent.

To take an example of a bond purchased at a premium, assume that you bought the bond at $1,020 and that it has just 10 years to run, at which time you will receive $1,000 for it. Thus you will lose $20 over the 10 years, or 2.00 a year, which you must deduct each year from the $100 interest you receive in order to arrive at your real average annual income, which is thus, of course, $98. Your average investment over the ten years was $1,020 + $1,000 ÷ 2, or $1,010. Thus your return—your approximate yield—is:

```
          .09707
   1010)98.000000
        90 90
         7 100
         7 070
           3000
           2020
            9800
            9090
```

or 9.71 percent.

The rates in both these examples are approximate and not mathematically exact, for reasons too complicated to explain here. For this reason, investment officers of financial institutions and others dealing with bonds use an elaborate book of bond tables to determine the true yield when they know the coupon rate, maturity, and proposed purchase price of a bond. A page of a bond table is shown in Table 13–11.

Assume you purchased a bond with a 10 percent coupon which has 13 years to run to maturity for a price of $971.80. If you had purchased the bond for $1,000, the coupon and the yield would have been identical—10 percent—as the table indicates; but since you purchased the bond at a considerable discount, your yield must obviously be higher than 10 percent. Looking down the 13 year column, you come to the figure $97.18 midway. Looking across to the left, you find the exact yield—10.40 percent. In similar fashion, somewhere in the 1,200 pages of this particular set of tables, you would be able to find the effective yield of any bond with a maturity of from six months to 50 years bearing a coupon rate of from 7 to 11.95 percent. Other sets of tables cover rates below 7 percent, still others cover maturities of from 50 to 100 years, and there is a special set of tables covering maturities of less than six months. There is, therefore, no need to be concerned with the exact details of computations of bond yields, since it is much more accurate and easier to use prepared bond tables. Bond experts and investment specialists do, and there is no reason why you should not do likewise.

Bond Prices and Interest Rates

The principal risk in high grade bonds is not related so much to the course of business activity as it is to the trend of interest rates. If you

TABLE 13–11
A Page of a Bond Yield Table (10 percent coupon)

LEHMAN BROTHERS HIGH YIELD TABLES SEMI-ANNUAL INTEREST PAYMENTS INTEREST RATE 10.000

YIELD	11 YRS EVEN	11 YRS 6 MOS	12 YRS EVEN	12 YRS 6 MOS	13 YRS EVEN	13 YRS 6 MOS	14 YRS EVEN	14 YRS 6 MOS	15 YRS EVEN	15 YRS 6 MOS	16 YRS EVEN	16 YRS 6 MOS
7.00	122.75	123.43	124.09	124.72	125.34	125.93	126.50	127.05	127.59	128.10	128.60	129.09
7.10	121.89	122.54	123.16	123.77	124.35	124.92	125.47	125.99	126.50	126.99	127.47	127.93
7.20	121.03	121.65	122.25	122.83	123.38	123.92	124.44	124.94	125.43	125.90	126.35	126.78
7.30	120.18	120.77	121.34	121.89	122.42	122.94	123.43	123.91	124.37	124.81	125.24	125.66
7.40	119.34	119.90	120.44	120.97	121.47	121.96	122.43	122.88	123.32	123.74	124.15	124.54
7.50	118.50	119.04	119.56	120.05	120.53	121.00	121.44	121.87	122.29	122.69	123.07	123.44
7.60	117.68	118.19	118.68	119.15	119.60	120.04	120.46	120.87	121.26	121.64	122.01	122.36
7.70	116.86	117.34	117.81	118.25	118.68	119.10	119.50	119.88	120.25	120.61	120.95	121.28
7.80	116.05	116.51	116.94	117.37	117.77	118.17	118.54	118.91	119.25	119.59	119.91	120.22
7.90	115.25	115.68	116.09	116.49	116.87	117.24	117.60	117.94	118.27	118.58	118.89	119.18
8.00	114.45	114.86	115.25	115.62	115.98	116.33	116.66	116.98	117.29	117.59	117.87	118.15
8.10	113.66	114.04	114.41	114.76	115.10	115.43	115.74	116.04	116.33	116.61	116.87	117.13
8.20	112.88	113.24	113.58	113.91	114.23	114.53	114.83	115.11	115.38	115.63	115.88	116.12
8.30	112.11	112.44	112.76	113.07	113.37	113.65	113.92	114.18	114.43	114.68	114.91	115.13
8.40	111.34	111.65	111.95	112.24	112.51	112.78	113.03	113.27	113.50	113.73	113.94	114.15
8.50	110.58	110.87	111.15	111.41	111.67	111.91	112.14	112.37	112.58	112.79	112.99	113.18
8.60	109.83	110.10	110.35	110.60	110.83	111.06	111.27	111.48	111.68	111.87	112.05	112.22
8.70	109.09	109.33	109.56	109.79	110.00	110.21	110.41	110.60	110.78	110.95	111.12	111.28
8.80	108.35	108.57	108.78	108.99	109.19	109.37	109.55	109.72	109.89	110.05	110.20	110.34
8.90	107.62	107.82	108.01	108.20	108.37	108.54	108.71	108.86	109.01	109.15	109.29	109.42
9.00	106.89	107.07	107.25	107.41	107.57	107.73	107.87	108.01	108.14	108.27	108.39	108.51
9.10	106.17	106.34	106.49	106.64	106.78	106.92	107.04	107.17	107.29	107.40	107.51	107.61
9.20	105.46	105.60	105.74	105.87	105.99	106.11	106.23	106.34	106.44	106.54	106.63	106.72
9.30	104.76	104.88	105.00	105.11	105.22	105.32	105.42	105.51	105.60	105.69	105.77	105.85
9.40	104.06	104.16	104.26	104.36	104.45	104.54	104.62	104.70	104.77	104.85	104.91	104.98
9.50	103.37	103.45	103.54	103.61	103.69	103.76	103.83	103.89	103.96	104.01	104.07	104.13
9.60	102.68	102.75	102.81	102.88	102.94	102.99	103.05	103.10	103.15	103.19	103.24	103.28
9.70	102.00	102.05	102.10	102.15	102.19	102.23	102.27	102.31	102.35	102.38	102.41	102.44
9.80	101.33	101.36	101.39	101.42	101.45	101.48	101.51	101.53	101.55	101.58	101.60	101.62
9.90	100.66	100.68	100.69	100.71	100.72	100.74	100.75	100.76	100.77	100.78	100.79	100.81
10.00	100.00	100.00	100.00	100.00	100.00	100.00	100.00	100.00	100.00	100.00	100.00	100.00
10.10	99.34	99.33	99.31	99.30	99.28	99.27	99.26	99.25	99.24	99.22	99.21	99.20
10.20	98.70	98.66	98.63	98.60	98.58	98.55	98.53	98.50	98.48	98.46	98.44	98.42
10.30	98.05	98.01	97.96	97.92	97.88	97.84	97.80	97.77	97.73	97.70	97.67	97.64
10.40	97.41	97.35	97.29	97.24	97.18	97.13	97.08	97.04	96.99	96.95	96.91	96.88
10.50	96.78	96.71	96.63	96.56	96.50	96.43	96.37	96.32	96.26	96.21	96.16	96.12
10.60	96.16	96.07	95.98	95.90	95.82	95.74	95.67	95.61	95.54	95.48	95.42	95.37
10.70	95.54	95.43	95.33	95.24	95.15	95.06	94.98	94.90	94.83	94.76	94.69	94.63
10.80	94.92	94.80	94.69	94.58	94.48	94.38	94.29	94.20	94.12	94.04	93.97	93.90
10.90	94.31	94.18	94.05	93.93	93.82	93.71	93.61	93.52	93.42	93.34	93.25	93.18
11.00	93.71	93.56	93.42	93.29	93.17	93.05	92.94	92.83	92.73	92.64	92.55	92.46
11.10	93.11	92.95	92.80	92.66	92.52	92.40	92.27	92.16	92.05	91.95	91.85	91.76
11.20	92.52	92.35	92.18	92.03	91.88	91.75	91.62	91.49	91.38	91.26	91.16	91.06
11.30	91.93	91.75	91.57	91.41	91.25	91.10	90.96	90.83	90.71	90.59	90.48	90.37
11.40	91.35	91.15	90.97	90.79	90.63	90.47	90.32	90.18	90.05	89.92	89.80	89.69
11.50	90.77	90.56	90.37	90.18	90.01	89.84	89.68	89.53	89.39	89.26	89.14	89.02

Source: Lehman Bros., *High Yield Tables*, p. 727.

hold high grade bonds and interest rates, which had been low, start to rise, and you cannot hold your bonds until maturity but are forced to sell them because you need funds, you can suffer a capital loss. Why is this, and how does it work? If interest rates start to rise (because of Federal Reserve open market activity, for example), the 10 percent rate on the bond, bought at par some years back, will no longer look so attractive as it once did to some holders of the issue, who now become aware of the fact that they can get 11 or 11.50 percent in more recent issues. They, therefore, sell the old issue to free their funds for investment in better yielding issues. This selling pressure forces the price of the old issue down, and it will continue to fall until its price in the market yields the new purchaser the same rate of return as the average new, higher level of rates in the market. Thus as the boom progresses and the demand for money grows and interest rates rise, high grade bond prices may fall as stock prices rise.

Usually, at the top of a boom when the central banking authorities are enforcing a tight money policy which has driven interest rates up and bond prices down, if your timing is good, switch from common stocks to high grade bonds just as the boom turns into recession. Tight money will be relaxed, interest rates will be allowed to fall, and high grade bond prices may rise. In fact the deeper the recession, the higher will go the prices of high grade bonds as investment demand switches to them and bids up their prices.

It isn't always so clear cut and simple, however. Figure 13–9 shows the trend of bond yields from 1929 to 1974. As you can see, bond yields rose

FIGURE 13–9
Corporate Bond Yields by Ratings 1929–1974

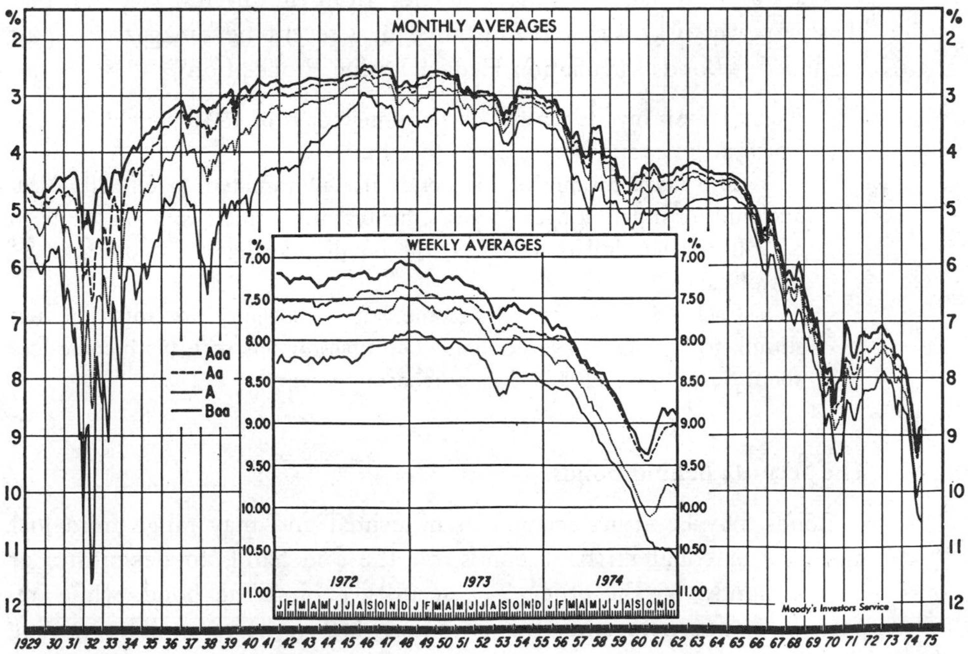

Source: Moody's Investors Service.

sharply during the recession years of 1969 and 1970 as well as in the boom years of 1967 and 1968. The pressures of inflation drove interest rates up in poor years as well as in good ones, and therefore prices of old bonds with low coupons fell sharply as new bonds were issued with higher and higher coupons. For example, in 1970 General Telephone and Electronics, had to offer a coupon of 9.75 percent to sell a debenture maturing in 1995. At the same time, another of its debentures issued in 1963 with a coupon of 4.50 percent maturing in 1988 sold as low as 58 ($580 for a $1,000 bond) in 1970. Because the 9.75 percent debenture was selling above par in 1971 and the 4.50 percent debenture way below par (100 or $1,000 per bond is par), both had a yield to maturity of over 8 percent.

Another example—A.T.&T., for AAA rated debentures, had to provide coupons of 8.75 percent in 1970 for a new issue of debentures due in the year 2000. In 1946 it had issued debentures with a coupon of only 2.625 percent (due in 1986). These, in 1970, sold as low as 51. Both debentures provided yields to maturity of over 7 percent in 1971. This illustrates very well the interest rate risk associated with bonds. The inflation and efforts to control it drove interest rates up in 1969–70 and again even more so in 1973–74. Borrowing corporations and governmental bodies had to pay much higher coupons on new issues and older outstanding bonds with lower coupons fell in price, even in a recession period!

The way in which bonds have suffered from the interest rate and purchasing power risks was well illustrated in a recent newsmagazine report headlined: "Bonds as Inflation Hedge: Losing Proposition"

> Example: An investor in the cheap money days of 1946 bought $10,000 worth of long-term bonds. Since that time—
>
> • The market value of his bonds has plummeted to $4,830. After allowing for inflation over 28 years, his real investment value has sunk to $1,960 in 1946 dollars. In effect, the bondholder has lost more than $4 out of each $5 investment.
>
> • Each $100 of interest income, after allowance for inflation, has shrunk to $40.60 in 1946 dollars. The investor has seen his income lose about $3 out of each $5 of its purchasing power.[19]

The Security behind Bonds

Bonds may be either secured or unsecured and may range from first mortgage or collateral trust bonds, on the one hand, to debentures or income bonds, on the other. The security behind the bond, while important, is not necessarily the governing factor, however. The earning

[19] *U.S. News & World Report*, June 17, 1974, p. 46.

power, financial status, and reputation of one company may result in its unsecured bonds being rated higher than the secured bonds of another company. For example, the debentures of A.T.&T. are rated higher than the first mortgage bonds of Indianapolis Power & Light. The debentures of Southern Bell Telephone have a higher rating than the first mortgage bonds of Missouri Power & Light Company.

In the case of secured bonds, the issuing corporation backs up its promise to pay interest and repay principal by a pledge of specific property, as evidenced by a mortgage bond, a collateral trust note, or an equipment trust certificate. In the case of unsecured bonds, such as debentures or income bonds, on the other hand, the issuing corporation merely promises to pay interest and repay principal, but there is no specific pledge of security to back up its promise.

Mortgage Bonds

Mortgage bonds are secured by a mortgage on part or all of a company's property. If the company defaults (fails to pay interest or repay principal), the bondholders, through the trustee appointed to represent them and look after their rights, may foreclose the mortgage and take over the pledged property.

When we discussed home ownership and home mortgages, it was stated that the mortgagee gets title (in such states as Massachusetts) or a lien (in other states) on the real estate to secure the promissory note which is given to him. Bond issues are usually large. It would be impossible to give every bondholder title to or a lien on part of the specific property used to secure the bonds. It is much more convenient to transfer the security to a trustee (often a bank) which will represent the bondholders and see that the issuing company does what it has agreed to do. The agreement of the issuing company with the bondholders is contained in a legal instrument called an *indenture*.

Some corporate mortgages have what is known as an *after-acquired clause*, which provides that all property thereafter acquired will become subject to the mortgage and automatically be pledged to secure the bond issue. This is so favorable a feature for the investor that it is not widely found. When there is an after-acquired property clause and the company wishes to put out another bond issue secured by a mortgage on its property, this second mortgage will be a *junior lien*, subordinate to the first mortgage, or *senior lien*, on the property. Usually, when corporations float junior issues, secured by junior liens, they do not clearly label them as such. They call them "general" or "consolidated" or some other ambiguous name, and the only way you can determine the security status of the bonds exactly is to read the bond indenture carefully—something which the average bondholder, unfortunately, usually never does.

When more bonds may be issued with the same security or under the same mortgage deed, the mortgage is said to be "open"; additional bonds will naturally dilute the security available for each bond. If the mortgage is "closed," no additional bonds may be issued with the same security, and each bond has, therefore, better protection.

Collateral Trust Bonds

Security for bonds need not be real estate, as in the case of mortgage bonds. Just as we may borrow at a bank and put up securities of one sort or another as collateral for the loan, it is possible for a corporation to issue bonds secured by the pledge of other stocks and bonds which it owns. A bond secured by a pledge of specific securities is known as a "collateral trust bond." Collateral trust bonds are issued mainly by holding companies, investment companies, and finance companies, which do not have much real property, as would a utility or a railroad, to pledge.

The securities or notes pledged are transferred to the trustee who acts for the bondholders. The income from these assets goes to the corporation as long as it continues to pay interest on the collateral trust bonds (or "notes," as they are sometimes called). If it should default on interest payments, the trustee can use the income from the securities held to reimburse the bondholders. Investment experts tell us, however, that the strength of a collateral trust bond lies not so much in the type of securities pledged as in the general financial standing of the companies whose securities are used as collateral.

Equipment Trust Obligations

A relatively safe type of bond investment is the equipment trust certificate, which is used to finance the purchase of rolling stock by railroads. Approximately one seventh of railroad debt is represented by these certificates. They owe their strength to the fact that they are secured by railroad rolling stock, which can be moved anywhere in the country. If the certificates are in default, the equipment may be sold to another railroad.

Under the Philadelphia Plan, title to equipment (freight cars, locomotives, passenger coaches) being bought by a railroad vests in a trustee who holds it for the benefit of certificate holders. The railroad makes a down payment (perhaps 20 percent), and the trustee issues equipment trust certificates to cover the balance of the purchase price of the equipment. The trustee then leases the equipment to the railroad under an agreement whereby the railroad obtains title to the equipment only when all obligations have been met. Sometime when you are at a railroad station, it may interest you to note that each piece of equipment financed by such an arrangement has a plate attached to it stating where the ownership lies (temporarily in the trustee).

Debentures

Debentures are unsecured bonds protected only by the general credit of the borrowing corporation. If there are no mortgage bonds, and debentures are the senior issues, they may rate very high. A.T.&T., for example, has only debentures outstanding. There are no bonds senior to these. Debentures may contain a "covenant of equal coverage," which means that if any mortgage bond is issued in the future, which ordinarily would take precedence over the debentures, the issuer agrees to secure the debentures equally. In some states the law requires that this be done.

All direct domestic obligations of federal, state, and municipal governments in the United States are debentures. Since this type of security is protected only by the general promise to pay and, in the event of default, the debenture holder is merely a general creditor, debentures can usually be sold only by corporations enjoying very high credit standings. The value of a debenture must be judged wholly in terms of the overall financial status and earnings outlook of the issuer, which is the best basis for evaluating any bond.

Income or Adjustment Bonds

Income or adjustment bonds are bonds on which interest is not mandatory but is paid only when earned and declared. Usually, income or adjustment bonds result from corporate reorganizations, under which it is desired to reduce fixed interest charges to a level which can be reasonably expected to be met. Former holders of junior liens are, therefore, as a result of the reorganization, given income or adjustment bonds to replace their former holdings. Several examples of income bonds are (*a*) the Atchison, Topeka, & Santa Fe Railroad adjustment 4s of 1995, issued in the railroad's reorganization of 1895; (*b*) the Erie Railroad 5s of 2020; and (*c*) the Lehigh Valley income 4s of 2003. The Atchison 4s are rated A, while the latter two are rated D. The Atchison issue is an exception.

Most income bonds are rated in the C category, because, as a group, they are regarded as speculative. In a few instances they are secured by general mortgages, but not in most cases. Some income bonds, as the Atchison issue, are cumulative, in that interest not paid on the due date accrues as a charge against future earnings and must be paid before any dividends may be paid on stock. In this sense they resemble cumulative preferred stock.

Guaranteed or Assumed Bonds

Particularly in the case of railroads and railroad terminals, you find one company guaranteeing the bonds of another. In the railroad consolidations of the last half of the nineteenth century there was much guaranteeing or assuming of bonds. For example, the Pennsylvania Railroad Company before its merger with the New York Central technically operated only from Philadelphia to Pittsburgh, but the Pennsylvania Railroad System included many leased lines, such as the United New Jersey (New York to Philadelphia) and the Pittsburgh, Fort Wayne, & Chicago (Pittsburgh to Chicago). The Pennsylvania Railroad Company guaranteed the outstanding bonds of these leased lines.

Terminal companies generally have their bonds guaranteed by the railroad companies principally using the terminal. For example, the Terminal Railroad Associates of St. Louis' Refunding and Improvement 2⅞s of 1985, rated AA by Standard & Poor's, are guaranteed by 15 railroads. The value of a guaranteed bond is determined not only by the credit of the guaranteeing company but also by the value, essentiality, and usefulness of its own property to the guaranteeing company. Leases are sometimes not renewed, and guaranties are allowed to lapse, in cases where the value of the underlying property proves to be less than anticipated.

Convertible Bonds

Convertible bonds are bonds which may be exchanged, at the option of the holder, for a specified amount of other securities (usually common stock) of the issuing corporation. Theoretically, this would appear to be an ideal security, since it affords, on the one hand, the relative safety of a fixed income creditor obligation and, on the other, an opportunity to share in the prospective profits of the company. Thus it would seem, at one and the same time, to provide relative safety as well as a hedge against inflation.

"Well, if you consider a four hour briefing on convertible subordinated debentures a good time—then I had a good time!"

The Commercial and Financial Chronicle

The value of convertible bonds in the market tends to rise as the price of the common into which they are convertible rises. On the other hand, in a declining market, the price declines until the conversion parity point is reached; that is, the conversion feature no longer has any value, and the bond, therefore, sells solely on the basis of its fixed income, safety status. Thus you may conclude that there are two considerations affecting the market value of a convertible bond: (*a*) its actual value as a fixed income obligation and (*b*) its potential value in terms of the stock into which it may be converted.[20]

[20] For further information, see *A Handbook to Convertible Securities* (New York: Kalb, Voorhis & Co., latest edition) as well as William Schwartz & Julius Spellman, *Guide to Convertible Securities* (New York, latest edition).

Callable Bonds

Callable bonds are bonds which may be redeemed by the issuing company prior to the maturity date. Usually the bonds require the company to pay a premium over their face value when called before maturity. Why should a corporation, when it has borrowed for a term of, say, 20 years, decide to retire its debt in a shorter period of time? Usually it does so because it finds that, due to a decline in interest rates, it can borrow more cheaply now. It therefore calls the old issue with the higher coupon rate and sells a new one at a lower rate. Some bonds are noncallable.

Because bonds are likely to be called when it is advantageous to the issuer and, therefore, disadvantageous to the bondholder, there is usually a premium paid over and above the maturity price when the bond is called. The call price may be 105, for example, if the redemption value at maturity is 100. Frequently, also, the premiums are on a sliding scale, with higher premiums paid for calls in the early life of the bond, when it has a long period to run, and lower premiums if the bond is called later in its existence.

Financial Analysis and Bond Evaluation

While all the technical aspects of bonds which have been described thus far are useful in judging the quality and soundness of an issue, the real basis for evaluation lies in the financial status and earning power of the borrowing corporation or government. The farsightedness and efficiency of the management, the outlook for the industry, the position of the particular firm in the industry, and the soundness of the company's internal finances as reflected in its balance sheet and income account, all must be carefully considered.

The security behind a bond is, in itself, no guaranty of soundness, since the value of pledged property is often dependent on the earning power of the corporation. If the corporation fails, its fixed assets may prove to be worth very little. A good example is the Seaboard—All Florida Railway's first-mortgage 6s, which sold in 1931 at 1 cent on the dollar soon after completion of the road. In selecting bonds, it is best to try to choose a company which will avoid trouble rather than seek to protect yourself in the event of trouble.

REAL ESTATE INVESTMENT

The lures of tax free income, high returns ranging from 12 to 18 percent, substantial capital gains, and, in addition, an excellent hedge

BILLION DOLLAR TRINKETS

One last myth about Manhattan real estate deserves to be exploded. Every school kid knows that crafty Peter Minuit put one over on the Manhattoes Indians in 1626 by buying their island for $24 worth of doodads. But, Salomon Bros.' Sidney Homer, author of *The History of Interest Rates*, provides figures that show that the Indians got the best of the deal. Had they taken a boat to Holland, invested the $24 in Dutch securities returning 6% per year and kept the money invested at 6%, they would now have $13 billion. With that sum they could buy back all the land on the island, and still have $4 billion left for trinkets. Or the Indians could keep the money invested at 6%, so it could continue yielding $780 million a year, without the risk of doing business amid urban decay.

The question isn't who owns New York. It's who the hell wants to?

From "Who Owns New York?" *Forbes Magazine*, June 1, 1971, p. 32.

against inflation, have combined to heighten interest over the last decade in real estate investment and speculation.

There are a wide and unfortunately bewildering variety of ways to invest or speculate in real estate. Generally, the main channels are buying your own home or apartment, investing in raw land or in mortgages, participating in real estate syndicates, buying shares in real estate companies, or investing in real estate investment trusts.

Raw Land

"From Waikiki to Paris, Price of Choice Land Climbs," reads a *New York Times* headline. The story tells of the rise of land prices at Waikiki beach to $150 per square foot. On the island of Oahu, the price of an average house was $20,000 in 1960 but rose to $35,000 in 1971. "So the tight little island of 607 square miles, a third the size of Long Island, is becoming tighter. Condominiums, hotels, homes, and industries rise on verdant hills, on lands that days before were cow pastures or sugar cane fields. A purchaser often seeks in vain for a square inch of beach front."[21]

Amfac, Inc. is Hawaii's biggest company, rich in land and other valuable assets. It recently sold eight beach front acres on the island of Maui for $1 million per acre. The land cost $10 an acre in 1893 when purchased by Amfac. Subsequently, it invested about $17,000 per acre for improvements.

[21] *New York Times*, September 26, 1971.

It owns 40 more acres next to the 8, and in all another 65,000 acres, not all beachfront, however.[22]

"Land Speculator's Play Disney's Money Machine—the new Florida playland has pushed land values to 500 times their former worth," wrote *Business Week*.[23] The 27,000 acre tract on which Disney World is located, some 25 miles southwest of Orlando, Florida, was assembled at an average price of $350 per acre. Land nearby rose to a range of $75,000 to $130,000 per acre for choice motel sites.

Forbes expressed the longer view.[24] "While there were only 40 million persons living on the nation's land a century ago, some 320 million mobile, affluent citizens are expected to share its 2.3 billion acres in the year 2000. The demand for our earth has boosted land prices 100 percent in the past decade alone, says the Urban Land Institute."

As cities grow and the urban pattern encroaches upon suburbia, land in the path of the expansion increases in value. Over time the sheer growth of population tends to enhance the value of raw land. Seemingly all you have to do is follow the bus line out, see where the vacant lots start and buy a few. It isn't this easy, however. Towns don't necessarily grow in all directions, and you may pick the wrong end of town. You can't borrow money on land from banks, insurance companies, or savings and loan associations. You either sink your own cash or you put up a down payment and give the seller a purchase money mortgage for the main amount. In Florida, for example, it is customary to put up 29 percent of the cost in cash and give a purchase money mortgage for the remainder. But you have to pay interest on the mortgage, of course, and usually at a rate of at least 8 percent. And you have to pay taxes on the idle, vacant land, and about a 10 percent sales commission to the real estate broker through whom you made the purchase. And you lose the return you could otherwise have earned by investing the money you put up as a cash down payment. Therefore if you have to hold the lot or lots for a while, waiting for the growth of population and enhancement of values to occur, it can cost you a good sum each year without any return. Some experts estimate that your lots must increase in value 12 to 15 percent a year to provide a gain equal to that you could obtain in other, more conventional, forms of investment. Also you may be locked in. You may want to sell and find no one who wants to buy. Or, on the other hand, you may be one of the

---

[22] See *Wall Street Journal*, April 17, 1974 and *Forbes*, June 1, 1974, p. 29.

[23] *Business Week*, September 11, 1971.

[24] "Real Estate: On The Brink? The Public Is Moving into Real Estate Again. Can Trouble Be Far Behind?" *Forbes* Magazine, July 1, 1970, p. 19.

fortunate ones, and double or triple your money in a few years. It's a tricky operation.[25]

Farm land has soared in value in recent years and country homes (second homes) have become very popular. Iowa farm land, which in the 1930s sold for $10 an acre has been bringing $600 to $800 an acre. It is estimated that a 600 acre Iowa corn and soybean farm now costs at least $480,000 (see Figure 13–10).

The land rush has reached an almost ludicrous pitch. In some areas there are more lots on the market than any conceivable housing demand can justify. New Mexico officials estimate that more than one million acres of the state have been laid out in small lot subdivisions—enough to house eight times the present population if the land was actually developed.[26]

Informed buyers can now avoid buying swampland or cliffs. The federal law that set up the Office of Interstate Land Sales Registration in the U.S. Department of Housing and Urban Development requires companies selling land to register with HUD and give each customer a factual property report on developments, under threat of criminal penalties. A property report similar to a securities prospectus must go to a buyer before sale. There, the buyer will find information on such things as water and sewer availability, existence of liens on the property, number of houses in the development currently occupied and the type of title the buyer will receive. A seller who fulfills HUD requirements and provides a property report is in the clear, even if the property is worthless. "If you designate the property for what it is," says the head of HUD's Office of Interstate Land Sales Registration, "you can sell it."[27]

Not too long ago, a popular book warned that buying country property had pitfalls as well as pleasures.[28] The gist of Price's message that most people's dream of a cottage in the country is just that, a dream. The reality requires about twice as much time, money, and effort as the average buyer expects to expend. There are no bargains left within two or three hours of a major city. The buyer must decide either to go further out—six or seven hours—or to make do with less land than is desired. Raw land

---

25 See "Buying Vacation Land—Nine Ways Not to Get Stung," *Changing Times*, August 1973; also "A New Way to Invest in Land," *Changing Times*, April 1973.

26 "Investors Speculating in Land Often Find Profits Are Elusive," *Wall Street Journal*, April 2, 1974, p. 1.

27 "The Crackdown on the Land Dodge," *Business Week*, March 10, 1973 p. 72.

28 Irving Price, *Buying Country Property: Pitfalls and Pleasures*, (New York: Harper & Row, 1972). See also "An Investor's Guide to Land Bargains," in "Personal Business," *Business Week*, June 22, 1974.

FIGURE 13–10
Farm Land Values per Acre in Dollars

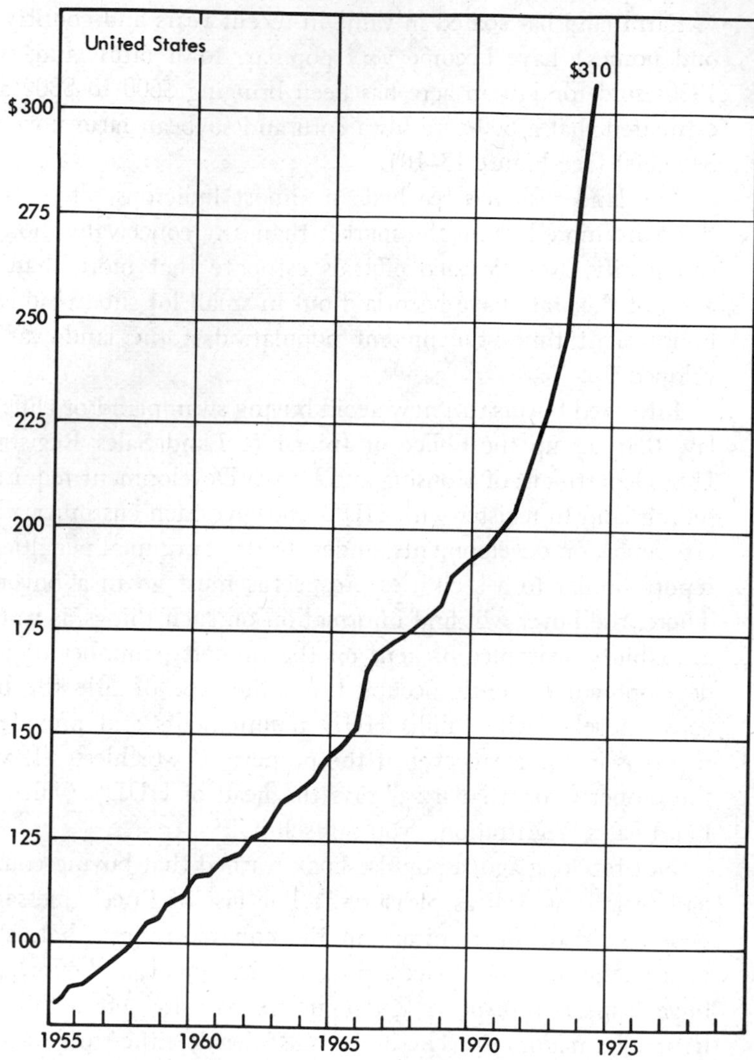

requires cash since it can rarely be financed. Houses, too, present problems. Buyers often say "I want a place that you can't see from the road, and that I can't see the road from." Price says, "What they forget is that this means they will probably be responsible for plowing a half mile of their own driveway when it snows." Yet despite the drawbacks it is estimated that 2 to 3 million families own country houses.

Forbes cast doubt on the satisfactions to be derived from the land boom. Prices aren't profits, it argues. "The fact is that your land can go

FIGURE 13–10 (continued)
Farm Land Values by Regions (per acre in dollars)

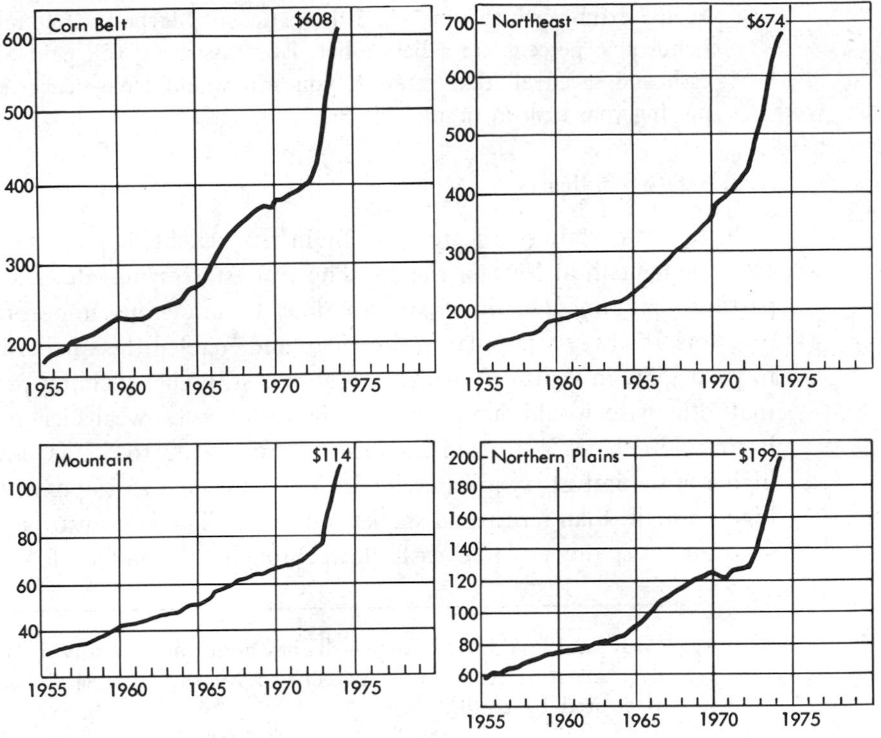

boom and you can still go bust. It happens every day"[29] An example follows:

> Let's assume you paid $100,000 for a rural parcel ten years ago and just sold it for double, $200,000. Did you make $100,000? Well, not quite. Like any sharp real estate investor you used leverage. You put $20,000 down, and the seller took back a 7 percent note with a $50,000 balloon payment due in 1974, a fairly common arrangement. In addition to the $100,000 price, over the years you paid $23,275 in interest on the note and $20,000 in real estate taxes, after 50 percent tax deductions against personal income. Then when you sold you got socked with the standard 10 percent realtor's commission on your land—in this case $20,000. Your total investment so far is $163,275; you're still $36,725 ahead. But there's one last item—the 30 percent capital gains tax on the $80,000 "profit" you made after commissions by selling your $100,000 parcel for $200,000. Uncle Sam gets $24,000.
>
> Don't look now, but you made only $12,275. Had you simply de-

[29] "Has the Land Boom Crested?" *Forbes,* June 15, 1974, pp. 32–38.

posited your $20,000 down payment in a risk free savings account ten years ago you woud have made about $6,240 after taxes. Was the $6,485 extra worth the risk? And the patience? Maybe tax free municipal bonds at 6 percent are a better bet. Even assuming you paid $100,000 cash and saved all that interest, you still would have been better off putting your cash in municipals.[30]

Real Estate Syndicates

In the real estate syndicate you obtain the benefit of professional real estate judgment, at least in theory. The real estate syndicate is a limited partnership formed to offer participations to numerous nonprofessional investors. It was very popular in the 1950s and enabled the smaller investor to participate in ventures involving higher cost, higher yielding properties that otherwise would have been available only to wealthier investors. Partnership shares were sold in units of from $500 to $5,000 and even higher in semiprivate syndicates. Yields ranged from 8 to 15 percent, much higher usually than returns on stocks and bonds. The key advantage of the syndicate was the tax free cash flow through accelerated depreciation.

> "Buy land," said Will Rogers. "They aren't making any more of it." Not true. At least 25 percent of Manhattan Island has been created by landfill.

Usually, half or more of syndicate yields came from depreciation and were a return of capital and not taxable as income. This advantage needs to be understood clearly because it lies at the bottom of the attractiveness of much real estate investment.

Changing Times cites an example, given in a speech before the New York Society of Security Analysts, to show how depreciation is used to achieve tax free income.

Assume that property has been bought for $1 million—$900,000 for the building and $100,000 for the land. Cash payment was $400,000 and a 6 percent mortgage was secured for the balance, or $600,000. Annual payments on the mortgage are $45,000 including principal and interest. Rent comes in at $100,000 a year, and operating expenses, including insurance, repairs, real estate taxes, and management, are $19,000. Here are two statements showing how a tax free income of $36,000 a year could be paid to owners of the building.

---

[30] *Forbes*, June 15, 1974, p. 33. On the other hand see, "Yes, Amateurs Do Make Money in Real Estate," *Changing Times*, March 1972.

Profit and Loss for Income Tax Purpose

Rent income		$100,000
Expenses:		
Mortgage interest	$36,000	
Depreciation (5%)	45,000	
Operating expenses	19,000	
Total Expenses		100,000
Net profit or loss		–0–

Cash Flow

Rent		$100,000
Cash disbursements:		
Mortgage (principal and interest)	$45,000	
Operating expenses	19,000	
Total Expenses		64,000
Balance for distribution		$ 36,000

As you can see, here is a property that madc no profit, and therefore paid no income tax, but was able to give its owners a 9 percent return on the cash investment of $400,000. This technique can be carried even further. If a faster rate of depreciation is used, the owners may not only get a tax free distribution but receive a tax loss in addition, which they may use to reduce their other income.

The syndicate appeared to be a way a small investor could participate in a high return, tax free real estate investment and avoid the headaches of property management and be in partnership with professional operators. While some of the earlier syndicates worked out well, later ones paid excessively high prices for properties, underestimated maintenance, overestimated income and after the first few years when the accelerated depreciation fell off, proved disappointing. The syndicates that were offered to the public, and required extensive sales efforts and numerous small investors, were likely to be the least attractive, because if they had really excellent prospects they would have been absorbed by big professional investors and never offered to the public.

Disadvantages of Syndicates

Most syndicates owned a single property which no matter how well chosen was more risky than diversified real estate investment. Also for the individual participant there was little liquidity. No formal market existed for the sale of a participating unit of the syndicate. Usually the contract made no provision for the repurchase or retirement of the participation. Furthermore, the property share in the syndicate could not be used for loans. Syndicators took much of the profit with little financial investment. One proposed syndicate listed in its prospectus the following details: For forming the syndicate and financing the estimated $50,000 organizational expenses, the promoters were to collect $612,350 in profit. An additional $265,650 in sales commission would go to their sales subsidiary. The subsidiary had agreed to hire the sellers of the building as "management consultants" at an annual fee of $20,000 for 25 years or $500,000. The prospectus conceded, "The services of the consultants may not be required more than one day each month nor more than 12 times in any fiscal year. No representation is made that there is any relationship between the consultants' services and the compensation they are to receive." Even if the sellers worked their full 12 days a year, their pay would be at the rate of $1,600 a day. The prospective investors shunned the deal and the prospectus was revised. Supervision by the SEC was avoided by limiting investment eligibility to residents of a single state. Only a very few states regulate intrastate syndicates.

A number of highly speculative syndicates collapsed in scandalous fashion in the early sixties and made investors wary. At the turn of the decade—1969–72—syndication regained some of its old popularity, especially in California. This was due partly to the tax reform act of 1969. Under prior tax law, tax savings could be achieved by the use of accelerated depreciation converting ordinary income into capital gains. Accelerated depreciation on real estate provided initial tax loss deductions and subsequent capital gains. The tax reform act of 1969 reduced the tax benefit opportunities in real estate, commercial and industrial, by restricting the use of accelerated depreciation methods and recapturing 100 percent of post–1969 accelerated depreciation. To encourage new residential rental property, however, exceptions to the new restrictions were granted for it. The revival of syndication centered on new residential rental properties.

The tax changes, coupled with a growing search for real estate tax shelters, led to a resurgence of the real estate syndicate in the early 1970s, especially 1972. Syndications were brought out by private developers, by banks, and even by brokerage houses. The results were no more satisfactory than in the earlier period. Properties were purchased at inflated values, costs were underestimated, and unrealistically high rates of rental were assumed. Smaller investors who went in as limited partners suffered heavy loses, in numerous cases.[31]

---

[31] See "Taxing Experience: Real Estate Shelters Sometimes Are Leaky, Investors Discover: Some Syndicates Collapse; 'Little Guys' are Victims of Inflated Costs and Fees," *Wall Street Journal*, December 4, 1973; see also Shirley L. Benzer, "New Shakeout in Real Estate Syndicates: Victims Are Investors in Housing Projects," *New York Times*, March 24, 1974.

Real Estate Companies

A number of real estate syndicates converted subsequently into publicly held companies to finance large property acquisitions. The owner of stock in a real estate corporation has all the advantages of the usual stockholder —liquidity, marketability, limited liability, plus that which accrues because funds are invested in a diversified portfolio representing various properties whose blend of earnings are combined in a single earnings package.

There are a number of different types of real estate companies from which to choose. There are diversified real estate companies such as City Investing, converted syndication corporations such as Basic Properties, First National Realty, and others; construction firms such as Tishman and Uris; hotel-motel firms such as Hilton, Sheraton, and Loew's; and land development firms as General Development, Deltona, Gulf American Land (absorbed by the GAC Corp.), Amrep and Horizon Corporation. While the returns, from investment in such companies are less than for syndicates, such investments have proved vulnerable to required changes in the accounting practices of the nation's retail land sales companies in response to a vigorous controversy over how the industry's earnings should be reported.[32]

In evaluating such companies it is more important to look to their cash flow before taxes than to their net income after taxes. Cash flow is depreciation plus net income. Depreciation in industrial firms is plowed back to replace old and worn equipment, but in real estate operations, well constructed and well maintained buildings have actually increased rather than decreased in value. Thus the depreciation allowed on them represents nontaxable earnings which can be paid out to investors. This results in large tax sheltered earnings and at times high dividends.

Great Lakes Carbon—thc namc would hardly suggest that it built and developed the $200 million Del Amo Center in southwest Los Angeles, but it did and it's typical of a trend in recent years. A number of large corporations in recent years have turned to real estate and have been devoting a percentage of their resources to developments, new towns, shopping centers, apartment houses, and other residential complexes and even to land acquisitions. Chrysler, Westinghouse, I.T.&T., Gulf & Western, the Norfolk & Western Railroad, Humble Oil, Standard of California, Weyerhauser, St. Regis Paper, International Paper, Gulf Life Insurance, Union Camp, Alcoa, American Hawaiian, Castle & Cooke, Sunset Inter-

---

[32] "Land Sales Companies Refigure Their Books," *Business Week*, May 12, 1973, p. 78.

national Petroleum, Boise Cascade, Aetna Insurance, Prudential, Connecticut General, even Hallmark Cards are all involved. U.S. Steel Realty Development Corporation is in a joint venture with Connecticut Mutual Life Insurance Co. for the development of 13,500 acres in Dade County, Florida.[33] Buying shares in one or more of these companies lets you participate to a degree in real estate and land appreciation and development. The results have varied, however. Some companies have done well in their real estate operations, others have done poorly and have withdrawn.

Real Estate Investment Trusts (REITs)

In recent years interest has shifted to the real estate investment trust primarily for tax purposes. The concept of the real estate investment trust goes back to 1886. But the trusts, which are unincorporated, increased rapidly in numbers as a result of a 1960 law which permits them to operate without paying taxes if they pay out 90 percent of their income to shareholders and meet certain other restrictions on operations and investments. The trusts, of which there are now over 200, are set up along the same lines as closed end investment companies—pooling money of small investors for placement in real estate ventures. They avoid making any promise on their return to shareholders and operate at a lower yield than syndicates. Trusts now yield anywhere from 6 to 12 percent on book value. A number of the REITs formed during 1970–72 have been sponsored by commercial banks, insurance companies, or mortgage banking concerns.

To qualify as a real estate investment trust there must be at least 100 shareholders and not more than 50 percent of the shares may be owned by five or fewer persons. These provisions are designed to insure that every trust will be broadly owned and not serve as a personal holding company for a few investors. At least 75 percent of gross income must be from investments related to real estate and not more than 25 percent of the total assets can be invested in other than real estate.

The trusts may not manage any property they own. Nor may they engage in developing land for sale. Capital gains on securities held less than six months and on properties held less than four years must constitute less than 30 percent of the trusts gross income. Thus the trust must place

---

[33] See Karl G. Pearson, "Big Business Discovers Real Estate," in *Michigan Business Review*, University of Michigan, Ann Arbor, March, 1971; see also, "On Investing in Land as a Way to Diversify," *New York Times*, November 16, 1969; "The Big Market in Land Stocks," *Fortune*, July, 1969; "Look Who's Rushing into Real Estate," *Fortune*, October, 1968. See also, Ira U. Cobleigh, *"All About Investing in Real Estate Securities,"* (New York: Weybright & Talley, 1971).

its emphasis on longer term investments in office buildings, apartments, shopping centers, leases, mortgages and so on.

Types of Trusts

There are several different kinds of trusts.

Blank Check Trusts—so called because they sell their shares to investors and then seek properties in which to invest.

Purchase Trusts—go to the public seeking funds to buy specified properties. Sometimes these are properties in which the promoters have interests. The SEC requires the offering prospectus to include a full description of the properties. This must be done whenever a trust offers new shares to the public.

Exchange Trusts—offer their shares in exchange for properties. This enables property owners to diversify their holdings and postpone any capital gains tax until they sell their shares of the trust.

Mortgage Trusts—do not buy properties but invest in mortgages and construction loans. They are, therefore, competing with all other financial institutions trying to invest mortgage money.

Another way of looking at the REITs is as real estate mutual funds, basically of two types—the equity trust and the mortgage trust. Equity trusts buy properties, income producing, and after expense and mortgage payments, pass the remaining income on to shareholders. "Mortgage" trusts which invest in first mortgages rather than properties, have been more popular with investors than equity trusts. One reason for their popularity was the early success of Continental Mortgage Investors and First Mortgage Investors, both formed in 1961. Both trusts are short term or interim lenders. They write construction and development first mortgages with an average life of about 12 months. Once a building is completed and occupied, the interim lenders are repaid with the proceeds of the permanent mortgages, known as "takeout" mortgages.

Table 13–12 covers the 20 largest real estate investment trusts with $8.6 billion of assets, or about 43 percent of the $20.2 billion of assets reported by the industry trade group, the National Association of Real Estate Investment Trusts. The tabulation makes clear the industry's present problems: extremely high leverage, an average of 51.5 percent of capital in short term borrowings, and share prices selling about 50 percent below book value. About 18–19 percent of the industry's invested assets are in a nonearning status, reducing income. The culprits were extremely high short term interest rates, a shortage of mortgage money, and a virtual collapse of building activity.

TABLE 13–12
The 20 Largest Real Estate Investment Trusts

Trust	Type*	First Public Offering	Assets (in millions)	Book Value per Share†	Share Price (7/23/74)	Premium or (Discount)	Yield	Capital Structure: Equity	Capital Structure: Long Term Debt	Capital Structure: Short Term Debt
Chase Manhattan Mtg. & Realty	I	1970	$912.0	$30.08	$15.63	(48.0%)	23.0%	15.0%	22.5%	62.5%
Continental Mortgage Investors	I	1962	828.1	8.63	2.13	(75.3)	0.0	18.2	26.5	55.3
First Mortgage Investors	I&L	1961	671.8	14.42	2.75	(80.9)	0.0	17.0	33.3	49.7
Great American Mtg. Investors	I	1969	478.8	17.08	5.88	(65.6)	40.8	15.3	28.2	56.5
Guardian Mortgage Investors	I	1969	479.4	28.43	9.38	(67.0)	21.3	17.6	21.5	60.9
Citizens & Southern Realty Inv.	I	1970	429.9	23.12	13.13	(43.2)	21.3	18.6	12.8	68.6
Connecticut General Mtg. & Realty	L,E	1970	446.9	23.13	13.25	(42.7)	13.6	25.5	40.0	34.5
Builders Investment Group	I	1971	423.6	22.63	10.00	(55.8)	21.3	15.8	17.0	67.2
Lomas & Nettleton Mtg. Investors	I	1969	416.2	33.27	18.38	(44.8)	21.8	30.0	7.6	62.4
Diversified Mortgage Investors	I,L	1969	390.8	20.07	4.75	(76.3)	14.3	38.2	35.0	26.8
C.I. Mortgage Group	I	1969	373.2	18.83	5.25	(72.1)	22.9	24.6	7.8	67.6
Saul (B.F.) Real Estate Inv. Tr.	I,E	1964	343.3	15.14	8.00	(47.2)	18.5	22.5	41.2	36.3
Cousins Mtg. & Equity Investments	I,L	1970	327.2	20.83	5.88	(71.8)	13.6	24.8	34.0	41.2
Continental Illinois Realty	I	1969	326.8	18.53	7.25	(60.9)	18.8	16.1	15.5	68.4
Equitable Life Mtg. & Rlty. Inv.	L	1970	318.6	24.14	14.88	(38.4)	13.4	43.1	25.3	31.6
IDS Realty Trust	I	1972	314.8	22.45	16.00	(28.7)	21.0	17.0	48.6	34.4
Barnett Mortgage Trust	I	1970	299.2	25.36	11.13	(56.1)	25.5	14.5	29.6	55.9
MassMutual Mtg. & Rlty. Inv.	L	1970	292.2	23.78	10.63	(55.3)	16.2	31.8	41.9	26.3
Wells Fargo Mortgage Investors	I	1970	282.4	18.31	9.00	(50.8)	22.2	25.9	0.0	74.1
MONY Mortgage Investors	L	1970	278.4	9.89	6.38	(35.5)	12.5	31.4	18.6	50.0

* E = Equity I = Interim mortgages, mainly construction loans. L = Long term mortgages.
† Book value per share assumes full conversion of all convertibles. Current yield is based upon the latest quarterly dividend.
Source: Kenneth D. Campbell, President, Audit Investment Research, Inc., 230 Park Avenue, New York, N.Y. 10017, August 1974.

The long term mortgage trusts may make loans for up to 30 years and are made at lower rates than for construction and development mortgage loans. The spread reflects the added risk the short term lender takes that the project might flounder before completion, or that the takeout money will not be forthcoming either because of changes in economic conditions or because of some contractual default by the builder. During 1973–74 the short term trusts were particularly hard hit. A few trusts combine mortgage and equity investments.

Procedures

All the trusts are users of borrowed capital. Some are permitted to mortgage up to two thirds of their total properties' market value. Others have set lower limits for themselves.

The trusts also vary in their treatment of depreciation. A few use accelerated depreciation but not for the same reason corporations do—i.e., to defer taxes. The trusts, which are not taxed on distributed earnings, do it to protect their shareholders from taxation. Because any distribution paid out of depreciation instead of net income is a return of capital, the shareholder owes no tax on it until the full cost of the shares is recovered or they are sold—at which point a capital gains tax is paid instead of straight income taxes.

Most trusts which favor straight line depreciation feel that the other method may lead to a cash bind since principal payments get bigger as the years go by, while depreciation allowances, under an accelerated schedule, get smaller and eventually no longer cover the mortgage amortization.

Most analysts believe the trusts should be bought primarily on the basis of yield, not promise of growth. Since trusts cannot grow by retained earnings because of the requirement that they distribute most of their income, they rely heavily on leverage to increase earnings. Mortgage trusts have no cash flow from depreciation, since they don't invest directly in real property. On the other hand their investment in mortgages makes them more "liquid" than equity trusts.[34]

---

[34] For further information, see "Sorting Out the Real Estate Investment Trusts," in Personal Investing, *Fortune*, August, 1970; see also, Peter A. Schulkin, "Conflicts of Interest in REIT's," in *Financial Analysts Journal*, May–June, 1971; Edmund J. Tunitis, *Real Estate Investment Trusts*, Financial Publishing Company, Boston, 1972; Leon Korobow and Richard J. Gelson, "Real Estate Investment Trusts: An Appraisal of their Impact on Mortgage Credit," in *Monthly Review, Federal Reserve Bank of New York*, August, 1971.

For an account of recent difficulties see "Falling Out: Real Estate Trusts Feud

Real estate trusts usually have but one class of stock. Management responsibility is vested in trustees. The shareholder has no voice in policy. In some cases he is allowed to elect trustees each year, elsewhere he may only have the right to remove a trustee by two-thirds vote or three-quarters vote and elect a replacement. Sometimes he has no vote at all.

As compared to the real estate syndicate, the real estate investment trust provides much greater liquidity for the investor. Usually shares can be sold either on organized exchanges or over the counter. It provides greater diversification by investing in a number of properties, not just one or two as in the case of the syndicate. As compared to real estate companies, the real estate investment trust must pay out 90 percent of its net income. The real estate company does not have to do this. The REIT is not subject to the corporate income tax whereas the real estate company is.

As compared to direct investment in common stock or shares of investment companies, investing in real estate investment trusts raises some difficult questions. Did insiders unload properties at inflated prices on the trust? Is the trust paying a reasonable price for the properties it acquires or in which it invests? Real estate values are harder to measure than values in securities. What kind of management fee is being charged? Is this fair and reasonable? Who are the trustees? Are they competent, experienced in real estate investment, and honest? You should try and have answers to all these questions before you invest in a real estate investment trust.

INVESTING IN ART AND COLLECTORS' ITEMS

One of the earliest French impressionist paintings earned its artist, Claude Monet, only $80 in 1866. In 1926 it was purchased by a Pennsylvania minister, the Reverend Theodore Pitcairn, for $11,000. He sold it at auction in 1968 for $1.4 million.

In 1944 a Jackson Pollack could be bought for $100. By 1953 it was

---

with Advisers over Their Obligations," *Wall Street Journal,* March 13, 1975; also "Too Much Too Soon: How Two Realty Trusts Gave Backers Big Gains—And Then Big Losses," *Wall Street Journal,* March 14, 1975.

Additional material is available from Audit Investment Research, Inc. 230 Park Avenue, New York, N.Y. 10017. It publishes the *Realty Trust Review,* the only investment advisory service covering REITs. See also, Kenneth G. Campbell, *The Real Estate Investment Trusts: America's Newest Billionaires,* Audit Investment Research, 1971. The industry trade association, National Association of Real Estate Investment Trusts, provides industry data, a yearbook of member trusts, and other information. Its address is: 1101 Seventeenth Street, N.W., Washington, D.C. 20036.

$2,000; in 1960, $50,000 and in 1970, $100,000. In 1973 *Blue Poles* was sold for $2 million.

The late Edward G. Robinson sold his collection (after 25 years) of 58 paintings and 1 sculpture to Stavros Niarchos, the Greek shipping magnate, through Knoedler & Co. for $3.2 million. It had cost him about $1 million to assemble.

Fashions and tastes change. Prices began soaring in 1973–74 for a group that had been largely neglected—twentieth century American paintings. A two day auction by Sotheby Parke Bernet of 219 works from the estate of the late Edith Halpert, a leading New York gallery owner and sponsor of United States artists since the 1920s, was expected to bring about $2.5 million. It hit $3.7 million. Japanese buyers developed a yen for works by Yasuo Kuniyoshi, a naturalized U.S. citizen born in Japan. His *Little Joe with Cow,* which was painted in 1923 and sold for $300, went for a record $220,000.[35]

Investors in art, antiques, rare books, and stamps have had greater appreciation over the years than those in common stocks. In an exchange of letters, Richard Rush, leading art connoisseur and chronicler, advised that: "Between 1950 and 1955 art prices doubled. Then they tripled between 1955 and 1960 so that in a decade they went up six times. Between 1960 and 1970 they tripled again so in 20 years they increased 18 times, despite the fact that 1970 was a recession year. From 1970 to 1974 they increased about 2½ times."

The *London Times*—Sotheby index of old masters pictures (overall) rose sevenfold between 1951 and 1969. Dutch landscapes increased 8 times while Italian eighteenth century works rose 9½ times. The index of impressionist paintings (overall) rose 15½ times between 1951 and 1970. Within this category Monet's increased 22½ times and Boudin's 19 times.[36]

Some buy art as a status symbol, some as a hedge against inflation, some for capital gains—attempting to buy a painting for a "song" today to sell for a fortune tomorrow. Who does the buying? One survey shows that only 15 percent of the buyers in the United States are wealthy collectors. The largest percentage of buyers—about 50 percent—are high

---

[35] See "The Art Market's Hot New Group," *Business Week,* March 24, 1973, p. 61. See also "Ars Gratia Pecuniae," *Forbes,* August 1, 1973, p. 46; and "Now Art Investors Turn Their Taste to Prints," *U.S. News & World Report,* March 25, 1974, p. 54; "The Art Market vs. The Stock Market," *Financial World,* May 23, 1973.

[36] James O. and Joanne T. Winjum, "The Art Investment Market," University of Michigan *Business Review,* Ann Arbor, November 1974; Richard H. Rush, "The New Investment Boom," *The Wall Street Transcript,* April 15, 1974; Geraldine Keen, "Lasting Impressionists," *London Times,* February 13, 1971. Also by Geraldine Keen, "Old Masters' Pictures," *London Times,* May 19, 1970.

salaried, while 35 percent of those buying paintings are medium or low salaried.[37]

Most paintings are sold for $1,000 or less. Finds are rare, but when they occur they are usually so well publicized that the impression gets around that they occur all the time. A Franz Hals was sold in the Netherlands in 1963 for $7. It was bought by a Russian-born cabaret pianist, Leonid Hostinov, at an auction in Arnheim, Holland. He resold it for $84,000 and the German woman who purchased it, resold it at auction two years later for $205,800. On the other hand, one of the world's wealthiest men, John Paul Getty, found an obscure Raphael, heavily repainted, and bought it at auction for £40, about $200 at the time. It was cleaned and restored and valued at $1 million.

The *London Times*—Sotheby's analysis of the art market warned investors against pulling out of the stock market and plunging into art, however. "Apart from the fact that pictures pay no dividends, it is not possible to buy a painting one day and sell it at auction the next," the *Times* said. "If a picture is resold too quickly in the salesroom it usually drops in price." It takes about five years for some schools to "mature" on the market, the analysis noted. The art market, it advised, is not for the short term investor.

So popular has art investing become that several mutual funds for investment in art were started. Typical of the pressure for art investment was the investor who told his broker: "Forget Polaroid and Burroughs. I want a piece of that Monet-Picasso action." One of the most noted of the some 20 mutual funds formed around the world for investment in art is one named Artemis, after the Greek goddess of hunting. Incorporated in Luxembourg, it was founded by two prestigious European bankers who went into it, part time, to get richer—Baron Leon Lambert of the Banque Lambert of Brussels and Baron Elie de Rothschild of the Rothschild Bank of Paris. One of its record purchases was of an 1888 oil painting by Seurat for $1,033,200 at auction at Christie's of London. Some funds are private, some are public.[38]

---

[37] For further information, see "The Art of Investing in Art," *Changing Times*, February, 1974. *The Economics of Taste: The Rise and Fall of Picture Prices, 1760–1960* (London: Barrie, 1961), and its sequel *The Art Market in the 1960's* (New York: Humanities Press, 1971), both by Gerald Reitlinger. See also Richard Rush, *Art as an Investment* (Englewood Cliffs, N.J.: Prentice-Hall, Inc., 1961), and its sequel, *Antiques as an Investment* (New York: Prentice-Hall, Inc., 1968), by the same author. Also, Robert Wraight, *The Art Game* (New York: Simon & Schuster, 1966) and Geraldine Keen, *Money and Art* (New York: G. P. Putnam's Sons, 1971).

[38] See "Art for the Sake of Speculation," *Forbes*, July 4, 1970; See also, "Now There are Mutual Funds for Art," *New York Times*, November 7, 1969, and "Two European Bankers Backing New Art Fund," *New York Times*, June 30, 1970.

Rare books have appreciated even more than old masters. The *London Times*—Sotheby index for old books (overall) rose 11½ times between 1951 and 1969.[39] For the last decade and a half, rare book prices, with few exceptions, have climbed at a startling rate. Franz Pick, who chronicles the yearly changes in auction prices of rare books and manuscripts, found figures up 40 to 50 percent in 1966, 50 to 60 percent in 1967, 60 percent in 1968, and 30 percent in 1969 and 1970, with a continuing spiral over the past five years. Most collectors hold onto their acquisitions. It is the disposal of private collections—usually after the collector's death—that makes most of the rare book market. There are, however, occasions where individuals do sell affording added insight into the market. Thus, in 1970, Arthur A. Houghton, Jr., president of Steuben Glass, and a book collector, sold a fifteenth century Gutenberg Bible to a book dealer, H. P. Kraus, for which Mr. Kraus subsequently asked $2.5 million. Mr. Houghton acquired the Bible in the 1950s for a reported $150,000. His sales price was not disclosed.

Just as some paintings have declined in price due to loss of popularity of the painter or the school, books too at times decline in price. In the 1920s, for example, first editions of some of Bernard Shaw's works cost about $350. Today they can be purchased for $50. John Galsworthy's prices went into the thousands then; $100 would be a common price now.[40]

The stamp market is another interesting investment market. There are some 25 million collectors, and the market is international in scope. Values are appreciating as much as 20 to 30 percent a year. Over the last decade, collections of American stamps have increased in value an average of 10 percent a year, while a good Japanese stamp collection rose 1,000 percent over the decade. Two 1847 stamps from the island of Mauritius (in the Indian Ocean) sold for $380,000. A New Orleans stamp dealer bought them. Only 14 such stamps were ever printed, and they had a typographical error in them which added to their rarity. Consider the recent sale of a piece of reddish purple paper with a face value of one penny. This last surviving first British Guiana stamp sold at auction for $280,000. The buyer was the representative of a syndicate of investors who felt that the best place for spare funds was in stamps.[41] A 24 cent 1918 U.S. airmail stamp with an upside down airplane is worth some $25,000

---

[39] Geraldine Keen, "A Boom in Books for Collectors," in the *London Times*, July 3, 1970. Sylvia O'Neill Dorn, *The Insider's Guide to Antiques, Art and Collectibles*, Garden City, N.Y.: Doubleday, 1974.

[40] "Appreciating Rare Books, *New York Times*, August 15, 1971.

[41] "Stamp Collecting: Rich Man's Hobby Lures Investors," in "Personal Business," *Business Week*, November 20, 1971; See also "Investing in Stamps," *Changing Times*, September 1974.

today. The same stamp without the upside down error is worth only $10. Watch out, however, for purposely manufactured errors. You can be taken. Postage stamps are a traditional hedge against inflation. It would be better to have a nest egg in the upside down U.S. airmail than in the safest bond. The stamp would provide no current income, but its appreciation over a period of time would more than make up for this current shortcoming, if you can afford to do without the income.

Small fortunes are being made by appreciation in various types of antiques, such as seventeenth century English silver tankards, French eighteenth century furniture, Chippendale furniture, Oriental rugs, snuff boxes, Boehm porcelain birds, Chinese vases, and English glass. An original Chippendale china cabinet brought $125,000 at a sale in Britain in 1968. In 1973, the American dealer who bought it turned down an offer of $400,000. In the face of continuing inflation, he expected to sell it for at least $500,000.

Sylvia Porter notes that a pair of Boehm porcelain song sparrows rose from $2,000 to $18,000 and then to over $45,000 in little more than a decade.[42] An eighteenth century Paul Revere tea set brought $70,000 in an auction at Parke-Bernet Galleries. A 5-inch sugar tongs brought an amazing $5,250. Some American silver antique pieces have more than doubled in price over the last five years.

All these rather esoteric types of investments have one thing in common. You have to know the field to buy safely, or if you don't you can be taken badly. That doesn't mean you have to be an expert. Reliable experts are available to consult, but if you know little about the field you run a substantial risk. Forgeries, imitations, fakes, and the like, abound. Each market is somewhat obscure and relatively unpublicized. And if you are among the uninitiated, you may not know how to locate a reputable expert. Start carefully. Study the field. Invest a minimum to start. Even the experts, especially in art and antiques, have sometimes been fooled.[43]

GOLD AND SILVER

In 1971 when the official United States price of gold was $35 an ounce, the world market price was $41 an ounce. In 1974 the official price was $42 an ounce while the market price reached $180 an ounce. Since Americans

[42] Sylvia Porter, "Your Dollar, Investments III: The Antiques," *New York Post*, June 18, 1969, and Robert Metz, "Market Place: Buying Antiques as Investments," *New York Times*, October 16, 1971; see also, Gerald Reitlinger, *The Economics of Taste, The Rise and Fall of the Objets d'Art Market Since 1750* (New York: Henry Holt & Co., 1965), vol. 2, and Scott, Amoret, and Christopher, *Antiques As an Investment* (New York: International Publications Service, 1967).

[43] David L. Goodrich, *Art Fakes in America* (New York: Viking, 1973); see also W. Crawley, *Is It Genuine?*, New York: Hart Publishing Co. 1972.

were forbidden to own gold until 1975, the pursuit of gold as an inflation hedge, led to collecting gold coins and buying gold stocks (shares in gold mining companies).[44]

In response to rising gold prices, the price of the *London Financial Times* average of gold mining stocks increased six fold between 1972 and 1974.

For more than 3,500 years collecting gold or gold coins has been a fascinating pursuit, no less in contemporary than in ancient times. As Ira C. Cobleigh has noted: "Millions of people owe their lives to gold coins, secretly stashed away, which have enabled them to survive in times of famine, political upheaval, or natural disaster, to escape persecution or death; or to flee to safer lands by buying off guards, officials, or border sentinels. Gold has always opened myriads of doors, closed to those who had nothing, lost everything, or held only depreciating or worthless paper money."[45]

In the seventies, hoarding gold has been popular worldwide, as fear of inflation and depreciated paper currencies swept across nations. The French, mindful of 14 devaluations in this century are estimated to be hoarding $6 billion in gold bars, jewelry, and coins. Among Swiss bankers, Indian merchants, Japanese industrialists, and nervous Americans, holding gold or gold coins has become increasingly popular. The world famous gold coins—Napoleons, Sovereigns, Double Eagles, Mexican 50 pesos, Dutch Guilders—are in good supply but prices have risen more than 100 percent during the early 1970s.

It was illegal for Americans to own gold bullion from 1934 to the end of 1974, but legal to own gold coins of numismatic value minted before 1934. The latent demand of Americans for gold spilled over into the gold coin market and prices of select coins rose to substantial premiums above the intrinsic gold content of these coins. For example, premiums on gold coins, legal for U.S. citizens, residents, or corporations to own for "numismatic purposes" were as shown in Table 13–13. Premiums keep changing all the time. The premium is the amount of extra money you pay for a coin over and above the current market value of its actual gold content.

In 1974 a $20 U.S. Double Eagle (1909 St. Gaudins) was worth about

---

[44] "Investing in Gold," *Changing Times*, August 1974; see also "Investing in Gold: Five Sides of the Coin," *Money*, September 1974; *Gold: A Special Report*, Merrill Lynch Pierce Fenner & Smith, Inc., New York, 1974. A free copy may be obtained by writing to the firm at One Liberty Plaza, 165 Broadway, New York, N.Y. 10006.

[45] See Ira U. Cobleigh, *Buy Gold and Coin Money*, (New York: Goldfax, 1972), and *Golden Profits from Golden Coins*, New York: Goldfax, 1974. See also Harry Browne, *You Can Profit from a Monetary Crisis*, (New York: Macmillan Publishing Co., 1974); also Donald J. Hoppe, *How to Invest in Gold Stocks and Avoid the Pitfalls*, (New Rochelle, N.Y.: Arlington House, 1972).

TABLE 13–13
Premium on Gold Coins—1974

Nation	*Coin*	*Ounces of Gold*	*Premium*
Germany	20 mark	.23045	80%
Great Britain	Sovereign	.23540	50
Mexico	50 Peso	1.20563	25
Netherlands	10 Guilder	.19444	50
Switzerland	10 Franc	.09333	575
Switzerland	20 Franc	.18666	75
United States	$20 Liberty (Double Eagle)	.96746	70
United States	$10 Liberty (Eagle)	.48373	75
United States	$5 Liberty (Half Eagle)	.24187	120

Source: *How to "Wheel and Deal" in Gold and Silver*, C. M. Allen, New York 1974, p. 53–54.

$500. A $20 U.S. Double Eagle (1863) had a value of $275, as compared with about $65 in 1971. There were about 52,500 of the former minted but 966,570 of the latter. Hence the numismatic value of the former was higher. The $5 Half Eagle (1834) was valued at $550 while the 2.50 Quarter Eagle (1848) of which only 13,771 were minted, sold for $425.

When it became legal, once again, at the end of 1974, for U.S. citizens to own gold bullion, the "gold rush of 1975" failed to materialize. The expected surge to gold was anticipated due to a desire to preserve capital and hedge against inflation. In the flight from currency to goods which usually marks a period of sharp inflation, there is also an awareness that over the ages gold has been a store of value, independent of any government or monetary authority. It is no one's liability, no one's promise to pay. Despite efforts in recent years to get away from gold standards and to relegate gold to a place of no importance in monetary systems, for Europeans and Asians it retained its age old attraction as a means of preserving capital—by-passing depreciating paper money and loss of purchasing power and has remained a traditional way of coping with inflation.

The failure of Americans to become excited about gold ownership, when it became legally permissible, was probably due to a variety of reasons. First, gold paid no return at all. Second, there is a bewildering variety of ways to buy it, gold bullion or bars, gold coins, gold commodity futures, shares in gold funds, or gold mining company stocks, to name the major ways. Third, it is costly to buy and own gold. Local sales and use taxes are payable in many states—they amount to 8 percent in New York City. Gold must be insured, shipped, and stored at the purchaser's expense. Premiums—fabrication charges—of 2 to 7 percent must be paid on the relatively small purchases within the reach of the typical investor, and before gold can be resold it almost always must be assayed, its quality and fineness determined, a service for which charges begin at $30. The standard 400 ounce gold bars are expensive. They sell for about $77,000 at current world prices. As one banker put it: "We want every customer to realize that gold is expensive to buy, expensive to store, expensive to insure, and expensive to sell. Besides it pays no return and it usually doesn't appreciate while you own it."

The extent of the rise in gold bullion prices may be seen in Figure 13–11. Gold bullion rose to a peak of $180 an ounce in late February 1974, fell off to $129 an ounce in early July and rose again to $187 in December 1974. The stock price of the preeminent U.S. gold producer, Homestake Mining, rose from $9 a share in 1972 to 69⅝ in 1974, a gain of over 650 percent.

Engelhard Minerals & Chemicals Corp. provided the following advice to prospective buyers of gold bullion or coins:

> Gold bullion should have a known refiners mark, assaying its weight and fineness.
>
> The buyer should realize that the difference between the offering price and daily newspaper quotes for a given amount of gold is the

FIGURE 13–11
Official and Market Prices of Gold, 1968–1974

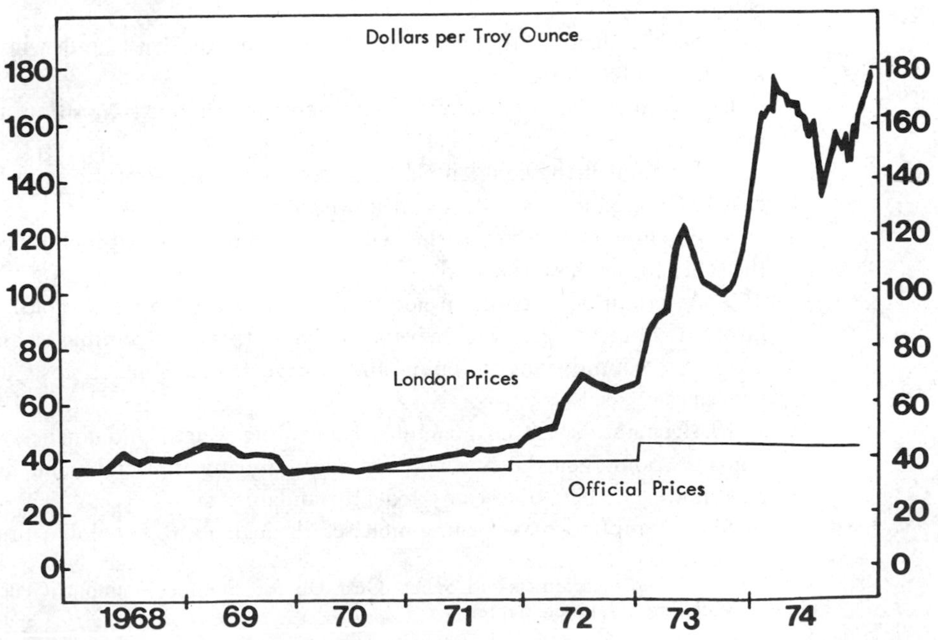

Source: Merrill Lynch, Pierce, Fenner, & Smith Inc.

seller's commission and premium (if any) and should shop around for the best deal.

Coins of no numismatic value are worth only the price of their bullion—despite the fact that they sell at a premium—and counterfeits and restrikes (newly minted coins bearing fake back dates) abound.

Get a guarantee.

If you are a nervous investor, stay clear of highly leveraged margin accounts.

Prudence is especially advised where dealing with companies stipulating that the customer must only resell a purchase to the original seller; the customer is usually at a disadvantage in such instances.

Remember an investment in gold bullion or gold coin pays no return and may involve carrying, storage, and insurance charges.[46]

"Consumers may find that the purchase of gold is more of a minefield than a gold mine unless they are familiar with the risks," the President's special assistant for consumer affairs advised in setting forth, in conjunction with the Federal Trade Commission, the following guidelines:

1. Be wary of unsolicited correspondence or calls from strangers offering to sell you gold or gold investments.
2. Be skeptical of promises of spectacular profits. Ask yourself: Why am I being offered this golden opportunity?
3. Resist pressures to make hurried, uninformed investment decisions.
4. Be suspicious of claims of new, secret or exotic processes to extract gold.
5. Seek independent advice from a person you trust and who is knowledgeable.
6. Consider the risks in relation to your own financial position and needs.
7. Find out if the company has registered with the Securities and Exchange Commission or state securities agency.
8. Attempt to determine the seller's mark-up, or how much it cost the seller to purchase the gold.
9. Ascertain what costs, in addition to the quoted price of gold, are involved. For example, you may be required to pay a refining charge, assay fees, commissions, shipping and storage fees, insurance costs and sales tax.
10. Demand a written guarantee concerning weight and fineness, or pureness. Some gold bears a refiner's mark assaying its weight and fineness; however, there aren't any federal standards.
11. Attempt to make your purchases through local, reputable firms.

[46] "Bullion Boom? Nation's Gold Sellers Gear Up for 'Stampede' among General Public," *Wall Street Journal*, September 4, 1974.

(Firms including the term "exchange" in their name shouldn't be assumed to constitute an association or group of firms that provide a public market for buyers and sellers.)

12. Obtain in writing the terms of your purchase, for example, when and how the gold will be delivered and stored, including what security precautions will be taken to ensure that your gold isn't shaved or that counterfeit gold isn't substituted.

13. Ask whether the gold will be segregated and stored in your name (not the seller's or supplier's). Make sure you receive a written receipt showing that the requisite amount of gold is being stored for your account by a reputable concern.

14. Ask whether there will be a ready market for the gold in the form being offered to you. You may have to pay to have your gold reassayed, recast into a different shape, size and-or transported to a distant market before you can sell it.[47]

Silver

U.S. citizens have been free to buy, sell, and hoard silver bullion or silver coins and many have sought to hedge against inflation or capital gains via silver. Silver is traded on both the New York Commodity Exchange and the Chicago Board of Trade. Silver coins in bags of $10,000 face value are traded on the New York Mercantile Exchange. People began intensive hoarding of silver coins in the mid 1960s. In 1965 the U.S. government stopped minting coins of 90 percent silver. In 1967 the price of silver rose above the mint price of $1.29 an ounce and a free market in silver developed. In 1968 the government no longer redeemed silver certificates (paper money) for silver bullion and in 1969 the government sold over two billion ounces of silver from its stockpile. Unlike gold, silver has numerous industrial uses and industrial demand in the first half of the 1970s has tended to out run supply with the price rising to above $6.00 an ounce. Buying silver contracts on the commodity exchanges requires knowledge of the mechanics and procedures of commodity trading, which takes time, effort, and is a complicated business.[48] Numerous coin dealing firms have sprung up to sell bags of silver coins to the public, on margin (you put up only part of the purchase price) and at excessively high prices. When you buy bags of silver on margin you do not get delivery of the bags. The coin exchange holds them and some exchanges have al-

[47] See "White House Issues 14 'Golden Rules' on Bullion Investing," *Wall Street Journal*, December 10, 1974; also *Gold Purchasing and Investing*, Federal Trade Commission, Washington, December 9, 1974.

[48] Bruce G. Gould, *Dow Jones-Irwin Guide to Commodities Trading*, (Homewood, Ill.: Dow Jones-Irwin, Inc., 1973).

legedly not used the margin money to buy coins but instead have speculated in silver futures.[49]

After exploring in detail the possible pitfalls of investing in silver, *Forbes* sounded a general warning:

> One thing is certain. Silver is not gold. Silver is certainly not recession-proof; in the middle of the Depression silver sold for 24 cents, its lowest price in a century. And, unlike gold, silver is not easily portable. A 10 pound bar of gold, which you could pack in your suitcase, would be worth $28,000 at recent prices; the same amount of silver would be worth only about $700. Which makes silver undesirable either for a quick getaway or for stuffing under your mattress.[50]

Of investing in silver coins, bars and bullion, *Changing Times* says: "It's strictly speculative at best and sometimes it's a waste of money," and "investing in silver is a speculative investment: if you do it, you'd be wise to use only money you can afford to lose."[51]

SUGGESTED READINGS

1. Jerome B. Cohen, Edward D. Zinbarg and Arthur Zeikel, *Investment Analysis and Portfolio Management.* (rev. ed.) Homewood, Ill.: Richard D. Irwin, Inc., 1973.
2. New York Stock Exchange, *The Language of Investing: A Glossary.* A free copy may be obtained by writing to the Exchange at 11 Wall Street, New York, N.Y. 10005.
3. Louis Engel, *How to Buy Stocks.* New York: Bantam Books, paperbound. A free copy may be obtained by writing to Merrill Lynch, Pierce, Fenner & Smith, at One Liberty Plaza, 165 Broadway, New York, N.Y. 10006.
4. Irving Price, *Buying Country Property.* New York: Harper & Row, 1972.
5. *In Changing Times, The Kiplinger Magazine:*
   "Eleven Ways to Size Up a Stock," August 1972.
   "Should You Invest in New Stock Issues?" September 1972.
   "A New Way to Invest in Land," April 1973.
   "Buying Stocks: Does the Small Investor Have a Chance?" June 1973.
   "How Do Brokers Treat the Small Investor?" July 1973.
   "Put Some of Your Money into Government Securities?" April 1974.

---

[49] See "Texas Judge Enjoins Coin Dealer's Sales after Finding Securities Law Violations," *Wall Street Journal*, April 19, 1974; See also "Elusive Gains: Small Investors Flock to Bags of Silver Coins but Pricing Is Tricky: Dealers' Quotes, Some Find, Provide Some Surprises," *Wall Street Journal*, February 4, 1974.

[50] "The Silver Slickers," *Forbes*, May 1, 1974, pp. 18–19.

[51] See "Investing in Silver Coins, Bags and Bullion," *Changing Times*, July 1974; see also "Are Silver Coins a Good Investment?" *Changing Times*, January 1974.

"Who Protects You Against Stock Market Frauds?" April 1974.
"Which Stock Market Index Do You Read?" June 1974.
"Investing in Gold," August 1974.
"Investing in Silver Coins, Bars, & Bullion," July 1974.
"Are Silver Coins a Good Investment?" January, 1974.

6. Burton G. Malkiel, *A Random Walk Down Wall Street*. New York: W. W. Norton & Co., Inc., 1973.
7. *What Everybody Ought to Know about This Stock and Bond Business*, published by Merrill Lynch, Pierce, Fenner & Smith, New York. A free copy may be obtained by writing to this firm at One Liberty Plaza, 165 Broadway, New York, N.Y. 10006.
8. *The Exchange*, a monthly magazine published by the New York Stock Exchange. For a sample copy write to New York Stock Exchange, 11 Wall Street, New York, N.Y. 10005.
9. Harry G. Sauvain, *Investment Management*, 4th ed., Englewood Cliffs, N.J.: Prentice-Hall, Inc. 1973.
10. *Gold: A Special Report*, Merrill Lynch, Pierce, Fenner & Smith, Inc., New York, 1974. A free copy may be obtained by writing to the firm at One Liberty Plaza, 165 Broadway, New York, N.Y. 10006.
11. James H. Lorie & Mary T. Hamilton, *The Stock Market*. Homewood, Ill.: Richard D. Irwin, Inc., 1973.
12. *The Bond Book*. New York: Merrill Lynch, Pierce, Fenner & Smith. A free copy may be obtained by writing to the firm at One Liberty Plaza, 165 Broadway, New York, N.Y. 10006.
13. New York Stock Exchange, *Understanding Convertible Securities*. A free copy may be obtained by writing to the Exchange at 11 Wall Street, New York, N.Y. 10005.
14. New York Stock Exchange, *Understanding Bonds and Preferred Stocks*. A free copy may be obtained by writing to the Exchange at 11 Wall Street, New York, N.Y. 10005.
15. *The Story of Municipal Bonds: Investing for Tax-Free Income*. New York: Merrill Lynch, Pierce, Fenner & Smith. A free copy may be obtained by writing to the firm at One Liberty Plaza, 165 Broadway, New York, N.Y. 10006.
16. Adam Smith, *The Money Game* (1968) and *Supermoney* (1972), New York: Random House.
17. Jean Young & Jim Young, *Peoples Guide to Country Real Estate*, New York: Praeger Publishers, 1973.
18. C. Colburn Hardy, *Your Investments, 1975–76*, New York: Thomas Y. Crowell, 1975.
19. Hugh C. Sherwood, *How to Invest in Bonds*, Walker Publishing Co., New York, 1974.

20. A. M. Watkins, "Breaking Ground as a Real Estate Investor," *Money*, December 1973.
21. Ira U. Cobleigh, *All About Investing in Real Estate Securities*. New York: Weybright & Talley, 1971.
22. Geraldine Keen, *Money and Art*. New York: G. P. Putnam's Sons, 1971.
23. *Merrill Lynch Looks at Tax Sheltered Investments*. A free copy may be obtained by writing to the firm at One Liberty Plaza, 165 Broadway, New York, N.Y. 10006.
24. "Should You Buy Gold?" *Money*, September 1974; see also "The Gold Rush of '74," *Money*, May 1974.
25. Sylvia O'Neill Dorn, *The Insider's Guide to Antiques, Art and Collectibles*, Garden City, N.Y.: Doubleday, 1974.
26. Kenneth D. Campbell (ed.), *The Real Estate Trusts: America's Newest Billionaires*. New York: Audit Investment Research, 1971.

CASE PROBLEMS

1. Jane and Bob, a young married couple, are both working. She intends to continue to do so for another three or four years. They have been living on his salary ($8,500 a year), placing most of her $5,500 a year take home pay in their savings account, in which they have about $5,000. They now plan to invest about $2,000 and her current income in securities. Bob is buying a 20 payment life insurance policy and their Blue Cross–Blue Shield insurance out of his salary. What kind of an investment program would you suggest for them?

2. Jack Rothwell, a lawyer, age 45, is married and has three children (ages 12, 14, and 15). He has a current income of $25,000 a year. During the years he has built up considerable savings through insurance and investments (in stocks). He decided to buy some bonds, primarily as a hedge against downward fluctuations in the business cycle, and partly to round out his investment program. What types of bonds would best meet his needs?

3. Paul and Dorothy have been married a year. Paul is studying for his doctorate in history, which he expects to receive in two years, and has just been hired at a neighboring institution as a half time instructor. His wife has a full time job. They have been living on Dorothy's salary and have been able to add $30 to their savings bank account each month. They rent a small apartment, are covered by Blue Cross–Blue Shield, and have a small amount of life insurance. Should they consider investing the additional income from Paul's new position in stocks? Why? Why not?

4. John Blake is 55 years old; his wife is 50. Their two sons have graduated from college and have good jobs. Blake is earning $10,000 and hopes to retire after another 10 years, at which time he will receive a pension of $5,000 a year. He owns his home and has sufficient life, health, and general insurance.

They have emergency funds in the savings bank. He has just inherited $50,000 which he wishes to invest, along with some additional money he believes he can save, since he will no longer have any college bills for his boys. He thinks he knows a good deal about investing, although he has never actually done any himself. He asks for your suggestions.

5. Tom and Polly are a young married couple with two children (ages 2 and 4). Thus far the family has lived on his salary; he feels that he has enough health insurance protection which he obtained through his company. In addition he is covered by a $20,000 straight life insurance policy (paid up at age 65), which seems adequate. He has just received a $25,000 inheritance from his uncle and wants to invest it in growth stocks. Help him select five growth stocks and justify your choices.

6. Terry and Judy have recently moved to Scarsdale with their two young children, since Terry has been transferred to the New York office of his company. He has group life and health insurance through his firm and a tidy sum in the bank. They have just bought a house, but do not know how long his firm will want him to remain at the home office. They feel they can afford to invest about $1,200–$1,300 a year. What suggestions can you give them?

7. The Dew Drop Inn Company, Inc., is a chain of restaurants in a large city. It is a family held corporation, and its capitalization consists of 1,000 shares of common stock divided equally among five brothers. The stock is not for sale on the market but is valued on the books at $100 per share. All the owners agree that this price represents a fair value. Business opportunities look good. The company wishes to expand and finance this expansion by offering rights in the ratio of 5 to 1 at $80 for each new share. One brother, Larry, cannot afford to retain his equity in the company. He wants to know how much he should receive when he offers to sell his rights to his brothers and what percentage of the business he will retain.

8. Bryan has been buying the common stocks of companies which, after careful study, he expected would experience a healthy growth. He is now worth $50,000. In two more years, he must retire without pension from his $15,000 a year job. Although his three children are grown up and independent, his wife (age 62) is bedridden, thus causing large medical expenses. Under the circumstances, would you advise any change in his investment practices? Explain and justify.

9. When Dorothy Lingham finally had $8,000 which she felt she could invest in securities, it was toward the end of a long period of prosperity which she thought could only be followed by several years of recession. Under the circumstances, what investment policy would be most suitable for her consideration?

10. Amos and Natalie Hopkins have just made the final payment on their home. They have three children (ages 9, 14, and 17). Amos runs the local

hardware store (he owns the inventory and the building) and has kept about $5,000 on deposit for several years to meet the needs of the business. For several years he has been carrying $50,000 of straight life insurance on his life. Now he feels that they can invest about $3,000 yearly in stocks and bonds. If you were in his position, what kind of an investment program would you develop?

11. Samuel Lincoln is a trustee. He is to pay the income of a $250,000 estate annually to John Brown for life. Upon Brown's death he is to turn over the principal of the estate to a designated college. Lincoln has an opportunity to invest the $250,000 in high grade 6 percent bonds, which he can buy to yield 7 percent. Should he do so? Why, why not?

12. Saul Levine is 30, married, and earns $11,000 a year. His wife has inherited $75,000 and they are debating how to invest it. He favors real estate. She prefers blue chip common stocks for their safety and marketability. He argues that returns over time are higher in real estate and that it is a better hedge against inflation. With whom would you side in this debate? Why? How would you suggest investing the $75,000?

13. Kickham, age 32, has a wife (age 30) and three children (ages 3, 4, and 6). He is the manager of a local factory, where he earns $16,000 a year. He owns his home and an automobile, in addition to having saved $7,000 in the local savings and loan association. On his savings he is now earning 5.5 percent per annum. He has been reading about common stocks and real estate as a hedge against inflation. Do you believe that he should invest part or all of his savings in common stocks or real estate? If so, what kind of investment program do you think would suit his needs?

14

How to Buy and Sell Securities

The Public is always wrong.
Wall Street maxim

"If you want to make your pile, you have got to be in style," wrote Eldon Grimm a leading analyst in the *Financial Analysts Journal.* Styles in common stock, he pointed out, change almost as rapidly as women's fashions. You have to be alert to changing fancies in the market if you would do well in common stocks, he concluded after a fascinating review of some extremes of mass emotion in the market. For example, during World War I, Bethlehem Steel was in high fashion. It soared from $10 a share in 1914 to $200 just one year later. In the twenties, talking pictures and radio absorbed the country. Warner Bros. Pictures (your grandparents may remember Al Jolson in *The Singing Fool*) skyrocketed from 9¾ in 1927 to 138 in 1928. RCA rose from 12½ in 1922 to 573 in 1929. Airplane stocks boomed with the first trans Atlantic flight. Wright Aeronautical rose from 9⅝ in 1924 to 289 in 1928. Ever hear of the Auburn car? Its stock rose from 78 in 1928 to 514 in 1929 and then dropped to 60 in 1930.

During the Great Depression and the early New Deal days, gold and liquor stocks were in high style. The price of the old Homestake Mining stock went from 81 in 1931 to 544 in 1936. Alaska Juneau rose from 4½ in 1930 to 33 in 1933. With the repeal of Prohibition, National Distillers zoomed from 13 in 1932 to 124 a year later.

During World War II airline shares boomed. The old stock of American Airlines rose from 7½ in 1937 to 94½ eight years later. Eastern Airlines increased from 16¾ to 134 in some seven years. TWA went up from 7⅝ in 1942 to 79 in 1945.

The post–World War II period saw television, electronics, aircraft, and aluminum, among others, rise to great popularity. Motorola went from 8¾ to 185. General Dynamics, which had ranged from 1 to 11 between 1929 and 1949, rose from 4 in 1949 to 68⅝ in 1957. Over the same period Minnesota Mining and Manufacturing jumped from 8¼ to 101. Aluminum Company of America rose from 46 in 1949 to the equivalent of 352 in 1955, and Reynolds Metals moved up from 19 to the equivalent of $300 over the same period. Subsequently the ephemeral popularity of Metrecal as a dieting fad sent Mead Johnson shares from $40 to over $200. The advent of the computer age pushed IBM from $40 to $600 and Control Data from $20 to over $174. The profitability of the first jets sent airline stocks soaring—Delta Airlines from 5 to 97 and Northwest Airlines from 7 to 171.

In recent years the spotlight has touched on office equipment—Burroughs climbed from 22⅛ to 252; leisure—Walt Disney from 5 to 201¾, and back down to 16⅝; franchise restaurants—McDonald's from 1 to 76⅞, and then down to 21¼; furniture—Levitz from 1 to 61, and then down to 1½; recreation vehicles—Skyline from ⅜ to 74, then back to 10¼; cosmetics—Avon Products from 8½ to 140 and then off to 18⅝; photography—Polaroid from 10¼ to 149½, and then down to 14⅛; beverages—Coca Cola from 12¼ to 150; health care—Johnson & Johnson from 6 to 133; offshore drilling—Vetco from 4⅝ to 61⅞ and Ocean Drilling from 2⅞ to 70½; oil drilling equipment—Halliburton from 14 to 189; pharmaceuticals—Schering Plough from 7¾ to 141½, Warner Lambert from 17 to 109, Upjohn from 28¾ to 132, then back down to 34⅜.

Now lest performances of this type cause you to rush into the market, a word of caution. It's a rare investor who was able to pick more than a few of these successes. And even more rare was the investor who timed the style changes correctly. It's just about impossible to buy at the low and sell at the high. You're not that omniscient. Don't try. Syntex offers a good example. From an adjusted price of 5 in 1963, the stock zoomed to a peak of 124¾ in the early part of 1966. By the time of 1970, it was down to 18⅛ but recovered to a high of 128½ in 1973 and then fell to 27¾ in 1974.

A hot issue during one period may be a dud during the next. Itek shares, for example, rose from 9 to 172 and then fell back to 4⅞. Bausch & Lomb rose from 5 to 97 and then went down to 17¾. Mattel shot up from 1 to 52, then fell back to 2¼. Teledyne rose from 3⅞ to 60¼ and then fell to 7⅝. Kalvar rose to 176½ and then fell to 3½! Tropicana Products went from 4¼ to 60⅜ and then down to 6½. MGIC Investments rose

"Don't laugh. Did you buy Control Data at eight?"

Drawing by Robert Day; © 1964 the New Yorker Magazine, Inc.

from 1⅝ to 98⅞ and then fell to 6⅛. Tampax went from 8½ to 136 and then dropped to 29.

Some wise rules for successful investment were offered by Edgar Scott, formerly president of the Philadelphia Stock Exchange and a governor of the New York Stock Exchange. His list of do's and don'ts includes:

1. Don't pay attention to irresponsible tips. Tipsters have surprisingly little money of their own and if they are convinced that they know of a stock that will go up 10 points in 10 days, let them lose their own money, not yours.

2. Don't open an account with a brokerage house until you have satisfied yourself that it is thoroughly reputable.

3. Don't approach the market with the hallucination that you can buy

at the bottom and sell at the top. That is as rare as a hole in one, even for the most experienced brains in the business. Wise investing consists of selecting securities which represent real present and *future* values; then buying them at some reasonable stage in their price cycle.

4. Don't be stubborn about your own errors of judgment. If a stock fails to fulfill the promise you thought you saw in it, sell it—at a loss if necessary. Quick action in such cases often cuts losses which would otherwise grow larger.

5. Don't become blindly attached to a stock because it has done well for you. Take your profits and find a new, better situation. You seldom lose money taking a profit.

6. Don't be swayed by a loquacious salesman peddling an unseasoned stock. Of course, you would have made millions if you had gone in with Henry Ford, but you might also have bought Stutz, Hupmobile or one of the other 20 odd automobile companies which disappeared in the twenties.

7. Do take your time. Check up on all the available facts about a contemplated investment.

8. Do be clear about your particular purpose. What is your objective? Until you know what you are looking for, there is little chance of finding it.

9. Get in the habit of reading the financial section of a newspaper, or other good financial publication.

10. Do, in the process of forming your considered judgment, seek information and ideas from qualified people and sources of financial information.

11. Do remember that not every transaction will be successful. That is true of any business. If an investor or trader in securities tells you he never takes a loss, pay him no heed, for the truth is not in him.

Diversification

There is an old adage that it is never wise to put all one's eggs in one basket; this is an excellent rule to follow in investment. It means much more, however, than simply investing in several companies rather than in one. It means, first of all, a proper blending of common stocks, preferreds, and bonds in the light of your investment objectives and of the business cycle. For example, if yours is a young family, after you have provided adequately for insurance and after you have established an emergency fund to fall back on by a savings bank deposit or by government savings bond purchases, they your surplus savings can to a large extent go into good growth (common) stocks and convertible bonds in the upward phase of the business cycle and then, toward the top of the cycle, be shifted gradually, in part, to high grade bonds.

An elderly couple, to take a second example, dependent upon the income from a savings accumulation of a lifetime, might put 75 percent of their fund in good grade income stocks (common) and 25 percent in bonds in the upward phase of the cycle and then shift the proportion increasingly to high grade bonds as it became apparent that the downtrend either would soon begin or had begun, until the percentages were reversed: 75 percent in high grade bonds, 25 percent in common stock. Or, if an increase in the rate of inflation is accompanied by a decline in both the bond and stock markets, a timely switch into short term high rate money market instruments, such as Treasury bills, floating rate notes, certificates of deposit, may be advisable. Why ride IBM down from 350 to 150, or a high grade bond from 101 to 70, when you can get 8 percent on a Treasury bill or 11 percent on a certificate of deposit (see Figure 14–1)?

Diversification of this sort among types of securities involves close attention to the trend of the business cycle and a nice precision in investment timing. As we shall see, if the individual is too busy or too unsure to feel reasonably confident and competent in judging trends, there are mechanical formulas for investment which help.

The second phase of diversification is selecting and differentiating among industries. Industry selection, as practiced by an increasing group of investors and investment managers, recognizes that "the market" is composed of many industrial groups of securities and that economic pressures and influences bear unequally on the various industries at any given period, resulting in dissimilar and often divergent market action. For example, if you had invested $1,000 in shipping and coal stocks in August 1939, and had held the stocks through the period ending July 1952, your capital would have grown to $6,570—a 557 percent gain. But had you invested the same $1,000 in shipping and coal stocks, then switched into printing and publishing and radio broadcasting, and then into petroleum and chemical stocks, your capital would have increased to $38,260, or a 3,726 percent gain in the same period. This illustration, employing hindsight, covers a period in which the market advanced. In a declining period, your experience could easily be one that showed a percentage gain by shifting as against a percentage loss by sitting tight.

The third aspect of diversification is to pick the best companies within the industry. In any industry, whether it is declining or advancing, there are a few companies doing better than average. For proper diversification you will want to find which companies these are and then invest in them.

FIGURE 14–1
A Shopping List of Yield (percent)

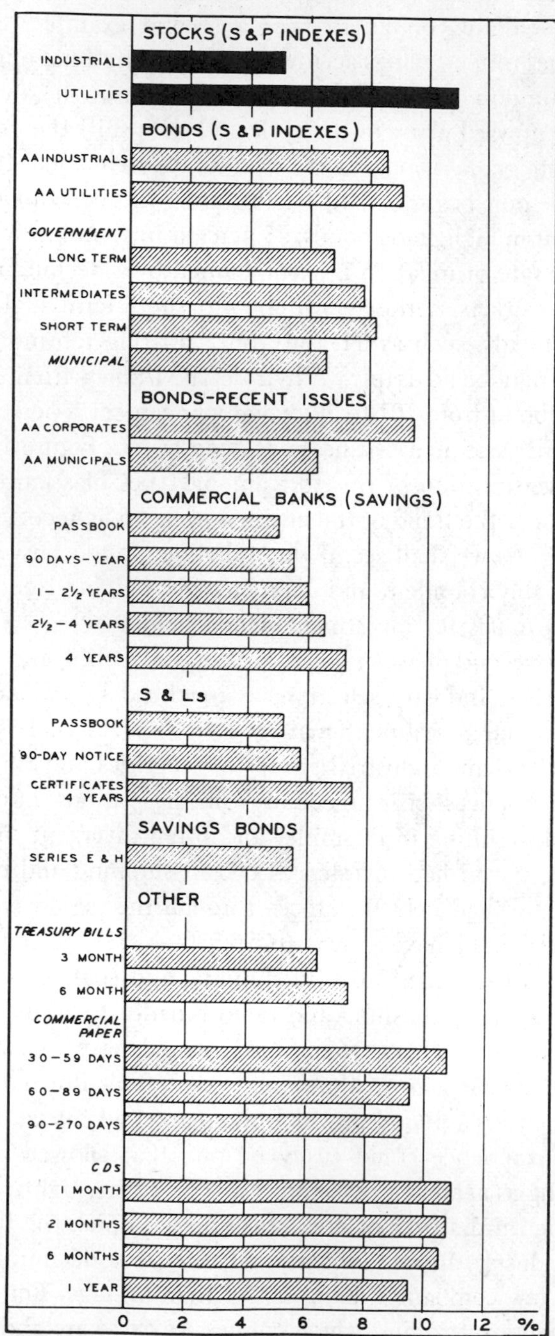

Source: Standard & Poor's *Outlook*, October 7, 1974.

Investment Timing

One of the most difficult aspects of investments is to know when to buy and when to sell. There are three broad approaches to this problem: (*a*) fundamental value approaches; (*b*) technical indicators of market timing; and (*c*) mechanical formulas.

At the outset, however, you should be aware of objective studies of stock market forecasting, which have indicated that stock prices cannot be successfully forecast consistently based on any recurrent pattern. Market movements are random and most stock market "experts" have been wrong more often than right. Almost no one, for example, forecast the stock market setback in the spring of 1962 or in 1969 or in 1973–74. But forecasting or evaluation techniques have a certain usefulness, even if they are correct only 60 or 70 percent of the time. They provide a kind of blurry radar which prevents flying blind.

Fundamental value approaches depend on earnings, yields, and the relationship of both to prices. While basic economic factors such as business conditions, government fiscal and tax policies, interest rates, and so forth, are taken into consideration, analysis centers on price/earnings ratios, yields, profits, cash flow, and so on.

The yield on a share of common stock is the effective return to the investor and is based on two factors: the price paid for the share, and the dividend received. For example, if you bought A.T.&T. stock at $40 per share and received a $3.40 per year dividend per share, the yield would be:

$$\begin{array}{r} .085 \\ 40\overline{)3.40} \\ \underline{3.20} \\ 200 \\ \underline{200} \\ 0 \end{array}$$

or 8.5 percent per annum. When stock prices go up, unless dividends are raised proportionately, yields fall. Conversely, when stock prices fall, unless dividends are reduced as fast or faster, yields increase. In past bull markets, whenever stock prices rose to a point where current stock yields came down close to 3 percent, bull market peaks have been reached and stock prices tended subsequently to come down. In bear markets, when stock prices fall and current yields on stocks rise, when they go above 6 percent, buying has generally proved worthwhile. Low points in bear markets seem to have been reached in the past when common stock yields were 6 to 8 percent. In the same fashion price/earnings ratios can be used as broad gauged indicators of market levels. They are not absolute but merely approximate

FIGURE 14–2
Multiples Take a Plunge: Price/Earnings Ratios and Yields of Moody's Industrials

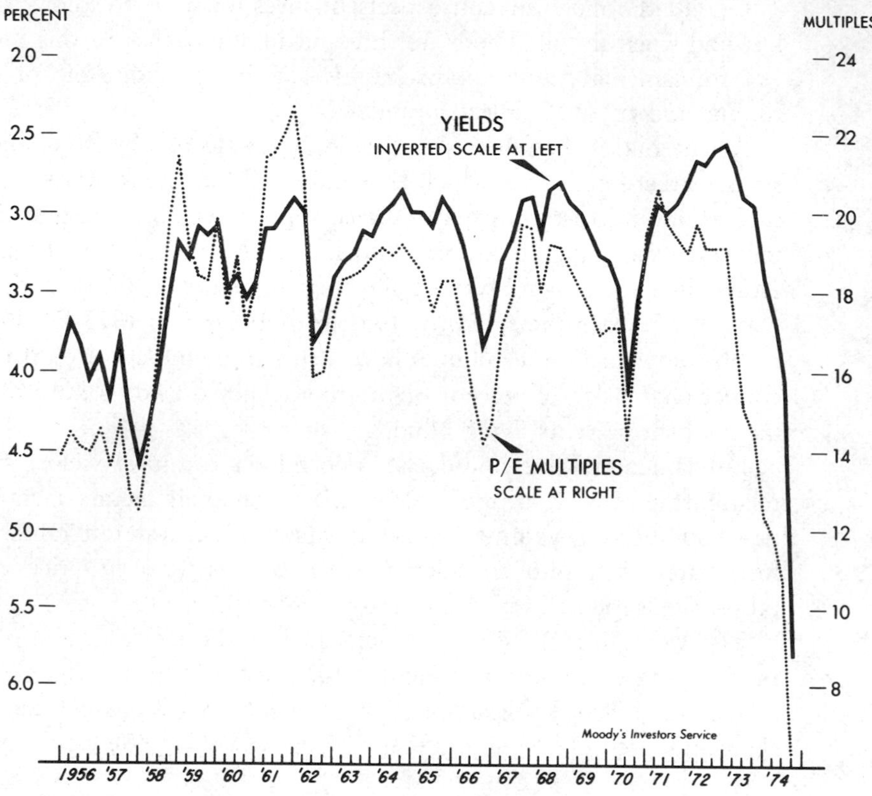

Source: Data: Moody's Investors Service, Inc.

indicators. They suggest general buying or general selling ranges. They are not precise timing devices (see Figure 14–2).

In the attempt to find more precise and less vague timing indicators, a bewildering variety of technical approaches have been developed, starting way back with the Dow Theory, which has been found to be far from infallible, and including everything from odd lot indexes, breadth of trading and volume of trading indicators, to Barron's "smart-money" Confidence Index and the Speculation Index.[1]

[1] For explanations of these technical approaches see Peter L. Bernstein and David Bostian, Jr., *How to Forecast the Stock Market* in *Methods and Techniques of Business Forecasting*, ed. by William Butler, Robert Kavesh, and Robert Platt, Englewood Cliffs, N.J.: Prentice-Hall, Inc., 1974; also R. D. Edwards and John Magee, *Technical Analysis of the Market* latest ed.; New York: John Magee, Inc., latest edition; Investor Intelligence, *Encyclopedia of Stock Market Techniques* (New York, latest edition); and James H. Dines, *How the Average Investor Can Use Technical Analysis for Stock Profits*, New York: James H. Dines Corp., 1973.

Since individual indicators have given false signals from time to time in the past, the idea occurred to use a consensus of indicators for greater reliability. There are now a number of services using the consensus technique. One of the most interesting is the Indicator Digest, which achieved some prominence as a result of the "sell" signal which it gave in early 1962, thereby anticipating correctly the subsequent sharp drop in the market later in the spring of 1962. It also was effective in 1969 and 1970 and in 1973–74.

Indicator Digest uses a consensus of 12 technical indicators at any one time, varying several of them depending on whether a bull or bear market is under way. These are then given weights of 1 or ½ for a total weight of 10. Whenever the composite total is 6 or more, a favorable signal is being given and stocks should be purchased. If the score sinks to 4 or less, this is an unfavorable signal and stocks should be sold. The action of the Composite Indicator Index over recent years is shown in the bottom part of Figure 14–3. The top part of this figure shows the range of closing prices of the Dow-Jones Industrial average. There are several services using somewhat similar consensus techniques but they are not always in agreement. Thus it's still a very difficult investment problem to know when to buy and when to sell.

Formula Plan Investing

Some solve this dilemma by resorting to mechanical formula plans which provide in advance for automatic buying and selling action. Dr. Barnes, an investment authority, declares:

> In most cases, they compel caution in bull markets and bravery in bear markets. They automatically (even if only partially) achieve the investment target of buying cheap and selling dear. They impel you to sell as prices rise and force you to buy as prices decline. Formula plans can definitely improve the batting average of most investors. While they deliberately avoid maximum theoretical profits, they more than make up for this by substantially cutting potential losses. Only the exceptional investor or speculator can hope to out perform a good formula plan in the long run.

In the uptrend of the market, the average person hates to sell and take his profit because he is afraid the market will continue to rise and that he will, by selling, miss additional gain. Thus he misses the top, for which he aims but never achieves, and continues to hold well into the downturn. He hesitates to sell during the early stages of the downturn because he sees the profit he has missed by not selling at the peak (which only

FIGURE 14–3
Indicator Digest Average and Composite Index 1964–1974

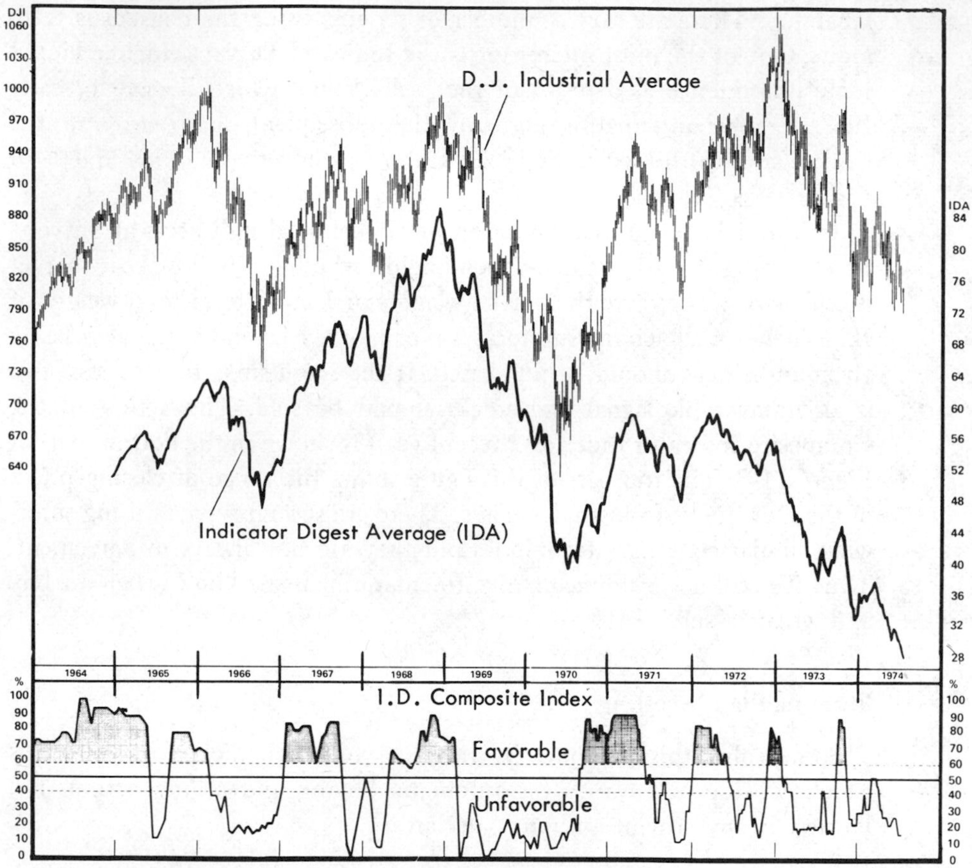

Source: Courtesy of Indicator Digest, Inc., Palisades Park, New Jersey 07650.

hindsight permits him to recognize as a peak), and he holds, hoping the market will reverse itself and return to the peak. It usually does not, but he holds on the downturn until, well on the downside, he grows tired of holding watching the retrogression and sells. In this way emotion and bad judgment play a large role in lack of investment success. A variety of formula plans have been devised to overcome to a large extent this human element in investing. A description of one or two will suffice to indicate the nature of formula-plan investing.

Dollar Averaging

This is the simplest type of formula plan. It is nothing more than the regular purchase of securities in equal dollar amounts, but the potential results of strict compliance with the plan are startling. The very obvious fact that the same amount of money will buy a greater number of shares of any stock when the price is low than it will when the price is high is the basis of the success of dollar averaging. You put the same fixed amount of money periodically into the same stock or stocks regardless of the price of the stock. Your fixed amount of money buys more shares when the stock is low, less shares when it is high. The important thing is to stick to your schedule—to buy, even though the price keeps falling, which, psychologically, is usually hard to do. This brings your average cost down, and any subsequent rise will yield a handsome profit.

Dollar averaging over a period of time will result in the average *cost* of all shares purchased being *lower* than the average *price* at which the shares were bought. An example may serve to show why this is so. Assume that $500 is invested at quarterly intervals in a certain stock and that the first two purchases are made at prices of $100 and $50, as shown in Table 14–1. Thus the average price is $75, but the average cost is $66.66. More

TABLE 14–1

Price	*Shares Purchased Each Time*	*Total Shares Purchased*	*Average Price*	*Average Cost of Shares Purchased*
100	5	5	$100	$100.00
50	10	15	75	66.66

shares were bought at 50, and that is why average cost is lower than average price.

An excellent example of dollar cost averaging is given by Louis Engel in his interesting book.[2] He asks you to assume that you buy $500 worth of a given stock when it is selling at $10 a share, another $500 worth six months later when it is $9, another $500 worth at $8, and so on while the stock falls to $5, then rises to $15, and settles back to $10. If you sold out at this point, you would have a profit of about 10 percent, despite the fact that you paid an average price of $10 and sold out at exactly the same price. In case you do not believe it, here are the figures (Table 14–2), assuming that, since you cannot buy fractional shares, you buy whatever number of shares yields a total cost nearest $500. As shown in the table, you paid $10,489, but your shares are worth $11,510, for a profit of $1,021. If you had sold out at $15, your profit would have been $6,108. Even if you had

---

[2] Louis Engel, *How to Buy Stocks—a Guide to Successful Investing* (paperbound ed.; New York: Bantam Books, latest edition). A free copy may be obtained by writing to Merrill Lynch, Pierce, Fenner & Smith, One Liberty Plaza, 165 Broadway, New York, N.Y., 10006.

TABLE 14–2
An Example of Dollar Cost Averaging in Buying Stocks

Price per Share	*Number of Shares Purchased*	*Cost of Shares*	*Number of Shares Owned*	*Cumulative Cost of Shares*	*Total Value of Shares*
$10	50	$500	50	$ 500	$ 500
9	55	495	105	995	945
8	63	504	168	1,499	1,344
7	71	497	239	1,996	1,673
6	84	504	323	2,500	1,938
5	100	500	423	3,000	2,115
6	84	504	507	3,504	3,042
7	71	497	578	4,001	4,046
8	63	504	641	4,505	5,128
9	55	495	696	5,000	6,264
10	50	500	746	5,500	7,460
11	45	495	791	5,995	8,701
12	42	504	833	6,499	9,996
13	38	494	871	6,993	11,323
14	36	504	907	7,497	12,698
15	33	495	940	7,992	14,100
14	36	504	976	8,496	13,664
13	38	494	1,014	8,990	13,182
12	42	504	1,056	9,494	12,672
11	45	495	1,101	9,989	12,111
10	50	500	1,151	10,489	11,510

Source: Louis Engel, *How to Buy Stocks—a Guide to Successful Investing* (paperbound ed.; New York: Bantam Books).

undertaken only the first half of the purchases, and the price had fallen to $5 and then returned to $10, at which point you closed out, you would have had a profit of $1,960, or almost 35 percent on your money. Clearly, dollar cost averaging is a very useful technique if it enables you to make a 35 percent profit on a stock which declines after you start buying it and then merely returns but does not go above the price you originally paid for it. You must, however, have both the courage and the funds to continue buying in a declining market (see also Figure 14–4).

What to Buy

Even if you use a formula plan or dollar cost averaging to solve the problem of when to buy, you still face the problem of what to buy. The first approach to the solution of this problem is to pick the industries or industry whose outlook seems most attractive. After that you can give attention to the problem of what companies or company within the industry to choose. Most of the large stockbrokerage houses and all of the large financial services devote considerable effort to the problem of in-

FIGURE 14–4
How Dollar Cost Averaging Can Work for You

Illustrated below are three hypothetical examples started at different points in varying business cycles. These examples have been simplified and exaggerated to demonstrate more clearly the principles of dollar-cost averaging. Of course, there are numerous variations. So in actual practice the investor should take into consideration the period of his overall program, the amount of his regular investments, the fluctuations in the values of securities.

In a declining market

	Regular investment	*Share price*	*Shares acquired*
	$ 300	$25	12
	$ 300	$15	20
	$ 300	$20	15
	$ 300	$10	30
	$ 300	$ 5	60
Totals	$1,500	$75	137

Average price per share.........($75 ÷ 5) = $15.00
Dollar-cost average per share ($1500 ÷ 137) = $10.95

This example shows the importance of continued investments in a declining market. When the share value dropped from $25 to 5, the greatest number of shares were acquired. So any recovery above the dollar cost average of $10.95 would establish a profit for the investor.

In a steady market

	Regular investment	*Share price*	*Shares acquired*
	$ 300	$12	25
	$ 300	$15	20
	$ 300	$12	25
	$ 300	$15	20
	$ 300	$12	25
Totals	$1,500	$66	115

Average price per share.........($66 ÷ 5) = $13.20
Dollar-cost average per share ($1500 ÷ 115) = $13.04

Even in a relatively steady market, dollar cost averaging works to the advantage of the investor. As the example shows, the actual per share cost is 16¢ less than the average price of $13.20 per share.

In a rising market

	Regular investment	*Share price*	*Shares acquired*
	$ 300	$ 5	60
	$ 300	$15	20
	$ 300	$10	30
	$ 300	$15	20
	$ 300	$25	12
Totals	$1,500	$70	142

Average price per share.........($70 ÷ 5) = $14.00
Dollar-cost average per share ($1500 ÷ 142) = $10.57

As the example shows, the dollar-cost average per share of the five regular investments is $10.57. When compared to the current $25 per share value, it does demonstrate the importance of fluctuations in prices to the success of dollar-cost averaging.

Source: The Keystone Company of Boston.

dustry selection and analysis. For example, Merrill Lynch, Pierce, Fenner & Smith, the largest brokerage house, issues reports on individual industries it favors, from time to time. Each report has an introduction which explains why the industry is being recommended as an investment opportunity and then goes on to select favored companies within the industry which the firm recommends.

Choosing the Industry

Some industries over a period of time do better than the market; some do less well. For example, over the 10 year period, January 1, 1964–December 31, 1973, the investment results of stocks of 50 industries ranged from + 297 to − 65 percent. The stocks of 19 industries were above average, the stocks of 31 industries were below average, but the average gain was 46 percent. As Figure 14–5 shows, gold mining shares and machinery stocks performed best, while apparel shares and automobile stocks had the poorest records. The divergence of industry group performance in 1974 is shown in Table 14–3. Sugarbeet refiners stocks as a group rose 99.4 percent over the year, turning in the best industry record, while real estate investment trusts were at the very bottom for a decline of 78.9 percent.

The successful investor learns how to avoid the lower than market average stocks and chooses the above market average industry groups. Discrimination in this respect makes a very big difference in your investment experience. Standard & Poor's believes that the industry approach is the greatest single factor in investment success. The "Fan" chart, shown in Figure 14–6 indicates how various industry groups performed pricewise during the period of the big bull market which started in April 1942, and ended in May 1946. Which industrial group would you have picked in April 1942? Probably aircraft, since you would have expected aircraft manufacturers to benefit most from the war. You would probably never have given a thought to printing and publishing. Yet aircraft had the worst comparative performance, as the "fan" chart shows: you would have gained only 50 percent; while printing and publishing had the best: you would have gained over 1,000 percent. Would you have picked paper over steel? Or floor coverings over chemicals?

The diverse trends of various industry groups over the last 15 years may be seen in Figure 14–7, pages 714–17. Note the superior performance of gold stocks (p. 714) as compared to the utility stocks p. 714; the better performance of the drug group (p. 715), as compared to the poorer performance of the chemical stocks (p. 715); the steady rise of liquor stocks

FIGURE 14–5
Stocks of Fifty Industries, January 1, 1964—December 31, 1973

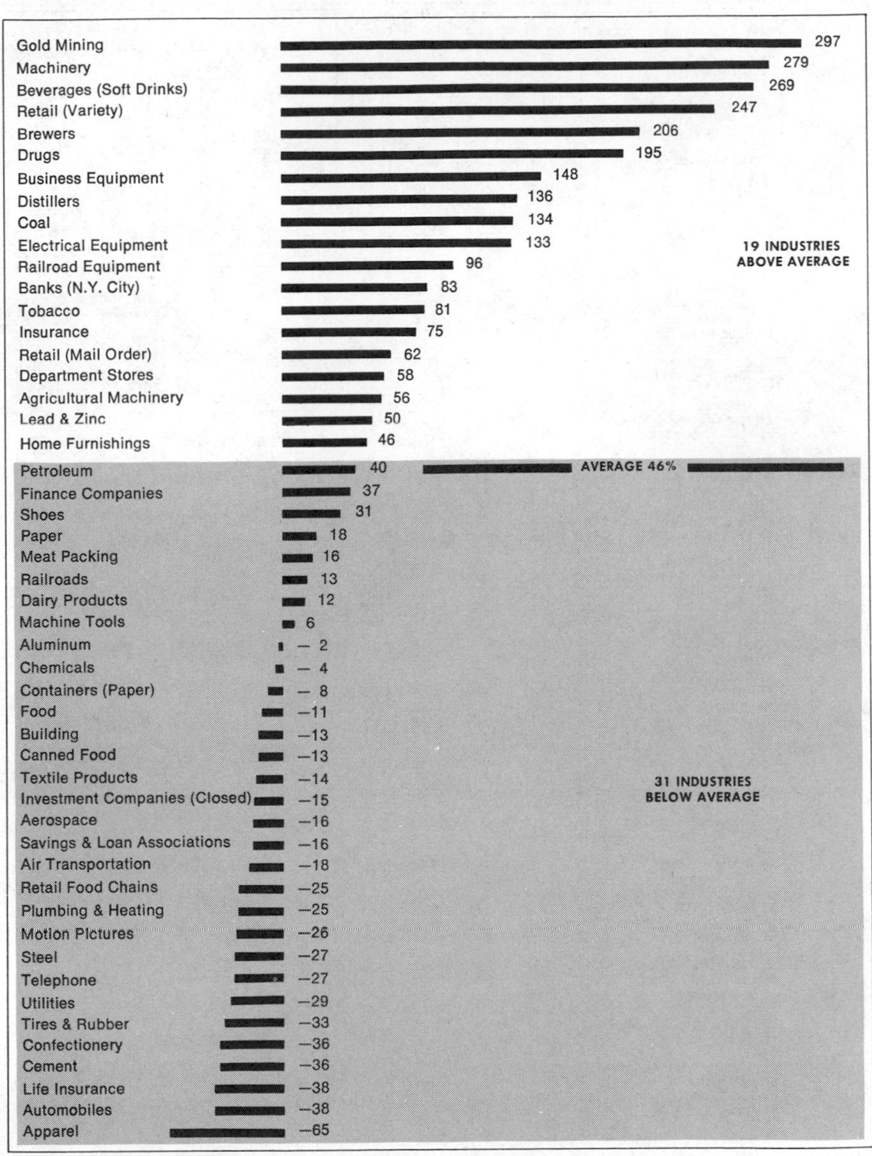

Source: Johnson Investment Company Charts.

TABLE 14–3
Stock Group Performances in 1974

*Rank	1973 Dec. 31	1974 Dec. 31	% Change	1974 Range High	1974 Range Low
1 Sugar Beet Refiners	14.09	28.10	+ 99.4	35.80	14.12
2 Motion Pictures	34.52	49.54	+ 43.5	50.24	35.05
3 Mobile Homes	36.88	50.12	+ 35.9	66.45	35.06
4 Heating & Plumbing	18.55	22.91	+ 23.5	27.00	18.28
5 Atomic Energy	35.79	40.30	+ 12.6	42.52	24.53
6 Coal: Bituminous	281.13	306.06	+ 8.9	382.11	234.95
7 Metal & Glass Con.	26.29	27.92	+ 6.2	30.53	23.61
8 Steel	43.83	43.40	− 1.0	51.17	40.97
9 Tobac.-Cigarette Mfrs.	57.78	56.70	− 1.9	61.10	45.07
10 Steel—excl. U.S. Steel	44.53	43.61	− 2.1	49.63	40.71
11 Nat. Gas Distributors	55.74	52.46	− 5.9	61.39	41.02
12 Meat Packing	34.54	31.78	− 8.0	41.87	29.18
13 Gold Mining	102.53	93.71	− 8.6	147.14	87.54
14 Chem.—excl. du Pont	49.29	45.02	− 8.7	56.68	43.00
15 Aerospace	35.14	31.57	− 10.2	42.72	30.61
16 Roofing & Wallboard	46.73	41.91	− 10.3	62.52	37.84
17 Canned Foods	78.75	70.59	− 10.4	91.76	57.45
18 Radio TV Broadcasters	177.98	158.94	− 10.7	232.48	150.74
19 Discount Stores	6.35	5.64	− 11.2	7.75	4.52
20 Tires & Rubber Goods	116.21	102.63	− 11.7	146.64	98.54
21 Soaps	170.94	149.22	− 12.7	188.45	125.61
22 Telephone	22.90	19.66	− 14.1	24.04	18.09
23 Food Chains	48.66	41.11	− 15.5	60.35	40.01
24 Food Composite	60.12	49.36	− 17.9	65.70	41.68
25 Dairy Products	76.54	61.83	− 19.2	85.26	54.09
26 Agricultural Mach.	56.14	45.35	− 19.2	56.81	35.19
27 Nat. Gas Pipelines	108.95	87.84	− 19.4	112.55	68.79
28 Drugs	220.87	177.05	− 19.8	226.51	144.12
29 Packaged Foods	83.67	66.80	− 20.2	89.82	54.61
30 Chemicals	60.85	48.22	− 20.8	68.80	47.20
31 Textile Products	40.41	31.67	− 21.6	48.98	30.14
32 Oil—Integ. Domestic	171.10	133.51	− 22.0	172.41	104.44
33 15 RAILROADS	**45.80**	**35.59**	**− 22.3**	**47.36**	**29.38**
34 Confectionery	22.85	17.75	− 22.3	26.91	17.08
35 Building Composite	36.37	28.16	− 22.6	46.54	26.56
36 Oil Well Mach. & Serv.	800.94	616.84	− 23.0	796.82	451.06
37 Metal Fabricating	67.17	51.61	− 23.2	79.14	49.26
38 Textiles-Synthetic Fib.	47.30	35.73	− 24.5	54.69	35.27
39 Truckers	85.83	64.65	− 24.7	101.63	61.78
40 Finance Companies	89.21	66.02	− 26.0	91.85	48.24
41 Lead & Zinc	19.86	14.67	− 26.1	22.29	13.73
42 Publishing	106.48	78.30	− 26.5	120.39	75.63
43 Home Furnishings	21.17	15.48	− 26.9	30.35	14.85
44 Paper Containers	111.14	81.07	− 27.1	124.02	77.82
45 Auto Parts-Orig. Equip.	48.11	35.04	− 27.2	57.25	33.08
46 S & L Holding Cos.	16.31	11.87	− 27.2	19.67	7.34
47 Auto—excl. Gen. Mot.	22.20	16.14	− 27.3	28.15	15.15
48 High Grade Common	84.08	60.77	− 27.7	88.77	55.92
49 Consumer Goods	87.76	63.33	− 27.8	93.92	58.01
50 Life Insurance	200.43	144.05	− 28.1	207.01	114.58
51 Oil Composite	152.21	109.12	− 28.3	153.81	93.77
52 60 UTILITIES	**46.91**	**33.54**	**− 28.5**	**49.44**	**29.37**
53 Property-Liability Ins.	114.96	81.98	− 28.7	116.73	56.72
54 500 COMPOSITE	**97.55**	**68.56**	**− 29.7**	**99.80**	**62.28**
55 425 INDUSTRIALS	**109.14**	**76.47**	**− 29.9**	**111.65**	**69.53**
56 Low Priced	76.67	53.23	− 30.6	95.14	53.23
57 Hospital Supplies	45.05	31.28	− 30.6	44.81	24.35
58 Machinery Composite	224.47	155.52	− 30.7	222.70	121.79
59 Const. Mat. Hand Mach.	325.18	225.39	− 30.7	322.20	190.40
60 Forest Products	20.22	13.97	− 30.9	23.26	12.81
61 Oil-Integ. International	134.43	92.94	− 30.9	135.97	85.15
62 Metals Misc.	66.46	45.37	− 31.7	71.76	43.71
63 Automobile	59.53	40.61	− 31.8	70.72	38.68
64 Paper	214.51	146.01	− 31.9	221.11	138.59
65 Copper	44.36	30.13	− 32.1	45.77	27.18
66 Shoes	26.56	17.99	− 32.3	31.01	15.78
67 Teleph.—excl. AT&T	37.00	24.97	− 32.5	37.78	24.51
68 Capital Goods	110.67	74.50	− 32.7	111.33	70.56
69 Distillers	185.40	124.47	− 32.9	196.96	115.68
70 Electric Companies	32.85	22.03	− 32.9	34.17	20.41
71 Industrial Mach.	142.00	93.31	− 34.3	139.69	77.89
72 Conglomerates	10.08	6.55	− 35.0	11.33	6.41
73 Invest. Cos., closed end	52.00	33.82	− 35.0	54.41	31.81
74 Auto Trucks & Parts	37.67	24.30	− 35.5	47.12	23.81
75 Toys	5.93	3.82	− 35.6	7.58	3.63
76 New York City Banks	69.57	44.69	− 35.8	69.33	39.30
77 Retail Stores Comp.	106.45	67.85	− 36.3	118.17	66.26
78 Variety Stores	66.18	41.90	− 36.7	73.68	38.97
79 Department Stores	150.83	95.15	− 36.9	169.20	93.74
80 Office & Bus. Equip.	1174.10	739.54	− 37.0	1198.48	725.15
81 Specialty Mach.	27.44	17.24	− 37.2	27.76	15.27
82 Leisure Time	13.18	8.22	− 37.6	17.51	8.17
83 Auto Parts—After Mkt.	49.86	31.04	− 37.7	50.37	27.74
84 Air Transport	38.72	23.73	− 38.7	51.05	23.06
85 Textiles-Apparel Mfrs.	17.38	10.59	− 39.1	21.27	9.64
86 Banks, Outside N.Y.C.	105.50	64.29	− 39.1	111.81	55.87
87 Electronics	640.72	389.68	− 39.2	712.00	380.74
88 Mail Ord. & Gen Chains	193.65	117.29	− 39.4	215.75	109.50
89 Multi-Line Ins.	12.77	7.53	− 41.0	12.95	5.86
90 Aluminum	94.95	55.78	− 41.3	100.07	52.52
91 Household Appliances	170.27	98.54	− 42.1	188.64	91.11
92 Vending & Food Svc.	27.06	15.61	− 42.3	30.02	15.46
93 Electrical Equipment	289.56	166.28	− 42.6	298.70	158.31
94 Small Loans	92.75	51.66	− 44.3	98.85	48.28
95 Railroad Equipment	56.36	31.30	− 44.5	57.15	29.55
96 Cosmetics	71.64	38.04	− 46.9	71.68	28.56
97 Major Electronics	96.35	50.95	− 47.1	97.46	47.76
98 Cement	25.58	13.36	− 47.8	28.54	12.63
99 Oil—Crude Producers	357.18	185.26	− 48.1	365.45	153.11
100 Machine Tools	34.85	17.69	− 49.2	37.88	16.35
101 Office & Bus. Equip.—excl. I.B.M.	366.86	186.24	− 49.2	381.10	182.43
102 Air Freight	34.54	17.23	− 50.1	33.71	15.23
103 Air Conditioning	20.35	10.12	− 50.3	25.52	9.61
104 Restaurants	26.41	12.69	− 52.0	28.29	11.80
105 Real Estate	13.92	6.49	− 53.4	16.41	6.01
106 Offshore Drilling	76.53	35.47	− 53.7	77.49	25.38
107 Hotel/Motel	23.51	10.57	− 55.0	30.07	9.70
108 Soft Drinks	148.56	66.35	− 55.3	146.85	59.05
109 Pollution Control	22.71	7.03	− 69.0	24.57	6.35
110 Brewers	140.14	39.39	− 71.9	139.82	39.39
111 Steam Generating	338.34	94.37	− 72.1	332.46	88.35
112 Real Estate Inv. Trusts	6.06	1.28	− 78.9	6.45	1.19

ANNUAL RANGES AND CLOSES

	425 Industrials High	425 Industrials Low	425 Industrials Close	Rails High	Rails Low	Rails Close
1974	111.65	69.53	76.47	47.36	29.38	35.59
1973	134.54	103.37	109.14	45.80	32.50	45.80
1972	132.95	112.19	131.87	48.31	40.40	44.26
1971	115.84	99.36	112.72	48.32	35.03	44.61
1970	102.87	75.58	100.90	38.94	24.65	35.40

	Utilities High	Utilities Low	Utilities Close	500 Stock Composite High	500 Stock Composite Low	500 Stock Composite Close
1974	49.44	29.37	33.54	99.80	62.28	68.56
1973	61.57	43.91	46.91	120.24	92.16	97.55
1972	62.99	52.95	61.05	119.12	101.67	118.05
1971	64.81	54.48	59.83	104.77	90.16	102.09
1970	61.71	47.67	61.71	93.46	69.29	92.15

Source: Standard & Poor's, *The Outlook*, January 6, 1975.

FIGURE 14–6
Stock Prices (percentage increase from April 1942, to May 1946)

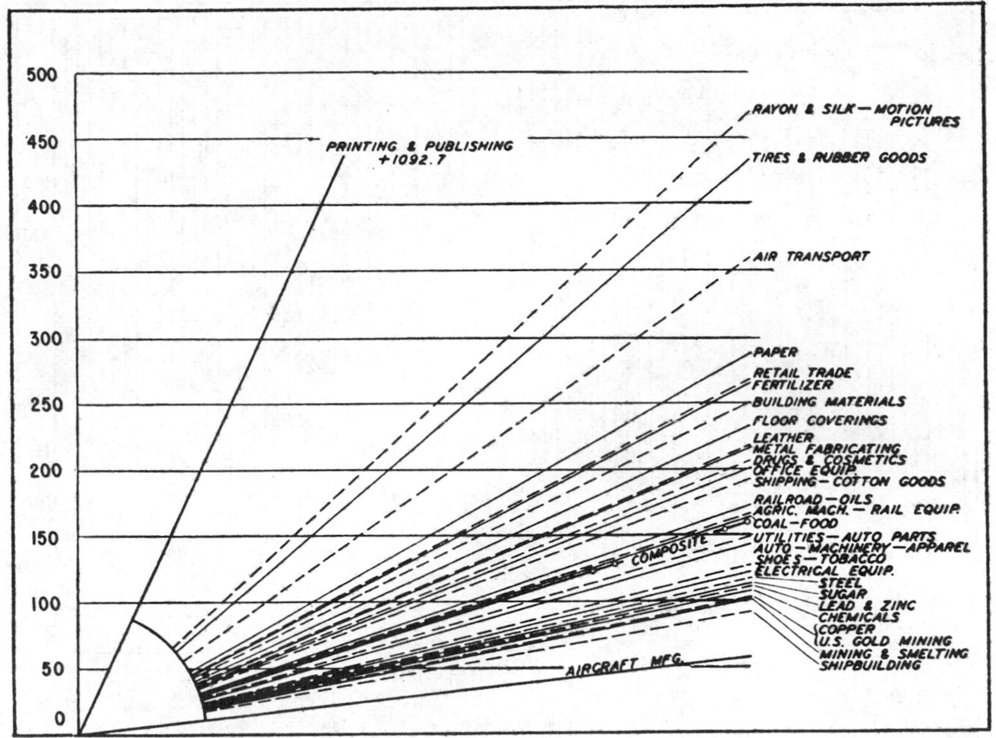

Source: Standard & Poor's.

(p. 716) as compared to the erratic performance of machinery stocks (p. 716); and the rise and decline in office equipment stocks (p. 717) and motion picture shares (p. 717).

For the average investor there are neither time nor resources available to undertake an original analysis. In such cases the best solution is to have one's name placed on the mailing list to receive the publications of three or four of the leading brokerage houses which have large research departments competent to make industry analyses. Also, such an investor can consult one or more of the large financial services—Moody's, Standard & Poor's, Value Line—in any library and carefully read their industry outlook summaries.

Standard & Poor's relies heavily on an industry approach. An excellent S & P. series is *Industry Surveys,* covering some 45 industries. In each case a *Basic Analysis* is issued, usually annually, followed by supplementary sections entitled *Current Analysis and Outlook,* issued at varying intervals

FIGURE 14–7
The Stock Picture

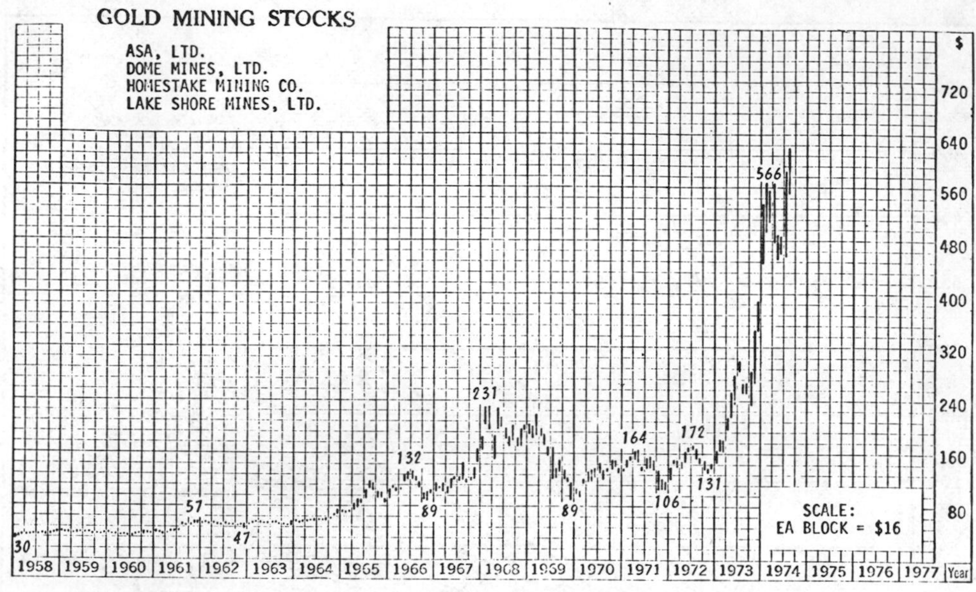

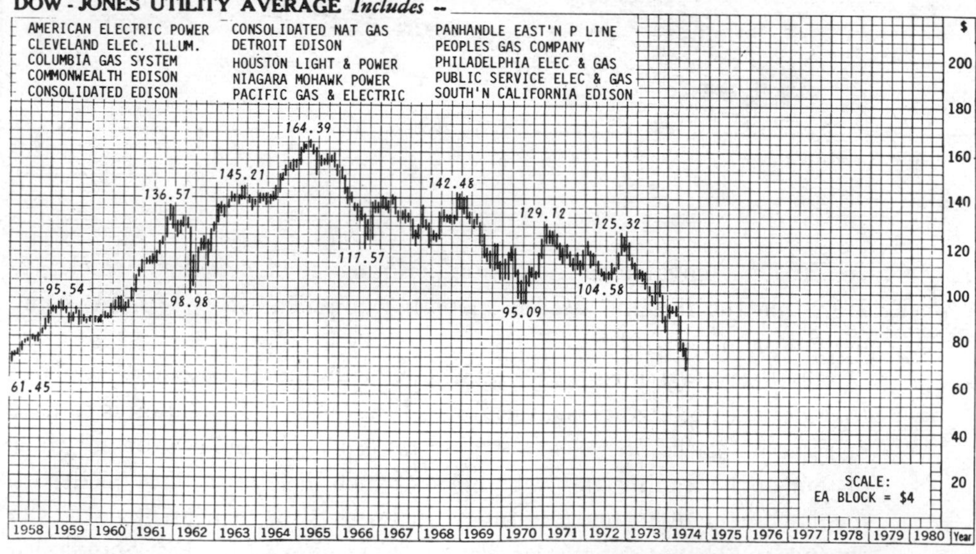

FIGURE 14–7 (continued)

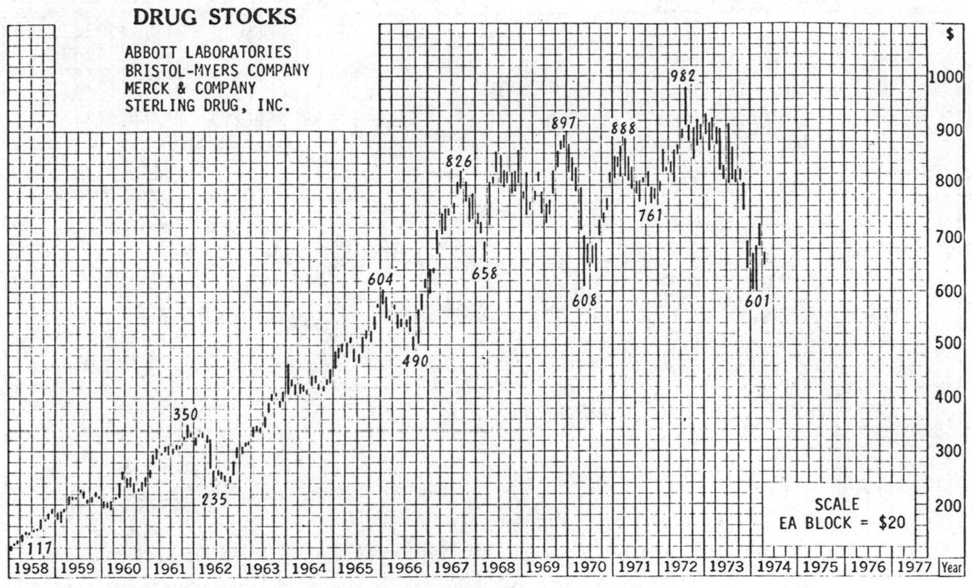

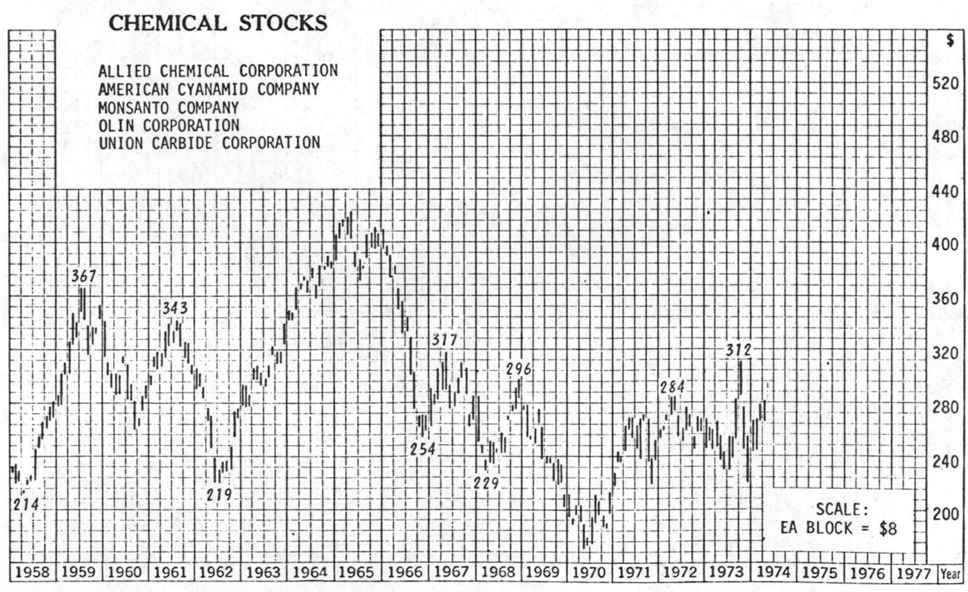

FIGURE 14–7 (continued)

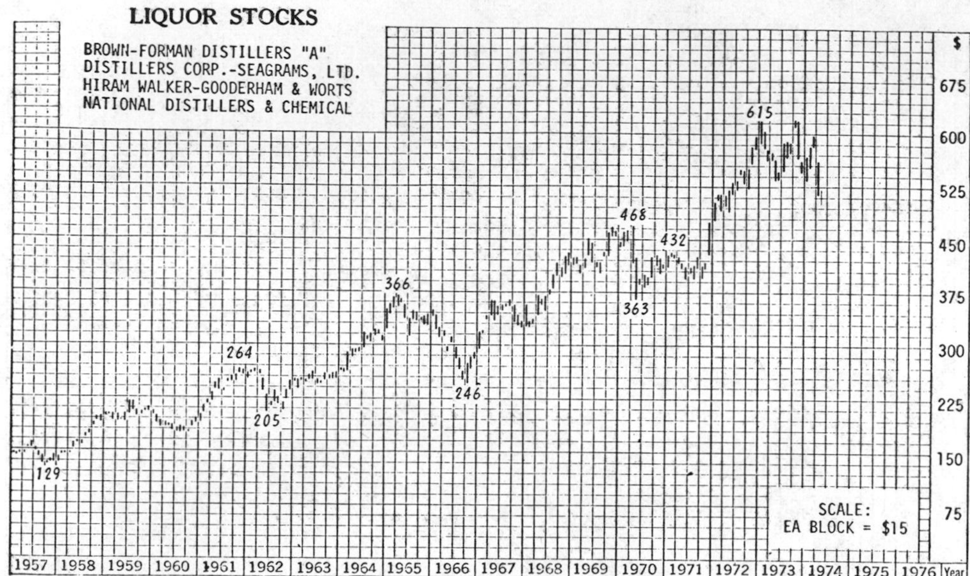

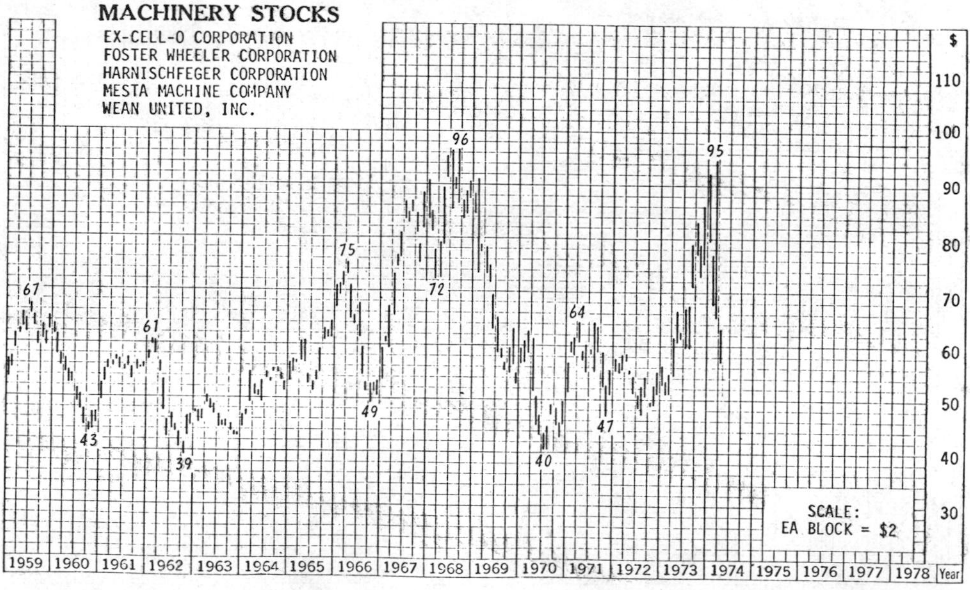

FIGURE 14–7 (concluded)

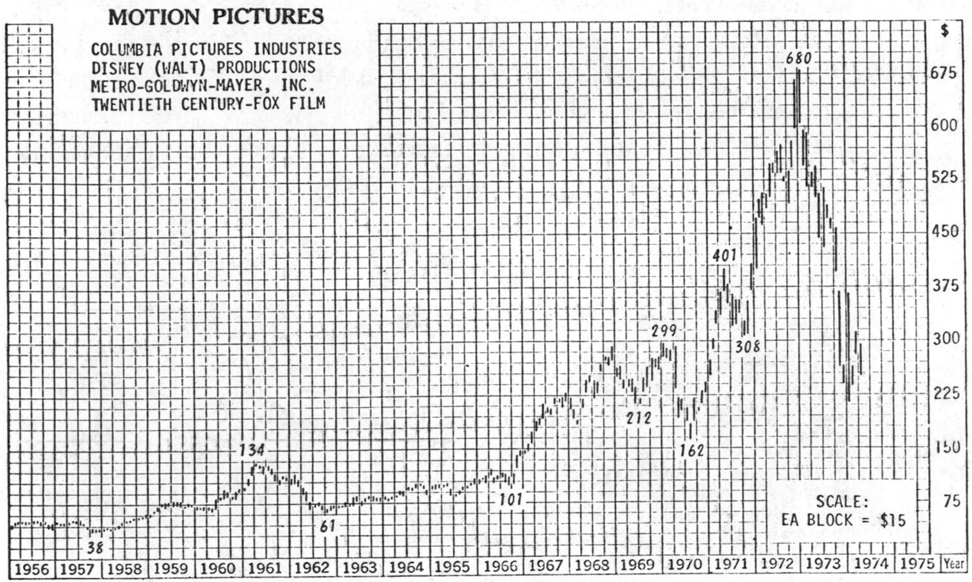

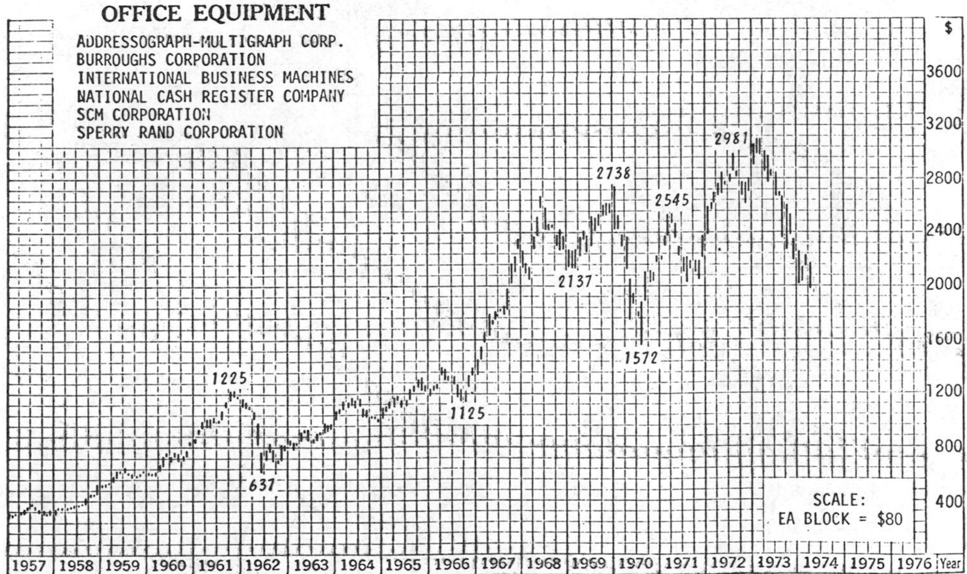

Source: © M. C. Horsey & Co., Publishers, 120 South Boulevard, Salisbury, Md. 21801.

during the year, usually quarterly. Summaries are published from time to time in the weekly *Outlook*.

The "Relative Price Movements of Leading Stock Groups" are charted so that performance relative to the Standard & Poor's 425 Stock Industrial Index may be seen at a glance (see Figure 14–8). If you read enough of these special studies and industry analyses, you will in a short time acquire

FIGURE 14–8
Stock Group Movements (ratio scale 1941–43 = 10)

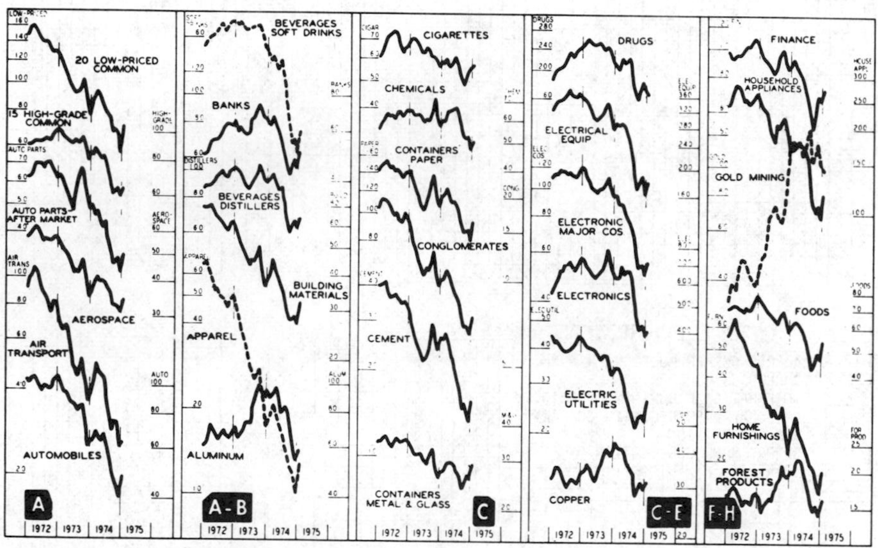

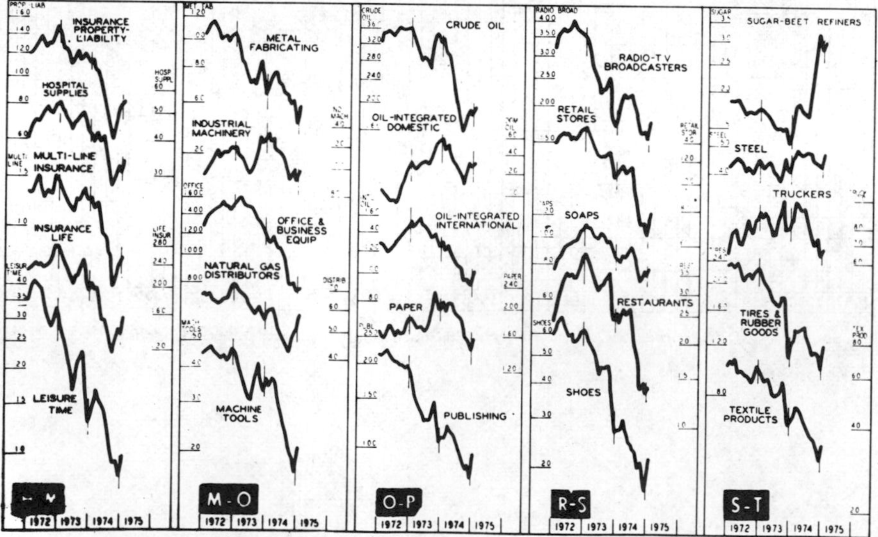

Source: Standard & Poor's, *Outlook*, February 10, 1975.

a "feel" for the contrasting patterns and soon be able to select the industry or industries in which you want to invest.

Choosing the Company

Your next step, once you have chosen the industry, is to select the company or companies. Again the average investor has neither the time nor the technical know-how to study and analyze a large number of individual companies in order to choose two or three. If by chance you do have the time and the accounting competence to look into balance sheets and income accounts, then you can engage in ratio and financial analysis, and come up with your own conclusions. Then you can check these against the opinions of the leading services in arriving at a final decision. But if you are the average investor, a balance sheet or an income account will frighten you away, while a 10K (the annual detailed financial report the company files with the SEC) will horrify you. Under these circumstances, you can do several things. You can rely on the company analyses and recommendations of the leading services (to be described in the next chapter), or you can find out what the big institutional investors, such as insurance companies, savings banks, mutual funds, and college endowment funds, are buying and selling, and pick and choose from among their most frequent selections.

For example, one financial house publishes a semiannual survey of "The Favorite Fifty," the 50 listed stocks most popular with investment company managers. The first 10 were International Business Machines, Exxon, American Telephone & Telegraph, Philip Morris, Atlantic Richfield, Burroughs Corporation, Eastman Kodak, Xerox, Kerr-McGee, and Schlumberger, Inc. By dollar value 25.8 percent of total funds were in oil and natural gas stocks, 20.9 percent in chemicals and drugs, 16.4 percent in office equipment, 5.9 percent in utilities, 4.5 percent in finance, and so on. Other tabulations are available of the investment preferences of insurance companies, trust companies, savings banks, endowment funds, etc. It is always useful to check your own judgment, however derived, against these lists.

Special Situations

One method of investment for the adventurous investor is to look for and take advantage of "special situations." This involves finding a clearly undervalued situation before the general public does; or profiting from possibilities inherent in a merger or reorganization, a recapitalization or liquidation; or finding a cumulative preferred with large back dividends whose earnings are just about to increase sufficiently to pay off the accumulation.

Of special situations, one leading expert declares:

> Special situations are investments in stocks or bonds that reflect *Corporate Action,* meaning activities occurring within the administrative scope of the corporation rather than at the business level. Their built-in potential for capital gains is the hallmark distinguishing true special situations from run of the mill investments. Apart from Corporate Action, which is the common denominator of all special situations, we can usually find the following identifying characteristics:
>
> 1. Profits develop independently of the trend of the securities market.
> 2. Risks are at a minimum (reflecting prior knowledge of anticipated profit).
> 3. Corporate action is in the development stage.
> 4. The securities are undervalued.
> 5. Information is available inviting comprehensive analysis.
>
> In short, a true special situation is an investment in securities . . . where risks are at a minimum and achievement of the expected profit a calculated probability, regardless of the trend of the securities market.[3]

Most analysts regard undervalued and special situations in the same category. Northern Pacific Railroad common was so recommended some years back. Before World War II it had sold as low as 3¾. By 1949 it reached 17; in 1951 it was 31¼; and then, in a little more than a year, it rose to a high of 94. This last spurt was due to the fact that oil was discovered in the Williston Basin, which stretches from the Dakotas and eastern Montana into Manitoba and Saskatchewan. Northern Pacific had large landholdings in the Basin.

Philadelphia and Reading in the early fifties was losing money in anthracite coal. Its sales and earnings dropped, reaching a deficit of $2.60 a share. The common stock sold at from $6 to $10 a share (adjusted). New management took over in 1955 and began a major acquisition and diversification program. The stock rose from 17 in 1956 to 131½ in 1959.

A service recommended U.S Foil Company, Class "B" common stock as a special, undervalued situation. It was pointed out that U.S Foil is a holding company whose chief investment is 48 percent of the shares of the common stock of Reynolds Metal Corporation. If the value of its other assets were disregarded, U.S Foil held, after deduction of the value of its

---

[3] Maurece Schiller, *Fortunes in Special Situations in the Stock Market,* American Research Council, Larchmont, N.Y., latest edition.

own preferred stock, approximately one share of Reynolds for each share of its own common. At the price at the time of the recommendation, the investor could have acquired an equity in Reynolds at about 28 percent below the market price. When its whole portfolio was considered, U.S Foil "B" was selling at a discount from its net asset value per share of about 40 percent. Over the years U.S Foil, Class B stock went from 25 cents a share (adjusted) to a high of $60.75.[4]

Market neglect may result in a special situation. Wall Street may fail for a time to recognize dynamic changes in a company and retain a former less promising corporate image after the upsurge has taken place. For example, up to the early 1960s, Burroughs was a stodgy maker of adding machines and electromechanical accounting equipment. At that time it transformed itself into a highly successful producer of electronic data processing equipment. Earnings per share rose from 71 cents to $5.90 and the stock price rose from a low of 11½ (adjusted for stock splits) to a high of 252¾ in 1973.

A variety of developments may make a special situation. Resolution of a court action is one example. Because the market "withdraws from the unknown," pending litigation can often depress a stock price out of proportion to the possible real impact of an adverse decision. But favorable decisions can become bonanzas for investors who have correctly anticipated the outcome. For example, Hartford Fire Insurance Company's common held at about 40 up until May 1970, while Connecticut's State Insurance Commission considered I.T.&T.'s application to acquire the company. Then it was granted. Eight months after the favorable ruling, Hartford Fire Insurance shares had increased over 60 percent to 67.

One final example of the many variations of special situation investing must suffice. A distribution of assets takes place and a subsidiary "spin-off" to shareholders gives them more in dollar value for stocks in two separate companies than in the original one. For example, the offshore oil construction company, J. Ray McDermott, was selling at 32 on April 28, 1970, when it made a tax free distribution of its exploratory subsidiary, Transocean Oil, to stockholders at the rate of .88 shares of Transocean for each share of McDermott stock. Nine months later, on February 1, 1971, McDermott stood at 36, Transocean at 16—over a 60 percent gain for shareholders.

---

[4] Two investment services, Forbes and Value Line, issue periodic special situation recommendations. See "Over the Counter Special Situation Service," The Value Line Investment Survey, New York. See also "Forbes Special Situation Survey," 60 Fifth Ave., New York, N.Y., 10011. A new special situation service was begun in 1971 by Anametrics, Inc., 299 Park Ave., New York, N.Y. 10017.

Markets, Exchanges, and Brokers

Although stocks and bonds are usually sold initially to the investing public by investment bankers, they are later bought and sold by investors in the over the counter market or on the organized stock exchanges. The person who wishes to buy or sell such securities should seek out a reliable stockbroker who, for a commission, will act as agent and handle the details of the transaction. Whereas an investment banker is a dealer who buys securities in the hope that they can be resold at a profit, the broker, as such, buys no securities but merely earns commissions by representing other persons who wish to buy or sell securities. Stockbrokers are, therefore, often called "commission brokers."

The Over the Counter Market

The over the counter market has no one place in which buyers and sellers of securities (or their agents) make it a practice to meet to transact business. It has no common meeting place and is not housed in any one location; yet it is national in scope and local as well. Its segments are tied together by a vast system of telephone and computer electronic connections. All securities transactions that are not made on organized stock exchanges take place in the over the counter securities markets. In this market, buyers and sellers contact each other commonly by telephone or telegraph. Buyers, through their brokers, telephone likely prospective sellers, concentrate on the seller offering to sell at the lowest price, and negotiate in the hope of obtaining a still lower price. Sellers, on the other hand, contact prospective buyers, concentrate on the buyer bidding the highest price, and endeavor to obtain an even higher price. In the over the counter market, securities are traded whether or not they have been listed or accepted for trading on the organized stock exchanges.

Buyers and sellers consist of securities dealers, institutions, estates, corporations, wealthy individuals, and people in all walks of life. Today the over the counter securities market consists of more than 3,800 securities houses employing over 100,000 registered representatives. The over the counter market is primarily a "negotiation" market. Buyers and sellers seek each other out and negotiate prices.[5]

Of the 1.7 million corporations in the United States it is estimated that

---

[5] For further information, see "How Over the Counter Securities Are Traded," Merrill Lynch, Pierce, Fenner & Smith, Inc. A free copy may be obtained by writing to the firm at One Liberty Plaza (165 Broadway), New York, N.Y. 10006. See also *The O–T–C Chart Manual*, published bimonthly by *Trendline*, a division of Standard & Poor's Corporation. There is also an *Over-the-Counter Securities Review*.

about 3 percent, or 55,000, have stock in the public's hands. In a year's time, the National Quotation Bureau, which collects and publishes over the counter securities prices, quotes prices on about 40,000 issues. It quotes prices daily on about 8,000 over the counter stocks—a larger number than are listed on the country's major exchanges. Companies range from Steak & Brew Corporation, whose stock sells at about $1 a share, to General Reinsurance, whose shares are priced at around $120 each.

In 1971 a new development occurred in the over the counter securities market. It was the advent of NASDAQ (pronounced Naz' dak), a remarkable new communications system that makes dealers' quotes on over the counter stocks instantly available in brokerage offices across the nation. The system was planned by the National Association of Securities Dealers, the over the counter industry's self-regulatory body. The term NASDAQ is an acronym for the associations initials and "automatic quotations." Bunker-Ramo Corporation produced and designed the computer hardware and software. While NASDAQ at the outset covered some 2,400 issues, it is being expanded to cover more unlisted issues as well as "third market" issues—that is, listed stocks traded over the counter. It now reports on about 3,000 issues. The advantage of NASDAQ for the individual investor in O–T–C securities is that there is a much more reliable bid and asked quotation by actual market markers continuously. Drop in at your broker's office and ask for a demonstration of the NASDAQ machine and system. Say you are thinking of buying 100 shares of General Reinsurance.[6]

The Organized Stock Exchanges

The stock exchange, on the other hand, is an "auction" market. Trading is conducted in the manner of a two sided auction, with competition among both buyers and sellers. The buyer making the highest bid buys, and the seller with the lowest offer sells, when the two agree on price. Stock exchanges are centers for trading in securities that are listed with them.

On the organized stock exchanges, only those securities are traded which have been listed. To secure the privileges of listing, the company issuing the securities must fill out an application to list the securities and must satisfy the particular exchange that the security is one which should prop-

---

[6] See "The Higher Meaning of NASDAQ," in Personal Investing in *Fortune*, April 1971. See also, Ira V. Cobleigh, "The New Dimensions of the O-T-C Market" in the *Commercial & Financial Chronicle*, October 21, 1971. A free copy of "The NASDAQ Revolution: How Over the Counter Securities are Traded" may be obtained from Merrill Lynch, Pierce, Fenner & Smith Inc., One Liberty Plaza (165 Broadway), New York, N.Y. 10006.

erly be traded there. Only members of the exchange are permitted to trade on its "floor." To become a member, one buys a "seat" on the exchange. A seat, or membership, on the New York Stock Exchange has sold for as high as $625,000 (1929) and for as low as $17,000 (1942). The current price is about $75,000.

The second largest exchange is the American Stock Exchange. In addition, there are 11 regional exchanges outside New York City. The three principal regional exchanges are the Midwest Stock Exchange (MSE), the Pacific Coast Stock Exchange (PCSE), and the Philadelphia–Baltimore–Washington (PBWSE) Exchange. In a recent year, of the number of shares sold on registered exchanges, the NYSE accounted for 75.7 percent, the ASE for 12.9 percent and the regional exchanges for 11.4 percent. By market value of shares traded the NYSE accounted for 82.3 percent, the ASE for 5.9 percent and the regional exchanges for 11.9 percent.

Types of Members

There are now 1,366 members of the New York Stock Exchange. A member may be a partner or officer in one of the brokerage concerns which, by virtue of his exchange membership, is known as a "member firm." Today there are 523 such firms. From the founding of the exchange in 1792 until May 1953, membership in the exchange was limited to individuals, and member firms were limited to partnerships. Then the exchange constitution was amended to permit corporations to become member firms, provided the corporation is engaged primarily in the securities business as a dealer or broker. There are now over 260 member corporations.

About half the members are partners or officers in firms doing business with the public—so called "commission houses." These members execute customers' orders to buy and sell on the exchange, and their firms receive the commissions on those transactions. Many firms have more than one member.

About one third of all members are specialists—so called because they specialize in "making a market" for one or more stocks. Carrying out his function of "making a market," the specialist must often risk his own capital by buying at a higher price than the public may be willing to pay at that moment. For instance: let us say that the best offer to sell XYZ stock is at $35 a share and that the best bid to buy is at $34. The specialist would be expected, under normal conditions, to bid 34½ in order to narrow the temporary spread between supply and demand. In a rising market the specialist may be expected to sell stock from his own account at a price lower than that at which the public will sell.

A specialist restricts his business to a particular stock or group of stocks at one trading post on the floor of the exchange. Primarily he acts as agent for other brokers who cannot remain at one post until prices specified by their customers' buy and sell orders—either below or above prevailing prices—are reached. Part of the commission the customer pays his own broker goes to the specialist for his services. Much of the specialist's earnings comes from commissions on orders executed for other brokers.

The exchange sets specific requirements for specialists regarding market experience and the amount of capital they must have. The specialist must assume full responsibility for all orders turned over to him. He is expected to maintain a fair and orderly market in the stocks in which he specializes. This function is essential to the smooth operation of a national securities exchange. He must always subordinate his personal interests in the market to that of his customers. The specialist cannot buy or sell in the exchange market at any price for his own account until he has executed all public orders held by him at that price.

Some members are odd lot dealers. They serve investors who purchase or sell a few shares at a time rather than in the conventional 100 share unit, known as a "round lot." The odd lot member acts as a dealer, not as a broker, buying odd lots of stock from, or selling odd lots of stock to, other members doing a public business. In most stocks, an "odd lot" is any number of shares from 1 to 99. The price at which the odd lot dealer fills an order is determined by the price of the next round lot sale on the floor. Odd lot dealers do not deal directly with the public.

Then there are floor brokers, whose function is to assist the commission brokers. Floor brokers are still popularly known as "$2.00 brokers," although the commission they receive for their services has long been above that amount.

All members—whatever their function—must, of course, own a "seat" on the exchange—a term that traces back to early years, when the brokers did remain seated while the president called the list of securities. The price of a stock exchange membership is determined by how much a candidate will pay and the amount the owner of the membership will accept. The Board of Directors maintains complete control over admissions of new members.

Pay Cash or Buy on Margin?

Transactions in securities may be for cash or on margin. Although securities (like merchandise) can be bought for cash, it is commonly the practice for one who wishes to deal in securities to open an account with a stockbroker in much the same manner as he opens an account with a commercial bank. Then he gives orders for securities to be bought and/or sold and charged or credited to his account, whether or not the transactions are for cash or on margin.

Margin transactions involve credit. The buyer of securities on margin puts up part of the necessary cash himself and borrows from his broker the balance necessary to pay for the securities bought. The broker may in turn borrow from a commercial bank. The Federal Reserve Board has authority to specify how much of the total purchase price the buyer must himself provide (and, consequently, how much of it may be borrowed both by the customer and by the broker). Lately the Board has required the buyer to pay for at least 50 percent of the total purchase price. This means that the buyer may borrow 50 percent of the price of the securities acquired. By thus restricting the amount of credit (borrowing) permitted, a control or brake is applied to the amount of gain or loss to which a given investor may be exposed. In other words, foolish excesses in the quest for gain are discouraged. Prior to the crash in the stock market in 1929, it was usual to buy stocks with a margin payment of 10 or 20 percent. The chance for substantial gain (or loss) under those circumstances was much greater than it is today, as can be seen from Table 14–4:

TABLE 14–4
Relative Gain or Loss under Different Margin Requirements

Requirement for Margin	*Funds Advanced by Buyer*	*Amount of Credit Needed*	*Number of Shares Purchased at $50 Each*	*Per-share Change in Market Value*	*Profit (+) and Loss (−) Involved*
10%	$1,000	$9,000.00	200.00	±$5	±$1,000.00
20	1,000	4,000.00	100.00	± 5	± 500.00
50	1,000	1,000.00	40.00	± 5	± 200.00
75	1,000	333.33	26.67	± 5	± 133.33
100	1,000	0.00	20.00	± 5	± 100.00

Only one tenth of the profit or loss is possible when one uses only his own money, as compared with the possibilities when his own money is merely one tenth of the total funds used. By operating with other people's money, the opportunity for profit or loss is greatly magnified, especially with the very low margins. With a 50 percent margin, the chance for profit or loss is only twice what it would be if only one's own money were used; as the margin is reduced below 50 percent, the possible profit or loss is expanded several times. Of course, borrowed money generally has an interest expense connected with it.

How an Order Is Handled

How does a transaction take place on the floor of the New York Stock Exchange? Here are four considerations to keep in mind:

1. When you buy, you buy from another person.
2. When you sell, you sell to another person.
3. The Stock Exchange itself neither buys nor sells, nor sets prices.
4. The Exchange provides the marketplace.

Let us say that a Dr. R. J. Phillips of Baltimore has sold his summer place. After talking things over with a New York Stock Exchange member firm, he decides to buy common shares in American Telephone and Telegraph Company. He asks the member firm's registered representative to find out for him what A.T.&T. shares are selling for on the exchange.

Employing an electronic interrogation device which has instant access to a computer center that receives current market information from the exchange's Market Data System, the representative reports that "Telephone" is quoted at "45 to a quarter." This means that, at the moment, the highest bid to buy A.T.&T. is $45 a share, the lowest offer to sell is $45.25 a share.

Dr. Phillips learns that 100 shares will cost him approximately $4,500, plus a commission of $62.50.

The Order Enters the Market

Dr. Phillips tells the registered representative to go ahead. The latter writes out an order to buy 100 shares of A.T.&T. "at the market" and has it wired to his firm's partner on the floor of the exchange. "At the market" means the best price available to his broker on the floor at that time. Each stock is assigned a specific location at one of the 18 trading posts, and all bids and offers in a stock must take place at the location. The floor partner hurries over to Post 15 where "T" is traded.

About the same time, a Seattle hardware man, let us say his name is James Greenway, decided he would sell his 100 shares of A.T.&T. to get funds to enlarge his store. He called his broker, got a "quote," and told his broker to sell. That order, too, was relayed to the floor over a direct wire. Greenway's broker also hurried to the "T" post. Just as he entered the A.T.&T. "crowd," he heard Phillips' broker calling out, "How's A.T.&T.?" Someone answers, "45 bid, offered at a quarter."

Phillips' broker could, without further thought, buy the 100 A.T.&T. offered at $45.25, and Greenway's broker could sell his 100 at $45. In that event, if their customers had been looking over their shoulders, the cus-

BP GAF MTC HER FLY AHP

$\frac{7}{8}$ 2s$14\frac{1}{2}$ 3s19 3s$45\frac{1}{8}$ 2s34 2s$36\frac{3}{8}$

Symbolism on the Ticker

HER has joined HE and HIS on the New York Stock Exchange, and that's not bad grammar. HER is the ticker symbol for Helena Rubinstein, which was listed last month. HE is Hawaiian Electric and HIS is Henry I. Siegel Co., a sportswear manufacturer that uses HIS as a brand name.

Assignment of a symbol for Helena Rubinstein was quite simple; the company brought the designation with it from the Amex where it was previously traded. For other companies it's not so easy. There are 26 possible one-letter symbols, 676 with two letters and 17,576 with three letters.

Not all of these are available for use. The letter Q, for example, is banned because it is used to designate companies that are in receivership or bankruptcy proceedings.

Certain combinations of letters are also arbitrarily eliminated from consideration as symbols. For instance, the negatives. If a company called Detroit Outdoor Graphics were to be assigned its initials, it is a safe assumption that stockholders would be less than delighted to see DOG trot across the tape each time the stock was traded.

Other combinations are pre-empted because of their associations in the public's mind. It is absolutely certain that if a Nelson Battleship Corp. were to be listed, its symbol would not be NBC, even though no listed stock bears that designation.

The matter of good taste is also considered. SEX and SIN may be well represented in the world around us but they do not appear on the symbol roster.

Further, once a company receives a symbol on being listed on one exchange, no other company listing on another exchange will get the same symbol.

"Clarity is the key. Our aim in choosing symbols is to avoid confusion on the part of the investing public, member firms and, very importantly, on the trading floor," says a Big Board staff member. Thus, regularly used trading abbreviations—such as GTC, meaning "good till canceled" —are eliminated.

These considerations, and a few others, narrow the number of available two-letter symbols to well under 500, of which about 200 are in use. About 15,000 three-letter combinations are usable.

Within the framework of these considerations—and there will be more in a moment—how does the Exchange staff go about its process of selection?

Initials are good for a start—M, EK and FCB, representing Marcor, Eastman Kodak, and Foote, Cone & Belding. With the number of issues already on the list, however, initials may not be easy to come by.

First syllables come in for heavy use. METromedia, HALliburton, SEAtrain and MADison Fund are examples. But the dozens of companies that have names beginning with General, Consolidated, American, National, etc., have to go elsewhere for their symbols.

Next comes what might be called "the Speedwriting school" of symbols. Symbols are designed so that the letters visually create aural suggestions of corporate names. These include XRX for Xerox, SLZ for Schlitz, and SNE for Sony, which could not be given SNY because it is a symbol on another exchange.

When Cooper Laboratories, then an over-the-counter company, merged with Chemway, a Big Board corporation recently, the deal required a new listing for the surviving company, Cooper. An initial listing by Exchange staff showed 100 possible letter combinations to represent Cooper, but 71 were discarded under the various guidelines. Twenty-six of the remainder were cast aside in the interest of trading floor efficiency, which takes into account possible transpositions of letters, phonetic similarity to other symbols, the problems inherent in the symbol being written as small letters instead of capitals, and the wide range of variations in individual handwriting.

The remaining three were CLA, CLB and COO. After they were cleared with the other exchanges, reviewed by other staff members and approved by two senior floor governors, they were passed on to the company.

The company made its selection, and on Monday, May 3, the first 100 shares of COO crossed the tape.

Source: *The Exchange*, September 1971, pp. 23–24.

tomers probably would have said, "Why didn't you try to get a better price for us?" The customers would have been right. That's what a broker is expected to do. Every broker is charged with the responsibility of getting the best possible price for his customer. He must exercise his experience, knowledge, and brokerage skill. He must make split-second decisions. Here's how Phillips' and Greenway's brokers might figure as each tries to get the best price for his customer.

PHILLIP'S BROKER: I can't buy my 100 at 45. Someone has already bid 45, and no one will sell at that price. Guess I'd better bid 45⅛.

GREENWAY'S BROKER: Looks like I can't sell my 100 at 45¼; someone has already tried to get that price. I'd better try to get 45⅛.

Greenway's broker hears Phillips' broker bid 45⅛ and instantly shouts, "Sold 100 at 45⅛." They have agreed on a price, and the transaction takes place.

Here is the auction market in operation. This procedure is repeated over and over again every day on the floor of the exchange.

The two brokers complete their verbal agreement by noting each other's names and reporting the transaction back to their phone clerks so that their customers can be notified. In the meantime, an exchange employee at the post pencil-marks a special card to indicate the stock symbol, the number of shares, and the price, and places it in an "optical card reader." The card reader scans the pencil marks with its photoelectric eye and transmits the information to the Market Data System computer. The computer records the information in its memory bank and transmits the details of the transaction to some 12,000 tickers and display devices in the United States, Canada, and Europe. It appears as T 45⅛. The number of shares in a round lot transaction is specified only when more than 100 shares are involved.

Thus, within a few minutes, Dr. Phillips has arranged to exchange the proceeds from the sale of a summer cottage for 100 shares in the world's largest telephone company; Jim Greenway has sold his shares in that company for money to expand his own business.[7]

Less than 100 Shares—Odd Lots

But, you may ask, what if Dr. Phillips had only $1,000 to invest in A.T.&T. stock rather than $4,500? In other words, could he buy only 22 shares instead of 100?

---

[7] See *Understanding the New York Stock Exchange* (New York: New York Stock Exchange). A free copy may be obtained by writing to the Publications Division, New York Stock Exchange, 11 Wall St., New York, N.Y., 10005.

Yes, he could buy only one share if he wanted. In most stocks, an order to buy or sell less than 100 shares is an odd lot order. These orders are serviced by odd lot members, who act as dealers in odd lots on the floor of the exchange. The mere fact that most stocks on the exchange are traded in units of 100 shares does not prevent the investor of modest means from buying or selling any number of shares desired.

If Dr. Phillips had ordered only 22 shares of A.T.&T. common, his broker would have given the order to an odd lot dealer at the Telephone trading post. There is at least one odd lot dealer at each post. The dealer would fill the order at a price based on the next round lot transaction in A.T.&T. common. Assuming this next round lot trade is made at 45⅛ a share, the odd lot dealer would sell 22 shares of A.T.&T. from his own inventory to Dr. Phillips' broker at 45¼. The additional one eighth point, or 12½ cents per share, is designed to cover expenses incident to the odd lot dealer's operations.

Much the same procedure would have been followed if Jim Greenway had had only 15 or 28 or 99 shares of A.T.&T. common to sell. His broker, too, would have given the sell order to an odd lot dealer. If the next 100 share transaction in A.T.&T. were at 45⅛ a share, the dealer would have bought Jim's stock for $45 a share. In neither instance could the odd lot dealer refuse either to sell 22 shares to Dr. Phillips' broker or to buy the odd lot offered by Greenway's broker.

Pay as You Go Investing

Every investor faces two basic problems: when to buy and what to buy? The Monthly Investment Plan of the member firms of the New York Stock Exchange, by affording the investor a way to buy common stock systematically by the dollars' worth and to average costs over a period, provides a practical, though somewhat costly, approach to the problem of when to buy.

You can invest any amount from $40 to $1,000 per month or per quarter to purchase any one stock. Your money is invested promptly no matter whether you are buying shares at $180 or at $18 each. The exact number of shares (and fraction of a share figured to four decimal places) bought for you with each payment is credited to your account by your stock broker. For example, if Dr. Phillips decides to invest $100 a month in A.T.&T. and it is selling for $45 a share, his $100 (at the odd lot price) buys 2.22 shares. Dividends paid by the company apply to his full shares and any fractional share. He can have the dividends mailed to him or automatically reinvested in A.T.&T. and his account charged for the commissions.

The plan is noncontractual, which means that he is at liberty to stop his payments whenever he chooses without penalty. Since he is buying only a $100 worth of stock each month, his transaction is an odd lot purchase and he is charged a commission plus the regular odd lot differential. This is, of course, a costly way to buy stock. It would be much less expensive for him to buy 100 shares at a time, if he could afford it. It's like buying anything on the installment plan. It costs more than if you buy it outright.

Since he is buying shares by the dollar's worth—putting in the same amount each month—he is engaging in dollar cost averaging. If the market price of A.T.&T. declines, his $100 buys more shares; if the price advances, his $100 buys fewer shares. Under this theory, as we have seen, investors may benefit from a temporary decline in the price of the stock they are accumulating, provided its long-range price trend is upward and periodic purchases are continued in good times and bad.

"MIP"—the Monthly Investment Plan—was inaugurated in January 1954, by members of the New York Stock Exchange to meet the needs of individuals who wish to invest in NYSE listed stocks regularly out of current income.[8]

Recently several new plans have been developed for tapping the funds of the small investor. One is Merrill Lynch's *Sharebuilder Plan*. Another is Chase Manhattan's *Automatic Stock Investment Plan.* Under the Shareholder Plan you invest by the dollar instead of by the share. You decide how many dollars worth of a stock you want to buy. For example, suppose you want to buy IBM which is selling for about $180 a share. You have only $90 to invest. Just place an order for $90 worth of IBM and Merrill Lynch will credit about a half share to your account. Or, if you have more money, you can buy one and a half shares, or 3.3 shares. As soon as your check is in Merrill Lynch's hands they'll buy the stock you ordered at the opening of the market on the *next* business day. Or, if you want to sell, they will execute your order on the morning after you let them have the stock. Merrill Lynch holds the securities of all Sharebuilder Plan members in its own vaults. By launching its Sharebuilder Plan, Merrill Lynch was able to lower brokerage commission charges on investments of $2,000 or less. For example, on the purchase or sale of $100 worth of stock, the old

---

[8] *How to Invest on a Budget—the Monthly Investment Plan* may be obtained by writing to the Publications Division, New York Stock Exchange, 11 Wall St., New York, N.Y., 10005.

NYSE commission was $7.04. Merrill Lynch's Sharebuilder Plan commission is $4.50.

As little as $20 a month will purchase stock under the Chase Manhattan Automatic Stock Investment Plan. Any amount from $20 to $500 a month is deducted from your checking account to buy stock in one or more of 25 leading corporations. By adding investments of many checking account customers, the brokerage costs should be lower than if an individual purchase was made. There is a small service fee plus a proportionate share of commission charges. The bank holds the stock. You must, of course, have a checking account at the bank to participate. A number of large banks have similar plans.

Types of Orders

Dr. Phillips, as we have seen, gave the registered representative a market order to buy A.T.&T. And Jim Greenway placed a market order when he wanted to sell Telephone. This is the procedure used by most investors. Some other kinds of orders are:

A *limit order* specifies a price. If an order is entered to buy a stock at $35, for example, it cannot be executed at a price higher than $35. If an order is entered to sell at $35, it cannot be executed below that price. In all cases the broker will, of course, do his best to get a better price.

Stop orders, sometimes known as "stop loss orders," are designed to limit losses or protect profits. To illustrate: if you bought stock at $35 a share, you could enter an order to sell at "30 stop." In the event the stock should decline to $30, your order automatically becomes a market order and is executed at about $30, depending upon the market in the stock at that time.[9]

Stop orders are also used to protect profits after a stock has risen in price. If stock bought at $35 a share should rise to $55, for example, the customer could enter a stop order to sell at $50. Should the stock decline to $50 or below, the stop order would automatically become a market order, and the stock would be sold at the best obtainable price.

When he gives his broker a limit or stop order, the customer can specify that it is to be good for only one day; this is known as a *day order*. Or he can give a *week order* or a *month order*. If the order is not executed during the period designated, it automatically expires.

If the customer wants his order to hold good indefinitely, he gives his

---

[9] See *The Stop Order: A Guide for the Careful Investor*. A free copy may be obtained by writing to the Publication Division, New York Stock Exchange, 11 Wall St., New York, N.Y. 10005.

broker a *good till canceled order*. This type of order is carried as an open order—until the broker is able to execute it at the specified price, or until the customer cancels it.

Long and Short

A person may be long on certain securities which he holds and short on certain securities which he has sold before he has acquired them. If he sells from his holdings, we have a *long sale*, according to the terminology of the market. If he sells shares that he does not have (and through his broker borrows the shares to make delivery to the buyer), he is engaged in a *short sale*. Margin requirements of the Federal Reserve Board apply to both long and short sales. Short sales are subject to certain restrictions.

Short Selling. Short selling in the securities market is selling shares you do not own and borrowing the number of shares you sell in order to make delivery to the purchaser. When you buy the stock later to return to the lender, you hope to do so at a lower price, thus making a profit. Short selling may not be used as a device to depress security prices artificially, and there are rigid rules to enforce this prohibition. No short sale of a stock is permitted except on a rising price. For instance, there might be six separate transactions in a given stock at a price of $45 a share. However, no stock could be sold short at $45 unless the price before the six transactions at $45 had been $44⅞ or less.

Delivery

Delivery of securities to buyers must, according to the rules and practices of the business, be made with dispatch. On transactions which are designated as "cash," delivery must be made to the purchaser's broker on the very day of the transaction. However, the usual, or "regular" way, of making delivery requires transmission to the buyer's broker by the fifth full business day following the transaction. In recent years, as brokerage houses have been inundated by rising volume and back office breakdowns and delays these rules have often not been observed. Automation, which was thought to be the answer to the problem has not seemed to help in many cases.

Quotations

Stocks are usually quoted at eighths of a point (28⅛, 28¼, 28⅜, 28½, 28⅝, 28¾, and so on). The newspaper stock table, a segment of which appears in Figure 14–9, isn't nearly as complicated as it looks. Let's take the line marked with the arrow, which is A.T.&T. (American Telephone and Telegraph Company). The first two columns before the company's name give the 1974–75 year to date high and low price of its stock. Thus the high was $53, and the low was $39⅝. The figure after the company's name ($3.40) is the annual dividend paid on each share of stock. The next number, 9 is the price/earnings ratio. This is the number of times the price of the stock sells in relation to annual earnings (not dividends). A p/e of 9 means an investor is paying $9 for each dollar of earnings. The next figure, 2020 means 202,000 shares of the stock were traded during the day shown. Next, the 46¾, is the high price (trade) for the day; 46⅛ was the low price for the day. The stock closed—last sale of the day—at 46⅜, down ⅞, or 87½ cents from the closing price the *previous* day it was traded.

Why Stock Prices Change

It is rare indeed when an active issue does not change in price during the day, even if only an eighth of a point, or 12½ cents a share. Why should a share of stock change in value so frequently? A share of stock represents part ownership in, say, a giant utility which supplies a metropolis with power, or a railroad which daily hauls thousands of tons of freight and thousands of passengers. It seems unlikely that Commonwealth Edison Company or Pacific Gas & Electric, to name two corporations, becomes any more or any less valuable from one day to the next. But shares in them do. The answer is supply and demand.

A corporation has just so many shares outstanding. If you want to buy 25, 100, 500, or 5,000 shares of any stock listed on the New York Stock Exchange, you must buy them from someone who owns that number of shares. If you want to sell, you must find someone who wants to buy your shares. The exchange brings together those who want to buy and those who want to sell.

An investor's decision to buy or sell a stock reflects his opinion of its value in relation to personal investment needs and his financial position. His opinion may be influenced, literally, by anything from the state of his digestion to a crisis abroad. Facts sway him; so do fears, hopes, his appraisal of the future, and the past. Earnings reports and prospects may disturb him or elate him. An increased or an omitted dividend may clinch his decision. These opinions—of investors all over the nation—are reflected hour by hour, day by day, on the trading floor of the New York Stock Exchange.

FIGURE 14–9

Thursday's Volume

17,110,000 Shares; 182,600 Warrants

Volume since Jan. 1:	1975	1974	1973
Total shares	190,402,250	187,871,919	219,808,500
Total warrants ..	1,974,400	1,281,200	2,944,100

MOST ACTIVE STOCKS

	Open	High	Low	Close	Chg.	Volume
Data Genl	12¼	12¼	9⅛	10⅝	−1⅜	428,900
Kresge SS	24½	24⅞	24	24¼	− ¼	273,100
Gulf Resrc	11½	12¼	11½	12¼	+ ½	224,100
Am Tel&Tel	46¼	46¾	46⅛	46⅜	− ⅞	202,000
Comw Edis	25⅜	25⅝	25	25⅜	+ ⅛	183,500
Brit Pet	6	6⅛	6	6⅛	+ ¼	162,500
Alcoa	28⅝	28⅝	28¼	28⅝	......	161,400
Alcan Alu	20⅞	20⅞	19	19⅝	−1⅛	143,300
Southern Co	10¾	10⅞	10½	10⅝	− ⅛	136,500
Fairch Cam	18⅝	18¾	18	18¼	− ¼	130,800

Average closing price of most active stocks: 20.21.

1974-75– High	Low	Stocks	Div.	P-E Ratio	Sales in 100s	High	Low	Close	Net Chg.
		– A–A–A –							
61¼	30½	Abbt Lb	1.32	12	65	47¼	46½	47¼	+ ¾
61¼	28¾	ACF In	2.60	8	11	38½	38⅛	38⅛	− ⅛
14⅝	7	AcmeClev	1	7	16	10⅛	10	10⅛	+ ⅛
5⅝	1⅜	AdmDg	.04e	3	21	2⅛	1⅞	2	− ⅛
13¼	7⅜	AdmEx	.77e	...	30	9⅛	8⅝	8⅝	− ½
5¼	1¾	Adms Millis		...	4	2¾	2⅝	2¾	......
11¾	3	Addressog		...	62	4¼	4	4⅛	− ⅛
11⅞	6½	AdvInv	.30e	...	120	9⅛	8¾	8¾	......
31	15⅛	AetnaLf	1.08	7	159	24⅜	24	24¼	− ⅛
13⅞	5⅜	Ahmans	.20	5	39	9⅜	9⅛	9⅜	+ ⅛
4¾	1⅜	Aileen Inc		5	18	2⅛	2	2⅛	......
58	35⅝	AirPrd	.20b	16	107	49⅜	47¼	49	+ 2⅛
14⅞	10	AircoInc	.90	5	49	12⅞	12⅝	12¾	− ⅛
2⅜	1	AJ Industris		...	3	1⅜	1⅜	1⅜	+ ⅛
24	8¾	Akzona	1.20	4	10	13⅜	13	13⅜	+ ⅛
15	7¼	Ala Gas	1.18	15	10	10½	10	10½	+ ¾
103¾	69½	AlaP	pf8.28	...	z200	76¼	76¼	76¼	+ ¾
88½	70	AlaP	pf8.16	...	z20	74½	74½	74½	+ 1
29⅛	5⅜	Alaska Intrs		...	94	10¼	9⅞	10	+ ¼
24⅝	12⅞	AlbanyIn	.60	5	7	17	16¾	17	+ ½
11⅜	4	AlbertoC	.36	20	6	5½	5¼	5½	+ ¼
17¾	10	Albertsn	.60	7	12	12¾	12⅜	12¾	+ ⅜
41	18¼	AlcanAl	1.40	4	1433	20⅞	19	19⅝	− 1⅛
9⅜	6¼	AlcoStd	.48	4	48	8⅜	8⅛	8⅜	+ ⅛
32⅞	12⅛	AlconLb	.20	18	53	17	16⅝	17	+ ⅝
7⅝	2	Alexdrs	.10e	10	10	3½	3¼	3¼	− ¼
23½	2½	AlisnM	2.84e	2	15	5¾	5½	5½	− ¼
12⅛	6¼	AllegCp	.45e	3	22	8	7⅞	8	......
32¾	20⅛	AllgLud	1.60	3	15	21⅝	21⅝	21⅝	......
41	29⅝	AllgLud	pf 3	...	11	33½	32⅞	33⅜	+ 1
21¼	11¾	AllgPw	1.52	9	476	16¾	16¼	16⅝	+ ⅛
9⅝	3⅝	AllenGrp	.40	4	11	4¾	4⅝	4¾	− ⅛
54¼	23	AlldCh	1.80	5	359	28¼	27¾	28	+ ¼
22⅝	8⅜	AlldMnt	.54	7	16	11⅛	10¾	11⅛	+ ⅞
17½	11¼	AlldProd	1	4	5	14	14	14	......
25⅝	15¼	AlldStr	1.50	5	12	19⅝	19½	19⅝	+ ⅛
4⅞	1⅝	Alld Supmkt		...	13	3⅜	3¼	3⅜	+ ¼
10¾	6⅛	AllisChal	.26	4	106	7⅝	7⅛	7½	− ⅛
7¾	3½	AllrtAut	.56	6	7	5¾	5⅝	5¾	+ ⅛
17⅜	6¾	Alpha Pl	.72	4	2	8½	8⅜	8½	+ ⅛
51¾	25⅞	Alcoa	1.34	6	1614	28⅝	28¼	28⅝	......
35	21½	AmalSug	2a	3	17	30½	29⅞	30⅛	+ ⅜
52⅞	28¾	Amax	1.75	5	46	32¼	32	32⅛	− ¼
129	77	Amax	pf5.25	...	5	81⅝	80⅝	81⅝	+ ½
12	5⅞	AMBAC	.50	4	28	7⅝	7¼	7½	......
5	2⅝	Amcord	.24	4	7	3⅝	3⅝	3⅝	......
22	11⅝	Amerce	1.20	3	2	15	15	15	+ ¼
39	25	Amrc	pf2.60	...	4	28	28	28	......
40	12¾	A Hess	.30b	2	487	16⅝	16	16⅛	− ½
89¼	39⅝	A Hes	pf3.50	...	52	44	43½	43¾	+ ⅛
16¼	5¾	AAirFilt	.44	7	62	8⅞	8⅝	8⅞	+ ¼
13¾	[illegible]	Aml Airlin		12	162	6⅛	6	6	− ⅛
[illegible]	[illegible]	AmShip	[illegible]					[illegible]	
27⅜	13	A Smelt	1.50	3	136	16	15⅝	15⅞	− ¼
15⅝	7¾	AmStand	.80	4	94	10½	10⅛	10½	+ ⅜
59	37½	A Std	pf4.75	...	2	45	45	45	......
13⅝	5½	AmSteril	.28	8	54	6⅝	6⅜	6⅝	+ ⅛
34¾	22⅝	AmStores	2	4	11	30	29½	29¾	+ ¼
4⅞	5-16	AT&T	wt	...	957	11-16	9-16	9-16	− ⅛
→ 53	39⅝	AmT&T	3.40	9	2020	46¾	46⅛	46⅜	− ⅞
60	44⅜	AmT&T	pf 4	...	71	51	50¼	50¾	− ½
49	39¼	ATT	pfB3.74	...	22	44⅛	43¾	44⅛	+ ¼
48¼	38½	ATT	pfA3.64	...	18	42½	42	42⅜	......
10¾	6¼	AWatWk	.64	5	7	8½	8⅜	8⅜	......
16	10	AW	5pf1.25	...	z120	12½	12½	12½	+ ½
15	10¾	AW	prf 1.25	...	z120	13	13	13	......
13⅛	8½	Ameron	.90	3	9	9⅜	9¼	9⅜	+ ⅛
4¾	2¼	AmesD	.10e	3	44	3⅜	3¼	3⅜	......
14⅞	9¼	Ametek	1	6	64	12½	12¼	12¼	− ⅛
24	9	AMF In	1.24	6	124	11⅞	11⅝	11⅞	......

Source: *Wall Street Journal*, January 17, 1975.

Every day nearly 600 newspapers across the country publish a price record of stocks traded on the New York Stock Exchange, or tell about the market's action in a news column. Many papers do both. Eighty percent of all dailies in large U.S. cities regularly publish stock market news.

When most people want to buy, the general market will rise. When most people want to sell, the market will decline. Individual stocks, of course, may move independently of the main body of shares. And they frequently do, reflecting developments peculiar to a company or an industry. When it is reported that the market "advanced," it means really that a majority of issues went up—not every stock.

What Are Bull and Bear Markets?

Sometimes a great many people will decide, more or less at the same time, perhaps just on the basis of the general business outlook, that it is a good idea to buy stocks—all kinds of stocks. Such general buying action raises the average price of all stocks. If the price rise is big enough and lasts long enough, we have what is called a "bull market." A "bear market" is just the opposite. The average price of all stocks drops because of widespread selling. To be "bullish" or "bearish" simply is to believe that stocks are going up or down.

Incidentally, it is a simple business to keep track of whether the market as a whole is moving up or down, because almost every major newspaper in the country publishes daily the average price of some group of key stocks and reports whether that average is moving up or down. The Dow-Jones averages are the best known of these indexes, but certainly not the most accurate.

Marketability and Organized Exchanges

Investment of liquid funds in both short and long term capital commitments is enhanced if there is a wide market for both new and seasoned securities. Most people are unable to invest their money and forget it, even though, in the case of a few foolish ones, that may be their wish. They never know when a need may arise for current funds. Unless they can readily sell investments and convert back to a liquid (cash) position, intelligent persons hesitate to part with their money for investments, no matter how sound. The great function of the organized exchange is that it provides the marketability and liquidity desired. You never have to worry about being able to sell a security listed on an organized exchange. Even if no other person wants to buy your shares, the specialists usually will.

The speed with which orders are executed is extraordinary. It takes only a few seconds to send a customer's order from any branch office to the broker's main office located in the same city as the exchange. A few minutes suffice to put through an order either on the floor of the exchange or, for that matter, in the over the counter market.

Customers' Accounts

To open an account at a stockbrokerage firm is a procedure which is comparable to opening an account at a commercial bank. Having opened an account and deposited a sufficient amount of money with the broker, orders may be given in person or by meal, telephone, telegraph, or cable. The customer receives a confirmation from the broker for each order completed. Monthly statements are sent to customers showing the details of all transactions and any other facts, such as dividends collected for and credited to customers' accounts, interest charges on borrowings, and customers' deposits and withdrawals.

Not only do customers have cash deposits with brokerage houses, they frequently leave their securities in the custody of the brokerage firm. In such instances this is done for convenience in buying and selling and often such securities are held in "Street names," that is in the name of the brokerage house and not in the customer's name. The federal government has created the *Securities Investor Protection Corporation* (SIPC) to insure customers of brokerage houses against losses due to the financial failure of brokerage firms. Insurance is afforded up to $20,000 for cash balances and up to $50,000 for securities held by a brokerage firm per customer account.

The new corporation is a membership corporation. All broker-dealers registered with the Securities and Exchange Commission are automatically members. The same is true of all members of national securities exchanges. Firms that do only mutual fund, insurance, or investment advisory business are not covered. The insurance fund is being built up by assessments on member firms, and is backed by a billion dollar line of credit from the U.S. Treasury. Most brokerage houses will now provide you with a booklet entitled "An Explanation of the Securities Investor Protection Act of 1970." After a description of the protection afforded, it contains a series of questions and answers about the extent and nature of coverage.

Services of Securities Houses

Securities houses perform a variety of services for their customers. They open branches in communities where large numbers of investors and speculators reside. They stand ready to supply current quotations on securities and to put through transactions promptly. It is common practice for them to furnish news of, and opinions about, happenings in the world of finance. Inquiries concerning investment and tax problems of individuals are usually answered. Recommendations for the inclusion or exclusion of specific securities in portfolios of individual investors are offered as part of ordinary, everyday services.

Research departments which study financial facts about individual businesses and which make and publish studies of industries and companies are common. Some of them publish instructional material on the financial structure of corporations and the interpretation of published financial statements. Some brokerage houses even go so far as to conduct formal seminars or lectures for customers and prospective customers on various phases of the financial world. The New York Stock Exchange supports the efforts of its members by publishing a monthly magazine and running educational advertisements in the press. It has produced and makes available for free distribution color films, which describe the investment process and the operation of the Exchange.[10] Also, any visitor who applies at the Visitors' Gallery entrance to the Exchange, at 20 Broad Street, will be taken on a guided tour of exchange facilities and be permitted to watch operations on the floor of the exchange from the second floor balcony.

Commission Rates and Discount Brokers

The rate structure changes so fast these days that almost anything that is written is outdated by publication time. The SEC pressed to have all rates made negotiable or competitive, and this occurred in the spring of 1975. Competition among brokerage houses on rates has increased.

The *Wall Street Journal* ad of one discount broker reads: "Commissions —Ours: $22 maximum per 100 shares. Theirs $50 average per 100 shares." The ad reads on: "Let's say you want to buy or sell 200 shares of U.S. Steel. You can either go to a conventional exchange member broker or you can come to us. If you go to them, it will cost you about $130 in commissions. If you come to us, it will cost you $44, maximum." The discount brokers specialize in "third market" trading in listed securities. To keep costs down they pare services. They have no research staffs, for example, offer no advice, keep paper work to a minimum. To appeal to larger investors a number of the discount brokers offer volume discounts based on the number of shares you trade in the course of a year. Discount

[10] Requests for films, which are available free of charge, should be sent to the local office of any member firm of the New York Stock Exchange.

brokers include Burke, Christensen & Lewis Securities, Inc. of Chicago; C. W. Clayton & Co. of Boston; Columbia Securities of Denver; Daley, Coolidge and Co. of Cleveland; First Columbia Corp. of Seattle; Kahn and Co. of Memphis; Odd Lot Securities, Ltd. of New York City; Rose & Co. of Chicago; Source Securities of New York City; Stockcross, Inc. of Boston; and Thrift Trading of Minneapolis. All are members of both the National Association of Securities Dealers and of the Securities Investor Protection Corp., meaning customer accounts are insured up to $50,000 if the firm is liquidated.[11]

Stock Gifts to Minors

It is possible in most states and the District of Columbia to make stock gifts to minors. The Uniform Gifts to Minors Act, adopted by the National Conference of Commissioners on Uniform State Laws provides:

> The donor registers the securities either in his own name, the name of an adult member of the child's family, or the name of the child's guardian, as custodian for the minor.
>
> The gift to the minor is irrevocable.
>
> The custodian may buy, sell, collect dividends or reinvest, subject only to the restrictions of normal prudence.
>
> The gift is exempt from gift tax up to the donor's annual exclusion of $3,000 (or $6,000 for a married couple).
>
> The income from the gift will be taxable to the child.

Previously gifts of stock and other securities to minors were subject to severe legal restrictions. An adult could, it was true, simply register an issue in a child's name—but once done the action was irrevocable. The security had to remain untouched until the minor reached 21. Not even parents (or the minor) could sell, exchange, or otherwise dispose of the security to take advantage of changing market conditions. Legally, dividends also could not be touched but accrued to the minor.

The Uniform Act made possible an outright gift to a minor by registering the security in the name of an adult (parent, for example) as "custodian for a minor." Of crucial importance is the fact that the custodian has the right to sell the stock, reinvest the proceeds, collect dividends, and in general manage the investment until the owner becomes 21. The gift is still irrevocable, but the securities are no longer frozen and may be traded.[12]

---

[11] See "*Now the Small Investor Can Save on Broker's Fees*", *Changing Times*, September 1974; "Buying Stocks at Cut Rate Commissions, *Money*, March 1974.

[12] See *Gifts of Securities or Money to Minors—A Guide to Laws in 50 States*, Association of Stock Exchange Firms, now called the Securities Industry Association, 120 Broadway, New York, N.Y., 10005, latest edition.

Controls—from Within

Over the years, the New York Stock Exchange—largely through experience—has evolved a complex system of rules for self-control. But the underlying principles have remained the same, namely, (1) securities may be bought and sold on the exchange only at prices openly and fairly arrived at; (2) regulations for trading on the floor of the exchange repeatedly stress the importance of the open market—"open" in the sense that secret deals are prohibited; (3) bids and offers are made in multiples of the unit of trading (ordinarily 100 shares), and the highest bid and the lowest offer have precedence. Bids and offers must be called out loud. Transactions are immediately reported across the country. No trades are allowed on the exchange floor before or after trading hours, which are from 10 A.M. to 4 P.M., Monday through Friday.

The relations of stock exchange member firms and corporations and their clients must meet a rigid set of requirements. Member firms must inform their customers, monthly or at other set periods, of the condition of their accounts, and all customers of a stock exchange member firm must be supplied with copies of the firm's financial statement upon request. Member firms must have adequate capital and must answer at least three financial questionnaires of the exchange every year. One of these reports is based on a surprise audit by independent public accountants. Unfortunately however, this has not kept firms from falling by the wayside. In addition, stock exchange examiners visit member firms' offices and spot-check their books and records to see that exchange, federal, and state regulations are being followed. Member firms also must report weekly on their positions as underwriters of securities and must disclose borrowings or loans by the firm or by individual partners.

Controls—from Without

The Securities Acts of 1933 and 1934 ushered in a new era in American finance. The 1933 act provides for full and fair disclosure of the character of new issues of securities publicly offered in interstate and foreign commerce and through the mails, and for the prevention of fraud in the sale of such securities. The 1934 act provides for the regulation of securities exchanges and of over the counter markets operating in interstate and foreign commerce and through the mails, to prevent inequitable and unfair practices. The Securities and Exchange Commission, with headquarters in Washington and offices in other cities, administers the acts.

The 1934 act makes mandatory:

1. Adequate disclosure of information about a listed security

2. Registration with the SEC of all securities listed on national securities exchanges
3. The banning of all manipulative operations, such as pools, wash or faked sales, false and misleading statements, etc.
4. The prohibition of "actual or apparent active trading in any security, or raising or depressing the price for the purpose of inducing the purchase or sale of it by others"

In addition, the SEC prescribes rules for periodic reports covering dealings in their stock by officers, directors, and principal stockholders of companies whose securities are listed on an exchange.

Government controls also regulate the flow of credit into the securities market. This section of the Securities Exchange Act of 1934 is administered by the Federal Reserve Board, as this agency has jurisdiction over the use of credit and regulates the flow of credit in the banking system. Brokers may borrow only from a source approved by the Federal Reserve, which also determines how much credit a broker may extend to a customer to purchase or carry listed securities.

With the computer and automation, vast changes in the structure and organization of securities trading lie ahead. The SEC's Institutional Investors Study and the Martin report suggest new procedures and new techniques and with them will undoubtedly come new forms of regulation designed to protect the investor. The brokerage industry and the organized exchanges are in a state of flux. That the small investor will benefit from the forthcoming changes is not at all clear.

SUGGESTED READINGS

1. Louis Engel, *How to Buy Stocks—a Guide to Successful Investing.* Paperbound edition. New York: Bantam Books. A free copy may be obtained upon request to Merrill Lynch, Pierce, Fenner & Smith, One Liberty Plaza (165 Broadway), New York, N.Y. 10006.
2. *Over-the-Counter Securities.* New York: Merrill Lynch, Pierce, Fenner & Smith. A free copy may be obtained by writing to the firm at One Liberty Plaza (165 Broadway), New York, N.Y. 10006.
3. *New York Stock Exchange Fact Book.* NYSE annual. A free copy of the latest edition may be obtained by writing to the Publications Division, New York Stock Exchange, 11 Wall St., New York, N.Y. 10005.
4. James Dines, *How the Average Investor Can Use Technical Analysis for Stock Profits,* Dines Chart Corp., New York, 1974.
5. *Encyclopedia of Stock Market Techniques.* Larchmont, N.Y.: Investors Intelligence, Inc., latest edition.

6. Mark Weaver, *The Technique of Short Selling*. Rev. ed. New Jersey: Investors Library, Inc., latest edition.
7. Maurece Schiller, *Special Situations*. Larchmont, N.Y.: American Research Council, latest edition.
8. *What Is Margin?* Merrill Lynch, Pierce, Fenner & Smith. Latest edition. A free copy may be obtained by writing to the firm at One Liberty Plaza (165 Broadway) New York, N.Y. 10006.
9. "The NASDAQ Revolution: How Over-the-Counter Securities are Traded," Merrill Lynch, Pierce, Fenner, and Smith, New York. A free copy may be obtained by writing to the firm at One Liberty Plaza (165 Broadway), New York, N.Y., 10006.
10. Paul F. Jessup, *Competing for Stock Market Profits*. New York: John Wiley & Sons 1974.
11. Louis Rukeyser, *How to Make Money in Wall Street*, Garden City, N.Y.: Doubleday & Co., 1974.
12. Maurice L. Farrell (ed.), *Dow Jones Investors Handbook*. Princeton, N.J.: Dow Jones Books, 1975.
13. John W. Bowyer Jr., *Investment Analysis & Management*, 4th ed., Homewood, Ill.: Richard D. Irwin, Inc., 1972.
14. *Facts You Should Know about Securities*. Latest edition. Educational Division, Better Business Bureau, 1107 17th St. N.W. Washington, D.C. 20036.
15. *Facts You Should Know about Security and Commodity Exchanges*. Latest edition. Educational Division, Better Business Bureau, 1107 17th St. N.W. Washington, D.C. 20036.
16. In *Changing Times:*
    "How Do Brokers Treat The Small Investor?," July 1973.
    "What If your Broker Goes Broke?," August 1973.
    "Ten Ways to Buy Stock a Little at a Time," November 1973.
    "Which Stock Market Index Do you Read?" June 1974.
    "Brokers' Commissions: Now the Small Investor Can Save," September 1974.
    "Is It Time to Buy Stocks?," January 1975.
17. In *Money:*
    "What Your Broker Doesn't Know Can Hurt You," September 1973.
    "Buying Stocks at Cut Rate Commissions," March 1974.
    "Stocks for the Times of Your Life," April 1974.
    "Investing in Yesterday's Tortoises," November 1974.
18. Publications available from the New York Stock Exchange; single copies free on request:*

---

* Requests for free single copies of publications should be sent to: New York Stock Exchange, Publications Division, 11 Wall St., New York, N.Y., 10005.

How to Get Help When You Invest—Primer for prospective and new investors providing basic information on investing.

How to Invest on a Budget—Describes the story of the Monthly Investment Plan, how it works, what it costs, how to start a plan.

Investment Clubs . . . What Are They? . . . How Are They Started?—Information on the organization and operation of investment clubs.

Understanding the New York Stock Exchange—Comprehensive and easy-to-read description of the functions of the Stock Exchange and Member Firms.

Now, About the Specialist—Tells about the activities and responsibilities of the specialist, and Exchange regulations and policies governing his operations.

The Language of Investing, A Glossary—Definitions of stock market terms.

Understanding Financial Statements—Comprehensive booklet for educators, students, and investors. Explains basic techniques used in investment analysis.

Does It Make Sense for Me to Buy Stocks?—Answers nine questions most often asked about investing.

Understanding Bonds and Preferred Stocks—An explanation of the investment characteristics of senior securities and their role in a balanced investment program.

Growth Leaders on the Big Board—An investment guide featuring a list of hundreds of common stocks which have shown a five-year compound growth rate in earnings per share of at least 5 percent. Grouped by industry and by growth rate for convenient comparison. Semi-Annual.

Subscription Publications:

The Exchange—Monthly magazine for the NYSE provides, in everyday language, facts, figures, and articles of current interest to present and potential shareowners. ($4.50 per year; $8 for two years.)

New York Stock Exchange Monthly Review—A compilation of current business and financial statistics, including record highs and lows for each series. ($2.50 for 12 issues.)

Films:*

The Lady and the Stock Exchange—An amusing drama produced in color by Paramount and starring Janet Blair. Emphasizes the right versus the wrong way to start investing. (27 minutes)

Market in Motion—This award-winning exchange film reflects the role of the Big Board and its member firms in an expanding economy. In color (13 minutes).

---

* Requests for these films should be sent to the local office of any Member Firm of the NYSE or to Modern Talking Picture Service, with offices in major cities. Films loaned free of charge.

What Makes Us Tick—An animated Technicolor short about the investment process, the NYSE, listed corporations and their stockholders. (12 minutes)

Working Dollars—A cartoon film in full color, showing how Fred Finchley puts his dollars to work through MIP. (13 minutes)

At the Market—Designed for the professional investment manager. In color (22 minutes)*

CASE PROBLEMS

1. Nancy is a recent college graduate. She has a good job with a firm in the San Francisco area. Her salary allows her to make small weekly contributions to her savings account, which by now, with the help of a graduation gift from her parents, is equal to a year's salary. She feels that she would like to invest part of it in securities. What things should she consider? What would you advise her to do?

2. Bert (35), an alumnus of a graduate school of business, has a secure job with a manufacturing firm. He is married and has two children (ages 5 and 3). His home and automobile are paid for. Ten years ago Bert inherited a dryland wheat farm, which for years, because of drought and poor crops, barely produced a sufficient income to cover taxes and cost of operation. Three years ago oil was discovered on his farm and it is now yielding an annual net income of $25,000. Bert wants to invest this extra income in securities. What would you advise him to do?

3. Winters has just received a promotion with a substantial increase in salary. He feels that the time has come to begin to build an investment fund. In his opinion he can afford to invest $500 every three months. Since he does not have enough capital to secure the services of an investment counselor, and since the idea of a mutual fund does not appeal to him, he has decided to try the dollar averaging formula plan. While this plan helps him to decide *how* to invest, it does not tell him in *what* stocks he should invest. How can he obtain this information?

4. Jane and Ted Lyons have been married six years. They live in a rented, furnished apartment and carry no insurance. They have saved about $3,000. Both work and are covered by social security and pension plans. Jane wants to invest their savings in shares of the stock of the American Telephone and Telegraph Company. What do you think about it?

5. Mandel started his own business 10 years ago. By now he owns the business (including buildings), his home, an automobile, and savings accounts of $8,000. He is currently earning about $15,000 a year. His family consists of a

* Available, free of charge, through any Member Firm, or contact Institutional Investors' Department, New York Stock Exchange, 11 Wall St., New York, N.Y., 10005.

wife and two young children. Now he thinks that he should invest $5,000 of his savings in good common stocks. Do you agree?

6. Robbins is 32 years old. He lives with his wife (age 30) and two children (ages 6 and 8). For the last few years the family has been living comfortably on his income (average, $17,000 a year) from a small business which he owns and which has taken all of his time and attention. At his mother's death he inherits $50,000, which he would like to invest in securities. What advice can you give him concerning the investment of this money at present?

7. Sharon knows by experience that it is not good to "put all of one's eggs into one basket." Having $75,000 to invest, she decides to buy approximately $1,000 worth of each of 75 "blue chip" stocks, selected pretty much at random. Can you improve upon her plan?

8. Archer has accumulated $25,000 in savings banks and savings and loan associations. He was always afraid of investing in stocks because he thought the stock market was subject to such abuses that investment therein was unsafe. He has been led to believe, however, that most of the abuses have now been eliminated by regulation. Now he is beginning to think that his money would be about as safe in securities as it would be in savings banks. He is a married man in his 40s with four children (ages 12, 14, 17, and 19). His job pays him, steadily, $20,000 a year. He thinks that hereafter he will invest $2,000 a year ($500 a quarter) in common stocks, leaving his already accumulated $25,000 and the earnings thereon where they are. What is your opinion of this plan?

9. Balcom has $1,800 of surplus savings. With this money he can buy shares in a small local company or shares in a large company, national in scope. At the present rate of dividends, he will receive 4 percent on his investment in either company. Does one investment look better to you than the other?

10. Zettelli is a real estate broker whose earnings fluctuate widely from year to year, although they have averaged $25,000 annually over the last 10 years. He and his wife live comfortably on $17,000 a year. They own their home and have a nest egg of $10,000 in the bank. He is intrigued by dollar averaging, believing that he could not fail to be successful if he followed it in the stock market. However, he thinks that his fluctuating earnings bar his using it. What advice would you give him?

11. After Bisbee put aside $2,000 for emergencies, he decided to invest his remaining savings, $1,000, in a common stock selling at $100 a share. Since he realized that his $1,000 would permit him to buy only 10 shares outright and he believed strongly that shares in this company would advance sharply in price, he decided to buy 20 shares on a 50 percent margin. Do you agree with him?

15

Obtaining Investment Information

Investigate before you invest.
Better Business Bureau

THE "Bawl Street Journal" is the annual lampoon of the financial community. Although it's all in fun, many a true word is said in jest. "If you believe your stockbroker is an idiot talk to one of ours," advertized one brokerage house. "If you think smoking is hazardous to your health, try our research," announced another firm. "Trust us to get you to the bottom of things," said one firm, while, in similar vein, another announced, "Our modern day computers provide our customers with up to the minute reporting on their losses." "Our analysts are all psychos. You'll find one to match your personality." "Our representatives are fired with enthusiasm," read two others. "Now that logical reasoning is no longer required in this crazy market we have more confidence in our recommendations", announced one firm. "Let us review your holdings with an aim at increasing our commissions," said another jokingly. "If you are looking for laughs come in and see us! Some of our offerings are hilarious," said a new issue house: "We sincerely hope that the market catches up with our predictions before the SEC does," advertised one house, while another announced: "Get our research bulletin: Rarely do so many who know so little say so much." Wall Street poking fun at itself but highlighting a very real problem. Which of many sources of information should the small investor use? Where to go for accurate, useful information?

Before buying stocks and bonds, an intelligent investor should accumulate a good deal of information concerning the securities in which he is interested. It is common to undertake the inquiry in three steps:

(1) Are general business conditions such that it is a propitious time to invest? Should one buy or sell short? (2) What is the condition and what are the prospects of the industry in which one proposes to invest? Which are the best growth industries? Which are the best defensive industries? (3) What is the status of, and what has the future in store for, the particular company in the industry in which the investor is interested? Or which is the company with the best prospects in the industry? Although the job may be too extensive for the average small investor to do adequately, a general outline of where to look and what to look for may be given if one has the time, the patience, and the intelligence to do it.

Large Investors

Large investors, such as investment companies, banks, and insurance companies, have extensive research organizations which study all available facts before a commitment is made in a given security. They keep track of conditions pertaining to specific securities as long as they hold those securities; they continue to hold the securities only because the facts indicate that it is the wise thing to do. When conditions develop which indicate that securities should be sold, the decision to sell is based on facts. Research is kept constantly up to date. Experience proves that it is not satisfactory to buy a security (after investigation), put it away in a vault, and forget about it. Such a procedure almost invariably ends in a result which is less advantageous than constant watchfulness would have produced. The larger organizations can afford to buy and read the services published by specialists. While these services may be too expensive for the average small investor to buy, any good public library or university business school library will have them available for reference and use.

Typical Investors

Unfortunately, most small investors expect to obtain for nothing the facts on which to form a judgment. Sometimes they act on the basis of tips, without even finding out whether there is any merit in the tip. Often they rely on offhand information received from a banker or somebody in a stockbrokerage house. Even though the individuals who give the information may be able persons, the casual, offhand remark or advice may not fit the particular investment problem of the listener. Banks or brokerage houses may give some useful information and advice as to where more can be found, but the individual must expect to do a lot of digging. The broker, as the name implies, earns a living by bringing buyers and sellers together, effecting purchases and sales. Some of the large brokerage houses have competent research departments. It is to their advantage to make sound recommendations, for they will not long retain a customer who loses money acting on their advice, and they know it. Also, the more farsighted brokerage houses know that the younger, small investor of today may become the larger investor of tomorrow, and a few of these houses are now actively catering to the small investor.

Use an Investment Counselor?

For the investor with $50,000 or more who feels that investing is too much of a job personally, the investment counselor is available to furnish necessary information and make decisions as to buying and selling. For a relatively small percentage of the market value of a list of investments, usually 0.5 percent annually, or 1 percent depending on the size of the portfolio, one may hire an investment counsel who maintains a staff and makes a business of furnishing advice for a fee. Since they cannot afford to furnish much information for little compensation, they usually cannot afford to work for clients who do not have at least $50,000 to invest, and they are therefore not available to the smaller investor. However, some of the smaller investment counseling firms will take accounts of $10,000 size. The fee involved is usually worth the cost, because investment counselors today must register with and are regulated by the SEC. This does not guarantee, of course, that the advice they give is good, but it does insure that it is not fraudulent; and the investment counselor usually obtains business by recommendations of satisfied and pleased clients. Leading investment counseling firms include Scudder-Stevens & Clark, Calvin Bullock, Loomis-Sayles, Lehman Brothers. Also, the leading financial services—Moody's, Standard & Poor's, and Value Line—all have investment counseling departments.

Recently there has been a trend toward accommodating the small investor, both by banks and by financial services. First National City Bank of New York will accept investment advisory accounts with a $10,000 value minimum. The cost of its advice is 1 percent a year on the market value of the investment, with a $250 minimum charge. The Marine Midland Banks will give investment advice on accounts as low as $8,000. The fee is 0.75 percent a year with a $160 minimum charge. Danforth Associates, of Wellesley Hills, Massachusetts, takes clients with as little as $5,000, charging a fee of 2 percent a year on portfolios up to $25,000 in value and 0.25 percent on additional amounts over that, with a $100 a year minimum fee.[1]

General Business Conditions

To keep abreast of general business conditions and be informed on trends and developments is not at all difficult. The financial section of a good newspaper, such as the *New York Times*, or a magazine, such as *Business Week*, will, if read regularly, build a feeling of awareness of what is happening and a background to understand it. The *Survey of Current Business*, published monthly by the U.S. Department of Commerce, is also helpful. Specialized daily or weekly financial newspapers, such as the *Wall Street Journal, Financial World, Forbes, Journal of Commerce, Commercial and Financial Chronicle*, and *Barron's* are invaluable. The Federal Reserve System publishes a "National Summary of Business Conditions" each month in its *Federal Reserve Bulletin*. Upon request, a mimeographed copy of this summary will be mailed in advance of publication. There is no charge for this. Your name will be placed on the Federal Reserve's mailing list for this summary if you write to the Publications Services, Board of Governors, Federal Reserve System, Washington, D.C. 20551. Each month the U.S. government's Council of Economic Advisers prepares and issues *Economic Indicators*. This may be obtained from the Superintendent of Documents, U.S. Government Printing Office, Washington, D.C. The Council also prepares the very useful annual *Economic Report of the President*, analyzing current economic trends in the country.

Business Conditions Digest, published monthly by the Bureau of the Census of the U.S. Department of Commerce is based on the National Bureau of Economic Research leading, coincident, and lagging indicators approach. The publication is divided into two parts—the first on charts, the second on backup tables. There are six sections in each part covering National Income and Gross National Product, Cyclical Indicators, Anticipations and Intentions, Other Key Indicators, Analytical Measures (including Actual and Potential GNP, Analytical Ratios, Diffusion Indices, and Rate of Change Analysis) and International Comparisons. If you possess some degree of economic and statistical competence, you will find this a very valuable tool.

There are many other publications which are useful to a person who is

[1] "Now the Small Investor Can Have an Adviser," *Business Week*, February 23, 1974, pp. 75–79.

attempting to keep abreast of general business conditions. *Sources of Business Information* (rev. ed.), by Edwin R. Coman, Jr., may assist you in locating some of these; *Business Service Checklist* of the U.S. Department of Commerce and the *List of Selected U.S. Government Publications* (appearing twice a month), obtainable from the Superintendent of Documents, Washington, D.C., are also worth knowing about. Once you become acquainted with some of these sources of information, you will inevitably be led by them to others. After you have been studying business information for a time, you will probably be bothered not so much by the difficulty of obtaining information but rather by the difficulty of making intelligent choice as to what part of the mass of available material should receive your attention and what part should be dismissed from consideration.

Industry Information

As to the essentials of an industry, much can be learned from the *Industry Surveys* of Standard & Poor's. These are excellent, brief, yet comprehensive studies, revised annually. Trade associations are sources of information about the various industries; a list of them may be found in *National Organizations of the United States,* Vol. I of the Encyclopedia of Associations.[2] The *Record* of the Conference Board publishes excellent studies on particular industries. There are a large number of industry journals, some issued by the trade associations, some published commercially. Each usually issues an annual or review of the year number, which provides much useful information. Examples are *Advertising Age, Chemical Week, Electronic News, Computers and Automation, Construction Review, Data Processing Magazine, Drug and Cosmetic Industry, Engineering News Record, Iron Age, Oil and Gas Journal, Paper Trade Journal, Printing, Railway Age, Canner,* and others. The student who wishes further information and does not know how to acquire it can usually obtain help from the librarians at any good public or university library.

Information about Particular Companies

The various financial services, such as Moody's, Standard & Poor's, and Value Line (to be described later), publish a wealth of information about particular companies, and there is no excuse for anyone investing in a corporation without first having looked it up in one of the services and

[2] Gale Research Co., Detroit, 1975, rev. ed.

learned all the basic facts about its finances, operations, and outlook. In most cases, the services not only provide the basic financial and economic facts about the company but also give a recommendation as to whether the company's stock (or bond) should be bought, sold, or held. An example of a company analysis is shown in Figure 15–1.

Whenever a company floats a new issue of securities, it is required by law (with certain exceptions) to file a *registration statement* and *prospectus* with the Securities and Exchange Commission. The registration statement contains all the pertinent financial, economic, and legal information about the company, its officers, and its operations that any investor might need and want to know in arriving at a decision on whether to buy the company's securities. A copy of the registration statement may be purchased at cost. The prospectus is a summarized or abridged version of the information contained in the registration statement. A copy must be given to every prospective purchaser of the company's new issue of securities. Frequently, in seeking information about a company, if there has been a recent new issue, examination of the registration statement and prospectus at the nearest SEC office will yield a wealth of information about the company and its operations.

If you have the technical competence, the best way, of course, to find out about a company's financial status and position is to analyze its balance sheet and income account yourself. You can usually obtain copies of the latest balance sheet and income account by writing to the company. Normally, unless it is a closed or family corporation, it will make its balance sheet and income account public. All corporations whose securities are listed on organized exchanges and the larger ones traded over the counter are required to make their financial statements available. They, and all corporations which have issued new securities, have registered them with the SEC, and have at least a million dollars worth of such securities still outstanding, must file *Form 10K* with the SEC. This is a detailed financial statement, prepared annually in accordance with SEC specifications. It can be consulted either at the office of the exchange on which the company is listed or at the local branch of the SEC.

Brokerage Houses

Most of the leading brokerage houses not only publish a wealth of information in the form of analyses worked up by their own research departments but also distribute free of charge, on request to customers, company analyses prepared by the standard financial services. They also have available in their offices, for examination and use by customers, the various manuals and compilations of the leading financial services.

FIGURE 15–1

T[1] **American Tel. & Tel.** 182

Stock—	Price Jan. 23'75	Dividend	Yield
COMMON	47⅛	[2]$3.40	[2]7.2%
$4 CONV. PREFERRED	51¼	4.00	7.8
WARRANTS	⅝	None	None

RECOMMENDATION: AT&T is dominant in communications, not only through its telephone subsidiaries but also through Western Electric and Bell Telephone Laboratories. On November 20, 1974, the Justice Department filed an antitrust suit charging AT&T with monopolizing the market for telecommunications services and equipment, and seeking the break up of the company. Although the suit will probably put a damper on the COMMON and CONVERTIBLE PREFERRED stocks for some time ahead, long-term holdings need not be disturbed as any ultimate resolution should not impair underlying values. Each WARRANT entitles the holder to buy one common share at $52 through May 15, 1975.

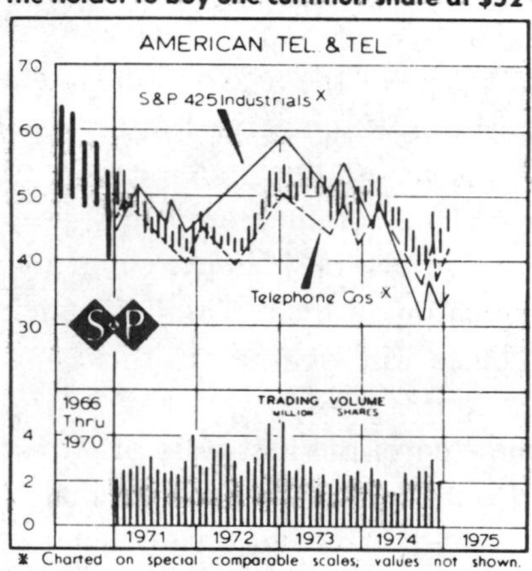

X Charted on special comparable scales, values not shown.

[3]OPERATING REVENUES (Million $)

Quarter:	1974	1973	1972	1971	1970
Feb.	6,234	5,511	4,884	4,382	4,062
May	6,514	5,815	5,139	4,581	4,243
Aug.	6,588	5,915	5,262	[5]4,632	4,284
Nov.	6,677	6,044	5,417	4,699	4,279

Revenues for the 12 months ended November 20, 1974, advanced 12%, year to year, aided by rate increases. The operating ratio eased to 81.9%, from 82.2%, and operating income rose 13%. After 19% greater interest deductions, net income was up 9.1%. The smaller gain in share earnings, to $5.33 from $4.97 (before $0.08 special credit), reflected greater preferred dividend requirements.

Based on preliminary figures, share earnings for 1974 were $5.27 (after $0.05 charge for additional depreciation recorded in December), versus the $4.98 of 1973.

[3,4]COMMON SHARE EARNINGS ($)

Quarter:	1974	1973	1972	1971	1970
Feb.	1.27	1.16	0.97	1.01	0.98
May	1.40	1.28	1.07	1.06	1.03
Aug.	1.33	[6]1.28	1.10	[6]0.95	0.96
Nov.	1.33	1.27	1.15	0.94	1.00

PROSPECTS

Despite the recession, share earnings for 1975 are expected to compare favorably with 1974's $5.27 (preliminary), reflecting anticipated rate increases and productivity improvements. The dividend is expected to continue at $0.85 quarterly.

RECENT DEVELOPMENTS

On January 3, 1975, AT&T filed with the FCC for $717 million (7.2%) of interstate rate increases ($433 million after taxes). These rates--that would become effective on March 4 on an interim basis unless the FCC delays them 90 additional days--are designed to provide a 10%-11% return on interstate investment (13.5%-14% on common equity), versus 8.2% currently earned and 8.5%-9% authorized by the FCC in January, 1973.

On November 20, 1974, the Justice Department filed an antitrust suit charging AT&T with monopolizing the market for telecommunications services and equipment through the use of illegal methods against competitors, mainly in the area of business services. The suit sought divestiture of Western Electric and its division into two or more companies, and the divestiture of AT&T's Long Lines Department or the sale of some or all of the 23 local telephone companies served by Long Lines. The suit may not come to trial for at least three years, and court proceedings could continue for many more years unless a negotiated settlement is reached. AT&T has indicated that it will contest the suit with all its resources.

DIVIDEND DATA

Payments in the past 12 months were:

Amt of Divd $	Date Decl	Ex divd Date	Stock of Record	Payment Date
0.77	Feb. 20	Feb. 21	Feb. 27	Apr. 1'74
0.77	May 15	May 24	May 31	Jul. 1'74
0.85	Aug. 21	Aug. 23	Aug. 29	Oct. 1'74
0.85	Nov. 20	Nov. 25	Dec. 2	Jan. 2'75

[1]Listed N.Y.S.E.; com. also listed Boston, Midwest, PBW & Pacific S.Es. & traded Cincinnati & Detroit, S.Es.; pfd. also listed PBW S.E. [2]Indicated rate. [3]Consol. [4]Based on avge. shs. [5]Gives effect to Calif. Supreme Court refund order to Pacific Tel. & Tel. in this & subseq. periods. [6]Excl. $0.08 sp. cr.

STANDARD N.Y.S.E. STOCK REPORTS STANDARD & POOR'S CORP.

Published at Ephrata, Pa. Editorial & Executive Offices, 345 Hudson St., New York, N.Y. 10014

Vol. 42, No. 20 Wednesday, January 29, 1975 Sec. 2

FIGURE 15–1 (continued)

182 AMERICAN TELEPHONE & TELEGRAPH COMPANY

[1]INCOME STATISTICS (Million $) AND PER SHARE ($) DATA

Year Ended Dec. 31	Revenues Local	Revenues Toll	[3]Gross	% of Gr. Revs. Depr. & Maint.	% of Gr. Revs. Taxes	[2]Oper. Ratio	[7]Fxd. Chgs. & Pfd. Divs. Tms. Earns.	[8]Net Inc.	Common Share ($) Data [4][6]Earns.	Common Share ($) Data Divs. Paid	Common Share ($) Data Price Range	Earns. Ratios HI LO
1975--	------	------	------	---	---	---	---	------	---	0.85	------	-----
1974--	------	------	------	---	---	---	---	------	[9]5.27	3.16	53 -39⅝	10- 8
1973--	11,418.5	11,278.5	23,527.3	34.7	18.5	82.2	2.47	2,946.7	4.98	2.80	55 -45⅜	11- 9
1972--	10,362.9	9,771.4	20,904.1	35.1	18.2	82.9	2.50	2,532.1	4.34	2.65	53½ -41⅛	12- 9
1971--	9,135.5	8,632.8	18,442.1	35.5	18.0	83.4	2.66	2,202.0	3.92	2.60	53⅞ -40¾	14-10
1970--	8,456.0	7,874.1	16,954.9	34.8	19.3	83.4	3.25	2,192.2	3.99	2.60	53⅞ -40⅜	14-10
1969--	7,774.4	7,297.8	15,683.8	33.5	22.3	83.6	4.70	2,198.7	4.00	2.40	58⅛ -48⅛	15-12
1968--	7,184.1	6,341.2	14,100.0	32.7	23.4	83.3	5.34	2,051.8	3.75	2.40	58⅜ -48	16-13
1967--	6,737.7	5,737.9	13,009.2	32.5	22.1	82.2	5.95	2,049.4	3.79	2.20	62¾ -49¾	17-13
1966--	6,354.7	5,274.4	12,138.3	32.3	22.4	82.2	6.76	1,978.9	3.69	2.20	63½ -49¾	17-13
1965--	5,961.3	4,613.7	11,061.8	32.4	22.1	82.4	6.74	1,796.1	3.41	2.00	70½ -60⅛	21-18
1964--	5,633.7	4,205.5	10,306.0	31.6	23.1	82.6	6.47	1,658.6	3.24	1.95	75 -65⅜	23-20

[1]PERTINENT BALANCE SHEET STATISTICS (Million $)

Dec. 31	Gross Prop.	Capital Expend.	%Depr. of Gross Prop.	[6]%Earn. on Net Prop.	[5]Funded Debt	% Funded Debt of Net Prop.	% Funded Debt of Gross Rev.	% Funded Debt of Invest. Cap.	Total Invest. Cap.	[6][7]%Earn. on Inv. Cap.	Net Inc. per Tel.	($) Book Val. Com. Sh.
1973--	74,005	9,300	20.9	7.1	28,371	48.4	120.6	45.2	62,748	7.6	26.69	54.90
1972--	67,082	8,300	21.6	6.8	26,020	49.5	124.5	45.7	56,969	7.2	24.05	50.95
1971--	60,568	7,564	22.1	6.5	22,828	48.4	123.8	44.7	51,112	7.0	21.96	47.36
1970--	54,813	7,159	22.4	6.6	20,454	48.1	120.6	44.2	46,286	7.0	22.70	45.53
1969--	49,244	5,731	22.8	6.8	15,868	41.7	101.2	38.9	40,792	7.1	23.72	43.96
1968--	44,975	4,742	22.7	6.8	13,430	38.8	95.2	36.0	37,366	7.0	23.31	42.24
1967--	41,476	4,310	22.1	7.2	11,901	36.8	91.5	34.1	34,905	7.3	24.46	40.63
1966--	38,354	4,193	21.7	7.2	10,352	34.5	85.3	32.2	32,178	7.4	24.77	38.91
1965--	35,334	3,918	21.4	7.0	9,082	32.7	82.1	30.5	29,727	7.3	23.67	37.10
1964--	32,544	3,519	21.4	7.0	8,725	34.1	84.6	31.0	28,136	7.2	23.03	35.39

[1]Data for 1973 as originally reported; data for each yr. prior to 1973 as taken from subsequent yr.'s Annual Report. [2]After depr. & taxes. [3]Aft. deduct. uncollectible revs. [4]Based on avge. shs. [5]Incl. interim debt to be refinanced. [6]Based on bk. value, may differ from return on rate base. [7]Fixed chgs. only prior to 1971; aft. 1969 reflects change in FPC method of accounting for allowance for funds used during construction. [8]Bef. spec. cr. of $0.08 a sh. in 1973. [9]Company estimate.

Fundamental Position

A holding company, American Telephone & Telegraph, through its telephone subsidiaries comprising the Bell System, controlled 110,337,000 phones at year-end 1973, about 80% of the nation's total. Non-controlling stock interests are held in other telephone operating companies. Approximately 48% of system revenues was derived from local service and 48% toll. The parent directly operates long-distance lines (through its Long Lines Department) connecting regional units and independent systems.

Equipment is purchased largely from 100%-owned Western Electric Co., an important contributor to earnings. Research is done for AT&T and Western Electric on a non-profit basis by Bell Telephone Laboratories.

Auxiliary services of AT&T include private line telephone services, and transmission of data and radio and TV programs. Overseas service to 237 countries is provided through cable, radio, and satellite circuits.

Rapid depreciation is used for tax purposes with normalization. Savings from investment tax credits are amortized over the life of the property giving rise to the credit.

Rate increase requests pending on the state level totaled $2.152 billion as of early January, 1975, of which $1.377 billion was filed during the last quarter of 1974. During 1974 $503 million was granted, of which $126 million was booked in that year.

Dividends paid in each year since 1885, averaged 61% of earnings in 1969-73.

Employees: 1,003,000. Shareholders: 2,-991,620.

Finances

Capital outlays for 1975 are estimated at $9.9 billion (cut back from $10.5 billion), versus $10 billion indicated for 1974. Financing in 1975 is to total around $3.3 billion, against $4.2 billion in 1974, including $600 million of (parent) debt scheduled for January 28.

CAPITALIZATION

LONG TERM DEBT: $29,538,326,000.
INTERIM DEBT: $1,782,211,000.
MINORITY INTEREST: $827,427,000.
$4 CUM CONV. PREFERRED STOCK: 27,-446,769 shs. ($1 par; $50 stated value); red. at $51 thru July 31, 1975, $50.50 thru July 31, 1976, then $50; conv. into approx. 1.05 com.
$77.50 PREFERRED STOCK: 625,000 shs. ($1 par; $1,000 stated value). Privately held.
$3.74 CUM. PREFERRED STOCK: 10,000,000 shs. ($1 par; $50 stated value); red. thru each Jan. 31: 1975, $53.74; 1976, $53.63; 1977, $53.53; then less to $50.11 in 2009.
$3.64 CUM. PREFERRED STOCK: 10,000,-000 shs. ($1 par; $50 stated value); red. thru each Apr. 30: 1975, $53.54; 1976, $53.43; then less to $50.10 in 2008.
COMMON STOCK: 558,370,000 shs. ($16,-2/3 par).
WARRANTS: 31,313,301 each to purchase 1 com. sh. at $52 thru May 15, 1975. (Terms and trading basis should be checked in detail).

Incorporated in N.Y. in 1885. **Office**— 195 Broadway, NYC 10007. **Pres**— R. D. Lilley. **Secy**— F. A. Hutson, Jr. **VP-Treas**— W. L. Mobraaten. **Dirs**— J. D. deButts (Chrmn), W. M. Batten, L. D. Brace, E.W. Carter, C. B. Cleary, A. K. Davis, E. B. Hanify, J. V. Herd, W. A. Hewitt, J. H. Holland, B. K. Johnson, J. R. Killian, Jr., R. D. Lilley, W. L. Lindholm, D. S. MacNaughton, W. J. McGill, J. I. Miller, W. B. Murphy, T. F. Patton, J. Taylor, R. Warner, Jr. **Transfer Agents**—Company's offices; 195 Broadway, NYC; New England Tel. & Tel. Co., Boston; Illinois Bell Telephone Co., Chicago; Pacific Tel. & Tel., San Francisco. **Registrars**—Bankers Trust Co., NYC; Old Colony Trust Co., Boston; First National Bank, Chicago; Wells Fargo Bank, San Francisco.

The following large brokerage houses all have competent research departments and will make available studies, reports, and analyses upon request:

1. Merrill Lynch, Pierce, Fenner & Smith, Inc.
   One Liberty Plaza (165 Broadway)
   New York, N.Y. 10006
2. Bache & Co.
   100 Gold Street
   New York, N.Y. 10004
3. Paine, Webber, Jackson & Curtis, Inc.
   140 Broadway
   New York, N.Y. 10005
4. Kidder, Peabody & Co.
   10 Hanover Square
   New York, N.Y. 10005
5. Blyth Eastman Dillon
   One Chase Manhattan Plaza
   New York, N.Y. 10005
6. Hornblower & Weeks, Hemphill, Noyes
   8 Hanover St.
   New York, N.Y. 10004
7. Oppenheimer & Co.
   One New York Plaza
   New York, N.Y. 10004
8. Shields Model Roland
   44 Wall Street
   New York, N.Y. 10005
9. W. E. Hutton & Co.
   14 Wall St.
   New York, N.Y. 10005
10. Wertheim & Co.
    One Chase Manhattan Plaza
    New York, N.Y. 10005
11. Loeb, Rhoades & Co.
    42 Wall St.
    New York, N.Y. 10005
12. Smith, Barney & Co.
    20 Broad St.
    New York, N.Y. 10004
13. Reynolds Securities, Inc.
    120 Broadway
    New York, N.Y. 10005
14. Shearson Hayden Stone, Inc.
    767 Fifth Avenue
    New York, N.Y. 10022

These and many other brokerage houses are glad either to answer specific questions or to send their weekly or monthly publications upon request.

The Financial Services

In recent years so many financial and investment services have sprung up that it is almost as difficult to know which to use for what as it is to pick the right stock at the right time. The three leaders in the field are:

Standard & Poor's Corporation, 345 Hudson St., New York, N.Y., 10014
Moody's Investors Service, 99 Church St., New York, N.Y., 10007
The Value Line Investment Survey, 5 East 44th St., New York, N.Y. 10017

They publish a wide variety of financial and investment data, some of it so expensive and technical, such as the bond service, that the average investor seldom sees or hears of it. Basic, however, are the reference books —Standard & Poor's *Corporation Records* and Moody's *Manuals*. These are big, thick volumes for each year and by fields—industrials, rails, utilities, governments, etc. Each volume contains reports on thousands of corporations (or governmental bodies), giving the history and full financial data for a period of years. These volumes are kept up to date by current supplements—Standard & Poor's six volume *Corporation Records* are supplemented with a daily bulletin, while five Moody's *Manuals* are kept up to date by a biweekly report. A good library or a brokerage office will have both the basic volumes and the supplements.

All of the agencies have a bulletin service on all the leading companies. On one page (both sides) is condensed all the pertinent financial information about the company, its outlook, and prospects for its stock. An example of the Standard & Poor's bulletin is shown in Figure 15–1. Standard & Poor's has a special survey reviewing conditions industry by industry. It is called *Industry Surveys* and covers 45 leading industries, plus a summary of Canadian industries, together with over 1,200 of their constituent companies. The larger brokerage houses subscribe to at least one of these services and make them available to customers or prospective customers.

The Standard & Poor's *Stock Guide* is a pocket-size condensed handbook, issued monthly, containing a thumbnail sketch of essential facts about a given stock. Several thousand common and preferred stocks, listed and O–T–C, are covered. Two pages of one of these handbooks are shown in Figure 15–2. They are given away free of charge by some brokerage houses as a service to customers. Ask your broker for a copy.

Both Moody's and Standard & Poor's publish weekly or monthly bond guides. Moody's, for example, issues a weekly *Bond Survey*, a bimonthly *Bond Record;* and one page summaries of individual bond situations.

Some parts of both the Standard & Poor's and Moody's service are aimed primarily at the smaller investor. Standard & Poor's issues a weekly magazine, *The Outlook*, a daily *Facts and Forecast Service*, and an *Investment Advisory Survey*, which consists of a confidential bulletin featuring a supervised list of recommended investments. The master list of recommended issues grouped in four categories is shown in Figure 15–3. This appears from time to time in *The Outlook*.

In addition, there is the Standard & Poor's *Stock Summary*, a monthly digest on more than 1,922 widely traded stocks with 40 columns of information on each stock.

An interesting and useful newer publication is Standard & Poor's *Earnings Forecaster*, a weekly report of current earnings' estimates on over

FIGURE 15–2

STANDARD & POOR'S CORPORATION

INDEX	Ticker Symbol	STOCKS NAME OF ISSUE (Call Price of Pfd. Stocks)	Market	Earns &Div Ranking	Par Val.	Inst. Hold Cos	Inst. Hold Shs. (000)	PRINCIPAL BUSINESS	PRICE RANGE 1960-72 High	1960-72 Low	1973 High	1973 Low	1974 High	1974 Low	Aug. Sales in 100s	August, 1974 Last Sale Or Bid High	Low	Last	% Div. Yield	P-E Ratio
1	WY	Weyerhaeuser Co	[1]NYS,Bo,Ci,De,MW,PB	B+	1⅞	252	14242	Timber products: cartons	31⅛	5⅝	41⅛	22⅛	46	30½	10751	37¼	30½	32¼	e2.5	12
2	WFI	Wheelabrator-Frye	NYS,Bo,MW,PB.PS	NR	30¢	22	1076	Environ controls,ink,graphic	32⅞	8¼	23¼	9⅝	17½	8⅛	903	11¾	8⅛	9½	4.2	7
3	WLE	Wheeling & Lake Erie	NYS([10])	A	100	...	...	Leased by Norf & Westn RR	122	64	77	64	68	62	2	68	65½	60B	9.6	..
4	WHX	Wheeling Pitts Steel	NYS,Bo,PB,PS	NR	10	6	35	Large U.S. steel producer	62¾	9¾	21⅝	10¼	23¼	13¼	946	21¾	18	19¾	...	2
5	Pr B	6% cm Pr Pfd ([51]106)vtg	NYS([10])	B	100	...	...	fully integrated, producing	75½	44	64¾	54	61½	53¾	17	56	53¾	54¼	11.1	..
6	Pr	$5 cm Pfd (105 fr '75) vtg	NYS([10])	B	No	...	...	flat-rolled products	101½	35½	53½	43	51¾	45½	17	47½	46	46½	10.8	..
7	WPP	Whippany Paper Board	ASE	B	10¢	...	...	Paperboards for containers	19½	7⅜	11	7½	13	7¾	46	11¾	10⅞	11	5.5	11
8	WHR	Whirlpool Corp	NYS,Bo,MW,PB	A	1	67	4677	Home laundry eq, refrig etc	40⅛	3⅝	37½	23¼	29¾	12⅝	4696	24	12⅝	14⅝	5.5	9
9	WCB	Whitaker Cable	ASE	B	1	1	1	Electric wiring assemblies	13⅝	1¾	11¼	5⅜	6¾	4½	62	4⅞	4½	4¾	7.2	4
10	WSW	White Consol Indus	NYS,Bo,MW,PB	B	1	26	1695	Mach & eq: valves, controls:	35¾	1	21⅞	8⅝	12¼	8	1363	9⅞	8	8¼	8.5	3
11	Pr A	$3.00 cm A Pfd ([53]51)vtg	NYS	B	50	5	32	distr ind'l suppl: sew mach:	42	29½	45	39	41½	36⅝	11	37¾	36⅝	36⅝B	8.2	..
12	Pr C	$3.00 cm C Pfd ([54]52)vtg	NYS	B	50	2	68	household appl'n'c's heat'g	40½	28½	41½	34	38¾	29½	64	31½	30¼	30⅝	9.8	..
13	WH	White Motor	NYS,Bo,MW,PB,PS	B	1	18	847	Trucks:const'n,ind'l,farm eq	57½	9⅝	16	8⅛	14¼	8¾	1081	12⅝	10⅛	10⅞	3.7	3
14	WSHI	White Shield	OTC	NR	5¢	1	6	Oil/gas expl:toll collect eq	28	⅛	8⅛	1⅜	6	1⅛	1467	2⅜	1¾	1⅞B	...	d
15	WHT	Whitehall Corp	ASE	B—	10¢	3	52	Earth sciences: electr: aero	17⅜	⅜	4⅞	1⅞	2¾	1⅝	130	2	1⅝	1¾	...	4
16	WTG	Whiting Corp	ASE	B+	5	1	4	Mat'l handl'g eq: chem proc'g	43⅜	4½	19⅝	15	21⅞	15	65	17⅞	16	17⅛	8.2	4
17		Whitney Holding	OTC	...	No	5	51	Owns Whitney Nat'l Bk, N.O.	96	33½	102	93	107	99	....	105	103	104B	†3.8	12
18	WKR	Whittaker Corp	NYS,Bo,MW,PB,PS	B—	1	2	144	Metals,textiles & chemicals	45⅞	¾	7¾	1⅞	2⅞	1⅞	1680	2⅜	2	2⅛	...	8
19	WS	Wrrt (Purch 1 com at $50)	[2]ASE,Bo,MW	...	....	...	...	marine & recreation prod	10⅛	2	2¾	½	1	⅜	345	½	⅜	½	...	..
20	WRO	Wichita Indus	ASE,Bo	C	1	...	...	Ind'l controls:engr:oil,gas	11⅞	⅞	2½	1	2½	1⅛	246	2	1⅛	1⅝	...	10
21	WIX	Wickes Corp	NYS,MW,PS	A—	2½	22	461	Retail lumber/bldg supp:mfg	58⅜	7⅛	28⅜	10⅝	15⅞	10	1126	12½	10	10⅜	9.6	5
22	WIE	Wieboldt Stores	NYS	B	No	...	...	Dept store, Chic & suburbs	20¾	1⅛	7⅝	5⅜	6¼	3⅛	253	4⅛	3⅛	3¼	8.6	4
23	WCON	Wien Air Alaska	OTC	NR	1	3	128	Alaska intrastate airline	14¼	2¾	8⅜	4⅜	7⅞	5	366	5⅝	5	5B	...	11
24	WIEN	Wiener Corp	OTC	B	1	...	...	Retail shoe & apparel stores	26	4	17½	5¾	8	4⅜	80	6	4¾	4¾B	4.5	4
25	WILL	Wiley (John) & Sons	OTC	NR	1	9	160	College text, reference books	46¾	7¼	19¼	5½	9¼	6	61	7½	7	7½B	8.0	4
26	WMTT	Willamette Indus	OTC	B+	50¢	6	21	Mfr wood and paper products	31⅝	14¼	25¼	16¼	21¾	11	1279	14¾	11	11¼B	s6.4	4
27	WG	Willcox & Gibbs	ASE	NR	1	1	1	Apparel/textile supplies,eq	20⅝	3⅜	4⅜	2⅛	4½	2¼	353	3⅛	2½	2⅞B	3.5	4
28	WMH	Williamhouse-Regency	ASE	B+	10¢	8	123	Fine paper pr:plastics,publ	42⅛	1⅜	16⅝	5½	8⅛	4¾	194	6¾	5⅜	5⅞	5.1	3
29	WMS	Williams & Co	PB,Bo	NR	1	...	...	Dstr indust'l supplies: metals	19	10	14⅜	12	13½	11	9	11¼	11	11¼	†9.3	3
30	WMB	Williams Cos	NYS,Bo,PB,PS	B	1	134	2868	Const, operates pipelines:	52⅞	2 1/16	74	39	77	45⅜	5030	59¾	47⅝	59⅜	1.0	8
31	WS	A Wrrt (Purch 1 com at $20)	NYS,PB,PS	...	....	20	266	marketing: ag chems:steel	34¾	14½	54⅛	19	56⅞	27⅛	3278	39⅞	29	39¾	...	..
32	Pr	$0.80 cm Cv A Pfd ([60]37)vtg	NYS,PS	BB	No	3	42	dstr:LP-Gas:investing	50½	16	65⅛	35¼	69	42	251	53	43½	52½	1.5	..
33	WOC	Wilshire Oil Of Texas	ASE,Bo,PB,TS,VS	B	1	1	40	E'ltr'cs dstr,oil&gas,bank	14¼	1⅜	7¼	3⅞	7¾	5	751	5⅝	5	5⅛	2.0	8
34	WLB	Wilson Brothers	ASE,PS	B	1	...	...	Men's shirts, sportswear etc.	11⅜	1½	5⅞	2¾	3⅝	2¾	148	3⅛	2¾	2⅞	10.4	5
35	WILN	Wilson (H.J.)	OTC	NR	No	6	382	Discount stores: catalog	37	8½	31¾	7½	10¼	4¾	90	6¼	4¾	5B	...	4
36	WILS	Wilson Freight	OTC	NR	No	1	3	Interstate motor freight	14	3⅛	8¼	4¼	8¾	4¼	64	5¾	4⅞	5B	†6.6	3
37	WLTK	Wiltek Inc	OTC	NR	33⅓¢	1	15	Data communications equip	20½	1⅛	17½	6½	8¼	3	29	3¾	3	3B	...	7
38	WNK	Winkelman Stores	ASE,De	B	3	...	...	Ladies specialty stores	19	4⅝	10¾	5⅜	7⅛	5⅝	57	6⅞	6⅜	6⅞	7.3	4
39	WIN	Winn-Dixie Stores	NYS,PB	A+	1	26	414	Food supermkts: southeast	42	14⅛	41¾	29¼	44⅜	22¾	1071	36¼	22¾	27	4.9	11
40	B	Cl B Com Accum Cv vtg	NYS	...	1	...	...		49	18¾	48¾	35¼	53¾	38	6	47	38	30B	...	..
41	WGO	Winnebago Indus	NYS,Bo,Ci,MW,PB,PS	NR	50¢	6	108	Mfr recreation vehicles: equip	48¼	1	27½	2⅞	7⅝	3⅛	2396	6½	4⅞	5⅛	...	d
42	WSTO	Winn's Stores	OTC	NR	1¼	2	22	Retail variety stores, Texas	37½	6⅞	27	10½	14	8	38	9¾	8½	8½B	6.5	4
43	WNST	Winston (N K) Corp	OTC	Liq	No	...	...	Large-scale prop development	11¼	1	10⅛	4⅞	10⅜	5⅜	142	6	5⅜	5⅜B	...	5
44	WNM	Winston Mills	ASE	NR	10¢	...	...	Textiles-double-knit fabrics	24¾	1¾	7⅞	2⅛	3⅜	1⅛	58	1⅝	1⅛	1⅛	...	4
45	WJCK	Winter (Jack)	OTC	NR	1	...	...	Apparel mfr: fabric stores	11½	1¼	8¾	5⅛	9¾	6¼	343	9	7	7¼B	6.9	2

Uniform Footnote Explanations—See Page 1. Other: [1]PS. [2]PB,PS. [51]To 12-4-74, scale to $100 in'79. [52]®$2.40,'73. [53]To 12-31-74, scale to $50 in'75. [54]To 3-31-75, scale to $50 in'78. [55]Whitney Nat'l Bank,adj to hold'g co shrs. [56]1/10 Wrrt. [57]Fiscal Dec'69:4 Mo Apr $d0.33. [58]®$0.65,'73. [59]®$4.27,'73. [60]Fr 10-16-76, scale to $35 in '78. [61]®$0.46,'73. [62]®$1.89,'73. [63]Incr.each year to 1.54 shs fr 1-1-81. [64]Co plans fiscal year change to August. [65]®$1.03,'74. [66]®$2.33,'73.

COMMON AND PREFERRED STOCKS

INDEX	Some Divs. Ea. Yr. Since	DIVIDENDS — Latest Payment — Per $	Date	Ex. Div.	$ So Far 1974	Total Ind. Rate	$ Paid 1973	FINANCIAL POSITION — Mil-$ — Cash& Equiv.	Curr. Assets	Curr. Liabs.	Balance Sheet Date	CAPITALIZATION Long Term Debt Mil-$	Shs. 000 Pfd.	Com.	Ended	$ Per Shr—EARNINGS—$ Per Shr — Years — 1970	1971	1972	1973	1974	Last 12 Mos.	INTERIM EARNINGS OR REMARKS Period	$—Per Share—$ 1973	1974	INDEX
1◆	1933	Q0.20	9-3-74	7-29	0.60	d0.80	†0.47	24.7	478.	349.	12-30-73	526.	...	128588	Dc	0.93	0.82	1.17	2.74	E2.70	2.62	6 Mo Jun	1.58	1.46	1
2◆	1951	Q0.10	7-31-74	7-8	0.20	0.40	0.40	29.1	133.	62.2	12-31-73	45.0	...	7978	Dc	□0.08	□0.65	•1.01	△1.26	E1.45	1.37	6 Mo Jun	0.51	0.62	2
3	1939	Q1.43¾	8-1-74	6-28	4.31¼	5.75	5.75	...	...	...		9.10	116	340	Divs. payable at $5.75 rate under lease										3
4	1974	0.35	10-1-74	9-6	0.35	Nil	....	31.5	313.	134.	12-31-73	★150.	566	3654	Dc	0.49	△0.44	△2.78	△4.10	....	9.35	6 Mo Jun	1.50	6.75	4
5	1969	Q1.50	10-1-74	9-6	6.00	6.00	6.00	...	...	...		....	238	...	Dc	20.37	19.74	55.48	75.86	....	....				5
6	1968	Q1.25	10-1-74	9-6	5.00	5.00	5.00	...	...	...		....	328	...	Dc	10.41	9.95	35.83	50.60	....	....				6
7	1961	Q0.15	9-16-74	8-26	0.45	0.60	0.60	5.66	20.1	6.41	6-30-73	2.36	...	±2427	Je	±0.35	±0.28	□±0.02	±0.71	....	1.00	9 Mo Mar	±0.48	±0.77	7
8◆	1929	Q0.20	9-14-74	8-26	0.60	0.80	0.682	16.5	511.	262.	12-31-73	73.5	...	36047	Dc	□1.00	1.41	1.91	2.41	E1.70	1.83	6 Mo Jun	1.16	0.58	8
9◆	1937	Q0.08½	9-30-74	9-9	0.25½	0.34	0.34	1.04	17.8	6.86	5-31-73	7.89	...	1225	My	0.67	•0.44	•1.10	1.34	P1.29	1.29				9
10◆	1967	Q0.17½	9-20-74	8-26	0.50	0.70	0.55	28.1	403.	125.	12-31-73	204.	p1444	11073	Dc	□2.05	1.55	2.22	[52]△2.70	E2.75	2.83	6 Mo Jun	△1.37	1.50	10
11	1966	Q0.75	8-1-74	7-9	2.25	3.00	3.00	Mand red'p 5% ea Aug 1				....	219	...	Dc	17.95	14.52	19.72	24.14	....	....	Whitin Mach Wks merger			11
12	1968	Q0.75	8-1-74	7-9	2.25	3.00	3.00	Mand red'p 5% ea March 1				....	1152	...	Dc	17.95	14.52	19.72	24.14	....	....	Bullard Co merger			12
13	1974	Q0.10	9-24-74	9-4	0.30	0.40	....	15.3	432.	211.	12-31-73	148.	158	8241	Dc	d3.27	□0.19	•0.79	•[52]2.46	E3.25	3.02	6 Mo Jun	△1.23	1.79	13
14	.....	h....	3-29-69	1-10	....	Nil	....	p12.8	18.0	11.9	12-31-73	3.37	...	5701	Dc	d0.69	□d0.80	△0.08	□d0.33	....	d0.26	6 Mo Jun	d0.08	•d0.01	14
15	.....	None Paid			....	Nil	....	0.66	9.47	5.12	12-31-73	5.00	...	1970	Dc	0.13	0.48	0.48	0.42	....	0.47	6 Mo Jun	0.25	0.30	15
16	1936	Q0.35	7-26-74	6-28	1.00	1.40	1.15	0.86	23.4	11.3	4-30-74	0.34	...	584	Ap	1.80	1.75	1.31	1.79	2.97	3.99	3 Mo Jul	0.44	1.46	16
17	1885	†1.00	7-1-74	6-14	†3.50	4.00	†4.00	Book Value $77.12			12-31-73	....	...	1114	Dc	△[55]8.57	△[55]7.31	△7.50	△8.96	....	8.96				17
18	.....	[56]....	5-5-69	3-17	....	Nil	....	19.7	376.	228.	10-31-73	182.	386	20560	Oc	□0.27	□0.38	□0.37	□d0.19	E0.25	0.22	9 Mo Jul	□d0.03	0.38	18
19	.....	Terms&trad.basis should be checked in detail						Warrants expire May 5,1979				....	...	4956	Oc	....	....	....	....	....	....				19
20	.....	h....	10-11-63	9-16	....	Nil	....	0.23	0.86	1.08	12-31-73	0.45	...	1764	Dc	d0.05	0.01	△d0.07	0.03	....	0.17	6 Mo Jun	0.01	•0.15	20
21	1895	Q0.25	12-9-74	11-1	1.00	1.00	1.00	15.0	344.	170.	1-26-74	121.	...	9706	Ja	1.08	1.65	2.03	2.20	E2.00	2.37	6 Mo Jul	1.15	□1.32	21
22◆	1967	Q0.07	7-1-74	6-11	0.20¼	0.28	s0.244	3.04	39.9	23.2	2-2-74	19.6	8	3064	Ja	0.64	0.46	△0.76	△0.83	E0.75	0.68	6 Mo Jul	0.18	0.03	22
23	.....	0.02¼	1-2-68	11-28	....	Nil	....	0.40	8.91	7.34	6-30-74	15.7	...	3743	Dc	0.04	0.04	0.02	0.18	....	0.44	12 Mo Jun	0.04	0.44	23
24◆	1969	Q0.053	10-10-74	9-19	0.213	0.213	0.213	1.05	7.52	3.59	12-31-73	4.00	...	755	Dc	0.61	0.85	1.07	1.20	....	1.26	6 Mo Jun	0.62	0.68	24
25	1904	Q0.15	7-15-74	7-3	0.37	0.60	0.42	4.47	30.0	11.0	4-30-74	....	...	1542	Ap	[57]1.59	1.65	□1.37	1.61	□1.86	2.04	3 Mo Jul	0.56	0.74	25
26◆	1962	Q0.18	9-6-74	8-16	0.50	0.72	s0.531	15.9	70.4	39.4	12-31-73	88.7	...	11582	Dc	0.97	1.15	1.85	2.88	....	3.04	6 Mo Jun	1.67	1.83	26
27	1974	0.05	7-15-74	5-24	0.05	0.10	....	1.32	26.8	18.4	12-31-73	★10.2	266	±2668	Dc	□0.34	△d0.09	△0.47	∫[58]0.67	....	0.74	6 Mo Jun	0.30	0.37	27
28	1973	Q0.07½	9-16-74	8-26	0.19½	0.30	0.21	4.37	26.8	5.11	6-30-73	6.27	...	2986	Je	1.26	□1.15	1.30	1.50	P1.73	1.73				28
29	1918	Q0.25	9-10-74	8-26	0.75	1.05	†1.02	1.17	33.4	13.1	12-31-73	....	...	1113	Dc	1.60	△1.07	△1.69	2.63	....	3.41	6 Mo Jun	1.27	2.05	29
30	1974	Q0.15	9-30-74	9-3	0.35	0.60	....	180.	376.	132.	12-31-73	400.	1131	9205	Dc	△3.29	△3.33	3.94	[59]4.65	E7.00	◉5.63	6 Mo Jun	◉2.47	◉3.83	30
31	.....	Terms&trad.basis should be checked in detail						Warrants expire Jan 1, 1976				....	...	1976	Dc	....	....	....	....	....	....				31
32	1969	Q0.20	9-30-74	9-3	0.60	0.80	0.80	Conv into 0.9 shrs common				....	1131	...	Dc	19.79	24.50	32.65	42.82	....	....	Mgr of Edgcomb Steel			32
33◆	1974	0.05	8-5-74	6-28	0.10	0.10	4%Stk	1.79	9.25	4.90	12-31-73	8.18	...	6985	Dc	□0.12	△0.09	0.20	•[61]0.48	....	0.66	6 Mo Jun	•0.19	0.37	33
34◆	1970	Q0.07½	7-1-74	6-10	0.22½	0.30	0.296	1.57	16.4	4.24	12-31-73	5.57	...	2546	Dc	0.46	0.60	0.68	△0.54	....	0.57	6 Mo Jun	0.25	0.28	34
35◆	.....	None Paid			....	Nil	....	1.25	25.6	11.2	12-31-73	10.1	...	2450	Je	0.48	0.61	0.75	1.04	....	1.31	9 Mo Mar	0.90	1.17	35
36◆	1961	Q0.07	7-11-74	6-14	0.20	0.33	†0.29	1.63	7.99	5.74	12-31-73	11.8	...	1692	Dc	▲0.56	■1.08	▲1.16	▲1.60	....	1.68	24 Wk Jun	0.64	0.72	36
37◆	.....	None Since Public			....	Nil	....	0.37	15.2	4.54	10-31-73	★15.0	...	1322	Oc	•0.14	•0.16	□0.25	∫□0.30	....	0.41	6 Mo Apr	0.07	0.18	37
38	1959	Q0.12½	8-19-74	7-23	0.32½	0.50	0.40	1.01	18.1	10.1	1-26-74	0.97	...	1037	Ja	0.22	0.70	1.29	1.47	....	1.62	6 Mo Jul	0.57	0.72	38
39◆	1934	M0.11	9-30-74	9-9	0.96	1.32	1.23	51.4	202.	82.8	6-30-73	2.99	...	±19161	Je	1.45	1.73	1.98	[62]2.12	E2.50	2.48	40 Wk Apr	1.54	1.90	39
40◆	.....	None Paid			....	Nil	....	Cv into 1.225 to 12-31-74[63]				....	...	6368	Je	....	....	....	....	....	....				40
41◆	.....	None Paid			....	Nil	....	1.56	54.5	24.9	2-23-74	....	...	25214	Fb	0.19	0.56	□0.77	□d0.25	[64]....	d0.40	3 Mo May	0.16	0.01	41
42◆	⑦63	Q0.13¾	7-29-74	7-9	0.41¼	0.55	0.52½	0.33	12.0	4.08	12-31-73	0.22	...	1000	Dc	1.29	1.61	1.79	1.84	....	2.05	6 Mo Jun	0.71	0.92	42
43	.....	None Paid			....	Nil	....	0.96	...	...	2-28-74	3.80	...	2292	Fb	d0.81	d0.86	d0.62	•[65]1.11	....	1.18	3 Mo May	△d0.08	□d0.01	43
44	.....	None Paid			....	Nil	....	4.02	16.8	11.2	12-1-73	4.45	...	1536	Nv	△0.90	△1.94	□0.60	∫0.70	....	0.25	6 Mo May	0.51	0.06	44
45◆	1972	Q0.12½	10-31-74	10-11	0.36¼	0.50	0.12	2.79	21.2	9.72	12-31-73	0.75	1	2500	Dc	0.64	0.44	1.12	[66]2.41	....	3.00	6 Mo Jun	1.00	1.59	45

◆ **Stock Splits & Divs By Line Reference Index** [1]2-for-1,'73. [2]Reverse 1-for-3,'72. [8]3-for-1,'72. [9]3-for-2,'72. [10]Adj to 5%,'72. [22]Adj to 5%,'73. [24]50%, '71. [26]Adj to 3%,'73. [33]Adj for 4%,'73. [34]2-for-1,'71:4-for-3,'72. [35]2-for-1,'72. [36]2-for-1,'72. [37]3-for-1,'72. [39]3-for-2,'72. [40]3-for-2,'72. [41]2-for-1,'71,'72. [42]2-for-1,'71. [45]5-for-4 Jan'74,2-for-1 Jul'74.

Source: Standard & Poor's *Stock Guide*.

FIGURE 15–3

MASTER LIST OF RECOMMENDED ISSUES

GROUP 1: FOUNDATION STOCKS FOR LONG-TERM GAIN

These issues are basic building blocks for the portfolio. They offer the prospect of long-term appreciation, along with moderate but growing income. The investor seeking to build an estate should start with stocks from this list, augmenting them with issues from other groups according to his objectives and temperament.

Earnings Per Share ($) 1973	E1974	E1975	Indicated Div. $	1973-75 Price Range	Recent Price	P/E Ratio	Yield %		Annual Growth Rates—for Latest 5 Years— Sales	Earn.	Div.	▼Price Action vs. Mkt. 5-26-70 to 1-11-73	Since 1-11-73	Last Ref. Page
2.36	A2.55	2.80	1.24	37⅜-22¼	30	10.7	4.1	Campbell Soup (July)	8%	8%	3%	0.74	1.53	381
[1]1.61	[1]2.40	[1]2.75	[1]0.90	19⅜-10⅝	15	5.5	6.0	Canadian Pacific	5	22	4	0.94	1.53	478
[4]2.14	[4]P2.55	[4]3.00	0.80	51½-20⅞	29	9.7	2.8	Citicorp	—	[4]16	7	1.62	1.21	491
2.94	6.40	7.00	1.40	103¾-54⅞	55	7.9	2.6	→Dow Chemical	12	28	4	1.44	1.83	414
10.90	13.00	10.50	5.30	70 -46½	67	6.4	7.9	Exxon Corp.	12	19	2	0.99	1.26	434
3.21	3.35	3.45	1.60	75⅞-30	34	9.9	4.7	General Electric	7	18	2	1.37	0.79	390
8.34	2.60	3.25	3.40	84⅝-28⅞	35	10.8	9.7	General Motors	10	4	3	0.78	0.74	403
3.60	6.50	5.00	2.00	57 -31⅝	37	7.4	5.4	International Paper	7	19	3	0.83	1.50	383
3.70	3.75	4.25	1.92	50⅜-26⅞	34	8.0	5.7	→Kraftco Corp.	8	6	2	0.80	1.24	415
2.82	3.50	4.00	1.60	40½-16⅜	27	6.8	5.9	Lone Star Gas	8	16	6	1.22	1.16	415
6.90	9.35	9.25	2.40	75¾-39⅜	44	4.8	5.5	Monsanto	7	34	2	1.06	1.41	439
3.68	A3.85	4.40	1.80	120 -67	80	18.2	2.3	Procter & Gamble (June)	12	10	7	1.60	1.19	403
3.66	7.50	7.00	1.80	55 -34⅞	36	4.0	5.5	→Standard Oil (Ind.)	10	21	3	1.34	1.71	415
5.50	9.50	9.00	1.98	56¾-27¼	44	6.3	4.1	Union Oil of Calif.	10	17	3	0.96	1.52	406

GROUP 2: STOCKS WITH PROMISING GROWTH PROSPECTS

These stocks promise to enjoy well above average growth rates in earnings per share for the foreseeable future. Stocks in the second category carry a higher degree of risk, but by the same token offer greater reward potential. Income is not a consideration here.

Established Growth

Earnings Per Share ($) 1973	E1974	E1975	Indicated Div. $	1973-75 Price Range	Recent Price	P/E Ratio	Yield %		Latest 5-Year Growth Rates Sales	Earn.	No. of Earn. Gains '69-'73	Interim ▪Earn. Trend	▼Price Action vs. Mkt. 5-26-70 to 1-11-73	Since 1-11-73	Last Ref. Page
1.25	1.40	1.50	0.80	48¾- 26⅛	30	20.0	2.7	Amer. Home Products	12%	12%	5	+ 13	1.34	1.26	478
3.16	3.70	4.05	1.52	71¾- 30⅝	50	12.3	3.0	Bristol-Myers	10	10	4	+ 18	0.83	1.21	401
4.05	3.60	3.70	[6]1.56	151¾- 57⅝	63	17.0	2.5	Eastman Kodak	9	11	5	− 17	1.44	0.74	401
10.79	13.00	13.75	6.00	365¼-150½	163	11.9	3.7	Int. Business Machines	10	14	5	+ 24	0.97	0.84	390
3.96	A4.33	3.65	1.85	123¼- 41½	51	13.9	3.6	Sears, Roebuck (Jan.)	8	9	5	− 18	1.33	0.72	431
1.52	A2.29	2.65	0.40	64¼- 23⅛	35	13.2	1.1	•Syntex (July)	16	28	4	+ 30	2.04	1.52	466

More Speculative Growth

Earnings Per Share ($) 1973	E1974	E1975	Mill. Shs. Outst.	1973-75 Price Range	Recent Price	P/E Ratio	Yield %		Latest 5-Year Growth Rates Sales	Earn.	No. of Earn. Gains '69-'73	Interim ▪Earn. Trend	▼Price Action vs. Mkt. 5-26-70 to 1-11-73	Since 1-11-73	Last Ref. Page
1.45	A1.69	1.95	16.9	44¾- 20⅜	30	15.4	1.3	→Becton, Dickinson (Sept.)	14%	11%	4	+ 17%	0.72	1.22	413
1.05	2.25	3.60	18.6	26 - 11¼	29	8.1	2.4	MAPCO	18	33	5	+221	3.63	2.36	414
4.65	7.25	11.00	9.9	77 - 39	56	5.1	1.1	Williams Companies	26	15	5	+ 48	1.90	1.79	461

EARNINGS are for calendar years or for fiscal years ending as indicated after names. Unless otherwise noted, they are based on common and common share equivalents, excluding nonrecurring items and including restatements. A—Actual. E—Estimated. P—Preliminary. *Of the following year.

INDICATED DIVIDENDS include actual or possible extras. PRICE/EARNINGS RATIOS are based on latest shown estimated or actual earnings.

Stocks are listed on the New York Stock Exchange, except as indicated. •American Stock Exchange.

▼A figure above 1.0 indicates that the stock outperformed the S & P industrial stock price index in this period. It is computed by taking the ratio of the stock's price at the end of the period vs. the beginning of the period and dividing it by the corresponding ratio of the index.

▪This column compares share earnings of the latest six months with those of the corresponding year-earlier period.

1,400 companies by S & P and other leading investment organizations and brokerage firms. Continuously updated, it provides a quick check of the various estimates against one another. The source of each estimate is given.[3]

[3] So extensive have S & P services become that it now issues a brochure entitled: *Standard & Poor's Services and Publications Cover Every Financial Information Need.* A free copy may be obtained by writing to the firm at 345 Hudson Street, New York,

FIGURE 15–3 (continued)

GROUP 3: CYCLICAL/SPECULATIVE STOCKS

This group comprises stocks selected for high reward potentials stemming from a variety of considerations—including emerging opportunities, turnaround situations, stocks to benefit from cyclical upswings, and the like. Readers can expect to see more frequent changes in this list than in the others. The risk factor in some of the issues in this group may be high and the stocks recommended may not be suitable for those concerned with income or with investment grade securities.

Earnings Per Share ($) 1973	E1974	E1975	Indicated Div. $	1973-75 Price Range	Recent Price	P/E Ratio	Yield %		Remarks
4.19	P4.65	4.65	1.80	51¼-20	23	4.9	7.8	**Bendix (Sept.)**	Cost efficiency aiding earnings.
[3]4.01	[3]7.00	[3]7.75	1.70	49⅞-26¾	40	5.2	4.3	**Burlington Northern**	Oil, gas, coal and land holdings add to potentials.
[5]4.84	[5]3.75	[5]5.00	2.60	43⅝-23⅛	35	7.0	7.4	**Continental Corp.**	Expected upturn in underwriting brightens 1975 prospects.
1.84	4.75	6.00	0.60	29½-12½	26	4.3	2.3	**→Eastern Gas & Fuel**	Sustained strength in coal markets supporting earnings growth.
1.58	A3.59	9.00	1.28	40¾-15¼	33	3.7	3.9	**→Int. Minerals (June)**	Worldwide fertilizer shortage enhances prospects.
2.20	A3.52	4.40	1.50	58⅜-24¼	44	10.0	3.4	**Joy Mfg.(Sept.)**	Coal mining gear in strong demand due to energy shortage.
2.52	2.30	1.60	0.15	24⅜- 6¾	10	6.3	1.5	**Louisiana-Pacific**	Marketing flexibility enhances long-term prospects.
3.13	A2.80	2.85	1.10	47⅜-10¼	13	4.6	8.5	**Macy (R.H.) (July)**	Internal profit improvement progams enhancing potential.
†3.00	†3.45	†3.60	0.72	46¼-13⅝	17	4.7	4.2	**NCR Corp.**	Speculative appeal based on new products, labor cost savings.
4.48	4.60	N.E.	1.70	47 -20	26	5.7	6.5	**PPG Industries**	Modest valuation underrates favorable long-range outlook.
3.03	3.80	4.25	0.80	39⅞-20	26	6.1	3.1	**Raytheon**	Energy-related services spurring earnings gains.
2.88	4.75	3.90	1.40	37½-18	20	5.1	7.0	**St. Regis Paper**	Aided by a strong asset base, broad product mix.
1.28	[7]2.40	2.35	0.30	52⅛-13	20	8.5	1.5	**Sante Fe Int.**	North Sea oil adds plus to offshore drilling, construction.
[3]4.47	[3]6.00	[5]6.50	2.12	52¾-29¾	42	6.5	5.1	**Southern Railway**	Aided by area growth, profit-oriented management.

GROUP 4: LIBERAL INCOME WITH INFLATION PROTECTION

If high yield alone were the goal, it would be simple to devise a list of high-quality bonds yielding 8% or more. But the individual who must rely to a major extent on his investments for income must take into account the prospect of continuing inflation. Accordingly, this group presents a list of quality high-yielding stocks which in our opinion offer the prospect of dividend growth at least sufficient to compensate for inflation over a period of time.

Earnings Per Share ($)			Indicated	1973-75	Recent	P/E	Yield		Dividend History				Inflation	Last
1973	E1974	E1975	Div. $	Price Range	Price	Ratio	%		10-Year Growth Rate	No. of Ann. Incr. 1965-74	[9]10-Year Avg. Payout	Latest Increase	Hedge Ratio††	Ref. Page
4.98	5.35	5.60	3.40	55 -39⅝	48	8.6	7.1	**American Tel. & Tel.**	4%	7	61%	10- 1-74	1.04	985
[4]5.02	[4]P6.47	[4]7.10	2.88	54⅞-27¾	32	4.5	9.0	**Chemical N. Y.**	5	6	51	1- 1-71	1.03	439
8.34	11.25	8.50	3.20	75½-30⅝	35	4.1	9.1	**Mobil Oil**	8	9	42	6-10-74	1.44	390
5.89	7.20	7.60	2.88	55¾-36½	53	7.0	5.4	**Reynolds (R.J.) Indust.**	4	9	50	12- 5-74	1.07	415
[3]3.77	[3]4.50	[3]4.65	2.24	44⅝-25	28	6.0	8.0	**Southern Pacific**	4	9	52	9-16-74	1.07	431
4.75	[8]6.00	5.00	2.00	43⅝-20	23	4.6	8.7	**Texaco**	6	9	46	3- 8-74	1.16	383

††A figure of 1.0 indicates that dividend growth exactly offset the impact of inflation in the 1964-73 period; a higher ratio indicates the degree to which the growth in annual dividend payments exceeded the rise in the Consumer Price Index in this period.

[1]Canadian currency. [3]Consolidated, GAAP accounting basis. [4]Net operating earnings. [5]Assumes conv. of pfd. shares. [6]Excluding extras. [7]Includes $0.49 a share from sale of minor portion of Thistle Field interest. [8]Reflects change to LIFO accounting. [9]Ratio calculated through 1974, with 1974 earnings on an estimated basis. †Fully diluted.

Changes since December 9: →Additions: In Group 1, Dow Chemical, Kraftco Corp., Standard Oil (Indiana); in Group 2, Becton, Dickinson; in Group 3, Eastern Gas & Fuel, International Minerals. **Deletions:** From Group 3, Allied Chemical, Rockower Bros. **Other Changes:** Mobil Oil transferred from Group 1 to Group 4.

Source: Standard & Poor's, *The Outlook,* January 13, 1975.

Moody's *Stock Survey,* a weekly letter, reviews market conditions and analyzes various investment opportunities. *Moody's Handbook of Common Stocks,* contains charts and summary reports on 1,010 common stocks. It contains a 19 year "Price Action Profile" chart, with earnings and dividends, for each of the stocks; 10 year comparative statistics (income, profit margins, payout, price/earnings ratio, yield); a brief description of the company's history and its products, and Moody's analytical characterization of the stock. The *Handbook* is published quarterly (see Figure 15–4). It also

N.Y. 10014. There are also offices in leading cities across the country. Moody's also publishes a brochure describing its services. It is entitled: *How to Use Moody's Special Library Service of Financial Publications and Investment Services;* a free copy may be obtained by writing to Moody's Investor Service, 99 Church Street, New York, N.Y. 10007.

FIGURE 15–4

Here is an actual listing from Moody's *Handbook* with the vital facts you'll find for each of 1,010 stocks.

GENERAL MOTORS CORPORATION

LISTED	SYMBOL	INDICATED DIV.	RECENT PRICE	PRICE RANGE (1974)	YIELD
NYSE	GM	$3.40	35	56 - 35	9.7%

COMPANY HAS ACHIEVED AN ABOVE AVERAGE LONG-TERM EARNINGS RECORD AMONG AUTOMOTIVE MANUFACTURERS. THE HIGH GRADE COMMON OFFERS A LIBERAL YIELD.

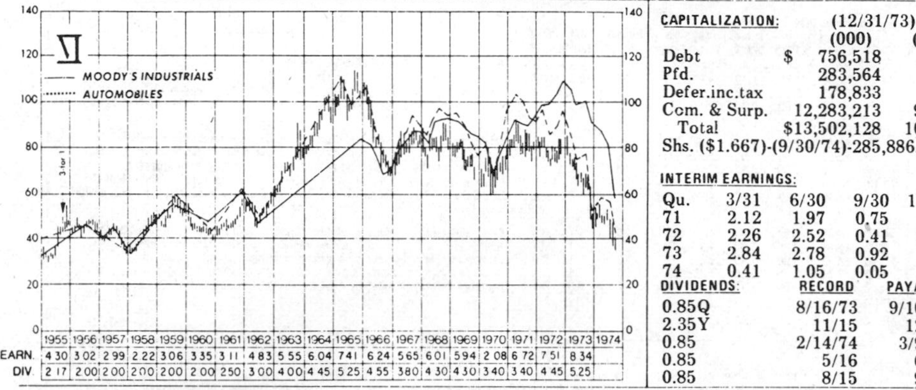

	1955	1956	1957	1958	1959	1960	1961	1962	1963	1964	1965	1966	1967	1968	1969	1970	1971	1972	1973	1974
EARN.	4 30	3 02	2 99	2 22	3 06	3 35	3 11	4 83	5 55	6 04	7 41	6 24	5 65	6 01	5 94	2 08	6 72	7 51	8 34	
DIV.	2 17	2 00	2 00	2 00	2 00	2 00	2 50	3 00	4 00	4 45	5 25	4 55	3 80	4 30	4 30	3 40	3 40	4 45	5 25	

CAPITALIZATION: (12/31/73)

	(000)	(%)
Debt	$ 756,518	5.6
Pfd.	283,564	2.1
Defer.inc.tax	178,833	1.3
Com. & Surp.	12,283,213	91.0
Total	$13,502,128	100.0%

Shs. ($1.667)-(9/30/74)-285,886,274

INTERIM EARNINGS:

Qu.	3/31	6/30	9/30	12/31
71	2.12	1.97	0.75	1.88
72	2.26	2.52	0.41	2.32
73	2.84	2.78	0.92	1.80
74	0.41	1.05	0.05	

DIVIDENDS:	RECORD	PAYABLE
0.85Q	8/16/73	9/10/73
2.35Y	11/15	12/10
0.85	2/14/74	3/9/74
0.85	5/16	6/10
0.85	8/15	9/10

BACKGROUND:

The world's largest automotive manufacturer, GM's worldwide factory sales of passenger cars and trucks in 1973 totaled 8.7 mill. units. 77% of worldwide dollar sales in 1973 represented U.S. operations, 8% Canadian and overseas 15%. Through a dealer organization of about 13,000, GM penetrated 52.5% of the domestic passenger car market. In 1973, the Chevrolet division accounted for over 44% of the Company's 5.3 mill. U.S. passenger car factory sales. Principal overseas manufacturing locations are West Germany (Opel), England (Vauxhall) and Australia (Holden). Because of the energy shortage, GM is stepping up production of Chevrolet Vega and compact models.

RECENT DEVELOPMENTS:

Net income for the first nine months of 1974 of $442.3 mill. declined 76.5% as sales fell 17.3%. Net income in the third quarter fell 93.8%. During the period, production was hurt by strikes at some GM assembly plants and at outside suppliers, which caused parts shortages. Also, for the first nine months, beside lower volume, earnings were reduced by inflationary increases of materials, components, and wages, which were only partially recovered by price increases. Sales of $35.8 bill. increased 17.8% in 1973 while net income gained 10.9%.

PROSPECTS:

Sales for passenger cars are not expected to show a rebound from 1974's low level until later in 1975. Tentatively, some improvement in 1975 earnings is anticipated over the $3.25 a share estimated for 1974. Truck sales are expected to continue strong. Besides lower volume of passenger cars and a shift to smaller, more economical units, profit margins may continue to be restricted by costs of product improvements including government-mandated equipment, together with rising labor and material costs.

STATISTICS:

YEAR	GROSS REVS. ($ MILL.)	OPER. PROFIT MARGIN %	NET INCOME ($ 000)	WORK CAP. ($ MILL.)	SENIOR CAPITAL ($ MILL.)	NO. SHS. OUT. (000)	EARN. PER SH. $	DIV. PER SH. $	DIV. PAY. %	PRICE RANGE	PRICE X EARN.	AVG. YIELD %
64	16,997	18.4	1,734,782	3,651	515.5	285,185	6.04	4.45	74	102^5 - 77^2	14.9	4.9
65	20,734	19.0	2,125,606	3,685	515.1	285,066	7.41	5.25	71	113^6 - 91^2	13.8	5.1
66	20,209	16.0	1,793,392	3,606	571.0	285,172	6.24	4.55	73	108^2 - 65^5	13.9	5.2
67	20,026	14.5	1,627,276	4,006	628.4	285,703	5.65	3.80	67	89^3 - 67^4	13.9	4.8
68	22,755	14.9	1,731,915	4,230	567.8	285,795	6.01	4.30	72	89^7 - 72^5	13.5	5.3
69	24,295	13.6	1,710,695	4,352	600.6	285,763	5.94	4.30	72	83^3 - 65^4	12.5	5.8
70	18,752	3.5	609,087	3,010	565.8	286,057	2.08	3.40	—	81^3 - 59^4	33.9	4.8
71	28,264	12.9	1,935,709	4,530	899.2	286,225	6.72	3.40	51	91^1 - 73^3	12.2	4.1
72	30,435	13.3	2,162,807	5,565	1,074.4	287,617	7.51	4.45	59	84^6 - 71^2	10.4	5.7
73	35,798	11.9	2,398,103	6,197	1,040.1	287,617	8.34	5.25	63	84^5 - 44^7	7.8	8.1

TAX FREE IN PENNA.

INCORPORATED: Oct. 13, 1916--Delaware

PRINCIPAL OFFICE: 3044 W. Grand Blvd. Detroit, Mich. 48202

ANNUAL MEETING: Fourth Friday in May

NUMBER OF STOCKHOLDERS: 1,283,260

TRANSFER AGENT: Company office in New York; Bank of America, San Francisco, Calif.; Wilmington Trust Co., Delaware

REGISTRAR: Chase Manhattan Bank, N.Y.; Bank of Delaware, Wilmington, Del.; Wells Fargo Bank, San Francisco, Calif.

INSTIT. HOLDINGS: NO.: 703; SHS.: 14,819,010

OFFICERS

CHAIRMAN: R.C. Gerstenberg

PRESIDENT: E.N. Cole

SECRETARY: C. Thomas

TREASURER: F.A. Smith

Source: *Moody's Handbook of Common Stocks*, Second Quarter 1974 edition.

has an Investors' Advisory Service, offering subscribers a review of their present holdings plus recommendations about what to buy or sell.

Both Moody's and Standard & Poor's now use computers extensively in investment analysis and investment information retrieval. Standard & Poor's has a variety of computer derived and automated financial services. These include *Compustat,* which is a comprehensive corporate data bank with up to 20 years of annual financial statistics and 10 years of quarterly information for each of several thousand companies, on magnetic tape. Also *Comparative Analysis,* tailor made comparative studies of approximately 3,000 companies, supplemented by continuously updated, computer printout financial summaries. And *Financial Dynamics,* a computerized financial data library, updated daily, covering almost a thousand companies and 115 industries. Services such as these, however, are primarily for the experts and the professionals.

THE VALUE LINE (5 East 44th St., New York, N.Y., 10017) has an interesting technique, which may be seen in Figure 15–5. It publishes standard charts showing the stock performance of the leading companies and then adds a line indicating how the service believes the stock is likely to move over the next 12 months and over the next 3 to 5 years. The charts and text are revised quarterly. In addition, this service supplies reports recommending "special situations," a fortnightly letter of market comment and advice, a report on the Value Line's model fund, and a *Convertible Survey* covering warrants, convertible bonds, and convertible preferreds. It also publishes a weekly selection and opinion report.

THE AMERICAN INSTITUTE FOR ECONOMIC RESEARCH (Great Barrington, Mass.) in the investment field publishes a weekly *Research Report,* a semimonthly *Investment Bulletin,* and special studies from time to time. The *Investment Bulletin* covers three typical investment plans, all designed for the long term, although with different objectives. It recommends purchases or sales of securities for each plan and explains the reasons for its recommendation.

BABSON'S REPORTS (Wellesley Hills, Mass.) are designed for the investor who has at least $10,000, half for investment in common stock. The weekly *Babson Report* comments on market trends, but, in addition, the subscriber's investment situation is analyzed and purchases or sales are suggested. The subscriber gets a one page report on each company's stock owned—a red bordered report if Babson's thinks it is not particularly sound, a green border if it is all right.

INDICATOR DIGEST, INC. (Palisades Park, New Jersey 07650) covers stock market timing by reviewing and interpreting a large number of stock market indicators. It also, in its bimonthly review, covers industry group

FIGURE 15–5

A Performance rank
B Safety rank
C Beta

These three reflect thousands of hours of research. They express Value Line's evaluation of practically everything you need to know to select a stock for purchase or sale or for holding according to Value Line's recommended strategy.

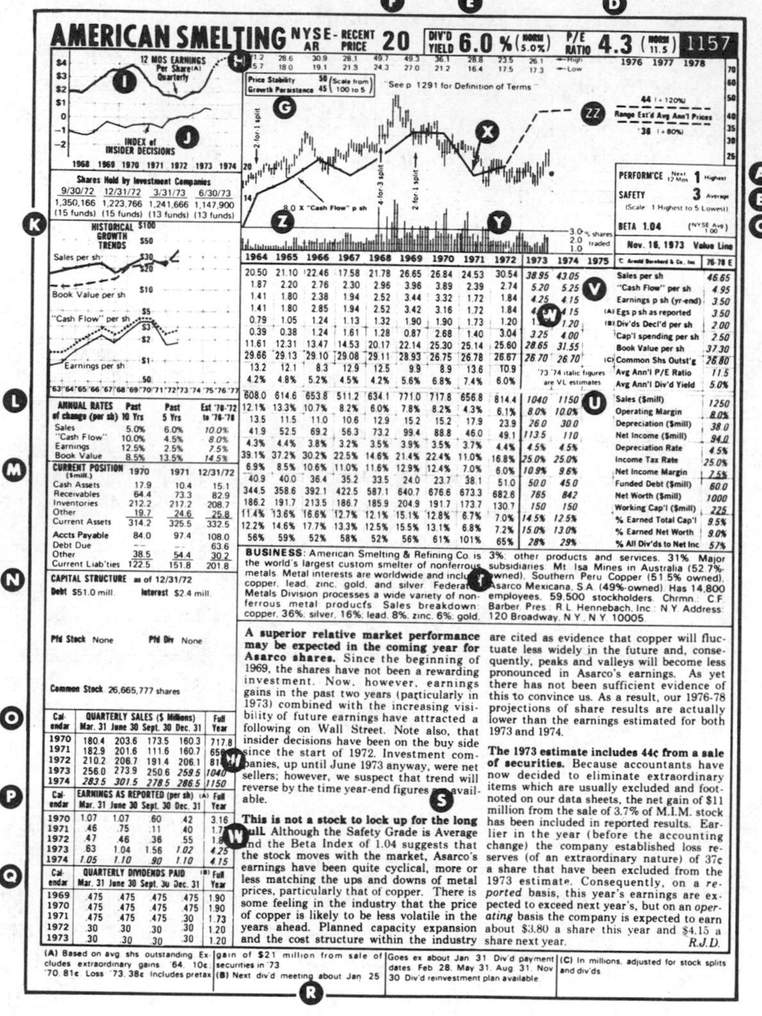

AMERICAN SMELTING NYSE-AR RECENT PRICE **20** DIV'D YIELD **6.0%** (NORM 5.0%) P/E RATIO **4.3** (NORM 11.5) **1157**

High	[illegible]	28.6	30.9	28.1	49.7	49.3	36.1	28.8	23.5	26.1
Low	[illegible]	18.0	19.1	21.3	24.3	27.0	21.2	16.4	17.5	17.3

PERFORM'CE Next 12 Mos **1** Highest
SAFETY **3** Average
(Scale: 1 Highest to 5 Lowest)
BETA 1.04 (NYSE Avg 1.00)
Nov. 16, 1973 Value Line

Shares Held by Investment Companies

9/30/72	12/31/72	3/31/73	6/30/73
1,350,166 (15 funds)	1,223,766 (15 funds)	1,241,666 (13 funds)	1,147,900 (13 funds)

1964	1965	1966	1967	1968	1969	1970	1971	1972	1973	1974	1975	© Arnold Bernhard & Co., Inc.	76-78 E
20.50	21.10	22.46	17.58	21.78	26.65	26.84	24.53	30.54	38.95	43.05		Sales per sh	46.65
1.87	2.20	2.76	2.30	2.96	3.96	3.89	2.39	2.74	5.20	5.25		"Cash Flow" per sh	4.95
1.41	1.80	2.38	1.94	2.52	3.44	3.32	1.72	1.84	4.25	4.15		Earnings p sh (yr-end)	3.50
1.41	1.80	2.85	1.94	2.52	3.42	3.16	1.72	1.84	4.[illegible]	4.15		(A) Egs p sh as reported	3.50
0.79	1.05	1.24	1.13	1.32	1.90	1.90	1.73	1.20	1.[illegible]	1.20		(B) Div'ds Decl'd per sh	2.00
0.39	0.38	1.24	1.61	1.28	0.87	2.68	1.40	3.04	3.25	4.00		Cap'l spending per sh	2.50
11.61	12.31	13.47	14.53	20.17	22.14	25.30	25.14	25.60	28.65	31.55		Book Value per sh	37.30
29.66	29.13	29.10	29.08	29.11	28.93	26.75	26.78	26.67	26.70	26.70		(C) Common Shs Outst'g	26.80
13.2	12.1	8.3	12.9	12.5	9.9	8.9	13.6	10.9	'73 '74 italic figures			Avg Ann'l P/E Ratio	11.5
4.2%	4.8%	5.2%	4.5%	4.2%	5.6%	6.8%	7.4%	6.0%	are VL estimates			Avg Ann'l Div'd Yield	5.0%
608.0	614.6	653.8	511.2	634.1	771.0	717.8	656.8	814.4	1040	1150		Sales ($mill)	1250
12.1%	13.3%	10.7%	8.2%	6.0%	7.8%	8.2%	4.3%	6.1%	8.0%	10.0%		Operating Margin	8.0%
13.5	11.5	11.0	10.6	12.9	15.2	15.2	17.9	23.9	26.0	30.0		Depreciation ($mill)	38.0
41.9	52.5	69.2	56.3	73.2	99.4	88.8	46.0	49.1	113.5	110		Net Income ($mill)	94.0
4.3%	4.4%	3.8%	3.2%	3.5%	3.9%	3.5%	3.7%	4.4%	4.5%	4.5%		Depreciation Rate	4.5%
39.1%	37.2%	30.2%	22.5%	14.6%	21.4%	22.4%	11.0%	16.8%	25.0%	25.0%		Income Tax Rate	25.0%
6.9%	8.5%	10.6%	11.0%	11.6%	12.9%	12.4%	7.0%	6.0%	10.9%	9.6%		Net Income Margin	7.5%
40.9	40.0	36.4	35.2	33.5	24.0	23.7	38.1	51.0	50.0	45.0		Funded Debt ($mill)	60.0
344.5	358.6	392.1	422.5	587.1	640.7	676.6	673.3	682.6	765	842		Net Worth ($mill)	1000
186.2	191.7	213.5	186.7	185.9	204.9	191.7	173.7	130.7	150	150		Working Cap'l ($mill)	225
11.4%	13.6%	16.6%	12.7%	12.1%	15.1%	12.8%	6.7%	7.0%	14.5%	12.5%		% Earned Total Cap'l	9.5%
12.2%	14.6%	17.7%	13.3%	12.5%	15.5%	13.1%	6.8%	7.2%	15.0%	13.0%		% Earned Net Worth	9.0%
56%	59%	52%	58%	52%	56%	61%	101%	65%	28%	29%		% All Div'ds to Net Inc	57%

ANNUAL RATES of change (per sh)	Past 10 Yrs	Past 5 Yrs	Est '70-'72 to '76-'78
Sales	5.0%	6.0%	10.0%
"Cash Flow"	10.0%	4.5%	8.0%
Earnings	12.5%	2.5%	7.5%
Book Value	8.5%	13.5%	14.5%

CURRENT POSITION ($mill.)	1970	1971	12/31/72
Cash Assets	17.9	10.4	15.1
Receivables	64.4	73.3	82.9
Inventories	212.2	217.2	208.7
Other	19.7	24.6	25.8
Current Assets	314.2	325.5	332.5
Accts Payable	84.0	97.4	108.0
Debt Due	--	--	63.6
Other	38.5	54.4	30.2
Current Liab'ties	122.5	151.8	201.8

CAPITAL STRUCTURE as of 12/31/72
Debt $51.0 mill. **Interest** $2.4 mill.

Pfd Stock None **Pfd Div** None

Common Stock 26,665,777 shares

Calendar	QUARTERLY SALES ($ Millions) Mar. 31	June 30	Sept. 30	Dec. 31	Full Year
1970	180.4	203.6	173.5	160.3	717.8
1971	182.9	201.6	111.6	160.7	65[illegible]
1972	210.2	206.7	191.4	206.1	81[illegible]
1973	256.0	273.9	250.6	259.5	1040
1974	283.5	301.5	278.5	286.5	1150

Calendar	EARNINGS AS REPORTED (per sh) (A) Mar. 31	June 30	Sept. 30	Dec. 31	Full Year
1970	1.07	1.07	.60	.42	3.16
1971	.46	.75	.11	.40	1.7[illegible]
1972	.47	.46	.36	.55	1.8[illegible]
1973	.63	1.04	1.56	1.02	4.25
1974	1.05	1.10	.90	1.10	4.15

Calendar	QUARTERLY DIVIDENDS PAID (B) Mar. 31	June 30	Sept. 30	Dec. 31	Full Year
1969	.475	.475	.475	.475	1.90
1970	.475	.475	.475	.475	1.90
1971	.475	.475	.475	.30	1.73
1972	.30	.30	.30	.30	1.20
1973	.30	.30	.30	.30	1.20

BUSINESS: American Smelting & Refining Co. is the world's largest custom smelter of nonferrous metals. Metal interests are worldwide and include copper, lead, zinc, gold, and silver. Federated Metals Division processes a wide variety of nonferrous metal products. Sales breakdown: copper, 36%; silver, 16%; lead, 8%; zinc, 6%; gold, 3%; other products and services, 31%. Major subsidiaries: Mt. Isa Mines in Australia (52.7%-owned), Southern Peru Copper (51.5% owned), Asarco Mexicana, S.A. (49%-owned). Has 14,800 employees, 59,500 stockholders. Chrmn.: C.F. Barber. Pres.: R.L. Hennebach, Inc.: N.Y. Address: 120 Broadway, N.Y., N.Y. 10005.

A superior relative market performance may be expected in the coming year for Asarco shares. Since the beginning of 1969, the shares have not been a rewarding investment. Now, however, earnings gains in the past two years (particularly in 1973) combined with the increasing visibility of future earnings have attracted a following on Wall Street. Note also, that insider decisions have been on the buy side since the start of 1972. Investment companies, up until June 1973 anyway, were net sellers; however, we suspect that trend will reverse by the time year-end figures are available.

This is not a stock to lock up for the long pull. Although the Safety Grade is Average and the Beta Index of 1.04 suggests that the stock moves with the market, Asarco's earnings have been quite cyclical, more or less matching the ups and downs of metal prices, particularly that of copper. There is some feeling in the industry that the price of copper is likely to be less volatile in the years ahead. Planned capacity expansion and the cost structure within the industry are cited as evidence that copper will fluctuate less widely in the future and, consequently, peaks and valleys will become less pronounced in Asarco's earnings. As yet there has not been sufficient evidence of this to convince us. As a result, our 1976-78 projections of share results are actually lower than the earnings estimated for both 1973 and 1974.

The 1973 estimate includes 44¢ from a sale of securities. Because accountants have now decided to eliminate extraordinary items which are usually excluded and footnoted on our data sheets, the net gain of $11 million from the sale of 3.7% of M.I.M. stock has been included in reported results. Earlier in the year (before the accounting change) the company established loss reserves (of an extraordinary nature) of 37¢ a share that have been excluded from the 1973 estimate. Consequently, on a *reported* basis, this year's earnings are expected to exceed next year's, but on an *operating* basis the company is expected to earn about $3.80 a share this year and $4.15 a share next year.

R.J.D.

(A) Based on avg shs outstanding. Excludes extraordinary gains: '64, 10¢; '70, 81¢. Loss: '73, 38¢. Includes pretax gain of $21 million from sale of securities in '73. (B) Next div'd meeting about Jan. 25. Goes ex about Jan. 31. Div'd payment dates: Feb. 28, May 31, Aug. 31, Nov. 30. Div'd reinvestment plan available. (C) In millions, adjusted for stock splits and div'ds.

D Price/Earnings ratio
E Dividend yield
F Recent price
G Indicies of price stability and growth Persistence
H Annual price range
I 12 months earnings per share plotted quarterly
J Index of insider decisions
K Historical growth trends
L Annual rates of change
M Current position
N Capital structure
O Quarterly sales (company basis)
P Earnings (per share) as reported
Q Quarterly dividend paid (per share)
R Dividend record
S Stock comment
T Business comment
U Statistical milestones (company basis)
V Statistical milestones (per share basis)
W Estimates of sales, earnings, dividends, etc.
X Value line
Y Percentage of outstanding shares traded monthly
Z "Cash flow" multiple used to describe historical price/earnings relationship
ZZ Estimated range of average annual prices. 1976–78

Source: Value Line.

selection in relation to market timing and occasionally has individual company selections related to phase of the market.

The Dines Letter is a weekly publication of stock market advice and information. It features current market trend changes based on technical indicators but also includes recommendations for purchase and sale of individual stocks based on six long range lists grouped in the following categories: High Quality; Speculative and Depressed; High Income; Growth; Precious Metals; and Short Sales. For short term traders there is a separate trading list each week.

America's Fastest Growing Companies, published by JOHN S. HEROLD, INC. (35 Mason Street, Greenwich, Conn. 06830) provides a constantly revised list of growth companies, together with relevant, factual data and comment. Some 150 companies are selected and listed based solely on growth in net income per common share. Companies are delisted when earnings decline or fail to measure up to expectations. Transactions of the Connecticut Capital Company, an investment partnership and a growth stock investment operation, are reported each month showing changes and resulting profits or losses.

In addition to *America's Fastest Growing Companies* there are several other growth stock services. One is the GROWTH STOCK OUTLOOK, INC. (Chevy Chase, Maryland 20015). Its *Growth Stock Outlook Report* is published twice a month. It seeks out and recommends young companies in the incubation stage. Another is the DANFORTH ASSOCIATES (Wellesley Hills, Massachusetts 02181), which publishes the *Growth Stock Letter.* This is a weekly report on growth stocks, adding to and deleting from "The Growth Stock Portfolio."

THE UNITED BUSINESS AND INVESTMENT SERVICE (210 Newbury St., Boston, Mass., 02116) issues a comprehensive *Weekly Report* on business, investment, and stock market conditions. In addition, regular reports are issued on all stocks on the service's supervised lists. A summary of the opinion of eight other advisory services is given, and subscribers are offered an inquiry and advisory service.

Chart Services

There are a number of chart services, of which four leading ones are: M. C. HORSEY & Co. (79 Wall St., New York, N.Y., 10005 and 120 South Blvd. Salisbury, Maryland 21801), CHARTCRAFT, INC. (Larchmont, N.Y. 10538), TRENDLINE 345 Hudson Street, New York, N.Y. 10014), and DINES CHART CORPORATION (18 East 41 St., New York, N.Y. 10017). These companies publish chart books, which portray graphically, by means of a separate chart for each stock, the monthly movement of prices and sales volume over a period of years for individual stocks. Horsey issues *The Stock Picture,* a book of over 1,700 charts (see Figure 15–6). Twice a year it also publishes *Selected Stocks,* which gives added detail and 25 year coverage of some 255 stocks. Chartcraft, Inc., publishes a monthly chart book containing over 2,700 point and figure charts (see Figure 15–7). A point and figure chart shows only one thing, price movement. It does not take into account volume of trading, or time in the usual sense. Unless the price of the stock changes, by one point, or three points, no

FIGURE 15–6

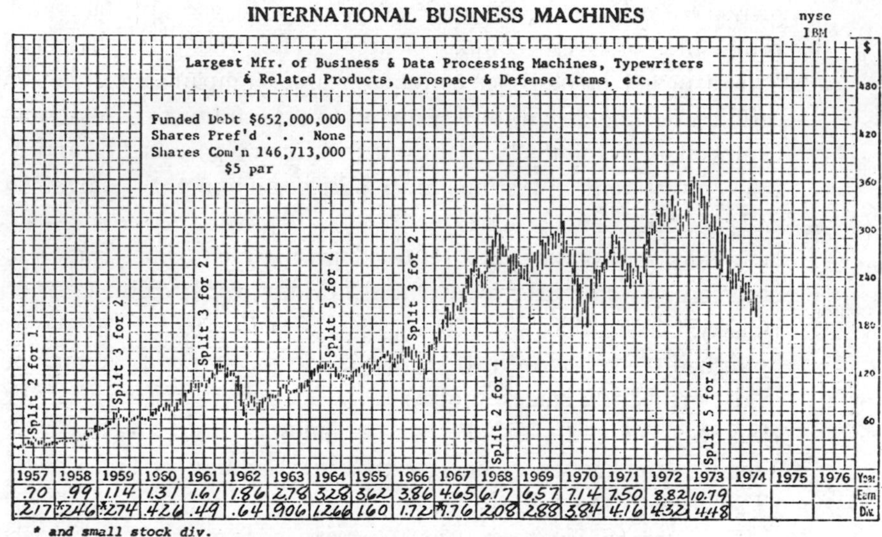

Source: M. C. Horsey & Company, Inc., *The Stock Picture*, May, 1974.

entry is made on the chart even though weeks and months may go by. Xs are used when the price is going up and Os when the price is going down. When the stock changes price direction, a new column is started. Figure 15–8 is a three-unit point and figure chart. The trend lines are drawn at 45° angles (not connecting particular points on the chart).[4]

Trendline, now a division of Standard & Poor's, publishes three chartbooks. One, called *Daily Basis Stock Charts,* shows the market behavior

---

[4] For more detail, see *How to Use the Three-Point Reversal Method of Point and Figure Stock Market Trading,* by A. W. Cohen, Chartcraft, Inc., Larchmont, New York. See also, *How Charts Can Help You in the Market,* by William L. Jiler, Trendline, New York, latest edition.

FIGURE 15–7

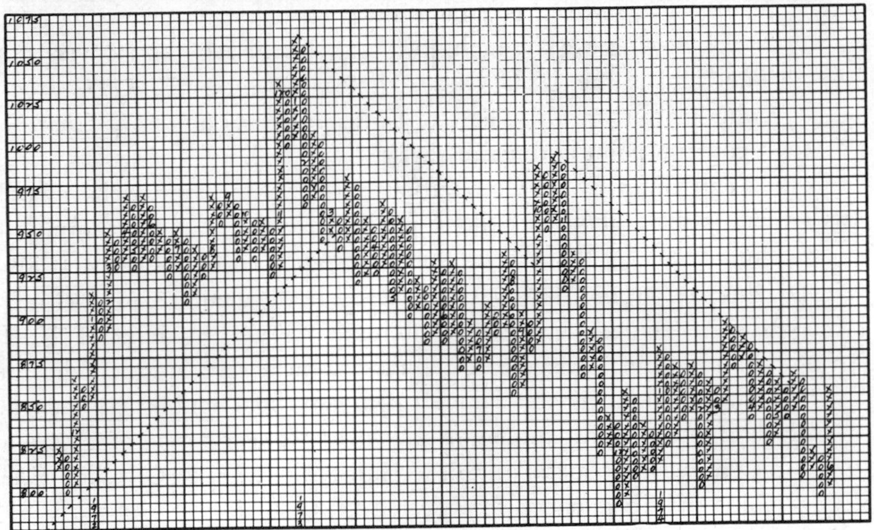

Source: Chartcraft, Inc.

FIGURE 15–8

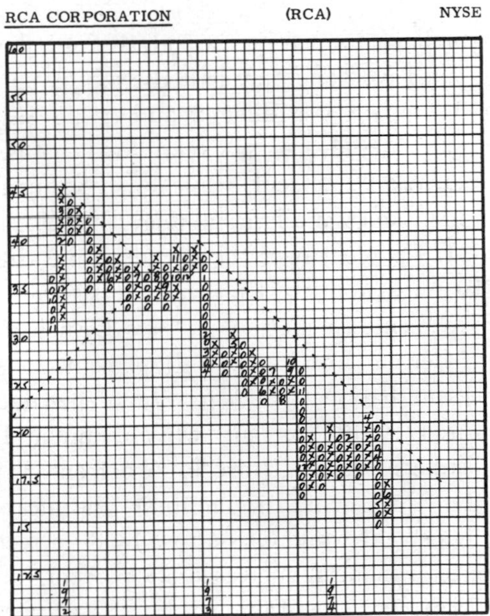

Source: Chartcraft, Inc.

of about 750 NYSE and ASE stocks plotted on a daily basis and issued every Friday after the close of the market. A second, called *Current Market Perspectives,* is a monthly book of charts on nearly 1,000 listed issues showing weekly, high, low, and close. Each chart covers four years. The third is the *OTC Chart Manual* covering 840 OTC stocks. It is published bimonthly. Chartcraft also publishes an *OTC Chartbook,* but it contains point and figure charts.

The Dines Chart Corporation also publishes three chart books. The first is the *Paflibe Chartbook* published every Monday morning. It contains about 2,000 charts of companies grouped by industry. It also shows Dines listing of America's Smartest Managements, Dines listing of Unusual Earnings Upswings, Automatic Group Analysis of 80 Industry Groups from strongest to weakest, and 60 technical indicators. The second volume is the Dines *Crosschart* book published monthly. The charts are all point and figure and cover a longer period of time than those in the *Paflibe* book. The third volume is the Dines *OTClibe Chartbook,* point and figure charts for selected OTC stocks.

These are but some of the many sources of information for the investor who would be informed. The annual cost of any of these services can be deducted from investors' income under the personal income tax.

Choosing the Company

Once you have decided on the industry or industries in which you want to invest, you have done only half the job. Even within a given industry, selecting a company is a difficult and trying task. Assume you picked a given industry a decade ago, say, retail food chains. Over the decade Winn-Dixie Stores rose 99 percent, while First National Stores fell 64 percent. Perhaps you picked something more cyclical, like machinery. Clark Equipment rose 123 percent over the decade while Allis-Chalmers dropped 45 percent. In dairy products, Kraftco increased by 17 percent, while Borden fell by 35 percent. In motion pictures Disney rose 1,113 percent, while Twentieth Century-Fox dropped 51 percent. In paper, Scott fell 62 percent while International Paper rose by 62 percent! In life insurance Gulf Life increased by 101 percent, while Franklin Life fell by 27 percent. Among distillers, National rose by 6 percent, while American Distilling declined by 27 percent. In plumbing and heating American Standard dropped 39 percent while Crane rose by 39 percent. In savings and loans First Charter Financial increased 23 percent, but Financial Federation dropped 73 percent (see Table 15–1). Even if you feel reasonably sure of your industry choice, selecting the better performing company requires additional effort and skill.

"No annual report, no net earnings, no dividends—what a chance to get in on the ground floor!"

Edgar Allen, Jr., The Commercial and Financial Chronicle

Direct Financial Information

To the average person who has not had an accounting course, the mere sight of a balance sheet or income statement inspires awe and fear. Yet, to invest wisely, you should know how to read and understand a financial statement. It is not difficult at all, and the mathematics involved is no more than one learns in grade school. This ability to read and understand a financial report is a "must" today for anyone going into business; and for the average investor, putting in a few hours to study the subject may pay dividends in the future.[5]

[5] A free copy of *How to Read a Financial Report* may be obtained by writing to Merrill Lynch, Pierce, Fenner & Smith, One Liberty Plaza (165 Broadway), New York, N.Y., 10006. For greater detail, see Roy A. Foulke, *Practical Financial Statement Analysis* (New York: McGraw-Hill Book Co., latest edition). Also a free copy of *Understanding Financial Statements* may be obtained by writing to the Publications Division of the New York Stock Exchange, 11 Wall Street, New York, N.Y. 10005.

TABLE 15–1

One Hundred Stocks of the Fifty Industries (January 1, 1964—December 31, 1973)

Industry	Stock	Change
AEROSPACE	Boeing Co.	— 31%
	General Dynamics	— 16
AGRICULTURAL MACHINERY	Deere & Company	+ 44
	International Harvester	— 14
AIRLINES	American Airlines	— 50
	Eastern Airlines	— 64
ALUMINUM	Aluminum Co. of America	+ 6
	Reynolds	— 40
APPAREL	Cluett Peabody	— 68
	Genesco	— 81
AUTOMOBILES	General Motors	— 41
	American Motors	— 51
BANKS (N.Y.C.)	Chase Manhattan	+ 37
	Bankers Trust	— 23
BEVERAGES (Soft Drinks)	Coca-Cola	+338
	Pepsico	+182
BREWERS	Falstaff Brewing	— 87
	Anheuser-Busch, Inc.	+546
BUILDING	National Gypsum	— 46
	U.S. Gypsum	— 59
BUSINESS EQUIPMENT	IBM	+134
	National Cash Register	— 13
CEMENT	General Portland	— 43
	Alpha Portland	+ 24
CHEMICALS	Union Carbide	— 43
	Allied Chemical	— 5
COAL	Eastern Gas & Fuel	+178
	Pittston Co.	+221
CONTAINERS (Paper)	Federal Paperboard	— 21
	Standard Packaging	— 89
DAIRY PRODUCTS	Kraftco	+ 17
	Borden Co.	— 35
DEPARTMENT STORES	Federated Dept. Stores	+ 3
	Allied Stores	— 6
DISTILLERS	National Dist. & Chem.	+ 6%
	American Distilling	— 27
DRUGS	American Home Prod.	+297
	Gillette	+ 15
ELECTRICAL EQUIPMENT	General Electric	+ 45
	Westinghouse	+ 50
FINANCE COMPANIES	Heller (W.E.) Co.	+196
	CIT Financial	+ 3
FOOD	General Foods	— 47
	Libby McNeil	— 64
FOOD (Canned)	H. J. Heinz	+116
	Campbell Soup	— 22
GOLD MINING	Dome Mines	+502
	Homestake Mining	+221
HOME FURNISHINGS	Simmons Co.	+ 21
	Armstrong Cork	— 20
INSURANCE	Hanover Insurance	— 52
	Lincoln National Corp	— 3
INVESTMENT COS. (Closed)	Tricontinental Corp.	+ 11
	Atlas Corp.	— 42
LEAD and ZINC	St. Joseph's Lead	+110
	NL Industries	— 68
LIFE INSURANCE	Gulf Life	+101
	Franklin Life Ins.	— 27
MACHINE TOOLS	Monarch Machine Tools	— 14
	Cinn. Milacron	+ 29
MACHINERY	Clark Equipment	+123
	Allis-Chalmers	— 45
MEAT PACKING	Iowa Beef	+403
	Esmark	+ 14
MOTION PICTURES	(Walt) Disney	+1113
	Twentieth Century-Fox	— 51
PAPER	Int'l Paper	+ 62
	Scott Paper	— 62
PETROLEUM	Texaco	— 12%
	Continental Oil	+ 81
PLUMBING and HEATING	American Standard	— 39
	Crane Co.	+ 39
RAILROAD EQUIPMENT	ACF Industries, Inc.	+ 87
	General Signal	+252
RAILROADS	Southern Pacific	+ 10
	Southern Railway	+ 64
RETAIL (Mail Order)	Sears, Roebuck	+ 64
	Marcor, Inc.	+ 18
RETAIL STORES (Food Chains)	Winn-Dixie Stores	+ 99
	First National Stores	— 64
RETAIL (Variety)	Grant (W.T.)	— 9
	Woolworth, F. W.	— 25
SAVINGS & LOANS	First Charter Financial	+ 23
	Financial Federation	— 73
SHOES	Interco, Inc.	+100
	Genesco	— 81
STEEL	Bethlehem Steel	+ 7
	U.S. Steel	— 29
SULPHUR	Texas Gulf Sulphur	+290
	Freeport Sulphur	+ 45
TELEPHONE	General Tel. & El.	— 21
	Pacific Tel. & Tel.	— 50
TEXTILE PRODUCTS	Burlington Ind.	— 4
	Cone Mills	+ 1
TIRE and RUBBER	Goodyear Tire & Rubber	— 26
	Goodrich (B. F.)	— 53
TOBACCO	Liggett and Myers	— 21
	Reynolds Tobacco	— 4
UTILITIES	Commonwealth Edison	— 41
	Niagara Mohawk	— 50

The average gain of these 100 stocks was 42%. Only 29 out of the 100 were above average, and while 71 were below average, 54 of these actually declined during this period.

Source: Johnson's Investment Company Charts.

Ratios, Standards, and Investment Judgment

There are a considerable number of ratios used in investment analysis which combine items from both the balance sheet and the income account. Standards of average or acceptable performance have been established for many of these ratios, and a study and knowledge of them, if time affords, will provide the prospective investor with useful tools of analysis.

Consider briefly nine basic financial relationships derived from balance sheets or income accounts. These you should understand.

1. *Net Income to Net Worth or Rate of Return on Stockholders' Equity.* You divide net income after taxes by the total of preferred stock, common stock, and surplus accounts. This is one of most significant of all the financial ratios. It tells you how much the company is earning on the stockholders' investment. The higher the ratio, the more favorable. On the average, U.S. corporations tend to earn 9–10 percent on stockholders' equity. Comparable figures for a large number of industries are provided quarterly by the government[6] and annually by the First National City Bank of New York.[7] By using these two sources you can compare figures of companies you are interested in with the average for the industry or for other industries.

2. *Times Fixed Charges Earned or Interest Coverage.* You divide net income before taxes by the annual interest requirements (fixed charges). Sometimes interest coverage after taxes is shown but since interest is a claim prior to income taxes, it is therefore better practice to compute interest coverage before provision for income taxes. This ratio shows how well protected by earnings—or how poorly—is the bondholders' interest. Ordinarily, a manufacturing company's interest coverage is regarded as satisfactory at 5 times; among public utilities a 3 to 4 times coverage is satisfactory.

3. *Earnings per Share (preferred stock).* This ratio is found by merely dividing the net income by the number of shares of preferred stock. You use net income after interest and after taxes. This ratio shows the earnings protection for the preferred dividend. A coverage of about 4 times is usually considered adequate for industrial companies.

4. *Combined or Overall Coverage.* You divide the adjusted operating profit (net income before interest but after taxes) by the total of interest and preferred dividends. This is a more conservative method than merely considering the net income available for the preferred stock. A preferred stock of an industrial company with average earnings (before interest on bonds but after taxes) for five years of not less than 4 times the combined interest and preferred dividend requirements is usually regarded as satisfactory. For a public utility preferred, earnings of around 3 times the combined requirements make the stock high grade.

5. *Earnings per Share (common stock) or Yield on Common Stock.* The buyer of common stock is often more concerned with the earnings

[6] See *Quarterly Financial Report for Manufacturing Corporations*, Federal Trade Commission—Securities and Exchange Commission, Washington, D.C.: U.S. Government Printing Office.

[7] See "Review of Corporate Profits in (year)," in the April issue each year of *The Monthly Economic Letter*, First National City Bank of New York. A free copy may be obtained by writing to the bank at 399 Park Avenue, New York, N.Y., 10022.

per share of the stock than with the dividend. It is usually earnings per share, or rather, prospective earnings per share, that influence stock prices. The income statement does not show the earnings available for common stock, if a company has preferred stock outstanding. You must subtract the preferred dividend from net income after taxes. You then divide this residual net income by the number of shares of common stock outstanding. This gives you earnings per share. For example, net income after taxes amounts to $5 million. The preferred dividend requires $1 million. Thus $4 million remains for the 500,000 common shares outstanding. Earnings per share are thus $8.00 ($4 million divided by 500,000 shares).

6. *Dividends per Share (common stock).* This too, is a simple computation. You divide the dividends paid on the common stock by the number of shares. In the example above, assume the company pays $2 million of the $4 million available. With 500,000 shares outstanding each share receives a dividend of $4. Dividend payout varies from company to company depending on stability of earnings, need for new capital, the directors' judgment as to the outlook for earnings, etc. On the average, industrial companies pay out between 50 and 60 percent of earnings as dividends. Growth companies pay out less because of their greater need for capital for expansion. Utilities pay out more because of their stability of earnings and because they depend more on debt.

7. *Book Value per Share of Common Stock.* This is found by adding the stated or par value of the common stock to the surplus accounts and dividing the total by the number of shares. To illustrate:

Common stock	$ 5,000,000
Capital surplus	1,000,000
Earned surplus	14,000,000
Total	$20,000,000

Number of shares 500,000
Book value per share = $40

Another method of calculating book value, called the long way, is to deduct from total assets (exclusive of such intangibles as goodwill and patents) all liabilities and preferred stock, if any. The remainder is divided by the number of common shares and the result is the book value per share or net tangible assets per share of common stock.

For industrial companies, book value per share does not mean very much. It is not as important as earnings and prospective earnings. Usually the largest category of assets is plant and equipment and aside from salvage value, such assets are worth only what they can earn.

On the other hand, the book value of the common stock of such money corporations as banks, insurance companies, and investment companies is more significant. The assets of these companies are in securities or in other forms that can usually be readily turned into cash. The book value of public utility common stock is also important, since these regulated companies are entitled by law to earn a fair return on their investment, which is made up largely of fixed assets. Their rates, and hence, earnings are based on the value of their investment in plant and equipment.

8. *Price/Earnings Ratio.* This is simply the earnings per share of the common stock divided into the market price. For example, if the company earns $8 per share and the stock sells for 96, the price/earnings ratio is 12. The stock is selling at 12 times earnings. What is the right price/earnings ratio? No one can really say. All we can do is study trends over time, and average levels. It used to be said that a stock should sell at 10 times earnings but this is now regarded as too general. In a bear market many stocks will sell at 5 to 7 times earnings, while in bull markets the average level would be about 15 to 18 times earnings. Some growth stocks have sold at 40 to 50 times earnings. Buyers are anticipating and paying for sharply higher expected or projected earnings.

9. *Dividend Return (dividend yield or income).* This is determined by dividing the annual dividend per share by the price of the stock. For example, if there is a $4.00 per share dividend on common which sells for $96, the dividend return is 4.1 + % ($4.00 divided by $96).

Some of the more important ratios[8] used by leading security analysts in forming judgments and making investment decisions follow.

Profitability ratios include:

1. Earnings per dollar of capital funds (return on capital),
2. Sales per dollar of capital funds (sales ratio).
3. Profit per dollar of sales (return on sales).

The best gauge of the success of a company is the percentage earned (though not necessarily paid out) on its invested capital.

Credit ratios include:

4. The working capital ratio—current assets to current liabilities.
5. The common stock ratio—the total capital fund at book value to the common stock component thereof.
6. Senior charge coverage ratio—the balance of earnings available for senior charges divided by the fixed charges.

---

[8] For a discussion of these frequently used financial ratios, see "Key Ratios in Security Analysis" in Benjamin Graham, David L. Dodd, and Sidney Cottle, *Security Analysis* (4th ed.; New York: McGraw-Hill Book Co., Inc., 1962), pp. 231–38.

Ratios which help to judge the *growth* of a company over a period of time include:

7. Dollar sales—annual rate of growth.
8. Net profits in dollars to total capital.
9. Earnings per share.

Ratios which indicate the *stability* of earnings of a company over a period of years include:

10. Minimum coverage of senior charges—times earnings cover senior charges in poorest years.
11. Maximum earnings decline—percentage decline in income in given poor years to average income in a normal base period. This is very useful in comparing the volatility of earnings as among companies.

The percentage of available earnings paid out in common dividends affects the market's evaluation of the stock. This ratio is the

12. Payout ratio: divide earnings per share into the dividend paid per share.

Then there are a number of ratios which are useful in judging the *price of an issue*—whether it is too high or too low. These include:

13. Sales per dollar of common, at market.
14. Earnings per dollar of common, at market (earnings yield).
15. Dividends per dollar of common, at market (dividend yield).
16. Net assets (equity) per dollar of common at market (asset ratio).

While the use of all of the ratios may be too difficult for the average investor, the application of three or four of the more significant ones to a given stock or bond investment possibility will provide safeguards and permit the avoidance of costly mistakes. If you have no time at all or cannot understand balance sheets, income accounts, and ratio analysis, then at least you can consult one or more of the financial services which do understand and use these tools. They will give you the essence of their judgment, boiled down in a few simple words. Thus you save time and profit from the hours of work which their skilled analysts devote to the task. You need not even buy the service, since one or more will be found in any good library. There is really no excuse for hit or miss investing based on tips, rumor, or flights of fancy and imagination.[9]

---

[9] For a fantastic example, see Andrew Tobias, *The Funny Money Game* (Chicago: Playboy Press, 1971).

SUGGESTED READINGS

1. *How to Read a Financial Report*. New York: Merrill Lynch, Pierce, Fenner & Smith, latest edition. A free copy can be obtained by writing to this firm at One Liberty Plaza (165 Broadway), New York, N.Y. 10006.
2. New York Stock Exchange, *Understanding Financial Statements*. A free copy may be obtained from Publications Division, New York Stock Exchange, 11 Wall Street, New York, N.Y. 10005.
3. *The Outlook*, published weekly by Standard & Poor's Corporation, 345 Hudson St., New York, N.Y. 10014. A free sample copy will be sent on request.
4. *Moody's Stock Survey*, published weekly by Moody's Investor's Service, 99 Church St., New York, N.Y. 10007. A free sample copy will be sent on request.
5. James B. Woy (cd.), *Investment Information: A Detailed Guide to Selected Sources*. Management Information Guides Series No. 19. Detroit: Gale Research Co., latest edition.
6. (*a*) "Now the Small Investor Can Have an Adviser," *Business Week*, February 23, 1974
   (*b*) "Stockbrokers Who Won't Turn Down Small Orders," *Changing Times*, October 1972.
   (*c*) "Rating the Investment Advisory Services," *Money*, October 1973.
7. Roy A. Foulke, *Practical Financial Statement Analysis*. New York: McGraw-Hill Book Co., latest edition.
8. C. Norman Stabler, *How to Read the Financial News*. New York: Harper & Row, latest edition. See also John G. Forrest, *Financial News: How to Read and Interpret It. New York Times*, latest edition.
9. *Business Conditions Digest*, Bureau of the Census, U.S. Department of Commerce, Washington, D.C., issued monthly.
10. New York Stock Exchange, *Investors' Notebook: A Guide to the Working Language of Wall Street*, Vols. 1, 2, 3, & 4. Free copies may be obtained by writing to the Publications Division of the Exchange, 11 Wall Street, New York, N.Y. 10005.
11. William L. Jiler, *How Charts Can Help You in the Market*. New York: Trendline, Standard & Poor's, latest edition.
12. A. W. Cohen, *How to Use the Three-Point Reversal Method of Point and Figure Stock Market Trading*. Larchmont, N.Y.: Chartcraft, Inc., latest edition.
13. George A. Chestnutt, Jr., *Stock Market Analysis: Facts and Principles*. Greenwich, Conn.: Chestnutt Corporation, latest edition.
14. Richard A. Brealey, *An Introduction to Risk and Return from Common Stock*. Cambridge, Mass.: M.I.T. Press, 1969.

15. Richard A. Brealey, *Security Prices In a Competitive Market: More About Risk and Return from Common Stock*. Cambridge, Mass.: M.I.T. Press, 1971.

CASE PROBLEMS

1. Max Kugelfuss is a young bachelor, a teacher with a Ph.D., and a man earning a moderately good income. Since he has no outstanding financial obligations, he decides to invest some of his savings. He hears about some oil stock in a Canadian company which is for sale at 50 cents a share. Before he decides to buy 1,000 shares, what facts do you think he should consider? How can he find out more facts about the company?

2. Jim Jefferson, age 23, is advised by his father to buy a few shares in the stock market in order to learn about investments. He recently graduated from college and is earning $9,000 per year. In school he majored in liberal arts and had no investment training. His savings are such that he feels that he can invest $1,000 initially in stock. He asks you to advise him how he should proceed. What would you suggest?

3. A friend tells you that he has just heard that Skyline, Fleetwood, and Redman are "sleeper stocks," that he is going to buy shares in all three and that you should do likewise. Research these stocks, using at least five sources of information. Evaluate them. Do you agree with your friend or not? Why?

4. Your barber tells you that he has heard from a customer of his that Thermal Power and Pioneer Hi-Bred International, Inc. are "hot buys." With your usual judicious skepticism you decide to look into the situation, to investigate before you invest. What sources of information will you use? After using them, what conclusions do you come to regarding these "tips"?

5. Your mother-in-law to be wants to give her daughter a gift of $25,000 of stock as a wedding gift for choosing such an attractive and intelligent son-in-law. To be polite she asks your advice as to what stocks she should buy for your fiancee. She indicates that she is quite conservative and favors only the bluest of the blue chips. Write her a letter giving your suggestions for this $25,000 blue chip investment program, citing facts, figures, and sources to back your choices.

6. Elinore Bush has been a college professor for 10 years. Her retirement fund is with the Teachers Insurance and Annuity Association in New York and has been invested (along with the funds of other teachers) in bonds. The Association has also set up an organization (CREF) which invests its funds in common stock. She is asked whether she wants part of her past and future retirement payments handed to that organization or whether she prefers to have her entire retirement fund invested in bonds as heretofore. What are your thoughts on the subject?

7. Aaron Rudstein has been asked to invest $10,000 in the common stock of the Better Homes Mortgage Corporation, which buys old houses, restores them, and then endeavors to sell them at a profit. To persuade him to invest, he is given the financial statements of the company for the last five years. His study of these statements reveals that the company's inventory of houses for sale was carried at cost for the first four years but that in the latter year the company carried this inventory at the total figure for which the company expected to sell them. How should Aaron react to this change? Why?

8. Your wealthy father-in-law elect learns that you are studying personal finance and is impressed. He says he is interested in investing in the "leisure" industry, mentioning stocks such as Ramada Inns, Holiday Inns, Howard Johnson, McDonalds, Marriott, Hilton, Loew's, and others. He asks that you research the "industry" and advise him. Using sources of information that you consider relevant and reliable, gather the facts you require and prepare a brief report not to exceed five pages.

9. Arthur Byron's $25,000 endowment policy has matured. He is 45 years of age and has a wife (age 43) and one child (age 15). His other assets are a home (cost, $25,000 but probably worth $40,000), subject to a mortgage of $5,000, and $2,000 in banks. He is principal of the local high school, at a salary of $18,500 a year. He asks you to advise him as to the most effective use of the proceeds of the endowment policy. Develop an investment portfolio or program for him, supplying facts, figures, and sources.

10. A friend, who is specializing in computer sciences, is trying to decide whether to invest in one of the following companies: Augat, Inc., Data General, Digital Equipment, General Automation, International Systems & Controls, Modular Computer System, Watkins Johnson. Your help is asked to check these out and possibly select one for investment. Which one would you select? Why?

16

Investment Companies—Mutual Funds

An investment trust is known by the companies it keeps.

Herbert Prochnow

BELOW IS a pre-Civil War menu of a once famous restaurant. When dinner cost 12 cents, an average weekly wage was $6. Secular (long run) inflation has carried us very far from the 12 cent dinner and the $6 weekly wage. If we project from the $6 dinner and $150 weekly wage of today, what will prices and wages be in the year 1985?

DELMONICO'S

RESTAURANT.

494·PEARL·STREET.

BILL OF FARE.

Cup Tea or Coffee,	1	Pork Chops,	4
Bowl " "	2	Pork and Beans,	4
Crullers,	1	Sausages,	4
Soup,	2	Puddings,	4
Fried or Stewed Liver,	3	Liver and Bacon,	5
" " Heart,	3	Roast Beef or Veal,	5
Hash,	3	Roast Mutton,	5
Pies,	4	Veal Cutlet,	5
Half Pie,	2	Chicken Stew,	5
Beef or Mutton Stew,	4	Fried Eggs,	5
Corn Beef and Cabbage,	4	Ham and Eggs,	10
Pigs Head " "	4	Hamburger Steak,	10
Fried Fish,	4	Roast Chicken,	10
Beef Steak,	4		

Regular Dinner 12 Cents.

Smith & Handford Printers 23 and 25 Dey St N. Y.

"If you are afraid of inflation, buy mutual fund shares." This was the basic appeal which sold 6 million investors almost $50 billion of mutual fund shares over the last 30 years. So great was the versatility of the funds' appeals (see Figure 16–1) that they were able to persuade people to buy mutual fund shares instead of life insurance, to cash bonds and withdraw

FIGURE 16–1

FORTUNES FLOW THROUGH YOUR HANDS
BUT HOW MUCH HAVE YOU KEPT SO FAR?

TOTAL EARNINGS...

Average Monthly Income	5 Years	10 Years	15 Years	20 Years	25 Years	30 Years
$ 500	30,000	60,000	90,000	120,000	150,000	180,000
600	36,000	72,000	108,000	144,000	180,000	216,000
700	42,000	84,000	126,000	168,000	210,000	252,000
800	48,000	96,000	144,000	192,000	240,000	288,000
900	54,000	108,000	162,000	216,000	270,000	324,000
1,000	60,000	120,000	180,000	240,000	300,000	360,000
1,200	72,000	144,000	216,000	288,000	360,000	432,000
1,500	90,000	180,000	270,000	360,000	450,000	540,000
2,000	120,000	240,000	360,000	480,000	600,000	720,000
3,000	180,000	480,000	720,000	960,000	1,200,000	1,440,000

YOU ARE ____________ YEARS OLD.

YOU HAVE WORKED HARD FOR ____________ YEARS.

YOUR TOTAL EARNINGS FOR THAT PERIOD WERE $ ____________

YOU HAVE $ ____________ LEFT TO SHOW FOR YOUR WORK.

ARE YOU SATISFIED?

Source: Keystone Custodian Funds, Inc.

savings in order to buy mutual fund shares for "safety of principal in old age and retirement." Few other financial institutions had so rapid a growth in recent years as the open end investment company, as the mutual fund is technically called.

Kinds of Investment Companies

An investment company is simply a financial institution whose aim is to gather the savings of many individuals and invest them in a diversified portfolio of securities. If the investments were made chiefly in bonds and mortgages, the portfolio would not be unlike that of mutual savings banks, savings and loan associations, or life insurance companies. However, investment companies typically invest far more extensively in common stocks than do these other institutions.

It cannot be emphasized too much that all sorts of investment companies exist. Some of them, such as the American Research and Development Corporation, have as their prime purpose investment in relatively new and untried undertakings, which by their very nature can be only speculative. At the other extreme, some investment companies invest only in high grade bonds. Investors can find investment companies which limit their investments to the type of securities in which they wish to participate, be they blue chip common stocks, speculative common stocks, preferred stocks, high grade bonds, more speculative bonds, a balanced fund of stocks and bonds or a short term liquid asset current income fund. Companies can be found which emphasize as objectives high income or capital appreciation; others stress primarily the preservation of principal. Of course, preservation of principal may be sought either from the point of view of maintaining the number of dollars in the original investment or from the point of view of maintaining the purchasing power of the original investment.

The Investment Companies Act of 1940 requires a statement by each company of its basic investment policies. Once stated, policies may not be changed without stockholder approval. Thus the investor can tell fairly quickly the aim and investment objective of any company in which he is interested. For example, one of the more seasoned mutual funds, Fundamental Investors, has as its objective: "Long term growth of capital and income." Its policy is to invest in "principally common stocks but other securities or cash may be held under flexible policy." The fund with one of the best capital gains records over the last decade, Keystone Custodian Funds—S4, has as its objective, "Growth of capital." Its policy is stated as ". . . Speculative situations in newer and smaller companies, particularly those believed to be in the early phases of growth, when appropriate are favored. Income is *not* an objective. . . ." On the other hand, Wellington Fund has as its objective: ". . . Conservation of principal, reasonable income return and profits without undue risk. . . ." It is a balanced fund, holding bonds and preferred and common stock. The Dreyfus Liquid Assets Fund, formed in 1974, "is a no load, diversified, open end investment company whose objective is maximization of current income to the extent consistent with preservation of capital. The company pursues this objective by investing in money market obligations. . . ."

Not only do investment companies vary widely according to objectives and policy, but very great disparities exist in investment results. In many cases, the management more than earns its fee; in some others, it would seem as though the managers should pay the investors for the privilege of learning how to invest with the use of public funds. Indeed, the most difficult problem for the small investor is to learn how to distinguish the competent, ably managed funds from the less effective ones.

How Investment Companies Obtain Their Funds

Like other corporations, investment companies obtain the money with which to operate by selling their securities—common stock, preferred stock, and bonds—to the public. Before 1940, bonds were sold more commonly than they are today. Since 1940 the Federal Investment Company Act of 1940 has required open end companies, to have a single capital structure—only one class of security outstanding, usually common stock.

Open End Investment Companies

There are two principal types of investment companies—open end and closed end. An open end investment company is one whose shares are redeemable at any time at approximate asset value. In most cases, new shares are offered for sale continuously at asset value plus a fixed percentage as selling charge.

Open end investment companies offer additional shares of their stock for sale at all times, and, furthermore, they will repurchase previously issued stock from investors at any time. They are usually called "mutual funds." They sell their own shares at prices which will net the fund an amount equal to the net asset value of each share outstanding at the time of sale. This means that the investor must pay 6 to 9 percent more than the net asset value to buy shares, since, of course, it costs money to get the shares sold.

The large majority of open end investment companies appraise the market value of portfolios daily—after the close of the markets in New York—and thus arrive at a figure for net asset value per share on which the published bid and offered prices are based. Net asset value is then the worth of a mutual fund share as determined by dividing the total market value of its portfolio by the number of its own shares outstanding.

The surcharge of 6 to 9 percent is worthy of comment. Usually it is the only cost the investor incurs in making this type of investment. When he sells, he usually receives the net asset value of his shares without deduction. But even this slight cost will wipe out earnings of 3 or 4.5 percent per year for a couple of years, should the investor decide not to retain the investment. If there is doubt as to whether the investment can be retained for at least five years, the investor might well consider whether it might not be more profitable to accept the current per annum return from a savings bank or savings and loan association than to buy shares in an open end investment company. It is the surcharge of 6 to 9 percent which encourages brokerage firms to push the sales of open end investment company shares.

If a mutual fund has a surcharge—or "loading charge," as it is usually called in the trade—of say, 8 percent, this means that if you invest $10,000 in a fund, you get only $9,200 of net asset value, while $800 of your money goes to the broker or other financial middleman who solicited and obtained your order. Some have held that this contrasts unfavorably with New York Stock Exchange commission rates, when a "round lot" (usually 100 shares of stock) is purchased. Proponents of mutual funds reply that this is a fallacious and misleading comparison because two entirely unlike things are being compared. A share in an investment company, they hold, is not an ordinary "security." In addition to representing a pro rata share of ownership in a fund, it is in effect, they contend, a service contract. But, of course, you also pay, out of dividends earned and due you, an annual management fee for this service.

A number of funds, such as Scudder, Stevens and Clark, and also Loomis-Sayles, both of Boston, the T. Rowe Price Growth Stock Fund of Baltimore, the De Vegh Fund of New York, have no loading charge at all (see Table 16–1). They are, however, as a result, not very popular with brokerage houses which push mutual funds.

The actual percentage sales charges of the "load" funds are in fact somewhat higher than stated. This is because the sales charge is stated as a percent of the total purchase price including the sales charge or "load" itself. Thus, the mutual fund purchaser who buys $10,000 in mutual funds and pays an 8.5 percentage load or $850 is paying 8.5 percent on $10,000, but the net asset value of the shares he receives is only $9,150. A charge of $850 for $9,150 of mutual fund shares is 9.3 percent, not 8.5 percent.[1] New mutual funds with scaled sales charges now make such differences ex-

[1] See Securities and Exchange Commission, *Public Policy Implications of Investment Company Growth* (Washington, D.C., 1966), p. 52–53; see also, J. Finley Lee, Jr., *The Role of Investment Companies in Portfolio Management* (Bryn Mawr, Pa.: American College of Life Underwriters, 1969), p. 6.

TABLE 16–1
No Load Funds

Common Stock Funds
Afuture Fund
American Investors Fund
David L. Babson Investment Fund
De Vegh Mutual Fund
Drexel Equity Fund
Energy Fund
Farm Bureau Mutual Fund
Janus Fund
Financial Industrial Fund
Guardian Mutual Fund
Hartwell Growth Fund
Hartwell Leverage Fund
Ivy Fund
The Johnson Mutual Fund
Mathers Fund
Mutual Shares Corp.
National Industries Fund
The Nassau Fund
Nelson Fund
The One William Street Fund
Penn Square Mutual Fund
Pro Fund
Rowe Price New Era Fund
Rowe Price New Horizons Fund
T. Rowe Price Growth Stock Fund
Scudder Special Fund
Sherman Dean Fund
Stein Roe & Farnham Stock Fund
Naess & Thomas Special Fund
Variable Stock Fund
Smith Barney Equity Fund
Loomis-Sayles Capital Development Fund

Balanced Funds
Dodge & Cox Fund
Loomis-Sayles Mutual Fund
Northeast Investors Trust
The Prudential Fund of Boston
Financial Industrial Income Fund
Scudder, Stevens & Clark Balanced Fund
Stein Roe & Farnham Balanced Fund

Bond Funds
Alliance Bond Fund
California Fund for Investing in U.S. Gov't. Securities
Capital Preservation
Rowe Price New Income Fund

*Money Market Funds**
J. B. Cabot Short-Term Fund
Current Interest
Daily Income Fund
Dreyfus Liquid Assets
Fidelity Daily Income
Money Market Management
Reserve Fund

* Money market funds, as *Forbes* states, unlike most mutual funds, aren't tied to the stock market. They are tied to interest rates. They offer not a slice of American industry but a slice of high interest rates. The majority of them are packages of short term debt maturing in 90 days and less. For small investors they offer an attractive alternative to savings accounts. They were paying returns ranging from 8.5 percent to 11.5 percent (as of mid–1974). Minimum initial investments range from $1 to $5,000. For further information see "Playing the Money Market," *Forbes*, August 15, 1974, p. 67.

plicit, as the data taken from a recent fund prospectus indicates (see Table 16–2).

Obligatory repurchase of its shares by a corporation is relatively uncommon. Savings and loan associations and credit unions indulge in the practice, but investment companies, as far as is known, provide the only other corporate example. Savings and loan associations always repurchase without penalty (except for unearned dividends or interest), and investment companies usually do; but the potential investor is an investment company will do well to check to see whether any redemption fee will be charged by his company if he wishes to sell. Since open end investment companies repurchase their shares on demand, they must constantly be selling at least as many shares as are redeemed in order to have the neces-

TABLE 16–2

Amount of Purchase	Sales Charge as a Percentage of Offering Price	Sales Charge as a Percentage of Amount Invested
Less than $25,000	8.5%	9.3%
$25,000 or more but less than $50,000	6.0	6.4
$50,000 or more but less than $100,000	4.0	4.2
$100,000 or more but less than $250,000	3.0	3.1
$250,000 or more but less than $500,000	2.0	2.1
$500,000 and over	1.0	1.0

sary redemption money; otherwise they will be forced to liquidate some of the investments they hold to obtain it, perhaps at an inauspicious time.

It is these open end investment companies which have enjoyed the greatest growth in the past. From 1940 through 1972, the number of publicly offered mutual funds grew from approximately 70 to more than 600; mutual fund assets grew from under $500 million to more than $59 billion, (see Table 16–3). Shareholders accounts rose from 300,000 to about 10.6 million, representing an estimated 8.5 million individual shareholders. The 1973–74 period showed a sharp decline in assets, down $24 billion in two years. By the end of 1974, 121 mutual funds had assets exceeding $50 million, 18 funds had assets greater than $500 million and 8 funds had assets of more than $1 billion each.

TABLE 16–3
Shareholder Accounts and Total Net Assets, 1940–74 (assets in 000's of dollars)

Calendar Year End	Number of Reporting	Number of Accounts	Assets
1974	431	10,144,678	$35,776,793
1973	421	10,330,862	$46,518,535
1972	410	10,635,287	59,830,646
1971	392	10,900,952	55,045,328
1970	361	10,690,312	47,618,100
1969	269	10,391,534	48,290,733
1968	240	9,080,168	52,677,188
1967	204	7,904,132	44,701,302
1966	182	7,701,656	34,829,353
1965	170	6,709,343	35,220,243
1960	161	4,897,600	17,025,684
1955	125	2,085,325	7,837,524
1950	98	938,651	2,530,563
1945	73	497,875	1,284,185
1940	68	296,056	447,959

Note: Figures for shareholder accounts represent combined totals for member companies. Duplications have not been eliminated. Figures are only for member companies of the Investment Company Institute.

Source: Investment Company Institute.

Who Owns Mutual Funds? And Why?

Seventy (70) percent of total U.S. households did *not* know about mutual funds, according to an Investment Company Institute Survey)[2] Only about 7.8 percent of total U.S. households owned at least one mutual fund as of 1970. Of total U.S. households, 4.9 million were fund owners; 58.1 million were not. Only about 18 percent of people with incomes under $8,000 were aware of funds compared to more than 75 percent of those with incomes of $25,000 or more.

The average person who knows about funds is in his early 40s, married, has some college education, and is earning about $13,500 a year. The typical person who does not know about funds is a few years older, did not finish high school, and earns less than $8,000 per year. There are, however, 13 million householders with income of more than $10,000 a year who were unaware of funds. According to this survcy, only about 15 percent of the aware people with incomes under $8,000 own mutual funds compared with about 50 percent of those with incomes of $25,000 or more.

To check people's perception of mutual funds and other financial assets, investors were asked to rate the risk and gain associated with various assets from 1 to 10. Figure 16–2 summarizes the averages of the risk/gain responses. Risk is plotted on the vertical axis from 1 to 10 (low to high). Gain is shown on the horizontal scale.

Over the counter stocks—designated by the letter O at the top of the chart—were referred to mainly by upper income people. Their perception of the risk associated with this type of asset averaged 9, close to the upper limit. Their perception of gain was a more modest 5. Thus, people perceived investing in over the counter stocks to be very risky relative to expected gain.

Mutual funds, designated by M—at the center of the chart—were generally favorably perceived. They were seen to be somewhat higher in potential gain than O-T-C stocks, and considerably less risky. Common stocks were seen as slightly more profitable than funds but were riskier.[3]

Another study by the Survey Research Center classified investors into four categories: (*a*) Group I, those who own stock only, no mutual fund shares; (*b*) Group II, those who own both stocks and mutual fund shares but have less than about 35 percent in funds; (*c*) Group III, those who

[2] *The Public's Attitude Toward Mutual Funds* (Washington, D.C.: Investment Company Institute, 1971). A free copy may be obtained by writing to the Institute at 1775 K Street, N.W., Washington, D.C. 20006.

[3] For those interested in a more technical and detailed exposition of the risk/reward relationship, see Richard A. Brealey, *An Introduction to Risk and Return from Common Stocks* (Cambridge, Mass.: M.I.T. Press, 1969).

FIGURE 16–2
Perception of Risk/Gain (means: 10 point scale)

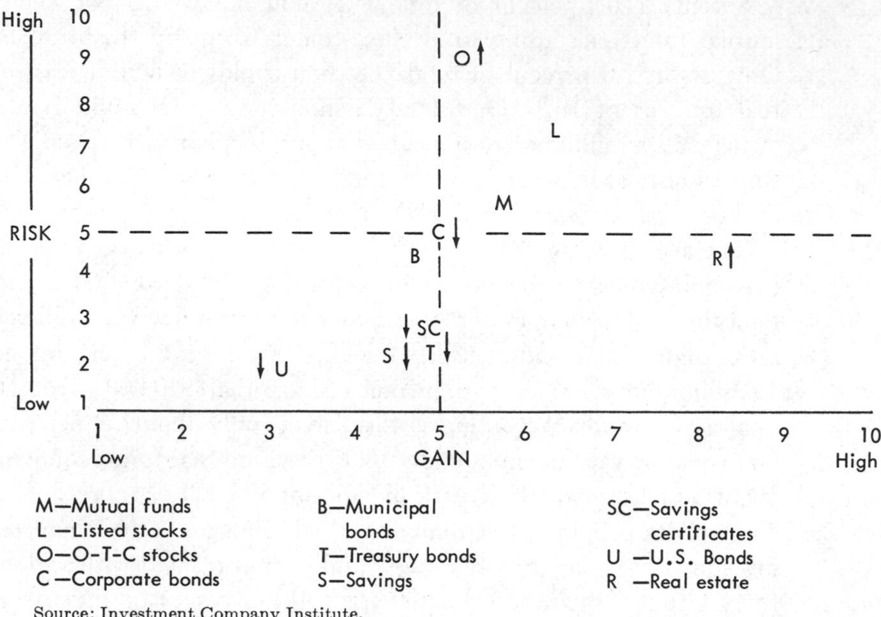

own both stocks and mutual funds and have about 35 percent or more in funds; (*d*) Group IV, those who own mutual fund shares only. The results of the study are shown in Tables 16–4 and 16–5. Of all security owners surveyed, 64 percent owned only stocks, no mutual funds; 25 percent owned both stocks and mutual funds; 11 percent owned only mutual funds, no stocks directly.

Various characteristics of the owners of securities in the four groups are

TABLE 16–4
An Analysis of Ownership

		Security Owners with Income before Taxes of:		
Ownership of either Stocks or Mutual Fund Shares	*All Owners*	*Less than 10,000*	*$10,000 –24,999*	*$25,000 and over*
Group I own only stocks	64%	69	62%	56%
Group II own both, less than 35% in mutual funds	12	6	12	28
Group III own both, 35–99% in mutual funds	13	11	15	12
Group IV own only mutual funds	11	14	11	4
Total	100%	100%	100%	100%

Source: *Institutional Investor*, February 1971 and Survey Research Center, University of Michigan.

TABLE 16–5
Some Characteristics of Ownership

	I Own Only Stocks	II Own Both, MF less than 35%	III Own Both, MF 35–99%	IV Own Only MF
Income				
Under $5,000	11%	*	5%	10%
$5000–7,499	12	8%	11	12
$7500–9,999	16	10	12	22
$10,000–14,999	32	34	34	39
$15,000–24,999	20	22	28	14
$25,000 and over	9	26	10	3
Total	100%	100%	100%	100%
Median income	$11,800	$14,700	$13,300	$10,800
Age				
Under 35	25%	16%	14%	30%
35–44	21	22	27	28
45–54	22	25	26	20
55–64	17	26	20	14
65 and over	15	11	13	8
Total	100%	100%	100%	100%
Median age	46	49	47	41
Education				
11 grades or less	20%	10%	13%	15%
12 grades	31	19	33	24
Some college	21	21	20	23
BA degree	20	30	20	24
Advanced degree	8	20	14	14
Total	100%	100%	100%	100%
Occupation				
Professional, technical workers, managers, officials	38%	48%	42%	46%
Self-employed	6	10	10	7
Clerical, sales workers	13	12	15	13
Craftsmen, foremen	12	11	11	7
Operatives, laborers, service workers	13	1	8	17
Not employed (retired, student, housewife)	18	18	14	10
Total	100%	100%	100%	100%
Number of cases	690	122	132	120

* Less than 0.5%.
Source: *Institutional Investor*, and Survey Research Center, University of Michigan.

presented in Table 16–5. Group II contains the largest number and Group IV the smallest proportion of people with high incomes. Younger people are most frequent in Group IV, which contains an unusually small proportion of older people. Differences in education are not substantial, but Group II contains the largest proportion of highly educated people.

TABLE 16–6
Why People Do or Do Not Invest in Mutual Funds

	Under $5,000	*$5– $10,000*	*$10– $15,000*	*$15,000 and Over*
A. Main reason(s) for investing in mutual funds				
Good investment—safe	32%	22%	39%	42%
Profit—dividends—savings	13	32	35	26
Long-term growth	—	19	15	17
In the hands of pros	5	7	16	22
Diversified investments	11	2	7	14
Security—retirement	5	8	5	6
Opportunity to buy on monthly plan	10	2	4	3
Protection against inflation	—	3	2	2
Inherited—gift	11	4	1	6
Talked into it by good salesman	—	5	4	4
B. Main reason(s) for not investing in mutual funds				
No money to invest—can't afford	60%	51%	40%	19%
Not interested	13	15	17	15
Prefer savings—other investments	9	10	16	34
More risk than stocks	4	4	4	3
Management fees too high	1	1	4	15
Don't know	16	22	21	17
C. What commission rate are you now paying on your mutual fund purchases?				
0 to 5%	6%	17%	24%	15%
6 to 8%	11	22	18	28
Over 9%	19	16	10	7
D. And what commission rate do you think would be a fair rate?				
0 to 5%	30%	44%	35%	48%
6 to 8%	0	11	17	7
Over 8%	0	1	3	2

Source: Louis Harris & Associates for *Newsweek.*

Light on why people invest in mutual funds was shed by a study by Louis Harris and Associates for *Newsweek* magazine. It found that the dominant interest of mutual fund investors is long term growth combined with safety as a means of saving. See Table 16–6 (A). Generally speaking, people decline to invest in mutual funds for the same reasons they stay out of the stock market. It is interesting to note that among the higher income category a sizable number feel that management fees are "too high." See Table 16–6 (B). Most mutual fund investors seemed to feel that their money was being managed pretty well. Many mutual fund holders think a "fair rate" of commission would be one lower than they are actually paying.[4] See Table 16–6 (C and D).

---

[4] "Public Attitudes Toward Money and Its Management," Louis Harris & Associates for *Newsweek,* latest survey.

Types of Open End Companies

There is no hard and fast classification of mutual funds. Objectives often are so broadly stated as to defy classification. Portfolio holdings change over time with changing conditions. As *FundScope*, a leading publication in the mutual fund field, declares: "Mutual funds cannot be unitized. Classifications are necessarily somewhat arbitrary and are not intended to imply that all funds under the same heading have identical purposes or policies. It is possible that certain funds in different groups can be compared more properly than some which fall into the same category."

FundScope, in its many tabulations, classifies funds into seven categories with a number of subcategories. *Group 1* broadly is headed "growth" funds. There is *Group 1–dcs*—diversified common stock funds or diversified common stock growth funds such as Fidelity Trend, Ivest, Fidelity Capital, T. Rowe Price Growth Stock Fund, Mathers, Value Line Fund, Keystone S–3. *Group 1–pf* are the "performance funds" or the "go go" funds. They include, among many others the Enterprise Fund, the Oppenheimer Fund, the Axe-Houghton Stock Fund, the Rowe Price New Horizons Fund, and others. *Group 1–spl* are the specialized common stock growth funds, such as the Chemical Fund, the Energy Fund, the Technology Fund, the Oceanography Fund, the Axe Science Fund, and others.

Group 2 includes the Canadian-International Funds.

Group 3 includes growth with income common stock funds, both diversified common stock funds and flexibly diversified funds, aiming at both growth and income. Examples would be Penn Square, Istel, Babson, Dreyfus, Pioneer and Keystone S–1, to name but a few.

Group 4 are income and growth funds, with the subtle difference between categories 3 and 4 merely a matter of emphasis of objective, more on growth with some income, or more on income with some growth. Examples include Pine Street, Washington, Financial Income, Southwestern, Channing Income.

Group 5 are the balanced funds, with three aspects: growth, income and stability combining stocks and bonds. Examples are the Wellington Fund, Axe-Houghton A, Stein Balanced, Channing Balanced, Dodge Cox Balanced, Nationwide, Whitehall, and American Business.

Group 6 are the income funds, such as Decatur, Puritan, Provident, Value Line Income, American Express Income, and others.

Group 7 are bond preferred stock funds, such as the Harbor Fund, Keystone Bond Funds and so on.[5]

---

[5] For more information see "1974 Mutual Fund Guide," *FundScope* (April 1974), 1900 Avenue of the Stars, Los Angeles, Calif. 90067.

The most simple classification, however, would be (*a*) balanced funds, (*b*) growth (including performance) funds, (*c*) growth and income funds, and (*d*) income funds.

Usually the bond–stock fund is called a *balanced* fund. This has been described as any fund which at all times holds at least 20 to 25 percent (although never more than 75 to 80 percent) of its assets in cash and good grade or high grade senior securities for defensive purposes and which invests the remainder in common stocks or other equity type securities. Balanced funds appear suitable for investors who want to turn over to investment company management fairly complete responsibility for their invested capital and who prefer a "middle of the road" course to one that assumes greater risks in the hope of greater profits or higher income. Examples are Wellington Fund, Eaton & Howard Balanced Fund, and the George Putnam Fund of Boston.

Diversified bond–stock, or balanced, funds normally invest some portion of their assets in bonds or preferred stocks, or both, in addition to a portion which is invested in common stocks. On the average, the funds in the bond–stock classification follow more conservative investment policies than do those which normally limit their holdings to common stocks. They tend to have a lower average return, less capital gain in a rising market, less volatility, better defenses in a falling market, more stability of income, and greater safety of principal than do the stock funds.

The largest group of funds—over 50 percent by net assets—are the *diversified common stock funds*. These have all, or almost all, of the money they hold in common stock, but they are by no means alike, either in investment objective or in performance. Some invest primarily in the better known stocks of large corporations—the standard type of good quality shares frequently described as "blue chips." Others may specialize in "growth company" shares. Some concentrate on shares of less well-known firms, where greater opportunities for profits are believed to exist. Some *performance* funds provide a means of buying into a diversified list of low priced or highly volatile shares. Some diversified common stock funds place greater stress on growth with stability, while others emphasize volatile capital appreciation. Generally they appeal to those investors who concentrate funds in common stock, taking risks to achieve capital gains with or without stability. Examples are Affiliated Fund; Dreyfus Fund; Fundamental Investors; Keystone Custodian Funds S1 (high grade), T. Rowe Price Growth Stock Fund, Keystone S3 (growth), and Keystone S4 (lower priced); Massachusetts Investors Growth Stock Fund; Investors Stock Fund; Massachusetts Investors Trust, Mathers Fund, the Oppenheimer Fund, the Rowe Price New Horizons Fund.

Bonds and preferred stock mutual funds are designed for diversification in senior securities and continuous professional supervision. Examples of bond funds are the Keystone Custodian Funds B1 (high grade), Keystone B2 (medium grade), United Bond Fund, Keystone B4 (discount bonds). Preferred stock funds include National Securities Preferred Stock Series. Because of the sharp rise in interest rates and bond yields, a number of new bond funds were started in the first half of the 1970s.

The specialized common stock funds provide diversification only within a single industry or a group of industries. The holdings of each fund are restricted to securities related to a particular industry, such as insurance, or banks, or a group of industries such as chemicals, energy sources, technology, and oceanography. Examples of industry type common stock funds include Chemical Fund, Inc., Life Insurance Investors, Energy Fund, Technology Fund, United Science Fund, and a few others.

Closed End Investment Companies

The closed end investment company is one with a relatively fixed amount of capital, generally all raised at formation, whose securities are traded on an organized securities exchange or in the over the counter market in the same way as ordinary corporate securities. They issue authorized stock at a given time and wait before they float another issue, if at all. Stock is not usually redeemed by them for their shareholders. Investors who wish to purchase issued shares of closed end companies must purchase them from those who are already stockholders, through their brokers on the exchanges (if it is listed) or via the over the counter market. Tri-Continental Corp., The Lehman Corp., Adams Express, the Madison Fund, Inc., and the Japan Fund, Inc., are examples of leading closed end investment companies.[6]

Shares of closed end companies differ from those of open end companies in the way they are priced. Open end company shares are bought and sold on the basis of their net asset value, whereas the prices of closed end shares are governed entirely by the supply and demand of the shares in the open market. Closed end company shares are usually traded at discounts from their asset value, although a few command premiums.

The resale market for shares of open end investment companies lies primarily in the companies themselves, for they are pledged to redeem their shares. In good times, when the sale of their new shares to the public is producing more money than is needed to buy in old shares offered for

[6] For a list of closed end investment companies, write to *Association of Closed-End Investment Companies,* 330 Madison Avenue, New York, N.Y. 10017.

redemption, there is apt to be no problem; but in times when investment company shares are difficult to sell, the only way that open end investment companies can secure money with which to redeem their own outstanding shares is by selling the investments in their portfolio. To sell at such times may upset dollar averaging and automatic formula timing. In addition, wholesale selling of good securities by many investment companies can only serve to depress the prices at which they can be sold.

The closed end investment companies do not have this problem, because they do not, and cannot be required to, repurchase their shares. Many closed end investment companies have their shares listed on the security exchanges, where active trading secures for them a wide market. Some closed end companies have a multiple capital structure. Besides common stock, they may have preferred stocks, bonds, or bank loans (or all three) outstanding. In such cases, the common stock, possesses a special quality generally known as "leverage."

Leverage

"Leverage" is the special force created by the use of borrowed money or other senior capital which magnifies changes in the assets and earnings available for junior issues. More simply, it is just a case of making money with the use of other people's money. The degree of leverage depends on the ratio of senior securities and bank borrowings to the total resources of the corporation and the relationship of the rate of interest paid on senior securities and bank borrowings to the rate of return which is earned on all the assets of the corporation. If the common stockholders have the use of money furnished by others at a given rate of return and can earn a high rate of return on all the money, including their own, the earnings of the common shareholders will be magnified as compared with what they would be if only their own money were used. The important thing for the potential investor in an investment company to remember is that there is the possibility of greater earnings (and also greater loss) if leverage is present. Such leverage is now rarely found in the diversified closed end investment companies.

Dual Purpose Funds

To take advantage of the concept of leverage, a new type of closed end fund was formed in the late 1960s. Known as the dual purpose fund, it issues two different kinds of stock: income shares and capital shares. The income shares receive all of the income from the entire portfolio purchased by the fund but none of the capital gains. On the other hand, the capital shares receive all of the capital gains, if any, from the entire fund but none of the income. Thus there is theoretically two for one leverage. For example the capital shares have the use of twice the capital they contributed, equivalent to buying stock on a 50 percent margin. The capital shareholders have been using the income shareholders' funds to achieve capital gains, and instead of paying interest, as would be the case if the money had been borrowed, they give up the right to income earned on the capital they have contributed. We may call this *capital leverage.*

There is also *income leverage* because the income shareholders have not only a stated minimum dividend as in the case of preferred stock but also the right to receive all additional income the fund may earn. They receive not only the income earned from the capital contributed by all income shares but also the income earned from the capital contributed by the capital shares as well.

Thus the dual purpose funds seek to combine in one fund two basic investment objectives, high income and significant capital gains. An investor can buy either the income shares alone or the capital shares alone, or both, if desired. Income shares offer only income, capital shares only capital gains. If the fund is not able to pay the minimum dividend in any given year, the amount not paid is carried forward to the next year. Payments above the stated minimum in later years can be applied against any dividend arrearages.

Seven dual funds are in existence today, all started in 1967. Six are traded on the New York Stock Exchange and one over the counter. The dual purpose funds are: American Dualvest Fund, Gemini Fund, Hemisphere Fund, Income and Capital Shares, Leverage Fund of Boston, Putnam Duofund, and, Scudder Duovest. Dual purpose funds are closed end investment companies. Their shares are limited to the amount originally issued and are traded in the market with price determined by supply and demand for the shares. The net asset value of the shares may be more or less than market price, at a given time. If net asset value is less than market price, the shares sell at a premium. If net asset value is more than market price, the shares sell at a discount, which has been the case for the most part, thus far.

Dual purpose funds, unlike other closed end funds, have a limited life —from 12 to 18 years. At the end of these periods, the income shares are paid a stated redemption price plus any dividend arrearages out of the fund's total assets. The remaining assets are distributed to the capital shareholders.

Types of Closed End Investment Companies

At one time a number of closed end investment companies were highly leveraged and therefore speculative. In recent years leverage has declined in importance as closed end companies have reduced or eliminated senior capital.

Most of the larger closed end companies, such as Lehman Corporation, Madison Fund, U.S. & Foreign Securities, now have only common stock outstanding. They are also diversified in their investment policy in that they do not specialize in any one industry or field. There are a few specialized closed end companies such as National Aviation Corporation and the Petroleum Corporation of America. Then there are venture capital investment companies such as American Research and Development Corporation, the Diebold Venture Capital Corporation, the Value Line Development Capital Corporation, and others. Some closed end companies concentrate their investments in specific areas of the world as American–South African Investment Company, and Japan Fund.

Two newer types of closed end investment companies are the real estate investment trust (REIT), discussed in Chapter 13, and the small business investment company (SBIC). There are now well over 350 SBICs in operation, of which only a small percentage are publicly owned.

Most of the new bond funds formed in the early 1970s were closed end. Some disappointed stock investors cashed in their holdings and turned to bond funds which seemed to provide a high, stable and less risky return, seemingly. A large proportion of the newer bond funds were organized and are managed by banks or insurance companies. The banks and insurance companies customarily invest large amounts in bonds. They have the technical know-how and adding a bond fund required relatively little added expense. The majority of the funds invested principally in higher grade bonds. Some invested in tax exempt state and municipal bonds. These are known as tax free bond funds. The regular variety paid a 7.5 to 8 percent return which was regarded as attractive at the time the funds were organized.[7]

Methods of Purchase

There are three basic ways to purchase mutual fund shares: regular account, accumulation plan, and contractual plan.

Regular Account. This is a lump sum purchase. A specific amount of money is invested at one time. The sales fee, or "loading charge" of 7.5 or 8

[7] For further information see "Closed End Bond Funds: Investing for Income," *Changing Times*, September 1973.

percent is assessed against your total purchase. Thus, if you invest $10,000, $800 goes to dealers or distributors, and you buy $9,200 worth of shares. Most funds now reduce the loading charge for larger purchases (see Table 16–2, p. 782).

A few days after you place the order, you should receive a certificate in your name for the proper number of shares. Dividend checks are sent to you in the mail, usually quarterly, though some funds will arrange to pay monthly dividends. Or you can arrange to reinvest your dividends to purchase additional shares. If the fund distributes realized capital gains, as many do from time to time, you can either take them as cash or you can reinvest them in additional shares.

Accumulation Plans. These are of two types, informal (or voluntary) and contractual. The informal or voluntary plan starts with an application stating the amount of the initial purchase, which must be from $100 to $500, depending on the particular fund, and an indication of the amounts to be invested periodically thereafter and the dates on which payments will be made. There is usually a minimum of $25 or $50 required for the periodic payment, but there is no compulsion to adhere to the amount stated in the application, provided the payment tendered does not fall below the minimum required. A confirmation of each purchase is sent to the investor but stock certificates are not sent unless specifically requested.

An informal accumulation plan differs in many respects from the contractual plan to be described. Each purchase is an entity in itself. There is no specified duration of the plan. It lasts as long as the purchaser wishes to continue making further payments. There is no built in element of compulsion to continue payments in order to minimize the effect of the sales charge. In the voluntary accumulation plan the load is based only on the individual payment and is deducted from each payment. Thus the voluntary plan combines the advantage of the dollar cost averaging principle with the "load" arrangements of the regular account. It does not have the penalty arrangement of the contractual plan. The investor can liquidate his account, if he wishes, just as he can in the case of shares bought the regular way. In many funds the informal accumulation plan can be used as an open account by investors, who instead of making regular payments of stated amounts at indicated future dates, prefer to make irregular additions at varying times. The voluntary accumulation plan allows the investor maximum flexibility in contrast to the contractual plan.

The Contractual Plan. There has been a very rapid growth in contractual plans over the last decade partly because they are exceedingly favorable to the salesmen. They are accumulation plans with a built-in financial incentive to carry out the agreed upon future purchases and payments. Under a contractual plan, the purchaser agrees to make regular monthly or quarterly payments toward the purchase of mutual fund shares, over a period of years, usually 10. The plan is set up in such a way as to discourage the purchaser from discontinuing payments, especially in the early years. This is achieved by providing that a substantial part of the total sales commission on the entire plan be deducted in the first year. Under the Investment Company Act the specific provisions with respect to contractual plans limit the sales charge on them to a maximum of 9 percent of the total investment over the life of the plan but permit the deduction for sales charges of up to 50 percent of the first year's investment. Thus, if you purchase a 10 year, $10,000 plan and pay in $1,000 the first year, assuming the "load" is 8 percent, or $800 on the $10,000, your $1,000 the first year will bring only $500 worth of shares because $500 of the $800 commission will be deducted from the first year's $1,000 investment. The balance of the sales charge, amounting to $300, must be apportioned evenly over the remaining installments.

You can easily see the great disadvantage of discontinuing the plan in any early year. If you discontinue the plan at the end of the first year, for example, assuming the price of the shares have not changed, you would receive back only $500 of your $1,000 investment. The remaining $500 went to the distribution organization. How sharply must the shares rise and how much capital gain and dividend distribution must there be to enable your $500, which was all that was actually put to work of your first year's $1,000, to double itself? It is quite unlikely to double within a year or two. Thus the financial pressure of the contractual plan. For this reason it has sometimes been called "a penalty plan or a "front end load plan." The more polite term, preferred by the mutual funds, is, however, "contractual" plan, because it formalizes the buyer's agreement to make periodic payments.

Continued criticism of the "front end load" led to an amendment to the Investment Companies Act in 1970 to provide for the use of one or the other of two sales charge arrangements in contractual plans.[8]

(*a*) Either the company can, as before, deduct up to 50 percent of the first 12 monthly payments for sales commissions. If it does, then the shareholder has the right during the first 45 days to cash in the shares, securing a complete refund of the sales commissions. Or, during the first 18 months, the shares can be cashed in and a refund of the sales charges that exceed 15 percent of total payments obtained. The 15 percent would be lost, however.

(*b*) Or, if a plan deducts no more than 20 percent from payments during any one year and no more than an average of 16 percent from the first

[8] It should be noted that the states of California, Illinois, Ohio, and Wisconsin prohibit the sale of contractual arrangements.

48 monthly payments, then it doesn't have to extend the 18 month refund right, only the 45 day one.

Capital gains and dividend distributions paid on the shares owned are automatically reinvested and thus used to purchase additional shares, an important factor in adding to the longer term value of the accumulation. Keep in mind, however, that such capital gains and dividends, even though they are reinvested, are taxable annually to the shareholder.

A useful form of insurance has been developed to provide, in the case of the purchaser's death before completion of the plan, the funds to cover the difference between the intended total investment and the amount already paid. Known as "plan completion insurance" the maximum coverage with any plan company is $45,000 and in many cases $30,000. The cost of the insurance is deducted from the investor's regular monthly payments. Investors must be able to prove insurability. A medical examination is usually required. Insurance rates charged are usually low, based on group term policies and partly on the age of the investor.

Bear in mind that the insurance does not guarantee the purchaser's estate any fixed sum of money. All it does is provide for the fulfilment of the plan and therefore the delivery of the number of shares that could be bought based on the agreed upon investment and the net asset value of the shares at time of purchase. The value of the shares delivered to the estate may be more or less than the total amount invested, depending on market conditions at the time of the purchaser's death.

Withdrawal Plans

Many mutual funds provide withdrawal plans for those who desire a regular quarterly or monthly income, especially for retirement purposes. A minimum amount, usually $5,000 or $10,000, is customarily required to start a withdrawal plan. As in the case of an annuity, this may be paid in over a long period of time via either regular payments or an accumulation plan, or it may be paid in as a lump sum at a given point when the individual decides to retire. The monthly or quarterly payments made by the fund to the individual may be drawn from capital as well as from investment income and from capital gains. It may be more or less per month, per quarter, or per annum than the capital earns via income and capital gains. How fast or slowly you wish to use up your capital depends on the monthly or quarterly payment specified and on the performance of the fund. There are now about 252,000 withdrawal accounts operational.[9]

---

9 For the latest figure, see *The Mutual Fund Fact Book*, latest edition. A free copy may be obtained by writing to the Investment Company Institute at 1775 K Street, N.W., Washington, D.C. 20006.

The advantage of a withdrawal plan is that in a successful fund you can obtain steady income and preserve or enhance your capital as well. Or in retirement you can eat into capital to maximize your drawing. The limitations are that if you select a poorly performing fund, your capital will melt away rapidly. Also, there is the ever present risk that in retirement you will outlive your capital. Unlike an annuity which guarantees you either a fixed or variable income for life, a mutual fund withdrawal plan will last only as long as your capital lasts. If the underlying stocks in the mutual fund decline in value, instead of growing, your capital can diminish and eventually be used up.

Thus the risk of outliving your capital makes a mutual fund withdrawal plan more suitable as a supplement to a pension or an annuity rather than as the sole source of retirement income. Withdrawal plans are also useful for paying for a college education or helping to pay off a mortgage.[10]

The most important ingredient of a successful withdrawal plan is having the "right" mutual fund. The "right" one, of course, is one that will keep your money growing fast enough so that your shares will never be worth any less than when you started. Some mutual fund 6 percent withdrawal plans started a decade ago showed capital appreciation of 50 percent or more despite withdrawals each month. Others had sharp decreases in assets, in some cases 50 percent or more.

One method of selecting a withdrawal plan from among the hundreds of funds of varying performance that offer them is to obtain a copy of the latest edition of *A Guide to Mutual Fund Withdrawal Plans*.[11] The current edition shows the results of a $10,000, $50 a month withdrawal plan over the prior decade.

The Portfolio

Since 1940 in the open end company, management has had wide discretion as to the securities to be carried in the portfolio. This is known as the "management" type of operation, and the managers deduct an annual fee from accumulated earnings to cover their services. The fee is usually stated as a percentage of asset value. For example, if a fund charges 1 percent per year of asset value and its assets are $20 million, the management fee is $200,000. If the fund earned a 5 percent return on its $20 million of assets, or $1 million, then the management fee would be 20 percent of annual in-

---

[10] See "Withdrawal Programs," *FundScope*, June 1974.

[11] Published by Wiesenberger Services, Inc., One New York Plaza, New York, N.Y. 10004.

come. It is usually never stated in this fashion, however, the funds preferring to state it as a percentage of asset value, not of annual income.

Most mutual funds publish, quarterly, a list showing their holdings of securities; and perhaps more than any other type of financial institution their portfolio and their operations are largely open to public scrutiny. The securities they hold, as of the last quarter, can usually be easily ascertained, either by writing to the fund itself or by consulting such sources as the annual edition of *Investment Companies,* published each year by Arthur Wiesenberger and Company, or *Vickers Guide to Investment Company Portfolios.* Observation of changes in portfolios over a period of years will provide interesting insights into changing patterns of investment and will tell the small, amateur investor what the investment managers are thinking and doing. For example, industry preferences over a period of time by investment company managers may be seen from Tables 16–7 and 16–8.

Earnings

From their investments, both closed and open end companies have two sorts of income. In addition to the ordinary interest and dividends earned, there is often a profit secured by selling securities at more than their cost. These latter profits (capital gains) are often thought of as a nice, juicy melon to be cut and enjoyed. Income taxes on capital gains are much less for many wealthier investors than the taxes they have to pay on ordinary income; the result is that some managements feel an especial urge to attempt to achieve them.

This is especially true since for many funds expenses run quite high. For example, according to the "Tablistics" section of *Johnson's Charts,* expenses expressed as a percent of income, rather than as a percent of asset value (Johnson shows it both ways), run from a low of 4.4 percent for the Affiliated Fund) to a high of 536 percent (for the Doll Fund, Inc.). A goodly number of funds have expenses running in excess of 50 percent of income. This seems quite high and before investing in high expense funds, you should investigate the causes for the high charges, since they eat into prospective dividend distributions and in due course affect capital gains.

Payments from both sources are made to the investor in the same way, and frequently in the same check. The companies are required by law, however, to state the source of distributions from anything other than net investment income. The distinction between dividends from net investment income and distributions from capital gains is important and should be thoroughly understood. Investment companies differ in their view of how shareholders should regard capital gains distributions; some maintain that

TABLE 16–7
Vickers Favorite Fifty

RANK BY $ VALUE				STOCKS	$ Value (Millions)	No. Fds. Holding	Number of Shares Held	Net Change In Holdings	% Outst. Stk. Held by Fds.
Dec. 31 1969	Dec. 31 1973	Sept. 30 1974	Dec. 31 1974						
1	1	1	1	INTERNATIONAL BUSINESS MACHINES	1301	421	7,746,400	+261,400	5.3
7	2	2	2	EXXON CORPORATION	665	227	10,290,000	-223,400	4.6
3	4	3	3	AMERICAN TELEPHONE & TELEGRAPH	550	194	12,322,800	-766,700	2.2
18	5	5	4	PHILIP MORRIS, INC.	447	104	9,309,200	+135,900	16.7
9	8	8	5	ATLANTIC RICHFIELD COMPANY	335	143	3,688,200	-118,300	7.9
6	7	7	6	BURROUGHS CORPORATION	330	146	4,369,400	-112,900	11.2
5	6	6	7	EASTMAN KODAK COMPANY	301	200	4,790,400	+78,000	3.0
2	3	4	8	XEROX CORPORATION	283	189	5,502,900	-439,500	6.9
-	9	15	9	KERR-McGEE CORPORATION	261	84	3,649,600	-181,100	14.6
-	37	28	10	SCHLUMBERGER, LTD.	240	109	2,220,400	+188,300	6.0
39	-	17	11	R. J. REYNOLDS INDUSTRIES	234	82	4,473,800	+345,000	10.6
-	45	21	12	STANDARD OIL COMPANY (INDIANA)	233	107	5,359,300	+838,100	3.8
13	10	9	13	TEXACO INC.	233	122	11,164,100	-812,900	4.1
-	32	19	14	SCHERING-PLOUGH CORPORATION	232	98	4,425,000	+444,900	8.2
41	-	13	15	UNION CARBIDE CORPORATION	227	131	5,481,800	-277,400	8.9
-	-	12	16	DOW CHEMICAL COMPANY	218	115	3,957,900	-138,000	4.3
20	41	25	17	MERCK & COMPANY	217	118	3,262,500	+131,400	4.4
25	24	32	18	CONTINENTAL OIL COMPANY	201	69	4,496,400	+188,400	8.9
26	17	10	19	FORD MOTOR COMPANY	199	94	5,955,400	-204,800	6.4
8	12	11	20	GENERAL MOTORS CORPORATION	196	141	6,387,100	+300,600	2.2
-	11	26	21	McDONALD'S CORPORATION	190	104	6,466,200	+83,100	16.2
-	20	35	22	HALLIBURTON COMPANY	189	93	1,375,300	+80,000	7.2
-	22	33	23	CITICORP	185	93	6,525,200	+340,400	5.3
-	-	-	24	**FEDERAL NATIONAL MORTGAGE ASSN.	183	67	9,941,500	+410,800	21.1
-	25	34	25	UNION PACIFIC CORPORATION	178	62	2,595,800	+118,700	11.4
-	40	47	26	GETTY OIL COMPANY	174	50	1,100,200	+35,600	5.9
49	16	20	27	WEYERHAEUSER COMPANY	174	72	6,350,800	-392,900	5.0
-	-	-	28	**BRISTOL-MYERS COMPANY	173	66	3,462,300	+306,000	11.0
34	36	46	29	WARNER-LAMBERT COMPANY	170	72	6,539,300	+374,700	8.3
-	28	41	30	SYNTEX CORPORATION	169	99	4,299,200	+53,400	20.9
16	23	16	31	MINNESOTA MINING & MANUFACTURING	167	115	3,614,000	+5,300	3.2
31	-	44	32	AMERICAN HOME PRODUCTS	167	97	5,009,200	+660,100	3.2
-	15	40	33	PHILLIPS PETROLEUM COMPANY	166	89	3,826,900	+128,400	5.1
14	13	27	34	GENERAL ELECTRIC COMPANY	161	139	4,837,200	-56,800	2.7
-	-	37	35	ELI LILLY & COMPANY	159	76	2,337,600	-42,300	3.4
47	18	22	36	STANDARD OIL COMPANY OF CALIFORNIA	158	80	7,092,400	-203,200	4.2
-	43	-	37	**DEERE & COMPANY	157	76	3,685,400	+113,400	12.5
-	19	-	38	**AETNA LIFE & CASUALTY COMPANY	155	79	6,480,200	+323,000	12.3
22	26	31	39	MOBIL OIL CORPORATION	153	119	4,258,400	-162,200	4.2
36	50	-	40	**PFIZER INC.	151	83	4,581,000	+370,200	6.5
43	14	14	41	E. I. DU PONT DE NEMOURS	150	99	1,624,500	-214,500	3.4
-	-	23	42	U. S. STEEL CORPORATION	150	77	3,939,800	-212,900	7.3
-	-	18	43	MONSANTO COMPANY	149	84	3,664,800	-192,700	10.8
28	21	42	44	S. S. KRESGE COMPANY	142	92	6,402,900	-79,600	5.2
-	38	29	45	GENERAL TELEPHONE & ELECTRONICS	139	100	8,254,100	+266,100	6.5
40	29	30	46	INTERNATIONAL PAPER COMPANY	138	88	3,859,100	-233,700	8.8
-	-	39	47	JOHNSON & JOHNSON	135	82	1,666,000	-24,600	2.9
-	-	-	48	*WILLIAMS COMPANIES (new)	128	80	3,926,000	+225,400	20.6
-	49	38	49	BETHLEHEM STEEL CORPORATION	126	48	5,079,400	-92,500	11.7
11	42	-	50	**AVON PRODUCTS, INC.	126	80	4,377,700	+498,600	7.5

*NEWCOMER **RETURNEE DISPLACED: Alcan Aluminium Ltd. - Aluminum Co. of America -
Digital Equipment Corp. - Hercules, Inc. - Procter & Gamble Co. - Sperry Rand Corp. - Texas Instruments, Inc.

SUMMARY OF FAVORITE FIFTY BY INDUSTRY

dollar value of stocks by industry to total dollar value of favorite fifty

	12/31/74	9/30/74	12/31/73	12/31/69
OIL & NATURAL GAS	25.8%	24.0%	26.2%	14.6%
CHEMICALS & DRUGS	20.9	19.1	11.7	12.1
OFFICE EQUIPMENT	16.4	20.7	20.6	27.7
UTILITIES	5.9	6.5	5.7	4.5
FINANCE	4.5	1.4	4.7	2.4
LEISURE	4.2	4.5	6.7	8.0
MOTORS	3.4	4.3	3.8	4.0
STEEL	2.4	2.8	1.1	-
MISCELLANEOUS	16.5	16.7	19.5	26.7
	100.0%	100.0%	100.0%	100.0%

Source: Vickers Guide to Investment Company Portfolios.

TABLE 16–8
100 Stocks Ranked by Number of Investment Companies

Rank	Stock	No. of Inv. Cos. Holding	Rank	Stock	No. of Inv. Cos. Holding	Rank	Stock	No. of Inv. Cos. Holding	Rank	Stock	No. of Inv. Cos. Holding
1.	I.B.M.	421	26.	Amer. Home Prods.	97	51.	Sperry Rand	72	76.	CBS Inc.	58
2.	Exxon Corp.	227	27.	Sears Roebuck	96	52.	Upjohn Co.	72	77.	Hercules Inc.	57
3.	Eastman Kodak	200	28.	Citicorp	93	53.	Warner-Lambert	72	78.	Mapco	56
4.	A. T. & T.	194	29.	Halliburton Co.	93	54.	Weyerhaeuser Co.	72	79.	Fed. Dept. Stores	55
5.	Xerox Corp.	189	30.	Kresge (S.S.)	92	55.	Gulf Oil	70	80.	Hughes Tool	55
6.	Burroughs Corp.	146	31.	Ford Motor	90	56.	Continental Oil	69	81.	Air Prods. & Chem.	54
7.	Atlantic Richfield	143	32.	Phillips Petroleum	89	57.	Imperial Oil 'A'	68	82.	Coca-Cola	54
8.	General Motors	141	33.	Intl. Paper	88	58.	Kennecott Copper	68	83.	Delta Airlines	52
9.	General Electric	139	34.	Procter & Gamble	85	59.	Fedl. Natl. Mtg.	67	84.	Penney (J. C.)	52
10.	Union Carbide	131	35.	Kerr-McGee	84	60.	McDermott (J. Ray)	67	85.	Vetco Offshore	52
11.	Texaco Inc.	122	36.	Monsanto	84	61.	Alum. Co. of Amer.	66	86.	Canadian Pacific	51
12.	Mobil Oil	119	37.	Pfizer Inc.	83	62.	Bristol-Myers	66	87.	Jim Walter	51
13.	Merck & Co.	118	38.	Digital Equipment	82	63.	Intl. Tel. & Tel.	65	88.	Dome Petroleum	50
14.	Intl. Nickel 'A'	116	39.	Johnson & Johnson	82	64.	Tenneco Inc.	65	89.	Getty Oil	50
15.	Dow Chemical	115	40.	Reynolds (R.J.)	82	65.	Polaroid	64	90.	Amer. Broadcasting	49
16.	M.M.M.	115	41.	Avon Products	80	66.	Texas Utilities	64	91.	IU Intl.	49
17.	Schlumberger Ltd.	109	42.	Std. Oil, Calif.	80	67.	Pittston Co.	63	92.	Northwest Air	49
18.	Alcan Aluminium	107	43.	Williams Cos.	80	68.	Travelers Corp.	63	93.	United Aircraft	49
19.	Std. Oil (Indiana)	107	44.	Aetna Life & Cas.	79	69.	Raytheon Co.	62	94.	Bethlehem Steel	48
20.	McDonald's Corp.	104	45.	U. S. Steel	77	70.	Union Pacific	62	95.	Gillette Co.	48
21.	Philip Morris	104	46.	Deere & Co.	76	71.	Std. Oil (Ohio)	61	96.	Santa Fe Ind.	48
22.	Genl. Tel. & Elec.	100	47.	Lilly (Eli)	76	72.	Intl. Min. & Chem.	60	97.	Seagram Co.	48
23.	du Pont (E. I.)	99	48.	Texas Instruments	73	73.	Goodyear	59	98.	Utah Intl.	48
24.	Syntex	99	49.	UAL Inc.	73	74.	Motorola	59	99.	Safeway Stores	47
25.	Schering-Plough	98	50.	Caterpillar Tractor	72	75.	Baxter Labs.	58	100.	Squibb Corp.	47

Source: Vickers Associates, Inc., 226 New York Avenue, Huntington, N.Y. 11743.

they should never be thought of as spendable income, while others believe it is all right to consider small payments from that source as an earned addition to dividend income. The more conservative view is that capital gains realized in rising markets must be conserved to offset capital loss which are inevitable in falling markets.

Measuring Performance

There are generally two views of the performance record of investment companies, especially of the mutual funds. One is the salesman's view, which makes mutuals appear incomparable. The exhibit is usually a formidable looking chart that shows the 10 year rise in per share asset value. This is normally unaccompanied by an explanation that rising stock prices over the prior decade caused a swelling book value for many investment portfolios. Nor is there any indication that a given sum of money, such as $10,000, invested at compound interest over a decade would appreciate significantly solely by reason of the compounding process (see Figure 16–3).

The second, more sober, view was expressed by *Forbes* magazine when it declared: "The real truth lies somewhere between these two extremes and it varies widely from fund to fund. Some mutuals have achieved results far better than the average small investor could accomplish for himself. Others just equal blind chance. And a third and sizeable group show few results but expensive managements."

The customary presentation is to assume that $10,000 was invested in

FIGURE 16–3
Quarterly Compounding Table

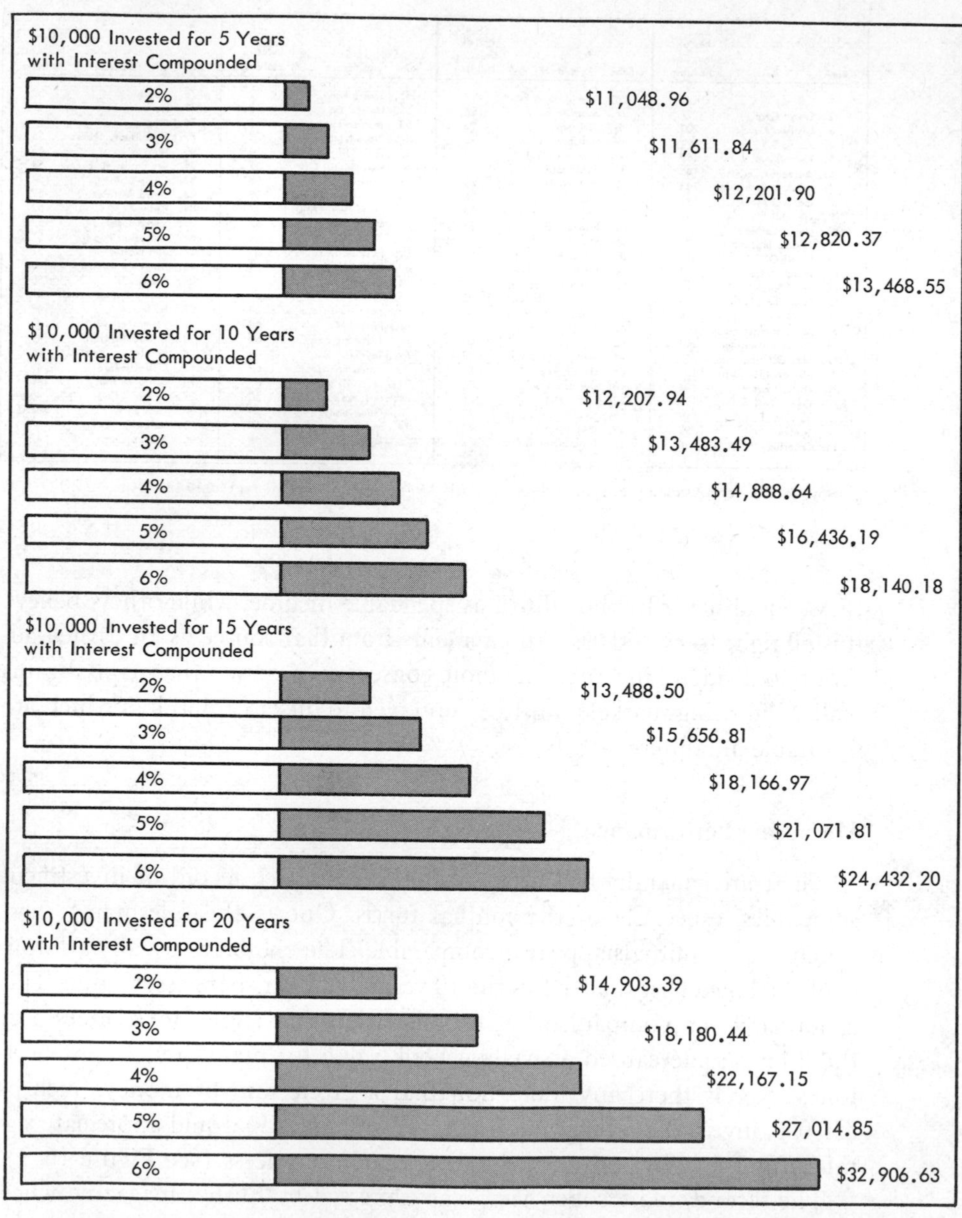

a given fund 10 or 15 years back, or when the fund was started, and then show what happened to the investment by the end of the selected period. In many cases the results are truly impressive. For example, in the case of a leading no load fund, the T. Rowe Price Growth Stock Fund, an assumed investment of $10,000 made when the fund was started in April 1950, would, by December 31, 1974, with dividends reinvested and with capital gains accepted in additional shares, have amounted to $114,482. In the case of a leading load fund, the Oppenheimer Fund, an initial investment of $10,000 at the time the fund was started in April 1959, would, by December 31, 1974, again assuming all dividends were reinvested and all capital gains taken as additional shares, have amounted to $24,986 (see Figures 16–4 and 16–5). These are, of course, fine performances, and it is the use of statistics such as these that have brought total investment in mutual funds from $400 million in 1941 to a peak of $59 billion in 1972, now down to $35 billion. But both funds turned in two of the better performances. A good many funds did not do as well, and a number did not match the capital appreciation of standard stock indexes, such as Dow-Jones or Standard & Poor's. It is this type of comparison which brings us to the second view.

Another view compares the performance of a given fund with the investment results which would have followed had the same amount of money been placed across the board directly in the stocks comprising, say, the Dow-Jones Industrial average. In 1949 one of the longest and greatest bull markets in U.S. history began. From December 31, 1949, to January 11, 1973, the Dow-Jones Industrial average rose from 200 to 1051, a rise of 425 percent. Only a minority of the funds equaled or exceeded this performance. Many of the funds, despite their professional management, did not do as well.

This type of comparison—contrasting, for example, the Standard & Poor's Stock Index performance with that of any given fund—can be undertaken at a glance by using *Johnson's Charts*, published annually by Hugh A. Johnson, Buffalo, New York. This volume has a chart for each major fund and also overlays of the Standard & Poor's Index and of the performance of the stock of a number of individual companies such as General Motors or Exxon or Xerox. You simply place the overlay on the chart of a given fund, and you can see a comparison or contrast of performance at a glance. It is a very useful volume, and any prospective investor in mutual funds should study it carefully before buying. It helps materially in the difficult process of deciding which fund to select. Individual funds can be compared to the average of all balanced funds or the average of all growth stock funds or of all income funds.

The variety of ways by which *Johnson's Charts* enable you to compare and measure market performance may be seen by reviewing the following figures. Figure 16–6 shows the 10 year performance of the Johnson growth fund average. You can compare any individual fund performance with the average. For example, Figure 16–7 shows the comparable results for the Rowe Price New Horizons Fund. Clearly this fund performed better than the average. Tables are also provided showing performance results for 10 year, 15 year, 20 year, and 25 year periods. These are useful for evaluating the performance record for the stock funds shown in *Johnson's Charts*.

FIGURE 16–4
Illustration of a $10,000 Assumed Investment in Shares of Oppenheimer Fund, Inc. 1959–1974

This chart covers the period from the Fund's inception on April 30, 1959 to December 31, 1974. The period was one of widely fluctuating common stock prices, but security prices, with some exceptions, were higher at the end of this period than at the beginning. The results shown should not be considered as a representation of the dividend income or capital gain or loss which may be realized from an investment made in the Fund today. Initial net asset value is the amount received by the Fund after deducting from the cost of the investment the sales charge as described in the prospectus. No adjustment has been made for any income taxes payable by the investor or income reinvested or security profits distributions taken in shares.

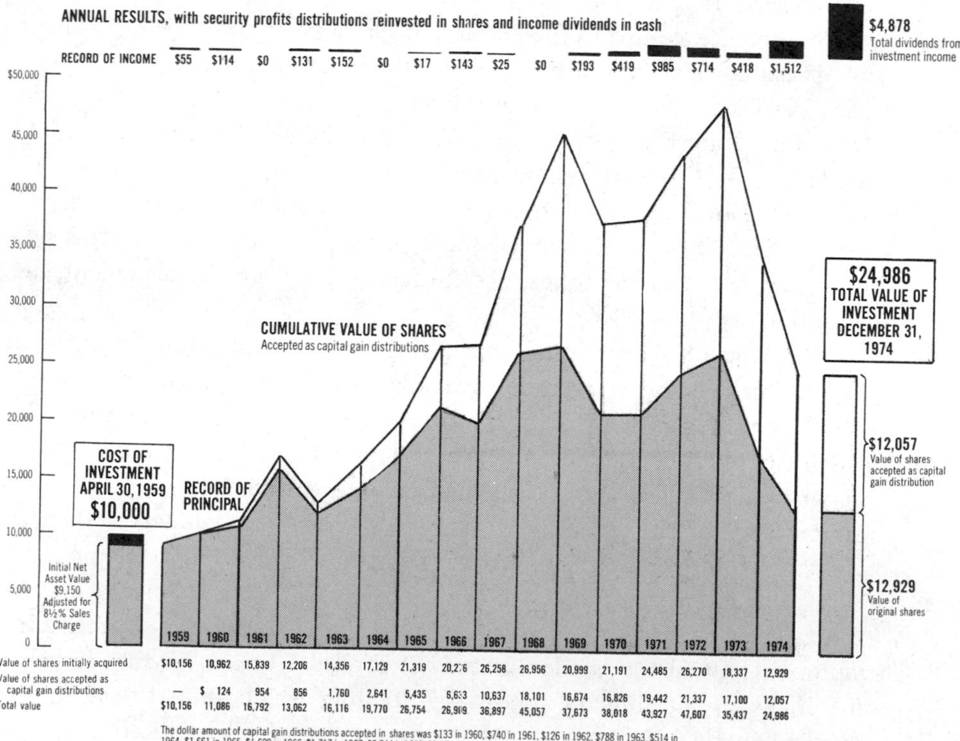

	1959	1960	1961	1962	1963	1964	1965	1966	1967	1968	1969	1970	1971	1972	1973	1974
Value of shares initially acquired	$10,156	10,962	15,839	12,206	14,356	17,129	21,319	20,2[illegible]6	26,258	26,956	20,999	21,191	24,485	26,270	18,337	12,929
Value of shares accepted as capital gain distributions	—	$ 124	954	856	1,760	2,641	5,435	6,6[illegible]3	10,637	18,101	16,674	16,826	19,442	21,337	17,100	12,057
Total value	$10,156	11,086	16,792	13,062	16,116	19,770	26,754	26,9[illegible]9	36,897	45,057	37,673	38,018	43,927	47,607	35,437	24,986

The dollar amount of capital gain distributions accepted in shares was $133 in 1960, $740 in 1961, $126 in 1962, $788 in 1963, $514 in 1964, $1,661 in 1965, $1,629 in 1966, $1,717 in 1967, $5,744 in 1968, $2,971 in 1969, $468 in 1972, and $2,696 in 1973. Total $19,187.

Source: The Oppenheimer Fund, Inc.

FIGURE 16–5
Illustration of an Assumed Investment of $10,000

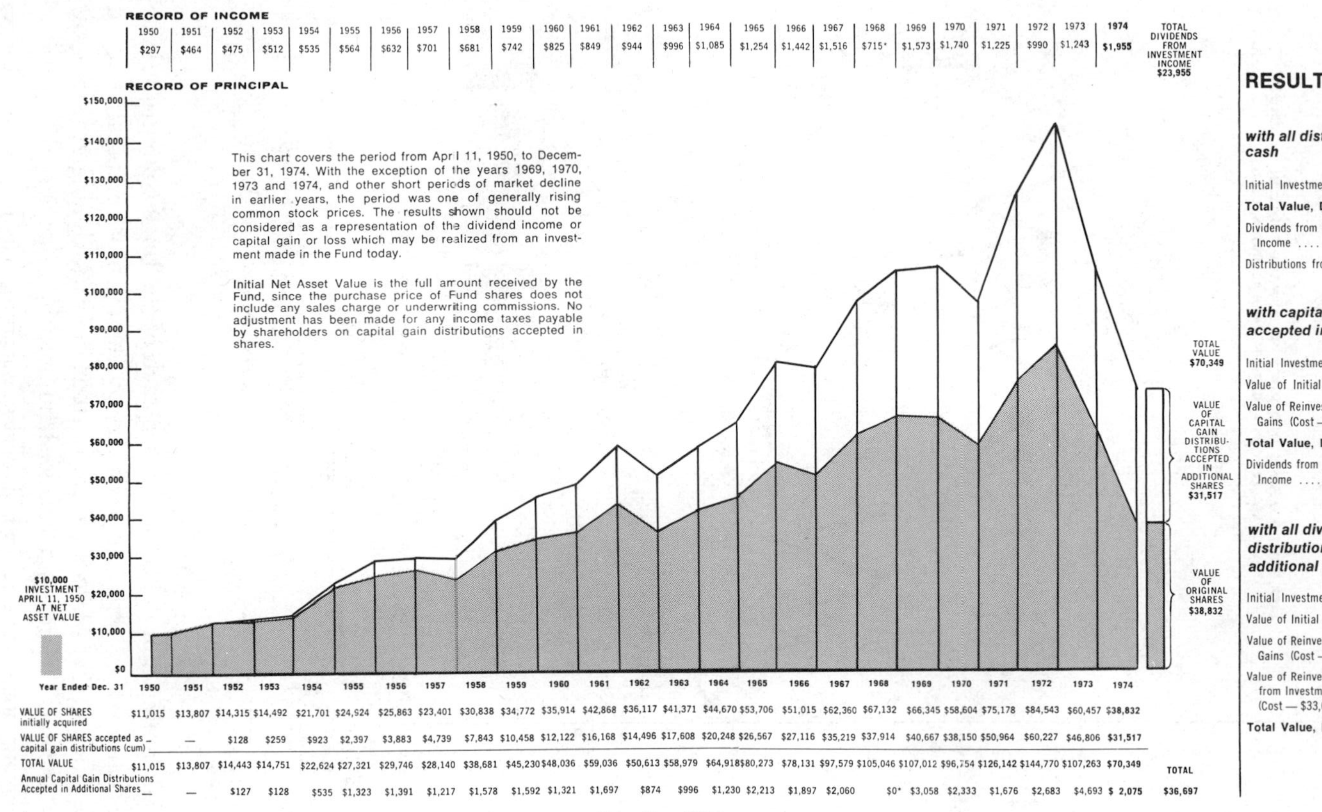

Record of Income

1950	1951	1952	1953	1954	1955	1956	1957	1958	1959	1960	1961	1962
$297	$464	$475	$512	$535	$564	$632	$701	$681	$742	$825	$849	$944

1963	1964	1965	1966	1967	1968	1969	1970	1971	1972	1973	1974	TOTAL DIVIDENDS FROM INVESTMENT INCOME
$996	$1,085	$1,254	$1,442	$1,516	$715*	$1,573	$1,740	$1,225	$990	$1,243	$1,955	$23,955

Year Ended Dec. 31	1950	1951	1952	1953	1954	1955	1956	1957	1958	1959	1960	1961	1962
VALUE OF SHARES initially acquired	$11,015	$13,807	$14,315	$14,492	$21,701	$24,924	$25,863	$23,401	$30,838	$34,772	$35,914	$42,868	$36,117
VALUE OF SHARES accepted as capital gain distributions (cum)	—	—	$128	$259	$923	$2,397	$3,883	$4,739	$7,843	$10,458	$12,122	$16,168	$14,496
TOTAL VALUE	$11,015	$13,807	$14,443	$14,751	$22,624	$27,321	$29,746	$28,140	$38,681	$45,230	$48,036	$59,036	$50,613
Annual Capital Gain Distributions Accepted in Additional Shares	—	—	$127	$128	$535	$1,323	$1,391	$1,217	$1,578	$1,592	$1,321	$1,697	$874

Year Ended Dec. 31	1963	1964	1965	1966	1967	1968	1969	1970	1971	1972	1973	1974	TOTAL
VALUE OF SHARES initially acquired	$41,371	$44,670	$53,706	$51,015	$62,360	$67,132	$66,345	$58,604	$75,178	$84,543	$60,457	$38,832	
VALUE OF SHARES accepted as capital gain distributions (cum)	$17,608	$20,248	$26,567	$27,116	$35,219	$37,914	$40,667	$38,150	$50,964	$60,227	$46,806	$31,517	
TOTAL VALUE	$58,979	$64,918	$80,273	$78,131	$97,579	$105,046	$107,012	$96,754	$126,142	$144,770	$107,263	$70,349	
Annual Capital Gain Distributions Accepted in Additional Shares	$996	$1,230	$2,213	$1,897	$2,060	$0*	$3,058	$2,333	$1,676	$2,683	$4,693	$ 2,075	$36,697

* In 1968, payments of capital gain distributions for the year and income dividends for the last six months were shifted to a February, 1969 date.

RESULTS . . .

with all distributions taken in cash

Initial Investment, April 11, 1950	$ 10,000
Total Value, Dec. 31, 1974	**$ 38,832**
Dividends from Investment Income	$ 17,031
Distributions from Capital Gains	$ 25,512

with capital gain distributions accepted in additional shares

Initial Investment, April 11, 1950	$ 10,000
Value of Initial Investment	$ 38,832
Value of Reinvested Capital Gains (Cost — $36,697)	$ 31,517
Total Value, Dec. 31, 1974	**$ 70,349**
Dividends from Investment Income	$ 23,955

with all dividends and distributions accepted in additional shares

Initial Investment, April 11, 1950	$ 10,000
Value of Initial Investment	$ 38,832
Value of Reinvested Capital Gains (Cost — $52,479)	$ 43,298
Value of Reinvested Dividends from Investment Income (Cost — $33,609)	$ 32,352
Total Value, Dec. 31, 1974	**$114,482**

Source: T. Rowe Price Growth Stock Fund, Inc.

FIGURE 16–6
Johnson Growth Fund Average (January 1, 1964—December 31, 1973)

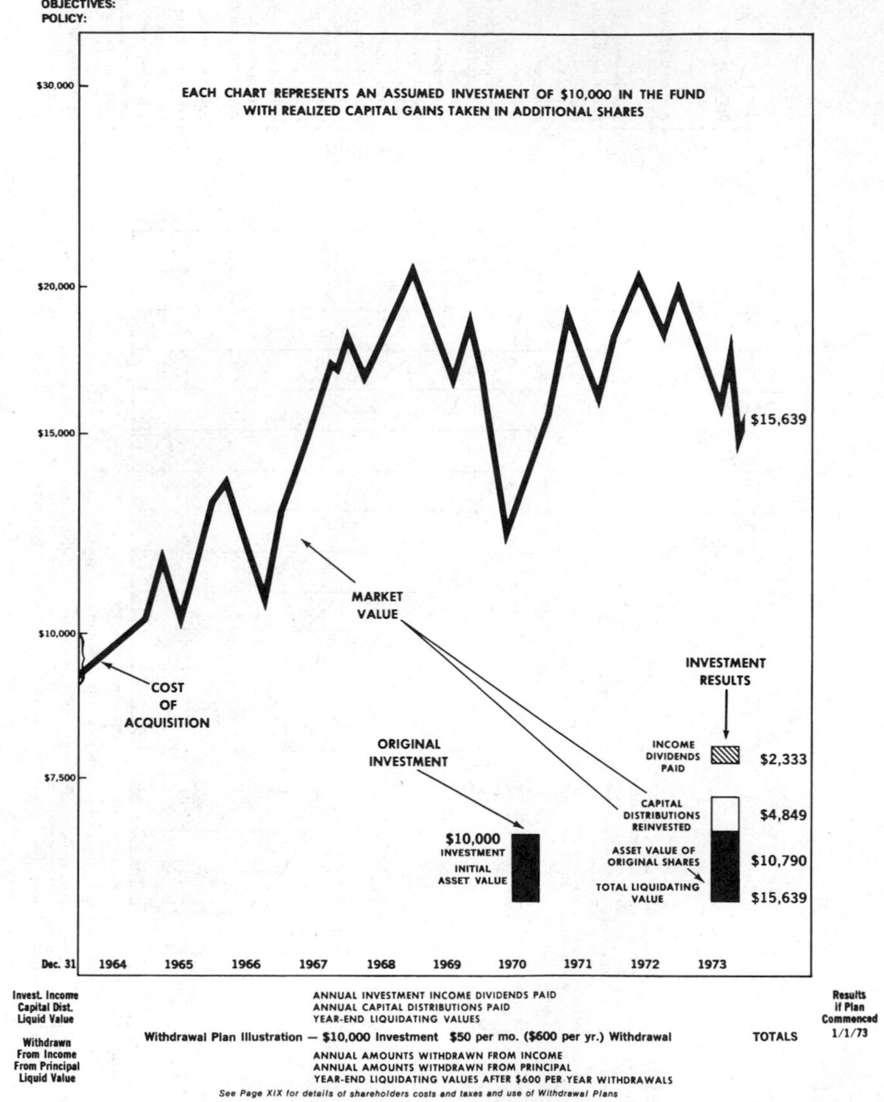

Source: Reproduced by permission of *Johnson's Investment Company Charts.*

Running your eye up and down each of the three columns headed "liquidating value" will give you a very quick notion of comparative results. Bear in mind that while these are all stock funds (including growth, growth and income, income, and balanced funds), the objectives may vary and thus you should turn to the "tablistics" section, which tabulates the essential

FIGURE 16–7
Rowe Price New Horizons Fund, Inc. (January 1, 1964—December 31, 1973)

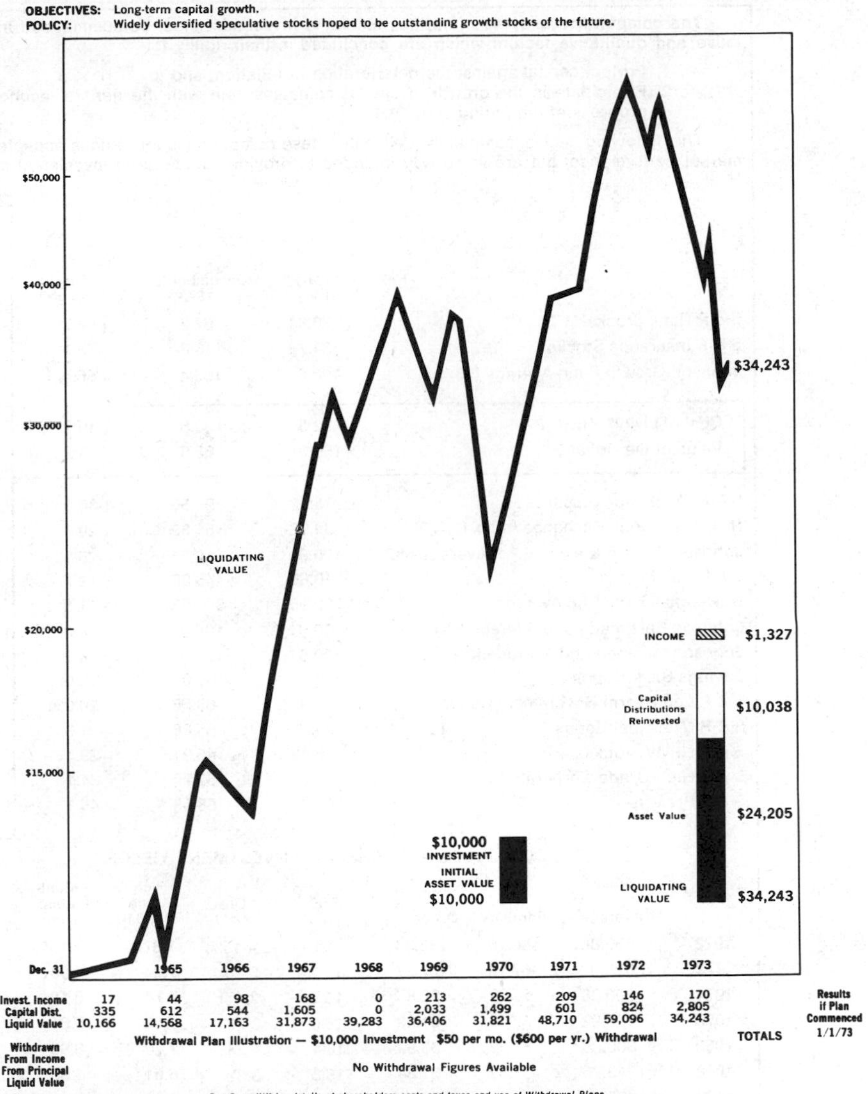

Dec. 31		1965	1966	1967	1968	1969	1970	1971	1972	1973
Invest. Income	17	44	98	168	0	213	262	209	146	170
Capital Dist.	335	612	544	1,605	0	2,033	1,499	601	824	2,805
Liquid Value	10,166	14,568	17,163	31,873	39,283	36,406	31,821	48,710	59,096	34,243

Withdrawal Plan Illustration — $10,000 Investment $50 per mo. ($600 per yr.) Withdrawal

Withdrawn
From Income
From Principal
Liquid Value

No Withdrawal Figures Available

See Page XIX for details of shareholders costs and taxes and use of Withdrawal Plans

Source: Reproduced by permission of *Johnson's Investment Company Charts*.

characteristics and facts about each fund covered. An interesting set of comparisons is also provided for the four Johnson Stock Fund Averages, with the leading stock indexes, Dow-Jones Industrials, the New York Stock Exchange Index, and the Standard & Poor's 500 Stock Index. This comparison is shown in Figure 16–8.

FIGURE 16–8
Securities Markets of the Period

The comparative anaylsis of various media of investment must be summarized in the quantitative and qualitative factors which are concluded in their ability to;

1) Protect capital against the deterioration of inflation, and to,
2) Participate in the growth of capital commensurate with the general economic progress of the period.

The following tables completely delineate these comparisons for various accepted indices of market performance, but are in no way intended to provide standards of investment management.

	January 1, 1964	December 31, 1973	% Change	% Change Adjusted for Value of the Dollar
S & P Bank Stocks	36.84	67.3	+82.7%	+22.0%
S & P Insurance Stocks	64.72	113.3	+75.1	+17.0
Johnson Growth Fund Average (73)	100.0	156.4	+56.4	+ 4.5
Cost of Living Index	92.5	138.5	+49.7	—
Value of the Dollar	100.0	66.8	−33.2	—
S & P Stock Index (500)	75.02	97.55	+30.0	−13.2
New York Stock Exchange Index (1,478)	39.92	51.82	+29.8	−13.3
Johnson Growth & Income Fd. Average (40)	100.0	12.51	+25.1	−16.4
S & P Rail Stocks	40.65	45.80	+12.7	−24.7
Dow-Jones Industrial Average (30)	762.95	850.86	+11.5	−25.6
Johnson Balanced Fund Average (19)	100.0	108.8	+ 8.8	−27.3
Johnson Income Fund Average (21)	100.0	104.2	+ 4.2	−30.4
Savings Bank Deposit	100.0	100.0	0.0	−33.2
S & P Long-Term Government Bonds	86.95	69.58	−20.0	−46.6
S & P Municipal Bonds	109.9	85.86	−21.9	−47.8
S & P Utility Stocks	66.42	46.91	−29.4	−52.8
S & P High-Grade Corporate Bonds	95.24	62.75	−34.1	−56.0
S & P Preferred Stocks	161.2	88.58	−45.1	−63.3

DOW-JONES AVERAGE AND INVESTMENT YIELDS

	Year End Average	Earnings	Dividends	P/E Ratio	D-J Yield	High Grade Bonds	Municipal Bonds	Government Bonds
1973	850.86	$86.16	$35.33	9.9	4.15%	7.67%	5.14%	6.13%
1972	1,020.02	67.13	32.27	15.2	3.16	7.24	5.08	5.68
1971	890.20	55.09	30.87	15.9	3.47	7.14	5.19	5.72
1970	838.92	52.49	31.53	16.0	3.76	7.38	5.81	6.31
1969	800.36	57.02	33.90	13.4	4.24	7.76	6.93	6.91
1968	943.75	57.89	31.34	16.3	3.32	6.51	4.93	5.83
1967	905.11	53.87	30.19	16.8	3.33	6.12	4.51	5.43
1966	785.69	57.67	31.89	13.6	4.00	5.39	3.78	4.63
1965	969.26	54.25	28.63	17.9	2.95	4.71	3.56	4.46
1964	874.13	46.75	25.80	18.7	2.95	4.35	3.13	4.17
1963	762.95	41.15	23.41	18.5	3.07	4.36	3.32	4.18
% Change	+11.5%	+109.4%	+50.9%					

FIGURE 16–8 (continued)

No fund can go in all directions at the same time, or be all things to all men. The degree of market fluctuations will primarily reflect the kind and quality of the securities prescribed in the investment policy and the ability of management to contend with general economic conditions of industry and the securities markets. The charts are drawn to logarithmic scale to show actual market fluctuations as well as year-end liquidating value.

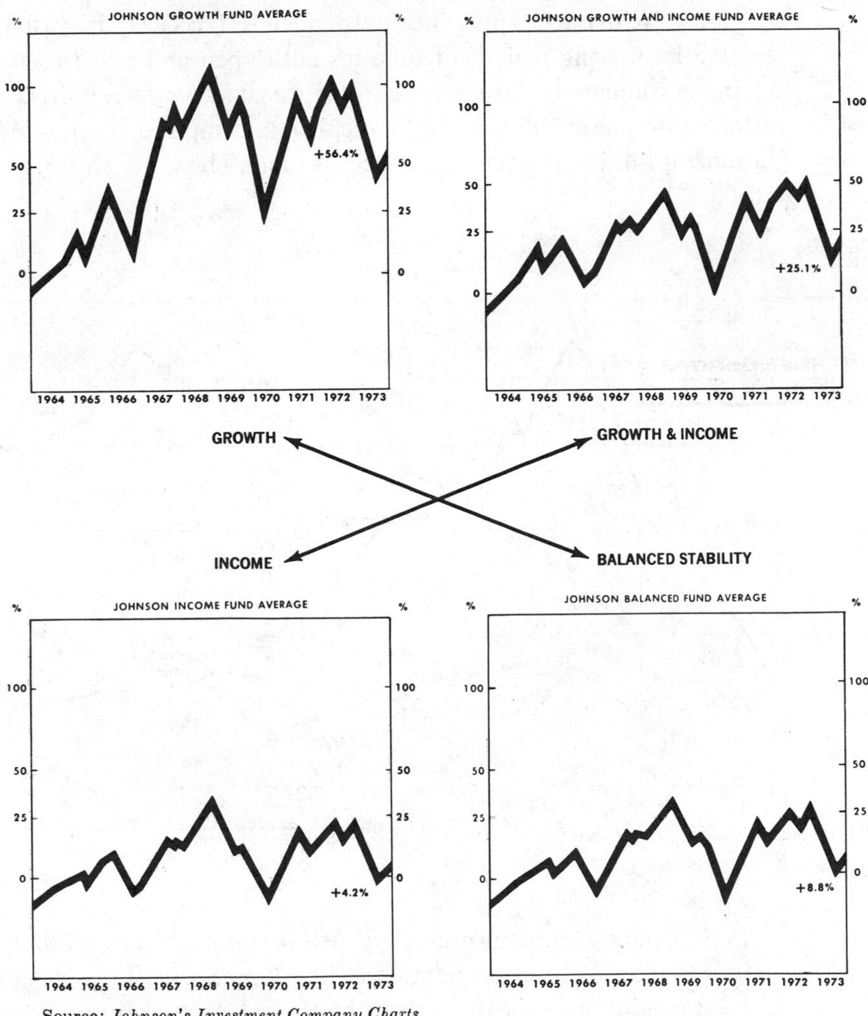

Source: *Johnson's Investment Company Charts.*

Wiesenberger's *Investment Companies* annual also compares and contrasts funds according to their performance record in a variety of ways. Funds are classified by objective and a 10 year illustration of a $10,000 investment is developed on a basis which permits comparison. In addition the approximate percent net change in net asset value per share with capital gains (reinvested) plus income dividends (received in cash) is calculated for varying periods of time for both open end and closed end investment companies. A 10 year performance chart for each individual fund listed is also presented. Finally, Wiesenberger computes composite indexes of mutual fund performance by type of fund. These are shown in Figure 16–9.

FIGURE 16–9

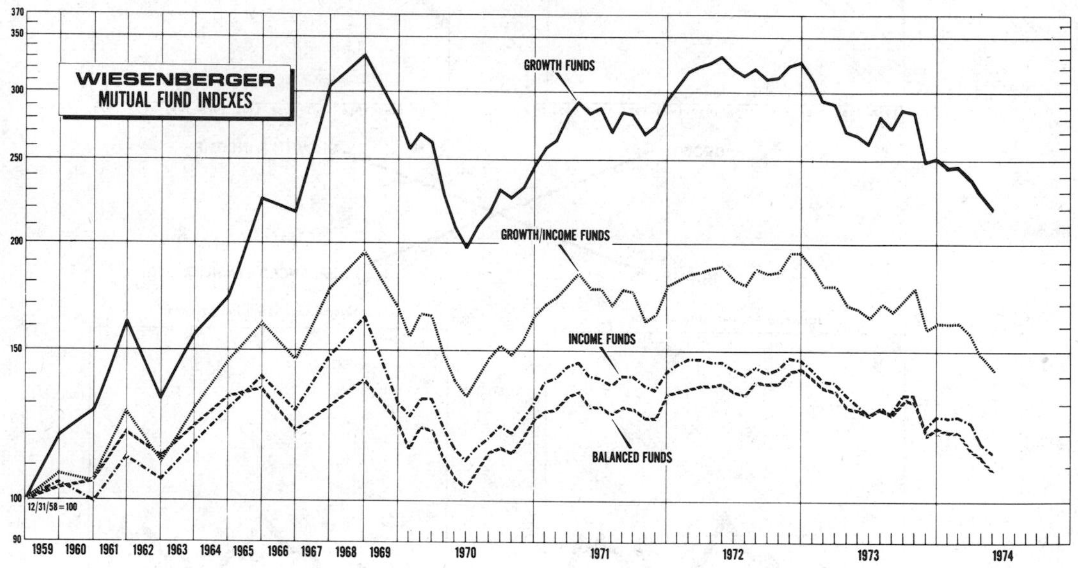

Source: Wiesenberger Services, Inc.

Performance is also measured by Arthur Lipper, from week to week, month to month, and year to year, and by *FundScope*. Lipper's computer assisted tabulation, appears in three parts: (*a*) mutual fund performance analysis—year to date ranking; (*b*) mutual fund performance analysis—alphabetical listing; and (*c*) mutual fund performance analysis—ranking by objective, assets, and year percent change. The Lipper procedure is to rate the funds in terms of changes in net asset values, comparing the funds. While the percentage changes in net asset value may be compared to the major stock price indices given at the top of each tabulation, Lipper does not explicitly measure performance in this way. The method is

FIGURE 16–10
Ten year Results Ranked by Groups by FundScope*

ALL COSTS DEDUCTED INCLUDING SALES COMMISSION AND REDEMPTION FEE, IF ANY.

(★) Above Median (★★) In "Top 10%"

If Fund Is No-Load, Name Appears In Bold Face

Fund	Group	Inv. Obj.	Cash [1] Dividends	Rank	Liquid. [2] Value	Rank
Int'l Investors	2	G	$2,889	98	$41,783★★	1
Pr N Horizons	1-pf	G	1,327	163	35,668★★	2
Enterprise	1-pf	G	3,463★	67	30,684★★	3
Security Eq	1-pf	G	2,217	130	28,251★★	4
Istel Fund	3-dcs	G-I-S	3,592★	61	26,741★★	5
O-T-C Fund	1-spl	G	3,137★	92	26,379★★	6
Axe-H Stock	1-pf	G-S-I	3,619★	59	25,797★★	7
Inv Research	1-dcs	G	1,820	150	25,188★★	8
Ivy Fund	1-pf	G-I-S	3,031	94	24,563★★	9
Johnston	1-dcs	G-I-S	2,449	122	24,450★★	10
Fin Income	4-fd	I-G	6,489★★	3	24,182★★	11
Putnam Inv	1-dcs	G-I	2,585	115	23,975★★	12
Loomis Cap	1-pf	G	2,192	132	23,779★★	13
Pioneer Fund	3-dcs	G-I-S	4,281★	33	23,352★★	14
Babson Fund	3-dcs	G-I	2,630	112	22,661★★	15
Harbor Fund	7-i	I-S-G	6,582★★	2	21,734★★	16
Oppenheimer	1-pf	G	1,654	155	21,682★★	17
Inv Co Amer	3-dcs	G-I	4,038★	43	21,257★★	18
deVegh Mut	3-fd	G	3,590★	62	21,140★	19
Canadian	2	G-I	2,876	99	21,137★	20
Decatur	6-fd	I	6,364★★	5	21,014★	21
Price, TR Gr	1-dcs	G-I	2,168	134	20,889★	22
Scudder Spl	1-pf	G	3,627★	58	20,866★	23
Imperial Gr	1-pf	G	1,313	164	20,622★	24
Provident	6-fd	I-G-S	6,595★★	1	20,446★	25
Putnam Growth	1-dcs	G	2,729	107	20,211★	26
Hedbg-Gordon	1-dcs	G	2,866	100	19,793★	27
Puritan	6-fd	I-S	5,609★★	13	19,736★	28
Founders Gr	1-pf	G	2,493	120	19,727★	29
Nat Investors	1-dcs	G-I-S	2,342	123	19,715★	30
One William	1-dcs	G-I	2,469	121	19,554★	31
Security Inv	4-fd	I-G-S	5,883★★	7	19,519★	32
Guardian	3-fd	G-I	3,712★	53	19,506★	33
Fidelity Cap	1-dcs	G	3,290★	81	19,467★	34
Axe-Science	1-spl	G-S-I	2,626	113	19,464★	35
Stein Stock	1-dcs	G-I	2,256	126	19,407★	36
MIF Fund	4-dcs	I	4,767★	23	19,209★	37
Pine Street	4-dcs	I-G	4,122★	41	19,115★	38
Wash Mutual	4-dcs	I-G	4,538★	27	18,985★	39
Com Stk-SBM	1-dcs	G	1,903	145	18,958★	40
Pligrowth	1-dcs	G	2,549	117	18,948★	41
Fidelity Fund	3-dcs	G-I	3,988★	44	18,904★	42
Windsor	1-dcs	G-I	3,898★	48	18,876★	43
Energy Fund	1-spl	G	3,204★	87	18,868★	44
Mass Inv Gr	1-dcs	G-I-S	2,153	136	18,755★	45
E & E Mutual	1-dcs	G-I	49	183	18,691★	46
Keystone S-3	1-dcs	G	2,083	140	18,332★	47
Stein Bal	5-gis	G-I	3,202★	90	18,323★	48
Fidelity Trend	1-dcs	G	2,788	102	18,269★	49
Channing Inc	4-fd	I-G	5,428★★	14	18,125★	50
Colonial Gr	1-dcs	G	2,061	141	18,119★	51
Financial Ind	3-dcs	G-I	3,359★	77	17,950★	52
Super Inv Inc	5-isg	I	5,130★★	17	17,892★	53
Franklin Gr	1-dcs	G	1,559	157	17,853★	54
Ivest Fund	1-dcs	G	1,464	160	17,823★	55
Vance S Cmn	1-dcs	G-I-S	2,163	135	17,761★	56
Imperial Cap	1-dcs	G-I	2,747	106	17,739★	57
Putnam, Geo	5-gis	G-I-S	3,663★	55	17,703★	58
Chase Fund	1-pf	G	1,770	153	17,691★	59
Lexington Res	1-dcs	G	1,416	162	17,690★	60
Loomis Mut	3-fd	G-I-S	3,639★	57	17,658★	61
Delaware	3-dcs	G-I-S	3,974★	45	17,657★	62
Am Mutual	3-fd	G-I-S	4,154★	39	17,623★	63
Broad Street	4-dcs	I-G-S	3,656★	56	17,606★	64
Northeast	6-fd	I-G	6,152★★	6	17,524★	65
Axe-Hought A	5-gis	S-G-I	4,402★	32	17,502★	66
Technology	1-spl	G-I	2,950	95	17,500★	67
Keystone K-2	1-pf	G	1,553	159	17,457★	68
Penn Square	3-dcs	G	4,133★	40	17,360★	69
Eaton Income	6-fd	I	5,116★★	18	17,000★	70
Admiralty Inc	6-fd	I-S	5,866★★	8	16,992★	71
Stein Capital	1-pf	G	1,780	152	16,960★	72
Whitehall	5-sig	S-I-G	3,671★	54	16,854★	73
Bayrock Gr	1-dcs	G	1,115	166	16,696★	74
Compos B&S	4-dcs	I-S-G	4,263★	35	16,627★	75
Paramount	3-fd	G	4,104★	42	16,616★	76
United Income	4-dcs	I-G	3,204★	87	16,577★	77
Foursquare	3-dcs	G-I	3,238★	86	16,562★	78
Growth Ind	1-dcs	G-I	2,217	130	16,553★	79
Affiliated	3-fd	G-I-S	4,488★	29	16,550★	80
Founders Inc	6-fd	I-G	5,103★	19	16,544★	81
Colonial Fund	4-fd	I-G	4,233★	37	16,531★	82
Massachusetts	5-sig	S-I-G	3,615★	60	16,505★	83
Steadman Assoc	4-fd	I-G	5,662★★	10	16,474★	84
Dreyfus	3-dcs	G-I	3,152★	91	16,449★	85
Variable Stk	1-dcs	G	2,310	124	16,425★	86
Dividend Shrs	3-dcs	G-I	3,369★	74	16,372★	87
Colonial Eq	1-pf	G	1,862	147	16,319★	88
Philadelphia	1-dcs	G-I	2,521	118	16,292★	89
Drexel Equity	1-dcs	G	3,117	93	16,182★	90
Crown W Div	4-dcs	I-G	3,802★	51	16,181★	91
Am Growth	1-dcs	G-I-S	2,777	104	16,179★	92
Sigma Invest	3-dcs	G-I-S	3,128	NRN	16,147★	NRN
MEDIAN			**3,145**		**16,131**	
Bullock	3-dcs	G-I	3,249★	85	16,083	93
Shareholders	4-fd	I-G-S	4,637★	25	16,027	94
Founders Mut	3-dcs	G-I	3,322★	79	16,014	95
Nat Industries	1-dcs	G-I	2,039	142	16,001	96
Keystone S-2	4-dcs	I-G	3,315★	80	15,999	97
Value L Inc	6-fd	I	5,639★★	12	15,991	98
USLIFE Com	4-dcs	I-G	4,229★	38	15,974	99
Newton	1-pf	G	1,845	149	15,930	100
Boston Found	5-sgi	S-G-I	4,564★	NRN	15,834	NRN
Am Exp Inc	6-fd	I	5,021★	20	15,783	101
Safeco Equity	3-dcs	G-I	3,468★	65	15,702	102
Keystone S-1	3-dcs	G-I	2,142	137	15,626	103
Knickerb Fd	4-fd	I-G-S	3,413★	70	15,563	104
Axe-Hought B	5-igs	S-I-G	4,242★	36	15,459	105
USLIFE Balanced	5-igs	I-S-G	4,414★	31	15,446	106
New World	3-dcs	G-I	2,780	103	15,425	107
Franklin Inc	6-fd	I	5,794★★	9	15,396	108
Knickerb Gr	1-pf	G-I-S	828	170	15,224	109
Nation-Wide	5-sig	S	4,269★	34	15,224	109
Mann, Horace	1-dcs	G	1,923	144	15,223	111
Corporate Ldrs	4-dcs	S-I-G	3,466★	66	15,040	112
Channing Spl	1-pf	G	861	169	15,018	113
Am Nat'l Gr	1-pf	G	2,169	133	15,015	114
Selected Am	3-dcs	G-I	3,203★	89	15,013	115
Unified	3-dcs	G-I	2,725	109	14,976	116
Inv Tr Boston	3-dcs	G-I-S	2,917	97	14,973	117
Investors Var	1-dcs	G	2,254	127	14,867	118
Composite Fd	3-fd	G-I-S	3,889★	49	14,828	119
Investors Sel	7-is	S	4,905★	21	14,808	120
Putnam Income	6-fd	I	4,757★	24	14,753	121
Wisconsin	3-dcs	G-I	3,070	NRN	14,733	NRN
Commerce	1-dcs	G-I	2,238	128	14,671	122
Am Exp Inv	5-igs	S-I	3,942★	46	14,637	123
Pioneer Ent	1-pf	G	1,742	154	14,561	124
Twenty C Inc	4-dcs	I-G	3,363★	76	14,499	125
Keystone B-4	7-i	I	6,413★★	4	14,461	126
Scudder Bal	5-gis	S-I-G	3,375★	72	14,300	127
Am Exp Stk	3-dcs	G-S	3,290★	81	14,281	128
Channing Bal	5-gis	G-I-S	3,912★	47	14,197	129
Am Business	5-sig	G-S-I	4,529★	28	14,191	130
Mass Inv Tr	3-dcs	G-I-S	3,348★	78	14,180	131
Keystone S-4	1-pf	G	961	168	14,178	132
Nassau	3-fd	G-I-S	3,251★	84	14,167	133
Inc Fd Boston	6-fd	I-S	5,657★★	11	14,164	134
Twenty C Gr	1-pf	G	347	182	14,142	135
Commw Tr C	4-fd	S-I-G	3,744★	52	14,095	136
Eaton Bal	5-igs	I-S	3,573★	63	14,043	137
Am Investors	1-pf	G	751	172	13,903	138
Scudder Com	1-dcs	G-I	2,642	111	13,853	139
Bondstock	3-dcs	G-I	3,407★	71	13,782	140
Eaton Stock	3-dcs	G-I	2,671	110	13,702	141
Anchor Income	4-fd	I-S-G	4,450★	30	13,699	142
Steadman Inv	3-dcs	G-I	1,933	143	13,621	143
Investors Stk	3-dcs	G-I	2,762	105	13,620	144
Mutual Trust	6-fd	I-S	4,780★	22	13,548	145
Keystone K-1	6-fd	I	5,354★★	15	13,542	146
Channing Com	3-dcs	G-I	3,253★	83	13,536	147
Sovereign	4-dcs	I-G-S	3,432★	68	13,460	148
Value L Fund	1-dcs	G-I	2,219	129	13,371	149
United Sci	1-spl	G	2,087	139	13,360	150
Wall Street	1-dcs	G-I	2,506	119	13,285	151
Keystone B-2	7-is	I-S	5,322★★	16	13,223	152
Channing Gr	1-dcs	G	1,556	158	13,198	153
First Inv Fd	3-fd	G-I	2,796	101	13,059	154
Anchor Growth	1-dcs	G	1,805	151	12,983	155
MIF Growth	1-dcs	G	2,614	114	12,965	156
Investors Mut	5-isg	I-S-G	3,553★	64	12,916	157
United Accum	1-dcs	G-I	2,306	125	12,868	158
Hamilton Fund	3-dcs	G-I	3,375★	72	12,814	159
Keystone B-1	7-si	S-I	4,607★	26	12,561	160
Fundamental	3-dcs	G-I	2,949	96	12,527	161
Crown W Dal	1-pf	G	1,903	145	12,314	162
Century Shares	1-ins	G-I-S	1,581	156	12,263	163
Liberty	4-fd	S-I-G	3,810★	50	12,208	164
Wellington	5-sig	S-I-G	3,368★	75	12,177	165
Vance S Inv	NC	NC	3,418★	69	11,911	166
Fund of Amer	1-dcs	S-I-G	1,435	161	11,815	167
Founders Spl	1-pf	G	524	178	11,800	168
Sigma Trust	5-sig	S-I-G	3,698★	NRN	11,735	NRN
MidAmerica	1-dcs	G	1,854	148	11,679	169
Steadman AIF	1-pf	G	1,268	165	11,039	170
Varied Ind	3-dcs	G-I	2,577	116	10,668	171
Beacon Inv	1-dcs	G-I	2,115	138	10,191	172
Landmark Gr	1-dcs	G	658	174	9,917	173
Value L Spl	1-pf	G	538	177	9,848	174
Life Ins Inv	1-ins	G	787	171	9,659	175
Admiralty Insur	1-ins	G	518	179	9,611	176
Revere	1-pf	G	401	181	9,153	177
Cap Inv Gr	1-pf	G-I	727	173	8,675	178
Equity Prog	1-pf	G	963	167	8,562	179
Growth Fd Am	1-pf	G	542	176	8,239	180
Admiralty Gr	1-pf	G	416	180	7,847	181
Franklin Util	1-spl	G-I	2,726	108	7,691	182
Capital Shares	1-dcs	G	629	175	6,026	183
RANKING RANGES			**1 to 183**		**1 to 183**	
Total Funds			459		459	
Tabulated			186		186	
Total NA's			47		47	
Total X's			226		226	

[1] Ten-year total of dividends from investment income paid in cash, based on initial $10,000 investment with capital gain distributions reinvested in stock.

[2] Based on initial $10,000 investment, represents liquidating value at end of ten-year period assuming all distributions reinvested in stock.

MUTUAL FUND GROUP CLASSIFICATIONS

1) **GROWTH FUNDS:** (dcs) Diversified Common Stocks; (hf) Hedge Funds: funds that always are "hedged" — that is, always have a long and short position; (ins) Specialized, Insurance Stock Funds; (pf) "Performance" Funds: greater emphasis on volatile issues, and/or lesser known, lower priced, OTC issues, foreign securities, and/or use of leverage, short sales, puts, calls, warrants, hedging, and/or other practices generally regarded as more speculative; (spl) Specialized and/or semi-specialized, commodities, mutual fund holding companies, industry funds, area funds, etc.
2) **CANADIAN** and/or **INTERNATIONAL SECURITIES.** (Growth Funds).
3) **GROWTH, WITH INCOME:** (dcs) Diversified Common Stocks; (fd) Flexibly Diversified.
4) **INCOME, AND GROWTH:** (dcs) Diversified Common Stocks; (fd) Flexibly Diversified.
5) **GROWTH, INCOME AND STABILITY** (Balanced Funds): (G-I-S) Growth-Income, Stability; (I-G-S) Income-Growth, Stability; (S-I-G) Stability-Income, Growth.
6) **INCOME FUNDS** (Flexibly Diversified).
7) **BOND** and **PREFERRED STOCK FUNDS:** (S-I) Stability-Income; (I-S) Income-Stability; (I) Income

NC) **NOT CLASSIFIED.** Will be classified soon as essential information available.

* Ranked by order of performance for 10 year liquidating value of $10,000 investment, 1964–1973.
Source: Reproduced with permission from the April, 1974, issue of *FundScope*.

instead to compare the changes in the net asset value of each fund tabulated.

FundScope publishes so many variations of mutual fund performance that you simply have to read the over 400 pages of its annual mutual fund guide to grasp the scope of its coverage. Figure 16–10 provides one of many tabulations—this one illustrative of 10 year performance, based on liquidating values. It is an interesting summary table. Keep in mind, however, that outstanding or poor past performance is no assurance of future outstanding or poor performance, as *FundScope* itself warns on a number of pages.

Each year *Forbes* magazine publishes a special report on mutual fund performance. It asks and answers such questions as: How well did the fund do in keeping up with (or ahead of) the stock market? How big is the fund? How much income? How do its costs compare? "How Good Are The Mutual Funds?" *Forbes* asks, and answers: "There are funds of every size and shape, from the breezily speculative to stodgy bond funds. Yet no mat-

FIGURE 16–11
Forbes Fund Ratings—1974

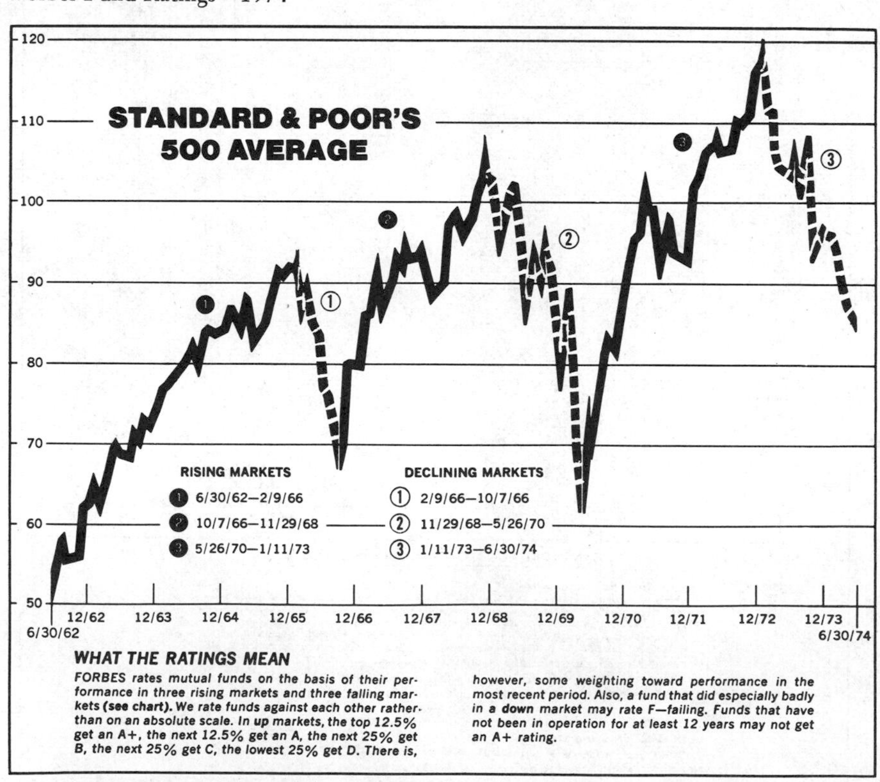

Source: *Forbes*, August 15, 1974.

ter what its aim, a fund can be no better than its management. Herewith *Forbes* takes their measure—and finds some topnotch, many just pedestrian, and some sadly wanting."

The *Forbes* ratings are described in Figure 16–11 and shown in part in Figure 16–12. *Forbes* rates the funds on two scores: their abilities in rising

FIGURE 16–12
Forbes Fund Ratings, 1974

PERFORMANCE RATINGS			DOLLAR RESULTS						
In UP Markets	In DOWN Markets		Latest 12 Months	12-Year Average Annual Growth Rate	Dividend Return	Total Assets 6/30/74 in Millions	Total Assets % Change 1974 vs. 1973	Maximum Sales Charge	Annual Expenses Per $100
–	–	Standard & Poors 500 Stock Average	–17.5%	3.8%	4.1%				
C	C	FORBES Stock Fund Average	–17.2%	4.0%	3.3%				
		STOCK FUNDS (LOAD)							
		Admiralty Funds							
B	F	Growth Series	–16.6%	–0.8%	1.4%	$12.1	–25.8%	8.75%	$1.50
D	B	Income Series	–15.7	1.2	8.1	4.6	–28.1	8.75	1.26
C	D	Insurance Series	–9.7	1.8	5.0	2.3	–23.3	8.75	1.24
D	D	Advisers Fund	–13.6	0.3	4.5	1.8	–14.3	8.50	1.50
D	B	Affiliated Fund	–4.5	3.3	5.5	1,272.8	–8.5	7.50	0.37
• • C	F	All American Fund (started 2/64)	–28.8	–	1.3	1.3	–31.6	8.50	0.99
• B	• C	Allstate Enterprises Stock Fund (started 2/70)	–20.0	–	0.7	168.9	–19.3	7.00	0.73
• B	• • D	Alpha Fund (started 5/68)	–25.4	–	2.1	24.3	–24.8	8.50	0.95
• B	• • C	AMCAP Fund (started 4/67)	–14.3	–	3.2	47.0	–26.2	8.50	0.70
• D	• A	American Birthright Trust (started 5/70)	2.3	–	none	17.3	121.8	9.00	1.00
• • D	C	American Diversified Investors Fund (started 12/64)	–21.0	–	4.2	2.0	–16.7	8.50	1.12
• C	• B	American Equity Fund (started 1/69)	–9.1	–	0.1	2.3	.0	8.75	1.50
		American Express Funds							
B	F	Capital	–24.7	2.7	2.6	111.4	–27.8	8.50	0.76
• D	• C	Special (started 4/69)	–14.1	–	1.8	32.1	–22.3	8.50	0.98
C	D	Stock	–17.9	2.3	4.0	42.5	–27.1	8.50	0.72
B	C	American Growth Fund	–16.9	5.3	3.4	11.8	–20.3	8.50	1.00
• A	• • B	American Ins. & Ind. Fund (started 12/65)	–16.6	–	1.1	3.4	30.8	8.50	1.00
• D	• B	American Leaders Fund (started 2/69)	–16.6	–	3.5	1.0	–28.6	1.50	1.62
C	B	American Mutual Fund	–7.7	4.3	5.1	289.9	–12.6	8.50	0.60
A	F	American National Growth Fund	–14.9	4.3	2.9	10.5	2.9	8.50	0.86
B	F	Anchor Growth Fund	–20.4	2.5	3.2	229.9	–27.2	8.75	0.65
• B	• D	Audax Fund (started 2/70)	–22.0	–	0.9	2.8	–22.2	8.50	1.13
A	D	Axe-Houghton Stock Fund	–6.7	9.4	3.1	60.5	–16.0	8.50	0.95
B	F	Axe Science Corp.	–6.3	5.6	2.0	32.2	–13.7	8.00	0.88
B	D	Bayrock Growth Fund	–24.4	2.6	none	11.0	66.7	8.50	1.51
• C	• C	Berkshire Capital Fund (started 12/68)	–24.8	–	5.2	2.4	–14.3	8.50	1.42
• D	• F	Berkshire Growth Fund	–26.0	–	1.1	1.3	–18.8	8.50	1.45
• B	• C	BLC Growth Fund (started 10/69)	–18.5	–	1.5	6.5	–9.7	8.50	1.00
• C	• B	BLC Income Fund (started 10/69)	–10.9	–	5.5	5.2	–3.7	8.50	1.01
D	D	Bondstock Corp.	–18.8	1.4	5.9	18.0	–19.3	8.50	0.78
• C	• • C	Boston Mutual Equity Growth Fund (started 1/69)	–17.0	–	2.2	2.0	–13.0	8.50	1.01
C	B	Broad Street Investing Corp.	–16.4	4.4	4.3	309.1	–20.4	8.50	0.31
D	D	The Brown Fund of Hawaii	–22.6	1.0	2.8	3.7	–32.7	3.00	1.40
C	C	Bullock Fund	–13.4	3.8	3.8	117.5	–20.2	8.67	0.43
• • D	A	Capamerica Fund (started 2/65)	–7.7	–	5.9	2.1	.0	8.75	1.50
C	F	Capital Investors Growth Fund	–1.7	1.7	none	1.3	–7.1	8.75	1.50
D	F	Capital Shares	–22.8	–3.3	2.9	23.2	–27.7	8.75	1.27
C	D	Century Shares Trust	–23.4	1.5	4.8	67.5	–29.0	8.50	0.48
• B	• • C	CG Fund (started 2/68)	–16.0	–	2.2	90.1	.3	7.50	0.75

• Fund rated for one period only; maximum allowable rating A
• • Fund rated for two periods only; maximum allowable rating A

EXPLANATION OF COLUMN HEADINGS

*The Performance Ratings are based on the following **UP** and **DOWN** markets: **UP**, 6/30/62–2/9/66; 10/7/66–11/29/68; 5/26/70–1/11/73. **DOWN**, 2/9/66–10/7/66; 11/29/68–5/26/70; 1/11/73–6/30/74. In determining both the performance ratings and the percentage figures in the Dollar Results section, all capital gains distributions have been reinvested, but income dividends have not. All results are based on investments at net asset value and do not allow for sales charges. In the Dollar Results section, the latest 12 months covers the period from June 30, 1973 to June 30, 1974; the 12-year average annual growth rate covers the period from June 30, 1962 to June 30, 1974. Dividend Return is based on June 30, 1974 net asset value and the income payout for the preceding 12-month period. Annual expenses include management fees and operating expenses as a percentage of average net assets.*

Source: *Forbes*, August 15, 1974.

markets and their resistance in declining markets. In up markets it ranks funds from A plus to D; in down markets from A to F. To get a high rating, a fund must have shown an ability to make money, not just in one rising market, but in several different ones. To get an A plus rating, for example, a fund must have ranked among the top one eighth (12.5 percent) of all funds and have done so consistently in all three of the bull markets *Forbes* measures. That's hard to do. While the top 12.5 percent of funds get an A plus rating, the next 12.5 percent get an A rating.[12]

That As and A pluses in up markets were frequently attained at the expense of Cs, Ds, and, Fs in down markets is hardly surprising, since you can't achieve major gains without taking risks.[13] What is surprising, however, is the number of funds that did poorly in both up and down markets. In the case of funds with C and D ratings in both bull and bear markets, managements were not performing adequately. One page of the Forbes ratings may be seen in Figure 16–12.

A study of the ratings seems to prove that it's about as difficult to pick the better mutual funds over the long haul as it is to pick a good common stock.

Investment Company Act of 1940

Because of abuses in investment company management earlier, Congress, after an exhaustive five year study by the SEC, passed the Investment Company Act of 1940. This act required full disclosure and aimed to prevent the speculation and manipulation by management which had been prevalent. Since the act requires a minimum capital of $100,000 before the stock of an investment company may be offered for sale to the public, it serves to discourage companies without some potential financial strength from trying to come into existence.

The law provides for more conservative capital structures for investment companies. Under the rules of the Securities and Exchange Commission, open end investment companies incorporated after 1940 may issue only common stock, but they may enjoy limited leverage through the medium of bank borrowings. Assets must, however, cover bank loans at least three times. With the exception of refunding operations, the act provides that funded debt (or bank loans) created after 1940 by closed end companies

---

[12] The *Forbes* rating system is described in detail annually in the August 15 issue of the magazine, when new ratings are issued.

[13] For an excellent technical analysis of risk and performance in the mutual fund field, see Irwin Friend, Marshall Blume, and Jean Crockett, *Mutual Funds and Other Institutional Investors: A New Perspective* (A Twentieth Century Fund Study [New York: McGraw-Hill Book Co., 1970]). See especially Chapter 3, "Investment Performance of Mutual Funds."

must be covered by assets at least three times as large, and their new issues of preferred stocks must be covered twice by assets.

According to the act, investment policies of an investment company must be stated clearly and specifically, and policies once declared cannot be changed without the stockholders' consent. This effectively prevents the sudden conversion of a diversified list of marketable securities into a non-diversified list. The law requires semiannual reports on investment company operations, but the majority of companies publish quarterly statements. Sale of management contracts is discouraged by a provision of the act that such contracts are automatically terminated if transferred. Many regulations govern investment companies' boards of directors, sales of securities, advertising, and the like, and such safeguards have helped greatly to strengthen public respect for and confidence in investment companies.

After some years of controversy over mutual fund fees, Congress passed the Investment Company Amendments Act of 1970. The main features of this new law were as follows:

(*a*) The *investment advisor* of a mutual fund has a fiduciary obligation as far as compensation is concerned. This means that the mutual fund shareowner can sue to recover if it is felt that the investment advisor's fees are too high. While the shareholder's right to sue is limited to the issue of excessive compensation, the Securities and Exchange Commission is given much more extensive powers over investment advisors, both in terms of regulation and in the authority to sue.

(*b*) As to the *sales charge*, the National Association of Securities Dealers is empowered to regulate sales charges. The SEC is given standby authority to step into the picture if it finds that the rates authorized by the NASD are too high. The SEC can also exempt smaller companies from the NASD sales charge regulations.

(*c*) Contractual plans with their "front end" loads have been, as indicated earlier, a subject of controversy. The new law attempts to ameliorate the situation. Under it, the investor who withdraws from a contractual plan within 45 days is entitled to a refund in full of any sales charge paid. If canceled within 18 months, the investor will be entitled to a refund of 85 percent of the sales charge paid.

A mutual fund can avoid these refund provisions by electing instead that not more than 20 percent of the total commission be allocated to payments made during each of the first three years of the periodic payment contract, and that no more than 64 percent of the total sales load be charged to payments during the first four years.

(*d*) Banks and savings and loan associations are *not* allowed to set up and sell their own mutual funds. Insurance companies are, however.

Income Taxes

Earnings of ordinary corporations are subject to income tax. Then the persons who receive dividends out of corporate earnings are also taxed. This is double taxation—the same income taxed twice. If an investment company received this already taxed dividend income, paid a tax on it, and paid dividends to its own shareholders, who were again taxed, we would have triple taxation of the same income.

The Internal Revenue Law permits investment companies which are irrevocably registered as regulated investment companies, and which agree to distribute at least 90 percent of the dividends and interest received from the securities they own, to avoid triple taxation on the earnings distributed, although they must pay the ordinary corporate income tax on any such earnings retained. They enjoy a like exemption on long term capital gains distributed, but they are subject to the usual tax on such gains retained. The latter provision may be harmful in that capital gains cannot be retained (without incurring the tax) to offset capital losses, which are bound to occur sooner or later.

Thus, under the Internal Revenue Code, investment companies which qualify as such are *not* taxed on any of their income or capital gains which they pay out. The investor in shares of open or closed end investment companies is taxed at the same rates as if he had realized the income and capital gains—paid him by the investment company—from his own direct investments.

Invest in Common Stock Directly or Buy Mutual Fund Shares?

Well managed investment companies may be in a position to handle the problems of selection, timing, and diversification of security purchases and sales more effectively than an individual with moderate resources. Which securities to buy and which to sell are difficult problems which can perhaps best be answered by analysts who have had sufficient training in such areas as accounting, economics, and finance and who have had years of experience. Not only do investment companies have their own staffs, skilled in such work, but they can use outside research whenever it is deemed necessary. With the best of resources at one's command, wise selection of securities is not easy; for the individual with few of these resources at hand, it is quite difficult. Not only is it necessary to choose the right securities to buy or sell but it is equally as important to time the purchases and sales correctly. If you feel unable to do this for yourself, you can pass the problem along to an investment company to do it for you. In this way you may secure the advantages of such techniques as dollar averaging and automatic formula timing.

But even if you turn to the investment company to solve your investment problems, there still remains one major problem which you cannot unload in this fashion. You must make at least one judgment and one decision—and it is a major one—yourself: you must decide which of the many and diverse investment companies, with their very different objectives and unequal performances, you wish to choose. This is a decision which you should not let a salesperson make for you. It is a most important judgment and should only be arrived at after considerable investigation and study. If you do decide to buy mutual fund shares, don't let yourself be sold; decide for yourself after you have all the facts.

Forbes declared:

> Nevertheless, in the light of events the average investor can draw some useful conclusions. Probably the most basic lesson is simply this: mutual fund investing is not the simple procedure that many salesmen try to make it. The funds, obviously, differ radically from one another in investment slant and management dexterity.
>
> To invest intelligently, therefore, the investor must make a choice. Does he want a "growth" stock for the long pull? A diversified commitment in a single promising industry? A changing approach which gives management full power to switch money around as conditions change? Or a low geared stake in stocks through a balanced fund?

Bear in mind that the no load funds, some of which have performed well, have no salespeople and if you wait to be persuaded the better no load funds may never come to your attention. You do not need an intermediary to buy no loads. You can order shares yourself by mail or telephone. Similarly, no load mutual funds, as well as load funds, will buy your shares directly from you.[14]

Mutual Funds and Insurance

Occasionally one hears of an unscrupulous mutual fund salesperson who attempts to persuade elderly persons to cash in their life insurance and use the proceeds to buy mutual fund shares. While there is a place in a total financial program for both life insurance and investment company shares, the latter are no substitute for the former when matters of death, family security, and protection of dependents are involved. Insurance is the quickest way for a young person to create an estate. It provides the older one with income should he live, or death benefits that are certain for his dependents, should he die. Insurance should be the keystone for meeting the basic needs of your family in case of your death. Mutual fund investment based on the fluctuating market price of common stock is too uncertain

[14] "Why the No-Load Funds Keep Growing," *Changing Times*, October 1973.

where maximum security is required. It would be most unwise to liquidate a basic insurance protection program to allow investment in mutual shares. If and when resources permit expansion and diversification in a financial program, then common stock investment can be undertaken, either directly or through mutual funds.

The formerly clear line between insurance and mutual funds has become blurred in recent years. The larger insurance companies have been forming mutual funds. Brokerage houses are selling life insurance as well as mutual funds. And the mutual funds are now offering various types of insurance. As we have noted, insurance is available to enable a contractual plan purchaser to have a plan completed by insurance payments in the event of his or her death prior to the completion of the plan. Also, some mutual funds have started programs under which an investor will be able to purchase insurance against long term loss on investments in mutual fund shares.

For example, suppose you made an investment of $10,000 in mutuals on July 1, 1972, and took insurance for a 15 year term. The critical date would then be July 1, 1987. If on that date the redemption value of your investment is less than $10,000, the insurance company must pay you the difference. Essentially the insurance is protection against a sharp market drop such as occurred in the spring of 1970 or in 1973–74. This insurance is designed only for the long-term investor—one who is prepared to stay with an investment in mutuals for 10 years or more. Otherwise he loses his insurance coverage and is not entitled to any refund of the premiums paid. Another limitation is that the investor must be prepared to forego current income from the investment in mutuals. The insured investor must reinvest all dividends and capital gains from his mutuals.[15]

To enable investors to buy life insurance and mutual funds at the same time with a limited amount of money, a new concept known as "funding" has developed. The idea is quite simple. You buy mutual fund shares and then use them as collateral to borrow money to pay for the life insurance. Thus, you get both but only lay out the money for one. If you buy $750 worth of mutual shares, you can borrow, say, $300 against them to buy life insurance. If you buy $10,000 of mutual fund shares, you can borrow $4,000 to buy insurance. The rule of thumb is that you must maintain a ratio of mutual fund shares at least 2.5 times the amount of the loan for insurance.

Prospectuses are available from "funding" companies set up to handle

---

[15] For further information, see "Mutual Funds to Offer Insurance Against Long-Term Loss," in Kalb, Voorhis & Co., *Financial Planning Workbook*, 1975.

mutual fund insurance programs. Such plans may represent a risky and costly affair, beyond your financial resources. They require careful investigation. Above all, beware of the salesperson who tries to convince you to cancel your policy to buy his policy or to borrow on it to buy mutual funds. There are so many new twists and gimmicks being developed that you have to be alert constantly to keep from being out dated and uninformed.

SUGGESTED READINGS

1. *Investment Companies,* latest annual edition. Arthur Wiesenberger & Co. One New York Plaza, New York, N.Y. 10004.
2. *Johnson's Investment Company Charts,* latest annual edition. Hugh A. Johnson Investment Co., Rand Building, Buffalo, N.Y. 14203.
3. In *Changing Times:*
   "Invest in Bonds the Mutual Fund Way," July 1972.
   "Why So Many Lawsuits Against Mutual Funds?" November 1972.
   "Why the No-Load Funds Keep Growing," October 1973.
   "Money Market Funds," April 1974.
   "Mutual Funds That Invest in the 'Money Market.' " November 1974.
   "Closed-End Bond Funds: Investing for Income," September 1973.
   "Mutual Funds: How to Find the Best Performers," July 1974.
4. In *Money:*
   "The Route to the Right Mutual Fund," November 1972.
   "Matching You and Your Mutual Fund," August 1974.
   "The Negative Load Funds," March 1973.
   "When to Split Up with Your Mutual Fund," January 1974.
   "The T. Rowe Price Earnings System," January 1973.
5. *Mutual Funds Almanac,* The Hirsch Organization, Inc., Six Deer Trail, Old Tappan, New Jersey 07675.
6. *Mutual Fund Fact Book,* issued annually by the Investment Company Institute. A free copy may be obtained by writing to the Institute at 1775 K Street, N.W., Washington, D.C. 20006.
7. "Which Funds Were Top Performers? 1964–1973 Annual Results Ranked," in *FundScope,* March, 1974. A sample copy of this monthly magazine of the mutual fund industry may be obtained by writing to *FundScope,* Suite 700, 1900 Avenue of the Stars, Los Angeles, Calif. 90067.
8. *Mutual Fund Guide,* issued annually in the April issue of *FundScope,* Los Angeles, Calif.
9. *Vickers Guide to Investment Company Portfolios,* latest annual edition. Vickers Associates, Inc., 226 New York Avenue, Huntington, New York, 11743.

10. Irwin Friend, Marshall Blume, Jean Crockett, *Mutual Funds and Other Institutional Investors: A New Perspective.* A Twentieth Century Fund Study. New York: McGraw-Hill Book Co., 1970.
11. Lucille Tomlinson, *How to Start, Operate and Manage Mutual Funds.* New York: President's Publishing House, 1971.
12. *Investment Trusts and Funds from the Investor's Point of View.* Great Barrington, Mass.: American Institute for Economic Research, latest annual edition.
13. *Census of Mutual Fund Shareowners and Potential Shareowners.* Washington, D.C.: Investment Company Institute, 1971.
14. "Forbes Mutual Fund Survey," issued annually in the August 15 issue of *Forbes.* A reprint may be obtained by writing to *Forbes* at 60 Fifth Avenue, New York, N.Y. 10011.

CASE PROBLEMS

1. Robert and Alice Quint have one son (age 8), for whose education they are building a college fund. Whenever they can afford it, they buy a share of the common stock of the American Telephone and Telegraph Company and add it to the fund. What do you think of their plan? Can you suggest a better one?

2. The John Dohertys, who live next door to the Quints, have a daughter (age 6) whom they want to be able to send to college. They make regular monthly payments to a savings and loan association with an eye to building a fund of $10,000 for their daughter's education. Do you like this plan more than that of the Quints? Why? Why not?

3. James Layton received the prospectus of a mutual fund (it happened to be that of a specialized common stock fund). He read the prospectus and was impressed by the growth in the value of the shares and by the earnings per share which it had achieved in the years since 1960. He thought he would withdraw $12,000 of his savings from the savings department of his local commercial bank and invest the money in these shares. His total savings amounted to $18,000. In two years, Layton was due to retire; he and his wife would have to depend on his savings for much of their support in retirement. Do you think he was making a good move? Why? Why not?

4. Lionel Batson has worked hard all his life. At age 40 he owns his $24,000 home, has $5,000 in savings banks, and has a steady job which now pays $18,000 a year and promises to pay much more. He has a wife (age 38) and two children (ages 16 and 13). Upon the death of his mother, he inherits $25,000 from her. For the first time in his life he thinks that he is in a position to "buy common stocks and make some money," "buy a stake in American industry"; but (not having had any experience) he debates whether to invest

directly or through an investment company. One evening while you are at his house, he engages you in conversation on this topic. What advice would you give him?

5. Peter Putnam has just started at his first career job. He is earning $750 a month and since he is still a bachelor, he finds he can save and invest $100 a month. He knows he knows nothing about investments and therefore he decides to buy investment company shares. He asks all his friends what they would recommend. The suggestions include Wellington Fund; T. Rowe Price Growth Stock Fund; Scudder, Stevens & Clark Common Stock Fund; Lehman Corp.; Doll Fund; Tri-Continental, Dreyfus Fund, Keystone S 4 Fund, The Oppenheimer Fund, and Keystone B 1. Since you have taken a course in personal finance and are presumably knowledgeable he asks you to help him by evaluating the characteristics and performance trends of each of these funds and selecting the one you think best for his purposes. Help him.

6. Arthur Haskins, Jr., is a bachelor (age 31). He lives in Rio de Janeiro, Brazil, where he has been working for the last eight years for a New York bank. Promotion for him is expected to be rapid. Some of his savings he invests in Brazil, where he gets a very good return. He feels that he is too far away from North America to invest directly in stocks there. What type of mutual fund, if any, do you think he should consider? Which particular one would you recommend? Why?

7. Jonathan Swift is a man (age 30) of little education. He has saved his money and invested it in wholly owned common stocks which he selected by noting what the mutual funds appeared to be buying (from their lists, published quarterly). Once he bought, he continued to hold. He made a practice of never investing more than $1,000 in the stock of any one company. After 8 years of this sort of program, he finds that original investments of $8,000 are now worth $12,000 and that he has averaged a 5.5 percent return on his investments. What is your opinion of his plan?

8. Janet Clarkson is a secretary for a lawyer, who pays her $250 a week. At age 40 she has been in his employment for 22 years. She lives in an apartment with her mother (whom she supports). She has $6,000 in various savings banks and $12,000 of straight life insurance. In addition, she manages to save about $15 a week. It is her desire to retire when she is age 62. She expects to draw a social security monthly retirement benefit but no pension. She intends to put future savings into a mutual fund. What sort of fund would you advise her to seek? Why?

9. The Adams family owns its home, has $5,000 in the bank for emergencies, has all the life insurance which it thinks it should carry, and is now considering the investment of $3,000 of other savings. Mr. Adams, who is a research worker for a chemical company, thinks that it is prudent to buy some shares of common stock in two or three good companies. Mrs. Adams thinks

that it would be better to buy the shares of an investment company. Which of them do you believe is right? Why?

10. John and Elizabeth Raynhauer have just saved their first $1,000 since they were married. John especially fears the results of inflation. He wants to invest their $1,000 emergency fund in the common stock of some good company. Elizabeth, who has had a course in personal finance, feels that it should be put in a savings bank. If it is to be invested in common stock, she feels that this should be done by buying shares in a no load investment company. What would you advise? Why?

11. At age 28 Peter Dane finds himself still single and doing rather well as a loan officer in the commercial bank for which he works. He lives with his mother in the family home. Except for owning the home the mother is without funds. Since Peter's salary has just been increased to $13,000 annually, he is considering an investment of about $2,500 a year in a mutual fund. He asks you to help him decide whether to invest in a balanced fund, or a diversified commonstock fund. Also he wonders whether an accumulation plan or a contractual plan would be best for him. All of Peter's savings to date ($7,000) are in an account in the savings department of the bank where he works. Advise him.

17

Estate Planning: Wills, Trusts, Estates; Death and Gift Taxes

If your riches are yours, why don't you take them with you to the other world?
Benjamin Franklin

RESIDING in a small village was a lawyer who was famous throughout the state for drawing up wills. When a wealthy man died, there was much speculation as to the value of his estate, and the town gossip set about to find out. He went to see the lawyer, and after a few preliminary remarks about the deceased, said rather bluntly:

"I understand you made his will. Would you mind telling me how much he left?"

"Not at all," answered the attorney, resuming his writing, "he left everything he had."

ESTATE PLANNING

Estate planning has been called an "old trade with a new name." At one time it appeared to involve merely will making, but today it is recognized that making a will is just one part of a more elaborate process that should run for most of a person's adult lifetime.

Estate planning is a process of arranging a person's affairs to produce the most effective disposition of his or her capital and income. It is an attempt to work out an arrangement which best suits the financial requirements, personalities, and welfare of those concerned and at the same time produces the most economical method of disposition. The tools of estate planning include:

1. *Outright gifts during life.* Too often this aspect is ignored. Gifts may include cash, securities, real estate, life insurance, annuities, and more.
2. *Gifts in trust created during owner's lifetime.* This is particularly useful as a device for endowing minor children.
3. *Annuities.* These can be used in many ways to assist in estate planning.
4. *Life insurance.* Contrary to popular belief, life insurance proceeds, except under certain circumstances are part of one's *taxable* estate.
5. *Passing property by will.* When personal property is passed, it is called a "bequest"; when real property is involved, it is called a "devise."
6. *Trusts created at death.* Just as you can create a trust or trusts during your lifetime, you can also create one by will at death.
7. *Special devices and mechanisms.* There are a variety of devices, such as use of a business, which attorneys, experienced in estate planning, have developed.
8. *Social security benefits* (as discussed in Chapter 9) provide goodly sums to the widow with dependent children and again when she reaches 60.
9. *Pensions at retirement* including the *Keogh plan* (discussed in Chapter 9) for the self-employed through U.S. government securities, savings accounts, mutual funds, and life insurance.

All these tools, or several of them combined, are involved in estate planning. You can either use them wisely or you can do nothing. Not making an estate plan *is* making an estate plan, in a way, but one you may not really want to make. If you do nothing, the state takes over. Your property passes to those people and in such proportions as the state legislature has decreed.

What Happens if You Do Not Leave a Will

If you die and leave no will, you are said to have died "intestate." In effect, the state makes your will for you, and your property passes in accordance with the fixed provisions of the law of the state in which you are domiciled. No matter how small or large your estate, not leaving a will causes much trouble and inconvenience for your survivors. A woman who died in Pennsylvania in 1936 left lawyers there a lot of work and a legacy of disappointment to a lot of other people. She left more than $17 million, but no will. Because some 26,000 persons claimed kinship, there were over 2,000 hearings in the probate court. The testimony of 1,100 witnesses filled 390 volumes and 115,000 pages. The estate was not settled until 1952—16 years after the owner's death.

But, you may say, no one would be interested in a small estate, and why does one have to make a will if one has very little to leave? Assume that you are married, have one small child, and leave $18,000—but no will. Your wife, under the laws of many states, will receive only one third of your estate. The child will inherit two thirds, but since it is a minor, a guardian will have to be appointed by the probate (or surrogate's) court. It may very well be that your wife will be that guardian; yet she will be anything but a free agent in the handling of your child's money. She will have to provide a bond; she will be under constant supervision of the court; she will have to file annual accountings. All told, guardianship is an expensive and cumbersome procedure. It can be avoided by a properly drawn will.

How Property Passes if There Is No Will

While the statutes of descent and distribution which govern the disposition of one's estate if there is no will vary from state to state, it is possible to give a general impression of what is usually found in them, as follows:

1. On death of unmarried man or woman (or widow or widower)
   a. In the absence of children or their descendants, property goes one half to each parent or entirely to the surviving parent.
   b. In the absence of children or their descendants, and parents, property goes equally to brothers and sisters. Children of a deceased brother or sister divide equally their parent's share.
   c. In the absence of children or their descendants, parents, brothers, sisters, or their descendants, property is divided among next of kin.
   d. In the absence of all relatives, property escheats to the state of the domicile of the deceased.
2. On death of married man or woman
   a. In the absence of children or their descendants, a stipulated amount (perhaps $5,000 or $10,000) and half of the remaining balance go to the surviving spouse, with the remainder going to the parents of the deceased; in the absence of parents, the surviving spouse is apt to take the entire estate.
   b. In the presence of children or their descendants, either one third or one half goes to the surviving spouse, and the balance is

divided equally among the children, descendants of a child dividing their parent's share equally. The amount herein stipulated for the surviving spouse is in addition to the life interest in real estate granted by the homestead statutes. An option may be given the surviving spouse of taking an amount mentioned in a will or provided by rights of dower and curtesy, if it is larger than would be secured under the statutes of descent and distribution. The right of dower is the wife's right to one third of the income for life from her husband's real estate after his death; curtesy is a like right giving a husband one third of the income for life from his wife's real estate after her death. In some states these rights no longer exist; in others they have been written into law in the form of a wife's (or husband's) right to elect to take the intestate share against the will rather than accept the share provided in the will.

3. On death of widow or widower with children or their descendants, children take the property equally, descendants of deceased children dividing equally their parents' share.

The estate law of each state may have a table showing the way in which property passes in intestacy under differing and varying relationships. Table 17–1 shows the pattern for New York, New Jersey, and Connecticut.

The Inadequacies of Intestacy

The will written for every man and woman *by law* is rarely an acceptable substitute for the will that the law permits every legally competent person to write for himself. The state, whose laws of intestacy are inflexible and cannot be adapted to the needs of your dependents, will distribute your property in a manner which you might not think desirable.

For example, assume that you are married and have one child, age four. The real asset of your estate is your retail business, which you own individually and which pays a good living. You die without leaving a will, and, upon her petition to the probate or surrogate's court, your wife is appointed guardian for the child. A special guardian will also be appointed by the court to check on your wife's disposition of the estate—on her accounting to the court. She may wish to continue the business; but the special guardian will insist that the business be sold in order to liquidate and settle the estate. If retained, it would provide a good living; when sold, it brings only a moderate sum, which, when invested, will not provide a good living. Yet the special guardian and the court will require that the business be sold, since you left no will granting the power to continue the

TABLE 17–1
How an Estate Is Distributed if There Is No Will

Surviving Heirs	*New York*	*New Jersey*	*Connecticut*
Spouse and one child	$2,000 and ½ to spouse ½ to child	To wife—life use of ½ the realty plus ⅓ of personal property outright. Child or children take rest	⅓ to wife ⅔ to child
Spouse and two or more children	⅓ to spouse ⅔ to children	Same as above	Same as above
Child or children, but no spouse	All to children	All to children	All to children
Spouse and parent(s), but no children	$25,000 plus ½ the balance to spouse. Rest to parent or parents	All to wife	$5,000 plus ½ of balance to wife. Rest to parent or parents
Grandchildren	Grandchildren and more remote descendants do not share unless their parent is dead. Then each set of grandchildren divides the share their parent would have taken if alive		
Wife, and brothers and sisters or their descendants	$10,000 plus ½ the balance to wife. Rest to brothers and sisters or their descendants	All to wife	All to wife
Wife, and uncles, cousins, etc. (no descendant, parent, brother, sister, nephew, niece)	All to wife	All to wife	All to wife
No wife and no children	All to parent or parents or, if none, to brothers and sisters or their descendants	Equally to parent or parents and brothers and sisters or their descendants	All to parent or parents or, if none, to brothers and their descendants

Notes: A surviving husband takes the same share of his wife's estate as she would of his. Descendants of a brother and sister (for example nieces or nephews) take their parent's share only if the parent is not alive to take his or her share. If there are no relatives closer than cousins, the property normally goes to the "distributees" or "next of kin," usually the closest surviving relatives, for example, surviving first cousins (but if there are surviving first cousins, descendants of deceased first cousins will not share).

Source: Irving Trust Company.

business. By a simple will with such power, you could have left your wife a going business and a good income.

To take a second example: Assume that you are age 60 and that your wife is age 54. You have one son, age 30, who is employed, earning a good income but who likes a good time and is a spendthrift. You die without leaving a will. Your wife, who has no other means of support and who may be too old to go to work after being a housewife for so many years, gets only one third of your $90,000 estate; the son, who does not need it and who will probably squander it, gets two thirds, or $60,000. Obviously, you would not have intended this division; but, in the absence of a will, that is how your estate is divided.

A third example may interest you. Tom and Ethel Young have no children; Tom's father is living and is quite wealthy. Ethel has no resources of her own. Yet, on Tom's death, since there was no will, Ethel received $5,000 plus half of the remainder of Tom's estate, while Tom's father received the other half. The father had no need of the funds; the wife did, but the law is inflexible.

If you die intestate (without a will), an administrator for your estate must be appointed by the court, and a bond equal to the size of the estate must be posted. The wrong person may be selected to administer the estate. The court may pick your widow, who knows little about money matters, whereas you would have made your brother, who has been your business partner for years, your executor had you bothered to make a will. No tax savings devices will be available to your estate if you do not leave a will. There is no room for charitable dispositions. Your estate will not be distributed among your heirs in accordance with either sentiment or need. Your parents, or other persons you may have in mind, however much they may need or deserve your help, may not receive anything from your estate.

For example, assume that your wife is quite wealthy in her own right and that her parents are very well off too. Your parents, on the other hand, are poor, retired, not well, and wholly dependent upon you for support. Moreover, they do not, unfortunately, get along with your wife, nor she with them. You have two small children. You die and leave no will. All your property goes to your wife and children; nothing goes to your parents. Your wife could easily take care of herself and the children from her own resources, but, because you left no will, your death leaves your parents destitute.

The Young Family and "Guardianship"

You are young and carefree, and nothing could be further from your mind than death, wills, and estates. Who cares—why bother? But consider one young and carefree family.

Jim and Mary Fantini had been married for three years. They had a son, aged one. On a family summer vacation, they were in an automobile accident. Jim was killed. Mary was in the hospital for a month. Miraculously, the little boy was unhurt. Jim had no will. With the house they owned, the estate amounted to about $70,000. They lived in a state where the law said that in the case of death of a husband and no will, one third must go to the widow, two thirds to the child.

When Mary recovered she was shocked to learn that she could not administer her child's money, or even act as guardian without consent of the court. She had to apply to the court to administer the estate and post a bond, the premium cost of which was $210. Then she had to apply for legal guardianship of her son and post another bond, at an additional cost of $380. Because she had to sell the house, she had to secure court approval to do so. There were additional fees, including payments to lawyers, totaling $750 more. The first year, then, her expenses came to almost $1,400.

That isn't the end, however, for her lengthy legal involvement with the court will continue until the boy reaches 18. Each year she will have to post bonds, and the fees will be about $500 per annum. Altogether, Jim's not having drawn a will cost Mary and her son about $10,000 of a modest estate. It could have financed the boy's college education. And it was all so unnecessary. A simple will drawn by Jim, leaving everything to Mary and naming her executor to serve without bond, would have avoided most of the involvement with the court and eliminated almost all the cost.

Modern Estate Planning

The limitations and inadequacies of intestacy are so apparent, and inequities which frequently arise as a result are so glaring, that the informed person today plans the disposal of his lifetime accumulation and the protection and welfare of his family in the light of their special circumstances. Just as modern insurance programing, when coupled with social security and annuities, provides for planned security in old age and retirement, so modern estate planning permits you to use your resources to protect your wife, your children, and your parents in the best possible way in the light of your circumstances. Your business and investments can be left in the most competent hands, estate expenses and death taxes can be minimized, and family protection can be maximized through a carefully planned, flexible, and liquid estate program. Trusts may be established for those not competent to handle funds themselves, double estate taxes can be avoided, and your life insurance and real property can be tied in with other assets, such as stocks and bonds, so that forced sales, with costly shrinkage of values shortly after death, can be eliminated.

A man of means does a grave injustice to his family if he does not sit down with a competent lawyer specializing in estate planning and with an official of the trust department of his commercial bank to discuss a co-ordinated plan for the disposal of his assets upon death.

The information needed to plan intelligently for estate purposes is shown in Figure 17–1. Before you discuss your problem with your lawyer, you should set down all the facts required in this form so that both of you will have all the essential information available. Figure 17–2 is a graphic illustration of what a completed estate plan will look like. In an actual case, of course, exact facts and figures will be described precisely. You can-

FIGURE 17–1
Getting the Facts for Estate Planning

Statement of Facts

The following suggests some of the facts concerning yourself and your dependents which you ought to take into consideration to formulate a sound plan. It is not necessary to prepare the statement before discussing the subject with us but having it available would be helpful. All information which we may receive is held in confidence.

(Approximate amounts are sufficient)

NAME..

PRESENT ADDRESS.................................... LEGAL RESIDENCE....................................

YOUR BUSINESS INTERESTS

(a) ....Corporation ....Partnership ....Proprietorship

(b) Kind of business..

(c) Who owns control?..

(d) Do you desire to have your business continued after your death?..

(e) What plans have you made to have it continued?..

....

(f) Describe any written contracts, business insurance agreements or other arrangements you have made for the disposition of your business interests:..

....

(g) Give any other important details with respect to your business:..

....

YOUR APPROXIMATE WORTH

	Net Value	Annual Income
(a) Value of business interest	$....................	
(b) Salary, commissions, fees, income from business, etc.		$....................
(c) Stocks	$....................	$....................
(d) Bonds	$....................	$....................
(e) Mortgages	$....................	$....................
(f) Real Estate	$....................	$....................
(g) Other property and income	$....................	$....................
TOTAL NET WORTH AND INCOME	$....................	$....................

Describe any trust interests you may have: (including powers of appointment)..

....

How much of your net annual income is available for investment each year?..

FIGURE 17–1 (continued)

YOUR LIFE INSURANCE

How Payable:

	Lump Sum Payment	Insurance Company Plan	Trust Company Plan	Other Plan
(a) To named beneficiary	$..........	$..........	$..........	$..........
(b) To estate	$..........			

Approximate annual net premiums $..........

Have you made a will?.......... Has your wife made a will?..........

YOUR WIFE'S NET ESTATE

Wife's total separate net worth $..........

Approximate annual income of wife $..........

YOUR HEIRS AND DEPENDENTS

NAME	RELATIONSHIP	AGES, if children
....	....	....
....	....	....
....	....	....
....	....	....

What approximate minimum annual income will be required to maintain your family in its present standard of living after your death? $..........

Please state to whom you wish the income of your estate to be paid after your death.

NAME	Amount or Percentage of Annual Income
....	....
....	....
....	....
....	....

Within legal limits, any desired disposition of an estate can be made. On the following pages there are two charts indicating two different plans for the distribution of an estate.

Source: *Planning Your Estate,* City Bank Farmers Trust Co.

FIGURE 17–2
A Completed Estate Plan

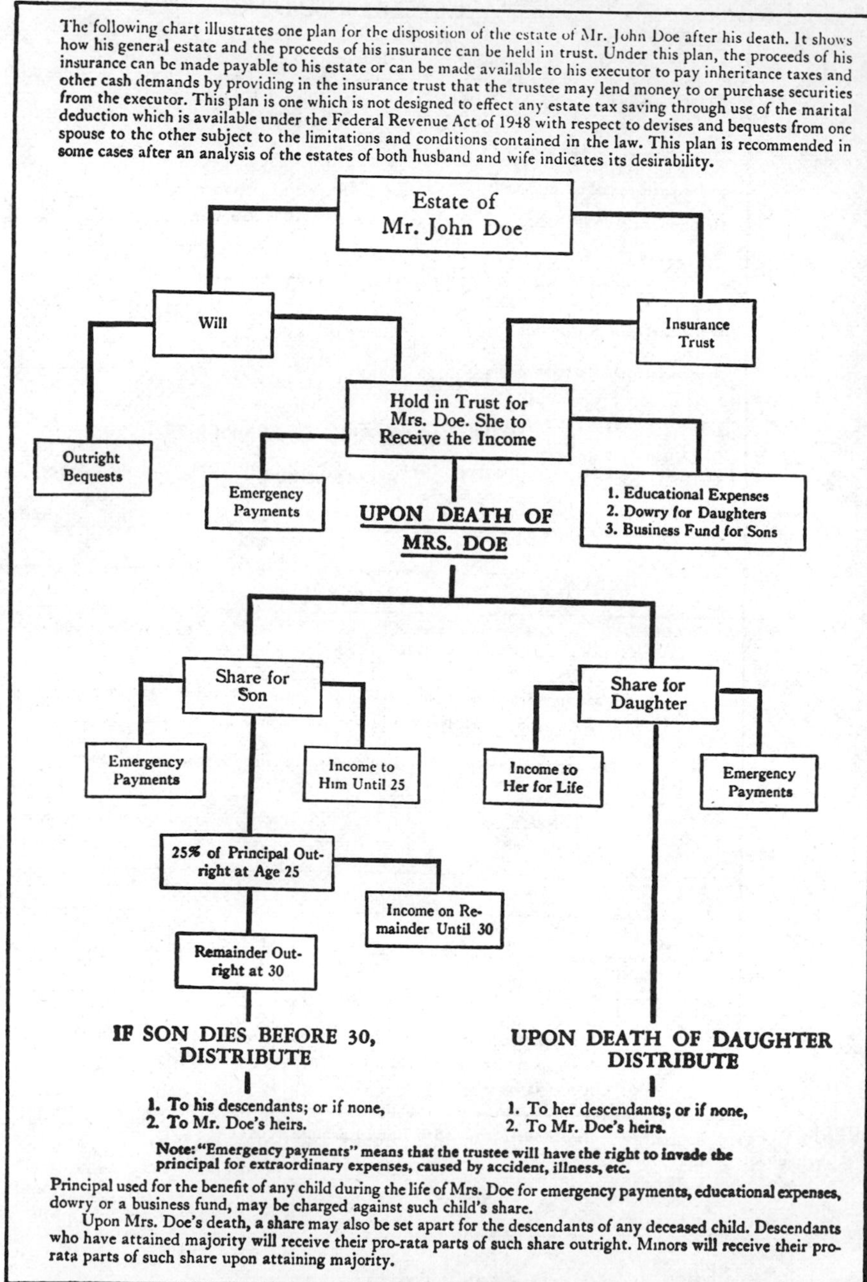
The following chart illustrates one plan for the disposition of the estate of Mr. John Doe after his death. It shows how his general estate and the proceeds of his insurance can be held in trust. Under this plan, the proceeds of his insurance can be made payable to his estate or can be made available to his executor to pay inheritance taxes and other cash demands by providing in the insurance trust that the trustee may lend money to or purchase securities from the executor. This plan is one which is not designed to effect any estate tax saving through use of the marital deduction which is available under the Federal Revenue Act of 1948 with respect to devises and bequests from one spouse to the other subject to the limitations and conditions contained in the law. This plan is recommended in some cases after an analysis of the estates of both husband and wife indicates its desirability.

Note: "Emergency payments" means that the trustee will have the right to invade the principal for extraordinary expenses, caused by accident, illness, etc.

Principal used for the benefit of any child during the life of Mrs. Doe for emergency payments, educational expenses, dowry or a business fund, may be charged against such child's share.

Upon Mrs. Doe's death, a share may also be set apart for the descendants of any deceased child. Descendants who have attained majority will receive their pro-rata parts of such share outright. Minors will receive their pro-rata parts of such share upon attaining majority.

Source: *Planning Your Estate*, City Bank Farmers Trust Co.

not leave a planned estate, however, without a will. The central feature of estate planning is the will.

YOUR "LAST WILL AND TESTAMENT"

The expression "last will and testament" is historical and comes from the time when a distinction was drawn between a "testament" (a term derived from the Latin) which disposed of personal property, and a "will" (a term derived from the Anglo-Saxon) which disposed of real property. The word *will* is the current modern equivalent of both, although the heading of a will customarily employs the longer form. Some states make a distinction as to the descent of real property, on the one hand, and personal property, on the other.

Why Make a Will?

Aside from the fact that if you die without a will your estate will be distributed according to the intestate laws, the provisions of which are necessarily general and inflexible, there are a number of other valid reasons why a will is decidedly advisable—in fact, almost necessary. *It is well to remember that if you die intestate—*

1. Your family will find itself unnecessarily involved in certain court procedures, of which, the chances are, it has little or no knowledge.
2. Your knowledge of the property that you own and your advice as to its disposition cannot be passed on. It dies with you.
3. Indifference on your part is indicated. It is, therefore, not unlikely that this indifference will be transferred to those who administer your estate.
4. You lose the privilege of naming your executor—and this may be a very costly loss indeed.
5. You lose the privilege, afforded by the laws of most states, of naming a guardian for your minor children. This is vital, particularly if your spouse should not survive you.
6. In some instances, if you leave no immediate family, your failure to leave a will may result in the passage of your property to persons in whom you have no particular interest, or even in its escheat to the state.
7. The procedure involved in intestacy is likely to increase the shrinkage of your estate.
8. You lose the opportunity of minimizing estate and inheritance taxes, as can often be done by a carefully planned will.

In *contrast*, a will gives you the advantage of specifying—

1. To whom your property should go.
2. When it should go.
3. In what amounts it should go.
4. How it should be safeguarded.
5. By whom it should be handled.

Disposition of Property by Will

Usually a person may dispose of his property by will as he wishes. We have already seen one possible exception to this rule, in that, if a husband or wife leaves his spouse less in his will than she would have under the statutes of descent and distribution or under the laws of dower and curtesy, the surviving spouse may elect to take the larger amount granted by the statutes or laws. That is, one spouse may not usually, in most states, disinherit the other, although it is possible to disinherit children. Another exception is provided by the homestead laws, which are found in nearly every state. The purpose of such laws is to provide a roof over her head for a wife in spite of her husband's possible desire to deprive her of it.

Certain provisions or bequests in wills may be against "public policy" and hence will be invalidated. For example, a man who had lived in a certain house during all of his adult life provided that his home be boarded up for 20 years after his death and then be given free of charge for two years to any deserving young married couple. The probate court held that, while it recognized the sentimental purpose, the closing of a needed dwelling for 20 years was against public policy. Also, a condition in a will to the effect that a person who has never married shall only receive a bequest providing he or she remain unmarried for life is usually against public policy, since it is thought that marriage and the founding of families is in the best interest of society. While it is impossible to prevent a person who has never married from getting married, you are usually permitted to restrict a person from remarrying a second or third time on pain of losing the gift set forth in your will. It is also possible in some states to insert provisions that your beneficiaries marry only persons of certain religions. A mother bequeathed her wealth to her daughter only on condition the daughter divorce her husband or was widowed at the time the will was probated. The court held that the will was valid.

Certain property will pass automatically on death and is not subject to disposition by will. This may be because of the nature of the property or the technical legal title by which it is held; because the testator is married; or for a combination of reasons. For example, if property is held by two persons as joint tenants with right of survivorship, or by husband and wife as tenants by the entirety, and one of them dies, the survivor becomes sole owner of the property, regardless of the will of the decedent.

Validity of Wills

It is the generally accepted rule that the validity of a will which bequeathes personal property depends upon the law of the state or country where the deceased had his domicile (home); whereas the validity of a will which devises real estate depends on the law of the state or country where the real estate is located (its "situs"). Most states have loosened the principles of local sovereignty in order to give validity to wills made in other states and countries. Many have adopted the Uniform Wills Act or similar statutes. The power to dispose of property by will is neither a natural nor a constitutional right. It depends wholly upon statute, i.e., it may be given, revoked, or circumscribed by act of the legislature.

"Domicile" is a very important concept in wills, especially from a tax standpoint. A person may have a number of residences; there is usually but one domicle. This is based on intent and is judged by such things as where the person voted, paid taxes, and so on. In the famous *Dorrance* case, both New Jersey and Pennsylvania claimed that John T. Dorrance (sole stockholder in the Campbell Soup Company) had been domiciled in their respective states. The U.S. Supreme Court refused to take jurisdiction, and both states assessed and collected death taxes on his estate, New Jersey $12 million, Pennsylvania $14 million.

Formalities in Wills

There are several steps in the ritual required to make a valid will. While these may seem excessively precise to you, remember that the law insists on these steps to prevent fraud, as safeguards for the protection of all concerned. A will must be in writing, and the more important aspects of the ritual with which the maker must comply are outlined in the following paragraphs.

Signature of Testator. A valid will must be signed by the maker. Although the signature may be made satisfactorily by pen, pencil, or typewriter, it is only common sense to write it in ink, by hand. The signature should be placed right after the last sentence of the will itself. The will must be signed *at the end* to prevent fraud—to eliminate the possibility that someone might add a typed paragraph either before or after the signature and thus change the terms and intent of the will. A surprisingly large number of cases are brought to court to determine whether the signature was at the end of a will, particularly where a rather confusing printed form was used by a testator (maker of a will) who tried to write his own will. Where the signature of the decedent was not at the end, the will was denied "probate." That is, it was held no valid will, and the testator's property was divided up, when he died, as if he had died "intestate," i.e., without a will. It is a further legal requirement that the signature be written in the presence of the subscribing witnesses. Confusion is avoided if the testator's signature agrees in all respects with his name as given elsewhere in the will. To avoid question as to other pages of the will, the testator's signature, or at least his initials, should be written on each of the other pages, customarily in the margin. This is also to prevent fraud—to prevent the substitution of a new typed page for one of the originals.

Witnesses. State statutes generally require at least two or three witnesses to a will. The witnesses should also be of full age and of sound mind. It is also good if they are healthy, and younger than the testator. Usually a will is not needed for some years after it is made. In case of dispute later, it is helpful if the witnesses are then living and still mentally able, so that they can give any necessary testimony. No beneficiary under a will or spouse of a beneficiary should sign as a witness, since any bequest may be lost by doing so.

Witnesses should see the testator write his signature or be told by him that the signature is his. They should see each other sign, and the will itself should state that all witnesses signed in the presence of each other. If the addresses of witnesses are added, it may help later in locating them. Although the witnesses need not read the will, and the testator may not want them to read it, the testator should tell them that he wants them to witness his signature to his last will and testament.

Absence of Alterations. Alterations should not be made in a will after it has been signed and witnessed. Any alterations made prior to signatures should be incorporated in a fair copy, free of erasures or any other changes which later might be the cause of misunderstanding. Once a will has been completed, changes can be effected through a codicil or addition, executed with all the formalities of the will itself.

A few examples of errors will serve to show the importance of the ritual. An intelligent, literate woman bought a will form at a stationery store, on which she wrote her wishes for the disposal of her property. There was not enough room for her to write all she wanted above the dotted lines for signatures of maker and witnesses, so she continued her writing below. She and the witnesses signed on the dotted lines. Everything seemed in order. There was no question but that she was of sound mind at the time;

no doubt as to how she wished to dispose of her property; no dispute that the witnesses saw her sign, knew she meant the document to be her will, and signed as witnesses. Nor is there anything necessarily wrong with a will made out on a printed form. But she hadn't signed it at the end; and, in the state where she lived, the law required that a will be signed at the end. The court would not permit the document to be given effect as her will—could not consider the writing above the signature as a will and ignore what followed—inasmuch as she had written it all as a single, consecutive expression of her wishes.

Mr. Thomas asked two friends if they would come over to the home of his sister, Mrs. Conway, to witness the signing of her will. Two or three days later he drove them to her house. They waited in the living room while Mr. Thomas went into the dining room. In a few minutes the two witnesses were called into the dining room; then Mrs. Conway was wheeled in. Mr. Thomas told her to "sign this paper here," and she did. Then the witnesses signed. Later, after Mrs. Conway's death, this paper was offered for probate; but the court would not accept it as her will. The witnesses testified that, at the time of signing, Mrs. Conway had not shown, either by word or deed, that she knew it was her will. Neither she nor anyone else in her presence had asked the witnesses to sign as witnesses to her will.

Thus a will is not valid unless, at the time the witnesses sign, the maker of the will, in the presence of the witnesses, "declares" or gives a definite indication that it is his will. The example given illustrates the reason for this requirement: Mrs. Conway was age 85 and infirm at the time of signing. The requirement—like the others for a valid will—is intended to protect anyone from being imposed upon in making what may be a last, and hence irrevocable, will.

The well-known commentator Drew Pearson wrote seven wills from 1919 to 1962 by hand on hotel stationery, telegraph paper, and university letterhead, but only one was witnessed. It was that one—written in 1938 in Council Bluffs, Iowa—that was accepted as valid by the District of Columbia Registrar of Wills. The family and friends are convinced that the 1962 will represented what Mr. Pearson really wanted, but it was the 1938 one that was probated.[1]

Terminology

Occasionally a student will complain, "I do not understand why such unintelligible terms as 'intestate,' 'testamentary,' 'corpus,' 'issue,' 'per stirpes,' 'power of appointment,' and the like have to be used in talking—

[1] *New York Times,* September 12, 1969.

or writing—about wills and trusts. Why don't you use language I can understand?"

When it comes to using legal words in legal situations such as wills and trusts represent, there is a good reason why lawyers use them. Over the years, through definition by statute and interpretation by the courts, these terms have acquired precise meanings—meanings that might take pages of words to explain fully. Technical words and terms are a means of exact and comprehensive expression; and when properly used in wills and trust agreements, they are a protection to the people whose interests are served and can be an economy, too, in the avoiding of litigation. You should, therefore, understand a few of these terms.

Administrator. This is the term applied to the person appointed by the court to administer an estate of a person who died intestate.

Administration Expenses. The cost of settling an estate—court costs; the fees of executors, attorneys, and appraisers; and other expenses.

Ancillary. An ancillary executor is subordinate to the one named in your will and is appointed to dispose of property in another state or country which does not permit your chosen executor to represent you.

Beneficiary. A beneficiary is one who is named in the will as a recipient of property under it.

Bequeath. In connection with wills, this is a word with a technical legal meaning, the giving of a bequest of personal property (as contrasted with real property), the recipient being a *legatee.*

Codicil. An addition to a will or a change executed with the same formalities as required in the will itself.

Decedent. The deceased, or deceased person.

Devise. This is the gift of real property (not personal property) to a person known as the "devisee."

Estate. Your estate is all you own—real estate, cash, stocks, bonds, and other property. You can pass these on by will, subject to the deduction of debts, estate and inheritance taxes, and administration expenses.

Exculpatory Clause. "None of my Executors or Trustees shall be liable for any act or omission in connection with the administration of my estate or any of the trusts or powers hereunder nor for any loss or injury to any property held in or under my estate or any of said trusts or powers, except only for his or her actual fraud; and none of my Executors or Trustees shall be responsible for any act or omission of any other Executor or Trustee."

Executor. The person named in a will and appointed to administer an estate according to the provisions of a will.

Holographic Will. Such a will is written entirely in the handwriting of the person making the will.

Intestate. This term refers to one who dies without leaving a valid will.

Legatee. This is a person who receives personal property under a will, as contrasted with a "devisee," one who receives real property.

Letters Testamentary. The court's certificate of the probate of a will and the executor's authority to act under it.

Nuncupative Will. Such a will is an oral disposition of personal property made by a person during a fatal illness or by a soldier or sailor during battle. It should be put in writing by witnesses as soon as possible and offered promptly for probate. This is the only sort of oral will commonly held to be valid.

Personal Property. This is all property which is not real estate.

Probate. This is the name of courts having jurisdiction of wills and of the court's procedure in proving the validity of wills. "Probating a will" means presentation of proof to the court after your death of the legality of your last will and testament, whereupon the court grants authority to the executor to carry out your intentions as expressed in the will.

Real Estate. Land and the buildings thereon.

Surrogate. This term (used in New York) means the same as "probate judge."

Testate. A person leaving a valid will is said to have died "testate."

Testator. A person who makes and leaves a will.

Trust. A trust puts your money or other property into the hands of a trustee (either financial institution or individual, or both) for management and disposition of income and of principal as you direct in your will or trust agreement. There are "living trusts," "insurance trusts," and "testamentary trusts," to be described later. A person who receives the income from a trust during his or her lifetime is known as a "life tenant" or "life beneficiary," while the person who receives the principal of the trust after the death of the life tenant is a "remainderman."

Common Provisions

Since the purpose of a will is to direct the distribution of an estate to the person or persons whom the testator wishes to have it, the following comments may prevent omission of important provisions which might otherwise be overlooked. It is common to mention the testator's just debts and funeral expenses, which must be paid before anything can be left for anyone else. Customarily, notice is given to creditors; they have a reasonable time in which to submit their claims for payment. The testator may find it desirable to state in his will the type of funeral and burial services he wishes in order that a great deal more or a great deal less than he thinks appropriate will not be paid for them.

Distribution of real and personal property to family, relatives, friends,

Names Clipped From Will Restored by Surrogate

BUFFALO, N.Y. (UPI)—Surrogate Thomas J. O'Donnell recently told nine persons they could not be cut out of the will of a relative even though they literaly were.

One paragraph of the will of Mrs. Lillian G. Briggs of suburban Kenmore, who died Feb. 21, 1962 was scissored out. It provided for bequests to nine relatives. The will was contested.

In what Surrogate O'Donnel called "a rare move," he accepted a carbon copy of the will and awarded $6,000 to the relatives. It was not determined who did the cutting.

and charities should be set out in clear and concise terms; in connection therewith, disposition of personal effects should be dealt with in such a way as to avoid dispute. It is usually advisable for the testator to nominate the person of his choice as executor; and if there are minor children, it may be expedient to nominate a guardian for them. The will can set up any trusts thought advantageous for spouse, children, or others and can make special provision for anything else the testator desires.

Too much care cannot be devoted to the drawing of a will; in spite of care, ambiguities are frequently found in them, and dissatisfaction and unfairness often result. When distributing property by will, the property already owned by the beneficiaries and any money coming to them as beneficiaries of life insurance policies should be taken into consideration in order to achieve an equitable overall result.

If individual pieces of property are left to each of several children, there is always the question as to whether some pieces of property may increase in value by the time of the testator's death, whereas others may decline in value, thus effecting an unequal distribution. It might be better to give each child an equal interest in all properties or the proceeds from the sale of them all. Some years ago, a certain wealthy individual left stipulated amounts to several charities, thinking that he was leaving such a substantial estate that there would be plenty left over for his family. A depression in the stock market, however, so depleted the assets that, after the designated amounts were distributed to the charities, little remained for the family.

What Is in a Will?

There are five principal sections to a will: the opening recitation, the dispositive clauses, the administrative clauses, a testimonium clause, and an attestation clause. Each has a special and important function.

The opening recitation tells who you are, where you live, may say that you are of sound mind and competent to make a will (though saying it does not prove it is so), may revoke all previous wills, direct that all just debts and funeral expenses be paid, and give instructions as to burial (though this latter feature is better done in a separate letter of instruction rather than in a will, since the will may not be opened until after the funeral). A typical introductory clause is as follows:

> IN THE NAME OF GOD, AMEN. I, Joseph Tagget, of the Borough of Manhattan, City, County, and State of New York, being of sound mind and memory, but also aware of the uncertainties of this life, do hereby make, publish and declare this to be my Last Will and Testament. I hereby revoke all wills and codicils made by me at any time heretofore.

The dispositive clauses are the heart of the will. They indicate who is to get what. There are four types of legacies: specific, general, demonstrative, and residuary. There are also lapsed and preferred legacies. A *specific* legacy occurs when a particular piece of property in an estate is set aside and given to a named individual: you bequeath your gold watch to your son, Thomas. A *general* legacy exists when you leave a given sum of money, such as $5,000, to an individual. A cash bequest is payable out of the general assets of the estate. When the testator does not leave sufficient property to pay all the general legacies, the specific legatees would nevertheless receive the particular items bequeathed to them, whereas general legacies would be proportionately diminished and abated. In fact, where it is necessary to raise money to pay debts, the general legacies will first completely abate before recourse is had to the sale of items specifically bequeathed. In other words, a specific bequest has priority over a general or cash bequest.

A *demonstrative* legacy is usually one of a stated amount of money coupled with a specification in the will of a source of funds for its payment. In the case of a true demonstrative legacy, if the indicated source of funds is nonexistent—or to the extent that it is insufficient—the legacy is payable out of general assets, like a general legacy. This has, however, occasioned considerable litigation, so that many lawyers prefer to avoid demonstrative legacies completely.

A *residuary* legacy, as the term implies, is payable from the remainder of the estate after administration expenses, debts, and specific, general, and demonstrative legacies have been paid. Danger exists, as pointed out previously, when you may make a will with a number of specific and general legacies and then leave the remainder—the bulk of your estate—as a residuary legacy to your spouse or child. A shrinkage of the assets of the estate may sharply reduce the residuary legacies without impairing or touching the specific and general bequests. Since this, of course, was not your intent, you can guard against such an eventuality by inserting an abatement clause, which provides that if the entire net estate, or residuary estate, is less than a certain amount, or shrinks a certain percentage from value at the time the will was drawn, then the general legacies shall be reduced proportionately or eliminated altogether. When you leave your residuary estate to your nearest and dearest, such an abatement clause should always be used.

A *lapsed* legacy occurs when the legatee predeceases the testator. To provide for such contingencies, the will should make provision for alternate disposition. A *preferred* legacy is, of course, one where the testator in his will indicates that preference shall be given in the event that the estate is insufficient to satisfy all legacies in full.

The third major part of the will is the section which contains the administrative clauses. These set up the machinery for carrying out all your instructions. Here you name your post-mortem agents, your executors, and your guardians (if you have any minor children). The executor is the person (or persons, since there can be more than one) or institution (since it can be a trust company) responsible for having the will approved by the court, locating heirs and property, paying bills, distributing bequests, and so on. You may select anyone—your spouse, a business partner, your brother or sister, your lawyer, your banker—as your executor; but you will want to ask them if they will accept, and you will want to be reasonably sure that they are able to handle the complicated business of settling an estate and are young enough so that they are not likely to predecease you. You may also wish to name an alternate or substitute executor in case your first choices decline to serve or die. The guardian you appoint for your minor child may, of course, be your spouse, in which case you will want to provide that this service be without bond and with absolute discretion in the handling of any funds you may leave to the child. If you own and operate a business, you will want to give your executor very broad powers if you want the business continued, because otherwise he will either be forced to liquidate it or may not have sufficient authority to operate it efficiently. These are all highly technical matters, the settlement of which should never be attempted without the advice of a lawyer.

The fourth part of a will is the testamonium clause. Actually this is very simple. It ends the will and says that, in approval of the foregoing, you are signing your name. Do not sign your name, however, until the witnesses are present. The testamonium clause is likely to read: "In Witness Whereof, I have hereunto set my hand (and seal, in some states) this 5th day of May 1974."

MR. KELLY'S "HUMOROUS" WILL

"For years I have been reading Last Wills and Testaments, and I have never been able to clearly understand any of them at one reading. Therefore, I will attempt to write my own Will with the hope that it will be understandable and legal. Kids will be called 'kids' and not 'issue' and it will not be cluttered up with 'parties of the first part,' 'per stirpes,' 'perpetuities,' 'quasi judicial,' 'to wit' and a lot of other terms that I am sure are only used to confuse those for whose benefit it is written."

So begins the Last Will of John B. Kelly of Philadelphia, one-time bricklayer, founder of two of the country's largest brick contracting firms, former Olympic rowing champion, and father of H. S. H. Princess Grace of Monaco.

It was typed on twelve full-size legal sheets, prompting his parting observation: "If I don't stop soon, this will be as long as Gone With the Wind."

Finally, there is what the lawyers call the "attestation clause." This is the clause for witnesses, so that a record will exist reciting the circumstances under which the signing of the will was witnessed and by whom. Remember that they must hear you announce that this is your will, see you sign it, and then sign in the presence of each other as well as in your presence.

Probate

The purpose of probate is to insure that the will which has your signature is genuine and that its execution will precisely carry out your intent. But before that can be done the executor must satisfy the Surrogates Court that your debts are paid, as well as state and federal taxes, and that any one who has a claim against the estate has been notified. Please note on pages 843–46 all the other time consuming duties that must be handled. Creditors have from four months to a year to make a claim. While the executor must settle federal estate taxes within nine months after death, the Internal Revenue Service and state tax authorities may then take several months to a year to indicate their acceptance. Only then can distribution be made from the estate. Any contest creates delay. And while legal and court costs and taxes shrink an estate, the need for cash mounts during the time that probate freezes funds. Studies made in Wisconsin show that the average time spent in probate was 12 to 15 months—on estates averaging about $30,000.

It has been suggested that a Uniform Probate Code, a proposed model law that has been fashioned by legal experts over a ten year period, would if adopted by the states, enable uncontested wills to be put into effect as quickly as five days after death. It would free the executor to pay bills, taxes, and legacies without the courts' formalities. It would simplify legal procedures for unchallenged small estates and those which are administered by members of the family.

Duties of an Executor

One institution entitled a section such as this, describing the functions of an executor, as "How (Not) to Give a White Elephant." There was once, it declared, a wily rajah, who punished all those who earned his

the important role of executor

disfavor by giving them a "sacred" white elephant. Refusal was out of the question; working the dedicated beast was taboo. The eating habits of elephants being what they are, these ponderous, idle pachyderms eventually ate the recipients out of house and home, which was the potentate's plan. And so it is that Webster's dictionary describes a white elephant as "a property requiring much care and expense and yielding little profit." High on the list of modern day white elephants is the job of executor when it is bestowed on an inexperienced individual. The path winds through a veritable jungle of laws and regulations, where today's executor can be held personally liable for failure to exercise "reasonable care, diligence, and prudence."

The duties of an executor have been described in detail as follows:[2]

Locates and Reads Will

1. Carries out burial instructions if arrangements have not previously been handled by relatives.
2. Arranges for living expenses of family, where necessary.

Takes Preliminary Steps to Safeguard Assets

1. Retains counsel to probate will.
2. Confers with persons familiar with decedent's affairs.
3. Examines checkbooks, books of account, and other records pertaining to assets, where such records are available.
4. Obtains immediate information as to decedent's business interests.
5. Notifies postmaster, banks, safe deposit companies, and other depositaries, of death.
6. Makes preliminary inventory.

Probates the Will

This proceeding is judicial. It consists of petitioning the court through your attorney to admit the will to probate and to issue letters testamentary to the executor named in the will, as authority to carry out the testator's wishes. The proper parties must be notified, and the required proof must be submitted by witnesses to satisfy the court that the will is valid and that any attempts to contest the probate should be resisted. Appointment of a temporary administrator is possible if delay of probate occurs because of a contest or for other reasons.

Assembles the Estate Property

1. Life insurance—obtains proofs and collects.
2. Household and personal effects—makes proper provision for their care.
3. Securities and mortgages
   a. Locates safe deposit box.
   b. Removes contents in presence of representative of state tax commission.
   c. Obtains tax waivers and collects securities in custody of others.
   d. Liquidates indebtedness if any securities have been used as collateral.
4. Real estate
   a. Inspects and reports on condition of property.
   b. Ascertains status of taxes, mortgages against property, and leases.
   c. Arranges for management and collection of rents.

---

[2] Adapted from *Executor and Testamentary Trustee*, City Bank Farmers Trust Co., New York, no date.

   d. Files exemplified copy of will in counties where real estate is situated.
5. Cash—obtains tax waivers and collects.
6. Miscellaneous assets
   a. Collects money due decedent, bank accounts, and interests in other estates or trusts, present or future.
   b. Adjust conflicting claims and liquidates them.
7. Inventory—makes complete list of property.
8. Ancillary administration—takes necessary steps to obtain property located outside the state.

Has Appraisals Made

Has appraisals made to establish value as of date of death, when necessary.

Manages Assets

Sets up a separate set of accounts for estate. Segregates assets specifically bequeathed and arranges for any income thereon to be held separately, pending distribution. Sets up accounts as follows:

1. Household and personal effects—determines best time and method for disposal of personal property, with special consideration to valuable collections.
2. Business interests—investigates and determines policy as to continuance, liquidation, or sales of business after securing information about the particular lines of business affected, always having due regard to the testator's wishes.
3. Securities and mortgages
   a. Examines desirability of investments.
   b. Determines propriety of retention or sale. Varying factors should be considered, sometimes one and sometimes others, e.g.:
      (1) Funds for taxes.
      (2) Other cash requirements.
      (3) Investment powers in will.
      (4) Market conditions.
      (5) Results of statistical research.
      (6) Taxable gains or losses.
      (7) Ultimate disposition of estate.
4. Real estate
   a. Investigates, leases, encumbrances, condition of buildings, and determines rental revenue.
   b. Considers anticipated conditions of locality and neighborhood and, where desirable, consults with real estate specialists.

c. If circumstances require a sale, lists property with leading brokers.

Settles Claims and Debts

1. Claims
   a. Advertises for claims when required by law.
   b. Considers propriety of claims and rejects those deemed improper.
2. Nature of claims and expenses encountered
   a. Bills for current expenses
   b. Funeral expenses.
   c. Taxes or adjustment of taxes.
   d. Unmatured charitable subscriptions and pledges.
   e. Liability as endorser or maker of promissory notes.
   f. Liability on leases; special partnership or business contracts.
   g. Administration expenses and legal fees.

Settles Taxes

The procedure for proper assessment and payment of modern taxes is highly technical. Special forms of information and tax returns must be prepared and filed with the respective taxing authorities.

1. Income taxes
   a. Federal, state, and local. Considers propriety of all claims for taxes and, where practicable, resists those deemed improper.
   b. On income before death: files necessary returns and pays taxes due; makes final settlement with tax authorities.
   c. On income after death: files necessary returns and pays taxes, if any.
2. Estate and gift and inheritance taxes
   a. Federal
      (1) Files preliminary notice.
      (2) Makes return and pays taxes.
      (3) Makes final adjustment after review and audit.
   b. State of domicile
      (1) Obtains waivers for transfer of securities.
      (2) Considers payment in time to obtain discount.
      (3) Institutes proceedings for fixing tax.
      (4) Final adjustment of tax payment.
   c. Foreign states and countries—takes necessary steps to file returns and pay taxes so that property affected can be released for transfer.
3. Real estate and other miscellaneous taxes—attends to adjustment

of all outstanding taxes, including state, city, and local property and other miscellaneous taxes.

Accounts to Court and Distributes Net Estate

1. Payment of legacies
   a. Pays legacies.
   b. Delivers specific bequests.
   c. Obtains final receipts and releases from legatees.
2. Audit of administration of estate and accounting
   a. Causes a detailed statement of account of its acts as executor to be prepared and submitted either to the interested parties or for judicial settlement by the appropriate court.
   b. Upon the settlement of the account to the satisfaction of the interested parties and such court, distributes the balance of the estate remaining in the hands of the executor as required by the terms of the will.
3. Establishment of trust funds
   a. Turns over securities or cash or other property to trustee to constitute corpus of any trust provided for in will.
   b. Adjusts income due trust fund from date of decedent's death.

Executors are, of course, compensated for such services, but an inexperienced person would either spend an excessive amount of time at the task or perform it inadequately. For this reason, if you appoint your spouse as executor, you may wish to name your lawyer as coexecutor in order to take adequate care of such involved matters as probating the will, settling the estate, meeting claims, providing for estate taxes, and filing an accounting with the court. Choose your executors carefully—not on the basis of friendship alone, but on the basis of competence and ability to handle money matters. When you have chosen them, tell them where you keep your will and give them each an unsigned copy of it.

Fees for independent executors, such as those appointed by courts, are fixed by state law. A typical example of the sliding scale usually used would be the following:

4 percent on the first $25,000 of the estate,
3.5 percent on the next $125,000,
3 percent on the next $150,000, and
2 percent on any amount in excess of $300,000.

Thus, for a $50,000 estate, an executor could charge $1,875; for a $100,000 estate $3,625; and for a $200,000 estate, $6,875. Only in the very large estates does the fee really pay for the time and problems involved. On a $1 million estate, for example, the fee would be $23,875. While executors' commissions vary from state to state, the fee is generally 3 percent of estates over $500,000, with the percentage charge increasing up to 5 percent as the size of the estate decreases.

Four years after his suicide, three executors of the estate of Mark Rothko, leading abstract expressionist painter, are involved in a $32 million estate suit with international art galleries and famed art centers, a phalanx of lawyers, a guardian for a minor child and the Attorney General of New York State taking sides. One of the executors is opposed to the other two. Rothko's daughter, when she came of age two years ago, brought suit to dismiss the executors because they had sold all 800 of his paintings in an exclusive deal to one gallery, alleging that two of the executors had a relationship with the gallery, and they had thereby "wasted the assets" of the estate. One art dealer testified that the 100 paintings bought by the gallery for $1.8 million were worth $6,420,000 at the artist's death and have now risen in value to $14,613,000.

Simultaneous Deaths (Common Disasters)

You often read about a husband and wife who die in the same accident. In the absence of a will, all the property would probably pass to their children. If there were no children, there would probably be an argument as to which person died first. The same sort of difficulty could arise if each had left a will. If it was established that the husband died first, the wife would take whatever her husband willed her; and this property, together with any other she owned, would pass as stipulated in her will, except that her husband would not be living and could not receive anything left to him in that will. In the absence of a will, any property she left would go to her relatives, to the exclusion of his.

Gross inequities often result. For example, Johnson and his wife are traveling, and there is an accident. Johnson is killed instantly. Mrs. Johnson dies a few hours later. Neither had wills. What happens to Johnson's quite substantial estate? All of it would go to his wife's relatives. Johnson's father, mother, brother, sister—even his own children by a former wife—would receive nothing. If there is no will and it cannot be determined who died first, there may be endless and very costly litigation between the two sides of the family to determine which inherits.

To prevent unwanted results as far as possible, it may be helpful for a will to state how the property is to be disposed of if both husband and wife die at the same time. A well drawn will usually contains a *common disaster clause*. Such a clause may read: "Any person who shall have died at the same time as I, or in a common disaster with me, or under such circumstances that it is difficult or impossible to determine which died first, shall be deemed to have predeceased me."

If the will contains only one bequest—for example, a gift of all property to the testator's wife and, if she does not survive the testator, then to the testator's daughter—a useful wording of a common disaster clause would be as follows: "All of my property, I give, devise, and bequeath to my wife, Mina, and if she does not survive me or if she and I die at the same time or in a common disaster or under such circumstances that it is difficult or impossible to determine which died first, then to my daughter Carla, if she survives me."

A Child Is Born—a Will Is Broken

It is sometimes possible for children not mentioned in a will to argue successfully that they were inadvertently forgotten when the will was made and that they should receive part of the estate. If the testator wishes to leave practically nothing to one or more of his children, he can do so by naming them and leaving each $1; this will show definitely that they were not forgotten. It would also be well if the testator explained why he was, in effect, cutting them off.

Often a husband wishes to give the wife control of the entire estate and therefore disinherits a child or children on the assumption that his wife will care for the child. Such a clause might read: "As it is my wish that my wife shall have the entire control of my estate, I have deliberately omitted any provision for bequests to my children, Dorothy and Anne, since I am confident that my wife will make all necessary provisions for them." If your spouse, however, is a financially irresponsible type or is very likely to remarry upon your death and possibly neglect the children or not provide adequately for them, then such a clause is inappropriate, and the children should be separately and carefully protected by preferred legacies.

You may have drawn a will leaving all to your wife, explaining that you are leaving nothing to your little daughter because you are confident that your wife will provide for her. Several years later a son is born. Then the husband dies. The son may be entitled to one third of his father's estate. The widow receives two thirds. The daughter gets nothing. Why? Because the law in most states provides that when a child is born after a will is made, that child is entitled to take his "intestate share" as if no will existed—unless some provision has been made in advance for afterborn children, or unless it is clear from the language of the will that no provision for them is intended. A useful rule for every family is: Whenever a child is born, have both parents' wills checked by the family lawyer.

Review of Wills

Here is a streamlined statement of facts in a court case: Mrs. J owned 75 shares of General Electric stock when she executed her will. The will gave a niece "Seventy five shares (75 sh.) of common stock of General Electric Company." Between the time the will was signed and Mrs. J died, General Electric effected a three for one stock split. As a result, there were 225 shares of General Electric in Mrs. J's estate at the time of her death.

In the same will Mrs. J bequeathed "ninety (90) shares of International Paper Company stock" to a nephew. After the will was signed, the company paid dividends in its own stock. As a consequence, there were 104 shares in Mrs. J's estate at her death.

Was the niece entitled to 75 shares of General Electric or 225?

Was the nephew entitled to 90 shares of International Paper or 104?

A court proceeding was necessary to decide what Mrs. J intended. It was finally held that the niece was entitled to all 225 shares of General Electric. But it was also held that the nephew was entitled to only 90 shares of the Paper Company; the balance went to the person to whom Mrs. J willed her residuary estate.

Here trouble and expense could have been avoided by wording the will in a way that would have anticipated the possibility of stock splits and dividends. But a review of the will after the extra stock had been received would have revealed its weakness.

We live in a dynamic, not a static, world. A will which makes a sensible distribution of property at one time may result in a foolish distribution at another, later time. When a will has been made, therefore, it should not be put aside and overlooked for many years. It is good practice to review its stipulations at regular intervals to ascertain whether any of the provisions should be changed. A variety of causes may signal the need for review; change in the size of the estate, changes in the family—a marriage, a birth, a death, a significant change in the assets of a family member, or a move to another state.

The safest way to make changes is to have a new will drawn, although a codicil to the old will may be effective.

A *codicil* is an instrument which amends or changes a will. An example will indicate how it is drawn. Assume that you want to change your executor:

> I, Joseph F. Tarren, of the County of Confusion, City of Confusion, State of Confusion, do hereby make, publish and declare this Codicil to my Last Will and Testament:

> I hereby ratify each and every provision of my will executed the 24th day of September 1974, except insofar as such will is inconsistent with the terms of this instrument.
>
> I hereby direct that Henry Takelittle be substituted as my executor, in place of Thomas Graball.
>
> In witness whereof I have hereunto set my hand (and seal) this 20th day of January 1975.

The same formality must be employed in executing and witnessing a codicil as was done with the will. You need not have the same witnesses, but you must have the same number. You must announce to the witnesses that the instrument is the codicil to your will. Then you must sign, and they must sign, all in the presence of one another. You should then fasten the codicil securely to the will itself.

Revocation of Wills

The safest way to revoke a will is to tear it up and burn the pieces in the presence of informed witnesses. If it is burned, canceled, torn, or otherwise destroyed by the testator or by another person in the testator's presence and at his order, the law will consider it revoked. A new will under a later date and stating the testator's intention to revoke prior wills will revoke them. A later will which is inconsistent with the provisions of previous wills serves as a revocation of the earlier wills to the extent that it is inconsistent with them.

Where to Keep a Will

Being valuable documents, wills should be kept with other important papers. Above all, they should be left where they will come into the hands of persons who will see that they are presented to the court for probate. Frequently they are left for safekeeping with one's attorney; logically, they should be left with one's executor to be.

A safe deposit box is not recommended as a place to keep a will because when the person dies the safe deposit box is sealed by the safe deposit company. It may be opened only upon application to the probate court, and then only in the presence of a representative of the Estate Tax Division of the state's Tax Department. It must then be resealed, and the contents may not again be touched until the will is probated and the executor is given authority and access to the box. It is better, therefore, to keep your will either in a strongbox at home or with your lawyer or executor. Of course, if your spouse also has a personal safe deposit box, you can keep your wills in each other's box.

Letter of Last Instructions

You should give your executor or your lawyer a letter of last instructions, which is separate and apart from your will. This letter, to be opened upon your death, should contain the following:

1. A statement as to where your will may be found.
2. Instructions as to funeral and burial. You may wish to specify for example, that, as a veteran, you be buried in a certain national cemetery rather than in the family burial plot.
3. Where your birth or baptismal certificate, social security card, marriage or divorce certificate, naturalization and citizenship papers, and discharge papers from the armed forces may be found. The latter is important if you wish to be buried in a national cemetery, which is the privilege of any veteran.
4. Where your membership certificates in any lodges or fraternal organizations which provide death or cemetery benefits may be found.
5. A list of the locations of any safe deposit boxes you may have, and where the keys may be found.
6. A list of your insurance policies, and where they may be found.
7. A statement concerning any pension systems to which you belonged and from which your estate may be entitled to receive a death benefit.
8. A list of all bank accounts, checking and savings, and their locations.
9. A list of all stocks and bonds you own, and where they may be found.
10. A statement of all real property owned by you.
11. A list of all other property—personal, business, and others.
12. Instructions or directions concerning your business in the event your will suggests or provides that it be continued.
13. A statement of reasons for actions taken in your will, such as disinheritances. It is sometimes better to place the explanation in a separate letter available to the court, rather than in your will, to avoid a complicated will and expensive litigation in connection therewith.

A useful supplement to a letter of instruction is shown in Figure 17–3.

FIGURE 17–3
Estate Organizer

PERSONAL INVENTORY OF

____
(name)

IN REGARD TO MYSELF AND MY FAMILY:

I was born on ______________________
at ______________________
____

Birth was ________ was not ________ recorded
Birth certificate is located at ______________________
____

(If naturalized citizen, fill out below)
My United States citizenship papers are located at
____

I was married on ______________________
________ at ______________________
____

My marriage certificate is located at ______________________
______________________, ______________________

My wife's maiden name was ______________________
____

and our children are (list names and date of birth)
______________________; ______________________
______________________; ______________________
______________________; ______________________
______________________; ______________________

(If divorced or legally separated, fill out below)
I was divorced ________ legally separated ________
on ______________________
at ______________________. Documents
relating to this are located at ______________________
____
____

Military Service. I served
in ______________________
from ______________________
to ______________________
My serial number was ______________________
and my military papers are located at ______________________
____

I have ________ have not ________ a safe deposit box(es) located at ______________________
____

Keys are located at ______________________
The following person(s) have access to the box
____
____
____

I have ________ have not ________ a cemetery plot located at ______________________
____

The deed is located at ______________________
____

• • •

IN REGARD TO MY EMPLOYMENT:

At present, I am employed by ______________________
____

located at ______________________
____

I commenced this employment on ______________________
______________________, ______________________

My Social Security number is ______________________
and my card is located at ______________________
____
____

FIGURE 17–3 (continued)

I am eligible for the following benefits including pension and profit sharing:
(1)________
(2)________
(3)________
(4)________

• • •

IN REGARD TO MY ASSETS:
(All assets listed are owned by me individually unless otherwise noted)
I have the following bank accounts:
Checking No.________
Bank ________
Branch ________
Savings No.________
Bank ________
Branch ________
Passbooks are located at ________

Stocks and Bonds:
My stocks are ________
My broker is ________
Address ________
Company ________

Shares	*Company*	*Acct. or Cert. No.*

Certificates located at ________
I do ________ do not ________ own bonds.

Certificates are located at ________

I own interests in the following joint property:
Bank accounts
(1)________
Joint owner ________
(2)________
Joint owner ________
Stocks, bonds, real estate:
(1)________
Joint owner ________
(2)________
Joint owner ________
Amount of life insurance and annuities:

Company	*Amount*	*Type*

Policies are located at ________
My insurance agent is ________
located at ________
________ , ________

I do ________ do not ________ own real estate.
It is located at ________

Documents pertaining thereto are located at ________

I own the following personal property:
Automobile(s) — Yes ________ No ________
Certificate of title located at ________

Household furnishings — Yes ________ No ________
Located at ________

Miscellaneous assets not previously noted, including jewelry, stamps, art and coin collection:
Located at ________

Located at ________

Located at ________

Located at ________

• • •

IN REGARD TO MY LIABILITIES:
My mortgages and other major debts are listed below:
Description ________

Description ________

Description ________

Description ________

• • •

IN REGARD TO MY WILL:
The original executed copy is located at ________

It is dated ________ ,19 ____
An original executed codicil is located at ________

It is dated ________ ,19 ____
The attorney who drew the will is ________

located at ________

This memorandum was completed on the ________
________ day of ________
19 ____ , by ________
whose legal residence is ________

It has been annually reviewed as follows:
(1)________
(2)________
(3)________

Note: Copies of the Estate Organizer are available on request from Oppenheimer Management Corporation, One New York Plaza, New York, N.Y. 10004.

TRUSTS

"The Federal Tax Court ruled today that trust funds amounting to $64,000 set up for the two children of Joe Louis must be used to pay part of the $1,199,437 he owed the government in back taxes.

"The judge estimated that during his long reign as heavyweight champion from 1937 to 1948, Mr. Louis made about $4,600,000. But when he retired, the judge said, he was $500,000 in debt. . . ." Thus ran a newspaper account. Fortunately most trusts have happier outcomes than those Joe Louis established. In some circles they are used very extensively. *Fortune* remarked, "If you don't have a trust fund in Boston, it's as if you didn't have clothes on."

A trust is an agreement whereby the person who establishes the trust—the settlor or grantor—gives property to a trustee or trustees for the benefit of the beneficiary or beneficiaries of the trust. Individuals, and institutions such as trust companies and banks, act as trustees. According to the desire of the grantor, a trust may be revocable or irrevocable. Formerly it was the practice to choose an individual or individuals as trustees. Then it was necessary to choose honest, able, responsible people for this important undertaking. The advent of the trust company brought a continued life not enjoyed by individuals. Sooner or later an individual is sure to die; a trust company usually enjoys a perpetual charter. Furthermore, the large volume of trust business handled by such institutions gives them an experience and organization beyond the scope of the individual. By teaming an institution and an individual as cotrustees, many of the advantages of each may be secured for a trust.

Life Tenants and Remaindermen

Those who receive incomes from trusts during their lifetimes only are known as "life tenants"; those beneficiaries who get the corpus or principal of the trust upon the death of the life tenants are called "remaindermen."

Living Trusts

A living trust, or trust *inter vivos*, or voluntary trust is in effect while the grantor is still living; in fact, he may be a beneficiary. Any person having enough property to warrant it can set up such a trust for his own protection. Unless there is a minimum of $10,000 or $20,000, there will be difficulty in finding competent trustees who are willing to undertake the responsibility. The trustee takes the legal title to the property and administers it to preserve the principal and earn a relatively safe income with it, although both principal and income may be distributed currently under the agreement, in which case the beneficiary would be very much like an annuitant.

In addition to the advantage of putting the property into skillful hands, there are some tax advantages in setting up living trusts. If the settlor really parts definitely with the property put into the trust by (1) making the trust irrevocable, (2) receiving no income, and (3) not retaining the power to change the beneficiary, although he will be answerable for gift taxes when the trust is established, no estate or inheritance taxes will be levied on this property when he dies. Should the settlor retain the power to revoke the trust, receive the income, or change the beneficiary, he has in important respects not really parted with his property at all. He still has it under his control and could not reasonably expect to obtain an estate tax advantage. Important income tax advantages may still result, however. That is because the income produced by the capital is taxable to the beneficiary, who normally would be in a lower bracket. The living trust, also known as a Clifford trust, must run a minimum of ten years.

There would be no tax advantage in setting up a living trust for the education of children because tax laws state that any money spent to take care of one's legal obligation is taxed to the person who has that obligation. A trust created through a will is regarded differently from a tax viewpoint.

The U.S. Tax Court approved an arrangement of 20 meticulously managed separate trusts irrevocably set up by two parents to accumulate income during the lives of their son and daughter-in-law and be paid to the grandchildren at specified ages. The use of the trusts as tax avoidance was conceded, but the 20 separate accounts, checkbooks, and 20 separate yearly tax returns made them acceptable as a taxable entity.

A valid trust may be established orally as to personal property if the words used indicate clearly that the legal title is to be held by one person for the benefit of another; but a writing is required for real property, and a writing is always preferable for the purpose of eliminating dispute as to the agreement. It should go without saying that the drawing of a trust instrument is a technical undertaking which should be left to an experienced lawyer; an ordinary individual drawing such an instrument could raise difficulties involving far more money than a lawyer would have charged to create an effective instrument.

Testamentary Trusts

A testamentary trust is a trust under the will of a deceased person, becoming effective at death. Trustee and executor may or may not be the same person. The purpose of such a trust is to lodge the property in skillful hands so that it may be advantageously administered for the beneficiaries. If the same money were handled by an inexperienced person, the chances of doing as well with it, either from the viewpoint of income or of safety of principal, would probably not be bright.

This type of trust is often set up so that a widow (a life tenant) may receive the income for life and the children (the remaindermen) may have the principal upon her death. In the absence of a widow, the income may be left to the children for a number of years, usually during their minority, at the end of which time the corpus (principal) of the trust is to be paid to them. It is possible to incorporate a provision in the trust agreement whereby the trustee may use part of the principal to supplement the income should income alone be inadequate. Testamentary trusts are often useful as a means of reducing taxes, as will be shown later.

The Trust Term Rule against Perpetuities

In nearly all, if not all, states there is a public policy against the continuance of trusts or suspension of powers of alienation beyond periods defined by certain rules. The common law rule fixed the period at lives in being plus 21 years, but this has been modified in some states. For example, in several states a trust under a will can be created for a term measured by the lives of not more than two persons who are named in the will and who are living at the testator's death; these are the so called "measuring lives."[3]

The persons whose lives are specified in the will as the measuring lives need not necessarily be, although they most frequently are, the same persons as those who are to receive the income from the trust. Furthermore, the rule against perpetuities does not limit the number of beneficiaries but only the duration of the trust. Thus, a trust can be created to continue during the life of A and thereafter during the life of B, with a direction that the income during the continuance of the trust

---

[3] In New York the law now provides that a testamentary trust may run for the duration of any number of lives as long as the individuals are all alive when the testator dies. The only restriction is that a trust cannot be measured by such a large number of lives that it would be "unreasonably difficult" to establish when it came to an end.

be paid to X, Y, and Z and as many other persons as the testator desires to receive the income during the continuance of the trust.

In the above example, although A and B must be persons in being at the date of death, X, Y, and Z need not be, since they are not measuring lives. In other words, there is no objection to creating a trust for the payment of income to a person born after the date of the testator's death, provided that such person's life is not a measuring life. In such a case, the measuring life must be that of a person specified in the will who is living at the testator's death. Therefore, a testator can establish a trust directing that the income shall be paid to his widow during her lifetime and that, after her death, the trust shall continue during the life of their daughter who was living at the time of the father's (testator's) death. The income from the trust may go to the daughter or be divided among such of the testator's grandchildren as are living at the date of the widow's death. Even though some of the grandchildren may not have been born at the date of the testator's death, they will nevertheless be entitled to share in the income of the trust so long as B, the daughter—the second measuring life—lives. Upon the daughter's death, the trust terminates, and the grandchildren—the remaindermen—receive specified shares of the corpus or principal of the trust.

Powers of Appointment

A frequent and valid criticism of the conventional type of trust created in a will is that the beneficiary of the income is given no control over the disposition of the trust property and that, in many cases, it would be better to allow the beneficiary to exercise such control in order to provide for conditions which the testator cannot foresee when the will is drawn.

For example, consider the conventional type of trust created for a son or daughter, with directions for the payment of the income to him (or her) during his or her lifetime, the principal to be distributed to his children living at his death in equal shares, per stirpes.[4] This trust leaves

---

[4] There is a significant difference between per stirpes and per capita. An example will make the very real difference clear.

Let us say that the will of John Adams created three trusts for his three children, Arthur, Barry, and Catherine. The sons marry and, in the course of time, have children. Arthur has one son, Albert. Barry is blessed with three daughters, Barbara, Betty, and Brenda. But Catherine, who outlives both her brothers, dies without ever having children. According to Mr. Adams' will, the principal of the trust for Catherine, if she leaves no descendants, is to be paid to the "issue, *per stirpes*" of Mr. Adams who survive Catherine.

The word "issue" has the same general meaning as "descendants." In this case, the no room for any provision for the son's widow. The principal of the trust bypasses her completely. If the son has little property of his own to dispose of at his death, his widow must be content to see the principal of the trust pass to her children or more remote descendants. Perhaps the testator considers this appropriate, but he might recognize that it would be desirable to allow his son to make the decision as to whether it would be appropriate to provide for his widow out of the principal of the trust, the income of which was enjoyed by the son during his married life.

Furthermore, the trust vests the principal in the son's children in equal shares, *per stirpes*. It is reasonable to suppose, however, that when the son dies, the economic status of his children will vary. Some may have married wealthy spouses. Some may have been disabled by chronic illness. Some may have predeceased the son, leaving children of their own, with little property for their support and education. Nevertheless, under the rigid plan provided in the will, the principal of the trust must be distributed without regard to the differing needs of the remaindermen.

If the testator is disposed to allow the son to determine how to meet these problems, the creation of a power of appointment offers an excellent solution. In general, *a power of appointment* is a provision in a will granting another the power to decide, after the will-maker's

---

"issue" are the grandchildren (and their descendants, if any). *Per stirpes* means that the issue take through their ancestors—that is, in the proportion their parents would have taken. Under this scheme the principal of Catherine's trust is split into two equal shares for the two ancestors—Arthur and Barry. Arthur's only son stands in Arthur's place and will take one share. Barry's three girls stand in his place and divide the other share. Thus, under the *per stirpes* division, the grandson gets one half the trust principal, but each granddaughter gets only one sixth.

The *per stirpes* provision is traditional. But many people, having been told how it works have this reaction: "I don't like that kind of distribution—I am equally fond of all my grandchildren. I would like them to share equally."

Is the answer, then, a direction that the trust principal be paid to "issue, *per capita* and not *per stirpes*"? Perhaps, but maybe not. The possibility of the birth of great-grandchildren would have to be considered. They would usually be deemed "issue" and would be entitled to a share if the division were on a *per capita* basis. Thus, in Mr. Adams' case, if there had been three great-grandchildren, in addition to the four grandchildren, each of the seven would have taken the same amount under a *per capita* division.

The "issue, *per capita*" division is not as often used. It seems inappropriate to give a grand-grandchild (who may have been born long after the will maker dies) the same share his parent gets. An alternative that combines both the *per stirpes* and *per capita* methods of division may be better. It would take the form of a direction to pay the trust principal "in equal shares to my grandchildren surviving the termination of the trust, the share of any grandchild who dies before such event, to be divided among his issue, *per stirpes*." That direction has the advantage of equalizing the shares of the grandchildren while at the same time making provision for the offspring of a grandchild who might die before the trust ends.

death, how property left in trust shall eventually be distributed. For example, in the case above, the father (the testator) would give the son a power of appointment, which would allow the son to specify, in his will, how and to whom the principal of the trust should be distributed upon his death. The son does not own the principal of the trust, but he is permitted on his death to decide how it should be distributed. A typical power of appointment clause in a will would read: "Upon the death of my said son, my Trustees shall pay over the then principal of the trust in such shares, and in such manner, outright or in lesser estates, in trust or otherwise, as my said son may by his last will and testament appoint. . . ."

Power of Invasion

Future developments cannot be foreseen, especially during a trust term which may run for many years. Furthermore, no one can predict whether the investments of a trust will retain their value or will depreciate. Hence, inadequacy of income is a contingency which must be faced and covered in the drafting of the trust, particularly where the initial corpus of the trust is not large and where the purpose of the trust is to support the testator's immediate family.

For example, assume that a married man with children (testator) has accumulated $100,000, and, up to the time of his death, is earning $15,000 a year. When he dies, he leaves a widow and young children. In his will he has directed that his entire estate be held in trust, with income to be paid to his wife during her life and the principal to be divided among his children on her death. Assume that his net estate is $90,000, which forms the principal of the trust. On the basis of the present yield of so called "trust investments," this might produce no more than $5,000 per year. From this there must be deducted trustee's commissions and any income tax payable by the widow, which means that the amount available for the support of her family will be only a small proportion of her husband's income at the time of his death.

In this hypothetical example the principal, although much needed for the support and education of the young children, cannot be used by the trustee because the will contains no permissive language to that effect. The hardship which will arise in such a situation is obvious and might have been avoided by appropriate language allowing an invasion of the principal.

There are many ways of taking care of such a situation. The testator can provide that if, in any year, the income from the trust fund is less than a stated amount, the deficiency is to be made up out of the principal. Or the testator may prefer to leave it to the discretion of the trustee to determine how much of the principal shall be paid over to the wife from time to time, in order to enable her to support her family. Or, alternatively, the testator may wish to vest this discretion in his wife, giving her the right to require the trustee to pay over whatever amounts of principal she may request. Various combinations are possible.

Life Insurance Trusts

Life insurance is being used increasingly in estate planning and in a variety of ways. For example, it is used:

1. To increase the estate. You can increase the size of your estate by adding to your insurance protection. If a trust is set up during a policyholder's lifetime and it pays the premium and provides that the interest goes to the spouse, principal to the children at the spouse's death, estate taxes can be avoided.
2. To solve the problem of liquidity. On your death a variety of charges must be paid, debts settled, taxes paid, and so on. Life insurance will provide your estate with immediate liquid funds to meet these liabilities. It sidesteps the delay of probate for these insurance funds.
3. To keep your business going. You can have a trust created with the proceeds of your insurance, and it can buy assets from the estate or lend money to the estate, and by this means provide the liquid cash to keep your business going.
4. To provide staggered or long term income. Rather than have your beneficiaries paid a lump sum you may wish the funds paid out over a period of time either as interest from a trust, or as interest and principal under the annuity method.
5. To provide management. A great many people accumulate more money through life insurance these days than in any other way. It would be a disaster if, upon their deaths, their beneficiaries were forced to administer the proceeds of these policies, because in many cases they have not the experience and training to do so effectively. Fortunately, several options are open. The insured can, before death, stipulate that the proceeds be payable to a trustee for the benefit of the loved ones. If this is not done, the beneficiaries may find that they can leave the funds with the insurance company and receive an annuity for a period of years. Or they can accept the proceeds of the policies and turn them over to a trustee of their own choosing under a trust agreement acceptable to them.

Choosing a Trustee

Care must be taken when choosing a trustee. Be sure that the individual or an institution appointed is capable of handling the trust in the best interests of the beneficiaries and can be fully trusted to do so. There are some arguments for the choice of an individual. The main one is that the settlor knows just who is going to handle his money in behalf of his beneficiaries. The weakness in this argument lies in the fact that the person appointed may die, thereby necessitating a successor. It may be difficult for ordinary persons to locate a qualified individual who will bother with the administration of limited funds.

For reasons such as these, more and more persons in ordinary circumstances are turning toward corporate trustees—trust companies and the trust departments of commercial banks. Permanency of corporate trustees, their experience and familiarity with legal details, the fact that they are unlikely to abscond, and the possibility that they can often be more easily found than experience individuals—all of these considerations have led to a great growth of trust business in institutions.

Sometimes the results are not satisfactory despite professional handling, as in a *New York Times* story[5] about two trusts created in 1919 and 1920. In 1920 their combined sums equaled $383,800; in March 1971, they were worth only $252,767. Even at the low 2.5 percent interest up to 1940, and the continued current interest since, it was figured that trusts should have been worth $664,785.

The trust account department of a well-known bank which managed the trusts had sold at a loss the 500 shares of Jersey Standard acquired in 1924. Most of the other holdings suffered similarly, and the money was invested in low yield government and municipal bonds. A professional, too, may fail to utilize prudently the wealth left in his trust.

Duties of Trustees

When a trustee has been chosen, what may be expected of him? It is his duty to strive diligently to preserve the principal of the trust estate, to keep it invested to the best of his ability, and to secure as good a return on the investment as is reasonably possible. He is engaged in a fiduciary undertaking and must observe the stipulations of the trust agreement to the utmost. Where the trust agreement allows him a choice, he must exercise the choice within the requirements of law. In

[5] *New York Times*, June 2, 1971. See also "Huge Sums Managed by Bank Trust Units Stir Up Controversy," *Wall Street Journal*, January 7, 1975.

some states, trustees may invest only in securities named on an approved list issued by the state. In the absence of statutory restrictions, the trustee must abide by the common law, which differs among the states. However, it is universally required that the trustee act in good faith and prudently.

The usual trust estate earns only a conservative, moderate income. In recent years there has been a growing movement to permit trustees to combat inflation by investing in common stocks, which, at one time at least, were considered too speculative for trust estates. Compensation of trustees depends upon the size of the trust estate and the income; it differs in the various states. If beneficiaries are dissatisfied with the actions of trustees, they may petition a court to (1) remove the trustee and appoint another, (2) cause the trustee to do certain things or refrain from doing others, (3) nullify any wrongful doings of the trustee, (4) assess money damages against the trustee, or (5) punish the trustee for criminal acts.

The Advantages of Trusts

It is obviously undesirable to bequeath or devise property directly to a minor, because a minor cannot receive or manage his or her property. Such a gift would require the appointment of a guardian. A guardian is usually required to file a bond; must make an annual accounting to the court; has to obtain a court order before any property can be used for the minor's maintenance; and is limited to so called "legal investments" in investing any of the minor's funds. Then, too, the sale of a minor's real estate requires approval of the court, and it is an expensive and lengthy proceeding to obtain the necessary permission. All these difficulties can be avoided by creating a trust for the infant's benefit.

In the case of a widow, a trust may be advantageous to free her from the responsibility and worry involved in the investment and administration of funds, which can better be entrusted to other, more experienced hands. Also, she is shielded from the consequences of dissipating, by improvident investments or gifts, any money left to her outright.

A trust is likewise advantageous where a testator feels that other beneficiaries, in addition to his widow, ought to be protected from financial worry in general and from their own financial irresponsibility in particular. In many states the income from such a trust may be protected against garnishment or attachment by creditors of the beneficiary and even against voluntary assignments by the beneficiary. These are the so called "spendthrift trusts."

Tax Advantages of the Trust

One of the main reasons, today, for creating trusts is the tax advantage. If a testator leaves his estate to his widow outright, an estate tax will be payable on his death. When the widow dies, there is a further estate tax on what she leaves, including the property received from her husband. Assuming that she leaves her property to her children and that this property continues to be owned by the children until their deaths, their estates, in turn, will pay estate taxes thereon (subject to a tax credit with respect to the property inherited from her if their deaths occur within five years after her death).

Thus, three sets of estate taxes will have been paid in the course of the transmission of the original property left by the testator. If, on the other hand, the property is left in trust, with the income payable to the widow, for her life and thereafter in further trusts, with the income payable to the children for their respective lives, and the principal of the trust for each child to be paid outright to that child's issue on the death of such child, only one estate tax will be payable; namely, on the death of the testator.

THE ESTATE TAX

The federal estate tax is a tax on the right to transfer property, including not only transfers taking effect at death but also certain *inter vivos* transfers, such as one made in contemplation of death. The federal estate tax, like all death duties, is not a tax on property. Nor is it an inheritance tax, which is imposed on the right to receive property. Instead, it is a tax on the right to transmit property at death, and it is measured by the value of the property. To prevent avoidance of the tax, a transfer which is deemed to be in lieu of a testamentary disposition—as, for example, a gift made in contemplation of death—is also subject to the estate tax.

The starting point in computing federal estate tax liability is the gross estate. The gross estate of a decedent is the total value of the property, whether real or personal, tangible or intangible, except real property situated outside the United States. Once the property that makes up gross estate has been determined, the next step is the valuation of such property. The executor or administrator has the option of valuing the estate either at the date of the decedent's death or six months from date of death. Estate taxes due the federal government, which are much heavier than those due the state where you live, are payable within nine months after death. State estate and inheritance tax laws vary as to the time of payment, usually from 1 year to 18 months.

Settlement of the estate requires a need for immediate cash for taxes, estate administration expenses, and funeral costs, and it may be necessary to sell assets (stocks, business, property) to realize funds. Under the law these may qualify for long term capital treatment—rather than as short term gains—regardless of the time element involved.

Talk of estates and estate planning is regarded by the young as irrelevant, since they lack both age and assets. Such thinking is not valid, however; age is not the only cause of death, and you may have more assets than you think.

If you work for a company that provides group insurance based on three times your annual salary, your financial estate could begin with $45,000 (assuming your salary is $15,000). Other items, even without counting all personal possessions, might bring the total up to $63,000:

Insurance on job	$45,000
Personal insurance	10,000
Car	3,000
Bank savings	5,000
Total	$63,000

Surely you would want to plan where that $63,000 should go?

Your Gross Estate—What Is Included?

Estate tax laws refer to the "gross estate." This means the fair market value of all the real and personal property which you own at your death. In addition to your house and its contents, cash, stocks, bonds, mortgages (owned by you), notes (held by you), jewelry, automobile, and all other such property, the following are also included:

1. Life insurance on your life is taxable (no matter how payable) if you pay the premiums on the policy directly or indirectly, or if you possess "incidents of ownership in the policies," such as the right to change the beneficiaries, to borrow on the policies, or to collect cash surrender values. If your wife pays the premiums out of money you give her for household expenses, you are considered to have paid indirectly. Most people labor under the illusion that because life insurance proceeds are not taxable under the personal income tax, they are also exempt from the federal estate tax. This is not the case.

If you do not retain any "incidents of ownership," that is, for example, the right to borrow on the policy, or receive dividends, or elect settlement options, or name the beneficiary, you can have someone else take out a policy on your life, or you can assign your policy to someone else and the principal at your death may not be taxed to your estate, even if you continued to pay all the premiums on the policy directly.

2. Another illusion is that if all your property is in joint ownership with rights of survivorship, your estate will not have to pay taxes on it. The property passes outside your will, just as does insurance to a named beneficiary, but both are subject to the federal estate tax. Property of any kind which you own jointly with someone else, with right of survivorship, is taxable to the extent of your contribution to its purchase price or other interest therein. Under the federal law, and generally under state laws, when the first joint owner dies, it is presumed that he or she supplied all of the purchase price of the jointly owned property, so that all is considered taxable in the deceased joint owner's estate, except to the extent that it can be proved that the survivor contributed to the purchase.

3. Gifts made within three years of your death, unless your executor can prove they were not made in contemplation of death, are taxable.

4. Trusts you have created in your lifetime wherein you have reserved certain rights or powers or wherein the enjoyment of the trust property by the beneficiaries depends on their surviving you are taxable. For example, bank accounts which you establish in trust for your children are taxable, since you can add to them or withdraw at will. For tax purposes, it is the same as if the bank accounts were solely in your name.

5. All other forms of property, or rights in property, are taxable, such as powers of appointment (which powers require special scrutiny to determine whether the value of the trust property they control is taxable or not; for the most part, general powers of appointment are taxable, limited powers are not).

The Limitations of Joint Ownership

Owning property jointly with a wife may be a convenient way of handling a family checking account, but if you carry the idea much further, say the estate planning experts, you are inviting trouble. Why?

Under joint ownership with the right of survivorship, property is not co-owned half and half, but is owned entirely by each. There is a risk of one party acting independently—although the other may be in disagreement—or in ignorance. There are several different forms of joint ownership, some of which do not pass property outside of probate and have varying limitations and advantages depending on state laws.

Life insurance is best *not* owned jointly. If each spouse owns insurance on the other, pays for it out of separate income, surrenders the right to change beneficiaries or borrow against the cash value, then it will be outside the taxable part of the estate of the first to die.

Joint property ordinarily passes outside a will, not under it, and is a simplified method of transmitting property at death, avoiding months of probate delays and probate costs as well as decreasing attorney fees. However, if a husband establishes a trust with their joint assets to maximize family protection and minimize taxes, his wife will either have to pay a gift tax or lower her gift tax exemption to let him do this with what previously had been her share. The gift tax law likewise states that when a person who does not contribute to a joint bank account, makes a withdrawal, a gift has occurred. This is also true in the cashing of a United States savings bond.

In Connecticut the law holds that one half of the joint tenancy property is subject to inheritance tax on the death of either party. It does not matter if the other contributed nothing.

Under joint ownership your property may wind up wholly or partly in the wrong hands. A middle aged man puts his property into joint ownership with his wife. They have no children, but the husband has an aged parent still living, and the wife has two brothers. The husband dies unexpectedly. A short time later the wife dies without having made a will. Since the joint property was entirely the wife's at her death, it all goes to her brothers (under state law). Probably, both husband and wife would have wanted to care for the husband's parent as well.

Will joint tenancy avoid taxes at death? No! On the contrary it often attracts higher tax or expensive tax complications—particularly in the usual case where the money or property all came from the husband originally. Suppose, for instance, that the wife dies first. If everything is in joint names, and the amount is substantial, the husband will have to report the property in the estate tax return on her estate. Then he will have the job of proving that it was all his money or property in the first place. If he cannot, he will be in the unhappy position of paying a tax to get his own money back. On the other hand, if both contributed to the joint estate, he has the job of tracing the contributions of each.

Your Net Estate—What Is Included?

The federal estate tax law allows certain exemptions and deductions in determining the "net estate," which is the base on which the tax is computed. An overall, basic exemption of $60,000 is allowed by the federal law. Most state estate or inheritance tax laws allow similar deductions and also exemptions of varying amounts, usually depending on the relationship of your beneficiaries.

Among the permissible deductions are funeral expenses and claims, loans, and mortgages against your property. Expenses for the administration of your estate, including fees for legal services and commissions of your executor, are deductible, and this reduces the net cost of these services to your estate. Bequests to qualified charities and other tax-exempt institutions are deductible. There may be circumstances under which property which you recently inherited—property previously taxed to another estate *within five years of your death*—may also be deducted. The most important deduction, if your wife or husband survives you, is the "marital deduction."

The Marital Deduction—What It Means

Under the marital deduction feature of the tax laws, a specified portion of a married person's estate may pass to the surviving spouse free of federal (since 1948) and state (New York, for example, since 1950) death taxes when particular requirements of the law are met. A husband or wife may leave up to one half of his or her adjusted gross estate (gross estate less debts, claims, and admininstration expenses but before exemptions or charitable bequests) to a surviving spouse as an outright legacy or in trust, providing the survivor receives all the income at least annually and has the unrestricted power to dispose of the property during his or her lifetime or upon death, by will or otherwise.

The marital deduction makes a very real difference in your estate tax liability, as may be seen in Table 17–2. It may be much more than all other deductions put together. In some cases it may wipe out your tax entirely. For example, you leave an estate of $100,000. Your marital deduction is $50,000, thereby bringing your net estate down to $50,000, or $10,000 less than the $60,000 exemption; there is, therefore, no tax liability. Assume that your estate is $300,000 and that you leave your property in such a way that the marital deduction amounts to the maximum allowed—$150,000. With the $60,000 exemption subtracted, only $90,000 remains to be taxed; and on this the tax is $17,500. On the $300,000 estate without the marital deduction, it would be $59,100.

If you cut the estate in half, you always reduce the tax by more than half. The marital deduction, or any other deduction, comes "off the top"

TABLE 17–2
A Sample Computation of Estate Taxes with and without Using the Marital Deduction

Gross estate:		
Real estate	$ 50,000	
Jewelry, automobile, etc.	15,000	
Cash and securities	370,000	
Savings account	5,000	
Life insurance	100,000	$540,000
Deductions:		
Debts and funeral expenses	$ 10,000	
Administration expenses*	30,000	40,000
Adjusted gross estate		$500,000
Using Marital Deduction		
Adjusted gross estate		$500,000
Less:		
Maximum marital deduction (one half adjusted gross estate)	$250,000	
Charitable bequests	50,000	300,000
Net estate (before exemptions)		$200,000
Estate Taxes:		
Federal		31,500
New York State		2,500
Total		$ 34,000
Without Using Marital Deduction		
Adjusted gross estate		$500,000
Less:		
Charitable bequests		50,000
Net estate (before exemptions)		$450,000
Estate Taxes:		
Federal		$102,100
New York State		11,500
Total		$113,600

* Administration expenses include the executor's commissions and attorney's fees, both of which are deductible for estate tax purposes. The amount in any particular case depends on the number of executors and your attorney's charges. In making estimates, an arbitrary figure of 5–6 percent may be used to illustrate the aggregate of such expenses.

Source: Morgan Guaranty Trust Company of New York.

of the estate, where the rates are highest. Thus, if there is a surviving spouse, the specific exemption plus the marital deduction totals $120,000, and a 10 percent estimate for other deductions and credits would make the estate tax inapplicable to estates of less than $132,000. The savings which result from the marital deduction at different estate levels may be seen in Table 17–3.

TABLE 17–3
Estate Tax Savings Due to Marital Deduction

Net Estate before $60,000 Exemption	*Tax without Marital Deduction**	*Tax with Marital Deduction**	*Tax Saving*
$ 100,000	$ 4,800	......	$ 4,800
150,000	17,500	$ 1,050	16,450
200,000	31,500	4,800	26,700
250,000	45,300	10,700	34,600
500,000	116,500	45,300	71,200
750,000	191,800	80,500	111,300
1,000,000	270,300	116,500	153,800
2,500,000	830,000	351,400	478,600
5,000,000	2,038,800	830,000	1,208,800
10,000,000	4,975,000	2,038,800	2,936,200

* After maximum credit for state inheritance taxes.

The Credit for State Death Taxes

The federal estate tax is really a little more complicated than it has been made to appear in the presentation above, since in reality two federal estate taxes are actually imposed, namely, the basic estate and the additional estate tax. The federal estate tax payable is the sum of the net basic estate tax and the net additional estate tax. The function of the basic estate tax is the computation of the amount of credit allowable for estate, inheritance, or death taxes paid to the states and to foreign countries. A credit of up to 80 percent of the basic estate tax is allowed for death taxes paid to a state. The basic tax remaining after the credit for state taxes, plus the additional estate tax, add up to the total estate tax. The effective rates of the total tax, allowing maximum credit for state taxes, may be seen in Table 17–4 (also see Figure 17–4).

State Inheritance and Estate Taxes

An inheritance tax differs from an estate tax in that the former is levied on the right of the beneficiary to receive a bequest and is based on his or her share, while the estate tax is levied on all the property of the person dying and must be paid out of the estate by the executor.

All states, except Nevada, levy either inheritance or estate taxes. In some states they are known as succession taxes. Don't hurry to Nevada. It won't help. The federal estate tax is constructed to equalize state practices by allowing a credit against the federal tax for the amount

TABLE 17–4
Federal Estate Tax Burden on Representative Net Estates

*Amount of Net Estate**	*Maximum Gross Tax*†	*Maximum Credit for State Taxes*	*Net Total Tax*	*Effective Rate*‡
$ 5,000	$ 150	$ 40	$ 110	2.2%
20,000	1,600	160	1,440	7.2
50,000	7,000	400	6,600	13.2
100,000	20,700	1,200	19,500	19.5
200,000	50,700	3,600	47,100	23.5
600,000	180,700	18,000	162,700	27.1
1,000,000	325,700	38,800	286,900	28.7
5,000,000	2,468,200	402,800	2,065,400	41.3
10,000,000	6,088,200	1,082,800	5,005,400	50.0
50,000,000	36,888,200	7,482,800	29,405,400	58.8

* Includes amount of net estate after all deductions and exemptions.
† Totals are for both the basic and additional tax.
‡ Based on net tax.

paid to the state. Thus, if you pay nothing to the state, you receive no credit and your federal tax is just that much higher.

Most states—Colorado, Illinois, Indiana, Kansas, Maine, Pennsylvania, Texas, Virginia, West Virginia, and Wisconsin, for example—have inheritance taxes. Only a few, New York, for example, have estate taxes. Some states, such as Ohio, have both.

The state inheritance tax is usually levied at a much lower rate than the federal estate tax—1 to 20 percent in most cases. The rate varies with (*a*) the degree of relationship between the decedent and the beneficiary, and (*b*) the size of the bequest. In Kansas, for example, a widow is given a $75,000 personal exemption, a child only a $15,000 exemption. In Ohio a widow, or a child under 21, have only a $5,000 exemption, and a son or daughter over 21 receives only a $3,500 exemption. Practices vary so widely that it is useless to attempt to generalize. This is especially true of rates, kinds of property taxed, and types exempt. Usually the states are not only lower in rates but also more generous in their exemptions on types of property taxed than is the federal government. The chief tax officer of your state can provide you with a copy of your state inheritance or estate tax law.

If you were a sculptor who sold 80 works during 1940–1963 and had an average income of not more than $4,000 a year, would you expect your estate to face a tax deficiency of $2.4 million plus interest of about $250,000? This is what happened to sculptor David Smith. Two years before his death, his work suddenly found a market and five pieces were sold for a total of $108,000—although none within the last five months of his life. But these high prices had to be considered when valuing the

FIGURE 17–4
Average Estate Settlement Costs

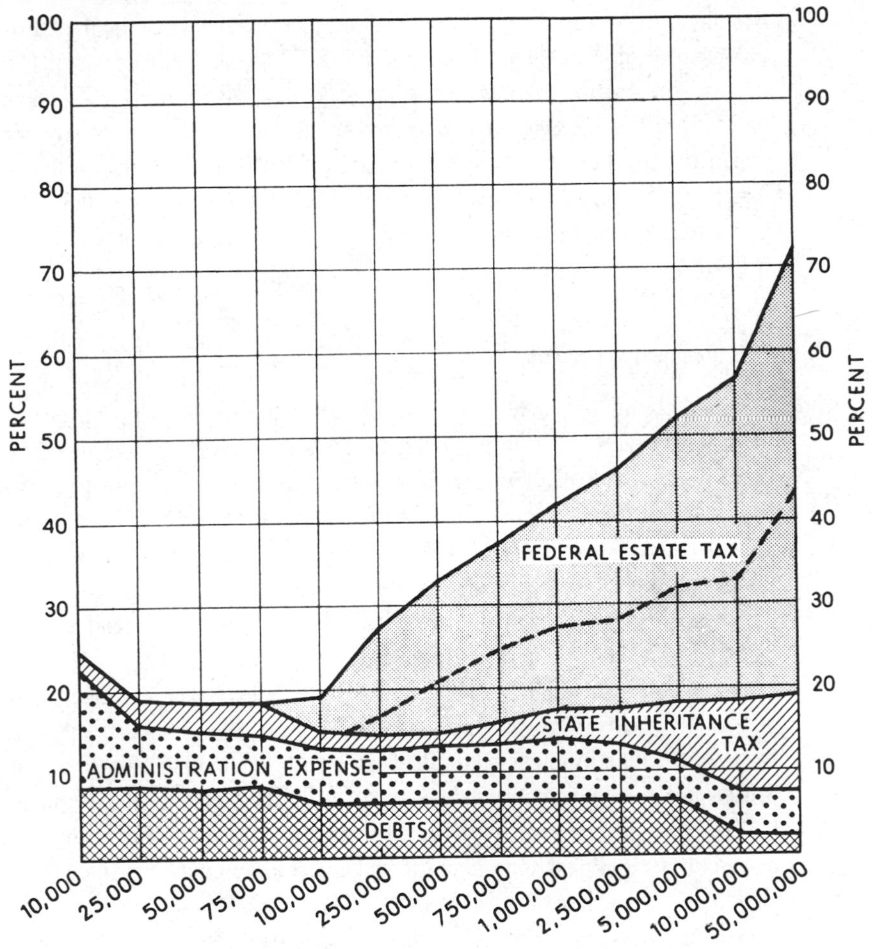

This graph was prepared by the Estate Recording Company, an independent statistical organization, from a survey of the court records of over 10,000 estates probated in all parts of the United States. "Debts" comprise mortgages payable, income and real estate taxes, and everything else the decedent owed; "Administration Expense" includes funeral costs, fees, court costs, and miscellaneous charges; "State Inheritance Tax" is the average found as a result of this study.

The broken line indicates the extent of the Federal Estate Tax in those estates where the full marital deduction was taken but in those estates where no marital deduction was taken the complete Federal Estate Tax applied.

Source: Reproduced by courtesy of Estate Recording Company, San Diego, Calif. 92105 remaining 425 works for tax purposes. The executors assumed an increased value for them, but took into consideration commission costs and the lack of ready buyers. They filed an estate tax return showing an evaluation of $714,000 with a tax of $240,000. Three years later, just before the statute of limitations expired, the IRS made its own valuation of $2.4 million. To pay the assessment all of Smith's work would have to go on the market at once, with probable loss. The executors filed a protest. After two years of negotiation, the U.S. Tax Court ruled that the estate had only to pay an additional levy of $69,000 instead of the original $2.4 million asked by the IRS.

The Federal Gift Tax

The federal gift tax is commonly regarded as a supplement to estate taxes to prevent avoidance of the latter by transfers of property during the owner's lifetime. A gift, however, must be in the nature of a windfall. It must be unearned; otherwise, it is taxable as income. "Gifts" are broadly defined under the federal law as all gratuitous transfers of property, direct or indirect, real or personal. Four types of gifts must be distinguished to determine whether they are taxable under the gift or estate levies: (1) a gift to take effect at death; (2) a gift *causa mortis* (in anticipation of death); (3) a gift *inter vivos* (during life); and (4) a fictitious sale or exchange in which the property is transferred for a consideration less than its true value. The first two cases are taxed under the estate tax, the latter two under the gift tax. The rates of the federal gift tax are fixed at three fourths of those of the additional estate tax, so that it is less expensive to give property away during your lifetime than it is to part with it on death.

What Gifts Are Taxed? All gifts and transfers of property, real and personal, including life insurance policies and certain transfers of property to joint ownership, are subject to the tax. Where, however, a person creates a joint bank account, having the right to regain the entire fund without the consent of the other joint owner, the gift does not occur until the latter withdraws for his or her own benefit from the fund; and the gift is the amount so withdrawn. Gifts to qualified charitable, religious, educational, and other tax exempt institutions are deductible for gift tax purposes as well as for income tax purposes. The tax is computed on the total gifts made during the calendar year—but gift tax returns must be filed and paid quarterly on the fifteenth day of the second month following the close of the calendar quarter in which the gift was made.

What May Be Excluded. The first $3,000 given to any one person during any calendar year is excluded from the amount of the gifts for the year. Thus, $3,000 a year may be given to each of one or more persons without incurring a gift tax for that year. In addition to this annual exclusion there is an overall specific exemption of $30,000 against all taxable gifts which a person may make during a lifetime. This exemption may be used entirely in one year or be spread over a period of years until it is exhausted.

For example, if a person makes a gift of $10,000 to another in one year, $3,000 of the gift will be free from the tax under the annual exclusion, and the balance of $7,000 may be applied against the $30,000 exemption, leaving $23,000 of the exemption to be used in subsequent years. No gift tax will be due as the result of such a gift, but it must be reported on a gift tax return.

To take another example, if a person makes gifts of $5,000 to each of two others in one year, $3,000 of each gift will be free from tax under the annual exclusion, and the balance of $2,000 of each gift (or a total of $4,000) may be applied against the $30,000 exemption, leaving $26,000 of the exemption to be used in subsequent years. No gift tax would be due as the result of such gifts, but they, too, must be reported. Not only the donor but also the recipient of a gift (except qualified public and charitable organizations) must report it.

The Marital Deduction. As in the case of the federal estate tax, the federal gift tax also provides for a marital deduction. If you make a gift to your wife or she makes a gift to you, there may be deducted one half of the value of the gift before applying the annual exclusion and the specific exemption. The marital deduction is available only if the gift meets tests similar to those necessary to obtain the marital deduction for federal estate tax purposes, as previously described.

Joint Gifts by Husband and Wife. Gifts made to third persons by you or your wife may be treated for gift tax purposes as made one half by you and one half by your wife if each of you consents to this procedure, in writing, on the gift tax returns. Thus, you and your wife report only one half of the gift in your respective gift tax returns, and the annual exclusion and the specific exemption are then used by each of you separately. However, if you and your wife elect to treat any one gift to another person as made jointly, then all gifts made to other persons by either of you during that calendar year must be treated the same way.

It is thus possible for a husband and wife to make a joint outright gift of $66,000 to one person without incurring gift tax liability if no

TABLE 17–5
Federal Gift Tax

Amount of Gift	A Federal Gift Tax (unmarried donor)	B Federal Gift Tax (married donors to third parties)	C Federal Gift Tax (married donor to spouse)
$ 30,000	$ 0	$ 0	$ 0
60,000	2,250	0	0
100,000	9,225	2,400	1,200
150,000	20,025	8,850	4,425
200,000	31,275	18,450	9,225
250,000	42,525	28,950	14,475
300,000	54,075	40,050	20,025
350,000	66,075	51,300	25,650
400,000	78,075	62,550	31,275
450,000	90,075	73,800	36,900
500,000	102,075	85,050	42,525
600,000	127,650	108,150	54,075
700,000	153,900	132,150	66,075
800,000	180,450	156,150	78,075
900,000	208,200	180,150	90,075
1,000,000	235,950	204,150	102,075
1,500,000	386,700	334,050	167,025
2,000,000	554,775	471,900	235,950
2,500,000	737,625	617,250	308,625
3,000,000	935,475	773,400	386,700
5,000,000	1,836,975	1,475,250	737,625
10,000,000	4,549,050	3,673,950	1,836,975

Amount of Gift: This column represents the amount of gift *after* deducting the annual exclusion or exclusions but *before* deducting the lifetime exemption or exemptions.

Column **A** Gift tax payable on gifts to third parties where donor is unmarried or prescribed consent of spouse has not been given.

Column **B** Combined gift tax payable on gifts by married donors to third parties where prescribed consents have been given.

Column **C** Gift tax payable on gifts by one spouse to the other.

Source: Manufacturers Hanover Trust Company, New York, N.Y.

previous gifts of more than the allowable annual exclusions have been made by either in the past. However, one result of such a gift would be that the present specific exemption of both husband and wife would no longer be available against any subsequent gifts to the same person or to others. You save taxes by splitting gifts, of course. For example, assume that a man puts $200,000 into a trust for the benefit of his daughter. If he were taxed on the whole gift, his tax would be $30,600. By splitting the gift, however, so that he gives $100,000 and his wife gives the same amount, the aggregate tax is only $17,190.

Why Gifts Save Tax. There are several reasons why gifts during a lifetime save taxes. In the first place, the federal gift tax rates are lower than the federal estate tax rates. Federal gift tax rates may be seen in Table 17–5. Secondly, by making gifts, you divide the taxation of your property between estate tax and gift tax. This is a saving, because each tax—the gift tax and the estate tax—has its own exemption and its own rising scale of rates. It keeps the property out of the high brackets.

Finally, a gift may save on income taxes. Assume that you want to help your married son. You give him stocks and bonds (which you formerly owned) which will now yield him a monthly income of $100. By making the gift, your annual income subject to taxes is $1,200 less than it would have been had you held the securities in your own name and paid out the $100 a month to your son.

Relationship of Gift Tax to Estate Tax. If the maker of a gift lives three years after making it, the estate is not required to pay an estate tax on the property which was the subject of the gift. On the other hand, a gift made within three years of death is, for estate tax purposes, presumed to have been made in contemplation of death, unless it can be proved that the gift was in fact not so made. Even though a gift tax has been paid on a transfer of property, such property may also be subject to the estate tax. To help the taxpayer in such situations, the federal estate tax law allows a "gift tax credit" to be taken off the estate tax. The credit is the amount of the gift tax that was paid.

Since gifts made during a lifetime may be considered as coming from the top estate tax bracket of an individual, sizable tax savings may result from a program of lifetime gifts. For example, if Thomas Farmer has a net estate of $200,000, which he wishes to transfer to his son (since his wife is independently wealthy), the estate tax (if it passed at his death) would be:

Net estate	$200,000
Minus $60,000 exemption	140,000
Federal estate tax on $140,000	32,700

If, however, he decided to transfer the major portion of the estate by gifts, say over a 10 year period, taking advantage of marital option to split the gift, the tax results would be as follows:

Gift Tax Computation

Outright gifts of $60,000 against lifetime exemption ($30,000 each parent)	$ 60,000
Ten years annual exclusion of $6,000 ($3,000 each parent)	60,000
Total gifts	$120,000
Gift tax	0
Final estate at father's death	$ 80,000
Net estate after exemption	20,000
Federal estate tax on $20,000	1,600

Gifts to Children. Sentiment, dreams, and tax savings all combine to make this a popular form of gift giving. The procedure for giving securities or money to minors is regulated by law in each of the 50 states, the District of Columbia, Virgin Islands, and the Canal Zone. These factors must be remembered in making such a gift.

1. It is irrevocable—and the custodian must act for the minor and not for himself.
2. There is no way the donor can reclaim the gift before the minor comes of age. The property is the minor's.
3. All that is required is registration of the securities in the name of the custodian for the minor. There is no other legal technicality.

The custodial property may be used for the support, maintenance, education, and general use of the minor as the custodian with discretion deems suitable and proper.

The tax benefits allow the donor to shift income to a lower bracket and therefore taxable at lower rates. Parents of such minors continue to enjoy the tax exemptions for the minor regardless of his income, if they contribute more than half of his support, and he is under 19, or a full time student. However, if income from the gift is used to discharge the legal obligation of any person to support the minor, that sum is taxable to that person as income.

CONCLUSION

What are the highlights of this complicated business of estate planning?

1. Everyone should make a will regardless of the size of the estate.
2. Everyone should leave a letter of last instructions.

3. Every individual has an exemption of $60,000 before federal estate taxes accrue.
4. Because of the marital deduction one half of a husband's or wife's estate already belongs to the survivor and is therefore not subject to the estate tax.
5. A person may give up to $3,000 a year to as many individuals as desired without its being subject to gift or estate taxes.
6. A husband and wife can together give up to $6,000 under the conditions stated in 5.
7. An individual may give away as much as $30,000 without its being subject to gift or estate taxes. This is a lifetime exemption. It is in addition to the annual $3,000 exclusion.
8. A husband and wife together have a $60,000 lifetime exclusion, from the gift tax.
9. For a person of means, estate taxes are minimized by making gifts during one's lifetime to the full extent of the gift tax exemptions.
10. Gift tax rates, even when they apply, are three quarters of estate tax rates.
11. Insurance, handled in certain ways, aids in estate planning and may, under special circumstances, not be subject to the estate tax.
12. The trust is a very effective way of passing an estate on to children, or even grandchildren, and minimizing estate taxes.

Of the many complex and involved financial problems one inevitably faces through life: insurance, debts, mortgage financing, taxes, investments—all of which we have now surveyed—none is more difficult or technical than wills, trusts, estates, and death and gift taxes. Nowhere is it more saving of time and trouble to pay the fee of a lawyer or other expert for careful, competent, precise, and correct advice. Invariably, a shortsighted attempt to save a fee will result in a much more serious loss.

All that this book has attempted is to provide the framework and background to enable you to talk more intelligently about your personal financial problems with the various experts—lawyers, accountants, insurance agents, bank mortgage officers, internal revenue agents, trust officers, and others—whom you will encounter in due course in your "three score and ten." It would be a real disservice to deal with all these complicated matters on your own. Remember: "Many persons might have attained to wisdom had they not assumed that they already possessed it"—SENECA.

SUGGESTED READINGS

1. *A Guide to Federal Estate and Gift Taxation,* Publication No. 448. Available from the Superintendent of Documents, U.S. Government Printing Office, Washington, D.C.

2. "How to Do More for Your Family," *Monthly Bulletin,* Irving Trust Company, New York, N.Y.

3. *Changing Times, The Kiplinger Magazine*
   "Maybe Joint Ownership is Right for You—Maybe Not," June 1974.
   "Suppose You Die Without A Will," January 1974.
   "Settling An Estate Could Be Cheaper & Faster," November 1972.
   "When Your Wife is a Widow What Then?" June, 1971.
   "Yes—Single People Do Need to Plan Their Estates, February, 1971.

4. *Gifts of Securities or Money to Minors; A Guide to Laws in 50 States.* Securities Industry Association, 120 Broadway, New York, N.Y. 10005, annual.

5. "The New Law for Filing and Paying Federal Estate and Gift Taxes," Personal Trust Division, Manufacturers Hanover Trust Co., New York, 1971.

6. Millie Considine and Ruth Pool, *Wills: A Dead Giveaway,* New York: Doubleday, 1974.

7. "How Trusts Can Help in Financial Planning," *U.S. News and World Report* January 21, 1974.

8. "Taxes and Estates"—*Monthly Bulletin,* Chemical Bank, New York.

9. John T. Creedon, *Some Uses of Life Insurance in Estate Planning,* American Law Institute, 1974.

10. Richard S. Ziegler and Patrick F. Flaherty, *Estate Planning for Everyone —The Whole Truth from Planning to Probate.* New York: Funk & Wagnalls 1974.

11. John Barnes, *Who Will Get Your Money,* New York: Wm. Morrow & Co., 1972.

12. *What Does She Do Now?,* Life Insurance Marketing and Research Association, Hartford, Conn., 1974. A free copy may be obtained on request.

13. Commerce Clearing House Editorial Staff, *Federal Estate and Gift Taxes Explained, Including Estate Planning.* Chicago, Ill., latest edition.

14. Maurice B. Goudzwaard and Keith V. Smith, "How Trustmen View Their Objectives," *Institutional Investor,* February 1972.

15. Gail McKnight Beckman, "Estate Planning: A Women's Perspective," *Trusts & Estates,* March 1975.

16. Richard W. Desmond, "The Taxation of Estate Income," *Trusts & Estates,* November 1974.

CASE PROBLEMS

1. Norman Roberts is 28 years old and an employee of a large advertising concern. He is married and the father of a year old son. He has life insurance payable to his wife, owns a car, and recently was given by his parents a small ranch house worth about $20,000. He has stock in his name totaling about $10,000, and has a joint savings account with his wife in which they have deposited about $4,000. It has not occurred to him to make a will, but his wife suggests that he should do so. Norman is not impressed, saying that what he has would automatically go to her. How would you advise them?

2. Jack Lobart was a successful young engineer who, as an employee of a large electronics corporation, drew a salary of about $20,000 yearly. He died when he was in his late thirties, leaving an estate totaling about $150,000, primarily the result of several successful investments. In his will, he directed that a trust be created, with the income to be paid to his wife during her lifetime and the principal to be divided equally among their children after her demise. His wife was left with three children, whose ages ranged from 9 to 17. The net estate, on which she was dependent for support, amounted to about $130,000. This estate yielded an income of about $6,000. From this sum, far beneath her accustomed income, income taxes and trustee commissions had to be deducted. Although she needs and will continue to need a larger sum for the support and education of the children, Mrs. Lobart has no way of obtaining any of the principal, because her husband's will contained no provision to that effect. The trustee, her late husband's brother, sympathizes with her predicament, but is unable to help her obtain more money under the will. How could Jack Lobart have avoided such a situation?

3. John Smith, aged 26, was killed in an accident, leaving a blind wife and two children (ages 1 and 3). Having just begun his career, John left very little money. His father, Fred Smith, a widower, has cancer and the doctors give him only a year to live. His will, as it stood at the time of the accident, named his son as sole heir. His estate amounts to about $400,000. Fred Smith now wishes to rewrite the will so as to aid his daughter-in-law and his grandchildren. What are your suggestions?

4. Mr. Jones is extremely wealthy. He is married, but has no children. He has, however, a permanently crippled unmarried younger sister, whose support he has assumed. For the last few years Miss Jones has been living with her brother and his wife. For business reasons, Mr. Jones is to move to another part of the country. His sister would prefer to remain in their home town. She has friends with whom she can live, and Mr. Jones would like to make her financially secure for the years to come. What might be sensible financial arrangements?

5. Martin Morse, a 60 year old businessman, has a net estate of $75,000. His son is earning a good income, but his daughter is a widow with two small

children. She is living on social security and a barely adequate pension. Mr. Morse would like to help her now and also to finance her children's education. What would be a good way of accomplishing this?

6. John Randall, age 64, has never made a will and does not see any reason for making one. His wife, age 55, and his five children, four of whom have large incomes, are still living. Randall's net estate is worth about $100,000. His only son is concerned that, upon Randall's death intestate, his entire estate would not go to Mrs. Randall, who would have no other income. Mr. Randall refuses to speak to a lawyer about the matter, but his son thinks that his father may listen to him. What points should the son bring to the attention of the father?

7. Branch Burlingame (age 49) is a successful account executive in an advertising agency. He makes $40,000 a year and has a wife (age 45) and three children: a son, age 27, and two daughters, ages 16 and 17. In addition to a mortgage free home worth $50,000, which will go to his wife upon his death, and substantial annuities and insurance coverage to send his daughters to college and provide himself and his family with a comfortable income after his retirement, he has assets of $300,000. Burlingame would like to have this money go to his wife and daughters; he does not get along well with his son and does not want him to receive any of this money. What are your suggestions?

8. Allen Rubens has a large income and pays heavy income taxes. Besides his wife, he supports his daughter-in-law and her three children by sending them $800 monthly, since his son was killed in Vietnam. How can he reduce his tax liability and accomplish the same goals?

9. Peter Tompkins inserted in his will a specific legacy of old gold coins, worth $3,000, to a local museum; a demonstrative legacy of $8,000 to his grandson, to be taken from $10,000 deposited in a savings bank; and residuary legacies of $57,000, all to be taken from his estate, which he believed was worth $68,000. After his death it was found that burial expenses, debts, and taxes absorbed $10,000. At his death he still owned the gold coins, and his savings account amounted to $14,000. The balance of his estate consisted of stocks and bonds, which brought $32,000 upon their sale. The residuary legacies were for $20,000 to his grown, successful son and $37,000 to his elderly, crippled wife. Tompkins and his wife had been living for years on his $28,000 annual salary. How did the will affect the way the money left was distributed?

10. Frank Corbett made his wife beneficiary of $100,000 of straight life insurance on his life. She died when their three children were 3, 6, and 7 years of age. He has built up a successful grocery business (netting $24,000 a year), owns his own home free and clear (worth $27,000), has $9,000 in various banks, and owns $35,000 of securities, yielding 5 percent. This morning he

was almost run down by an automobile as he went to work. Accordingly, he begins thinking of the future and his three children. He wonders whether he should go to the local lawyer and have a will drawn. What should he do about estate planning?

11. Gerald Craig lived and died in your state. Although he made and signed a will, he had no witnesses to it. His estate amounted to $90,000. He left a wife (age 61), who was accustomed to living on a scale befitting an annual income of $25,000, and an unsuccessful son 33 years of age, who has a wife and three young children. How will his property be distributed?

12. Lucretia Smith, a widow, inherited $150,000. She wanted to retain $100,000 and give $25,000 to her son and her daughter, but they were only 8 and 10 years of age. How should she do this?

13. When widower Peter Turgeon died, he left a residence worth $25,000; a summer home worth $10,000, which all his children liked very much; and $25,000 invested in stocks and bonds. He was survived by two sons and two daughters, all of whom he loved equally well. What would have been a suitable disposition of his property in his will?

Index

B

I

J–K

L

P

Q–R

S

This book has been set in 10 point and 9 point Electra, leaded 3 points. Chapter numbers are set in 42 point Weiss Series II; chapter titles are set in 18 point Scotch Roman. The size of the type page is 30 by 46 picas.